Distances and j

The mileage chart shows distances in r
AA-recommended routes. Using motor
normally the fastest route, though not n

The journey times, shown in hours and ~~minutes~~, are average off-peak
driving times along AA-recommended routes. These times should be used
as a guide only and do not allow for unforeseen traffic delays, rest breaks
or fuel stops.

For example, the 378 miles (608 km) journey between Glasgow and
Norwich should take approximately 7 hours 28 minutes.

Journey times

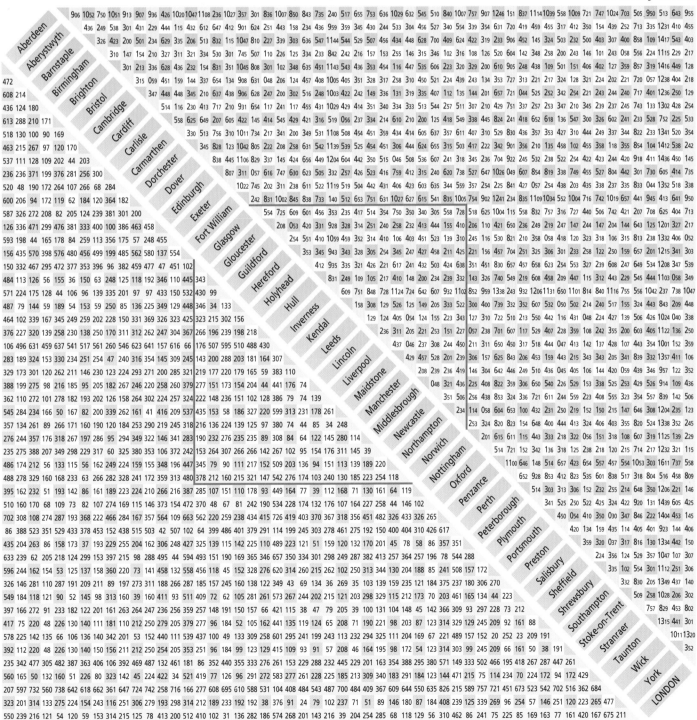

Distances in miles (one mile equals 1.6093 km)

GREAT BRITAIN
ROAD ATLAS

33rd edition June 2018

© AA Media Limited 2018

Original edition printed 1986.

Cartography: All cartography in this atlas edited, designed and produced by the Mapping Services Department of AA Publishing (A05623).

This atlas contains Ordnance Survey data © Crown copyright and database right 2018 and Royal Mail data © Royal Mail copyright and database right 2018.

Contains public sector information licensed under the Open Government Licence v3.0

Ireland mapping contains data from openstreetmap.org © OpenStreetMap contributors

Publisher's Notes: Published by AA Publishing (a trading name of AA Media Limited, whose registered office is Fanum House, Basing View, Basingstoke, Hampshire RG21 4EA, UK. Registered number 06112600).

ISBN: 978 0 7495 7955 5 (leather)
ISBN: 978 0 7495 7954 8 (standard)

A CIP catalogue record for this book is available from The British Library.

Disclaimer: The contents of this atlas are believed to be correct at the time of the latest revision, it will not contain any subsequent amended, new or temporary information including diversions and traffic control or enforcement systems. The publishers cannot be held responsible or liable for any loss or damage occasioned to any person acting or refraining from action as a result of any use or reliance on material in this atlas, nor for any errors, omissions or changes in such material. This does not affect your statutory rights.

The publishers would welcome information to correct any errors or omissions and to keep this atlas up to date. Please write to the Atlas Editor, AA Publishing, The Automobile Association, Fanum House, Basing View, Basingstoke, Hampshire RG21 4EA, UK. **E-mail:** *roadatlasfeedback@theaa.com*

Acknowledgements: AA Publishing would like to thank the following for information used in the creation of this atlas: Cadw, English Heritage, Forestry Commission, Historic Scotland, National Trust and National Trust for Scotland, RSPB, The Wildlife Trust, Scottish Natural Heritage, Natural England, The Countryside Council for Wales. Award winning beaches from 'Blue Flag' and 'Keep Scotland Beautiful' (summer 2017 data): for latest information visit *www.blueflag.org* and *www.keepscotlandbeautiful.org*. Road signs are © Crown Copyright 2018. Reproduced under the terms of the Open Government Licence. Transport for London (Central London Map), Nexus (Newcastle district map).

Ireland mapping: Republic of Ireland census 2011 © Central Statistics Office and Northern Ireland census 2011 © NISRA (population data); Irish Public Sector Data (CC BY 4.0) (Gaeltacht); Logainm.ie (placenames); Roads Service and Transport Infrastructure Ireland

Printer: Leo Paper Products, China

Contents

Map pages and distance chart	**inside front cover**
Route planning	**II–XVII**
Route planner	II–VII
Channel hopping and the Isle of Wight	VIII–IX
Ferries to Ireland and the Isle of Man	X
Scotland and North Sea ferries	XI
Caravan and camping sites in Britain	XII–XV
Traffic signs	XVI–XVII
Motorways	**XVIII–XXV**
Restricted junctions	XVIII–XXI
M25 London Orbital motorway	XXII
M6 Toll motorway	XXIII
Smart motorways	XXIV–XXV
Map pages	**XXVI**
Road map symbols	**1**
Road maps	**2–173**
Britain 1:200,000 scale	2–169
Some islands are shown at slightly smaller scales	
Ireland 1:1,000,000 scale	170–173
District maps	**174–185**
Birmingham	174–175
Glasgow	176–177
London	178–181
Manchester	182–183
Tyne & Wear	184–185
Street map symbols	**186**
Towns, ports and airports	**187–237**
Town plans	188–234
Major airports	235–237
Port plans	VIII–XI
Channel Tunnel terminals	27
Central London	**238–253**
Central London street map	238–247
Central London index	248–253
Index to place names	**254–302**
County, administrative area map	254
Place name index	255–302
Map pages and distance chart	**inside back cover**

Scale 1:200,000
or 3.16 miles to 1 inch

REPUBLIC
OF
IRELAND

Legend:
- Motorway
- Toll motorway
- Primary route dual carriageway
- Primary route single carriageway
- Other A road
- or V | Vehicle ferry
- Fast vehicle ferry or catamaran
- National Park
- **16** Atlas page number

Page numbers: 66, 68, 70, 54, 56, 55, 42, 44, 46, 40, 28, 30, 32, 16, 18, 20, 8, 10, 4, 6, 2

Isles of Scilly inset (page 2)

Channel Islands inset

WALES
SNOWDONIA
PEMBROKESHIRE COAST
BRECON BEACONS
DARTMOOR
EXMOOR
Cardigan Bay
Bristol Channel
ENGLISH [CHANNEL]

Place names:
Holyhead, Anglesey, Llandudno, Colwyn Bay, Rhyl, Widnes, Runcorn, Knutsford, Manche[ster], Bangor, Conwy, Abergele, Holywell, John Lennon, Ellesmere Port, Northwich, Maccle[sfield], Caernarfon, Bethesda, Denbigh, Mold, Queensferry, Chester, Betws-y-Coed, Ruthin, Nantwich, Crewe, Kidsgrove, STO[KE], Pwllheli, Porthmadog, Wrexham, Whitchurch, Newcastle-under-Lyme, Abersoch, Bala, Llangollen, Market Drayton, Oswestry, Newport, St[afford], Barmouth, Dolgellau, Welshpool, Shrewsbury, Cannoc[k], Machynlleth, Telford, WOLVERHAMPTON, Church Stretton, Bridgnorth, Dudley, Newtown, Stourbridge, Halesowe[n], Aberystwyth, Llangurig, Kidderminster, Rhayader, Bromsgrove, Knighton, Ludlow, Aberaeron, New Quay, Tregaron, Llandrindod Wells, Leominster, Worcester, Cardigan, Lampeter, Kington, Great Malvern, Newcastle Emlyn, Builth Wells, Hay-on-Wye, Hereford, Ledbury, Llandovery, Brecon, Ross-on-Wye, Tewkesb[ury], Carmarthen, Llandeilo, Abergavenny, Gloucester, St Clears, Fishguard, Monmouth, Stroud, St Davids, Haverfordwest, Llanelli, Neath, Merthyr Tydfil, Chepstow, Milford Haven, Swansea, Cwmbran, Newport, Pembroke Dock, Pembroke, Port Talbot, Pontypridd, Avonmouth, Tenby, Bridgend, CARDIFF, BRISTOL, Cardiff, Clevedon, Weston-super-Mare, Bath, Ilfracombe, Lynton, Minehead, Cheddar, Frome, Lundy, Exmoor, Wells, Shepton Mallet, Trowb[ridge], Barnstaple, Bridgwater, Glastonbury, War[minster], Bideford, Great Torrington, South Molton, Taunton, Wincanton, Yeovil, Shaftesbury, Bude, Hatherleigh, Tiverton, Ilminster, Sherborne, Holsworthy, Crediton, Chard, Crewkerne, Blandford Forum, Okehampton, Exeter, Honiton, Axminster, Bridport, Launceston, Exmouth, Dawlish, Lyme Regis, Dorchester, Wadebridge, Tavistock, Teignmouth, Newton Abbot, Weymouth, Cornwall Newquay, Bodmin, Buckfastleigh, Torquay, Fortuneswell, Newquay, Liskeard, Paignton, Lostwithiel, Saltash, PLYMOUTH, Totnes, Redruth, Fowey, Torpoint, Dartmouth, Truro, St Austell, Kingsbridge, Camborne, Penzance, Land's End, Falmouth, Helston, Lizard

Ferry routes:
Rosslare, Roscoff / Santander (Apr–Oct), Guernsey Jersey St-Malo

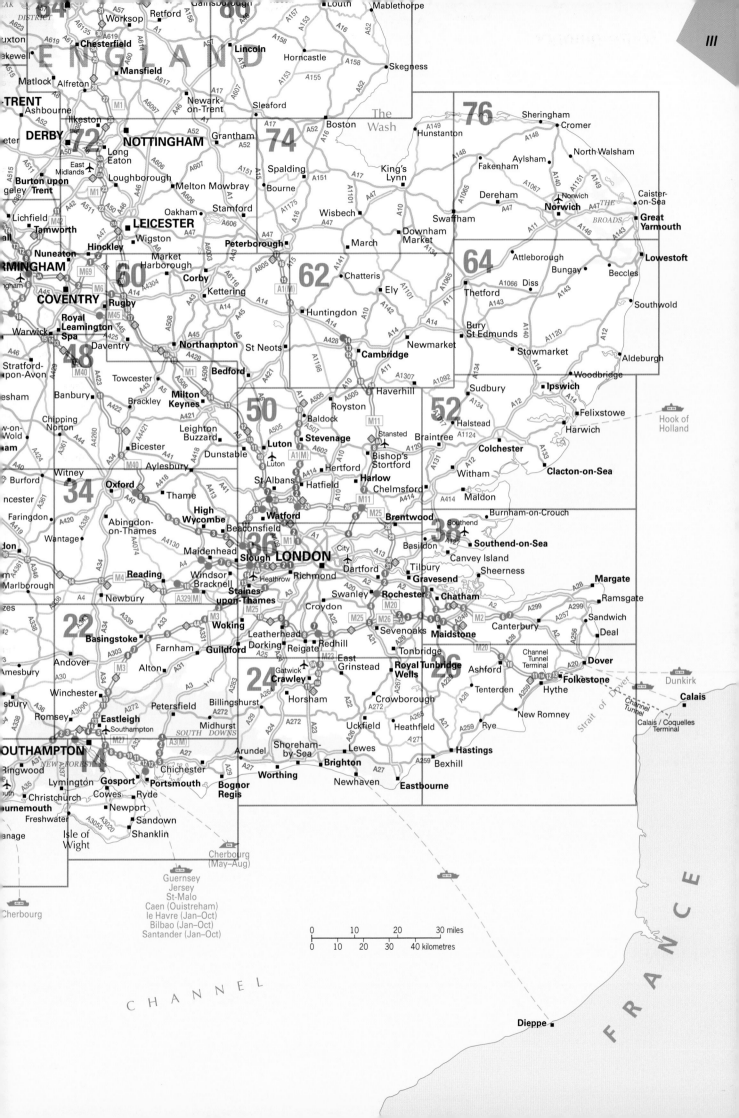

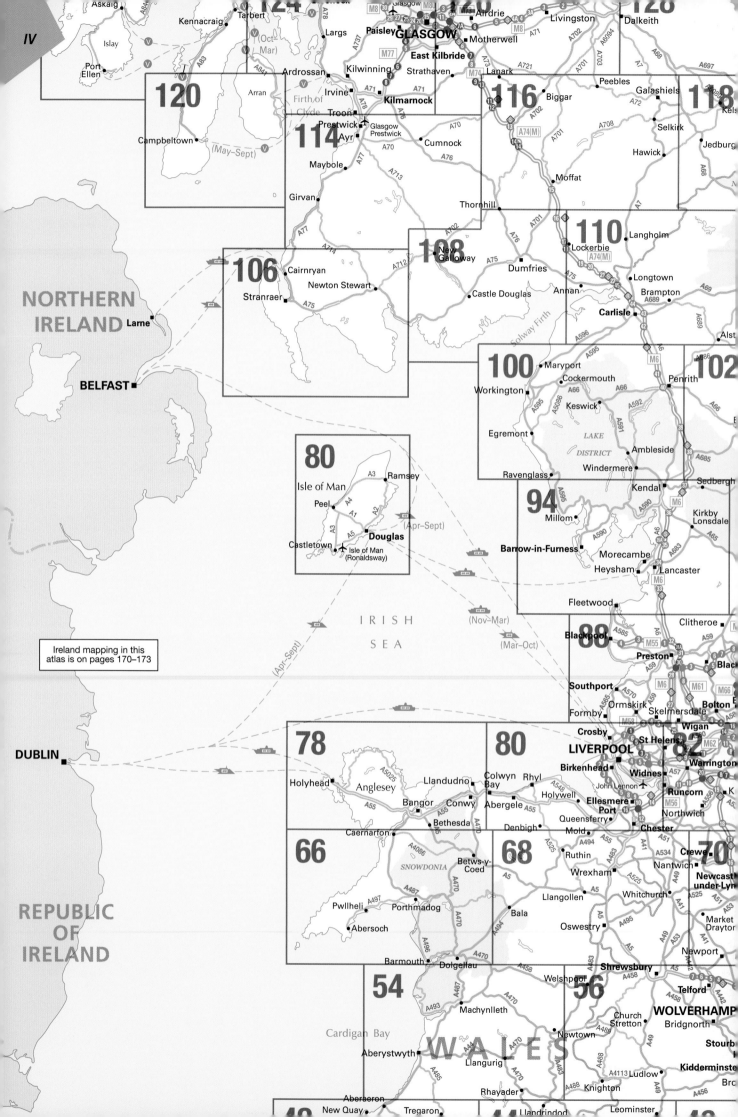

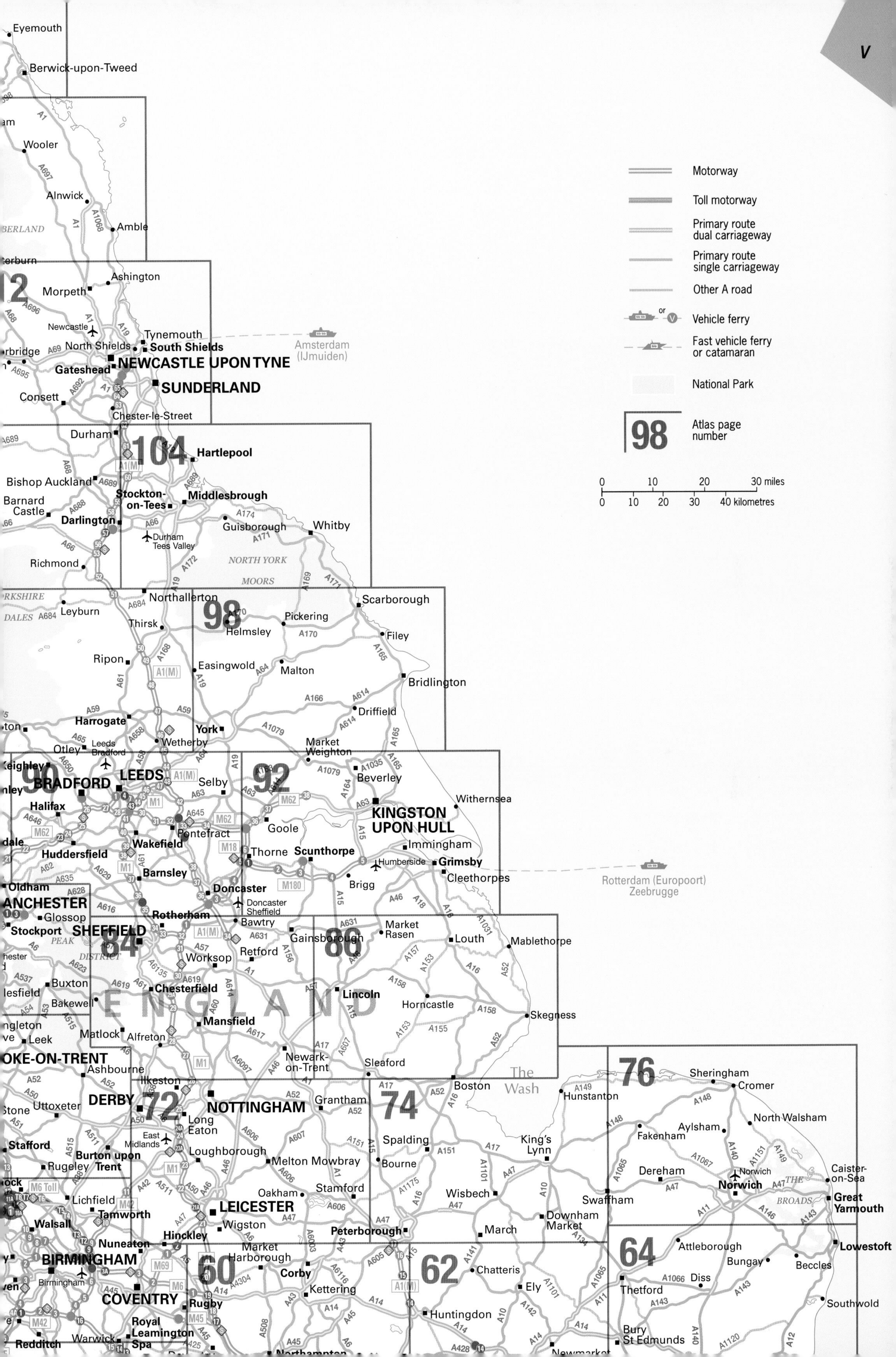

Legend

- Motorway
- Toll motorway
- Primary route dual carriageway
- Primary route single carriageway
- Other A road
- Vehicle ferry *or* V
- Fast vehicle ferry or catamaran
- National Park
- **98** Atlas page number

| 0 | 10 | 20 | 30 miles |
| 0 | 10 | 20 | 30 | 40 kilometres |

104

98

92

90

84

86

76

72

74

64

60

62

Eyemouth
Berwick-upon-Tweed
Wooler
Alnwick
Amble
BERLAND
Morpeth
Ashington
Newcastle
Tynemouth
North Shields
South Shields
NEWCASTLE UPON TYNE
Gateshead
SUNDERLAND
Consett
Chester-le-Street
Durham
Bishop Auckland
Hartlepool
Barnard Castle
Stockton-on-Tees
Middlesbrough
Darlington
Durham Tees Valley
Guisborough
Whitby
Richmond
NORTH YORK MOORS
Leyburn
Northallerton
Scarborough
DALES
Thirsk
Helmsley
Pickering
Filey
Ripon
Easingwold
Malton
Bridlington
Driffield
Harrogate
Otley
Leeds Bradford
York
Wetherby
Market Weighton
BRADFORD
LEEDS
Selby
Beverley
Keighley
Halifax
KINGSTON UPON HULL
Withernsea
Goole
Huddersfield
Wakefield
Pontefract
Thorne
Scunthorpe
Immingham
Barnsley
Humberside
Grimsby
MANCHESTER
Oldham
Doncaster
Cleethorpes
Glossop
Doncaster Sheffield
Brigg
Stockport
SHEFFIELD
Rotherham
Bawtry
Market Rasen
Louth
Mablethorpe
PEAK DISTRICT
Retford
Worksop
Gainsborough
Buxton
Chesterfield
Horncastle
Skegness
Bakewell
Lincoln
ENGLAND
Leek
Matlock
Alfreton
Mansfield
Newark-on-Trent
Sleaford
STOKE-ON-TRENT
Ashbourne
Ilkeston
The Wash
Boston
Sheringham
Cromer
Uttoxeter
DERBY
NOTTINGHAM
Grantham
Hunstanton
North Walsham
Stafford
Long Eaton
East Midlands
Spalding
King's Lynn
Aylsham
Fakenham
Burton upon Trent
Loughborough
Bourne
Dereham
Norwich
Caister-on-Sea
Rugeley
Melton Mowbray
Wisbech
Swaffham
THE BROADS
Lichfield
Oakham
Stamford
Downham Market
Great Yarmouth
Walsall
LEICESTER
March
Tamworth
Wigston
Peterborough
Attleborough
Lowestoft
Nuneaton
Hinckley
Market Harborough
Thetford
Bungay
Beccles
BIRMINGHAM
Corby
Chatteris
Diss
Birmingham
COVENTRY
Rugby
Kettering
Ely
Southwold
Redditch
Royal Leamington Spa
Huntingdon
Bury St Edmunds
Warwick
Northampton
Newmarket

Amsterdam (IJmuiden)
Rotterdam (Europoort) Zeebrugge

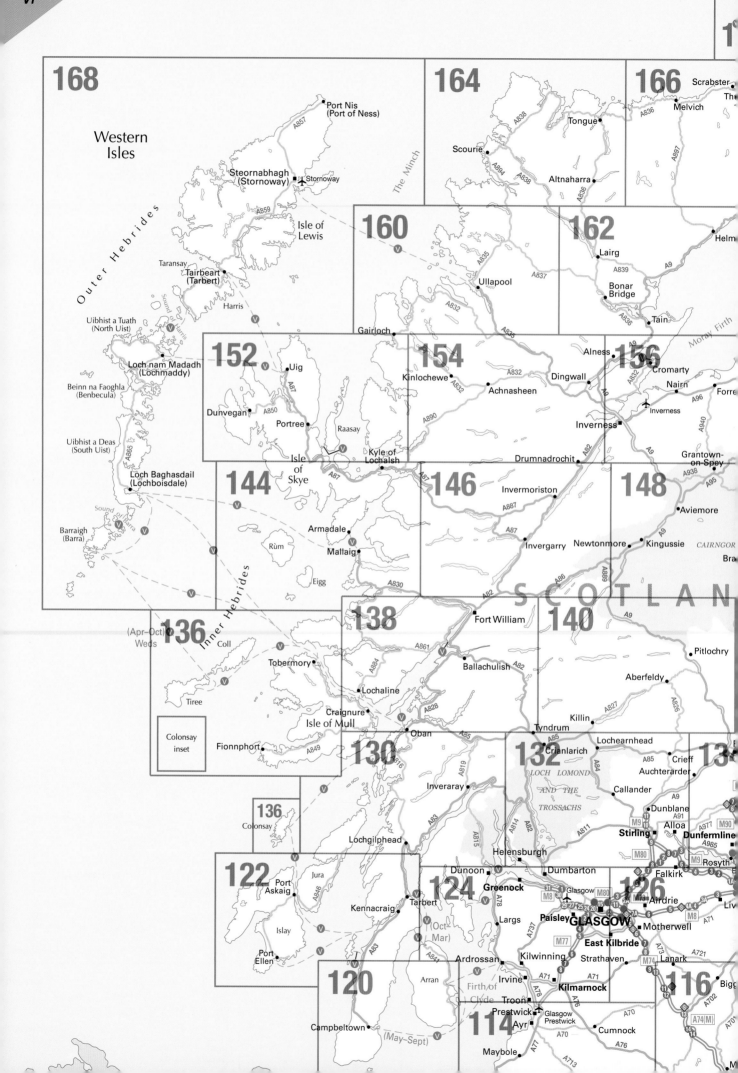

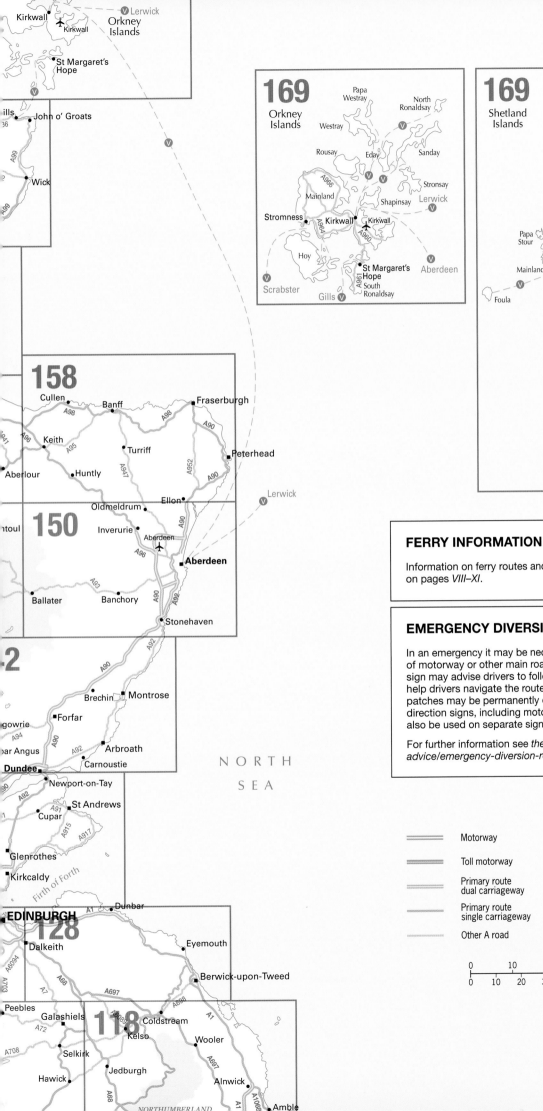

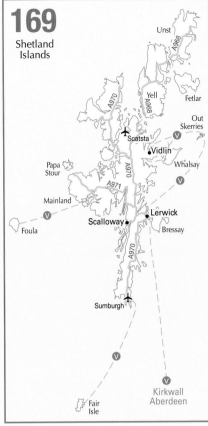

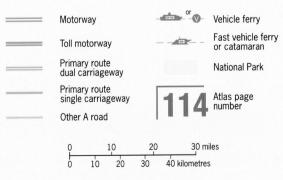

FERRY INFORMATION

Information on ferry routes and operators can be found on pages *VIII–XI*.

EMERGENCY DIVERSION ROUTES

In an emergency it may be necessary to close a section of motorway or other main road to traffic, so a temporary sign may advise drivers to follow a diversion route. To help drivers navigate the route, black symbols on yellow patches may be permanently displayed on existing direction signs, including motorway signs. Symbols may also be used on separate signs with yellow backgrounds.

For further information see *theaa.com/breakdown-cover/ advice/emergency-diversion-routes*

Motorway	Vehicle ferry
Toll motorway	Fast vehicle ferry or catamaran
Primary route dual carriageway	National Park
Primary route single carriageway	**114** Atlas page number
Other A road	

0   10   20   30 miles
0 10 20 30 40 kilometres

Channel hopping and the Isle of Wight

For business or pleasure, hopping on a ferry across to France, the Channel Islands or Isle of Wight has never been easier.

The vehicle ferry services listed in the table give you all the options, together with detailed port plans to help you navigate to and from the ferry terminals. Simply choose your preferred route, not forgetting the fast sailings (see).
Bon voyage!

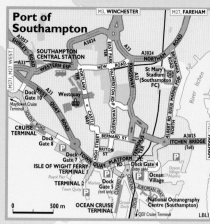

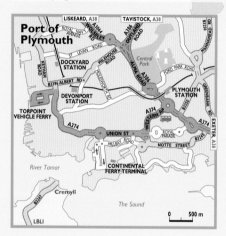

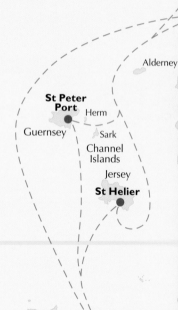

ENGLISH CHANNEL AND ISLE OF WIGHT FERRY CROSSINGS

From	To	Journey time	Operator website
Dover	Calais	1 hr 30 mins	dfdsseaways.co.uk
Dover	Calais	1 hr 30 mins	poferries.com
Dover	Dunkirk	2 hrs	dfdsseaways.co.uk
Folkestone	Calais (Coquelles)	35 mins	eurotunnel.com
Lymington	Yarmouth (IOW)	40 mins	wightlink.co.uk
Newhaven	Dieppe	4 hrs	dfdsseaways.co.uk
Plymouth	Roscoff	6–8 hrs	brittany-ferries.co.uk
Poole	Cherbourg	4 hrs 15 mins	brittany-ferries.co.uk
Poole	Guernsey	3 hrs	condorferries.co.uk
Poole	Jersey	4 hrs 40 mins	condorferries.co.uk
Poole	St-Malo	7–12 hrs (via Channel Is.)	condorferries.co.uk
Portsmouth	Caen (Ouistreham)	6–7 hrs	brittany-ferries.co.uk
Portsmouth	Cherbourg	3 hrs (May–Aug)	brittany-ferries.co.uk
Portsmouth	Fishbourne (IOW)	45 mins	wightlink.co.uk
Portsmouth	Guernsey	7 hrs	condorferries.co.uk
Portsmouth	Jersey	8–11 hrs	condorferries.co.uk
Portsmouth	le Havre	8 hrs (Jan–Oct)	brittany-ferries.co.uk
Portsmouth	St-Malo	9–11 hrs	brittany-ferries.co.uk
Southampton	East Cowes (IOW)	1 hr	redfunnel.co.uk

The information listed is provided as a guide only, as services are liable to change at short notice. Services shown are for vehicle ferries only, operated by conventional ferry unless indicated as a fast ferry service (). Please check sailings before planning your journey.

Travelling further afield? For ferry services to Northern Spain see *brittany-ferries.co.uk*.

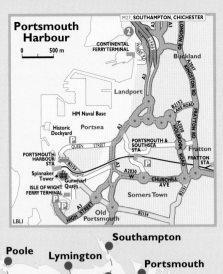
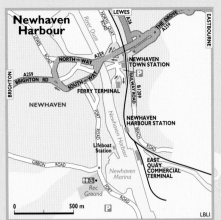
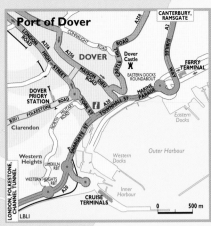
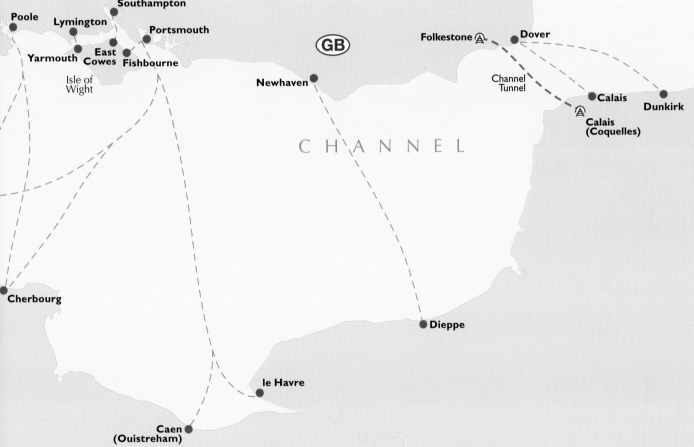
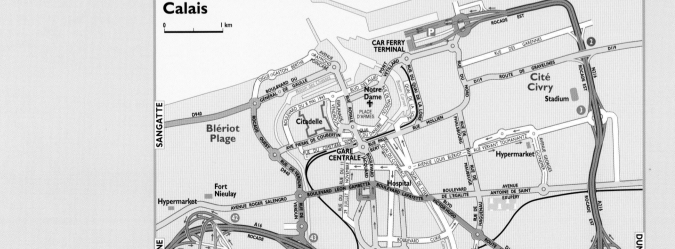

Ferries to Ireland and the Isle of Man

With so many sea crossings to Ireland and the Isle of Man the information provided in the table to the right will help you make the right choice.

IRISH SEA FERRY CROSSINGS

From	To	Journey time	Operator website
Cairnryan	Belfast	2 hrs 15 mins	stenaline.co.uk
Cairnryan	Larne	2 hrs	poferries.com
Douglas	Belfast	2 hrs 45 mins (April–Sept)	steam-packet.com
Douglas	Dublin	2 hrs 55 mins (April–Sept)	steam-packet.com
Fishguard	Rosslare	3 hrs 15 mins	stenaline.co.uk
Heysham	Douglas	3 hrs 45 mins	steam-packet.com
Holyhead	Dublin	1 hr 50 mins	irishferries.com
Holyhead	Dublin	3 hrs 15 mins	irishferries.com
Holyhead	Dublin	3 hrs 15 mins	stenaline.co.uk
Liverpool	Douglas	2 hrs 45 mins (Mar–Oct)	steam-packet.com
Liverpool	Dublin	8 hrs–8 hrs 30 mins	poferries.com
Liverpool (Birkenhead)	Belfast	8 hrs	stenaline.co.uk
Liverpool (Birkenhead)	Douglas	4 hrs 15 mins (Nov–Mar)	steam-packet.com
Pembroke Dock	Rosslare	4 hrs	irishferries.com

The information listed is provided as a guide only, as services are liable to change at short notice. Services shown are for vehicle ferries only, operated by conventional ferry unless indicated as a fast ferry service ( ). Please check sailings before planning your journey.

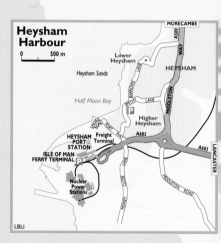

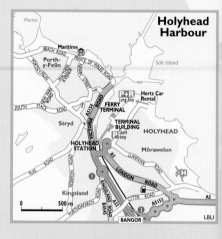

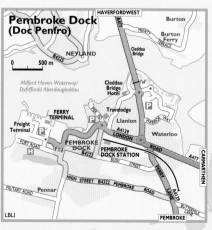

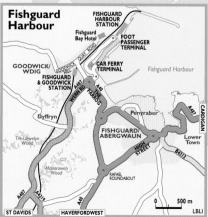

SCOTLAND FERRIES

From	To	Journey time	Operator website
Scottish Islands/west coast of Scotland			
Gourock	Dunoon	20 mins	western-ferries.co.uk
Glenelg	Skye	20 mins (Easter–Oct)	skyeferry.co.uk
Numerous and varied sailings from the west coast of Scotland to Scottish islands are provided by Caledonian MacBrayne. Please visit calmac.co.uk for all ferry information, including those of other operators.			
Orkney Islands			
Aberdeen	Kirkwall	6 hrs	northlinkferries.co.uk
Gills	St Margaret's Hope	1 hr	pentlandferries.co.uk
Scrabster	Stromness	1 hr 30 mins	northlinkferries.co.uk
Lerwick	Kirkwall	5 hrs 30 mins	northlinkferries.co.uk
Inter-island services are operated by Orkney Ferries. Please see orkneyferries.co.uk for details.			
Shetland Islands			
Aberdeen	Lerwick	12 hrs 30 mins	northlinkferries.co.uk
Kirkwall	Lerwick	7 hrs 45 mins	northlinkferries.co.uk
Inter-island services are operated by Shetland Island Council Ferries. Please see shetland.gov.uk/ferries for details.			

Please note that some smaller island services are day dependent and reservations are required for some routes. Book and confirm sailing schedules by contacting the operator.

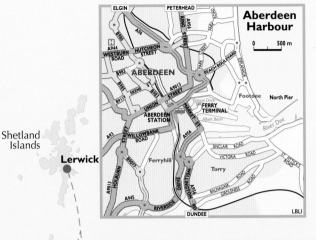
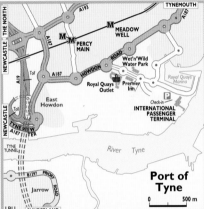
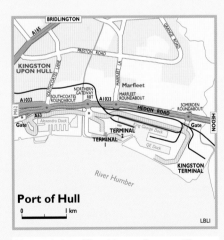

For a port plan of Harwich see atlas page 53

NORTH SEA FERRY CROSSINGS

From	To	Journey time	Operator website
Harwich	Hook of Holland	7–8 hrs	stenaline.co.uk
Kingston upon Hull	Rotterdam (Europoort)	12 hrs	poferries.com
Kingston upon Hull	Zeebrugge	12 hrs	poferries.com
Newcastle upon Tyne	Amsterdam (IJmuiden)	15 hrs 30 mins	dfdsseaways.co.uk

The information listed on this page is provided as a guide only, as services are liable to change at short notice. Services shown are for vehicle ferries only, operated by conventional ferry. Please check sailings before planning your journey.

Caravan and camping sites in Britain

These pages list the top 300 AA-inspected Caravan and Camping (C & C) sites in the Pennant rating scheme. **Five Pennant Premier sites are shown in green, Four Pennant sites are shown in blue.**

Listings include addresses, telephone numbers and websites together with page and grid references to locate the sites in the atlas. The total number of touring pitches is also included for each site, together with the type of pitch available. The following abbreviations are used: **C = Caravan CV = Campervan T = Tent**

To find out more about the AA's Pennant rating scheme and other rated caravan and camping sites not included on these pages please visit ***theAA.com***

ENGLAND

Alders Caravan Park
Home Farm, Alne, York
YO61 1RY
Tel: 01347 838722 **97 R7**
alderscaravanpark.co.uk
Total Pitches: 87 (C, CV & T)

Andrewshayes Holiday Park
Dalwood, Axminster
EX13 7DY
Tel: 01404 831225 **10 E5**
andrewshayes.co.uk
Total Pitches: 150 (C, CV & T)

Apple Tree Park C & C Site
A38, Claypits, Stonehouse
GL10 3AL
Tel: 01452 742362 **32 E3**
appletreepark.co.uk
Total Pitches: 65 (C, CV & T)

Appuldurcombe Gardens Holiday Park
Appuldurcombe Road, Wroxall, Isle of Wight
PO38 3EP
Tel: 01983 852597 **14 F10**
appuldurcombegardens.co.uk
Total Pitches: 130 (C, CV & T)

Atlantic Bays Holiday Park
St Merryn, Padstow
PL28 8PY
Tel: 01841 520855 **4 D7**
atlanticbaysholidaypark.co.uk
Total Pitches: 70 (C, CV & T)

Ayr Holiday Park
St Ives, Cornwall
TR26 1EJ
Tel: 01736 795855 **2 E5**
ayrholidaypark.co.uk
Total Pitches: 40 (C, CV & T)

Back of Beyond Touring Park
234 Ringwood Road, St Leonards, Dorset
BH24 2SB
Tel: 01202 876968 **13 J4**
backofbeyondtouringpark.co.uk
Total Pitches: 80 (C, CV & T)

Bagwell Farm Touring Park
Knights in the Bottom, Chickerell, Weymouth
DT3 4EA
Tel: 01305 782575 **11 N8**
bagwellfarm.co.uk
Total Pitches: 320 (C, CV & T)

Bardsea Leisure Park
Priory Road, Ulverston
LA12 9QE
Tel: 01229 584712 **94 F5**
bardsealeisure.co.uk
Total Pitches: 83 (C & CV)

Barlings Country Holiday Park
Barlings Lane, Langworth
LN3 5DF
Tel: 01522 753200 **86 E5**
barlingscountrypark.co.uk
Total Pitches: 84 (C, CV & T)

Barn Farm Campsite
Barn Farm, Birchover, Matlock
DE4 2BL
Tel: 01629 650245 **84 B8**
barnfarmcamping.com
Total Pitches: 62 (C, CV & T)

Bath Chew Valley Caravan Park
Ham Lane, Bishop Sutton
BS39 5TZ
Tel: 01275 332127 **19 Q3**
bathchewvalley.co.uk
Total Pitches: 45 (C, CV & T)

Bay View Holiday Park
Bolton le Sands, Carnforth
LA5 9TN
Tel: 01524 732854 **95 K7**
holgates.co.uk
Total Pitches: 100 (C, CV & T)

Beaconsfield Farm Caravan Park
Battlefield, Shrewsbury
SY4 4AA
Tel: 01939 210370 **69 P11**
beaconsfieldholidaypark.co.uk
Total Pitches: 60 (C & CV)

Beech Croft Farm
Beech Croft, Blackwell in the Peak, Buxton
SK17 9TQ
Tel: 01298 85330 **83 P10**
beechcroftfarm.co.uk
Total Pitches: 30 (C, CV & T)

Bellingham C & C Club Site
Brown Rigg, Bellingham
NE48 2JY
Tel: 01434 220175 **112 B4**
campingandcaravanningclub.co.uk/bellingham
Total Pitches: 64 (C, CV & T)

Beverley Park C & C Park
Goodrington Road, Paignton
TQ4 7JE
Tel: 01803 661961 **7 M7**
beverley-holidays.co.uk
Total Pitches: 172 (C, CV & T)

Bingham Grange Touring & Camping Park
Melplash, Bridport
DT6 3TT
Tel: 01308 488234 **11 K5**
binghamgrange.co.uk
Total Pitches: 150 (C, CV & T)

Blackmore Vale C & C Park
Sherborne Causeway, Shaftesbury
SP7 9PX
Tel: 01747 851523 **20 F10**
blackmorevalecaravanpark.co.uk
Total Pitches: 13 (C, CV & T)

Blue Rose Caravan Country Park
Star Carr Lane, Brandesburton
YO25 8RU
Tel: 01964 543366 **99 N11**
bluerosepark.com
Total Pitches: 58 (C & CV)

Briarfields Motel & Touring Park
Gloucester Road, Cheltenham
GL51 0SX
Tel: 01242 235324 **46 H10**
briarfields.net
Total Pitches: 72 (C, CV & T)

Broadhembury C & C Park
Steeds Lane, Kingsnorth, Ashford
TN26 1NQ
Tel: 01233 620859 **26 H4**
broadhembury.co.uk
Total Pitches: 110 (C, CV & T)

Brompton Caravan Park
Brompton-on-Swale, Richmond
DL10 7EZ
Tel: 01748 824629 **103 N10**
bromptoncaravanpark.co.uk
Total Pitches: 177 (C, CV & T)

Budemeadows Touring Park
Widemouth Bay, Bude
EX23 0NA
Tel: 01288 361646 **16 C11**
budemeadows.com
Total Pitches: 145 (C, CV & T)

Burnham-on-Sea Holiday Village
Marine Drive, Burnham-on-Sea
TA8 1LA
Tel: 01278 783391 **19 K5**
haven.com/burnhamonsea
Total Pitches: 781 (C, CV & T)

Burrowhayes Farm C & C Site & Riding Stables
West Luccombe, Porlock, Minehead
TA24 8HT
Tel: 01643 862463 **18 A5**
burrowhayes.co.uk
Total Pitches: 120 (C, CV & T)

Burton Constable Holiday Park & Arboretum
Old Lodges, Sproatley, Hull
HU11 4LJ
Tel: 01964 562508 **93 L3**
burtonconstable.co.uk
Total Pitches: 105 (C, CV & T)

Caister-on-Sea Holiday Park
Ormesby Road, Caister-on-Sea, Great Yarmouth
NR30 5NH
Tel: 01493 728931 **77 Q9**
haven.com/caister
Total Pitches: 949 (C & CV)

Caistor Lakes Leisure Park
99a Brigg Road, Caistor
LN7 6RX
Tel: 01472 859626 **93 K10**
caistorlakes.co.uk
Total Pitches: 36 (C & CV)

Cakes & Ale
Abbey Lane, Theberton, Leiston
IP16 4TE
Tel: 01728 831655 **65 N9**
cakesandale.co.uk
Total Pitches: 55 (C, CV & T)

Calloose C & C Park
Leedstown, Hayle
TR27 5ET
Tel: 01736 850431 **2 F7**
calloose.co.uk
Total Pitches: 109 (C, CV & T)

Camping Caradon Touring Park
Trelawne, Looe
PL13 2NA
Tel: 01503 272388 **5 L11**
campingcaradon.co.uk
Total Pitches: 75 (C, CV & T)

Capesthorne Hall
Congleton Road, Siddington, Macclesfield
SK11 9JY
Tel: 01625 861221 **82 H10**
capesthorne.com
Total Pitches: 50 (C & CV)

Carlyon Bay C & C Park
Bethesda, Cypress Avenue, Carlyon Bay
PL25 3RE
Tel: 01726 812735 **3 R3**
carlyonbay.net
Total Pitches: 180 (C, CV & T)

Carnon Downs C & C Park
Carnon Downs, Truro
TR3 6JJ
Tel: 01872 862283 **3 L5**
carnon-downs-caravanpark.co.uk
Total Pitches: 150 (C, CV & T)

Carvynick Country Club
Summercourt, Newquay
TR8 5AF
Tel: 01872 510716 **4 D10**
carvynick.co.uk
Total Pitches: 47 (C & CV)

Castlerigg Hall C & C Park
Castlerigg Hall, Keswick
CA12 4TE
Tel: 017687 74499 **101 J6**
castlerigg.co.uk
Total Pitches: 68 (C, CV & T)

Cayton Village Caravan Park
Mill Lane, Cayton Bay, Scarborough
YO11 3NN
Tel: 01723 583171 **99 M4**
caytontouring.co.uk
Total Pitches: 310 (C, CV & T)

Charris C & C Park
Candy's Lane, Corfe Mullen, Wimborne
BH21 3EF
Tel: 01202 885970 **12 G5**
charris.co.uk
Total Pitches: 45 (C, CV & T)

Cheddar Mendip Heights C & C Club Site
Townsend, Priddy, Wells
BA5 3BP
Tel: 01749 870241 **19 P4**
campingandcaravanningclub.co.uk/cheddar
Total Pitches: 90 (C, CV & T)

Chy Carne Holiday Park
Kuggar, Ruan Minor, Helston
TR12 7LX
Tel: 01326 290200 **3 J10**
chycarne.co.uk
Total Pitches: 30 (C, CV & T)

Clippesby Hall
Hall Lane, Clippesby, Great Yarmouth
NR29 3BL
Tel: 01493 367800 **77 N9**
clippesby.com
Total Pitches: 120 (C, CV & T)

Cofton Country Holidays
Starcross, Dawlish
EX6 8RP
Tel: 01626 890111 **9 N8**
coftonholidays.co.uk
Total Pitches: 450 (C, CV & T)

Concierge Camping
Ratham Estate, Ratham Lane, West Ashling, Chichester
PO18 8DL
Tel: 01243 573118 **15 M5**
conciergecamping.co.uk
Total Pitches: 15 (C, CV & T)

Coombe Touring Park
Race Plain, Netherhampton, Salisbury
SP2 8PN
Tel: 01722 328451 **21 L9**
coombecaravanpark.co.uk
Total Pitches: 50 (C, CV & T)

Corfe Castle C & C Club Site
Bucknowle, Wareham
BH20 5PQ
Tel: 01929 480280 **12 F8**
campingandcaravanningclub.co.uk/corfecastle
Total Pitches: 80 (C, CV & T)

Cornish Farm Touring Park
Shoreditch, Taunton
TA3 7BS
Tel: 01823 327746 **18 H10**
cornishfarm.com
Total Pitches: 50 (C, CV & T)

Cosawes Park
Perranarworthal, Truro
TR3 7QS
Tel: 01872 863724 **3 K6**
cosawestouringandcamping.co.uk
Total Pitches: 59 (C, CV & T)

Cote Ghyll C & C Park
Osmotherley, Northallerton
DL6 3AH
Tel: 01609 883425 **104 E11**
coteghyll.com
Total Pitches: 77 (C, CV & T)

Country View Holiday Park
Sand Road, Sand Bay, Weston-super-Mare
BS22 9UJ
Tel: 01934 627595 **19 K2**
cvhp.co.uk
Total Pitches: 190 (C, CV & T)

Crealy Meadows C & C Park
Sidmouth Road, Clyst St Mary, Exeter
EX5 1DR
Tel: 01395 234888 **9 P6**
crealymeadows.co.uk
Total Pitches: 120 (C, CV & T)

Crows Nest Caravan Park
Gristhorpe, Filey
YO14 9PS
Tel: 01723 582206 **99 M4**
crowsnestcaravanpark.com
Total Pitches: 49 (C, CV & T)

Deepdale Backpackers & Camping
Deepdale Farm, Burnham Deepdale
PE31 8DD
Tel: 01485 210256 **75 R2**
deepdalebackpackers.co.uk
Total Pitches: 80 (CV & T)

Diamond Caravan & Camping Park
Islip Road, Bletchingdon
OX5 3DR
Tel: 01869 350909 **48 F11**
diamondpark.co.uk
Total Pitches: 37 (C, CV & T)

Dolbeare Park C & C
St Ive Road, Landrake, Saltash
PL12 5AF
Tel: 01752 851332 **5 P9**
dolbeare.co.uk
Total Pitches: 60 (C, CV & T)

Dornafield
Dornafield Farm, Two Mile Oak, Newton Abbot
TQ12 6DD
Tel: 01803 812732 **7 L5**
dornafield.com
Total Pitches: 135 (C, CV & T)

East Fleet Farm Touring Park
Chickerell, Weymouth
DT3 4DW
Tel: 01305 785768 **11 N9**
eastfleet.co.uk
Total Pitches: 400 (C, CV & T)

Eden Valley Holiday Park
Lanlivery, Nr Lostwithiel
PL30 5BU
Tel: 01208 872277 **4 H10**
edenvalleyholidaypark.co.uk
Total Pitches: 56 (C, CV & T)

Exe Valley Caravan Site
Mill House, Bridgetown, Dulverton
TA22 9JR
Tel: 01643 851432 **18 B8**
exevalleycamping.co.uk
Total Pitches: 48 (C, CV & T)

Fields End Water Caravan Park & Fishery
Benwick Road, Doddington, March
PE15 0TY
Tel: 01354 740199 **62 E2**
fieldsendcaravans.co.uk
Total Pitches: 52 (C, CV & T)

Flower of May Holiday Park
Lebberston Cliff, Filey, Scarborough
YO11 3NU
Tel: 01723 584311 **99 M4**
flowerofmay.com
Total Pitches: 503 (C, CV & T)

Flusco Wood
Flusco, Penrith
CA11 0JB
Tel: 017684 80020 **101 N5**
fluscowood.co.uk
Total Pitches: 36 (C & CV)

Freshwater Beach Holiday Park
Burton Bradstock, Bridport
DT6 4PT
Tel: 01308 897317 **11 K6**
freshwaterbeach.co.uk
Total Pitches: 750 (C, CV & T)

Globe Vale Holiday Park
Radnor, Redruth
TR16 4BH
Tel: 01209 891183 **3 J5**
globevale.co.uk
Total Pitches: 138 (C, CV & T)

Golden Cap Holiday Park
Seatown, Chideock, Bridport
DT6 6JX
Tel: 01308 422139 **11 J6**
wdlh.co.uk
Total Pitches: 108 (C, CV & T)

Golden Coast Holiday Park
Station Road, Woolacombe
EX34 7HW
Tel: 01271 872302 **16 H3**
woolacombe.com
Total Pitches: 431 (C, CV & T)

Golden Sands Holiday Park
Quebec Road, Mablethorpe
LN12 1QJ
Tel: 01507 477871 **87 N3**
haven.com/goldensands
Total Pitches: 1672 (C, CV & T)

Golden Square C & C Park
Oswaldkirk, Helmsley
YO62 5YQ
Tel: 01439 788269 **98 C5**
goldensquarecaravanpark.com
Total Pitches: 129 (C, CV & T)

Goosewood Holiday Park
Sutton-on-the-Forest, York
YO61 1ET
Tel: 01347 810829 **98 B8**
flowerofmay.com
Total Pitches: 100 (C & CV)

Green Acres Caravan Park
High Knells, Houghton, Carlisle
CA6 4JW
Tel: 01228 675418 **110 H8**
caravanpark-cumbria.com
Total Pitches: 35 (C, CV & T)

Greenhill Farm C & C Park
Greenhill Farm, New Road, Landford, Salisbury
SP5 2AZ
Tel: 01794 324117 **21 Q11**
greenhillfarm.co.uk
Total Pitches: 160 (C, CV & T)

Greenhill Leisure Park
Greenhill Farm, Station Road, Bletchingdon, Oxford
OX5 3BQ
Tel: 01869 351600 **48 E11**
greenhill-leisure-park.co.uk
Total Pitches: 92 (C, CV & T)

Grouse Hill Caravan Park
Flask Bungalow Farm, Fylingdales, Robin Hood's Bay
YO22 4QH
Tel: 01947 880543 **105 P10**
grousehill.co.uk
Total Pitches: 175 (C, CV & T)

Gunvenna Holiday Park
St Minver, Wadebridge
PL27 6QN
Tel: 01208 862405 **4 F6**
gunvenna.com
Total Pitches: 75 (C, CV & T)

Haggerston Castle Holiday Park
Beal, Berwick-upon-Tweed
TD15 2PA
Tel: 01289 381333 **119 K2**
haven.com/haggerstoncastle
Total Pitches: 1340 (C & CV)

Harbury Fields
Harbury Fields Farm, Harbury,
Nr Leamington Spa
CV33 9JN
Tel: 01926 612457 **48 C2**
harburyfields.co.uk
Total Pitches: 59 (C & CV)

Haw Wood Farm Caravan Park
Hinton, Saxmundham
IP17 3QT
Tel: 01502 359550 **65 N7**
hawwoodfarm.co.uk
Total Pitches: 60 (C, CV & T)

Heathfield Farm Camping
Heathfield Road, Freshwater,
Isle of Wight
PO40 9SH
Tel: 01983 407822 **13 P7**
heathfieldcamping.co.uk
Total Pitches: 75 (C, CV & T)

Heathland Beach Caravan Park
London Road, Kessingland
NR33 7PJ
Tel: 01502 740337 **65 Q4**
heathlandbeach.co.uk
Total Pitches: 63 (C, CV & T)

Hele Valley Holiday Park
Hele Bay, Ilfracombe
EX34 9RD
Tel: 01271 862460 **17 J2**
helevalley.co.uk
Total Pitches: 50 (C, CV & T)

Hendra Holiday Park
Newquay
TR8 4NY
Tel: 01637 875778 **4 C9**
hendra-holidays.com
Total Pitches: 548 (C, CV & T)

Herding Hill Farm
Shield Hill, Haltwhistle
NE49 9NW
Tel: 01434 320175 **111 P7**
herdinghillfarm.co.uk
Total Pitches: 22 (C, CV & T)

Hidden Valley Park
West Down, Braunton,
Ilfracombe
EX34 8NU
Tel: 01271 813837 **17 J3**
hiddenvalleypark.com
Total Pitches: 100 (C, CV & T)

Highfield Farm Touring Park
Long Road, Comberton,
Cambridge
CB23 7DG
Tel: 01223 262308 **62 E9**
highfieldfarmtouringpark.co.uk
Total Pitches: 120 (C, CV & T)

Highlands End Holiday Park
Eype, Bridport, Dorset
DT6 6AR
Tel: 01308 422139 **11 K6**
wdlh.co.uk
Total Pitches: 195 (C, CV & T)

Hill Cottage Farm C & C Park
Sandleheath Road, Alderholt,
Fordingbridge
SP6 3EG
Tel: 01425 650513 **13 K2**
hillcottagefarmcampingand
caravanpark.co.uk
Total Pitches: 95 (C, CV & T)

Hill of Oaks & Blakeholme
Windermere
LA12 8NR
Tel: 015395 31578 **94 H3**
hillofoaks.co.uk
Total Pitches: 43 (C & CV)

Hillside Caravan Park
Canvas Farm, Moor Road,
Knayton, Thirsk
YO7 4BR
Tel: 01845 537349 **97 P3**
hillsidecaravanpark.co.uk
Total Pitches: 50 (C & CV)

Holiday Resort Unity
Coast Road, Brean Sands, Brean
TA8 2RB
Tel: 01278 751235 **19 J4**
hru.co.uk
Total Pitches: 1114 (C, CV & T)

Hollins Farm C & C
Far Arnside, Carnforth
LA5 0SL
Tel: 01524 701767 **95 J5**
holgates.co.uk
Total Pitches: 12 (C, CV & T)

Hylton Caravan Park
Eden Street, Silloth
CA7 4AY
Tel: 016973 31707 **109 P10**
stanwix.com
Total Pitches: 90 (C, CV & T)

Island Lodge C & C Site
Stumpy Post Cross,
Kingsbridge
TQ7 4BL
Tel: 01548 852956 **7 J9**
islandlodgesite.co.uk
Total Pitches: 30 (C, CV & T)

Isle of Avalon Touring Caravan Park
Godney Road,
Glastonbury
BA6 9AF
Tel: 01458 833618 **19 N7**
avaloncaravanpark.co.uk
Total Pitches: 120 (C, CV & T)

Jacobs Mount Caravan Park
Jacobs Mount, Stepney Road,
Scarborough
YO12 5NL
Tel: 01723 361178 **99 L3**
jacobsmount.com
Total Pitches: 156 (C, CV & T)

Jasmine Caravan Park
Cross Lane, Snainton,
Scarborough
YO13 9BE
Tel: 01723 859240 **99 J4**
jasminepark.co.uk
Total Pitches: 68 (C, CV & T)

Kenneggy Cove Holiday Park
Higher Kenneggy, Rosudgeon,
Penzance
TR20 9AU
Tel: 01736 763453 **2 F8**
kenneggycove.co.uk
Total Pitches: 40 (C, CV & T)

Kennford International Caravan Park
Kennford, Exeter
EX6 7YN
Tel: 01392 833046 **9 M7**
kennfordinternational.co.uk
Total Pitches: 87 (C, CV & T)

King's Lynn C & C Park
New Road, North Runcton,
King's Lynn
PE33 0RA
Tel: 01553 840004 **75 M7**
kl-cc.co.uk
Total Pitches: 150 (C, CV & T)

Kneps Farm Holiday Park
River Road, Stanah,
Thornton-Cleveleys, Blackpool
FY5 5LR
Tel: 01253 823632 **88 D2**
knepsfarm.co.uk
Total Pitches: 40 (C & CV)

Knight Stainforth Hall Caravan & Campsite
Stainforth, Settle
BD24 0DP
Tel: 01729 822200 **96 B7**
knightstainforth.co.uk
Total Pitches: 100 (C, CV & T)

Ladycross Plantation Caravan Park
Egton, Whitby
YO21 1UA
Tel: 01947 895502 **105 M9**
ladycrossplantation.co.uk
Total Pitches: 130 (C, CV & T)

Lady's Mile Holiday Park
Dawlish, Devon
EX7 0LX
Tel: 01626 863411 **9 N9**
ladysmile.co.uk
Total Pitches: 570 (C, CV & T)

Lakeland Leisure Park
Moor Lane,
Flookburgh
LA11 7LT
Tel: 01539 558556 **94 H6**
haven.com/lakeland
Total Pitches: 977 (C, CV & T)

Lamb Cottage Caravan Park
Dalefords Lane, Whitegate,
Northwich
CW8 2BN
Tel: 01606 882302 **82 D11**
lambcottage.co.uk
Total Pitches: 45 (C & CV)

Langstone Manor C & C Park
Moortown, Tavistock
PL19 9JZ
Tel: 01822 613371 **6 E4**
langstone-manor.co.uk
Total Pitches: 40 (C, CV & T)

Lanyon Holiday Park
Loscombe Lane, Four Lanes,
Redruth
TR16 6LP
Tel: 01209 313474 **2 H6**
lanyonholidaypark.co.uk
Total Pitches: 25 (C, CV & T)

Lebberston Touring Park
Filey Road, Lebberston,
Scarborough
YO11 3PE
Tel: 01723 585723 **99 M4**
lebberstontouring.co.uk
Total Pitches: 125 (C & CV)

Lickpenny Caravan Site
Lickpenny Lane, Tansley,
Matlock
DE4 5GF
Tel: 01629 583040 **84 D9**
lickpennycaravanpark.co.uk
Total Pitches: 80 (C & CV)

Lime Tree Park
Dukes Drive, Buxton
SK17 9RP
Tel: 01298 22988 **83 N10**
limetreeparkbuxton.com
Total Pitches: 106 (C, CV & T)

Lincoln Farm Park Oxfordshire
High Street, Standlake
OX29 7RH
Tel: 01865 300239 **34 C4**
lincolnfarmpark.co.uk
Total Pitches: 90 (C, CV & T)

Littlesea Holiday Park
Lynch Lane, Weymouth
DT4 9DT
Tel: 01305 774414 **11 P9**
haven.com/littlesea
Total Pitches: 861 (C, CV & T)

Long Acres Touring Park
Station Road, Old Leake, Boston
PE22 9RF
Tel: 01205 871555 **87 L10**
long-acres.co.uk
Total Pitches: 40 (C, CV & T)

Longnor Wood Holiday Park
Newtown, Longnor, Nr Buxton
SK17 0NG
Tel: 01298 83648 **71 K2**
longnorwood.co.uk
Total Pitches: 47 (C, CV & T)

Lower Polladras Touring Park
Carleen, Breage, Helston
TR13 9NX
Tel: 01736 762220 **2 G7**
lower-polladras.co.uk
Total Pitches: 39 (C, CV & T)

Lowther Holiday Park
Eamont Bridge, Penrith
CA10 2JB
Tel: 01768 863631 **101 P5**
lowther-holidaypark.co.uk
Total Pitches: 180 (C, CV & T)

Manor Wood Country Caravan Park
Manor Wood, Coddington,
Chester
CH3 9EN
Tel: 01829 782990 **69 N3**
cheshire-caravan-sites.co.uk
Total Pitches: 45 (C, CV & T)

Marton Mere Holiday Village
Mythop Road, Blackpool
FY4 4XN
Tel: 01253 767544 **88 C4**
haven.com/martonmere
Total Pitches: 782 (C & CV)

Mayfield Park
Cheltenham Road, Cirencester
GL7 7BH
Tel: 01285 831301 **33 K3**
mayfieldpark.co.uk
Total Pitches: 105 (C, CV & T)

Meadowbank Holidays
Stour Way, Christchurch
BH23 2PQ
Tel: 01202 483597 **13 K6**
meadowbank-holidays.co.uk
Total Pitches: 41 (C, CV & T)

Middlewood Farm Holiday Park
Middlewood Lane, Fylingthorpe,
Robin Hood's Bay, Whitby
YO22 4UF
Tel: 01947 880414 **105 P10**
middlewoodfarm.com
Total Pitches: 100 (C, CV & T)

Minnows Touring Park
Holbrook Lane,
Sampford Peverell
EX16 7EN
Tel: 01884 821770 **18 D11**
minnowstouringpark.co.uk
Total Pitches: 59 (C, CV & T)

Moon & Sixpence
Newbourn Road, Waldringfield,
Woodbridge
IP12 4PP
Tel: 01473 736650 **53 N2**
moonandsixpence.eu
Total Pitches: 50 (C & CV)

Moor Lodge Park
Blackmoor Lane,
Bardsey, Leeds
LS17 9DZ
Tel: 01937 572424 **91 K2**
moorlodgecaravanpark.co.uk
Total Pitches: 12 (C & CV)

Moss Wood Caravan Park
Crimbles Lane, Cockerham
LA2 0ES
Tel: 01524 791041 **95 K11**
mosswood.co.uk
Total Pitches: 25 (C, CV & T)

Naburn Lock Caravan Park
Naburn
YO19 4RU
Tel: 01904 728697 **98 C11**
naburnlock.co.uk
Total Pitches: 100 (C, CV & T)

New Lodge Farm C & C Site
New Lodge Farm, Bulwick, Corby
NN17 3DU
Tel: 01780 450493 **73 P11**
newlodgefarm.com
Total Pitches: 72 (C, CV & T)

Newberry Valley Park
Woodlands, Combe Martin
EX34 0AT
Tel: 01271 882334 **17 K2**
newberryvalleypark.co.uk
Total Pitches: 110 (C, CV & T)

Newlands Holidays
Charmouth, Bridport
DT6 6RB
Tel: 01297 560259 **10 H6**
newlandsholidays.co.uk
Total Pitches: 240 (C, CV & T)

Newperran Holiday Park
Rejerrah, Newquay
TR8 5QJ
Tel: 01872 572407 **3 K3**
newperran.co.uk
Total Pitches: 357 (C, CV & T)

Ninham Country Holidays
Ninham, Shanklin, Isle of Wight
PO37 7PL
Tel: 01983 864243 **14 G10**
ninham-holidays.co.uk
Total Pitches: 135 (C, CV & T)

North Morte Farm C & C Park
North Morte Road, Mortehoe,
Woolacombe
EX34 7EG
Tel: 01271 870381 **16 H2**
northmortefarm.co.uk
Total Pitches: 180 (C, CV & T)

Northam Farm Caravan & Touring Park
Brean, Burnham-on-Sea
TA8 2SE
Tel: 01278 751244 **19 K3**
northamfarm.co.uk
Total Pitches: 350 (C, CV & T)

Oakdown Country Holiday Park
Gatedown Lane, Weston,
Sidmouth
EX10 0PT
Tel: 01297 680387 **10 D6**
oakdown.co.uk
Total Pitches: 150 (C, CV & T)

Old Hall Caravan Park
Capernwray, Carnforth
LA6 1AD
Tel: 01524 733276 **95 L6**
oldhallcaravanpark.co.uk
Total Pitches: 38 (C & CV)

Ord House Country Park
East Ord, Berwick-upon-Tweed
TD15 2NS
Tel: 01289 305288 **129 P9**
ordhouse.co.uk
Total Pitches: 79 (C, CV & T)

Otterington Park
Station Farm, South Otterington,
Northallerton
DL7 9JB
Tel: 01609 780656 **97 N3**
otteringtonpark.com
Total Pitches: 67 (C & CV)

Oxon Hall Touring Park
Welshpool Road, Shrewsbury
SY3 5FB
Tel: 01743 340868 **56 H2**
morris-leisure.co.uk
Total Pitches: 105 (C, CV & T)

Padstow Touring Park
Padstow
PL28 8LE
Tel: 01841 532061 **4 E7**
padstowtouringpark.co.uk
Total Pitches: 150 (C, CV & T)

Park Cliffe C & C Estate
Birks Road, Tower Wood,
Windermere
LA23 3PG
Tel: 015395 31344 **94 H2**
parkcliffe.co.uk
Total Pitches: 60 (C, CV & T)

Parkers Farm Holiday Park
Higher Mead Farm,
Ashburton, Devon
TQ13 7LJ
Tel: 01364 654869 **7 K4**
parkersfarmholidays.co.uk
Total Pitches: 100 (C, CV & T)

Park Foot C & C Estate
Howtown Road,
Pooley Bridge
CA10 2NA
Tel: 017684 86309 **101 N6**
parkfoottullswater.co.uk
Total Pitches: 454 (C, CV & T)

Parkland C & C Site
Sorley Green Cross, Kingsbridge
TQ7 4AF
Tel: 01548 852723 **7 J9**
parklandsite.co.uk
Total Pitches: 50 (C, CV & T)

Penrose Holiday Park
Goonhavern, Truro
TR4 9QF
Tel: 01872 573185 **3 K3**
penroseholidaypark.com
Total Pitches: 110 (C, CV & T)

Pentire Haven Holiday Park
Stibb Road, Kilkhampton, Bude
EX23 9QY
Tel: 01288 321601 **16 C9**
pentirehaven.co.uk
Total Pitches: 120 (C, CV & T)

Perran Sands Holiday Park
Perranporth, Truro
TR6 0AQ
Tel: 01872 573551 **4 B10**
haven.com/perransands
Total Pitches: 1012 (C, CV & T)

Petwood Caravan Park
Off Stixwould Road,
Woodhall Spa
LN10 6QH
Tel: 01526 354799 **86 G8**
petwoodcaravanpark.com
Total Pitches: 98 (C, CV & T)

Polmanter Touring Park
Halsetown, St Ives
TR26 3LX
Tel: 01736 795640 **2 E6**
polmanter.co.uk
Total Pitches: 270 (C, CV & T)

Porthtowan Tourist Park
Mile Hill, Porthtowan, Truro
TR4 8TY
Tel: 01209 890256 **2 H4**
porthtowantouristpark.co.uk
Total Pitches: 80 (C, CV & T)

Quantock Orchard Caravan Park
Flaxpool, Crowcombe,
Taunton
TA4 4AW
Tel: 01984 618618 **18 F7**
quantock-orchard.co.uk
Total Pitches: 60 (C, CV & T)

Ranch Caravan Park
Station Road, Honeybourne,
Evesham
WR11 7PR
Tel: 01386 830744 **47 M6**
ranch.co.uk
Total Pitches: 120 (C, CV & T)

Ripley Caravan Park
Knaresborough Road,
Ripley, Harrogate
HG3 3AU
Tel: 01423 770050 **97 L8**
ripleycaravanpark.com
Total Pitches: 60 (C, CV & T)

River Dart Country Park
Holne Park, Ashburton
TQ13 7NP
Tel: 01364 652511 **7 J5**
riverdart.co.uk
Total Pitches: 170 (C, CV & T)

River Valley Holiday Park
London Apprentice, St Austell
PL26 7AP
Tel: 01726 73533 **3 Q3**
rivervalleyholidaypark.co.uk
Total Pitches: 45 (C, CV & T)

Riverside C & C Park
Marsh Lane, North Molton Road,
South Molton
EX36 3HQ
Tel: 01769 579269 **17 N6**
exmoorriverside.co.uk
Total Pitches: 58 (C, CV & T)

Riverside Caravan Park
High Bentham, Lancaster
LA2 7FJ
Tel: 015242 61272 **95 P7**
riversidecaravanpark.co.uk
Total Pitches: 61 (C & CV)

Riverside Holiday Park
Southport New Road, Southport
PR9 8DF
Tel: 01704 228886 **88 E7**
riversideleisurecentre.co.uk
Total Pitches: 615 (C & CV)

Riverside Meadows Country Caravan Park
Ure Bank Top, Ripon
HG4 1JD
Tel: 01765 602964 **97 M6**
flowerofmay.com
Total Pitches: 80 (C, CV & T)

Robin Hood C & C Park
Green Dyke Lane, Slingsby
YO62 4AP
Tel: 01653 628391 **98 E6**
robinhoodcaravanpark.co.uk
Total Pitches: 32 (C, CV & T)

Rose Farm Touring & Camping Park
Stepshort, Belton,
Nr Great Yarmouth
NR31 9JS
Tel: 01493 780896 **77 P11**
rosefarmtouringpark.co.uk
Total Pitches: 145 (C, CV & T)

Rosedale C & C Park
Rosedale Abbey, Pickering
YO18 8SA
Tel: 01751 417272 **105 K11**
flowerofmay.com
Total Pitches: 100 (C, CV & T)

Ross Park
Park Hill Farm, Ipplepen,
Newton Abbot
TQ12 5TT
Tel: 01803 812983 **7 L5**
rossparkcaravanpark.co.uk
Total Pitches: 110 (C, CV & T)

Rudding Holiday Park
Follifoot, Harrogate
HG3 1JH
Tel: 01423 870439 **97 M10**
ruddingholidaypark.co.uk
Total Pitches: 86 (C, CV & T)

Run Cottage Touring Park
Alderton Road, Hollesley,
Woodbridge
IP12 3RQ
Tel: 01394 411309 **53 Q3**
runcottage.co.uk
Total Pitches: 45 (C, CV & T)

Rutland C & C
Park Lane, Greetham, Oakham
LE15 7FN
Tel: 01572 813520 **73 N8**
rutlandcaravanandcamping.co.uk
Total Pitches: 130 (C, CV & T)

St Helens Caravan Park
Wykeham, Scarborough
YO13 9QD
Tel: 01723 862771 **99 K4**
sthelenscaravanpark.co.uk
Total Pitches: 250 (C, CV & T)

St Ives Bay Holiday Park
73 Loggans Road,
Upton Towans, Hayle
TR27 5BH
Tel: 01736 752274 **2 F6**
stivesbay.co.uk
Total Pitches: 507 (C, CV & T)

St Mabyn Holiday Park
Longstone Road, St Mabyn,
Wadebridge
PL30 3BY
Tel: 01208 841677 **4 H7**
stmabynholidaypark.co.uk
Total Pitches: 120 (C, CV & T)

Salcombe Regis C & C Park
Salcombe Regis, Sidmouth
EX10 0JH
Tel: 01395 514303 **10 D7**
salcombe-regis.co.uk
Total Pitches: 110 (C, CV & T)

Sand le Mere Holiday Village
Southfield Lane, Tunstall
HU12 0JF
Tel: 01964 670403 **93 P4**
sand-le-mere.co.uk
Total Pitches: 89 (C & CV)

Sandy Balls Holiday Village
Sandy Balls Estate Ltd, Godshill,
Fordingbridge
SP6 2JZ
Tel: 01442 508850 **13 L2**
sandyballs.co.uk
Total Pitches: 225 (C, CV & T)

Searles Leisure Resort
South Beach Road,
Hunstanton
PE36 5BB
Tel: 01485 534211 **75 N3**
searles.co.uk
Total Pitches: 413 (C, CV & T)

Seaview Holiday Park
Preston, Weymouth
DT3 6DZ
Tel: 01305 832271 **11 Q8**
haven.com/seaview
Total Pitches: 347 (C, CV & T)

Seaview International Holiday Park
Boswinger, Mevagissey
PL26 6LL
Tel: 01726 843425 **3 P5**
seaviewinternational.com
Total Pitches: 201 (C, CV & T)

Severn Gorge Park
Bridgnorth Road, Tweedale,
Telford
TF7 4JB
Tel: 01952 684789 **57 N3**
severngorgepark.co.uk
Total Pitches: 12 (C & CV)

Shamba Holidays
East Moors Lane, St Leonards,
Ringwood
BH24 2SB
Tel: 01202 873302 **13 K4**
shambaholidays.co.uk
Total Pitches: 150 (C, CV & T)

Shrubbery Touring Park
Rousdon, Lyme Regis
DT7 3XW
Tel: 01297 442227 **10 F6**
shrubberypark.co.uk
Total Pitches: 120 (C, CV & T)

Silverbow Park
Perranwell, Goonhavern
TR4 9NX
Tel: 01872 572347 **3 K3**
silverbowpark.co.uk
Total Pitches: 90 (C, CV & T)

Silverdale Caravan Park
Middlebarrow Plain,
Cove Road, Silverdale,
Nr Carnforth
LA5 0SH
Tel: 01524 701508 **95 K5**
holgates.co.uk
Total Pitches: 80 (C, CV & T)

Skelwith Fold Caravan Park
Ambleside, Cumbria
LA22 0HX
Tel: 015394 32277 **101 L10**
skelwith.com
Total Pitches: 150 (C & CV)

Skirlington Leisure Park
Driffield, Skipsea
YO25 8SY
Tel: 01262 468213 **99 P10**
skirlington.com
Total Pitches: 930 (C & CV)

Somers Wood Caravan Park
Somers Road, Meriden
CV7 7PL
Tel: 01676 522978 **59 K8**
somerswood.co.uk
Total Pitches: 48 (C & CV)

South Lytchett Manor C & C Park
Dorchester Road, Lytchett
Minster, Poole
BH16 6JB
Tel: 01202 622577 **12 G6**
southlytchettmanor.co.uk
Total Pitches: 150 (C, CV & T)

South Meadows Caravan Park
South Road,
Belford
NE70 7DP
Tel: 01668 213326 **119 M4**
southmeadows.co.uk
Total Pitches: 83 (C, CV & T)

Stanmore Hall Touring Park
Stourbridge Road, Bridgnorth
WV15 6DT
Tel: 01746 761761 **57 N6**
morris-leisure.co.uk
Total Pitches: 129 (C, CV & T)

Stanwix Park Holiday Centre
Greenrow, Silloth
CA7 4HH
Tel: 016973 32666 **109 P10**
stanwix.com
Total Pitches: 337 (C, CV & T)

Stowford Farm Meadows
Berry Down,
Combe Martin
EX34 0PW
Tel: 01271 882476 **17 K3**
stowford.co.uk
Total Pitches: 700 (C, CV & T)

Stroud Hill Park
Fen Road, Pidley, St Ives
PE28 3DE
Tel: 01487 741333 **62 D5**
stroudhillpark.co.uk
Total Pitches: 60 (C, CV & T)

Sumners Ponds Fishery & Campsite
Chapel Road, Barns Green,
Horsham
RH13 0PR
Tel: 01403 732539 **24 D5**
sumnersponds.co.uk
Total Pitches: 86 (C, CV & T)

Swiss Farm Touring & Camping
Marlow Road,
Henley-on-Thames
RG9 2HY
Tel: 01491 573419 **35 L8**
swissfarmcamping.co.uk
Total Pitches: 140 (C, CV & T)

Tanner Farm Touring C & C Park
Tanner Farm, Goudhurst Road,
Marden
TN12 9ND
Tel: 01622 832399 **26 B3**
tannerfarmpark.co.uk
Total Pitches: 120 (C, CV & T)

Tattershall Lakes Country Park
Sleaford Road, Tattershall
LN4 4LR
Tel: 01526 348800 **86 H9**
tattershall-lakes.com
Total Pitches: 186 (C, CV & T)

Tehidy Holiday Park
Harris Mill, Illogan,
Portreath
TR16 4JQ
Tel: 01209 216489 **2 H5**
tehidy.co.uk
Total Pitches: 18 (C, CV & T)

Tencreek Holiday Park
Polperro Road, Looe
PL13 2JR
Tel: 01503 262447 **5 L11**
dolphinholidays.co.uk
Total Pitches: 355 (C, CV & T)

Teversal C & C Club Site
Silverhill Lane, Teversal
NG17 3JJ
Tel: 01623 551838 **84 G8**
campingandcaravanning
club.co.uk/teversal
Total Pitches: 126 (C, CV & T)

The Laurels Holiday Park
Padstow Road, Whitecross,
Wadebridge
PL27 7JQ
Tel: 01209 313474 **4 F7**
thelaurelsholidaypark.co.uk
Total Pitches: 30 (C, CV & T)

The Old Brick Kilns
Little Barney Lane, Barney,
Fakenham
NR21 0NL
Tel: 01328 878305 **76 E5**
old-brick-kilns.co.uk
Total Pitches: 65 (C, CV & T)

The Old Oaks Touring Park
Wick Farm, Wick,
Glastonbury
BA6 8JS
Tel: 01458 831437 **19 P7**
theoldoaks.co.uk
Total Pitches: 98 (C, CV & T)

The Orchards Holiday Caravan Park
Main Road, Newbridge,
Yarmouth, Isle of Wight
PO41 0TS
Tel: 01983 531331 **14 D9**
orchards-holiday-park.co.uk
Total Pitches: 160 (C, CV & T)

The Quiet Site
Ullswater,
Watermillock
CA11 0LS
Tel: 07768 727016 **101 M6**
thequietsite.co.uk
Total Pitches: 100 (C, CV & T)

The Ranch Caravan Park
Cliffe Common,
Selby
YO8 6PA
Tel: 01757 638984 **91 R4**
theranchcaravanpark.co.uk
Total Pitches: 44 (C, CV & T)

Thornwick Bay Holiday Village
North Marine Road,
Flamborough
YO15 1AU
Tel: 01262 850569 **99 Q6**
haven.com/parks/yorkshire/
thornwick-bay
Total Pitches: 225 (C, CV & T)

Thorpe Park Holiday Centre
Cleethorpes
DN35 0PW
Tel: 01472 813395 **93 P9**
haven.com/thorpepark
Total Pitches: 1491 (C, CV & T)

Treago Farm Caravan Site
Crantock,
Newquay
TR8 5QS
Tel: 01637 830277 **4 B9**
treagofarm.co.uk
Total Pitches: 90 (C, CV & T)

Tregoad Park
St Martin, Looe
PL13 1PB
Tel: 01503 262718 **5 M10**
tregoadpark.co.uk
Total Pitches: 200 (C, CV & T)

Treloy Touring Park
Newquay
TR8 4JN
Tel: 01637 872063 **4 D9**
treloy.co.uk
Total Pitches: 223 (C, CV & T)

Trencreek Holiday Park
Hillcrest, Higher Trencreek,
Newquay
TR8 4NS
Tel: 01637 874210 **4 C9**
trencreekholidaypark.co.uk
Total Pitches: 194 (C, CV & T)

Trethem Mill Touring Park
St Just-in-Roseland,
Nr St Mawes, Truro
TR2 5JF
Tel: 01872 580504 **3 M6**
trethem.com
Total Pitches: 84 (C, CV & T)

Trevalgan Touring Park
Trevalgan, St Ives
TR26 3BJ
Tel: 01736 791892 **2 D6**
trevalgantouringpark.co.uk
Total Pitches: 135 (C, CV & T)

Trevedra Farm C & C Site
Sennen, Penzance
TR19 7BE
Tel: 01736 871818 **2 B8**
trevedrafarm.co.uk
Total Pitches: 100 (C, CV & T)

Trevella Park
Crantock, Newquay
TR8 5EW
Tel: 01637 830308 **4 C10**
trevella.co.uk
Total Pitches: 165 (C, CV & T)

Trevornick
Holywell Bay,
Newquay
TR8 5PW
Tel: 01637 830531 **4 B10**
trevornick.co.uk
Total Pitches: 688 (C, CV & T)

Truro C & C Park
Truro
TR4 8QN
Tel: 01872 560274 **3 K4**
trurocaravanandcamping
park.co.uk
Total Pitches: 51 (C, CV & T)

Tudor C & C
Shepherds Patch, Slimbridge,
Gloucester
GL2 7BP
Tel: 01453 890483 **32 D4**
tudorcaravanpark.com
Total Pitches: 75 (C, CV & T)

Twitchen House Holiday Park
Mortehoe Station Road,
Mortehoe, Woolacombe
EX34 7ES
Tel: 01271 872302 **16 H3**
woolacombe.com
Total Pitches: 569 (C, CV & T)

Two Mills Touring Park
Yarmouth Road,
North Walsham
NR28 9NA
Tel: 01692 405829 **77 K6**
twomills.co.uk
Total Pitches: 81 (C, CV & T)

Ulwell Cottage Caravan Park
Ulwell Cottage, Ulwell,
Swanage
BH19 3DG
Tel: 01929 422823 **12 H8**
ulwellcottagepark.co.uk
Total Pitches: 77 (C, CV & T)

Vale of Pickering Caravan Park
Carr House Farm,
Allerston, Pickering
YO18 7PQ
Tel: 01723 859280 **98 H4**
valeofpickering.co.uk
Total Pitches: 120 (C, CV & T)

Wagtail Country Park
Cliff Lane, Marston,
Grantham
NG32 2HU
Tel: 01400 251955 **73 M2**
wagtailcountrypark.co.uk
Total Pitches: 76 (C & CV)

Waldegraves Holiday Park
Mersea Island,
Colchester
CO5 8SE
Tel: 01206 382898 **52 H9**
waldegraves.co.uk
Total Pitches: 30 (C, CV & T)

Warcombe Farm C & C Park
Station Road, Mortehoe,
Woolacombe
EX34 7EJ
Tel: 01271 870690 **16 H2**
warcombefarm.co.uk
Total Pitches: 250 (C, CV & T)

Wareham Forest Tourist Park
North Trigon,
Wareham
BH20 7NZ
Tel: 01929 551393 **12 E6**
warehamforest.co.uk
Total Pitches: 200 (C, CV & T)

Waren C & C Park
Waren Mill, Bamburgh
NE70 7EE
Tel: 01668 214366 **119 N4**
meadowhead.co.uk
Total Pitches: 150 (C, CV & T)

Warren Farm Holiday Centre
Brean Sands, Brean,
Burnham-on-Sea
TA8 2RP
Tel: 01278 751227 **19 J3**
warren-farm.co.uk
Total Pitches: 975 (C, CV & T)

Watergate Bay Touring Park
Watergate Bay,
Tregurrian
TR8 4AD
Tel: 01637 860387 **4 D8**
watergatebaytouringpark.co.uk
Total Pitches: 171 (C, CV & T)

Waterrow Touring Park
Wiveliscombe,
Taunton
TA4 2AZ
Tel: 01984 623464 **18 E9**
waterrowpark.co.uk
Total Pitches: 44 (C, CV & T)

Wayfarers C & C Park
Relubbus Lane, St Hilary,
Penzance
TR20 9EF
Tel: 01736 763326 **2 F7**
wayfarerspark.co.uk
Total Pitches: 32 (C, CV & T)

Wells Touring Park
Haybridge, Wells
BA5 1AJ
Tel: 01749 676869 **19 P5**
wellstouringpark.co.uk
Total Pitches: 72 (C, CV & T)

Wheathill Touring Park
Wheathill, Bridgnorth
WV16 6QT
Tel: 01584 823456 **57 L8**
wheathillpark.co.uk
Total Pitches: 25 (C & CV)

XV

**Whitecliff Bay
Holiday Park**
Hillway Road, Bembridge,
Whitecliff Bay
PO35 5PL
Tel: 01983 872671 **14 H9**
wight-holidays.com
Total Pitches: 653 (C, CV & T)

**Whitefield Forest
Touring Park**
Brading Road, Ryde,
Isle of Wight
PO33 1QL
Tel: 01983 617069 **14 H9**
whitefieldforest.co.uk
Total Pitches: 90 (C, CV & T)

Whitemead Caravan Park
East Burton Road, Wool
BH20 6HG
Tel: 01929 462241 **12 D7**
whitemeadcaravanpark.co.uk
Total Pitches: 105 (C, CV & T)

**Widdicombe Farm
Touring Park**
Marldon, Paignton
TQ3 1ST
Tel: 01803 558325 **7 M6**
widdicombefarm.co.uk
Total Pitches: 180 (C, CV & T)

Wild Rose Park
Ormside,
Appleby-in-Westmorland
CA16 6EJ
Tel: 017683 51077 **102 C7**
harrisonholidayhomes.co.uk
Total Pitches: 226 (C & CV)

**Wilksworth Farm
Caravan Park**
Cranborne Road,
Wimborne Minster
BH21 4HW
Tel: 01202 885467 **12 H4**
wilksworthfarmcaravanpark.co.uk
Total Pitches: 85 (C, CV & T)

**Willowbank Holiday Home
& Touring Park**
Coastal Road, Ainsdale,
Southport
PR8 3ST
Tel: 01704 571566 **88 C8**
willowbankcp.co.uk
Total Pitches: 87 (C & CV)

Wolds View Touring Park
115 Brigg Road,
Caistor
LN7 6RX
Tel: 01472 851099 **93 K10**
woldsviewtouringpark.co.uk
Total Pitches: 60 (C, CV & T)

Wood Farm C & C Park
Axminster Road,
Charmouth
DT6 6BT
Tel: 01297 560697 **10 H6**
woodfarm.co.uk
Total Pitches: 175 (C, CV & T)

Wooda Farm Holiday Park
Poughill, Bude
EX23 9HJ
Tel: 01288 352069 **16 C10**
wooda.co.uk
Total Pitches: 200 (C, CV & T)

Woodclose Caravan Park
High Casterton,
Kirkby Lonsdale
LA6 2SE
Tel: 015242 71597 **95 N5**
woodclosepark.com
Total Pitches: 22 (C, CV & T)

Woodhall Country Park
Stixwold Road, Woodhall Spa
LN10 6UJ
Tel: 01526 353710 **86 G8**
woodhallcountrypark.co.uk
Total Pitches: 115 (C, CV & T)

**Woodland Springs Adult
Touring Park**
Venton, Drewsteignton
EX6 6PG
Tel: 01647 231695 **8 G6**
woodlandsprings.co.uk
Total Pitches: 81 (C, CV & T)

Woodlands Grove C & C Park
Blackawton,
Dartmouth
TQ9 7DQ
Tel: 01803 712598 **7 L8**
woodlands-caravanpark.com
Total Pitches: 350 (C, CV & T)

Woodovis Park
Gulworthy, Tavistock
PL19 8NY
Tel: 01822 832968 **6 C4**
woodovis.com
Total Pitches: 50 (C, CV & T)

**Woolacombe Bay
Holiday Park & Spa**
Sandy Lane,
Woolacombe
EX34 7AH
Tel: 01271 872302 **16 H3**
woolacombe.com
Total Pitches: 355 (C, CV & T)

SCOTLAND

**Auchenlarie
Holiday Park**
Gatehouse of Fleet
DG7 2EX
Tel: 01556 506200 **107 P7**
swalwellholidaygroup.co.uk
Total Pitches: 451 (C, CV & T)

Beecraigs C & C Site
Beecraigs Country Park,
The Visitor Centre,
Linlithgow
EH49 6PL
Tel: 01506 844516 **127 J3**
beecraigs.com
Total Pitches: 36 (C, CV & T)

**Blair Castle
Caravan Park**
Blair Atholl, Pitlochry
PH18 5SR
Tel: 01796 481263 **141 L4**
blaircastlecaravanpark.co.uk
Total Pitches: 226 (C, CV & T)

**Brighouse Bay
Holiday Park**
Brighouse Bay, Borgue,
Kirkcudbright
DG6 4TS
Tel: 01557 870267 **108 D11**
gillespie-leisure.co.uk
Total Pitches: 190 (C, CV & T)

Cairnsmill Holiday Park
Largo Road, St Andrews
KY16 8NN
Tel: 01334 473604 **135 M5**
cairnsmill.co.uk
Total Pitches: 62 (C, CV & T)

Craig Tara Holiday Park
Ayr
KA7 4LB
Tel: 0800 975 7579 **114 F4**
haven.com/craigtara
Total Pitches: 1144 (C & CV)

**Craigtoun Meadows
Holiday Park**
Mount Melville,
St Andrews
KY16 8PQ
Tel: 01334 475959 **135 M4**
craigtounmeadows.co.uk
Total Pitches: 56 (C, CV & T)

Faskally Caravan Park
Pitlochry
PH16 5LA
Tel: 01796 472007 **141 M6**
faskally.co.uk
Total Pitches: 430 (C, CV & T)

Gart Caravan Park
The Gart, Callander
FK17 8LE
Tel: 01877 330002 **133 J6**
theholidaypark.co.uk
Total Pitches: 128 (C & CV)

Glen Nevis C & C Park
Glen Nevis, Fort William
PH33 6SX
Tel: 01397 702191 **139 L3**
glen-nevis.co.uk
Total Pitches: 380 (C, CV & T)

Glenearly Caravan Park
Dalbeattie
DG5 4NE
Tel: 01556 611393 **108 H8**
glenearlycaravanpark.co.uk
Total Pitches: 39 (C, CV & T)

**Hoddom Castle
Caravan Park**
Hoddom, Lockerbie
DG11 1AS
Tel: 01576 300251 **110 C6**
hoddomcastle.co.uk
Total Pitches: 200 (C, CV & T)

**Huntly Castle
Caravan Park**
The Meadow, Huntly
AB54 4UJ
Tel: 01466 794999 **158 D9**
huntlycastle.co.uk
Total Pitches: 90 (C, CV & T)

Invercoe C & C Park
Ballachulish, Glencoe
PH49 4HP
Tel: 01855 811210 **139 K6**
invercoe.co.uk
Total Pitches: 66 (C, CV & T)

Loch Ken Holiday Park
Parton, Castle Douglas
DG7 3NE
Tel: 01644 470282 **108 E6**
lochkenholidaypark.co.uk
Total Pitches: 40 (C, CV & T)

**Lomond Woods
Holiday Park**
Old Luss Road, Balloch,
Loch Lomond
G83 8QP
Tel: 01389 755000 **132 D11**
holiday-parks.co.uk
Total Pitches: 115 (C & CV)

**Milton of Fonab
Caravan Park**
Bridge Road,
Pitlochry
PH16 5NA
Tel: 01796 472882 **141 M6**
fonab.co.uk
Total Pitches: 154 (C, CV & T)

River Tilt Caravan Park
Blair Atholl,
Pitlochry
PH18 5TE
Tel: 01796 481467 **141 L4**
rivertiltpark.co.uk
Total Pitches: 30 (C, CV & T)

**Sands of Luce
Holiday Park**
Sands of Luce, Sandhead,
Stranraer
DG9 9JN
Tel: 01776 830456 **106 F7**
sandsofluceholidaypark.co.uk
Total Pitches: 80 (C, CV & T)

Seaward Caravan Park
Dhoon Bay,
Kirkcudbright
DG6 4TJ
Tel: 01557 870267 **108 E11**
gillespie-leisure.co.uk
Total Pitches: 25 (C, CV & T)

**Seton Sands
Holiday Village**
Longniddry
EH32 0QF
Tel: 01875 813333 **128 C4**
haven.com/setonsands
Total Pitches: 640 (C & CV)

**Silver Sands
Holiday Park**
Covesea, West Beach,
Lossiemouth
IV31 6SP
Tel: 01343 813262 **157 N3**
silver-sands.co.uk
Total Pitches: 140 (C, CV & T)

Skye C & C Club Site
Loch Greshornish, Borve,
Arnisort, Edinbane,
Isle of Skye
IV51 9PS
Tel: 01470 582230 **152 E7**
campingandcaravanning
club.co.uk/skye
Total Pitches: 105 (C, CV & T)

**Thurston Manor
Leisure Park**
Innerwick, Dunbar
EH42 1SA
Tel: 01368 840643 **129 J5**
thurstonmanor.co.uk
Total Pitches: 120 (C & CV)

Trossachs Holiday Park
Aberfoyle
FK8 3SA
Tel: 01877 382614 **132 G8**
trossachsholidays.co.uk
Total Pitches: 66 (C, CV & T)

Witches Craig C & C Park
Blairlogie,
Stirling
FK9 5PX
Tel: 01786 474947 **133 N8**
witchescraig.co.uk
Total Pitches: 60 (C, CV & T)

WALES

**Bron Derw Touring
Caravan Park**
Llanrwst
LL26 0YT
Tel: 01492 640494 **67 P2**
bronderw-wales.co.uk
Total Pitches: 48 (C & CV)

**Bron-Y-Wendon
Caravan Park**
Wern Road, Llanddulas,
Colwyn Bay
LL22 8HG
Tel: 01492 512903 **80 C9**
northwales-holidays.co.uk
Total Pitches: 130 (C & CV)

**Caerfai Bay Caravan
& Tent Park**
Caerfai Bay, St Davids,
Haverfordwest
SA62 6QT
Tel: 01437 720274 **40 E6**
caerfaibay.co.uk
Total Pitches: 106 (C, CV & T)

**Cenarth Falls
Holiday Park**
Cenarth,
Newcastle Emlyn
SA38 9JS
Tel: 01239 710345 **41 Q2**
cenarth-holipark.co.uk
Total Pitches: 30 (C, CV & T)

Daisy Bank Caravan Park
Snead, Montgomery
SY15 6EB
Tel: 01588 620471 **56 E6**
daisy-bank.co.uk
Total Pitches: 80 (C, CV & T)

Dinlle Caravan Park
Dinas Dinlle,
Caernarfon
LL54 5TW
Tel: 01286 830324 **66 G3**
thornleyleisure.co.uk
Total Pitches: 175 (C, CV & T)

Eisteddfa
Eisteddfa Lodge, Pentrefelin,
Criccieth
LL52 0PT
Tel: 01766 522696 **67 J7**
eisteddfapark.co.uk
Total Pitches: 100 (C, CV & T)

Fforest Fields C & C Park
Hundred House,
Builth Wells
LD1 5RT
Tel: 01982 570406 **44 G4**
fforestfields.co.uk
Total Pitches: 120 (C, CV & T)

Fishguard Bay Resort
Garn Gelli, Fishguard
SA65 9ET
Tel: 01348 811415 **41 J3**
fishguardbay.com
Total Pitches: 102 (C, CV & T)

Greenacres Holiday Park
Black Rock Sands,
Morfa Bychan,
Porthmadog
LL49 9YF
Tel: 01766 512781 **67 J7**
haven.com/greenacres
Total Pitches: 945 (C & CV)

Hafan y Môr Holiday Park
Pwllheli
LL53 6HJ
Tel: 01758 612112 **66 G7**
haven.com/hafanymor
Total Pitches: 875 (C & CV)

**Hendre Mynach Touring
C & C Park**
Llanaber Road,
Barmouth
LL42 1YR
Tel: 01341 280262 **67 L11**
hendremynach.co.uk
Total Pitches: 240 (C, CV & T)

Home Farm Caravan Park
Marian-glas,
Isle of Anglesey
LL73 8PH
Tel: 01248 410614 **78 H8**
homefarm-anglesey.co.uk
Total Pitches: 102 (C, CV & T)

Islawrffordd Caravan Park
Tal-y-bont, Barmouth
LL43 2AQ
Tel: 01341 247269 **67 K10**
islawrffordd.co.uk
Total Pitches: 105 (C, CV & T)

Kiln Park Holiday Centre
Marsh Road,
Tenby
SA70 8RB
Tel: 01834 844121 **41 M10**
haven.com/kilnpark
Total Pitches: 849 (C, CV & T)

Pencelli Castle C & C Park
Pencelli, Brecon
LD3 7LX
Tel: 01874 665451 **44 F10**
pencelli-castle.com
Total Pitches: 80 (C, CV & T)

**Penisar Mynydd
Caravan Park**
Caerwys Road, Rhuallt,
St Asaph
LL17 0TY
Tel: 01745 582227 **80 F9**
penisarmynydd.co.uk
Total Pitches: 71 (C, CV & T)

Plassey Holiday Park
The Plassey, Eyton,
Wrexham
LL13 0SP
Tel: 01978 780277 **69 L5**
plassey.com
Total Pitches: 90 (C, CV & T)

Pont Kemys C & C Park
Chainbridge,
Abergavenny
NP7 9DS
Tel: 01873 880688 **31 K3**
pontkemys.com
Total Pitches: 65 (C, CV & T)

**Presthaven Sands
Holiday Park**
Gronant, Prestatyn
LL19 9TT
Tel: 01745 856471 **80 F8**
haven.com/presthavensands
Total Pitches: 1102 (C, CV & T)

Red Kite Touring Park
Van Road, Llanidloes
SY18 6NG
Tel: 01686 412122 **55 L7**
redkitetouringpark.co.uk
Total Pitches: 66 (C & CV)

River View Touring Park
The Dingle, Llanedi,
Pontarddulais
SA4 0FH
Tel: 01635 844876 **28 G3**
riverviewtouringpark.com
Total Pitches: 60 (C, CV & T)

Riverside Camping
Seiont Nurseries, Pont Rug,
Caernarfon
LL55 2BB
Tel: 01286 678781 **67 J2**
riversidecamping.co.uk
Total Pitches: 73 (C, CV & T)

**The Trotting Mare
Caravan Park**
Overton, Wrexham
LL13 0LE
Tel: 01978 711963 **69 L7**
thetrottingmare.co.uk
Total Pitches: 65 (C, CV & T)

Trawsdir Touring C & C Park
Llanaber, Barmouth
LL42 1RR
Tel: 01341 280999 **67 K11**
barmouthholidays.co.uk
Total Pitches: 70 (C, CV & T)

Trefalun Park
Devonshire Drive, St Florence,
Tenby
SA70 8RD
Tel: 01646 651514 **41 L10**
trefalunpark.co.uk
Total Pitches: 90 (C, CV & T)

Tyddyn Isaf Caravan Park
Lligwy Bay, Dulas, Isle of Anglesey
LL70 9PQ
Tel: 01248 410203 **78 H7**
tyddynisaf.co.uk
Total Pitches: 80 (C, CV & T)

White Tower Caravan Park
Llandwrog, Caernarfon
LL54 5UH
Tel: 01286 830649 **66 H3**
whitetowerpark.co.uk
Total Pitches: 52 (C & CV)

CHANNEL ISLANDS

Fauxquets Valley Campsite
Castel, Guernsey
GY5 7QL
Tel: 01481 255460 **10 b2**
fauxquets.co.uk
Total Pitches: 120 (CV & T)

Rozel Camping Park
Summerville Farm, St Martin,
Jersey
JE3 6AX
Tel: 01534 855200 **11 c1**
rozelcamping.com
Total Pitches: 100 (C, CV & T)

Signs giving orders

**Signs with red circles are mostly prohibitive.
Plates below signs qualify their message.**

Entry to
20mph zone

End of
20mph zone

Maximum
speed

National speed
limit applies

School crossing
patrol

Stop and
give way

Give way to
traffic on
major road

Manually operated temporary
STOP and GO signs

No entry for
vehicular traffic

No vehicles
except bicycles
being pushed

No cycling

No motor
vehicles

No buses
(over 8
passenger
seats)

No
overtaking

No
towed
caravans

No vehicles
carrying
explosives

No vehicle or
combination of
vehicles over
length shown

No vehicles
over
height shown

No vehicles
over
width shown

Give priority to
vehicles from
opposite
direction

No right turn

No left turn

No
U-turns

No goods vehicles
over maximum
gross weight
shown (in tonnes)
except for loading
and unloading

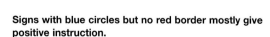

WEAK BRIDGE
No vehicles
over maximum
gross weight
shown
(in tonnes)

Permit holders only
Parking
restricted to
permit holders

RED ROUTE
No stopping
during
period indicated
except for buses

URBAN CLEARWAY
Monday to Friday
am 8.00 - 9.30 pm 4.30 - 6.30
No stopping during
times shown
except for as long
as necessary to set
down or pick up
passengers

No waiting

No stopping
(Clearway)

**Signs with blue circles but no red border mostly give
positive instruction.**

Ahead only

Turn left ahead
(right if symbol
reversed)

Turn left
(right if symbol
reversed)

Keep left
(right if symbol
reversed)

Vehicles may
pass either
side to reach
same
destination

Mini-roundabout
(roundabout
circulation – give
way to vehicles
from the
immediate right)

Route to be
used by pedal
cycles only

Segregated
pedal cycle
and pedestrian
route

Minimum speed

End of minimum
speed

Buses and
cycles only

Trams only

TRAMWAY LOOK BOTH WAYS
Pedestrian
crossing
point over
tramway

One-way traffic
(note: compare
circular 'Ahead
only' sign)

With-flow bus and
cycle lane

Contraflow bus lane

With-flow pedal cycle lane

Warning signs

Mostly triangular

STOP 100 yds
Distance to
'STOP' line
ahead

Dual
carriageway
ends

Road narrows on
right (left if
symbol reversed)

Road
narrows on
both sides

GIVE WAY 50 yds
Distance to
'Give Way'
line ahead

Crossroads

Junction on
bend ahead

T-junction with
priority over
vehicles from
the right

Staggered
junction

Traffic merging
from left ahead

The priority through route is indicated by the broader line.

Double bend first
to left (symbol
may be reversed)

Bend to right
(or left if symbol
reversed)

Roundabout

Uneven road

REDUCE SPEED NOW
Plate below
some signs

Two-way
traffic crosses
one-way road

Two-way traffic
straight ahead

Opening or
swing bridge
ahead

Low-flying aircraft
or sudden
aircraft noise

Falling or
fallen rocks

Traffic signals
not in use

Traffic signals

Slippery road

Steep hill
downwards

Steep hill
upwards

Gradients may be shown as a ratio i.e. 20% = 1:5

Tunnel ahead

Trams crossing ahead

Level crossing with barrier or gate ahead

Level crossing without barrier or gate ahead

Level crossing without barrier

School crossing patrol ahead (some signs have amber lights which flash when crossings are in use)

Frail (or blind or disabled if shown) pedestrians likely to cross road ahead

Pedestrians in road ahead

Zebra crossing

Overhead electric cable; plate indicates maximum height of vehicles which can pass safely

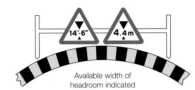
Available width of headroom indicated

Sharp deviation of route to left (or right if chevrons reversed)

Light signals ahead at level crossing, airfield or bridge

Miniature warning lights at level crossings

Cattle

Wild animals

Wild horses or ponies

Accompanied horses or ponies

Cycle route ahead

Risk of ice

Traffic queues likely ahead

Distance over which road humps extend

Other danger; plate indicates nature of danger

Soft verges

Side winds

Hump bridge

Worded warning sign

Quayside or river bank

Risk of grounding

Direction signs

Mostly rectangular

Signs on motorways – blue backgrounds

At a junction leading directly into a motorway (junction number may be shown on a black background)

On approaches to junctions (junction number on black background)

Route confirmatory sign after junction

Downward pointing arrows mean 'Get in lane'
The left-hand lane leads to a different destination from the other lanes.

The panel with the inclined arrow indicates the destinations which can be reached by leaving the motorway at the next junction

Signs on primary routes - green backgrounds

On approaches to junctions

At the junction

Route confirmatory sign after junction

On approaches to junctions

On approach to a junction in Wales (bilingual)

Blue panels indicate that the motorway starts at the junction ahead.
Motorways shown in brackets can also be reached along the route indicated.
White panels indicate local or non-primary routes leading from the junction ahead.
Brown panels show the route to tourist attractions.
The name of the junction may be shown at the top of the sign.
The aircraft symbol indicates the route to an airport.
A symbol may be included to warn of a hazard or restriction along that route.

Signs on non-primary and local routes - black borders

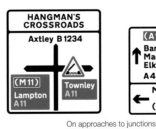
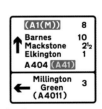
On approaches to junctions

At the junction

Direction to toilets with access for the disabled

Green panels indicate that the primary route starts at the junction ahead.
Route numbers on a blue background show the direction to a motorway.
Route numbers on a green background show the direction to a primary route.

Emergency diversion routes

In an emergency it may be necessary to close a section of motorway or other main road to traffic, so a temporary sign may advise drivers to follow a diversion route. To help drivers navigate the route, black symbols on yellow patches may be permanently displayed on existing direction signs, including motorway signs. Symbols may also be used on separate signs with yellow backgrounds.

For further information visit:
theaa.com/breakdown-cover/advice/emergency-diversion-routes

Note: The signs shown in this road atlas are those most commonly in use and are not all drawn to the same scale. In Scotland and Wales bilingual versions of some signs are used, showing both English and Gaelic or Welsh spellings. Some older designs of signs may still be seen on the roads. A comprehensive explanation of the signing system illustrating the vast majority of road signs can be found in the AA's handbook Know Your Road Signs. Where there is a reference to a rule number, this refers to The Highway Code.

Restricted junctions

Motorway and primary route junctions which have access or exit restrictions are shown on the map pages thus:

M1 London - Leeds

Northbound
Access only from A1 (northbound)

Southbound
Exit only to A1 (southbound)

Northbound
Access only from A41 (northbound)

Southbound
Exit only to A41 (southbound)

Northbound
Access only from M25 (no link from A405)

Southbound
Exit only to M25 (no link from A405)

Northbound
Access only from A414

Southbound
Exit only to A414

Northbound
Exit only to M45

Southbound
Access only from M45

Northbound
Exit only to M6 (northbound)

Southbound
Exit only to A14 (southbound)

Northbound
Exit only, no access

Southbound
Access only, no exit

Northbound
Access only from A42

Southbound
No restriction

Northbound
No exit, access only

Southbound
Exit only, no access

Northbound
Exit only, no access

Southbound
Access only, no exit

Northbound
Exit only to M621

Southbound
Access only from M621

Northbound
Exit only to A1(M) (northbound)

Southbound
Access only from A1(M) (southbound)

M2 Rochester - Faversham

Westbound
No exit to A2 (eastbound)

Eastbound
No access from A2 (westbound)

M3 Sunbury - Southampton

Northeastbound
Access only from A303, no exit

Southwestbound
Exit only to A303, no access

Northbound
Exit only, no access

Southbound
Access only, no exit

Northeastbound
Access from M27 only, no exit

Southwestbound
No access to M27 (westbound)

M4 London - South Wales

For junctions 1 & 2 see London district map on pages 178–181

Westbound
Exit only to M48

Eastbound
Access only from M48

Westbound
Access only from M48

Eastbound
Exit only to M48

Westbound
Exit only, no access

Eastbound
Access only, no exit

Westbound
Exit only, no access

Eastbound
Access only, no exit

Westbound
Exit only to A48(M)

Eastbound
Access only from A48(M)

Westbound
Exit only, no access

Eastbound
No restriction

Westbound
Access only, no exit

Eastbound
No access or exit

Westbound
Exit only to A483

Eastbound
Access only from A483

M5 Birmingham - Exeter

Northeastbound
Access only, no exit

Southwestbound
Exit only, no access

Northeastbound
Access only from A417 (westbound)

Southwestbound
Exit only to A417 (eastbound)

Northeastbound
Exit only to M49

Southwestbound
Access only from M49

Northeastbound
No access, exit only

Southwestbound
No exit, access only

M6 Toll Motorway

See M6 Toll motorway map on page *XXIII*

M6 Rugby - Carlisle

Northbound
Exit only to M6 Toll

Southbound
Access only from M6 Toll

Northbound
Exit only to M42 (southbound) and A446

Southbound
Exit only to A446

Northbound
Access only from M42 (southbound)

Southbound
Exit only to M42

Northbound
Exit only, no access

Southbound
Access only, no exit

Northbound
Exit only to M54

Southbound
Access only from M54

Northbound
Access only from M6 Toll

Southbound
Exit only to M6 Toll

Northbound
No restriction

Southbound
Access only from M56 (eastbound)

Northbound
Exit only to M56 (westbound)

Southbound
Access only from M56 (eastbound)

Northbound
Access only, no exit

Southbound
Exit only, no access

Northbound
Exit only, no access

Southbound
Access only, no exit

Northbound
Access only from M61

Southbound
Exit only to M61

Northbound
Exit only, no access

Southbound
Access only, no exit

Northbound
Exit only, no access

Southbound
Access only, no exit

M8 Edinburgh - Bishopton

For junctions 7A to 28A see Glasgow district map on pages 176–177

Westbound
Exit only, no access

Eastbound
Access only, no exit

Westbound
Access only, no exit

Eastbound
Exit only, no access

Westbound
Access only, no exit

Eastbound
Exit only, no access

M9 Edinburgh - Dunblane

Northwestbound
Access only, no exit

Southeastbound
Exit only, no access

Northwestbound
Exit only, no access

Southeastbound
Access only, no exit

Northwestbound
Access only, no exit

Southeastbound
Exit only to A905

Northwestbound
Exit only to M876
(southwestbound)

Southeastbound
Access only from M876
(northeastbound)

M11 London - Cambridge

Northbound
Access only from A406
(eastbound)

Southbound
Exit only to A406

Northbound
Exit only, no access

Southbound
Access only, no exit

Northbound
Exit only, no access

Southbound
No direct access,
use jct 8

Northbound
Exit only to A11

Southbound
Access only from A11

Northbound
Exit only, no access

Southbound
Access only, no exit

Northbound
Exit only, no access

Southbound
Access only, no exit

M20 Swanley - Folkestone

Northwestbound
Staggered junction; follow
signs - access only

Southeastbound
Staggered junction; follow
signs - exit only

Northwestbound
Exit only to M26
(westbound)

Southeastbound
Access only from M26
(eastbound)

Northwestbound
Access only from A20

Southeastbound
For access follow signs -
exit only to A20

Northwestbound
No restriction

Southeastbound
For exit follow signs

Northwestbound
Access only, no exit

Southeastbound
Exit only, no access

M23 Hooley - Crawley

Northbound
Exit only to A23
(northbound)

Southbound
Access only from A23
(southbound)

Northbound
Access only, no exit

Southbound
Exit only, no access

M25 London Orbital Motorway

See M25 London Orbital motorway map on
page *XXII*

M26 Sevenoaks - Wrotham

Westbound
Exit only to clockwise
M25 (westbound)

Eastbound
Access only from
anticlockwise M25
(eastbound)

Westbound
Access only from M20
(northwestbound)

Eastbound
Exit only to M20
(southeastbound)

M27 Cadnam - Portsmouth

Westbound
Staggered junction; follow
signs - access only from
M3 (southbound). Exit
only to M3 (northbound)

Eastbound
Staggered junction; follow
signs - access only from
M3 (southbound). Exit
only to M3 (northbound)

Westbound
Exit only, no access

Eastbound
Access only, no exit

Westbound
Staggered junction; follow
signs - exit only to M275
(southbound)

Eastbound
Staggered junction; follow
signs - access only from
M275 (northbound)

M40 London - Birmingham

Northwestbound
Exit only, no access

Southeastbound
Access only, no exit

Northwestbound
Exit only, no access

Southeastbound
Access only, no exit

Northwestbound
Exit only to M40/A40

Southeastbound
Access only from
M40/A40

Northwestbound
Exit only, no access

Southeastbound
Access only, no exit

Northwestbound
Access only, no exit

Southeastbound
Exit only, no access

Northwestbound
Access only, no exit

Southeastbound
Exit only, no access

M42 Bromsgrove - Measham

See Birmingham district map on pages
174–175

M45 Coventry - M1

Westbound
Access only from A45
(northbound)

Eastbound
Exit only, no access

Westbound
Access only from M1
(northbound)

Eastbound
Exit only to M1
(southbound)

M48 Chepstow

Westbound
Access only from M4
(westbound)

Eastbound
Exit only to M4
(eastbound)

Westbound
No exit to M4 (eastbound)

Eastbound
No access from M4
(westbound)

M53 Mersey Tunnel - Chester

Northbound
Access only from M56
(westbound). Exit only to
M56 (eastbound)

Southbound
Access only from M56
(westbound). Exit only to
M56 (eastbound)

M54 Telford - Birmingham

Westbound
Access only from M6
(northbound)

Eastbound
Exit only to M6
(southbound)

M56 Chester - Manchester

For junctions 1,2,3,4 & 7 see Manchester
district map on pages 182–183

Westbound
Access only, no exit

Eastbound
No access or exit

Westbound
No exit to M6
(southbound)

Eastbound
No access from M6
(northbound)

Westbound
Exit only to M53

Eastbound
Access only from M53

Westbound
No access or exit

Eastbound
No restriction

M57 Liverpool Outer Ring Road

Northwestbound
Access only, no exit

Southeastbound
Exit only, no access

Northwestbound
Access only from A580
(westbound)

Southeastbound
Exit only, no access

M58 Liverpool - Wigan

Westbound
Exit only, no access

Eastbound
Access only, no exit

M60 Manchester Orbital

See Manchester district map on pages
182–183

M61 Manchester - Preston

Northwestbound
No access or exit

Southeastbound
Exit only, no access

Northwestbound
Exit only to M6
(northbound)

Southeastbound
Access only from M6
(southbound)

M62 Liverpool - Kingston upon Hull

Westbound
Access only, no exit

Eastbound
Exit only, no access

Westbound
No access to A1(M)
(southbound)

Eastbound
No restriction

M65 Preston - Colne

Northeastbound
Exit only, no access

Southwestbound
Access only, no exit

Northeastbound
Access only, no exit

Southwestbound
Exit only, no access

M66 Bury

Northbound
Exit only to A56
(northbound)

Southbound
Access only from A56
(southbound)

Northbound
Exit only, no access

Southbound
Access only, no exit

M67 Hyde Bypass

Westbound
Access only, no exit

Eastbound
Exit only, no access

Westbound
Exit only, no access

Eastbound
Access only, no exit

Westbound
Exit only, no access

Eastbound
No restriction

M69 Coventry - Leicester

Northbound
Access only, no exit

Southbound
Exit only, no access

M73 East of Glasgow

Northbound
No exit to A74 and A721

Southbound
No exit to A74 and A721

Northbound
No access from or exit to
A89. No access from M8
(eastbound)

Southbound
No access from or exit to
A89. No exit to M8
(westbound)

M74 and A74(M) Glasgow - Gretna

Northbound
Exit only, no access

Southbound
Access only, no exit

Northbound
Access only, no exit

Southbound
Exit only, no access

Northbound
No access from A74 and
A721

Southbound
Access only, no exit to
A74 and A721

Northbound
Access only, no exit

Southbound
Exit only, no access

Northbound
No access or exit

Southbound
Exit only, no access

Northbound
No restriction

Southbound
Access only, no exit

Northbound
Access only, no exit

Southbound
Exit only, no access

Northbound
Exit only, no access

Southbound
Access only, no exit

Northbound
Exit only, no access

Southbound
Access only, no exit

M77 Glasgow - Kilmarnock

Northbound
No exit to M8
(westbound)

Southbound
No access from M8
(eastbound)

Northbound
Access only, no exit

Southbound
Exit only, no access

Northbound
Access only, no exit

Southbound
Exit only, no access

Northbound
Access only, no exit

Southbound
No restriction

Northbound
Exit only, no access

Southbound
Exit only, no access

M80 Glasgow - Stirling

For junctions 1 & 4 see Glasgow district map
on pages 176–177

Northbound
Exit only, no access

Southbound
Access only, no exit

Northbound
Access only, no exit

Southbound
Exit only, no access

Northbound
Exit only to M876
(northeastbound)

Southbound
Access only from M876
(southwestbound)

M90 Edinburgh - Perth

Northbound
No exit, access only

Southbound
Exit only to A90
(eastbound)

Northbound
Exit only to A92
(eastbound)

Southbound
Access only from A92
(westbound)

Northbound
Access only, no exit

Southbound
Exit only, no access

Northbound
Exit only, no access

Southbound
Access only, no exit

Northbound
No access from A912
No exit to A912
(southbound)

Southbound
No access from A912
(northbound).
No exit to A912

M180 Doncaster - Grimsby

Westbound
Access only, no exit

Eastbound
Exit only, no access

M606 Bradford Spur

Northbound
Exit only, no access

Southbound
No restriction

M621 Leeds - M1

Clockwise
Access only, no exit

Anticlockwise
Exit only, no access

Clockwise
No exit or access

Anticlockwise
No restriction

Clockwise
Access only, no exit

Anticlockwise
Exit only, no access

Clockwise
Exit only, no access

Anticlockwise
Access only, no exit

Clockwise
Exit only to M1
(southbound)

Anticlockwise
Access only from M1
(northbound)

M876 Bonnybridge - Kincardine Bridge

Northeastbound
Access only from M80
(northbound)

Southwestbound
Exit only to M80
(southbound)

Northeastbound
Exit only to M9
(eastbound)

Southwestbound
Access only from M9
(westbound)

A1(M) South Mimms - Baldock

Northbound
Exit only, no access

Southbound
Access only, no exit

Northbound
No restriction

Southbound
Exit only, no access

Northbound
Access only, no exit

Southbound
No access or exit

A1(M) Pontefract - Bedale

Northbound
No access to M62
(eastbound)

Southbound
No restriction

Northbound
Access only from M1
(northbound)

Southbound
Exit only to M1
(southbound)

A1(M) Scotch Corner - Newcastle upon Tyne

Northbound
Exit only to A66(M)
(eastbound)

Southbound
Access only from A66(M)
(westbound)

Northbound
No access. Exit only to
A194(M) & A1
(northbound)

Southbound
No exit. Access only from
A194(M) & A1
(southbound)

A3(M) Horndean - Havant

Northbound
Access only from A3

Southbound
Exit only to A3

Northbound
Exit only, no access

Southbound
Access only, no exit

A38(M) Birmingham Victoria Road (Park Circus)

Northbound
No exit

Southbound
No access

A48(M) Cardiff Spur

Westbound
Access only from M4
(westbound)

Eastbound
Exit only to M4
(eastbound)

Westbound
Exit only to A48
(westbound)

Eastbound
Access only from A48
(eastbound)

A57(M) Manchester Brook Street (A34)

Westbound
No exit

Eastbound
No access

A58(M) Leeds Park Lane and Westgate

Northbound
No restriction

Southbound
No access

A64(M) Leeds Clay Pit Lane (A58)

Westbound
No exit (to Clay Pit Lane)

Eastbound
No access (from Clay Pit
Lane)

A66(M) Darlington Spur

Westbound
Exit only to A1(M)
(southbound)

Eastbound
Access only from A1(M)
(northbound)

A74(M) Gretna - Abington

Northbound
Exit only, no access

Southbound
No exit

A194(M) Newcastle upon Tyne

Northbound
Access only from A1(M)
(northbound)

Southbound
Exit only to A1(M)
(southbound)

A12 M25 - Ipswich

Northeastbound
Access only, no exit

Southwestbound
No restriction

Northeastbound
Exit only, no access

Southwestbound
Access only, no exit

Northeastbound
Exit only, no access

Southwestbound
Access only, no exit

Northeastbound
Access only, no exit

Southwestbound
Exit only, no access

Northeastbound
No restriction

Southwestbound
Access only, no exit

Northeastbound
Exit only, no access

Southwestbound
Access only, no exit

Northeastbound
Access only, no exit

Southwestbound
Exit only, no access

Northeastbound
Exit only, no access

Southwestbound
Access only, no exit

Northeastbound
Exit only (for Stratford
St Mary and Dedham)

Southwestbound
Access only

A14 M1 - Felixstowe

Westbound
Exit only to M6 & M1
(northbound)

Eastbound
Access only from M6 &
M1 (southbound)

Westbound
Exit only, no access

Eastbound
Access only, no exit

Westbound
Exit only to M11
(for London)

Eastbound
Access only, no exit

Westbound
Exit only to A14
(northbound)

Eastbound
Access only, no exit

Westbound
Access only, no exit

Eastbound
Exit only, no access

Westbound
Exit only to A11
Access only from A1303

Eastbound
Access only from A11

Westbound
Access only from A11

Eastbound
Exit only to A11

Westbound
Exit only, no access

Eastbound
Access only, no exit

Westbound
Access only, no exit

Eastbound
Exit only, no access

A55 Holyhead - Chester

Westbound
Exit only, no access

Eastbound
Access only, no exit

Westbound
Access only, no exit

Eastbound
Exit only, no access

Westbound
Exit only, no access

Eastbound
No access or exit.

Westbound
No restriction

Eastbound
No access or exit

Westbound
Exit only, no access

Eastbound
No access or exit

Westbound
Exit only, no access

Eastbound
Access only, no exit

Westbound
Exit only to A5104

Eastbound
Access only from A5104

Refer also to atlas pages 36–37 and 50–51

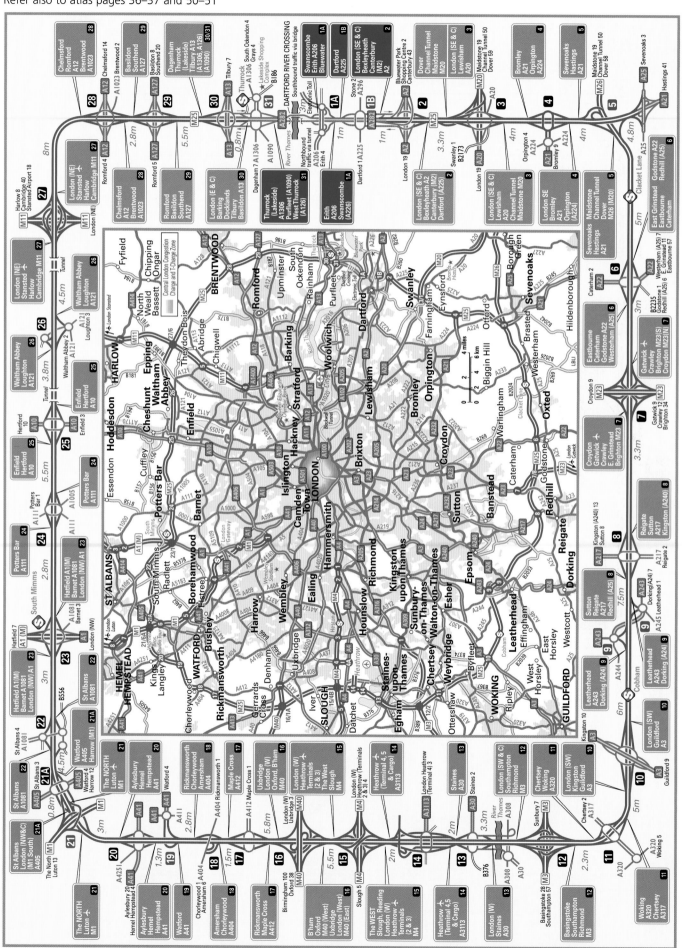

Refer also to atlas pages 58–59

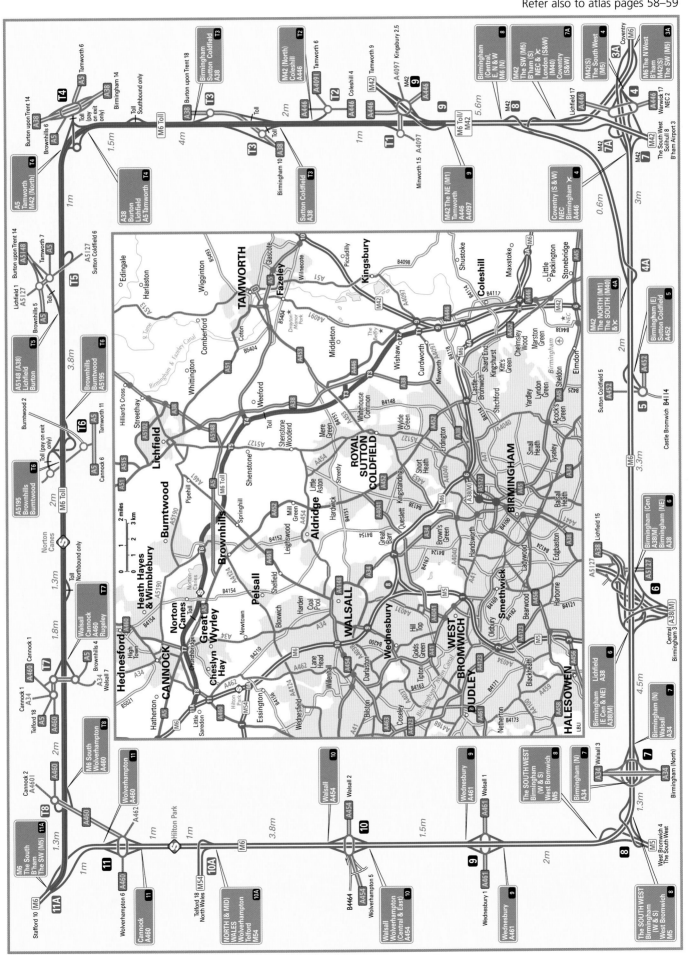

Smart motorways

Since Britain's first motorway (the Preston Bypass) opened in 1958, motorways have changed significantly. A vast increase in car journeys over the last 60 years has meant that motorways quickly filled to capacity. To combat this, the recent development of **smart motorways** uses technology to monitor and actively manage traffic flow and congestion.

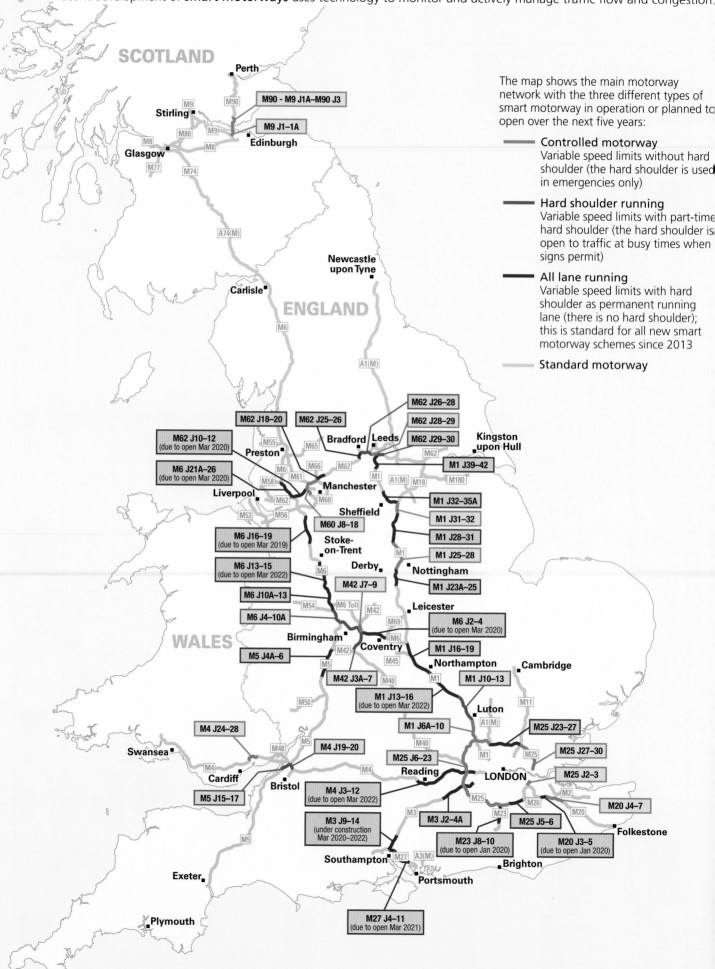

The map shows the main motorway network with the three different types of smart motorway in operation or planned to open over the next five years:

Controlled motorway
Variable speed limits without hard shoulder (the hard shoulder is used in emergencies only)

Hard shoulder running
Variable speed limits with part-time hard shoulder (the hard shoulder is open to traffic at busy times when signs permit)

All lane running
Variable speed limits with hard shoulder as permanent running lane (there is no hard shoulder); this is standard for all new smart motorway schemes since 2013

Standard motorway

Smart motorways (*Intelligent Transport Systems* in Scotland) are the responsibility of Highways England, Transport Scotland and Transport for Wales

How they work

Smart motorways utilise various active traffic management methods, monitored through a regional traffic control centre:

- Traffic flow is monitored using CCTV
- Speed limits are changed to smooth traffic flow and reduce stop-start driving
- Capacity of the motorway can be increased by either temporarily or permanently opening the hard shoulder to traffic

- Warning signs and messages alert drivers to hazards and traffic jams ahead
- Lanes can be closed in the case of an accident or emergency by displaying a red X sign
- Emergency refuge areas are located regularly along the motorway where there is no hard shoulder available

In an emergency

On a smart motorway there is often no hard shoulder so in an emergency you will need to make your way to the nearest **emergency refuge area** or motorway service area.

Emergency refuge areas are lay-bys marked with blue signs featuring an orange SOS telephone symbol. The telephone connects to the regional control centre and pinpoints your location. The control centre will advise you on what to do, send help and assist you in returning to the motorway.

If you are unable to reach an emergency refuge area or hard shoulder (if there is one) move as close to the nearside (left hand) boundary or verge as you can.

If it is not possible to get out of your vehicle safely, or there is no other place of relative safety to wait, stay in your vehicle with your seat-belt on and dial 999 if you have a mobile phone. If you don't have a phone, sit tight and wait to be rescued. Once the regional traffic control centre is aware of your situation, via the police or CCTV, they will use the smart motorway technology to set overhead signs and close the lane to keep traffic away from you. They will also send a traffic officer or the police to help you.

Sign indicating presence of emergency refuge areas ahead

This sign is located at each emergency refuge area

Signs

Motorway signals and messages advise of abnormal traffic conditions ahead and may indicate speed limits. They may apply to individual lanes when mounted overhead or, when located on the central reservation or at the side of the motorway, to the whole carriageway.

Where traffic is allowed to use the hard shoulder as a traffic lane, each lane will have overhead signals and signs. A red cross (with no signals) displayed above the hard shoulder indicates when it is closed. When the hard shoulder is in use as a traffic lane the red cross will change to a speed limit. Should it be necessary to close any lane, a red cross with red lamps flashing in vertical pairs will be shown above that lane. Prior to this, the signal will show an arrow directing traffic into the adjacent lane.

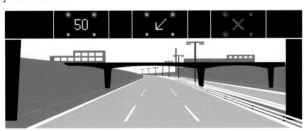

These signals are mounted above the carriageway with a signal for each traffic lane; each signal has two pairs of lamps that flash. You should obey the signal for your lane

Move to adjacent lane (arrow may point downwards to the right)

Leave motorway at next exit

Red lamps flashing from side to side in pairs, together with a red cross, mean 'do not proceed in the traffic lane directly below'. More than one lane may be closed to traffic

Where variable speed limit signs are mounted over individual lanes and the speed limit is shown in a red ring, the limit is mandatory. You will be at risk of a driving offence if you do not keep to the speed limit. Speed limits that do not include the red ring are the maximum speeds advised for the prevailing conditions.

Speed limits of 60, 50 and 40mph are used on all types of smart motorways. When no speed limit is shown the national speed limit of 70mph is in place (this is reduced to 60mph for particular vehicles such as heavy or articulated goods vehicles and vehicles towing caravans or trailers).

Quick tips

- Never drive in a lane closed by a red X
- Keep to the speed limit shown on the gantries
- A solid white line indicates the hard shoulder – do not drive in it unless directed or in the case of an emergency
- A broken white line indicates a normal running lane

- Exit the smart motorway where possible if your vehicle is in difficulty. In an emergency, move onto the hard shoulder where there is one, or the nearest emergency refuge area
- Put on your hazard lights if you break down

Motoring information

M4 Motorway with number	**S** Primary route service area	Road tunnel	**F** International freight terminal	
Toll T4 Toll motorway with toll station	**BATH** Primary route destination	**Toll** Road toll, steep gradient (arrows point downhill)	**H** 24-hour Accident & Emergency hospital	
6 Motorway junction with and without number	**A1123** Other A road single/dual carriageway	**5** Distance in miles between symbols	**C** Crematorium	
5 Restricted motorway junctions	**B2070** B road single/dual carriageway	**or V** Vehicle ferry	**P+R** Park and Ride (at least 6 days per week)	
Fleet S R Motorway service area, rest area	Minor road more than 4 metres wide, less than 4 metres wide	Fast vehicle ferry or catamaran	City, town, village or other built-up area	
Motorway and junction under construction	Roundabout	Railway line, in tunnel	**628 ▲ 637 Lecht Summit** Height in metres, mountain pass	
A3 Primary route single/dual carriageway	Interchange/junction	Railway/tram station, level crossing	Snow gates (on main routes)	
11 Primary route junction with and without number	Narrow primary/other A/B road with passing places (Scotland)	Tourist railway	National boundary	
3 Restricted primary route junctions	Road under construction	Airport (major/minor), heliport	County, administrative boundary	

Touring information To avoid disappointment, check opening times before visiting

Scenic route	Garden	Waterfall	Motor-racing circuit	
Tourist Information Centre	Arboretum	Hill-fort	Air show venue	
Tourist Information Centre (seasonal)	Country park	Roman antiquity	Ski slope (natural, artificial)	
Visitor or heritage centre	Agricultural showground	Prehistoric monument	National Trust site	
Picnic site	Theme park	**1066** Battle site with year	National Trust for Scotland site	
Caravan site (AA inspected)	Farm or animal centre	Steam railway centre	English Heritage site	
Camping site (AA inspected)	Zoological or wildlife collection	Cave or cavern	Historic Scotland site	
Caravan & camping site (AA inspected)	Bird collection	Windmill, monument	Cadw (Welsh heritage) site	
Abbey, cathedral or priory	Aquarium	Beach (award winning)	Other place of interest	
Ruined abbey, cathedral or priory	RSPB site	Lighthouse	Boxed symbols indicate attractions within urban areas	
Castle	National Nature Reserve (England, Scotland, Wales)	Golf course (AA listed)	World Heritage Site (UNESCO)	
Historic house or building	Local nature reserve	Football stadium	National Park and National Scenic Area (Scotland)	
Museum or art gallery	Wildlife Trust reserve	County cricket ground	Forest Park	
Industrial interest	Forest drive	Rugby Union national stadium	Sandy beach	
Aqueduct or viaduct	National trail	International athletics stadium	Heritage coast	
Vineyard, brewery or distillery	Viewpoint	Horse racing, show jumping	Major shopping centre	

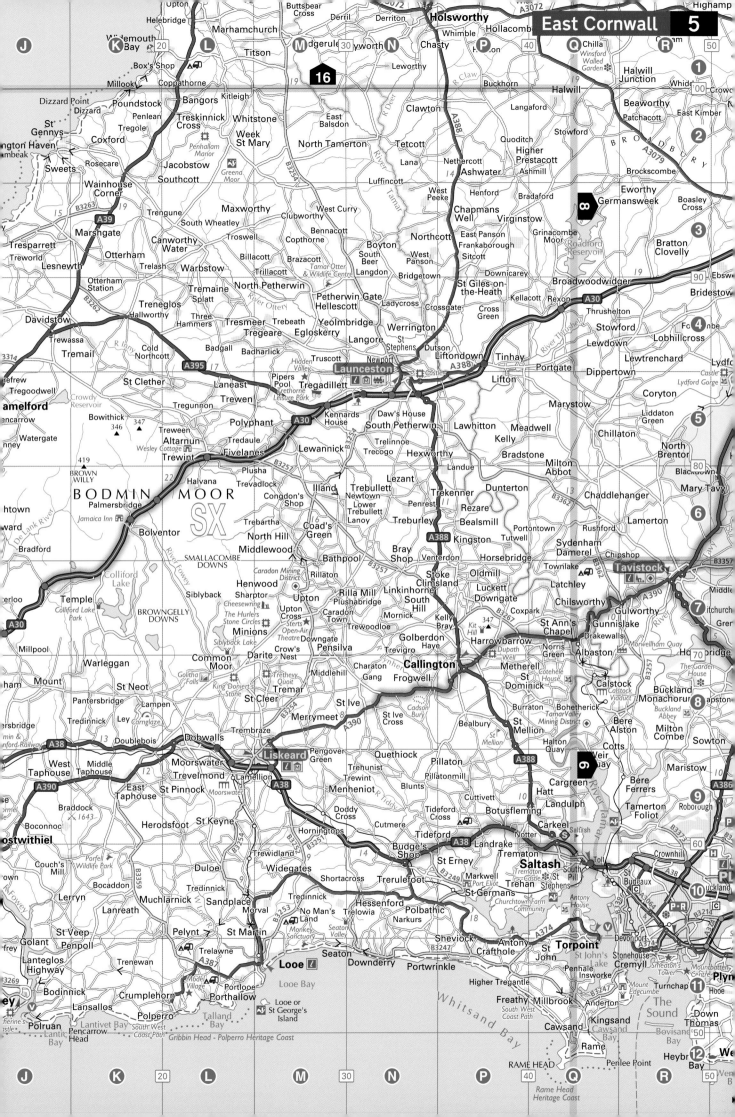

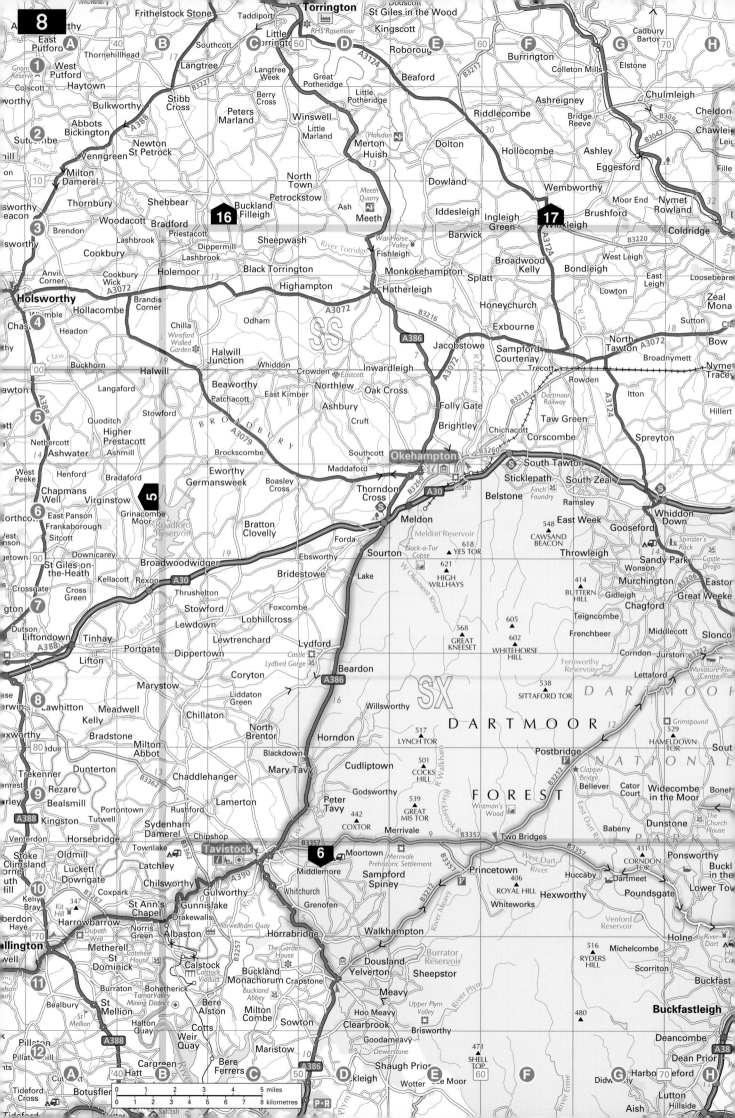

Town plan: Exeter p.202

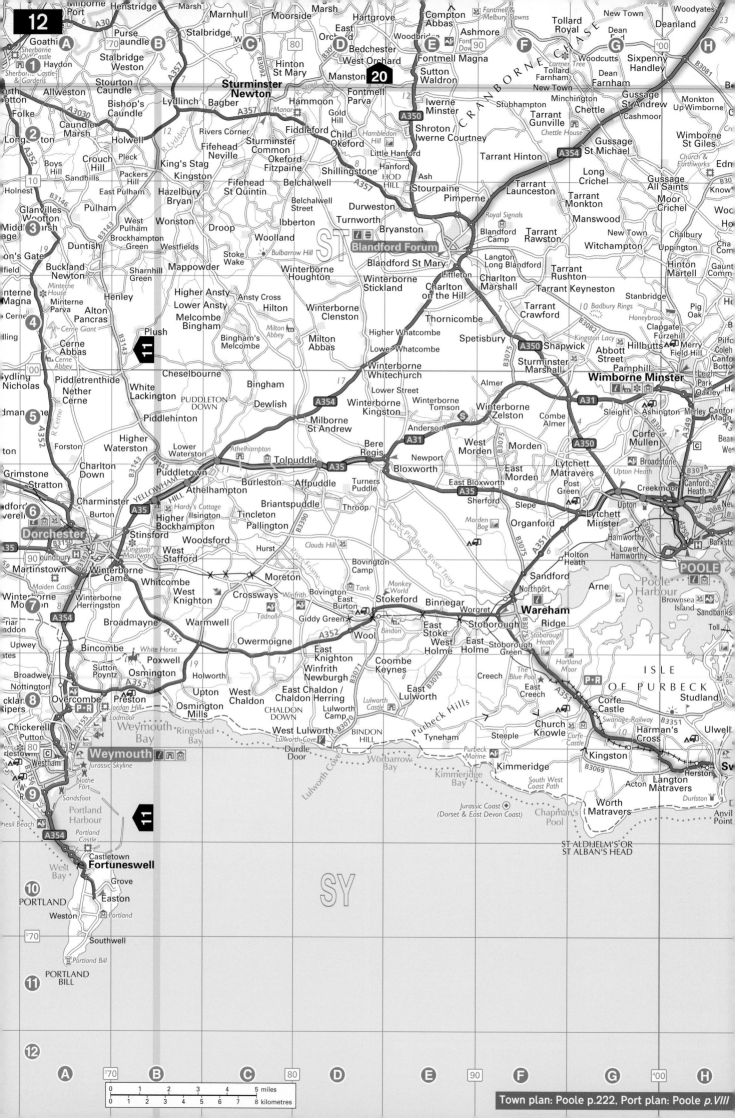

16

A · B · 20 · C · D · 30 · E · F · 40 · G · H

1
50
2
North West
Point
*Lundy
Heritage Coast* LUNDY
▲142 *Marisco*
*Marine
Reserve* Shutter Point
Surf Point
3
40
4
5
30
6
SS HARTLAND POINT *Shipload
Bay*
Damehole
Point Titchberry Brownsham
Stoke *Hartland Abbey
& Gardens*
Hartland Quay Hartland B3248 Velly
Speke's Mill
Mouth Milford *Docton
Mill* Philham Higher
Clovelly
Elmscott Edistone *Milky Way*
Hardisworthy Tosberry Woolfardisworthy
South
Hole
7
20
Welcombe
Mead Darracott
Gooseham
Mill Woolley Meddon
Morwenstow Gooseham
Eastcott East
Youlstone Dinworthy
Higher Sharpnose Point *16* West Youlstone
*South West
Coast Path* Shop A39 Bradworthy
Woodford Kimworthy
Lower Sharpnose Point Tamar
Lakes Alfardisworthy
Steeple Point Kilkhampton Sutcombemill
Stibb Thurdon Soldon
8
9
*Sandy
Mouth* Poughill Bush
1643 Dunsdon
Northcott
Mouth Maer Hersham
Castle Bude Flexbury Grimscott Lana
Bude
Bay i Bude Stratton Launcells
Launcells
Cross Kingford
Lynstone Red Post Pancrasweek
Upton A3072 Buttsbear
Cross
Helebridge Derril
Widemouth Bay Marhamchurch Derriton
Box's Shop Titson Bridgerule Pyworthy
Millook Coppathorne Leworthy
Dizzard Point Poundstock Bangors Kitleigh
Dizzard Penlean Treskinnick
Cross Whitstone
St Gennys Tregole Week
St Mary
Crackington Haven
Cambeak Coxford
Sweets

10

11

'00

12

'10

BARNSTAPLE
OR
BIDEFORD BAY

Bull
Point Lee
Bay
Rockham
Bay Mortehoe
Morte
Point
Woolacombe Trim
Morte
Bay Chapel Wo
Baggy
Point Pickwell North
Bucklα
Putsborough
Croyde Bay Georgeham Nethe
Croyde B3231 Darracott
Croyde
Saunton Lobb

North Devon
Heritage Coast Braunton Wra
Braunton
Burrows
Isley
Marsh Yello
Northam
Burrows Crow
Point 9
Appledore Inst
Westward Ho! Northam To
Pa
B3236 West
Eastleigh
The Big
Sheep Pillhe
Abbotsham East-the-Water
*Hartland
Heritage Coast* Bideford i
Ford
Fairy Cross Yeo
Vale Landcross
Horns Woodtown
Clovelly Cross Littleham
Buck's Goldworthy Saltrens
Mills 10 A386
Buck's Parkham Cabbacott
Cross Cranford Buckland Monkleigh
Parkham Brewer Frithelstock
Ash Melbury
Frithelstock Stone Taddiport
Ashmansworthy Lit
East Southcott Torri
Putford Langtree
Thornehillhead 17 Langt
West Wee
Gnome
Reserve Putford B3227
Colscott Haytown Stibb
Bradworthy Bulkworthy Cross Peters
Marland
Abbots A388
Sutcombe Bickington Newton Berry
Venngreen St Petrock Cross
River Milton
Soldon Damerel
Cross Thornbury Shebbear
Holsworthy Woodacott Buckland
Beacon Filleigh
Brendon Bradford
Waldon Lashbrook Priestacott Shee
Chilsworthy Cookbury Lashbrook Dippermill
Anvil Cookbury Holemoor Black To
Corner Wick A3072
Holsworthy Brandis
Whimble Hollacombe Corner
Headon Chilla Odham
Chasty Winsford Walled
Garden Halwill
Junction Whid
East Buckhorn Halwill
Balsdon Clawton A388 Langaford Beaworthy
North Tamerton Patchacott Eas
Tetcott A3079
Nethercott Stc G d
Lana Quoditch BROADB
Higher Ashmill
Prestacott

R Dee
R Claw

5 ◄

0 1 2 3 4 5 miles
0 1 2 3 4 5 6 7 8 kilometres

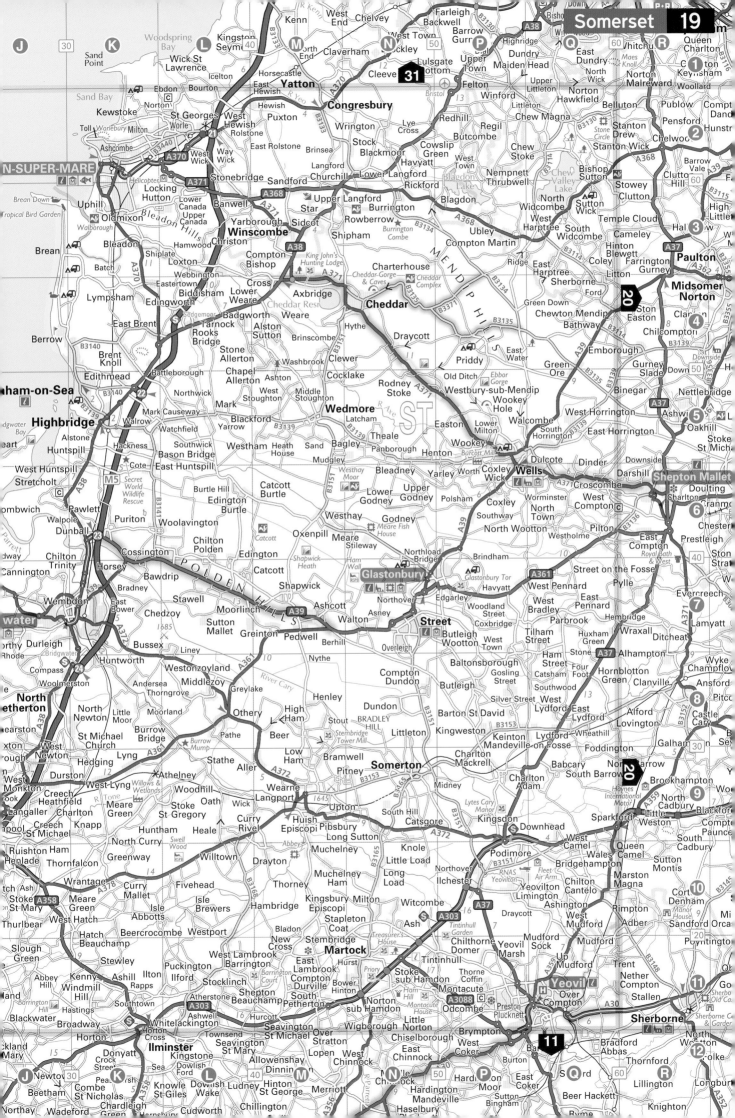

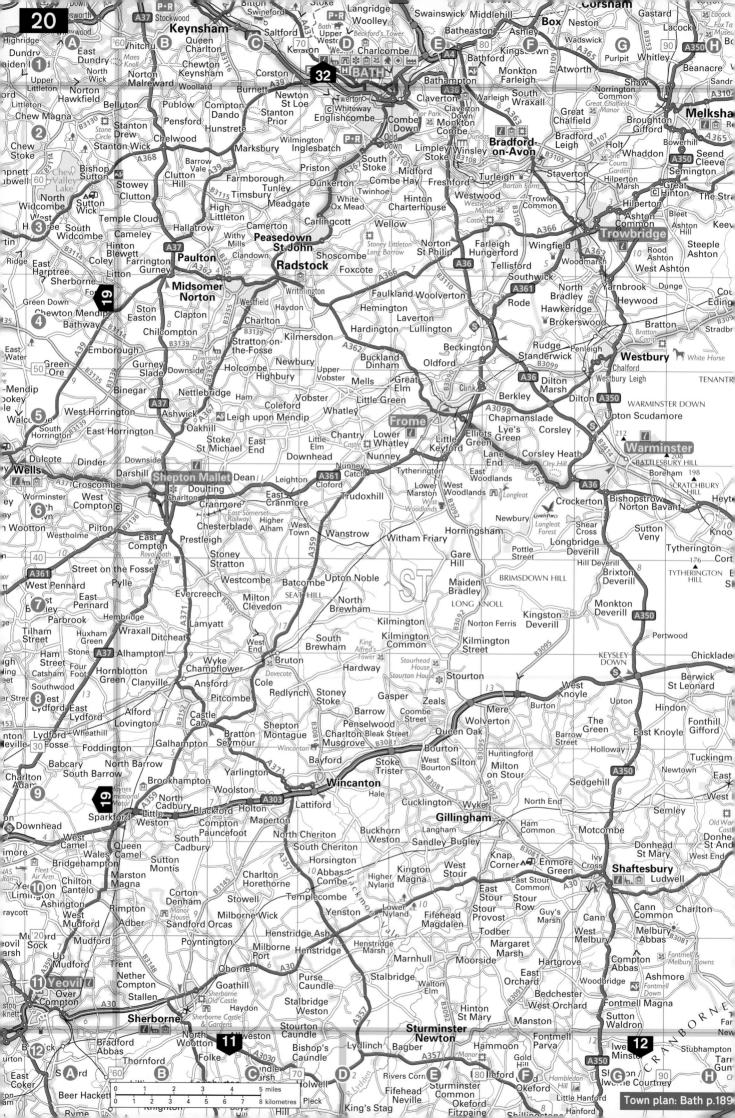

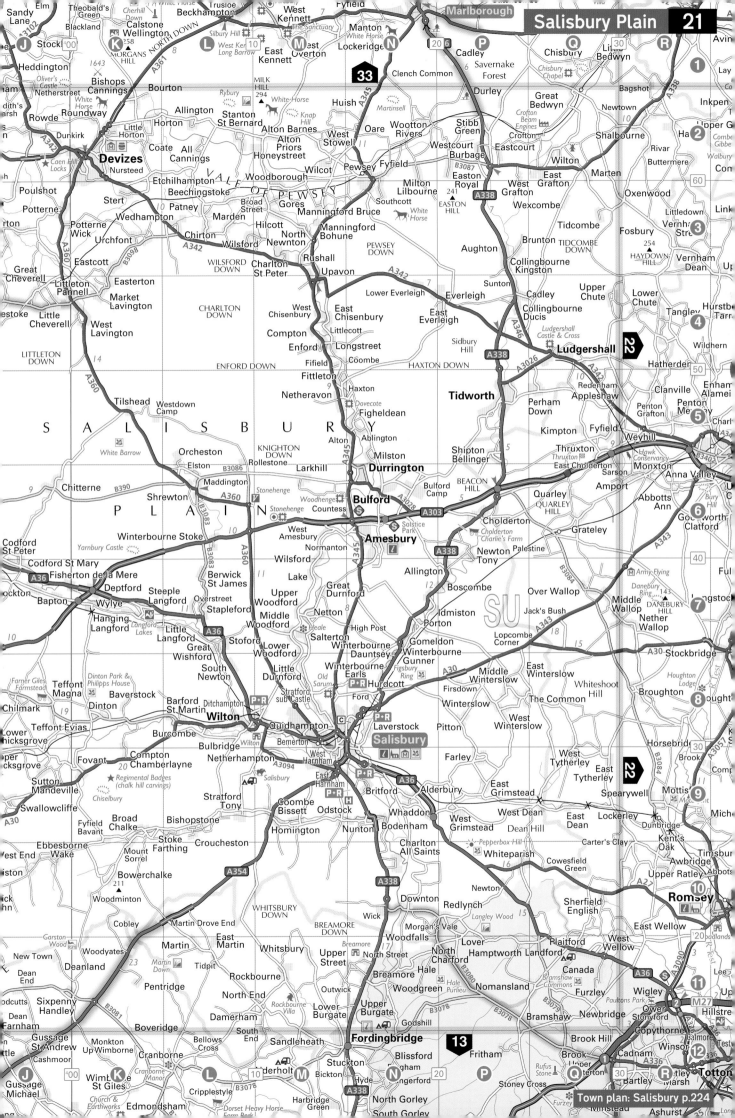

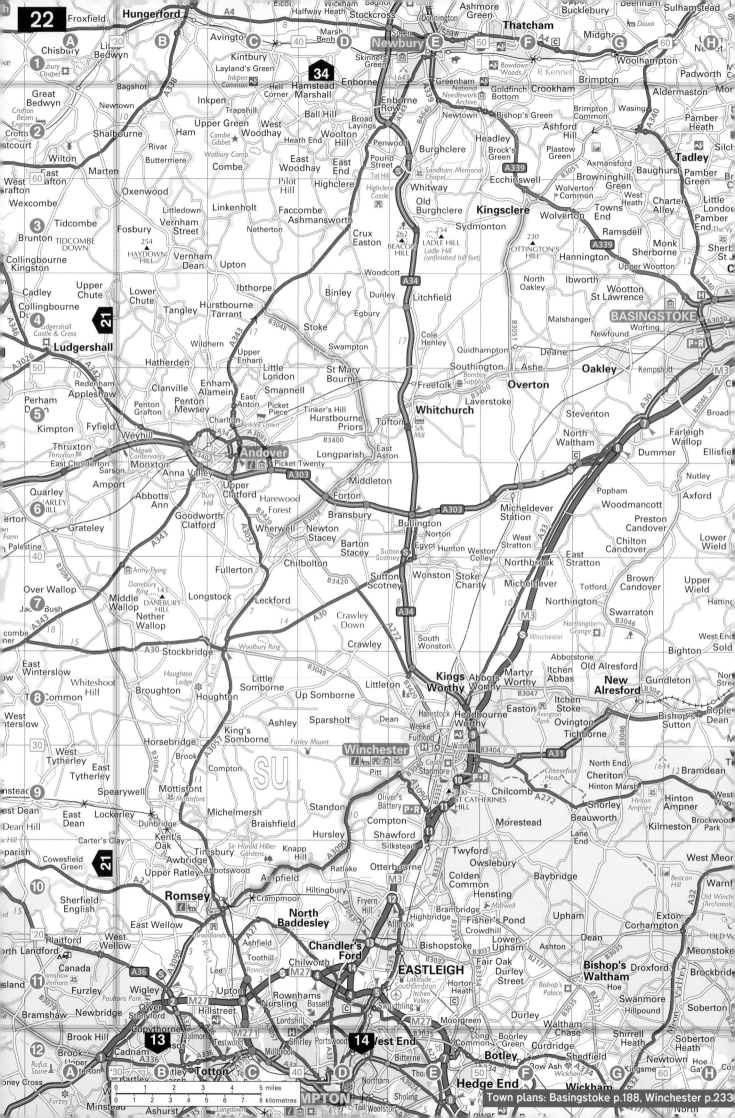

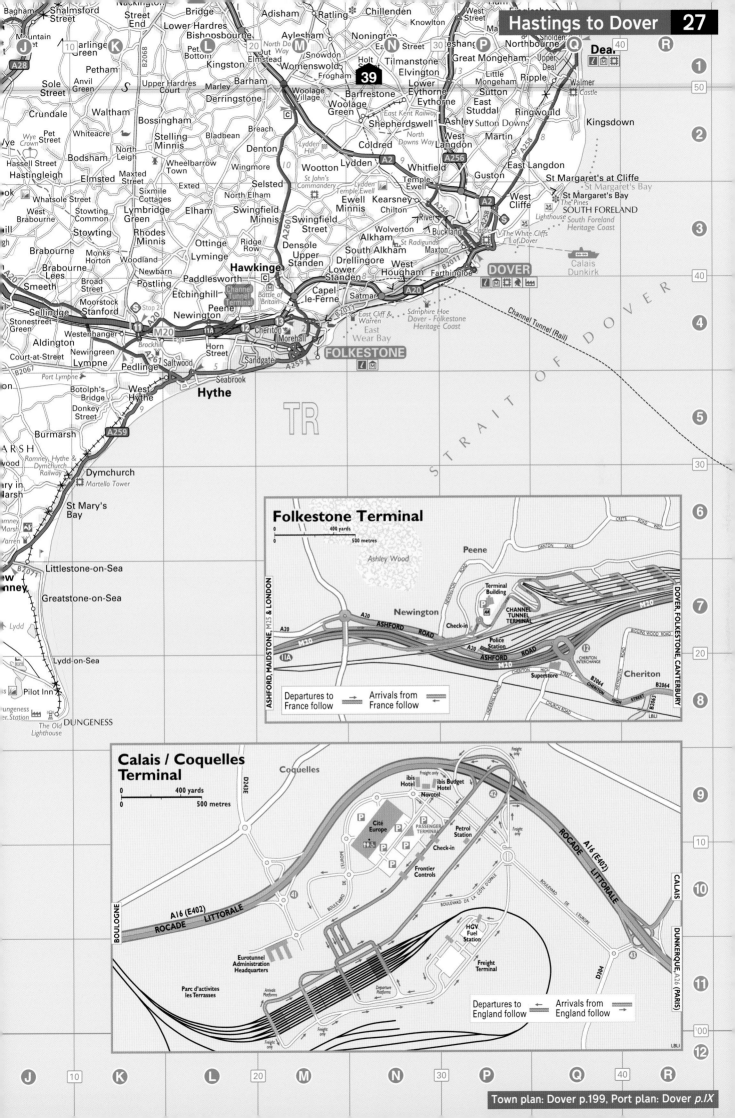

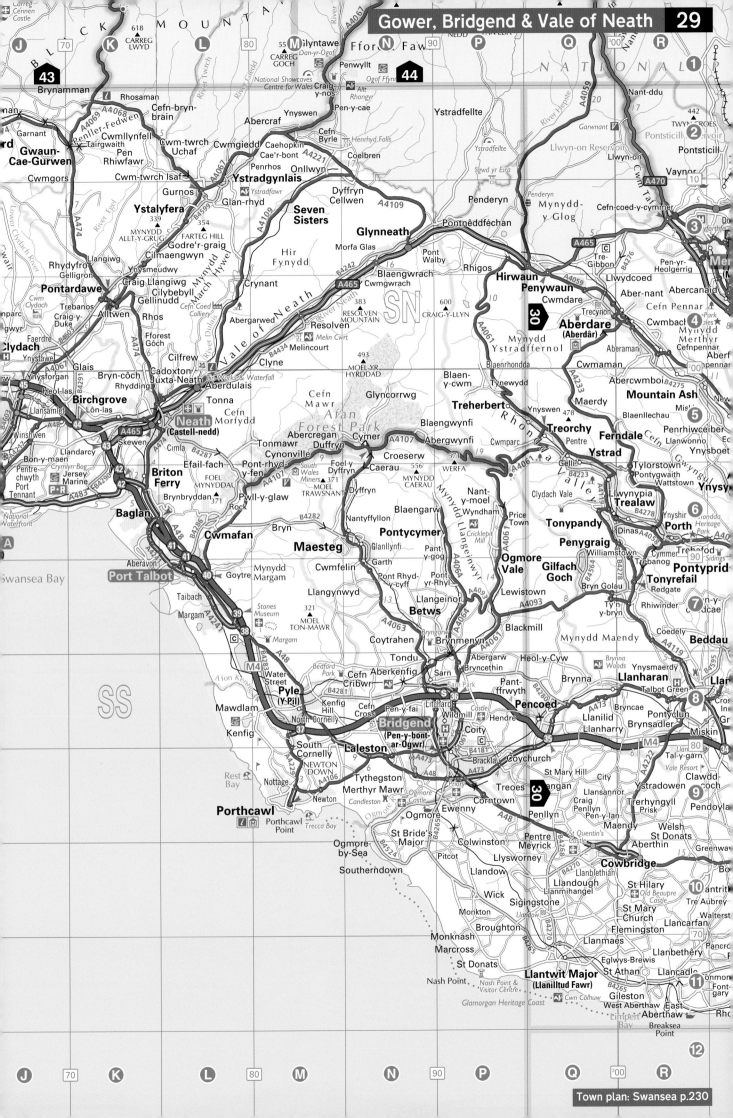

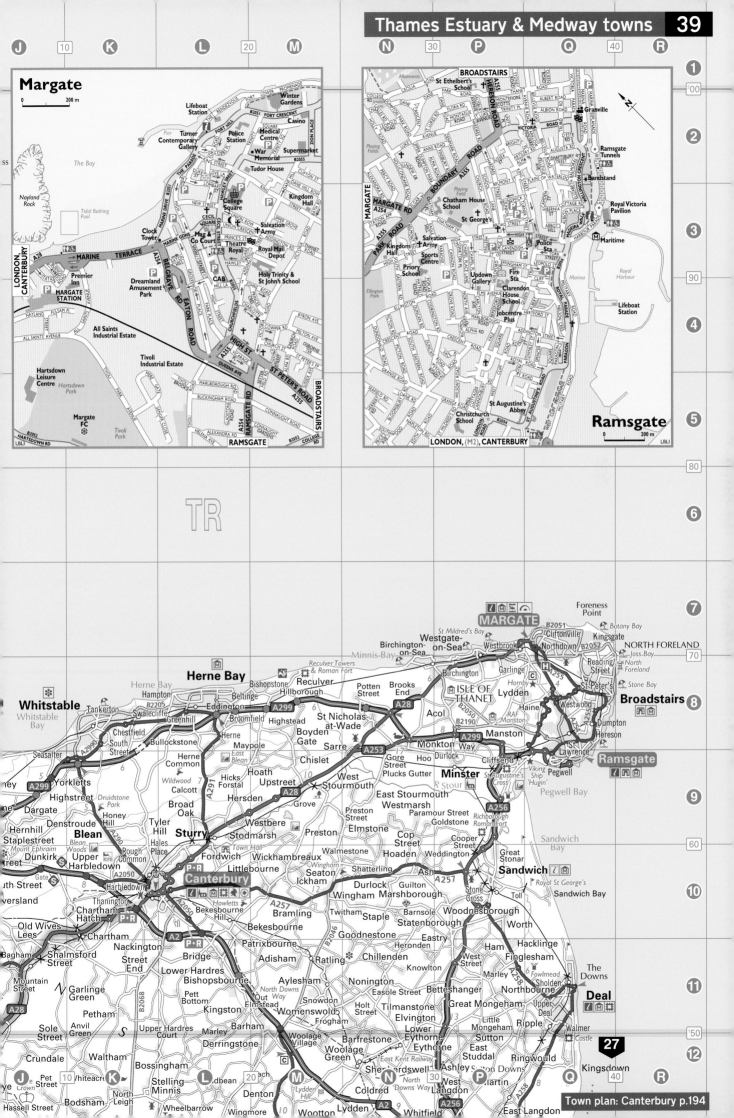

Margate

0   200 m

The Bay

Nayland Rock

Tidal Bathing Pool

Lifeboat Station
Turner Contemporary Gallery
Winter Gardens
Police Station
Casino
Medical Centre
Supermarket
War Memorial
Tudor House
Kingdom Hall
Clock Tower
College Square
Mag & Co Court
Theatre Royal
Salvation Army
Royal Mail Depot
Holy Trinity & St John's School
CAB
LONDON, CANTERBURY
Premier Inn
MARGATE STATION
Dreamland Amusement Park
All Saints Industrial Estate
Tivoli Industrial Estate
Hartsdown Leisure Centre
Hartsdown Park
Margate FC
Tivoli Park
RAMSGATE
BROADSTAIRS
HIGH ST
ST PETERS ROAD
QUEENS AVE

Ramsgate

0   200 m

BROADSTAIRS
St Ethelbert's School
Allotments
Granville
Ramsgate Tunnels
Bandstand
Royal Victoria Pavilion
Maritime
Royal Harbour
Marina
MARGATE RD
Chatham House School
St George's
Salvation Army
Kingdom Hall
Priory School
Sports Centre
Updown Gallery
Police Sta.
Fire Sta.
Clarendon House School
Jobcentre Plus
Ellington Park
St Augustine's Abbey
Christchurch School
Lifeboat Station
LONDON, (M2), CANTERBURY

TR

Foreness Point
MARGATE
St Mildred's Bay
Botany Bay
Westgate-on-Sea
Birchington-on-Sea
Minnis Bay
Cliftonville
Kingsgate
NORTH FORELAND
Westbrook
Northdown
Joss Bay
North Foreland
Whitstable
Whitstable Bay
Herne Bay
Bishopstone
Reculver Towers & Roman Fort
Hampton
Beltinge
Hillborough
Potten Street
Brooks End
Birchington
Garlinge
Reading Street
St Peter's
Stone Bay
Broadstairs
Tankerton
Swalecliffe
Greenhill
Eddington
Broomfield
Highstead
St Nicholas-at-Wade
Acol
ISLE OF THANET
Lydden
Haine
Westwood
Dumpton
Hereson
Chestfield
South Street
Bullockstone
Herne
Maypole
Boyden Gate
Sarre
Monkton
Manston
RAF Manston
St Lawrence
Ramsgate
Seasalter
East Blean
Chislet
Hoo
Durlock
Cliffsend
Viking Ship 'Hugin'
Pegwell
Yorkletts
Highstreet
Druidstone Park
Wildwood Park
Hicks Forstal
Calcott
Hoath
Upstreet
West Stourmouth
Gore Street
Plucks Gutter
Minster
St Augustine's Cross
Pegwell Bay
Dargate
Honey Hill
Tyler Hill
Broad Oak
Hersden
Grove
Westbere
Preston
East Stourmouth
Westmarsh
Paramour Street
Goldstone
Richborough Roman Fort
Sandwich Bay
Hernhill
Staplestreet
Blean
Blean Woods
Rough Common
Upper Harbledown
Fordwich
Stodmarsh
Preston Street
Elmstone
Cop Street
Hoaden
Cooper Street
Great Stonar
Sandwich
Royal St George's
Denstroude
Dunkirk
Mount Ephraim
Harbledown
Sturry
Wickhambreaux
Walmestone
Weddington
Sandwich Bay
Canterbury
Howletts
Bekesbourne Hill
Littlebourne
Seaton
Ickham
Shatterling
Ash
Guilton
Marshborough
Woodnesborough
The Downs
Old Wives Lees
Chartham Hatch
Bridge
Bekesbourne
Bramling
Twitham
Staple
Wingham
Statenborough
Worth
Chartham
Nackington
Street End
Lower Hardres
Bishopsbourne
Patrixbourne
Adisham
Ratling
Chillenden
Knowlton
West Street
Barnsole
Goodnestone
Eastry
Heronden
Ham
Hacklinge
Finglesham
Northbourne
Deal
Mountain Street
Garlinge Green
Pett Bottom
Kingston
Aylesham
Nonington
Easole Street
Snowdon
Holt Street
Betteshanger
Great Mongeham
Marley
Sholden
Shalmsford Street
Petham
Out Way
Elmstead
Womenswold
Barham
Frogham
Tilmanstone
Elvington
Little Mongeham
Upper Deal
Sutton
Ripple
Walmer
Kingsdown
Sole Street
Anvil Green
Upper Hardres Court
Marley
Woolage Village
Barfrestone
Lower Eythorne
Eythorne
East Studdal
Ringwould
Walmer Castle
Crundale
Waltham
Bossingham
Stelling Minnis
Denton
Woolage Green
East Kent Railway
Shepherdswell
Ashley
West Langdon
Martin
Bosham
Bodsham
North Leigh
Wheelwright
Wingmore
Lydden Hill
Lydden
Whitfield
East Langdon
Hassell Street
Whiteacre
Bladbean
Stelling Minnis
Coldred
North Downs Way
Wootton

Town plan: Canterbury p.194

27

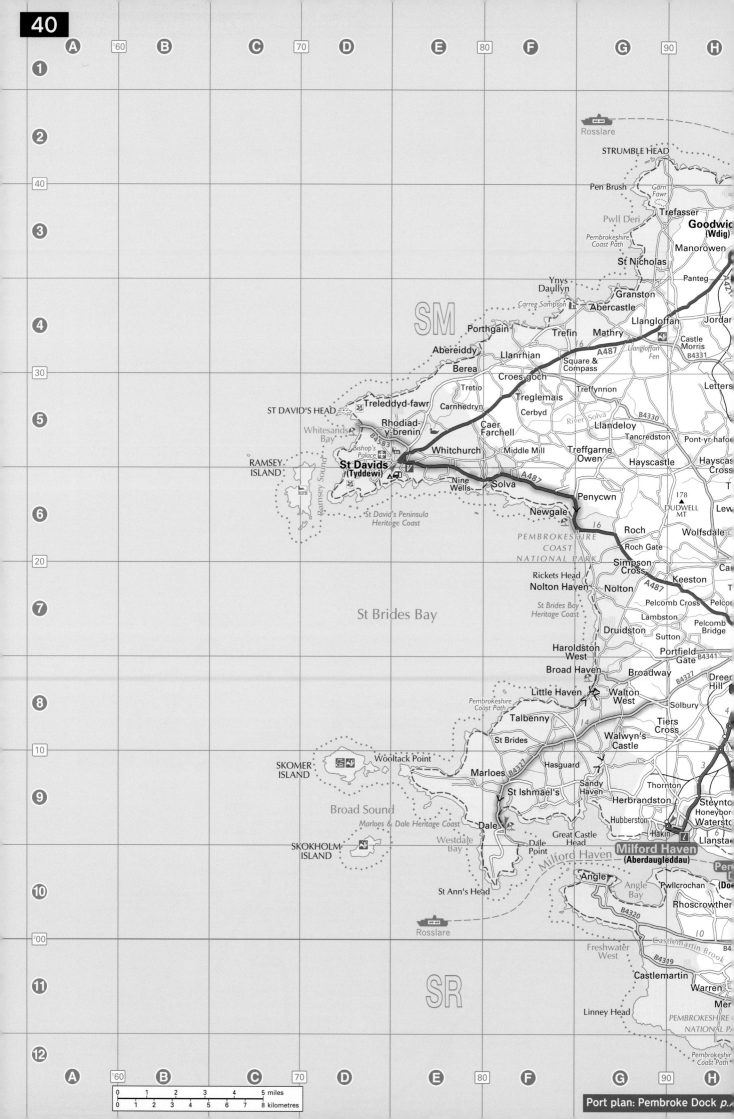

A '60 B C 70 D E 80 F G 90 H

1

2

Rosslare

40

STRUMBLE HEAD

Pen Brush
Garn
Fawr

3

Trefasser

Goodwic
(Wdig)

Pwll Deri

Manorowen

Pembrokeshire
Coast Path

St Nicholas

Panteg

Ynys
Daullyn

Granston

Abercastle

SM

Carreg Sampson

Llangloffan

Jordan

4

Porthgain

Trefin

Mathry

Castle
Morris

Abereiddy

Llangloffan
Fen

16

A487

Llanrhian

B4331

Berea

Croes-goch

Treffynnon

Letters

30

Tretio

Treglemais

St David's Head

Treleddyd-fawr

Carnhedryn

Cerbyd

River Solva

B4330

5

Rhodiad-
y-brenin

Caer
Farchell

Llandeloy

Whitesands
Bay

Tancredston

Pont-yr-hafo

B4583

Middle Mill

Treffgarne
Owen

Bishop's
Palace

Whitchurch

Hayscastle

Hayscas
Cross

RAMSEY
ISLAND

St Davids
(Tyddewi)

Nine
Wells

Solva

A487

178
DUDWELL
MT

T

6

Newgale

Penycwn

Lew

St David's Peninsula
Heritage Coast

Roch

Wolfsdale

PEMBROKESHIRE
COAST
NATIONAL PARK

16

Roch Gate

Simpson
Cross

Ca

Rickets Head

Keeston

Nolton Haven

Nolton

A487

7

St Brides Bay

St Brides Bay
Heritage Coast

Pelcomb Cross

Pelcom

Lambston

Druidston

Sutton

Pelcomb
Bridge

Haroldston
West

Portfield
Gate

B4341

Broad Haven

Broadway

B4327

Dreer
Hill

8

Pembrokeshire
Coast Path

Little Haven

Walton
West

Solbury

Talbenny

14

Tiers
Cross

10

St Brides

Walwyn's
Castle

SKOMER
ISLAND

Wooltack Point

Marloes

Hasguard

Thornton

B4327

9

Broad Sound

St Ishmael's

Sandy
Haven

Herbrandston

Steynto
Honeybo
Waterst

Marloes & Dale Heritage Coast

Dale

Hubberston

Hakin

Llansta

SKOKHOLM
ISLAND

Westdale
Bay

Great Castle
Head

Dale
Point

Milford Haven
(Aberdaugleddau)

Pen

Milford Haven

(Do

10

St Ann's Head

Angle

Angle
Bay

Pwllcrochan

Rhoscrowther

B4320

10

200

Freshwater
West

B4
B4319

SR

11

Castlemartin

Warren

Linney Head

Mer

PEMBROKESHIRE
NATIONAL P

12

Pembrokesh
Coast Path

A '60 B C 70 D E 80 F G 90 H

0 1 2 3 4 5 miles
0 1 2 3 4 5 6 7 8 kilometres

Port plan: Pembroke Dock p.

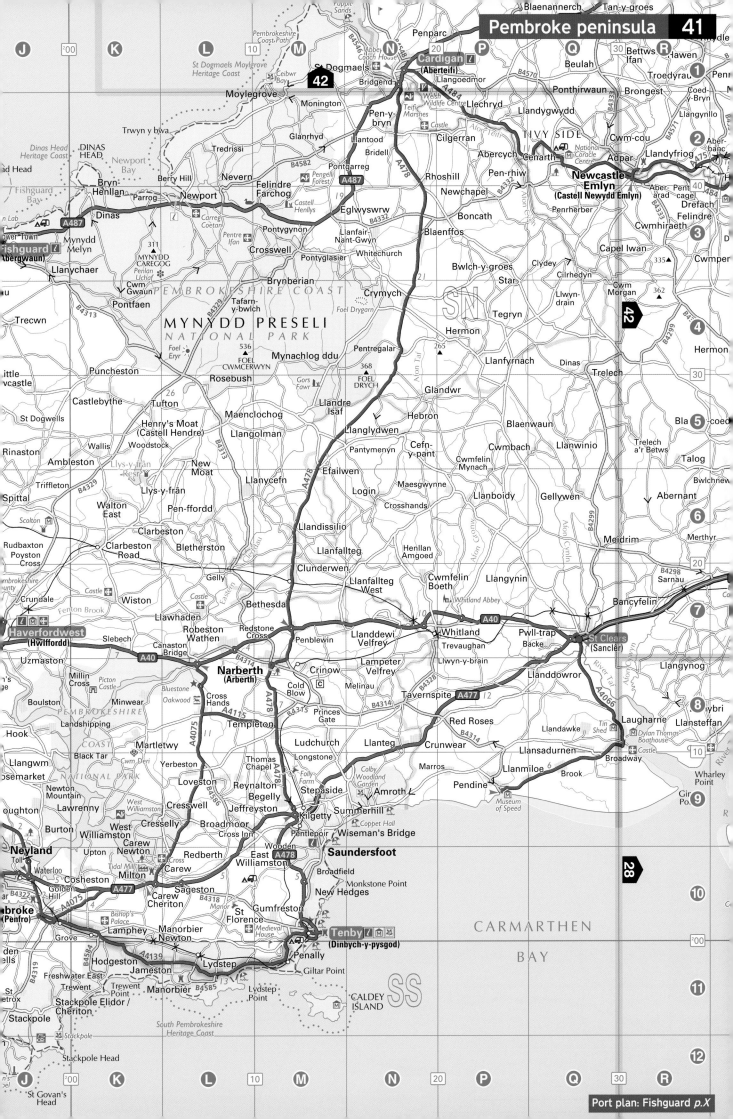

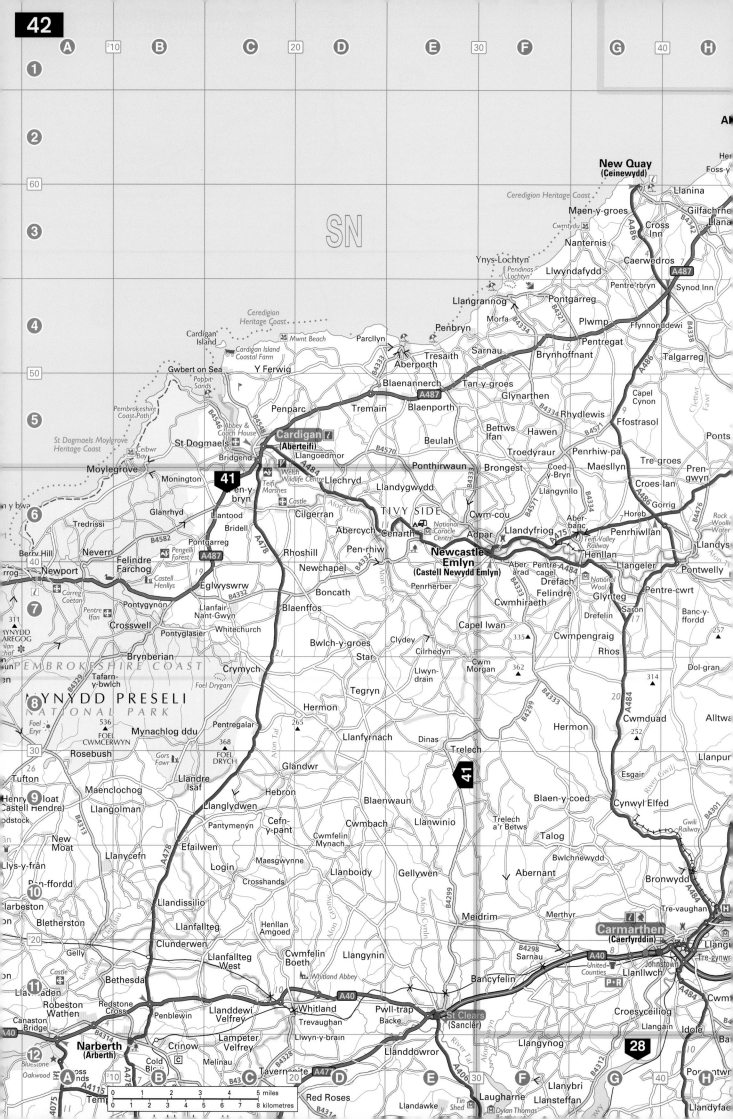

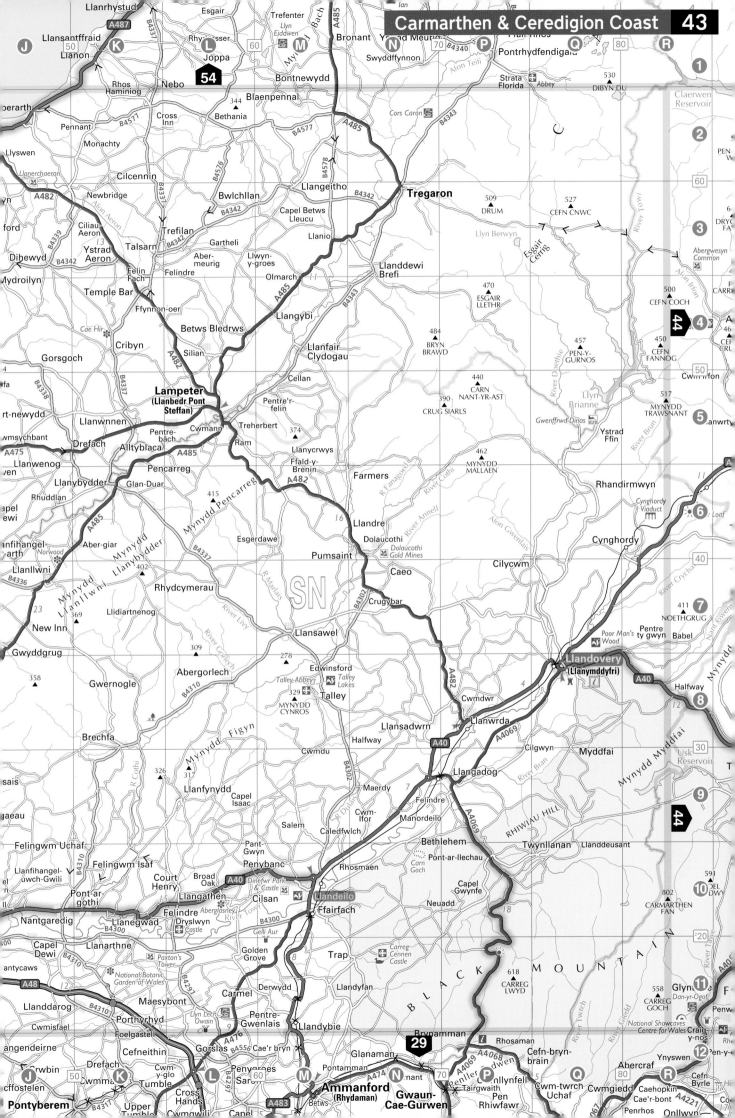

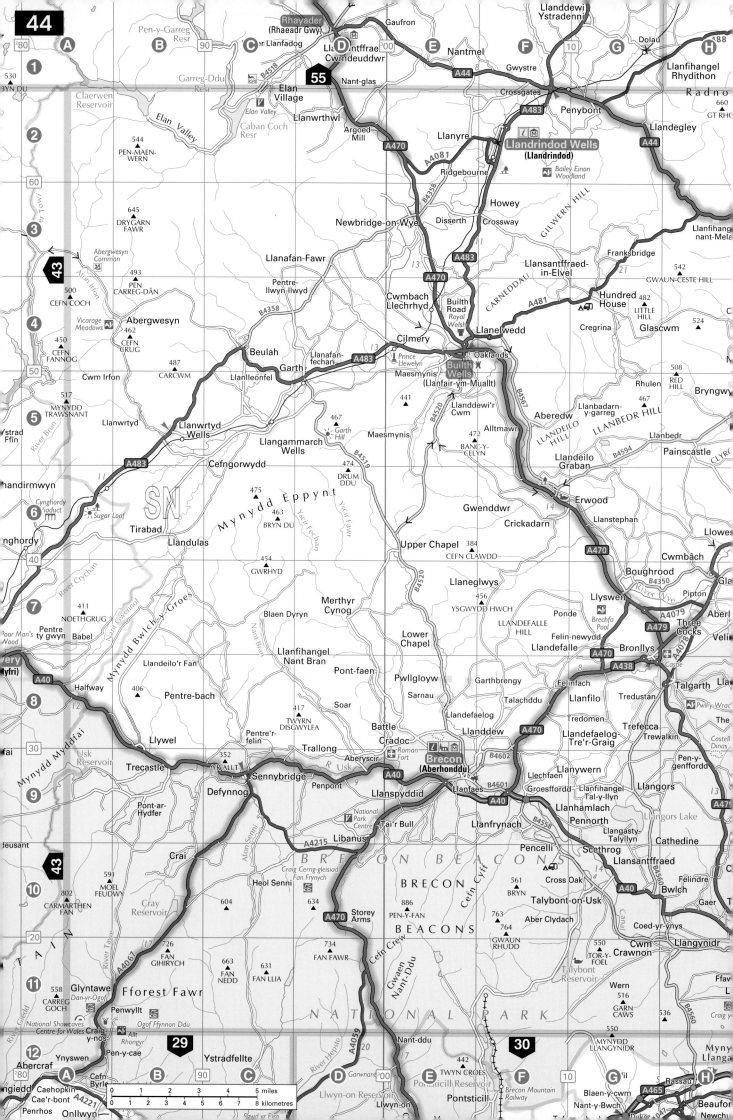

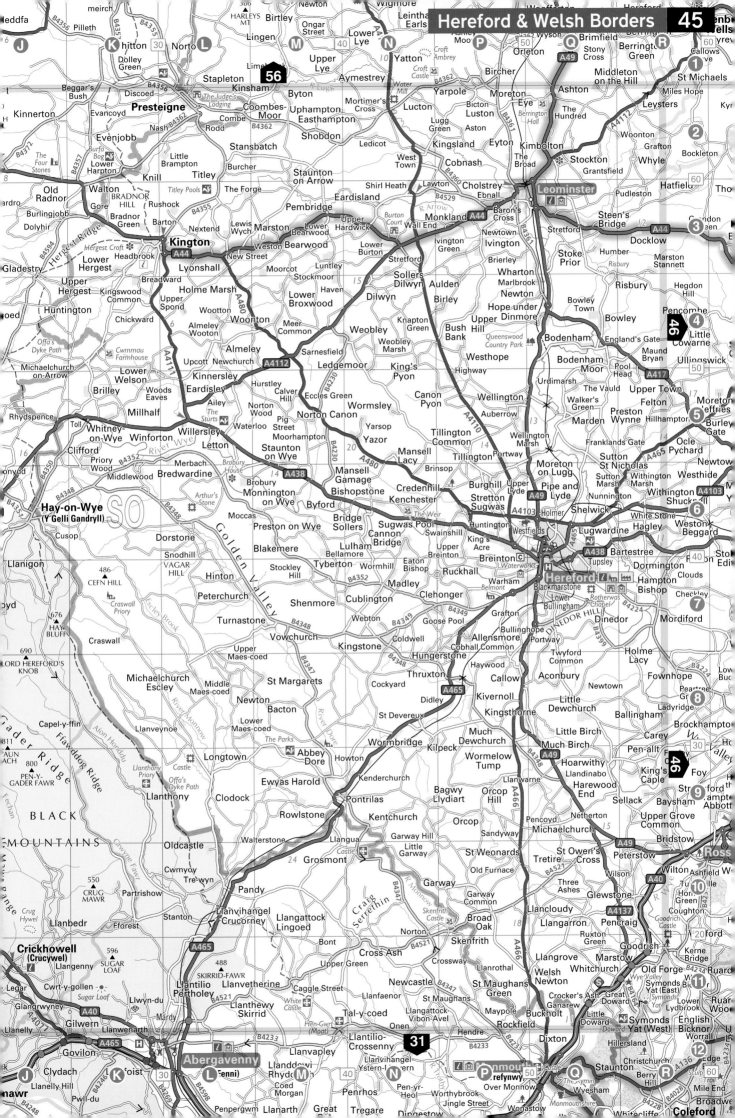

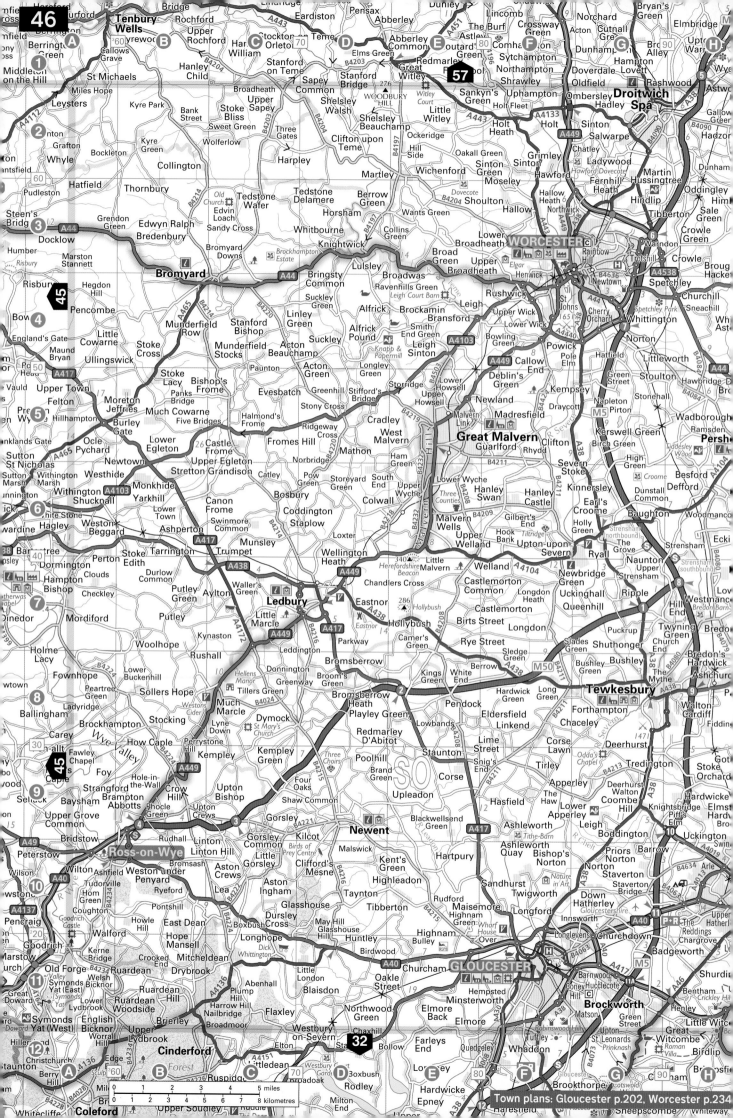

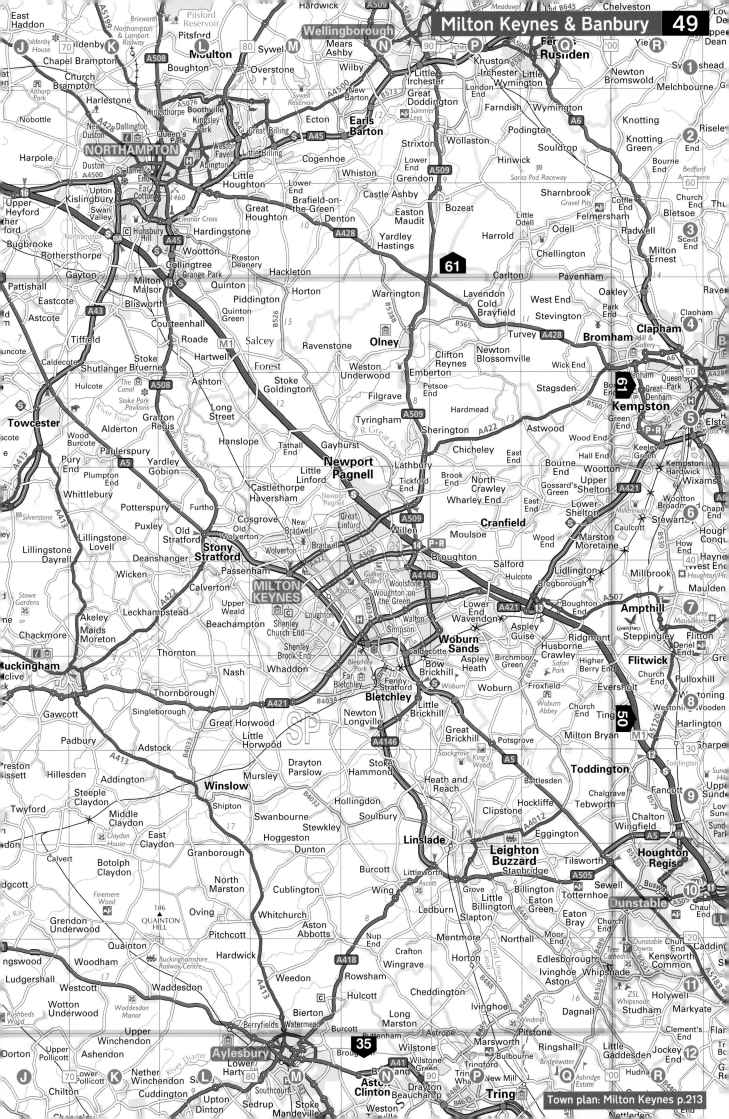

Harwich International Port

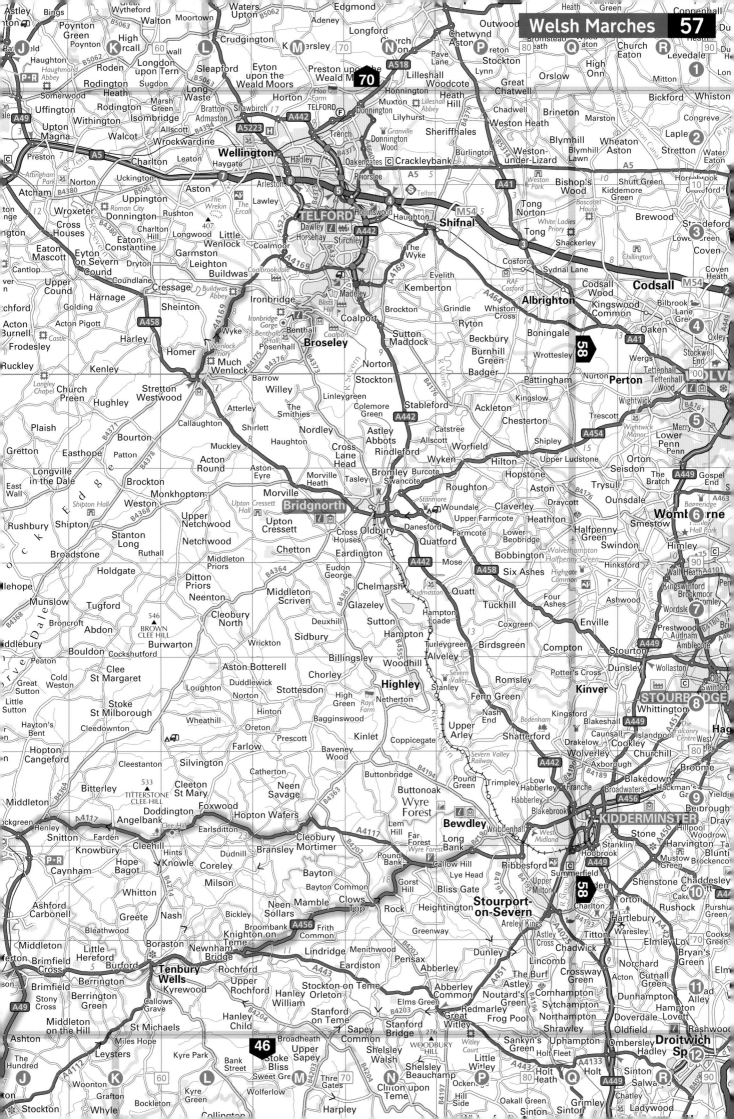

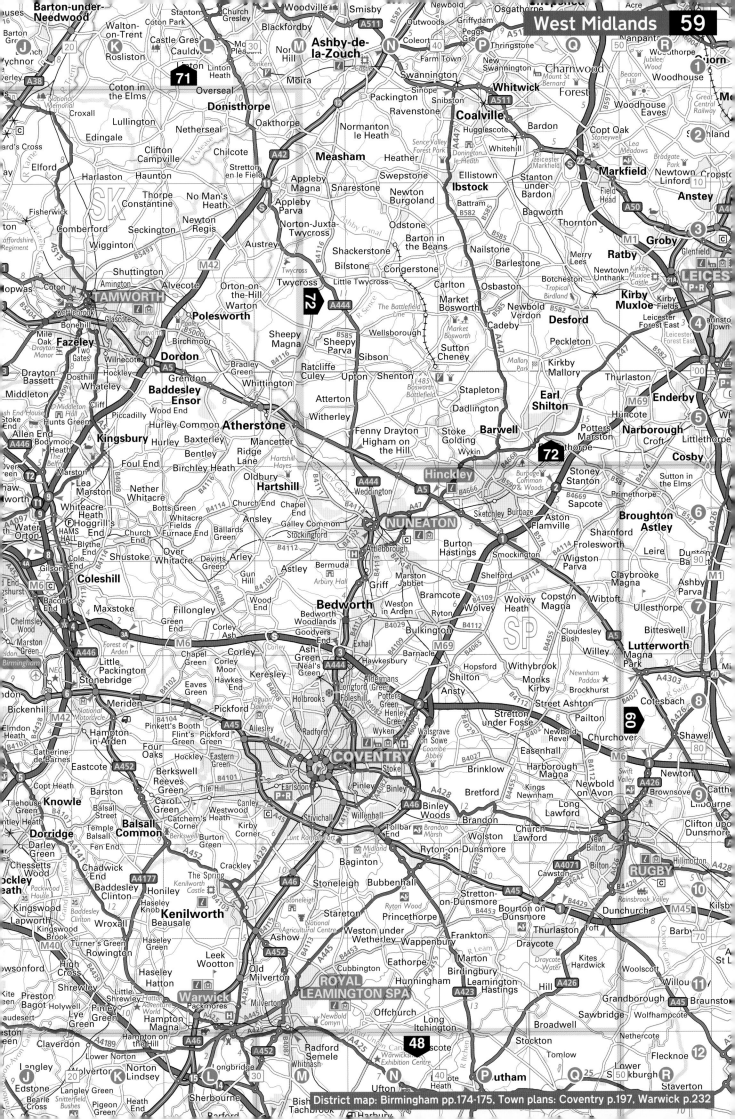

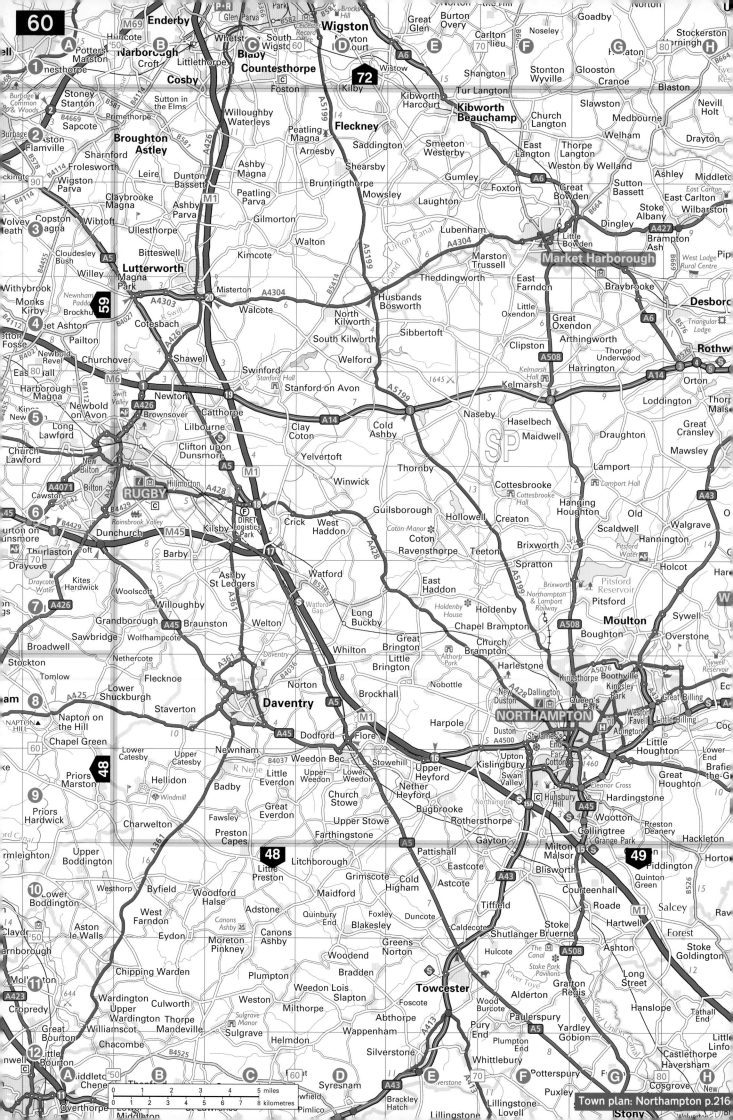

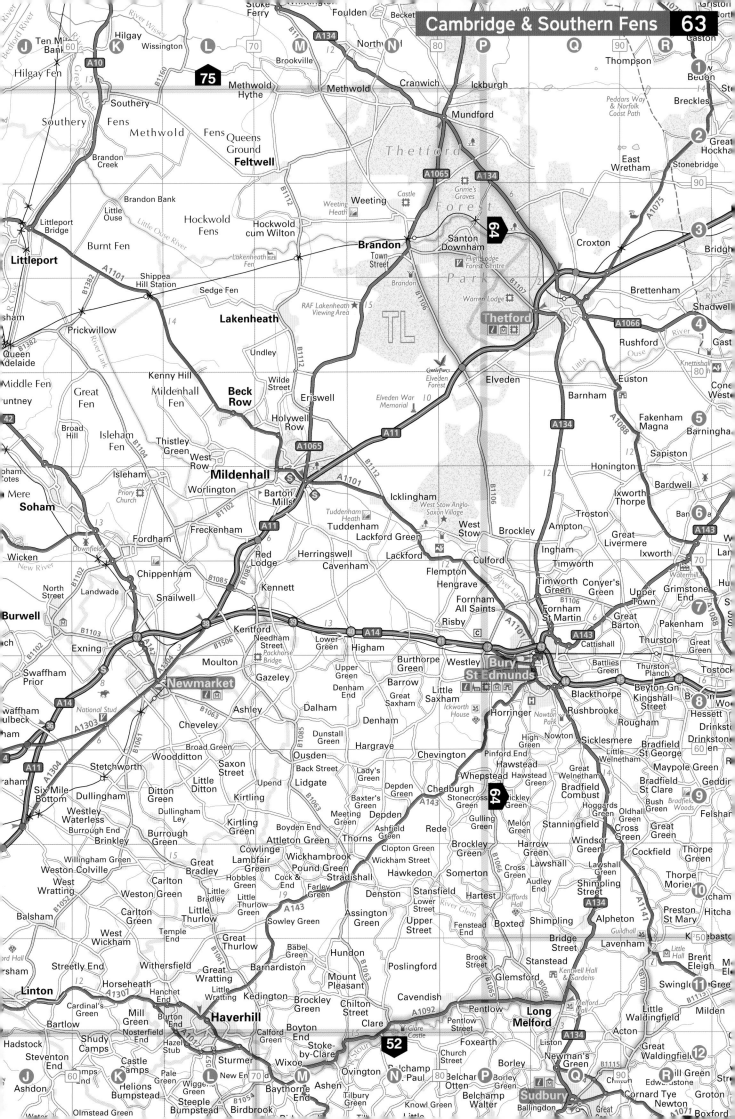

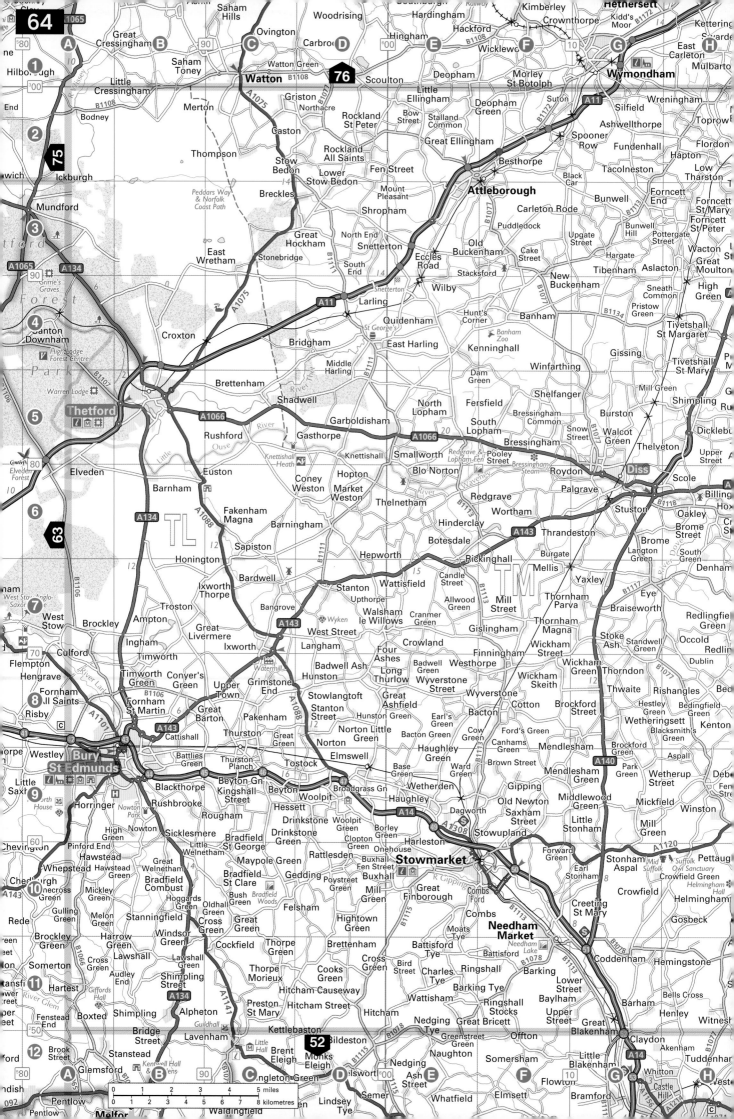

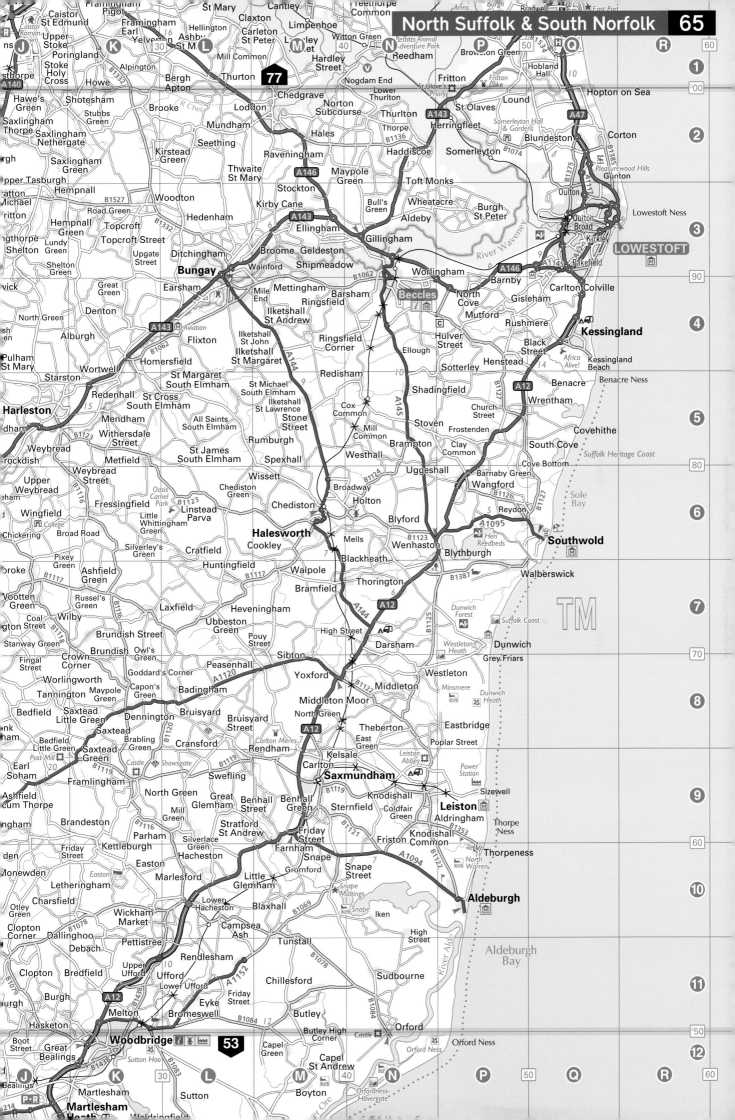

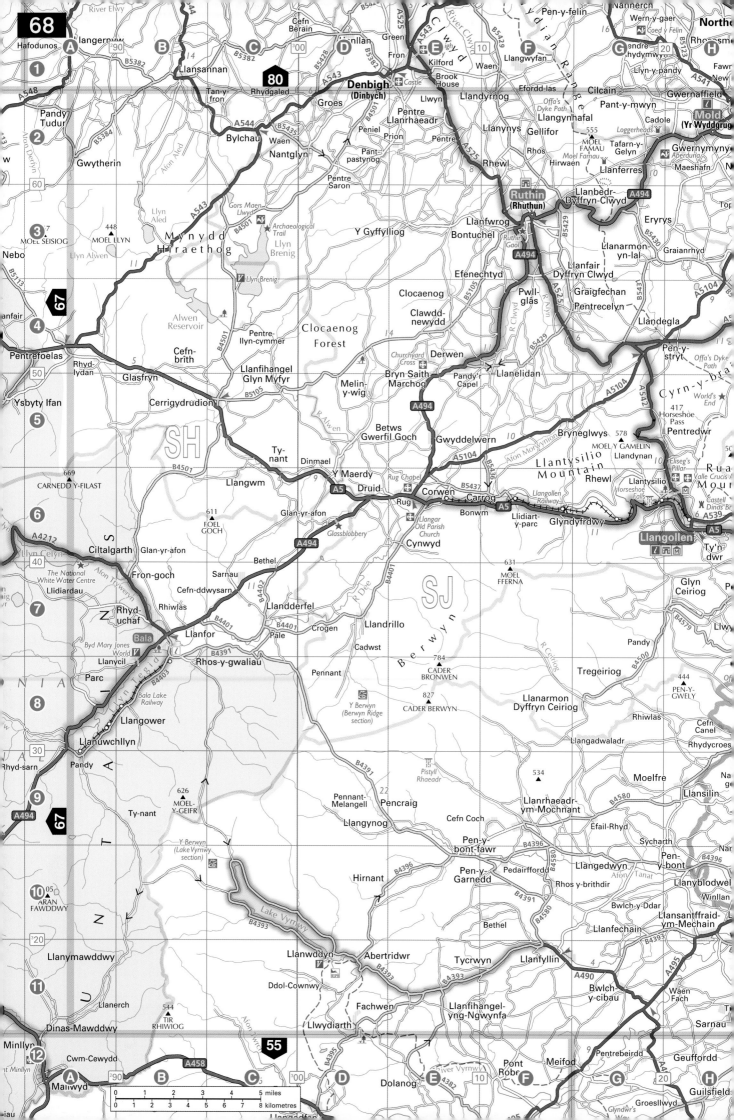

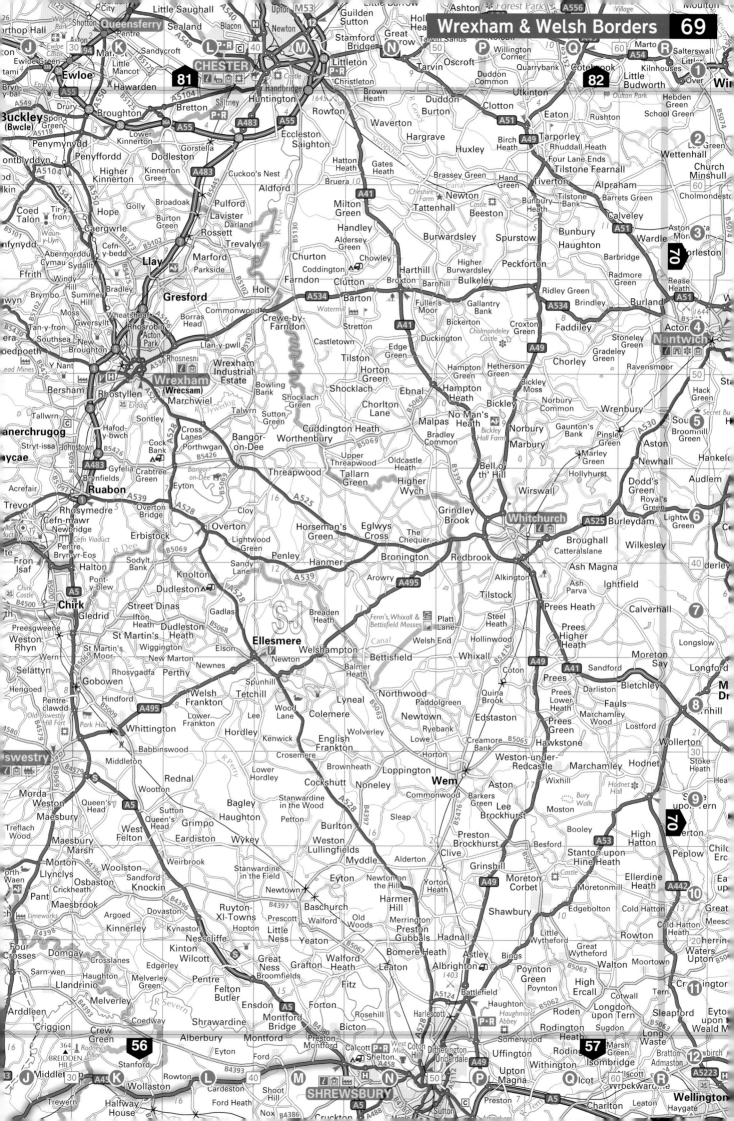

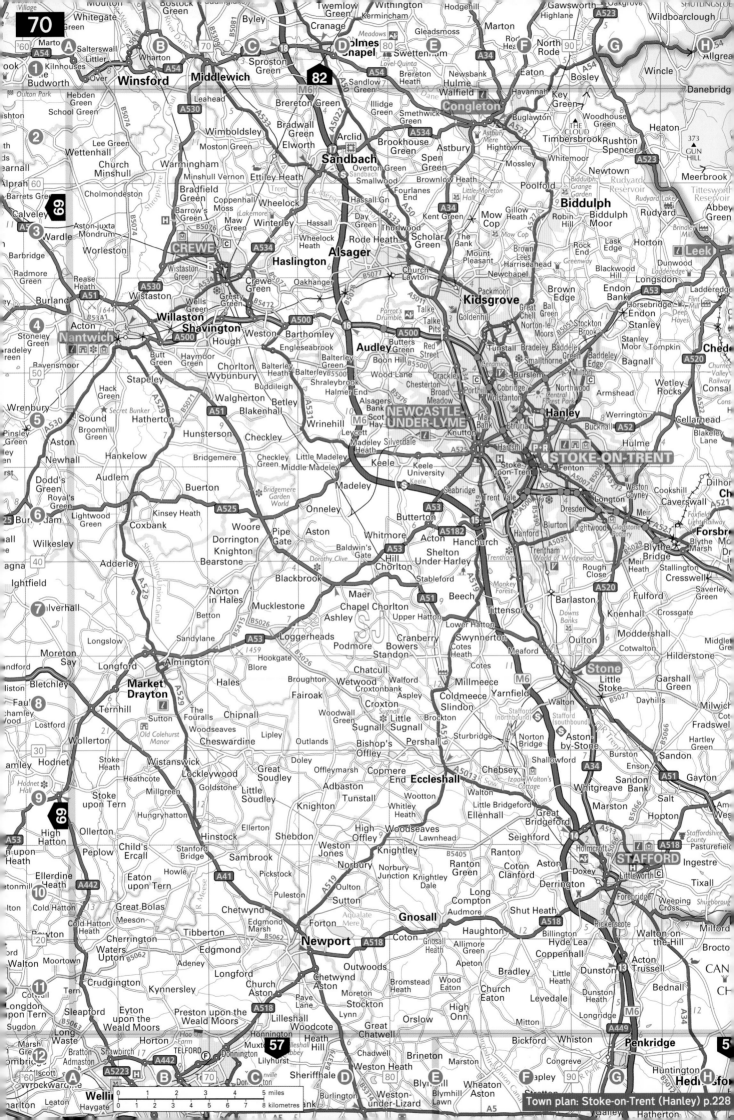

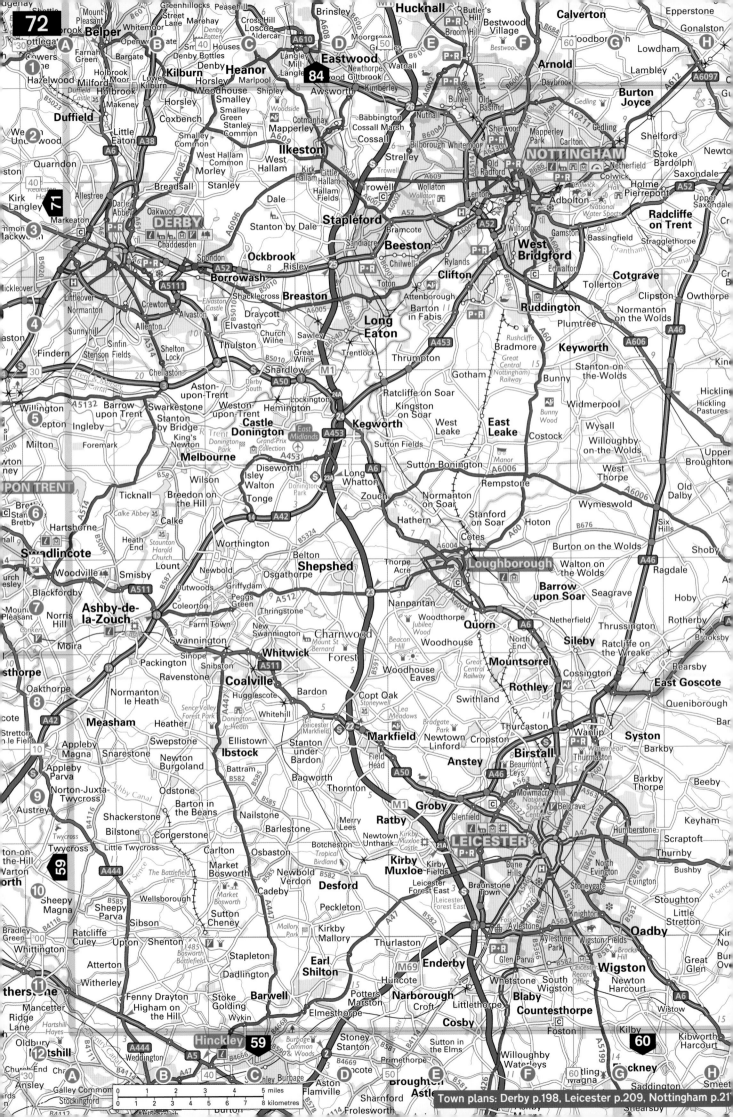

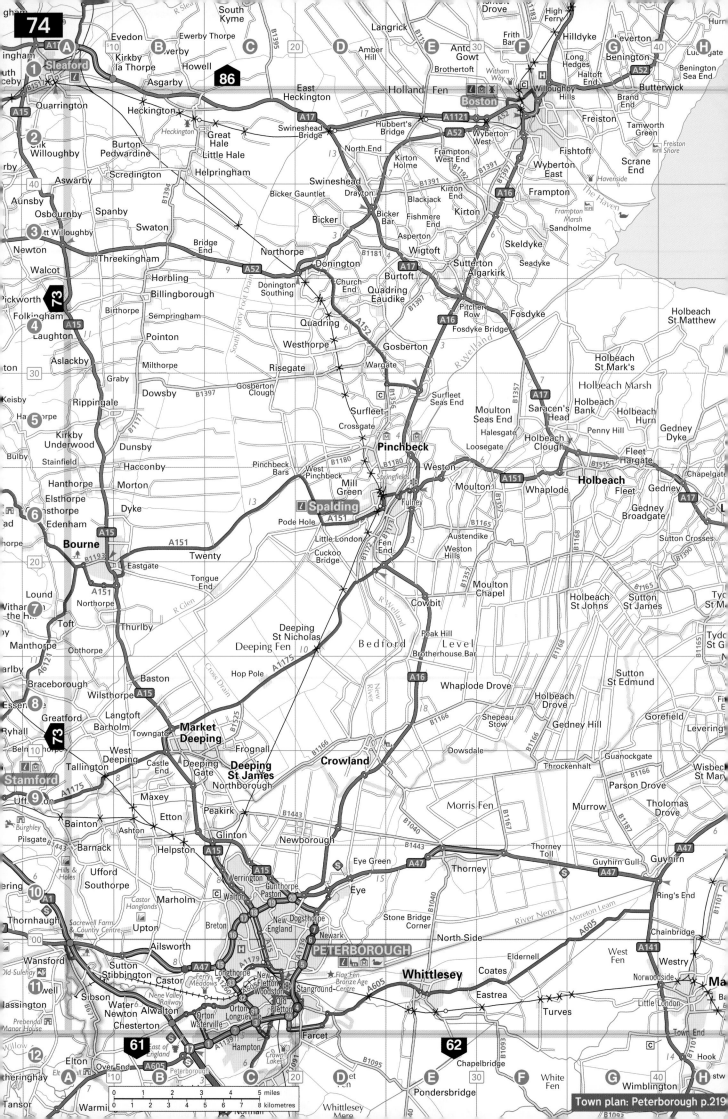

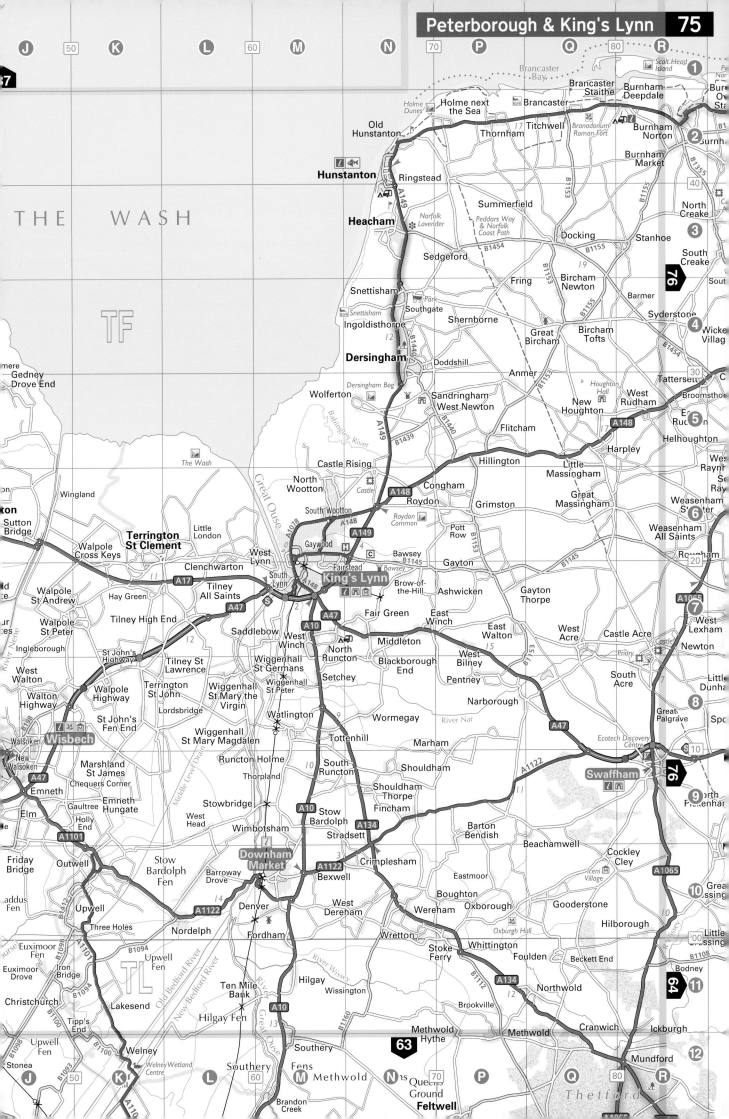

THE WASH

TF

THE WASH

Scolt Head Island
Brancaster Bay
Brancaster Staithe
Burnham Deepdale
Burnham Overy Staithe
Holme next the Sea
Holme Dunes
Brancaster
Titchwell
Thornham
Branodunum Roman Fort
Burnham Norton
Burnham Market
Old Hunstanton
Hunstanton
Ringstead
Summerfield
Docking
Stanhoe
North Creake
South Creake
Heacham
Norfolk Lavender
Peddars Way & Norfolk Coast Path
Sedgeford
Fring
Bircham Newton
Barmer
Syderstone
Wicken Village
Snettisham
Park
Southgate
Shernborne
Great Bircham
Bircham Tofts
Ingoldisthorpe
Dersingham
Doddshill
Anmer
Houghton Hall
New Houghton
West Rudham
Tattersett
Broomsthorpe
East Rudham
Wolferton
Dersingham Bog
Sandringham
West Newton
Flitcham
Harpley
Helhoughton
Castle Rising
North Wootton
Castle
Hillington
Congham
Little Massingham
Great Massingham
West Raynham
Weasenham St Peter
South Wootton
A148
Roydon
Roydon Common
Grimston
Great Massingham
Weasenham All Saints
Rougham
Terrington St Clement
Little London
West Lynn
A1078
Gaywood
Pott Row
Gayton
Walpole Cross Keys
Clenchwarton
South Lynn
King's Lynn
Bawsey
Brow-of-the-Hill
Ashwicken
Gayton Thorpe
West Acre
Castle Acre
West Lexham
Newton
Little Dunham
Tilney All Saints
Fairstead
Fair Green
East Winch
West Walton
Hay Green
Saddlebow
West Winch
Middleton
East Walton
West Bilney
West Acre
South Acre
Great Palgrave
Walpole St Andrew
Tilney High End
St John's Highway
North Runcton
Blackborough End
Pentney
Walpole St Peter
Ingleborough
Tilney St Lawrence
Wiggenhall St Germans
Setchey
Narborough
Ecotech Discovery Centre
West Walton
Walpole Highway
Terrington St John
Lordsbridge
Wiggenhall St Mary the Virgin
Wiggenhall St Peter
Watlington
Wormegay
River Nar
Swaffham
Walton Highway
St John's Fen End
Wiggenhall St Mary Magdalen
Tottenhill
Marham
Shouldham
Wisbech
Walsoken
Runcton Holme
Thorpland
South Runcton
Shouldham Thorpe
Fincham
Barton Bendish
Beachamwell
Cockley Cley
Iceni Village
New Walsoken
Marshland St James
Chequers Corner
Stowbridge
West Head
Stow Bardolph
Stradsett
Crimplesham
Eastmoor
Oxborough
Gooderstone
Emneth
Gaultree
Emneth Hungate
Barroway Drove
Wimbotsham
Bexwell
West Dereham
Boughton
Oxburgh Hall
Hilborough
Elm
Holly End
Stow Bardolph Fen
Downham Market
Wereham
Friday Bridge
Outwell
Denver
Fordham
Wretton
Stoke Ferry
Whittington
Foulden
Beckett End
Bodney
Upwell
Three Holes
Nordelph
Hilgay
Wissington
Northwold
Euximoor Fen
Iron Bridge
Upwell Fen
Ten Mile Bank
Hilgay Fen
Brookville
Methwold
Cranwich
Ickburgh
Christchurch
Lakesend
Old Bedford River
New Bedford River
River Wissey
Methwold Hythe
Mundford
Tipp's End
Welney
Welney Wetland Centre
Southery
Southery Fens
Queens Ground
Feltwell
Thetford
Brandon Creek

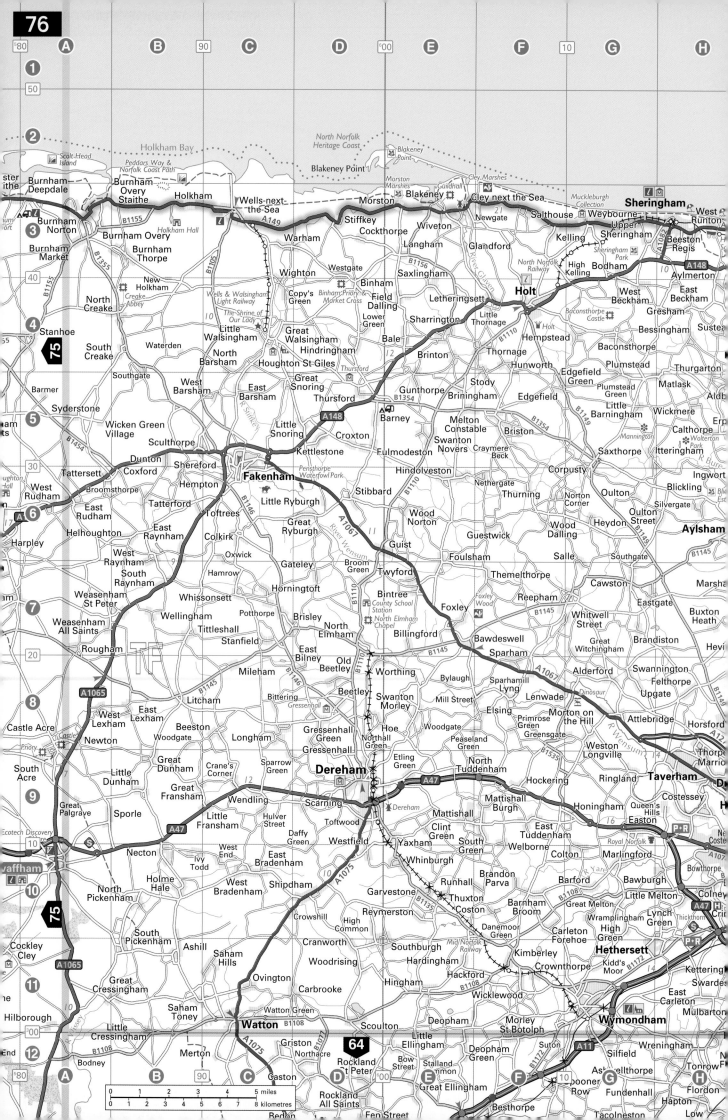

Isle of Man

0 1 2 3 4 5 miles
0 1 2 3 4 5 6 7 8 kilometres

NX

POINT OF AYRE

The Lhen
Rue Point
Point Cranstal
Cranstal
Bride
Ayres
A10
A16
Jurby Head
Andreas
Shellag Point
Jurby
A19
Sandygate
Regaby
B7
Ramsey
Bay
St Judes
Ballachurry Fort
The Cronk
Sulby
The Grove
Ramsey
(Rhumsaa)
Ballaugh
Churchtown
Port e Vullen
Manx Electric Railway
Orrisdale
Curraghs
Glen Auldyn
Maughold
Orrisdale Head
Dreemskerry
Maughold
Head
ISLE OF
Ancient Crosses
Ravensdale
NORTH
BARRULE
Ballajora
Kirk Michael
565
Corrany
Ballafayle
Glen Dhoo
MAN
Cashtal yn Ard
Cooildarry
488
Block Eary
Glen Mona
R.Neb
Sulby
Reservoir
621
SNAEFELL
466
SLIEAU LHEAN
Dhoon
Bay
Barregarrow
The Bungalow
Great
Laxey
Wheel
B10
Snaefell
Mountain Railway
King Orry's Grave
ELLAN
Cronk-
y-Voddy
487
COLDEN
Laxey
Laxey Head
Knocksharry
St Patrick's Isle
Millennium
Way
Ballafeannagh
Peel Castle
544
BEINN PHOTT
Old
Laxey
VANNIN
TT Circuit
Peel
(Purt ny-hinshey)
479
SLIEAU RUY
Creg ny Baa
Cloven Stones
Laxey
Bay
Contrary Head
Corrins Folly
Greeba
Baldwin
Manx Electric Railway
Patrick
Tynwald Hill
St John's
Clay Head
A1
Glen Maye
Crosby
Glen
Vine
Onchan
Glen Moye
Lower
Foxdale
Strang
Graudle Glen
Railway
Dalby
Niarbyl
Eairy
Union Mills
Cronkbourne
Norse
Houses
Onchan Head
Foxdale
Braaid
Niarbyl Bay
Round
Table
483
SOUTH
BARRULE
Closeclark
DOUGLAS
(DOOLISH)
Belfast
443
Douglas
Head
CRONK NY
ARREY LAA
Ballamodha
St Marks
Heysham
Fleshwick
Bay
Millennium
Way
Santon
Ballakilpheric
Grenaby
Isle of Man
Steam Railway
Liverpool
Port Soderick
Ballakelly
Colby
Ballabeg
Milners Tower
Silverdale Glen
Santon Head
Cronk ny
Merriu
Bradda Head
Ballasalla
Cregneash
Howe
Port Erin
Port
St Mary
Castletown
Derbyhaven
Birkenhead
CALF OF
MAN
Meayll
Circle
The
Sound
A5
Dublin
Derby Fort
Spanish Head
Close ny
Chollagh
Castletown
Bay
Scarlett
Point
Herring Tower
LIVERPOOL
BAY
Caigher
Point
Dreswick Point

SC

Manx Heritage site

SH

Point of Ayr

Little Ormes Head
Penrhyn
Bay
Penrhyn-
side
Llandrillo-
yn-Rhos
Rhôs-on-Sea
Colwyn Bay
(Bae Colwyn)
Old
Colwyn
A55
Esgyryn
Mochdre
Llandudno
Junction
Llansanffraid
Glan Conwy
Llanelian-
yn-Rhôs
Bryn-
y-Maen
Llysfaen
Rhyd-
y-foel
Llanddulas
A547
Pensarn
Abergele
Towyn
Dolwen
Dawn
Betws-
yn-Rhos
Trofarth
Graig
Tal-y-Cafn
Eglwysbach
Pentre'r
Felin
Llanfair
Talhaiarn
Pentre Isaf
River Elwy
Llangernyw
Hafodunos
Llannefydd
Cefn
Berain
Maenan
Llansannan
Tan-y-
fron
Rhydgaled
Henllan
Groes
Peniel
L'doget
Pandy
Tudur
Nantglyn
Prestatyn
Talacre
Gwespyr
Gronant
Ffynnongroyw
Llanasa
Picton
Rhyl
Gwaenysgor
Kinmel Bay
Meliden
Rhewl-
fawr
Axton
Trelogan
Mostyn
Kinmel
Bay
Abergele Roads
Miniature
Railway
Dyserth
Trelawnyd
Berthengam
Tre-
Mostyn
Glan-y-
Rhuddlan
Cwm
Walwen
Maen
Achwyfan
Cross
Downing
Whitford
Greenfield
Valley
St Winefride's
Well
Pengwern
Bodelwyddan
Rhuallt
Offa's
Dyke
Pen-y-cefn
Lloc
Gorsedd
Carmel
St George
St Asaph
Rhuallt
Pantasaph
Calcot
Bodelwyddan
Castle
Babell
Brynford
Glascoed
Tremeirchion
Graig
Caerwys
Mynydd-
llan
Dolp
Groesffordd
Marli
Sodom
Afon-wen
Ddol
Y Ddol Uchaf
Lixwm
Rhes
Trefnant
Bodfari
Pen-y-felin
Ysceifiog
Walwen
Nanner
Denbigh
Friary
Green
Fron
Kilford
Llangwyfan
Wer
Denbigh
(Dinbych)
Llandyrnog
Clwydian Range
Offa's
Dyke
Path
Brook
House
Fforidd-las
Cilcain
Llanrhaeadr
Bylch
Peniel
Waen
Prion
Pant-
pastynog
Groes
MOEL
FAMAU
555
Rhos
Moel-y-Gelyn
Hirwaen
Llanferres

0 1 2 3 4 5 miles
0 1 2 3 4 5 6 7 8 kilometres

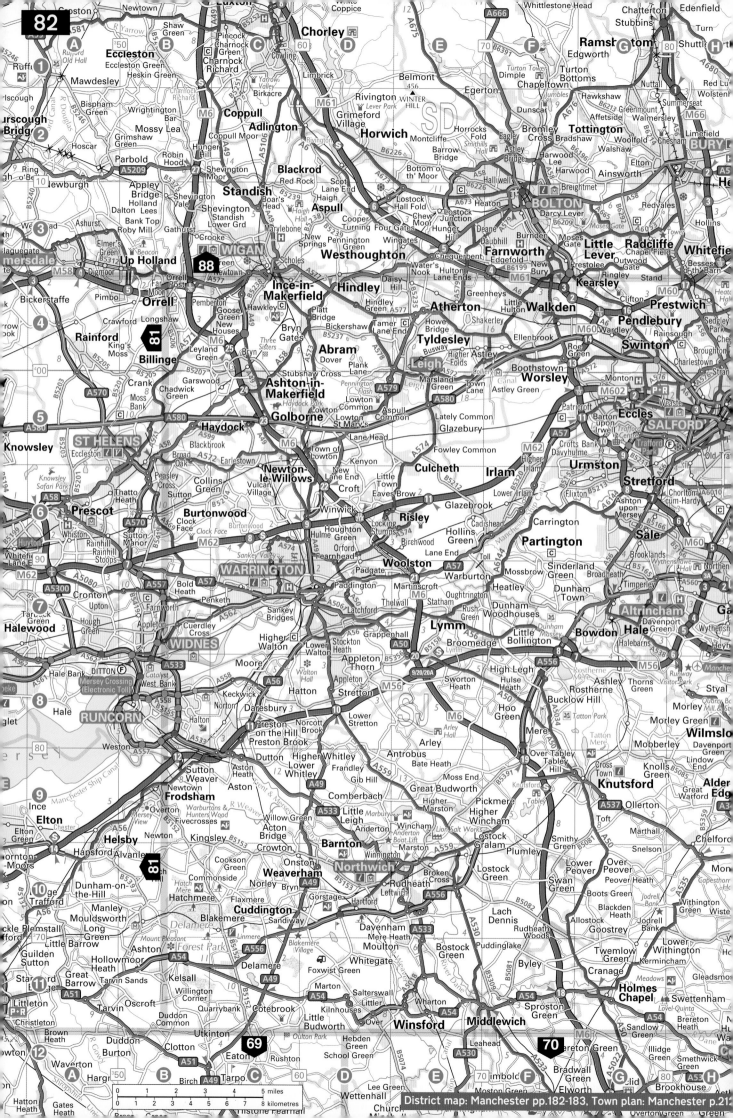

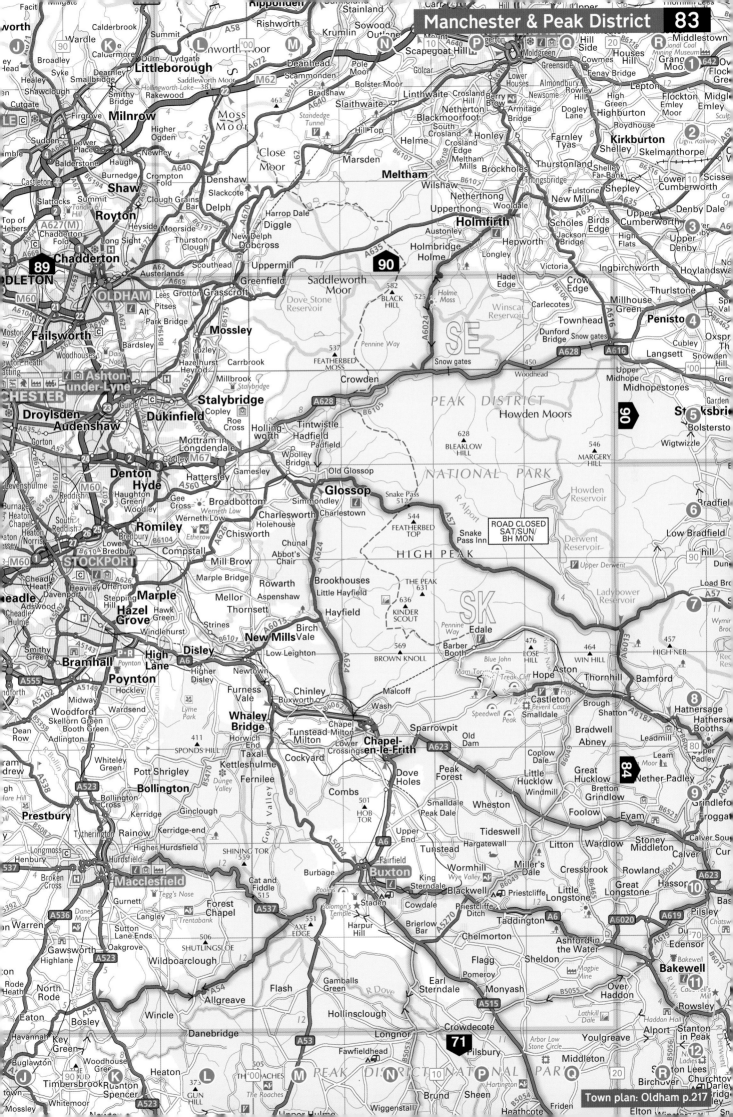

North Thoresby
Eskham
North Somercotes
Churchthorpe
West End
Grainthorpe
QB1201
A16
30
Fulstow
Skidbrooke North End
Saltfleet
Covenham St Bartholomew
Lincolnshire Wolds Railway
Conisholme
93
Church End
South Somercotes
Skidbrooke
Saltfleetby - Theddlethorpe Dunes
Covenham St Mary
Yarburgh
Little Grimsby
Alvingham
Saltfleetby St Clement
Utterby
Fotherby
North Cockerington
Saltfleetby All Saints
Keddington Corner
Rushmoor
North End
Saltfleetby St Peter
Theddlethorpe St Helen
Keddington
South Cockerington
Grimoldby
Stewton
Theddlethorpe All Saints
Seal Sanctuary & Wildlife Centre
Louth
Manby
Mablethorpe
Little Carlton
Great Carlton
Legbourne
A157
North Reston
Gayton le Marsh
Trusthorpe
Sutton on Sea
Little Cawthorpe
South Reston
Withern
Strubby
Thorpe
Sandilands
A16
Muckton
Tothill
Authorpe
Woodthorpe
Maltby le Marsh
Hagnaby
Hannah
Burwell
Claythorpe
Beesby
Saleby
Belleau
Watermill & Wildfowl
Markby
Asserby
White Pit
Swaby
Aby
Thoresthorpe
Asserby Turn
Huttoft
Calceby
Ailby
Bilsby
Thurlby
South Thoresby
Haugh
Alford
Anderby Creek
Rigsby
A1104
Farlesthorpe
Anderby
Driby
Well
Cumberworth
Mumby
Authorpe Row
Chapel Point
Mawthorpe
Ulceby
Helsey
A1028
Bonthorpe
Hogsthorpe
Chapel St Leonards
Sutterby
Willoughby
Langton
Claxby
Slackholme End
Aswardby
Dalby
Skendleby
Hasthorpe
Sloothby
Habertoft
Addlethorpe
Fantasy Island
A158
Hagworthingham
Partney
Scremby
Welton le Marsh
Ingoldmells
Raithby
A16
Candlesby
Lincolnshire Coast Light Railway
Ingoldmells Point
Spilsby
Ashby by Partney
Gunby
Orby
Winthorpe
Hundleby
Monksthorpe
Natureland Seal Sanctuary
Halton Holegate
Great Steeping
Bratoft
Burgh le Marsh
A158
Skegness
Toynton All Saints
Northcote
Irby in the Marsh
West Keal
Halton Fenside
Little Steeping
Firsby
Croft
Seacroft
East Keal
Toynton St Peter
Keal Cotes
Toynton Fen Side
Fendike Corner
Thorpe St Peter
Wainfleet Haven
Stickford
Wainfleet Bank
Wainfleet All Saints
Gibraltar
New Leake
Wainfleet St Mary
A52
New Bolingbroke
Stickney
Midville
Eastville
Lincolnshire
Friskney
Gibraltar Point
East Fen
Friskney Eaudike
A16
Lade Bank
Wrangle Common
75

TF

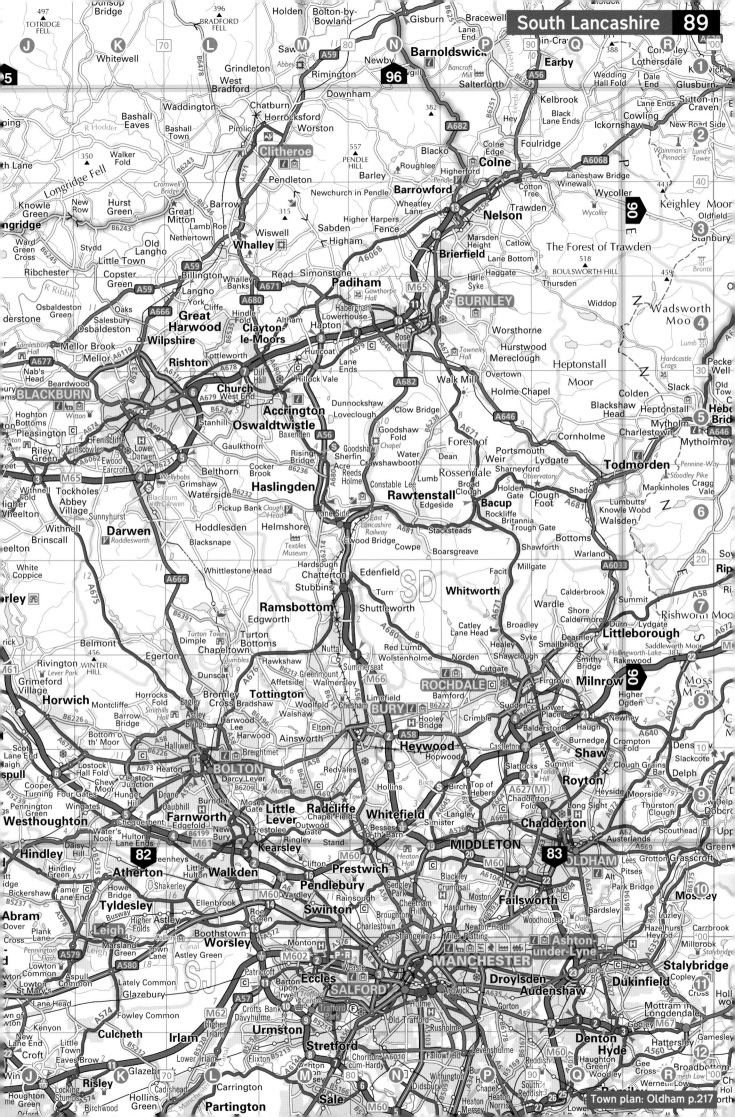

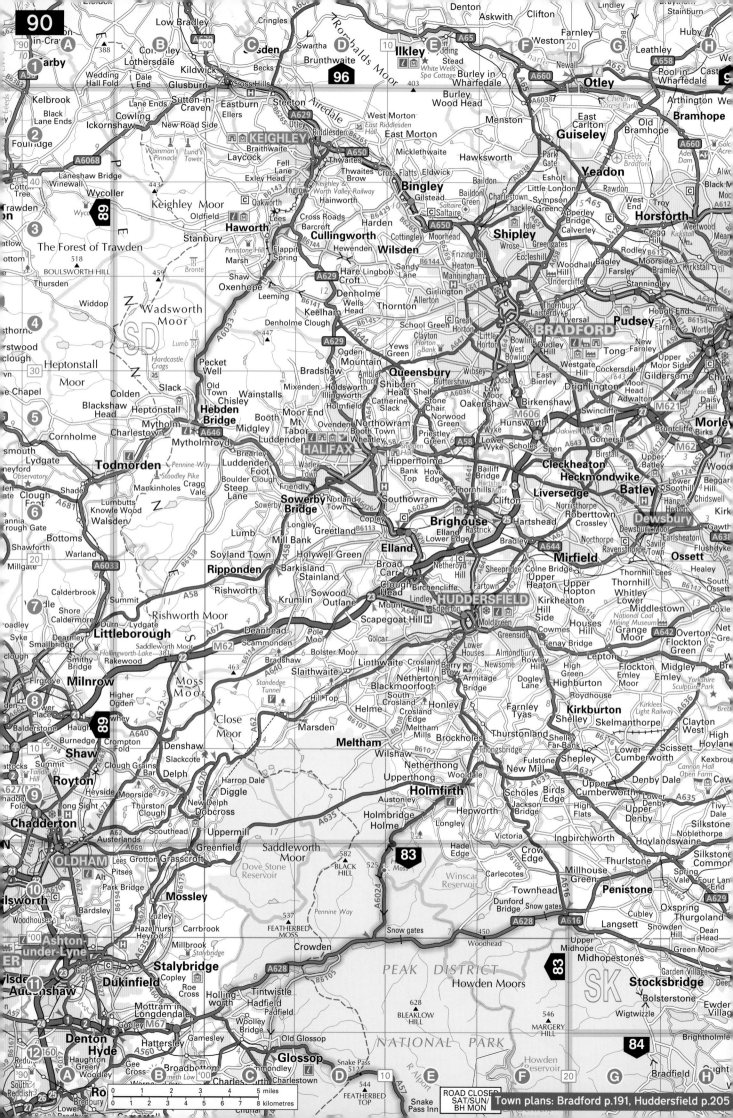

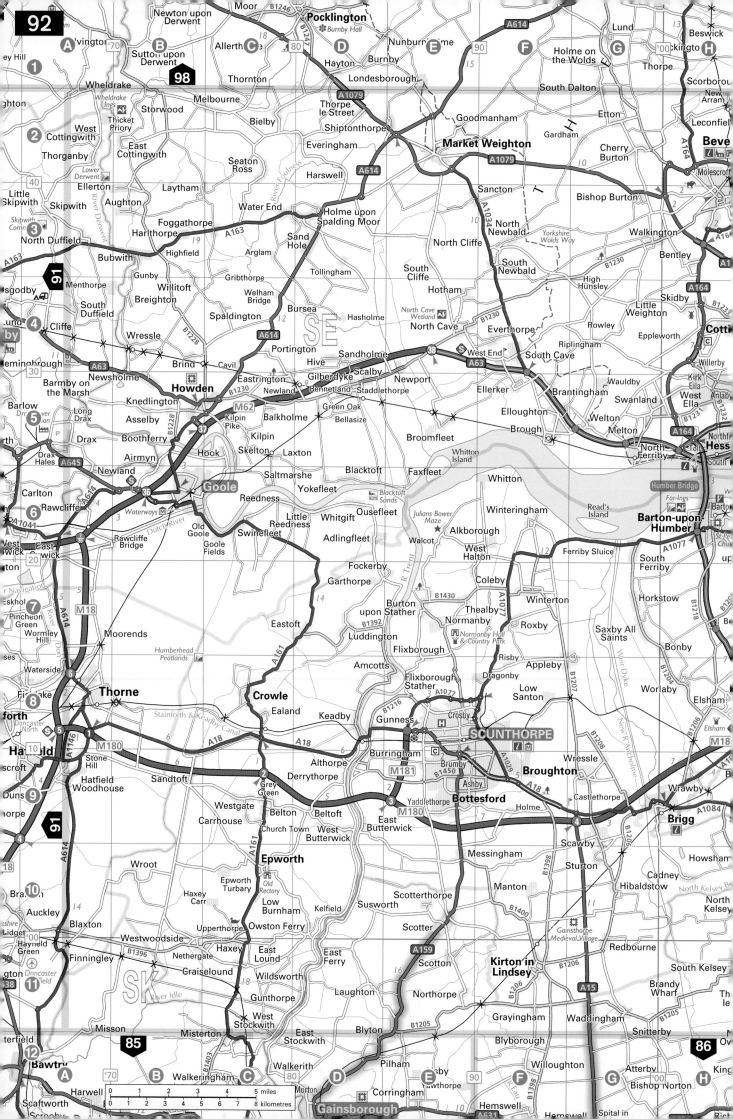

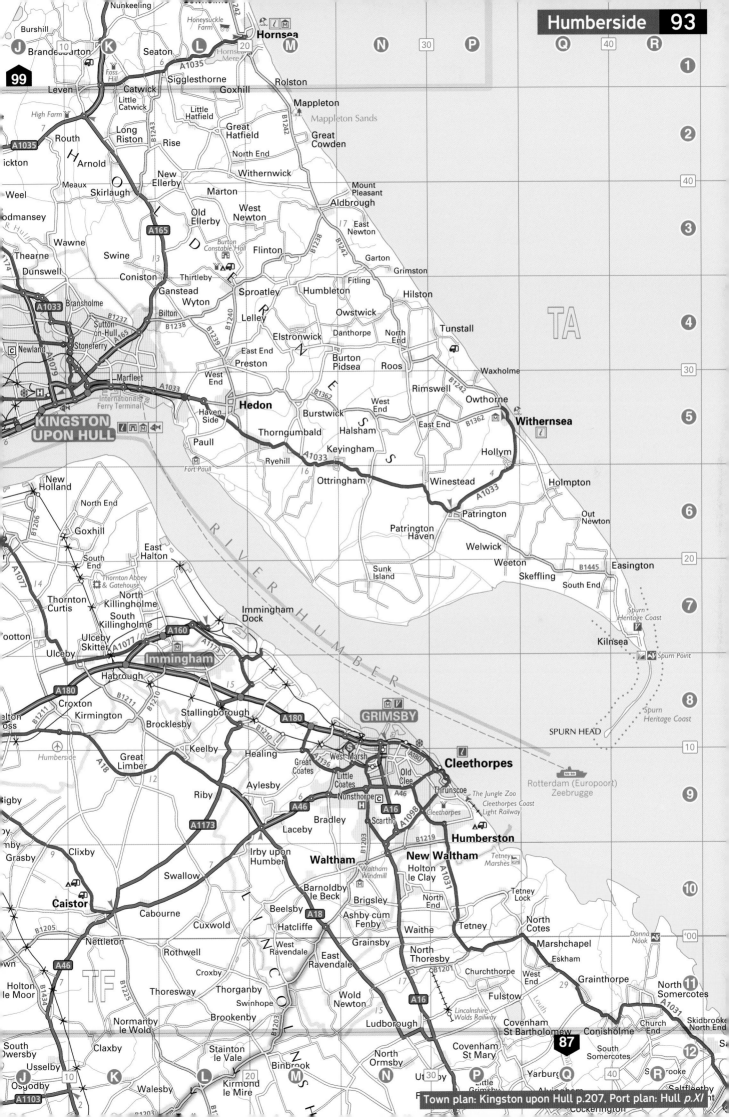

Heysham Harbour

0   500 m

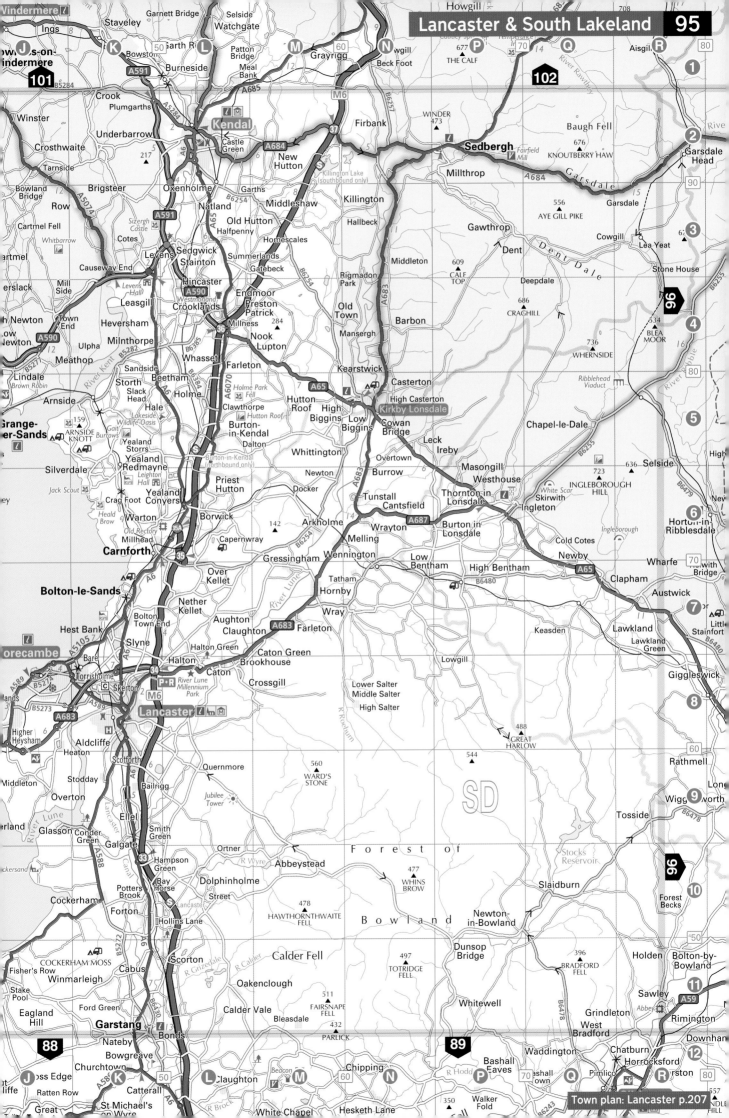

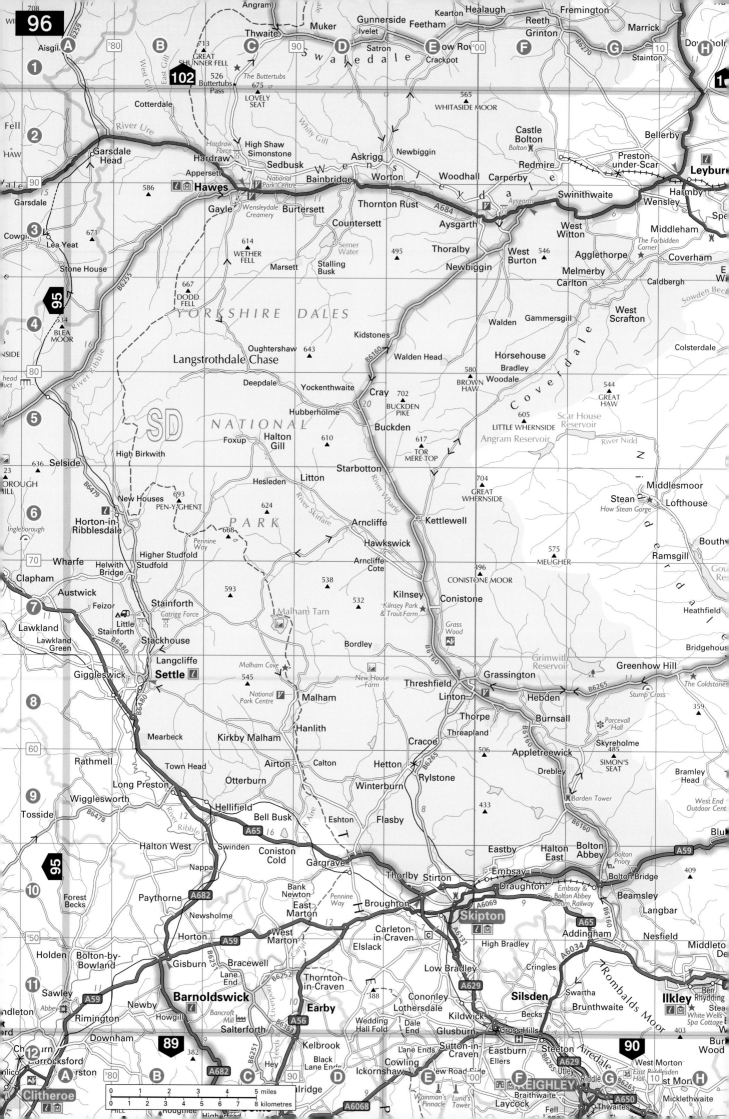

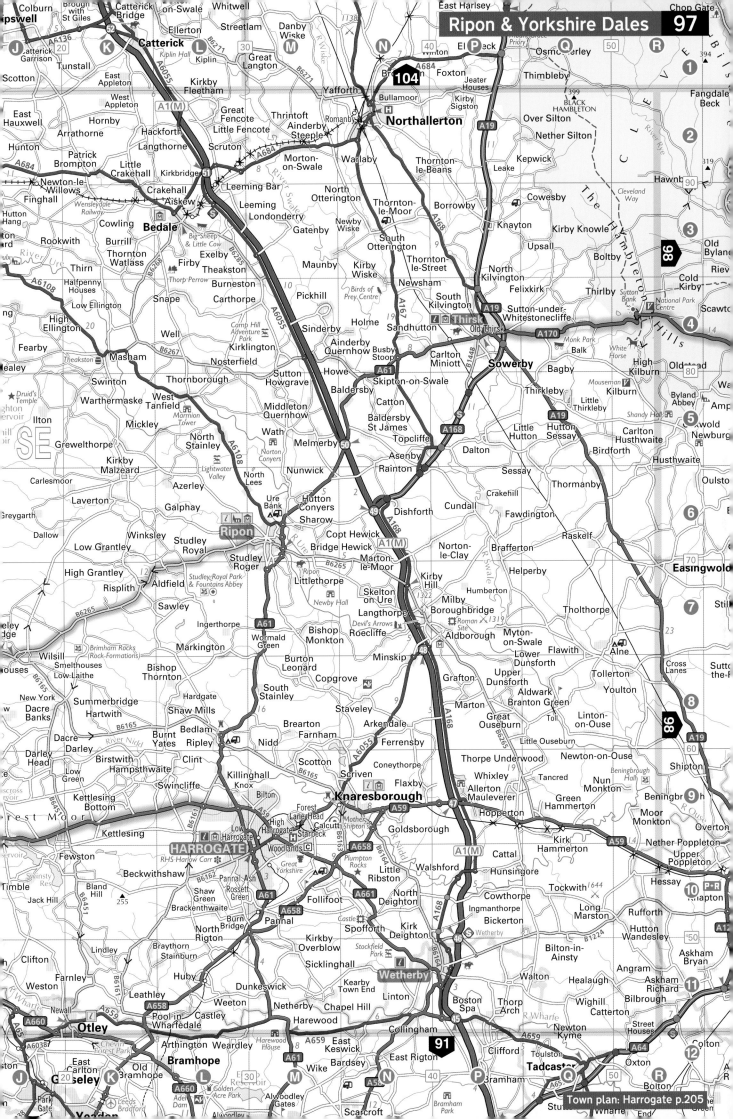

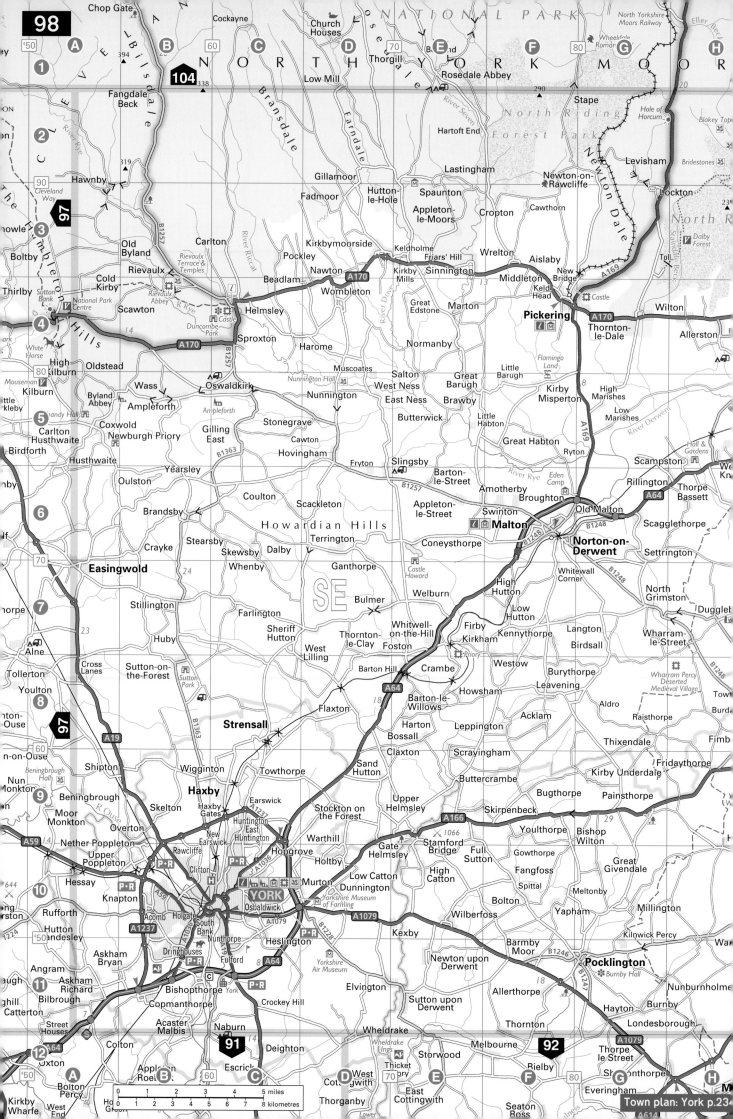

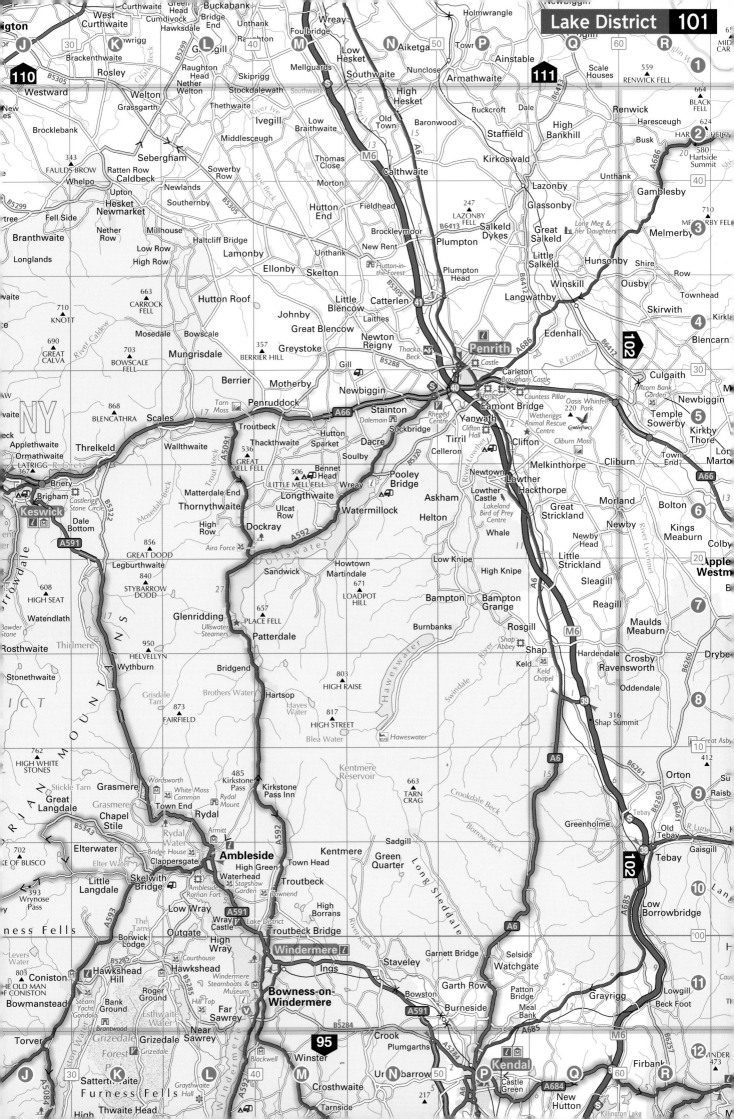

J · 70 · K · L · 80 · M · N · 90 · P · Q · ⁵⁰⁰ · R

① ② ③ ④ ⑤ ⑥ ⑦ ⑧ ⑨ ⑩ ⑪ ⑫

40
30
20
10
⁵⁰⁰
00

NZ

Saltburn-by-the-Sea
Saltburn Smugglers
New Brotton
Brotton
Skelton
New Skelton
Carlin How
North Skelton
Kilton
Skinningrove
Hummersea Scar
Upton
Boulby
Loftus
Staithes
Captain Cook & Staithes
Port Mulgrave
Lingdale
Kilton Thorpe
Liverton Mines
Dalehouse
Easington
Hinderwell
North Yorkshire and Cleveland Heritage Coast
Woodhill
Liverton
Handale
Roxby
Newton Mulgrave
Runswick Bay
Stanghow
Borrowby
Runswick
Kettleness
Goldsborough
A171
Moorsholm
B1366
Scaling
B1266
Ellerby
Lythe
Overdale Wyke
Gerrick
Scaling Dam
Mickleby
A174
Sandsend
Sandsend Wyke
West Barnby
East Barnby
Raithwaite
Whitby ℹ Ⓜ
Ugthorpe
Dunsley
Newholm
Abbey
Saltwick Bay
The Moors National Park Centre 301
Stonegate
Hutton Mulgrave
Ruswarp
Stainsacre
Danby
Aislaby
Briggswath
Sneaton
High Hawsker
Castleton
Ainthorpe
Lealholm
Lealholm Side
A171
Sleights
Ugglebarnby
Low Hawsker
B1447
Ness Point or North Cheek
River Esk
The Green
Egton
Esk Dale
Iburndale
Sneatonthorpe
Raw
Robin Hood's Bay
erdale
Glaisdale
Grosmont
Littlebeck
Fylingthorpe
Robin Hood's Bay
Danby Bottom
Egton Bridge
Key Green
B1416
Street
Old Peak or South Cheek
NORTH YORK MOORS
Beck Hole
A171
Ravenscar
326 PIKE HILL
Goathland
Staintondale
369
Shire Horse Centre
NATIONAL PARK
North Yorkshire Moors Railway
292
Hayburn Wyke
rch ses
Rosedale
Low Bell End
Eller Beck
Harwood Dale
Cloughton Newlands
Thorgill
NORTH YORK MOORS
Wheeldale Roman Road
Cloughton Wyke
Mill
Rosedale Abbey
River Seven
290
NORTH RIDING
Stape
Hole of Horcum
Blakey Topping
99
Cloughton
Cromer Point
North Riding For t P k
Crosscliff
Toll
Cleveland Way
J · 70 · K rtoft End · L t P · 80 · M · N · 90 · P Bickley · Q Bur ⁰⁰ton · R
Lastingham
Levisham
Bridestones
Dalby
Langdale
Hackness
Broxa
Silpho
Suffield

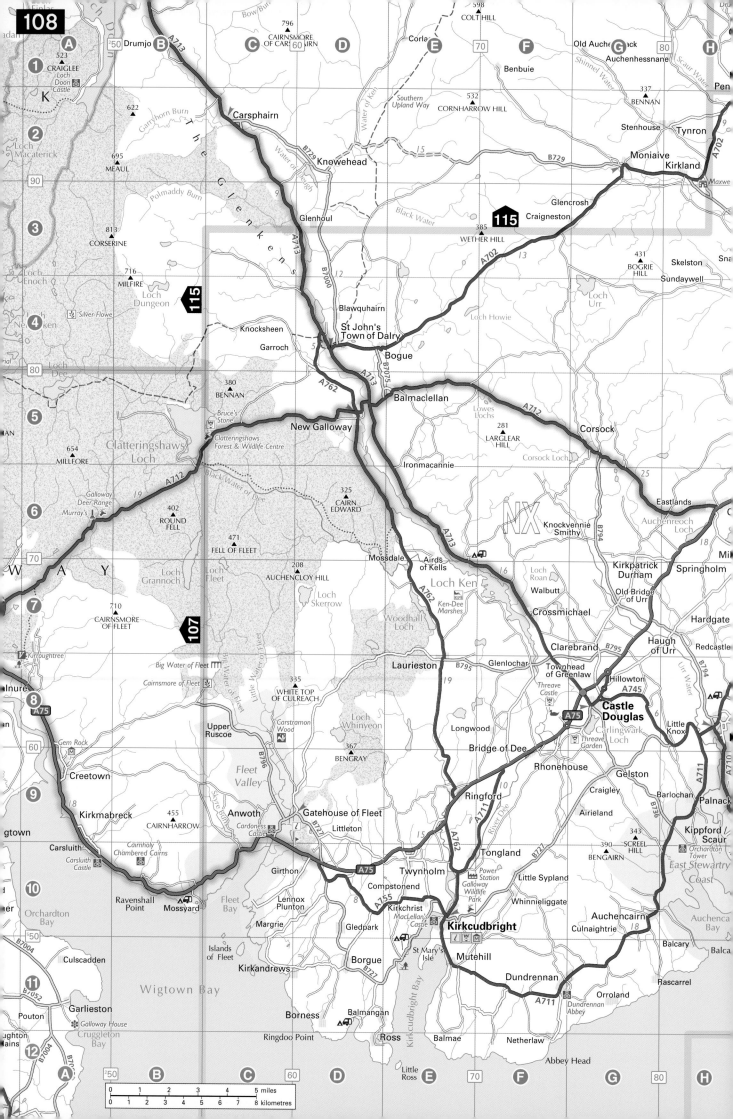

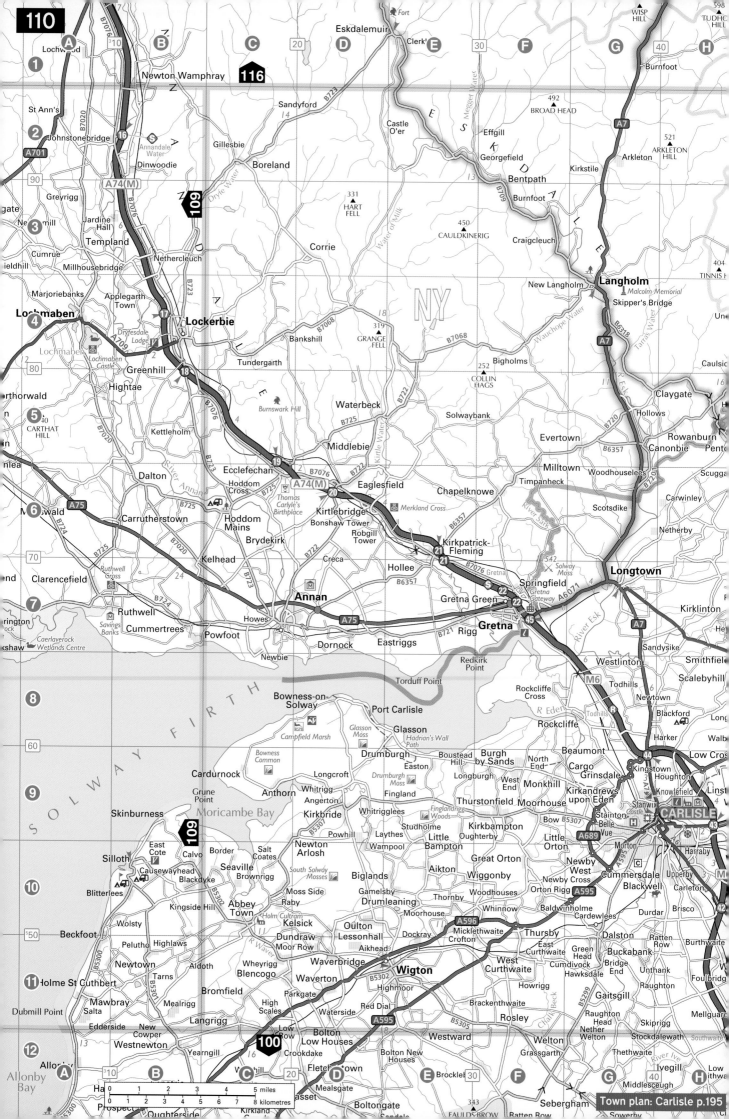

J   50   K   L   M   60   N   70   P   Q   HINDHC LAW   80   R   Horsley   1

433 SAUGHTREE FELL
Myredykes
PEEL FELL
OH ME EDGE
Kielderhead
A06 Camp

Hermitage Castle
Hermitage
7

Newlands
Riccarton
60

Kielder Burn
118
513 MONKSIDE
Pennine Way
Troughen   2

Steele Road
403 LOCH KNOWE
Observatory
Skyspace
Toll
Kielder
Kielder Castle
Tarset Burn
Black Middens Bastle House
Highgreen Manor
90
B6320   3

Castleton
B6399
B6357
413 WILSON'S PIKE
Kielder Water
Kielder Water
Waterside
397 EARLS SEAT
307 WHITE HILL
Gatehouse
Falstone
Greenhaugh
112
9   3

Newcastleton
513 GLENDHU HILL
Kershope Burn
Lewis Burn
Kielder Water
Tower Knowe
Stannersburn
Hott
Laneheaad
Charlton   4

275 BLINKBONNY HEIGHT
Forest
Hesleyside
Bellingh
V

Kershopefoot
NORTHUMBERLAND
Red

Sleetbeck
atlowdy
Baileyhead
Blackpool Gate
Oakshaw Ford
519 SIGHIY CRAG
492 BLACK KNOWE
395 BOLTS LAW
Chirdon Burn
NATIONAL
Stonehaugh
Wark
Park E   5

Haggbeck
Roadhead
B6318
355 BARRON'S PIKE
Bewcastle
WARK FOREST
Churnsike Lodge
325 ROUND TOP
PARK
Simonbu   6

Lyneholmford
Stapleton
265 GREEN RIGG
313 SPY RIGG
Black Fell
Warks Burn
Pennine Way
Greenlee Lough
Broomlee Lough
Hadrian's Path
70
Br   6

Boltonfellend
Kirkcambeck
River Irthing
Greenlee Lough
Crag Lough
Housesteads Fort
Grindon Hill
ewbro   7

Hethersgill
Nickies Hill
Triermain
B6318
Gilsland
Walltown Crags!
Hadrian's Wall
Roman Army
Cawfields
Vindolanda (Chesterholm)
The Sill   7

Walton
Birdoswald Fort
Pike Hill
Upper Denton
Milecastle
Greenhead
Once Brewed
Birkshaw Westwood
Westend Town
Chesterwood
Haydon Bridge

Hadrian's Wall Path
Banks
East Turret
Greenhead
Haltwhistle
Henshaw
Thorngrafton
Bardon Mill

Newtown
Burtholme
Lanercost Priory
Lanercost
Low Row
A69
9
DENTON FELL 255
Pennine Way
Haltwhistle
Melkridge
Redburn
Beltingham
Ridley
Deanraw
Langley
Elringto
Castle
B6305
8

aversdale
Brampton
Irthington
Milton
Hallbankgate
Park
Rowfoot
Plenmeller
Allen Banks & Staward Gorge
B6304
60

dwall
A689
M
Kirkhouse
Farlam
Talkin
Talkin Tarn
Geltsdale
Tindale
A689
Midgeholme
Coanwood
Lambley
Stonehouse
Wolf Hills
Fellhouse Fell
Whitfield
Catt   9

h Crosby East
Low Gettbridge
Hayton
Forest Head
Halton Lea Gate
Eals
Whitfield Hall
Thornley Gate
Allendale

Corby idge
Burnrigg
How Mill
Castle Carrock
621 COLD FELL
522 GLENDUE FELL
Knarsdale
A686
17
Ninebanks
112
10

ick den
Fenton
Heads Nook
Great Corby
Wetheral Priory Gatehouse
Faugh
River Gelt
NY
R South Tyne
Keirsleywell Row
Limestone Brae

whinton
Cumwhitton
483 CUMREW FELL
521 GELTSDALE MIDDLE
584 THREE PIKES
Slaggyford
Blagill
572 HARTLEY MOOR
11

Hornsbygate
Cumrew
Newbiggin
Croglin Water
657 MIDDLE CARRICK
Kirkhaugh
Ayle
B6294
Carr Shield

ugh
Aiketgate
Hornsby
Holmwrangle
Croglin
The Hub
Alston
Raise
Nenthall

High Hesket
Nunclose
Armathwaite
Scale Houses
559 RENWICK FELL
664 BLACK FELL
Gilderdale Forest
102
Nenthead
A689
12

J   50   K   L   60   M   N   70   P   Q   80   R   Lanehead
1   Baronwood   Staffield   Hi Bank   Renwick   Haresough   624 HARTSIDE HEIGHT   Alston Moor   Garrigill   Kill   Killhope Mining   Cornri
Kirkoswald   A686   20   Hartside Summit   Shield Water   Aj

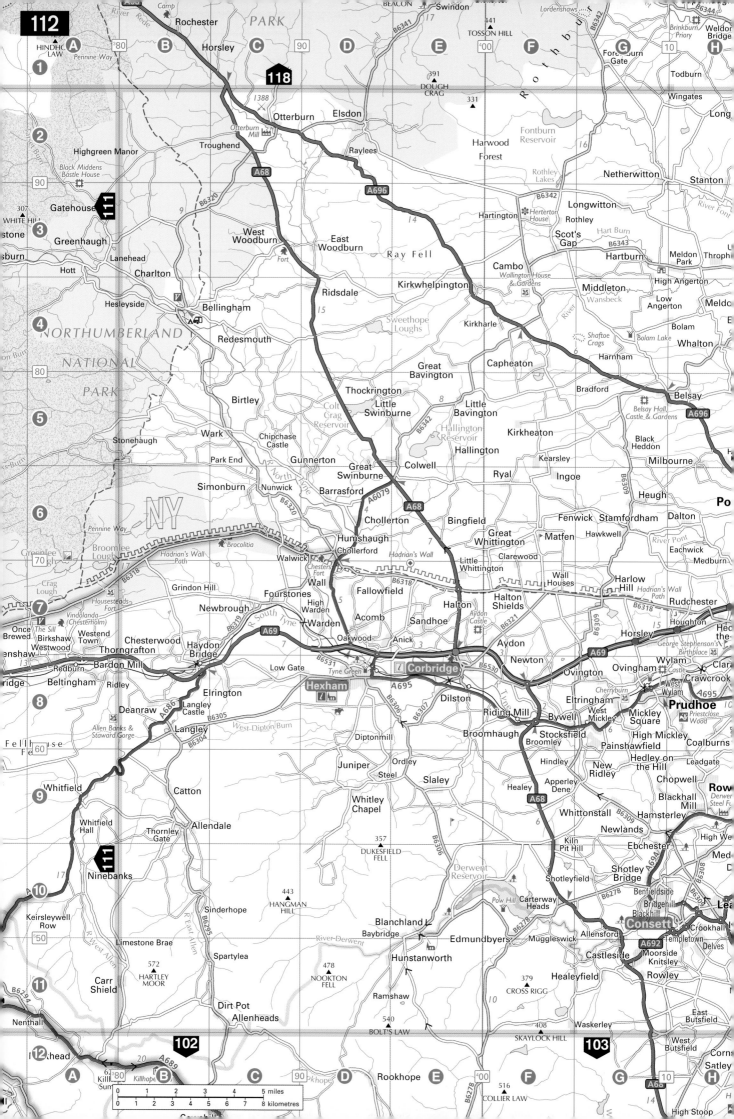

Port of Tyne

TYNEMOUTH
THE NORTH
NEWCASTLE
A193
A1058
A187
PERCY MAIN
M MEADOW WELL
M
HOWDON ROAD
Wet'n'Wild Water Park
Toll
A19
A187
East Howdon
Royal Quays Outlet
Premier Inn
Royal Quays Marina
Check-in
Toll
TYNE VIEW
A187
Tyne Tunnel
P
Check-in
INTERNATIONAL PASSENGER TERMINAL
River Tyne
PRIORY ROAD
B1297
Jarrow
LBLI
SUNDERLAND
0   500 m

West Thirston
Broomhill
Red Row
Druridge Bay
Eshott
Helm
West Chevington
Druridge
Druridge Bay
Causey Park
Stobswood
Widdrington
North Northumberland Heritage Coast
Causey Park Bridge
Earsdon
Tritlington
Ulgham
Widdrington Station
Linton
Ellington
Cresswell
Fenrother
Hebron
Longhirst
Lynemouth
A1
Pegswood
Woodhorn
Beacon Point
QE2
Woodhorn Demesne
Ashington
Hepscott
Bothal
Hirst
North Seaton
Newbiggin-by-the-Sea
Morpeth
Sheepwash
Scotland Gate
Stakeford
North Seaton Colliery
Tranwell
Clifton
Guide Post
Bomarsund
Cambois
Choppington
Nedderton
East Sleekburn
North Blyth
Bedlington
Cowpen
Blyth
Stannington Station
Bebside
Newsham
East Hartford
New Delaval
Shotton
Shankhouse
New Hartley
Seaton Sluice
Stannington
East Cramlington
Seaton
Cramlington
Seghill
Seaton Delaval
Hartley
Berwick Hill
Brenkley
Big Waters
Holywell
St Mary's
Dinnington
Seaton Burn
Annitsford
Prestwick
Burradon
Earsdon
Dudley
Wide Open
Camperdown
Monkseaton
Whitley Bay
Brunswick Village
Killingworth
Backworth
Cullercoats
NZ
High Callerton
Woolsington
Great Park
Shiremoor
Murton
Hazlerigg
Forest Hall
New York
Tynemouth
Black Callerton
Kenton Bankfoot
Rising Sun
Tynemouth Priory & Castle
Amsterdam (IJmuiden)
North Gosforth
South Gosforth
Longbenton
North Shields
Callerton
Fawdon
Jesmond
Willington
SOUTH SHIELDS
Westerhope
Kenton
Wallsend
Int. Ferry Terminal
Newburn
Heaton
Westoe
NEWCASTLE UPON TYNE
Walker
Jarrow
Tyne Tunnel
Harton
Stella
Byker
Hebburn
Marsden
Scotswood
Elswick
Monkton
Marsden Bay
Blaydon
Dunston
Felling
Souter Lighthouse & The Leas
Winlaton
Metro Centre
Wardley
Cleadon
Whitburn Coastal Park
Derwent Walk
GATESHEAD
Boldon Colliery
West Boldon
Souter Point
Winlaton Mill
Whickham
Team Valley
Wrekenton
Whitburn
Sunniside
Watergate Forest
Low Fell
Bowes Railway
East Boldon
Whitburn Bay
Gibside
Street Gate
A1
Lamesley
Angel of the North
A194(M)
Hylton Castle
Seaburn
Sheep Hill
Marley Hill
Tanfield Railway
Springwell
Usworth
Wetland Centre
Castletown
Fulwell
Southwick
Roker
Byermoor
Kibblesworth
Birtley
Portobello
South Hylton
Monkwearmouth
Causey Arch
Tanfield
High Urpeth
WASHINGTON
Pennywell
SUNDERLAND
Tanfield Lea
Beamish
Urpeth
Ouston
Perkinsville
Offerton
Hendon
Stanley
West Pelton
Pelton
Fatfield
Penshaw
Herrington
High Newport
Grangetown
Catchgate
Oxhill
Grange
Pelton Fell
Penshaw Monument
New Silksworth
Tunstall
Ryhope
Durham Heritage Coast
The Villa Middles
Newfield
Shiney Row
Philadelphia
Chester-le-Street
Craghead
Houghton Gate
Bournmoor
New Herrington
Newbottle
Seaham
South Moor
Quaking Houses
Fence Houses
High Dubmire
Houghton-le-Spring
Seaton
Maiden Law
Waldridge
Great Lumley
Colliery Row
Holmside
Edmondsley
Chester Moor
West Rainton
Hetton-le-Hole
Murton
Dalton-le-Dale
Burnhope
Nettlesworth
Plawsworth
East Rainton
Hetton Lyons
Parkside
Cold Hesleden
Ornsby Hill
Sacriston
Kimblesworth
Leamside
Low Moorsley
Dalton Park
Lanchester
Witton Gilbert
Pity Me
High Moorsley
South Hetton
Easington Colliery
Quebec
Langley Park
Adventure Valley
Pittington
Hawthorn
Easington
Esh Win
Framwellgate Moor
Hallgarth
Haswell
Easington
Pittle Thorpe
Bearpark
Crook Hall
Gilesgate Moor
Carrville
Durn
Haswell Plough
Durham Heritage Coast
River Browney
Diggerland
Littletown
Shotton
Usha Moor
Bowburn
DURHAM
Broompark
New Brancepeth

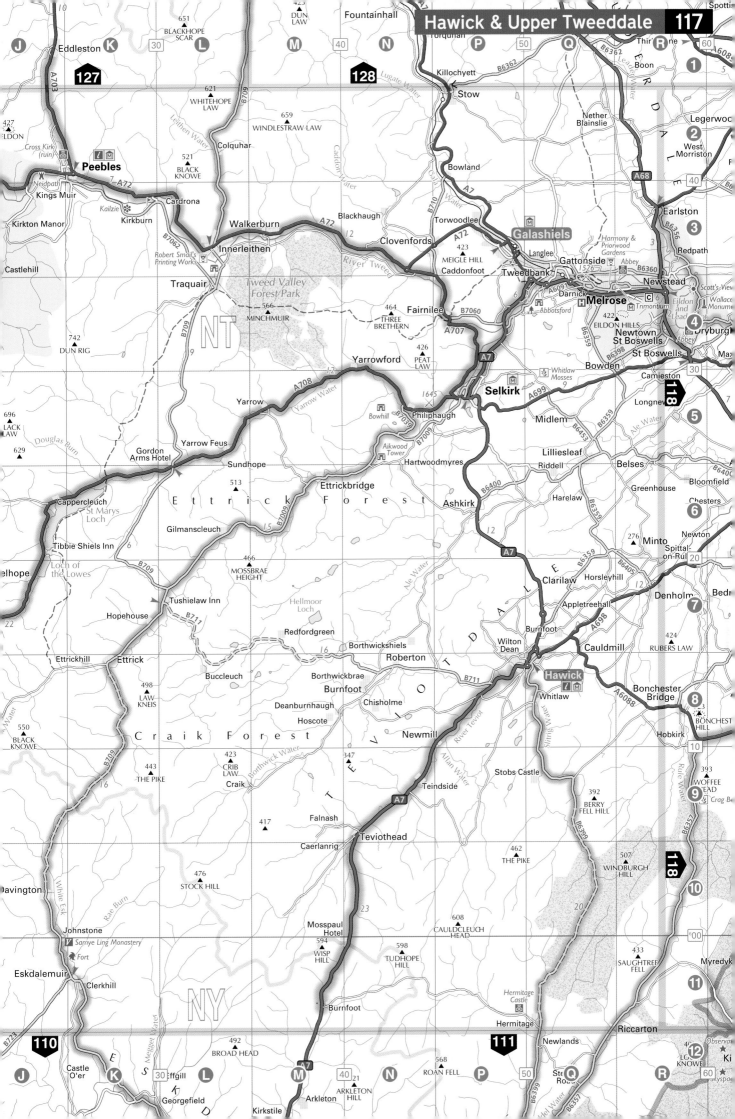

Sound of Bute

St Blane's Church

Faitlie Roads

Kilbirnie

Glengarnock

B784

Garrochty

Garroch Head

Little Cumbrae Island

Hunterston Power Station

Drakemyre

Highfield

Barr

Thor

Dalry

Munnoch

B780

B780

Munnoch

Chalmadale

A841

Portencross

Farland Head

B7048

B781

West Kilbride

Seamill

Dalgarven

Auchen

Dalgarven Mill

Sannox

CU N

B714

B778

Corrie

834 TEAL ABHAIL

874 GOATFELL

Merkland Point

Brodick Castle, Garden & Country Park

Ardrossan

Horse Isle

A737

A78

Kilwinning

Fergushill

A78

B785

eslie

Stevenston

A738

A738

A78

Ardeer

A78

Girdle Toll

Cun

Pe

Spring

Dreghorn

40

Saltcoats

Glen Rosa

Brodick Bay

124

Brodick

Strathwhillan

Corriegills

FIRTH

Irvine Bay

Irvine

Maritime

Fullarton

Gailes

Dryb

512 CHRUACH

REAC

A841

H

Clauchlands Point

Lamlash

Margnaheglish

Lamlash Bay

Cordon

Holy Island

OF

Barassie

Castle

Loans

CLYDE

Drodale

4

Auchencairn

Kingscross

Knockenkelly

Carn Ban

Whiting Bay

Whiting Bay

Troon

Royal Troon

A759

Lady Isle

M ton

Prestwick

New Prestwick

B743

Whitlet

A71

Glenashdale

Largymore

Largybeg

Dippen

Dippen Head

Ayr Bay

NS

Wallace

A7

Ayr

orrylin Cairn

Bennan

Kildonan

Heads of Ayr

Heads of Ayr

Burns Cottage

Doonfoot

A79

Belmon

ilmory

Bennan Head

Pladda

Robert B

Birthplace

Alloway

Heads of Ayr

Fisherton

A719

Culroy

Minishant

Dunure

Drumshang

Croy Brae (Electric Brae)

Knoweside

114

Culzean Bay

Culzean Castle & Country Park

Maidenhead Bay

Maidens

Pennyglen

Whitefaulds

B7023

A719

22

Maybole

Crossraguel Abbey

Kirkoswald

Souter Johnnie's Cottage

B7023

Grimmet

10

Kirkm

Threave

Crosshill

Turnberry

Turnberry

Turnberry Bay

12

Roan of Craigoch

Ailsa Craig

340

Dipple

Kilgrammie

Wallacetown

Dailly

B741

Water of Girvan

NX

Old Dailly

Penkill

B7035

B734

EFFIN F

Linfern Loc

429

Girvan

Dounepark

A77

B734

Dalquhairn

River Stincha

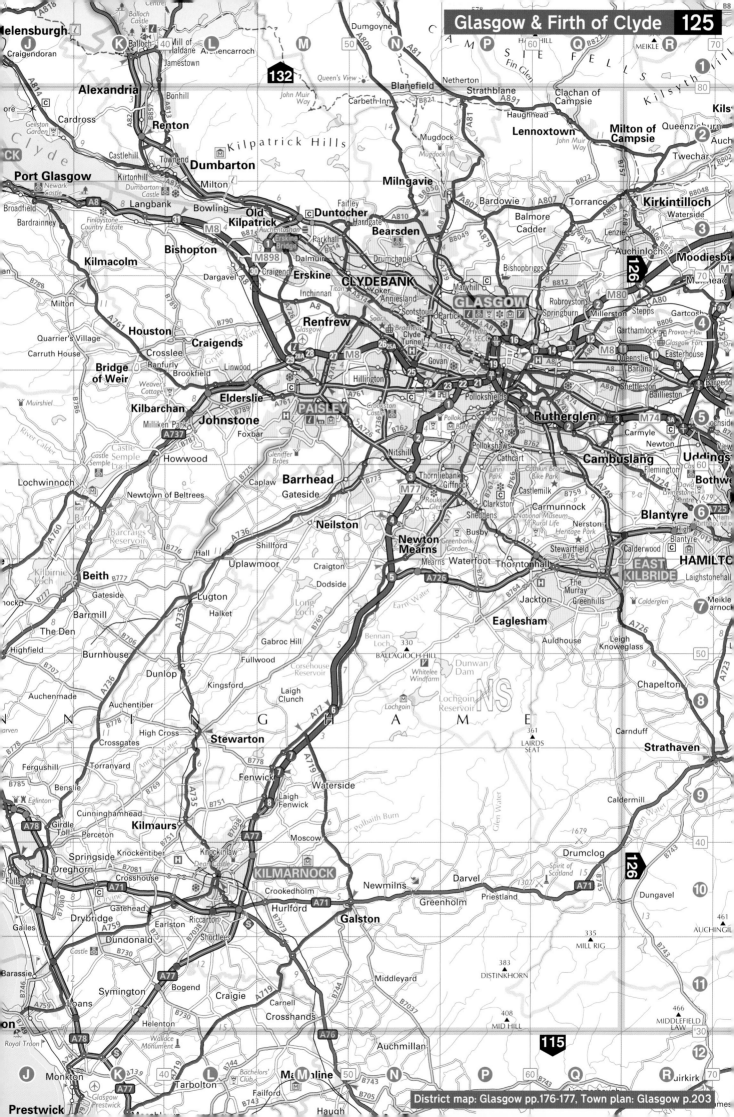

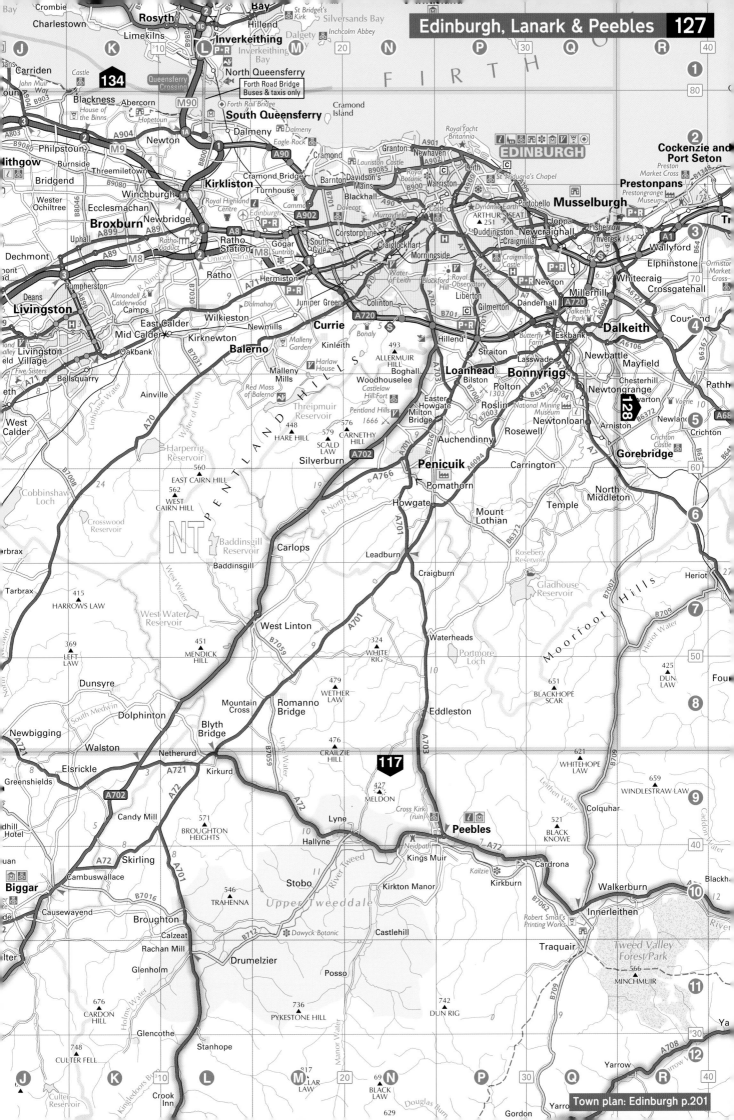

J K 80 L M 90 N P '00 Q R 10

① 90
②
③
80
④

Barns Ness
East Barns
Chapel Point
Skateraw
ick
Crowhill
Torness Power-Station
Thorntonloch

319
OCKLAW HILL
Reed Point
Dunglass Collegiate Church
Cove
Pease Bay
Siccar Point
ldhamstocks
Cockburnspath
⑤ 70

91
ART AW
Ecclaw
Pease Dean
A1107
Fast Castle Head
ST ABB'S HEAD
196
BROWN RIG
Coldingham Loch
⑥

Abbey St Bathans
Southern Upland Way
Butterdean
Grantshouse
Houndwood
Coldingham
St Abbs
Coldingham Bay
A1107
mford
Eye Water
Quixwood
21
Heugh Head
Cairncross
B6438
22
Eyemouth
⑦ 60

Edin's Hall Broch
325
COCKBURN LAW
14
262
HORSELEY HILL
Reston
B6438
A1
Ayton
B6355
Burnmouth
NU

Primrosehill
Cumledge
Marygold
Lintlaw
Preston
Auchencrow
B6355
Chirnside
B6437
B6355
Lamberton
Marshall Meadows Bay
⑧

B6365
A6112
Edrom Church
Edrom
15
Chirnsidebridge
Broadhaugh
Foulden
Foulden Tithe Barn
1333
North Northumberland Heritage Coast

Duns
Manderston
A6105
Allanton
Edington
Whiteadder Water
Hutton
A6105
Berwick-upon-Tweed
Gavinton
Blackadder
B6437
B6460
Whitsome
Hilton
Paxton
Paxton
B6461
Tweedmouth
Spittal
⑨ 50

Polwarth
Nisbet Hill
Sinclair's Hill
Loanend
East Ord
Huds Head
Fogo
A6112
13
Horndean
Horncliffe
Murton
Unthank
Scremerston
A1

Charterhall
B6437
Ladykirk
Castle
Norham
Thornton
Cheswick
⑩
7
6
Swinton
B6470
A698
Shoreswood
West Allerdean
Ancroft
CAUSEWAY FLOODED AT HIGH TIDE

118
B6460
Leitholm
10
Simprim
A6112
Upsettlington
Grindon
Felkington
Bowsden
119
Haggerston
Goswick
⑪
Lambden
Eccles
11
B6461
15
The Hirsel
Lennel
15
Donaldson's Lodge
Shellacres
Grindonrigg
Duddo
B6525
Berrington
Beal
Fenham
Lindis Pri

Coldstream
B6461
Birgham
Carham
Wark
hidlaw
West earmouth
Cornhill-on-Tweed
Castle
Etal
Heatherslaw Light Railway
Heatherslaw Corn Mill
B6353
Lowick
West Kyloe
Fenwick
Buckton
⑫
Ednam
Kelso
B6350
Hadden
East Learmouth
E xton
90
Crookl.
N
Ford
Lady Water Hall
P
Q
R
10
fiel
Detchant
Holburn
Flodden
1513
Kimmerston
14

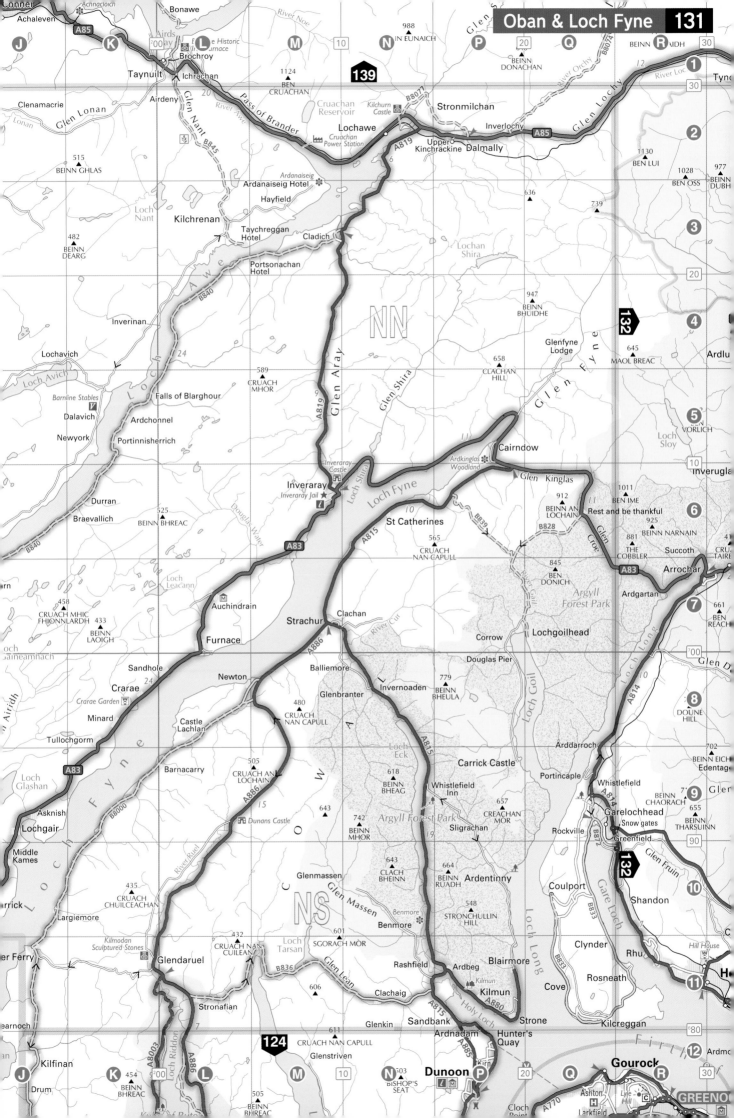

J K L M N P Q R

1
30
143
BUDDON NESS

Birkhill
Fintry
Whitfield
Earth-House
Barry
Carnoustie
Camperdown
Gourdie
Downie
Baldovie
B961
A92
B962
A930
Carnoustie
Denhead of Gray
K
40
A90
Claypotts
Castle
50
M
Monifieth
N
Iff
J
Lochee
Ancrum's
Outdoor
Centre
L
Barnhill
P
Invergowrie
H
B960
HMS
Unicorn
**Broughty
Ferry**
nvie
Mills Observatory
A85
DUNDEE
Broughty
Castle
Kingoodie
Dundee
Discovery
Point
A92
North Carr
Lightship
Tayport
2
30
Invergowrie
gan
Tay Bridge
**Newport-
on-Tay**
Tentsmuir Point
B946
Morton Locks
Wormit
Tentsmuir
A914
Scottish National
Golf Centre
Tentsmuir
Forest & Beach
Balmerino
Abbey
Kirkton
Tentsmuir Point
Coultra
Bottomcraig
Gauldry
St Michaels
3
20
Hazelton
Walls
Kilmany
Lucklawhill
13
Leuchars
Creich
Rathillet
Logie
A919
ST ANDREWS
BAY
Brunton
A92
16
Balmullo
uthrie
Denbrae
13
Guardbridge
Moonzie
10
River Eden
Kincaple
St Andrews
Castle
4
Cupar
Dairsie
A91
St Andrews
Kemback
Strathkinness
B939
Botanic
Brownhills
tham
Cupar
Muir
A913
Blebocraigs
Craigtoun
A917
Boarhills
5
Bow of
Fife
Denhead
B940
10
Springfield
Deer
Centre
Ceres
Baldinnie
Cameron
Reservoir
Dunino
Kingsbarns
Cambo
ydbank
Scotstarvit
Tower
Craigrothie
A914
Bridgend
Pitscottie
B940
12
Radernie
A915
Kingsmuir
Scotland's
Secret Bunker
B940
Balcomie
Links
FIFE NESS
Pitlessie
Struthers
Peat
Inn
New
Gilston
Lathones
Lochty
Carnbee
B9171
Easter Pitkierie
4
6
10
Balmalcolm
Woodside
Largoward
A915
Kellie
Castle
Wester
Pitkierie
A917
Crail
248
Langdykke
B927
Praytis
Arncroach
B9171
Newton of
Balcormo
B9131
Kilrenny
Cellardyke
CLATTO
HILL
Upper
Largo
Colinsburgh
B942
B941
B942
Anstruther
Fisheries
7
Baintown
Bonnybank
Lundin
Mill
6
Drumeldrie
Kilconquhar
6
Pittenweem
Scoonie
5
Lower
Largo
A917
Kennoway
A915
Lundin
Links
St Monans
700
Windygates
Leven
Innerleven
Leven
Largo Bay
Earlsferry
Elie
Isle of May
Milton of
Balgonie
Methilhill
Methil
8
nie
Buckhaven
A955
East Wemyss
Coaltown of Wemyss
9
ig Castle
NT
West Wemyss
15
8
A955
90
128
10
Craigleith
Bass Rock
Fidra
Eyebroughy
Yellowcraig
North Berwick
Scottish Seabird
Tantallon Castle
11
Dirleton Castle
& Gardens
A198
Dirleton
NORTH
BERWICK
LAW
Cleghornie
Muirfield
Gullane Bay
8
Whitekirk
Gullane Point
Gullane
John Muir
Way
Fenton
Barns
Kingston
A198
12
80
Aberlady Bay
Prora
B1377
East
Fortune
Tyninghame
John Muir
Belhaven
Bay
Dunbar
Craigilaw Point
Aberlady
Luffness
Drem
B1347
Museum
of Flight
Markle
Tyne Mouth
Belhaven
West B
A1087
Gosford
Preston Mill
& Phantassie
Doocot
A198
60
Q
**Cockenzie and
Port Seton**
Seton
Collegiate
Church
Spittal
A198
M
Balle
50 off
Chesters
Hill Fo
N
Athelstaneford
B1347
East
Linton
P
A1
70
kbur
165E
Longniddry
Preston
Market Cross
A6137
Hailes
Castle
Spott

136

A   B   C   D   E   F   G   H

°90   '00   10   20

70

1

2

Eilean Mòr

Rubha
Mòr

Rubh'
Sgor-

3

Cliad
Bay

B8072   Bousd   Sorisd

60

Arnabost

Grishipoll
Clabhach   Loch
Cliad   B8071

NL

4

Hogh Bay   Ballyhaugh   Arinagour   COLL

Bagh a Chaisteil
(Castlebay)   Totronald

Arileod   Coll   Acha   Eilean
Ornsay

Uig

5

Calgary Point   Rubha
Fàsachd

50   Feall
Bay   Crossapol
Bay

Gunna

6

Caoles   Rubha Dubh

Rubha Port
Bhiosd   Clachan
Mor   Balephetrish
Bay   B8069   Ruaig

Loch
Bhasapoll   B8068

Haugh
Bay   Ballevullin   Cornoigmore   Kenovay   Gott
Bay

Tiree

Kilkenneth   B8068   Scarinish

Middleton   Moss   Heylipoll   B8065   TIREE

7   Barrapoll   Crossapol

Loch a
Phuill   B8067   Balemartine   Hynish Bay

Mannal

40   Rinn
Thorbhais   TRESHNISH
ISLES   Lunga

Hynish

Balephuil
Bay   Colonsay

8   NM   Bac Mòr or Dutchman

Bac Beag

1   Eilean
Dubh

'00   Balnahard   Rudh' a' Geodha

9   Kiloran Bay   Oban

COLONSAY

2   Kiloran

Kilchattan

30   B8087

Scalasaig

10   B8086   NR

3   Machrins

Colonsay   B8085

Garvard   IONA   Iona Abbey
& Nunne

'90   Baile Mòr

Oronsay   Rubha
Bàn   MacLean's Cross

11   Dubh Eilean   Port Askaig

ORONSAY   Eilean
4   Ghaoideamal   Sound

0   1   2   3 miles

0   1   2   3   4   5 kilometres

'20   Soa Island

12   Errai

A   B   C   D   E   F   G   H
°90   '00   10   20

a   b   '40   c   d

0   1   2   3   4   5 miles
0   1   2   3   4   5   6   7   8 kilometres

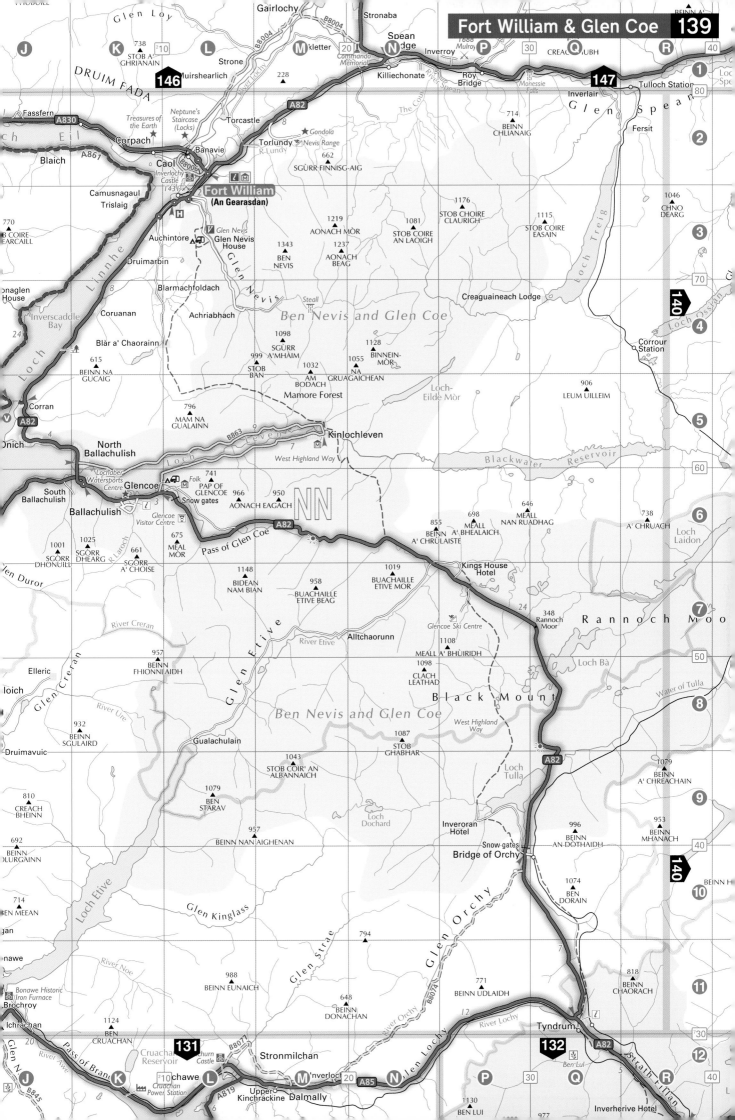

Glen Loy
Gairlochy
Stronaba
B8004
Spean Lodge
N
BEINN A'
B8004
Mkletter
M
1688 Mulroy
P
30
CREAG DUBH
Q
R
1
DRUIM FADA
738
K
STOB A'
GHRIANAIN
²10
Strone
L
Muirshearlich
228
146
Killiechonate
Commando
Memorial
Inverroy
Roy
Bridge
Monessie
Falls
147
Inverlair
Tulloch Station
Glen Spean
80
Fassfern
A830
J
Neptune's
Staircase
(Locks)
Treasures
of the Earth
Torcastle
8
Gondola
Nevis Range
714
BEINN
CHLIANAIG
Fersit
2
h Eil
Corpach
A861
Banavie
B8006
Torlundy
R Lundy
662
SGÙRR FINNISG-AIG
1046
CHNO
DEARG
Blaich
Caol
Inverlochy
Castle
[431]
Fort William
(An Gearasdan)
H
1219
AONACH MÒR
1081
STOB COIRE
AN LAOIGH
1176
STOB CHOIRE
CLAURIGH
1115
STOB COIRE
EASAIN
Loch Treig
70
3
Camusnagaul
Trislaig
Auchintore
Glen Nevis
House
1343
BEN
NEVIS
1237
AONACH
BEAG
B COIRE
EARCAILL
770
Druimarbin
Glen Nevis
Blarmachfoldach
Steall
Ben Nevis and Glen Coe
Creaguaineach Lodge
140
Loch Ossian
4
onaglen
House
Coruanan
Achriabhach
1098
SGÙRR
A'MHAIM
999
STOB
BAN
1032
AM
BODACH
1055
NA
GRUAGAICHEAN
1128
BINNEIN-
MÒR
Corrour
Station
24
Inverscaddle
Bay
Blàr a' Chaorainn
615
BEINN NA
GUCAIG
796
MAM NA
GUALAINN
Mamore Forest
Loch-
Eilde Mòr
906
LEUM UILLEIM
70
60
5
Corran
V
A82
Onich
4
North
Ballachulish
B863
Loch Leven
7
Kinlochleven
West Highland Way
M
Blackwater
Reservoir
South
Ballachulish
Lochaber
Watersports
Centre
Glencoe
741
PAP OF
GLENCOE
966
AONACH EAGACH
950
NN
855
BEINN
A' CHRULAISTE
698
MEALL
A' BHEALAICH
646
MEALL
NAN RUADHAG
738
A' CHRUACH
6
Loch
Laidon
Ballachulish
Glencoe
Visitor Centre
3
Snow gates
Folk
Museum
675
MEALL
MÒR
A82
Pass of Glen Coe
Kings House
Hotel
7
Glen Duror
1001
SGÒRR
DHONUILL
1025
SGÒRR
DHEARG
661
SGÒRR
A' CHOISE
1148
BIDEAN
NAM BIAN
958
BUACHAILLE
ETIVE BEAG
1019
BUACHAILLE
ETIVE MOR
Glencoe Ski Centre
348
Rannoch
Moor
Rannoch Moo
Elleric
River Creran
River Etive
Alltchaorunn
1108
MEALL A' BHÙIRIDH
24
Loch Bà
50
8
loich
Glen Creran
River Ure
957
BEINN
FHIONNLAIDH
Glen Etive
1098
CLACH
LEATHAD
Black Mount
Water of Tulla
Druimavuic
932
BEINN
SGULAIRD
Gualachulain
Ben Nevis and Glen Coe
1087
STOB
GHABHAR
West Highland
Way
1079
BEINN
A' CHREACHAIN
9
40
692
BEINN
OLURGAINN
1043
STOB COIR' AN
ALBANNAICH
1079
BEN
STARAV
Loch
Dochard
Inveroran
Hotel
Loch Tulla
A82
996
BEINN
AN-DOTHAIDH
953
BEINN
MHANACH
140
714
EN MEEAN
957
BEINN NAN AIGHENAN
Snow gates
Bridge of Orchy
1074
BEN
DORAIN
BEINN A'
10
40
jan
Glen Kinglass
Glen Orchy
nawe
810
CREACH
BHEINN
River Noe
988
BEINN EUNAICH
794
771
BEINN UDLAIDH
818
BEINN
CHAORACH
11
730
Bonawe Historic
Iron Furnace
Brochroy
648
BEINN
DONACHAN
River Orchy
River Lochy
Tyndrum
Ichrachan
1124
BEN
CRUACHAN
Cruachan
Reservoir
B8077
burn Castle
131
Stronmilchan
B8074
Glen Lochy
12
132
A82
Strath
20
Glen A
Pass of Brand
River Awe
chawe
Cruachan
Power Station
L
A819
Upper
Kinchrackine
Dalmally
M
n'verloc
20
A85
N
P
30
Q
R
40
J
B845
K
1130
BEN LUI
Inverherive Hotel
977

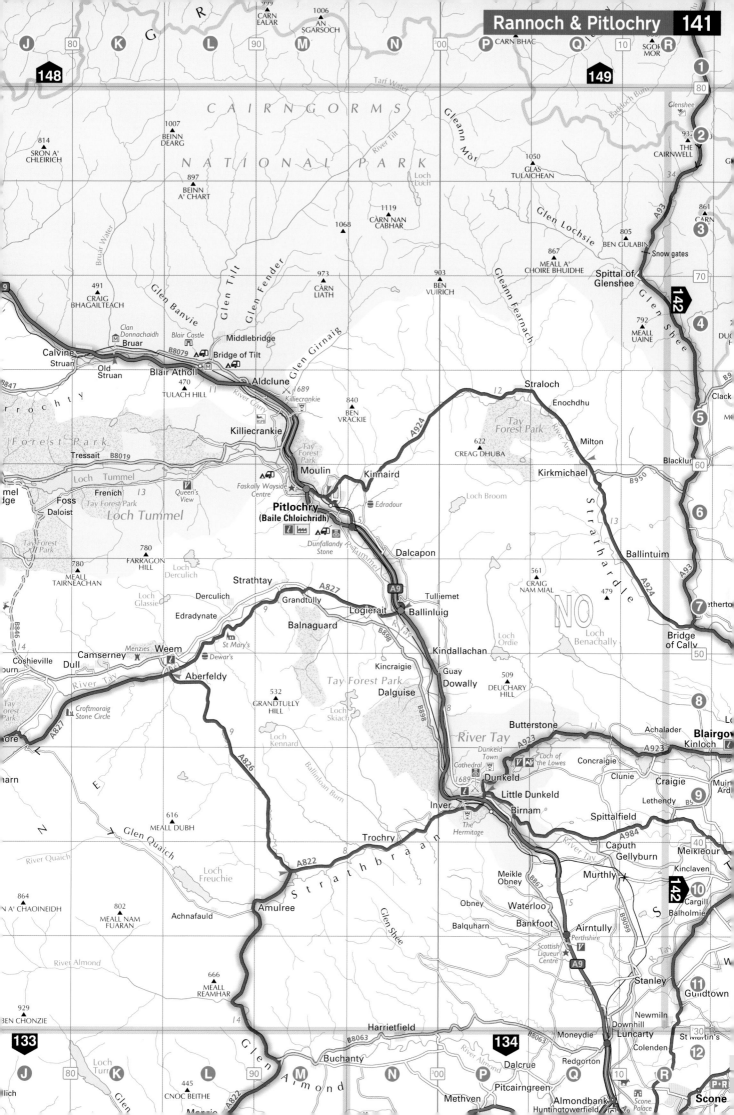

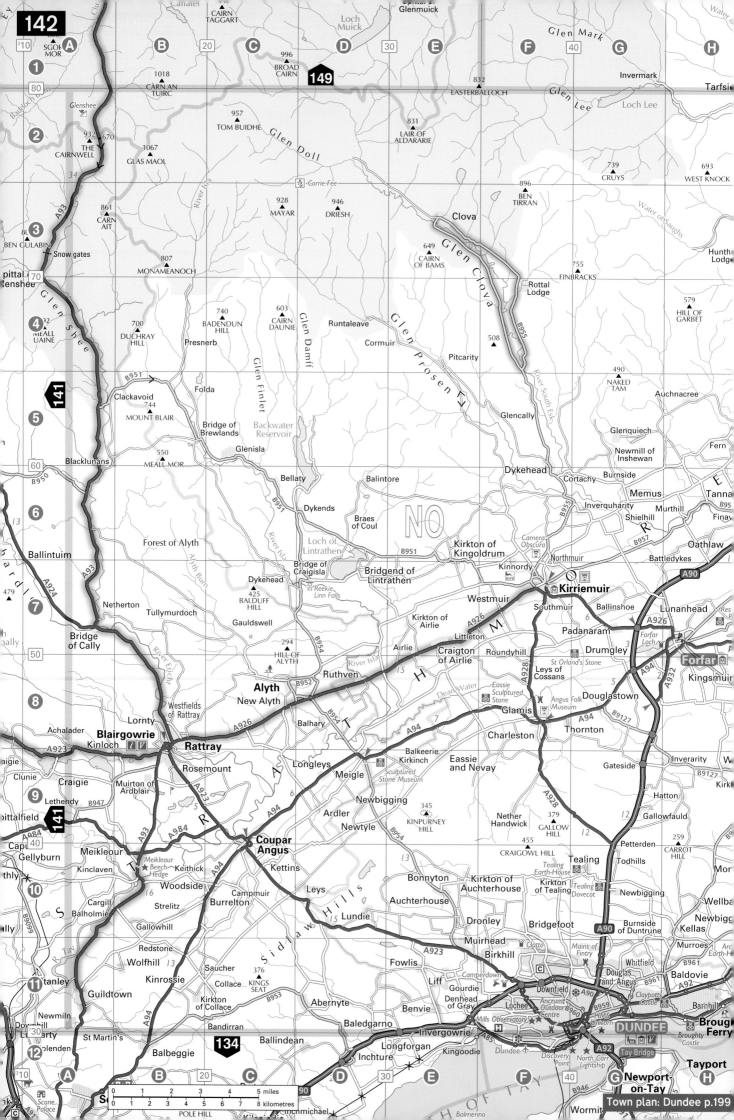

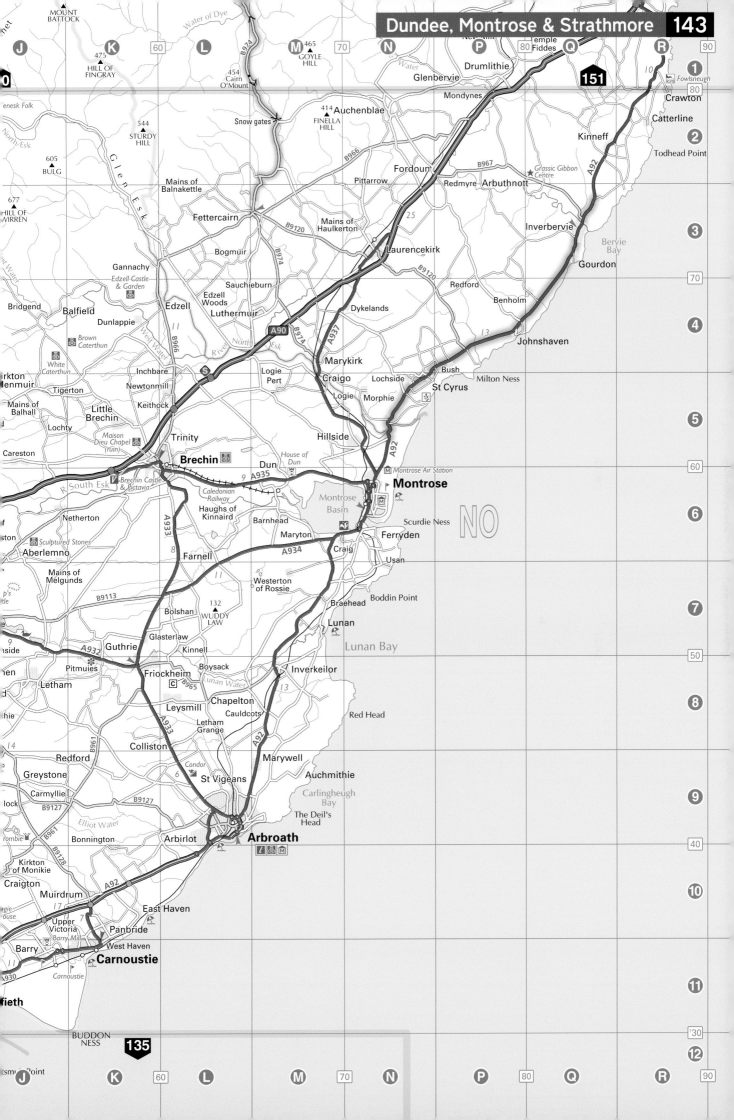

144

152

Rubha nan Clach

Fernilea
Carbost
Drynoch
Merkadale

369 ARNAVAL

Talisker 40

A863

S K Y E

444 BEN LEE
Pei

conser

Talisker Bay

Talisker

Glen Eynort

Glen Drynoch

Sligachan

773 GLAMAIG

A87

Minginish

Glen Brittle

369 BEINN BHREAC

447 BEINN BHREAC

Grula

Fairy Pools

965 SGURR NAN GILLEAN

Forest

Loch Eynort

974 SGÙRR A' GHEADAIDH

The Cuillin Hills

434 AN CRUACHIN

Glenbrittle

Bualintur

Cuillin Hills

1009 SGÙRR ALASDAIR

Loch Coruisk

927 BLAVEN

Loch na Crèithéach

Loch Brittle

225 CEANN NA BEINNE

894 GARS BHEINN

34
B
MEA

Rubha an Dùnain

Soay Sound

139 BEINN BHREAC

Loch Scavaig

Elg

Mol-chlach

Elgo

SOAY

Rubh' Aonghais

Loch Baghasdail (Lochboisdale)

C U I L L I N   S O U N D

NG

CANNA

210 CÀRN A' GHAILL

Garrisdale Point

A'Chill

Canna Harbour

Sanday

Kilmory Bay

Rubha Shamhnan Insir

Sound of Canna

302 MULLACH MÒR

Rubha na Roinne

A' Bhrìdeanach

570 ORVAL

Kinloch

Loch Scresort

Oigh-sgeir

RÙM

810 ASKIVAL

Harris Bay

763 SGÙRR NAN GILLEAN

The Small Isles

Rubha nam Meirleach

Sound of Rùm

NM

Bay of Laig

Cleadale

Rubha an Fhasaidh

Laig

299 AN CRUACHAN

EIGG

Kildonnan

393 AN SGÙRR

Galmisdale

Sound of Eigg

Eilean Chathastail

Eilean nan Each

MUCK

Port Mòr

0   1   2   3   4   5 miles
0   1   2   3   4   5   6   7   8 kilometres

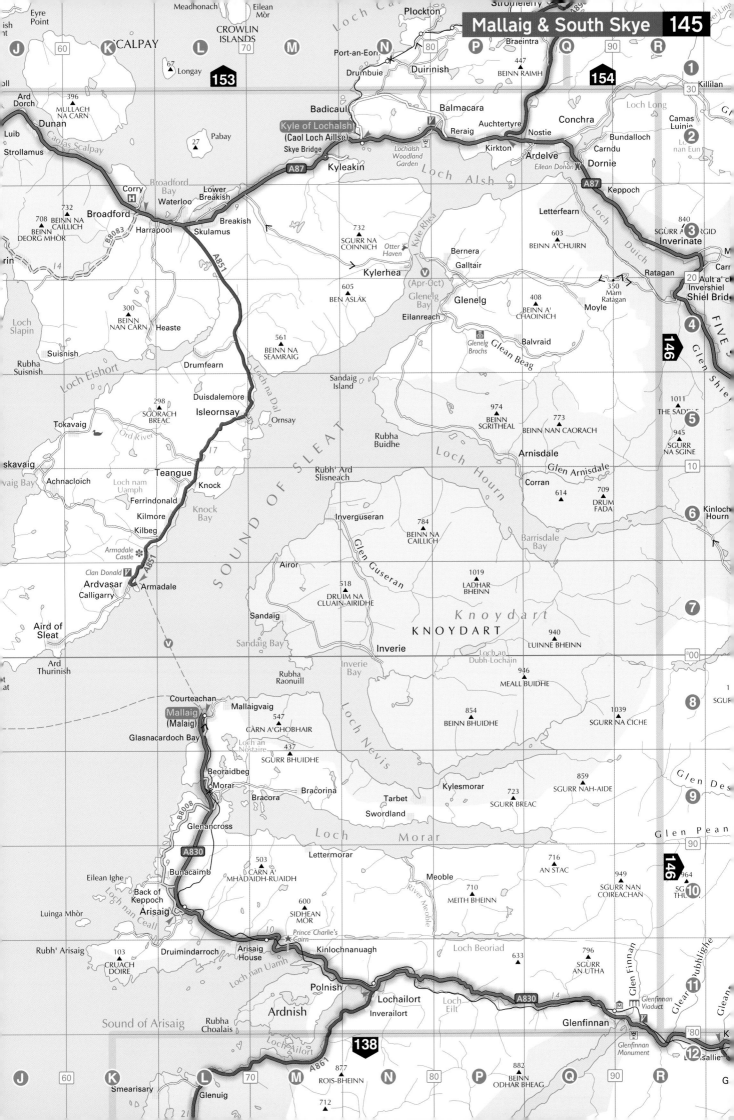

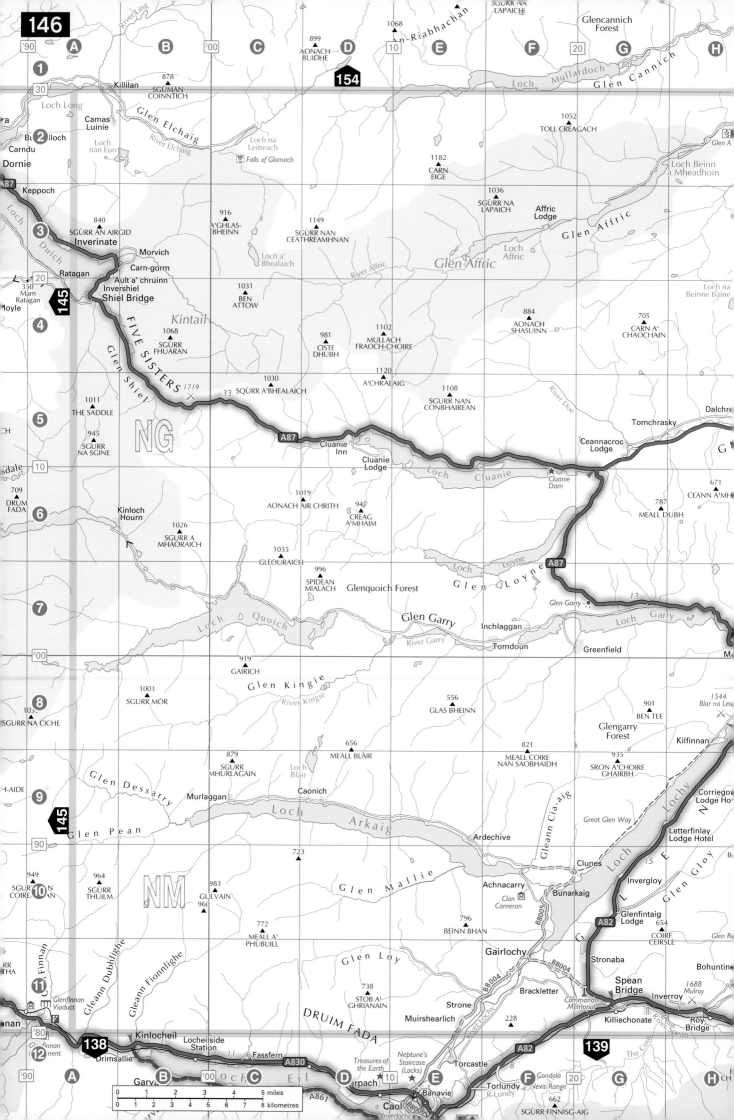

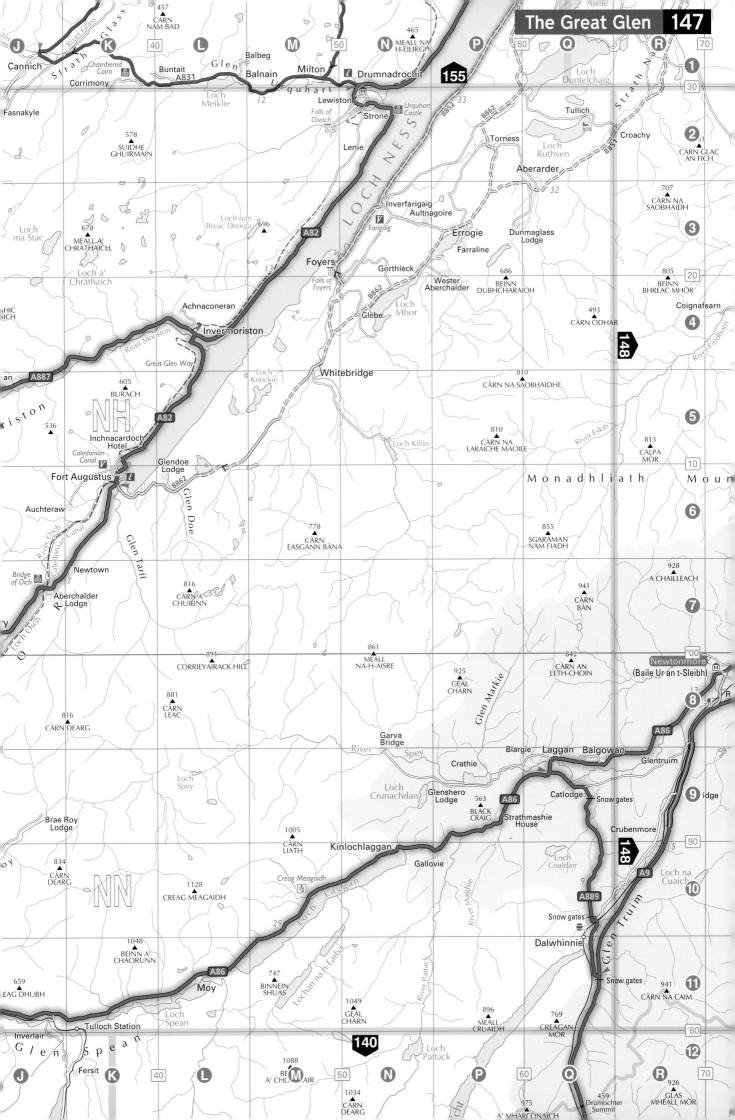

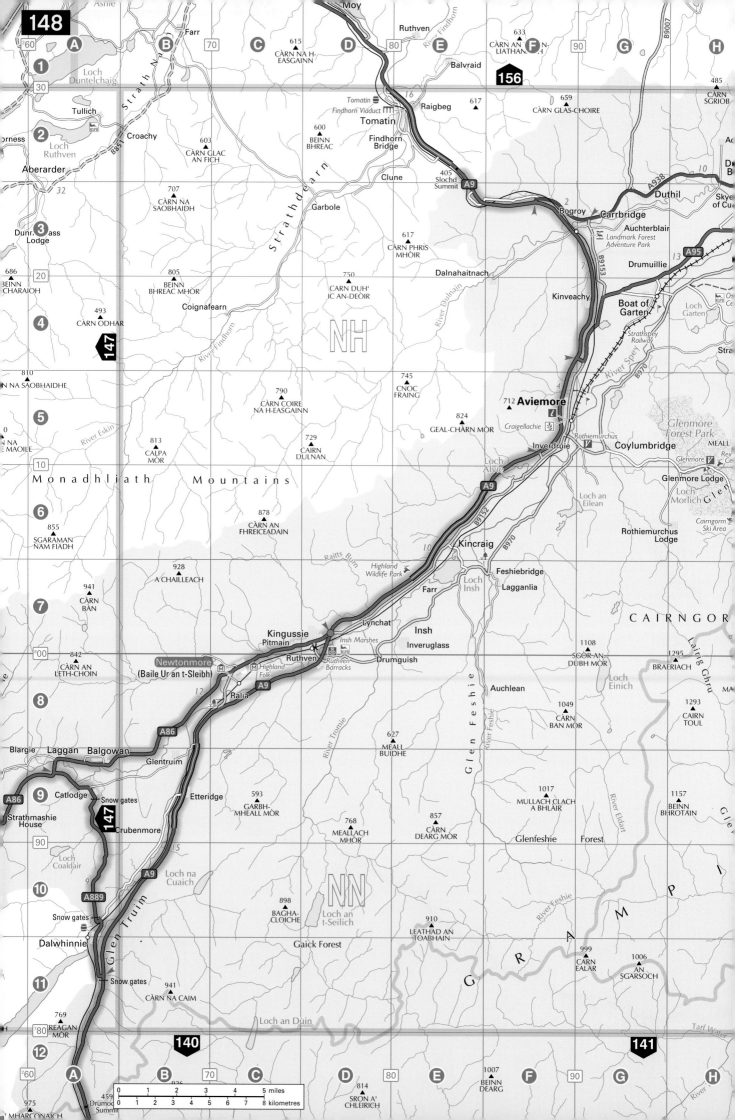

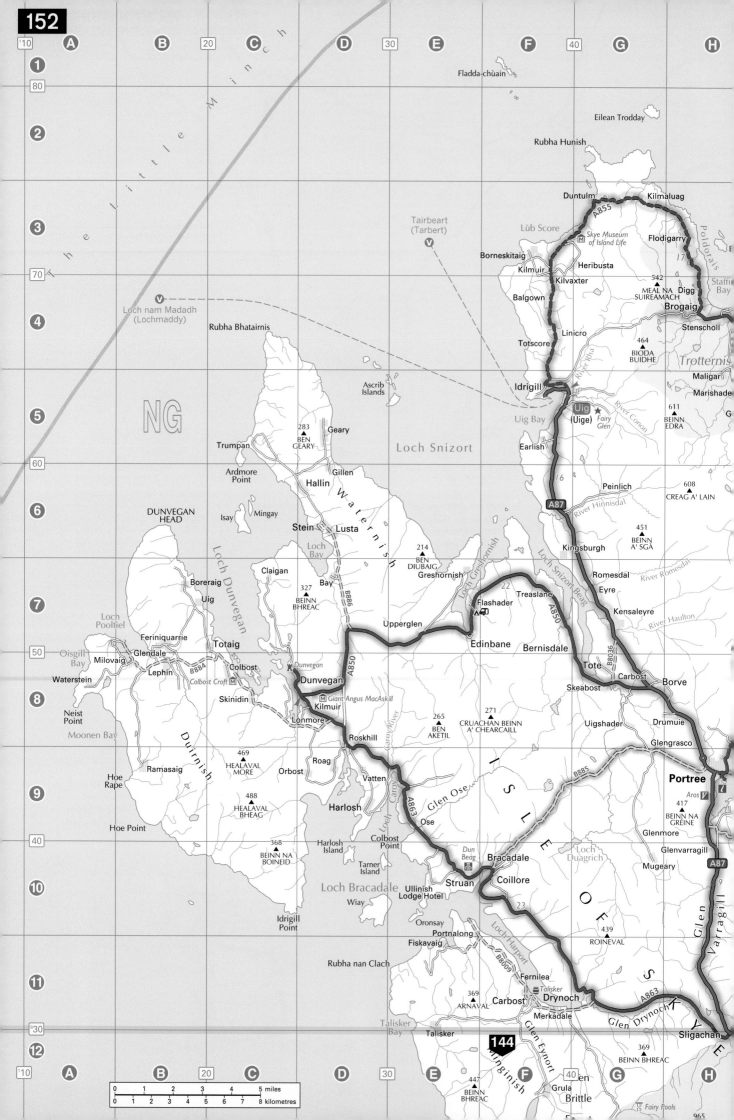

CNOC BREAC

J   K   60   L   M   70   N   B8021   P   80   Q   R   90   250   ALL NA

North Erradale

Garden

Poolewe   Londubh

Big Sand   160   A832   Strath

Smithstown   Auchtercairn   Heritage

Longa Island   Lonemore   Gairloch   Charlestown   421   MEALL AN DOIREIN

Loch Gairloch   Eilean Horrisdale

Port Henderson   B8056

Badachro   Opinan

South Erradale   Loch Bad an Sgalaig   70   Talla

Redpoint   Loch Ghaineamhach   154   Loch na A-Oidh

Loch a' Ghodhainn   875   855

619   BEINN AN EÒI

Red Point   BAOSBHEINN

BEINN BHREAC   Loch a' Bhealaich

NG   Loch Torridon   985   914

'lt Rock   Rubha na Fearn   Lower Diabaig   BEINN ALLIGIN   BEINN DEARG   60

ishader

Valtos   Rubha nam Brathairean   Fearnmore

Culnaknock   Òb Chuaig   Fearnbeg   Loch Diabaig   Allt na Shuas   Inveralligin

Tote   Arrina   Kenmore   Torridon House   Torr

Cuaig   Upper Loch Torridon

RONA   Callakille   Ardheslaig   Shieldaig

Loch Shieldaig   Annat

Lonbain   492   AN GARBH-MHEALL   Western ross

Eilean Tigh   493   CROIC-BHEINN   Loch Damph   902   B 50 DAMPH MA

Eilean Fladday   River Applecross   A896   Glenshieldaig Forest

Manish Point   Loch Arnish   Torran   Loch Lundie

Arnish   895   730

Brochel   BEINN BHAN   SGURR A GHARAIDH

RAASAY   V   Rassal Ashwood

Applecross Bay   626   Pass of the Cattle   774

Applecross   Bealach-Na-Ba   SGÙRR A'CHAORACHAIN

Milton

Camusteel   Kishorn   A896   Kirkton

444   DÙN CAAN   Camusterrach   40

Oskaig   Aird Dhubh   Kishorn   Ardarroch   Lochcarron

amastianavaig   Culduie   154   Slumbay

Tianavaig Bay   310   Toscaig   Achintraid

Ollach   BEINN NA LEAC   Eilean Meadhonach   Kishorn Island   394   BAD A CHREAMHA

Clachan   Inverarish   Eyre Point   Ardaneaskan   Strome   Ardnarff

raes   Peinchorran   Suisnish Point   Eilean Mòr   Loch Carron   Stromeferry   A890

CROWLIN ISLANDS   Plockton

773   Moll   67 Longay   Port-an-Eorna   Braeintra

AMAIG   A87   Ard Dorch   396 MULLACH NA CARN   Drumbuie   Duirinish   Achmore   11

Dunan   60   Badicaul   447 BEINN RAIMH   30

145   Balmacara   Conchra   90

J   K   L   L   M Pabay   70   N   P   Q   R

Strollamus   Skye Bridge   Rera   Auchtertyre   Nostie   Ardelve   Carndu

564   Kyleakin   Lochalsh Woodland Garden   Kirkton   Dornie

GLAS BHEIN

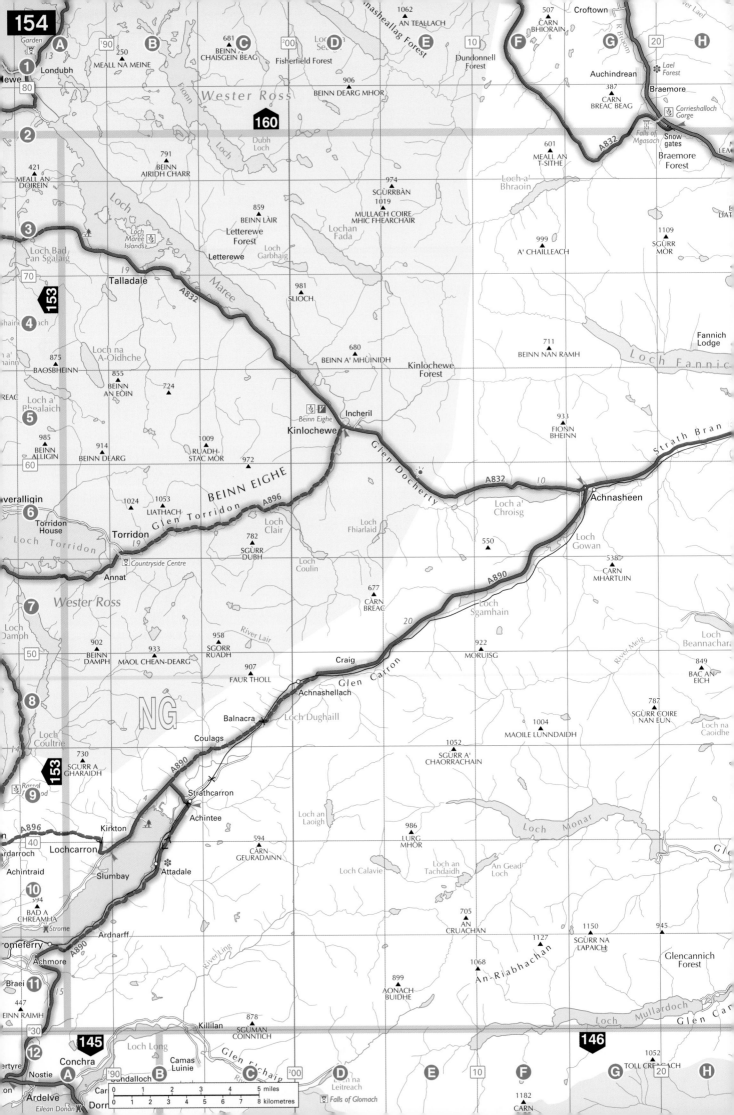

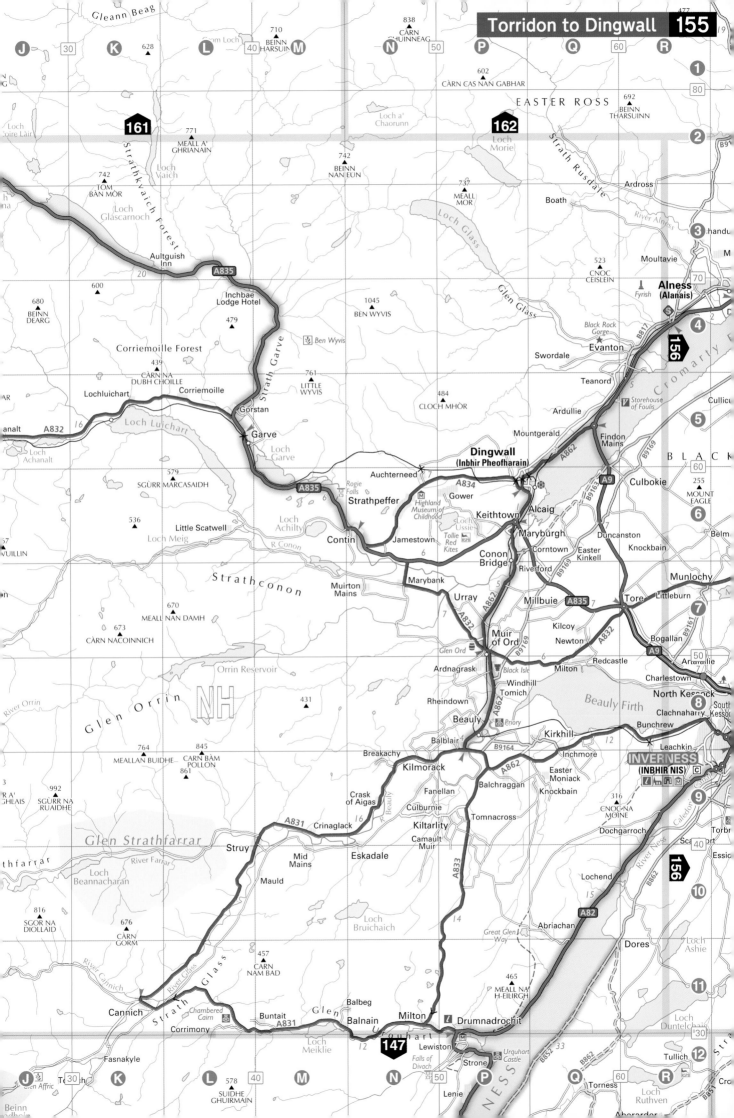

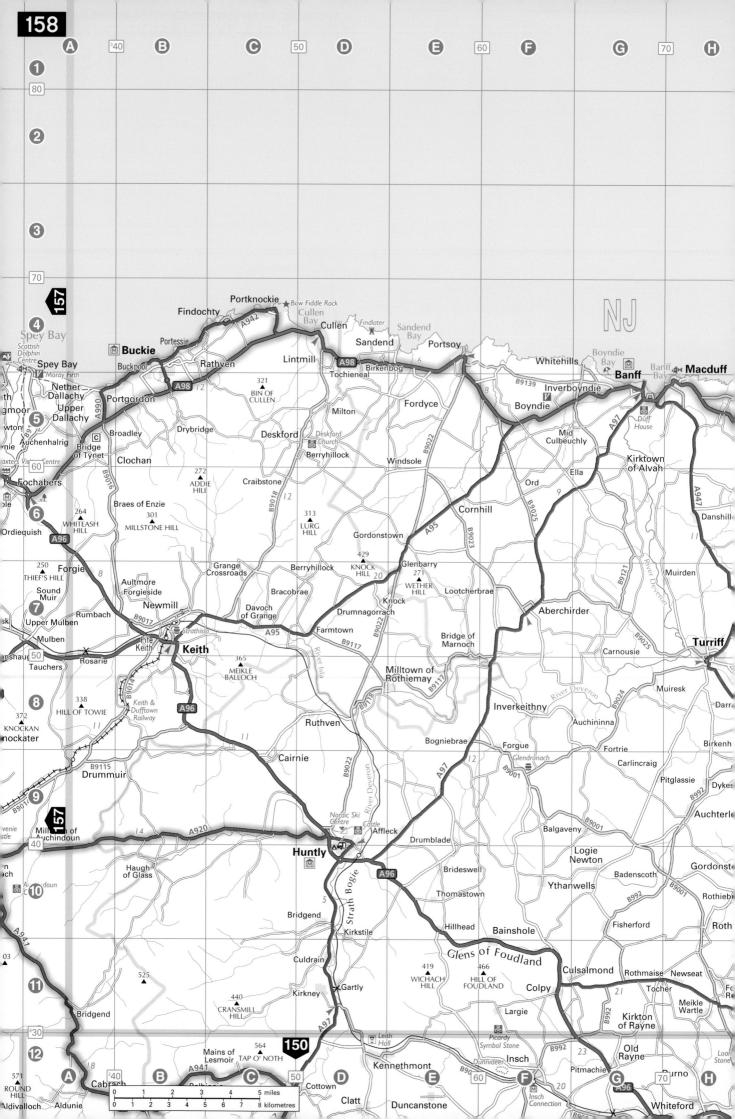

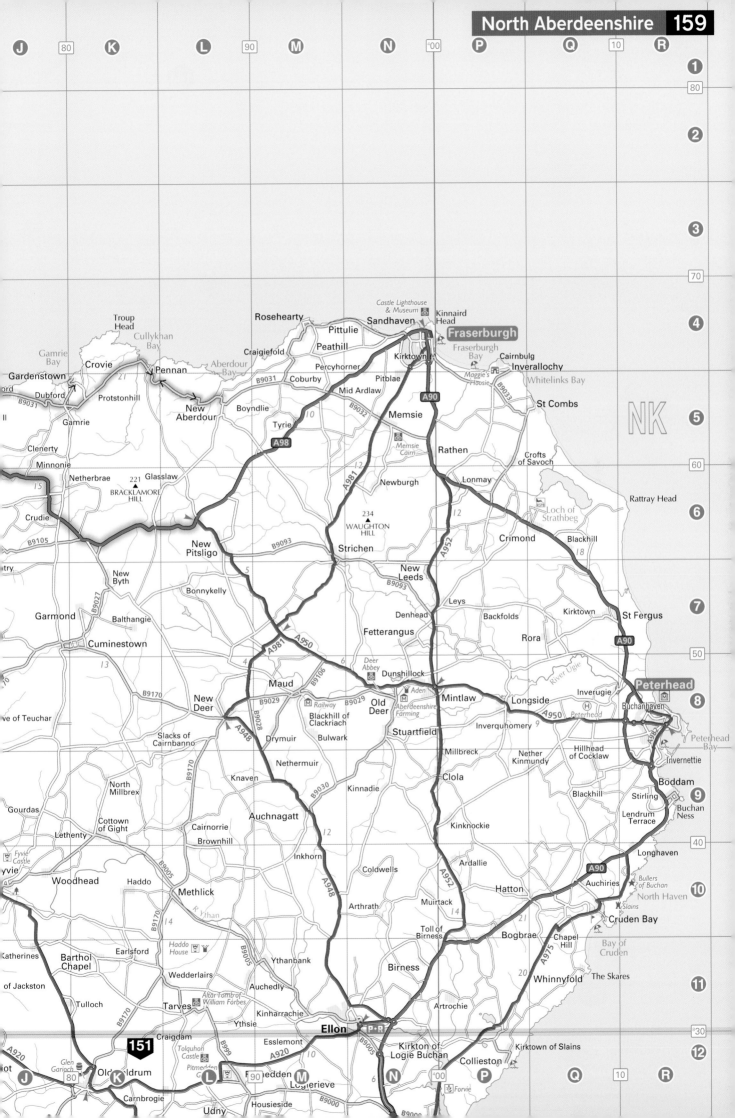

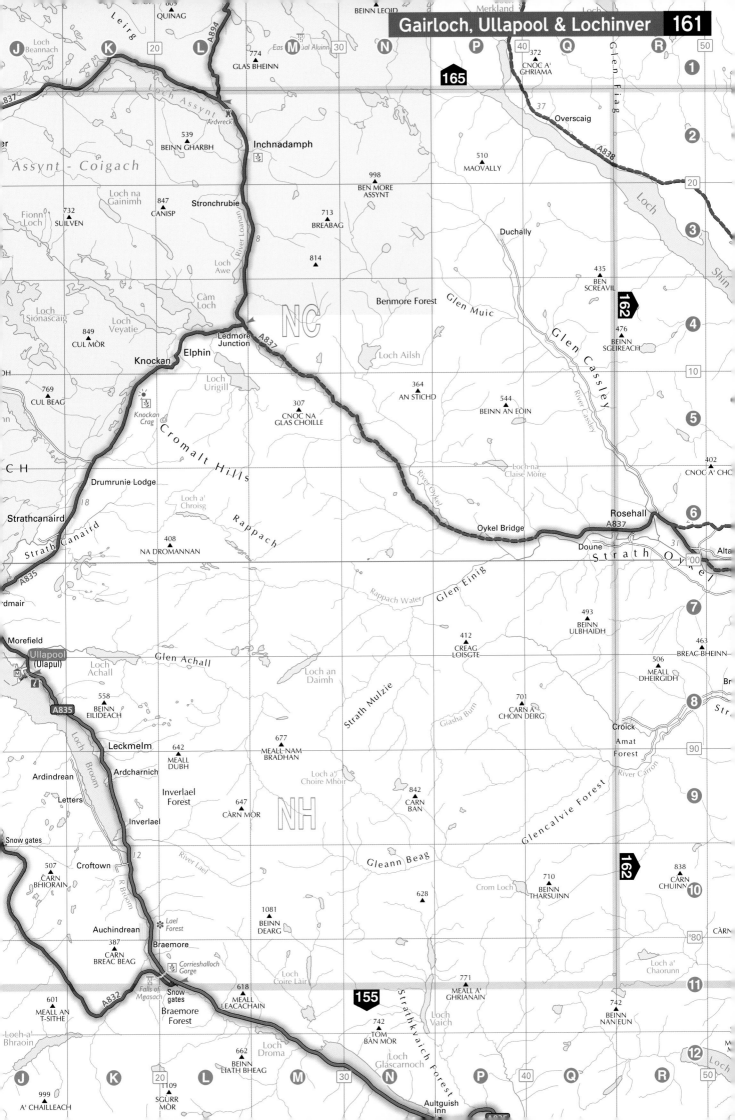

J K 20 L M 30 N P 40 372 Q R 50

165

1
2
3
4
10
5
6
7
8
90
9
162
10
80
11
12

Leirg
805
QUINAG
BEINN LEOID
Merkland
Eas Mual Aluinn 30
CNOC A' GHRIAMA
Overscaig
Glen Fiag
Loch
774
GLAS BHEINN
539
BEINN GHARBH
Inchnadamph
Ardvreck
Loch Assynt
A894
A838
510
MAOVALLY
Loch Shin

Assynt - Coigach
998
BEN MORE ASSYNT
Duchally
847
CANISP
Stronchrubie
River Loanan
713
BREABAG
435
BEN SCREAVIL

732
SUILVEN
Loch na Gainimh
Loch Awe
814
162

Fionn Loch
Loch Awe
8
Càm Loch
Benmore Forest
Glen Muic
476
BEINN SGEIREACH

Loch Sionascaig
Loch Veyatie
Ledmore Junction
NC
Loch Ailsh
Glen Cassley

849
CUL MÒR
A837
364
AN STICHD
544
BEINN AN EÒIN
River Cassley

769
CUL BEAG
Knockan Elphin
Loch Urigill
307
CNOC NA GLAS CHOILLE
Loch na Claise Mòire
402
CNOC A' CHC

Knockan Crag
Cromalt Hills
River Oykel
Rosehall
A837

Drumrunie Lodge
Rappach
Oykel Bridge
Doune
Strath Oykel
Alta
800
31

Strathcanaird
18
408
NA DROMANNAN
Glen Einig

Strath Canaird
Rappach Water
493
BEINN ULBHAIDH
463
BREAC BHEINN

A835
dmair
412
CREAG LOISGTE
506
MEALL DHEIRGIDH

Morefield
Glen Achall
Loch an Daimh
Br

Ullapool (Ulapul)
Loch Achall
Strath Mulzie
701
CARN A' CHOIN DEIRG
Croick
Amat Forest
Str

A835
558
BEINN EILIDEACH
Giasha Burn
River Carron
90

Leckmelm
642
MEALL DUBH
677
MEALL-NAM-BRADHAN
842
CARN BAN
Glencalvie Forest

Ardcharnich
Loch a' Choire Mhòir

Ardindrean
Inverlael Forest
647
CÀRN MÒR
NH

Letters
Inverlael
Gleann Beag
162

Snow gates
River Lael
628
710
BEINN THARSUINN
Crom Loch
838
CARN CHUINN

507
CÀRN BHIORAIN
Croftown
12
R Broom

Auchindrean
1081
BEINN DEARG
771
MEALL A' GHRIANAIN
Loch a' Chaorunn
80

387
CARN BREAC BEAG
Braemore
Lael Forest
742
BEINN NAN EUN

Corrieshalloch Gorge
618
MEALL LEACACHAIN
Loch Coire Làir
155
Strathvaich Forest

601
MEALL AN T-SITHE
A832
Falls of Measach
Snow gates
Braemore Forest
Loch Droma
742
TOM BÀN MÒR
Loch Vaich

Loch a' Bhraoin
662
BEINN LIATH BHEAG
Loch Glascarnoch

999
A' CHAILLEACH
T109
SGÙRR MÒR
Aultguish Inn

J K 20 L M 30 N P 40 Q R 50

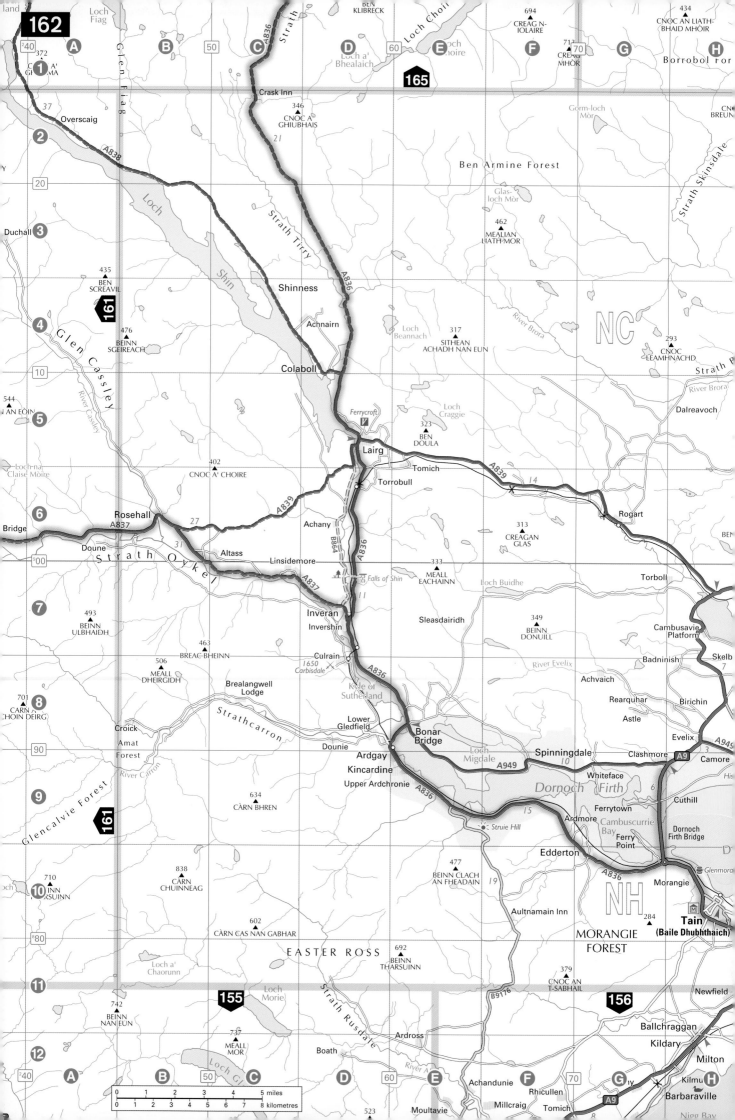

167

Langwell Forest

NA FEARNA

705
MORVEN

518
CNOC AN
EIREANNAICH

626
SCARABEN

Snow gates

Knockelly

Omscraigs

Borgue

Newport

Langwell
House

Berriedale

202
CNOC DAIL-
CHAIRN

Strath Free

Loch
Ascaig

Suisgill

Learable Hill
Cairns, Stone Row
& Stone Circles

388
CREAG NAM FIÀDH

Kildonan Lodge

Kildonan 416
BEINN
DUBHAIN

A897

Torrish

River Helmsdale

554
CREAG
SCALABSDALE

Strath of Kildonan

337
OC NA H-
SE MOIRE

421
CNOC NAN CRÙBAG MÒR

624
BEINN
DHORAIN

591
BEINN NA
MEILICH

Glen Loth

401
CNOC NA
MAOILE

404
CREAG
THORARAIDH

A9

Badbea
Historic Village

Ord of Caithness

Snow gates

Navidale

Timespan

West
Helmsdale

East Helmsdale

Helmsdale

Gartymore

Portgower

ND

Lothmore

539
COL-
BHEINN

Lothbeg

Loch
Brora

21

nacoil

Dalchalm

Clynelish

Brora

378
CAGAR
FEOSAIG

Doll

Backies

A9

Carn
Liath

Dunrobin
Castle

RAGGIE

hives

Golspie

33

eet

benny

Embo

Street

al Dornoch

och

noch

Firth

point

Innis Mhor

Tarbat Ness

Wilkhaven

Portmahomack

Inver

Arboll

B9165

Rockfield

NJ

Toulvaddie

Lochslin

Loch
Eye

Rhynie

Hill of
Fearn

Balmuchy

Hilton of Cadboll
Chapel (ruin)

Fearn

Tullich

B9166

Hilton

rabella

Shandwick

Balintore

Ankerville

Shandwick Bay

tca

B9040

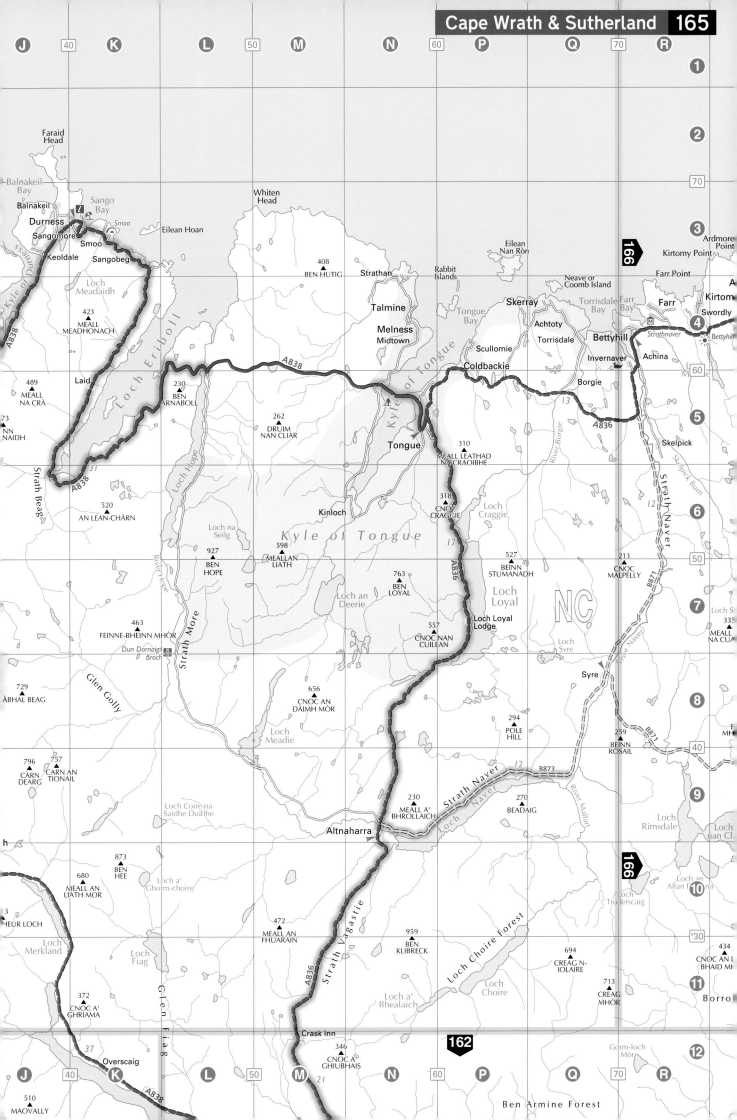

J 40   K   L 50   M   N 60   P   Q 70   R

1
2
70
166
3

Faraid
Head

Balnakeil
Bay

Balnakeil
Durness
Sangomore
Smoo
Keoldale
Sango
Bay
Smoo
Eilean Hoan
Sangobeg

Whiten
Head

408
BEN HUTIG
Strathan
Talmine
Melness
Midtown

Eilean
Nan Ròn
Rabbit
Islands
Neave or
Coomb Island

Skerray
Achtoty
Torrisdale
Scullomie
Coldbackie

Torrisdale
Bay
Farr
Bay

Farr Point
Farr
Swordly
Bettyhill
Invernaver
Achina

Kirtomy Point
Kirtom
Ardmore
Point

Loch
Meadaidh
423
MEALL
MEADHONACH

489
MEALL
NA CRÀ
Laid

230
BEN
ARNABOLL

A838

Loch Eriboll

262
DRUIM
NAN CLIAR

Tongue

310
MEALL LEATHAD
NA CRAOIBHE

Borgie
13
A836
Skelpick

73
NN
NAIDH

Strath Beag
A838
37

520
AN LEAN-CHÀRN

Loch Hope

Kinloch

318
CNOC
CRAGGIE

Loch
Craggie

NC
Loch
Loyal

Strath Naver
Skelpick Burn
12

Kyle of Tongue
598
MEALLAN
LIATH

927
BEN
HOPE

Loch na
Seilg

763
BEN
LOYAL
17

A836

527
BEINN
STUMANADH

213
CNOC
MALPELLY
50

B871
335
MEALL
NA CUA

463
FEINNE-BHEINN MHOR

Loch an
Deerie

Loch Loyal
Lodge

557
CNOC NAN
CUILEAN

Loch S

Dun Dornaigil
Broch

Glen Golly
Strath More

656
CNOC AN
DÀIMH MÒR

Loch
Syre

Syre
River Naver

8
40
B871
259
BEINN
ROSAIL
E
MH

729
ÀBHAL BEAG

Loch
Meadie

294
POLE
HILL

796
CÀRN
DEARG
757
CARN AN
TIONAIL

Loch Coire na
Saidhe Duibhe

230
MEALL A'
BHROLLAICH

Strath Naver
12
B873
270
BEADAIG

Loch Naver

River Mallart

9
Loch
Rimsdale
Loch
nan Cl

h

873
BEN
HEE
680
MEALL AN
LIATH MOR

Loch a'
Ghorm-choire

Altnaharra

166
Loch
Truderscaig
Loch an
Altan F na
10
30

3
HEUR LOCH

Loch
Merkland

Loch
Fiag

472
MEALL AN
FHUARAIN

A836

Strath Vagastie

959
BEN
KLIBRECK

Loch Choire Forest

694
CREAG N-
IOLAIRE

434
CNOC AN
BHAID MH

372
CNOC A'
GHRIAMA

Glen Fiag

Loch a'
Bhealaich

Loch
Choire

713
CREAG
MHOR

11
Borro

510
MAOVALLY

Overscaig
37
A838

Crask Inn
346
CNOC A'
GHIUBHAIS
21

162

Gorm-loch
Mòr
12

Ben Armine Forest

J 40   K   L 50   M   N 60   P   Q 70   R

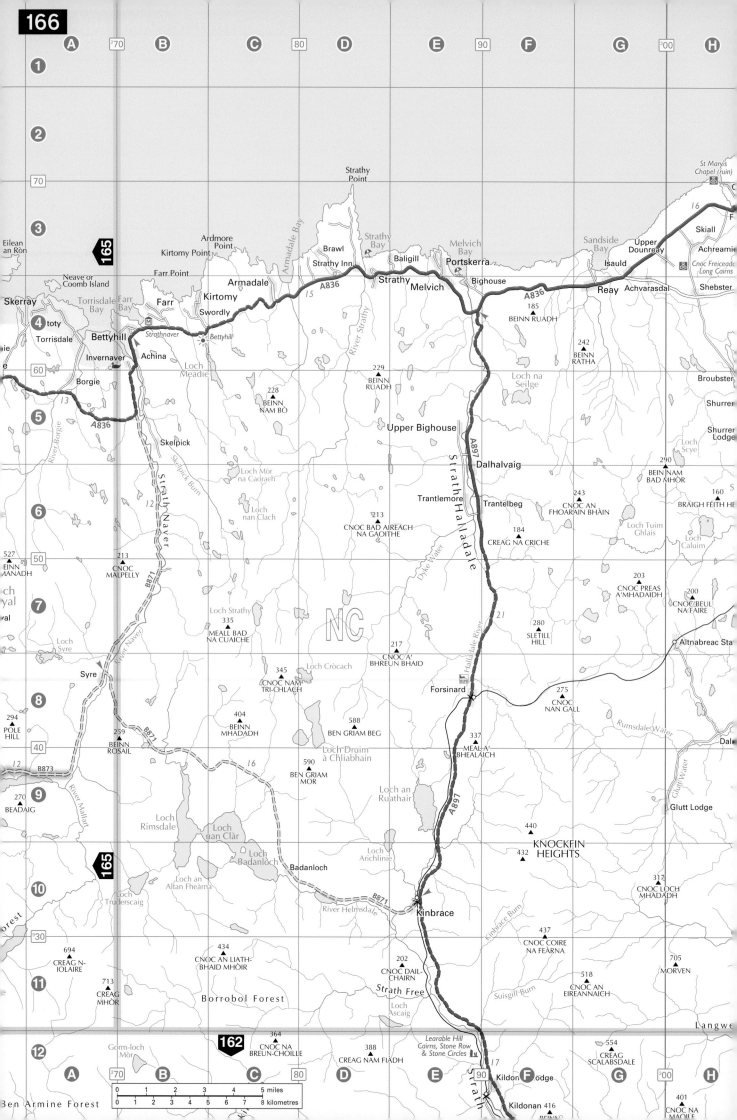

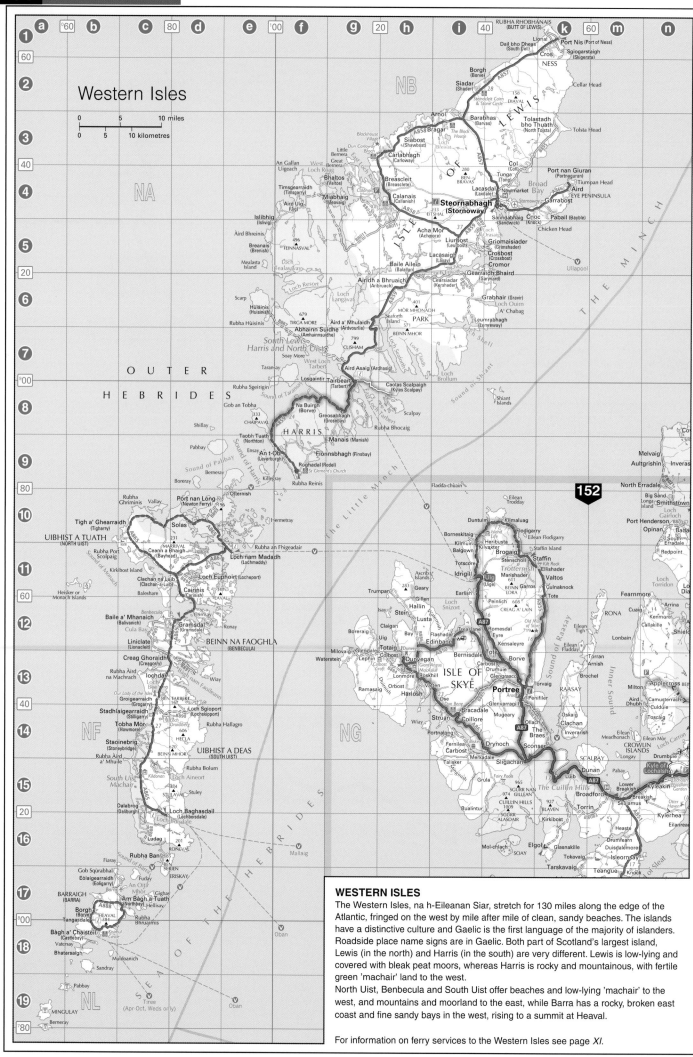

Western Isles

0   5   10 miles
0   5   10 kilometres

WESTERN ISLES

The Western Isles, na h-Eileanan Siar, stretch for 130 miles along the edge of the Atlantic, fringed on the west by mile after mile of clean, sandy beaches. The islands have a distinctive culture and Gaelic is the first language of the majority of islanders. Roadside place name signs are in Gaelic. Both part of Scotland's largest island, Lewis (in the north) and Harris (in the south) are very different. Lewis is low-lying and covered with bleak peat moors, whereas Harris is rocky and mountainous, with fertile green 'machair' land to the west.

North Uist, Benbecula and South Uist offer beaches and low-lying 'machair' to the west, and mountains and moorland to the east, while Barra has a rocky, broken east coast and fine sandy bays in the west, rising to a summit at Heaval.

For information on ferry services to the Western Isles see page XI.

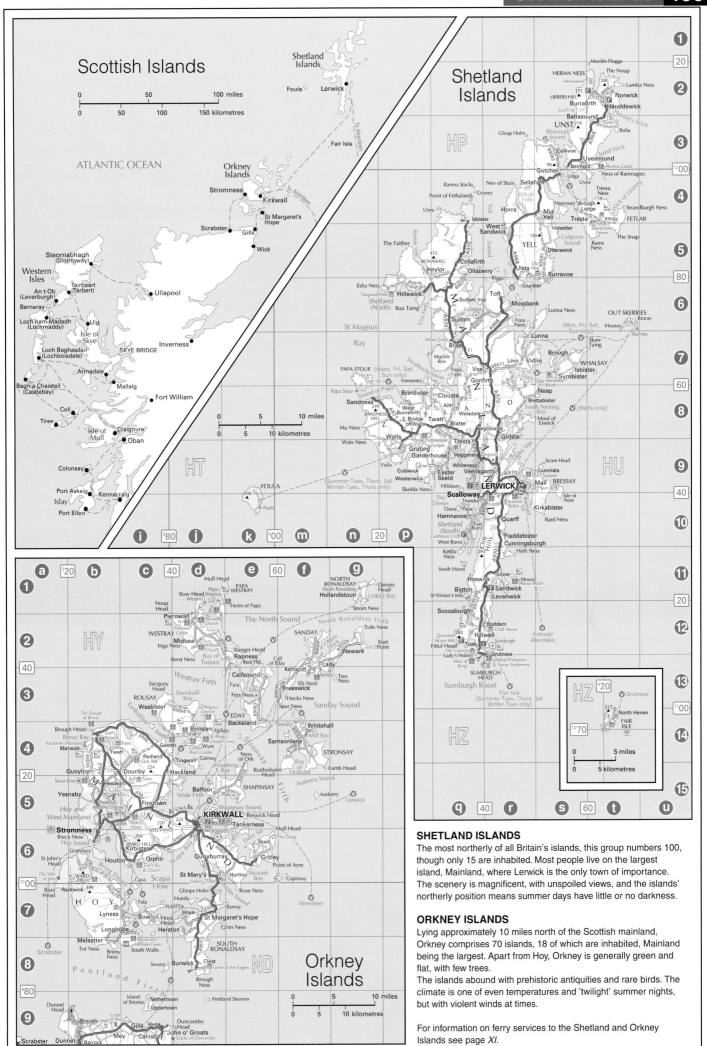

SHETLAND ISLANDS
The most northerly of all Britain's islands, this group numbers 100, though only 15 are inhabited. Most people live on the largest island, Mainland, where Lerwick is the only town of importance. The scenery is magnificent, with unspoiled views, and the islands' northerly position means summer days have little or no darkness.

ORKNEY ISLANDS
Lying approximately 10 miles north of the Scottish mainland, Orkney comprises 70 islands, 18 of which are inhabited, Mainland being the largest. Apart from Hoy, Orkney is generally green and flat, with few trees.
The islands abound with prehistoric antiquities and rare birds. The climate is one of even temperatures and 'twilight' summer nights, but with violent winds at times.

For information on ferry services to the Shetland and Orkney Islands see page XI.

IRISH
SEA

173

To reflect the distances shown on road signs,
distances are shown in miles in Northern Ireland
and kilometres in the Republic of Ireland.

16 kilometres = 10 miles

M1	Toll-free motorway
M1 Toll	Toll motorway and plaza
3	Motorway junctions with and without number
3	Restricted motorway junctions
Gorey S	Motorway service area
N7	National primary route (Republic of Ireland)
N81	National secondary route (Republic of Ireland)
R116	Regional road (Republic of Ireland)
7	Distance in kilometres between symbols (Republic of Ireland)
A2	Primary route (Northern Ireland)
A42	A road (Northern Ireland)

B176	B road (Northern Ireland)
7	Distance in miles between symbols (Northern Ireland)
	Minor road
Toll	Road tunnel, with toll
	Road under construction
	Scenic route
	International boundary
or V	Vehicle ferry
	Fast vehicle ferry or catamaran
	Gaeltacht (Irish language area)

For key to touring information see page 1

Ireland index

Abbeydorney....C12
Abbeyfeale....D12
Abbeyleix....G11
Adare....D12
Adrigole....C14
Aghalee....J5
Ahascragh....E9
Ahoghill....J4
Allenwood....H9
Allihies....B15
An Bun Beag....E4
An Charraig....E5
An Cheathrú Rua....C9
An Clochán Liath....E4
An Coireán....B14
An Daingean....B13
An Fál Carrach....F3
Annahilt....J6
Annalong....J7
Annascaul....B13
An Rinn....G13
An Spidéal....D9
Antrim....J5
Ardagh....D12
Ardara....E5
Ardee....H8
Ardfert....C12
Ardfinnan....F12
Ardglass....K6
Ardmore....F14
Ardnacrusha....E11
Arklow....J11
Armagh....H6
Armoy....J3
Arvagh....G7
Ashbourne....J9
Ashford....J10
Askeaton....D12
Athboy....H8
Athea....D12
Athenry....E9
Athleague....E8
Athlone....F9
Athy....H10
Augher....G6
Aughnacloy....H6
Aughrim....E9
Aughrim....J11
Avoca....J11

Bagenalstown....H11
Baile an Fheirtéaraigh....B13
Baile Chláir....D9
Baile Mhic Íre....D14
Bailieborough....H7
Balbriggan....J8
Ballacolla....G11
Ballaghaderreen....D7
Ballina....D7
Ballina....E11
Ballinafad....E7
Ballinagar....G9
Ballinamallard....G6
Ballinamore....F7
Ballinasloe....E9
Ballincollig....E14
Ballindaggan....H12
Ballingarry....D12
Ballingarry....D14
Ballinlough....E8
Ballinrobe....D8
Ballinspittle....E15
Ballintra....F5
Ballivor....H9
Ballon....H11
Ballybay....H7
Ballybofey....F5
Ballybunion....C12
Ballycanew....J11
Ballycarry....K5
Ballycastle....J3

Ballycastle....C6
Ballyclare....J5
Ballyclerahan....F12
Ballyconneely....B9
Ballyconnell....G7
Ballycotton....F14
Ballycumber....F9
Ballydehob....C15
Ballydesmond....D13
Ballyfarnan....E7
Ballyferriter....B13
Ballygally....J4
Ballygar....E9
Ballygawley....H6
Ballygawley....E6
Ballygowan....K5
Ballyhack....H13
Ballyhaise....G7
Ballyhalbert....K5
Ballyhaunis....E8
Ballyheige....C12
Ballyjamesduff....G8
Ballyliffin....G3
Ballylongford....C12
Ballymacarbry....F13
Ballymahon....F8
Ballymakeery....D14
Ballymena....J4
Ballymoe....E8
Ballymoney....H4
Ballymore....F9
Ballymore Eustace....H10
Ballymote....E7
Ballynacarrigy....G8
Ballynahinch....J6
Ballynure....J5
Ballyporeen....F13
Ballyragget....G11
Ballyshannon....F5
Ballyvaughan....D10
Ballywalter....K5
Balrothery....J8
Baltimore....C15
Baltinglass....H10
Banagher....F10
Banbridge....J6
Bandon....E14
Bangor....K5
Bangor Erris....C7
Bansha....F12
Bantry....C14
Barna....D9
Béal an Mhuirthead....B6
Béal Átha an Ghaorthaidh....D14
Bearna....D9
Belcoo....F6
Belfast....J5
Belgooly....E14
Bellaghy....H4
Belleek....F6
Belmullet....B6
Belturbet....G7
Benburb....H6
Bennettsbridge....G12
Beragh....G5
Bessbrook....J6
Birr....F10
Blacklion....F6
Blackwater....J12
Blarney....E14
Blessington....H10
Borris....H12
Borris-in-Ossory....F10
Borrisokane....F10
Borrisoleigh....F11
Boyle....E7
Bray....J10
Bridgetown....H13
Brittas....J9
Broadford....E11

Broadford....D12
Broughshane....J4
Bruff....E12
Bunbeg....E4
Bunclody....H11
Buncrana....G3
Bundoran....E6
Bunnyconnellan....D7
Bushmills....H3
Buttevant....E13
Bweeng....E13

Cadamstown....E12
Caherconlish....E12
Caherdaniel....B14
Cahersiveen....B14
Cahir....F12
Caledon....H6
Callan....G12
Camp....B13
Carndonagh....G3
Cappawhite....F12
Cappoquin....F13
Carlanstown....H8
Carlingford....J7
Carlow....H11
Carna....C9
Carnew....J11
Carnlough....J4
Carraig Airt....F3
Carraroe....C9
Carrickart....F3
Carrick....E5
Carrickfergus....K5
Carrickmacross....H7
Carrickmore....G5
Carrick-on-Shannon....F7
Carrick-on-Suir....G12
Carrigaline....E14
Carrigallen....F7
Carriganimmy....D13
Carrigtwohill....E14
Carryduff....J5
Cashel....F12
Castlebar....D8
Castlebellingham....J7
Castleblakeney....F9
Castleblayney....H7
Castlebridge....J12
Castlecomer....G11
Castleconnell....E11
Castlederg....G5
Castledermot....H11
Castlegregory....B13
Castleisland....C13
Castlemaine....C13
Castlemartyr....F14
Castlepollard....G8
Castlerea....E8
Castlerock....H3
Castletownbere....B15
Castletownroche....E13
Castletownshend....D15
Castlewellan....J6
Cathair Dónall....B14
Causeway....C12
Cavan....G7
Celbridge....H9
Charlestown....D7
Charleville....E12
Cill Charthaigh....E5
Clady....H4
Clane....H9
Clara....F10
Claregalway....D9
Claremorris....D8
Clashmore....F13
Claudy....G4
Cleggan....B8
Clifden....B9

Cliffoney....E6
Cloghan....F10
Clogheen....F13
Clogher....G6
Clogherhead....J8
Clogh Mills....J4
Clonakilty....D15
Clonaslee....G10
Clondalkin....J9
Clonea....G13
Clones....G7
Clonmany....G3
Clonmel....F12
Clough....K6
Cloughjordan....F10
Cloyne....F14
Coachford....D14
Coagh....H5
Coalisland....H5
Cobh....E14
Coleraine....H3
Collinstown....G8
Collon....H8
Collooney....E7
Comber....K5
Cong....D9
Conga....D9
Convoy....F4
Cookstown....H5
Cootehill....G7
Cork....E14
Corrofin....D10
Courtmacsherry....E15
Courtown....J11
Craigavon....H6
Craughwell....E9
Creeslough....F4
Croithlí....E4
Crolly....E4
Crookhaven....C15
Crookstown....D14
Croom....E12
Crosshaven....E14
Crossmaglen....H7
Crossmolina....D7
Crumlin....J5
Crusheen....D10
Culdaff....G3
Cullybackey....J4
Culmore....G4
Curracloe....J12
Curry....E7
Cushendall....J3
Cushendun....J3

Daingean....G9
Daingean Uí Chúis....B13
Delvin....G8
Derrinturn....H9
Derry....G4
Derrygonnelly....F6
Derrylin....G6
Dervock....H3
Dingle....B13
Doagh....J5
Donabate....J9
Donaghadee....K5
Donaghmore....H8
Donegal....F5
Donemana....G4
Doolin....C10
Doonbeg....C11
Downings....F3
Downpatrick....K6
Dowra....F6
Draperstown....H5
Drimoleague....D14
Drogheda....J8
Droichead Nua....H10
Dromahair....E6
Dromara....J6
Dromore....J6

Dromcollogher....D12
Dromiskin....J7
Drommahane....E13
Dromod....F8
Dromore....J6
Dromore....G5
Dromore West....D6
Drumaness....K6
Drumfries....G3
Drumkeeran....F7
Drumlish....F8
Drumquin....F6
Drumshanbo....C12
Duagh....C12
Dublin....J9
Duleek....J8
Dunboyne....J9
Dundalk....J7
Dundonald....K5
Dundrum....F12
Dunfanaghy....F3
Dungannon....H5
Dungarvan....G13
Dungiven....H4
Dunglow....E4
Dún Laoghaire....J9
Dunlavin....H10
Dunleer....J8
Dunloy....J4
Dunmanway....D14
Dunmore....E8
Dunmore East....H13
Dunshaughlin....H9
Durrow....G11
Durrow....G9
Durrus....C15
Dysart....E9

Easky....D6
Edenderry....H9
Edgeworthstown....G8
Eglinton....G4
Elphin....F8
Enfield....H9
Ennis....D11
Enniscorthy....H12
Enniscrone....D6
Enniskean....D14
Enniskillen....F6
Ennistymon....D10
Eyrecourt....F10

Fahan....G4
Falcarragh....F3
Fanore....D10
Farranfore....C13
Feakle....E11
Fenagh....F7
Fenit....B13
Ferbane....E13
Fermoy....E13
Ferns....J12
Fethard....F12
Fethard....H13
Fintona....G6
Fivemiletown....G6
Foxford....D7
Foynes....D12
Freemount....D13
Frenchpark....E8
Freshford....G11

Galbally....E12
Galway....D9
Garrison....F6
Garvagh....H4
Gilford....J6
Glandore....D15
Glaslough....H6
Glassan....F9
Gleann Cholm Cille....E5
Glenamaddy....E8

Glenarm....J4
Glenavy....J5
Glenbeigh....B13
Glencolumbkille....E5
Glenealy....J10
Glengarriff....C14
Glenties....E5
Glin....D12
Golden....F12
Goresbridge....H11
Gorey....J11
Gort....D10
Gortin....G5
Gowran....H11
Graiguenamanagh....H12
Granard....G8
Grange....E6
Greencastle....H3
Greencastle....G5
Greenore....J7
Greyabbey....K5
Greystones....J10
Gulladuff....H4

Hacketstown....H11
Headford....D9
Hillsborough....J6
Hilltown....J6
Holycross....F11
Holywood....K5
Hospital....E12
Howth....J9

Inagh....D11
Inch....B13
Inishcrone....D6
Innishannon....E14
Irvinestown....F6

Johnstown....G11

Kanturk....D13
Keadue....F7
Keady....H6
Kealkill....C14
Keel....B7
Kells....H8
Kenmare....C14
Kesh....F5
Kilbeggan....G9
Kilcar....E5
Kilcock....H9
Kilconnell....E9
Kilcoole....J10
Kilcormac....F10
Kilcullen....H10
Kildare....H10
Kildorrery....E13
Kilfenora....D10
Kilgarvan....C14
Kilkee....C11
Kilkeel....J7
Kilkenny....G11
Kill....H9
Kill....G13
Killala....D6
Killaloe....E11
Killarney....C13
Killashandra....G7
Killenaule....F12
Killinick....J13
Killorglin....C13
Killough....K6
Killucan....G9
Killurin....G10
Killybegs....E5
Killyleagh....K6
Kilmacanogue....J10
Kilmacrenan....F4
Kilmacthomas....G13
Kilmaganny....G12
Kilmaine....D8

Kilmallock....E12
Kilmanagh....G11
Kilmichael....D14
Kilmihil....C11
Kilmore Quay....H13
Kilmuckridge....J12
Kilpedder....J10
Kilrea....H4
Kilrush....C11
Kilsheelan....G12
Kiltimagh....D8
Kilworth....E13
Kingscourt....H7
Kinlough....E6
Kinnegad....G9
Kinnitty....F10
Kinsale....E14
Kinvara....D10
Kircubbin....K5
Knock....D8
Knockcroghery....F8

Lahinch....C10
Lanesborough....F8
Laragh....J10
Larne....K4
Lauragh....C14
Laurencetown....F10
Leap....D15

Leenaun....C8
Leighlinbridge....H11
Leixlip....H9
Letterfrack....B8
Letterkenny....F4
Lifford....G4
Limavady....H4
Limerick....E11
Lisbellaw....F6
Lisburn....J5
Liscarroll....D13
Lisdoonvarna....C10
Lismore....F13
Lisnaskea....G6
Listowel....C12
Londonderry....G4
Longford....F8
Longwood....H9
Loughbrickland....J6
Loughglinn....E8
Loughrea....E10
Louisburgh....C8
Lucan....J9
Lurgan....J6
Lusk....J9

Macroom....D14
Maghera....H4
Magherafelt....H5

Maguiresbridge..........G6
Maigh Cuilinn..........D9
Malahide..........J9
Málainn Mhóir..........E5
Malin..........G3
Malin More..........E5
Mallow..........E13
Manorhamilton..........F6
Markethill..........H6
Maynooth..........H9
Mayobridge..........H7
Midleton..........F14
Milford..........F4
Millstreet..........D13
Milltown..........C13
Miltown Malbay..........C11
Mitchelstown..........E13
Moate..........F9
Mohill..........F7
Monaghan..........H6
Monasterevin..........G10
Moneymore..........H5
Monivea..........E9
Mooncoin..........G13
Mountbellew..........E9
Mountmellick..........G10
Mountrath..........G10
Moville..........G3
Moy..........H6

Moycullen..........D9
Mucklagh..........G9
Muff..........G4
Muine Bheag..........H11
Mullagh..........H8
Mullaghmore..........E6
Mullinahone..........G12
Mullinavat..........G12
Mullingar..........G9
Mulranny..........C7
Murrisk..........C8
Murroe..........E11

Naas..........H10
Na Dúnaibh..........F3
Naul..........J8
Navan..........H8
Nenagh..........E11
Newbawn..........H12
Newbliss..........G7
Newbridge..........H10
Newcastle..........J6
Newcastle West..........D12
New Inn..........F12
Newmarket..........D13
Newmarket-on-Fergus..........D11
Newport..........C7

Newport..........E11
New Ross..........H12
Newry..........J6
Newtownabbey..........J5
Newtownards..........K5
Newtownbutler..........G7
Newtown-cunningham..........G4
Newtownforbes..........F8
Newtownhamilton..........H6
Newtownmount-kennedy..........J10
Newtownstewart..........G5
Nobber..........H8

Oilgate..........H12
Oldcastle..........G8
Omagh..........G5
Omeath..........J7
Oranmore..........D9
Oughterard..........D9

Pallas Green..........E12
Partry..........D8
Passage East..........H13
Passage West..........E14
Patrickswell..........E12
Pettigo..........F5
Piltown..........G13

Plumbridge..........G5
Pomeroy..........H5
Portadown..........H6
Portaferry..........K6
Portarlington..........G10
Portavogie..........K6
Portballintrae..........H3
Portglenone..........H4
Port Laoise..........G10
Portlaw..........G13
Portmagee..........B14
Portmarnock..........J9
Portnoo..........E4
Portrush..........H3
Portstewart..........H3
Portumna..........E10
Poyntzpass..........J6
Prosperous..........H9

Quin..........D11

Ramelton..........F4
Randalstown..........J5
Raphoe..........G4
Rasharkin..........H4
Rathangan..........H10
Rathcoole..........J9
Rathcormac..........E13
Rathdowney..........G11

Rathdrum..........J10
Rathfriland..........J6
Rathkeale..........D12
Ráth Luirc..........E12
Rathmore..........D13
Rathnew..........J10
Rathvilly..........H11
Ratoath..........J9
Recess..........C9
Rhode..........G9
Ringaskiddy..........E14
Ringville..........G13
Riverchapel..........J11
Riverstick..........E14
Rochfortbridge..........G9
Rockcorry..........H7
Roscommon..........F8
Roscrea..........F10
Rosscarbery..........D15
Rosses Point..........E6
Rosslare..........J13
Rosslare Harbour..........J13
Rosslea..........G6
Rossnowlagh..........E5
Rostrevor..........J7
Roundstone..........B9
Roundwood..........J10
Rush..........J9

Saintfield..........K6
Sallins..........H9
Scarriff..........E11
Scartaglin..........C13
Schull..........C15
Seskinore..........G5
Shannon..........D11
Shannonbridge..........F9
Shercock..........H7
Shillelagh..........H11
Sixmilebridge..........D11
Skerries..........J8
Skibbereen..........D15
Slane..........H8
Sligo..........E6
Sneem..........B14
Spanish Point..........C11
Spiddal..........D9
Sraith Salach..........C9
Stewartstown..........H5
Stoneyford..........G12
Strabane..........G4
Stradbally..........G10
Stradone..........G7
Strandhill..........E6
Stranorlar..........F5
Strokestown..........F8

Summerhill..........H9
Swan..........G11
Swanlinbar..........F6
Swinford..........D7
Swords..........J9

Taghmon..........H12
Tagoat..........J13
Tallaght..........J9
Tallow..........F13
Tandragee..........J6
Tarbert..........C12
Templemore..........F11
Termonfeckin..........J8
Thomastown..........G12
Thurles..........F11
Timoleague..........D15
Tinahely..........J11
Tipperary..........F12
Tobercurry..........E7
Tobermore..........H4
Toomevara..........F11
Toormore..........C15
Tower..........E14
Tralee..........C13
Tramore..........G13
Trim..........H8
Tuam..........D9
Tubbercurry..........E7

Tulla..........D11
Tullamore..........G9
Tullow..........H11
Tulsk..........E8
Turlough..........D7

Urlingford..........G11
Virginia..........G8

Warrenpoint..........J7
Waterford..........G13
Watergrasshill..........E13
Waterville..........B14
Wellingtonbridge..........H13
Westport..........C8
Wexford..........J12
Whitegate..........E14
Whitehead..........K5
Wicklow..........J10
Woodenbridge..........J11
Woodford..........E10

Youghal..........F14

171

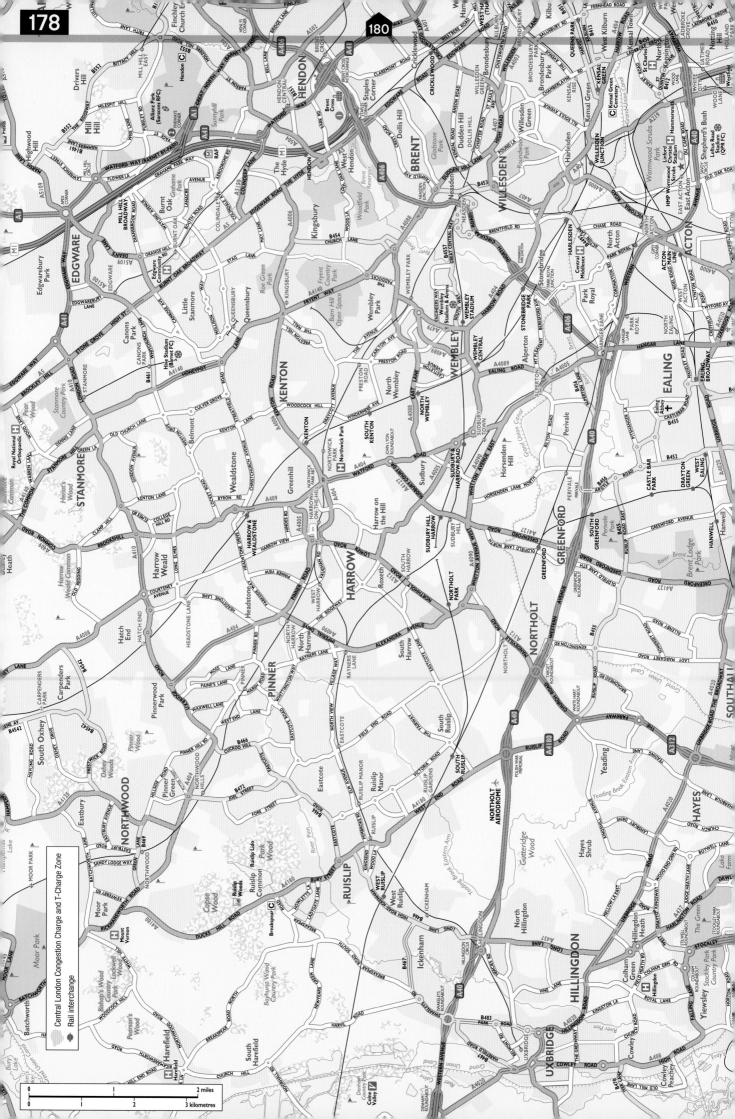

NORTH

SEA

Street map symbols

Town, port and airport plans

Motorway and junction	One-way, gated/ closed road	Railway station	Car park
Primary road single/ dual carriageway and numbered junction	Restricted access road	Light rapid transit system station	Park and Ride (at least 6 days per week)
A road single/ dual carriageway and numbered junction	Pedestrian area	Level crossing	Bus/coach station
B road single/ dual carriageway	Footpath	Tramway	Hospital
Local road single/ dual carriageway	Road under construction	Airport, heliport	24-hour Accident & Emergency hospital
Other road single/ dual carriageway, minor road	Road tunnel	Railair terminal	Beach (award winning)
Building of interest	Lighthouse	Theatre or performing arts centre	City wall
Ruined building	Castle	Cinema	Escarpment
Tourist Information Centre	Castle mound	Abbey, chapel, church	Cliff lift
Visitor or heritage centre	Monument, statue	Synagogue	River/canal, lake
World Heritage Site (UNESCO)	Post Office	Mosque	Lock, weir
Museum	Public library	Golf course	Viewpoint
English Heritage site	Shopping centre	Racecourse	Park/sports ground
Historic Scotland site	Shopmobility	Nature reserve	Cemetery
Cadw (Welsh heritage) site	Football stadium	Aquarium	Woodland
National Trust site	Rugby stadium	Agricultural showground	Built-up area
National Trust Scotland site	County cricket ground	Toilet, with facilities for the less able	Beach

Central London street map (see pages 238–247)

London Underground station	London Overground station
Docklands Light Railway (DLR) station	Central London Congestion Charge and T-Charge Zone boundary

Royal Parks

Green Park	Park open 5am–midnight. Constitution Hill and The Mall closed to traffic Sundays and public holidays 8am–dusk.
Grosvenor Square Garden	Park open 7:30am–dusk.
Hyde Park	Park open 5am–midnight. Park roads closed to traffic midnight–5am.
Kensington Gardens	Park open 6am–dusk.
Regent's Park	Park open 5am–dusk. Park roads closed to traffic midnight–7am, except for residents.
St James's Park	Park open 5am–midnight. The Mall closed to traffic Sundays and public holidays 8am–dusk.
Victoria Tower Gardens	Park open dawn–dusk.

Traffic regulations in the City of London include security checkpoints and restrict the number of entry and exit points.

Note: Oxford Street is closed to through-traffic (except buses & taxis) 7am–7pm Monday–Saturday.

Central London Congestion Charge Zone (CCZ)
The charge for driving or parking a vehicle on public roads in this Central London area, during operating hours, is £11.50 per vehicle per day in advance or on the day of travel. Alternatively you can pay £10.50 by registering with CC Auto Pay, an automated payment system. Drivers can also pay the next charging day after travelling in the zone but this will cost £14. Payment permits entry, travel within and exit from the CCZ by the vehicle as often as required on that day.

The CCZ operates between 7am and 6pm, Mon–Fri only. There is no charge at weekends, on public holidays or between 25th Dec and 1st Jan inclusive.

For up to date information on the CCZ, exemptions, discounts or ways to pay, visit www.tfl.gov.uk/modes/driving/congestion-charge

T-Charge (Toxicity Charge)
All vehicles in Central London need to meet minimum exhaust emission standards or pay a £10 daily Emission Surcharge. It applies to the same area covered by the Congestion Charge and operates during the same hours (between 7am and 6pm Monday to Friday). The surcharge is in addition to the Congestion Charge.

The minimum emmission standards are Euro 4/IV for both petrol and diesel vehicles (different standards may apply to certain specialist vehicle types). The surcharge will largely apply to pre-2006 vehicles.

For further information visit www.tfl.gov.uk/t-charge

The Ultra Low Emission Zone (ULEZ) is planned to replace the T-Charge in April 2019 with even stricter standards. For details visit www.tfl.gov.uk/ultra-low-emission-zone

Town Plans

Aberdeen	188	Guildford	204	Plymouth	220
Basingstoke	188	Harrogate	205	Poole	222
Bath	189	Huddersfield	205	Portsmouth	221
Birmingham	190	Inverness	206	Preston	222
Blackpool	189	Ipswich	206	Ramsgate	39
Bournemouth	191	Kingston upon Hull	207	Reading	223
Bradford	191	Lancaster	207	Royal Tunbridge Wells	223
Brighton	192	Leeds	208	Salisbury	224
Bristol	192	Leicester	209	Sheffield	224
Cambridge	193	Lincoln	209	Shrewsbury	225
Canterbury	194	Liverpool	210	Southampton	226
Cardiff	194	Llandudno	79	Southend-on-Sea	225
Carlisle	195	LONDON	238-247	Stirling	227
Cheltenham	195	Luton	211	Stockton-on-Tees	227
Chester	196	Maidstone	211	Stoke-on-Trent (Hanley)	228
Colchester	196	Manchester	212	Stratford-upon-Avon	228
Coventry	197	Margate	39	Sunderland	229
Darlington	197	Middlesbrough	214	Swansea	230
Derby	198	Milton Keynes	213	Swindon	230
Doncaster	198	Newcastle upon Tyne	215	Taunton	231
Dover	199	Newport	214	Torquay	231
Dundee	199	Newquay	4	Warwick	232
Durham	200	Northampton	216	Watford	232
Eastbourne	200	Norwich	216	Winchester	233
Edinburgh	201	Nottingham	217	Wolverhampton	233
Exeter	202	Oldham	217	Worcester	234
Glasgow	203	Oxford	218	York	234
Gloucester	202	Perth	219		
Great Yarmouth	204	Peterborough	219		

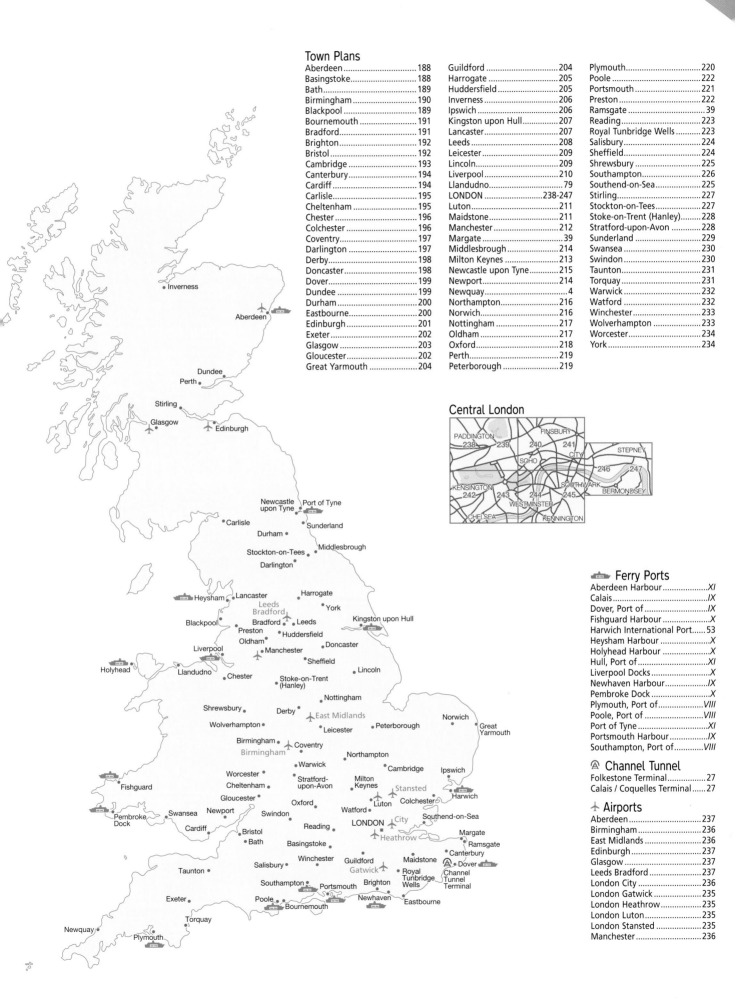

Central London

PADDINGTON 238 239 240 241 STEPNEY
SOHO CITY
KENSINGTON 242 243 244 245 SOUTHWARK 246 247 BERMONDSEY
CHELSEA WESTMINSTER KENNINGTON

Ferry Ports

Aberdeen Harbour	XI
Calais	IX
Dover, Port of	IX
Fishguard Harbour	X
Harwich International Port	53
Heysham Harbour	X
Holyhead Harbour	X
Hull, Port of	XI
Liverpool Docks	X
Newhaven Harbour	IX
Pembroke Dock	X
Plymouth, Port of	VIII
Poole, Port of	VIII
Port of Tyne	XI
Portsmouth Harbour	IX
Southampton, Port of	VIII

Channel Tunnel

Folkestone Terminal	27
Calais / Coquelles Terminal	27

Airports

Aberdeen	237
Birmingham	236
East Midlands	236
Edinburgh	237
Glasgow	237
Leeds Bradford	237
London City	236
London Gatwick	235
London Heathrow	235
London Luton	235
London Stansted	235
Manchester	236

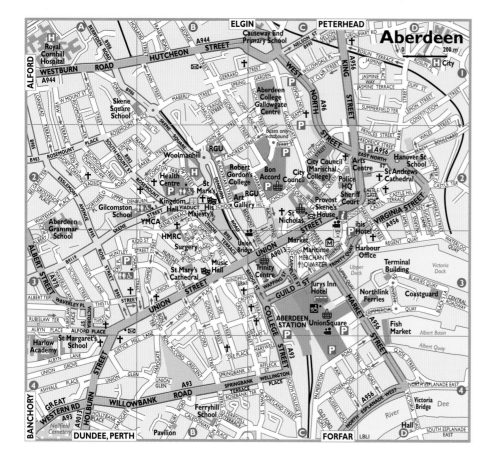

Aberdeen

Aberdeen is found on atlas page **151 N6**

Affleck Street	C4	Maberly Street	B1
Albert Street	A3	Marischal Street	D2
Albury Road	B4	Market Street	C3
Alford Place	A3	Nelson Street	C1
Ann Street	B1	Palmerston Road	C4
Beach Boulevard	D2	Park Street	D1
Belgrave Terrace	A2	Portland Street	C4
Berryden Road	A1	Poynernook Road	C4
Blackfriars Street	B2	Regent Quay	D3
Blaikies Quay	D3	Richmond Street	A2
Bon Accord Crescent	B4	Rose Place	A3
Bon Accord Street	B3	Rose Street	A3
Bridge Street	C3	Rosemount Place	A2
Caledonian Place	B4	Rosemount Viaduct	A2
Carmelite Street	C3	St Andrew Street	B2
Chapel Street	A3	St Clair Street	C1
Charlotte Street	B1	School Hill	C2
College Street	C3	Skene Square	B2
Constitution Street	D1	Skene Street	A3
Crimon Place	B3	Skene Terrace	B2
Crown Street	B3	South College Street	C4
Dee Street	B3	South Esplanade East	D4
Denburn Road	B2	South Mount Street	A2
Diamond Street	B3	Spa Street	B2
East North Street	D2	Springbank Street	B4
Esslemont Avenue	A2	Springbank Terrace	B4
Gallowgate	C1	Summer Street	B3
George Street	B1	Summerfield Terrace	D1
Gilcomston Park	B2	Thistle Lane	A3
Golden Square	B3	Thistle Place	A3
Gordon Street	B3	Thistle Street	A3
Great Western Road	A4	Trinity Quay	C3
Guild Street	C3	Union Bridge	B3
Hadden Street	C3	Union Grove	A4
Hanover Street	D2	Union Street	B3
Hardgate	B4	Union Terrace	B2
Harriet Street	C2	Upper Denburn	A2
Holburn Street	A4	Victoria Road	D4
Huntley Street	A3	Victoria Street	A3
Hutcheon Street	B1	View Terrace	A1
Jasmine Terrace	D1	Virginia Street	D2
John Street	B2	Wapping Street	C3
Justice Mill Lane	A4	Waverley Place	A3
King Street	C1	Wellington Place	C4
Langstane Place	B3	West North Street	C1
Leadside Road	A2	Westburn Road	A1
Loanhead Terrace	A1	Whitehall Place	A2
Loch Street	C1	Willowbank Road	A4

Basingstoke

Basingstoke is found on atlas page **22 H4**

Alencon Link	C1	London Street	C3
Allnutt Avenue	D2	Lower Brook Street	A2
Basing View	C1	Lytton Road	D3
Beaconsfield Road	C4	Market Place	B3
Bounty Rise	A4	May Place	C3
Bounty Road	A4	Montague Place	C4
Bramblys Close	A3	Mortimer Lane	A2
Bramblys Drive	A3	New Road	B3
Budd's Close	A3	New Road	C2
Castle Road	C4	New Street	B3
Chapel Hill	B1	Penrith Road	A3
Chequers Road	C2	Rayleigh Road	A2
Chester Place	A4	Red Lion Lane	C3
Churchill Way	B2	Rochford Road	A2
Churchill Way East	D1	St Mary's Court	C2
Churchill Way West	A2	Sarum Hill	A3
Church Square	B2	Seal Road	C2
Church Street	B2	Solby's Road	A2
Church Street	B3	Southend Road	A2
Cliddesden Road	C4	Southern Road	B4
Clifton Terrace	C1	Stukeley Road	A3
Cordale Road	A4	Sylvia Close	B4
Council Road	B4	Timberlake Road	B2
Crossborough Gardens	D3	Victoria Street	B3
Crossborough Hill	D3	Victory Roundabout	A2
Cross Street	B3	Vyne Road	B1
Devonshire Place	A4	Winchcombe Road	A4
Eastfield Avenue	D2	Winchester Road	A4
Eastrop Lane	D2	Winchester Street	B3
Eastrop Roundabout	C1	Winterthur Way	A1
Eastrop Way	D2	Worting Road	A3
Essex Road	A2	Wote Street	C3
Fairfields Road	B4		
Festival Way	C2		
Flaxfield Court	A2		
Flaxfield Road	A3		
Flaxfield Road	B3		
Frances Road	A4		
Frescade Crescent	A4		
Goat Lane	C2		
Hackwood Road	C4		
Hamelyn Road	A4		
Hardy Lane	A4		
Hawkfield Lane	A4		
Haymarket Yard	C3		
Joices Yard	B3		
Jubilee Road	B4		
London Road	D3		

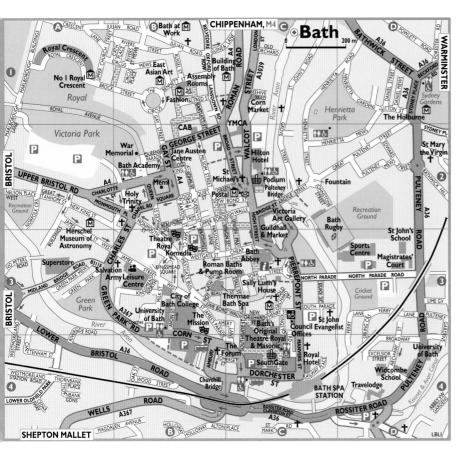

Bath

Bath is found on atlas page 20 D2

Archway Street	D4	Lower Borough Walls	B3
Argyle Street	C2	Lower Bristol Road	A3
Avon Street	B3	Lower Oldfield Park	A4
Bartlett Street	B1	Manvers Street	C3
Barton Street	B2	Midland Bridge Road	A3
Bathwick Street	D1	Milk Street	B3
Beauford Square	B2	Milsom Street	B2
Beau Street	B3	Monmouth Place	A2
Beckford Road	D1	Monmouth Street	B2
Bennett Street	B1	New Bond Street	B2
Bridge Street	C2	New King Street	A2
Broad Street	C2	New Orchard Street	C3
Broadway	D4	Norfolk Buildings	A3
Brock Street	A1	North Parade	C3
Chapel Road	B2	North Parade Road	D3
Charles Street	A3	Old King Street	B2
Charlotte Street	A2	Oxford Row	B1
Cheap Street	C3	Pierrepont Street	C3
Cheltenham Street	A4	Princes Street	B2
Circus Mews	B1	Pulteney Road	D2
Claverton Street	C4	Queen Square	B2
Corn Street	B4	Queen Street	B2
Daniel Street	D1	Railway Place	C4
Dorchester Street	C4	Rivers Street	B1
Edward Street	D2	Roman Road	C1
Ferry Lane	D3	Rossiter Road	C4
Gay Street	B1	Royal Avenue	A1
George Street	B2	Royal Crescent	A1
Great Pulteney Street	C2	St James's Parade	B3
Great Stanhope Street	A2	St John's Road	C1
Green Park Road	A3	Saw Close	B3
Green Street	B2	Southgate Street	C4
Grove Street	C2	South Parade	C3
Guinea Lane	B1	Stall Street	C3
Henrietta Gardens	D1	Sutton Street	D1
Henrietta Mews	C2	Sydney Place	D1
Henrietta Road	C1	The Circus	B1
Henrietta Street	C2	Thornbank Place	A4
Henry Street	C3	Union Street	B2
High Street	C2	Upper Borough Walls	B2
Hot Bath Street	B3	Upper Bristol Road	A2
James Street West	B3	Upper Church Street	A1
John Street	B2	Walcot Street	C2
Julian Road	B1	Wells Road	A4
Kingsmead North	B3	Westgate Buildings	B3
Kingston Road	C3	Westgate Street	B3
Lansdown Road	B1	Westmoreland Station Road	A4
London Street	C1	York Street	C3

Blackpool

Blackpool is found on atlas page 88 C3

Abingdon Street	B1	Havelock Street	C4
Adelaide Street	B3	High Street	C1
Albert Road	B3	Hornby Road	B3
Albert Road	C3	Hornby Road	D3
Alfred Street	C2	Hull Road	B3
Ashton Road	D4	Kay Street	C4
Bank Hey Street	B2	Kent Road	C4
Banks Street	B1	King Street	C2
Belmont Avenue	C4	Leamington Road	D2
Bennett Avenue	D3	Leicester Road	D2
Bethesda Road	C4	Leopold Grove	C2
Birley Street	B2	Lincoln Road	D2
Blenheim Avenue	D4	Livingstone Road	C3
Bonny Street	B4	Lord Street	B1
Buchanan Street	C1	Louise Street	C4
Butler Street	C1	Milbourne Street	C1
Caunce Street	D1	Montreal Avenue	D3
Cedar Square	C2	New Bonny Street	B3
Central Drive	C4	New Larkhill Street	C1
Chapel Street	B4	Palatine Road	C4
Charles Street	C1	Palatine Road	D3
Charnley Road	C3	Park Road	D2
Cheapside	B2	Park Road	D4
Church Street	B2	Peter Street	D2
Church Street	C2	Pier Street	B4
Church Street	D2	Princess Parade	B1
Clifton Street	B2	Promenade	B1
Clinton Avenue	D4	Queen Street	B1
Cookson Street	C2	Raikes Parade	D2
Coop Street	B4	Reads Avenue	C3
Coronation Street	C3	Reads Avenue	D3
Corporation Street	B2	Regent Road	C2
Dale Street	B4	Ribble Road	C4
Deansgate	B2	Ripon Road	D3
Dickson Road	B1	Seasiders Way	B4
Edward Street	C2	Selbourne Road	D1
Elizabeth Street	D1	South King Street	C2
Fairhurst Street	D1	Springfield Road	B1
Fisher Street	C1	Stanley Road	C3
Fleet Street	C3	Talbot Road	B2
Foxhall Road	B4	Talbot Road	C1
Freckleton Street	D4	Topping Street	C2
General Street	B1	Vance Road	B3
George Street	C1	Victoria Street	B2
Gorton Street	D1	Victory Road	D1
Granville Road	D2	West Street	B2
Grosvenor Street	C1	Woolman Road	D4
Harrison Street	D4	York Street	B4

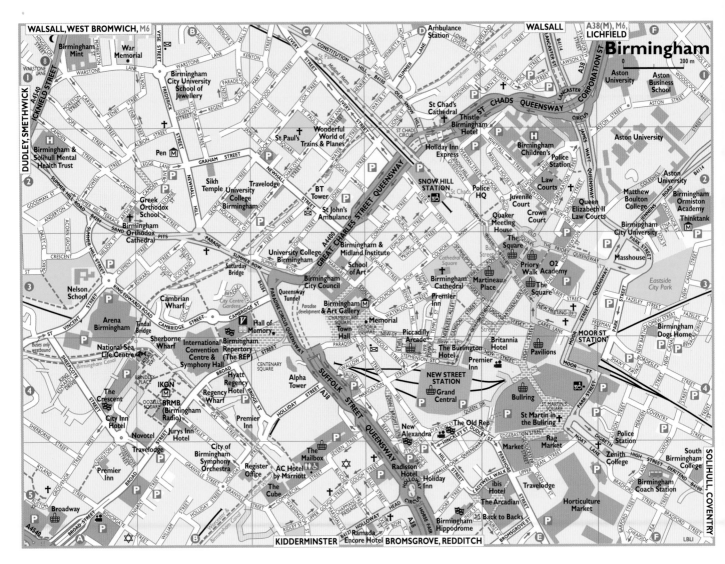

Birmingham

Birmingham is found on atlas page **58 G7**

Acorn Grove ... A2	Caroline Street ... B1	Etna Street ... F2	Kenyon Street ... B1	Oozells Square ... B4	Snow Hill Queensway ... D2
Albert Street ... E3	Carrs Lane ... E3	Exeter Street ... D5	King Edward's Drive ... A4	Oxford Street ... F5	Spencer Street ... B1
Albert Street ... F3	Carver Street ... A1	Fazeley Street ... F3	King Edwards Road ... A3	Parade ... B3	Staniforth Street ... E1
Albion Street ... B2	Chamberlain Square ... C3	Fleet Street ... C3	Ladywell Walk ... D5	Paradise Circus	Station Street ... D5
Allison Street ... F4	Chapmans Passage ... C5	Fox Street ... F3	Lancaster Circus ... E1	Queensway ... C3	Steelhouse Lane ... E2
Anderton Street ... A2	Charlotte Street ... B3	Frederick Street ... B1	Lancaster Street ... E1	Paradise Street ... C4	Stephenson Street ... D4
Arthur Place ... A2	Cheapside ... F5	Freeman Street ... E3	Lawson Street ... E1	Park Street ... E4	Suffolk Street Queensway ... C4
Aston Street ... F1	Cherry Street ... D3	Gas Street ... B4	Legge Lane ... B2	Pemberton Street ... A1	Summer Hill Road ... A2
Atlas Way ... B4	Church Street ... D2	George Street ... B2	Lighthouse Avenue ... A3	Pershore Street ... E5	Summer Hill Street ... A2
Banbury Street ... F3	Civic Close ... B3	Gloucester Street ... E5	Lionel Street ... C3	Pinfold Street ... D4	Summer Hill Terrace ... A2
Barford Street ... F5	Clement Street ... A3	Goodman Street ... A2	Livery Street ... C1	Pope Street ... A1	Summer Lane ... D1
Bartholomew Street ... F3	Cleveland Street ... D1	Gough Street ... C5	Louisa Street ... B3	Powell Street ... A2	Summer Row ... B3
Barwick Street ... D3	Coleshill Street ... F2	Graham Street ... B2	Loveday Street ... E1	Price Street ... E1	Swallow Street ... C4
Bath Street ... E1	Colmore Circus	Granville Street ... B5	Lower Loveday Street ... D1	Princip Street ... E1	Temple Row ... D3
Beak Street ... D4	Queensway ... E2	Great Charles Street	Lower Temple Street ... D4	Printing House Street ... E2	Temple Row West ... D3
Benacre Drive ... F4	Colmore Row ... D3	Queensway ... C3	Ludgate Hill ... C2	Queens Drive ... D4	Temple Street ... D3
Bennetts Hill ... D3	Commercial Street ... C5	Grosvenor Street ... F2	Margaret Street ... C3	Queensway Tunnel ... C3	Tenby Street ... A1
Berkley Street ... B4	Constitution Hill ... C1	Grosvenor Street West ... A5	Marshall Street ... C5	Rea Street ... F5	Tenby Street North ... A1
Bishopgate Street ... A5	Cornwall Street ... D3	Hall Street ... B1	Martineau Way ... E3	Regent Parade ... B1	Tennant Street ... A5
Blucher Street ... C5	Corporation Street ... E1	Hampton Street ... D1	Mary Ann Street ... C1	Regent Place ... B1	The Priory Queensway ... E3
Bond Street ... C1	Corporation Street ... E3	Helena Street ... B3	Mary Street ... C1	Regent Street ... B1	Thorp Street ... D5
Bordesley Street ... F4	Coventry Street ... F4	Henrietta Street ... C1	Meriden Street ... F4	Ridley Street ... C5	Tindal Bridge ... B3
Bow Street ... D5	Cox Street ... C1	High Street ... E4	Mill Lane ... F5	Ruston Street ... A5	Trent Street ... F4
Bradford Street ... F5	Dale End ... E3	High Street Deritend ... F5	Moat Lane ... E4	Ryland Street ... A5	Union Street ... E3
Bridge Street ... B4	Daley Close ... A3	Hill Street ... C4	Moor Street ... E4	St Chads Queensway ... E1	Upper Dean Street ... E5
Brindley Drive ... B3	Dalton Street ... E2	Hinckley Street ... D4	Moor Street	St Jude's Pass ... D5	Upper Gough Street ... C5
Brindley Place ... B4	Dean Street ... E5	Holland Street ... B2	Queensway ... E4	St Marks Crescent ... A3	Vesey Street ... E1
Broad Street ... A5	Digbeth ... E4	Holliday Street ... B5	Moreton Street ... A1	St Martin's Square ... E4	Victoria Square ... C3
Bromsgrove Street ... E5	Dudley Street ... D4	Holloway Circus ... D5	Navigation Street ... C4	St Paul's Square ... C1	Vittoria Street ... B1
Brook Street ... C2	Eden Place ... C3	Holloway Head ... C5	Needless Alley ... D3	St Philip's Place ... D3	Vyse Street ... B1
Brunel Street ... C4	Edgebaston Street ... E4	Holt Street ... F1	Nelson Street ... A3	St Vincent Street ... A3	Warstone Lane ... A1
Bull Street ... E3	Edmund Street ... D3	Horse Fair ... D5	New Bartholomew Street ... F4	Sand Pitts ... A2	Washington Street ... C5
Cambridge Street ... B3	Edward Street ... B3	Hospital Street ... D1	New Canal Street ... F4	Saturday Bridge ... B3	Waterloo Street ... D3
Camden Drive ... B2	Ellis Street ... D5	Hurst Street ... E5	Newhall Hill ... B2	Scotland Street ... B3	Water Street ... C2
Camden Street ... A2	Essington Street ... A5	Icknield Street ... A1	Newhall Street ... C2	Severn Street ... C5	Weaman Street ... D2
Cannon Street ... D3	Ethel Street ... D4	Inge Street ... D5	New Meeting Street ... E3	Shadwell Street ... D1	Whittall Street ... E2
		James Street ... B2	New Street ... D3	Shaw's Passage ... F4	William Street ... B5
		James Watt Queensway ... E2	Newton Street ... E3	Sheepcote Street ... A4	Woodcock Street ... F1
		Jennens Road ... F2	Northwood Street ... C1	Sherborne Street ... A4	
		John Bright Street ... D4	Old Snow Hill ... D1	Sloane Street ... B2	
			Old Square ... E3	Smallbrook Queensway ... D5	

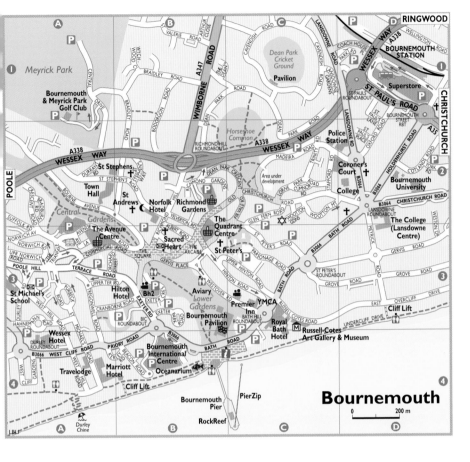

Bournemouth

Bournemouth is found on atlas page **13 J6**

Albert Road	B3	Old Christchurch Road	C2
Avenue Lane	A3	Orchard Street	A3
Avenue Road	A3	Oxford Road	D2
Bath Hill Roundabout	C3	Park Road	D1
Bath Road	B4	Parsonage Road	C3
Beacon Road	B4	Poole Hill	A3
BIC Roundabout	B3	Priory Road	A4
Bodorgon Road	B2	Purbeck Road	A3
Bourne Avenue	A2	Richmond Gardens	B2
Bournemouth Street		Richmond Hill	B3
Roundabout	D1	Richmond Hill Roundabout	B2
Bradburne Road	A2	Russell Cotes Road	C3
Braidley Road	B1	St Michael's Road	A3
Cavendish Road	C1	St Paul's Lane	D1
Central Drive	A1	St Paul's Place	D2
Christchurch Road	D2	St Paul's Road	D1
Coach House Place	D1	St Pauls Roundabout	D1
Commercial Road	A3	St Peter's Road	C3
Cotlands Road	D2	St Peter's Roundabout	C3
Cranborne Road	A3	St Stephen's Road	A2
Crescent Road	A2	St Stephen's Way	B2
Cumnor Road	C2	St Valerie Road	B1
Dean Park Crescent	B2	Stafford Road	C2
Dean Park Road	B2	Suffolk Road	A2
Durley Road	A3	Terrace Road	A3
Durley Roundabout	A4	The Arcade	B3
Durrant Road	A2	The Deans	B1
East Overcliff Drive	D3	The Square	B3
Exeter Crescent	B3	The Triangle	A3
Exeter Park Road	B3	Tregonwell Road	A3
Exeter Road	B3	Trinity Road	C2
Fir Vale Road	C2	Undercliff Drive	D3
Gervis Place	B3	Upper Hinton Road	C3
Gervis Road	D3	Upper Norwich Road	A3
Glen Fern Road	C2	Upper Terrace Road	A3
Grove Road	C3	Wellington Road	D1
Hahnemann Road	A3	Wessex Way	A2
Hinton Road	B3	West Cliff Gardens	A4
Holdenhurst Road	D2	West Cliff Road	A4
Kerley Road	A4	West Hill Road	A3
Lansdowne Gardens	C1	Weston Drive	D2
Lansdowne Road	C1	Westover Road	B3
Lansdowne Roundabout	D2	Wimborne Road	B1
Lorne Park Road	C2	Wootton Gardens	C2
Madeira Road	C2	Wootton Mount	C2
Meyrick Road	D3	Wychwood Close	B1
Norwich Avenue	A3	Yelverton Road	B2
Norwich Road	A3	York Road	D2

Bradford

Bradford is found on atlas page **90 F4**

Aldermanbury	B3	Lower Kirkgate	C2
Bank Street	B2	Lumb Lane	A1
Barkerend Road	D2	Manchester Road	B4
Barry Street	B2	Manningham Lane	A1
Bolling Road	C4	Manor Row	B1
Bolton Road	C2	Market Street	B3
Bridge Street	C3	Midland Road	B1
Broadway	C3	Morley Street	A4
Burnett Street	D2	Neal Street	B4
Canal Road	C1	Nelson Street	B4
Carlton Street	A3	North Brook Street	C1
Centenary Square	B3	Northgate	B2
Chandos Street	C4	North Parade	B1
Chapel Street	D3	North Street	C2
Cheapside	B2	North Wing	D1
Chester Street	A4	Otley Road	D1
Church Bank	C2	Paradise Street	A2
Claremont	A4	Peckover Street	D2
Croft Street	C4	Piccadilly	B2
Darfield Street	A1	Pine Street	C2
Darley Street	B2	Princes Way	B3
Drewton Road	A2	Randall Well Street	A3
Dryden Street	D4	Rawson Road	A2
Duke Street	B2	Rawson Square	B2
East Parade	D3	Rebecca Street	A2
Edmund Street	A4	St Blaise Way	C1
Edward Street	C4	Sawrey Place	A4
Eldon Place	A1	Senior Way	B4
Filey Street	D3	Shipley Airedale Road	C1
George Street	C3	Stott Hill	C2
Godwin Street	B2	Sunbridge Road	A2
Grattan Road	A2	Tetley Street	A3
Great Horton Road	A4	Thornton Road	A3
Grove Terrace	A4	Trafalgar Street	B1
Hallfield Road	A1	Tyrrel Street	B3
Hall Ings	B4	Upper Park Gate	D2
Hamm Strasse	B1	Upper Piccadilly	B2
Holdsworth Street	C1	Valley Road	C1
Houghton Place	A1	Vicar Lane	C3
Howard Street	A4	Wakefield Road	D4
Hustlergate	B3	Wapping Road	D1
Infirmary Street	A1	Water Lane	A2
John Street	B2	Wellington Street	C2
Lansdowne Place	A4	Westgate	A2
Leeds Road	D3	Wharf Street	C1
Little Horton	A4	White Abbey Road	A1
Little Horton Lane	B4	Wigan Street	A2
Longcroft Link	A2	Wilton Street	A4

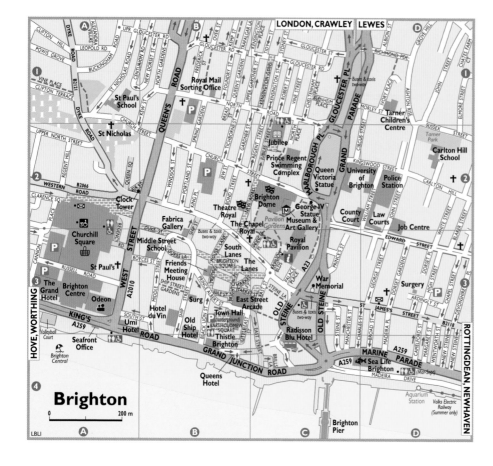

Brighton

Brighton is found on atlas page **24 H10**

Ardingly Street	D3	Madeira Place	D4
Ashton Rise	D1	Manchester Street	C4
Bartholomew Square	B3	Margaret Street	D4
Black Lion Street	B3	Marine Parade	D4
Blaker Street	D3	Market Street	B3
Bond Street	B2	Marlborough Place	C2
Boyces Street	A3	Meeting House Lane	B3
Brighton Place	B3	Middle Street	B3
Broad Street	D4	Morley Street	D1
Buckingham Road	A1	New Dorset Street	B1
Camelford Street	D4	New Road	B2
Cannon Place	A3	New Steine	D4
Carlton Hill	D2	Nile Street	B3
Centurion Road	A1	North Gardens	B1
Chapel Street	D3	North Place	C2
Charles Street	C4	North Road	B1
Cheltenham Place	C1	North Street	B2
Church Street	A1	Old Steine	C3
Church Street	B2	Portland Street	B2
Circus Street	C2	Powis Grove	A1
Clifton Hill	A1	Prince Albert Street	B3
Clifton Terrace	A1	Prince's Street	C3
Devonshire Place	D3	Queen's Gardens	B1
Dukes Lane	B3	Queen Square	A2
Duke Street	B2	Queen's Road	B2
East Street	C3	Regency Road	A2
Edward Street	D3	Regent Hill	A2
Elmore Street	D1	Regent Street	C2
Foundry Street	B1	Robert Street	C1
Frederick Street	B1	St James's Street	D3
Gardner Street	B2	St Nicholas Road	A1
George Street	D3	Ship Street	B3
Gloucester Place	C1	Spring Gardens	B1
Gloucester Road	B1	Steine Street	C4
Gloucester Street	C1	Sussex Street	D2
Grand Junction Road	B4	Sydney Street	C1
Grand Parade	C2	Tichborne Street	B2
High Street	D3	Tidy Street	C1
Ivory Place	D1	Upper Gardner Street	B1
John Street	D2	Upper Gloucester Road	A1
Jubilee Street	C2	Upper North Street	A2
Kensington Gardens	C1	Vine Street	C1
Kensington Street	C1	Wentworth Street	D4
Kew Street	B1	Western Road	A2
King's Road	A3	West Street	A3
Kingswood Street	C2	White Street	D3
Leopold Road	A1	William Street	D2
Little East Street	B4	Windsor Street	B2

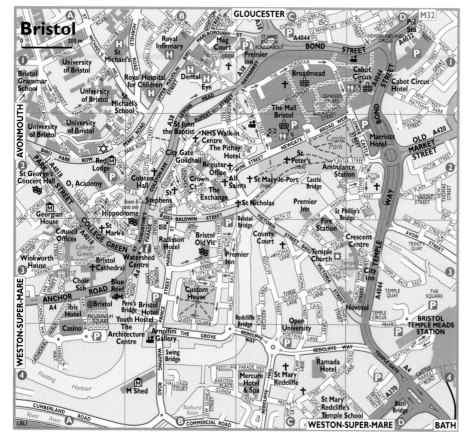

Bristol

Bristol is found on atlas page **31 Q10**

Anchor Road	A3	Passage Street	C2
Avon Street	D3	Pembroke Street	C1
Baldwin Street	B2	Penn Street	C1
Bath Bridge	D4	Pero's Bridge	B3
Bond Street	C1	Perry Road	A2
Bond Street	D2	Philadelphia Street	C2
Broadmead	C1	Portwall Lane	C4
Broad Plain	D2	Prewett Street	C4
Broad Quay	B3	Prince Street	B3
Broad Street	B2	Queen Charlotte Street	B3
Broad Weir	C2	Queen Square	B3
Canons Way	A3	Redcliffe Hill	C4
Canynge Street	C3	Redcliffe Parade West	B4
Castle Street	C2	Redcliffe Way	C4
College Green	A3	Redcliff Mead Lane	C4
Colston Avenue	B2	Redcliff Street	C3
Colston Street	B2	Royal Fort Road	A1
Commercial Road	B4	Rupert Street	B2
Corn Street	B2	St Augustine's Parade	B3
Countership	C3	St George's Road	A3
Cumberland Road	A4	St Matthias Park	D1
Deanery Road	A3	St Michael's Hill	A1
Denmark Street	A3	St Stephen's Street	B2
Explore Lane	A3	St Thomas Street	C3
Fairfax Street	C2	Small Street	B2
Ferry Street	C3	Somerset Street	C4
Friary	D3	Southwell Street	A1
Frogmore Street	A2	Tankards Close	A1
Great George Street	A3	Telephone Avenue	B3
Great George Street	D1	Temple Back	C3
Guinea Street	B4	Temple Back East	D3
Haymarket	C1	Temple Gate	D4
Hill Street	A2	Temple Street	C3
Horfield Road	B1	Temple Way	D3
Houlton Street	D1	The Grove	B4
Jacob Street	D2	The Horsefair	C1
King Street	B3	The Pithay	C2
Lewins Mead	B2	Tower Hill	C2
Lodge Street	A2	Trenchard Street	A2
Lower Castle Street	D2	Tyndall Avenue	A1
Lower Church Lane	A2	Union Street	C1
Lower Maudlin Street	B1	Upper Maudlin Street	B1
Marlborough Hill	B1	Victoria Street	C2
Marlborough Street	B1	Wapping Road	B4
Marsh Street	B3	Welsh Back	C3
Newgate	C2	Whitson Street	B1
Old Market Street	D2	Wine Street	C2
Park Street	A2	Woodland Road	A1

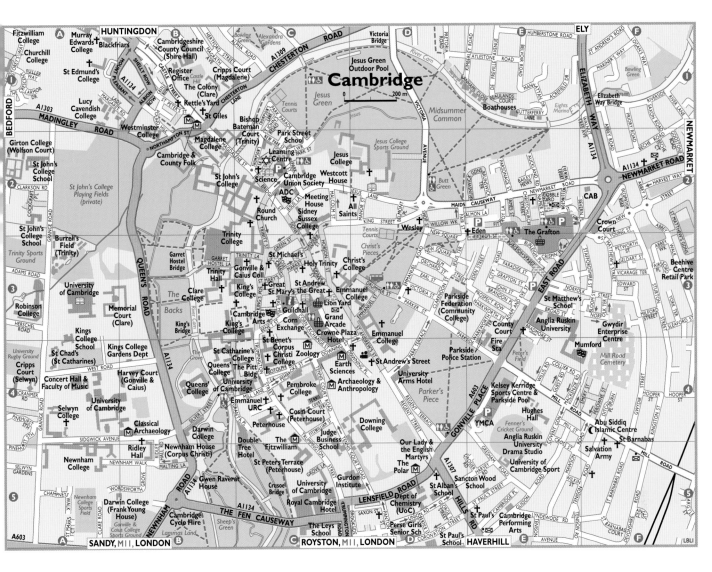

Cambridge

Cambridge is found on atlas page **62 G9**

Abbey Road	F1	
Abbey Street	F2	
Abbey Walk	F3	
Acrefield Drive	E1	
Adam and Eve Street	E3	
Albion Row	B1	
Alpha Road	C1	
Auckland Road	E2	
Aylestone Road	E2	
Bailey Mews	E2	
Banhams Close	D1	
Beaulands Court	E1	
Beche Road	F2	
Belmont Place	D2	
Belvoir Road	E1	
Bene't Street	C3	
Bloom Street	F3	
Bradmore Street	E3	
Brandon Place	E3	
Bridge Street	C2	
Broad Street	E3	
Brookside	D5	
Brunswick Gardens	E2	
Brunswick Terrace	E2	
Burleigh Place	E3	
Burleigh Street	E3	
Cambridge Place	E5	
Castle Row	B1	
Castle Street	B1	
Champneys Walk	A5	
Chesterton Lane	B1	
Chesterton Road	C1	
Christchurch Street	E2	
City Road	E3	
Clarendon Street	D3	
Cobble Yard	E2	

Collier Road	E4	
Corn Exchange Street	C3	
Coronation Street	D4	
Covent Garden	E4	
Crispin Place	E3	
Cross Street	E4	
Crusoe Bridge	B5	
Cutler Ferry Close	E1	
Cutterferry Lane	E1	
De Freville Avenue	E1	
Devonshire Road	F5	
Ditchburn Place	F4	
Downing Place	C4	
Downing Street	C4	
Drosier Road	D5	
Drummer Street	D3	
Earl Street	D3	
East Road	E3	
Eden Street	E3	
Eden Street Back	E3	
Edward Street	F3	
Elizabeth Way	F1	
Elm Street	D3	
Emery Street	F4	
Emmanuel Road	D3	
Emmanuel Street	D3	
Evening Court	E2	
Fairsford Place	F3	
Fair Street	D2	
Fitzroy Lane	E2	
Fitzroy Street	E3	
Fitzwilliam Street	C4	
Garret Hostel Bridge	B3	
Garret Hostel Lane	B3	
Geldart Street	F3	
George IV Street	D5	

Glisson Road	E5	
Godstone Road	F2	
Gonville Place	D4	
Grange Road	A3	
Grange Road	A4	
Granta Place	B4	
Green Street	C3	
Gresham Road	E5	
Gwydir Street	F4	
Harvest Way	F2	
Harvey Road	E5	
Hertford Street	B1	
Hills Road	D5	
Hobson Street	C3	
Humberstone Road	E1	
James Street	E2	
Jesus Lane	C2	
Jesus Terrace	D3	
John Street	E3	
Kimberley Road	E1	
King's Bridge	B3	
King's Parade	C3	
Kingston Street	F4	
King Street	D2	
Lady Margaret Road	A1	
Lensfield Road	D5	
Logan's Way	F1	
Lwr Park Street	C2	
Lyndewode Road	E5	
Mackenzie Road	E4	
Madingley Road	A1	
Magdalene Street	B2	
Magrath Avenue	B1	
Malcolm Street	C2	
Malting Lane	B5	
Manhattan Drive	E1	
Manor Street	D2	
Mariner's Way	F1	
Market Street	C3	
Mawson Road	E5	

Milford Street	F3	
Mill Lane	C4	
Mill Road	E4	
Mill Street	E4	
Mortimer Road	E4	
Mount Pleasant	B1	
Napier Street	E2	
Newmarket Road	E2	
Newnham Road	B5	
Newnham Walk	A5	
New Park Street	C2	
New Square	D3	
New Street	F2	
Norfolk Street	E3	
Norfolk Terrace	F3	
Northampton Street	B2	
Occupation Road	F2	
Orchard Street	D3	
Panton Street	D5	
Paradise Street	E3	
Parker Street	D3	
Park Parade	C1	
Parkside	D3	
Park Street	C2	
Park Terrace	D4	
Parsonage Street	E2	
Peas Hill	C3	
Pembroke Street	C4	
Perowne Street	F4	
Petworth Street	F3	
Pound Hill	B1	
Priory Road	F1	
Prospect Row	E3	
Queen's Road	B3	
Regent Street	D4	
Regent Terrace	D4	
River Lane	F1	
Riverside	F1	
St Andrew's Road	F1	
St Andrew's Street	D3	
St Barnabas Road	F5	

St Mary's Street	C3	
St Matthew's Gardens	F2	
St Matthew's Street	F3	
St Paul's Street	E5	
St Peter's Street	B1	
Salmon Lane	E2	
Saxon Road	F1	
Saxon Street	D5	
Severn Place	F2	
Shelly Row	B1	
Shop Street	D2	
Sidgwick Avenue	A4	
Sidney Street	C2	
Silver Street	B4	
Staffordshire Street	F3	
Sturton Street	F3	
Sussex Street	C3	
Tenison Avenue	E5	
Tenison Road	E5	
Tennis Court Road	C4	
Tennis Court Terrace	C4	
The Fen Causeway	B5	
Thompson's Lane	C2	
Trinity Lane	C3	
Trinity Street	C2	
Trumpington Road	C5	
Trumpington Street	C4	
Union Road	D5	
Vicarage Terrace	F4	
Victoria Avenue	D1	
Victoria Bridge	D1	
Victoria Street	D3	
Warkworth Street	E3	
Warkworth Terrace	E4	
Wellington Street	E2	
West Road	A4	
Wilkin Street	E5	
Willis Road	E4	
Willow Walk	D2	
Wordsworth Grove	A5	
Young Street	F3	

University Colleges

Christ's College	C3
Clare College	A3
Clare College	B1
Clare College	B3
Corpus Christi College	C4
Darwin College	B4
Downing College	D4
Emmanuel College	C3
Emmanuel College	D3
Fitzwilliam College	A1
Girton College (Wolfson Court)	A2
Gonville & Caius College	C3
Gonville & Caius College	B4
Jesus College	C2
King's College	B3
Lucy Cavendish College	A1
Magdalene College	B2
Murray Edwards College	A1
Newnham College	A5
Pembroke College	C4
Peterhouse	C4
Queens' College	B4
Robinson College	A3
St Catharine's College	C4
St Edmund's College	A1
St John's College	B2
Selwyn College	A4
Sidney Sussex College	C2
Trinity College	B3
Westminster College	B1

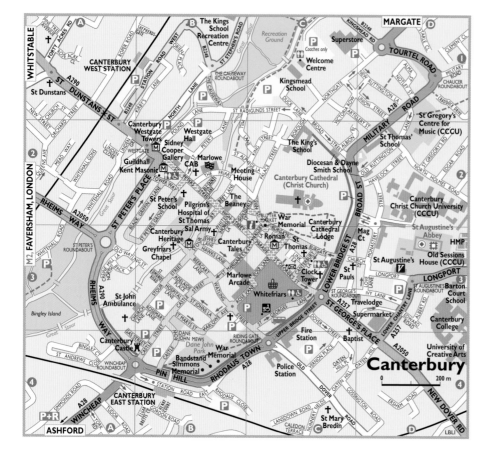

Canterbury

Canterbury is found on atlas page **39 K10**

Adelaide Place	B3	Nunnery Fields	C4
Albion Place	C2	Oaten Hill	C4
Alma Street	D1	Old Dover Road	C4
Artillery Street	C1	Old Ruttington Lane	D2
Beercart Lane	B3	Orchard Street	A2
Best Lane	B2	Palace Street	C2
Black Griffin Lane	A3	Parade	C3
Borough	C2	Pin Hill	B4
Broad Street	D2	Pound Lane	B2
Burgate	C3	Queens Avenue	B2
Butter Market	C2	Rheims Way	A3
Canterbury Lane	C3	Rhodaus Town	B4
Castle Row	B4	Rose Lane	C3
Castle Street	B3	Rosemary Lane	B3
Cossington Road	C4	St Alphege Lane	C2
Dover Street	C3	St Dunstans Street	A1
Duck Lane	C1	St Edmunds Road	B3
Edgar Road	D2	St George's Lane	C3
Edward Road	D3	St George's Place	C3
Ersham Road	D4	St George's Street	C3
Gas Street	A4	St Gregory's Road	D2
Gordon Road	B4	St Johns Lane	C3
Guildhall Street	B2	St Margaret's Street	B3
Havelock Street	D2	St Marys Street	B3
Hawks Lane	B3	St Peter's Grove	B3
High Street	B2	St Peter's Lane	B2
Hospital Lane	B3	St Peter's Place	A3
Ivy Lane	C3	St Peters Street	B2
Jewry Lane	B3	St Radigunds Street	B1
King Street	C2	Station Road East	C4
Kirby's Lane	B1	Station Road West	A1
Lansdown Road	C4	Stour Street	B3
Linden Grove	A2	Sturry Road	D1
Longport	D3	Sun Street	C2
Love Lane	D3	The Causeway	B1
Lower Bridge Street	C3	The Friars	B2
Lower Chantry Lane	D4	Tourtel Road	D1
Marlowe Avenue	B3	Tower Way	B2
Mead Way	A2	Tudor Road	A4
Mercery Lane	C3	Union Street	D1
Military Road	D2	Upper Bridge Street	C4
Mill Lane	B1	Vernon Place	C4
Monastery Street	D3	Victoria Row	C1
New Dover Road	D4	Watling Street	B3
New Ruttington Lane	D1	Whitehall Gardens	A2
North Lane	B1	Whitehall Road	A2
Northgate	C1	Wincheap	A4
Notley Street	D1	York Road	A4

Cardiff

Cardiff is found on atlas page **30 G9**

Adam Street	C3	Museum Avenue	B1
Adams Court	D2	Museum Place	B1
Adamscroft Place	D3	Newport Road	D1
Atlantic Wharf	D4	Newport Road Lane	D2
Boulevard de Nantes	B1	North Luton Place	D2
Bridge Street	C3	North Road	A1
Brigantine Place	D4	Oxford Lane	D1
Bute Street	C4	Oxford Street	D1
Bute Terrace	C3	Park Grove	B1
Callaghan Square	B4	Park Lane	B1
Caroline Street	B3	Park Place	B1
Castle Lane	D1	Park Street	A3
Castle Street	A2	Pellett Street	C3
Central Link	D3	Pendyris Street	A4
Charles Street	B2	Quay Street	A3
Churchill Way	C2	Queen Street	B2
City Hall Road	A1	Richmond Crescent	C1
City Road	D1	Richmond Road	C1
Crockherbtown Lane	B2	St Andrew's Crescent	B1
Custom House Street	B4	St Andrew's Lane	C1
David Street	C3	St Andrew's Place	B1
Davis Street	D3	St John Street	B2
Duke Street	A2	St Mary Street	B3
Dumfries Place	C2	St Peter's Street	C1
East Bay Close	D3	Salisbury Road	C1
East Grove	D1	Sandon Street	C3
Fford Churchill	C2	Saunders Road	B4
Fitzalan Place	D2	Schooner Way	D4
Fitzalan Road	D2	Stuttgarter Strasse	B1
Fitzhamon Embankment	A4	The Friary	B2
Glossop Road	D1	The Hayes	B3
Greyfriars Road	B2	The Parade	D1
Guildford Street	C3	The Walk	C1
Guildhall Place	A3	Trinity Street	B3
Havelock Street	B3	Tudor Street	A4
Hayes Bridge Road	B3	Tyndall Street	D4
Heol Siarl	B2	Vere Street	D1
Herbert Street	C4	Wesley Lane	B2
High Street	B3	West Canal Wharf	B4
High Street Arcade	B2	West Grove	C1
Hills Street	B3	Westgate Street	A3
King Edward VII Avenue	A1	Wharton Street	B3
Knox Road	D2	Windsor Lane	C2
Lloyd George Avenue	C4	Windsor Place	C1
Mary Ann Street	C3	Windsor Road	D3
Mill Lane	B4	Womanby Street	A3
Moira Place	D2	Wood Street	A4
Moira Terrace	D2	Working Street	B3

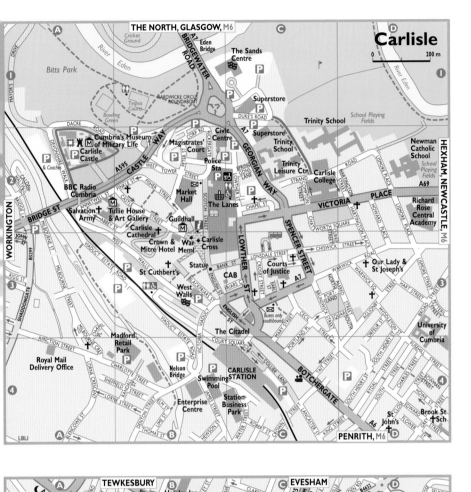

Carlisle

Carlisle is found on atlas page **110 G9**

Abbey Street	A2	Howard Place	D2
Aglionby Street	D3	Howe Street	D4
Annetwell Street	A2	James Street	B4
Bank Street	B3	John Street	A3
Blackfriars Street	B3	Junction Street	A4
Blencowe Street	A4	King Street	C4
Botchergate	C4	Lancaster Street	C4
Bridge Lane	A2	Lime Street	B4
Bridge Street	A2	Lismore Place	D2
Bridgewater Road	B1	Lismore Street	D3
Broad Street	D3	Lonsdale Street	C3
Brunswick Street	C3	Lorne Crescent	A4
Caldew Maltings	A2	Lorne Street	A4
Castle Street	B2	Lowther Street	C3
Castle Way	B2	Mary Street	C3
Cecil Street	C3	Mayor's Drive	A1
Chapel Place	A3	Milbourne Crescent	A3
Chapel Street	C2	Milbourne Street	A3
Charles Street	D4	Myddleton Street	D3
Charlotte Street	B4	North Alfred Street	D3
Chatsworth Square	C2	Orfeur Street	D3
Chiswick Street	C3	Peter Street	B2
Close Street	D4	Petteril Street	D3
Collier Lane	C4	Portland Place	C4
Compton Street	C2	Portland Square	C3
Corp Road	B2	Randall Street	B4
Court Square	B4	Rickergate	B2
Crosby Street	C3	Rigg Street	A3
Crown Street	C4	Robert Street	C4
Currie Street	C3	Rydal Street	D4
Dacre Road	A1	Scotch Street	B2
Denton Street	B4	Shaddongate	A3
Devonshire Walk	A2	Sheffield Street	A4
Duke's Road	C1	South Alfred Street	D3
Edward Street	D4	South Henry Street	D4
Elm Street	B4	Spencer Street	C2
English Street	B3	Spring Gardens Lane	C2
Finkle Street	B2	Strand Road	C2
Fisher Street	B2	Tait Street	C4
Flower Street	D4	Thomas Street	B4
Friars Court	C3	Viaduct Estate Road	A3
Fusehill Street	D4	Victoria Place	C2
Georgian Way	C2	Victoria Viaduct	B4
Grey Street	D4	Warwick Road	D3
Hartington Place	D2	Warwick Square	D3
Hartington Street	D2	Water Street	C4
Hart Street	D3	West Tower Street	B2
Hewson Street	B4	West Walls	B3

Cheltenham

Cheltenham is found on atlas page **46 H10**

Albion Street	C2	Montpellier Parade	B4
All Saints' Road	D2	Montpellier Spa Road	B4
Ambrose Street	B1	Montpellier Street	A4
Argyll Road	D4	Montpellier Terrace	A4
Back Montpellier Terrace	A4	Montpellier Walk	A4
Bath Road	B4	New Street	A1
Bath Street	C3	North Street	B2
Bayshill Road	A3	Old Bath Road	D4
Bayshill Villas Lane	A3	Oriel Road	B3
Bennington Street	B1	Parabola Lane	A3
Berkeley Street	C3	Parabola Road	A3
Burton Street	A1	Park Street	A1
Carlton Street	D3	Pittville Circus	D1
Church Street	B2	Pittville Circus Road	D1
Clarence Parade	B2	Pittville Street	B2
Clarence Road	C1	Portland Street	C1
Clarence Street	B2	Prestbury Road	C1
College Road	C4	Priory Street	D3
Crescent Terrace	B2	Promenade	B3
Devonshire Street	A1	Queens Parade	A3
Duke Street	D3	Regent Street	B2
Dunalley Street	B1	Rodney Road	B3
Evesham Road	C1	Royal Well Lane	A2
Fairview Road	C2	Royal Well Road	B2
Fairview Street	D2	St Anne's Road	D2
Fauconberg Road	A3	St Anne's Terrace	D2
Glenfall Street	D1	St George's Place	B2
Grosvenor Street	C3	St George's Road	A2
Grove Street	A1	St George's Street	B1
Henrietta Street	B1	St James' Square	A2
Hewlett Road	D3	St James Street	C3
High Street	A1	St Johns Avenue	C2
High Street	C2	St Margaret's Road	B1
Imperial Lane	B3	St Paul's Street South	B1
Imperial Square	B3	Sandford Street	C3
Jersey Street	D1	Selkirk Street	D1
Jessop Avenue	A2	Sherborne Street	C2
Keynsham Road	D4	Station Street	A1
King Street	A1	Suffolk Parade	B4
Knapp Road	A1	Swindon Road	B1
Lansdown Road	A4	Sydenham Villas Road	D3
Leighton Road	D2	Trafalgar Street	B4
London Road	D3	Union Street	D2
Malden Road	D1	Wellington Street	C3
Market Street	A1	Winchcombe Street	C2
Milsom Street	A1	Winstonian Road	D2
Monson Avenue	B1	Witcombe Place	C3
Montpellier Grove	B4	York Street	D1

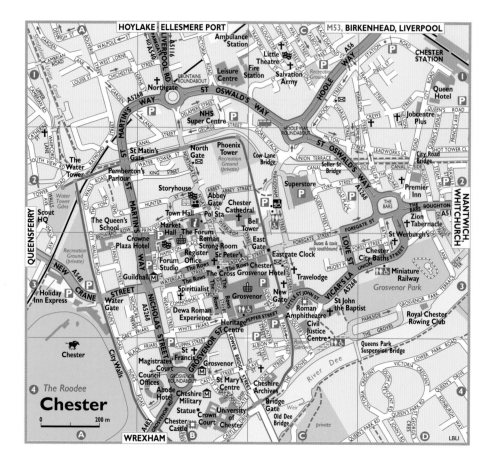

Chester

Chester is found on atlas page **81 N11**

Albion Street	C4	Nicholas Street	B3
Bath Street	D2	Northgate Street	B2
Black Diamond Street	C1	Nun's Road	A3
Boughton	D2	Parkgate Road	B1
Bouverie Street	A1	Park Street	C3
Bridge Street	B3	Pepper Street	C3
Brook Street	C1	Princess Street	B2
Canal Side	C2	Priory Place	C3
Castle Street	B4	Queen's Park Road	C4
Charles Street	C1	Queen's Road	D1
Chichester Street	A1	Queen Street	C2
City Road	D2	Raymond Street	A2
City Walls Road	A2	Russell Street	D2
Commonhall Street	B3	St Anne Street	C1
Cornwall Street	C1	St John's Road	D4
Crewe Street	D1	St John Street	C3
Cuppin Street	B4	St Martin's Way	A2
Dee Hills Park	D2	St Mary's Hill	B4
Dee Lane	D2	St Olave Street	C4
Delamere Street	B1	St Oswald's Way	B1
Duke Street	C4	St Werburgh Street	B2
Eastgate Street	B3	Samuel Street	C2
Egerton Street	C1	Seller Street	D2
Foregate Street	C2	Shipgate Street	B4
Forest Street	C3	Souter's Lane	C3
Francis Street	D1	South View Road	A2
Frodsham Street	C2	Stanley Street	A3
Garden Lane	A1	Station Road	C1
George Street	B2	Steam Mill Street	D2
Gloucester Street	C1	Steele Street	C4
Gorse Stacks	C2	Talbot Street	C1
Grosvenor Park Terrace	D3	Tower Road	A2
Grosvenor Road	B4	Trafford Street	C1
Grosvenor Street	B4	Trinity Street	B3
Hamilton Place	B3	Union Street	D3
Hoole Way	C1	Union Terrace	C2
Hunter Street	B2	Upper Cambrian Road	A1
King Street	B2	Vicar's Lane	C3
Leadworks Lane	D2	Victoria Crescent	D4
Little St John Street	C3	Victoria Road	B1
Liverpool Road	B1	Volunteer Street	C3
Lorne Street	A1	Walpole Street	A1
Love Street	C3	Walter Street	C1
Lower Bridge Street	B4	Watergate Street	B3
Lower Park Road	D4	Water Tower Street	B2
Milton Street	C2	Weaver Street	B3
New Crane Street	A3	White Friars	B3
Newgate Street	C3	York Street	C2

Colchester

Colchester is found on atlas page **52 G6**

Abbey Gates	C3	Middleborough	B1
Alexandra Road	A3	Middleborough Roundabout	A1
Alexandra Terrace	A4	Military Road	D4
Balkerne Hill	A3	Mill Street	D4
Beaconsfield Avenue	A4	Napier Road	C4
Burlington Road	A3	Nicholsons Green	D3
Butt Road	A4	North Bridge	B1
Castle Road	D1	Northgate Street	B1
Cedar Street	B3	North Hill	B1
Chapel Street North	B3	North Station Road	B1
Chapel Street South	B3	Nunn's Road	B1
Church Street	B3	Osborne Street	C3
Church Walk	B3	Papillon Road	A3
Circular Road East	C4	Pope's Lane	A2
Circular Road North	B4	Portland Road	C4
Creffield Road	A4	Priory Street	D3
Cromwell Road	C4	Queen Street	C3
Crouch Street	A3	Rawstorn Road	A2
Crouch Street	B3	Roman Road	D1
Crowhurst Road	A2	St Alban's Road	A3
Culver Street East	C2	St Augustine Mews	D2
Culver Street West	B2	St Botolph's Circus	C3
East Hill	D2	St Botolph's Street	C3
East Stockwell Street	C2	St Helen's Lane	C2
Essex Street	B3	St John's Avenue	B3
Fairfax Road	C4	St John's Street	B3
Flagstaff Road	C4	St Julian Grove	D3
Garland Road	A4	St Mary's Fields	A2
George Street	C2	St Peter's Street	B1
Golden Noble Hill	D4	Salisbury Avenue	A4
Gray Road	A3	Sheepen Place	A1
Headgate	B3	Sheepen Road	A1
Head Street	B2	Short Wyre Street	C3
Henry Laver Court	A2	Sir Isaac's Walk	B3
High Street	B2	South Street	B4
Hospital Road	A4	Southway	B3
Hospital Lane	A3	Stanwell Street	C3
Land Lane	D2	Trinity Street	B3
Lewis Gardens	D2	Walsingham Road	B3
Lexden Road	A3	Wellesley Road	A3
Lincoln Way	D1	Wellington Street	B3
Long Wyre Street	C2	West Stockwell Street	B1
Lucas Road	C4	West Street	B4
Magdalen Street	D3	Westway	A1
Maidenburgh Street	C1	Whitehall Road	C4
Maldon Road	A4	Wickham Road	A4
Manor Road	A3	William's Walk	C2
Mersea Road	C4	Winnock Road	D4

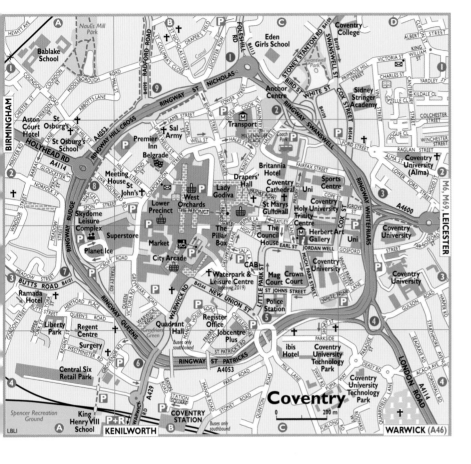

Coventry

Coventry is found on atlas page **59 M9**

Abbotts Lane	A1	Much Park Street	C3
Acacia Avenue	D4	New Union Street	B3
Alma Street	D2	Norfolk Street	A2
Barras Lane	A2	Paradise Street	D4
Bayley Lane	C2	Park Road	B4
Bird Street	C1	Parkside	C4
Bishop Street	B1	Primrose Hill Street	D1
Broadgate	B2	Priory Row	C2
Butts Road	A3	Priory Street	C2
Butts Street	A3	Puma Way	C4
Canterbury Street	D1	Quarryfield Lane	D4
Chester Street	A2	Queen's Road	A3
Cheylesmore	C3	Queen Victoria Road	B3
Cornwall Road	D4	Quinton Road	C4
Corporation Street	B2	Radford Road	B1
Coundon Road	A1	Raglan Street	D2
Cox Street	D1	Regent Street	A4
Cox Street	D2	Ringway Hill Cross	A2
Croft Road	A3	Ringway Queens	A3
Earl Street	C3	Ringway Rudge	A3
Eaton Road	B4	Ringway St Nicholas	B1
Fairfax Street	C2	Ringway St Patricks	B4
Foleshill Road	C1	Ringway Swanswell	C1
Gloucester Street	A2	Ringway Whitefriars	D2
Gosford Street	D3	St Johns Street	C3
Greyfriars Lane	B3	St Nicholas Street	B1
Greyfriars Road	B3	Salt Lane	C3
Grosvenor Road	A4	Seagrave Road	D4
Gulson Road	D3	Spon Street	A2
Hales Street	C2	Starley Road	A3
Hertford Place	A3	Stoney Road	B4
High Street	C3	Stoney Stanton Road	C1
Hill Street	B2	Strathmore Avenue	D3
Holyhead Road	A2	Swanswell Street	C1
Jordan Well	C3	The Burges	B2
Lamb Street	B2	Tower Street	B1
Leicester Row	B1	Trinity Street	C2
Little Park Street	C3	Upper Hill Street	B2
London Road	D4	Upper Wells Street	A4
Lower Ford Street	D2	Victoria Street	D1
Lower Holyhead Road	A2	Vine Street	D1
Manor House Road	B4	Warwick Road	B3
Manor Road	B4	Warwick Road	B4
Meadow Street	A3	Westminster Road	A4
Meriden Street	A1	White Friars Street	D3
Middleborough Road	A1	White Street	C1
Mile Lane	C4	Windsor Street	A3
Mill Street	A1	Yardley Street	D1

Darlington

Darlington is found on atlas page **103 Q8**

Abbey Road	A3	Maude Street	A2
Albert Street	D4	Melland Street	D3
Appleby Close	D4	Neasham Road	D4
Barningham Street	B1	Northgate	C2
Bartlett Street	B1	North Lodge Terrace	B2
Beaumont Street	B3	Northumberland Street	B4
Bedford Street	C4	Oakdene Avenue	A4
Beechwood Avenue	A4	Outram Street	A2
Blackwellgate	B3	Parkgate	D3
Bondgate	B2	Park Lane	D4
Borough Road	D3	Park Place	C4
Brunswick Street	C3	Pendower Street	B1
Brunton Street	D4	Pensbury Street	D4
Chestnut Street	C1	Polam Lane	B4
Cleveland Terrace	A4	Portland Place	A3
Clifton Road	C4	Powlett Street	B3
Commercial Street	A2	Priestgate	C3
Coniscliffe Road	A4	Raby Terrace	B3
Corporation Road	B1	Russell Street	C2
Crown Street	C2	St Augustine's Way	B2
Dodds Street	B1	St Cuthbert's Way	C2
Duke Street	A3	St Cuthbert's Way	C4
Easson Road	B1	St James Place	D4
East Mount Road	D1	Salisbury Terrace	A1
East Raby Street	B3	Salt Yard	B3
East Street	C3	Scarth Street	A4
Elms Road	A2	Skinnergate	B3
Elwin Lane	B4	Southend Avenue	A4
Feethams	C4	Stanhope Road North	A2
Fife Road	A3	Stanhope Road South	A3
Four Riggs	B2	Stonebridge	C3
Freeman's Place	C2	Sun Street	B2
Gladstone Street	B2	Swan Street	C4
Grange Road	B4	Swinburne Road	A3
Greenbank Road	A1	Trinity Road	A2
Greenbank Road	B2	Tubwell Row	B3
Hargreave Terrace	C4	Uplands Road	A3
Haughton Road	D2	Valley Street North	C2
High Northgate	C1	Vane Terrace	A2
High Row	B3	Victoria Embankment	C4
Hollyhurst Road	A1	Victoria Road	B4
Houndgate	B3	Victoria Road	C4
John Street	C1	West Crescent	A2
John Williams Boulevard	D3	West Powlett Street	A3
Kendrew Street	B2	West Row	B3
Kingston Street	B1	West Street	B4
Langholm Crescent	A4	Woodland Road	A2
Larchfield Street	A3	Yarm Road	D3

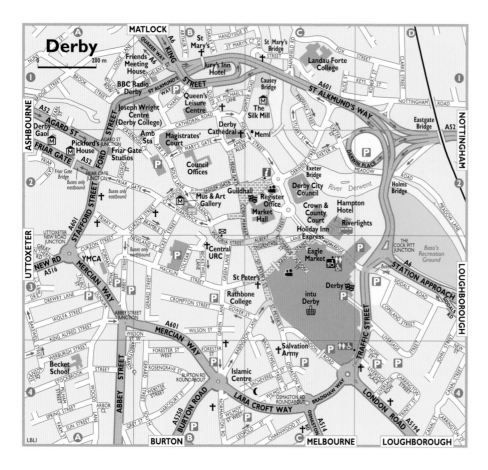

Derby

Derby is found on atlas page **72 B3**

Abbey Street	A4	King Alfred Street	A3
Agard Street	A1	King Street	B1
Albert Street	C3	Lara Croft Way	B4
Babington Lane	B4	Leopold Street	B4
Back Sitwell Street	C4	Liversage Row	D4
Becket Street	B3	Liversage Street	D3
Bold Lane	B2	Lodge Lane	A1
Bradshaw Way	C4	London Road	C3
Bramble Street	B2	Macklin Street	B3
Bridge Street	A1	Mansfield Road	C1
Brook Street	A1	Meadow Lane	D2
Burton Road	B4	Meadow Road	D2
Canal Street	D4	Mercian Way	B3
Carrington Street	D4	Morledge	C2
Cathedral Road	B1	Newland Street	A3
Cavendish Court	A2	New Road	A3
Chapel Street	B1	New Street	D4
Clarke Street	D1	Nottingham Road	D1
Copeland Street	D3	Osmaston Road	C4
Corn Market	B2	Phoenix Street	C1
Crompton Street	B3	Queen Street	B1
Curzon Street	A2	Robert Street	D1
Curzon Street	A3	Rosengrave Street	B4
Darwin Place	C2	Sacheverel Street	C4
Derwent Street	C2	Sadler Gate	B2
Drewry Lane	A3	St Alkmund's Way	C1
Duke Street	C1	St Helen's Street	B1
Dunkirk	A3	St Mary's Gate	B2
East Street	C3	St Peter's Street	C3
Exchange Street	C3	Siddals Road	D3
Exeter Place	C2	Sowter Road	C1
Exeter Street	C2	Spring Street	A4
Ford Street	A2	Stafford Street	A3
Forester Street West	B4	Station Approach	D3
Forman Street	A3	Stockbrook Street	A4
Fox Street	C1	Strand	B2
Friary Street	A2	Stuart Street	A4
Full Street	B1	Sun Street	A4
Gerard Street	B3	The Cock Pitt	D3
Gower Street	B3	Thornton Lane	C3
Green Lane	B3	Traffic Street	D4
Grey Street	A4	Trinity Street	D4
Handyside Street	B1	Victoria Street	B2
Harcourt Street	B4	Wardwick	B2
Iron Gate	B2	Werburgh Street	A4
John Street	D4	Wilmot Street	C4
Jury Street	B2	Wolfa Street	A3
Keys Street	D1	Woods Lane	A4

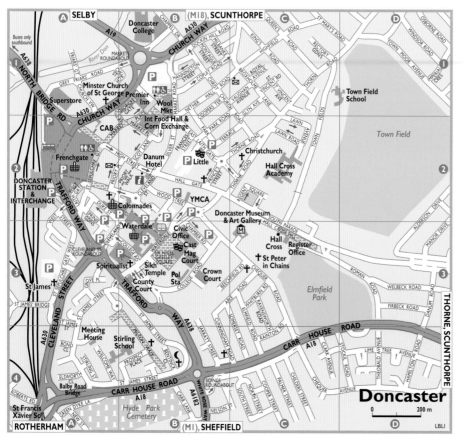

Doncaster

Doncaster is found on atlas page **91 P10**

Alderson Drive	D3	Nelson Street	B4
Apley Road	B3	Nether Hall Road	B1
Balby Road Bridge	A4	North Bridge Road	A1
Beechfield Road	B3	North Street	C4
Broxholme Lane	C1	Osborne Road	D1
Carr House Road	C4	Palmer Street	B2
Carr Lane	B4	Park Road	B2
Chamber Road	B3	Park Terrace	B2
Chequer Avenue	C4	Prince's Street	B2
Chequer Road	C3	Priory Place	A2
Childers Street	C4	Prospect Place	B4
Christ Church Road	B1	Queen's Road	C1
Church View	A1	Rainton Road	C4
Church Way	B1	Ravensworth Road	C3
Clark Avenue	C4	Rectory Gardens	C1
Cleveland Street	A4	Regent Square	C2
College Road	B3	Roman Road	D3
Cooper Street	C4	Royal Avenue	C1
Coopers Terrace	B2	St Georges Gate	B2
Copley Road	B1	St James Street	A3
Cunningham Road	B3	St Mary's Road	C1
Danum Road	D3	St Sepulchre Gate	A2
Dockin Hill Road	B1	St Sepulchre Gate West	A3
Duke Street	A2	St Vincent Avenue	C1
East Laith Gate	B2	St Vincent Road	C1
Elmfield Road	C3	Scot Lane	B2
Firbeck Road	D3	Silver Street	B2
Frances Street	B2	Somerset Road	B3
Glyn Avenue	C1	South Parade	C3
Green Dyke Lane	A4	South Street	C4
Grey Friars' Road	A1	Spring Gardens	A2
Hall Cross Hill	C2	Stirling Street	A4
Hall Gate	B2	Stockil Road	C4
Hamilton Road	D4	Theobald Avenue	D4
Hannington Street	B1	Thorne Road	C2
High Street	A2	Town Fields	C2
Highfield Road	C1	Town Moor Avenue	D1
Jarratt Street	B4	Trafford Way	A2
King's Road	C1	Vaughan Avenue	C1
Lawn Avenue	C2	Waterdale	B3
Lawn Road	C2	Welbeck Road	D3
Lime Tree Avenue	D4	Welcome Way	A4
Manor Drive	D3	West Laith Gate	A2
Market Place	A2	West Street	A3
Market Road	B1	Whitburn Road	B4
Milbanke Street	B1	White Rose Way	B4
Milton Walk	B4	Windsor Road	D1
Montague Street	B1	Wood Street	B2

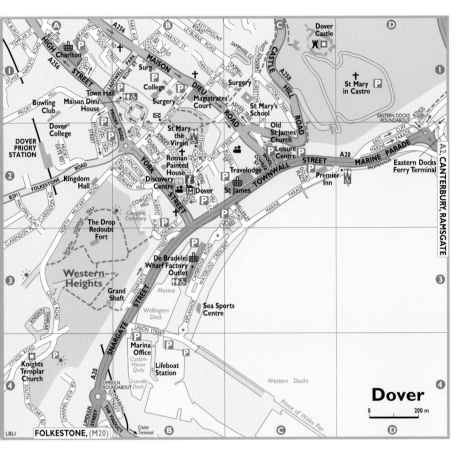

Dover

Dover

Dover is found on atlas page **27 P3**

Adrian Street	B3	Marine Parade	D2
Albany Place	B2	Military Road	B2
Ashen Tree Lane	C1	Mill Lane	B2
Athol Terrace	D1	New Street	B2
Biggin Street	B2	Norman Street	A2
Cambridge Road	B3	North Downs Way	A3
Camden Crescent	C2	North Military Road	A3
Castle Hill Road	C1	Park Avenue	B1
Castlemount Road	B1	Park Street	B1
Castle Street	B2	Pencester Road	B2
Centre Road	A3	Peter Street	A1
Channel View Road	A4	Priory Gate Road	A2
Church Street	B2	Priory Hill	A1
Citadel Road	A4	Priory Road	A1
Clarendon Place	A3	Priory Street	B2
Clarendon Road	A2	Promenade	D2
Cowgate Hill	B2	Queen's Gardens	B2
Crafford Street	A1	Queen Street	B2
De Burgh Hill	A1	Russell Street	B2
Douro Place	C2	Samphire Close	C1
Dour Street	A1	Saxon Street	A2
Durham Close	B2	Snargate Street	A4
Durham Hill	B2	South Military Road	A4
East Cliff	D2	Stembrook	B2
Eastern Docks		Taswell Close	C1
Roundabout	D2	Taswell Street	B1
Effingham Street	A2	Templar Street	A1
Elizabeth Street	A4	The Viaduct	A4
Esplanade	B3	Tower Hamlets Road	A1
Folkestone Road	A2	Townwall Street	C2
Godwyne Close	B1	Union Street	B3
Godwyne Road	B1	Victoria Park	C1
Harold Street	B1	Waterloo Crescent	B3
Harold Street	B1	Wellesley Road	C2
Heritage Gardens	C1	Wood Street	A1
Hewitt Road	A1	Woolcomber Street	C2
High Street	A1	York Street	B2
King Street	B2		
Knights Templar	A3		
Ladywell	A1		
Lancaster Road	B2		
Laureston Place	C1		
Leyburne Road	B1		
Limekiln Roundabout	A4		
Limekiln Street	A4		
Maison Dieu Road	B1		
Malvern Road	A2		
Marine Parade	C2		

Dundee

Dundee is found on atlas page **142 G11**

Albert Square	B2	Laurel Bank	B1
Bank Street	B2	Lochee Road	A1
Barrack Road	A1	McDonald Street	D2
Barrack Road	B2	Meadowside	B2
Bell Street	B2	Miln Street	A2
Blackscroft	D1	Murraygate	C2
Blinshall Street	A1	Nethergate	A4
Blinshall Street	A2	North Lindsay Street	B2
Bonnybank Road	C1	North Marketgait	B1
Brown Street	A2	North Victoria Road	C1
Candle Lane	C2	Old Hawkhill	A3
Castle Street	C2	Panmure Street	B2
Chapel Street	C2	Perth Road	A4
City Square	C3	Princes Street	D1
Commercial Street	C2	Prospect Place	B1
Constable Street	D1	Queen Street	C1
Constitution Crescent	A1	Reform Street	B2
Constitution Road	A1	Riverside Drive	B4
Constitution Road	B2	Riverside Esplanade	C3
Court House Square	A2	Roseangle	A4
Cowgate	C1	St Andrews Street	C1
Cowgate	D1	Scrimgeour Place	A1
Crichton Street	C3	Seabraes Lane	A4
Dock Street	C3	Seagate	C2
Douglas Street	A2	Session Street	A2
Dudhope Street	B1	South Castle Street	C3
East Dock Street	D2	South Commercial Street	D3
East Marketgait	C1	South Crichton Street	C3
East Whale Lane	D1	South Marketgait	B3
Euclid Crescent	B2	South Tay Street	B3
Euclid Street	B2	South Union Street	C3
Exchange Street	C3	South Victoria Dock Road	D3
Forebank Road	C1	South Ward Road	B2
Foundry Lane	D1	Sugarhouse Wynd	C1
Gellatly Street	C2	Tay Road Bridge	D3
Greenmarket	B4	Tay Square	B3
Guthrie Street	A2	Thomson Avenue	C3
Hawkhill	A3	Trades Lane	C2
High Street	C3	Union Street	B3
Hilltown	B1	Union Terrace	B1
Hilltown Terrace	B1	Ward Road	B2
Hunter Street	A3	Weavers Yard	D1
Infirmary Brae	A1	West Marketgait	A2
Johnston Street	B2	West Port	A3
King Street	C1	West Victoria Dock Road	D2
Kirk Lane	C1	Whitehall Crescent	C3
Laburn Street	A1	Whitehall Street	C3
Ladywell Avenue	C1	Yeaman Shore	B3

Durham

Durham is found on atlas page **103 Q2**

Albert Street	A1
Alexandria Crescent	A2
Allergate	A2
Atherton Street	A2
Back Western Hill	A1
Bakehouse Lane	C1
Baths Bridge	C2
Bow Lane	C3
Boyd Street	C4
Briardene	A3
Church Lane	C3
Church Street	C4
Church Street Head	C4
Clay Lane	A3
Claypath	C1
Court Lane	C3
Crossgate	A2
Crossgate Peth	A3
Douglas Villas	D1
Elvet Bridge	C2
Elvet Crescent	C3
Elvet Waterside	C2
Finney Terrace	C1
Flass Street	A2
Framwelgate	B1
Framwelgate Bridge	B2
Framwelgate Waterside	B1
Freeman Place	B1
Gilesgate	C1
Green Lane	D3
Grove Street	A3
Hallgarth Street	C3
Hawthorn Terrace	A2
Highgate	B1
High Road View	C4
High Street	C2
Hillcrest	C1
Holly Street	A2
John Street	A2
Keiper Heights	C1
Kingsgate Bridge	C3
Leazes Lane	D1
Leazes Lane	D2
Leazes Place	C1
Leazes Road	B1
Margery Lane	A3
Market Square	B2
Mavin Street	C3

Mayorswell Close	D1
Milburngate Bridge	B1
Millburngate	B2
Millennium Place	B1
Mowbray Street	A2
Neville Street	A2
New Elvet	C2
New Elvet Bridge	C2
New Street	A2
North Bailey	B3
North Road	A1
Old Elvet	C3
Oswald Court	C3
Owengate	B2
Palace Green	B2
Palmers Garth	C3
Pelaw Rise	C1
Pimlico	A3
Potters Bank	B4
Prebends' Bridge	B3
Princes' Street	A1
Providence Row	A1
Quarryheads Lane	A3
Redhills Lane	A2
Renny Street	D1
Saddler Street	C2
St Hild's Lane	D1
Silver Street	B2
South Bailey	B3
South Road	C4
South Street	A3
Station Approach	A1
Stockton Road	C4
Summerville	A3
Sutton Street	A2
Tenter Terrace	A1
Territorial Lane	C2
The Avenue	A2
The Hall Garth	D3
Waddington Street	A1
Wear View	C1
Whinney Hill	D3
Willow Tree Avenue	D4

Eastbourne

Eastbourne is found on atlas page **25 P11**

Arlington Road	A2
Ashford Road	B2
Ashford Road	C1
Ashford Square	B1
Avenue Lane	A1
Belmore Road	C1
Blackwater Road	A4
Bolton Road	B3
Bourne Street	C1
Burlington Place	B3
Burlington Road	C3
Camden Road	A3
Carew Road	B1
Carlisle Road	A4
Carlisle Road	B4
Cavendish Avenue	C1
Cavendish Place	C1
Ceylon Place	C2
Chiswick Place	B3
College Road	B3
Colonnade Gardens	D2
Commercial Road	B1
Compton Street	B4
Compton Street	C3
Cornfield Lane	B3
Cornfield Road	B2
Cornfield Terrace	B3
Devonshire Place	B3
Dursley Road	C1
Elms Road	C3
Enys Road	A1
Eversfield Road	A1
Furness Road	A3
Gildredge Road	B2
Grand Parade	C3
Grange Road	A3
Grassington Road	A3
Grove Road	A3
Hardwick Road	B3
Hartfield Lane	A1
Hartfield Road	A1
Hartington Place	C3
Howard Square	C4
Hyde Gardens	B2
Hyde Road	A2
Ivy Terrace	A2
Jevington Gardens	A4
Junction Road	B2

Langney Road	D1
Langney Road	C2
Lascelles Terrace	B4
Latimer Road	D1
Leaf Road	B1
Lismore Road	B2
Longstone Road	C1
Lushington Road	B3
Marine Parade	D2
Marine Road	D1
Mark Lane	B2
Meads Road	A3
Melbourne Road	C1
Old Orchard Road	A2
Old Wish Road	A4
Pevensey Road	C2
Promenade	C3
Queen's Gardens	D2
Saffrons Road	A2
St Anne's Road	A1
St Aubyn's Road	D1
St Leonard's Road	B1
Seaside	D1
Seaside Road	C2
Southfields Road	A2
South Street	A3
South Street	B3
Spencer Road	B3
Station Parade	A2
Station Street	B2
Susan's Road	C2
Sutton Road	B2
Sydney Road	C1
Terminus Road	A2
Terminus Road	C3
The Avenue	A1
Tideswell Road	B2
Trinity Place	C3
Trinity Trees	B3
Upper Avenue	B1
Upperton Gardens	A1
Upperton Road	A1
West Street	A3
West Terrace	A2
Willowfield Road	D1
Wilmington Square	B4
Wish Road	B3
York Road	A3

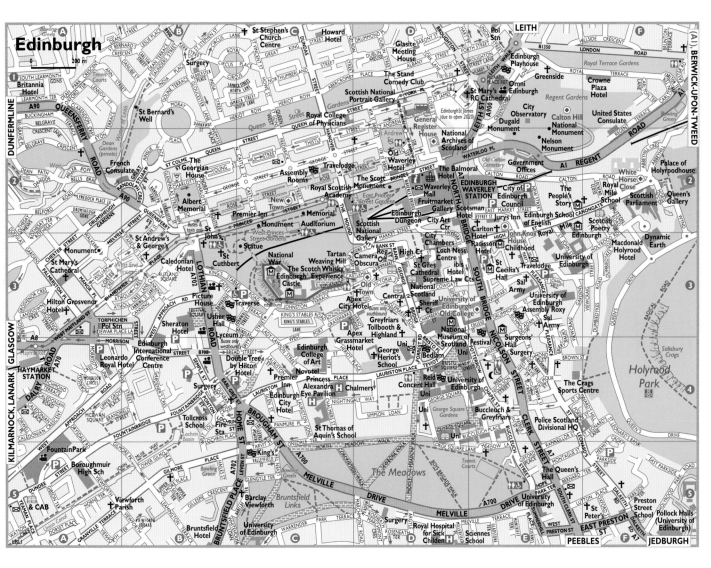

Edinburgh

Edinburgh is found on atlas page **127 P3**

Abbeyhill	F2	Chapel Street	E4
Abercromby Place	C1	Charlotte Square	B2
Adam Street	E3	Chester Street Gardens	A3
Albany Street	D1	Circus Lane	B1
Ann Street	A1	Circus Place	B1
Argyle Place	D5	Clarendon Crescent	A1
Atholl Crescent Lane	A3	Clerk Street	E4
Bank Street	D3	Cockburn Street	D2
Barclay Terrace	C5	Coronation Walk	C5
Belford Road	A2	Cowan's Close	E4
Belgrave Crescent	A2	Cowgate	D3
Bernard Terrace	E5	Dalkeith Road	F5
Boys Brigade Walk	D5	Dalry Road	A4
Brandfield Street	A4	Danube Street	B1
Bread Street	B4	Davie Street	E4
Bristo Place	D4	Dean Park Crescent	A1
Brougham Street	C4	Dean Street	A1
Broughton Street	D1	Dewar Place Lane	A3
Broughton Street Lane	E1	Douglas Gardens	A3
Brunton Terrace	F1	Doune Terrace	B1
Bruntsfield Place	B5	Drummond Street	E3
Buccleuch Place	D4	Dublin Street	D1
Buccleuch Street	E4	Dumbiedykes Road	F3
Caledonian Place	A4	Dunbar Street	B4
Caledonian Road	A4	Dundas Street	C1
Caledonian Street	A4	Dundee Street	A5
Calton Road	E2	Earl Grey Street	B4
Candlemaker Row	D3	Easter Road	F1
Canning Street	B3	East Market Street	E2
Canongate	E2	East Parkside	F5
Carlton Terrace	F1	East Preston Street	F5
Castle Hill	C3	Elder Street	D1
Castle Street	C2	Forrest Road	D4
Castle Terrace	B3	Forth Street	D1
Chalmers Street	C4	Fountainbridge	A4
Chambers Street	D3	Frederick Street	C2

Gardener's Crescent	B4	Jeffrey Street	E2
George IV Bridge	D3	Johnston Terrace	C3
George Square	D4	Keir Street	C4
George Square Lane	D5	Kerr Street	B1
George Street	B2	King's Stables Road	B3
George Street	C2	Lady Lawson Street	C3
Gifford Place	E5	Lansdowne Crescent	A3
Gillespie Crescent	B5	Lauriston Gardens	C4
Gilmore Park	A5	Lauriston Place	C4
Gilmore Place	B5	Lauriston Street	C4
Gilmour Street	E4	Lawnmarket	D3
Glenfinlas Street	B2	Leamington Terrace	B5
Gloucester Lane	B1	Leith Street	E1
Granville Terrace	A5	Leith Walk	E1
Great King Street	C1	Lennox Street	A1
Great Stuart Street	B2	Leven Place	C5
Greenmarket	C3	Lochrin Place	B4
Greenside Row	E1	Lochrin Street	B4
Grindlay Street	B3	London Road	E1
Grosvenor Street	A3	Lothian Road	B3
Grove Street	A4	Lower Gilmore Place	B5
Haddon's Court	C4	Lutton Place	E5
Hanover Street	C2	Lynedoch Place Lane	A2
Haymarket Terrace	A4	Manor Place	A3
Heriot Row	C1	Marchmont Crescent	D5
Hermits Croft	F5	Marchmont Road	D5
High Street	D3	Market Street	D2
High Street	E3	Meadow Lane	E5
Hillside Crescent	E1	Melville Drive	C5
Hill Street	C2	Melville Street	A3
Holyrood Park Road	F5	Melville Terrace	D5
Holyrood Road	E3	Middle Meadow Walk	D5
Home Street	C4	Millerfield Place	D5
Hope Street	B2	Miller Row	A2
Horse Wynd	F2	Moncrieff Terrace	E5
Howden Street	E4	Montague Street	E5
Howe Street	C1	Moray Place	B1
India Place	B1	Morrison Link	A4
India Street	B1	Morrison Street	A4
Jamaica Street South Lane	B1	Mound Place	D3
Jawbone Walk	D5	Nelson Street	C1

New Street	E2	St Patrick Street	E4
Nicolson Square	E4	St Stephen Street	B1
Nicolson Street	E4	St Vincent Street	C1
Nightingale Way	C4	Saunders Street	B1
North Bridge	D2	Sciennes	E5
North Castle Street	C2	Semple Street	B4
North Meadow Walk	C5	Shandwick Place	A3
North St Andrew Street	D1	Simpson Loan	D4
North St David Street	D1	South Bridge	E3
Northumberland Street	C1	South Charlotte Street	B2
Oxford Street	F5	South Clerk Street	E5
Palmerston Place	A3	South Learmonth Gardens	A1
Panmure Place	C4	South St Andrew Street	D2
Pleasance	E3	South St David Street	D2
Ponton Street	B4	Spittal Street	C4
Potterrow	E4	Stafford Street	B3
Princes Street	C2	Tarvit Street	C5
Queens Drive	F3	The Mound	C2
Queensferry Road	A1	Thistle Street	C2
Queensferry Street	B2	Torphichen Street	A3
Queen Street	B2	Union Street	E1
Radical Road	F3	Upper Gilmore Place	B5
Ramsay Lane	C3	Victoria Street	D3
Randolph Crescent	B2	Viewcraig Gardens	E3
Randolph Lane	B2	Viewcraig Street	F3
Rankeillor Street	E5	Viewforth	A5
Regent Road	E2	Walker Street	A3
Richmond Place	E3	Warrender Park Terrace	C5
Rose Street	B2	Waterloo Place	D2
Rosebeath Place	D5	Waverley Bridge	D2
Rothesay Place	A3	West Approach Road	A4
Royal Circus	B1	West Maitland Street	A3
Royal Terrace	E1	West Nicolson Street	E4
St Andrew Square	D1	West Port	C4
St Bernard's Crescent	A1	West Richmond Street	E4
St Colme Street	B2	West Toll Cross	B4
St James Place	D1	William Street	A3
St Leonard's Bank	F4	Yeaman Place	A5
St Leonard's Hill	E4	York Lane	D1
St Leonard's Lane	F4	York Place	D1
St Leonard's Street	E4	Young Street	B2

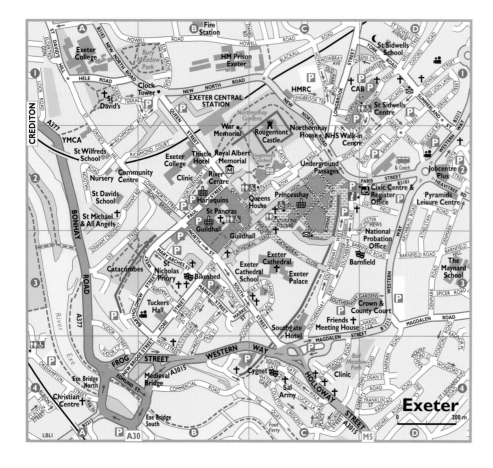

Exeter

Exeter is found on atlas page **9 M6**

Acland Road	D1	King William Street	D1
Archibald Road	D3	Longbrook Street	C1
Athelstan Road	D3	Lower North Street	B2
Bailey Street	C2	Magdalen Road	D3
Bampfylde Lane	C2	Magdalen Street	C4
Bampfylde Street	D2	Market Street	B3
Barnfield Road	D3	Martins Lane	C2
Bartholomew Street West	B3	Mary Arches Street	B3
Bear Street	C3	Musgrave Row	C2
Bedford Street	C2	New Bridge Street	A4
Belgrave Road	D2	New North Road	A1
Blackall Road	C1	Northernhay Street	B2
Bonhay Road	A2	North Street	B3
Bude Street	D2	Old Park Road	C1
Bull Meadow Road	C4	Oxford Road	D1
Castle Street	C2	Palace Gate	C3
Cathedral Close	C3	Paris Street	D2
Cathedral Yard	B3	Paul Street	B2
Cedars Road	D4	Preston Street	B4
Cheeke Street	D1	Princesshay	C2
Chichester Mews	C3	Queens Crescent	D1
Commercial Road	B4	Queen's Terrace	A1
Coombe Street	B3	Queen Street	B2
Deanery Place	C3	Radford Road	D4
Dean Street	D4	Red Lion Lane	D1
Denmark Road	D3	Richmond Court	A2
Dinham Crescent	A3	Richmond Road	A2
Dinham Road	A2	Roberts Road	C4
Dix's Field	D2	Roman Walk	C2
Eastgate	C2	St David's Hill	A1
Edmund Street	A4	Sidwell Street	D1
Elm Grove Road	B1	Sidwell Street	D1
Exe Street	A3	Smythen Street	B3
Fairpark Road	D4	Southernhay East	C3
Fore Street	B3	Southernhay Gardens	C3
Franklin Street	D4	Southernhay West	C3
Friernhay Street	B3	South Street	B3
Frog Street	A4	Spicer Road	D3
George Street	B3	Summerland Street	D1
Guinea Street	B3	Temple Road	C3
Haldon Road	A2	Tudor Court	A4
Heavitree Road	D2	Tudor Street	A3
Hele Road	A1	Verney Street	D1
High Street	C2	Well Street	D1
Holloway Street	C4	Western Way	B4
Howell Road	B1	West Street	B4
Iron Bridge	B2	Wonford Road	D4
King Street	B3	York Road	D1

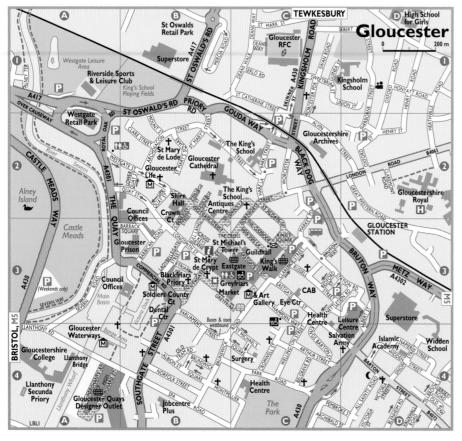

Gloucester

Gloucester is found on atlas page **46 F11**

Albert Street	D4	Millbrook Street	D4
Albion Street	B4	Montpellier	B4
All Saints' Road	D4	Napier Street	D4
Alvin Street	C2	Nettleton Road	C3
Archdeacon Street	B2	New Inn Lane	C3
Arthur Street	C4	Norfolk Street	B4
Barbican Road	B3	Northgate Street	C3
Barrack Square	B3	Old Tram Road	B4
Barton Street	D4	Over Causeway	A1
Bedford Street	C3	Oxford Road	D1
Belgrave Road	C4	Oxford Street	D2
Berkeley Street	B3	Park Road	C4
Black Dog Way	C2	Park Street	C2
Blenheim Road	D4	Parliament Street	B3
Brunswick Road	B4	Pembroke Street	C4
Brunswick Square	B4	Pitt Street	B2
Bruton Way	D3	Priory Road	B1
Bull Lane	B3	Quay Street	B2
Castle Meads Way	A2	Royal Oak Road	A2
Clarence Street	C3	Russell Street	C3
Clare Street	B2	St Aldate Street	C2
College Court	B2	St Catherine Street	C1
Commercial Road	B3	St John's Lane	B3
Cromwell Street	C4	St Mark Street	C1
Cross Keys Lane	B3	St Mary's Square	B2
Deans Walk	C1	St Mary's Street	B2
Eastgate Street	C3	St Michael's Square	B3
Gouda Way	B1	St Oswald's Road	B1
Great Western Road	D2	Sebert Street	C1
Greyfriars	B3	Severn Road	A3
Hampden Way	C3	Sherborne Street	D2
Hare Lane	C2	Sinope Street	C4
Heathville Road	D2	Southgate Street	B4
Henry Road	D1	Spa Road	B4
Henry Street	D2	Station Road	C3
High Orchard Street	A4	Swan Road	C2
Honyatt Road	D1	Sweetbriar Street	C1
Kings Barton Street	C4	The Cross	B3
Kingsholm Road	C1	The Oxebode	C2
King's Square	C3	The Quay	A2
Ladybellegate Street	B3	Union Street	C1
Llanthony Road	A4	Upper Quay Street	B2
London Road	D2	Vauxhall Road	C4
Longsmith Street	B3	Wellington Street	C4
Market Parade	C3	Westgate Street	A2
Merchants' Road	A4	Widden Street	D4
Mercia Road	B1	Worcester Parade	C2
Metz Way	D3	Worcester Street	C2

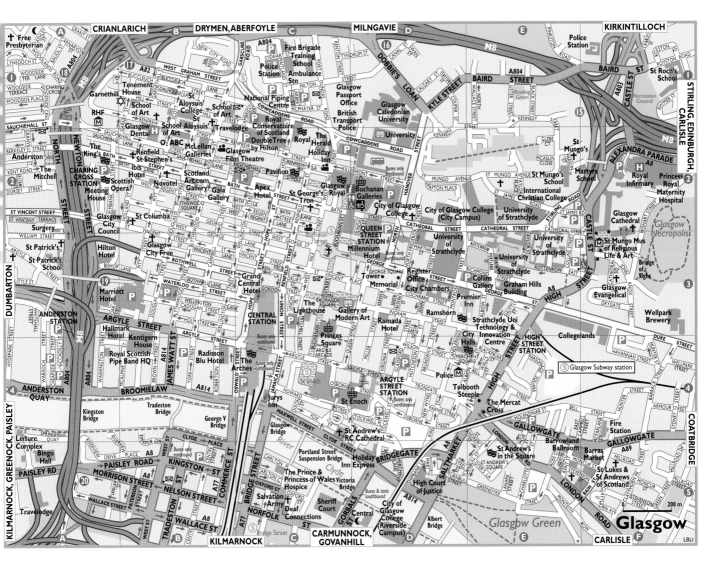

Glasgow

Glasgow is found on atlas page **125 P4**

Albert Bridge	D5	Candleriggs	D4	Gallowgate	E4
Albion Street	D4	Carlton Place	C5	Garnethill Street	B1
Albion Street	E3	Carnarvon Street	A1	Garnet Street	B2
Alexandra Parade	F2	Castle Street	F1	Garscube Road	C1
Anderston Quay	A4	Castle Street	F2	Garth Street	D3
Argyle Arcade	C4	Cathedral Square	F3	George Square	D3
Argyle Street	A3	Cathedral Street	D2	George Street	E3
Armour Street	F4	Centre Street	B5	George V Bridge	B4
Ashley Street	A1	Chalmer Street	F5	Glasgow Bridge	C5
Bain Street	F5	Charing Cross	A1	Glassford Street	D4
Baird Street	E1	Charles Street	F1	Glebe Court	E2
Baliol Street	A1	Charlotte Street	E5	Gorbals Street	C5
Barrack Street	F4	Cheapside Street	A4	Gordon Street	C3
Bath Lane	B2	Claythorn Avenue	F5	Grafton Place	D2
Bath Street	A2	Claythorn Park	F5	Granville Street	A2
Bell Street	E4	Clyde Place	B4	Greendyke Street	E5
Berkeley Street	A2	Clyde Street	C4	Green Street	F5
Blackfriars Street	E4	Cochrane Street	D3	Hanover Street	D3
Black Street	E1	Collins Street	E3	High Street	E4
Blythswood Square	B2	Commerce Street	B5	Hill Street	B1
Blythswood Street	B3	Couper Street	D1	Holland Street	B2
Bothwell Lane	B3	Cowcaddens Road	C1	Holm Street	B3
Bothwell Street	B3	Dalhousie Lane	B1	Hope Street	C3
Bridgegate	D5	Dixon Street	C4	Howard Street	C4
Bridge of Sighs	F3	Dobbie's Loan	D1	Hunter Street	F4
Bridge Street	C5	Dorset Street	A2	Hutcheson Street	D4
Broomielaw	B4	Douglas Street	B3	Hydepark Street	A4
Brown Street	B4	Drury Street	C3	Ingram Street	D3
Brunswick Street	D4	Drygate	F3	Jamaica Street	C4
Buccleuch Lane	B1	Duke Street	F4	James Watt Street	B4
Buccleuch Street	B1	Dundas Street	D3	John Knox Street	F3
Buchanan Street	C4	Dunlop Street	D4	John Street	D3
Cadogan Street	B3	Dyer's Lane	E5	Kennedy Street	D2
Calgary Street	D1	East Campbell Street	E4	Kennedy Street	E1
Cambridge Street	C1	Elmbank Street	A2	Kent Road	A2
Canal Street	D1	Fox Street	C4	Kent Street	E5
				Killermont Street	C2
				King Street	D4
				Kingston Bridge	A5
				Kingston Street	B5
				Kyle Street	D1

Lanark Street	E5	Paterson Street	B5	Steel Street	D5
Larbert Street	C1	Pinkston Road	E1	Stevenson Street	F5
Lister Street	E1	Pitt Street	B2	Stewart Street	C1
London Road	E4	Port Dundas Road	C1	Stirling Road	E2
Maitland Street	C1	Portland Street		Stockwell Place	D4
Martha Street	D3	Suspension Bridge	C5	Stockwell Street	D4
Mart Street	D5	Queen Street	C4	Suffolk Street	E5
Maxwell Street	C4	Renfield Lane	C3	Sydney Street	F4
McAlpine Street	B4	Renfield Street	C3	Taylor Place	E2
McAslin Close	E2	Renfrew Lane	C2	Taylor Street	E2
McFarlane Street	F4	Renfrew Street	B1	Tradeston Bridge	B4
McPhater Street	C1	Renton Street	C1	Tradeston Street	B5
Merchant Lane	D5	Rhymer Street	F1	Trongate	D4
Miller Street	D4	Richmond Street	E3	Turnbull Street	D5
Millroad Drive	F5	Riverview Drive	A4	Tyndrum Street	C1
Millroad Street	F5	Robertson Street	B4	Union Street	C3
Milton Street	C1	Rose Street	B2	Virginia Street	D4
Mitchell Street	C4	Ross Street	E5	Wallace Street	A5
Moir Street	E5	Rottenrow	E3	Walls Street	E4
Molendinar Street	E4	Rottenrow East	E3	Warroch Street	A4
Moncur Street	E5	Royal Exchange Square	C3	Washington Street	A4
Monteith Row	E5	Royston Road	F1	Waterloo Street	B3
Montrose Street	D3	Royston Square	F1	Wellington Lane	B3
Morrison Street	A5	St Andrew's Square	E5	Wellington Street	B3
Nelson Street	B5	St Andrew's Street	E4	Wellpark Street	F4
New City Road	B1	St James Road	E2	West Campbell Street	B3
Newton Street	A2	St Mungo Avenue	D2	West George Lane	B2
New Wynd	D4	St Vincent Lane	B3	West George Street	B2
Norfolk Street	C5	St Vincent Place	C3	West Graham Street	B1
North Frederick Street	D3	St Vincent Street	A2	West Nile Street	C3
North Hanover Street	D3	St Vincent Terrace	A2	West Regent Lane	C2
North Portland Street	E3	Saltmarket	D5	West Regent Street	B2
North Street	A2	Sauchiehall Lane	A2	West Street	B5
North Wallace Street	E1	Sauchiehall Lane	A1	William Street	A3
Osborne Street	C4	Sauchiehall Street	B2	Wilson Street	D4
Oswald Street	C4	Scott Street	B1	Wishart Street	F3
Oxford Street	C5	Shipbank Lane	D5	Woodlands Road	A1
Paisley Road	A5	Shuttle Street	E3	Woodside Crescent	A1
Parnie Street	D4	South Frederick Street	D3	Woodside Terrace	A1
Parsonage Square	E4	Springfield Quay	A4	Woodside Terrace Lane	A1
Parson Street	E2	Stafford Street	D1	York Street	B4

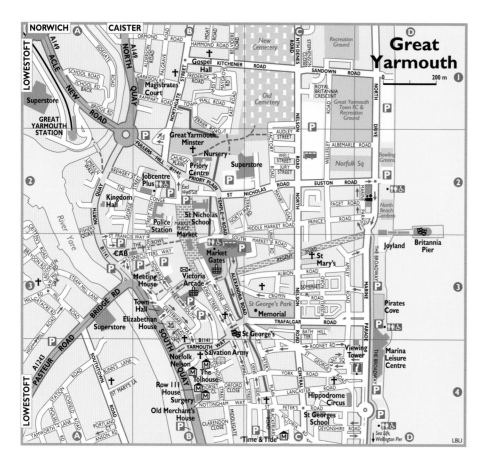

Great Yarmouth

Great Yarmouth is found on atlas page **77 Q10**

Acle New Road	A1	North Drive	D1
Albemarle Road	C2	North Market Road	C2
Albion Road	C3	North Quay	A2
Alderson Road	B1	Northgate Street	B1
Alexandra Road	B3	Nottingham Way	B4
Apsley Road	C3	Ormond Road	B1
Belvidere Road	B1	Paget Road	C2
Blackfriars Road	C4	Palgrave Road	B1
Brewery Street	A2	Pasteur Road	A4
Breydon Road	A3	Prince's Road	C2
Bridge Road	A1	Priory Plain	B2
Bridge Road	A3	Queen Street	B4
Bunn's Lane	A4	Rampart Road	B1
Church Plain	B2	Regent Road	C3
Critten's Road	A3	Rodney Road	C4
Crown Road	C3	Russell Road	C3
Dene Side	B3	St Francis Way	A3
Devonshire Road	C4	St George's Road	C4
East Road	B1	St Nicholas Road	B2
Euston Road	C2	St Peter's Plain	C4
Factory Road	C2	St Peter's Road	C4
Ferrier Road	B1	Sandown Road	C1
Fishers Quay	A2	Saw Mill Lane	A3
Frederick Road	B1	School Road	A1
Fullers Hill	B2	School Road Back	A1
Garrison Road	B1	Sidegate Road	A1
Gatacre Road	A3	South Market Road	C3
George Street	A2	South Quay	B3
Greyfriars Way	B3	Southtown Road	A4
Hammond Road	B1	Station Road	A4
High Mill Road	A3	Steam Mill Lane	A3
Howard Street North	B2	Stephenson Close	C1
Howard Street South	B3	Stonecutters Way	B3
King Street	B3	Tamworth Lane	A4
Kitchener Road	B1	Temple Road	B2
Ladyhaven Road	A3	The Broadway	D3
Lancaster Road	C4	The Conge	A2
Lichfield Road	A4	The Rows	B3
Limekiln Walk	A2	Tolhouse Street	B4
Manby Road	C2	Town Wall Road	B1
Marine Parade	D3	Trafalgar Road	C3
Maygrove Road	B1	Union Road	C3
Middle Market Road	C2	Victoria Road	C4
Middlegate	B4	Wellesley Road	C2
Moat Road	B1	West Road	B1
Nelson Road Central	C3	Wolseley Road	C3
Nelson Road North	C1	Yarmouth Way	B4
North Denes Road	C1	York Road	C4

Guildford

Guildford is found on atlas page **23 Q5**

Abbot Road	C4	Millmead	B3
Angel Gate	B3	Millmead Terrace	B4
Artillery Road	B1	Mount Pleasant	A4
Artillery Terrace	C1	Nightingale Road	D1
Bedford Road	A2	North Street	B3
Bridge Street	A3	Onslow Road	C1
Bright Hill	C3	Onslow Street	B2
Brodie Road	D3	Oxford Road	C3
Bury Fields	B4	Pannells Court	C2
Bury Street	B4	Park Street	B3
Castle Hill	C4	Pewley Bank	D3
Castle Street	C3	Pewley Fort Inner Court	D4
Chapel Street	B3	Pewley Hill	C3
Chertsey Street	C2	Pewley Way	D3
Cheselden Road	D2	Phoenix Court	B3
Church Road	B1	Porridge Pot Alley	B4
College Road	B2	Portsmouth Road	A4
Commercial Road	B2	Poyle Road	D4
Dene Road	D2	Quarry Street	B3
Denmark Road	D2	Sandfield Terrace	C2
Drummond Road	B1	Semaphore Road	D3
Eagle Road	C1	South Hill	C3
Epsom Road	D2	Springfield Road	C1
Falcon Road	C1	Station Approach	D1
Farnham Road	A3	Stoke Fields	C1
Fort Road	C4	Stoke Grove	C1
Foxenden Road	D1	Stoke Road	C1
Friary Bridge	A3	Swan Lane	B3
Friary Street	B3	Sydenham Road	C3
George Road	B1	Testard Road	A3
Guildford Park Road	A2	The Bars	C2
Harvey Road	D3	The Mount	A4
Haydon Place	C2	The Shambles	B3
High Pewley	D4	Tunsgate	C3
High Street	C3	Upperton Road	A3
Jeffries Passage	C3	Victoria Road	D1
Jenner Road	D2	Walnut Tree Close	A1
Laundry Road	B2	Ward Street	C2
Leapale Lane	B2	Warwicks Bench	C4
Leapale Road	B2	Wherwell Road	A3
Leas Road	B1	William Road	B1
London Road	D2	Wodeland Avenue	A3
Mareschal Road	A4	Woodbridge Road	B1
Market Street	C3	York Road	B1
Martyr Road	C2		
Mary Road	A1		
Millbrook	B3		
Mill Lane	B3		

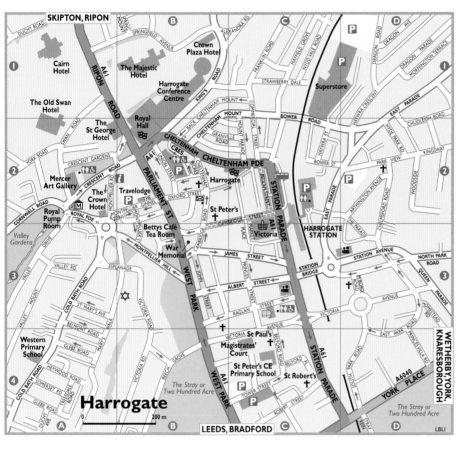

Harrogate

Harrogate is found on atlas page **97 M9**

Albert Street	C3	Montpellier Road	A2
Alexandra Road	B1	Montpellier Street	B2
Arthington Avenue	D2	Mornington Terrace	D1
Back Cheltenham Mount	B2	Mount Parade	C2
Beech Grove	B4	North Park Road	D3
Belford Place	C4	Nydd Vale Road	C1
Belford Road	C4	Oxford Street	B2
Belmont Road	A3	Park View	D2
Beulah Street	C2	Parliament Street	C3
Bower Road	C1	Princes Street	C3
Bower Street	C2	Princes Villa Road	D4
Cambridge Road	B3	Queen Parade	D3
Cambridge Street	C2	Raglan Street	C3
Chelmsford Road	D3	Ripon Road	A1
Cheltenham Crescent	B2	Robert Street	C4
Cheltenham Mount	B2	Royal Parade	A2
Cheltenham Parade	B2	St Mary's Avenue	A3
Chudleigh Road	D2	St Mary's Walk	A4
Cold Bath Road	A3	Somerset Road	A4
Commercial Street	C1	South Park Road	D4
Cornwall Road	A2	Springfield Avenue	B1
Crescent Gardens	A2	Spring Mount	B1
Crescent Road	A2	Station Avenue	D3
Dragon Avenue	D1	Station Bridge	C3
Dragon Parade	D1	Station Parade	C2
Dragon Road	D1	Strawberry Dale	C1
Duchy Avenue	A4	Stray Rein	D4
Duchy Road	A1	Swan Road	A2
East Parade	C2	The Ginnel	B2
East Park Road	D4	The Parade	D2
Esplanade	A3	Tower Street	C4
Franklin Road	C1	Treesdale Road	A4
Glebe Road	A4	Union Street	B2
Granville Road	B2	Valley Drive	A3
Haywra Street	C2	Valley Mount	A3
Heywood Road	A4	Valley Road	A3
Homestead Road	D3	Victoria Avenue	B4
Hyde Park Road	D2	Victoria Road	B3
Hywra Crescent	D2	West Park	B3
James Street	B3	West Park Street	B4
John Street	B3	Woodside	D2
King's Road	B1	York Place	D4
Kingsway	D2	York Road	A2
Market Place	C3		
Marlborough Road	D3		
Mayfield Grove	C1		
Montpellier Gardens	B2		
Montpellier Hill	B3		

Huddersfield

Huddersfield is found on atlas page **90 E7**

Albion Street	B4	New North Road	A2
Alfred Street	C4	New Street	B4
Back Union Street	C1	Northgate	C1
Bankfield Road	A4	Northumberland Street	C2
Bath Street	B1	Old Leeds Road	D2
Belmont Street	A1	Old South Street	B3
Brook Street	C2	Outcote Bank	B4
Byram Street	C2	Oxford Street	C1
Cambridge Road	B1	Page Street	C4
Carforth Street	D4	Park Avenue	A2
Castlegate	B1	Park Drive South	A2
Chancery Lane	B3	Peel Street	C4
Chapel Hill	B4	Portland Street	A2
Chapel Street	B4	Princess Street	B4
Church Street	C2	Prospect Street	A4
Clare Hill	B1	Quay Street	D2
Claremont Street	B1	Queen Street	C3
Cloth Hall Street	B3	Queen Street South	C4
Cross Church Street	C3	Queensgate	C4
Dundas Street	B3	Railway Street	B2
Elizabeth Queen Gardens	A2	Ramsden Street	B3
Elmwood Avenue	A1	Rook Street	B1
Firth Street	D4	St Andrew's Road	D2
Fitzwilliam Street	A2	St George's Square	B2
Fitzwilliam Street	B2	St John's Road	B1
Gasworks Street	D1	St Peter's Street	C2
Great Northern Street	C1	Southgate	C2
Greenhead Road	A3	Spring Grove Street	A4
Half Moon Street	B3	Spring Street	A3
High Street	B3	Springwood Avenue	A3
Highfields Road	A1	Stadium Way	D1
John William Street	B2	Station Street	B2
King Street	C3	Trinity Street	A2
King's Mill Lane	D4	Turnbridge Road	D2
Kirkgate	C3	Union Street	C1
Leeds Road	C2	Upper George Street	A3
Lincoln Street	D3	Upperhead Row	B3
Lord Street	C2	Viaduct Street	B2
Lower Fitzwilliam Street	C1	Victoria Lane	C3
Lynton Avenue	A3	Wakefield Road	D3
Manchester Road	A4	Water Street	A3
Market Place	C3	Watergate	D2
Market Street	B3	Waverley Road	A2
Merton Street	A3	Wentworth Street	A2
Milford Street	B4	Westgate	B3
Mountjoy Road	A1	William Street	C1
New North Parade	B2	Wood Street	C2
New North Road	A1	Zetland Street	C3

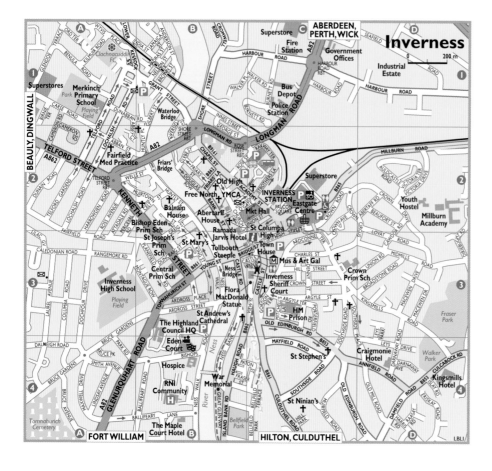

Inverness

Inverness is found on atlas page **156 B8**

Abertaff Road D2	Glenurquhart Road A4
Academy Street..............B2	Gordon Terrace C3
Anderson Street..............B1	Grant Street..............B1
Annfield Road..............D4	Great Glen Way..............B4
Ardconnel Terrace C3	Harbour Road C1
Ardross Street..............B3	Harris Road..............D4
Argyle Street..............C3	Harrowden Road A2
Argyle Terrace..............C3	Haugh Road..............B4
Ballifeary Lane..............A4	High Street..............C3
Ballifeary Road..............B4	Hill Park..............C4
Bank Street..............B2	Hill Street..............C3
Bellfield Terrace..............C4	Huntly Street..............B2
Benula Road..............A1	Innes Street..............B1
Birnie Terrace..............A1	Kenneth Street..............A2
Bishops Road..............B4	King Street..............B3
Bridge Street..............B3	Kingsmills Road..............D3
Broadstone Road..............D3	Laurel Avenue..............A3
Bruce Gardens..............A4	Lindsay Avenue..............A4
Bruce Park..............A4	Lochalsh Road..............A2
Burnett Road..............C1	Longman Road..............C2
Caledonian Road..............A3	Lovat Road..............C3
Cameron Road..............A2	Lower Kessock Street..............A1
Cameron Square..............A2	Maxwell Drive..............A4
Carse Road..............A1	Mayfield Road..............D3
Castle Road..............B3	Midmills Road..............D3
Castle Street..............C3	Millburn Road..............D2
Chapel Street..............B2	Mitchell's Lane..............C3
Charles Street..............C3	Muirfield Road..............C3
Columba Road..............A3	Ness Bank..............B4
Crown Circus..............C2	Old Edinburgh Road..............C3
Crown Drive..............D2	Park Road..............A4
Crown Road..............C2	Planefield Road..............B3
Crown Street..............C3	Porterfield Road..............C3
Culcabock Road..............D4	Raasay Road..............D4
Culduthel Road..............C4	Rangemore Road..............A3
Dalneigh Road..............A4	Ross Avenue..............A2
Damfield Road..............D4	Seafield Road..............D1
Darnaway Road..............D4	Shore Street..............B1
Denny Street..............C3	Smith Avenue..............A4
Dochfour Drive..............A3	Southside Place..............C4
Dunabban Road..............A1	Southside Road..............C4
Dunain Road..............A2	Telford Gardens..............A2
Duncraig Street..............B3	Telford Road..............A2
Eriskay Road..............D4	Telford Street..............A2
Fairfield Road..............A3	Tomnahurich Street..............B3
Falcon Square..............C2	Union Road..............D3
Friars' Lane..............B2	Walker Road..............C1
Glendoe Terrace..............A1	Young Street..............B3

Ipswich

Ipswich is found on atlas page **53 L3**

Alderman Road..............A3	Key Street..............C3
Anglesea Road..............B1	King Street..............B2
Argyle Street..............D2	London Road..............A2
Austin Street..............C4	Lower Brook Street..............C3
Barrack Lane..............A1	Lower Orwell Street..............C3
Belstead Road..............B4	Museum Street..............B2
Berners Street..............B1	Neale Street..............C1
Black Horse Lane..............B2	Neptune Quay..............D3
Blanche Street..............D2	New Cardinal Street..............B3
Bolton Lane..............C1	Newson Street..............A1
Bond Street..............D3	Northgate Street..............C2
Bramford Road..............A1	Norwich Road..............A1
Bridge Street..............C4	Old Foundry Road..............C2
Burlington Road..............A2	Orchard Street..............D2
Burrell Road..............B4	Orford Street..............A1
Cardigan Street..............A1	Orwell Place..............C3
Carr Street..............C2	Orwell Quay..............D4
Cecil Road..............B1	Portman Road..............A3
Cemetery Road..............D1	Princes Street..............A3
Chancery Road..............A4	Quadling Street..............B3
Charles Street..............B1	Queen Street..............B3
Christchurch Street..............D1	Ranelagh Road..............A4
Civic Drive..............B2	Russell Road..............A3
Clarkson Street..............A1	St George's Street..............B1
Cobbold Street..............C2	St Helen's Street..............D2
College Street..............C3	St Margaret's Street..............C2
Commercial Road..............A4	St Matthews Street..............B2
Constantine Road..............A3	St Nicholas Street..............B3
Crown Street..............B2	St Peter's Street..............B3
Cumberland Street..............A1	Silent Street..............B3
Dalton Road..............A2	Sir Alf Ramsey Way..............A3
Dock Street..............C4	Soane Street..............C2
Duke Street..............D4	South Street..............A1
Eagle Street..............C3	Star Lane..............C4
Elm Street..............B2	Stoke Quay..............C4
Falcon Street..............B3	Suffolk Road..............D1
Fonnereau Road..............B1	Tacket Street..............C3
Foundation Street..............C3	Tavern Street..............B2
Franciscan Way..............B3	Tower Ramparts..............B2
Geneva Road..............A1	Tuddenham Avenue..............D1
Grafton Way..............B3	Turret Lane..............B3
Great Gipping Street..............A2	Upper Orwell Street..............C3
Great Whip Street..............C4	Vernon Street..............C4
Grey Friars Road..............B3	West End Road..............A3
Grimwade Street..............D3	Westgate Street..............B2
Handford Road..............A2	Willoughby Road..............B4
Hervey Street..............D1	Wolsey Street..............B3
High Street..............B1	Woodbridge Road..............D2

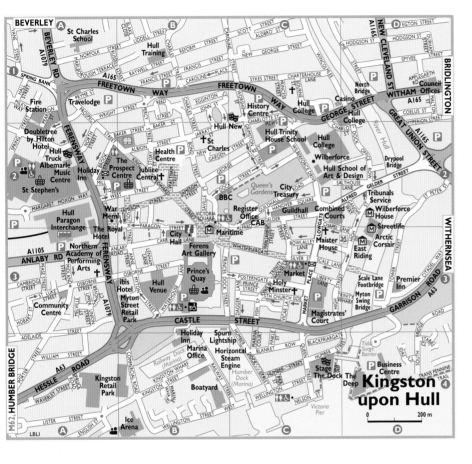

Kingston upon Hull

Kingston upon Hull is found on atlas page **93 J5**

Adelaide Street	A4	Market Place	C3
Albion Street	B2	Mill Street	A2
Alfred Gelder Street	C2	Myton Street	B3
Anlaby Road	A3	New Cleveland Street	D1
Baker Street	B2	New Garden Street	B2
Beverley Road	A1	New George Street	C1
Blackfriargate	C4	Norfolk Street	A1
Blanket Row	C4	Osborne Street	B3
Bond Street	B2	Osborne Street	A3
Brook Street	A2	Paragon Street	B2
Caroline Street	B1	Percy Street	B1
Carr Lane	B3	Porter Street	A3
Castle Street	B3	Portland Place	A2
Chapel Lane	C2	Portland Street	A2
Charles Street	B1	Posterngate	C3
Charterhouse Lane	C1	Princes Dock Street	B3
Citadel Way	D3	Prospect Street	A1
Commercial Road	B4	Queen Street	C4
Dagger Lane	C3	Railway Street	B4
Dock Office Row	D2	Raywell Street	B1
Dock Street	B2	Reform Street	B1
Durham Street	D1	Russell Street	A1
Egginton Street	B1	St Luke's Street	A3
Ferensway	A2	St Peter Street	D2
Freetown Way	A1	Saville Street	B2
Gandhi Way	D2	Scale Lane	C3
Garrison Road	D3	Scott Street	C1
George Street	B2	Silver Street	C3
George Street	D1	South Bridge Road	D4
Great Union Street	D1	South Church Side	C3
Grimston Street	C2	South Street	B2
Guildhall Road	C2	Spring Bank	A1
Hanover Square	C2	Spyvee Street	D1
Hessle Road	A4	Sykes Street	C1
High Street	C3	Tower Street	D3
Hodgson Street	D1	Upper Union Street	A3
Humber Dock Street	C4	Victoria Square	B2
Humber Street	C4	Waterhouse Lane	B3
Hyperion Street	D1	Wellington Street	C4
Jameson Street	B2	Wellington Street West	B4
Jarratt Street	B2	West Street	A2
King Edward Street	B2	Whitefriargate	C3
Kingston Street	B4	Wilberforce Drive	C2
Liddell Street	B1	William Street	A4
Lime Street	C1	Wincolmlee	C1
Lister Street	A4	Witham	D1
Lowgate	C3	Worship Street	C1
Margaret Moxon Way	A2	Wright Street	A1

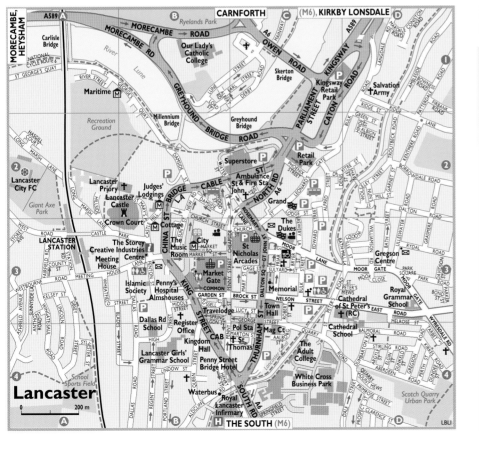

Lancaster

Lancaster is found on atlas page **95 K8**

Aberdeen Road	D4	Lincoln Road	A3
Aldcliffe Road	B4	Lindow Street	B4
Alfred Street	C2	Lodge Street	C2
Ambleside Road	D1	Long Marsh Lane	A2
Balmoral Road	D4	Lune Street	B1
Bath Street	D3	Market Street	B3
Blades Street	A3	Meeting House Lane	A3
Bond Street	D3	Middle Street	B3
Borrowdale Road	D2	Moor Gate	D3
Brewery Lane	C3	Moor Lane	C3
Bridge Lane	B2	Morecambe Road	B1
Brock Street	C3	Nelson Street	C3
Bulk Road	D2	North Road	C2
Bulk Street	C3	Owen Road	C1
Cable Street	B2	Park Road	D3
Castle Hill	B3	Parliament Street	C2
Castle Park	A3	Patterdale Road	D2
Caton Road	C2	Penny Street	B4
Cheapside	C3	Portland Street	B4
China Street	B3	Primrose Street	D4
Church Street	B2	Prospect Street	D4
Common Garden Street	B3	Quarry Road	C4
Dale Street	D4	Queen Street	B4
Dallas Road	B3	Regent Street	B4
Dalton Road	D2	Ridge Lane	D1
Dalton Square	C3	Ridge Street	D1
Damside Street	B2	Robert Street	C3
Derby Road	C1	Rosemary Lane	C2
De Vitre Street	C2	St George's Quay	A1
Dumbarton Road	D4	St Leonard's Gate	C2
East Road	D3	St Peter's Road	C4
Edward Street	C3	Sibsey Street	A3
Fairfield Road	A3	South Road	C4
Fenton Street	B3	Station Road	A3
Gage Street	C3	Stirling Road	D4
Garnet Street	D2	Sulyard Street	C3
George Street	C3	Sun Street	B3
Grasmere Road	D3	Thurnham Street	C4
Great John Street	C3	Troutbeck Road	D2
Gregson Road	D4	Ulleswater Road	D3
Greyhound Bridge Road	B1	West Road	A3
High Street	B4	Westbourne Road	A3
Kelsey Street	A3	Wheatfield Street	A3
Kentmere Road	D2	Williamson Road	D3
King Street	B3	Wingate-Saul Road	A3
Kingsway	C1	Wolseley Street	D2
Kirkes Road	D4	Woodville Street	D3
Langdale Road	D1	Wyresdale Road	D3

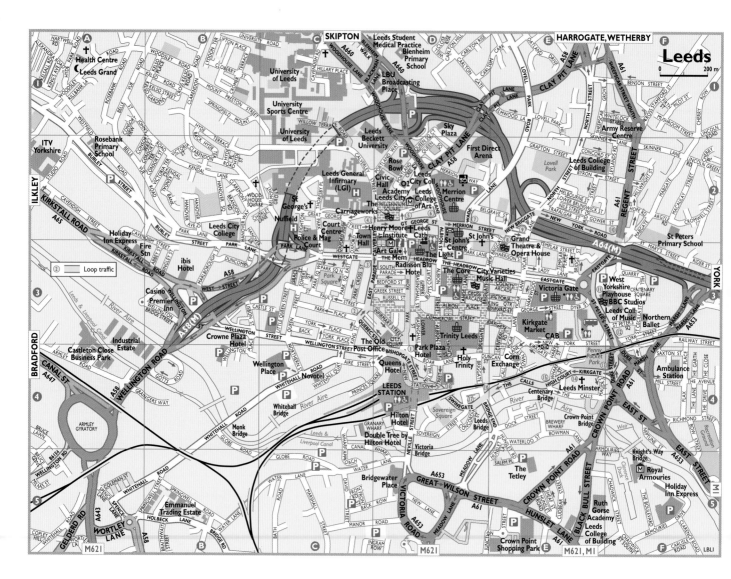

Leeds

Leeds is found on atlas page **90 H4**

Abbey Street...............B3	Calverley Street............C2	Duke Street...............F4	King's Avenue.............A1	Northern Street.............C4	Springfield Mount..........B1
Aire Street................C4	Canal Street..............A4	Duncan Street.............D4	King Street................C3	North Street...............E2	Springwell Road...........B5
Albion Place..............D3	Canal Wharf..............C4	Duncombe Street..........B3	Kirkgate..................E3	Oxford Place...............C3	Springwell Street..........B5
Albion Street.............D2	Carlton Carr..............D1	Dyer Street...............E3	Kirkstall Road.............A2	Oxford Row................C3	Studio Road...............A2
Alexandra Road...........A1	Carlton Hill..............D1	Eastgate.................E3	Lady Lane.................D3	Park Cross Street..........C3	Swinegate................D4
Argyle Road..............F2	Carlton Rise..............D1	East Parade...............C3	Lands Lane................D3	Park Lane.................B2	Templar Street.............E3
Armley Gyratory...........A4	Castle Street..............B3	East Street...............F4	Leighton Street............C2	Park Place................C3	The Avenue...............F4
Armley Road..............A4	Cavendish Road...........C1	Elmwood Lane............E1	Leylands Road.............F2	Park Row.................D3	The Boulevard............F5
Armouries Drive...........F5	Cavendish Street..........A2	Flax Place................F4	Lifton Place...............B1	Park Square East...........C3	The Calls.................E4
Armouries Way............E4	Centenary Square..........F3	Front Street...............C5	Lincoln Green Road.........E1	Park Square North..........C3	The Headrow..............D3
Back Hyde Terrace.........B2	Central Road..............E3	Geldered Road............A5	Lisbon Street..............B3	Park Square West..........C3	Thoresby Place............C2
Back Row.................C5	Chadwick Street..........F5	George Street.............E3	Little Queen Street.........B3	Park Street................C3	Trafalgar Street...........E2
Bath Road................C5	Cherry Row...............F1	Globe Road...............B4	Lovell Park Hill............E1	Pilot Street...............F1	Upper Basinghall Street....D3
Bedford Street............D3	Chorley Lane.............B2	Gotts Road...............B4	Lovell Park Road...........E1	Portland Crescent..........D2	Vicar Lane................E3
Belgrave Street............D2	City Square...............D3	Gower Street.............E2	Lower Basinghall Street.....D3	Portland Way..............D2	Victoria Road.............D5
Belle Vue Road............A1	Claremont................B2	Grace Street..............C3	Lower Brunswick Street.....E2	Princes Square............C4	Victoria Street............B2
Belmont Grove...........C2	Clarence Road............F5	Grafton Street............E2	Lyddon Terrace...........B1	Quarry Hill...............F3	Victoria Terrace..........B2
Benson Street............F1	Clarendon Road..........B1	Graingers Way...........A4	Mabgate.................F3	Quebec Street.............C3	Wade Lane...............D2
Bingley Street............B3	Clay Pit Lane.............D2	Great George Street.......C2	Macaulay Street...........F3	Queen Square.............D2	Water Lane...............B5
Bishopgate Street..........D4	Cloberry Street...........B1	Great Wilson Street........D5	Manor Road...............C5	Queen Square Court.......D2	Waterloo Street...........E4
Black Bull Street..........E5	Commercial Street.........D3	Greek Street..............D3	Mark Lane................D3	Queen Street.............C3	Wellington Bridge Street...B3
Blackman Lane............C1	Concord Street............E2	Hanover Avenue..........B2	Marlborough Street........B3	Railway Street.............F3	Wellington Road...........A4
Blenheim Walk............C1	Consort Street............B2	Hanover Lane............B2	Marshall Street............C5	Regent Street.............F2	Wellington Road...........A5
Boar Lane................D4	Consort View.............A1	Hanover Square..........B2	Marsh Lane...............F4	Richmond Street..........F4	Wellington Street..........B3
Bowman Lane.............E4	County Arcade............E3	Harewood Street.........E3	Maude Street..............E4	Rider Street...............F3	Westfield Road............A1
Bow Street...............F4	Cromer Terrace...........B1	Harper Street.............E4	Meadow Lane.............D5	Rillbank Lane..............A1	Westgate.................C3
Brandon Road............B2	Cromwell Street..........F2	Harrison Street............E3	Melbourne Street..........E2	Rosebank Road...........A1	West Street...............B3
Bridge End...............D4	Cross Arcade.............E3	Hartwell Road.............A1	Merrion Street............D2	St Cecilla Street...........F3	Wharf Approach...........C4
Bridge Road..............B5	Cross Kelso Road..........B1	High Court...............E4	Merrion Way..............D2	St John's Road.............A1	Wharf Street..............E4
Bridge Street.............E2	Cross Stamford Street......F1	Holbeck Lane.............B5	Millennium Square.........D2	St Mary's Street...........F3	Whitehall Quay............C4
Bridge Street.............E3	Crown Point Road.........E5	Hope Road...............F2	Mill Street................F3	St Paul's Street............C3	Whitehall Road............A5
Briggate.................D4	Crown Street.............E4	Hunslet Road.............E4	Millwright Street..........F2	St Peter's Square...........F3	Whitehall Road............B3
Burley Street.............A2	Cudbear Street...........E5	Hunslet Road.............E5	Mount Preston Street.......B1	St Peter's Street...........E3	Whitelock Street...........F1
Butts Court...............D3	David Street..............C5	Hyde Park Road..........A1	Mushroom Street.........F1	Salem Place...............E5	Willow Terrace Road.......C1
Byron Street..............E2	Dock Street...............E4	Hyde Street...............B2	Neptune Street............F4	Saxton Street.............F4	Woodhouse Lane..........C1
Call Lane................E4	Duke Street...............F4	Hyde Terrace.............B1	Neville Street..............D4	Sheepscar Grove..........E1	Woodhouse Square........B2
		Infirmary Street..........D3	New Briggate.............E3	Sheepscar Street South.....F1	Woodsley Road...........A1
		Junction Street...........D5	New Lane.................D5	Skinner Lane..............F2	Wortley Lane..............A5
		Kelso Road...............B1	New Station Street.........D4	South Parade.............D3	Wortley Lane..............A5
		Kendal Lane..............B2	New York Road...........E2	Sovereign Street...........D4	York Place................C3
		King Edward Street........E3	New York Street...........E3	Spence Lane...............A5	York Street................F3

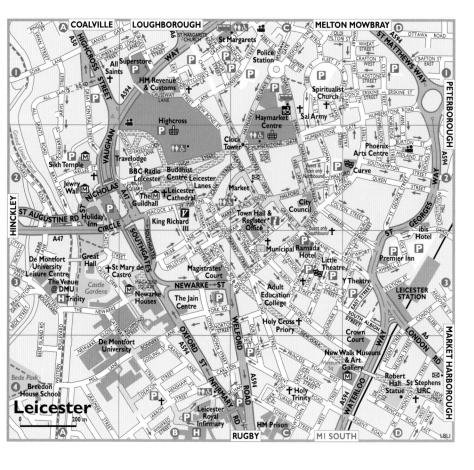

Leicester

Leicester is found on atlas page **72 F10**

Albion Street	C3	Infirmary Road	B4
All Saints Road	A1	Jarrom Street	B4
Bath Lane	A2	Jarvis Street	A1
Bedford Street	C1	King Street	C3
Belgrave Gate	C1	Lee Street	C1
Belvoir Street	C3	London Road	D3
Bishop Street	C3	Lower Brown Street	B3
Bonners Lane	B4	Magazine Square	B3
Bowling Green Street	C3	Mansfield Street	B1
Burgess Street	B1	Market Place South	B2
Burton Street	D2	Market Street	C3
Calais Hill	C3	Mill Lane	A4
Campbell Street	D3	Morledge Street	D1
Cank Street	B2	Newarke Street	B3
Castle Street	A3	New Walk	C3
Charles Street	C1	Oxford Street	B3
Chatham Street	C3	Peacock Lane	B2
Cheapside	C2	Pocklington Walk	B3
Church Gate	B1	Princess Road East	D4
Clyde Street	D1	Princess Road West	C4
Colton Street	C2	Queen Street	D2
Conduit Street	D3	Regent Road	C4
Crafton Street West	D1	Regent Street	D4
Deacon Street	B4	Richard III Road	A2
De Montfort Street	D4	Rutland Street	C2
Dover Street	C3	St Augustine Road	A2
Duke Street	C3	St George Street	D2
Duns Lane	A3	St Georges Way	D2
East Bond Street Lane	B1	St James Street	C1
Erskine Street	D1	St Matthews Way	D1
Fleet Street	C1	St Nicholas Circle	A2
Friar Lane	B3	Sanvey Gate	A1
Gallowtree Gate	C2	Soar Lane	A1
Gateway Street	A3	South Albion Street	D3
Granby Street	C2	Southampton Street	D2
Grasmere Street	A4	Southgates	B3
Gravel Street	B1	Station Street	D3
Great Central Street	A1	The Newarke	A3
Greyfriars	B2	Tower Street	C4
Halford Street	C2	Vaughan Way	A2
Haymarket	C2	Waterloo Way	D4
Highcross Street	A1	Welford Road	C4
Highcross Street	B2	Welles Street	A2
High Street	B2	Wellington Street	C3
Hill Street	C1	Western Boulevard	A4
Horsefair Street	B3	West Street	C4
Humberstone Gate	C2	Wharf Street South	D1
Humberstone Road	D1	Yeoman Street	C2

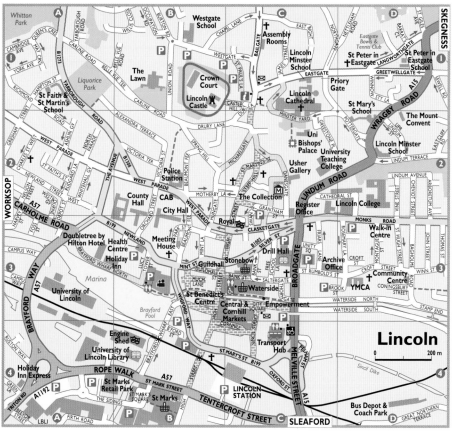

Lincoln

Lincoln is found on atlas page **86 C6**

Alexandra Terrace	B2	Montague Street	D3
Arboretum Avenue	D2	Motherby Lane	B2
Bagholme Road	D3	Nelson Street	A2
Bailgate	C1	Newland	B3
Bank Street	C3	Newland Street West	A2
Beaumont Fee	B3	Northgate	C1
Belle Vue Terrace	A1	Orchard Street	B3
Brayford Way	A4	Oxford Street	C4
Brayford Wharf East	B4	Park Street	B3
Brayford Wharf North	A3	Pelham Street	C4
Broadgate	C3	Pottergate	D2
Burton Road	B1	Queen's Crescent	A1
Carholme Road	A2	Richmond Road	A1
Carline Road	A1	Rope Walk	A4
Cathedral Street	C2	Rosemary Lane	D3
Chapel Lane	B1	Rudgard Lane	A2
Charles Street West	A2	St Hugh Street	D3
Cheviot Street	D2	St Mark Street	B4
City Square	C3	St Martin's Street	C2
Clasketgate	C3	St Mary's Street	B4
Cornhill	B4	St Rumbold's Street	C3
Croft Street	D3	Saltergate	C3
Danesgate	C2	Silver Street	C3
Depot Street	A3	Sincil Street	C4
Drury Lane	B2	Spring Hill	B2
East Bight	C1	Steep Hill	C2
Eastgate	C1	Swan Street	C3
Free School Lane	C3	Tentercroft Street	B4
Friars Lane	C3	The Avenue	A2
Grantham Street	C2	Thorngate	C3
Greetwellgate	D1	Triton Road	A4
Gresham Street	A2	Union Road	B1
Guildhall Street	B3	Unity Square	C3
Hampton Street	A1	Victoria Street	B2
High Street	B3	Victoria Terrace	B2
Hungate	B3	Vine Street	D2
John Street	D3	Waterside North	C3
Langworthgate	D1	Waterside South	C3
Lindum Road	C2	Westgate	B1
Lindum Terrace	D2	West Parade	A2
Lucy Tower Street	B3	Whitehall Grove	A2
May Crescent	A1	Wigford Way	B3
Melville Street	C4	Winnow Sty Lane	D1
Michaelgate	C2	Winn Street	D3
Minster Yard	C2	Wragby Road	D2
Mint Lane	B3	Yarborough Road	A1
Mint Street	B3	York Avenue	A1
Monks Road	D3		

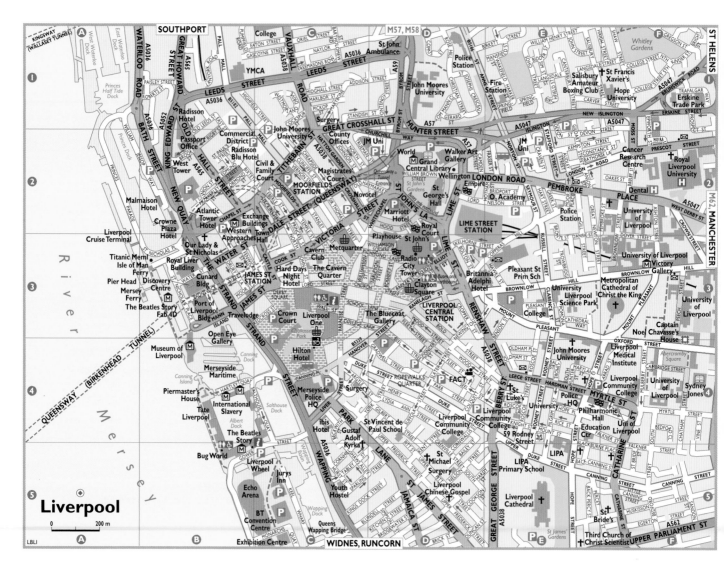

Liverpool

Liverpool is found on atlas page **81 L6**

Addison Street.................C1
Anson Street...................E2
Argyle Street..................C4
Arrad Street....................F4
Ashton Street..................F2
Audley Street..................E2
Back Canning Street........E5
Baltimore Street..............E4
Bath Street.....................B2
Beckwith Street...............C4
Bedford Street South.......F5
Benson Street.................E3
Berry Street...................E4
Bidder Street..................E1
Birkett Street..................D1
Bixteth Street.................B2
Blackburne Place............E5
Blundell Street................C5
Bold Street.....................D3
Bosnett Street................D3
Bridgewater Street..........D5
Bridport Street...............E2
Brook Street...................B2
Brownlow Hill.................E3
Brownlow Street.............F3
Brunswick Road..............F1
Brunswick Street.............B3
Byrom Street..................D1
Cambridge Street............F4
Camden Street................D2
Canning Place.................C4
Canning Street................E5
Canterbury Street...........E1
Carver Street..................E1
Castle Street...................C3
Catharine Street..............F5

Cathedral Way................E3
Chapel Street..................B2
Chatham Street...............F4
Cheapside......................C2
Christian Street...............D1
Churchill Way.................D2
Church Street.................C3
Clarence Street...............E3
Cockspur Street..............C1
College Lane...................C3
College Street North........F1
College Street South........F1
Colquitt Street................D4
Constance Street.............E2
Cook Street....................C3
Copperas Hill.................E3
Cornhill.........................C5
Cornwallis Street.............D5
Craven Street.................E2
Cropper Street................D3
Crosshall Street...............C2
Crown Street..................F2
Dale Street (Queensway)...C2
Dansie Street..................E3
Daulby Street..................F2
Derby Square..................C3
Devon Street..................E2
Dover Street...................F3
Drury Lane.....................B3
Duke Street....................D4
East Street.....................B1
Eaton Street...................B1
Eberle Street...................C2
Edmund Street................B2
Egerton Street................F5
Elliot Street....................D3

Epworth Street...............F1
Erskine Street.................F1
Falkner Street.................E4
Fazakerley Street.............B2
Fenwick Street................B3
Fleet Street.....................D3
Fontenoy Street..............D1
Fraser Street...................E2
Gascoyne Street..............B1
Gilbert Street..................D4
Gildart Street..................E2
Gill Street......................E2
Gower Street..................B5
Gradwell Street...............D4
Great Crosshall Street......C1
Great George Street.........E5
Great Howard Street........B1
Great Newton Street........E2
Greek Street...................E2
Gregson Street................F1
Grenville Street South.......D5
Hackins Hey....................C2
Hanover Street................C4
Hardman Street...............E4
Harker Street..................E1
Hartley Quay..................B4
Hart Street.....................E2
Hatton Garden................C2
Hawke Street..................E3
Henry Street...................D4
Highfield Street...............B1
Hood Street...................D2
Hope Place.....................E5
Hope Street....................E5
Hotham Street................E2
Hunter Street.................D1
Huskisson Street.............F5
Islington........................D2
Jamaica Street................D5
James Street...................B3
Johnson Street................C2

Keel Wharf.....................C5
Kempston Street.............E2
Kent Street.....................D5
Kinder Street..................F1
King Edward Street..........B2
Kingsway (Wallasey Tunnel)..A1
Kitchen Street.................D5
Knight Street..................E4
Langsdale Street..............E1
Leece Street...................E4
Leeds Street...................B1
Lime Street.....................D2
Liver Street....................C4
London Road..................D2
London Road..................E2
Lord Nelson Street...........D2
Lord Street.....................C3
Lydia Ann Street.............D4
Mann Island...................B3
Mansfield Street..............E1
Marybone......................C1
Maryland Street..............E4
Midghall Street...............C1
Moorfields......................C2
Moor Street...................B3
Moss Street....................F1
Mount Pleasant..............E3
Mount Street..................E4
Mulberry Street...............E4
Myrtle Street...................F4
Naylor Street..................C1
Nelson Street..................D5
Newington.....................E4
New Islington..................E1
New Quay......................B2
North John Street............C3
Norton Street.................E2
Old Hall Street................B2
Oldham Street.................E4
Old Haymarket...............C2
Old Leeds Street..............B1

Ormond Street................B2
Oxford Street.................F4
Paisley Street..................B1
Pall Mall........................B1
Paradise Street................C3
Parker Street..................D3
Park Lane.......................C4
Parr Street.....................D4
Peech Street...................F3
Pembroke Place..............E2
Pembroke Street.............F2
Percey Street..................E5
Pilgrim Street..................E4
Pleasant Street................E3
Pomona Street................E3
Prescot Street.................F2
Princes Parade................A2
Prospect Street...............F1
Queensway
  (Birkenhead Tunnel).....A4
Ranelagh Street...............D3
Redcross Street...............C3
Renshaw Street...............D3
Richmond Lane...............C3
Rigby Street....................B2
Rodney Street.................E4
Roscoe Street.................E4
Rose Hill........................D1
Russell Street..................E3
St Anne Street................D1
St James Street...............D5
St John's Lane.................D2
St Josephs Crescent.........D1
St Nicholas Place.............B3
St Paul's Street................B2
Salisbury Street...............E1
Salthouse Quay...............C4
Sandon Street.................F5
School Lane....................C3
Seel Street.....................D4
Seymour Street...............E2

Shaw Street....................F1
Sir Thomas Street............C2
Skelhorne Street.............D3
Slater Street...................D4
Soho Street.....................E1
Sparling Street................C5
Springfield......................E1
Stafford Street................E2
Stanley Street..................C2
Strand Street..................B3
Suffolk Street..................D4
Tabley Street..................C5
Tarleton Street................D3
Temple Street.................C2
The Strand.....................B3
Tithe Barn Street.............C2
Trafalgar Way.................F1
Trowbridge Street...........E3
Trueman Street...............C2
Upper Duke Street...........E5
Upper Frederick Street.....D4
Upper Parliament Street....F5
Upper Pitt Street.............D5
Vauxhall Road.................C1
Vernon Street.................C2
Victoria Street................C3
Wakefield Street..............E1
Wall Street.....................C3
Wapping........................C5
Waterloo Road................A1
Water Street...................B3
West Derby Street............F2
Westmorland Drive..........C1
Whitechapel....................D2
William Brown Street........D2
William Henry Street.........E1
William Jessop Way..........A2
Williamson Square...........D3
Williamson Street.............C3
Wood Street...................D3
York Street.....................D3

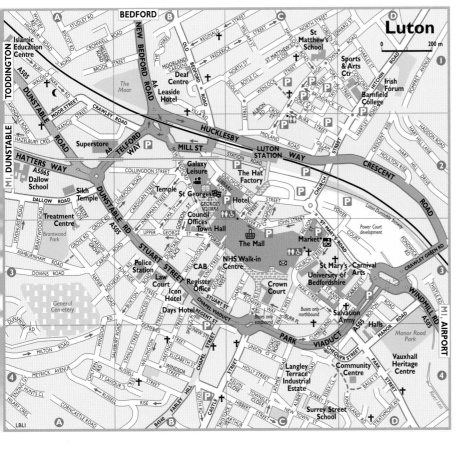

Luton

Luton is found on atlas page **50 C6**

Adelaide Street	B3	Hibbert Street	C4
Albert Road	C4	Highbury Road	A1
Alma Street	B2	High Town Road	C1
Arthur Street	C4	Hitchin Road	D1
Ashburnham Road	A3	Holly Street	C4
Biscot Road	A1	Hucklesby Way	B2
Brantwood Road	A3	Inkerman Street	B3
Brunswick Street	C1	John Street	C3
Burr Street	C2	King Street	B3
Bury Park Road	A1	Latimer Road	C4
Bute Street	C2	Liverpool Road	B2
Buxton Road	B3	Manor Road	D4
Cardiff Road	A3	Meyrick Avenue	A4
Cardigan Street	B2	Midland Road	C2
Castle Street	B4	Mill Street	B2
Chapel Street	B4	Milton Road	A4
Chapel Viaduct	B3	Moor Street	A1
Charles Street	D1	Napier Road	A3
Chequer Street	C4	New Bedford Road	B1
Church Street	C2	New Town Street	C4
Church Street	C3	Old Bedford Road	B1
Cobden Street	C1	Park Street	C3
Collingdon Street	B2	Park Street West	C3
Concorde Street	D1	Park Viaduct	C4
Crawley Green Road	D3	Princess Street	B3
Crawley Road	A1	Regent Street	B3
Crescent Road	D2	Reginald Street	B1
Cromwell Road	A1	Rothesay Road	A3
Cumberland Street	C4	Russell Rise	A4
Dallow Road	A2	Russell Street	B4
Dudley Street	C1	St Mary's Road	C3
Dumfries Street	B4	St Saviour's Crescent	A4
Dunstable Road	A1	Salisbury Road	A4
Farley Hill	B4	Stanley Street	B4
Flowers Way	C3	Station Road	C2
Frederick Street	B1	Strathmore Avenue	D4
George Street	B3	Stuart Street	B3
George Street West	B3	Surrey Street	C4
Gordon Street	B3	Tavistock Street	B4
Grove Road	A3	Telford Way	B2
Guildford Street	B2	Upper George Street	B3
Hart Hill Drive	D2	Vicarage Street	D3
Hart Hill Lane	D2	Waldeck Road	A1
Hartley Road	D2	Wellington Street	B4
Hastings Street	B4	Wenlock Street	C1
Hatters Way	A2	Windmill Road	D3
Havelock Road	C1	Windsor Street	B4
Hazelbury Crescent	A2	Winsdon Road	A4

Maidstone

Maidstone is found on atlas page **38 C10**

Albany Street	D1	Market Buildings	B2
Albion Place	D2	Marsham Street	C2
Allen Street	D1	Meadow Walk	D4
Ashford Road	D3	Medway Street	B3
Bank Street	B3	Melville Road	C4
Barker Road	B4	Mill Street	B3
Bedford Place	A3	Mote Avenue	D3
Bishops Way	B3	Mote Road	D3
Brewer Street	C2	Old School Place	D2
Broadway	A3	Orchard Street	C4
Broadway	B3	Padsole Lane	C3
Brunswick Street	C4	Palace Avenue	B3
Buckland Hill	A2	Princes Street	D1
Buckland Road	A2	Priory Road	C4
Camden Street	C1	Pudding Lane	B2
Chancery Lane	D3	Queen Anne Road	D2
Charles Street	A4	Reginald Road	A4
Church Street	C2	Rocky Hill	A3
College Avenue	B4	Romney Place	C3
College Road	C4	Rose Yard	B2
County Road	C1	Rowland Close	A4
Crompton Gardens	D4	St Anne Court	A2
Cromwell Road	D2	St Faith's Street	B2
Douglas Road	A4	St Luke's Avenue	D1
Earl Street	B2	St Luke's Road	D1
Elm Grove	D4	St Peters Street	A2
Fairmeadow	B1	Sandling Road	B1
Florence Road	A4	Sittingbourne Road	D1
Foley Street	D1	Square Hill Road	D3
Foster Street	C4	Stacey Street	B1
Gabriel's Hill	C3	Station Road	B1
George Street	C4	Terrace Road	A3
Greenside	D4	Tonbridge Road	A4
Hart Street	A4	Tufton Street	C2
Hastings Road	D4	Union Street	C2
Hayle Road	D4	Upper Stone Street	C4
Heathorn Street	D1	Victoria Street	A3
Hedley Street	C1	Vinters Road	D2
High Street	B3	Wat Tyler Way	C3
Holland Road	D1	Week Street	B1
James Street	C1	Well Road	C1
Jeffrey Street	C1	Westree Road	A4
King Street	C2	Wheeler Street	C1
Kingsley Road	D4	Woollett Street	C1
Knightrider Street	C4	Wyatt Street	C2
Lesley Place	A1		
London Road	A3		
Lower Stone Street	C3		

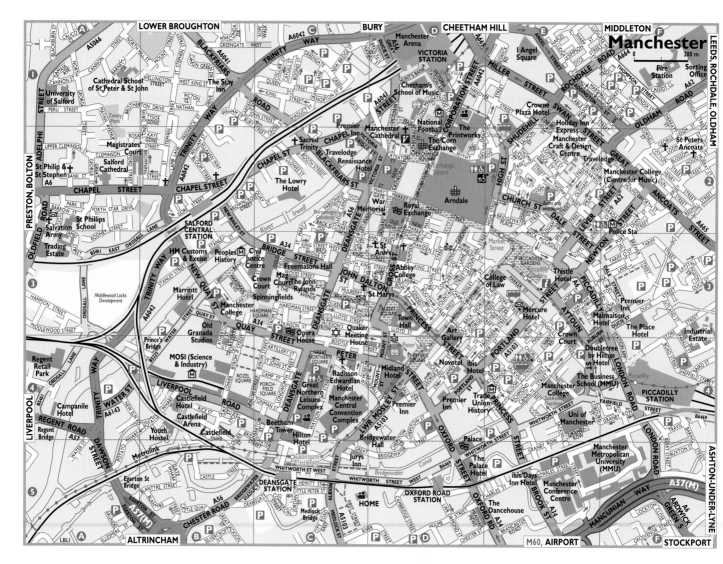

Manchester

Manchester is found on atlas page **82 H5**

Abingdon Street	E4	Browning Street	B2
Addington Street	E1	Brown Street	D3
Adelphi Street	A2	Bury Street	B1
Albion Street	C5	Byrom Street	B4
Angel Street	E1	Cable Street	E1
Ardwick Green South	F5	Cambridge Street	D5
Artillery Street	C4	Camp Street	C4
Atherton Street	B4	Canal Street	E4
Atkinson Street	C3	Cannon Street	A1
Auburn Street	E4	Canon Green Drive	B1
Aytoun Street	E3	Castle Street	B5
Back Piccadilly	E3	Cathedral Street	D2
Bank Street	A2	Chadderton Street	F1
Baring Street	F4	Chapel Street	A2
Barton Street	C4	Charles Street	E5
Berry Street	F4	Charlotte Street	D3
Blackfriars Road	B1	Chatham Street	E3
Blackfriars Street	C2	Cheapside	D3
Blantyre Street	B5	Chester Road	B5
Bloom Street	B2	China Lane	E3
Bloom Street	E4	Chorlton Street	E4
Blossom Street	F2	Church Street	E2
Boad Street	F4	City Road East	C5
Boond Street	C1	Cleminson Street	A2
Booth Street	D3	College Land	C2
Bootle Street	C4	Collier Street	C1
Brancaster Road	E5	Commercial Street	C5
Brazennose Street	C3	Copperas Street	E2
Brewer Street	F3	Cornell Street	F2
Bridge Street	C3	Corporation Street	D2
Bridgewater Place	E2	Cotton Street	F2
Bridgewater Street	B4	Crosskeys Street	F1
Bridgewater Viaduct	B5	Cross Street	C2
Brook Street	E5	Cross Street	D3
Brotherton Drive	A1	Dale Street	E2
Browncross Street	B2	Dantzic Street	D2
Dawson Street	A5	John Street	D1
Deansgate	C4	John Street	E2
Dickinson Street	D4	Joiner Street	E2
Duke Street	B4	Jutland Street	F3
Dulcie Street	F3	Kennedy Street	D3
East Ordsall Lane	A3	King Street	C1
Egerton Street	A5	King Street	C3
Exchange Square	D2	King Street West	C3
Fairfield Street	F4	Lamb Lane	B2
Faulkner Street	D4	Laystall Street	F3
Fennel Street	D1	Left Bank	B3
Ford Street	A2	Lena Street	F3
Fountain Street	D3	Lever Street	E2
Frederick Street	B2	Little Lever Street	E3
Garden Lane	B2	Little Peter Street	C5
Gartside Street	B3	Liverpool Road	B4
George Leigh Street	F2	Lloyd Street	C3
George Street	D4	London Road	F4
Gore Street	B2	Long Millgate	D1
Granby Row	E5	Longworth Street	C3
Gravel Lane	C1	Lower Byrom Street	B4
Great Ancoats Street	F2	Lower Mosley Street	C4
Great Bridgewater Street	C5	Lower Ormond Street	D5
Great Ducie Street	D1	Ludgate Street	E1
Great George Street	A2	Major Street	E4
Great Jackson Street	B5	Mancunian Way	E5
Great John Street	B4	Marble Street	D3
Greengate	C1	Market Street	D2
Greengate West	B1	Marsden Street	D3
Gun Street	F2	Marshall Street	E1
Hanover Street	D1	Mason Street	E1
Hardman Street	C3	Mayan Avenue	A1
Hewitt Street	C5	Medlock Street	C5
High Street	E2	Middlewood Street	A3
Hood Street	E3	Miller Street	E1
Hope Street	E3	Minshull Street	D4
Houndsworth Street	F2	Mirabel Street	C1
Hulme Street	D5	Mosley Street	D3
James Street	A3	Mount Street	B1
Jersey Street	F2	Mount Street	D4
John Dalton Street	C3	Museum Street	C4
Nathan Drive	B1	Sackville Street	E4
New Bailey Street	B2	St Anns Square	C2
New Bridge Street	C1	St Ann Street	C3
New Cathedral Street	D2	St James Square	C3
New Elm Road	A4	St James Street	D4
New George Street	E2	St Mary's Parsonage	C3
New Quay Street	B3	St Stephen Street	B2
Newton Street	E3	Store Street	F3
New York Street	E3	Sharp Street	E1
Nicholas Street	D3	Shudehill	E2
North George Street	A1	Silk Street	A1
North Hill Street	A1	Simpson Street	E1
North Star Drive	A2	South King Street	C3
Norton Street	C1	Spear Street	E3
Oldfield Road	A3	Spring Gardens	D3
Oldham Road	F1	Station Approach	F3
Oldham Street	E2	Swan Street	E1
Ordsall Lane	A4	Tariff Street	F3
Oxford Road	D5	Thomas Street	E2
Oxford Street	D4	Thompson Street	F1
Pall Mall	D3	Tib Lane	D3
Parker Street	E3	Tib Street	E2
Peru Street	A1	Todd Street	D1
Peter Street	C4	Tonman Street	C4
Piccadilly	E3	Travis Street	F3
Piccadilly Gardens	E3	Trinity Way	A4
Portland Street	D4	Turner Street	E2
Port Street	F3	Victoria Bridge Street	C2
Potato Wharf	A5	Victoria Station Approach	D1
Princess Street	D3	Victoria Street	D2
Quay Street	B3	Warwick Street	E1
Queen Street	C1	Watson Street	C4
Queen Street	C3	Well Street	D2
Redhill Street	F2	West King Street	B1
Regent Road	A4	West Mosley Street	D3
Reyner Street	D4	Whitworth Street	D5
Rice Street	B4	Whitworth Street West	C5
Richmond Street	E4	Windmill Street	C4
Rochdale Road	E1	Withy Grove	D2
Rodney Street	A3	Wood Street	C3
Rosamond Drive	A2	York Street	D3

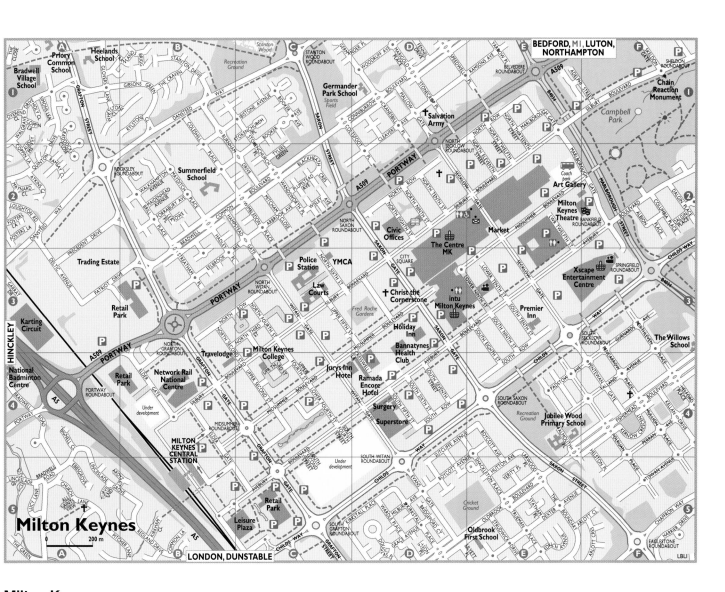

Milton Keynes

Milton Keynes is found on atlas page **49 N7**

Adelphi Street.................................E1
Albion Place...................................F2
All Saints View...............................A5
Arbrook Avenue.............................C2
Ardys Court...................................A5
Arlott Close....................................E5
Arlott Crescent.............................F5
Atkins Close...................................A2
Audley Mews..................................A2
Avebury Boulevard.........................C5
Bankfield Roundabout....................E2
Belvedere Roundabout....................E1
Bignell Close...................................A4
Blackheath Crescent......................C2
Booker Avenue..............................C1
Boycott Avenue..............................D5
Boycott Avenue..............................E4
Bradwell Common
    Boulevard..................................B2
Bradwell Road................................A4
Bradwell Road................................A5
Bridgeford Court............................D5
Brill Place......................................B2
Burnham Drive...............................B1
Chaffron Way.................................F5
Childs Way.....................................C5
Childs Way.....................................F3
Church Lane...................................A5
City Square.....................................D3
Cleavers Avenue.............................D1
Coleshill Place.................................B1
Coltsfoot Place...............................C1
Columbia Place...............................F2
Common Lane.................................B5
Conniburrow Boulevard.................C1
Coppin Lane....................................A2

Craddocks Close............................A1
Cranesbill Place...............................D1
Cresswell Lane................................D3
Dalgin Place....................................F2
Dansteed Way.................................A2
Dansteed Way.................................B1
Deltic Avenue.................................A3
Dexter Avenue...............................E5
Douglas Place..................................D5
Eaglestone Roundabout.................F5
Ebbsgrove.......................................A5
Edrich Avenue................................E5
Eelbrook Avenue............................B3
Elder Gate......................................B4
Evans Gate......................................D5
Falmouth Place...............................E4
Fennel Drive...................................D1
Fishermead Boulevard....................F4
Forrabury Avenue...........................B2
Fosters Lane...................................A2
Garrat Drive...................................A3
Germander Place............................C1
Gibsons Green.................................B1
Glovers Lane...................................A1
Grace Avenue.................................D5
Grafton Gate..................................B4
Grafton Street................................A1
Grafton Street................................C5
Gurnards Avenue............................F3
Hadley Place...................................B2
Hampstead Gate.............................B2
Harrier Drive.................................F5
Helford Place..................................F4
Helston Place..................................F4
Holy Close......................................A1
Hutton Avenue...............................E5

Ibistone Avenue.............................C1
Kellan Drive...................................F4
Kernow Crescent...........................F4
Kirkham Close................................B5
Kirkstall Place.................................C5
Larwood Place................................E5
Leasowe Place................................B2
Linceslade Grove............................A5
Loughton Road...............................A2
Lower Fourth Street.....................C4
Lower Ninth Street........................E3
Lower Tenth Street........................E3
Lower Twelfth Street.....................E2
Lucy Lane.......................................A5
Maidenhead Avenue.......................B2
Mallow Gate...................................D1
Marigold Place................................D1
Marlborough Gate..........................E1
Marlborough Gate..........................E2
Marlborough Street........................F2
Mayditch Place...............................B2
Maynard Close................................A2
Midsummer Boulevard....................C4
Midsummer Boulevard....................E2
Midsummer Roundabout.................B4
Milburn Avenue..............................D5
Mitcham Close................................C2
Mullion Place..................................F4
North Eighth Street........................D2
North Eleventh Street....................E1
North Fourth Street.......................C3
North Grafton
    Roundabout..............................B3
North Ninth Street.........................D2
North Row......................................B3
North Row......................................D2

North Saxon Roundabout..............C2
North Secklow
    Roundabout..............................D1
North Second Street......................B3
North Sixth Street..........................C3
North Tenth Street........................D2
North Third Street.........................C3
North Thirteenth Street................E1
North Twelfth Street.....................E1
North Witan Roundabout..............C3
Oldbrook Boulevard.......................E5
Overend Close................................A1
Padstow Avenue.............................E4
Patriot Drive..................................A3
Pencarrow Place.............................F3
Pentewan Gate...............................F4
Perran Avenue................................F4
Pitcher Lane...................................A5
Plumstead Avenue..........................C2
Polruan Place..................................F4
Porthleven Place............................F3
Portway..A4
Portway Roundabout......................A4
Precedent Drive.............................A3
Quinton Drive................................A2
Ramsay Close..................................A2
Ramsons Avenue.............................E1
Redland Drive.................................B5
Rooksley Roundabout.....................A2
Rylstone Close................................B1
Saxon Gate.....................................D2
Saxon Street...................................C1
Secklow Gate..................................D2
Shackleton Place............................E5
Sheldon Roundabout......................F1
Silbury Boulevard...........................B4

Silbury Roundabout........................B4
Simons Lea.....................................A1
Skeldon Gate..................................F1
South Eighth Street........................E3
South Fifth Street...........................D4
South Fourth Street.......................C4
South Grafton Roundabout............C5
South Ninth Street.........................E3
South Row......................................D4
South Saxon Roundabout...............E4
South Secklow Roundabout............E3
South Second Street.......................C5
South Seventh Street......................D4
South Sixth Street...........................D4
South Tenth Street.........................E3
South Witan Roundabout...............D5
Speedwell Place..............................D1
Springfield Roundabout..................F3
Stainton Drive................................B1
Stanton Wood
    Roundabout..............................C1
Statham Place.................................E5
Stokenchurch Place........................C1
Stonecrop Place..............................D1
Streatham Place.............................B3
Strudwick Drive.............................E5
Sutcliffe Avenue.............................D4
Talland Avenue...............................F4
The Boundary.................................E5
The Close..A1
The Craven.....................................B1
The Green.......................................A5
Towan Avenue................................F5
Tranlands Brigg...............................B1
Trueman Place................................E5
Turvil End.......................................A5

Tylers Green....................................C2
Tyson Place.....................................D5
Ulyett Place....................................D5
Upper Fifth Street..........................C3
Upper Fourth Street.......................C4
Upper Second Street......................C4
Upper Third Street.........................C4
Verity Place....................................E5
Walgrave Drive...............................A1
Walkhampton Avenue....................B2
Wandsworth Place..........................C2
Wardle Place..................................D5
Whetstone Close............................A1
Wimbledon Place...........................C2
Wisely Avenue................................C2
Witan Gate.....................................C3
Woodruff Avenue...........................D1
Yarrow Place...................................E1

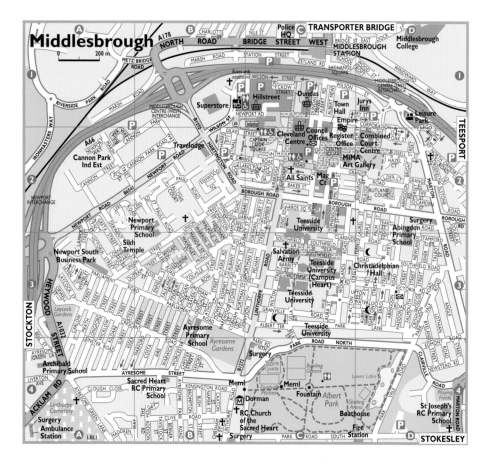

Middlesbrough

Middlesbrough is found on atlas page **104 E7**

Acklam Road	A4	Heywood Street	A3
Acton Street	C3	Ironmasters Way	A2
Aire Street	B4	Kensington Road	B4
Albert Road	C2	Kildare Street	A4
Amber Street	C2	Laurel Street	D3
Athol Street	B3	Lees Road	A2
Aubrey Street	D3	Linthorpe Road	B4
Ayresome Park Road	B4	Longford Street	A4
Ayresome Street	A4	Lorne Street	A3
Borough Road	C2	Lothian Road	D3
Bretnall Street	B2	Marsh Street	A2
Bridge Street East	C1	Marton Road	D2
Bridge Street West	C1	Melrose Street	D2
Bush Street	B4	Metz Bridge Road	A1
Cadogen Street	B3	Myrtle Street	D3
Camden Street	D2	Newlands Road	D3
Cannon Park Road	A2	Newport Road	A2
Cannon Park Way	A2	Palm Street	D3
Cannon Street	A2	Park Lane	D3
Carlow Street	A3	Park Road North	C4
Centre Square	C2	Park Vale Road	D4
Clairville Road	D4	Parliament Road	A3
Clarendon Road	C3	Pearl Street	C2
Clifton Street	B3	Pelham Street	D3
Corporation Road	D1	Portman Street	B3
Costa Street	B4	Princes Road	B3
Craven Street	B3	Riverside Park Road	A1
Crescent Road	A3	Ruby Street	C2
Croydon Road	D3	Russell Street	D2
Derwent Street	A2	St Pauls Road	B2
Diamond Road	B3	Southfield Road	C3
Egmont Road	D4	Station Street	C1
Emily Street	C2	Stowe Street	B3
Errol Street	D3	Tavistock Street	B4
Essex Street	A4	Tennyson Street	B3
Fairbridge Street	C2	Union Street	A3
Falmouth Street	D3	Victoria Road	C3
Finsbury Street	B3	Victoria Street	A3
Fleetham Street	B2	Warren Street	A2
Garnet Street	B2	Waterloo Road	D3
Glebe Road	B3	Waverley Street	B3
Grange Road	B2	Wembley Street	A3
Grange Road	D2	Wilson Street	B2
Granville Road	C3	Wilton Street	C2
Gresham Road	B3	Windsor Street	B2
Harewood Street	B3	Woodlands Road	C3
Harford Street	B4	Worcester Street	B4
Hartington Road	B2	Zetland Road	C1

Newport

Newport is found on atlas page **31 K7**

Albert Terrace	B3	Jones Street	B3
Allt-Yr-Yn Avenue	A2	Keynsham Avenue	C4
Bailey Street	B3	King Street	C4
Bedford Road	D2	Kingsway	C4
Blewitt Street	B3	Kingsway	C4
Bond Street	C1	Llanthewy Road	A3
Bridge Street	B2	Locke Street	B1
Bryngwyn Road	A3	Lower Dock Street	C4
Brynhyfryd Avenue	A4	Lucas Street	B1
Brynhyfryd Road	A4	Market Street	B2
Caerau Crescent	A4	Mellon Street	C4
Caerau Road	A3	Mill Street	B2
Cambrian Road	B2	North Street	B3
Caroline Street	D3	Oakfield Road	A3
Cedar Road	D2	Park Square	C4
Charles Street	C3	Queen's Hill	B1
Chepstow Road	D1	Queen's Hill Crescent	A1
Clarence Place	C1	Queen Street	B2
Clifton Place	B4	Queensway	B2
Clifton Road	B4	Risca Road	A4
Clyffard Crescent	A3	Rodney Road	C2
Clytha Park Road	A2	Rudry Street	D1
Clytha Square	C4	Ruperra Lane	C4
Colts Foot Close	A1	Ruperra Street	D4
Commercial Street	C4	St Edward Street	B3
Corelli Street	D1	St Julian Street	B4
Corn Street	C2	St Mark's Crescent	A2
Corporation Road	D2	St Mary Street	B3
Devon Place	B2	St Vincent Road	C2
Dewsland Park Road	B4	St Woolos Road	B3
Dumfries Place	D4	School Lane	C3
East Street	B3	Serpentine Road	A2
East Usk Road	C1	Skinner Street	C2
Factory Road	B1	Sorrel Drive	A1
Fields Road	A2	Spencer Road	A3
Friars Field	B4	Stow Hill	B3
Friars Road	B4	Stow Hill	B4
Friar Street	C3	Stow Park Avenue	A4
George Street	D4	Talbot Lane	C3
Godfrey Road	A2	Tregare Street	D1
Gold Tops	A2	Tunnel Terrace	A3
Grafton Road	C2	Upper Dock Street	C2
Granville Lane	D4	Upper Dock Street	C3
Granville Street	D4	Usk Way	D3
High Street	B2	Victoria Crescent	B3
Hill Street	C3	West Street	B3
John Frost Square	C3	Wyndham Stret	C1
John Street	D4	York Place	A4

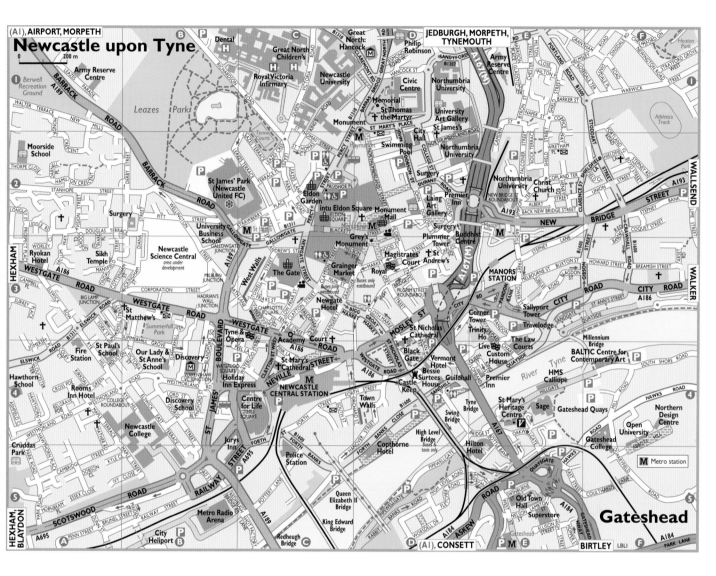

Newcastle upon Tyne

Newcastle upon Tyne is found on atlas page **113 K8**

Abbots Hill F4
Albert Street E2
Argyle Street E2
Askew Road D5
Avision Street A2
Back New Bridge Street E2
Barker Street E1
Barrack Road A1
Barras Bridge D1
Bath Lane B3
Belgrave Parade A4
Big Lamp Junction A3
Blackett Street C2
Blagdon Street E3
Blandford Square B4
Blandford Street B4
Bottle Bank E4
Boyd Street F2
Breamish Street F3
Bridge Street E4
Broad Chare E3
Brunel Street A5
Buckingham Street B3
Buxton Street E3
Byron Street E1
Cambridge Street A5
Camden Street E2
Campbell Place A3
Carliol Square D3
Charlotte Square C3
Chelmsford Green F1
Chester Street E1
City Road C3
Claremont Road D1
Clarence Street E2
Clayton Street C3

Clayton Street West C4
Cloth Market D3
Colby Court A4
College Roundabout A4
College Street D2
Cookson Close A3
Copland Terrace E2
Coppice Way E1
Coquet Street F2
Corporation Street B3
Cottenham Street A3
Coulthards Lane F5
Crawhall Road F2
Cross Parade A4
Cross Street C3
Darnell Place A2
Dean Street D3
Derby Street B2
Diana Street B3
Dinsdale Place F1
Dinsdale Road F1
Dobson Close A5
Douglas Terrace A2
Duke Street B4
Dunn Street A5
Durant Road D2
East Street E5
Edward Place A3
Eldon Square C2
Ellison Street E5
Elswick East Terrace B4
Elswick Road A3
Elswick Row A3
Essex Close A5
Falconar's Court C3
Falconer Street E2

Fenkle Street C3
Field Close F2
Fletcher Road D5
Forth Banks C4
Forth Banks Close D5
Forth Street C4
Friars Street C3
Gallowgate B2
Gallowgate Junction B3
Gateshead Highway E5
George Street B4
Gibson Street F3
Gladstone Terrace E1
Gloucester Terrace A4
Grainger Street C3
Grantham Road E1
Great North Road D1
Grey Street D3
Groat Market C3
Hamilton Crescent A2
Hanover Street C3
Harrison Place E1
Hawks Road E5
Hawthorn Place A4
Hawthorn Terrace A4
Helmsley Road E1
Henry Square E2
High Bridge D3
High Level Road D5
High Street E5
Hillgate E4
Hood Street D3
Hopper Street E5
Hornbeam Place A5
Houston Street A4
Howard Street F3
Hudson Street E5
Ivy Close A5
Jesmond Road West D1
John Dobson Street D2
Jubilee Road E3

King Edward Bridge C5
King Street E4
Kirkdale Green A4
Kyle Close A5
Lambton Street E5
Leazes Crescent C2
Leazes Lane C2
Leazes Park Road C2
Leazes Terrace C2
Liddle Road A2
Lime Street F2
Lombard Street E4
Longley Street A2
Lord Street B4
Low Friar Street C3
Maiden Street B5
Mansfield Street A3
Maple Street B5
Maple Terrace A4
Market Street D3
Mather Road A4
Melbourne Street E3
Mill Road F4
Milton Close E1
Milton Place E1
Monday Crescent A1
Mosley Street D3
Naper Street E1
Nelson Street C3
Nelson Street E5
Neville Street C4
New Bridge Street E2
Newgate Street C3
Newington Road F1
New Mills A1
Northumberland Road D2
Northumberland Street D2
Nun Street C3
Oakwellgate E4
Orchard Street C4
Ord Street B5

Oxford Street D2
Pandon E3
Pandon Bank E3
Park Lane F5
Park Road A5
Peel Lane B4
Penn Street A5
Percy Street C2
Pilgrim Street D2
Pink Lane C4
Pipewellgate D5
Pitt Street B2
Portland Road E1
Portland Road F1
Pottery Lane C5
Prospect Place A2
Prudhoe Place C2
Quarryfield Road F5
Quaysgate E5
Quayside F3
Quayside E4
Queen Street E4
Queen Victoria Road C1
Rabbit Banks Road D5
Railway Street B5
Red Barnes F2
Redheugh Bridge Road B5
Richardson Road B1
Rock Terrace E2
Rosedale Terrace E1
Rye Hill A4
St Andrew's Street C3
St Ann's Street F3
St James' Boulevard B4
St Mary's Place D1
St Nicholas Street D4
St Thomas' Court C2
St Thomas' Street C1
Sandgate E3
Sandhill D4
Sandyford Road D1

Scotswood Road A5
Shieldfield Lane F2
Shield Street E2
Shot Factory Lane C5
Simpson Terrace E2
Somerset Place A4
South Shore Road F4
South Street C4
Stanhope Street A2
Stepney Bank F2
Stepney Lane E3
Stepney Road E3
Stoddart Street F1
Stowell Street C3
Stratford Grove West F1
Strawberry Place C2
Summerhill Grove B3
Summerhill Street A3
Summerhill Terrace B4
Swinburne Street E5
Tarset Road F3
Terrace Place C2
Tindal Street A3
Tower Street E3
Tyne Bridge E4
Union Street F2
Vallum Way A3
Victoria Street B4
Walter Terrace A1
Warwick Street F1
Waterloo Square B4
Waterloo Street C4
Wellington Street B2
Westgate Road A3
Westmorland Road A4
West Street E5
West Walls C3
Worley Close A3
Worsdell Drive D5
Wretham Place E2
York Street A3

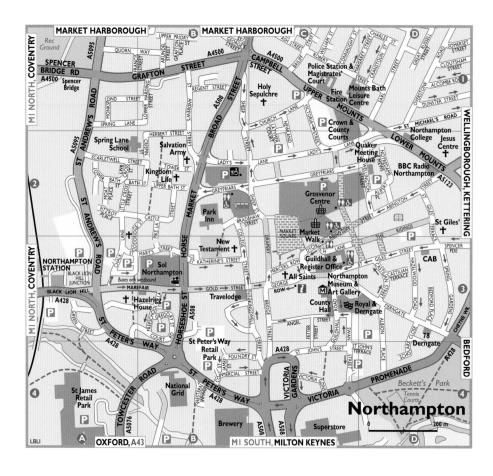

Northampton

Northampton is found on atlas page **60 G8**

Abington Street	C2	Little Cross Street	A2
Albert Place	D2	Lower Bath Street	A2
Albion Place	D3	Lower Cross Street	A2
Angel Street	C3	Lower Harding Street	B1
Arundel Street	B1	Lower Mounts	D2
Ash Street	C1	Marefair	A3
Bailiff Street	C1	Margaret Street	C1
Black Lion Hill	A3	Market Square	C2
Bradshaw Street	B2	Mercers Row	C2
Bridge Street	C3	Moat Place	A2
Broad Street	B1	Monkspond Street	A1
Campbell Street	C1	Newland	C2
Castilian Street	D3	Notredame Mews	D2
Castle Street	B2	Overstone Road	D1
Chalk Lane	A3	Pike Lane	B3
Cheyne Walk	D3	Quorn Way	A1
Church Lane	C1	Regent Street	B1
College Street	B2	Robert Street	C1
Commercial Street	B4	St Andrew's Road	A2
Connaught Street	C1	St Andrew's Street	B1
Court Road	B3	St Giles' Street	C2
Cranstoun Street	D1	St Giles' Terrace	D2
Crispin Street	B2	St John's Street	C4
Derngate	D3	St Katherine's Street	B3
Doddridge Street	A3	St Mary's Street	A3
Drapery	C3	St Michael's Road	D1
Dunster Street	D1	St Peter's Way	B4
Dychurch Lane	C3	Scarletwell Street	A2
Earl Street	D1	Scholars Close	D4
Fetter Street	C3	Sheep Street	B1
Fitzroy Place	A2	Sheep Street	C2
Foundry Street	B4	Spencer Bridge Road	A1
Francis Street	A1	Spencer Parade	D3
Freeschool Lane	B3	Spring Gardens	D3
George Row	C3	Spring Lane	A1
Gold Street	B3	Swan Street	C3
Grafton Street	A1	Tanner Street	A4
Great Russell Street	D1	The Ridings	D2
Green Street	A3	Towcester Road	A4
Gregory Street	B3	Tower Street	B2
Greyfriars	B2	Upper Bath Street	B2
Guildhall Road	C3	Upper Mounts	C2
Hazelwood Road	D3	Upper Priory Street	B1
Herbert Street	B2	Victoria Gardens	C4
Horse Market	B3	Victoria Promenade	C4
Horseshoe Street	B3	Victoria Street	C1
Kingswell Street	C3	Wellington Street	D2
Lady's Lane	B2	Western Wharf	B4

Norwich

Norwich is found on atlas page **77 J10**

All Saints Green	B4	Pottergate	A2
Bank Plain	C2	Prince of Wales Road	C2
Barn Road	A1	Princes Street	C2
Bedding Lane	C1	Quay Side	C1
Bedford Street	B2	Queens Road	B4
Ber Street	C4	Queen Street	C2
Bethel Street	A3	Rampant Horse Street	B3
Bishopgate	D1	Recorder Road	D2
Brigg Street	B3	Red Lion Street	B3
Calvert Street	B1	Riverside Road	D2
Castle Meadow	C3	Riverside Walk	D1
Cathedral Street	D2	Rose Lane	C3
Cattle Market Street	C3	Rouen Road	C3
Chantry Road	B3	Rupert Street	A4
Chapelfield East	A3	St Andrews Street	B2
Chapelfield North	A3	St Benedicts Street	A2
Chapelfield Road	A3	St Faiths Lane	D2
Cleveland Road	A3	St Georges Street	B1
Colegate	B1	St Giles Street	A2
Convent Road	A3	St Julians Alley	C4
Coslany Street	B2	St Marys Plain	B1
Cow Hill	A2	St Peters Street	B3
Davey Place	B3	St Stephens Road	B4
Dove Street	B2	St Stephens Square	A4
Duke Street	B1	St Stephens Street	B4
Elm Hill	C2	St Swithins Road	A2
Exchange Street	B2	St Verdast Street	D2
Farmers Avenue	C3	Surrey Street	B4
Ferry Lane	D2	Ten Bell Lane	A2
Fishergate	C1	Theatre Street	B3
Friars Quay	B1	Thorn Lane	C3
Gentlemans Walk	B3	Tombland	C2
Goldenball Street	C3	Unicorn Yard	A1
Grapes Hill	A2	Union Street	A3
Haymarket	B3	Unthank Road	A3
Heigham Street	A1	Upper Goat Lane	B2
King Street	C2	Upper King Street	C2
London Street	B2	Upper St Giles Street	A2
Lower Goat Lane	B2	Vauxhall Street	A3
Magdalen Street	C1	Walpole Street	A3
Market Avenue	C3	Wensum Street	C1
Mills Yard	A1	Wessex Street	A4
Mountergate	D3	Westlegate	B3
Music House Lane	D4	Westwick Street	A1
Muspole Street	B1	Wherry Road	D4
Norfolk Street	A4	Whitefriars	C1
Oak Street	A1	White Lion Street	B3
Palace Street	C1	Willow Lane	A2

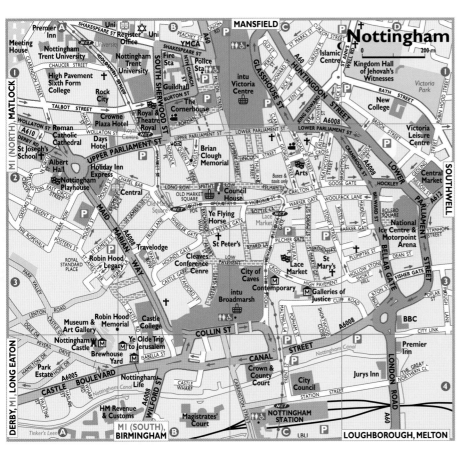

Nottingham

Nottingham is found on atlas page **72 F3**

Albert Street	B3	King Street	B2
Barker Gate	D2	Lenton Road	A3
Bath Street	D1	Lincoln Street	C2
Bellar Gate	D3	Lister Gate	B3
Belward Street	D2	London Road	D4
Broad Street	C2	Long Row	B2
Broadway	C3	Lower Parliament Street	C2
Bromley Place	A2	Low Pavement	B3
Brook Street	D1	Maid Marian Way	A2
Burton Street	B1	Market Street	B2
Canal Street	C4	Middle Hill	C3
Carlton Street	C2	Milton Street	B1
Carrington Street	C4	Mount Street	A3
Castle Boulevard	A4	Norfolk Place	B2
Castle Gate	B3	North Circus Street	A2
Castle Road	B3	Park Row	A3
Chapel Bar	B2	Pelham Street	C2
Chaucer Street	A1	Peveril Drive	A4
City Link	D3	Pilcher Gate	C3
Clarendon Street	A1	Popham Street	C3
Cliff Road	C3	Poultry	B2
Collin Street	B4	Queen Street	B2
Cranbrook Street	D2	Regent Street	A2
Cumber Street	C2	St Ann's Well Road	D1
Curzon Place	C1	St James's Street	A3
Derby Road	A2	St Marks Gate	C3
Exchange Walk	B2	St Marks Street	C1
Fisher Gate	D3	St Mary's Gate	C3
Fletcher Gate	C3	St Peter's Gate	B3
Forman Street	B1	Shakespeare Street	A1
Friar Lane	A3	Smithy Row	B2
Gedling Street	D2	South Parade	B2
George Street	C2	South Sherwood Street	B1
Glasshouse Street	C1	Spaniel Row	B3
Goldsmith Street	A1	Station Street	C4
Goose Gate	C2	Stoney Street	C2
Halifax Place	C3	Talbot Street	A1
Heathcote Street	C2	Thurland Street	C2
High Cross Street	C2	Trent Street	C4
High Pavement	C3	Upper Parliament Street	A2
Hockley	D2	Victoria Street	C2
Hollow Stone	D3	Warser Gate	C2
Hope Drive	A4	Weekday Cross	C3
Hounds Gate	B3	Wellington Circus	A2
Howard Street	C1	Wheeler Gate	B2
Huntingdon Street	C1	Wilford Street	B4
Kent Street	C1	Wollaton Street	A1
King Edward Street	C1	Woolpack Lane	C2

Oldham

Oldham is found on atlas page **83 K4**

Ascroft Street	B3	Napier Street East	A4
Bar Gap Road	B1	New Radcliffe Street	A2
Barlow Street	D4	Oldham Way	A3
Barn Street	B3	Park Road	B4
Beever Street	D2	Park Street	A2
Bell Street	D2	Peter Street	B3
Belmont Street	B1	Prince Street	D3
Booth Street	A3	Queen Street	C3
Bow Street	C3	Radcliffe Street	B1
Brook Street	D2	Ramsden Street	A1
Brunswick Street	B3	Regent Street	D2
Cardinal Street	C2	Rhodes Bank	C3
Chadderton Way	A1	Rhodes Street	C2
Chaucer Street	B3	Rifle Street	B1
Clegg Street	C3	Rochdale Road	A1
Coldhurst Road	B1	Rock Street	B2
Crossbank Street	B4	Roscoe Street	C3
Curzon Street	B2	Ruskin Street	A1
Dunbar Street	A1	St Hilda's Drive	A1
Eden Street	B2	St Marys Street	B2
Egerton Street	C2	St Mary's Way	B2
Emmott Way	C4	Shaw Road	D1
Firth Street	C3	Shaw Street	C1
Fountain Street	B2	Shore Street	D1
Franklin Street	B1	Siddall Street	C1
Gower Street	D2	Silver Street	B3
Grange Street	A2	Southgate Street	C3
Greaves Street	C3	South Hill Street	D4
Greengate Street	D4	Spencer Street	D2
Hardy Street	D4	Sunfield Road	B1
Harmony Street	C4	Thames Street	D1
Henshaw Street	B2	Trafalgar Street	A1
Higginshaw Road	C1	Trinity Street	B2
Highfield Street	A2	Tulbury Street	A1
High Street	B3	Union Street	B3
Hobson Street	B3	Union Street West	A4
Horsedge Street	C1	Union Street West	B3
John Street	A3	University Way	B4
King Street	B3	Wallshaw Street	D2
Lemnos Street	D2	Wall Street	B4
Malby Street	C1	Ward Street	A1
Malton Street	A4	Waterloo Street	C3
Manchester Street	A3	Wellington Street	B4
Market Place	B3	West End Street	A2
Marlborough Street	C4	West Street	B3
Middleton Road	A3	Willow Street	D2
Mortimer Street	D1	Woodstock Street	C4
Mumps	D2	Yorkshire Street	C3

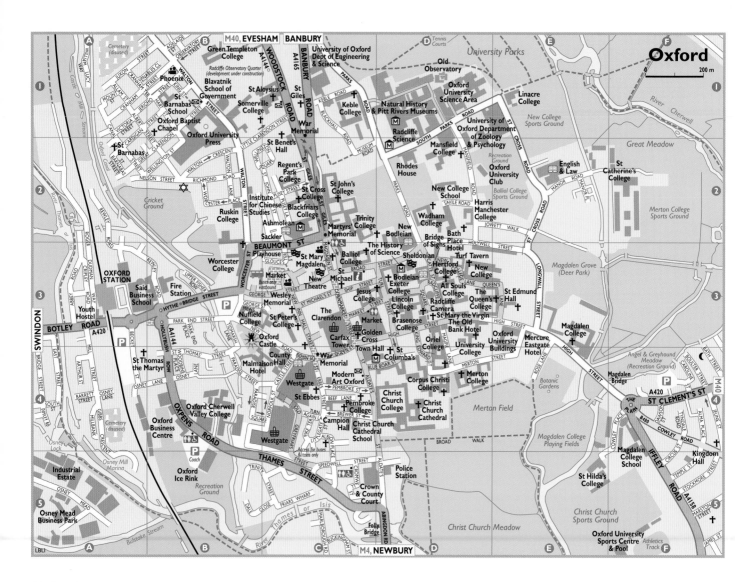

Oxford

Oxford is found on atlas page **34 F3**

Abbey Road...............A3	Cromwell Street...............C5	Marston Street...............F5	St Barnabas Street...............A2	**University Colleges**
Abingdon Road...............D5	Dale Close...............B5	Merton Street...............D4	St Clement's Street...............F4	
Adelaide Street...............B1	Dawson Street...............F4	Millbank...............A4	St Cross Road...............E1	
Albert Street...............A1	East Street...............A4	Mill Street...............A4	St Cross Road...............E2	All Souls College...............D3
Albion Place...............C4	Folly Bridge...............C5	Mount Street...............A1	St Ebbes Street...............C4	Balliol College...............C3
Allam Street...............A1	Friars Wharf...............C5	Museum Road...............C2	St Giles...............C2	Brasenose College...............D3
Alma Place...............F4	George Street...............B3	Nelson Street...............A2	St John Street...............C2	Christ Church College...............D4
Arthur Street...............A4	George Street Mews...............B3	New College Lane...............D3	St Michael's Street...............C3	Corpus Christi College...............D4
Banbury Road...............C1	Gibbs Crescent...............A4	New Inn Hall Street...............C3	St Thomas' Street...............B4	Exeter College...............D3
Barrett Street...............A4	Gloucester Street...............C3	New Road...............B3	Savile Road...............D2	Harris Manchester College...............D2
Bath Street...............F4	Great Clarendon Street...............A2	Norfolk Street...............C4	Ship Street...............C3	Hertford College...............D3
Beaumont Street...............C3	Hart Street...............B1	Observatory Street...............B1	South Parks Road...............D2	Jesus College...............C3
Becket Street...............A3	High Street...............D3	Old Greyfriars Street...............C4	South Street...............A4	Keble College...............C1
Beef Lane...............C4	High Street...............E4	Osney Lane...............A4	Speedwell Street...............C5	Linacre College...............E1
Blackhall Road...............C1	Hollybush Row...............B3	Osney Lane...............B4	Stockmore Street...............F5	Lincoln College...............D3
Blue Boar Street...............C4	Holywell Street...............D2	Osney Mead...............A5	Temple Street...............F5	Magdalen College...............E3
Bonn Square...............C4	Hythe Bridge Street...............B3	Oxpens Road...............B4	Thames Street...............C5	Mansfield College...............D2
Botley Road...............A3	Iffley Road...............F4	Paradise Square...............B4	The Plain...............F4	Merton College...............D4
Boulter Street...............F4	James Street...............F5	Paradise Street...............B4	Tidmarsh Lane...............B3	New College...............D3
Brewer Street...............C4	Jericho Street...............A1	Park End Street...............B3	Trinity Street...............B5	Nuffield College...............B3
Bridge Street...............A4	Jowett Walk...............D2	Parks Road...............C1	Turl Street...............D3	Oriel College...............D3
Broad Street...............C3	Juxon Street...............A1	Parks Road...............D2	Turn Again Lane...............C4	Pembroke College...............C4
Broad Walk...............D4	Keble Road...............C1	Pembroke Street...............C4	Tyndale Road...............F4	Ruskin College...............B2
Buckingham Street...............C5	King Edward Street...............D3	Pike Terrace...............C4	Upper Fisher Row...............B3	St Catherine's College...............F2
Canal Street...............A1	King Street...............B1	Pusey Lane...............C2	Venables Close...............A1	St Cross College...............C2
Cardigan Street...............A2	Little Clarendon Street...............B2	Pusey Street...............C2	Victoria Street...............A1	St Hilda's College...............E5
Caroline Street...............F4	Littlegate Street...............C4	Queen's Lane...............D3	Walton Crescent...............B2	St John's College...............C2
Castle Street...............C4	Longwall Street...............E3	Queen Street...............C4	Walton Lane...............B2	St Peter's College...............C3
Catte Street...............D3	Magdalen Bridge...............E4	Radcliffe Square...............D3	Walton Street...............B1	Somerville College...............B1
Circus Street...............F5	Magdalen Street...............C3	Rewley Road...............A2	Wellington Square...............B2	The Queen's College...............D3
Cornmarket Street...............C3	Magpie Lane...............D3	Rewley Road...............B3	Wellington Street...............B2	Trinity College...............C2
Cowley Place...............F4	Manor Place...............E2	Richmond Road...............B2	William Lucy Way...............A1	University College...............D3
Cowley Road...............F4	Manor Road...............E2	Roger Dudman Way...............A3	Woodbine Place...............B4	Wadham College...............D2
Cranham Street...............A1	Mansfield Road...............D2	Rose Lane...............E4	Woodstock Road...............C1	Worcester College...............B3
Cranham Terrace...............A1	Market Street...............C3	St Aldate's...............C4	Worcester Place...............B2	
Cripley Road...............A3	Marlborough Road...............C5	St Aldate's...............D5	Worcester Street...............B3	

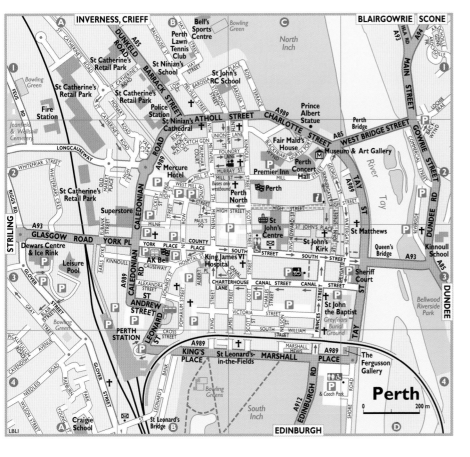

Perth

Perth is found on atlas page **134 E3**

Albert Place	B3		Melville Street	B1
Alexandra Street	B3		Mill Street	B2
Atholl Street	B1		Mill Street	C2
Back Wynd	D2		Milne Street	B2
Balhousie Street	B1		Monart Road	A1
Barossa Place	B1		Murray Street	B2
Barrack Street	B1		Needless Road	A4
Blackfriars Wynd	C2		New Row	B3
Black Watch Garden	B2		North Methven Street	B2
Caledonian Road	B2		North Port	C2
Caledonian Road	B3		North William Street	B2
Canal Street	C3		Old Market Place	A2
Cavendish Avenue	A4		Paul Street	B2
Charles Street	C3		Perth Bridge	D2
Charlotte Street	C2		Pickletullum Road	A4
Charterhouse Lane	B3		Pomarium Street	B3
Commercial Street	D2		Princes Street	C3
County Place	B3		Queen's Bridge	D3
Cross Street	B4		Raeburn Park	A4
Dundee Road	D3		Riggs Road	A2
Dunkeld Road	B1		Riverside	D3
Earls Dyke	A3		Rose Terrace	C1
Edinburgh Road	C4		St Andrew Street	B3
Elibank Street	A3		St Catherine's Road	A1
Feus Road	A1		St John's Place	C3
Foundry Lane	B2		St John Street	C3
George Street	C2		St Leonard's Bank	B4
Glasgow Road	A3		St Paul's Square	B2
Glover Street	A3		Scott Street	C3
Glover Street	A4		Shore Road	D4
Gowrie Street	D2		Skinnergate	C2
Gray Street	A3		South Methven Street	B2
Hay Street	B1		South Street	C3
High Street	B2		South William Street	C4
High Street	C2		Speygate	D3
Hospital Street	B3		Stormont Street	B1
Isla Road	D1		Tay Street	D2
James Street	C3		Tay Street	D4
King Edward Street	C3		Union Lane	B2
King's Place	B4		Victoria Street	C3
King Street	B3		Watergate	D2
Kinnoull Causeway	A3		West Bridge Street	D2
Kinnoull Street	C2		West Mill Wynd	B2
Leonard Street	B3		Whitefriars Crescent	A2
Lochie Brae	D1		Whitefriar Street	A2
Longcauseway	A2		Wilson Street	A4
Main Street	D1		York Place	A3
Marshall Place	C4		York Place	B3

Peterborough

Peterborough is found on atlas page **74 C11**

Albert Place	B3		New Road	C1
Bishop's Road	C3		Northminster	C1
Boongate	D1		North Street	B1
Bourges Boulevard	A1		Oundle Road	B4
Bridge Street	B3		Park Road	B1
Bright Street	A1		Peet Street	B1
Broadway	B2		Pipe Lane	D2
Brook Street	C1		Priestgate	A2
Cathedral Square	B2		Rivergate	B3
Cattle Market Street	B1		River Lane	A2
Chapel Street	C1		Russell Street	A1
Church Street	B2		St John's Street	C2
Church Walk	C1		St Peters Road	B3
City Road	C2		South Street	D2
Cowgate	B2		Star Road	D2
Craig Street	B1		Station Road	A2
Crawthorne Road	C1		Thorpe Lea Road	A3
Cromwell Road	A1		Thorpe Road	A2
Cross Street	B2		Trinity Street	B3
Cubitt Way	B4		Viersen Platz	B3
Deacon Street	A1		Vineyard Road	C3
Dickens Street	D1		Wake Road	D2
Eastfield Road	D1		Wareley Road	A4
Eastgate	D2		Wellington Street	D1
East Station Road	C4		Wentworth Street	B3
Embankment Road	C3		Westgate	A1
Exchange Street	B2			
Fengate Close	D2			
Field Walk	D1			
Fitzwilliam Street	B1			
Frank Perkins Parkway	D4			
Geneva Street	B1			
Gladstone Street	A1			
Granby Street	C2			
Hawksbill Way	B4			
Hereward Close	D2			
Hereward Road	D2			
King Street	B2			
Laxton Square	C2			
Lea Gardens	A3			
Lincoln Road	B1			
London Road	B4			
Long Causeway	B2			
Manor House Street	B1			
Mayor's Walk	A1			
Midgate	B2			
Morris Street	D1			
Nene Street	D2			

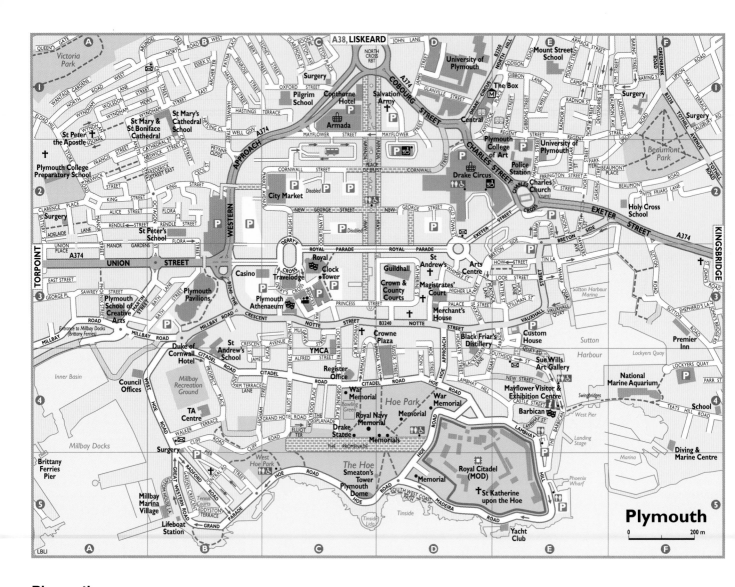

Plymouth

Plymouth is found on atlas page **6 D8**

Addison Road	E1	Clarence Place	A2	Greenbank Road	F1	May Terrace	F1	Raleigh Street	C2	Wharf Quay	E3
Adelaide Lane	A2	Cliff Road	B4	Hampton Street	E2	Millbay Road	A3	Regent Street	E1	Whimple Street	D3
Alfred Street	C4	Cobourg Street	D1	Harwell Street	B1	Moon Street	E2	Rendle Street	A2	White Friars Lane	F2
Alice Street	A2	Cornwall Street	C2	Hastings Street	B1	Mount Street	E1	Royal Parade	C3	Windsor Place	C3
Anstis Street	A2	Courtenay Street	C3	Hastings Terrace	B1	Mulgrave Street	C3	St James Place	B4	Wolsdon Street	A1
Archer Terrace	B1	Crescent Avenue	B3	Hawkers Avenue	E2	Neswick Street	A2	St John's Bridge Road	F3	Wyndham Lane	A1
Armada Street	E1	Custom House Lane	B5	Hetling Close	B1	New George Street	C2	St John's Road	F3	Wyndham Mews	A1
Armada Way	C2	Derry's Cross	C3	Hicks Lane	E3	New Street	E4	Salisbury Road	F1	Wyndham Square	A1
Armada Way	C4	Devonshire Street	E1	Higher Lane	D3	North Cross Roundabout	C1	Sawrey Street	A3	Wyndham Street East	A1
Arundel Crescent	A1	Drake Circus	D1	Hill Street	E2	North Hill	E1	Shepherd's Lane	F3	Zion Street	D4
Athenaeum Street	C3	East Street	A3	Hoe Approach	D4	North Road West	A1	Southside Street	D4	
Baring Street	F1	Ebrington Street	E2	Hoegate Street	D3	North Street	E2	South West Coast Path	D5	
Bath Lane	B3	Eddystone Terrace	B5	Hoe Road	C5	Notte Street	C3	Stillman Street	E3	
Bath Street	B3	Eldad Hill	A1	Hoe Street	D3	Octagon Street	B2	Stoke Road	A2	
Batter Street	E3	Elliot Place	C4	Holyrood Place	C4	Old Town Street	D2	Sussex Street	D3	
Battery Street	A2	Elliot Terrace	C4	How Street	E3	Osborne Place	C4	Sutton Road	F3	
Beaumont Avenue	F1	Essex Street	B1	Ilbert Street	B1	Oxford Street	C1	Sydney Street	B1	
Beaumont Place	E2	Eton Avenue	C1	James Street	D1	Palace Street	D3	Tavistock Place	D1	
Beaumont Road	F2	Eton Place	C1	John Lane	D1	Park Terrace	E2	Teats Hill Road	F4	
Bilbury Street	E2	Exeter Street	D2	King Street	A2	Parr Street	F4	The Barbican	E4	
Blackfriars Lane	D4	Exeter Street	E2	Ladywell Place	F1	Patna Place	B1	The Crescent	B3	
Boon's Place	C1	Flora Court	B2	Lambhay Hill	D4	Peacock Lane	D3	The Esplanade	C4	
Breton Side	D3	Flora Street	B2	Lambhay Street	E4	Penrose Street	B1	The Promenade	C4	
Buckwell Street	D3	Francis Street	A2	Leigham Street	B4	Phoenix Street	A3	Tin Lane	E3	
Camden Street	E1	Frederick Street East	B2	Leigham Terrace Lane	B4	Pier Street	B5	Tothill Avenue	F1	
Castle Street	E4	Friar's Parade	D4	Lipson Road	F1	Place de Brest	C2	Tothill Road	F2	
Cathedral Street	A2	Garden Crescent	B5	Lockyers Quay	F4	Plym Street	F1	Trafalgar Street	E2	
Catherine Street	D3	Gasking Street	E2	Lockyer Street	C3	Princess Street	C3	Union Place	A3	
Cecil Street	B1	George Place	A3	Looe Street	E3	Princess Way	C3	Union Street	A3	
Central Road	B5	Gibbon Lane	E1	Madeira Road	D5	Prospect Place	B4	Vauxhall Quay	E3	
Chapel Street	E1	Gibbons Street	E1	Manor Gardens	A3	Prynne Close	B2	Vauxhall Street	E3	
Charles Cross	E2	Gilwell Street	E1	Manor Street	A2	Quay Road	E4	Walker Terrace	B4	
Charles Street	D2	Glanville Street	D1	Market Avenue	C2	Queen's Gate	A1	Wantage Gardens	A1	
Citadel Road	B4	Grand Hotel Road	C4	Martin Street	A3	Radford Road	B5	Well Garden	B1	
Citadel Road	C4	Grand Parade	B5	Mayflower Street	C1	Radnor Place	E1	Western Approach	B2	
Claremont Street	C1	Great Western Road	B5	Mayflower Street	D1	Radnor Street	E1	West Hoe Road	A4	

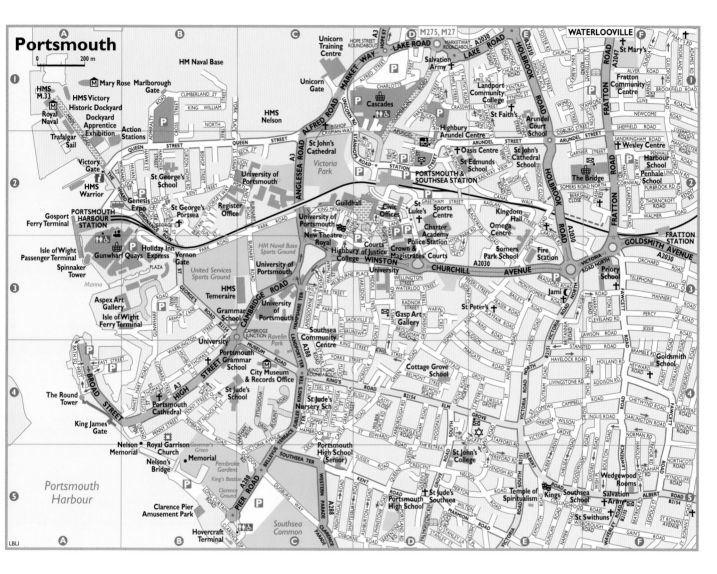

Portsmouth

Portsmouth is found on atlas page **14 H7**

Admiralty Road	B2	Cavendish Road	E5
Albany Road	E5	Central Street	E1
Albert Grove	E5	Charlotte Street	D1
Albert Road	E5	Chelsea Road	E5
Alec Rose Lane	D3	Chester Place	E5
Alexandra Road	E1	Chetwynd Road	F4
Alfred Road	C1	Churchill Avenue	D3
Alfred Street	D1	Church Road	E1
Alver Road	F1	Claremont Road	F2
Anglesea Road	C2	Clarence Parade	C5
Ariel Road	F2	Cleveland Road	F3
Armory Lane	B3	Clive Road	F1
Arundel Street	D2	Clock Street	B2
Arundel Street	E2	College Street	B2
Ashburton Road	D5	Collingwood Road	E5
Bailey's Road	E3	Commercial Road	D1
Bath Square	A4	Cornwall Road	F2
Bellevue Terrace	C5	Cottage Grove	D4
Belmont Place	D4	Cottage View	E2
Bishop Crispian Way	C2	Crasswell Street	D1
Bishop Street	B2	Cross Street	B2
Blackfriars Road	E2	Cumberland Street	B1
Blount Road	C4	Curzon Howe Road	B2
Boulton Road	F5	Darlington Road	F4
Bramble Road	F4	Drummond Road	E1
Bridgeside Close	E2	Duisburg Way	C5
Britain Street	B2	Duncan Road	E5
Broad Street	A4	Earlsdon Street	D3
Brookfield Road	F1	East Street	A4
Brunswick Street	C3	Eldon Street	D4
Buckingham Street	D1	Elm Grove	D4
Cambridge Road	C3	Elphinstone Road	D5
Campbell Road	E5	Exmouth Road	E5
Canal Walk	E2	Fawcett Road	F3
Carlisle Road	E2	Fawcett Road	F4
Castle Road	C4	Flint Street	C4
Foster Road	E1	Lake Road	D1
Fratton Road	F2	Landport Street	E1
Gain's Road	F5	Landport Terrace	C3
Garnier Street	E2	Landsdowne Street	C3
Goldsmith Avenue	E3	Lawrence Road	F5
Gold Street	C4	Lawson Road	F3
Goodwood Road	E5	Leopold Street	F5
Gordon Road	C5	Lincoln Road	F2
Great Southsea Street	C4	Little Southsea Street	C4
Green Road	D4	Livingstone Road	E4
Greetham Street	D2	Lombard Street	B4
Grosvenor Street	D3	Londesborough Road	F4
Grove Road North	D4	Lords Street	E1
Grove Road South	D5	Lorne Road	F4
Guildford Road	F1	Main Road	A1
Guildhall Walk	C2	Manners Road	F3
Gunwharf Road	B3	Margate Road	D4
Hambrook Street	C4	Market Way	C1
Hampshire Terrace	C3	Marmion Road	D5
Harold Road	F5	Mary Rose Street	D2
Havant Street	B2	Melbourne Place	C3
Havelock Road	E4	Merton Road	D5
Hawke Street	B2	Middle Street	D3
Hereford Road	E5	Milford Road	E2
Highbury Street	B4	Montgomerie Road	E3
High Street	B4	Moorland Road	F1
Holbrook Road	E1	Museum Road	C4
Holland Road	F4	Napier Road	E5
Hudson Road	D4	Newcome Road	D5
Hyde Park Road	D3	Nightingale Road	C5
Inglis Road	F4	Norfolk Street	D4
Jessie Road	F4	Norman Road	C5
Jubilee Terrace	C4	Olinda Street	F1
Kent Road	D5	Orchard Road	F3
Kent Street	B2	Ordnance Row	B2
King Albert Street	E1	Osborne Road	C5
King Henry I Street	C2	Outram Road	E4
King's Road	C4	Oxford Road	F5
King's Terrace	C4	Oyster Street	B4
King Street	C4	Pains Road	E3
King William Street	B1		
Palmerston Road	D5	Stamford Street	E1
Paradise Street	D1	Stanhope Road	D2
Park Road	B3	Stansted Road	E4
Pelham Road	D4	Station Street	D2
Pembroke Road	B4	Steel Street	C4
Penhale Road	F2	Stone Street	C4
Penny Street	B4	Sussex Road	D5
Percy Road	F3	Sutherland Road	F4
Pier Road	C5	Talbot Road	F4
Playfair Road	E3	Telephone Road	F3
Portland Road	D5	Temple Street	D1
Purbrook Road	F2	The Hard	A2
Queens Crescent	D5	The Retreat	D5
Queen Street	B2	The Thicket	D4
Raglan Street	E2	Thorncroft Road	F2
Railway View	E2	Tottenham Road	F1
Richmond Place	D5	Trevor Road	F4
Rivers Street	D3	Unicorn Road	C1
Rugby Road	E3	Upper Arundel Street	D2
Sackville Street	C3	Victoria Avenue	C5
St Andrews Road	E4	Victoria Grove	E4
St Bartholomews Gardens	E4	Victoria Road North	F3
St Davids Road	E4	Victoria Road North	F3
St Edwards Road	D4	Victoria Road South	E5
St Faith's Road	D1	Vivash Road	F2
St George's Road	B3	Walmer Road	F2
St George's Square	B2	Warblington Street	B4
St George's Way	B2	Warwick Crescent	D3
St James's Road	D3	Waterloo Street	D3
St James's Street	B2	Waverley Road	F5
St Nicholas Street	B4	Western Parade	C5
St Paul's Road	C3	West Street	A4
St Peters Grove	E4	White Hart Road	B4
St Thomas's Street	B4	Wilson Grove	E4
Sandringham Road	F2	Wiltshire Street	C3
Shaftesbury Road	C5	Winston Churchill Avenue	D3
Somers Road	D4	Wisborough Road	E5
Somers Road	E3	Woodpath	D4
Somers Road North	E2	Woodville Drive	C4
Southsea Terrace	C5	Yarborough Road	D4
Stafford Road	E4	Yorke Street	C4

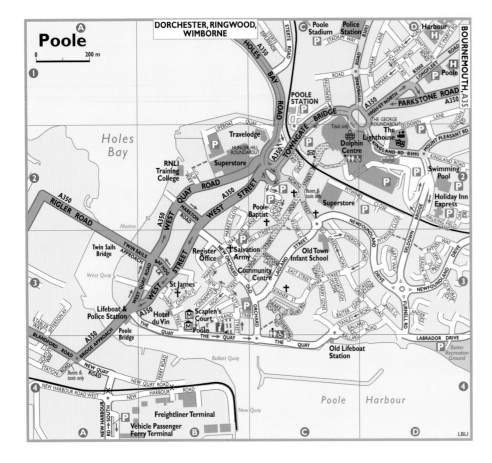

Poole

Poole is found on atlas page **12 H6**

Avenel Way	D3	New Orchard	B3
Baiter Gardens	C3	New Quay Road	A4
Ballard Close	C3	New Street	B3
Ballard Road	C4	North Street	C2
Bay Hog Lane	B3	Norton Way	A4
Blandford Road	A3	Oak Drive	D2
Bridge Approach	A4	Old Orchard	B3
Castle Street	B3	Parkstone Road	D1
Chapel Lane	C2	Perry Gardens	C3
Church Street	B3	Pitwines Close	C2
Cinnamon Lane	B3	Poole Bridge	A3
Colborne Close	D3	Rigler Road	A2
Dear Hay Lane	B3	St Mary's Road	D1
Denmark Lane	D1	Seager Way	D3
Denmark Road	D1	Seldown Bridge	D3
Drake Road	C3	Seldown Lane	D2
Durrell Way	D3	Seldown Road	D2
East Quay Road	C3	Serpentine Road	C1
East Street	C3	Shaftesbury Road	D1
Elizabeth Road	D1	Skinner Street	C3
Emerson Road	C3	Slip Way	B2
Ferry Road	B4	South Road	C3
Fisherman's Road	C3	Stabler Way	A3
Furnell Road	D3	Stadium Way	C1
Globe Lane	C2	Stanley Road	C3
Green Close	D3	Sterte Esplanade	C1
Green Road	C3	Sterte Road	C1
High Street	B3	Strand Street	B3
High Street North	D1	Thames Street	B3
Hill Street	C3	The Quay	B3
Holes Bay Road	C1	Towngate Bridge	C2
Jefferson Avenue	A3	Twin Sails Approach	A3
Kingland Road	D2	Twin Sails Bridge	A3
Labrador Drive	D4	Vallis Close	D3
Lagland Street	C3	Vanguard Road	C2
Lander Close	D3	Walking Field Lane	D2
Liberty Way	D3	Westons Lane	C3
Lifeboat Quay	B2	West Quay Road	B2
Longfleet Road	D1	West Street	B3
Maple Road	D1	Whatleigh Close	C3
Market Close	B2	Wimborne Road	D1
Market Street	B3		
Marston Road	B2		
Mount Pleasant Road	D2		
Newfoundland Drive	C2		
New Harbour Road	A4		
New Harbour Road South	A4		
New Harbour Road West	A4		

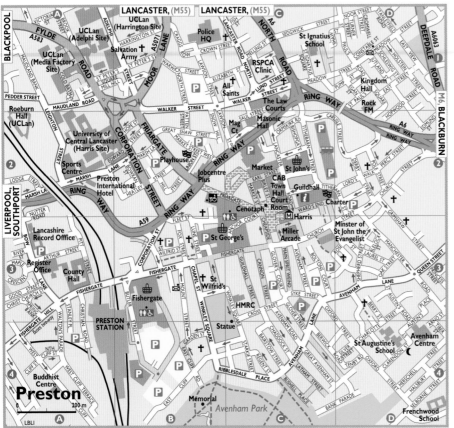

Preston

Preston is found on atlas page **88 G5**

Adelphi Street	A1	Holstein Street	D1
Arthur Street	A3	Hopwood Street	D2
Avenham Lane	C4	Jutland Street	D1
Avenham Road	C3	Lancaster Road	C2
Avenham Street	C3	Lancaster Road North	C1
Berwick Road	C4	Latham Street	C4
Birley Street	C2	Lawson Street	B1
Boltons Court	A3	Leighton Street	A2
Bow Lane	A3	Lund Street	C1
Butler Street	B3	Lune Street	B3
Cannon Street	C3	Main Sprit Weind	C3
Carlisle Street	C2	Manchester Road	D3
Chaddock Street	C4	Market Street	C2
Chapel Street	B3	Market Street West	B2
Charlotte Street	D4	Marsh Lane	A2
Cheapside	C3	Maudland Road	A1
Christ Church Street	A3	Meadow Street	C1
Church Street	C3	Moor Lane	B1
Clarendon Street	D4	Mount Street	B3
Corporation Street	B2	North Road	C1
Corporation Street	B3	Oak Street	D3
Craggs Row	B1	Ormskirk Road	C2
Cross Street	C3	Oxford Street	C3
Crown Street	B1	Pedder Street	A1
Deepdale Road	D1	Percy Street	D2
Derby Street	D2	Pitt Street	A3
Earl Street	C2	Pole Street	D2
East Cliff	B4	Pump Street	D1
East Street	D1	Queen Street	D3
Edmund Street	D2	Ribblesdale Place	B4
Edward Street	A2	Ring Way	B2
Elizabeth Street	B1	Rose Street	D3
Fishergate	B3	St Austin's Road	D3
Fishergate Hill	A4	St Paul's Road	D1
Fleet Street	B3	St Paul's Square	D1
Fox Street	B3	St Peter's Street	B1
Friargate	B2	Sedgwick Street	C1
Friargate	C2	Selborne Street	D4
Fylde Road	A1	Shepherd Street	D3
Glover's Court	C3	Snow Hill	B2
Glover Street	C3	Syke Street	C3
Great Avenham Street	C4	Tithebarn Street	C2
Great Shaw Street	B2	Walker Street	B1
Grimshaw Street	D2	Walton's Parade	A3
Guildhall Street	C3	Ward's End	C2
Harrington Street	B1	Warwick Street	B1
Heatley Street	B2	West Cliff	A4
Herschell Street	D4	Winkley Square	B3

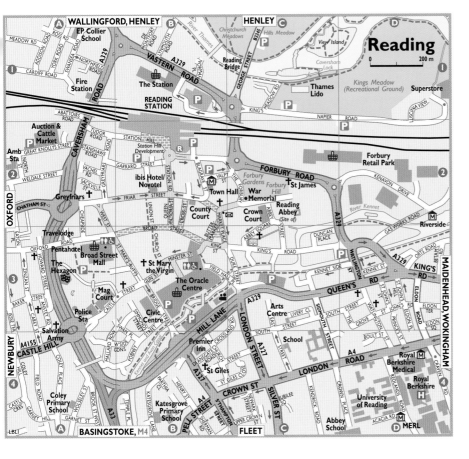

Reading

Reading is found on atlas page **35 K10**

Abbey Square............C3	King's Meadow Road............C1
Abbey Street............C2	King's Road............D3
Addison Road............A1	King Street............B3
Anstey Road............A3	Livery Close............C3
Baker Street............A3	London Road............C4
Blagrave Street............B2	London Street............C3
Boult Street............D4	Mallard Row............A4
Bridge Street............B3	Market Place............B2
Broad Street............B3	Mill Lane............B4
Brook Street West............A4	Minster Street............B3
Buttermarket............B3	Napier Road............C1
Cardiff Road............A1	Newark Street............C4
Carey Street............A3	Northfield Road............A1
Castle Hill............A4	Oxford Road............A3
Castle Street............A3	Parthia Close............B4
Caversham Road............A2	Pell Street............B4
Chatham Street............A2	Prince's Street............D3
Cheapside............A2	Queen's Road............C3
Church Street............B3	Queen Victoria Street............B2
Church Street............B4	Redlands Road............D4
Coley Place............A4	Ross Road............A1
Craven Road............D4	Sackville Street............A2
Crossland Road............B4	St Giles Close............B4
Cross Street............B2	St John's Road............D3
Crown Street............C4	St Mary's Butts............B3
Deansgate Road............B4	Sidmouth Street............C3
Duke Street............C3	Silver Street............C4
Duncan Place............C3	Simmonds Street............B3
East Street............C3	Southampton Street............B4
Eldon Road............D3	South Street............C3
Field Road............A4	Station Hill............B2
Fobney Street............B4	Station Road............B2
Forbury Road............C2	Swan Place............B3
Friar Street............B2	Swansea Road............A1
Garnet Street............A4	The Forbury............C2
Garrard Street............B2	Tudor Road............A2
Gas Works Road............D3	Union Street............B2
George Street............C1	Upper Crown Street............C4
Great Knollys Street............A2	Vachel Road............A2
Greyfriars Road............A2	Valpy Street............B2
Gun Street............B3	Vastern Road............B1
Henry Street............B4	Watlington Street............D3
Howard Street............A3	Weldale Street............A2
Katesgrove Lane............B4	West Street............A2
Kenavon Drive............D2	Wolseley Street............A4
Kendrick Road............C4	Yield Hall Place............B3
Kennet Side............C3	York Road............A1
Kennet Street............D3	Zinzan Street............A3

Royal Tunbridge Wells

Royal Tunbridge Wells is found on atlas page **25 N3**

Albert Street............C1	High Street............B4
Arundel Road............C4	Lansdowne Road............C2
Bayhall Road............D2	Lime Hill Road............B1
Belgrave Road............C1	Linden Park Road............A4
Berkeley Road............B4	Little Mount Sion............B4
Boyne Park............A1	London Road............A2
Buckingham Road............C4	Lonsdale Gardens............B2
Calverley Gardens............C3	Madeira Park............B4
Calverley Park............C2	Major York's Road............A4
Calverley Park Gardens............D2	Meadow Road............B1
Calverley Road............C2	Molyneux Park Road............A1
Calverley Street............C2	Monson Road............C2
Cambridge Gardens............D4	Monson Way............B2
Cambridge Street............D3	Mount Edgcumbe Road............A3
Camden Hill............D3	Mount Ephraim............A2
Camden Park............D3	Mount Ephraim Road............B1
Camden Road............C1	Mountfield Gardens............C3
Carlton Road............D2	Mountfield Road............C3
Castle Road............A2	Mount Pleasant Avenue............B2
Castle Street............B3	Mount Pleasant Road............B2
Chapel Place............B4	Mount Sion............B4
Christchurch Avenue............B3	Nevill Street............B4
Church Road............A2	Newton Road............B1
Civic Way............B2	Norfolk Road............C4
Claremont Gardens............C4	North Street............D2
Claremont Road............C4	Oakfield Court Road............D3
Clarence Road............B2	Park Street............D3
Crescent Road............C2	Pembury Road............D2
Culverden Street............B1	Poona Road............C4
Dale Street............C1	Prince's Street............D3
Dudley Road............B1	Prospect Road............D3
Eden Road............B4	Rock Villa Road............B1
Eridge Road............A4	Royal Chase............A1
Farmcombe Lane............C4	St James' Road............D1
Farmcombe Road............C4	Sandrock Road............D1
Ferndale............D1	Somerville Gardens............B1
Frant Road............A4	South Green............B3
Frog Lane............B4	Station Approach............B3
Garden Road............C1	Stone Street............D1
Garden Street............C1	Sutherland Road............C3
George Street............D3	Tunnel Road............C1
Goods Station Road............B1	Upper Grosvenor Road............B1
Grecian Road............C4	Vale Avenue............B3
Grosvenor Road............B1	Vale Road............B3
Grove Hill Gardens............C3	Victoria Road............C1
Grove Hill Road............C3	Warwick Park............B4
Guildford Road............C3	Wood Street............C1
Hanover Road............B1	York Road............B2

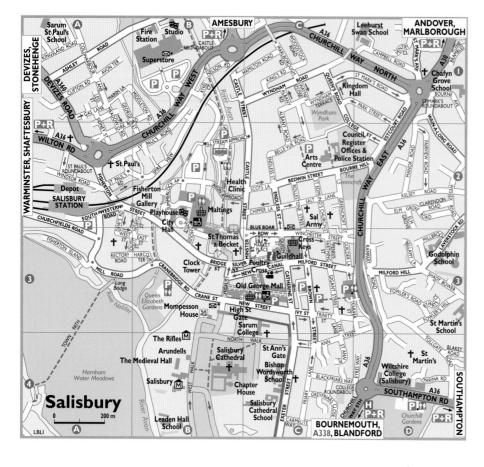

Salisbury

Salisbury is found on atlas page **21 M9**

Albany Road C1
Ashley Road A1
Avon Approach B2
Bedwin Street C2
Belle Vue Road C2
Blackfriars Way C4
Blue Boar Row C3
Bourne Avenue D1
Bourne Hill C2
Bridge Street B3
Brown Street C3
Campbell Road D1
Castle Street B1
Catherine Street C3
Chipper Lane C2
Churchfields Road A2
Churchill Way East D3
Churchill Way North C1
Churchill Way South C4
Churchill Way West B2
Clarendon Road D2
Clifton Road A1
Coldharbour Lane A1
College Street C1
Cranebridge Road B3
Crane Street B3
Devizes Road A1
Dew's Road A3
East Street B3
Elm Grove D2
Elm Grove Road D2
Endless Street C2
Estcourt Road D2
Exeter Street C4
Eyres Way D4
Fairview Road D2
Fisherton Street A2
Fowler's Road D3
Friary Lane C4
Gas Lane A1
George Street A1
Gigant Street C3
Greencroft Street C2
Guilder Lane C3
Hamilton Road C1
High Street B3
Ivy Street C3
Kelsey Road D2

Kingsland Road A1
King's Road C1
Laverstock Road D3
Malthouse Lane B3
Manor Road D2
Marlborough Road C1
Meadow Road A1
Middleton Road A1
Milford Hill D3
Milford Street C3
Mill Road A3
Minster Street C2
Nelson Road B1
New Canal B3
New Street B3
North Street B3
Park Street D1
Pennyfarthing Street C2
Queen's Road C1
Queen Street C3
Rampart Road D3
Rectory Road A3
Rollestone Street C2
St Ann Street C4
St Edmund's Church Street C2
St Mark's Avenue D1
St Mark's Road D1
St Paul's Road B2
Salt Lane C2
Scots Lane C2
Sidney Street A1
Silver Street B3
Southampton Road D4
South Street A3
South Western Road A2
Spire View B2
Summerlock Approach B2
Tollgate Road D4
Trinity Street C3
Wain-A-Long Road D1
Wessex Road D2
West Street A3
Wilton Road A2
Winchester Street C3
Windsor Road A2
Woodstock Road C1
Wyndham Road C1
York Road A2

Sheffield

Sheffield is found on atlas page **84 E3**

Angel Street C2
Arundel Gate C3
Arundel Street C4
Backfields B3
Bailey Street A2
Balm Green B3
Bank Street C2
Barkers Pool B3
Broad Lane A2
Broad Street D2
Brown Street C4
Cambridge Street B3
Campo Lane B2
Carver Street B3
Castlegate C1
Castle Street C2
Charles Street B4
Charter Row B4
Church Street B2
Commercial Street C2
Corporation Street B1
Cross Burgess Street B3
Cutlers Gate D1
Derek Dooley Way D1
Devonshire Street A3
Division Street A3
Dixon Lane C2
Duke Street D2
Exchange Street D2
Eyre Street B4
Fig Tree Lane C2
Fitzwilliam Street A4
Flat Street C3
Furnace Hill B1
Furnival Gate B4
Furnival Road D1
Furnival Street C4
Garden Street A2
George Street C2
Gibralter Street B1
Harmer Lane C3
Harts Head C2
Hawley Street B2
Haymarket C2
High Street C2
Holland Street A3
Hollis Croft A2
Holly Street B3

Howard Street C4
Hoyle Street A1
King Street C2
Lambert Street B1
Leopold Street B3
Mappin Street A3
Meetinghouse Lane C2
Mulberry Street C2
Newcastle Street A2
New Street C2
Norfolk Street C3
North Church Street B2
Orchard Street B3
Paradise Street B2
Pinstone Street B3
Pond Hill C3
Pond Street C3
Portobello Street A3
Queen Street B2
Rockingham Street A2
St James Street B2
Scargill Croft C2
Scotland Street A1
Sheaf Street D4
Shoreham Street C4
Shrewsbury Road D4
Silver Street B2
Smithfield A1
Snig Hill C2
Solly Street A2
South Street Park D3
Suffolk Road C4
Surrey Street C3
Talbot Street D4
Tenter Street B2
Townhead Street B2
Trafalgar Street A4
Trippet Lane B3
Union Street B4
Vicar Lane B2
Victoria Station Road D1
Waingate C2
Wellington Street A4
West Bar B2
West Bar Green B2
West Street A3
White Croft A2
York Street C2

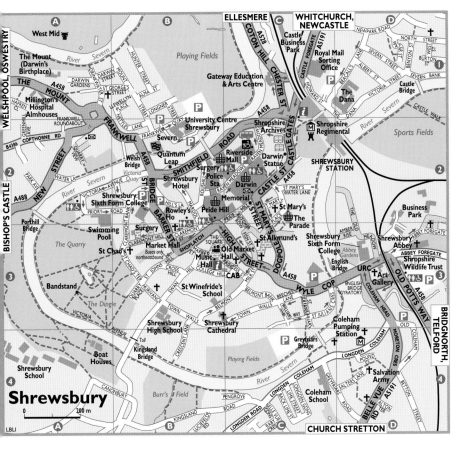

Shrewsbury

Shrewsbury is found on atlas page **56 H2**

Abbey Foregate	D3	Mardol	B2
Albert Street	D1	Market Street	B3
Alma Street	B1	Milk Street	C3
Amber Rise	D3	Moreton Crescent	D4
Barker Street	B2	Mount Street	B1
Beacall's Lane	D1	Murivance	B3
Beeches Lane	C3	Nettles Lane	B1
Belle Vue Gardens	C4	Newpark Road	D1
Belle Vue Road	D4	New Street	A2
Belmont	B3	North Street	D1
Belmont Bank	C3	Old Coleham	D3
Benyon Street	D1	Old Potts Way	D3
Betton Street	D4	Park Avenue	A2
Bridge Street	B2	Pengrove	C4
Burton Street	D1	Pound Close	D4
Butcher Row	C2	Pride Hill	C2
Canonbury	A4	Princess Street	B3
Castle Foregate	C1	Priory Road	A2
Castle Gates	C2	Quarry Place	B3
Castle Street	C2	Quarry View	A2
Chester Street	C1	Raven Meadows	B2
Claremont Bank	B3	Roushill	B2
Claremont Hill	B3	St Chad's Terrace	B3
Claremont Street	B3	St George's Street	A1
Coleham Head	D3	St Johns Hill	B3
College Hill	B3	St Julians Crescent	C3
Copthorne Road	A2	St Julians Friars	C3
Coton Hill	C1	St Mary's Place	C2
Crescent Lane	B4	St Mary's Street	C2
Cross Hill	B3	St Mary's Water Lane	C2
Darwin Gardens	A1	Salters Lane	D4
Darwin Street	A1	Severn Bank	D1
Dogpole	C3	Severn Street	D1
Drinkwater Street	A1	Shoplatch	B3
Fish Street	C3	Smithfield Road	B2
Frankwell	A2	Swan Hill	B3
Frankwell Quay	B2	The Dana	D1
Greenhill Avenue	A2	The Mount	A1
Greyfriars Road	C4	The Old Meadow	D3
High Street	C3	The Square	B3
Hill's Lane	B2	Town Walls	B3
Howard Street	C1	Victoria Avenue	A2
Hunter Street	B1	Victoria Street	D1
Kingsland Road	B4	Water Lane	A2
Lime Street	C4	Water Street	D1
Longden Coleham	C4	West Street	D1
Longden Road	C4	Williams Way	C3
Longner Street	B1	Wyle Cop	C3

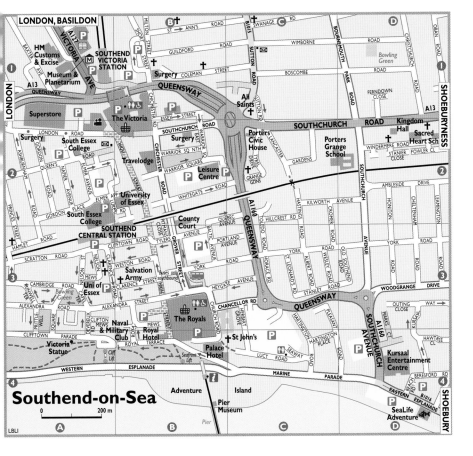

Southend-on-Sea

Southend-on-Sea is found on atlas page **38 E4**

Albert Road	C3	Lancaster Gardens	C2
Alexandra Road	A3	Leamington Road	D2
Alexandra Street	A3	London Road	A2
Ambleside Drive	D2	Lucy Road	C4
Ashburnham Road	A2	Luker Road	A2
Baltic Avenue	B3	Marine Parade	C4
Baxter Avenue	A1	Milton Street	B1
Beach Road	D4	Napier Avenue	A2
Boscombe Road	C1	Nelson Street	A3
Bournemouth Park Road	D1	Oban Road	D1
Cambridge Road	A3	Old Southend Road	D3
Capel Terrace	A3	Outing Close	D3
Chancellor Road	B3	Pitmans Close	B2
Cheltenham Road	D2	Pleasant Road	C3
Chichester Road	B1	Portland Avenue	B3
Christchurch Road	D1	Princes Street	A2
Church Road	B3	Prittlewell Square	A3
Clarence Road	A3	Quebec Avenue	B2
Clarence Street	B3	Queen's Road	A2
Clifftown Parade	A4	Queensway	A1
Clifftown Road	B3	Queensway	C3
Coleman Street	B1	Royal Terrace	B4
Cromer Road	C2	Runwell Terrace	A3
Devereux Road	A4	St Ann's Road	B1
Eastern Esplanade	D4	St Leonard's Road	C3
Elmer Approach	A2	Scratton Road	A3
Elmer Avenue	A2	Short Street	B1
Essex Street	B1	Southchurch Avenue	D2
Ferndown Close	D1	Southchurch Road	B2
Fowler Close	D2	Stanier Close	D2
Gordon Place	A2	Stanley Road	C3
Gordon Road	A2	Sutton Road	C1
Grange Gardens	C2	Swanage Road	C1
Grover Street	B3	Toledo Road	C2
Guildford Road	B1	Tylers Avenue	B3
Hamlet Road	A3	Tyrel Drive	C2
Hartington Place	C4	Victoria Avenue	A1
Hartington Road	C3	Warrior Square East	B2
Hastings Road	C2	Warrior Square North	B2
Hawtree Close	D4	Warrior Square	B2
Herbert Grove	C3	Wesley Road	C3
Heygate Avenue	B3	Western Esplanade	A4
High Street	B2	Weston Road	B3
Hillcrest Road	C2	Whitegate Road	B2
Honiton Road	D2	Wimborne Road	C1
Horace Road	C3	Windermere Road	B2
Kilworth Avenue	C2	Woodgrange Drive	D3
Kursaal Way	D4	York Road	B3

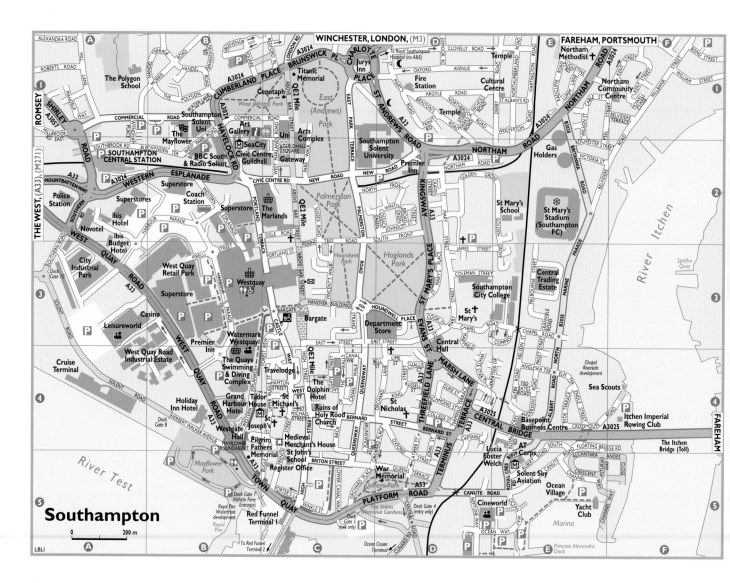

Southampton

Southampton is found on atlas page **14 D4**

Above Bar Street	C1
Albert Road North	E4
Albert Road South	E5
Alcantara Crescent	E5
Alexandra Road	A1
Anderson's Road	E4
Andes Close	F5
Anglesea Terrace	E4
Argyle Road	D1
Asturias Way	E5
Augustine Road	E1
Back Of The Walls	C4
Bargate Street	C3
Bedford Place	C1
Bell Street	D4
Belvidere Road	E2
Belvidere Terrace	F1
Bernard Street	C4
Blechynden Terrace	B2
Bond Street	F1
Brinton's Road	D1
Britannia Road	E1
Briton Street	C5
Broad Green	D2
Brunswick Place	C1
Brunswick Square	B1
Bugle Street	C5
Cable Street	E1
Canal Walk	C4
Canute Road	D5
Captains Place	D4
Carpathia Drive	D4
Castle Way	C3
Central Bridge	D4
Central Road	D5
Challis Court	D4

Channel Way	E5
Chapel Road	D3
Charlotte Place	C1
Civic Centre Road	B2
Clovelly Road	D1
Coleman Street	D3
College Street	D4
Commercial Road	A1
Cook Street	D3
Cossack Green	D2
Craven Street	D2
Crosshouse Road	E4
Cumberland Place	B1
Cunard Road	D5
Derby Road	E1
Devonshire Road	B1
Duke Street	D4
Eastgate Street	C4
East Park Terrace	C1
East Street	C3
Elm Terrace	E4
Endle Street	E4
Evans Street	D3
Exmoor Road	D1
Floating Bridge Road	E4
Forest View	C4
French Street	C5
Glebe Road	E4
Golden Grove	D2
Granville Road	E3
Grosvenor Square	B1
Hamtun Street	C4
Handel Road	B1
Handel Terrace	B1
Hanover Buildings	C3
Harbour Parade	B2

Hartington Road	E1
Havelock Road	B1
Herbert Walker Avenue	B4
High Street	C4
Hill Lane	A1
Houndwell Place	D3
Howell Close	F1
Itchen Bridge	F4
James Street	D3
Johnson Street	D2
John Street	D5
Kent Street	F1
King Street	D4
Kingsway	D2
Latimer Street	D5
Lime Street	D4
London Road	C1
Lower Canal Walk	C5
Lumpy Lane	C4
Mandela Way	A1
Marine Parade	E3
Marsh Lane	D4
Maryfield	D3
Mayflower Roundabout	B4
Melbourne Street	E3
Millbank Street	F1
Millbrook Road East	A1
Morris Road	B1
Mountbatten Way	A2
Nelson Street	E4
Neptune Way	D5
New Road	C2
Nichols Road	D1
Northam Road	D2
Northbrook Road	D1
North Front	C2

Northumberland Road	E1
Ocean Way	D5
Ogle Road	C2
Orchard Place	C5
Oxford Avenue	D1
Oxford Street	D4
Paget Street	E4
Palmerston Road	C2
Park Walk	C2
Peel Street	E1
Pirelli Street	B3
Platform Road	C5
Porter's Lane	C5
Portland Street	C3
Portland Terrace	B2
Pound Tree Road	C3
Queens Terrace	D5
Queensway	C4
Radcliffe Road	E1
Richmond Street	D4
Roberts Road	A1
Rochester Street	E2
Royal Crescent Road	E5
Russell Street	D4
Ryde Terrace	E4
St Alban's Road	D1
St Andrews Road	D1
St Marks Road	D1
St Mary's Place	D3
St Mary's Road	D1
St Mary Street	D2
St Michael Street	C4
Shirley Road	A1
Solent Road	A3
Southbrook Road	A2
Southern Road	A2

South Front	C2
Strand	C3
Sussex Road	C2
Ted Bates Road	E4
Terminus Terrace	D5
The Compass	D3
The Polygon	B1
Threefield Lane	D4
Town Quay	B5
Trinity Road	D1
Upper Bugle Street	C4
Victoria Street	E2
Vincent's Walk	C3
Water Lane	B1
Western Esplanade	A2
Western Esplanade	B4
West Marlands Road	C2
West Park Road	B2
West Quay Road	A2
West Street	C4
White Star Place	D4
William Street	F1
Wilson Street	E1
Winkle Street	C5
Winton Street	D2
Wolverton Road	E1
Wyndham Place	A1

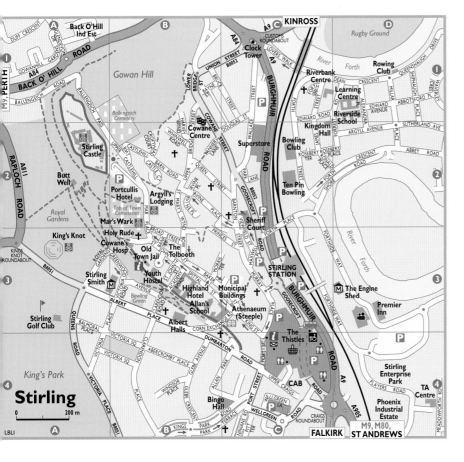

Stirling

Stirling is found on atlas page **133 M9**

Abbey Road	D2	James Street	C2
Abbotsford Place	D1	Kings Knot Roundabout	A3
Abercromby Place	B4	Kings Park Road	B4
Academy Road	B3	King Street	C3
Albert Place	A3	Lovers Walk	C1
Alexandra Place	D1	Lower Bridge Street	B1
Allan Park	B4	Lower Castlehill	B2
Argyll Avenue	D2	Mar Place	B2
Back O' Hill Road	A1	Maxwell Place	C3
Baker Street	B3	Meadowforth Road	D4
Ballengeich Road	A1	Millar Place	D1
Ballengeich Pass	A1	Morris Terrace	B3
Balmoral Place	A3	Murray Place	C3
Bank Street	B3	Ninians Road	C4
Barn Road	B2	Park Lane	C2
Barnton Street	C2	Park Terrace	B4
Bayne Street	B1	Players Road	D4
Bow Street	B3	Port Street	C4
Broad Street	B3	Princes Street	B3
Bruce Street	B1	Queenshaugh Drive	D1
Burghmuir Road	C1	Queens Road	A3
Castle Court	B2	Queen Street	B2
Clarendon Place	B4	Raploch Road	A2
Clarendon Road	B3	Ronald Place	C2
Corn Exchange Road	B3	Rosebery Place	C2
Cowane Street	B1	Rosebery Terrace	C2
Craigs Roundabout	C4	Royal Gardens	A3
Crofthead Court	B2	St John Street	B3
Customs Roundabout	C1	St Mary's Wynd	B2
Dean Crescent	D1	Shiphaugh Place	D1
Douglas Street	C2	Shore Road	C2
Dumbarton Road	B4	Spittal Street	B3
Edward Avenue	D1	Sutherland Avenue	D2
Edward Road	D1	Tannery Lane	B2
Forrest Road	D2	Union Street	B1
Forth Crescent	C2	Upper Bridge Street	B2
Forthside Way	C3	Upper Castlehill	A2
Forth Street	C1	Upper Craigs	C4
Forth Place	C3	Victoria Place	A4
Forth View	C1	Victoria Road	B3
Glebe Avenue	B4	Victoria Square	A4
Glebe Crescent	B4	Viewfield Street	C2
Glendevon Drive	A1	Wallace Street	C2
Goosecroft Road	C2	Waverley Crescent	D1
Gowanhill Gardens	A1	Wellgreen Lane	C4
Greenwood Avenue	A3	Wellgreen Road	C4
Harvey Wynd	B1	Whinwell Road	B2
Irvine Place	B2	Windsor Place	B4

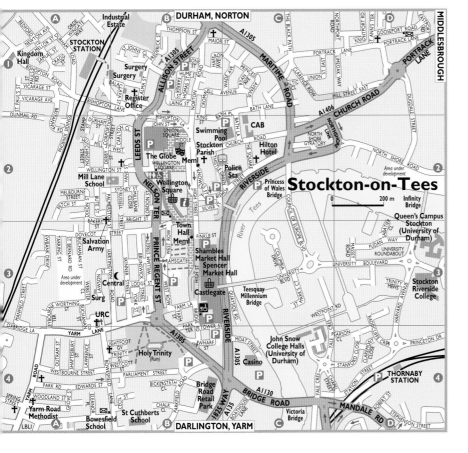

Stockton-on-Tees

Stockton-on-Tees is found on atlas page **104 D7**

1825 Way	B4	Massey Road	D3
Allison Street	B1	Melbourne Street	A2
Alma Street	B1	Middle Street	B2
Bath Lane	C1	Mill Street West	A2
Bedford Street	A1	Nelson Terrace	B2
Bishop Street	B2	North Shore Road	D2
Bishopton Lane	A1	Northport Road	D1
Bishopton Road	A1	Northshore Link	C2
Bowesfield Lane	A4	Norton Road	B1
Bridge Road	B3	Palmerston Street	A2
Bridge Road	C4	Park Road	A4
Bright Street	B2	Park Terrace	C3
Britannia Road	A1	Parkfield Road	B4
Brunswick Street	B3	Parliament Street	B4
Bute Street	A2	Portrack Lane	D1
Church Road	D1	Prince Regent Street	B3
Clarence Row	C1	Princess Avenue	C1
Corportion Street	A2	Princeton Drive	D4
Council of Europe		Quayside Road	C3
Boulevard	C2	Raddcliffe Crescent	D3
Cromwell Avenue	B1	Ramsgate	B3
Dixon Street	A2	Riverside	C3
Dovecot Street	A3	Russell Street	B2
Dugdale Street	D1	St Paul's Street	A1
Durham Road	A1	Silver Street	B2
Durham Street	A4	Skinner Street	B3
Edwards Street	A4	Station Street	D4
Farrer Street	B1	Sydney Street	B2
Finkle Street	B3	The Square	D2
Frederick Street	B1	Thistle Green	C2
Fudan Way	D3	Thomas Street	B1
Gooseport Road	D1	Thompson Street	B1
Hartington Road	A3	Tower Street	B4
Harvard Avenue	D3	Union Street East	C1
High Street	B2	University Boulevard	C3
Hill Street East	D1	Vane Street	B2
Hume Street	B1	Vicarage Street	A1
Hutchinson Street	A2	Wellington Street	A2
John Street	B2	West Row	B3
King Street	B2	Westbourne Street	A4
Knightport Road	D1	Westpoint Road	C3
Knowles Street	C2	Wharf Road	B4
Laing Street	B1	William Street	B3
Leeds Street	B2	Woodland Street	A4
Lobdon Street	B2	Worthing Street	A3
Lodge Street	B3	Yale Crescent	C4
Mandale Road	D4	Yarm Lane	A4
Maritime Road	C1	Yarm Road	A4

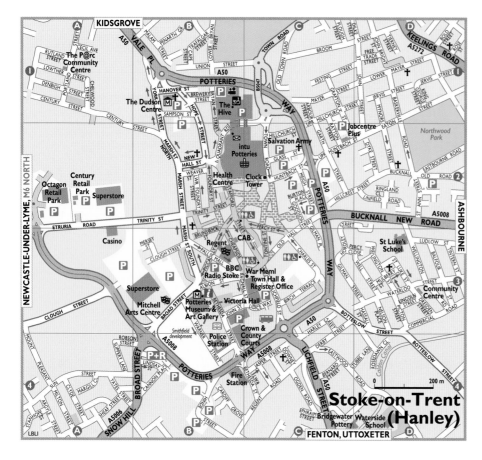

Stoke-on-Trent (Hanley)

Stoke-on-Trent (Hanley) is found on atlas page **70 F5**

Albion Street	B3	Linfield Road	D
Bagnall Street	B3	Lower Mayer Street	D
Balfour Street	D3	Lowther Street	A
Baskerville Road	D1	Ludlow Street	D
Bathesda Street	B4	Malam Street	B
Bernard Street	C4	Marsh Street	B
Bethesda Street	B3	Marsh Street North	B
Birch Terrace	C3	Marsh Street South	B
Botteslow Street	C3	Mayer Street	C
Broad Street	B4	Mersey Street	B
Broom Street	C1	Milton Street	A
Brunswick Street	B3	Mount Pleasant	A
Bryan Street	B1	Mynors Street	D
Bucknall New Road	C2	New Hall Street	B
Bucknall Old Road	D2	Ogden Road	C
Cardiff Grove	B4	Old Hall Street	C
Century Street	A1	Old Town Road	C
Charles Street	C3	Pall Mall	B
Cheapside	B3	Percy Street	B
Chelwood Street	A1	Piccadilly	B
Clough Street	A3	Portland Street	A
Clyde Street	A4	Potteries Way	B
Commercial Road	D3	Potteries Way	B
Denbigh Street	A1	Quadrant Road	B
Derby Street	C4	Regent Road	C
Dyke Street	D2	Rutland Street	A
Eastwood Road	C4	St John Street	D
Eaton Street	D2	St Luke Street	D
Etruria Road	A2	Sampson Street	B
Foundry Street	B2	Sheaf Street	A
Garth Street	C2	Slippery Lane	A
Gilman Street	C3	Snow Hill	A
Goodson Street	C2	Stafford Street	A
Grafton Street	C1	Sun Street	A
Hanover Street	B1	Tontine Street	C
Harley Street	C4	Town Road	C
Hillchurch	C2	Trafalgar Street	B
Hillcrest Street	C2	Trinity Street	B
Hinde Street	B4	Union Street	B
Hope Street	B1	Upper Hillchurch Street	C2
Hordley Street	C3	Upper Huntbach Street	C2
Huntbach Street	C2	Warner Street	B
Jasper Street	C4	Waterloo Street	D
Jervis Street	D1	Well Street	D
John Street	B3	Wellington Road	D
Keelings Road	D1	Wellington Street	D
Lichfield Street	C3	Yates Street	A
Lidice Way	C3	York Street	B

Stratford-upon-Avon

Stratford-upon-Avon is found on atlas page **47 P3**

Albany Road	A3	New Broad Street	B4
Alcester Road	A2	New Street	B4
Arden Street	B2	Old Red Lion Court	C2
Avenue Road	C1	Old Town	B4
Bancroft Place	C2	Orchard Way	A4
Birmingham Road	B1	Payton Street	C2
Brewery Street	B1	Percy Street	C1
Bridge Foot	D2	Rother Street	B3
Bridge Street	C2	Rowley Crescent	D1
Bridgeway	C2	Ryland Street	B4
Broad Street	B4	St Andrew's Crescent	A3
Brookvale Road	A4	St Gregory's Road	C1
Brunel Way	A2	St Martin's Close	A3
Bull Street	B4	Sanctus Drive	A4
Cedar Close	D1	Sanctus Road	B4
Chapel Lane	C3	Sanctus Street	B4
Chapel Street	C3	Sandfield Road	B4
Cherry Orchard	A4	Scholars Lane	B3
Cherry Street	B4	Seven Meadows Road	A4
Chestnut Walk	B3	Shakespeare Street	B1
Church Street	B3	Sheep Street	C3
Clopton Bridge	D3	Shipston Road	D3
Clopton Road	B1	Shottery Road	A3
College Lane	B4	Shrieves Walk	C3
College Mews	B4	Southern Lane	C3
College Street	B4	Swan's Nest	D3
Ely Gardens	B3	The Willows	B3
Ely Street	B3	Tiddington Road	D3
Evesham Place	B3	Town Square	D3
Evesham Road	A4	Tramway Bridge	D3
Garrick Way	A4	Tyler Street	C2
Great William Street	C1	Union Street	C2
Greenhill Street	B2	Warwick Court	C1
Grove Road	B3	Warwick Crescent	C1
Guild Street	C2	Warwick Road	C2
Henley Street	C2	Waterside	D1
High Street	C3	Welcombe Road	D1
Holtom Street	B4	Wellesbourne Grove	B3
John Street	C2	Western Road	B2
Kendall Avenue	B1	West Street	B4
Lock Close	C2	Willows Drive North	A2
Maidenhead Road	C1	Windsor Street	B2
Mansell Street	B2	Wood Street	B2
Mayfield Avenue	C1		
Meer Street	C2		
Mill Lane	C4		
Mulberry Street	C1		
Narrow Lane	B4		

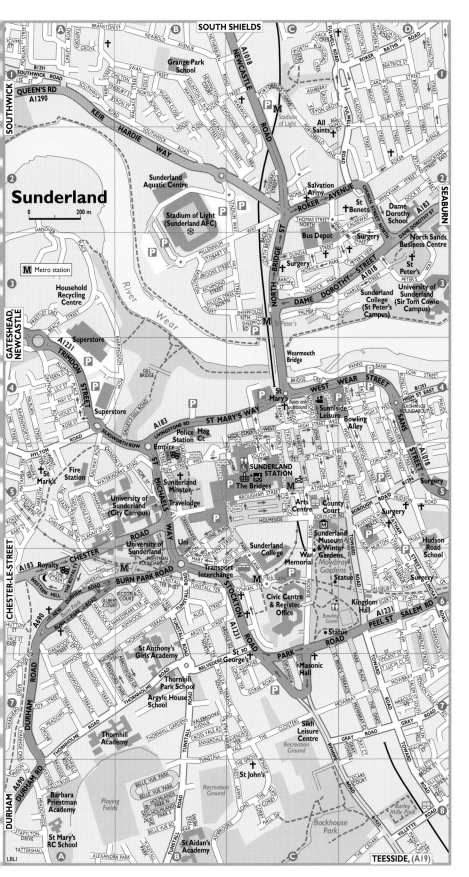

Sunderland

Sunderland is found on atlas page **113 N9**

Abbotsford Green	B7
Abbs Street	C2
Albion Place	B6
Alice Street	B6
Alliance Place	A4
Amberley Street	D6
Argyle Square	B6
Argyle Street	B6
Ashbrooke Road	B8
Ashmore Street	C7
Ashwood Street	A7
Ashwood Terrace	A7
Association Road	D1
Athenaeum Street	C5
Azalea Terrace North	B6
Azalea Terrace South	B7
Back North Bridge Street	C3
Beach Street	A3
Beaumont Street	D7
Bedford Street	C4
Beechwood Street	A6
Beechwood Terrace	A7
Belvedere Road	B7
Beresford Park	A7
Birchfield Road	A7
Borough Road	D5
Bridge Crescent	C4
Bridge Street	C4
Briery Vale Road	C7
Bright Street	D1
Brooke Street	B3
Brougham Street	C5
Burdon Road	C5
Burn Park Road	B6
Cardwell Street	D1
Carley Road	A1
Charles Street	D3
Chester Road	A6
Churchill Street	D6
Church Street North	D2
Clanny Street	A5
Cork Street	D4
Coronation Street	D5
Cowan Terrace	C6
Cross Vale Road	B7
Crozier Street	B1
Dame Dorothy Street	C3
Deptford Road	A4
Derby Street	B6
Derwent Street	B6
Devonshire Street	B1
Dock Street	D2
Dundas Street	C3
Durham Road	A7
Easington Street	B3
East Cross Street	D4
Eden House Road	A7
Egerton Street	D6
Eglinton Street	B1
Eglinton Street North	B1
Elmwood Street	A6
Ennerdale	B7
Farm Street	A1
Farringdon Row	B4
Fawcett Street	C4
Forster Street	D1
Fox Street	A7
Foyle Street	D5
Frederick Street	D5
Fulwell Road	C1
Galley's Gill Road	B4
Gladstone Street	D1
Gorse Road	C7
Gray Road	D7
Green Terrace	B5
Hampden Road	D1
Hanover Place	A2
Harlow Street	A5
Harrogate Street	D6
Hartington Street	D1
Havelock Terrace	A6
Hay Street	C3
Hendon Valley Road	D7
High Street East	D4
High Street West	B5
Holmeside	C5
Hope Street	B5
Howick Park	C3
Hudson Road	D5
Hylton Road	A5
Johnson Street	A5
John Street	C4
Keir Hardie Way	A1
Laura Street	D5
Lindsay Road	D6
Little Villiers Street	D4
Livingstone Road	B4
Low Street	D4
Mary Street	B6
Mauds Lane	D4
Meadowside	A8

Middle Street	C5
Milburn Street	A4
Millennium Way	B3
Monk Street	C2
Moreland Street	D1
Morgan Street	A1
Mowbray Road	D7
Netherburn Road	B1
Newbold Avenue	B1
Newcastle Road	C1
New Durham Road	A6
Nile Street	D4
Norfolk Street	D5
North Bridge Street	C3
Northcote Avenue	D6
North Street	B1
Oakwood Street	A6
Olive Street	B6
Otto Terrace	A7
Palmer's Hill Road	C3
Panns Bank	D4
Park Lane	C5
Park Place	D6
Park Road	C6
Pauls Road	D5
Peel Street	D6
Portobello Lane	C1
Queen's Road	A1
Railway Row	A5
Ravensworth Street	A4
Richmond Street	B3
Ripon Street	D1
Roker Avenue	C2
Roker Baths Road	D1
Rosedale Street	A5
Ross Street	B1
Russell Street	D4
Ryhope Road	C7
St Bede's Terrace	D7
St Mary's Way	B4
St Michaels Way	B5
St Peter's View	D3
St Thomas' Street	C5
St Vincent Street	D7
Salem Road	D6
Salem Street	D6
Salem Street South	D7
Salisbury Street	D6
Sans Street	D4
Selbourne Street	D1
Shakespeare Terrace	A6
Shallcross	A8
Sheepfolds Road	C3
Silksworth Row	A4
South Street	C5
Southwick Road	A1
Stadium Way	C2
Stansfield Street	D1
Station Street	C4
Stobart Street	B3
Stockton Road	C6
Swan Street	B1
Tatham Street	D5
Tatham Street Back	D5
The Avenue	C7
The Cloisters	C7
The Royalty	A6
Thomas Street North	C2
Thornhill Terrace	B6
Thornholme Road	A7
Toward Road	D5
Trimdon Street	A4
Tunstall Road	B7
Tunstall Terrace	B6
Tunstall Terrace West	B6
Tunstall Vale	B8
Union Street	C4
Valebrooke Avenue	B7
Villette Road	D8
Villiers Street	D4
Vine Place	B5
Wallace Street	B1
Warwick Street	C1
Waterloo Place	C5
Waterworks Road	A5
Wayman Street	B1
Wearhead Drive	A7
Westbourne Road	A5
Western Hill	A6
West Lawn	C8
West Street	C5
West Sunniside	D4
West Wear Street	C4
Wharncliffe Street	A5
Whickham Street	D2
Whickham Street East	D2
Whitburn Street	D3
William Street	D4
Wilson Street North	B3
York Street	C4
Zetland Street	D2

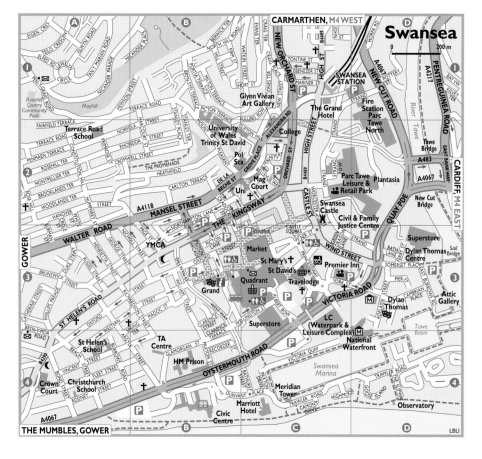

Swansea

Swansea is found on atlas page **29 J6**

Adelaide Street	D3	New Orchard Street	C1
Alexandra Road	C2	New Street	C1
Argyle Street	A4	Nicander Parade	A1
Bath Lane	D3	Nicholl Street	A3
Beach Street	A4	Norfolk Street	A2
Bond Street	A4	North Hill Road	B1
Brunswick Street	A3	Northampton Lane	A1
Burrows Road	A4	Orchard Street	C2
Caer Street	C3	Oxford Street	A3
Carlton Terrace	B2	Oystermouth Road	B4
Castle Street	C2	Page Street	B3
Catherine Street	A3	Park Street	B3
Clarence Street	B3	Paxton Street	B4
Clifton Hill	C2	Pentreguinea Road	D1
Constituion Hill	A2	Pen-Y-Graig Road	A1
Cradock Street	B2	Picton Lane	B3
Craig Place	C1	Pier Street	D3
Cromwell Street	A2	Primrose Street	A2
De La Beche Street	B2	Princess Way	C3
Dillwyn Street	B3	Quay Parade	D2
Duke Street	A3	Recorder Street	B4
Dunvant Place	B4	Rhondda Street	A2
East Bank Way	D2	Richardson Street	A3
East Burrows Road	D3	Rodney Street	A4
Ebenezer Street	C1	Rose Hill	A2
Elfed Road	A1	Russel Street	A2
Ferry Street	D3	St Helen's Road	A3
Firm Street	B1	Short Street	B1
Fleet Street	A4	Singleton Street	B3
George Street	A3	Somerset Place	D3
Glamorgan Street	B4	Strand	C1
Green Dragon Lane	C3	Tan Y Marian Road	A1
Grove Place	C2	Teilo Crescent	A1
Hanover Street	A2	Terrace Road	A2
Harcourt Street	B2	The Kingsway	B2
Heathfield	B2	Tontine Street	C1
Henrietta Street	A3	Trawler Road	C4
Hewson Street	A1	Victoria Quay	C4
High Street	C2	Victoria Road	C3
Hill Street	B1	Vincent Street	A4
Humphrey Street	A2	Walter Road	A3
Islwyn Road	A1	Watkin Street	C1
Llewelyn Circle	A1	Wellington Street	C3
Madoc Street	B3	West Way	B3
Mansel Street	B2	Western Street	A4
Mariner Street	C1	William Street	B3
Mount Pleasant	B2	Wind Street	C3
New Cut Road	D1	York Street	C3

Swindon

Swindon is found on atlas page **33 M8**

Albion Street	A4	Islington Street	C3
Alfred Street	C2	John Street	B3
Ashford Road	B4	King Street	B3
Aylesbury Street	B2	London Street	A3
Bathurst Road	C2	Manchester Road	C2
Beckhampton Street	C3	Market Street	B3
Bridge Street	B2	Maxwell Street	A3
Bristol Street	A3	Medgbury Road	C2
Broad Street	C2	Milford Street	B2
Cambria Bridge Road	A4	Milton Road	B3
Canal Walk	B3	Morley Street	B3
Carfax Street	C2	Morse Street	B4
Carr Street	B3	Newcastle Street	D3
Chester Street	A3	Newcombe Drive	A1
Church Place	A3	Newhall Street	B4
Cirencester Way	D1	Northampton Street	D3
Clarence Street	C3	North Star Avenue	B1
College Street	B3	Ocotal Way	D1
Commercial Road	B3	Park Lane	A3
Corporation Street	C2	Plymouth Street	C3
County Road	D2	Polaris Way	B1
Crombey Street	B4	Ponting Street	C2
Curtis Street	A4	Portsmouth Street	D3
Deacon Street	B4	Princes Street	C3
Dixon Street	B4	Prospect Hill	C4
Dover Street	C4	Queen Street	B3
Dowling Street	B4	Radnor Street	A4
Drove Road	D4	Regent Place	C3
Dryden Street	A4	Regent Street	B3
Eastcott Hill	C4	Rosebery Street	C2
East Street	B2	Salisbury Street	B3
Edgeware Road	B3	Sanford Street	B3
Elmina Road	C1	Sheppard Street	B2
Emlyn Square	A3	Southampton Street	D3
Euclid Street	C3	Stafford Street	B4
Faringdon Road	A3	Stanier Street	B4
Farnsby Street	B3	Station Road	B2
Fleet Street	B2	Swindon Road	C4
Fleming Way	C3	Tennyson Street	A3
Gladstone Street	C2	Theobald Street	A3
Gooch Street	C2	Victoria Road	C4
Graham Street	C2	Villett Street	B3
Great Western Way	A1	Westcott Place	A4
Groundwell Road	C3	Western Street	C4
Havelock Street	B3	Whitehead Street	B4
Hawksworth Way	A1	Whitney Street	B4
Haydon Street	B2	William Street	A4
Holbrook Way	B2	York Road	D3

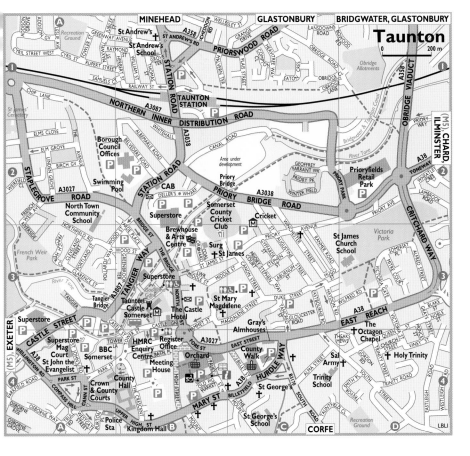

Taunton

Taunton is found on atlas page 18 H10

Albemarle Road	B2	Northern Inner	
Alfred Street	D3	Distribution Road	A1
Alma Street	C4	Northfield Road	A3
Belvedere Road	B2	North Street	B3
Billetfield	C4	Obridge Road	C1
Billet Street	C4	Obridge Viaduct	D2
Bridge Street	B2	Old Pig Market	B4
Canal Road	B2	Parkfield Road	A4
Cann Street	A4	Park Street	A4
Canon Street	C3	Paul Street	B4
Castle Street	A4	Plais Street	C1
Cheddon Road	B1	Portland Street	A3
Chip Lane	A1	Priorswood Road	B1
Church Street	D4	Priory Avenue	C3
Clarence Street	A3	Priory Bridge Road	B2
Cleveland Street	A3	Queen Street	D4
Compass Hill	A4	Railway Street	B1
Critchard Way	D2	Ranmer Road	C3
Cyril Street	A1	Raymond Street	A1
Deller's Wharf	B2	Rupert Street	A1
Duke Street	C3	St Andrew's Road	B1
Eastbourne Road	C3	St Augustine Street	C3
Eastleigh Road	D4	St James Street	B3
East Reach	D3	St John's Road	A4
East Street	C4	Samuels Court	A1
Fore Street	B4	South Road	C4
Fowler Street	A1	South Street	D4
French Weir Avenue	A2	Staplegrove Road	A2
Gloucester Road	C3	Station Road	B2
Grange Drive	C1	Stephen Street	C3
Grays Street	D3	Stephen Way	C3
Greenway Avenue	A1	Tancred Street	C3
Gyffarde Street	C3	The Avenue	A2
Hammet Street	B4	The Bridge	B3
Haydon Road	C3	The Crescent	B4
Herbert Street	B1	Thomas Street	B1
High Street	B4	Toneway	D2
Hugo Street	C3	Tower Street	B4
Hurdle Way	C4	Trinity Street	D4
Laburnum Street	C3	Upper High Street	B4
Lansdowne Road	C1	Victoria Gate	D3
Leslie Avenue	A1	Victoria Street	D3
Linden Grove	A2	Viney Street	D4
Lower Middle Street	B3	Wellington Road	A4
Magdalene Street	B3	Wilfred Road	C3
Mary Street	B4	William Street	B1
Maxwell Street	A1	Winchester Street	C2
Middle Street	B3	Wood Street	B3

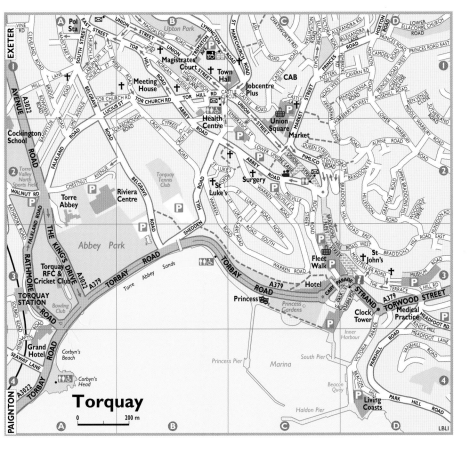

Torquay

Torquay is found on atlas page 7 N6

Abbey Road	B1	Mill Lane	A1
Alexandra Road	C1	Montpellier Road	D3
Alpine Road	C2	Morgan Avenue	B1
Ash Hill Road	C1	Museum Road	D3
Avenue Road	A1	Palm Road	B1
Bampfylde Road	A2	Parkhill Road	D4
Beacon Hill	D4	Pembroke Road	C1
Belgrave Road	A1	Pennsylvania Road	D1
Braddons Hill Road East	D3	Pimlico	C2
Braddons Hill Road West	C2	Potters Hill	C1
Braddons Street	D2	Princes Road	C1
Bridge Road	A1	Queen Street	C2
Camden Road	D1	Rathmore Road	A2
Cary Parade	C3	Rock Road	C2
Cary Road	C3	Rosehill Road	D1
Castle Lane	C1	St Efride's Road	A1
Castle Road	C1	St Luke's Road	B2
Cavern Road	D1	St Marychurch Road	C1
Chestnut Avenue	A2	Scarborough Road	B2
Church Lane	A1	Seaway Lane	A4
Church Street	A1	Shedden Hill Road	B3
Cleveland Road	A1	Solbro Road	A3
Croft Hill	B2	South Hill Road	D3
Croft Road	B2	South Street	A1
East Street	A1	Stentiford Hill Road	C2
Ellacombe Road	C1	Strand	D3
Falkland Road	A2	Sutherland Road	D1
Fleet Street	C3	Temperance Street	C2
Grafton Road	D2	The King's Drive	A3
Hennapyn Road	A4	The Terrace	D3
Higher Union Lane	B1	Torbay Road	A4
Hillesdon Road	D2	Tor Church Road	A1
Hoxton Road	D1	Tor Hill Road	B1
Hunsdon Road	D3	Torwood Road	D3
Laburnum Street	A1	Trematon Ave	B1
Lime Avenue	A2	Trinity Hill	D3
Lower Ellacombe		Union Street	B1
Church Road	D1	Upper Braddons Hill	D2
Lower Union Lane	C2	Vanehill Road	D4
Lower Warbury Road	D2	Vansittart Road	A1
Lucius Street	A1	Vaughan Parade	C3
Lymington Road	B1	Victoria Parade	D4
Magdalene Road	B1	Victoria Road	C1
Market Street	C2	Vine Road	A1
Meadfoot Lane	D4	Walnut Road	A2
Melville Lane	C2	Warberry Road West	C1
Melville Street	C2	Warren Road	B2
Middle Warbury Road	D1	Wellington Road	C1

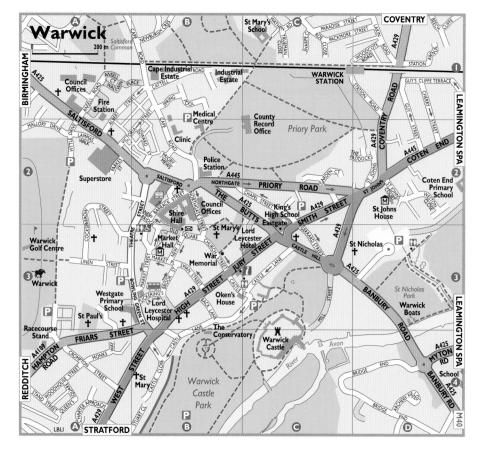

Warwick

Warwick is found on atlas page **59 L11**

Albert Street	A2	Old Square	B3
Ansell Court	A1	Packmore Street	C1
Ansell Road	A1	Paradise Street	C1
Archery Fields	D4	Parkes Street	A2
Back Lane	B3	Priory Mews	B2
Banbury Road	D3	Priory Road	C2
Barrack Street	B2	Puckering's Lane	B3
Beech Cliffe	D1	Queen's Square	A4
Bowling Green Street	B3	Roe Close	C1
Bridge End	D4	St Johns	D2
Brook Street	B3	St Johns Court	D2
Cape Road	B1	Saltisford	A1
Castle Close	B4	Sharpe Close	C1
Castle Hill	C3	Smith Street	C2
Castle Lane	B4	Spring Pool	B1
Castle Street	B3	Stand Street	A4
Cattell Road	B1	Station Avenue	D1
Chapel Street	C2	Station Road	D1
Charter Approach	A4	Stuart Close	B4
Cherry Street	D1	Swan Street	B3
Church Street	B3	Theatre Street	B3
Cocksparrow Street	A3	The Butts	B2
Coten End	D2	The Paddocks	D2
Coventry Road	D2	Trueman Close	C1
Crompton Street	A4	Victoria Street	A2
Edward Street	B2	Vittle Drive	A2
Friars Street	A4	Wallwin Place	A1
Garden Court	C2	Wathen Road	C1
Gerrard Street	C3	Weston Close	D2
Guy's Cliffe Terrace	D1	West Street	A4
Guy Street	D1	Woodcote Road	D1
Hampton Road	A4	Woodhouse Street	A4
High Street	B3		
Jury Street	B3		
Lakin Road	D1		
Lammas Walk	A2		
Linen Street	A3		
Mallory Drive	A2		
Market Place	B3		
Market Street	B3		
Mill Street	C3		
Monks Way	A4		
Myton Road	D4		
New Bridge	B2		
Newburgh Crescent	B1		
New Street	B3		
Northgate	B2		
Northgate Street	B2		

Watford

Watford is found on atlas page **50 D11**

Addiscombe Road	B3	Market Street	B4
Albert Road North	B2	Marlborough Road	B3
Albert Road South	B2	Merton Road	B4
Alexandra Road	A1	Mildred Avenue	A3
Anglian Close	D1	Monica Close	D1
Beechen Grove	C3	Nascot Street	B1
Brocklesbury Close	D2	New Road	D4
Burton Avenue	A4	New Street	C3
Cassiobury Drive	A2	Orphanage Road	C1
Cassio Road	A3	Park Avenue	A3
Charter Way	C3	Peace Prospect	A2
Chester Road	A4	Percy Road	B3
Chester Street	A4	Pretoria Road	A4
Clarendon Road	C1	Prince Street	C2
Cross Street	C2	Queen's Road	C2
Denmark Street	A1	Queen Street	C3
Derby Road	C3	Radlett Road	D2
Duke Street	C2	Raphael Drive	D1
Durban Road East	A4	Reeds Crescent	C1
Durban Road West	A4	Rickmansworth Road	A3
Earl Street	C3	Rosslyn Road	B3
Ebury Road	D2	St Albans Road	B1
Essex Road	A1	St John's Road	B1
Estcourt Road	C2	St Mary's Road	B4
Exchange Road	B3	St Pauls Way	D1
Farraline Road	B4	Shady Lane	B1
Feranley Street	B4	Shaftesbury Road	D2
Francis Road	B3	Smith Street	C4
Franklin Road	B1	Sotheron Road	C2
Gartlet Road	C2	Southsea Avenue	A4
Gaumont Approach	B2	Stanley Road	C3
George Street	C4	Station Road	B1
Gladstone Road	D3	Stephenson Way	D3
Granville Road	C4	Sutton Road	C2
Grosvenor Road	C3	The Avenue	A1
Halsey Road	B2	The Broadway	C3
Harwoods Road	A4	The Crescent	C4
Hempstead Road	A1	The Parade	B2
High Street	C3	Upton Road	B3
Hyde Road	A2	Vicarage Road	B4
Keele Close	C1	Water Lane	D4
King Street	C4	Wellington Road	B1
Lady's Close	C4	Wellstones	B3
Link Road	D1	Westland Road	B1
Loates Lane	C3	West Street	C4
Lord Street	C3	Whippendell Road	A4
Lower High Street	D4	Wiggenhall Road	B4
Malden Road	A1	Woodford Road	C1

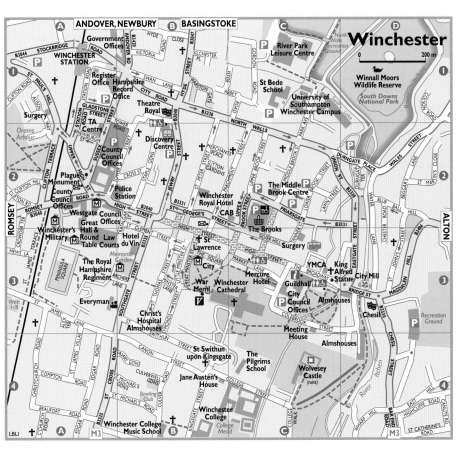

Winchester

Winchester is found on atlas page **22 E9**

Alex Terrace	A3	Market Lane	C3
Alison Way	A1	Marston Gate	B1
Andover Road	B1	Merchants Place	B2
Archery Lane	A3	Mews Lane	A3
Bar End Road	D4	Middle Brook Street	C2
Beaufort Road	A4	Minster Lane	B3
Beggar's Lane	D2	Newburgh Street	A2
Blue Ball Hill	D2	North Walls	C1
Bridge Street	D3	Parchment Street	B2
Canon Street	B4	Park Avenue	C2
Canute Road	D4	Romsey Road	A2
Chesil Street	D3	St Clement Street	B2
Chester Road	D2	St Cross Road	A4
Christchurch Road	A4	St George's Street	B2
City Road	B1	St James' Lane	A3
Clifton Hill	A2	St James Terrace	A3
Clifton Road	A1	St James' Villas	A4
Clifton Terrace	A2	St John's Street	D3
Colebrook Street	C3	St Martin's Close	D2
College Street	B4	St Michael's Gardens	B4
College Walk	C4	St Michael's Road	B4
Colson Road	D1	St Paul's Hill	A1
Compton Road	A4	St Peter Street	B2
Cross Street	B2	St Swithun Street	B3
Crowder Terrace	A3	St Thomas Street	B3
Culver Road	B4	Silchester Place	B1
Culverwell Gardens	B4	Silver Hill	C3
Durngate Place	D2	Southgate Street	B3
Durngate Terrace	D2	Staple Gardens	B2
Eastgate Street	D3	Station Road	A1
East Hill	D4	Stockbridge Road	A1
Edgar Road	A4	Sussex Street	A2
Friarsgate	C2	Sutton Gardens	B2
Friary Gardens	B4	Swan Lane	B1
Gladstone Street	A1	Symonds Street	B3
Gordon Road	C1	Tanner Street	C3
Great Minster Street	B3	The Broadway	C3
Highcliffe Road	D4	The Square	B3
High Street	B2	Tower Road	A1
Hyde Abbey Road	B1	Tower Street	A2
Hyde Close	B1	Trafalgar Street	B3
Hyde Street	B1	Union Street	C2
Jewry Street	B2	Upper Brook Street	C2
Kingsgate Street	B4	Upper High Street	A2
Lawn Street	C2	Victoria Road	B1
Little Minster Street	B3	Wales Street	D2
Lower Brook Street	C2	Water Lane	D3
Magdalen Hill	D3	Wharf Hill	D4

Wolverhampton

Wolverhampton is found on atlas page **58 D5**

Bath Avenue	A1	Peel Street	B3
Bath Road	A2	Penn Road	B4
Bell Street	B3	Piper's Row	D2
Berry Street	C2	Pitt Street	B3
Bilston Road	D3	Powlett Street	D4
Bilston Street	C3	Princess Street	C2
Birch Street	B2	Queen Square	B2
Broad Street	C2	Queen Street	C2
Castle Street	C3	Raby Street	D4
Chapel Ash	A3	Raglan Street	A3
Church Lane	B4	Red Lion Street	B2
Church Street	B4	Retreat Street	A4
Clarence Road	B2	Ring Road St Andrews	A2
Clarence Street	B2	Ring Road St Davids	D2
Cleveland Road	D4	Ring Road St Georges	C4
Cleveland Street	B3	Ring Road St Johns	B4
Corn Hill	D2	Ring Road St Marks	B3
Culwell Street	D1	Ring Road St Patricks	C1
Dale Street	A4	Ring Road St Peters	B2
Darlington Street	B3	Russell Street	A4
Dudley Road	C4	St George's Parade	C3
Dudley Street	C2	St John's Square	C4
Fold Street	B3	St Mark's Road	A3
Fryer Street	C2	St Mark's Street	A3
Garrick Street	C3	Salop Street	B3
Graiseley Street	A4	School Street	B3
Great Brickkiln Street	A4	Skinner Street	B3
Great Western Street	C1	Snow Hill	C3
Grimstone Street	D1	Stafford Street	C1
Horseley Fields	D2	Stephenson Street	A3
Hospital Street	D4	Stewart Street	B4
Lansdown Road	A1	Summer Row	B3
Lever Street	C4	Tempest Street	C3
Lichfield Street	C2	Temple Street	B3
Little's Lane	C1	Thomas Street	B4
Long Street	C2	Tower Street	C3
Lord Street	A3	Vicarage Road	D4
Mander Street	A4	Victoria Street	B3
Market Street	C3	Walsall Street	D3
Merridale Street	A4	Warwick Street	D3
Middle Cross	D3	Waterloo Road	B1
Mitre Fold	B2	Wednesfield Road	D1
Molineux Street	B1	Westbury Street	C2
New Hampton Road East	A1	Whitemore Hill	B1
North Street	B2	Whitmore Street	C2
Park Avenue	A1	Worcester Street	B4
Park Road East	B1	Wulfruna Street	C2
Park Road West	A2	Zoar Street	A4

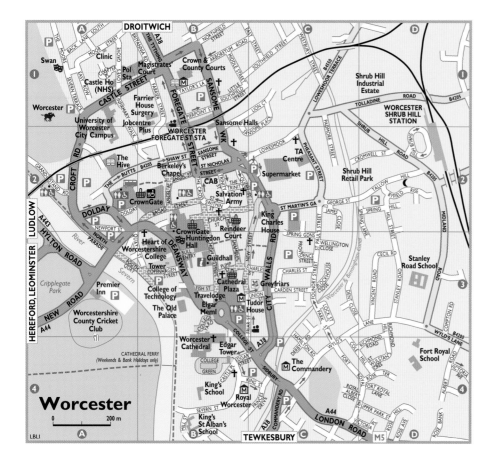

Worcester

Worcester is found on atlas page **46 G4**

Albert Road	D4	Middle Street	B1
Angel Street	B2	Midland Road	D2
Arboretum Road	B1	Mill Street	B4
Back Lane South	A1	Moor Street	A1
Blockhouse Close	C3	Newport Street	A2
Britannia Road	A1	New Road	A3
Broad Street	B2	New Street	C3
Byfield Rise	D2	Northfield Street	B1
Carden Street	C3	North Parade	A3
Castle Street	A1	Padmore Street	C1
Cathedral Ferry	A4	Park Street	C3
Cecil Road	D3	Pheasant Street	C2
Charles Street	C3	Pierpoint Street	B1
Charter Place	A1	Providence Street	C3
Church Street	B2	Pump Street	B3
City Walls Road	C3	Quay Street	A3
Cole Hill	C4	Queen Street	B2
College Street	B3	Richmond Road	D4
Commandery Road	C4	Rose Hill	D4
Compton Road	D3	Rose Terrace	D4
Copenhagen Street	B3	St Martin's Gate	C2
Croft Road	A2	St Nicholas Street	B2
Cromwell Street	D2	St Paul's Street	C3
Deansway	B3	St Swithin Street	B2
Dent Close	C3	Sansome Walk	B1
Derby Road	C4	Severn Street	B4
Dolday	A2	Severn Terrace	A1
East Street	B1	Shaw Street	B2
Edgar Street	B4	Shrub Hill Road	D2
Farrier Street	B1	Sidbury	C4
Fish Street	B3	Southfield Street	C1
Foregate Street	B1	Spring Hill	D2
Fort Royal Hill	C4	Stanley Road	D3
Foundry Street	C3	Tallow Hill	D2
Friar Street	C3	Taylor's Lane	B1
George Street	C2	The Butts	A2
Grandstand Road	A2	The Cross	B2
Hamilton Road	C3	The Moors	A1
High Street	B3	The Shambles	B2
Hill Street	D2	The Tything	B1
Hylton Road	A3	Tolladine Road	C1
King Street	B4	Trinity Street	B2
Little Southfield Street	B1	Union Street	C3
Lock Street	C3	Upper Park Street	D4
London Road	C4	Vincent Road	D3
Love's Grove	A1	Wellington Close	C3
Lowesmoor	C2	Westbury Street	C1
Lowesmoor Terrace	C1	Wyld's Lane	C3

York

York is found on atlas page **98 C10**

Aldwark	C2	Lower Ousegate	C3
Barbican Road	D4	Lower Priory Street	B3
Bishopgate Street	B4	Low Petergate	C2
Bishophill Senior	B3	Margaret Street	D3
Black Horse Lane	D2	Market Street	C2
Blake Street	B2	Micklegate	A3
Blossom Street	A4	Minster Yard	B1
Bootham	B1	Monkgate	C1
Bridge Street	B3	Museum Street	B2
Buckingham Street	B3	Navigation Road	D3
Cemetery Road	D4	New Street	B2
Church Street	C2	North Street	B2
Clifford Street	C3	Nunnery Lane	A3
College Street	C1	Ogleforth	C1
Colliergate	C2	Palmer Lane	D2
Coney Street	B2	Palmer Street	D2
Coppergate	C3	Paragon Street	D4
Cromwell Road	B4	Parliament Street	C2
Davygate	B2	Pavement	C2
Deangate	C1	Peasholme Green	D2
Dove Street	B4	Percy's Lane	D3
Duncombe Place	B2	Piccadilly	C3
Dundas Street	D2	Price's Lane	B4
Fairfax Street	B3	Priory Street	C3
Fawcett Street	D4	Queen Street	A3
Feasegate	C2	Rougier Street	B2
Fetter Lane	B3	St Andrewgate	C2
Finkle Street	C2	St Denys' Road	D3
Fishergate	D4	St Leonard's Place	B1
Foss Bank	D1	St Martins Lane	B3
Fossgate	C2	St Maurice's Road	C1
Foss Islands Road	D2	St Saviourgate	C2
George Street	D3	St Saviours Place	C2
Gillygate	B1	Scarcroft Road	A4
Goodramgate	C2	Shambles	C2
Hampden Street	B4	Skeldergate	B3
High Ousegate	C3	Spen Lane	C2
High Petergate	B1	Spurriergate	B2
Holgate Road	A4	Station Road	A3
Hope Street	D4	Stonegate	B2
Hungate	D2	Swinegate	C2
Jewbury	D1	The Stonebow	C2
Kent Street	D4	Toft Green	A3
King Street	C3	Tower Street	C3
Kyme Street	B4	Trinity Lane	B3
Lendal	B2	Victor Street	B4
Long Close Lane	D4	Walmgate	D3
Lord Mayor's Walk	C1	Wellington Road	D4

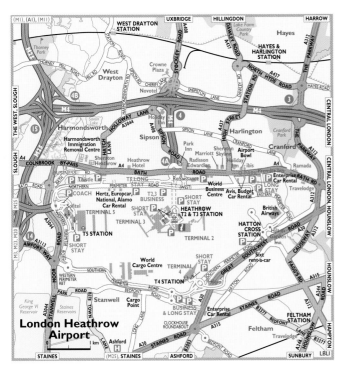

London Heathrow Airport – 17 miles west of central London, M25 junction 14 and M4 junction 4A

Satnav Location: TW6 1EW (Terminal 2), TW6 1QG (T3), TW6 3XA (T4), TW6 2GA (T5)
Information: visit www.heathrow.com
Parking: short-stay, long-stay and business parking is available.
Public Transport: coach, bus, rail and London Underground.
There are several 4-star and 3-star hotels within easy reach of the airport.
Car hire facilities are available.

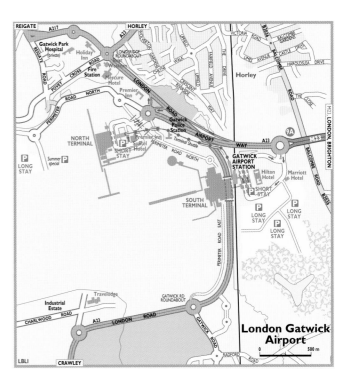

London Gatwick Airport – 29 miles south of central London, M23 junction 9A

Satnav Location: RH6 0NP (South terminal), RH6 0PJ (North terminal)
Information: visit www.gatwickairport.com
Parking: short and long-stay parking is available at both the North and South terminals.
Public Transport: coach, bus and rail.
There are several 4-star and 3-star hotels within easy reach of the airport.
Car hire facilities are available.

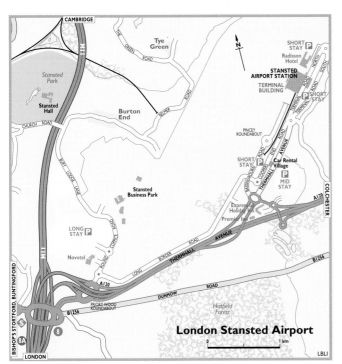

London Stansted Airport – 36 miles north-east of central London, M11 junction 8/8A

Satnav Location: CM24 1RW
Information: visit www.stanstedairport.com
Parking: short, mid and long-stay open-air parking is available.
Public Transport: coach, bus and direct rail link to London on the Stansted Express.
There are several hotels within easy reach of the airport.
Car hire facilities are available.

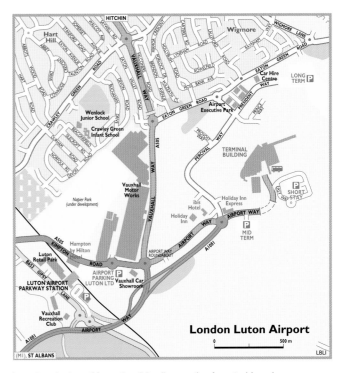

London Luton Airport – 34 miles north of central London

Satnav Location: LU2 9QT
Information: visit www.london-luton.co.uk
Parking: short-term, mid-term and long-stay parking is available.
Public Transport: coach, bus and rail.
There are several hotels within easy reach of the airport.
Car hire facilities are available.

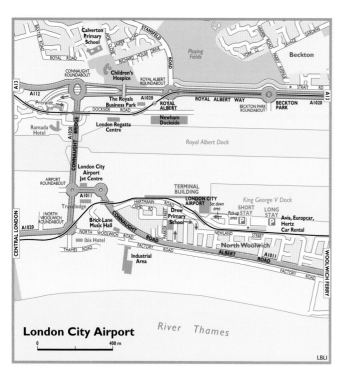

London City Airport – 8 miles east of central London

Satnav Location: E16 2PX
Information: visit *www.londoncityairport.com*
Parking: short and long-stay open-air parking is available.
Public Transport: easy access to the rail network, Docklands Light Railway and the London Underground.
There are 5-star, 4-star and 3-star hotels within easy reach of the airport.
Car hire facilities are available.

Birmingham Airport – 10 miles east of Birmingham, M42 junction 6

Satnav Location: B26 3QJ
Information: visit *www.birminghamairport.co.uk*
Parking: short and long-stay parking is available.
Public Transport: Air-Rail Link service operates every 2 minutes to and from Birmingham International Railway Station & Interchange.
There are several 4-star and 3-star hotels within easy reach of the airport.
Car hire facilities are available.

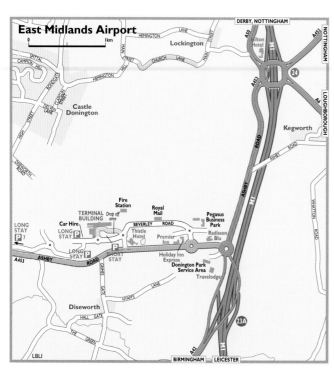

East Midlands Airport – 14 miles south-west of Nottingham, M1 junction 23A/24

Satnav Location: DE74 2SA
Information: visit *www.eastmidlandsairport.com*
Parking: short and long-stay parking is available.
Public Transport: bus and coach services to major towns and cities in the East Midlands.
There are several 3-star hotels within easy reach of the airport.
Car hire facilities are available.

Manchester Airport – 10 miles south of Manchester, M56 junction 5

Satnav Location: M90 1QX
Information: visit *www.manchesterairport.co.uk*
Parking: short and long-stay parking is available.
Public Transport: coach, bus and rail.
There are several 4-star and 3-star hotels within easy reach of the airport.
Car hire facilities are available.

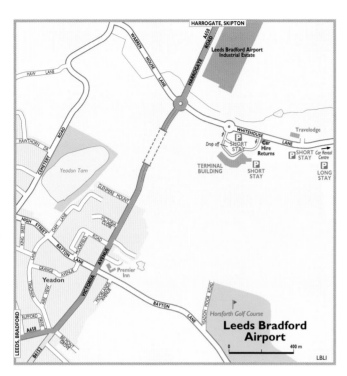

Leeds Bradford Airport – 8 miles north-east of Bradford and 8 miles north-west of Leeds

Satnav Location: LS19 7TU
Information: visit *www.leedsbradfordairport.co.uk*
Parking: short, mid-term and long-stay parking is available.
Public Transport: bus service operates every 30 minutes from Bradford, Leeds and Otley.
There are several 4-star and 3-star hotels within easy reach of the airport.
Car hire facilities are available.

Aberdeen Airport – 7 miles north-west of Aberdeen

Satnav Location: AB21 7DU
Information: visit *www.aberdeenairport.com*
Parking: short and long-stay parking is available.
Public Transport: regular bus service to central Aberdeen.
There are several 4-star and 3-star hotels within easy reach of the airport.
Car hire facilities are available.

Edinburgh Airport – 9 miles west of Edinburgh

Satnav Location: EH12 9DN
Information: visit *www.edinburghairport.com*
Parking: short and long-stay parking is available.
Public Transport: regular bus services to central Edinburgh, Glasgow and Fife and a tram service to Edinburgh.
There are several 4-star and 3-star hotels within easy reach of the airport.
Car hire and valet parking facilities are available.

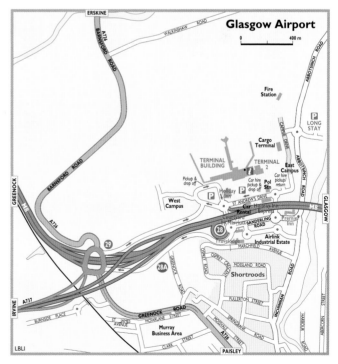

Glasgow Airport – 10 miles west of Glasgow, M8 junction 28/29

Satnav Location: PA3 2SW
Information: visit *www.glasgowairport.com*
Parking: short and long-stay parking is available.
Public Transport: regular coach services operate direct to central Glasgow.
There are several 3-star hotels within easy reach of the airport.
Car hire facilities are available.

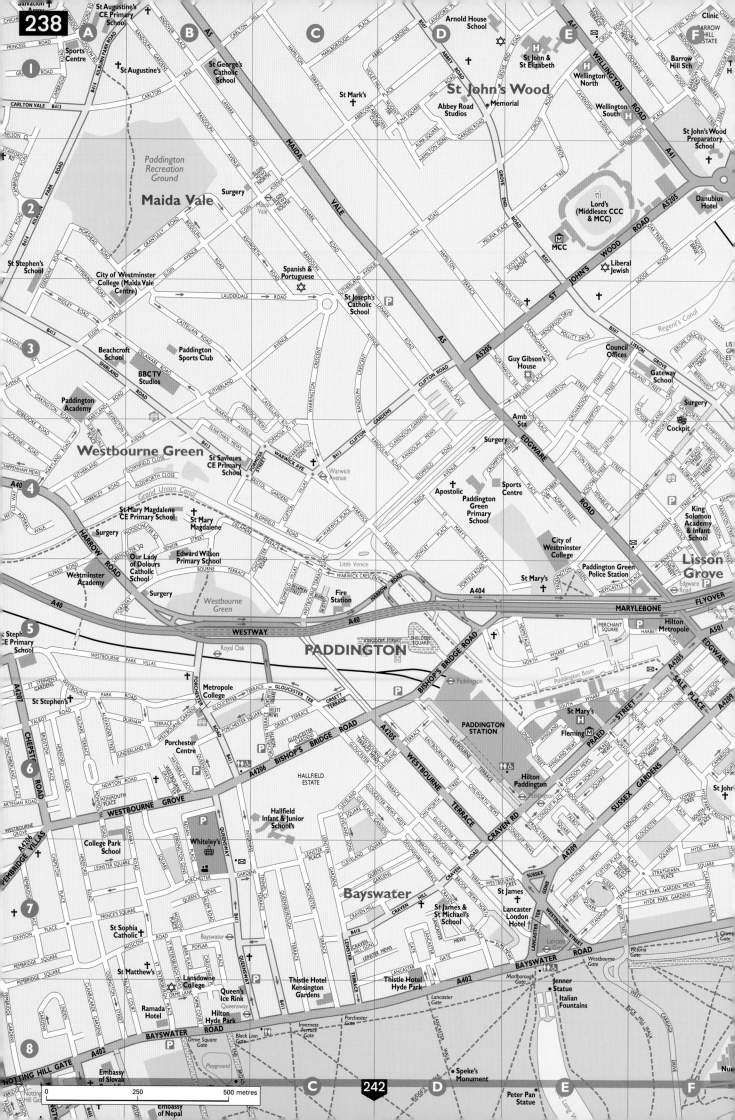

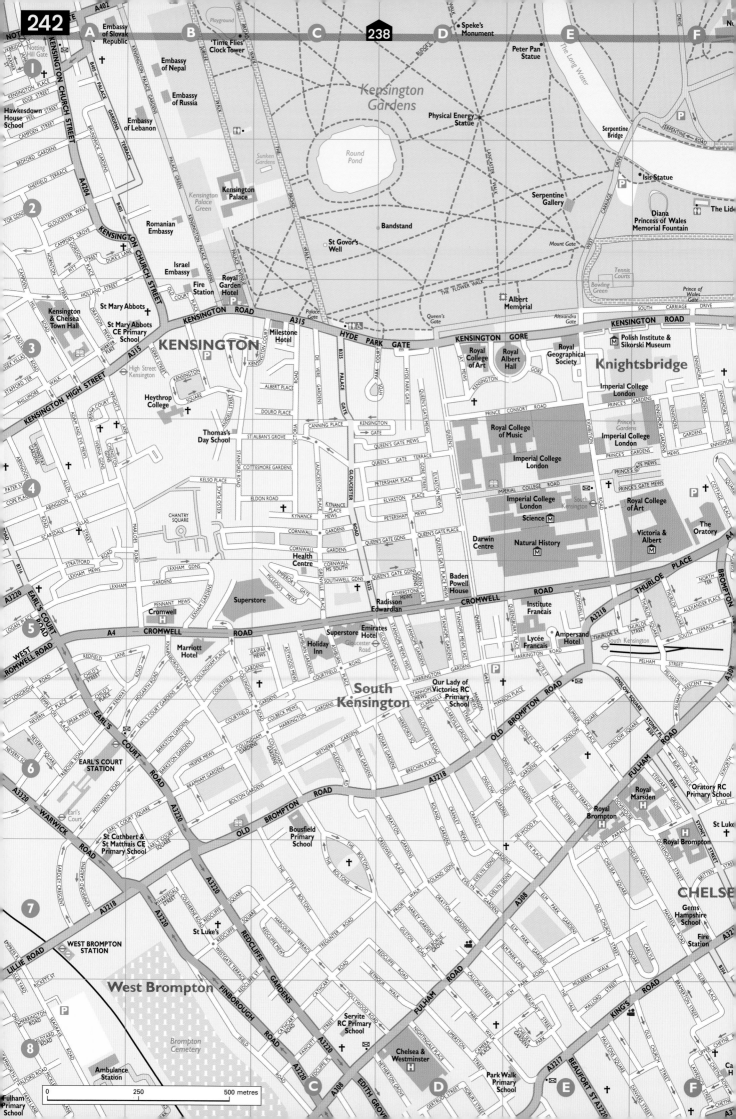

Central London index

This index lists street and station names, and top places of tourist interest shown in **red**. Names are listed in alphabetical order and written in full, but may be abbreviated on the map. Each entry is followed by its Postcode District and then the page number and grid reference to the square in which the name is found. Names are asterisked (*) in the index where there is insufficient space to show them on the map.

A

Abbey Gardens NW8 238 C1
Abbey Orchard Street SW1P 244 B4
Abbey Road NW8 238 D1
Abbey Street SE1 246 B7
Abchurch Lane EC4N 241 L7
Abercorn Close NW8 238 C1
Abercorn Place NW8 238 C1
Aberdeen Place NW8 238 E3
Aberdour Street SE1 245 M5
Abingdon Road W8 242 A4
Abingdon Street SW1P 244 C3
Abingdon Villas W8 242 A4
Ackroyd Drive E3 247 L1
Acorn Walk SE16 247 K5
Acton Street WC1X 240 E2
Adam and Eve Mews W8 242 A3
Adam's Row W1K 239 K8
Adam Street WC2N 240 D8
Addington Street SE1 244 E3
Addle Hill EC4V 241 H7
Adelina Grove E1 246 F1
Adeline Place WC1B 240 B5
Adler Street E1 246 D2
Admiral Place SE16 247 K5
Admiral Walk W9 238 A4
Adpar Street W2 238 E4
Agar Street WC2N 240 D8
Agdon Street EC1V 241 H3
Agnes Street E14 247 L2
Ainsty Street SE16 247 G6
Air Street W1B 240 A8
Alaska Street SE1 244 F2
Albany Road SE5 245 L8
Albany Street NW1 239 L1
Albemarle Street W1S 239 L8
Albermarle Way EC1V 241 H4
Alberta Street SE17 245 H6
Albert Bridge SW3 243 G8
Albert Embankment SE1 244 D7
Albert Gardens E1 247 H3
Albert Gate SW1X 243 H2
Albert Place W8 242 C3
Albion Gate W2 239 G7
Albion Place EC1M 241 H4
Albion Street SE16 247 G7
Albion Street W2 239 G7
Aldenham Street NW1 240 A1
Aldermanbury EC2V 241 K6
Alderney Mews SE1 245 K4
Alderney Street SW1V 243 L6
Aldersgate Street EC1A 241 J4
Aldford Street W1K 239 J8
Aldgate EC3M 246 B3
Aldgate ⊖ EC3N 246 B3
Aldgate East ⊖ E1 246 C2
Aldgate High Street EC3N 246 B3
Aldgate Square EC3N 246 B3
Aldsworth Close W9 238 B4
Aldwych WC2E 240 E7
Alexander Place SW7 242 F5
Alexander Street W2 238 A6
Alexandra Gate SW7 242 E3
Alfred Mews WC1E 240 B4
Alfred Place WC1E 240 B4
Alfred Road W2 238 A5
Alice Street SE1 245 M4
Alie Street E1 246 C3
Allen Street W8 242 A4
Allhallows Lane EC4R 241 L8
Allington Street SW1E 243 M4
Allitsen Road NW8 238 F1
Allsop Place NW1 239 H4
Alma Square NW8 238 D1
Alpha Place SW3 243 G8
Alsace Road SE17 245 M7
Alscot Road SE1 246 C8
Alvey Street SE17 245 M6
Ambergate Street SE17 245 H7
Amberley Road W9 238 A4
Ambrosden Avenue SW1P 244 A4
Amelia Street SE17 245 J6
America Square EC3N 246 B3
America Street SE1 245 J2
Ampton Street WC1X 240 E2
Amwell Street EC1R 240 F2
Anchorage Point E14 247 M6
Andover Place NW6 238 B1
Angel ⊖ N1 241 G1
Angela Hooper Place * SW1E 244 A4
Angel Junction N1 241 G1
Angel Lane EC4R 241 L8
Angel Street EC1A 241 J6
Ann Moss Way SE16 246 F8
Ann's Close SW1X 243 J3
Ansdell Street W8 242 B4
Antill Terrace E1 247 H2
Antizan Street E1 246 B2
Apple Tree Yard SW1Y 240 A8
Appold Street EC2A 241 M4
Apsley Gate W1J 243 J2
Apsley House & Wellington Museum W1J 243 K2
Aquinas Street SE1 245 G1
Arbour Square E1 247 H2
Archangels SE16 247 J7
Archer Street W1B 240 B7
Arch Street SE1 245 J4
Arden Estate N1 241 M1
Argyle Square WC1H 240 D2
Argyle Street WC1H 240 D2
Argyll Road W8 242 A3
Argyll Street W1F 239 M6
Arlington Street SW1A 243 M1
Arlington Way EC1R 241 G2
Arne Street WC2H 240 D6
Arneway Street SW1P 244 B5
Arnhem Place E14 247 M8
Arnold Estate SE1 246 C7
Arnside Street SE17 245 K8
Artesian Road W11 238 A6
Arthur Street EC4V 241 L7
Artichoke Hill E1W 246 E4
Artillery Lane E1 246 A1
Artillery Row SW1P 244 B4
Arundel Street WC2R 240 F7
Ashbridge Street NW8 238 F4
Ashburn Gardens SW7 242 C5
Ashburn Place SW7 242 C5
Ashby Street EC1V 241 H2
Asher Way E1W 246 D4
Ashfield Street E1 246 E2
Ashford Street N1 241 M2
Ashley Place SW1P 243 M4
Ashmill Street NW1 238 F4
Ashmole Street SW8 244 F8
Ashworth Road W9 238 B2
Assam Street E1 246 C2
Assembly Place E1 247 G1
Astell Street SW3 243 G6
Aston Street E14 247 K1
Astwood Mews SW7 242 C5
Atherstone Mews SW7 242 D5
Atterbury Street SW1P 244 C6
Attneave Street WC1X 240 F3
Augustus Street NW1 239 L1
Aulton Place SE11 245 G7
Austin Friars EC2N 241 L6
Australia Gate SW1A 243 M3
Austral Street SE11 245 H5
Aveline Street SE11 244 F7
Ave Maria Lane EC1A 241 H6
Avenue Dock Hill SE16 247 J6
Avery Farm Row SW1W 243 K6
Avery Row W1K 239 L7
Aybrook Street W1U 239 J5
Aylesbury Road SE17 245 L7
Aylesbury Street EC1R 241 H4
Aylesford Street SW1V 244 B7
Aylward Street E1 247 G2
Ayres Street SE1 245 K2

B

Babmaes Street SW1Y 240 B8
Bache's Street N1 241 L2
Back Church Lane E1 246 D3
Back Hill EC1R 241 G4
Bacon Grove SE1 246 B8
Bainbridge Street WC1A 240 C6
Bakers Mews W1U 239 J6
Baker's Row EC1R 241 G4
Baker Street NW1 239 H4
Baker Street W1U 239 J5
Baker Street ⊖ NW1 239 H4
Balcombe Street NW1 239 G3
Balderton Street W1K 239 J7
Baldwin's Gardens EC1N 240 F5
Baldwin Street EC1V 241 L2
Bale Road E1 247 J1
Balfe Street N1 240 D1
Balfour Mews W1K 239 K8
Balfour Place W1K 239 J8
Balfour Street SE17 245 K5
Baltic Street East EC1Y 241 J3
Baltic Street West EC1Y 241 J4
Balvaird Place SW1V 244 C7
Bank ⊖ ⊖ EC2R 241 L6
Bank End SE1 245 K1
Bankside SE1 241 J8
Banner Street EC1Y 241 K3
Banqueting House SW1A 244 C2
Banyard Road SE16 246 E8
Barbican ⊖ EC1A 241 J4
Barbican Estate EC2Y 241 J5
Barge House Street SE1 245 G1
Bark Place W2 238 B7
Barkston Gardens SW5 242 B6
Barley Corn Way E14 247 L4
Barlow/Congreve Estate SE17 245 M5
Barlow Place W1J 239 L7
Barlow Street SE17 245 L5
Barnardo Street E1 247 H3
Barnby Street NW1 240 A1
Barnes Street E14 247 J2
Barnham Street SE1 246 A6
Baron's Place SE1 245 G3
Baron Street N1 241 G1
Barrett Street W1U 239 K6
Barrow Hill Estate NW8 238 F1
Barrow Hill Road NW8 238 F1
Barter Street WC1A 240 D5
Bartholomew Close EC1A 241 J5
Bartholomew Lane EC2R 241 L6
Bartholomew Street SE1 245 L5
Bartlett Court EC4A 241 G6
Barton Street SW1P 244 C4
Basil Street SW3 243 H4
Basin Approach E14 247 K3
Basinghall Lane EC2V 241 K5
Basinghall Street EC2V 241 K5
Bastwick Street EC1V 241 J3
Bateman's Buildings W1D 240 B6
Bateman Street W1D 240 B6
Bath Street EC1V 241 K2
Bath Terrace SE1 245 J4
Bathurst Mews W2 238 E7
Bathurst Street W2 238 E7
Battle Bridge Lane SE1 245 M1
Batty Street E1 246 D2
Bayley Street WC1B 240 B5
Baylis Road SE1 244 F3
Bayswater ⊖ W2 238 B7
Bayswater Road W2 238 E7
Baythorne Street E3 247 L1
Beaconsfield Road SE17 245 M7
Beak Street W1F 240 A7
Bear Grove SE1 241 J8
Bear Lane SE1 245 H1
Beauchamp Place SW3 243 G4
Beaufort Gardens SW3 243 G4
Beaufort Street SW3 242 E8
Beaumont Place W1T 240 A3
Beaumont Street W1G 239 K4
Beccles Street E14 247 M3
Beckett Street SE1 245 L3
Beckway Street SE17 245 M6
Bedale Street SE1 245 L1
Bedford Avenue WC1B 240 C5
Bedfordbury WC2N 240 C7
Bedford Gardens W8 242 A2
Bedford Place WC1N 240 D4
Bedford Row WC1R 240 E4
Bedford Square WC1B 240 B5
Bedford Street WC2E 240 D7
Bedford Way WC1H 240 C3
Bedlow Close NW8 238 F3
Beech Street EC2Y 241 J4
Beeston Place SW1W 243 L4
Belgrave Mews North * SW1X 243 J3
Belgrave Mews South * SW1X 243 K4
Belgrave Place SW1X 243 J4
Belgrave Road SW1V 243 L5
Belgrave Road SW1V 244 A6
Belgrave Square SW1X 243 J3
Belgrave Street E1 247 J2
Belgrove Street WC1H 240 D2
Bell Lane E1 246 B1
Bell Street NW1 238 F4
Bell Yard WC2A 240 F6
Belvedere Road SE1 244 E2
Benjamin Street EC1M 241 H4
Ben Jonson Road E1 247 J1
Bennett Street SW1A 243 M1
Ben Smith Way SE16 246 D7
Benson Quay E1W 246 F4
Bentinck Mews W1U 239 K6
Bentinck Street W1U 239 K6
Bere Street E1W 247 H3
Bergen Square SE16 247 K8
Berkeley Mews W1H 239 H6
Berkeley Square W1J 239 L8
Berkeley Street W1J 239 L8
Bermondsey ⊖ ⊖ SE16 246 E7
Bermondsey Spa SE16 246 C8
Bermondsey Square SE1 246 A8
Bermondsey Street SE1 246 A6
Bermondsey Wall East SE16 246 E7
Bermondsey Wall Estate SE16 246 D7
Bermondsey Wall West SE16 246 C6
Bernard Street WC1N 240 D4
Berners Mews W1T 240 A5
Berners Place W1F 240 A6
Berners Street W1T 240 A5
Bernhardt Crescent NW8 238 F3
Berryfield Road SE17 245 J6
Berry Street EC1V 241 H3
Berwick Street W1F 240 A6
Bessborough Gardens SW1V 244 C6
Bessborough Street SW1V 244 B6
Betterton Street WC2H 240 D6
Bevenden Street N1 241 L2
Bevin Close SE16 247 J5
Bevington Street SE16 246 D7
Bevin Way WC1X 240 F1
Bevis Marks EC3A 246 A2
Bewley Street E1 246 F3
Bickenhall Street W1U 239 H4
Bidborough Street WC1H 240 C2
Biddulph Road W9 238 B2
Big Ben (Elizabeth Tower) SW1A 244 D3
Bigland Street E1 246 E3
Billiter Square EC3M 246 A3
Billiter Street EC3M 246 A3
Bina Gardens SW5 242 C6
Bingham Place W1U 239 J4
Binney Street W1K 239 K7
Birchfield Street E14 247 M3
Birchin Lane EC3V 241 L7
Birdcage Walk SW1H 244 A3
Birde Lane EC4Y 241 H6
Bird Street W1C 239 K6
Birkenhead Street N1 240 D1
Bishop's Bridge Road W2 238 C6
Bishopsgate EC2M 246 A2
Bishops Square E1 246 B1
Bishop's Terrace SE11 245 G5
Bittern Street SE1 245 J3
Blackall Street EC2A 241 M3
Blackburne's Mews W1K 239 J7
Blackfriars ⇌ ⊖ EC4V 241 H7
Blackfriars Bridge SE1 241 H8
Black Friars Lane EC4V 241 H7
Blackfriars Road SE1 245 H3
Blackhorse Court SE1 245 L4
Black Lion Gate W2 238 B8
Black Prince Road SE11 244 E6
Blackwood Street SE17 245 K6
Blandford Street W1U 239 H5
Blenheim Street W1S 239 L7
Bletchley Street N1 241 K1
Blomfield Mews W2 238 C5
Blomfield Road W9 238 C4
Blomfield Street EC2M 241 M5
Blomfield Villas W2 238 C5
Bloomfield Terrace SW1W 243 J6
Bloomsbury Square WC1A 240 D5
Bloomsbury Street WC1B 240 C5
Bloomsbury Way WC1A 240 C5
Blount Street E14 247 K2
Blue Ball Yard SW1A 243 M1
Bohn Road E1 247 J1
Bolsover Street W1W 239 L4
Bolton Gardens SW5 242 B6
Bolton Street W1J 243 L1
Bond Street ⊖ W1C 239 K6
Bondway SW8 244 D8
Bonhill Street EC2A 241 L4
Bonnington Square SW8 244 E8
Boot Street N1 241 M2
Borough ⊖ SE1 245 K3
Borough High Street SE1 245 K3
Borough Road SE1 245 H3
Boscobel Place SW1W 243 K5
Boscobel Street NW8 238 E4
Boss Street SE1 246 B6
Boston Place NW1 239 G3
Botolph Lane EC3R 241 M7
Boundary Lane SE17 245 K8
Boundary Row SE1 245 G2
Bourdon Street W1K 239 L7
Bourlet Close W1W 239 M5
Bourne Estate EC1N 240 F4
Bourne Street SW1W 243 J6
Bourne Terrace W2 238 B5
Bouverie Place W2 238 F6
Bouverie Street EC4Y 241 G6
Bowland Yard * SW1X 243 J3
Bow Lane EC4M 241 K6
Bowling Green Lane EC1R 241 G3
Bowling Green Place SE1 245 L2
Bowling Green Street SE11 244 F8
Bowling Green Walk N1 241 M2
Bowsell Street WC1N 240 D4
Bow Street WC2E 240 D7
Boyd Street E1 246 D3
Boyfield Street SE1 245 H3
Boyle Street W1S 239 M7
Boyson Road SE17 245 K8
Brackland Terrace SW3 243 H6
Brackley Street EC1Y 241 J4
Bradenham Close SE17 245 K8
Brad Street SE1 245 G2
Braganza Street SE17 245 H7
Braham Street E1 246 C3
Bramerton Street SW3 242 F7
Bramham Gardens SW5 242 B6
Branch Road E14 247 J3
Brandon Estate SE17 245 H8
Brandon Street SE17 245 K6
Brangton Road SE11 244 F7
Bray Crescent SE16 247 H6
Bray Place SW3 243 H6
Bread Street EC4M 241 K7
Bream's Buildings EC4A 240 F6
Brechin Place SW7 242 D6
Breezer's Hill E1W 246 D4
Brendon Street W1H 239 G5
Bressenden Place SW1W 243 L4
Brettell Street SE17 245 L7
Brewers Green SW1H 244 A3
Brewer Street W1F 240 A7
Brewhouse Lane E1W 246 F6
Brewhouse Walk SE16 247 J5
Brick Court WC2R 240 F7
Brick Lane E1 246 C1
Brick Street W1J 243 K2
Bridewell Place EC4V 241 H7
Bridgeman Street NW8 238 F1
Bridge Place SW1V 243 L5
Bridgeport Place E1W 246 D4
Bridge Street EC4V 241 J7
Bridge Street SW1A 244 D3
Bridgewater Street EC2Y 241 J4
Bridgeway Street NW1 240 A1
Bridle Lane W1F 240 A7
Bridstow Place W2 238 A6
Brightlingsea Place E14 247 L4
Brill Place NW1 240 C1
Briset Street EC1M 241 H4
Bristol Gardens W9 238 B4
Britannia Street WC1X 240 E2
Britannia Walk N1 241 L2
Britannia Way N1 241 K1
Britten Street SW3 242 F7
Britton Street EC1M 241 H4
Broadbent Street W1K 239 L7
Broadgate Circle EC2M 241 M5
Broadley Street NW8 238 F4
Broadley Terrace NW1 238 F4
Broadstone Place W1U 239 J5
Broad Walk NW1 239 K1
Broad Walk W2 239 H7
Broadwall SE1 245 G1
Broadway SW1H 244 B4
Broadwick Street W1F 240 A7
Brockham Street SE1 245 K4
Brodlove Lane E1W 247 H3
Bromley Street E1 247 J2
Brompton Road SW3 243 G4
Brompton Road SW7 242 F5
Brompton Square SW3 242 F4
Bronti Close SE17 245 K7
Brook Drive SE11 245 G5
Brooke Street EC1N 240 F5
Brook Gate W2 239 H8
Brook Mews North W2 238 D7
Brook's Mews W1K 239 K7
Brook Street W1K 239 K7
Brook Street W2 238 E7
Brown Heart Gardens W1K 239 K7
Browning Mews W1G 239 K5
Browning Street SE17 245 K6
Brownlow Mews WC1N 240 E3
Brownlow Street WC1V 240 E5
Brown Street W1H 239 G6
Brunel Road SE16 247 G6
Brune Street E1 246 B1
Brunswick Close SE1 246 A6
Brunswick Gardens W8 242 A1
Brunswick Place N1 241 L2
Brunswick Quay SE16 247 J8
Brunswick Square WC1N 240 D3
Brunswick Street WC1N 240 D3
Brunton Place E14 247 K3
Brushfield Street E1 246 B1
Bruton Lane W1J 239 L8
Bruton Place W1J 239 L7
Bruton Street W1J 239 L8
Bryan Road SE16 247 K6
Bryanstone Mews West W1H 239 G5
Bryanston Mews East W1H 239 H5
Bryanston Place W1H 239 G5
Bryanston Square W1H 239 H5
Bryanston Street W1C 239 H7
Buck Hill Walk W2 238 E8
Buckingham Gate SW1E 243 L3
Buckingham Mews SW1E 243 M3
Buckingham Palace SW1A 243 L3
Buckingham Palace Road SW1W 243 L5
Buckingham Place SW1E 243 M4
Buckland Street N1 241 L1
Buckle Street E1 246 C2
Bucknall Street WC2H 240 C6
Buckters Rents SE16 247 J5
Budge's Walk W2 242 D2
Bulleid Way SW1V 243 L5
Bulstrode Street W1U 239 K5
Bunhill Row EC1Y 241 L3
Burdett Estate E14 247 M1
Burdett Road E14 247 L2
Burdett Street SE1 244 F3
Burgess Street E14 247 M1
Burge Street SE1 245 L4
Burlington Arcade W1J 239 M8
Burlington Gardens W1S 239 M8
Burnhouse Place SW1W 243 J6
Burnsall Street SW3 243 G7
Burnside Close SE16 247 J5
Burrell Street SE1 245 H1
Burslem Street E1 246 D3
Burton Grove SE17 245 L7
Burton Street WC1H 240 C3
Burwood Place W2 239 G6
Bury Close SE16 247 H5
Bury Court EC3A 246 A2
Bury Place WC1A 240 D5
Bury Street EC3A 246 A2
Bury Street SW1Y 244 A1
Bury Walk SW3 242 F6
Bushell Street E1W 246 D5
Bush Lane EC4V 241 L7
Butcher Row E14 247 J3
Bute Street SW7 242 E5
Butler Place SW1H 244 B4
Butler's Wharf SE1 246 C6
Buttesland Street N1 241 L2
Byefield Close SE16 247 K6
Bylands Close SE16 247 J5
Byng Place WC1E 240 B4
Byng Street E14 247 M6
Byward Street EC3R 246 A4
Bywater Place SE16 247 K5
Bywater Street SW3 243 G6

C

Cabbell Street NW1 238 F5
Cable Street E1 246 F3
Cadiz Street SE17 245 K7
Cadogan Gardens SW3 243 H5
Cadogan Gate SW1X 243 H5
Cadogan Lane SW1X 243 J4
Cadogan Place SW1X 243 J4
Cadogan Square SW1X 243 H5
Cadogan Street SW3 243 G6
Caledonian Road N1 240 D1
Caledonia Street N1 240 D1
Cale Street SW3 242 F6
Callow Street SW3 242 D7
Calshot Street N1 240 E1
Calthorpe Street WC1X 240 E3
Cambridge Circus WC2H 240 C7
Cambridge Gardens NW6 238 A1
Cambridge Gate NW1 239 L3
Cambridge Road NW6 238 A1
Cambridge Road NW6 238 A2
Cambridge Square W2 238 F6
Cambridge Street SW1V 243 L6
Cambridge Terrace NW1 239 L2
Cambridge Terrace Mews NW1 239 L3
Camdenhurst Street E14 247 K2
Camera Place SW10 242 D8
Camomile Street EC3A 246 A2
Campden Grove W8 242 A2
Campden Hill Road W8 242 A2
Campden Street W8 242 A1
Camperdown Street E1 246 C3
Canada Estate SE16 247 G7
Canada Gate SW1A 243 M3
Canada Street SE16 247 H7
Canada Water ⊖ ⊖ SE16 247 G7
Canada Wharf SE16 247 L5
Canal Street SE5 245 L8
Canary Riverside E14 247 L4
Candle Street E1 247 K1
Canning Place W8 242 C4
Cannon Drive E14 247 M4
Cannon Street EC4N 241 K7
Cannon Street ⇌ ⊖ EC4R 241 K7
Cannon Street Road E1 246 E3
Canon Beck Road SE16 247 G6
Canon Row SW1A 244 D3
Canton Street E14 247 M3
Capeners Close * SW1X 243 J3
Capland Street NW8 238 E3
Capper Street WC1E 240 A4
Capstan Way SE16 247 K5
Carbis Road E14 247 L2
Carburton Street W1W 239 L4
Cardigan Street SE11 244 F6
Cardington Street NW1 240 A2
Carey Street WC2A 240 F6
Carlisle Avenue EC3N 246 B3
Carlisle Lane SE1 244 F4
Carlisle Place SW1P 243 M5
Carlisle Street W1D 240 B6
Carlos Place W1K 239 K7
Carlton Gardens SW1Y 244 B2
Carlton Hill NW6 238 B1
Carlton House Terrace SW1Y 244 B1
Carlton Street W1J 243 L1
Carlton Vale NW6 238 A1
Carlton Vale NW6 238 B1
Carlyle Square SW3 242 F7
Carmelite Street EC4Y 241 G7
Carnaby Street W1F 239 M7
Caroline Place W2 238 B7
Caroline Street E1 247 H3
Caroline Terrace SW1W 243 J5
Carpenter Street W1K 239 K7
Carrington Street W1J 243 L1
Carr Street E14 247 K1
Carteret Street SW1H 244 B3
Carter Lane EC4V 241 H7
Carter Place SE17 245 K7
Carter Street SE17 245 J7
Carthusian Street EC1M 241 J4
Carting Lane WC2R 240 D8
Cartwright Gardens WC1H 240 C2
Cartwright Street E1 246 C4
Casey Close NW8 238 F3
Casson Street E1 246 C1
Castellain Road W9 238 B3
Castlebrook Close SE11 245 G5
Castle Lane SW1E 243 M4
Catesby Street SE17 245 L6
Cathay Street SE16 246 F7
Cathcart Road SW10 242 C8

Cathedral Walk SW1E 243 M4
Catherine Place SW1E 243 M4
Catherine Street WC2E 240 D7
Cato Street W1H 239 G5
Causton Street SW1P 244 B6
Cavell Street E1 .... 246 F1
Cavendish Avenue NW8 .... 238 E1
Cavendish Place W1G 239 L6
Cavendish Square W1G 239 L6
Cavendish Street N1 .... 241 L1
Caversham Street SW3 .... 243 G8
Caxton Street SW1H 244 B4
Cayton Street EC1V 241 K2
Centaur Street SE1 .... 244 F4
Central Street EC1V 241 J1
Chadwell Street EC1R 241 G1
Chadwick Street SW1P 244 B4
Chagford Street NW1 .... 239 H4
Chalton Street NW1 .... 240 B1
Chambers Street SE16 .... 246 D7
Chamber Street E1 .... 246 C3
Chambers Wharf SE16 .... 246 D6
Chancel Street SE1 .... 245 H1
Chancery Lane WC2A 240 F5
Chancery Lane ⊖ WC1V 240 F5
Chandos Place WC2N 240 C8
Chandos Street W1G 239 L5
Chantry Square W8 .... 242 B4
Chapel Market N1 .... 240 F1
Chapel Street NW1 .... 238 F5
Chapel Street SW1X 243 K3
Chaplin Close SE1 .... 245 G3
Chapman Street E1 .... 246 E3
Chapter Road SE17 .... 245 H7
Chapter Street SW1P 244 B6
Chargrove Close SE16 .... 247 H6
Charing Cross ≿ ⊖ WC2N 244 D1
Charing Cross Road WC2H 240 B6
Charing Cross Road WC2N 240 C7
Charlbert Street NW8 .... 238 F1
Charles II Street SW1Y 240 B8
Charles Square N1 .... 241 M2
Charles Street W1J 243 K1
Charleston Street SE17 .... 245 K6
Charlotte Road EC2A 241 M3
Charlotte Street W1T 240 A4
Charlwood Place SW1V 244 A6
Charlwood Street SW1V 243 M7
Charlwood Street SW1V 244 A6
Charrington Street NW1 .... 240 B1
Charterhouse Square EC1M .. 241 H4
Charterhouse Street EC1M ... 241 G5
Chart Street N1 .... 241 L2
Chaseley Street E14 .... 247 J2
Chatham Street SE17 .... 245 L5
Cheapside EC2V 241 K6
Chelsea Bridge SW1W 243 K8
Chelsea Bridge Road SW1W .. 243 J7
Chelsea Embankment SW3 .... 243 G8
Chelsea Manor Gardens SW3 .. 242 F7
Chelsea Manor Street SW3 .... 243 G7
Chelsea Park Gardens SW3 ... 242 E8
Chelsea Physic Garden SW3 .. 243 H8
Chelsea Square SW3 .... 242 E7
Cheltenham Terrace SW3 ...... 243 H6
Chenies Mews WC1E 240 B4
Chenies Street WC1E 240 B4
Cheniston Gardens W8 .... 242 A4
Chepstow Place W2 .... 238 A7
Chepstow Road W2 .... 238 A6
Chequer Street EC1Y 241 K3
Cherbury Street N1 .... 241 L1
Cherry Garden Street SE16 ... 246 E7
Chesham Close SW1X 243 J4
Chesham Place SW1X 243 J4
Chesham Street SW1X 243 J4
Chester Close SW1X 243 K3
Chester Close North NW1 ..... 239 L2
Chester Close South NW1 ..... 239 L2
Chesterfield Gardens W1J 243 K1
Chesterfield Hill W1J 239 K8
Chesterfield Street W1J 243 K1
Chester Gate NW1 .... 239 L2
Chester Mews SW1X 243 K3
Chester Place NW1 .... 239 L1
Chester Road NW1 .... 239 K2
Chester Row SW1W 243 K5
Chester Square SW1W 243 K5
Chester Square Mews SW1W .. 243 K4
Chester Street SW1X 243 K4
Chester Terrace NW1 .... 239 L2
Chester Way SE11 .... 245 G6
Cheval Place SW7 .... 243 G4
Cheval Street E14 .... 247 M7
Cheyne Gardens SW3 .... 243 G8
Cheyne Row SW3 .... 242 F8
Cheyne Walk SW3 .... 242 F8
Chicheley Street SE1 .... 244 E2
Chichester Road NW6 .... 238 A1
Chichester Road W2 .... 238 C5
Chichester Street SW1V 244 A7
Chicksand Street E1 .... 246 C1
Chigwell Hill E1W 246 E4
Child's Place SW5 .... 242 A5
Child's Street SW5 .... 242 A5
Chiltern Street W1U 239 J4
Chilworth Mews W2 .... 238 D6
Chilworth Street W2 .... 238 D6
China Hall Mews SE16 .... 247 G8
Chinatown W1D 240 B7
Chippenham Mews W9 .... 238 A4
Chiswell Street EC1Y 241 K4
Chitty Street W1T 240 A4
Christchurch Street SW3 .... 243 G8
Christian Street E1 .... 246 D3
Christina Street EC2A 241 M3
Christopher Close SE16 .... 247 H6
Christopher Street EC2A 241 L4
Chudleigh Street E1 .... 247 H2
Chumleigh Street SE5 .... 245 M8
Churchill Gardens
  Road SW1V 243 L7
Churchill War Rooms SW1A ... 244 C3
Church Street NW8 .... 238 F4
Church Way NW1 .... 240 B2
Churchyard Row SE1 .... 245 H5
Churton Place SW1V 244 A6
Churton Street SW1V 244 A6
Circus Road NW8 .... 238 E1
Cirencester Square W2 .... 238 A5
City Garden Row N1 .... 241 J1
City Road EC1V 241 J1
City Road EC1V 241 L3
City Thameslink ≿ EC4M 241 H6
Clabon Mews SW1X 243 H5
Clack Street SE16 .... 247 G7
Clanricarde Gardens W2 .... 238 A8

Claremont Square N1 .... 240 F1
Clarence Gardens NW1 .... 239 L2
Clarence Mews SE16 .... 247 G6
Clarendon Gardens W9 .... 238 D4
Clarendon Gate W2 .... 238 F7
Clarendon Place W2 .... 238 F7
Clarendon Street SW1V 243 L6
Clareville Grove SW7 .... 242 D6
Clareville Street SW7 .... 242 D6
Clarges Mews W1J 243 L1
Clarges Street W1J 243 L1
Clark Street E1 .... 246 F2
Claverton Street SW1V 244 A7
Clave Street E1W 246 F5
Clay Street W1U 239 H5
Clayton Street SE11 .... 244 F8
Cleaver Square SE11 .... 245 G7
Cleaver Street SE11 .... 245 G7
Clegg Street E1W 246 F5
Clemence Street E14 .... 247 L2
Clements Lane EC4N 241 L7
Clement's Road SE16 .... 246 E8
Clenston Mews W1H 239 H6
Clere Street EC2A 241 L3
Clerkenwell Close EC1R 241 G3
Clerkenwell Green EC1R 241 G4
Clerkenwell Road EC1M 241 G4
Cleveland Gardens W2 .... 238 C6
Cleveland Mews W1T 239 M4
Cleveland Place SW1Y 244 A1
Cleveland Row SW1A 244 A2
Cleveland Square W2 .... 238 C6
Cleveland Street W1T 239 M4
Cleveland Terrace W2 .... 238 D6
Clifford Street W1S 239 M7
Clifton Gardens W9 .... 238 C4
Clifton Place SE16 .... 247 G6
Clifton Place W2 .... 238 E7
Clifton Road W9 .... 238 D3
Clifton Street EC2A 241 M3
Clifton Villas W9 .... 238 C4
Clink Street SE1 .... 245 K1
Clipper Close SE16 .... 247 H6
Clipstone Mews W1W 239 M4
Clipstone Street W1W 239 L4
Cliveden Place SW1W 243 J5
Cloak Lane EC4R 241 K7
Cloth Fair EC1A 241 J5
Cloth Street EC1A 241 J5
Cluny Place SE1 .... 246 A8
Cobb Street E1 .... 246 B2
Cobourg Street NW1 .... 240 A2
Coburg Close SW1P 244 A5
Cochrane Mews NW8 .... 238 E1
Cochrane Street NW8 .... 238 E1
Cock Lane EC1A 241 H5
Cockspur Street SW1Y 244 C1
Codling Close * E1W 246 D5
Coin Street SE1 .... 245 G1
Coke Street E1 .... 246 D2
Colbeck Mews SW7 .... 242 C6
Colebrook Row N1 .... 241 H1
Coleherne Road SW10 .... 242 B7
Coleman Street EC2R 241 L6
Cole Street SE1 .... 245 K3
Coley Street WC1X 240 F3
College Hill EC4R 241 K7
College Street EC4R 241 K7
Collett Road SE16 .... 246 D8
Collier Street N1 .... 240 E1
Collingham Gardens SW5 ..... 242 B6
Collingham Place SW5 .... 242 B5
Collingham Road SW5 .... 242 B5
Colnbrook Street SE1 .... 245 H4
Colombo Street SE1 .... 245 H1
Colonnade WC1N 240 D4
Coltman Street E14 .... 247 K2
Commercial Road E1 .... 246 D2
Commercial Road E14 .... 247 K3
Commercial Street E1 .... 246 B1
Compton Street EC1V 241 H3
Concert Hall Approach SE1 ... 244 E2
Conder Street E14 .... 247 K2
Conduit Mews W2 .... 238 E6
Conduit Place W2 .... 238 E6
Conduit Street W1S 239 L7
Congreve Street SE17 .... 245 M5
Connaught Close W2 .... 238 F7
Connaught Place W2 .... 239 G7
Connaught Square W2 .... 239 G6
Connaught Street W2 .... 239 G6
Cons Street SE1 .... 245 G2
Constitution Hill SW1A 243 L3
Content Street SE17 .... 245 K5
Conway Street W1T 239 M4
Cookham Crescent SE16 .... 247 H6
Cook's Road NW1 .... 245 H8
Coombs Street N1 .... 241 J1
Cooper's Lane Estate NW1 ... 240 B1
Cooper's Road SE1 .... 246 B3
Copenhagen Place E14 .... 247 L2
Cope Place W8 .... 242 A4
Copley Court SE17 .... 245 J8
Copley Street E1 .... 247 H2
Copperfield Road E3 .... 247 K1
Copperfield Street SE1 .... 245 J2
Copthall Avenue EC2R 241 L6
Coptic Street WC1A 240 C5
Coral Street SE1 .... 245 G3
Coram Street WC1H 240 C3
Cork Square E1W 246 E5
Cork Street W1S 239 M8
Corlett Street NW1 .... 238 F5
Cornhill EC3V 241 L6
Cornwall Gardens SW7 .... 242 C4
Cornwall Mews South SW7 ... 242 C5
Cornwall Road SE1 .... 244 F1
Cornwall Road SE1 .... 245 G2
Cornwall Street E1 .... 246 E3
Cornwall Terrace Mews NW1 .. 239 H4
Cornwood Drive E1 .... 247 G2
Coronet Street N1 .... 241 M2
Corporation Row EC1R 241 G3
Corsham Street N1 .... 241 L2
Cosser Street SE1 .... 244 F4
Cosway Street NW1 .... 239 G4
Cottage Place SW3 .... 242 F4
Cottesmore Gardens W8 .... 242 B4
Cottons Lane SE1 .... 245 M1
Coulson Street SW3 .... 243 H6
Counter Street SE1 .... 245 M1
County Street SE1 .... 245 K5
Courtenay Square SE11 .... 244 F7
Courtenay Street SE11 .... 244 F6
Courtfield Gardens SW5 .... 242 B5
Courtfield Mews * SW5 .... 242 C5
Courtfield Road SW7 .... 242 C5

Court Street E1 .... 246 E1
Cousin Lane EC4R 241 K8
Covent Garden ⊖ WC2E 240 D7
Covent Garden WC2E 240 D7
Coventry Street W1D 240 B8
Cowcross Street EC1M 241 H4
Cowper Street EC2A 241 L3
Crail Row SE17 .... 245 L5
Cramer Street W1U 239 J5
Crampton Street SE17 .... 245 J6
Cranbourn Street WC2H 240 C7
Cranleigh Street NW1 .... 240 A1
Cranley Gardens SW7 .... 242 D6
Cranley Mews SW7 .... 242 D6
Cranley Place SW7 .... 242 E6
Cranston Estate N1 .... 241 L1
Cranwood Street EC1V 241 L2
Craven Hill W2 .... 238 C7
Craven Hill Gardens W2 .... 238 C7
Craven Hill Gardens W2 .... 238 C7
Craven Road W2 .... 238 D7
Craven Street WC2N 244 D1
Craven Terrace W2 .... 238 D7
Crawford Passage EC1R 241 G3
Crawford Place W1H 239 G5
Crawford Street W1H 239 G5
Creechurch Lane EC3A 246 A3
Creed Lane EC4V 241 H7
Cresswell Place SW10 .... 242 D6
Cressy Place E1 .... 247 G1
Crestfield Street WC1H 240 D2
Crimscott Street SE1 .... 246 A8
Crispin Street E1 .... 246 B1
Cromer Street WC1H 240 D2
Crompton Street W2 .... 238 D4
Cromwell Mews * SW7 .... 242 E5
Cromwell Place SW7 .... 242 E5
Cromwell Road SW5 .... 242 B5
Cromwell Road SW7 .... 242 E5
Crondall Court N1 .... 241 M1
Crondall Street N1 .... 241 L1
Cropley Street N1 .... 241 K1
Crosby Row SE1 .... 245 L3
Cross Lane EC3R 246 A4
Crosswall EC3N 246 B3
Crowder Street E1 .... 246 E3
Crucifix Lane SE1 .... 246 A6
Cruikshank Street WC1X 240 F1
Crutched Friars EC3N 246 A3
Cuba Street E14 .... 247 M6
Cubitt Street WC1X 240 E2
Culford Gardens SW3 .... 243 H6
Culling Road SE16 .... 246 F7
Cullum Street EC3M 241 M7
Culross Street W1K 239 J8
Culworth Street NW8 .... 238 F1
Cumberland Gardens WC1X .. 240 F2
Cumberland Gate W2 .... 239 H7
Cumberland Market NW1 ..... 239 L2
Cumberland Street SW1V 243 L6
Cumberland Terrace NW1 .... 239 L1
Cumberland Terrace
  Mews NW1 .... 239 L1
Cumberland Wharf SE16 ...... 247 G6
Cumming Street N1 .... 240 E1
Cundy Street SW1W 243 K6
Cunningham Place NW8 .... 238 E3
Cureton Street SW1P 244 C6
Curlew Street SE1 .... 246 B6
Cursitor Street EC4A 240 F6
Curtain Road EC2A 241 M3
Curtain Road EC2A 241 M4
Curzon Gate W2 .... 243 K2
Curzon Street W1J 243 K1
Cuthbert Street W2 .... 238 E4
Cutler Street EC3A 246 A2
Cynthia Street N1 .... 240 F1
Cypress Place W1T 240 A4
Cyrus Street EC1V 241 H3

D

Dacre Street SW1H 244 B3
Dakin Place E1 .... 247 J1
Dallington Street EC1V 241 H3
Damien Street E1 .... 246 F2
Dane Street WC1R 240 E5
Dansey Place W1D 240 B7
Dante Road SE11 .... 245 H5
Danvers Street SW3 .... 242 F8
D'Arblay Street W1F 240 A6
Dartford Street SE17 .... 245 K8
Dartmouth Street SW1H 244 B3
Darwin Street SE17 .... 245 L5
Date Street SE17 .... 245 K7
Davenant Street E1 .... 246 D1
Daventry Street NW1 .... 238 F4
Davidge Street SE1 .... 245 H3
Davies Mews W1K 239 K7
Davies Street W1K 239 K7
Dawes Street SE17 .... 245 L6
Dawson Place W2 .... 238 A7
Deal Porters Way SE16 .... 247 G8
Deal Street E1 .... 246 D1
Dean Bradley Street SW1P 244 C5
Dean Close SE16 .... 247 H6
Deancross Street E1 .... 246 F3
Deanery Street W1K 243 K1
Dean Farrar Street SW1H 244 B3
Dean Ryle Street SW1P 244 C5
Dean's Buildings SE17 .... 245 L6
Dean Stanley Street SW1P 244 C4
Dean Street W1D 240 B6
Dean's Yard SW1P 244 C4
Decima Street SE1 .... 245 M4
Deck Close SE16 .... 247 J6
Defoe Close SE16 .... 247 K7
Delamere Street W2 .... 238 C5
Delamere Terrace W2 .... 238 B4
De Laune Street SE17 .... 245 H7
Delaware Road W9 .... 238 B3
Dellow Street E1 .... 246 F3
Delverton Road SE17 .... 245 H7
Denbigh Place SW1V 243 M6
Denbigh Street SW1V 243 M6
Denbigh Street SW1V 244 A6
Denman Street W1D 240 B7
Denmark Street WC2H 240 C6
Denny Close SE11 .... 245 G6
Denny Street SE11 .... 245 G6
Denyer Street SW3 .... 243 G5
Derby Gate SW1A 244 D3
Derby Street W1J 243 K1
Dering Street W1S 239 L6
Derry Street W8 .... 242 B3

De Vere Gardens W8 .... 242 C3
Deverell Street SE1 .... 245 L4
Devonport Street E1 .... 247 G3
Devonshire Close W1G 239 K4
Devonshire Mews
  South W1G 239 K4
Devonshire Mews West W1G .. 239 K4
Devonshire Place W1G 239 K4
Devonshire Place Mews W1G .. 239 K4
Devonshire Row EC2M 246 A2
Devonshire Square EC2M 246 A2
Devonshire Street W1G 239 K4
Devonshire Terrace W2 .... 238 D7
De Walden Street W1G 239 K5
Dickens Estate SE16 .... 246 D7
Dickens Square SE1 .... 245 K4
Dilke Street SW3 .... 243 H8
Dingley Place EC1V 241 K2
Dingley Road EC1V 241 J2
Discovery Walk E1W 246 E5
Disney Place SE1 .... 245 K2
Distaff Lane EC4V 241 J7
Distin Street SE11 .... 244 F6
Dockhead SE1 .... 246 C7
Dockley Road SE16 .... 246 D8
Dock Street E1 .... 246 D4
Doddington Grove SE17 .... 245 H7
Doddington Place SE17 .... 245 H8
Dodson Street SE1 .... 245 G3
Dod Street E14 .... 247 M2
Dolben Street SE1 .... 245 H2
Dolland Street SE11 .... 244 E7
Dolphin Square SW1V 244 A7
Dolphin Square SW1V 244 B7
Dombey Street WC1N 240 E4
Dominion Street EC2A 241 L5
Donegal Street N1 .... 240 F1
Dongola Road E1 .... 247 J1
Donne Place SW3 .... 243 G5
Doon Street SE1 .... 244 F1
Dora Street E14 .... 247 L2
Doric Way NW1 .... 240 B2
Dorset Rise EC4Y 241 G7
Dorset Square NW1 .... 239 H4
Dorset Street W1U 239 H5
Doughty Mews WC1N 240 E3
Doughty Street WC1N 240 E3
Douglas Street SW1P 244 B6
Douro Place W8 .... 242 B3
Douthwaite Square * E1W 246 D5
Dovehouse Street SW3 .... 242 E6
Dover Street W1J 243 L1
Dover Street W1S 239 L8
Dowgate Hill EC4R 241 K7
Downfield Close W9 .... 238 B4
Downing Street SW1A 244 C2
Down Street W1J 243 K2
Downtown Road SE16 .... 247 K6
D'Oyley Street SW1X 243 J5
Draco Street SE17 .... 245 J8
Drake Close SE16 .... 247 H6
Draycott Avenue SW3 .... 243 G5
Draycott Place SW3 .... 243 H6
Draycott Terrace SW3 .... 243 H5
Drayson Mews W8 .... 242 A3
Drayton Gardens SW10 .... 242 D6
Druid Street SE1 .... 246 A6
Druid Street SE1 .... 246 B6
Drummond Crescent NW1 .... 240 B2
Drummond Gate * SW1V 244 B6
Drummond Road SE16 .... 246 E8
Drummond Street NW1 .... 240 A3
Drury Lane WC2B 240 D6
Dryden Court SE11 .... 245 G5
Dryden Street WC2B 240 D6
Duchess Mews W1G 239 L5
Duchess Street W1B 239 L5
Duchy Street SE1 .... 245 G1
Duckett Street E1 .... 247 J1
Duck Lane W1F 240 B6
Dufferin Street EC1Y 241 K4
Duke of Wellington
  Place SW1W 243 K3
Duke of York Square SW3 ..... 243 H6
Duke of York Street SW1Y 244 A1
Duke Shore Wharf E14 .... 247 K4
Duke's Lane W8 .... 242 A2
Duke's Place EC3A 246 B2
Duke's Road WC1H 240 C2
Duke Street W1K 239 K7
Duke Street W1U 239 J6
Duke Street Hill SE1 .... 245 L1
Duke Street St James's SW1Y .. 244 A1
Dunbar Wharf E14 .... 247 L4
Duncannon Street WC2N 240 C8
Duncan Terrace N1 .... 241 H1
Dundee Street E1W 246 E5
Dundee Wharf E14 .... 247 L4
Dunelm Street E1 .... 247 H2
Dunlop Place SE16 .... 246 C8
Dunraven Street W1K 239 H7
Dunster Court EC3R 246 A3
Duplex Ride SW1X 243 H3
Durand's Wharf SE16 .... 247 L6
Durham Row E1 .... 247 J1
Durham Street SE11 .... 244 E7
Durham Terrace W2 .... 238 A6
Dyott Street WC1A 240 C6
Dysart Street EC2A 241 M4

E

Eagle Close EC1M 241 H4
Eagle Street WC1R 240 E5
Eardley Crescent SW5 .... 242 A7
Earlham Street WC2H 240 C7
Earl's Court ≿ ⊖ SW5 .... 242 A6
Earl's Court Gardens SW5 ..... 242 B6
Earl's Court Road SW5 .... 242 A6
Earl's Court Square SW5 .... 242 A6
Earlstoke Street EC1V 241 H2
Earl Street EC2A 241 M4
Earnshaw Street WC2H 240 C6
East Arbour Street E1 .... 247 H2
Eastbourne Mews W2 .... 238 D6
Eastbourne Terrace W2 .... 238 D6
Eastcastle Street W1W 240 A6
Eastcheap EC3M 241 M7
Eastfield Street E14 .... 247 K1
East India Dock Road E14 ..... 247 M3
East Lane SE16 .... 246 D6
Easton Street WC1X 240 F3
East Poultry Avenue EC1A 241 H5
East Road N1 .... 241 L2
East Smithfield E1W 246 C4

East Street SE17 .... 245 L6
Eaton Close SW1W 243 J5
Eaton Gate SW1W 243 J5
Eaton Lane SW1W 243 L4
Eaton Mews North SW1W 243 K5
Eaton Mews South SW1W 243 K5
Eaton Mews West SW1W 243 K5
Eaton Place SW1X 243 J4
Eaton Row SW1W 243 K4
Eaton Square SW1W 243 K5
Eaton Terrace SW1W 243 J5
Ebbisham Drive SW8 .... 244 E8
Ebury Bridge SW1W 243 K6
Ebury Bridge Road SW1W 243 K7
Ebury Mews SW1W 243 K5
Ebury Square SW1W 243 K5
Ebury Street SW1W 243 K5
Eccleston Bridge SW1W 243 L5
Eccleston Mews SW1X 243 K4
Eccleston Place SW1W 243 L5
Eccleston Square SW1V 243 L6
Eccleston Street SW1X 243 K4
Edbrooke Road W9 .... 238 A3
Edge Street W8 .... 238 A1
Edgware Road W2 .... 238 F5
Edgware Road ⊖ W2 .... 238 F5
Edinburgh Gate SW1X 243 H3
Edith Grove SW10 .... 242 C8
Edwards Mews W1H 239 J6
Egerton Crescent SW3 .... 242 F5
Egerton Gardens SW3 .... 242 F5
Egerton Terrace SW3 .... 243 G4
Eglington Court SE17 .... 245 J7
Elba Place SE17 .... 245 K5
Eldon Place EC2M 241 L5
Eldon Road W8 .... 242 B4
Eleanor Close SE16 .... 247 H6
Elephant & Castle SE1 .... 245 J4
Elephant & Castle ⊖ ⊖ SE1 .. 245 J5
Elephant Lane SE16 .... 246 F6
Elephant Road SE17 .... 245 J5
Elf Row E1W 247 G3
Elgar Street SE16 .... 247 K7
Elgin Avenue W9 .... 238 B2
Elgin Mews North W9 .... 238 C2
Elgin Mews South W9 .... 238 C2
Elia Mews N1 .... 241 H1
Elia Street N1 .... 241 H1
Elim Estate SE1 .... 245 M3
Elim Street SE1 .... 245 M3
Elizabeth Bridge SW1V 243 L6
Elizabeth Street SW1W 243 K5
Ellen Street E1 .... 246 D3
Elliott's Row SE11 .... 245 H5
Ellis Street SW1X 243 J5
Elmfield Way W9 .... 238 A4
Elm Park Gardens SW10 ...... 242 E7
Elm Park Lane SW3 .... 242 E7
Elm Park Road SW3 .... 242 E8
Elm Place SW7 .... 242 E7
Elms Mews W2 .... 238 D7
Elm Street WC1X 240 F4
Elm Tree Road NW8 .... 238 E2
Elnathan Mews W9 .... 238 B4
Elsa Street E1 .... 247 J1
Elsted Street SE17 .... 245 L6
Elvaston Mews SW7 .... 242 D4
Elvaston Place SW7 .... 242 D4
Elverton Street SW1P 244 B5
Ely Place EC1N 241 G5
Elystan Place SW3 .... 243 G6
Elystan Street SW3 .... 242 F6
Embankment ⊖ WC2N 244 D1
Embankment
  Gardens SW3 .... 243 H8
Embankment Place WC2N 244 D1
Emba Street SE16 .... 246 D7
Emerald Street WC1N 240 E4
Emerson Street SE1 .... 245 J1
Emery Hill Street SW1P 244 A5
Emery Street SE1 .... 245 G3
Emperor's Gate SW7 .... 242 C5
Empire Square SE1 .... 245 L3
Empress Place SW6 .... 242 A7
Endell Street WC2H 240 C6
Endsleigh Gardens WC1H 240 B3
Endsleigh Place WC1H 240 B3
Endsleigh Street WC1H 240 B3
Enford Street W1H 239 G5
English Grounds SE1 .... 245 M1
Enid Street SE16 .... 246 C8
Ennismore Gardens SW7 ...... 242 F3
Ennismore Gardens
  Mews SW7 .... 242 F3
Ennismore Mews SW7 .... 242 F3
Ennismore Street SW7 .... 242 F4
Ensign Street E1 .... 246 D4
Epworth Street EC2A 241 L3
Erasmus Street SW1P 244 C6
Errol Street EC1Y 241 K4
Essendine Road W9 .... 238 A3
Essex Street WC2R 240 F7
Essex Villas W8 .... 242 A3
Europa Place EC1V 241 J2
Euston ≿ ⊖ NW1 .... 240 B2
Euston Road NW1 .... 240 B3
Euston Square NW1 .... 240 A3
Euston Square ⊖ NW1 .... 240 A3
Euston Street NW1 .... 240 A2
Evelyn Gardens SW7 .... 242 D7
Evelyn Walk N1 .... 241 L1
Eversholt Street NW1 .... 240 A1
Everton Buildings NW1 .... 239 M2
Ewer Street SE1 .... 245 J2
Ewhurst Close E1 .... 247 G1
Exchange Square EC2A 241 M4
Exeter Street WC2E 240 D7
Exhibition Road SW7 .... 242 E3
Exmouth Market EC1R 241 G3
Exon Street SE17 .... 245 M6
Exton Street SE1 .... 244 F2
Eyre Street Hill EC1R 240 F4

F

Fairclough Street E1 .... 246 D3
Fair Street SE1 .... 246 B6
Falmouth Road SE1 .... 245 K4
Fann Street EC1M 241 J4
Fanshaw Street N1 .... 241 M1
Fareham Street W1D 240 B6
Farmer Street W8 .... 242 A1
Farm Lane SW6 .... 242 A8
Farm Street W1K 239 K8
Farnham Place SE1 .... 245 J1

Farrance Street E14 .... 247 M3
Farringdon ⊖ EC1M 241 G4
Farringdon Lane EC1R 241 G4
Farringdon Road EC1R 240 F3
Farringdon Street EC1M 241 H5
Farrins Rents SE16 .... 247 J5
Farrow Place E14 .... 247 K7
Farthing Fields * E1W 246 F5
Fashion Street E1 .... 246 B1
Faunce Street SE17 .... 245 H7
Fawcett Street SW10 .... 242 C8
Featherstone Street EC1Y 241 L3
Fenchurch Avenue EC3M 246 A3
Fenchurch Buildings EC3M 246 A3
Fenchurch Place EC3M 246 A3
Fenchurch Street EC3M 246 A3
Fenchurch Street ⇌ EC3M 246 A3
Fendall Street SE1 .... 246 B8
Fenning Street SE1 .... 245 M2
Fentiman Road SW8 .... 244 D8
Fernsbury Street WC1X 240 F1
Fetter Lane EC4A 241 G6
Fieldgate Street E1 .... 246 D2
Fielding Street SE17 .... 245 J7
Field Street WC1X 240 E1
Finborough Road SW10 .... 242 B8
Finch Lane EC3V 241 L6
Finland Street SE16 .... 247 K8
Finsbury Circus EC2M 241 L5
Finsbury Estate EC1R 241 G3
Finsbury Market EC2A 241 M4
Finsbury Square EC2A 241 L4
Finsbury Street EC2Y 241 L4
First Street SW3 .... 243 G5
Fishermans Drive SE16 .... 247 J6
Fisher Street WC1R 240 D5
Fisherton Street NW8 .... 238 E3
Fish Street Hill EC3R 241 L7
Fitzalan Street SE11 .... 244 F5
Fitzhardinge Street W1H 239 J6
Fitzroy Square W1T 239 M4
Fitzroy Street W1T 239 M4
Flamborough Street E14 .... 247 J3
Flank Street E1 .... 246 C4
Flaxman Terrace WC1H 240 C3
Fleet Street EC4A 241 G6
Fleming Road SE17 .... 245 H8
Fletcher Street E1 .... 246 D3
Flint Street SE17 .... 245 L6
Flitcroft Street WC2H 240 C6
Flockton Street SE16 .... 246 D7
Flood Street SW3 .... 243 G7
Flood Walk SW3 .... 243 G7
Floral Street WC2E 240 D7
Foley Street W1W 239 M5
Forbes Street E1 .... 246 D3
Fordham Street E1 .... 246 D2
Ford Square E1 .... 246 F2
Fore Street EC2Y 241 K5
Formosa Street W9 .... 238 C4
Forset Street W1H 239 G6
Forsyth Gardens SE17 .... 245 H8
Fort Street E1 .... 246 B1
Fortune Street EC1Y 241 K4
Forum Magnum Square SE1 .... 244 E3
Foster Lane EC2V 241 J6
Foulis Terrace SW7 .... 242 E6
Foundry Close SE16 .... 247 J5
Fournier Street E1 .... 246 B1
Fowey Close E1W 246 E5
Frampton Street NW8 .... 238 E4
Francis Street SW1P 244 A5
Frankland Close SE16 .... 246 F8
Franklin's Row SW3 .... 243 H6
Frazier Street SE1 .... 245 G3
Frean Street SE16 .... 246 C8
Frederick Close W2 .... 239 G7
Frederick Street WC1X 240 E2
Frederic Mews * SW1X 243 J3
Freemantle Street SE17 .... 245 M6
Friend Street EC1V 241 H2
Frith Street W1D 240 B6
Fulbourne Street E1 .... 246 E1
Fulford Street SE16 .... 246 F7
Fulham Road SW10 .... 242 D8
Fulham Road SW3 .... 242 F6
Furnival Street EC4A 240 F5
Fynes Street SW1P 244 B5

G

Gabriel's Wharf SE1 .... 245 G1
Gainsford Street SE1 .... 246 B6
Galleon Close SE16 .... 247 G6
Galsworthy Avenue E14 .... 247 K2
Galway Street EC1V 241 K2
Gambia Street SE1 .... 245 H2
Garden Road NW8 .... 238 D1
Garden Row SE1 .... 245 H4
Garden Street E1 .... 247 H1
Garden Terrace * SW1V 244 B6
Garden Walk EC2A 241 M3
Gard Street EC1V 241 J2
Garford Street E14 .... 247 M4
Garnault Place EC1R 241 G3
Garnet Street E1W 246 F4
Garrett Street EC1Y 241 K3
Garrick Street WC2E 240 C7
Garterway SE16 .... 247 H7
Garway Road W2 .... 238 B6
Gaspar Mews SW7 .... 242 C5
Gataker Street * SE16 .... 246 E8
Gate Mews SW7 .... 242 F3
Gateforth Street NW8 .... 238 F3
Gate Mews NW1 .... 239 L3
Gatesborough Street * EC2A 241 M3
Gate Street WC2A 240 E5
Gatliff Road SW1V 243 K7
Gaunt Street SE1 .... 245 J4
Gayfere Street SW1P 244 C4
Gaywood Street SE1 .... 245 H4
Gaza Street SE17 .... 245 H7
Gedling Place SE1 .... 246 C7
Gee Street EC1V 241 J3
George Mathers Road SE11 .... 245 H5
George Row SE16 .... 246 C7
George Street W1H 239 H6
George Yard W1K 239 K7
Geraldine Street SE1 .... 245 H4
Gerald Road SW1W 243 K5
Gerrard Street W1D 240 B7
Gerridge Street SE1 .... 245 G3
Gertrude Street SW10 .... 242 D8
Gibson Road SE11 .... 244 F5
Gilbert Place WC1A 240 C5

Gilbert Road SE11 .... 245 G5
Gilbert Street W1K 239 K7
Gildea Street W1W 239 L5
Gillingham Street SW1V 243 M5
Gill Street E14 .... 247 L3
Gilston Road SW10 .... 242 D7
Giltspur Street EC1A 241 H5
Gladstone Street SE1 .... 245 H4
Glamis Place E1W 247 G4
Glamis Road E1W 247 G4
Glasgow Terrace SW1V 243 M7
Glasshill Street SE1 .... 245 H3
Glasshouse Street W1B 240 A8
Glasshouse Walk SE11 .... 244 D7
Glasshouse Yard EC1 .... 241 J4
Glebe Place SW3 .... 242 F7
Gledhow Road SW5 .... 242 C6
Glentworth Street NW1 .... 239 H4
Globe Pond Road SE16 .... 247 J5
Globe Street SE1 .... 245 K3
Gloucester Court * EC3R 246 A4
Gloucester Gardens W2 .... 238 C6
Gloucester Mews W2 .... 238 D6
Gloucester Mews West W2 .... 238 C6
Gloucester Place W1U 239 H3
Gloucester Place NW1 .... 239 H3
Gloucester Place Mews W1U 239 H5
Gloucester Road SW7 .... 242 C4
Gloucester Road SW7 .... 242 D6
Gloucester Road ⊖ SW7 .... 242 C5
Gloucester Square W2 .... 238 F6
Gloucester Street SW1V 243 M7
Gloucester Terrace W2 .... 238 B5
Gloucester Terrace W2 .... 238 D6
Gloucester Walk W8 .... 242 A2
Gloucester Way EC1R 241 G2
Glyn Street SE11 .... 244 F7
Godfrey Street SW3 .... 243 G6
Goding Street SE11 .... 244 D7
Godliman Street EC4V 241 J6
Golden Close N1 .... 241 K1
Golden Jubilee Bridge WC2N 244 D1
Golden Lane EC1Y 241 J4
Golden Square W1F 240 A7
Goldington Street SE1 .... 246 E3
Goldney Road W9 .... 238 A4
Goldsmith Street EC2V 241 K6
Gomm Road SE16 .... 247 G8
Goodge Place W1T 240 A5
Goodge Street W1T 240 A5
Goodge Street ⊖ W1T 240 B5
Goodwin Close SE16 .... 246 C8
Gordon Place W8 .... 242 A2
Gordon Square WC1H 240 B3
Gordon Street WC1H 240 B3
Gore Street SW7 .... 242 D4
Goring Street * EC3A 246 A2
Gosfield Street W1W 239 L5
Goslett Yard WC2H 240 B6
Goswell Road EC1V 241 H1
Gough Street WC1X 240 F3
Goulston Street E1 .... 246 B2
Gower Mews WC1E 240 B5
Gower Place NW1 .... 240 A3
Gower Street WC1E 240 B3
Gower's Walk E1 .... 246 D2
Gracechurch Street EC3V 241 M7
Grafton Place NW1 .... 240 B2
Grafton Street W1S 239 L8
Grafton Way W1T 240 A4
Graham Street N1 .... 241 J1
Graham Terrace SW1W 243 J6
Granby Terrace NW1 .... 239 M1
Grand Avenue EC1A 241 H5
Grange Road SE1 .... 246 B8
Grange Walk SE1 .... 246 A8
Grange Yard SE1 .... 246 B8
Grantully Road W9 .... 238 B2
Granville Place W1H 239 J6
Granville Road NW6 .... 238 A1
Granville Square WC1X 240 F2
Grape Street WC2H 240 C6
Gravel Lane E1 .... 246 B2
Gray's Inn Road WC1X 240 D2
Gray's Inn Square WC1R 240 F5
Gray Street SE1 .... 245 G3
Great Castle Street W1G 239 L6
Great Central Street NW1 .... 239 G4
Great Chapel Street W1D 240 B6
Great College Street SW1P 244 C4
Great Cumberland
   Place W1H 239 H6
Great Dover Street SE1 .... 245 K3
Great Eastern Street EC2A 241 M3
Great George Street SW1P 244 C3
Great Guildford Street SE1 .... 245 J1
Great James Street WC1N 240 E4
Great Marlborough
   Street W1F 239 M7
Great Maze Pond SE1 .... 245 L2
Great New Portland
   Street WC2H 240 C7
Greatorex Street E1 .... 246 D1
Great Ormond Street WC1N 240 D4
Great Percy Street WC1X 240 F2
Great Peter Street SW1P 244 B4
Great Portland Street W1W 239 L4
Great Portland
   Street ⊖ W1W 239 L4
Great Pulteney Street W1F 240 A7
Great Queen Street WC2B 240 D6
Great Russell Street WC1B 240 C5
Great Scotland Yard SW1A 244 C1
Great Smith Street SW1P 244 C3
Great Suffolk Street SE1 .... 245 H2
Great Sutton Street EC1V 241 H4
Great Swan Alley EC2R 241 L6
Great Titchfield Street W1W 239 M4
Great Tower Street EC3M 241 M7
Great Tower Street EC3R 246 A4
Great Winchester
   Street EC2N 241 L6
Great Windmill Street W1D 240 B7
Greek Street W1D 240 B6
Greenacre Square SE16 .... 247 J6
Green Bank E1W 246 E5
Greenberry Street NW8 .... 238 F1
Greencoat Place SW1P 244 A5
Green Coat Row SW1P 244 A4
Greenfield Road E1 .... 246 D2
Greenham Close SE1 .... 244 F3
Green Park ⊖ W1J 243 M1
Green Street W1K 239 J7
Greenwell Street W1W 239 L4
Greet Street SE1 .... 245 G2
Grenade Street E14 .... 247 L4

Grendon Street NW8 .... 238 F3
Grenville Place SW7 .... 242 C5
Gresham Street EC2V 241 J6
Gresse Street W1T 240 B5
Greville Street EC1N 241 G5
Greycoat Place SW1P 244 B4
Greycoat Street SW1P 244 B4
Grigg's Place SE1 .... 246 A8
Grosvenor Bridge SW8 .... 243 L8
Grosvenor Crescent SW1X 243 J3
Grosvenor Crescent
   Mews SW1X 243 J3
Grosvenor Gardens SW1W 243 L4
Grosvenor Gardens Mews
   East SW1W 243 L4
Grosvenor Gardens Mews
   North SW1W 243 L4
Grosvenor Gardens Mews
   South * SW1W 243 L4
Grosvenor Gate W2 .... 239 H8
Grosvenor Hill W1K 239 L7
Grosvenor Place SW1X 243 K3
Grosvenor Road SW1V 243 L8
Grosvenor Square W1K 239 J7
Grosvenor Street W1K 239 K7
Grosvenor Terrace SE5 .... 245 J8
Grove End Road NW8 .... 238 D2
Guildhouse Street SW1V 243 M5
Guilford Street WC1N 240 D4
Guinness Square SE1 .... 245 M5
Gulliver Street SE16 .... 247 K8
Gunpowder Square EC4A 241 G6
Gun Street E1 .... 246 B1
Gunthorpe Street E1 .... 246 C2
Gutter Lane EC2V 241 J6
Guy Street SE1 .... 245 L3

H

Haberdasher Street N1 .... 241 L2
Haddonhall Estate SE1 .... 245 M4
Hainton Close E1 .... 246 F3
Halcrow Street * E1 .... 246 F2
Half Moon Street W1J 243 L1
Halford Road SW6 .... 242 A8
Halkin Place SW1X 243 J4
Halkin Street SW1X 243 K3
Hallam Street W1W 239 L5
Halley Street E14 .... 247 K1
Hallfield Estate W2 .... 238 C6
Hall Place W2 .... 238 E4
Hall Road NW8 .... 238 D2
Hall Street EC1V 241 H2
Halpin Place SE17 .... 245 M6
Halsey Street SW3 .... 243 G5
Hamilton Close NW8 .... 238 D2
Hamilton Close SE16 .... 247 K7
Hamilton Gardens NW8 .... 238 D2
Hamilton Place W1J 243 K2
Hamilton Terrace NW8 .... 238 C1
Hamlet Way SE1 .... 245 L3
Hammett Street EC3N 246 B4
Hampden Close N1 .... 240 B1
Hampden Gurney Street W2 .... 239 H6
Hampstead Road NW1 .... 239 M2
Hampton Street SE17 .... 245 J6
Hanbury Street E1 .... 246 C1
Hand Court WC1V 240 E5
Handel Street WC1N 240 D3
Hankey Place SE1 .... 245 L3
Hannibal Road E1 .... 247 G1
Hanover Square W1S 239 L6
Hanover Street W1S 239 L7
Hans Crescent SW3 .... 243 H3
Hanson Street W1W 239 M4
Hans Place SW1X 243 H4
Hans Road SW3 .... 243 G4
Hans Street SW1X 243 H4
Hanway Place W1T 240 B6
Hanway Street W1T 240 B6
Harbet Road W2 .... 238 F5
Harbour Street WC1N 240 E4
Harcourt Street W1H 239 G5
Harcourt Terrace SW10 .... 242 C7
Hardinge Street E1W 247 G3
Hardwick Street EC1R 241 G2
Hardwidge Street SE1 .... 245 M2
Hardy Close SE16 .... 247 H6
Harewood Place W1G 239 L6
Harewood Row NW1 .... 239 G4
Harewood Avenue NW1 .... 239 G4
Harford Street E1 .... 247 J1
Harleyford Road SE11 .... 244 E8
Harley Gardens SW10 .... 242 D7
Harley Place W1G 239 K5
Harley Street W1G 239 K4
Harmsworth Street SE17 .... 245 H7
Harold Estate SE1 .... 246 A8
Harper Road SE1 .... 245 K4
Harriet Street SW1X 243 H3
Harriet Walk SW1X 243 H3
Harrington Gardens SW7 .... 242 C6
Harrington Road SW7 .... 242 E5
Harrington Square NW1 .... 239 M1
Harrington Street NW1 .... 239 M2
Harrison Street WC1H 240 D2
Harrods SW1X 243 G4
Harrowby Street W1H 239 G6
Harrow Place E1 .... 246 B2
Harrow Road W2 .... 238 A4
Hart Street EC3R 246 A3
Hasker Street SW3 .... 243 G5
Hastings Street WC1H 240 C2
Hatfields SE1 .... 245 G1
Hatherley Grove W2 .... 238 B6
Hatteraick Road SE16 .... 247 G6
Hatton Garden EC1N 241 G5
Hatton Street W2 .... 238 E4
Hatton Wall EC1N 241 G4
Havering Street E1 .... 247 H3
Haverstock Street N1 .... 241 J1
Hawke Place * SE16 .... 247 H6
Haydon Street EC3N 246 B3
Hayes Place NW1 .... 239 G4
Hay Hill W1J 239 L8
Hayles Street SE11 .... 245 H5
Hayne Street EC1A 241 J4
Hay's Lane SE1 .... 245 M1
Hay's Mews W1J 239 L8
Haywood Place EC1R 241 H3
Headfort Place SW1X 243 K3
Head Street E1 .... 247 H2
Hearnshaw Street E14 .... 247 K2
Hearn Street EC2A 241 M4

Heathcote Street WC1N 240 E3
Heddon Street W1B 239 M7
Heddon Street W1S 240 A7
Hedger Street SE11 .... 245 H5
Heiron Street SE17 .... 245 J8
Hellings Street E1W 246 D5
Helmet Row EC1V 241 K3
Helsinki Square SE16 .... 247 L8
Henderson Drive NW8 .... 238 E3
Heneage Lane EC3A 246 A3
Heneage Street E1 .... 246 C1
Henrietta Place W1G 239 L6
Henrietta Street WC2E 240 D7
Henriques Street E1 .... 246 D2
Henshaw Street SE17 .... 245 L5
Herbal Hill EC1R 241 G4
Herbert Crescent SW1X 243 H4
Herbrand Street WC1H 240 C3
Hercules Road SE1 .... 244 F4
Hereford Road W2 .... 238 A6
Hereford Square SW7 .... 242 D6
Hermitage Street W2 .... 238 E5
Hermitage Wall E1W 246 D5
Hermit Street EC1V 241 H2
Heron Place SE16 .... 247 K5
Heron Quay E14 .... 247 M5
Herrick Street SW1P 244 C6
Hertford Street W1J 243 K2
Hertsmere Road E14 .... 247 M4
Hesper Mews SW5 .... 242 B6
Hessel Street E1 .... 246 E3
Hewett Street EC2A 241 M3
Heygate Street SE17 .... 245 J5
Hide Place SW1P 244 B6
High Holborn WC1V 240 E5
High Street
   Kensington ⊖ W8 .... 242 A3
Hildyard Road SW6 .... 242 A8
Hilliards Court E1W 246 F5
Hillingdon Street SE17 .... 245 J8
Hill Road NW8 .... 238 D1
Hills Place W1F 239 M6
Hill Street W1J 239 K8
Hinde Street W1U 239 K6
Hind Grove E14 .... 247 M3
Hindgrove Area E14 .... 247 M3
Hithe Grove SE16 .... 247 G8
HMS Belfast SE1 .... 246 A5
Hobart Place SW1W 243 K4
Hobury Street SW10 .... 242 D8
Hogarth Road SW5 .... 242 B6
Holbein Mews SW1W 243 J6
Holbein Place SW1W 243 J6
Holborn EC1N 241 G5
Holborn ⊖ WC2B 240 E5
Holborn Circus EC1N 241 G5
Holborn Viaduct EC1A 241 G5
Holford Street WC1X 240 F2
Holland Street SE1 .... 245 H1
Holland Street W8 .... 242 A3
Hollen Street W1F 240 A6
Holles Street W1C 239 L6
Hollywood Road SW10 .... 242 C8
Holyoak Road SE11 .... 245 H5
Holyrood Street SE1 .... 245 M2
Holyrood Street SE1 .... 246 A6
Holywell Row EC2A 241 M4
Homefield Street * N1 .... 241 M1
Homer Row W1H 239 G5
Homer Street W1H 239 G5
Hooper Street E1 .... 246 D3
Hopetown Street E1 .... 246 C1
Hopkins Street W1F 240 A7
Hopton Street SE1 .... 245 H1
Hopwood Road SE17 .... 245 L8
Hornton Place W8 .... 242 A3
Hornton Street W8 .... 242 A2
Horse & Dolphin Yard W1D 240 B7
Horseferry Road E14 .... 247 J3
Horseferry Road SW1P 244 B4
Horse Guards Avenue SW1A 244 C2
Horse Guards Parade SW1A 244 C2
Horse Guards Road SW1A 244 C2
Horselydown Lane SE1 .... 246 B6
Horsley Street SE17 .... 245 K8
Hosier Lane EC1A 241 H5
Hothfield Place SE16 .... 247 G8
Hotspur Street SE11 .... 244 F6
Houghton Street WC2A 240 E6
Houndsditch EC3A 246 A2
Houses of Parliament SW1A 244 D3
Howick Place SW1E 244 A4
Howland Street W1T 240 A4
Howland Way SE16 .... 247 K7
Howley Place W2 .... 238 D4
Hoxton Square N1 .... 241 M2
Hoxton Street N1 .... 241 M1
Hudson Place SW1V 243 M5
Hugh Mews SW1V 243 L6
Hugh Street SW1V 243 L6
Hugh Street SW1V 243 L6
Hull Close SE16 .... 247 J6
Hull Street EC1V 241 J2
Hungerford Bridge SE1 .... 244 E1
Hunter Close SE1 .... 245 M4
Hunter Street WC1N 240 D3
Huntley Street WC1E 240 A4
Huntsman Street SE17 .... 245 M6
Huntsworth Mews NW1 .... 239 H3
Hurley Crescent SE16 .... 247 H6
Hutching's Street E14 .... 247 M7
Hutton Street EC4Y 241 G7
Hyde Park ⊖ W2 .... 243 G1
Hyde Park Corner W1J 243 K2
Hyde Park Corner ⊖ W1J 243 K2
Hyde Park Court SW7 .... 242 D3
Hyde Park Crescent W2 .... 238 F6
Hyde Park Garden Mews W2 .... 238 F7
Hyde Park Gardens W2 .... 238 F7
Hyde Park Gate SW7 .... 242 C3
Hyde Park Gate SW7 .... 242 D3
Hyde Park Square W2 .... 238 F7
Hyde Park Street W2 .... 238 F7

I

Idol Lane EC3R 241 M7
Ifield Road SW10 .... 242 B8
Iliffe Street SE17 .... 245 J6
Iliffe Yard SE17 .... 245 J6
Imperial College Road SW7 .... 242 D4
Imperial War Museum SE1 .... 245 G4
India Street EC3N 246 B3
Ingestre Place W1F 240 A7
Inglebert Street EC1R 240 F2

Ingram Close SE11 .... 244 E5
Inner Circle NW1 .... 239 J2
Inverness Terrace W2 .... 238 B6
Inverness Terrace Gate W2 .... 238 C8
Invicta Plaza SE1 .... 245 H1
Inville Road SE17 .... 245 L7
Ironmonger Lane EC2V 241 K6
Ironmonger Row EC1V 241 K2
Irving Street WC2N 240 C8
Isambard Place SE16 .... 247 G6
Island Row E14 .... 247 K3
Iverna Court W8 .... 242 A4
Iverna Gardens W8 .... 242 A4
Ives Street SW3 .... 243 G5
Ivor Place NW1 .... 239 G4
Ixworth Place SW3 .... 242 F6

J

Jacob Street SE1 .... 246 C6
Jamaica Gate SE16 .... 246 F8
Jamaica Road SE1 .... 246 C7
Jamaica Road SE16 .... 246 E7
Jamaica Street E1 .... 247 G2
Jamaica Wharf SE1 .... 246 C6
James Street W1U 239 K6
James Street WC2E 240 D7
Jameson Street W8 .... 242 A1
Jamuna Close E14 .... 247 K1
Janeway Street SE16 .... 246 D7
Jardine Road E1W 247 J4
Java Wharf SE1 .... 246 C6
Jay Mews SW7 .... 242 D3
Jermyn Street SW1Y 240 A8
Jerome Crescent NW8 .... 238 F3
Jewery Street EC3N 246 B3
Joan Street SE1 .... 245 G2
Jockey's Fields WC1R 240 E4
Johanna Street SE1 .... 244 F3
John Adam Street WC2N 240 D8
John Carpenter Street EC4Y 241 G7
John Felton Road SE16 .... 246 D7
John Fisher Street E1 .... 246 C4
John Islip Street SW1P 244 C5
John Prince's Street W1G 239 L6
John Roll Way SE16 .... 246 D7
John Ruskin Street SE5 .... 245 J8
John Slip Street SW1P 244 C6
John's Mews WC1N 240 E4
Johnson's Place SW1V 244 A7
Johnson Street E1 .... 247 G3
John Street WC1N 240 E4
Joiner Street SE1 .... 245 L1
Jonathan Street SE11 .... 244 E6
Jubilee Place SW3 .... 243 G6
Jubilee Street E1 .... 247 G2
Jubilee Walk W8 .... 242 B1
Judd Street WC1H 240 C2
Junction Mews W2 .... 238 F5
Juxon Street SE11 .... 244 E5

K

Katherine Close SE16 .... 247 H5
Kean Street WC2B 240 E6
Keel Close SE16 .... 247 J6
Keeley Street WC2B 240 E6
Keeton's Road SE16 .... 246 E7
Kell Street SE1 .... 245 H3
Kelso Place W8 .... 242 B4
Kemble Street WC2B 240 E6
Kempsford Gardens SW5 .... 242 A7
Kempsford Road SE11 .... 245 G6
Kendall Place W1U 239 J5
Kendal Street W2 .... 239 G6
Kennet Street E1W 246 D5
Kenning Street SE16 .... 247 G6
Kennings Way SE11 .... 245 G7
Kennington ⊖ SE11 .... 245 H7
Kennington Lane SE11 .... 244 E7
Kennington Oval SE11 .... 244 E8
Kennington Park
   Gardens SE11 .... 245 G8
Kennington Park Place SE11 .... 245 G7
Kennington Park Road SE11 .... 245 G7
Kennington Road SE1 .... 244 F4
Kennington Road SE11 .... 245 G5
Kennnington Oval SE11 .... 244 F8
Kenrick Place W1U 239 J5
Kensington Church Street W8 .... 242 A1
Kensington Court W8 .... 242 B3
Kensington Gardens W2 .... 242 C1
Kensington Gardens
   Square W2 .... 238 B6
Kensington Gate W8 .... 242 C4
Kensington Gore SW7 .... 242 D3
Kensington High Street W8 .... 242 A4
Kensington Palace W8 .... 242 B2
Kensington Palace
   Gardens W8 .... 242 B1
Kensington Palace
   Gardens W8 .... 242 B2
Kensington Place W8 .... 242 A1
Kensington Road SW7 .... 242 B3
Kensington Road W8 .... 242 B3
Kensington Square W8 .... 242 B3
Kenton Street WC1N 240 C3
Kenway Road SW5 .... 242 A6
Keystone Close N1 .... 240 D1
Keyworth Street SE1 .... 245 H4
Kia Oval (Surrey County
   Cricket Ground) SE11 .... 244 F8
Kilburn Park Road NW6 .... 238 A2
Kildare Terrace W2 .... 238 A6
Killick Street N1 .... 240 E1
Kinburn Street SE16 .... 247 H6
Kinder Street E1 .... 246 E2
King & Queen Wharf SE16 .... 247 H5
King and Queen Street SE17 .... 245 K6
King Charles Street SW1A 244 C2
Kingdom Street W2 .... 238 C5
King Edward Street EC1A 241 J6
King Edward Walk SE1 .... 245 G4
King James Street SE1 .... 245 H3
Kingly Street W1F 239 M7
King's Arms Yard EC2R 241 L6
King's Bench Street SE1 .... 245 H2
Kingscote Street EC4V 241 H7
King's Cross ⊖ N1C 240 D1
King's Cross Road WC1X 240 E2
King's Cross Square N1C 240 D1
King's Cross St
   Pancras ⊖ N1C 240 D1

Kingsgate Walk * SW1E 244 A4
King's Head Yard SE1 .... 245 L1
King's Mews WC1N 240 F4
Kingsmill Terrace NW8 .... 238 E1
King Square EC1V 241 J2
King's Road SW3 .... 242 E8
King's Scholars
  Passage SW1P 243 M5
King's Stairs Close SE16 ..... 246 F6
King Street WC2E 240 D7
King Street W1Y 244 A1
King Street EC2V 241 K6
Kingsway WC2B 240 E6
King William Street EC4N 241 L7
Kinnerton Place
  North * SW1X 243 J3
Kinnerton Place
  South * SW1X 243 J3
Kinnerton Street SW1X 243 J3
Kinnerton Yard * SW1X 243 J3
Kipling Estate SE1 .... 245 L3
Kipling Street SE1 .... 245 L3
Kirby Estate SE16 .... 246 D7
Kirby Grove SE1 .... 245 M3
Kirby Street EC1N 241 G4
Knaresborough Place SW5 ...... 242 B5
Knightrider Street EC4V 241 H7
Knightsbridge SW1X 243 H3
Knightsbridge SW3 .... 243 H3
Knox Street W1H 239 H4
Kynance Mews SW7 .... 242 C4
Kynance Place SW7 .... 242 C4

L

Lackington Street EC2A 241 L4
Lafone Street SE1 .... 246 B6
Lagado Mews SE16 .... 247 H5
Lambeth Bridge SW1P 244 D5
Lambeth High Street SE1 ...... 244 E5
Lambeth Hill EC4V 241 J7
Lambeth North ⊖ SE1 .... 244 F3
Lambeth Palace Road SE1 ...... 244 E4
Lambeth Road SE1 .... 244 F4
Lambeth Walk SE11 .... 244 F5
Lamb's Conduit Street WC1N ... 240 E4
Lamb's Passage EC1Y 241 K4
Lamb Street E1 .... 246 B1
Lamb Way SE1 .... 246 A7
Lamlash Street SE11 .... 245 H5
Lanark Place W9 .... 238 D3
Lanark Road W9 .... 238 B1
Lancaster Gate W2 .... 238 D7
Lancaster Gate W2 .... 238 D8
Lancaster Gate ⊖ W2 .... 238 E7
Lancaster Mews W2 .... 238 E7
Lancaster Place WC2E 240 E7
Lancaster Street SE1 .... 245 H3
Lancaster Terrace W2 .... 238 E7
Lancaster Walk W2 .... 238 D8
Lancelot Place SW7 .... 243 G3
Lancing Street NW1 .... 240 B2
Lanesborough Place * SW1X 243 J3
Langdale Street E1 .... 246 E3
Langford Place NW8 .... 238 D1
Langham Place W1B 239 L5
Langham Street W1W 239 L5
Langham Street W1W 239 M5
Langley Lane SW8 .... 244 D8
Langley Street WC2H 240 C7
Langton Close WC1X 240 E3
Lanhill Road W9 .... 238 A3
Lansdowne Place SE1 .... 245 L4
Lant Street SE1 .... 245 J3
Larcom Street SE17 .... 245 K6
Lauderdale Road W9 .... 238 B3
Laud Street SE11 .... 244 E7
Launcelot Street SE1 .... 244 F3
Launceston Place W8 .... 242 C4
Laurence Pountney
  Lane EC4V 241 L7
Lavender Road SE16 .... 247 K5
Lavender Wharf SE16 .... 247 K4
Lavington Street SE1 .... 245 J1
Lawn Lane SW8 .... 244 D8
Lawrence Street SW3 .... 242 F8
Lawrence Wharf SE16 .... 247 L6
Law Street SE1 .... 245 L4
Laxton Place NW1 .... 239 L3
Laystall Street EC1R 240 F4
Leadenhall Street EC3A 246 A3
Leadenhall Street EC3V 241 M6
Leake Street SE1 .... 244 E2
Leather Lane EC1N 241 G4
Leathermarket Street SE1 ..... 245 M3
Leeke Street WC1X 240 E2
Leigh Street WC1H 240 C3
Lees Place W1K 239 J7
Leicester Square ⊖ WC2H 240 C7
Leicester Square WC2H 240 C7
Leicester Street WC2H 240 B7
Leigh Street WC1H 240 C3
Leinster Gardens W2 .... 238 C6
Leinster Mews W2 .... 238 C7
Leinster Place W2 .... 238 C7
Leinster Square W2 .... 238 A7
Leinster Terrace W2 .... 238 C7
Leman Street E1 .... 246 C3
Lennox Gardens SW1X 243 G4
Lennox Gardens Mews SW1X 243 G5
Leonard Street EC2A 241 L3
Leopold Estate E3 .... 247 M1
Leopold Street E3 .... 247 L1
Leroy Street SE1 .... 245 M5
Lever Street EC1V 241 J2
Lewisham Street SW1H 244 B3
Lexham Gardens W8 .... 242 A5
Lexham Mews W8 .... 242 A5
Lexington Street W1F 240 A7
Leyden Street E1 .... 246 B2
Leydon Close SE16 .... 247 H5
Library Street SE1 .... 245 H3
Lidlington Place NW1 .... 240 A1
Lilestone Street NW8 .... 238 F3
Lilley Close E1W 246 D5
Lillie Road SW6 .... 242 A7
Lillie Yard SW6 .... 242 A7
Limeburner Lane EC4M 241 H6
Lime Close E1W 246 D5
Limerston Street SW10 .... 242 D8
Limehouse ⊖ ⇌ E14 .... 247 J3
Limehouse Causeway E14 .... 247 L4
Limehouse Link E14 .... 247 L3
Limerston Street SW10 .... 242 D8
Lincoln's Inn Fields WC2A 240 E6
Linden Gardens W2 .... 238 A8

Lindley Street E1 .... 246 F1
Lindsay Square SW1V 244 B7
Lindsey Street EC1A 241 H4
Linhope Street NW1 .... 239 G3
Linsey Street SE16 .... 246 D8
Lisle Street WC2H 240 B7
Lisson Green Estate NW8 ...... 238 F3
Lisson Grove NW8 .... 239 G4
Lisson Grove NW8 .... 238 F3
Lisson Street NW1 .... 238 F4
Litchfield Street WC2H 240 C7
Little Argyll Street W1F 239 M6
Little Britain EC1A 241 J5
Little Chester Street SW1X ... 243 K4
Little George Street SW1P 244 C3
Little Marlborough
  Street W1F 240 A7
Little New Street EC4A 241 G6
Little Portland Street W1G ... 239 L6
Little Russell Street WC1A ... 240 C5
Little St James's Street SW1A . 243 M2
Little Sanctuary SW1A 244 C3
Little Somerset Street E1 .... 246 B3
Little Titchfield Street W1W . 239 M5
Liverpool Grove SE17 .... 245 K7
Liverpool Street EC2M 241 M5
Liverpool Street ⇌ ⊖ EC2M ... 241 M5
Lizard Street EC1V 241 K3
Llewellyn Street SE16 .... 246 D7
Lloyd Baker Street WC1X 240 F2
Lloyd's Avenue EC3N 246 B3
Lloyd Square WC1X 240 F2
Lloyds Row EC1R 241 G2
Lloyd's Street WC1X 240 F2
Locksley Estate E14 .... 247 L2
Locksley Street E14 .... 247 L1
Lockyer Street SE1 .... 245 L3
Lodge Road NW8 .... 238 F3
Loftie Street SE16 .... 246 D7
Logan Place W8 .... 242 A5
Lolesworth Close E1 .... 246 B1
Lollard Street SE11 .... 244 F5
Lollard Street SE11 .... 244 F6
Loman Street SE1 .... 245 J2
Lomas Street E1 .... 246 D1
Lombard Lane EC4Y 241 G6
Lombard Street EC3V 241 L7
London Bridge EC4R 241 L8
London Bridge SE1 .... 245 L1
London Bridge Street SE1 ..... 245 L1
London Dungeon SE1 .... 244 E2
London Eye SE1 .... 244 E2
London Mews W2 .... 238 E6
London Road SE1 .... 245 H4
London Street EC3R 246 A3
London Street W2 .... 238 E6
London Transport
  Museum WC2E 240 D7
London Wall EC2M 241 K5
London Zoo ZSL NW1 .... 239 J1
Long Acre WC2E 240 D7
Longford Street NW1 .... 239 L3
Long Lane EC1A 241 J5
Long Lane SE1 .... 245 L3
Longmoore Street SW1V 243 M5
Longridge Road SW5 .... 242 A5
Longville Road SE11 .... 245 H5
Long Walk SE1 .... 246 A8
Long Yard WC1N 240 E4
Lord North Street SW1P 244 C4
Lord's Cricket Ground NW8 .... 238 E2
Lorenzo Street WC1X 240 E1
Lorrimore Road SE17 .... 245 J7
Lorrimore Square SE17 .... 245 H8
Lothbury EC2R 241 L6
Loughborough Street SE11 ..... 244 F7
Lovat Lane EC3R 241 M7
Love Lane EC2V 241 K6
Lovell Place SE16 .... 247 K7
Lowell Street E14 .... 247 K2
Lower Belgrave Street SW1W ... 243 K4
Lower Grosvenor Place SW1W ... 243 K4
Lower James Street W1F 240 A7
Lower John Street W1F 240 A7
Lower Marsh SE1 .... 244 F3
Lower Road SE16 .... 247 G7
Lower Sloane Street SW3 ...... 243 J6
Lower Thames Street EC3R 246 A4
Lower Thames Street EC3R 241 M8
Lowndes Close * SW1X 243 J4
Lowndes Place SW1X 243 J4
Lowndes Square SW1X 243 H3
Lowndes Street SW1X 243 J4
Lucan Place SW3 .... 242 F5
Lucey Road SE16 .... 246 C8
Ludgate Circus EC4M 241 H6
Ludgate Hill EC4M 241 H6
Lukin Street E1 .... 247 G3
Lumley Street W1K 239 K7
Lupus Street SW1V 243 L7
Lupus Street SW1V 244 B7
Luton Street NW8 .... 238 E4
Luxborough Street W1U 239 J4
Lyall Mews SW1X 243 J4
Lyall Street SW1X 243 J4
Lyons Place NW8 .... 238 E3
Lytham Street SE17 .... 245 K7

M

Macclesfield Road EC1V 241 J2
Macclesfield Street * W1D 240 B7
Mace Close E1W 246 E5
Macklin Street WC2B 240 D6
Mackworth Street NW1 .... 239 M2
Macleod Street SE17 .... 245 K7
Madame Tussauds NW1 .... 239 J4
Maddox Street W1S 239 M7
Magdalen Street SE1 .... 245 M2
Magee Street SE11 .... 244 F8
Maguire Street SE1 .... 246 C6
Maida Avenue W9 .... 238 D4
Maida Vale W9 .... 238 C2
Maida Vale ⊖ W9 .... 238 C2
Maiden Lane SE1 .... 245 K1
Maiden Lane WC2E 240 D7
Major Road SE16 .... 246 D7
Makins Street SW3 .... 243 G6
Malet Street WC1E 240 B4
Mallord Street SW3 .... 242 E8
Mallory Street NW8 .... 238 F3
Mallow Street EC1V 241 K3
Malta Street EC1V 241 H3
Maltby Street SE1 .... 246 B7

Manchester Square W1U 239 J6
Manchester Street W1U 239 J5
Manciple Street SE1 .... 245 L3
Mandeville Place W1U 239 K6
Manette Street W1D 240 B6
Manilla Street E14 .... 247 M6
Manningford Close EC1V 241 H2
Manor Place SE17 .... 245 J7
Manresa Road SW3 .... 242 F7
Mansell Street E1 .... 246 C3
Mansfield Mews W1G 239 L5
Mansfield Street W1G 239 L5
Mansion House ⊖ EC4V 241 K7
Manson Mews SW7 .... 242 D5
Manson Place SW7 .... 242 D6
Mapleleaf Square SE16 .... 247 J6
Maples Place E1 .... 246 F1
Maple Street W1T 239 M4
Marble Arch ⊖ W1C 239 H7
Marchmont Street WC1H 240 C3
Margaret Street W1W 239 L6
Margaretta Terrace SW3 .... 242 F7
Margery Street WC1X 240 F3
Marigold Street SE16 .... 246 E7
Marine Street SE16 .... 246 C7
Market Mews W1J 243 K1
Market Place W1W 239 M6
Markham Square SW3 .... 243 G6
Markham Street SW3 .... 243 G6
Mark Lane EC3R 246 A4
Marlborough Gate W2 .... 238 E7
Marlborough Place NW8 .... 238 C1
Marlborough Road SW1A 244 A2
Marlborough Street SW3 .... 242 F6
Marloes Road W8 .... 242 B4
Marlow Way SE16 .... 247 H6
Maroon Street E14 .... 247 K2
Marshall Street W1F 240 A7
Marshalsea Road SE1 .... 245 K2
Marsham Street SW1P 244 C5
Marsh Wall E14 .... 247 M5
Martha's Buildings EC1V 241 K3
Martha Street E1 .... 246 F3
Martin Lane EC4R 241 L7
Maryland Road W9 .... 238 A4
Marylands Road W9 .... 238 A4
Marylebone ⇌ ⊖ NW1 .... 239 G4
Marylebone Flyover W2 .... 238 E5
Marylebone High Street W1U ... 239 K5
Marylebone Lane W1U 239 K6
Marylebone Road NW1 .... 239 G4
Marylebone Street W1G 239 K5
Marylee Way SE11 .... 244 F6
Masjid Lane E14 .... 247 M2
Mason Street SE17 .... 245 M5
Massinger Street SE17 .... 245 M6
Masters Street E1 .... 247 J1
Matlock Street E14 .... 247 J2
Matthew Parker Street SW1H ... 244 C3
Maunsel Street SW1P 244 B5
Mayfair Place W1J 243 L1
Mayflower Street SE16 .... 246 F7
Mayford Estate W1 .... 240 A1
Maynards Quay E1W 246 F4
May's Street WC2N 240 C8
McAuley Close SE1 .... 244 F4
McLeod's Mews SW7 .... 242 C5
Meadcroft Road SE11 .... 245 G8
Meadcroft Road SE11 .... 245 H8
Meadow Road SW8 .... 244 E8
Meadow Row SE1 .... 245 J5
Mead Row SE1 .... 244 F4
Meakin Estate SE1 .... 245 M4
Mecklenburgh Square WC1N 240 E3
Medway Street SW1P 244 B5
Meeting House Alley E1W 246 E5
Melbourne Place WC2A 240 F6
Melcombe Place NW1 .... 239 G4
Melcombe Street W1U 239 H4
Melina Place NW8 .... 238 D2
Melior Street SE1 .... 245 M2
Melton Street NW1 .... 240 A2
Memorial Gates SW1W 243 K3
Mepham Street SE1 .... 244 F2
Mercer Street WC2H 240 C7
Merchant Square W2 .... 238 E5
Merlin Street EC1R 240 F2
Mermaid Court SE1 .... 245 K2
Merrick Square SE1 .... 245 K4
Merrington Road SW6 .... 242 A8
Merrow Street SE17 .... 245 L7
Methley Street SE11 .... 245 G7
Meymott Street SE1 .... 245 G2
Micawber Street N1 .... 241 K1
Micklethwaite Lane SW6 .... 242 A8
Middlesex Street E1 .... 246 A1
Middlesex Street E1 .... 246 B2
Middle Street EC1A 241 J5
Middle Temple WC2R 241 G7
Middle Temple Lane EC4Y 240 F7
Middleton Drive SE16 .... 247 H6
Midhope Street WC1H 240 D2
Midland Road NW1 .... 240 C1
Midship Close SE16 .... 247 H6
Milborne Grove SW10 .... 242 D7
Milcote Street SE1 .... 245 H3
Miles Street SW8 .... 244 D8
Milford Lane WC2R 240 F7
Milk Street EC2V 241 K6
Milk Yard E1W 247 G4
Millbank SW1P 244 D4
Millennium Bridge SE1 .... 241 J8
Millennium Harbour E14 .... 247 M6
Milligan Street E14 .... 247 L4
Millman Mews WC1N 240 E4
Millman Street WC1N 240 E4
Mill Place E14 .... 247 K3
Millstream Road SE1 .... 246 B7
Mill Street SE1 .... 246 C6
Mill Street W1S 239 L7
Milner Street SW3 .... 243 G5
Milton Street EC2Y 241 K4
Milverton Street SE11 .... 245 G7
Mincing Lane EC3M 246 A4
Minera Mews SW1W 243 J5
Minories EC3N 246 B3
Mitchell Street EC1V 241 J3
Mitre Road SE1 .... 245 G2
Mitre Street EC3A 246 A3
Molyneux Street W1H 239 G5
Monck Street SW1P 244 C4
Monkton Street SE11 .... 245 G5
Monmouth Place W2 .... 238 A6
Monmouth Road W2 .... 238 A6
Monmouth Street WC2H 240 C6
Montague Close SE1 .... 245 L1
Montague Place EC3R 246 A3
Montague Place WC1E 240 C5
Montague Street WC1B 240 C5

Montagu Mansions W1U 239 H5
Montagu Mews North W1H 239 H5
Montagu Mews West W1H 239 H6
Montagu Place W1H 239 H5
Montagu Row W1U 239 H5
Montagu Square W1H 239 H5
Montagu Street W1H 239 H6
Montford Place SE11 .... 244 F7
Monthorpe Road E1 .... 246 C1
Montpelier Square SW7 .... 243 G3
Montpelier Street SW7 .... 243 G3
Montpelier Walk SW7 .... 242 G3
Montrose Place SW1X 243 K3
Monument ⊖ EC4R 241 L7
Monument Street EC3R 241 L7
Monument Street EC3R 241 M7
Monza Street E1W 247 G4
Moodkee Street SE16 .... 247 G7
Moore Street SW3 .... 243 H5
Moorfields EC2Y 241 L5
Moorgate EC2R 241 L6
Moorgate ⇌ ⊖ EC2Y 241 L5
Moor Lane EC2Y 241 K5
Moor Street W1D 240 C7
Mora Street EC1V 241 K2
Morecambe Street SE17 .... 245 K6
Moreland Street EC1V 241 H2
Moreton Place SW1V 244 A6
Moreton Street SW1V 244 B6
Moreton Terrace SW1V 244 A6
Morgan's Lane SE1 .... 245 M2
Morgan's Lane SE1 .... 246 A5
Morley Street SE1 .... 245 G3
Mornington Crescent NW1 ...... 239 M1
Mornington Place NW1 .... 239 L1
Mornington Terrace NW1 .... 239 L1
Morocco Street SE1 .... 246 A7
Morpeth Terrace SW1P 243 M5
Morris Street E1 .... 246 F3
Morshead Road W9 .... 238 A2
Mortimer Market W1E 240 A4
Mortimer Street W1T 240 A5
Mortimer Street W1W 239 M5
Morton Place SE1 .... 244 F4
Morwell Street WC1B 240 B5
Moscow Place W2 .... 238 B7
Moscow Road W2 .... 238 B7
Mossop Street SW3 .... 243 G5
Motcomb Street SW1X 243 J4
Mount Gate W2 .... 242 E2
Mount Mills EC1V 241 J3
Mount Pleasant WC1X 240 F4
Mount Row W1K 239 K8
Mount Street W1K 239 K8
Mount Street Mews W1K 239 K8
Mount Terrace E1 .... 246 E1
Moxon Street W1U 239 J5
Mulberry Street E1 .... 246 D2
Mulberry Walk SW3 .... 242 E8
Mulready Street NW8 .... 238 F4
Mundy Street N1 .... 241 M2
Munster Square W1 .... 239 L3
Munton Road SE17 .... 245 K5
Murphy Street SE1 .... 244 F3
Murray Grove N1 .... 241 K1
Musbury Street E1 .... 247 G2
Muscovy Street EC3N 246 A4
Museum of London EC2Y 241 J5
Museum Street WC1A 240 C5
Myddelton Passage EC1R 241 G2
Myddelton Square EC1R 241 G1
Myddelton Street EC1R 241 G3
Myrdle Street E1 .... 246 D2

N

Naoroji Street WC1X 240 F2
Napier Grove N1 .... 241 K1
Narrow Street E14 .... 247 K4
Nash Street NW1 .... 239 L2
Nassau Street W1W 239 M5
Nathaniel Close * E1 .... 246 C2
National Portrait
  Gallery WC2H 240 C8
Natural History Museum SW7 ... 242 E4
Neal Street WC2H 240 C6
Neathouse Place * SW1V 243 M5
Neckinger SE1 .... 246 C8
Needleman Street SE16 .... 247 H7
Nelson Close NW6 .... 238 A1
Nelson Place N1 .... 241 H1
Nelson Square SE1 .... 245 H2
Nelson Street E1 .... 246 D2
Nelson Terrace N1 .... 241 H1
Neptune Street SE16 .... 247 G7
Nesham Street E1W 246 D4
Netherton Grove SW10 .... 242 D8
Netley Street NW1 .... 239 M2
Nevern Place SW5 .... 242 A6
Nevern Square SW5 .... 242 A6
Neville Street SW7 .... 242 E6
Newark Street E1 .... 246 E2
New Atlas Wharf E14 .... 247 M8
New Burlington Place * SW1V .. 244 B7
New Bond Street W1S 239 L7
New Bond Street W1S 239 L8
New Bridge Street EC4V 241 H6
New Broad Street EC2M 241 M5
New Burlington Street W1S 239 M7
Newburn Street SE11 .... 244 F7
Newbury Street EC1A 241 J5
Newcastle Place W2 .... 238 E5
New Cavendish Street W1G 239 L5
New Change EC4M 241 J6
New Church Road SE5 .... 245 L8
Newcomen Street SE1 .... 245 K2
New Compton Street WC2H 240 C6
Newcourt Street NW8 .... 238 F1
Newell Street E14 .... 247 L3
New Fetter Lane EC4A 241 G6
Newgate Street WC1A 241 H6
New Goulston Street E1 .... 246 B2
Newham's Row SE1 .... 246 B7
Newington Butts SE1 .... 245 H5
Newington Causeway SE1 .... 245 J4
New Kent Road SE1 .... 245 K5
Newlands Quay E1W 246 F4
Newman Street W1T 240 A5
New North Place EC2A 241 M3
New North Road N1 .... 241 L1
New North Street WC1N 240 D4
New Oxford Street WC1A 240 B6
Newport Street SE11 .... 244 E5
New Quebec Street W1H 239 H6

New Ride SW7 .... 242 E3
New Road E1 .... 246 E2
New Row WC2N 240 C7
New Spring Gardens Walk SE1 .. 244 D7
New Square WC2A 240 F6
New Street EC2M 246 A2
New Street Square EC4A 241 G6
Newton Road W2 .... 238 A6
Newton Street WC2B 240 D5
New Union Street EC2Y 241 K5
Nicholas Lane EC3V 241 L7
Nicholson Street SE1 .... 245 H1
Nightingale Place SW10 .... 242 D8
Nile Street N1 .... 241 K2
Nine Elms Lane SW8 .... 244 C8
Noble Street EC2V 241 J6
Noel Road N1 .... 241 J1
Noel Street W1F 240 A6
Norbiton Road E14 .... 247 L2
Norfolk Crescent W2 .... 239 G6
Norfolk Place W2 .... 238 E6
Norfolk Square W2 .... 238 E6
Norman Street EC1V 241 J3
Norris Street SW1Y 240 B8
Northampton Road EC1R 241 G3
Northampton Square EC1V 241 H2
North Audley Street W1K 239 J7
North Bank NW8 .... 238 F2
Northburgh Street EC1V 241 H3
North Carriage Drive W2 ...... 238 F7
Northdown Street N1 .... 240 D1
Northey Street E14 .... 247 K4
North Gower Street NW1 .... 240 A2
Northington Street WC1N 240 E4
North Mews WC1N 240 E4
North Ride W2 .... 238 G7
North Row W1K 239 J7
North Tenter Street E1 .... 246 C3
North Terrace SW3 .... 242 F5
Northumberland Alley EC3N 246 B3
Northumberland
  Avenue WC2N 244 C1
Northumberland Place W2 ...... 238 A6
Northumberland
  Street WC2N 244 C1
North Wharf Road W2 .... 238 E5
Northwick Terrace NW8 .... 238 D3
Norway Gate SE16 .... 247 K7
Norway Place E14 .... 247 L3
Norwich Street EC4A 240 F5
Nottingham Place W1U 239 J4
Nottingham Street W1U 239 J4
Notting Hill Gate W11 .... 238 A8
Notting Hill Gate ⊖ W11 ..... 242 A1
Nugent Terrace NW8 .... 238 D1
Nutford Place W1H 239 G6

O

Oakden Street SE11 .... 245 G5
Oakington Road W9 .... 238 A3
Oak Lane E14 .... 247 L3
Oakley Close EC1V 241 H1
Oakley Gardens SW3 .... 243 G8
Oakley Square NW1 .... 240 A1
Oakley Street SW3 .... 242 F8
Oak Tree Road NW8 .... 238 F2
Oat Lane EC2V 241 J5
Occupation Road SE17 .... 245 J6
Ocean Square E1 .... 247 J1
Odessa Street SE16 .... 247 L7
Ogle Street W1W 239 M5
Old Bailey EC4M 241 H6
Old Barrack Yard SW1X 243 J3
Old Bond Street W1S 239 M8
Old Broad Street EC2N 241 M6
Old Brompton Road SW5 .... 242 B6
Old Brompton Road SW7 .... 242 D6
Old Burlington Street W1S 239 M7
Oldbury Place W1U 239 J4
Old Castle Street E1 .... 246 B2
Old Cavendish Street W1G 239 L6
Old Church Road E1 .... 247 H2
Old Church Street SW3 .... 242 E7
Old Compton Street W1D 240 B7
Old Court Place W8 .... 242 B3
Old Gloucester Street WC1N ... 240 D4
Old Jamaica Road SE16 .... 246 C7
Old Jewry EC2R 241 K6
Old Kent Road SE1 .... 245 M5
Old Marylebone Road NW1 ...... 239 G5
Old Montague Street E1 .... 246 C1
Old North Street WC1X 240 E5
Old Paradise Street SE11 ..... 244 E5
Old Park Lane W1J 243 K2
Old Pye Street SW1P 244 B4
Old Queen Street SW1H 244 B3
Old Square WC2A 240 F6
Old Street EC1V 241 J3
Old Street ⇌ ⊖ EC1Y 241 L3
Old Street Junction EC1Y 241 L3
Oliver's Yard EC1Y 241 L3
Olney Road SE17 .... 245 J8
O'Meara Street SE1 .... 245 K2
Omega Place N1 .... 240 D1
Onega Gate SE16 .... 247 K8
Ongar Road SW6 .... 242 A8
Onslow Gardens SW7 .... 242 D6
Onslow Square SW7 .... 242 E5
Onslow Square SW7 .... 242 E6
Ontario Street SE1 .... 245 J4
Ontario Way E14 .... 247 M4
Opal Street SE11 .... 245 H6
Orange Place SE16 .... 247 G8
Orange Square SW1W 243 K6
Orange Street E1W 246 D5
Orange Street WC2H 240 B8
Orb Street SE17 .... 245 L6
Orchardson Street NW8 .... 238 E4
Orchard Street W1H 239 J6
Ordehall Street WC1N 240 E4
Orient Street SE11 .... 245 H5
Orme Court W2 .... 238 B8
Orme Lane W2 .... 238 B8
Orme Square Gate W2 .... 238 B8
Ormond Close WC1N 240 D4
Ormonde Gate SW3 .... 243 H7
Ormond Yard SW1Y 240 A8
Orsett Mews W2 .... 238 C6
Orsett Street SE11 .... 244 E6
Orsett Terrace W2 .... 238 C5
Orton Street E1W 246 D5
Osbert Street SW1V 244 B6
Osborn Street E1 .... 246 C2
Oslo Square SE16 .... 247 K7

Osnaburgh Street NW1 .... 239 L3
Osnaburgh Terrace NW1 .... 239 L3
Ossington Buildings W1U 239 J5
Ossington Street W2 .... 238 A7
Ossulston Street NW1 .... 240 B1
Oswin Street SE11 .... 245 H5
Othello Close SE1 .... 245 H6
Otto Street SE17 .... 245 H8
Outer Circle NW1 .... 239 H3
Outer Circle NW1 .... 239 K1
Oval ⊖ SE11 .... 244 F8
Oval Way SE11 .... 244 E7
Ovington Square SW3 .... 243 G4
Ovington Street SW3 .... 243 G5
Owen Street EC1V 241 G1
Oxendon Street SW1Y 240 B8
Oxford Circus ⊖ W1B 239 M6
Oxford Road NW6 .... 238 A1
Oxford Square W2 .... 238 F6
Oxford Street W1C 239 L6
Oxford Street WC1A 240 A6

P

Pace Place E1 .... 246 E3
Pacific Wharf SE16 .... 247 H5
Paddington ⇌ ⊖ W2 .... 238 D6
Paddington Green W2 .... 238 E5
Paddington Street W1U 239 J5
Pageant Crescent SE16 .... 247 K5
Page Street SW1P 244 B5
Paget Street EC1V 241 H2
Pakenham Street WC1X 240 E3
Palace Avenue W8 .... 242 A1
Palace Court W2 .... 238 A7
Palace Gardens Terrace W8 .... 242 A1
Palace Gate W8 .... 242 C3
Palace Green W8 .... 242 B2
Palace Place SW1E 243 M4
Palace Street SW1E 243 M4
Pall Mall SW1Y 244 A1
Pall Mall East SW1Y 244 B1
Palmer Street SW1H 244 B3
Pancras Lane EC4N 241 K6
Pancras Road N1C 240 C1
Panton Street SW1Y 240 B8
Paradise Street SE16 .... 246 E7
Paradise Walk SW3 .... 243 H8
Pardoner Street SE1 .... 245 L4
Pardon Street EC1V 241 H3
Parfett Street E1 .... 246 D2
Paris Garden SE1 .... 245 G1
Park Crescent W1B 239 K4
Park Crescent
    Mews West W1G 239 K4
Parker's Row SE1 .... 246 C7
Parker Street WC2B 240 D6
Park Lane W1K 239 H7
Park Lane W2 .... 243 J1
Park Place SW1A 243 M1
Park Road NW1 .... 239 H3
Park Square East NW1 .... 239 L3
Park Square Mews NW1 .... 239 K3
Park Square West NW1 .... 239 K3
Park Street SE1 .... 245 K1
Park Street W1K 239 J7
Park Village East NW1 .... 239 L1
Park Walk SW10 .... 242 D8
Park West Place W2 .... 239 G6
Parliament Street SW1A 244 C2
Parry Street SW8 .... 244 D7
Passmore Street SW1W 243 J6
Paternoster Square EC1A 241 J6
Pater Street W8 .... 242 A4
Pattina Walk SE16 .... 247 K5
Paul Street EC2A 241 M3
Paultons Square SW3 .... 242 E8
Paveley Street NW1 .... 239 G3
Pavilion Road SW1X 243 H3
Pavilion Street SW1X 243 H4
Paxton Terrace SW1V 243 L7
Peabody Avenue SW1V 243 L7
Peabody Estate SE1 .... 245 J1
Peacock Street SE17 .... 245 J6
Pearl Street E1W 246 F5
Pearman Street SE1 .... 245 G3
Pear Tree Court EC1R 241 G3
Peartree Lane E1W 247 G4
Pear Tree Street EC1V 241 J3
Peel Street W8 .... 242 A1
Peerless Street EC1V 241 K2
Pelham Crescent SW7 .... 242 F6
Pelham Place SW7 .... 242 F5
Pelham Street SW7 .... 242 F5
Pelier Street SE17 .... 245 K8
Pemberton Row EC4A 241 G6
Pembridge Gardens W2 .... 238 A7
Pembridge Place W2 .... 238 A7
Pembridge Square W2 .... 238 A7
Pembridge Villas W11 .... 238 A7
Pembroke Close SW1X 243 J3
Penang Street E1W 246 F5
Penfold Place NW1 .... 238 E5
Penfold Street NW8 .... 238 E4
Pennant Mews W8 .... 242 B5
Pennington Street E1W 246 D4
Pennyfields E14 .... 247 M4
Penrose Grove SE17 .... 245 J7
Penrose Street SE17 .... 245 J7
Penryn Road SE16 .... 246 D7
Penton Place SE17 .... 245 H6
Penton Rise WC1X 240 E2
Penton Street N1 .... 240 F1
Pentonville Road N1 .... 240 E1
Penywern Road SW5 .... 242 A6
Pepper Street SE1 .... 245 J2
Pepys Street EC3N 246 A4
Percival Street EC1V 241 H3
Percy Circus WC1X 240 F2
Percy Street W1T 240 B5
Perkin's Rent SW1P 244 B4
Petersham Mews SW7 .... 242 D4
Petersham Place SW7 .... 242 C4
Peter Street W1F 240 B7
Peto Place NW1 .... 239 L3
Petticoat Lane E1 .... 246 B2
Petty France SW1H 244 A3
Petty Wales EC3R 246 A4
Petyward SW3 .... 243 G6
Phelp Street SE17 .... 245 L7
Phene Street SW3 .... 243 G8
Phillimore Walk W8 .... 242 A3
Philpot Lane EC3M 241 M7
Philpot Street E1 .... 246 E2
Phipp's Mews SW1W 243 L5

Phipp Street EC2A 241 M3
Phoenix Place WC1X 240 F3
Phoenix Road NW1 .... 240 B1
Phoenix Street WC2H 240 C6
Piccadilly W1J 243 L2
Piccadilly Arcade SW1Y 243 M1
Piccadilly Circus ⊖ W1B 240 A8
Piccadilly Circus W1J 240 B8
Pickard Street EC1V 241 J2
Picton Place W1U 239 K6
Pier Head E1W 246 E6
Pigott Street E14 .... 247 M3
Pilgrimage Street SE1 .... 245 L3
Pimlico ⊖ SW1V 244 B6
Pimlico Road SW1W 243 J6
Pinchin Street E1 .... 246 D3
Pindar Street EC2A 241 M4
Pindock Mews W9 .... 238 B3
Pine Street EC1R 240 F3
Pitfield Street N1 .... 241 M1
Pitsea Street E1 .... 247 H3
Pitt's Head Mews W1J 243 K2
Pitt Street W8 .... 242 A2
Pixley Street E14 .... 247 L2
Platina Street * EC2A 241 L3
Plover Way SE16 .... 247 K8
Plumbers Row E1 .... 246 D2
Plumtree Court EC4A 241 G5
Plympton Street NW8 .... 238 F4
Pocock Street SE1 .... 245 H2
Pollard Row E2 .... 247 H1
Pollen Street W1S 239 L7
Pollitt Drive NW8 .... 238 E3
Polperro Mews SE11 .... 245 G5
Polygon Road NW1 .... 240 B1
Pond Place SW3 .... 242 F6
Ponler Street E1 .... 246 E3
Ponsonby Place SW1P 244 C6
Ponsonby Terrace SW1P 244 C6
Ponton Road SW1V 244 B8
Pont Street SW1X 243 H4
Poolmans Street SE16 .... 247 H6
Pope Street SE1 .... 246 B7
Poplar Place W2 .... 238 B7
Poppin's Court EC4A 241 H6
Porchester Gardens W2 .... 238 B7
Porchester Gate W2 .... 238 C8
Porchester Place W2 .... 239 G6
Porchester Road W2 .... 238 B5
Porchester Square W2 .... 238 B6
Porchester Terrace W2 .... 238 C7
Porchester Terrace
    North W2 .... 238 C6
Porlock Street SE1 .... 245 L3
Porter Street NW1 .... 239 H4
Porteus Road W2 .... 238 D5
Portland Place W1B 239 L4
Portland Place W1B 239 L5
Portland Square E1W 246 E5
Portland Street SE17 .... 245 L7
Portman Close W1H 239 J6
Portman Mews South W1H 239 J6
Portman Square W1H 239 J6
Portman Street W1H 239 J6
Portpool Lane EC1N 240 F4
Portsea Place W2 .... 239 G6
Portsmouth Street WC2A 240 E6
Portsoken Street E1 .... 246 B3
Portugal Street WC2A 240 E6
Potier Street SE1 .... 245 L4
Potters Fields SE1 .... 246 B6
Pottery Street SE16 .... 246 F7
Poultry EC2V 241 K6
Powis Street WC1N 240 D4
Praed Mews W2 .... 238 E6
Praed Street W2 .... 238 E6
Pratt Walk SE1 .... 244 E5
Premier Place E14 .... 247 M4
Prescot Street E1 .... 246 C3
Preston Close SE1 .... 245 M5
Price's Street SE1 .... 245 H1
Prideaux Place WC1X 240 F2
Primrose Street EC2A 246 A1
Prince Albert Road NW8 .... 238 F1
Prince Consort Road SW7 .... 242 D3
Princelet Street E1 .... 246 C1
Prince of Wales Gate SW7 .... 242 F3
Princes Arcade SW1Y 240 A8
Prince's Gardens SW7 .... 242 E4
Prince's Gate Mews SW7 .... 242 E4
Prince's Riverside Road SE16 .... 247 H5
Prince's Square W2 .... 238 A7
Princess Road NW6 .... 238 A1
Princess Street SE1 .... 245 H4
Princes Street W1B 239 L6
Prince's Street EC2R 241 L6
Princeton Street WC1R 240 E5
Prioress Street SE1 .... 245 L4
Priory Green Estate N1 .... 240 E1
Priory Walk SW10 .... 242 D7
Proctor Street WC1V 240 E5
Prospect Place E1W 247 G4
Prospect Street SE16 .... 246 E7
Provident Court W1K 239 J7
Provost Street N1 .... 241 L1
Prusom Street E1W 246 F5
Pudding Lane EC3R 241 M7
Pumphouse Mews E1 .... 246 D3
Purbrook Street SE1 .... 246 A7
Purcell Street N1 .... 241 M1
Purchese Street NW1 .... 240 B1

Q

Quebec Way SE16 .... 247 J7
Queen Anne's Gate SW1H 244 B3
Queen Anne Street W1G 239 K5
Queen Elizabeth Street SE1 .... 246 B6
Queen Mother Gate W2 .... 243 J2
Queensborough Terrace W2 .... 238 C7
Queensbury Place SW7 .... 242 E5
Queen's Gardens W2 .... 238 C7
Queen's Gate SW7 .... 242 D3
Queen's Gate SW7 .... 242 D4
Queen's Gate Gardens SW7 .... 242 D5
Queen's Gate Mews SW7 .... 242 D4
Queen's Gate Place SW7 .... 242 D4
Queen's Gate Place
    Mews SW7 .... 242 D4
Queen's Gate Terrace SW7 .... 242 C4
Queen's Mews W2 .... 238 B7
Queen Square WC1N 240 D4
Queen's Row SE17 .... 245 L7
Queen Street EC4N 241 K7
Queen Street W1J 243 L1

Queen Street Place EC4R 241 K7
Queen's Walk SE1 .... 246 A5
Queen's Walk SW1A 243 M2
Queensway W2 .... 238 B6
Queensway ⊖ W2 .... 238 B8
Queen Victoria Street EC4V 241 J7
Quick Street N1 .... 241 H1

R

Raby Street E14 .... 247 K2
Radcliffe Road SE1 .... 246 B8
Radcot Street SE11 .... 245 G7
Radnor Mews W2 .... 238 E6
Radnor Place W2 .... 238 F6
Radnor Street EC1V 241 K3
Radnor Walk SW3 .... 243 G7
Railway Approach SE1 .... 245 L1
Railway Avenue SE16 .... 247 G6
Railway Street N1 .... 240 D1
Raine Street E1W 246 F5
Ralston Street SW3 .... 243 H7
Ramillies Place W1F 239 M6
Ramillies Street W1F 239 M6
Rampart Street E1 .... 246 E2
Rampayne Street SW1V 244 B6
Randall Road SE11 .... 244 D6
Randall Row SE11 .... 244 E6
Randolph Avenue W9 .... 238 B1
Randolph Crescent W9 .... 238 C3
Randolph Gardens NW6 .... 238 B1
Randolph Mews W9 .... 238 D4
Randolph Road W9 .... 238 C4
Ranelagh Grove SW1W 243 K6
Ranelagh Road SW1V 244 A7
Rangoon Street * EC3N 246 B3
Ranston Street NW8 .... 238 F4
Raphael Street SW7 .... 243 G3
Ratcliffe Cross Street E1W 247 J3
Ratcliffe Lane E14 .... 247 J3
Rathbone Place W1T 240 B5
Rathbone Street W1T 240 A5
Raven Row E1 .... 246 F1
Ravensdon Street SE11 .... 245 G7
Ravey Street EC2A 241 M3
Rawlings Street SW3 .... 243 G5
Rawstone Street EC1V 241 H2
Ray Street EC1R 241 G4
Reardon Place E1W 246 E5
Reardon Street E1W 246 E5
Rectory Square E1 .... 247 H1
Redan Place W2 .... 238 B6
Redburn Street SW3 .... 243 G7
Redcastle Close E1W 247 G4
Redcliffe Gardens SW10 .... 242 B7
Redcliffe Mews SW10 .... 242 C7
Redcliffe Place SW10 .... 242 C8
Redcliffe Road SW10 .... 242 D7
Redcliffe Square SW10 .... 242 B7
Redcliffe Street SW10 .... 242 B8
Redcross Way SE1 .... 245 K2
Redesdale Street SW3 .... 243 G7
Redfield Lane SW5 .... 242 A5
Redhill Street NW1 .... 239 L1
Red Lion Row SE5 .... 245 K8
Red Lion Square WC1R 240 E5
Red Lion Street WC2B 240 E5
Redman's Road E1 .... 247 G1
Red Place W1K 239 J7
Redriff Road SE16 .... 247 J8
Reedworth Street SE11 .... 245 G6
Reeves Mews W1K 239 J8
Regal Close E1 .... 246 D1
Regan Way N1 .... 241 M1
Regency Street SW1P 244 B5
Regent Place W1B 240 A7
Regent's Park ⊖ W1B 239 L4
Regent's Park NW1 .... 239 J1
Regent's Park Estate NW1 .... 239 L2
Regent Square WC1H 240 D2
Regent Street SW1Y 240 B8
Regent Street W1S 239 M7
Relton Mews SW7 .... 243 G4
Remington Street N1 .... 241 H1
Remnant Street WC2A 240 E6
Renforth Street SE16 .... 247 G7
Renfrew Road SE11 .... 245 H5
Rennie Street SE1 .... 245 H1
Rephidim Street SE1 .... 245 M4
Repton Street E14 .... 247 K2
Reveley Square SE16 .... 247 K7
Rex Place W1K 239 J8
Rhodeswell Road E14 .... 247 L2
Rich Street E14 .... 247 M3
Rickett Street SW6 .... 242 A8
Ridgemount Street WC1E 240 B4
Ridgemount Gardens WC1E 240 B4
Riding House Street W1W 239 M5
Riley Road SE1 .... 246 B7
Ripley's Believe It or Not! W1J 240 B8
Risborough Street SE1 .... 245 J2
Risdon Street SE16 .... 247 G7
Rissinghill Street N1 .... 240 F1
River Street EC1R 240 F2
Rivington Street EC2A 241 M3
Robert Adam Street W1U 239 J6
Roberts Close SE16 .... 247 J7
Robert Street NW1 .... 239 L2
Rochester Row SW1P 244 A5
Rochester Street SW1P 244 B5
Rockingham Street SE1 .... 245 J4
Rocliffe Street N1 .... 241 H1
Roding Mews E1W 246 D5
Rodmarton Street W1U 239 H5
Rodney Place SE17 .... 245 K5
Rodney Road SE17 .... 245 K5
Rodney Street N1 .... 240 E1
Roger Street WC1N 240 E4
Roland Gardens SW7 .... 242 D6
Roland Way SE17 .... 245 L7
Romford Street E1 .... 246 E2
Romilly Street W1D 240 B7
Romney Street SW1P 244 C5
Rood Lane EC3M 241 M7
Ropemaker Road SE16 .... 247 K7
Ropemaker Street EC2Y 241 L4
Roper Lane SE1 .... 246 B7
Rope Street SE16 .... 247 K8
Rope Walk Gardens E1 .... 246 E2
Rosary Gardens SW7 .... 242 D6
Roscoe Street EC1Y 241 K3
Rose Alley SE1 .... 245 K1
Rosebery Avenue EC1R 240 F3
Rosemoor Street SW3 .... 243 G6
Rose Street WC2E 240 C7

Rossmore Road NW1 .... 239 G3
Rotary Street SE1 .... 245 H3
Rotherhithe ⊖ SE16 .... 247 G6
Rotherhithe Street SE16 .... 247 G6
Rotherhithe Street SE16 .... 247 J4
Rotherhithe Tunnel SE16 .... 247 H5
Rothsay Street SE1 .... 245 M4
Rotten Row W2 .... 242 F2
Rouel Road SE16 .... 246 D8
Roupell Street SE1 .... 245 G2
Royal Albert Hall SW7 .... 242 E3
Royal Avenue SW3 .... 243 H6
Royal Hospital Road SW3 .... 243 H7
Royal Mint Street E1 .... 246 C4
Royal Oak ⊖ W2 .... 238 B5
Royal Oak Yard SE1 .... 246 A7
Royal Opera House WC2E 240 D7
Royal Road SE17 .... 245 H8
Royal Street SE1 .... 244 E3
Rudolph Road NW6 .... 238 A1
Rugby Street WC1N 240 E4
Rum Close E1W 246 F4
Rupack Street SE16 .... 246 F7
Rupert Street W1D 240 B7
Rushworth Street SE1 .... 245 H2
Russell Court SW1A 244 A2
Russell Square WC1B 240 C4
Russell Square ⊖ WC1B 240 D4
Russell Street WC2B 240 D7
Russia Dock Road SE16 .... 247 K6
Rutherford Street SW1P 244 B5
Rutland Gardens SW7 .... 243 G3
Rutland Gate SW7 .... 242 F3
Rutland Mews SW7 .... 242 F4
Rutland Street SW7 .... 243 G4
Ryder Street SW1Y 244 A1

S

Sackville Street W1S 240 A8
Saffron Hill EC1N 241 G4
Saffron Street EC1N 241 G4
Sail Street SE11 .... 244 E5
St Agnes Place SE11 .... 245 G8
St Alban's Grove W8 .... 242 B4
St Alban's Street SW1Y 240 B8
St Alphage Garden EC2Y 241 K5
St Andrews Hill EC4V 241 H7
St Andrew's Place NW1 .... 239 L3
St Andrew Street EC4A 241 G5
St Anne's Court W1F 240 B6
St Ann's Street SW1P 244 C4
St Anselm's Place W1K 239 K7
St Barnabas Street SW1W 243 K6
St Botolph Street EC3N 246 B2
St Bride Street EC4A 241 G6
St Chad's Street WC1H 240 D2
St Clare Street EC3N 246 B3
St Clements Lane WC2A 240 E6
St Cross Street EC1N 241 G4
St Dunstan's Hill EC3R 241 M8
St Dunstan's Lane EC3R 241 M7
St Elmos Road SE16 .... 247 J7
St Ermin's Hill SW1H 244 B3
St George's Circus SE1 .... 245 H3
St George's Drive SW1V 243 M6
St George's Estate E1 .... 246 D3
St George's Lane * EC3R 241 M7
St George's Road SE1 .... 245 G4
St George's Square SW1V 244 B7
St George Street W1S 239 L7
St Giles High Street WC2H 240 C6
St Helen's Place EC3A 241 M6
St James Market * SW1Y 240 B8
St James's Park ⊖ SW1H 244 B3
St James's Park SW1A 244 B3
St James's Place SW1A 243 M2
St James's Road SE16 .... 246 D8
St James's Square SW1Y 244 A1
St James's Street SW1A 243 M1
St James Walk EC1R 241 G3
St John's Lane EC1M 241 H4
St John's Place EC1M 241 H4
St John's Square EC1V 241 H4
St John Street EC1V 241 H3
St John's Wood High
    Street NW8 .... 238 F1
St John's Wood Road NW8 .... 238 E3
St Katharine's Way E1W 246 C5
St Leonard's Terrace SW3 .... 243 H7
St Loo Avenue SW3 .... 243 G8
St Luke's Close EC1V 241 K3
St Luke's Street SW3 .... 242 F6
St Manningtree E1 .... 246 C2
St Mark Street E1 .... 246 C3
St Martin's Lane WC2N 240 C7
St Martin's le Grand EC1A 241 J6
St Martin's Place WC2N 240 C8
St Mary at Hill EC3R 241 M8
St Mary Axe EC3A 246 A3
St Mary Church Street SE16 .... 246 F7
St Mary's Gardens SE11 .... 245 G5
St Mary's Terrace W2 .... 238 D4
St Mary's Walk SE11 .... 245 G5
St Matthew Street SW1P 244 B4
St Michael's Street W2 .... 238 F6
St Olav's Square SE16 .... 246 F7
St Oswald's Place SE11 .... 244 E7
St Oswulf Street * SW1P 244 C5
St Pancras
    International ⇌ N1C 240 C1
St Paul's ⊖ EC1A 241 J6
St Paul's Avenue SE16 .... 247 J5
St Paul's Cathedral EC4M 241 J6
St Paul's Churchyard EC4M 241 J6
St Paul's Way E3 .... 247 L1
St Petersburgh Mews W2 .... 238 B7
St Petersburgh Place W2 .... 238 B7
St Saviours Wharf SE1 .... 246 C6
St Stephen's Gardens W2 .... 238 A5
St Swithin's Lane EC4N 241 L7
St Thomas Street SE1 .... 245 L2
St Vincent Street W1U 239 J5
Salamanca Street SE1 .... 244 D6
Salem Road W2 .... 238 B7
Sale Place W2 .... 238 F5
Salisbury Court EC4Y 241 G6
Salisbury Place W1H 239 H4
Salisbury Street NW8 .... 238 F4
Salmon Lane E14 .... 247 J2
Salter Road SE16 .... 247 J5
Salter Street E14 .... 247 M4
Samford Street NW8 .... 238 F4
Sampson Street E1W 246 D5
Sancroft Street SE11 .... 244 F6

Sandford Row SE17 .... 245 L6
Sandland Street WC1R 240 E5
Sandpiper Close SE16 .... 247 L6
Sandwich Street WC1H 240 C2
Sandy's Row E1 .... 246 B1
Sans Walk EC1R 241 G3
Sardinia Street WC2A 240 E6
Savage Gardens EC3N 246 B3
Savile Row W1S 239 M7
Savoy Hill WC2R 240 E8
Savoy Place WC2R 240 D8
Savoy Street WC2E 240 E7
Sawyer Street SE1 .... 245 J2
Scala Street W1T 240 A5
Scandrett Street E1W 246 E5
Scarborough Street E1 .... 246 C3
Scarsdale Villas W8 .... 242 A4
Schooner Close * SE16 .... 247 H6
Science Museum SW7 .... 242 E4
Scoresby Street SE1 .... 245 H2
Scotch House Junction SW1X 243 H3
Scotland Place SW1A 244 C1
Scott Ellis Grove NW8 .... 238 E2
Scott Lidgett Crescent SE16 .... 246 D7
Scrutton Street EC2A 241 M3
Seaford Street WC1H 240 D2
Seagrave Road SW6 .... 242 A8
Sea Life London
    Aquarium SE1 .... 244 E3
Searles Road SE1 .... 245 L5
Sebastian Street EC1V 241 H2
Secker Street SE1 .... 245 F2
Sedan Way SE17 .... 245 M6
Sedding Street SW1X 243 J5
Seddon Street WC1X 240 E3
Seething Lane EC3N 246 A4
Sekforde Street EC1R 241 H3
Selfridges W1A 239 J6
Selsey Street E14 .... 247 M1
Selwood Place SW7 .... 242 E6
Semley Place SW1W 243 K6
Senior Street W2 .... 238 B4
Senrab Street E1 .... 247 H2
Serle Street WC2A 240 F6
Serpentine Bridge W2 .... 242 E1
Serpentine Road W2 .... 242 F2
Seth Street SE16 .... 247 G7
Settles Street E1 .... 246 D2
Seven Dials WC2H 240 C6
Seville Street SW1X 243 H3
Sevington Street W9 .... 238 A3
Seward Street EC1V 241 J3
Seymour Mews W1H 239 J6
Seymour Place W1H 239 G5
Seymour Street W1H 239 H6
Seymour Street W2 .... 239 G7
Seymour Walk SW10 .... 242 C7
Shad Thames SE1 .... 246 B6
Shad Thames SE1 .... 246 C6
Shadwell ⊖ ⊖ E1 .... 247 G3
Shadwell Gardens E1 .... 246 F3
Shaftesbury Avenue W1D 240 B7
Shaftesbury Avenue WC2H 240 C6
Shaftesbury Street N1 .... 241 K1
Shakespeare's Globe SE1 .... 241 J8
Shand Street SE1 .... 246 A6
Sharsted Street SE17 .... 245 H7
Shaw Crescent E14 .... 247 K2
Shawfield Street SW3 .... 243 G7
Sheffield Terrace W8 .... 242 A2
Sheldon Square W2 .... 238 D5
Shelmerdine Close E3 .... 247 M1
Shelton Street WC2H 240 C6
Shepherdess Walk N1 .... 241 K1
Shepherd Street W1J 243 K2
Sheraton Street W1F 240 B6
Sherborne Lane EC4N 241 L7
Sherwood Street W1D 240 A7
Ship and Mermaid Row SE1 .... 245 M2
Shipwright Road SE16 .... 247 K7
Shirland Road W9 .... 238 A3
Shoe Lane EC4A 241 G5
Shorter Street EC3N 246 B4
Shorts Gardens WC2H 240 C6
Short Street SE1 .... 245 G2
Shoulder of Mutton Alley E14 .... 247 K4
Shouldham Street W1H 239 G5
Shroton Street NW1 .... 238 F4
Siddons Lane W1H 239 H4
Sidmouth Street WC1N 240 D3
Sidney Square E1 .... 246 F2
Sidney Street E1 .... 246 F1
Silex Street SE1 .... 245 H3
Silk Street EC2Y 241 K4
Silver Walk SE16 .... 247 K5
Silvester Street SE1 .... 245 K3
Singer Street EC2A 241 L3
Sir John Soane's
    Museum WC2A 240 E5
Sir Simon Milton Square SW1V 243 L4
Skinner Place * SW1W 243 J6
Skinners Lane EC4V 241 K7
Skinner Street EC1R 241 G3
Slippers Place SE16 .... 246 F8
Sloane Avenue SW3 .... 243 G6
Sloane Court SW3 .... 243 J6
Sloane Court East SW3 .... 243 J6
Sloane Gardens SW1W 243 J6
Sloane Square SW1W 243 J5
Sloane Square ⊖ SW1W 243 J5
Sloane Street SW1X 243 H3
Sloane Terrace SW1X 243 H5
Smeaton Street E1W 246 E5
Smithfield Street EC1A 241 H5
Smith Square SW1P 244 C4
Smith Street SW3 .... 243 G7
Smith Terrace SW3 .... 243 G7
Smithy Street E1 .... 247 G1
Snowden Street EC2A 241 M4
Snow Hill EC1A 241 H5
Snowsfields SE1 .... 245 L2
Soho Square W1D 240 B6
Somerford Way SE16 .... 247 K7
Somers Crescent W2 .... 238 F6
Somerset House WC2R 240 E7
Somerstown Estate NW1 .... 240 B1
Sondes Street SE17 .... 245 L7
South & West Africa Gate SW1A 244 A3
Southall Place SE1 .... 245 L3
Southampton Buildings WC2A 240 F5
Southampton Place WC1A 240 D5
Southampton Row WC1B 240 D4
Southampton Street WC2E 240 D7
South Audley Street W1K 239 K8
South Carriage Drive SW1X 243 H3
South Carriage Drive SW7 .... 242 F3

This index lists places appearing in the main map section of the atlas in alphabetical order. The reference following each name gives the atlas page number and grid reference of the square in which the place appears. The map shows counties, unitary authorities and administrative areas, together with a list of the abbreviated name forms used in the index. The top 100 places of tourist interest are indexed in **red**, World Heritage sites in **green**, motorway service areas in **blue**, airports in blue *italic* and National Parks in green *italic*.

Scotland

Abers	**Aberdeenshire**
Ag & B	**Argyll and Bute**
Angus	**Angus**
Border	**Scottish Borders**
C Aber	**City of Aberdeen**
C Dund	**City of Dundee**
C Edin	**City of Edinburgh**
C Glas	**City of Glasgow**
Clacks	**Clackmannanshire (1)**
D & G	**Dumfries & Galloway**
E Ayrs	**East Ayrshire**
E Duns	**East Dunbartonshire (2)**
E Loth	**East Lothian**
E Rens	**East Renfrewshire (3)**
Falk	**Falkirk**
Fife	**Fife**
Highld	**Highland**
Inver	**Inverclyde (4)**
Mdloth	**Midlothian (5)**
Moray	**Moray**
N Ayrs	**North Ayrshire**
N Lans	**North Lanarkshire (6)**
Ork	**Orkney Islands**
P & K	**Perth & Kinross**
Rens	**Renfrewshire (7)**
S Ayrs	**South Ayrshire**
S Lans	**South Lanarkshire**
Shet	**Shetland Islands**
Stirlg	**Stirling**
W Duns	**West Dunbartonshire (8)**
W Isls	**Western Isles (Na h-Eileanan an Iar)**
W Loth	**West Lothian**

Wales

Blae G	**Blaenau Gwent (9)**
Brdgnd	**Bridgend (10)**
Caerph	**Caerphilly (11)**
Cardif	**Cardiff**
Carmth	**Carmarthenshire**
Cerdgn	**Ceredigion**
Conwy	**Conwy**
Denbgs	**Denbighshire**
Flints	**Flintshire**
Gwynd	**Gwynedd**
IoA	**Isle of Anglesey**
Mons	**Monmouthshire**
Myr Td	**Merthyr Tydfil (12)**
Neath	**Neath Port Talbot (13)**
Newpt	**Newport (14)**
Pembks	**Pembrokeshire**
Powys	**Powys**
Rhondd	**Rhondda Cynon Taff (15)**
Swans	**Swansea**
Torfn	**Torfaen (16)**
V Glam	**Vale of Glamorgan (17)**
Wrexhm	**Wrexham**

Channel Islands & Isle of Man

Guern	**Guernsey**
Jersey	**Jersey**
IoM	**Isle of Man**

England

BaNES	**Bath & N E Somerset (18)**
Barns	**Barnsley (19)**
Bed	**Bedford**
Birm	**Birmingham**
Bl w D	**Blackburn with Darwen (20)**
Bmouth	**Bournemouth**
Bolton	**Bolton (21)**
Bpool	**Blackpool**
Br & H	**Brighton & Hove (22)**
Br For	**Bracknell Forest (23)**
Bristl	**City of Bristol**
Bucks	**Buckinghamshire**
Bury	**Bury (24)**
C Beds	**Central Bedfordshire**
C Brad	**City of Bradford**
C Derb	**City of Derby**
C KuH	**City of Kingston upon Hull**
C Leic	**City of Leicester**
C Nott	**City of Nottingham**

C Pete	**City of Peterborough**
C Plym	**City of Plymouth**
C Port	**City of Portsmouth**
C Sotn	**City of Southampton**
C Stke	**City of Stoke-on-Trent**
C York	**City of York**
Calder	**Calderdale (25)**
Cambs	**Cambridgeshire**
Ches E	**Cheshire East**
Ches W	**Cheshire West and Chester**
Cnwll	**Cornwall**
Covtry	**Coventry**
Cumb	**Cumbria**
Darltn	**Darlington (26)**
Derbys	**Derbyshire**
Devon	**Devon**
Donc	**Doncaster (27)**
Dorset	**Dorset**
Dudley	**Dudley (28)**
Dur	**Durham**
E R Yk	**East Riding of Yorkshire**
E Susx	**East Sussex**
Essex	**Essex**
Gatesd	**Gateshead (29)**
Gloucs	**Gloucestershire**
Gt Lon	**Greater London**
Halton	**Halton (30)**
Hants	**Hampshire**
Hartpl	**Hartlepool (31)**
Herefs	**Herefordshire**
Herts	**Hertfordshire**
IoS	**Isles of Scilly**
IoW	**Isle of Wight**
Kent	**Kent**
Kirk	**Kirklees (32)**
Knows	**Knowsley (33)**
Lancs	**Lancashire**
Leeds	**Leeds**
Leics	**Leicestershire**
Lincs	**Lincolnshire**
Lpool	**Liverpool**
Luton	**Luton**

M Keyn	**Milton Keynes**
Manch	**Manchester**
Medway	**Medway**
Middsb	**Middlesbrough**
N Linc	**North Lincolnshire**
N Som	**North Somerset (34)**
N Tyne	**North Tyneside (35)**
N u Ty	**Newcastle upon Tyne**
N York	**North Yorkshire**
NE Lin	**North East Lincolnshire**
Nhants	**Northamptonshire**
Norfk	**Norfolk**
Notts	**Nottinghamshire**
Nthumb	**Northumberland**
Oldham	**Oldham (36)**
Oxon	**Oxfordshire**
Poole	**Poole**
R & Cl	**Redcar & Cleveland**
Readg	**Reading**
Rochdl	**Rochdale (37)**
Rothm	**Rotherham (38)**
Rutlnd	**Rutland**
S Glos	**South Gloucestershire (39)**
S on T	**Stockton-on-Tees (40)**
S Tyne	**South Tyneside (41)**
Salfd	**Salford (42)**
Sandw	**Sandwell (43)**
Sefton	**Sefton (44)**
Sheff	**Sheffield**
Shrops	**Shropshire**
Slough	**Slough (45)**
Solhll	**Solihull (46)**
Somset	**Somerset**
St Hel	**St Helens (47)**
Staffs	**Staffordshire**
Sthend	**Southend-on-Sea**
Stockp	**Stockport (48)**
Suffk	**Suffolk**
Sundld	**Sunderland**
Surrey	**Surrey**
Swindn	**Swindon**
Tamesd	**Tameside (49)**
Thurr	**Thurrock (50)**
Torbay	**Torbay**
Traffd	**Trafford (51)**
W & M	**Windsor & Maidenhead (52)**
W Berk	**West Berkshire**
W Susx	**West Sussex**
Wakefd	**Wakefield (53)**
Warrtn	**Warrington (54)**
Warwks	**Warwickshire**
Wigan	**Wigan (55)**
Wilts	**Wiltshire**
Wirral	**Wirral (56)**
Wokham	**Wokingham (57)**
Wolves	**Wolverhampton (58)**
Worcs	**Worcestershire**
Wrekin	**Telford & Wrekin (59)**
Wsall	**Walsall (60)**

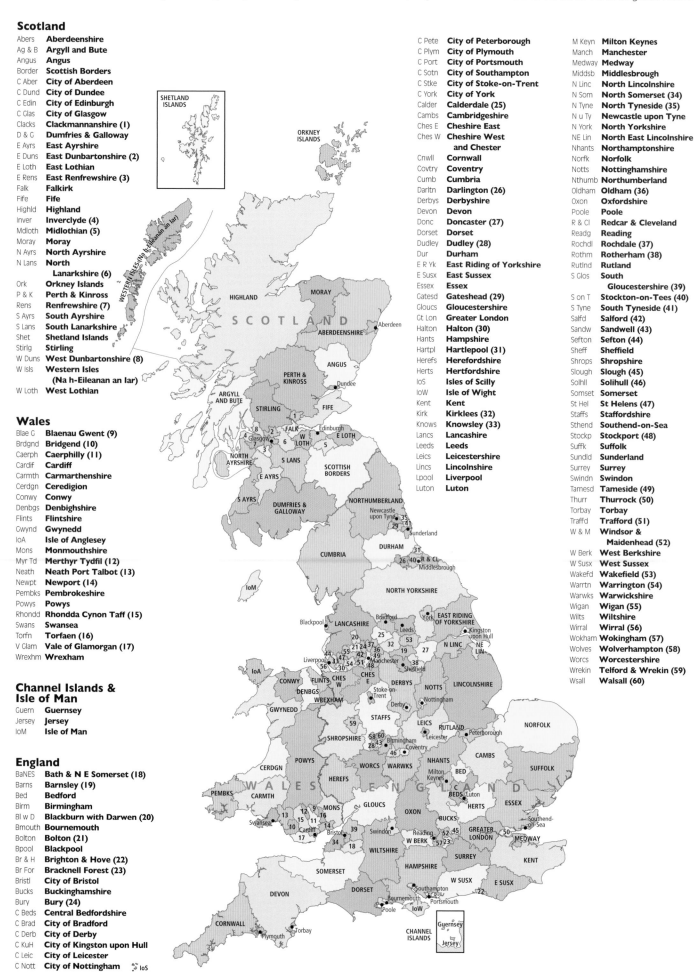

SHETLAND ISLANDS

ORKNEY ISLANDS

WESTERN ISLES (Na h-Eileanan an Iar)

SCOTLAND

HIGHLAND

MORAY

ABERDEENSHIRE

Aberdeen

ANGUS

PERTH & KINROSS

Dundee

ARGYLL AND BUTE

STIRLING

FIFE

FALK

Edinburgh

W LOTH

E LOTH

NORTH AYRSHIRE

Glasgow

S LANS

SCOTTISH BORDERS

E AYRS

S AYRS

DUMFRIES & GALLOWAY

NORTHUMBERLAND

Newcastle upon Tyne

Sunderland

CUMBRIA

DURHAM

R & Cl

Middlesbrough

IoM

NORTH YORKSHIRE

Blackpool

LANCASHIRE

Bradford

York

EAST RIDING OF YORKSHIRE

Kingston upon Hull

Leeds

Liverpool

Manchester

N LINC

NE LIN

Sheffield

IoA

CONWY

FLINTS

CHES E

CHES W

DERBYS

LINCOLNSHIRE

DENBGS

WREXHAM

Stoke-on-Trent

NOTTS

Derby

Nottingham

GWYNEDD

STAFFS

LEICS

RUTLAND

NORFOLK

SHROPSHIRE

Birmingham

Coventry

WARWKS

NHANTS

CAMBS

SUFFOLK

PEMBKS

POWYS

WORCS

Milton Keynes

BED

CERDGN

HEREFS

WALES

ENGLAND

BEDS

Luton

HERTS

ESSEX

CARMTH

MONS

GLOUCS

OXON

BUCKS

Swansea

Cardiff

Bristol

Southend-on-Sea

GREATER LONDON

MEDWAY

Reading

W BERK

Swindon

SURREY

KENT

WILTSHIRE

SOMERSET

HAMPSHIRE

W SUSX

E SUSX

DORSET

Southampton

DEVON

Bournemouth

Poole

Portsmouth

IoW

CORNWALL

Plymouth

Torbay

CHANNEL ISLANDS

Guernsey

Jersey

IoS

A

Abbas Combe Somset	20	D10
Abberley Worcs	57	P11
Abberley Common		
Worcs	57	N11
Abberton Essex	52	H8
Abberton Worcs	47	J4
Abberwick Nthumb	119	M8
Abbess Roding Essex	51	N8
Abbey Devon	10	C2
Abbey-Cwm-Hir Powys	55	P10
Abbeydale Sheff	84	D4
Abbey Dore Herefs	45	M8
Abbey Green Staffs	70	H3
Abbey Hill Somset	19	J11
Abbey St Bathans		
Border	129	K7
Abbeystead Lancs	95	M10
Abbey Town Cumb	110	C10
Abbey Valley		
Crematorium Derbys	84	F10
Abbey Village Lancs	89	J6
Abbey Wood Gt Lon	37	L5
Abbotrule Border	118	B8
Abbots Bickington		
Devon	16	F9
Abbots Bromley Staffs	71	K10
Abbotsbury Dorset	11	M7
Abbot's Chair Derbys	83	M6
Abbots Deuglie P & K	134	E5
Abbotsham Devon	16	G6
Abbotskerswell Devon	7	M5
Abbots Langley Herts	50	C10
Abbotsleigh Devon	7	L9
Abbots Leigh N Som	31	P10
Abbotsley Cambs	62	B9
Abbots Morton Worcs	47	K3
Abbots Ripton Cambs	62	B5
Abbot's Salford Warwks	47	L4
Abbotstone Hants	22	G8
Abbotswood Hants	22	C10
Abbots Worthy Hants	22	E8
Abbotts Ann Hants	22	B6
Abbott Street Dorset	12	G4
Abcott Shrops	56	F9
Abdon Shrops	57	K7
Abenhall Gloucs	46	C11
Aberaeron Cerdgn	43	J2
Aberaman Rhondd	30	D4
Aberangell Gwynd	55	J2
Aber-arad Carmth	42	F6
Aberarder Highld	147	Q2
Aberargie P & K	134	F4
Aberarth Cerdgn	43	J2
Aberavon Neath	29	K7
Aber-banc Cerdgn	42	G6
Aberbargoed Caerph	30	G4
Aberbeeg Blae G	30	H4
Abercanaid Myr Td	30	E4
Abercarn Caerph	30	H6
Abercastle Pembks	40	G4
Abercegir Powys	55	J4
Aberchalder Lodge		
Highld	147	J7
Aberchirder Abers	158	F7
Aber Clydach Powys	44	G10
Abercorn W Loth	127	K2
Abercraf Powys	29	M2
Abercregan Neath	29	M5
Abercwmboi Rhondd	30	D5
Abercych Pembks	41	P2
Abercynon Rhondd	30	E6
Aberdalgie P & K	134	D3
Aberdare Rhondd	30	D4
Aberdaron Gwynd	66	B9
Aberdeen C Aber	151	N6
Aberdeen Airport C Aber	151	M5
Aberdeen		
Crematorium C Aber	151	M6
Aberdesach Gwynd	66	G4
Aberdour Fife	134	F10
Aberdulais Neath	29	L5
Aberdyfi Gwynd	54	E5
Aberedw Powys	44	F5
Abereiddy Pembks	40	E4
Abererch Gwynd	66	F7
Aberfan Myr Td	30	E4
Aberfeldy P & K	141	L8
Aberffraw IoA	78	F11
Aberffrwd Cerdgn	54	F9
Aberford Leeds	91	L3
Aberfoyle Stirlg	132	G7
Abergarw Brdgnd	29	P8
Abergarwed Neath	29	M4
Abergavenny Mons	31	J2
Abergele Conwy	80	C9
Aber-giar Carmth	43	K6
Abergorlech Carmth	43	L8
Abergwesyn Powys	44	B4
Abergwili Carmth	42	H10
Abergwydol Powys	54	H4
Abergwynfi Neath	29	N5
Abergwyngregyn Gwynd	79	M10
Abergynolwyn Gwynd	54	F3
Aberhafesp Powys	55	P6
Aberhosan Powys	55	J5
Aberkenfig Brdgnd	29	N8
Aberlady E Loth	128	D4
Aberlemno Angus	143	J6
Aberllefenni Gwynd	54	H3
Aberllynfi Powys	44	H7
Aberlour, Charlestown		
of Moray	157	P9
Aber-Magwr Cerdgn	54	F10
Aber-meurig Cerdgn	43	L3
Abermorddu Flints	69	K3
Abermule Powys	56	B6
Abernant Carmth	42	F10
Aber-nant Rhondd	30	D4
Abernethy P & K	134	F4
Abernyte P & K	142	D11
Aberporth Cerdgn	42	E4
Abersoch Gwynd	66	E9
Abersychan Torfn	31	J4
Aberthin V Glam	30	D10
Abertillery Blae G	30	H4
Abertridwr Caerph	30	F7
Abertridwr Powys	68	D11
Abertysswg Caerph	30	F3
Aberuthven P & K	134	B4
Aberyscir Powys	44	D8
Aberystwyth Cerdgn	54	D8
Aberystwyth		
Crematorium Cerdgn	54	E8
Abingdon-on-Thames		
Oxon	34	E5
Abinger Common Surrey	36	D11
Abinger Hammer Surrey	36	C11
Abington Nhants	60	G8

Abington S Lans	116	C6
Abington Pigotts Cambs	50	H2
Abington Services S Lans	116	C6
Abingworth W Susx	24	D7
Ab Kettleby Leics	73	J6
Ab Lench Worcs	47	K4
Ablington Gloucs	33	M3
Ablington Wilts	21	N5
Abney Derbys	83	Q8
Above Church Staffs	71	J4
Aboyne Abers	150	E8
Abhainn Suidhe W Isls	168	f7
Abram Wigan	82	D4
Abriachan Highld	155	Q10
Abridge Essex	51	L11
Abronhill N Lans	126	D2
Abson S Glos	32	D10
Abthorpe Nhants	48	H5
Aby Lincs	87	M5
Acaster Malbis C York	98	B11
Acaster Selby N York	91	P2
Accrington Lancs	89	M5
Accrington		
Crematorium Lancs	89	M5
Acha Ag & B	136	F5
Achahoish Ag & B	123	N4
Achalader P & K	141	R8
Achaleven Ag & B	138	G11
Achanalt Highld	155	J5
Achandunie Highld	156	A3
Achany Highld	162	D6
Acharacle Highld	138	B4
Acharn Highld	138	C7
Acharn P & K	141	J9
Achavanich Highld	167	L8
Achduart Highld	160	G6
Achfary Highld	164	G9
A'Chill Highld	144	C6
Achiltibuie Highld	160	G5
Achina Highld	166	B4
Achinhoan Ag & B	120	E8
Achintee Highld	154	B9
Achintraid Highld	153	Q10
Achlean Highld	148	C9
Achleck Ag & B	137	M5
Achlyness Highld	164	G6
Achmelvich Highld	160	H2
Achmore Highld	153	R11
Achmore W Isls	168	i5
Achnacarnin Highld	164	B10
Achnacarry Highld	146	F10
Achnacloich Highld	145	J6
Achnaconeran Highld	147	L4
Achnacroish Ag & B	138	F9
Achnadrish House		
Ag & B	137	M5
Achnafauld P & K	141	L10
Achnagarron Highld	156	B3
Achnaha Highld	137	M2
Achnahaird Highld	160	G4
Achnahannet Highld	148	H2
Achnairn Highld	162	D4
Achnalea Highld	138	F5
Achnamara Ag & B	130	F10
Achnasheen Highld	154	G6
Achnashellach Highld	154	D8
Achnastank Moray	157	P11
Achosnich Highld	137	L2
Achranich Highld	138	C8
Achreamie Highld	166	H3
Achriabhach Highld	139	L4
Achriesgill Highld	164	G6
Achtoty Highld	165	Q4
Achurch Nhants	61	M4
Achvaich Highld	162	G8
Achvarasdal Highld	166	G4
Ackergill Highld	167	Q6
Acklam Middsb	104	E7
Acklam N York	98	F8
Ackleton Shrops	57	P5
Acklington Nthumb	119	P10
Ackton Wakefd	91	L6
Ackworth Moor Top		
Wakefd	91	L7
Acle Norfk	77	N9
Acock's Green Birm	58	H8
Acol Kent	39	P8
Acomb C York	98	B10
Acomb Nthumb	112	D7
Acombe Somset	10	D2
Aconbury Herefs	45	Q8
Acre Lancs	89	M6
Acrefair Wrexhm	69	J6
Acton Ches E	70	A4
Acton Dorset	12	G9
Acton Gt Lon	36	F4
Acton Shrops	56	E8
Acton Staffs	70	E6
Acton Suffk	52	E2
Acton Worcs	58	B11
Acton Beauchamp		
Herefs	46	C4
Acton Bridge Ches W	82	C9
Acton Burnell Shrops	57	J4
Acton Green Herefs	46	C4
Acton Park Wrexhm	69	K4
Acton Pigott Shrops	57	J4
Acton Round Shrops	57	L5
Acton Scott Shrops	56	H7
Acton Trussell Staffs	70	G11
Acton Turville S Glos	32	F8
Adbaston Staffs	70	D9
Adber Dorset	19	Q10
Adbolton Notts	72	F3
Adderbury Oxon	48	E7
Adderley Shrops	70	B7
Adderstone Nthumb	119	M4
Addiewell W Loth	126	H5
Addingham C Brad	96	G11
Addington Bucks	49	K9
Addington Gt Lon	37	J8
Addington Kent	37	Q9
Addiscombe Gt Lon	36	H7
Addlestone Surrey	36	C8
Addlestonemoor Surrey	36	C7
Addlethorpe Lincs	87	P7
Adeney Wrekin	70	B11
Adeyfield Herts	50	C9
Adfa Powys	55	P4
Adforton Herefs	56	F10
Adisham Kent	39	M11
Adlestrop Gloucs	47	P9
Adlingfleet E R Yk	92	D6
Adlington Ches E	83	K8
Adlington Lancs	89	J8
Admaston Staffs	71	J10
Admaston Wrekin	57	L2
Admington Warwks	47	P5
Adpar Cerdgn	42	F6
Adsborough Somset	19	J9
Adscombe Somset	18	G7
Adstock Bucks	49	K9
Adstone Nhants	48	G4

Adswood Stockp	83	J7
Adversane W Susx	24	C6
Advie Highld	157	L11
Adwalton Leeds	90	G5
Adwell Oxon	35	J5
Adwick le Street Donc	91	N9
Adwick upon Dearne		
Donc	91	M10
Ae Bridgend D & G	109	L3
Ae Bridgend D & G	109	M3
Afan Forest Park Neath	29	N5
Affetside Bury	89	M8
Affleck Abers	158	E9
Affpuddle Dorset	12	D6
Affric Lodge Highld	146	F3
Afon-wen Flints	80	G10
Afton Devon	7	L6
Afton IoW	13	P7
Agecroft Crematorium		
Salfd	82	H4
Agglethorpe N York	96	G3
Aigburth Lpool	81	M7
Aike E R Yk	99	L11
Aiketgate Cumb	111	J11
Aikhead Cumb	110	D11
Aikton Cumb	110	E10
Ailby Lincs	87	M5
Ailey Herefs	45	L5
Ailsworth C Pete	74	B11
Ainderby Quernhow		
N York	97	M4
Ainderby Steeple N York	97	M2
Aingers Green Essex	53	K7
Ainsdale Sefton	88	C8
Ainsdale-on-Sea Sefton	88	B8
Ainstable Cumb	111	K11
Ainsworth Bury	89	M8
Ainthorpe N York	105	K9
Aintree Sefton	81	M5
Ainville W Loth	127	L5
Aird Ag & B	130	F7
Aird D & G	106	E5
Aird W Isls	168	k4
Aird a' Mhulaidh W Isls	168	g6
Aird Asaig W Isls	168	g7
Aird Dhubh Highld	153	N9
Airdeny Ag & B	131	K2
Aird of Kinloch Ag & B	137	N10
Aird of Sleat Highld	145	J7
Airdrie N Lans	126	D4
Airdriehill N Lans	126	D4
Airds of Kells D & G	108	E6
Aird Uig W Isls	168	f4
Airidh a bhruaich W Isls	168	h6
Airieland D & G	108	G9
Airlie Angus	142	E7
Airmyn E R Yk	92	B6
Airntully P & K	141	Q10
Airor Highld	145	M6
Airth Falk	133	Q10
Airton N York	96	D9
Aisby Lincs	73	Q3
Aisby Lincs	85	Q2
Aisgill Cumb	102	E11
Aish Devon	6	H6
Aish Devon	7	L7
Aisholt Somset	18	G7
Aiskew N York	97	L3
Aislaby N York	98	F3
Aislaby N York	105	N9
Aislaby S on T	104	D8
Aisthorpe Lincs	86	B4
Aith Shet	169	q8
Akeld Nthumb	119	J5
Akeley Bucks	49	K7
Akenham Suffk	53	K2
Albaston Cnwll	5	Q7
Alberbury Shrops	56	F2
Albourne W Susx	24	G7
Albourne Green W Susx	24	G7
Albrighton Shrops	57	Q4
Albrighton Shrops	69	N11
Alburgh Norfk	65	K4
Albury Herts	51	K6
Albury Oxon	35	J3
Albury Surrey	36	B11
Albury End Herts	51	K6
Albury Heath Surrey	36	C11
Alby Hill Norfk	76	H5
Alcaig Highld	155	Q6
Alcaston Shrops	56	H7
Alcester Warwks	47	L3
Alcester Lane End Birm	58	G8
Alciston E Susx	25	M9
Alcombe Somset	18	C5
Alcombe Wilts	32	F11
Alconbury Cambs	61	Q5
Alconbury Weston		
Cambs	61	Q5
Aldborough N York	97	P7
Aldborough Norfk	76	H5
Aldbourne Wilts	33	Q9
Aldbrough E R Yk	93	M3
Aldbrough St John		
N York	103	P8
Aldbury Herts	35	Q2
Aldcliffe Lancs	95	K8
Aldclune P & K	141	L5
Aldeburgh Suffk	65	P10
Aldeby Norfk	65	N3
Aldenham Herts	50	D11
Alderbury Wilts	21	N9
Aldercar Derbys	84	F11
Alderford Norfk	76	H8
Alderholt Dorset	13	K2
Alderley Gloucs	32	E6
Alderley Edge Ches E	82	H9
Aldermans Green Covtry	59	N8
Aldermaston W Berk	34	G11
Alderminster Warwks	47	P5
Alder Moor Staffs	71	N9
Aldersey Green Ches W	69	N3
Aldershot Hants	23	N4
Alderton Gloucs	47	K8
Alderton Nhants	49	K5
Alderton Shrops	69	N10
Alderton Suffk	53	P3
Alderton Wilts	32	F8
Alderwasley Derbys	71	Q4
Aldfield N York	97	L7
Aldford Ches W	69	M3
Aldgate Rutlnd	73	P10
Aldham Essex	52	F6
Aldham Suffk	52	J2
Aldingbourne W Susx	15	P5
Aldingham Cumb	94	F6
Aldington Kent	27	J4
Aldington Worcs	47	L6
Aldington Corner Kent	27	J4
Aldivalloch Moray	150	B2
Aldochlay Ag & B	132	D9

Aldon Shrops	56	G9
Aldoth Cumb	109	P11
Aldreth Cambs	62	F6
Aldridge Wsall	58	G4
Aldringham Suffk	65	N9
Aldro N York	98	G8
Aldsworth Gloucs	33	N3
Aldsworth W Susx	15	L5
Aldunie Moray	150	B2
Aldwark Derbys	84	B9
Aldwark N York	97	Q8
Aldwick W Susx	15	P6
Aldwincle Nhants	61	M4
Aldworth W Berk	34	G9
Alexandria W Duns	125	K2
Aley Somset	18	G7
Alfardisworthy Devon	16	D9
Alfington Devon	10	C5
Alfold Surrey	24	B4
Alfold Bars W Susx	24	B4
Alfold Crossways Surrey	24	B3
Alford Abers	150	F4
Alford Lincs	87	N5
Alford Somset	20	B8
Alford Crematorium		
Lincs	87	M5
Alfreton Derbys	84	F9
Alfrick Worcs	46	D4
Alfrick Pound Worcs	46	D4
Alfriston E Susx	25	M10
Algarkirk Lincs	74	E3
Alhampton Somset	20	B8
Alkborough N Linc	92	D6
Alkerton Gloucs	32	E3
Alkerton Oxon	48	C6
Alkham Kent	27	N3
Alkington Shrops	69	P7
Alkmonton Derbys	71	M7
Allaleigh Devon	7	L8
Allanaquoich Abers	149	L9
Allanbank N Lans	126	E6
Allanton Border	129	M9
Allanton N Lans	126	E6
Allanton S Lans	126	C7
Allaston Gloucs	32	B4
Allbrook Hants	22	E10
All Cannings Wilts	21	L2
Allendale Nthumb	112	B9
Allenheads Nthumb	112	C11
Allensford Dur	112	G10
Allen's End Warwks	59	J5
Allen's Green Herts	51	L7
Allensmore Herefs	45	P7
Allenton C Derb	72	B4
Aller Devon	17	P6
Aller Somset	19	M9
Allerby Cumb	100	E3
Allercombe Devon	9	P6
Aller Cross Devon	17	N6
Allerford Somset	18	B5
Allerston N York	98	H4
Allerthorpe E R Yk	98	F11
Allerton C Brad	90	E4
Allerton Highld	156	D4
Allerton Lpool	81	M7
Allerton Bywater Leeds	91	L5
Allerton Mauleverer		
N York	97	P9
Allesley Covtry	59	M8
Allestree C Derb	72	A3
Allet Common Cnwll	3	K4
Allexton Leics	73	L10
Allgreave Ches E	83	L11
Allhallows Medway	38	D6
Allhallows-on-Sea		
Medway	38	D6
Alligin Shuas Highld	153	Q6
Allimore Green Staffs	70	F11
Allington Dorset	11	K6
Allington Kent	38	C10
Allington Lincs	73	M2
Allington Wilts	21	L2
Allington Wilts	21	P7
Allington Wilts	32	G9
Allithwaite Cumb	94	H5
Alloa Clacks	133	P9
Allonby Cumb	100	E2
Allostock Ches W	82	F10
Alloway S Ayrs	114	F4
Allowenshay Somset	10	H2
All Saints South		
Elmham Suffk	65	L5
Allscott Shrops	57	N5
Allscott Wrekin	57	L2
All Stretton Shrops	56	H5
Alltami Flints	81	K11
Alltchaorunn Highld	139	M7
Alltmawr Powys	44	F5
Alltwalis Carmth	42	H8
Alltwen Neath	29	K4
Alltyblaca Cerdgn	43	K5
Allweston Dorset	11	P2
Allwood Green Suffk	64	E7
Almeley Herefs	45	L4
Almeley Wooton Herefs	45	L4
Almer Dorset	12	F5
Almholme Donc	91	P9
Almington Staffs	70	C8
Almodington W Susx	15	M7
Almondbank P & K	134	D2
Almondbury Kirk	90	F8
Almondsbury S Glos	32	B8
Alne N York	97	Q7
Alness Highld	156	B4
Alnham Nthumb	119	J8
Alnmouth Nthumb	119	P8
Alnwick Nthumb	119	N8
Alperton Gt Lon	36	E4
Alphamstone Essex	52	E4
Alpheton Suffk	64	B11
Alphington Devon	9	M6
Alpington Norfk	77	K11
Alport Derbys	84	B8
Alpraham Ches E	69	Q3
Alresford Essex	53	J7
Alrewas Staffs	59	J2
Alsager Ches E	70	D3
Alsagers Bank Staffs	70	D5
Alsop en le Dale Derbys	71	M4
Alston Cumb	111	P11
Alston Devon	10	F4
Alstone Gloucs	47	J8
Alstone Somset	19	K5
Alstonefield Staffs	71	L3
Alston Sutton Somset	19	M4
Alswear Devon	17	N7
Alt Oldham	83	K4
Altandhu Highld	160	G3
Altarnun Cnwll	5	L5
Altass Highld	162	C6
Altcreich Ag & B	138	B10

Altgaltraig Ag & B	124	C3
Altham Lancs	89	M4
Althorne Essex	38	F2
Althorpe N Linc	92	D9
Altnabreac Station		
Highld	166	H7
Altnaharra Highld	165	N9
Altofts Wakefd	91	K6
Alton Derbys	84	E8
Alton Hants	23	K7
Alton Staffs	71	K6
Alton Wilts	21	N5
Alton Barnes Wilts	21	M2
Alton Pancras Dorset	11	Q4
Alton Priors Wilts	21	M2
Alton Towers Staffs	71	K6
Altrincham Traffd	82	G7
Altrincham		
Crematorium Traffd	82	F7
Altskeith Hotel Stirlg	132	F7
Alva Clacks	133	P8
Alvanley Ches W	81	P10
Alvaston C Derb	72	B4
Alvechurch Worcs	58	F10
Alvecote Warwks	59	K4
Alvediston Wilts	21	J10
Alveley Shrops	57	P8
Alverdiscott Devon	17	J6
Alverstoke Hants	14	H7
Alverstone IoW	14	G9
Alverthorpe Wakefd	91	J6
Alverton Notts	73	K2
Alves Moray	157	L5
Alvescot Oxon	33	Q4
Alveston S Glos	32	B7
Alveston Warwks	47	P3
Alvingham Lincs	87	L2
Alvington Gloucs	32	B4
Alwalton C Pete	74	B11
Alwinton Nthumb	118	H9
Alwoodley Leeds	90	H3
Alwoodley Gates Leeds	91	J2
Alyth P & K	142	C8
Am Bàgh a Tuath W Isls	168	c17
Ambergate Derbys	84	D10
Amber Hill Lincs	86	H11
Amberley Gloucs	32	G4
Amberley W Susx	24	B8
Amber Row Derbys	84	E9
Amberstone E Susx	25	N8
Amble Nthumb	119	Q10
Amblecote Dudley	58	C7
Ambler Thorn C Brad	90	D5
Ambleside Cumb	101	L10
Ambleston Pembks	41	K5
Ambrosden Oxon	48	H11
Amcotts N Linc	92	E8
America Cambs	62	F5
Amersham Bucks	35	Q5
Amersham Common		
Bucks	35	Q5
Amersham Old Town		
Bucks	35	Q5
Amersham on the Hill		
Bucks	35	Q5
Amerton Staffs	70	H9
Amesbury Wilts	21	N6
Amhuinnsuidhe W Isls	168	f7
Amington Staffs	59	K4
Amisfield D & G	109	M4
Amlwch IoA	78	G6
Ammanford Carmth	28	H2
Amotherby N York	98	E6
Ampfield Hants	22	D10
Ampleforth N York	98	B5
Ampney Crucis Gloucs	33	L4
Ampney St Mary Gloucs	33	L4
Ampney St Peter Gloucs	33	L4
Amport Hants	22	B6
Ampthill C Beds	50	B3
Ampton Suffk	64	B7
Amroth Pembks	41	N9
Amulree P & K	141	L10
Amwell Herts	50	E8
Anaheilt Highld	138	E5
Ancaster Lincs	73	P2
Ancells Farm Hants	23	M3
Anchor Shrops	56	B7
Ancroft Nthumb	129	P11
Ancrum Border	118	B6
Ancton W Susx	15	Q6
Anderby Lincs	87	P5
Anderby Creek Lincs	87	Q5
Andersea Somset	19	K8
Andersfield Somset	18	H8
Anderson Dorset	12	E5
Anderton Ches W	82	D9
Anderton Cnwll	6	C8
Andover Hants	22	C5
Andoversford Gloucs	47	K11
Andreas IoM	80	f2
Anelog Gwynd	66	B9
Anerley Gt Lon	36	H7
Anfield Lpool	81	M6
Anfield Crematorium		
Lpool	81	M6
Angarrack Cnwll	2	F6
Angarrick Cnwll	3	K6
Angelbank Shrops	57	K9
Angersleigh Somset	18	G11
Angerton Cumb	110	D9
Angle Pembks	40	G10
Anglesey IoA	78	G8
Anglesey Abbey Cambs	62	H8
Angmering W Susx	24	C10
Angram N York	97	R11
Angram N York	102	G11
Angrouse Cnwll	2	H10
Anick Nthumb	112	D7
Ankerville Highld	156	E3
Ankle Hill Leics	73	K7
Anlaby E R Yk	92	H5
Anmer Norfk	75	P5
Anmore Hants	15	J4
Annan D & G	110	C7
Annandale Water		
Services D & G	109	P2
Annaside Cumb	94	B3
Annat Highld	154	A7
Annathill N Lans	126	C3
Anna Valley Hants	22	C4
Annbank S Ayrs	114	H3
Anne Hathaway's		
Cottage Warwks	47	N4
Annesley Notts	84	H10
Annesley Woodhouse		
Notts	84	G10
Annfield Plain Dur	113	J10
Anniesland C Glas	125	N4
Annitsford N Tyne	113	L6
Annscroft Shrops	56	H3

Ansdell Lancs ...88 C5
Ansford Somset ...20 B8
Ansley Warwks ...59 M6
Anslow Staffs ...71 N9
Anslow Gate Staffs ...71 M10
Anslow Lees Staffs ...71 N10
Ansteadbrook Surrey ...23 P8
Anstey Hants ...23 K6
Anstey Herts ...51 K4
Anstey Leics ...72 F9
Anstruther Fife ...135 P7
Ansty W Susx ...24 G6
Ansty Warwks ...59 P8
Ansty Wilts ...21 J9
Ansty Cross Dorset ...12 C4
Anthill Common Hants ...14 H4
Anthonys Surrey ...36 B8
Anthorn Cumb ...110 C9
Antingham Norfk ...77 K5
An t-Ob W Isls ...168 f9
Antonine Wall ...126 E2
Anton's Gowt Lincs ...87 K11
Antony Cnwll ...5 Q11
Antrobus Ches W ...82 D9
Anvil Corner Devon ...16 F11
Anvil Green Kent ...27 K2
Anwick Lincs ...86 F10
Anwoth D & G ...108 C9
Aperfield Gt Lon ...37 K9
Apes Dale Worcs ...58 E10
Apethorpe Nhants ...73 Q11
Apeton Staffs ...70 F11
Apley Lincs ...86 F5
Apperknowle Derbys ...84 E5
Apperley Gloucs ...46 G9
Apperley Bridge C Brad ...90 F3
Apperley Dene Nthumb ...112 G9
Appersett N York ...96 C2
Appin Ag & B ...138 C8
Appleby N Linc ...92 G8
Appleby-in-Westmorland Cumb ...102 C6
Appleby Magna Leics ...59 M3
Appleby Parva Leics ...59 M3
Appleby Street Herts ...50 H10
Applecross Highld ...153 N9
Appledore Devon ...9 Q2
Appledore Devon ...16 H5
Appledore Kent ...26 G6
Appledore Heath Kent ...26 G5
Appleford Oxon ...34 F6
Applegarth Town D & G ...109 P4
Applehaigh Wakefd ...91 K8
Appleshaw Hants ...22 B5
Applethwaite Cumb ...101 J5
Appleton Halton ...81 Q7
Appleton Oxon ...34 D4
Appleton Warrtn ...82 D8
Appleton-le-Moors N York ...98 E3
Appleton-le-Street N York ...98 E6
Appleton Roebuck N York ...91 P2
Appleton Thorn Warrtn ...82 D8
Appleton Wiske N York ...104 C10
Appletreehall Border ...117 Q7
Appletreewick N York ...96 G8
Appley Somset ...18 E10
Appley Bridge Lancs ...88 G9
Apse Heath IoW ...14 G10
Apsley End C Beds ...50 D4
Apuldram W Susx ...15 M6
Arabella Highld ...156 E2
Arbirlot Angus ...143 L9
Arboll Highld ...163 K10
Arborfield Wokham ...35 L11
Arborfield Cross Wokham ...35 L11
Arborfield Green Wokham ...35 L11
Arbourthorne Sheff ...84 E3
Arbroath Angus ...143 L9
Arbuthnott Abers ...143 P2
Arcadia Kent ...26 E4
Archddu Carmth ...28 D4
Archdeacon Newton Darltn ...103 Q7
Archencarroch W Duns ...132 E11
Archiestown Moray ...157 N9
Archirondel Jersey ...11 c1
Arclid Ches E ...70 D2
Ardallie Abers ...159 P10
Ardanaiseig Hotel Ag & B ...131 M3
Ardaneaskan Highld ...153 Q10
Ardarroch Highld ...153 Q10
Ardbeg Ag & B ...122 F10
Ardbeg Ag & B ...124 D4
Ardbeg Ag & B ...131 P11
Ardcharnich Highld ...161 K9
Ardchiavaig Ag & B ...137 K12
Ardchonnel Ag & B ...131 K5
Ardchullarie More Stirlg ...132 H5
Arddarroch Ag & B ...131 Q9
Arddleen Powys ...69 J11
Ard Dorch Highld ...145 J2
Ardechive Highld ...146 E9
Ardeer N Ayrs ...124 H9
Ardeley Herts ...50 H5
Ardelve Highld ...145 Q2
Arden Ag & B ...132 D11
Ardens Grafton Warwks ...47 M4
Ardentallen Ag & B ...130 G3
Ardentinny Ag & B ...131 P10
Ardentraive Ag & B ...124 C3
Ardeonaig Stirlg ...140 G10
Ardersier Highld ...156 D7
Ardessie Highld ...160 H9
Ardfern Ag & B ...130 G7
Ardfernal Ag & B ...123 J5
Ardgartan Ag & B ...132 B7
Ardgay Highld ...162 D8
Ardgour Highld ...139 J3
Ardgowan Inver ...124 G3
Ardhallow Ag & B ...124 F3
Ardheslaig Highld ...168 g7
Ardindrean Highld ...161 K9
Ardingly W Susx ...24 H5
Ardington Oxon ...34 D7
Ardington Wick Oxon ...34 D7
Ardlamont Ag & B ...124 B4
Ardleigh Essex ...53 J6
Ardleigh Heath Essex ...52 H5
Ardler P & K ...142 D9
Ardley Oxon ...48 F9
Ardley End Essex ...51 M8
Ardlui Ag & B ...132 C4
Ardlussa Ag & B ...130 C10
Ardmair Highld ...161 J7
Ardmaleish Ag & B ...124 D4
Ardminish Ag & B ...123 K10
Ardmolich Highld ...138 C3
Ardmore Ag & B ...125 G3
Ardmore Highld ...162 G9

Ardnadam Ag & B ...131 P11
Ardnagrask Highld ...155 P8
Ardnamurchan Highld ...137 P2
Ardnarff Highld ...154 A10
Ardnastang Highld ...138 E5
Ardpatrick Ag & B ...123 N8
Ardrishaig Ag & B ...130 H10
Ardross Highld ...155 R3
Ardrossan N Ayrs ...124 G9
Ardsley Barns ...91 K9
Ardsley East Leeds ...91 J5
Ardslignish Highld ...137 P3
Ardtalla Ag & B ...122 G9
Ardtoe Highld ...138 A3
Arduaine Ag & B ...130 F5
Ardullie Highld ...155 Q5
Ardvasar Highld ...145 K7
Ardvorlich P & K ...133 J3
Ardvourlie W Isls ...168 g6
Ardwell D & G ...106 F8
Ardwick Manch ...83 J5
Areley Kings Worcs ...57 P10
Arevegaig Highld ...138 B4
Arford Hants ...23 M7
Arglam E R Yk ...92 C3
Argoed Caerph ...30 G5
Argoed Shrops ...69 K10
Argoed Mill Powys ...44 D2
Argos Hill E Susx ...25 N5
Argyll Forest Park Ag & B ...131 Q7
Aribruach W Isls ...168 h6
Aridhglas Ag & B ...137 J11
Arileod Ag & B ...136 F5
Arinagour Ag & B ...136 G4
Ariogan Ag & B ...130 H2
Arisaig Highld ...145 L10
Arisaig House Highld ...145 L11
Arkendale N York ...97 N8
Arkesden Essex ...51 L4
Arkholme Lancs ...95 M6
Arkleby Cumb ...100 F3
Arkleton D & G ...110 G2
Arkle Town N York ...103 K6
Arkley Gt Lon ...50 F11
Arksey Donc ...91 P9
Arkwright Town Derbys ...84 F6
Arle Gloucs ...46 H10
Arlecdon Cumb ...100 D7
Arlescote Warwks ...48 C5
Arlesey C Beds ...50 E3
Arleston Wrekin ...57 M2
Arley Ches E ...82 E8
Arley Warwks ...59 L6
Arlingham Gloucs ...32 D2
Arlington Devon ...17 L3
Arlington E Susx ...25 M9
Arlington Gloucs ...33 M3
Arlington Beccott Devon ...17 L3
Armadale Highld ...145 K7
Armadale Highld ...166 G4
Armadale W Loth ...126 G4
Armaside Cumb ...100 G5
Armathwaite Cumb ...111 K11
Arminghall Norfk ...77 K11
Armitage Staffs ...71 K11
Armitage Bridge Kirk ...90 E8
Armley Leeds ...90 H4
Armscote Warwks ...47 P6
Armshead Staffs ...70 G5
Armston Nhants ...61 N3
Armthorpe Donc ...91 Q10
Arnabost Ag & B ...136 G3
Arncliffe N York ...96 D6
Arncliffe Cote N York ...96 D6
Arncroach Fife ...135 N6
Arndilly House Moray ...157 P8
Arne Dorset ...12 G7
Arnesby Leics ...60 D2
Arngask P & K ...134 E5
Arnisdale Highld ...145 P5
Arnish Highld ...153 K8
Arniston Mdloth ...127 Q5
Arnol W Isls ...168 i3
Arnold E R Yk ...93 K2
Arnold Notts ...85 J11
Arnprior Stirlg ...133 J9
Arnside Cumb ...95 K5
Aros Ag & B ...137 P6
Arowry Wrexhm ...69 N7
Arrad Foot Cumb ...94 G4
Arram E R Yk ...92 H2
Arran N Ayrs ...120 H4
Arrathorne N York ...97 K2
Arreton IoW ...14 F9
Arrina Highld ...153 N6
Arrington Cambs ...62 D10
Arrochar Ag & B ...132 B7
Arrow Warwks ...47 L3
Arrowfield Top Worcs ...58 F10
Arscott Shrops ...56 G3
Artafallie Highld ...156 A8
Arthington Leeds ...90 H2
Arthingworth Nhants ...60 G4
Arthog Gwynd ...54 E2
Arthrath Abers ...159 N10
Arthursdale Leeds ...91 K3
Artrochie Abers ...159 P11
Arundel W Susx ...24 B9
Asby Cumb ...100 E6
Ascog Ag & B ...124 E5
Ascot W & M ...35 P11
Ascott Warwks ...48 B8
Ascott Earl Oxon ...48 B11
Ascott-under-Wychwood Oxon ...48 B11
Asenby N York ...97 N5
Asfordby Leics ...73 J7
Asfordby Hill Leics ...73 J7
Asgarby Lincs ...86 F11
Asgarby Lincs ...87 K7
Ash Devon ...7 L9
Ash Devon ...17 J10
Ash Dorset ...12 E2
Ash Kent ...37 P8
Ash Kent ...39 N10
Ash Somset ...19 J10
Ash Somset ...19 N10
Ash Surrey ...23 P4
Ashampstead W Berk ...34 G9
Ashampstead Green W Berk ...34 G9
Ashbocking Suffk ...64 H11
Ashbourne Derbys ...71 M5
Ashbrittle Somset ...18 E10
Ashburnham Place E Susx ...25 Q8
Ashburton Devon ...7 K4
Ashbury Devon ...8 D5
Ashbury Oxon ...33 Q7

Ashby N Linc ...92 E9
Ashby by Partney Lincs ...87 M7
Ashby cum Fenby NE Lin ...93 N10
Ashby de la Launde Lincs ...86 E9
Ashby Folville Leics ...73 J8
Ashby Magna Leics ...60 C2
Ashby Parva Leics ...60 B3
Ashby Puerorum Lincs ...87 K6
Ashby St Ledgers Nhants ...60 C7
Ashby St Mary Norfk ...77 L11
Ashchurch Gloucs ...46 H8
Ashcombe Devon ...9 M9
Ashcombe N Som ...19 K2
Ashcott Somset ...19 M7
Ashdon Essex ...51 N2
Ashdown Forest E Susx ...25 L4
Ashe Hants ...22 H4
Asheldham Essex ...52 G11
Ashen Essex ...52 B3
Ashendon Bucks ...35 K2
Asheridge Bucks ...35 P3
Ashfield Hants ...22 C11
Ashfield Herefs ...46 A10
Ashfield Stirlg ...133 M7
Ashfield cum Thorpe Suffk ...65 J9
Ashfield Green Suffk ...63 N9
Ashfield Green Suffk ...65 K7
Ashfold Crossways W Susx ...24 F5
Ashford Devon ...6 H9
Ashford Devon ...17 J4
Ashford Kent ...26 H3
Ashford Surrey ...36 C6
Ashford Bowdler Shrops ...57 J10
Ashford Carbonell Shrops ...57 J10
Ashford Hill Hants ...22 G2
Ashford in the Water Derbys ...83 Q11
Ashgill S Lans ...126 D7
Ash Green Surrey ...23 P5
Ash Green Warwks ...59 M8
Ashill Devon ...10 B2
Ashill Norfk ...76 B11
Ashill Somset ...19 K11
Ashingdon Essex ...38 E3
Ashington Nthumb ...113 L3
Ashington Poole ...12 H5
Ashington Somset ...19 Q10
Ashington W Susx ...24 D7
Ashkirk Border ...117 P6
Ashlett Hants ...14 E6
Ashleworth Gloucs ...46 F9
Ashleworth Quay Gloucs ...46 F9
Ashley Cambs ...63 L8
Ashley Ches E ...82 G8
Ashley Devon ...17 M9
Ashley Dorset ...13 K4
Ashley Gloucs ...32 H6
Ashley Hants ...13 N5
Ashley Hants ...22 C8
Ashley Kent ...27 P2
Ashley Nhants ...60 G2
Ashley Staffs ...70 D7
Ashley Wilts ...32 F11
Ashley Green Bucks ...35 Q3
Ashleyhay Derbys ...71 P4
Ashley Heath Dorset ...13 K4
Ashley Moor Herefs ...56 H11
Ash Magna Shrops ...69 Q7
Ashmansworth Hants ...22 D3
Ashmansworthy Devon ...16 E8
Ashmead Green Gloucs ...32 E5
Ashmill Devon ...5 P2
Ash Mill Devon ...17 P7
Ashmore Dorset ...20 H11
Ashmore Green W Berk ...34 F11
Ashorne Warwks ...48 B3
Ashover Derbys ...84 D8
Ashover Hay Derbys ...84 D8
Ashow Warwks ...59 M10
Ash Parva Shrops ...69 Q7
Ashperton Herefs ...46 B6
Ashprington Devon ...7 L7
Ash Priors Somset ...18 G9
Ashreigney Devon ...17 L9
Ash Street Suffk ...52 H2
Ashtead Surrey ...36 E9
Ash Thomas Devon ...9 P2
Ashton C Pete ...74 B9
Ashton Ches W ...81 Q11
Ashton Cnwll ...2 G8
Ashton Devon ...9 L8
Ashton Hants ...22 F11
Ashton Herefs ...45 Q2
Ashton Inver ...124 G2
Ashton Nhants ...49 L5
Ashton Nhants ...61 N3
Ashton Somset ...19 M5
Ashton Common Wilts ...20 G3
Ashton Hill Wilts ...20 H3
Ashton-in-Makerfield Wigan ...82 C5
Ashton Keynes Wilts ...33 K6
Ashton under Hill Worcs ...47 J7
Ashton-under-Lyne Tamesd ...83 K5
Ashton upon Mersey Traffd ...82 G6
Ashurst Hants ...13 P2
Ashurst Kent ...25 M3
Ashurst Lancs ...88 F9
Ashurst W Susx ...24 E7
Ashurstwood W Susx ...25 K3
Ash Vale Surrey ...23 N4
Ashwater Devon ...5 P2
Ashwell Herts ...50 G3
Ashwell Rutlnd ...73 M8
Ashwell End Herts ...50 G2
Ashwellthorpe Norfk ...64 G2
Ashwick Somset ...20 B5
Ashwicken Norfk ...75 P7
Ashwood Staffs ...58 C7
Askam in Furness Cumb ...94 E5
Askern Donc ...91 P8
Askerswell Dorset ...11 L6
Askett Bucks ...35 M3
Askham Cumb ...101 P6
Askham Notts ...85 M6
Askham Bryan C York ...98 B11
Askham Richard C York ...98 A11
Asknish Ag & B ...131 J9
Askrigg N York ...96 D2
Askwith N York ...97 J11
Aslackby Lincs ...74 A4
Aslacton Norfk ...64 H3
Aslockton Notts ...73 J3

Asney Somset ...19 N7
Aspall Suffk ...64 H9
Aspatria Cumb ...100 F2
Aspenden Herts ...51 J5
Aspenshaw Derbys ...83 M7
Asperton Lincs ...74 E3
Aspley Staffs ...70 E8
Aspley Guise C Beds ...49 P7
Aspley Heath C Beds ...49 P8
Aspley Heath Warwks ...58 G10
Aspull Wigan ...89 J9
Aspull Common Wigan ...82 D5
Asselby E R Yk ...92 B5
Asserby Lincs ...87 N5
Asserby Turn Lincs ...87 N5
Assington Suffk ...52 F4
Assington Green Suffk ...63 N10
Astbury Ches E ...70 E2
Astcote Nhants ...49 J4
Asterby Lincs ...87 J5
Asterley Shrops ...56 F4
Asterton Shrops ...56 F6
Asthall Oxon ...33 Q2
Asthall Leigh Oxon ...34 B2
Astle Highld ...162 G8
Astley Shrops ...69 P11
Astley Warwks ...59 M7
Astley Wigan ...82 F4
Astley Worcs ...57 P11
Astley Abbotts Shrops ...57 N5
Astley Bridge Bolton ...89 L8
Astley Cross Worcs ...57 P11
Astley Green Wigan ...82 F5
Aston Birm ...58 G7
Aston Ches E ...69 R5
Aston Ches W ...82 C9
Aston Derbys ...83 Q8
Aston Flints ...81 L11
Aston Herefs ...45 P2
Aston Herts ...50 G6
Aston Oxon ...34 B4
Aston Rothm ...84 G3
Aston Shrops ...57 Q6
Aston Shrops ...69 P9
Aston Staffs ...70 D6
Aston Staffs ...70 F10
Aston Wokham ...35 L3
Aston Wrekin ...57 L3
Aston Abbotts Bucks ...49 M10
Aston Botterell Shrops ...57 L8
Aston-by-Stone Staffs ...70 G8
Aston Cantlow Warwks ...47 M2
Aston Clinton Bucks ...35 N2
Aston Crews Herefs ...46 C10
Aston Cross Gloucs ...46 H8
Aston End Herts ...50 G6
Aston-Eyre Shrops ...57 M6
Aston Fields Worcs ...58 E11
Aston Flamville Leics ...59 Q6
Aston Heath Ches W ...82 C9
Aston Ingham Herefs ...46 C10
Aston juxta Mondrum Ches E ...70 A3
Aston le Walls Nhants ...48 E4
Aston Magna Gloucs ...47 N7
Aston Munslow Shrops ...57 J7
Aston-on-Carrant Gloucs ...46 H8
Aston on Clun Shrops ...56 F8
Aston Pigott Shrops ...56 E3
Aston Rogers Shrops ...56 E3
Aston Rowant Oxon ...35 K5
Aston Sandford Bucks ...35 L3
Aston Somerville Worcs ...47 K7
Aston-sub-Edge Gloucs ...47 M6
Aston Tirrold Oxon ...34 G7
Aston-upon-Trent Derbys ...72 C5
Aston Upthorpe Oxon ...34 G7
Astrop Nhants ...48 F7
Astrope Herts ...35 N2
Astwick C Beds ...50 F3
Astwith Derbys ...84 F8
Astwood M Keyn ...49 Q5
Astwood Worcs ...58 D11
Astwood Bank Worcs ...47 K2
Aswarby Lincs ...73 R3
Aswardby Lincs ...87 L6
Atcham Shrops ...57 J3
Atch Lench Worcs ...47 K4
Athelhampton Dorset ...12 C6
Athelington Suffk ...65 J7
Athelney Somset ...19 K9
Athelstaneford E Loth ...128 E4
Atherfield Green IoW ...14 E11
Atherington Devon ...17 K7
Atherington W Susx ...24 B10
Atherstone Somset ...19 L11
Atherstone Warwks ...59 M5
Atherstone on Stour Warwks ...47 P4
Atherton Wigan ...82 E4
Atley Hill N York ...103 Q10
Atlow Derbys ...71 N5
Attadale Highld ...154 B10
Attenborough Notts ...72 E4
Atterby Lincs ...86 C2
Attercliffe Sheff ...84 E3
Atterley Shrops ...57 L5
Atterton Leics ...72 B11
Attingham Park Shrops ...57 J2
Attleborough Norfk ...64 E2
Attleborough Warwks ...59 N6
Attlebridge Norfk ...76 G8
Attleton Green Suffk ...63 M10
Atwick E R Yk ...99 P10
Atworth Wilts ...32 G11
Auberrow Herefs ...45 P5
Aubourn Lincs ...86 B8
Auchbreck Moray ...149 N2
Auchedly Abers ...159 L11
Auchenblae Abers ...143 N2
Auchenbowie Stirlg ...133 M10
Auchencairn D & G ...108 G10
Auchencairn D & G ...109 L4
Auchencairn N Ayrs ...121 K6
Auchencrow Border ...129 M7
Auchendinny Mdloth ...127 P5
Auchengray S Lans ...126 H7
Auchenhalrig Moray ...157 R5
Auchenheath S Lans ...126 E8
Auchenhessnane D & G ...115 R8
Auchenlochan Ag & B ...124 B3
Auchenmade N Ayrs ...125 K8
Auchenmalg D & G ...106 H7
Auchentiber N Ayrs ...125 K8
Auchindrain Ag & B ...131 L7
Auchindrean Highld ...161 K10
Auchininna Abers ...158 G8
Auchinleck E Ayrs ...115 L3
Auchinloch N Lans ...126 B3
Auchinstarry N Lans ...126 C2

Auchintore Highld ...139 K3
Auchiries Abers ...159 Q10
Auchlean Highld ...148 F8
Auchlee Abers ...151 M8
Auchleven Abers ...150 G3
Auchlochan S Lans ...126 E10
Auchlossan Abers ...150 F7
Auchlyne Stirlg ...132 G2
Auchmillan E Ayrs ...115 K2
Auchmithie Angus ...143 M9
Auchmuirbridge Fife ...134 G7
Auchnacree Angus ...142 H5
Auchnagatt Abers ...159 M9
Auchnarrow Moray ...149 N3
Auchnotteroch D & G ...106 C5
Auchroisk Moray ...157 Q5
Auchterarder P & K ...133 Q5
Auchteraw Highld ...147 K5
Auchterblair Highld ...148 G3
Auchtercairn Highld ...153 Q3
Auchterderran Fife ...134 G8
Auchterhouse Angus ...142 E10
Auchterless Abers ...158 H9
Auchtermuchty Fife ...134 G5
Auchterneed Highld ...155 N6
Auchtertool Fife ...134 G9
Auchtertyre Highld ...145 P2
Auchtubh Stirlg ...132 H3
Auckengill Highld ...167 Q4
Auckley Donc ...91 Q10
Audenshaw Tamesd ...83 K5
Audlem Ches E ...70 B6
Audley Staffs ...70 D4
Audley End Essex ...51 M3
Audley End Essex ...52 D4
Audley End Suffk ...64 B11
Audley End House & Gardens Essex ...51 M3
Audmore Staffs ...70 E10
Audnam Dudley ...58 C7
Aughertree Cumb ...101 J3
Aughton E R Yk ...92 B3
Aughton Lancs ...88 D9
Aughton Lancs ...95 M7
Aughton Rothm ...84 G3
Aughton Wilts ...21 P3
Aughton Park Lancs ...88 E9
Auldearn Highld ...156 G6
Aulden Herefs ...45 P4
Auldgirth D & G ...109 K3
Auldhouse S Lans ...125 Q7
Ault a' chruinn Highld ...146 A3
Aultbea Highld ...160 B9
Aultgrishin Highld ...160 A9
Aultguish Inn Highld ...155 L3
Ault Hucknall Derbys ...84 G7
Aultmore Moray ...158 B7
Aultnagoire Highld ...147 N3
Aultnamain Inn Highld ...162 F10
Aunby Lincs ...73 Q8
Aunk Devon ...9 P4
Aunsby Lincs ...73 Q3
Aust S Glos ...31 Q7
Austendike Lincs ...74 E6
Austerfield Donc ...85 L2
Austerlands Oldham ...90 B9
Austhorpe Leeds ...91 K4
Austonley Kirk ...90 E9
Austrey Warwks ...59 L3
Austwick N York ...95 R7
Authorpe Lincs ...87 L4
Authorpe Row Lincs ...87 P6
Avebury Wilts ...33 M11
Avebury Trusloe Wilts ...33 L11
Aveley Thurr ...37 N4
Avening Gloucs ...32 G5
Averham Notts ...85 N10
Aveton Gifford Devon ...6 H9
Aviemore Highld ...148 F5
Avington W Berk ...34 C11
Avoch Highld ...156 C6
Avon Hants ...13 K5
Avonbridge Falk ...126 G3
Avon Dassett Warwks ...48 D4
Avonmouth Bristl ...31 P9
Avonwick Devon ...7 J7
Awbridge Hants ...22 B10
Awkley S Glos ...31 Q7
Awliscombe Devon ...10 C4
Awre Gloucs ...32 D3
Awsworth Notts ...72 D2
Axborough Worcs ...58 C9
Axbridge Somset ...19 M4
Axford Hants ...22 H6
Axford Wilts ...33 P10
Axmansford Hants ...22 G2
Axminster Devon ...10 F5
Axmouth Devon ...10 F6
Axton Flints ...80 G8
Aycliffe Dur ...103 Q6
Aydon Nthumb ...112 F7
Aylburton Gloucs ...32 B4
Ayle Nthumb ...111 P11
Aylesbeare Devon ...9 P6
Aylesbury Bucks ...35 M2
Aylesbury Crematorium Bucks ...49 M11
Aylesby NE Lin ...93 M9
Aylesford Kent ...38 B10
Aylesham Kent ...39 M11
Aylestone C Leic ...72 F10
Aylestone Park C Leic ...72 F10
Aylmerton Norfk ...76 H4
Aylsham Norfk ...76 H6
Aylton Herefs ...46 C7
Aylworth Gloucs ...47 M10
Aymestrey Herefs ...56 G11
Aynho Nhants ...48 F8
Ayot Green Herts ...50 F8
Ayot St Lawrence Herts ...50 E7
Ayot St Peter Herts ...50 F7
Ayr S Ayrs ...114 F3
Aysgarth N York ...96 F3
Ayshford Devon ...18 D11
Ayside Cumb ...94 H4
Ayston Rutlnd ...73 M10
Aythorpe Roding Essex ...51 N7
Ayton Border ...129 N7
Azerley N York ...97 L6

B

Babbacombe Torbay ...7 N5
Babbington Notts ...72 D2
Babbinswood Shrops ...69 K9
Babbs Green Herts ...51 J7
Babcary Somset ...19 Q9
Babel Carmth ...44 A7

Babel Green – Bean 257

Babel Green Suffk 63 M11
Babell Flints 80 H10
Babeny Devon 8 G9
Bablock Hythe Oxon 34 D4
Babraham Cambs 62 H10
Babworth Notts 85 L4
Bachau IoA 78 G8
Bache Shrops 56 H8
Bacheldre Powys 56 C6
Bachelor's Bump E Susx 26 D9
Backaland Ork 169 e3
Backbarrow Cumb 94 H4
Backe Carmth 41 Q7
Backfolds Abers 159 P7
Backford Ches W 81 M10
Backford Cross Ches W 81 M10
Backies Highld 163 J6
Back of Keppoch Highld 145 L10
Back o' th' Brook Staffs 71 K4
Back Street Suffk 63 M9
Backwell N Som 31 N11
Backworth N Tyne 113 M6
Bacon's End Solhll 59 J7
Baconsthorpe Norfk 76 G4
Bacton Herefs 45 M8
Bacton Norfk 77 L5
Bacton Suffk 64 F8
Bacton Green Suffk 64 E8
Bacup Lancs 89 P6
Badachro Highld 153 P3
Badanloch Highld 166 C10
Badbury Swindn 33 N8
Badby Nhants 60 C9
Badcall Highld 164 E8
Badcall Highld 164 F5
Badcaul Highld 160 G8
Baddeley Edge C Stke 70 G4
Baddeley Green C Stke 70 G4
Baddesley Clinton Warwks 59 K10
Baddesley Ensor Warwks 59 L5
Baddidarrach Highld 160 H2
Baddinsgill Border 127 L7
Badenscoth Abers 158 G10
Badentarbet Highld 160 G5
Badenyon Abers 149 Q4
Badersfield Norfk 77 K7
Badgall Cnwll 5 L4
Badgeney Cambs 74 H11
Badger Shrops 57 P5
Badger's Cross Cnwll 2 D7
Badgers Mount Kent 37 L8
Badgeworth Gloucs 46 H11
Badgworth Somset 19 L4
Badharlick Cnwll 5 M4
Badicaul Highld 145 N2
Badingham Suffk 65 L8
Badlesmere Kent 38 H11
Badlieu Border 116 F7
Badlipster Highld 167 M7
Badluarach Highld 160 F8
Badninish Highld 162 H8
Badrallach Highld 160 H8
Badsey Worcs 47 L6
Badshot Lea Surrey 23 N5
Badsworth Wakefd 91 M8
Badwell Ash Suffk 64 D8
Badwell Green Suffk 64 E8
Bagber Dorset 12 C2
Bagby N York 97 Q4
Bag Enderby Lincs 87 L6
Bagendon Gloucs 33 K3
Bagginswood Shrops 57 M8
Baggrow Cumb 100 G2
Bàgh a' Chaisteil W Isls 168 b18
Bagham Kent 39 J11
Bagillt Flints 81 J9
Baginton Warwks 59 M10
Baglan Neath 29 K6
Bagley Leeds 90 G3
Bagley Shrops 69 M9
Bagley Somset 19 N5
Bagmore Hants 23 J6
Bagnall Staffs 70 G4
Bagnor W Berk 34 E11
Bagshot Surrey 23 P2
Bagshot Wilts 34 B11
Bagstone S Glos 32 C7
Bagthorpe Notts 84 G10
Bagworth Leics 72 C9
Bagwy Llydiart Herefs 45 N9
Baildon C Brad 90 F3
Baildon Green C Brad 90 E3
Baile Ailein W Isls 168 h5
Baile a' Mhanaich W Isls 168 c12
Baile Mòr Ag & B 136 H11
Bailey Green Hants 23 J9
Baileyhead Cumb 111 K5
Bailiff Bridge Calder 90 E5
Baillieston C Glas 126 B5
Bailrigg Lancs 95 K9
Bainbridge N York 96 D2
Bainshole Abers 158 F10
Bainton C Pete 74 A9
Bainton E R Yk 99 K10
Bainton Oxon 48 G9
Baintown Fife 135 K7
Bairnkine Border 118 C7
Baker's End Herts 51 J7
Baker Street Thurr 37 P4
Bakewell Derbys 84 B7
Bala Gwynd 68 B7
Balallan W Isls 168 h5
Balbeg Highld 155 M11
Balbeggie P & K 134 F2
Balblair Highld 155 P8
Balblair Highld 156 C4
Balby Donc 91 P10
Balcary D & G 108 H11
Balchraggan Highld 155 P9
Balchreick Highld 164 E4
Balcombe W Susx 24 H4
Balcombe Lane W Susx 24 H4
Balcomie Links Fife 135 Q6
Baldersby N York 97 N5
Baldersby St James N York 97 N5
Balderstone Lancs 89 J4
Balderstone Rochdl 89 Q8
Balderton Notts 85 P10
Baldhu Cnwll 3 K5
Baldinnie Fife 135 L5
Baldinnies P & K 134 C4
Baldock Herts 50 F4
Baldock Services Herts 50 F3
Baldovie C Dund 142 H11
Baldrine IoM 80 f5
Baldslow E Susx 26 D9
Baldwin IoM 80 e5
Baldwinholme Cumb 110 F10
Baldwin's Gate Staffs 70 D7
Baldwin's Hill W Susx 25 J3
Bale Norfk 76 E4
Baledgarno P & K 142 D11
Balemartine Ag & B 136 B7
Balerno C Edin 127 M4
Balfarg Fife 134 H7
Balfield Angus 143 J4
Balfour Ork 169 d5
Balfron Stirlg 132 G10
Balgaveny Abers 158 G9
Balgonar Fife 134 C9
Balgowan D & G 106 F9
Balgowan Highld 147 Q9
Balgown Highld 152 F4
Balgracie D & G 106 C5
Balgray S Lans 116 B6
Balham Gt Lon 36 G6
Balhary P & K 142 D8
Balholmie P & K 142 A10
Baligill Highld 166 E3
Balintore Angus 142 D6
Balintore Highld 156 F2
Balintraid Highld 156 C3
Balivanich W Isls 168 c12
Balk N York 97 Q4
Balkeerie Angus 142 E9
Balkholme E R Yk 92 C5
Ballabeg IoM 80 c7
Ballachulish Highld 139 K6
Ballafesson IoM 80 b7
Ballajora IoM 80 g3
Ballakilpheric IoM 80 b7
Ballamodha IoM 80 c7
Ballanlay Ag & B 124 C5
Ballantrae S Ayrs 114 A11
Ballards Gore Essex 38 F3
Ballards Green Warwks 59 L6
Ballasalla IoM 80 c7
Ballater Abers 150 B8
Ballaugh IoM 80 d3
Ballchraggan Highld 156 D2
Ballencrieff E Loth 128 D4
Ballevullin Ag & B 136 B6
Ball Green C Stke 70 F4
Ball Haye Green Staffs 70 H3
Ball Hill Hants 22 D2
Ballidon Derbys 71 N4
Balliekine N Ayrs 120 G4
Balliemore Ag & B 131 N8
Balligmorrie S Ayrs 114 D9
Ballimore Stirlg 132 G4
Ballindalloch Moray 157 M10
Ballindean P & K 134 H2
Ballingdon Suffk 52 E3
Ballinger Common Bucks 35 P4
Ballingham Herefs 46 A8
Ballingry Fife 134 F8
Ballinluig P & K 141 N7
Ballinshoe Angus 142 G7
Ballintuim P & K 141 R6
Balloch Highld 156 C8
Balloch N Lans 126 C3
Balloch P & K 133 N4
Balloch S Ayrs 114 F8
Balloch W Duns 132 D11
Balls Cross W Susx 23 Q9
Balls Green E Susx 25 L3
Ball's Green Gloucs 32 G5
Ballygown Ag & B 137 L7
Ballygrant Ag & B 122 E6
Ballyhaugh Ag & B 136 F4
Balmacara Highld 145 P2
Balmaclellan D & G 108 E5
Balmae D & G 108 E12
Balmaha Stirlg 132 E9
Balmalcolm Fife 135 J6
Balmangan D & G 108 D11
Balmedie Abers 151 P4
Balmer Heath Shrops 69 M8
Balmerino Fife 135 K3
Balmerlawn Hants 13 P4
Balmichael N Ayrs 120 H5
Balmore E Duns 125 P3
Balmuchy Highld 163 K11
Balmule Fife 134 G10
Balmullo Fife 135 L3
Balnacoil Highld 163 J4
Balnacra Highld 154 C8
Balnacroft Abers 149 P9
Balnafoich Highld 156 B10
Balnaguard P & K 141 M7
Balnahard Ag & B 136 c2
Balnahard Ag & B 137 M9
Balnain Highld 155 M11
Balnakeil Highld 165 J3
Balne N York 91 P7
Balquharn P & K 141 P10
Balquhidder Stirlg 132 G3
Balsall Common Solhll 59 K9
Balsall Heath Birm 58 G8
Balsall Street Solhll 59 K9
Balscote Oxon 48 C6
Balsham Cambs 63 J10
Baltasound Shet 169 t3
Balterley Staffs 70 D4
Balterley Green Staffs 70 D4
Balterley Heath Staffs 70 C4
Baltersan D & G 107 M5
Balthangie Abers 159 K7
Baltonsborough Somset 19 P8
Balvicar Ag & B 130 F4
Balvraid Highld 145 P4
Balvraid Highld 156 E11
Balwest Cnwll 2 F7
Bamber Bridge Lancs 88 H5
Bamber's Green Essex 51 N6
Bamburgh Nthumb 119 N4
Bamburgh Castle Nthumb 119 N3
Bamford Derbys 84 B4
Bamford Rochdl 89 P8
Bampton Cumb 101 P7
Bampton Devon 18 C10
Bampton Oxon 34 B4
Bampton Grange Cumb 101 P7
Banavie Highld 139 L2
Banbury Oxon 48 E6
Banbury Crematorium Oxon 48 E6
Bancffosfelen Carmth 28 E2
Banchory Abers 150 H8
Banchory-Devenick Abers 151 N7
Bancycapel Carmth 28 D2
Bancyfelin Carmth 42 F11
Banc-y-ffordd Carmth 42 H7
Bandirran P & K 142 C11
Bandrake Head Cumb 94 G3
Banff Abers 158 G5
Bangor Gwynd 79 K10
Bangor Crematorium Gwynd 79 K10
Bangor-on-Dee Wrexhm 69 L5
Bangors Cnwll 5 L2
Bangor's Green Lancs 88 D9
Bangrove Suffk 64 C7
Banham Norfk 64 F4
Bank Hants 13 N3
Bankend D & G 109 M7
Bankfoot P & K 141 Q10
Bankglen E Ayrs 115 L5
Bank Ground Cumb 101 K11
Bankhead C Aber 151 N6
Bankhead S Lans 116 D2
Bank Newton N York 96 D10
Banknock Falk 126 D2
Banks Cumb 111 L8
Banks Lancs 88 D6
Banks Green Worcs 58 E11
Bankshill D & G 110 C4
Bank Street Worcs 46 B2
Bank Top Calder 90 E6
Bank Top Lancs 88 G9
Banningham Norfk 77 J6
Bannister Green Essex 51 Q6
Bannockburn Stirlg 133 N9
Banstead Surrey 36 G9
Bantham Devon 6 H10
Banton N Lans 126 C2
Banwell N Som 19 L3
Bapchild Kent 38 F9
Bapton Wilts 21 J7
Barabhas W Isls 168 i3
Barassie S Ayrs 125 J11
Barbaraville Highld 156 C3
Barber Booth Derbys 83 P8
Barber Green Cumb 94 H4
Barbieston S Ayrs 114 H4
Barbon Cumb 95 N4
Barbridge Ches E 69 R3
Barbrook Devon 17 N2
Barby Nhants 60 B6
Barcaldine Ag & B 138 H9
Barcheston Warwks 47 Q7
Barclose Cumb 110 H8
Barcombe E Susx 25 K8
Barcombe Cross E Susx 25 K7
Barcroft C Brad 90 C3
Barden N York 96 H2
Barden Park Kent 37 N11
Bardfield End Green Essex 51 P4
Bardfield Saling Essex 51 Q5
Bardney Lincs 86 F7
Bardon Leics 72 C8
Bardon Mill Nthumb 111 Q8
Bardowie E Duns 125 P3
Bardown E Susx 25 Q5
Bardrainney Inver 125 J3
Bardsea Cumb 94 G6
Bardsey Leeds 91 K2
Bardsey Island Gwynd 66 A10
Bardsley Oldham 83 K4
Bardwell Suffk 64 C7
Bare Lancs 95 K8
Bareppa Cnwll 3 K8
Barfad D & G 107 K4
Barford Norfk 76 G10
Barford Warwks 47 Q2
Barford St John Oxon 48 D8
Barford St Martin Wilts 21 L8
Barford St Michael Oxon 48 D8
Barfrestone Kent 39 N11
Bargate Derbys 84 E11
Bargeddie N Lans 126 B5
Bargoed Caerph 30 G5
Bargrennan D & G 107 L2
Barham Cambs 61 P5
Barham Kent 39 M11
Barham Suffk 64 G11
Barham Crematorium Kent 27 M2
Bar Hill Cambs 62 E8
Barholm Lincs 74 A8
Barkby Leics 72 G9
Barkby Thorpe Leics 72 G9
Barkers Green Shrops 69 P9
Barkestone-le-Vale Leics 73 K4
Barkham Wokham 35 L11
Barking Gt Lon 37 K4
Barking Suffk 64 F11
Barkingside Gt Lon 37 K3
Barking Tye Suffk 64 F11
Barkisland Calder 90 D7
Barkla Shop Cnwll 3 J3
Barkston Lincs 73 N2
Barkston Ash N York 91 M3
Barkway Herts 51 J3
Barlanark C Glas 126 B5
Barlaston Staffs 70 F7
Barlavington W Susx 23 Q11
Barlborough Derbys 84 G5
Barlby N York 91 Q4
Barlestone Leics 72 C9
Barley Herts 51 K3
Barley Lancs 89 N2
Barleycroft End Herts 51 K5
Barley Hole Rothm 91 K11
Barleythorpe Rutlnd 73 L9
Barling Essex 38 F4
Barlings Lincs 86 E6
Barlochan D & G 108 H9
Barlow Derbys 84 D6
Barlow Gatesd 113 J8
Barlow N York 91 Q5
Barmby Moor E R Yk 98 F11
Barmby on the Marsh E R Yk 92 A5
Barmer Norfk 75 R4
Barming Heath Kent 38 B10
Barmollack Ag & B 120 F3
Barmouth Gwynd 67 L11
Barmpton Darltn 104 B7
Barmston E R Yk 99 P9
Barnaby Green Suffk 65 P5
Barnacarry Ag & B 131 L9
Barnack C Pete 74 A9
Barnacle Warwks 59 N8
Barnard Castle Dur 103 L7
Barnard Gate Oxon 34 D2
Barnardiston Suffk 63 M11
Barnbarroch D & G 108 H9
Barnburgh Donc 91 M10
Barnby Suffk 65 P4
Barnby Dun Donc 91 Q9
Barnby in the Willows Notts 85 Q10
Barnby Moor Notts 85 L4
Barncorkrie D & G 106 E10
Barnehurst Gt Lon 37 L5
Barnes Gt Lon 36 F5
Barnes Street Kent 37 P11
Barnet Gt Lon 50 F11
Barnetby le Wold N Linc 93 J9
Barnet Gate Gt Lon 50 F11
Barney Norfk 76 D5
Barnham Suffk 64 B6
Barnham W Susx 15 Q6
Barnham Broom Norfk 76 F10
Barnhead Angus 143 M6
Barnhill C Dund 142 H11
Barnhill Ches W 69 N4
Barnhill Moray 157 L6
Barnhills D & G 106 C3
Barningham Dur 103 L8
Barningham Suffk 64 D6
Barnoldby le Beck NE Lin 93 M10
Barnoldswick Lancs 96 C11
Barnsdale Bar Donc 91 N8
Barns Green W Susx 24 D5
Barnsley Barns 91 J9
Barnsley Gloucs 33 L4
Barnsley Crematorium Barns 91 K9
Barnsole Kent 39 N10
Barnstaple Devon 17 K5
Barnston Essex 51 P7
Barnston Wirral 81 K8
Barnstone Notts 73 J3
Barnt Green Worcs 58 F10
Barnton C Edin 127 M3
Barnton Ches W 82 D10
Barnwell All Saints Nhants 61 M4
Barnwell St Andrew Nhants 61 N4
Barnwood Gloucs 46 G11
Baron's Cross Herefs 45 P3
Baronwood Cumb 101 P2
Barr S Ayrs 114 E9
Barra W Isls 168 b17
Barra Airport W Isls 168 c17
Barrachan D & G 107 L8
Barraigh W Isls 168 b17
Barrananaoil Ag & B 130 G6
Barrapoll Ag & B 136 A7
Barras Cumb 102 F8
Barrasford Nthumb 112 D6
Barregarrow IoM 80 d4
Barrets Green Ches E 69 Q3
Barrhead E Rens 125 M6
Barrhill S Ayrs 114 D11
Barrington Cambs 62 E11
Barrington Somset 19 L11
Barripper Cnwll 2 G6
Barrmill N Ayrs 125 K7
Barrock Highld 167 N2
Barrow Gloucs 46 G10
Barrow Lancs 89 L3
Barrow Rutlnd 73 M7
Barrow Shrops 57 M4
Barrow Somset 20 D8
Barrow Suffk 63 N8
Barroway Drove Norfk 75 L10
Barrow Bridge Bolton 89 K8
Barrow Burn Nthumb 118 G8
Barrowby Lincs 73 M3
Barrowden Rutlnd 73 N10
Barrowford Lancs 89 P3
Barrow Gurney N Som 31 P11
Barrow Haven N Linc 93 J6
Barrow Hill Derbys 84 F5
Barrow-in-Furness Cumb 94 E7
Barrow Island Cumb 94 D7
Barrow Nook Lancs 81 N4
Barrow's Green Ches E 70 B3
Barrow Street Wilts 20 F8
Barrow-upon-Humber N Linc 93 J6
Barrow upon Soar Leics 72 F7
Barrow upon Trent Derbys 72 B5
Barrow Vale BaNES 20 B2
Barry Angus 143 J11
Barry V Glam 30 F11
Barry Island V Glam 30 F11
Barsby Leics 72 H8
Barsham Suffk 65 M4
Barston Solhll 59 K9
Bartestree Herefs 45 R6
Barthol Chapel Abers 159 K11
Bartholomew Green Essex 52 B7
Barthomley Ches E 70 D4
Bartley Hants 13 P2
Bartley Green Birm 58 F8
Bartlow Cambs 63 J11
Barton Cambs 62 F9
Barton Ches W 69 M4
Barton Gloucs 47 L9
Barton Herefs 45 K3
Barton Lancs 88 D9
Barton Lancs 88 G3
Barton N York 103 P9
Barton Oxon 34 G3
Barton Torbay 7 N5
Barton Warwks 47 M4
Barton Bendish Norfk 75 P9
Barton End Gloucs 32 F5
Barton Green Staffs 71 M11
Barton Hartshorn Bucks 48 H8
Barton Hill N York 98 E8
Barton in Fabis Notts 72 E4
Barton in the Beans Leics 72 B9
Barton-le-Clay C Beds 50 C4
Barton-le-Street N York 98 E6
Barton-le-Willows N York 98 E8
Barton Mills Suffk 63 M6
Barton-on-Sea Hants 13 M6
Barton-on-the-Heath Warwks 47 Q8
Barton Park Services N York 103 P9
Barton St David Somset 19 P8
Barton Seagrave Nhants 61 J5
Barton Stacey Hants 22 D6
Barton Town Devon 17 M3
Barton Turf Norfk 77 M7
Barton-under-Needwood Staffs 71 M11
Barton-upon-Humber N Linc 92 H6
Barton upon Irwell Salfd 82 G5
Barton Waterside N Linc 92 H6
Barugh Barns 91 J9
Barugh Green Barns 91 J9
Barvas W Isls 168 i3
Barway Cambs 63 J5
Barwell Leics 72 C11
Barwick Devon 17 K10
Barwick Herts 51 J7
Barwick Somset 11 M2
Barwick in Elmet Leeds 91 L3
Baschurch Shrops 69 M10
Bascote Warwks 48 D2
Bascote Heath Warwks 48 C2
Base Green Suffk 64 E9
Basford Green Staffs 70 H4
Bashall Eaves Lancs 89 K2
Bashall Town Lancs 89 L2
Bashley Hants 13 M5
Basildon Essex 38 B4
Basildon & District Crematorium Essex 38 C4
Basingstoke Hants 22 H4
Basingstoke Crematorium Hants 22 G5
Baslow Derbys 84 C6
Bason Bridge Somset 19 K5
Bassaleg Newpt 31 J7
Bassendean Border 128 G10
Bassenthwaite Cumb 100 H4
Bassett C Sotn 22 D11
Bassingbourn-cum-Kneesworth Cambs 50 H2
Bassingfield Notts 72 G3
Bassingham Lincs 86 B9
Bassingthorpe Lincs 73 P5
Bassus Green Herts 50 H5
Basted Kent 37 P9
Baston Lincs 74 B8
Bastwick Norfk 77 N8
Batch Somset 19 K3
Batchworth Herts 36 C2
Batchworth Heath Herts 36 C2
Batcombe Dorset 11 N4
Batcombe Somset 20 C7
Bate Heath Ches E 82 E9
Batford Herts 50 D7
Bath BaNES 20 D2
Bathampton BaNES 32 E11
Bath, City of BaNES 20 E2
Bathealton Somset 18 E10
Batheaston BaNES 32 E11
Bathford BaNES 32 E11
Bathgate W Loth 126 H4
Bathley Notts 85 N9
Bathpool Cnwll 5 M7
Bathpool Somset 19 J9
Bath Side Essex 53 N5
Bathville W Loth 126 G4
Bathway Somset 19 Q4
Batley Kirk 90 G6
Batsford Gloucs 47 N8
Batson Devon 7 J11
Battersby N York 104 G9
Battersea Gt Lon 36 G5
Battisborough Cross Devon 6 F9
Battisford Suffk 64 F11
Battisford Tye Suffk 64 E11
Battle E Susx 26 C8
Battle Powys 44 E8
Battleborough Somset 19 K4
Battledown Gloucs 47 J10
Battledykes Angus 142 H6
Battlefield Shrops 69 P11
Battlesbridge Essex 38 C3
Battlesden C Beds 49 Q9
Battleton Somset 18 B9
Battlies Green Suffk 64 C9
Battram Leics 72 C9
Battramsley Cross Hants 13 P5
Batt's Corner Hants 23 M6
Baughton Worcs 46 G6
Baughurst Hants 22 G2
Baulds Abers 150 G9
Baulking Oxon 34 B6
Baumber Lincs 86 H6
Baunton Gloucs 33 K4
Baveney Wood Shrops 57 M9
Baverstock Wilts 21 K8
Bawburgh Norfk 76 H10
Bawdeswell Norfk 76 E7
Bawdrip Somset 19 K7
Bawdsey Suffk 53 P3
Bawsey Norfk 75 N6
Bawtry Donc 85 K2
Baxenden Lancs 89 M5
Baxterley Warwks 59 L5
Baxter's Green Suffk 63 N9
Bay Highld 152 D7
Bayble W Isls 168 k4
Baybridge Hants 22 F10
Baybridge Nthumb 112 E10
Baycliff Cumb 94 F6
Baydon Wilts 33 Q9
Bayford Herts 50 H9
Bayford Somset 20 D9
Bayhead W Isls 168 c11
Bay Horse Lancs 95 K10
Bayley's Hill Kent 37 M10
Baylham Suffk 64 G11
Baynard's Green Oxon 48 F9
Baysdale Abbey N York 104 H9
Baysham Herefs 45 R9
Bayston Hill Shrops 56 H3
Baythorne End Essex 52 B3
Bayton Worcs 57 M10
Bayton Common Worcs 57 N10
Bayworth Oxon 34 E4
Beach S Glos 32 D10
Beachampton Bucks 49 L7
Beachamwell Norfk 75 Q9
Beachley Gloucs 31 Q6
Beachy Head E Susx 25 N11
Beacon Devon 10 D3
Beacon End Essex 52 G7
Beacon Hill Kent 26 D5
Beacon Hill Notts 85 P10
Beacon Hill Surrey 23 N7
Beacon's Bottom Bucks 35 L5
Beaconsfield Bucks 35 P6
Beaconsfield Services Bucks 35 Q7
Beadlam N York 98 D4
Beadlow C Beds 50 D3
Beadnell Nthumb 119 P5
Beaford Devon 17 K8
Beal N York 91 N5
Beal Nthumb 119 L2
Bealbury Cnwll 5 P8
Bealsmill Cnwll 5 P6
Beam Hill Staffs 71 N9
Beamhurst Staffs 71 K7
Beaminster Dorset 11 K4
Beamish Dur 113 K10
Beamish Museum Dur 113 K10
Beamsley N York 96 G10
Bean Kent 37 N6

Beanacre Wilts....32 H11
Beanley Nthumb....119 L7
Beardon Devon....8 D8
Beardwood Bl w D....89 K5
Beare Devon....9 M4
Beare Green Surrey....24 E2
Bearley Warwks....47 N2
Bearley Cross Warwks....47 N2
Bearpark Dur....103 P2
Bearsden E Duns....125 N3
Bearsted Kent....38 D10
Bearstone Shrops....70 C7
Bearwood Birm....58 F7
Bearwood Herefs....45 M3
Bearwood Poole....12 H5
Beattock D & G....116 F10
Beauchamp Roding Essex....51 N9
Beauchief Sheff....84 D4
Beaudesert Warwks....59 J11
Beaufort Blae G....30 G2
Beaulieu Hants....14 C6
Beaulieu Road Station Hants....13 P3
Beauly Highld....155 P8
Beaumaris IoA....79 L9
Beaumaris Castle IoA....79 L9
Beaumont Cumb....110 F9
Beaumont Essex....53 L7
Beaumont Jersey....11 b2
Beaumont Hill Darltn....103 Q7
Beaumont Leys C Leic....72 F9
Beausale Warwks....59 K10
Beauworth Hants....22 G9
Beaworthy Devon....8 C5
Beazley End Essex....52 B6
Bebington Wirral....81 L8
Bebside Nthumb....113 L4
Beccles Suffk....65 N4
Becconsall Lancs....88 F6
Beckbury Shrops....57 P4
Beckenham Gt Lon....37 J7
Beckenham Crematorium Gt Lon....37 J7
Beckermet Cumb....100 D9
Beckett End Norfk....75 Q11
Beckfoot Cumb....94 D3
Beckfoot Cumb....100 G10
Beck Foot Cumb....102 B11
Beckfoot Cumb....109 N11
Beckford Worcs....47 J7
Beck Hole N York....105 M10
Beckingham Lincs....85 Q10
Beckingham Notts....85 N3
Beckington Somset....20 F4
Beckjay Shrops....56 F9
Beckley E Susx....26 E7
Beckley Hants....13 M5
Beckley Oxon....34 G2
Beck Row Suffk....63 L5
Becks C Brad....96 F11
Beck Side Cumb....94 E4
Beck Side Cumb....94 H4
Beckton Gt Lon....37 K4
Beckwithshaw N York....97 L10
Becontree Gt Lon....37 L3
Becquet Vincent Jersey....11 b1
Bedale N York....97 L3
Bedburn Dur....103 L4
Bedchester Dorset....20 G11
Beddau Rhondd....30 E7
Beddgelert Gwynd....67 K5
Beddingham E Susx....25 K9
Beddington Gt Lon....36 H7
Beddington Corner Gt Lon....36 G7
Bedfield Suffk....65 J8
Bedfield Little Green Suffk....65 J8
Bedford Bed....61 M11
Bedford Crematorium Bed....61 N10
Bedgebury Cross Kent....26 B5
Bedham W Susx....24 B6
Bedhampton Hants....15 K5
Bedingfield Suffk....64 H8
Bedingfield Green Suffk....64 H8
Bedlam N York....97 L8
Bedlington Nthumb....113 L4
Bedlinog Myr Td....30 E4
Bedminster Bristl....31 Q10
Bedminster Down Bristl....31 Q10
Bedmond Herts....50 C10
Bednall Staffs....70 H11
Bedrule Border....118 B7
Bedstone Shrops....56 F9
Bedwas Caerph....30 G7
Bedwellty Caerph....30 G4
Bedworth Warwks....59 N7
Bedworth Woodlands Warwks....59 M7
Beeby Leics....72 H9
Beech Hants....23 J7
Beech Staffs....70 F7
Beech Hill W Berk....23 J2
Beechingstoke Wilts....21 L3
Beedon W Berk....34 E9
Beedon Hill W Berk....34 E9
Beeford E R Yk....99 N10
Beeley Derbys....84 C7
Beelsby NE Lin....93 M10
Beenham W Berk....34 G11
Beenham's Heath W & M....35 M9
Beeny Cnwll....5 J3
Beer Devon....10 E7
Beer Somset....19 M8
Beercrocombe Somset....19 K10
Beer Hackett Dorset....11 N2
Beesands Devon....7 L10
Beesby Lincs....87 N4
Beeson Devon....7 L10
Beeston C Beds....61 Q11
Beeston Ches W....69 P3
Beeston Leeds....90 H4
Beeston Norfk....76 C8
Beeston Notts....72 E3
Beeston Regis Norfk....76 H3
Beeswing D & G....109 J7
Beetham Cumb....95 K5
Beetham Somset....10 F2
Beetley Norfk....76 D8
Began Cardif....30 H8
Begbroke Oxon....34 E2
Begdale Cambs....75 J9
Begelly Pembks....41 M9
Beggarington Hill Leeds....90 H6
Beggar's Bush Powys....45 K2
Beguildy Powys....56 B9
Beighton Norfk....77 M10
Beighton Sheff....84 F4

Beinn Na Faoghla W Isls....168 d12
Beith N Ayrs....125 K7
Bekesbourne Kent....39 L10
Bekesbourne Hill Kent....39 L10
Belaugh Norfk....77 K8
Belbroughton Worcs....58 D9
Belchalwell Dorset....12 C3
Belchalwell Street Dorset....12 C3
Belchamp Otten Essex....52 D3
Belchamp St Paul Essex....52 C3
Belchamp Walter Essex....52 D3
Belchford Lincs....87 J5
Belgrave C Leic....72 F9
Belhaven E Loth....128 H4
Belhelvie Abers....151 N4
Belhinnie Abers....150 D2
Bellabeg Abers....150 B5
Bellamore Herefs....45 M6
Bellanoch Ag & B....130 F9
Bellasize E R Yk....92 D5
Bellaty Angus....142 C6
Bell Bar Herts....50 G9
Bell Busk N York....96 D9
Belleau Lincs....87 M5
Bell End Worcs....58 D9
Bellerby N York....96 H2
Bellever Devon....8 G9
Belle Vue Cumb....110 G9
Belle Vue Wakefd....91 J7
Bellfield S Lans....126 E11
Bell Heath Worcs....58 D9
Bell Hill Hants....23 K10
Bellingdon Bucks....35 P3
Bellingham Nthumb....112 D4
Belloch Ag & B....120 C4
Bellochantuy Ag & B....120 C5
Bell o' th' Hill Ches W....69 P5
Bellows Cross Dorset....13 J2
Bells Cross Suffk....64 H11
Bellshill N Lans....126 C5
Bellshill Nthumb....119 M4
Bellside N Lans....126 E6
Bellsquarry W Loth....127 J4
Bells Yew Green E Susx....25 P3
Belluton BaNES....20 B2
Belmaduthy Highld....156 A6
Belmesthorpe Rutlnd....73 Q8
Belmont Bl w D....89 K7
Belmont Gt Lon....36 G8
Belmont S Ayrs....114 F4
Belmont Shet....169 s3
Belnacraig Abers....150 B4
Belowda Cnwll....4 F9
Belper Derbys....84 D11
Belper Lane End Derbys....84 D11
Belph Derbys....84 H5
Belsay Nthumb....112 G5
Belses Border....117 R5
Belsford Devon....7 K7
Belsize Herts....50 B10
Belstead Suffk....53 K3
Belstone Devon....8 F6
Belthorn Lancs....89 L6
Beltinge Kent....39 L8
Beltoft N Linc....92 D9
Belton Leics....72 C6
Belton Lincs....73 N3
Belton N Linc....92 C9
Belton Norfk....77 P11
Belton Rutlnd....73 L10
Belton House Lincs....73 N3
Beltring Kent....37 Q11
Belvedere Gt Lon....37 L5
Belvoir Leics....73 L4
Bembridge IoW....14 H9
Bemerton Wilts....21 M8
Bempton E R Yk....99 P6
Benacre Suffk....65 Q5
Benbecula W Isls....168 d12
Benbecula Airport W Isls....168 c12
Benbuie D & G....115 P8
Benderloch Ag & B....138 G10
Benenden Kent....26 D5
Benfieldside Dur....112 G10
Bengates Norfk....77 L6
Bengeo Herts....50 H8
Bengeworth Worcs....47 K6
Benhall Green Suffk....65 M9
Benhall Street Suffk....65 M9
Benholm Abers....143 Q4
Beningbrough N York....98 A9
Benington Herts....50 G6
Benington Lincs....87 L11
Benington Sea End Lincs....87 M11
Benllech IoA....79 J8
Benmore Ag & B....131 N10
Bennacott Cnwll....5 M3
Bennan N Ayrs....121 J7
Bennet Head Cumb....101 M6
Bennetland E R Yk....92 D5
Bennett End Bucks....35 L5
Ben Nevis Highld....139 M3
Benniworth Lincs....86 H4
Benover Kent....26 B2
Ben Rhydding C Brad....96 H11
Benslie N Ayrs....125 J9
Benson Oxon....34 H6
Bentfield Green Essex....51 M5
Benthall Shrops....57 M4
Bentham Gloucs....46 H11
Benthoul C Aber....151 L7
Bentley Donc....91 P9
Bentley E R Yk....92 H3
Bentley Hants....23 L6
Bentley Suffk....53 K4
Bentley Warwks....59 L5
Bentley Crematorium Essex....51 N11
Bentley Heath Herts....50 G11
Bentley Heath Solhll....59 J9
Benton Devon....17 M4
Bentpath D & G....110 F2
Bentwichen Devon....17 N5
Bentworth Hants....23 J6
Benvie Angus....142 E11
Benville Dorset....11 L4
Benwick Cambs....62 D2
Beoley Worcs....58 G11
Beoraidbeg Highld....145 L9
Bepton W Susx....23 N11
Berden Essex....51 L5
Berea Pembks....40 E4
Bere Alston Devon....6 C4
Bere Ferrers Devon....6 D6
Berepper Cnwll....2 G9
Bere Regis Dorset....12 D6
Bergh Apton Norfk....77 L11

Berhill Somset....19 M7
Berinsfield Oxon....34 G5
Berkeley Gloucs....32 C5
Berkeley Heath Gloucs....32 C5
Berkeley Road Gloucs....32 D4
Berkhamsted Herts....35 Q3
Berkley Somset....20 F5
Berkswell Solhll....59 K9
Bermondsey Gt Lon....36 H5
Bermuda Warwks....59 N7
Bernera Highld....145 P3
Bernisdale Highld....152 G7
Berrick Prior Oxon....34 H6
Berrick Salome Oxon....34 H6
Berriedale Highld....163 Q2
Berrier Cumb....101 L5
Berriew Powys....56 B4
Berrington Nthumb....119 K2
Berrington Shrops....57 J3
Berrington Worcs....57 K11
Berrington Green Worcs....57 K11
Berrow Somset....19 J4
Berrow Worcs....46 E8
Berrow Green Worcs....46 D3
Berry Brow Kirk....90 E8
Berry Cross Devon....16 H9
Berry Down Cross Devon....17 K3
Berryfields Bucks....49 L11
Berry Hill Gloucs....31 Q2
Berry Hill Pembks....41 L2
Berryhillock Moray....158 D5
Berryhillock Moray....158 D7
Berrynarbor Devon....17 K2
Berry Pomeroy Devon....7 L6
Berry's Green Gt Lon....37 K9
Bersham Wrexhm....69 K5
Bersted W Susx....15 P6
Berthengam Flints....80 G9
Berwick E Susx....25 M9
Berwick Bassett Wilts....33 L10
Berwick Hill Nthumb....113 J5
Berwick St James Wilts....21 L7
Berwick St John Wilts....20 H10
Berwick St Leonard Wilts....20 H8
Berwick Station E Susx....25 M9
Berwick-upon-Tweed Nthumb....129 P9
Bescaby Leics....73 L5
Bescar Lancs....88 D8
Besford Shrops....69 Q9
Besford Worcs....46 H6
Bessacarr Donc....91 Q10
Bessels Leigh Oxon....34 E4
Besses o' th' Barn Bury....89 N9
Bessingby E R Yk....99 P7
Bessingham Norfk....76 H4
Bestbeech Hill E Susx....25 P4
Besthorpe Norfk....64 F2
Besthorpe Notts....85 P8
Bestwood Village Notts....85 J11
Beswick E R Yk....99 L11
Betchcott Shrops....56 G5
Betchworth Surrey....36 F10
Bethania Cerdgn....43 L2
Bethania Gwynd....67 N6
Bethel Gwynd....68 C7
Bethel Gwynd....79 J11
Bethel IoA....78 F10
Bethel Powys....68 F10
Bethersden Kent....26 F3
Bethesda Gwynd....79 L11
Bethesda Pembks....41 L7
Bethlehem Carmth....43 N9
Bethnal Green Gt Lon....36 H4
Betley Staffs....70 D5
Betsham Kent....37 P6
Betteshanger Kent....39 P11
Bettiscombe Dorset....10 H4
Bettisfield Wrexhm....69 N7
Betton Shrops....70 B7
Betton Strange Shrops....57 J3
Bettws Newpt....31 J4
Bettws Cedewain Powys....55 Q5
Bettws Ifan Cerdgn....42 F5
Bettws-Newydd Mons....31 L3
Bettyhill Highld....166 B4
Betws Brdgnd....29 P7
Betws Carmth....28 H2
Betws Bledrws Cerdgn....43 L4
Betws Garmon Gwynd....67 J3
Betws Gwerfil Goch Denbgs....68 D5
Betws-y-Coed Conwy....67 P3
Betws-yn-Rhos Conwy....80 C10
Beulah Cerdgn....42 E5
Beulah Powys....44 C4
Bevendean Br & H....24 H9
Bevercotes Notts....85 L6
Beverley E R Yk....92 H3
Beverston Gloucs....32 G6
Bevington Gloucs....32 C5
Bewaldeth Cumb....100 H4
Bewcastle Cumb....111 L6
Bewdley Worcs....57 P9
Bewerley N York....97 J7
Bewholme E R Yk....99 P11
Bewlbridge Kent....25 Q4
Bexhill E Susx....26 B10
Bexley Gt Lon....37 L5
Bexleyheath Gt Lon....37 L5
Bexleyhill W Susx....23 P9
Bexon Kent....38 E10
Bexwell Norfk....75 M10
Beyton Suffk....64 C9
Beyton Green Suffk....64 C9
Bhaltos W Isls....168 f4
Bhatarsaigh W Isls....168 b18
Bibstone S Glos....32 C6
Bibury Gloucs....33 M3
Bicester Oxon....48 G10
Bickenhill Solhll....59 J8
Bicker Lincs....74 D3
Bicker Bar Lincs....74 D3
Bicker Gauntlet Lincs....74 D3
Bickershaw Wigan....82 D4
Bickerstaffe Lancs....81 N4
Bickerton Ches E....69 P4
Bickerton Devon....7 L11
Bickerton N York....97 Q10
Bickerton Nthumb....119 J10
Bickford Staffs....58 C2
Bickington Devon....7 L4
Bickington Devon....17 J5
Bickleigh Devon....6 E6
Bickleigh Devon....9 M3
Bickleton Devon....17 J5
Bickley Ches W....69 P5
Bickley Gt Lon....37 K7
Bickley N York....99 J2
Bickley Worcs....57 L10
Bickley Moss Ches W....69 P5

Bicknacre Essex....52 C11
Bicknoller Somset....18 F7
Bicknor Kent....38 E10
Bickton Hants....13 K2
Bicton Herefs....45 P2
Bicton Shrops....56 D8
Bicton Shrops....69 H10
Bidborough Kent....25 N2
Biddenden Kent....26 E4
Biddenden Green Kent....26 E4
Biddenham Bed....61 M10
Biddestone Wilts....32 G10
Biddisham Somset....19 L4
Biddlesden Bucks....48 H7
Biddlestone Nthumb....119 J9
Biddulph Staffs....70 F3
Biddulph Moor Staffs....70 G3
Bideford Devon....16 H6
Bidford-on-Avon Warwks....47 M4
Bidston Wirral....81 K6
Bielby E R Yk....92 C2
Bieldside C Aber....151 M7
Bierley IoW....14 F11
Bierton Bucks....49 M11
Big Balcraig D & G....107 L9
Bigbury Devon....6 H9
Bigbury-on-Sea Devon....6 H10
Bigby Lincs....93 J9
Biggar Cumb....94 D7
Biggar S Lans....116 E3
Biggin Derbys....71 M3
Biggin Derbys....71 P5
Biggin N York....91 N4
Biggin Hill Gt Lon....37 K9
Biggleswade C Beds....50 E2
Bigholms D & G....110 F4
Bighouse Highld....166 E4
Bighton Hants....22 H8
Biglands Cumb....110 E10
Bignor W Susx....15 Q4
Bigrigg Cumb....100 D8
Big Sand Highld....160 B9
Bigton Shet....169 q11
Bilborough C Nott....72 E2
Bilbrook Somset....18 D6
Bilbrook Staffs....58 C4
Bilbrough N York....98 A11
Bilbster Highld....167 N6
Bildershaw Dur....103 P6
Bildeston Suffk....52 G2
Billacott Cnwll....5 M3
Billericay Essex....37 Q2
Billesdon Leics....73 J10
Billesley Warwks....47 M3
Billingborough Lincs....74 B4
Billinge St Hel....82 B4
Billingford Norfk....64 H6
Billingford Norfk....76 F6
Billingham S on T....104 E6
Billinghay Lincs....86 G10
Billingley Barns....91 L10
Billingshurst W Susx....24 C5
Billingsley Shrops....57 N8
Billington C Beds....49 P10
Billington Lancs....89 L3
Billington Staffs....70 F10
Billockby Norfk....77 N9
Billy Row Dur....103 N3
Bilsborrow Lancs....88 G3
Bilsby Lincs....87 N5
Bilsham W Susx....15 Q6
Bilsington Kent....27 J4
Bilson Green Gloucs....32 C3
Bilsthorpe Notts....85 L8
Bilsthorpe Moor Notts....85 L8
Bilston Mdloth....127 P5
Bilston Wolves....58 E5
Bilstone Leics....72 B9
Bilting Kent....27 J2
Bilton E R Yk....93 L4
Bilton N York....97 M9
Bilton Nthumb....119 P8
Bilton Warwks....59 Q10
Bilton Banks Nthumb....119 P8
Bilton-in-Ainsty N York....97 Q11
Binbrook Lincs....86 H2
Binchester Blocks Dur....103 P4
Bincombe Dorset....11 P8
Binegar Somset....20 B5
Bines Green W Susx....24 E7
Binfield Br For....35 M10
Binfield Heath Oxon....35 K9
Bingfield Nthumb....112 G6
Bingham Notts....73 J3
Bingham's Melcombe Dorset....12 C4
Bingley C Brad....90 E3
Bings Shrops....69 P11
Binham Norfk....76 D4
Binley Covtry....59 N9
Binley Hants....22 D4
Binley Woods Warwks....59 N9
Binnegar Dorset....12 E7
Binniehill Falk....126 F3
Binscombe Surrey....23 Q5
Binsey Oxon....34 E3
Binstead IoW....14 G8
Binsted Hants....23 L6
Binsted W Susx....15 Q5
Binton Warwks....47 M4
Bintree Norfk....76 E7
Binweston Shrops....56 E4
Birch Essex....52 F8
Birch Rochdl....89 P9
Bircham Newton Norfk....75 Q4
Bircham Tofts Norfk....75 Q4
Birchanger Essex....51 M6
Birchanger Green Services Essex....51 M6
Birch Cross Staffs....71 L8
Birchencliffe Kirk....90 E7
Bircher Herefs....56 H11
Birchfield Birm....58 G6
Birch Green Herts....50 G8
Birch Green Essex....52 F8
Birchgrove Cardif....30 G9
Birchgrove Swans....29 K5
Birchgrove W Susx....25 K5
Birch Heath Ches W....69 P2
Birch Hill Ches W....81 Q10
Birchington Kent....39 N8
Birchington-on-Sea Kent....39 N8
Birchley Heath Warwks....59 L6
Birchmoor Warwks....59 L4
Birchmoor Green C Beds....49 Q8
Birch Services Rochdl....89 N9
Birch Vale Derbys....83 M7
Birch Wood Somset....10 E2
Birchwood Lincs....86 B7
Birch Wood Somset....10 E2

Birchwood Warrtn....82 E6
Bircotes Notts....85 K2
Birdbrook Essex....52 B3
Birdforth N York....97 Q5
Birdham W Susx....15 M6
Birdingbury Warwks....59 P11
Birdlip Gloucs....32 H2
Birdoswald Cumb....111 M7
Birdsall N York....98 G7
Birds Edge Kirk....90 G9
Birds Green Essex....51 N9
Birdsgreen Shrops....57 P7
Birdsmoorgate Dorset....10 H4
Bird Street Suffk....64 E11
Birdwell Barns....91 J10
Birdwood Gloucs....46 D11
Birgham Border....118 E3
Birichin Highld....162 H8
Birkacre Lancs....88 H8
Birkby N York....104 B10
Birkdale Sefton....88 C8
Birkenbog Abers....158 D4
Birkenhead Wirral....81 L7
Birkenhead (Queensway) Tunnel Lpool....81 L7
Birkenhills Abers....158 H8
Birkenshaw Kirk....90 G5
Birkhall Abers....149 Q9
Birkhill D & G....117 J7
Birkholme Lincs....73 P6
Birkin N York....91 N5
Birks Leeds....90 H5
Birkshaw Nthumb....111 Q7
Birley Herefs....45 P4
Birley Carr Sheff....84 D2
Birling Kent....37 Q8
Birling Nthumb....119 P9
Birling Gap E Susx....25 N11
Birlingham Worcs....46 H6
Birmingham Birm....58 G7
Birmingham Airport Solhll....59 J8
Birnam P & K....141 P9
Birness Abers....159 N11
Birse Abers....150 F8
Birsemore Abers....150 E8
Birstall Kirk....90 G5
Birstall Leics....72 F9
Birstwith N York....97 K9
Birthorpe Lincs....74 B4
Birtley Gatesd....113 L9
Birtley Herefs....56 F11
Birtley Nthumb....112 C5
Birtley Crematorium Gatesd....113 L9
Birts Street Worcs....46 E7
Bisbrooke Rutlnd....73 M11
Biscathorpe Lincs....86 H4
Biscovey Cnwll....3 R3
Bisham W & M....35 M7
Bishampton Worcs....47 J4
Bish Mill Devon....17 N6
Bishop Auckland Dur....103 P5
Bishopbridge Lincs....86 D2
Bishopbriggs E Duns....125 Q3
Bishop Burton E R Yk....92 G3
Bishop Middleham Dur....104 B4
Bishopmill Moray....157 N5
Bishop Monkton N York....97 M7
Bishop Norton Lincs....86 C2
Bishopsbourne Kent....39 L11
Bishops Cannings Wilts....21 K2
Bishop's Castle Shrops....56 E7
Bishop's Caundle Dorset....11 P2
Bishop's Cleeve Gloucs....47 J9
Bishop's Frome Herefs....46 C5
Bishops Gate Surrey....35 Q10
Bishop's Green Essex....51 P7
Bishop's Green Hants....22 F2
Bishop's Hull Somset....18 H10
Bishop's Itchington Warwks....48 C3
Bishops Lydeard Somset....18 G9
Bishop's Norton Gloucs....46 F10
Bishop's Nympton Devon....17 P7
Bishop's Offley Staffs....70 D9
Bishop's Stortford Herts....51 L6
Bishop's Sutton Hants....22 H8
Bishop's Tachbrook Warwks....48 B2
Bishop's Tawton Devon....17 K6
Bishopsteignton Devon....7 N4
Bishopstoke Hants....22 E11
Bishopston Swans....28 G7
Bishopstone Bucks....35 M2
Bishopstone E Susx....25 L10
Bishopstone Herefs....45 N6
Bishopstone Kent....39 M8
Bishopstone Swindn....33 P8
Bishopstone Wilts....21 L9
Bishopstrow Wilts....20 G6
Bishop Sutton BaNES....19 Q3
Bishop's Waltham Hants....22 G11
Bishop's Wood Staffs....58 B3
Bishopswood Somset....10 F2
Bishopsworth Bristl....31 Q11
Bishop Thornton N York....97 L8
Bishopthorpe C York....98 B11
Bishopton Darltn....104 C6
Bishopton Rens....125 L3
Bishopton Warwks....47 N3
Bishop Wilton E R Yk....98 F9
Bishton Newpt....31 L7
Bishton Staffs....71 J10
Bisley Gloucs....32 H3
Bisley Surrey....23 Q3
Bisley Camp Surrey....23 Q3
Bispham Bpool....88 C2
Bispham Green Lancs....88 F8
Bissoe Cnwll....3 K5
Bisterne Hants....13 K4
Bitchet Green Kent....37 N10
Bitchfield Lincs....73 P5
Bittadon Devon....17 J3
Bittaford Devon....6 H7
Bittering Norfk....76 C8
Bitterley Shrops....57 K9
Bitterne C Sotn....14 E4
Bitteswell Leics....60 B3
Bitton S Glos....32 C11
Bix Oxon....35 K8
Bixter Shet....169 q8
Blaby Leics....72 F11
Blackadder Border....129 L9
Blackawton Devon....7 L8
Blackbeck Cumb....100 D9
Blackborough Devon....10 B3
Blackborough End Norfk....75 N7

Black Bourton – Boythorpe 259

Black Bourton Oxon 33 Q4
Blackboys E Susx 25 M6
Blackbrook Derbys 84 D11
Blackbrook St Hel 82 B5
Blackbrook Staffs 70 D7
Blackbrook Surrey 36 E11
Blackburn Abers 151 L5
Blackburn Bl w D 89 K5
Blackburn Rothm 84 E2
Blackburn W Loth 126 H4
Blackburn with Darwen Services Bl w D 89 K6
Black Callerton N u Ty 113 J7
Black Car Norfk 64 F2
Black Corner W Susx 24 G3
Blackcraig E Ayrs 115 M6
Black Crofts Ag & B 138 G11
Black Cross Cnwll 4 E9
Blackden Heath Ches E 82 G10
Blackdog Abers 151 P5
Black Dog Devon 9 K3
Blackdown Devon 8 D9
Blackdown Dorset 10 H4
Blackdyke Cumb 109 P10
Blacker Barns 91 J9
Blacker Hill Barns 91 K10
Blackfen Gt Lon 37 L6
Blackfield Hants 14 D6
Blackford Cumb 110 G8
Blackford P & K 133 P6
Blackford Somset 19 M5
Blackford Somset 20 C9
Blackfordby Leics 72 A7
Blackgang IoW 14 E11
Blackhall C Edin 127 N3
Blackhall Dur 104 E3
Blackhall Colliery Dur 104 E3
Blackhall Mill Gatesd 112 H9
Blackhaugh Border 117 N3
Blackheath Essex 52 H7
Blackheath Gt Lon 37 J5
Blackheath Sandw 58 E7
Blackheath Suffk 65 N7
Blackheath Surrey 36 B11
Black Heddon Nthumb 112 G5
Blackhill Abers 159 Q6
Blackhill Abers 159 Q9
Blackhill Dur 112 G10
Blackhill of Clackriach Abers 159 M8
Blackhorse Devon 9 N6
Blackjack Lincs 74 E3
Blackland Wilts 33 K11
Black Lane Ends Lancs 89 Q2
Blacklaw D & G 116 E9
Blackley Manch 83 J4
Blackley Crematorium Manch 82 H4
Blacklunans P & K 142 A5
Blackmarstone Herefs 45 Q7
Blackmill Brdgnd 29 P7
Blackmoor Hants 23 L8
Black Moor Leeds 90 H3
Blackmoor N Som 19 N2
Blackmoorfoot Kirk 90 D8
Blackmoor Gate Devon 17 L3
Blackmore Essex 51 P10
Blackmore End Essex 52 B5
Blackmore End Herts 50 E7
Black Mountains 45 K9
Blackness Falk 127 K2
Blacknest Hants 23 L6
Blacknest W & M 35 Q11
Black Notley Essex 52 C7
Blacko Lancs 89 P2
Black Pill Swans 28 H6
Blackpool Bpool 88 C3
Blackpool Devon 7 L4
Blackpool Devon 7 M9
Blackpool Gate Cumb 111 K5
Blackpool Zoo Bpool 88 C3
Blackridge W Loth 126 F4
Blackrock Cnwll 2 H7
Blackrock Mons 30 H2
Blackrod Bolton 89 J8
Blacksboat Moray 157 M10
Blackshaw D & G 109 M7
Blackshaw Head Calder 90 B5
Blacksmith's Green Suffk 64 G8
Blacksnape Bl w D 89 L6
Blackstone W Susx 24 F7
Black Street Suffk 65 Q4
Black Tar Pembks 41 J9
Blackthorn Oxon 48 H11
Blackthorpe Suffk 64 C9
Blacktoft E R Yk 92 D6
Blacktop C Aber 151 M7
Black Torrington Devon 8 C3
Blackwall Derbys 71 P5
Blackwall Tunnel Gt Lon 37 J4
Blackwater Cnwll 3 J4
Blackwater Hants 23 M3
Blackwater IoW 14 F9
Blackwater Somset 19 J11
Blackwaterfoot N Ayrs 120 H6
Blackwell Cumb 110 H10
Blackwell Darltn 103 Q8
Blackwell Derbys 83 P10
Blackwell Derbys 84 F9
Blackwell Warwks 47 P6
Blackwell Worcs 58 E10
Blackwellsend Green Gloucs 46 E9
Blackwood Caerph 30 G5
Blackwood D & G 109 K3
Blackwood S Lans 126 D9
Blackwood Hill Staffs 70 G3
Blacon Ches W 81 M11
Bladbean Kent 27 L2
Bladnoch D & G 107 M7
Bladon Oxon 34 E2
Bladon Somset 19 M10
Blaenannerch Cerdgn 42 D5
Blaenau Ffestiniog Gwynd 67 N5
Blaenavon Torfn 31 J3
Blaenavon Industrial Landscape Torfn 30 H3
Blaen Dyryn Powys 44 C7
Blaenffos Pembks 41 N3
Blaengarw Brdgnd 29 P6
Blaengeuffordd Cerdgn 54 E8
Blaengwrach Neath 29 N3
Blaengwynfi Neath 29 N5
Blaenllechau Rhondd 30 D5
Blaenpennal Cerdgn 43 M2
Blaenplwyf Cerdgn 54 D9
Blaenporth Cerdgn 42 E5
Blaenrhondda Rhondd 29 P5
Blaenwaun Carmth 41 P5
Blaen-y-coed Carmth 42 F9
Blaen-y-cwm Blae G 30 F2
Blaenycwm Cerdgn 55 J9
Blaen-y-cwm Rhondd 29 P5
Blagdon N Som 19 P3
Blagdon Somset 18 H11
Blagdon Torbay 7 M6
Blagdon Hill Somset 18 H11
Blagill Cumb 111 P11
Blaguegate Lancs 88 F9
Blaich Highld 139 J2
Blain Highld 138 B4
Blaina Blae G 30 H3
Blair Atholl P & K 141 L4
Blair Drummond Stirlg 133 L8
Blairgowrie P & K 142 B8
Blairhall Fife 134 B10
Blairingone P & K 134 B8
Blairlogie Stirlg 133 N8
Blairmore Ag & B 131 P11
Blairmore Highld 164 E5
Blair's Ferry Ag & B 124 B4
Blaisdon Gloucs 46 D11
Blakebrook Worcs 57 Q9
Blakedown Worcs 58 C9
Blake End Essex 52 B7
Blakeley Lane Staffs 70 H5
Blakemere Ches W 82 C10
Blakemere Herefs 45 M6
Blakemore Devon 7 K6
Blakenall Heath Wsall 58 F4
Blakeney Gloucs 32 C3
Blakeney Norfk 76 E3
Blakenhall Ches E 70 C5
Blakenhall Wolves 58 D5
Blakeshall Worcs 58 B8
Blakesley Nhants 48 H4
Blanchland Nthumb 112 E10
Blandford Camp Dorset 12 F3
Blandford Forum Dorset 12 E3
Blandford St Mary Dorset 12 E3
Bland Hill N York 97 K10
Blanefield Stirlg 125 N2
Blankney Lincs 86 E8
Blantyre S Lans 126 B6
Blàr a' Chaorainn Highld 139 L4
Blargie Highld 147 Q9
Blarmachfoldach Highld 139 K4
Blashford Hants 13 L3
Blaston Leics 73 L11
Blatherwycke Nhants 73 P11
Blawith Cumb 94 F3
Blawquhairn D & G 108 D4
Blaxhall Suffk 65 M10
Blaxton Donc 91 R10
Blaydon Gatesd 113 J8
Bleadney Somset 19 N5
Bleadon N Som 19 K3
Bleak Street Somset 20 E8
Blean Kent 39 K9
Bleasby Lincs 86 F4
Bleasby Notts 85 M11
Bleasdale Lancs 95 M11
Bleatarn Cumb 102 D8
Bleathwood Herefs 57 K10
Blebocraigs Fife 135 L4
Bleddfa Powys 56 C11
Bledington Gloucs 47 P10
Bledlow Bucks 35 L4
Bledlow Ridge Bucks 35 L5
Bleet Wilts 20 G3
Blegbie E Loth 128 D7
Blencarn Cumb 102 B4
Blencogo Cumb 110 C11
Blendworth Hants 15 K4
Blenheim Palace Oxon 48 D11
Blennerhasset Cumb 100 G2
Bletchingdon Oxon 48 F11
Bletchingley Surrey 36 H10
Bletchley M Keyn 49 N8
Bletchley Shrops 69 R8
Bletchley Park Museum M Keyn 49 N8
Bletherston Pembks 41 L6
Bletsoe Bed 61 M9
Blewbury Oxon 34 F7
Blickling Norfk 76 H6
Blidworth Notts 85 J9
Blidworth Bottoms Notts 85 J10
Blindburn Nthumb 118 F8
Blindcrake Cumb 100 F4
Blindley Heath Surrey 37 J11
Blisland Cnwll 5 J7
Blissford Hants 13 L2
Bliss Gate Worcs 57 N10
Blisworth Nhants 49 K4
Blithbury Staffs 71 K11
Blitterlees Cumb 109 P10
Blockley Gloucs 47 N7
Blofield Norfk 77 L10
Blofield Heath Norfk 77 L9
Blo Norton Norfk 64 E6
Bloomfield Border 118 A6
Blore Staffs 70 C8
Blore Staffs 71 L5
Blounce Hants 23 K5
Blounts Green Staffs 71 K8
Blowick Sefton 88 D7
Bloxham Oxon 48 D7
Bloxholm Lincs 86 E10
Bloxwich Wsall 58 E4
Bloxworth Dorset 12 E6
Blubberhouses N York 97 J9
Blue Anchor Cnwll 4 E10
Blue Anchor Somset 18 D6
Blue Bell Hill Kent 38 B9
Blue John Cavern Derbys 83 P8
Blundellsands Sefton 81 L5
Blundeston Suffk 65 Q2
Blunham C Beds 61 Q10
Blunsdon St Andrew Swindn 33 M7
Bluntington Worcs 58 D10
Bluntisham Cambs 62 E6
Blunts Cnwll 5 N9
Blunts Green Warwks 58 H11
Blurton C Stke 70 F6
Blyborough Lincs 86 B2
Blyford Suffk 65 N6
Blymhill Staffs 57 Q2
Blymhill Lawn Staffs 57 Q2
Blyth Notts 85 K3
Blyth Nthumb 113 M4
Blyth Bridge Border 127 L8
Blythburgh Suffk 65 N6
Blyth Crematorium Nthumb 113 M4
Blythe Border 128 F10
Blythe Bridge Staffs 70 H6
Blythe End Warwks 59 K6
Blythe Marsh Staffs 70 H6
Blyth Services Notts 85 K3
Blyton Lincs 85 Q2
Boarhills Fife 135 P5
Boarhunt Hants 14 H5
Boarley Kent 38 C10
Boarsgreave Lancs 89 N6
Boarshead E Susx 25 M4
Boar's Head Wigan 88 H9
Boars Hill Oxon 34 E4
Boarstall Bucks 34 H2
Boasley Cross Devon 8 D6
Boath Highld 155 Q3
Boat of Garten Highld 148 G4
Bobbing Kent 38 E8
Bobbington Staffs 57 Q6
Bobbingworth Essex 51 M9
Bocaddon Cnwll 5 K10
Bocking Essex 52 C7
Bocking Churchstreet Essex 52 C6
Bockleton Worcs 46 A2
Boconnoc Cnwll 5 J9
Boddam Abers 159 R9
Boddam Shet 169 q12
Boddington Gloucs 46 G9
Bodedern IoA 78 E8
Bodelwyddan Denbgs 80 E9
Bodenham Herefs 45 Q4
Bodenham Wilts 21 N9
Bodenham Moor Herefs 45 Q4
Bodewryd IoA 78 G6
Bodfari Denbgs 80 F10
Bodffordd IoA 78 G9
Bodfuan Gwynd 66 E7
Bodham Norfk 76 G3
Bodiam E Susx 26 C6
Bodicote Oxon 48 E7
Bodieve Cnwll 4 F7
Bodinnick Cnwll 5 J11
Bodle Street Green E Susx 25 Q8
Bodmin Cnwll 4 H8
Bodmin Moor Cnwll 5 K6
Bodney Norfk 64 A2
Bodorgan IoA 78 F11
Bodsham Kent 27 K2
Bodwen Cnwll 4 G9
Bodymoor Heath Warwks 59 J5
Bogallan Highld 156 A7
Bogbrae Abers 159 P10
Bogend S Ayrs 125 L11
Boggs Holdings E Loth 128 C5
Boghall Mdloth 127 N4
Boghall W Loth 126 H4
Boghead S Lans 126 D9
Bogmoor Moray 157 R5
Bogmuir Abers 143 L3
Bogniebrae Abers 158 E8
Bognor Regis W Susx 15 P7
Bogroy Highld 148 G3
Bogue D & G 108 D4
Bohetherick Cnwll 5 Q8
Bohortha Cnwll 3 M7
Bohuntine Highld 146 H11
Bojewyan Cnwll 2 B7
Bokiddick Cnwll 4 H9
Bolam Dur 103 N6
Bolam Nthumb 112 H4
Bolberry Devon 6 H11
Bold Heath St Hel 82 B7
Boldmere Birm 58 H6
Boldon Colliery S Tyne 113 M8
Boldre Hants 13 P5
Boldron Dur 103 K8
Bole Notts 85 N3
Bolehill Derbys 84 C9
Bole Hill Derbys 84 D6
Bolenowe Cnwll 2 H6
Bolham Devon 18 C11
Bolham Water Devon 10 D2
Bolingey Cnwll 3 K3
Bollington Ches E 83 K9
Bollington Cross Ches E 83 K9
Bollow Gloucs 32 D2
Bolney W Susx 24 G6
Bolnhurst Bed 61 N9
Bolnore W Susx 24 H6
Bolshan Angus 143 L7
Bolsover Derbys 84 G6
Bolster Moor Kirk 90 D7
Bolsterstone Sheff 90 H11
Boltby N York 97 Q3
Boltenstone Abers 150 C5
Bolter End Bucks 35 L6
Bolton Bolton 89 L9
Bolton Cumb 102 B6
Bolton E Loth 128 E6
Bolton E R Yk 98 F10
Bolton Nthumb 119 M8
Bolton Abbey N York 96 G10
Bolton Bridge N York 96 G10
Bolton-by-Bowland Lancs 96 A11
Boltonfellend Cumb 111 J7
Boltongate Cumb 100 H2
Bolton-le-Sands Lancs 95 K7
Bolton Low Houses Cumb 100 H2
Bolton New Houses Cumb 100 H2
Bolton-on-Swale N York 103 Q11
Bolton Percy N York 91 N2
Bolton Town End Lancs 95 K7
Bolton upon Dearne Barns 91 M10
Bolventor Cnwll 5 K6
Bomarsund Nthumb 113 L4
Bomere Heath Shrops 69 N11
Bonar Bridge Highld 162 E8
Bonawe Ag & B 139 J11
Bonby N Linc 92 H7
Boncath Pembks 41 P3
Bonchester Bridge Border 118 A8
Bonchurch IoW 14 G11
Bondleigh Devon 8 G4
Bonds Lancs 88 F2
Bonehill Devon 8 H9
Bonehill Staffs 59 J4
Bo'ness Falk 134 C11
Boney Hay Staffs 58 F2
Bonhill W Duns 125 K2
Boningale Shrops 57 Q4
Bonjedward Border 118 C6
Bonkle N Lans 126 E6
Bonnington Angus 143 K10
Bonnington Kent 27 J4
Bonnybank Fife 135 K7
Bonnybridge Falk 126 E2
Bonnykelly Abers 159 L7
Bonnyrigg Mdloth 127 Q4
Bonnyton Angus 142 E10
Bonsall Derbys 84 C9
Bonshaw Tower D & G 110 D6
Bont Mons 45 M11
Bontddu Gwynd 67 M11
Bont-Dolgadfan Powys 55 K4
Bont-goch Cerdgn 54 F7
Bonthorpe Lincs 87 N6
Bontnewydd Cerdgn 54 E11
Bontnewydd Gwynd 66 H3
Bontuchel Denbgs 68 E3
Bonvilston V Glam 30 E10
Bonwm Denbgs 68 F6
Bon-y-maen Swans 29 J5
Boode Devon 17 J4
Booker Bucks 35 M6
Booley Shrops 69 Q9
Boon Border 128 F10
Boon Hill Staffs 70 E4
Boorley Green Hants 14 F4
Boosbeck R & Cl 105 J7
Boose's Green Essex 52 D5
Boot Cumb 100 G10
Booth Calder 90 C5
Boothby Graffoe Lincs 86 C9
Boothby Pagnell Lincs 73 P4
Boothferry E R Yk 92 B5
Booth Green Ches E 83 K8
Boothstown Salfd 82 F4
Booth Town Calder 90 D5
Boothville Nhants 60 G8
Bootle Cumb 94 C3
Bootle Sefton 81 L5
Boots Green Ches W 82 G10
Boot Street Suffk 53 M2
Booze N York 103 K10
Boraston Shrops 57 L11
Bordeaux Guern 10 c1
Borden Kent 38 E9
Borden W Susx 23 M10
Border Cumb 110 C10
Borders Crematorium Border 117 R4
Bordley N York 96 D7
Boreham Essex 52 C10
Boreham Wilts 20 G6
Boreham Street E Susx 25 Q8
Borehamwood Herts 50 E11
Boreland D & G 110 C2
Boreraig Highld 152 B7
Boreton Shrops 57 J3
Borgh W Isls 168 b17
Borgh W Isls 168 j2
Borgie Highld 165 Q5
Borgue D & G 108 D11
Borgue Highld 167 K11
Borley Essex 52 D3
Borley Green Essex 52 D3
Borley Green Suffk 64 D9
Borneskitaig Highld 152 F3
Borness D & G 108 D11
Boroughbridge N York 97 N7
Borough Green Kent 37 P9
Borras Head Wrexhm 69 L4
Borrowash Derbys 72 C4
Borrowby N York 97 P3
Borrowby N York 105 L7
Borrowstoun Falk 134 B11
Borstal Medway 38 B8
Borth Cerdgn 54 E6
Borthwickbrae Border 117 N8
Borthwickshiels Border 117 N7
Borth-y-Gest Gwynd 67 K7
Borve Highld 152 G8
Borve W Isls 168 b17
Borve W Isls 168 f8
Borve W Isls 168 j2
Borwick Lancs 95 L6
Borwick Lodge Cumb 101 K11
Borwick Rails Cumb 94 D5
Bosavern Cnwll 2 B7
Bosbury Herefs 46 C6
Boscarne Cnwll 4 G8
Boscastle Cnwll 4 H3
Boscombe Bmouth 13 K6
Boscombe Wilts 21 P7
Boscoppa Cnwll 3 Q3
Bosham W Susx 15 M6
Bosham Hoe W Susx 15 M6
Bosherston Pembks 41 J12
Boskednan Cnwll 2 C7
Boskenna Cnwll 2 C9
Bosley Ches E 83 K11
Bosoughan Cnwll 4 D9
Bossall N York 98 E8
Bossiney Cnwll 4 H4
Bossingham Kent 27 L2
Bossington Somset 18 A5
Bostock Green Ches W 82 E11
Boston Lincs 74 F2
Boston Crematorium Lincs 87 K11
Boston Spa Leeds 97 P11
Boswarthan Cnwll 2 C7
Boswinger Cnwll 3 P5
Botallack Cnwll 2 B7
Botany Bay Gt Lon 50 G11
Botcheston Leics 72 D10
Botesdale Suffk 64 E6
Bothal Nthumb 113 K3
Bothampstead W Berk 34 F9
Bothamsall Notts 85 L6
Bothel Cumb 100 G3
Bothenhampton Dorset 11 K6
Bothwell S Lans 126 C6
Bothwell Services S Lans 126 C6
Botley Bucks 35 Q4
Botley Hants 14 F4
Botley Oxon 34 E3
Botolph Claydon Bucks 49 K10
Botolphs W Susx 24 E9
Botolph's Bridge Kent 27 K5
Bottesford Leics 73 L3
Bottesford N Linc 92 E9
Bottisham Cambs 62 H8
Bottomcraig Fife 135 K3
Bottom of Hutton Lancs 88 F5
Bottom o' th' Moor Bolton 89 K8
Bottoms Calder 89 Q6
Bottoms Cnwll 2 B9
Botts Green Warwks 59 K6
Botusfleming Cnwll 5 Q9
Botwnnog Gwynd 66 D8
Bough Beech Kent 37 L11
Boughrood Powys 44 G7
Boughspring Gloucs 31 Q5
Boughton Nhants 60 G7
Boughton Norfk 75 P10
Boughton Notts 85 L7
Boughton Aluph Kent 26 H2
Boughton End C Beds 49 Q7
Boughton Green Kent 38 C11
Boughton Malherbe Kent 26 E2
Boughton Monchelsea Kent 38 C11
Boughton Street Kent 39 J10
Boulby R & Cl 105 L7
Boulder Clough Calder 90 C6
Bouldnor IoW 14 C9
Bouldon Shrops 57 J7
Boulmer Nthumb 119 Q8
Boulston Pembks 41 J8
Boultham Lincs 86 C7
Bourn Cambs 62 D9
Bourne Lincs 74 A6
Bournebridge Essex 37 M2
Bournebrook Birm 58 F8
Bourne End Bed 61 M8
Bourne End Bucks 35 N7
Bourne End C Beds 49 Q6
Bourne End Herts 50 B9
Bournemouth Bmouth 13 J6
Bournemouth Airport Dorset 13 K5
Bournemouth Crematorium Bmouth 13 K6
Bournes Green Gloucs 32 H4
Bournes Green Sthend 38 F4
Bournheath Worcs 58 E10
Bournmoor Dur 113 M10
Bournstream Gloucs 32 D6
Bournville Birm 58 F8
Bourton Dorset 20 E8
Bourton N Som 19 L2
Bourton Oxon 33 P7
Bourton Shrops 57 K5
Bourton Wilts 21 K2
Bourton on Dunsmore Warwks 59 P10
Bourton-on-the-Hill Gloucs 47 N8
Bourton-on-the-Water Gloucs 47 N10
Bousd Ag & B 136 H3
Boustead Hill Cumb 110 E9
Bouth Cumb 94 G3
Bouthwaite N York 96 H6
Bouts Worcs 47 K3
Boveney Bucks 35 P9
Boveridge Dorset 13 J2
Bovey Tracey Devon 9 K9
Bovingdon Herts 50 B10
Bovingdon Green Bucks 35 M7
Bovinger Essex 51 M9
Bovington Dorset 12 D7
Bovington Camp Dorset 12 D7
Bow Cumb 110 F9
Bow Devon 7 L7
Bow Devon 8 H4
Bow Gt Lon 37 J4
Bow Ork 169 c7
Bowbank Dur 102 H6
Bow Brickhill M Keyn 49 P8
Bowbridge Gloucs 32 G3
Bowburn Dur 104 B3
Bowcombe IoW 14 E9
Bowd Devon 10 C6
Bowden Border 117 R4
Bowden Devon 7 L9
Bowden Hill Wilts 32 H11
Bowdon Traffd 82 G7
Bower Highld 167 M4
Bowerchalke Wilts 21 K10
Bowerhill Wilts 20 H2
Bower Hinton Somset 19 N11
Bower House Tye Suffk 52 G3
Bowermadden Highld 167 M4
Bowers Staffs 70 E7
Bowers Gifford Essex 38 C4
Bowershall Fife 134 D9
Bower's Row Leeds 91 L5
Bowes Dur 103 J8
Bowgreave Lancs 88 F2
Bowhouse D & G 109 M7
Bowithick Cnwll 5 K5
Bowker's Green Lancs 81 N4
Bowland Border 117 P2
Bowland Bridge Cumb 95 J3
Bowley Herefs 45 Q4
Bowley Town Herefs 45 Q4
Bowlhead Green Surrey 23 P7
Bowling C Brad 90 F4
Bowling W Duns 125 L3
Bowling Bank Wrexhm 69 L5
Bowling Green Worcs 46 F4
Bowmanstead Cumb 101 K11
Bowmore Ag & B 122 D8
Bowness-on-Solway Cumb 110 D8
Bowness-on-Windermere Cumb 101 M11
Bow of Fife Fife 135 J5
Bowriefauld Angus 143 J8
Bowscale Cumb 101 L4
Bowsden Nthumb 119 J2
Bowston Cumb 101 N11
Bow Street Cerdgn 54 E7
Bow Street Norfk 64 E2
Bowthorpe Norfk 76 H10
Box Gloucs 32 G4
Box Wilts 32 F11
Boxbush Gloucs 32 D2
Boxbush Gloucs 46 C10
Box End Bed 61 M11
Boxford Suffk 52 G3
Boxford W Berk 34 D10
Boxgrove W Susx 15 P5
Box Hill Surrey 36 E10
Boxley Kent 38 C10
Boxmoor Herts 50 B9
Box's Shop Cnwll 16 C11
Boxted Essex 52 G5
Boxted Essex 52 H5
Boxted Suffk 64 A11
Boxted Cross Essex 52 H5
Boxwell Gloucs 32 F6
Boxworth Cambs 62 D8
Boyden End Suffk 63 M9
Boyden Gate Kent 39 M8
Boylestone Derbys 71 M7
Boyndie Abers 158 F5
Boyndlie Abers 159 M5
Boynton E R Yk 99 N7
Boysack Angus 143 L8
Boys Hill Dorset 11 P2
Boythorpe Derbys 84 E7

260 Boyton – Bromley

Boyton Cnwll 5 N3
Boyton Suffk 53 Q2
Boyton Wilts 21 J7
Boyton Cross Essex 51 P9
Boyton End Suffk 52 B3
Bozeat Nhants 61 K9
Braaid IoM 80 d6
Brabling Green Suffk 65 K9
Brabourne Kent 27 K3
Brabourne Lees Kent 27 J3
Brabstermire Highld 167 P3
Bracadale Highld 152 F10
Braceborough Lincs 74 A8
Bracebridge Heath Lincs 86 C7
Bracebridge Low Fields Lincs 86 C7
Braceby Lincs 73 Q3
Bracewell Lancs 96 C11
Brackenfield Derbys 84 E9
Brackenhirst N Lans 126 C4
Brackenthwaite Cumb 110 E11
Brackenthwaite N York 97 L10
Brackla Brdgnd 29 P9
Bracklesham W Susx 15 M7
Brackletter Highld 146 F11
Brackley Nhants 48 G7
Brackley Hatch Nhants 48 H6
Bracknell Br For 35 N11
Braco P & K 133 N6
Bracobrae Moray 158 D7
Bracon Ash Norfk 64 H2
Bracora Highld 145 M9
Bracorina Highld 145 M9
Bradaford Devon 5 P3
Bradbourne Derbys 71 N4
Bradbury Dur 104 B5
Bradden Nhants 48 H5
Braddock Cnwll 5 K9
Bradeley C Stke 70 F4
Bradenham Bucks 35 M5
Bradenstoke Wilts 33 K9
Bradfield Devon 9 Q3
Bradfield Essex 53 K5
Bradfield Norfk 77 K5
Bradfield Sheff 84 C2
Bradfield W Berk 34 H10
Bradfield Combust Suffk 64 B10
Bradfield Green Ches E 70 B3
Bradfield Heath Essex 53 K5
Bradfield St Clare Suffk 64 C10
Bradfield St George Suffk 64 C10
Bradford C Brad 90 F4
Bradford Cnwll 5 J6
Bradford Devon 16 G10
Bradford Nthumb 112 G5
Bradford Nthumb 119 N4
Bradford Abbas Dorset 11 M2
Bradford Leigh Wilts 20 F2
Bradford-on-Avon Wilts 20 F2
Bradford-on-Tone Somset 18 G10
Bradford Peverell Dorset 11 P6
Bradiford Devon 17 K5
Brading IoW 14 H9
Bradley Derbys 71 N5
Bradley Hants 22 H6
Bradley Kirk 90 F6
Bradley N York 96 F4
Bradley NE Lin 93 M9
Bradley Staffs 70 F11
Bradley Wolves 58 E5
Bradley Worcs 47 J2
Bradley Wrexhm 69 K4
Bradley Common Ches W 69 P5
Bradley Green Somset 19 J7
Bradley Green Warwks 59 L4
Bradley Green Worcs 47 J2
Bradley in the Moors Staffs 71 K6
Bradley Stoke S Glos 32 B8
Bradmore Notts 72 F4
Bradney Somset 19 K7
Bradninch Devon 9 N4
Bradninch Devon 17 L5
Bradnop Staffs 71 J3
Bradnor Green Herefs 45 K3
Bradpole Dorset 11 K6
Bradshaw Bolton 89 L8
Bradshaw Calder 90 D5
Bradshaw Kirk 90 D8
Bradstone Devon 5 P5
Bradwall Green Ches E 70 D2
Bradwell Derbys 83 Q8
Bradwell Devon 17 J3
Bradwell Essex 52 D7
Bradwell M Keyn 49 M6
Bradwell Norfk 77 Q11
Bradwell Crematorium Staffs 70 F5
Bradwell-on-Sea Essex 52 H10
Bradwell Waterside Essex 52 G10
Bradworthy Devon 16 E9
Brae Highld 156 B5
Brae Shet 169 q7
Braeface Falk 133 M11
Braehead Angus 143 M7
Braehead D & G 107 M7
Braehead S Lans 126 H7
Braeintra Highld 153 R11
Braemar Abers 149 M9
Braemore Highld 161 K11
Braemore Highld 167 J11
Brae Roy Lodge Highld 147 J9
Braeside Inver 124 G3
Braes of Coul Angus 142 D6
Braes of Enzie Moray 158 A6
Braeswick Ork 169 f3
Braevallich Ag & B 131 K6
Brafferton Darltn 103 Q6
Brafferton N York 97 P6
Brafield-on-the-Green Nhants 60 H9
Bragar W Isls 168 h3
Bragbury End Herts 50 G6
Braidwood S Lans 126 E8
Brailsford Derbys 71 P6
Brailsford Green Derbys 71 P6
Brain's Green Gloucs 32 C3
Braintree Essex 52 C7
Braiseworth Suffk 64 G7
Braishfield Hants 22 C9
Braithwaite C Brad 90 C2
Braithwaite Cumb 100 H6
Braithwell Donc 84 H2
Braken Hill Wakefd 91 L7
Bramber W Susx 24 E8
Brambridge Hants 22 E10
Bramcote Notts 72 E3
Bramcote Warwks 59 P7
Bramcote Crematorium Notts 72 E3
Bramdean Hants 22 H9
Bramerton Norfk 77 K11
Bramfield Herts 50 G7
Bramfield Suffk 65 M7
Bramford Suffk 53 K2
Bramhall Stockp 83 J8
Bramham Leeds 91 L2
Bramhope Leeds 90 H2
Bramley Hants 23 J3
Bramley Leeds 90 G3
Bramley Rothm 84 G2
Bramley Surrey 24 B2
Bramley Corner Hants 22 H3
Bramley Green Hants 23 J3
Bramley Head N York 96 H9
Bramling Kent 39 M10
Brampford Speke Devon 9 M5
Brampton Cambs 62 B6
Brampton Cumb 102 C6
Brampton Cumb 111 K8
Brampton Lincs 85 P5
Brampton Norfk 77 J7
Brampton Rothm 91 L10
Brampton Suffk 65 N5
Brampton Abbotts Herefs 46 B9
Brampton Ash Nhants 60 G3
Brampton Bryan Herefs 56 F10
Brampton-en-le-Morthen Rothm 84 G3
Bramshall Staffs 71 K8
Bramshaw Hants 21 Q11
Bramshill Hants 23 K2
Bramshott Hants 23 M8
Bramwell Somset 19 M9
Branault Highld 137 N2
Brancaster Norfk 75 Q2
Brancaster Staithe Norfk 75 Q2
Brancepeth Dur 103 P3
Branchill Moray 157 K7
Brand End Lincs 87 L11
Branderburgh Moray 157 N3
Brandesburton E R Yk 99 N11
Brandeston Suffk 65 J9
Brand Green Gloucs 46 D9
Brandis Corner Devon 16 G11
Brandiston Norfk 76 G7
Brandon Dur 103 P2
Brandon Lincs 86 B11
Brandon Nthumb 119 K7
Brandon Suffk 63 N3
Brandon Warwks 59 P9
Brandon Bank Norfk 63 K3
Brandon Creek Norfk 63 K2
Brandon Parva Norfk 76 F10
Brandsby N York 98 B6
Brandy Wharf Lincs 92 H11
Brane Cnwll 2 C8
Bran End Essex 51 Q5
Branksome Poole 12 H6
Branksome Park Poole 13 J6
Bransbury Hants 22 D6
Bransby Lincs 85 Q5
Branscombe Devon 10 D7
Bransford Worcs 46 E4
Bransgore Hants 13 L5
Bransholme C KuH 93 K4
Bransley Shrops 57 M9
Branson's Cross Worcs 58 G10
Branston Leics 73 L5
Branston Lincs 86 D7
Branston Staffs 71 N10
Branston Booths Lincs 86 E7
Branstone IoW 14 G10
Brant Broughton Lincs 86 B10
Brantham Suffk 53 K5
Branthwaite Cumb 100 E6
Branthwaite Cumb 101 J3
Brantingham E R Yk 92 F5
Branton Donc 91 Q10
Branton Nthumb 119 K7
Branton Green N York 97 P8
Branxton Nthumb 118 G3
Brassey Green Ches W 69 P2
Brassington Derbys 71 N4
Brasted Kent 37 L9
Brasted Chart Kent 37 L10
Brathens Abers 150 H8
Bratoft Lincs 87 N8
Brattleby Lincs 86 B4
Bratton Somset 18 B5
Bratton Wilts 20 H4
Bratton Wrekin 57 L2
Bratton Clovelly Devon 8 C6
Bratton Fleming Devon 17 L4
Bratton Seymour Somset 20 C9
Braughing Herts 51 J5
Braughing Friars Herts 51 K6
Braunston Nhants 60 B7
Braunston Rutlnd 73 L9
Braunstone Town Leics 72 F10
Braunton Devon 16 H4
Brawby N York 98 E5
Brawl Highld 166 D3
Braworth N York 104 F9
Bray W & M 35 P9
Braybrooke Nhants 60 G4
Braydon Wilts 33 K7
Braydon Brook Wilts 33 J6
Braydon Side Wilts 33 K7
Brayford Devon 17 M5
Bray's Hill E Susx 25 Q8
Bray Shop Cnwll 5 N7
Braystones Cumb 100 D9
Braythorn N York 97 K11
Brayton N York 91 Q4
Braywick W & M 35 N9
Braywoodside W & M 35 N9
Brazacott Cnwll 5 M3
Breach Kent 27 L2
Breach Kent 38 D8
Breachwood Green Herts 50 E6
Breaden Heath Shrops 69 M7
Breadsall Derbys 72 B3
Breadstone Gloucs 32 D4
Breadward Herefs 45 K4
Breage Cnwll 2 G8
Breakachy Highld 155 N9
Breakish Highld 145 L3
Breakspear Crematorium Gt Lon 36 C3
Brealangwell Lodge Highld 162 C8
Bream Gloucs 32 B3
Breamore Hants 21 N11
Brean Somset 19 J3
Breanais W Isls 168 e5
Brearley Calder 90 C5
Brearton N York 97 M8
Breascleit W Isls 168 h4
Breasclete W Isls 168 h4
Breaston Derbys 72 D4
Brechfa Carmth 43 K8
Brechin Angus 143 L5
Breckles Norfk 64 D3
Brecon Powys 44 E9
Brecon Beacons National Park 44 E10
Bredbury Stockp 83 K6
Brede E Susx 26 D8
Bredenbury Herefs 46 B3
Bredfield Suffk 65 K11
Bredgar Kent 38 E9
Bredhurst Kent 38 C9
Bredon Worcs 46 H7
Bredon's Hardwick Worcs 46 H7
Bredon's Norton Worcs 46 H7
Bredwardine Herefs 45 L6
Breedon on the Hill Leics 72 C6
Breich W Loth 126 H5
Breightmet Bolton 89 L9
Breighton E R Yk 92 B4
Breinton Herefs 45 P7
Bremhill Wilts 33 J10
Bremridge Devon 17 M6
Brenchley Kent 25 Q2
Brendon Devon 16 F10
Brendon Devon 17 P2
Brendon Hill Somset 18 D8
Brenfield Ag & B 123 P3
Brenish W Isls 168 e5
Brenkley N u Ty 113 K5
Brent Cross Gt Lon 36 F3
Brent Eleigh Suffk 52 F2
Brentford Gt Lon 36 E5
Brentingby Leics 73 K7
Brent Knoll Somset 19 K4
Brent Mill Devon 6 H7
Brent Pelham Herts 51 K4
Brentwood Essex 37 N2
Brenzett Kent 26 H6
Brenzett Green Kent 26 H6
Brereton Staffs 71 K11
Brereton Green Ches E 70 D2
Brereton Heath Ches E 82 H11
Brereton Hill Staffs 71 K11
Bressay Shet 169 s9
Bressingham Norfk 64 F5
Bressingham Common Norfk 64 F5
Bretby Derbys 71 P10
Bretby Crematorium Derbys 71 P10
Bretford Warwks 59 P9
Bretforton Worcs 47 L6
Bretherton Lancs 88 F6
Breton C Pete 74 C10
Brettabister Shet 169 r8
Brettenham Norfk 64 C5
Brettenham Suffk 64 D11
Bretton Derbys 84 B5
Bretton Flints 69 L2
Brewers End Essex 51 N6
Brewer Street Surrey 36 H10
Brewood Staffs 58 C3
Briantspuddle Dorset 12 D6
Brick End Essex 51 N5
Brickendon Herts 50 H9
Bricket Wood Herts 50 D10
Brick Houses Sheff 84 D4
Brickkiln Green Essex 52 B5
Bricklehampton Worcs 47 J6
Bride IoM 80 f1
Bridekirk Cumb 100 F4
Bridell Pembks 41 N2
Bridestowe Devon 8 D7
Brideswell Abers 158 E10
Bridford Devon 9 K7
Bridge Kent 39 L11
Bridge End Cumb 94 D4
Bridge End Cumb 110 G11
Bridge End Devon 6 H9
Bridge End Dur 103 K3
Bridge End Essex 51 Q4
Bridge End Lincs 74 B3
Bridgefoot Angus 142 F10
Bridgefoot Cumb 100 E5
Bridge Green Essex 51 L3
Bridgehampton Somset 19 Q10
Bridge Hewick N York 97 M6
Bridgehill Dur 112 G10
Bridgehouse Gate N York 97 J7
Bridgemary Hants 14 G6
Bridgemere Ches E 70 C5
Bridgend Abers 158 D10
Bridgend Ag & B 120 E4
Bridgend Ag & B 122 D7
Bridgend Angus 143 J4
Bridgend Brdgnd 29 P9
Bridgend Cerdgn 42 C5
Bridgend Cumb 101 M8
Bridgend D & G 116 F9
Bridgend Devon 6 F9
Bridgend Fife 135 K5
Bridgend Moray 158 A11
Bridgend P & K 134 E3
Bridgend W Loth 127 J2
Bridgend of Lintrathen Angus 142 D7
Bridge of Alford Abers 150 F4
Bridge of Allan Stirlg 133 M8
Bridge of Avon Moray 149 M3
Bridge of Avon Moray 157 M10
Bridge of Balgie P & K 140 E8
Bridge of Brewlands Angus 142 B5
Bridge of Brown Highld 149 L3
Bridge of Cally P & K 142 A7
Bridge of Canny Abers 150 H8
Bridge of Craigisla Angus 142 D7
Bridge of Dee D & G 108 F9
Bridge of Don C Aber 151 N6
Bridge of Dye Abers 150 H10
Bridge of Earn P & K 134 E4
Bridge of Ericht P & K 140 D6
Bridge of Feugh Abers 151 J9
Bridge of Gairn Abers 150 B8
Bridge of Gaur P & K 140 D6
Bridge of Marnoch Abers 158 E7
Bridge of Muchalls Abers 151 M9
Bridge of Orchy Ag & B 139 P10
Bridge of Tilt P & K 141 L4
Bridge of Tynet Moray 158 A5
Bridge of Walls Shet 169 p8
Bridge of Weir Rens 125 K4
Bridge Reeve Devon 17 M9
Bridgerule Devon 16 D11
Bridges Shrops 56 F5
Bridge Sollers Herefs 45 N6
Bridge Street Suffk 52 E2
Bridgetown Cnwll 5 N4
Bridgetown Somset 18 B8
Bridge Trafford Ches W 81 P10
Bridge Yate S Glos 32 C10
Bridgham Norfk 64 D4
Bridgnorth Shrops 57 N6
Bridgwater Somset 19 J7
Bridgwater Services Somset 19 K8
Bridlington E R Yk 99 P7
Bridport Dorset 11 K6
Bridstow Herefs 46 A10
Brierfield Lancs 89 N3
Brierley Barns 91 L8
Brierley Gloucs 46 B11
Brierley Herefs 45 P3
Brierley Hill Dudley 58 D7
Brierlow Bar Derbys 83 N11
Brierton Hartpl 104 E4
Briery Cumb 101 J6
Brigg N Linc 92 H9
Briggate Norfk 77 L6
Briggswath N York 105 N9
Brigham Cumb 100 E4
Brigham Cumb 101 J6
Brigham E R Yk 99 M10
Brighouse Calder 90 E6
Brighstone IoW 14 D10
Brightgate Derbys 84 C9
Brighthampton Oxon 34 C4
Brightholmlee Sheff 90 H11
Brightley Devon 8 F5
Brightling E Susx 25 Q6
Brightlingsea Essex 53 J8
Brighton Br & H 24 H10
Brighton Cnwll 3 N3
Brighton City Airport W Susx 24 E9
Brighton le Sands Sefton 81 L5
Brightons Falk 126 G2
Brightwalton W Berk 34 D9
Brightwalton Green W Berk 34 D9
Brightwalton Holt W Berk 34 D9
Brightwell Suffk 53 N3
Brightwell Baldwin Oxon 35 J5
Brightwell-cum-Sotwell Oxon 34 G6
Brightwell Upperton Oxon 35 J6
Brignall Dur 103 L8
Brig o'Turk Stirlg 132 G6
Brigsley NE Lin 93 N10
Brigsteer Cumb 95 K3
Brigstock Nhants 61 K3
Brill Bucks 35 J2
Brill Cnwll 3 J8
Brilley Herefs 45 K5
Brimfield Herefs 57 J11
Brimfield Cross Herefs 57 J11
Brimington Derbys 84 F6
Brimley Devon 9 K9
Brimpsfield Gloucs 32 H2
Brimpton W Berk 22 G2
Brimpton Common W Berk 22 G2
Brimscombe Gloucs 32 G4
Brimstage Wirral 81 L8
Brincliffe Sheff 84 D4
Brind E R Yk 92 B4
Brindham Somset 19 P7
Brindister Shet 169 p8
Brindle Lancs 88 H6
Brindley Ches E 69 Q4
Brineton Staffs 57 Q2
Bringhurst Leics 60 H2
Bringsty Common Herefs 46 D3
Brington Cambs 61 N5
Briningham Norfk 76 E5
Brinkely Notts 85 M10
Brinkhill Lincs 87 L6
Brinkley Cambs 63 K10
Brinklow Warwks 59 P9
Brinkworth Wilts 33 K8
Brinscall Lancs 89 J6
Brinscombe Somset 19 M4
Brinsea N Som 19 M2
Brinsley Notts 84 G11
Brinsop Herefs 45 N6
Brinsworth Rothm 84 F3
Brinton Norfk 76 E4
Brinyan Ork 169 d4
Brisco Cumb 110 H10
Brisley Norfk 76 C7
Brislington Bristl 32 B10
Brissenden Green Kent 26 F4
Bristol Bristl 31 Q10
Bristol Airport N Som 31 P11
Bristol Zoo Gardens Bristl 31 Q10
Briston Norfk 76 F5
Brisworthy Devon 6 F5
Britannia Lancs 89 P6
Britford Wilts 21 N9
Brithdir Caerph 30 F4
Brithdir Gwynd 67 P11
British Legion Village Kent 38 B10
Briton Ferry Neath 29 K6
Britwell Salome Oxon 35 J6
Brixham Torbay 7 N7
Brixton Devon 6 F8
Brixton Gt Lon 36 H5
Brixton Deverill Wilts 20 G7
Brixworth Nhants 60 F6
Brize Norton Oxon 33 Q3
Brize Norton Airport Oxon 33 Q3
Broad Alley Worcs 58 C11
Broad Blunsdon Swindn 33 M6
Broadbottom Tamesd 83 L6
Broadbridge W Susx 15 M5
Broadbridge Heath W Susx 24 D4
Broad Campden Gloucs 47 N7
Broad Carr Calder 90 D7
Broad Chalke Wilts 21 K9
Broad Clough Lancs 89 P6
Broadclyst Devon 9 N5
Broadfield Inver 125 J3
Broadfield Pembks 41 M10
Broadford Highld 145 K3
Broad Ford Kent 26 B4
Broadford Bridge W Susx 24 C6
Broadgairhill Border 117 J8
Broadgrass Green Suffk 64 D9
Broad Green Cambs 63 L8
Broad Green Essex 52 E7
Broad Green Worcs 46 E3
Broad Green Worcs 58 E10
Broadhaugh Border 129 M9
Broad Haven Pembks 40 G8
Broadheath Traffd 82 G7
Broadheath Worcs 57 M11
Broadhembury Devon 10 C4
Broadhempston Devon 7 L5
Broad Hill Cambs 63 J5
Broad Hinton Wilts 33 M9
Broadholme Lincs 85 Q6
Broadland Row E Susx 26 D8
Broadlay Carmth 28 C3
Broad Layings Hants 22 D2
Broadley Essex 51 K9
Broadley Lancs 89 P7
Broadley Moray 158 A5
Broadley Common Essex 51 K9
Broad Marston Worcs 47 M5
Broadmayne Dorset 12 B7
Broad Meadow Staffs 70 E5
Broadmere Hants 22 H5
Broadmoor Gloucs 46 B11
Broadmoor Pembks 41 L9
Broadnymett Devon 8 H4
Broad Oak Carmth 43 L10
Broad Oak Cumb 94 C2
Broadoak Dorset 11 J5
Broad Oak E Susx 25 P6
Broad Oak E Susx 26 D8
Broadoak Gloucs 32 C2
Broad Oak Hants 23 L4
Broad Oak Herefs 45 P10
Broad Oak Kent 39 L9
Broad Oak St Hel 82 B5
Broadoak Wrexhm 69 L3
Broad Road Suffk 65 K6
Broadsands Torbay 7 M7
Broad's Green Essex 51 Q8
Broadstairs Kent 39 Q8
Broadstone Mons 31 P4
Broadstone Poole 12 H5
Broadstone Shrops 57 J7
Broad Street E Susx 26 E8
Broad Street Essex 51 N7
Broad Street Kent 27 K3
Broad Street Kent 38 D10
Broad Street Medway 38 C7
Broad Street Wilts 21 M3
Broad Street Green Essex 52 E10
Broad Town Wilts 33 L9
Broadwas Worcs 46 E3
Broadwater Herts 50 F6
Broadwater W Susx 24 D10
Broadwaters Worcs 58 B9
Broadway Carmth 28 C3
Broadway Carmth 41 Q8
Broadway Pembks 40 G8
Broadway Somset 19 K11
Broadway Suffk 65 M6
Broadway Worcs 47 L7
Broadwell Gloucs 31 Q2
Broadwell Gloucs 47 P9
Broadwell Oxon 33 Q4
Broadwell Warwks 59 Q11
Broadwey Dorset 11 P8
Broadwindsor Dorset 11 J4
Broadwood Kelly Devon 8 F3
Broadwoodwidger Devon 5 Q4
Brobury Herefs 45 L6
Brochel Highld 153 K8
Brochroy Ag & B 139 J11
Brock Lancs 88 G2
Brockamin Worcs 46 E4
Brockbridge Hants 22 H11
Brockdish Norfk 65 J6
Brockencote Worcs 58 C10
Brockenhurst Hants 13 P4
Brocketsbrae S Lans 126 E10
Brockford Green Suffk 64 G8
Brockford Street Suffk 64 G8
Brockhall Nhants 60 D8
Brockham Surrey 36 E11
Brockhampton Gloucs 46 H9
Brockhampton Gloucs 47 K10
Brockhampton Hants 15 K5
Brockhampton Herefs 46 A8
Brockhampton Green Dorset 11 Q3
Brockholes Kirk 90 F8
Brockhurst Derbys 84 D8
Brockhurst Warwks 59 Q8
Brocklebank Cumb 101 K2
Brocklesby Lincs 93 K8
Brockley N Som 31 N11
Brockley Suffk 64 A7
Brockley Green Suffk 63 M11
Brockley Green Suffk 64 A11
Brockleymoor Cumb 101 N3
Brockmoor Dudley 58 D7
Brockscombe Devon 8 C5
Brock's Green Hants 22 F2
Brockton Shrops 56 E4
Brockton Shrops 56 E7
Brockton Shrops 57 K6
Brockton Shrops 57 N4
Brockton Staffs 70 E8
Brockweir Gloucs 31 P4
Brockwood Park Hants 22 H9
Brockworth Gloucs 46 G11
Brocton Cnwll 4 G8
Brocton Staffs 70 H11
Brodick N Ayrs 121 K4
Brodie Moray 156 H6
Brodsworth Donc 91 N9
Brogaig Highld 152 H4
Brogborough C Beds 49 Q7
Brokenborough Wilts 32 H7
Broken Cross Ches E 83 J10
Broken Cross Ches W 82 E10
Brokerswood Wilts 20 F4
Bromborough Wirral 81 M8
Brome Suffk 64 G6
Brome Street Suffk 64 H6
Bromeswell Suffk 65 L11
Bromfield Cumb 110 C11
Bromfield Shrops 56 H9
Bromham Bed 61 M10
Bromham Wilts 33 J11
Bromley Barns 91 J11
Bromley Dudley 58 D7
Bromley Gt Lon 37 K7
Bromley Shrops 57 N5

Bromley Common – Buttington 261

Bromley Common Gt Lon 37 K7
Bromley Cross Bolton 89 L8
Bromley Cross Essex 53 J6
Bromley Green Kent 26 G4
Bromlow Shrops 56 E4
Brompton Medway 38 C8
Brompton N York 104 C11
Brompton-by-Sawdon N York 99 J4
Brompton-on-Swale N York 103 P11
Brompton Ralph Somset 18 E8
Brompton Regis Somset 18 C8
Bromsash Herefs 46 C10
Bromsberrow Gloucs 46 D8
Bromsberrow Heath Gloucs 46 D8
Bromsgrove Worcs 58 E10
Bromstead Heath Staffs 70 D11
Bromyard Herefs 46 C4
Bromyard Downs Herefs 46 C3
Bronaber Gwynd 67 N8
Bronant Cerdgn 54 E11
Broncroft Shrops 57 J7
Brongest Cerdgn 42 F5
Bronington Wrexhm 69 N7
Bronllys Powys 44 G8
Bronwydd Carmth 42 H10
Bronydd Powys 45 J5
Bronygarth Shrops 69 J7
Brook Carmth 41 Q9
Brook Hants 13 N2
Brook Hants 22 B9
Brook IoW 14 C10
Brook Kent 27 J3
Brook Surrey 23 P7
Brook Surrey 36 C11
Brooke Norfk 65 K2
Brooke Rutlnd 73 L9
Brookenby Lincs 93 M11
Brook End Bed 61 N8
Brook End C Beds 61 Q11
Brook End Cambs 61 N6
Brook End M Keyn 49 P6
Brookfield Rens 125 L5
Brookhampton Oxon 34 H5
Brookhampton Somset 20 B9
Brook Hill Hants 13 N2
Brook House Denbgs 80 F11
Brookhouse Lancs 95 L8
Brookhouse Rothm 84 H3
Brookhouse Green Ches E 70 E2
Brookhouses Derbys 83 M7
Brookland Kent 26 G6
Brooklands Traffd 82 G6
Brookmans Park Herts 50 F10
Brooks Powys 55 Q5
Brooksby Leics 72 H7
Brooks End Kent 39 N8
Brooks Green W Susx 24 D6
Brook Street Essex 37 N2
Brook Street Kent 26 F5
Brook Street Suffk 52 D2
Brook Street W Susx 24 H5
Brookthorpe Gloucs 32 F2
Brookville Norfk 75 P11
Brookwood Surrey 23 Q3
Broom C Beds 50 E2
Broom Rothm 84 F2
Broom Warwks 47 L4
Broombank Worcs 57 M10
Broome Norfk 65 M3
Broome Shrops 56 G8
Broome Worcs 58 D9
Broomedge Warrtn 82 F7
Broome Park Nthumb 119 M8
Broomer's Corner W Susx 24 D6
Broomershill W Susx 24 C7
Broomfield Essex 52 B9
Broomfield Kent 38 D11
Broomfield Kent 39 L8
Broomfield Somset 18 H8
Broomfields Shrops 69 M11
Broomfleet E R Yk 92 E5
Broom Green Norfk 76 D7
Broomhall W & M 35 Q11
Broomhaugh Nthumb 112 F8
Broom Hill Barns 91 L10
Broom Hill Dorset 12 H4
Broom Hill Notts 84 H11
Broomhill Nthumb 119 P10
Broom Hill Worcs 58 D9
Broomhill Green Ches E 70 A5
Broomley Nthumb 112 F8
Broompark Dur 103 P2
Broom's Green Gloucs 46 D8
Broomsthorpe Norfk 76 A6
Broom Street Kent 38 H9
Brora Highld 163 L6
Broseley Shrops 57 M4
Brotherhouse Bar Lincs 74 E8
Brotherlee Dur 102 H3
Brothertoft Lincs 87 J11
Brotherton N York 91 M5
Brotton R & Cl 105 J7
Broubster Highld 166 H5
Brough Cumb 102 E8
Brough Derbys 83 Q8
Brough E R Yk 92 F5
Brough Highld 167 M2
Brough Notts 85 P9
Brough Shet 169 s7
Broughall Shrops 69 Q6
Brough Lodge Shet 169 s4
Brough Sowerby Cumb 102 E8
Broughton Border 116 G3
Broughton Bucks 35 M2
Broughton Cambs 62 C5
Broughton Flints 69 K2
Broughton Hants 22 B8
Broughton Lancs 88 G4
Broughton M Keyn 49 N7
Broughton N Linc 92 G9
Broughton N York 96 D10
Broughton N York 98 F6
Broughton Nhants 60 H5
Broughton Oxon 48 D7
Broughton Salfd 82 H4
Broughton Staffs 70 D8
Broughton V Glam 29 P10
Broughton Astley Leics 60 B2
Broughton Beck Cumb 94 F4
Broughton Gifford Wilts 20 G2
Broughton Green Worcs 47 J2
Broughton Hackett Worcs 46 H4
Broughton-in-Furness Cumb 94 E3
Broughton Mains D & G 107 N8
Broughton Mills Cumb 94 E2
Broughton Moor Cumb 100 E4
Broughton Poggs Oxon 33 P4
Broughton Tower Cumb 94 E3
Broughty Ferry C Dund 142 H11
Brough with St Giles N York 103 P11
Brow End Cumb 94 F6
Brownber Cumb 102 D9
Brown Candover Hants 22 G7
Brown Edge Lancs 88 D8
Brown Edge Staffs 70 G4
Brown Heath Ches W 69 N2
Brownheath Shrops 69 N9
Brownhill Abers 159 L9
Brownhills Fife 135 N4
Brownhills Wsall 58 F3
Brownieside Nthumb 119 N6
Browninghill Green Hants 22 G3
Brown Lees Staffs 70 F3
Brownlow Heath Ches E 70 E2
Brownrigg Cumb 100 D6
Brownrigg Cumb 110 C10
Brownsea Island Dorset 12 H7
Brown's Green Birm 58 G6
Brownsham Devon 16 D6
Browns Hill Gloucs 32 G4
Brownsover Warwks 60 B5
Brownston Devon 6 H8
Brown Street Suffk 64 F9
Brow-of-the-Hill Norfk 75 N7
Browston Green Norfk 77 P11
Broxa N York 99 J2
Broxbourne Herts 51 J9
Broxburn E Loth 128 H4
Broxburn W Loth 127 K3
Broxfield Nthumb 119 P7
Broxted Essex 51 N5
Broxton Ches W 69 N4
Broyle Side E Susx 25 L8
Bruan Highld 167 P9
Bruar P & K 141 K4
Bruchag Ag & B 124 E6
Bruera Ches W 69 M2
Bruern Abbey Oxon 47 Q10
Bruichladdich Ag & B 122 C7
Bruisyard Suffk 65 L8
Bruisyard Street Suffk 65 L8
Brumby N Linc 92 E9
Brund Staffs 71 L2
Brundall Norfk 77 L10
Brundish Suffk 65 K8
Brundish Street Suffk 65 K7
Brunery Highld 138 C3
Brunnion Cnwll 2 E6
Brunslow Shrops 56 F8
Brunswick Village N u Ty 113 K6
Bruntcliffe Leeds 90 H5
Brunthwaite C Brad 96 G11
Bruntingthorpe Leics 60 D3
Brunton Fife 135 J3
Brunton Nthumb 119 P6
Brunton Wilts 21 P3
Brushford Devon 17 M10
Brushford Somset 18 B9
Bruton Somset 20 C7
Bryan's Green Worcs 58 C11
Bryanston Dorset 12 E3
Bryant's Bottom Bucks 35 N5
Brydekirk D & G 110 C6
Bryher IoS 2 b2
Brymbo Wrexhm 69 J4
Brympton Somset 19 P11
Bryn Carmth 28 F4
Bryn Ches W 82 D10
Bryn Neath 29 M6
Bryn Shrops 56 D7
Bryn Wigan 82 C4
Brynamman Carmth 29 K2
Brynberian Pembks 41 M3
Brynbryddan Neath 29 L6
Bryn-bwbach Gwynd 67 L7
Bryncae Rhondd 30 C8
Bryncethin Brdgnd 29 P8
Bryncir Gwynd 66 H6
Bryn-côch Neath 29 K5
Bryncroes Gwynd 66 C8
Bryncrug Gwynd 54 E4
Bryn Du IoA 78 E10
Bryn-Eden Gwynd 67 N9
Bryneglwys Denbgs 68 F5
Brynfields Wrexhm 69 K6
Brynford Flints 80 H10
Bryn Gates Wigan 82 C4
Bryn Golau Rhondd 30 D7
Bryngwran IoA 78 F9
Bryngwyn Mons 31 L3
Bryngwyn Powys 44 H5
Bryn-Henllan Pembks 41 K3
Brynhoffnant Cerdgn 42 F4
Bryning Lancs 88 E5
Brynithel Blae G 30 H4
Brynmawr Blae G 30 G2
Bryn-mawr Gwynd 66 C8
Brynmenyn Brdgnd 29 P8
Brynmill Swans 28 H6
Brynna Rhondd 30 C8
Bryn-penarth Powys 55 Q4
Brynrefail Gwynd 67 K2
Brynrefail IoA 78 H7
Brynsadler Rhondd 30 D8
Bryn Saith Marchog Denbgs 68 E4
Brynsiencyn IoA 78 H11
Brynteg IoA 78 H8
Bryn-y-bal Flints 69 J2
Bryn-y-Maen Conwy 79 Q9
Bryn-yr-Eos Wrexhm 69 J6
Bualintur Highld 144 F3
Buarth-draw Flints 80 H9
Bubbenhall Warwks 59 N10
Bubwith E R Yk 92 B3
Buccleuch Border 117 L8
Buchanan Smithy Stirlg 132 F10
Buchanhaven Abers 159 R8
Buchanty P & K 133 Q2
Buchany Stirlg 133 L7
Buchlyvie Stirlg 132 H9
Buckabank Cumb 110 G11
Buckden Cambs 61 Q7
Buckden N York 96 D5
Buckenham Norfk 77 M10
Buckerell Devon 10 C4
Buckfast Devon 7 J5
Buckfastleigh Devon 7 J5
Buckhaven Fife 135 K8
Buckholt Mons 45 Q11
Buckhorn Devon 5 P2
Buckhorn Weston Dorset 20 E10
Buckhurst Hill Essex 37 K2
Buckie Moray 158 B4
Buckingham Bucks 49 J8
Buckland Bucks 35 N2
Buckland Devon 6 H10
Buckland Gloucs 47 L7
Buckland Hants 13 P5
Buckland Herts 51 J4
Buckland Kent 27 P3
Buckland Oxon 34 B5
Buckland Surrey 36 F10
Buckland Brewer Devon 16 G7
Buckland Common Bucks 35 P3
Buckland Dinham Somset 20 E4
Buckland Filleigh Devon 16 H10
Buckland in the Moor Devon 7 J4
Buckland Monachorum Devon 6 D5
Buckland Newton Dorset 11 P3
Buckland Ripers Dorset 11 P8
Buckland St Mary Somset 10 F2
Buckland-Tout-Saints Devon 7 K9
Bucklebury W Berk 34 G10
Bucklers Hard Hants 14 D6
Bucklesham Suffk 53 M3
Buckley Flints 69 J2
Buckley Green Warwks 59 J11
Bucklow Hill Ches E 82 F8
Buckminster Leics 73 M6
Bucknall C Stke 70 G5
Bucknall Lincs 86 G7
Bucknell Oxon 48 G9
Bucknell Shrops 56 F10
Buckpool Moray 158 B4
Bucksburn C Aber 151 M6
Buck's Cross Devon 16 F7
Bucks Green W Susx 24 C4
Buckshaw Village Lancs 88 H6
Bucks Hill Herts 50 C10
Bucks Horn Oak Hants 23 M6
Buck's Mills Devon 16 F7
Buckton E R Yk 99 P6
Buckton Herefs 56 F10
Buckton Nthumb 119 L3
Buckworth Cambs 61 P5
Budby Notts 85 K7
Buddileigh Staffs 70 C5
Bude Cnwll 16 C10
Budge's Shop Cnwll 5 N10
Budlake Devon 9 N4
Budle Nthumb 119 N3
Budleigh Salterton Devon 9 Q8
Budlett's Common E Susx 25 L6
Budock Water Cnwll 3 K7
Buerton Ches E 70 B6
Bugbrooke Nhants 60 E9
Bugford Devon 7 L8
Buglawton Ches E 70 F2
Bugle Cnwll 4 G10
Bugley Dorset 20 E10
Bugthorpe E R Yk 98 F9
Buildwas Shrops 57 L4
Builth Road Powys 44 E4
Builth Wells Powys 44 E4
Bulbourne Herts 35 P2
Bulbridge Wilts 21 L8
Bulby Lincs 73 R5
Bulford Wilts 21 N6
Bulford Camp Wilts 21 N6
Bulkeley Ches E 69 P4
Bulkington Warwks 59 N7
Bulkington Wilts 20 H3
Bulkworthy Devon 16 F9
Bullamoor N York 97 N2
Bull Bay IoA 78 G6
Bullbridge Derbys 84 E10
Bullbrook Br For 35 N11
Bullen's Green Herts 50 F9
Bulley Gloucs 46 E11
Bullgill Cumb 100 E3
Bullinghope Herefs 45 Q7
Bullington Hants 22 E6
Bullington Lincs 86 E5
Bullockstone Kent 39 L8
Bull's Green Herts 50 G7
Bull's Green Norfk 65 N3
Bulmer Essex 52 D3
Bulmer N York 98 D7
Bulmer Tye Essex 52 D4
Bulphan Thurr 37 P3
Bulstone Devon 10 D7
Bulstrode Herts 50 B10
Bulverhythe E Susx 26 C10
Bulwark Abers 159 M8
Bulwell C Nott 72 E2
Bulwick Nhants 61 L2
Bumble's Green Essex 51 K9
Bunacaimb Highld 145 L10
Bunarkaig Highld 146 F10
Bunbury Ches E 69 Q3
Bunbury Heath Ches E 69 Q3
Bunchrew Highld 155 R8
Buncton W Susx 24 D8
Bundalloch Highld 145 Q2
Bunessan Ag & B 137 K11
Bungay Suffk 65 L4
Bunker's Hill Lincs 87 J10
Bunnahabhain Ag & B 122 F5
Bunny Notts 72 F5
Buntait Highld 155 M11
Buntingford Herts 51 J5
Bunwell Norfk 64 G3
Bunwell Hill Norfk 64 G3
Bupton Derbys 71 N7
Burbage Derbys 83 M10
Burbage Leics 59 P6
Burbage Wilts 21 P2
Burcher Herefs 45 L2
Burchett's Green E Susx 25 Q4
Burchett's Green W & M 35 M8
Burcombe Wilts 21 L8
Burcot Oxon 34 G5
Burcot Worcs 58 E10
Burcote Shrops 57 N5
Burcott Bucks 49 M11
Burcott Bucks 49 N10
Burdale N York 98 H8
Bures Essex 52 F5
Burford Oxon 33 Q2
Burford Shrops 57 K11
Burg Ag & B 137 K6
Burgate Suffk 64 F6
Burgates Hants 23 L9
Burge End Herts 50 D4
Burgess Hill W Susx 24 H7
Burgh Suffk 65 J11
Burgh by Sands Cumb 110 F9
Burgh Castle Norfk 77 P10
Burghclere Hants 22 E2
Burghead Moray 157 L4
Burghfield W Berk 35 J11
Burghfield Common W Berk 35 J11
Burgh Heath Surrey 36 F9
Burgh Hill E Susx 26 B6
Burghill Herefs 45 P6
Burgh Island Devon 6 G10
Burgh le Marsh Lincs 87 P7
Burgh next Aylsham Norfk 77 J6
Burgh on Bain Lincs 86 H3
Burgh St Margaret Norfk 77 N9
Burgh St Peter Norfk 65 P3
Burghwallis Donc 91 N8
Burham Kent 38 B9
Buriton Hants 23 K11
Burland Ches E 69 R4
Burlawn Cnwll 4 F7
Burleigh Gloucs 32 G4
Burlescombe Devon 18 E11
Burleston Dorset 12 C6
Burlestone Devon 7 L9
Burley Hants 13 M4
Burley Rutlnd 73 M8
Burley Shrops 56 H8
Burleydam Ches E 69 R6
Burley Gate Herefs 46 A5
Burley in Wharfedale C Brad 97 J11
Burley Lawn Hants 13 M4
Burley Street Hants 13 M4
Burley Wood Head C Brad 90 F2
Burlingham Green Norfk 77 M9
Burlingjobb Powys 45 K3
Burlington Shrops 57 P2
Burlton Shrops 69 N9
Burmarsh Kent 27 K5
Burmington Warwks 47 Q7
Burn N York 91 P5
Burnage Manch 83 J6
Burnaston Derbys 71 P8
Burnbanks Cumb 101 P7
Burnbrae N Lans 126 F6
Burn Bridge N York 97 L10
Burnby E R Yk 98 G11
Burn Cross Sheff 91 J11
Burndell W Susx 15 Q6
Burnden Bolton 89 L9
Burnedge Rochdl 89 Q8
Burneside Cumb 101 P11
Burneston N York 97 M4
Burnett BaNES 32 C11
Burnfoot Border 117 N8
Burnfoot Border 117 Q7
Burnfoot D & G 109 L2
Burnfoot D & G 110 F3
Burnfoot D & G 117 M11
Burnfoot P & K 134 B7
Burnham Bucks 35 P8
Burnham N Linc 93 J7
Burnham Deepdale Norfk 75 R2
Burnham Green Herts 50 G7
Burnham Market Norfk 76 A3
Burnham Norton Norfk 76 A3
Burnham-on-Crouch Essex 38 F2
Burnham-on-Sea Somset 19 K5
Burnham Overy Norfk 76 A3
Burnham Overy Staithe Norfk 76 A3
Burnham Thorpe Norfk 76 B3
Burnhead D & G 116 B11
Burnhervie Abers 151 J4
Burnhill Green Staffs 57 P4
Burnhope Dur 113 J11
Burnhouse N Ayrs 125 K7
Burniston N York 99 L2
Burnley Lancs 89 N4
Burnley Crematorium Lancs 89 N4
Burnmouth Border 129 P7
Burn Naze Lancs 88 C2
Burn of Cambus Stirlg 133 L7
Burnopfield Dur 113 J9
Burnrigg Cumb 111 J9
Burnsall N York 96 F8
Burnside Angus 142 G6
Burnside Angus 143 J7
Burnside Fife 134 F6
Burnside Moray 157 M4
Burnside W Loth 127 K2
Burnside of Duntrune Angus 142 G11
Burntcommon Surrey 36 B10
Burntheath Derbys 71 N8
Burnt Heath Essex 53 J6
Burnt Hill W Berk 34 G10
Burnthouse Cnwll 3 K6
Burnt Houses Dur 103 M6
Burntisland Fife 134 G10
Burnt Oak E Susx 25 M5
Burnton E Ayrs 115 J6
Burntwood Staffs 58 G3
Burntwood Green Staffs 58 G3
Burnt Yates N York 97 L8
Burnworthy Somset 18 G11
Burpham Surrey 36 B10
Burpham W Susx 24 B9
Burradon N Tyne 113 L6
Burradon Nthumb 119 J9
Burrafirth Shet 169 t2
Burras Cnwll 2 H7
Burraton Cnwll 5 Q8
Burravoe Shet 169 s5
Burrells Cumb 102 C7
Burrelton P & K 142 C10
Burridge Devon 10 G3
Burridge Devon 17 K4
Burridge Hants 14 F4
Burrill N York 97 K3
Burringham N Linc 92 D9
Burrington Devon 17 L8
Burrington Herefs 56 G10
Burrington N Som 19 N3
Burrough End Cambs 63 K9
Burrough Green Cambs 63 K9
Burrough on the Hill Leics 73 K8
Burrow Lancs 95 N6
Burrow Somset 18 B6
Burrow Bridge Somset 19 L8
Burrowhill Surrey 23 Q2
Burrows Cross Surrey 36 C11
Burry Swans 28 E6
Burry Green Swans 28 E6
Burry Port Carmth 28 D4
Burscough Lancs 88 E8
Burscough Bridge Lancs 88 E8
Bursea E R Yk 92 D4
Burshill E R Yk 99 M11
Bursledon Hants 14 E5
Burslem C Stke 70 F5
Burstall Suffk 53 J3
Burstock Dorset 11 J4
Burston Norfk 64 G5
Burston Staffs 70 G8
Burstow Surrey 24 H2
Burstwick E R Yk 93 M5
Burtersett N York 96 C3
Burtholme Cumb 111 K8
Burthorpe Green Suffk 63 N8
Burthwaite Cumb 110 H11
Burthy Cnwll 4 E10
Burtle Hill Somset 19 L6
Burtoft Lincs 74 E3
Burton Ches W 69 P2
Burton Ches W 81 L10
Burton Dorset 11 P6
Burton Dorset 13 L6
Burton Nthumb 119 N4
Burton Pembks 41 J9
Burton Somset 11 L2
Burton Somset 18 G6
Burton Wilts 20 F8
Burton Wilts 32 F9
Burton Agnes E R Yk 99 N8
Burton Bradstock Dorset 11 K7
Burton-by-Lincoln Lincs 86 C6
Burton Coggles Lincs 73 P5
Burton Dassett Warwks 48 C4
Burton End Essex 51 M6
Burton End Suffk 63 L11
Burton Fleming E R Yk 99 M6
Burton Green Warwks 59 L9
Burton Green Wrexhm 69 K3
Burton Hastings Warwks 59 P7
Burton-in-Kendal Cumb 95 L5
Burton-in-Kendal Services Cumb 95 L5
Burton in Lonsdale N York 95 P6
Burton Joyce Notts 72 G2
Burton Latimer Nhants 61 K6
Burton Lazars Leics 73 K7
Burton Leonard N York 97 M8
Burton on the Wolds Leics 72 F6
Burton Overy Leics 72 H11
Burton Pedwardine Lincs 74 B2
Burton Pidsea E R Yk 93 M4
Burton Salmon N York 91 M5
Burton's Green Essex 52 D6
Burton upon Stather N Linc 92 E7
Burton upon Trent Staffs 71 N10
Burton Waters Lincs 86 B6
Burtonwood Warrtn 82 C6
Burtonwood Services Warrtn 82 C6
Burwardsley Ches W 69 P3
Burwarton Shrops 57 L7
Burwash E Susx 25 Q6
Burwash Common E Susx 25 P6
Burwash Weald E Susx 25 Q6
Burwell Cambs 63 J7
Burwell Lincs 87 L5
Burwen IoA 78 G6
Burwick Ork 169 d8
Bury Bury 89 N8
Bury Cambs 62 C4
Bury Somset 18 B9
Bury W Susx 24 B8
Bury End C Beds 50 D3
Bury Green Herts 51 L6
Bury St Edmunds Suffk 64 B9
Burythorpe N York 98 F8
Busby E Rens 125 P6
Busby Stoop N York 97 N4
Buscot Oxon 33 P5
Bush Abers 143 P4
Bush Cnwll 16 C10
Bush Bank Herefs 45 P4
Bushbury Wolves 58 D4
Bushbury Crematorium Wolves 58 D4
Bushby Leics 72 H10
Bushey Herts 50 D11
Bushey Heath Herts 36 D2
Bush Green Norfk 65 J4
Bush Green Suffk 64 C10
Bush Hill Park Gt Lon 50 H11
Bushley Worcs 46 G8
Bushley Green Worcs 46 G8
Bushmead Bed 61 P8
Bushmoor Shrops 56 G7
Bushton Wilts 33 L9
Busk Cumb 102 B2
Buslingthorpe Lincs 86 E3
Bussage Gloucs 32 G4
Bussex Somset 19 L7
Butcher's Cross E Susx 25 N5
Butcombe N Som 19 P2
Bute Ag & B 124 C4
Butleigh Somset 19 P8
Butleigh Wootton Somset 19 P7
Butler's Cross Bucks 35 M3
Butler's Hill Notts 84 H11
Butlers Marston Warwks 48 B4
Butley Suffk 65 M11
Butley High Corner Suffk 53 Q2
Buttercrambe N York 98 E9
Butterdean Border 129 K7
Butterknowle Dur 103 M5
Butterleigh Devon 9 N3
Butterley Derbys 84 F10
Buttermere Cumb 100 G7
Buttermere Wilts 22 B2
Butters Green Staffs 70 E4
Buttershaw C Brad 90 E5
Butterstone P & K 141 Q8
Butterton Staffs 70 E6
Butterton Staffs 71 K3
Butterwick Dur 104 C4
Butterwick Lincs 87 L11
Butterwick N York 98 E5
Butterwick N York 99 K6
Butt Green Ches E 70 B4
Buttington Powys 56 C3

Buttonbridge Shrops 57 N9
Buttonoak Shrops 57 P9
Buttsash Hants 14 D5
Buttsbear Cross Cnwll ..16 D11
Butt's Green Essex 52 C11
Buxhall Suffk 64 E10
Buxhall Fen Street Suffk ..64 E10
Buxted E Susx 25 L6
Buxton Derbys 83 N10
Buxton Norfk 77 J7
Buxworth Derbys 83 M8
Bwlch Powys 44 H10
Bwlchgwyn Wrexhm 69 J4
Bwlchllan Cerdgn 43 L3
Bwlchnewydd Carmth ..42 C10
Bwlchtocyn Gwynd 66 E9
Bwlch-y-cibau Powys ..68 G11
Bwlch-y-Ddar Powys 68 G10
Bwlchyfadfa Cerdgn 42 H5
Bwlch-y-ffridd Powys 55 P5
Bwlch-y-groes Pembks ..41 P3
Bwlchymyrdd Swans 28 G5
Bwlch-y-sarnau Powys ..55 N10
Byermoor Gatesd 113 J9
Byers Green Dur 103 P4
Byfield Nhants 48 F4
Byfleet Surrey 36 C8
Byford Herefs 45 M6
Bygrave Herts 50 G3
Byker N u Ty 113 L8
Byland Abbey N York ..98 A5
Bylaugh Norfk 76 E8
Bylchau Conwy 68 C2
Byley Ches W 82 F11
Bynea Carmth 28 F5
Byrness Nthumb 118 E10
Bystock Devon 9 P8
Bythorn Cambs 61 N5
Byton Herefs 45 M2
Bywell Nthumb 112 F8
Byworth W Susx 23 Q10

C

Cabbacott Devon 16 G7
Cabourne Lincs 93 K10
Cabrach Ag & B 122 G7
Cabrach Moray 150 B2
Cabus Lancs 95 K11
Cackle Street E Susx 25 L5
Cackle Street E Susx 25 Q7
Cackle Street E Susx 26 D8
Cadbury Devon 9 M3
Cadbury Barton Devon ..17 M8
Cadbury World Birm 58 F8
Cadder E Duns 125 Q3
Caddington C Beds 50 C7
Caddonfoot Border 117 P3
Cadeby Donc 91 N10
Cadeby Leics 72 C10
Cadeleigh Devon 9 M3
Cade Street E Susx 25 P6
Cadgwith Cnwll 3 J11
Cadham Fife 134 H7
Cadishead Salfd 82 F6
Cadle Swans 28 H5
Cadley Lancs 88 G4
Cadley Wilts 21 P4
Cadley Wilts 33 P11
Cadmore End Bucks 35 L6
Cadnam Hants 13 P2
Cadney N Linc 92 H10
Cadole Flints 68 H2
Cadoxton V Glam 30 F11
Cadoxton Juxta-Neath
  Neath 29 L5
Cadwst Denbgs 68 D7
Caeathro Gwynd 67 J2
Caehopkin Powys 29 M2
Caenby Lincs 86 C3
Caeo Carmth 43 N6
Caerau Brdgnd 29 N6
Caerau Cardif 30 F9
Cae'r-bont Powys 29 M2
Cae'r bryn Carmth 28 G2
Caerdeon Gwynd 67 M11
Caer Farchell Pembks ..40 E5
Caergeiliog IoA 78 E9
Caergwrle Flints 69 K3
Caerhun Conwy 79 P10
Caerlanrig Border 117 M10
Caerleon Newpt 31 K6
Caernarfon Gwynd 66 H2
Caernarfon Castle
  Gwynd 66 H2
Caerphilly Caerph 30 G7
Caersws Powys 55 N6
Caerwedros Cerdgn 42 G3
Caerwent Mons 31 N6
Caerwys Flints 80 G10
Caerynwch Gwynd 67 P11
Caggle Street Mons 45 M11
Caim IoA 79 L8
Cairinis W Isls 168 d11
Cairnbaan Ag & B 130 G9
Cairnbulg Abers 159 P4
Cairncross Border 129 M7
Cairncurran Inver 125 J3
Cairndow Ag & B 131 P5
Cairneyhill Fife 134 C10
Cairngarroch D & G 106 E8
Cairngorms National
  Park 149 K7
Cairnie Abers 158 C9
Cairnorrie Abers 159 L9
Cairnryan D & G 106 E4
Cairnty Moray 157 Q7
Caister-on-Sea Norfk ..77 Q9
Caistor Lincs 93 K10
Caistor St Edmund Norfk ..77 J11
Cakebole Worcs 58 C10
Cake Street Norfk 64 F3
Calais Street Suffk 52 G4
Calanais W Isls 168 h4
Calbourne IoW 14 D9
Calceby Lincs 87 L5
Calcot Flints 80 H10
Calcot Gloucs 33 L2
Calcot W Berk 35 J10
Calcots Moray 157 P5
Calcott Kent 39 L9
Calcott Shrops 56 G2
Calcutt N York 97 M9
Calcutt Wilts 33 M6
Caldbeck Cumb 101 K2
Caldbergh N York 96 G3
Caldecote Cambs 61 P3

Caldecote Cambs 62 D9
Caldecote Herts 50 F3
Caldecote Nhants 49 J4
Caldecote Highfields
  Cambs 62 E9
Caldecott Nhants 61 L7
Caldecott Oxon 34 E5
Caldecott Rutlnd 61 J2
Caldecotte M Keyn 49 N7
Calder Cumb 100 D10
Calderbank N Lans 126 D5
Calder Bridge Cumb ..100 D9
Calderbrook Rochdl 89 Q7
Caldercruix N Lans 126 E4
Calder Grove Wakefd ..91 J7
Caldermill S Lans 126 B9
Calder Vale Lancs 95 L11
Calderwood S Lans 126 B6
Caldey Island Pembks ..41 M11
Caldicot Mons 31 N7
Caldmore Wsall 58 F5
Caldwell N York 103 N8
Caldy Wirral 81 J7
Caledfwlch Carmth 43 N9
Calenick Cnwll 3 L5
Calf of Man IoM 80 a8
Calford Green Suffk 63 M11
Calfsound Ork 169 e3
Calgary Ag & B 137 K5
Califer Moray 157 K6
California Falk 126 G2
California Norfk 77 Q8
California Cross Devon ..7 J8
Calke Derbys 72 B6
Calke Abbey Derbys 72 B6
Callakille Highld 153 M6
Callaly Nthumb 119 J6
Callander Stirlg 133 J6
Callanish W Isls 168 h4
Callaughton Shrops 57 L5
Callerton N u Ty 113 J7
Callestick Cnwll 3 K3
Calligarry Highld 145 K2
Callington Cnwll 5 P8
Callingwood Staffs 71 M10
Callow Herefs 45 P8
Callow End Worcs 46 F4
Callow Hill Wilts 33 K8
Callow Hill Worcs 47 K2
Callow Hill Worcs 57 N10
Callows Grave Worcs ..57 K11
Calmore Hants 13 P2
Calmsden Gloucs 33 K3
Calne Wilts 33 J10
Calow Derbys 84 F6
Calshot Hants 14 E6
Calstock Cnwll 6 C5
Calstone Wellington
  Wilts 33 K11
Calthorpe Norfk 76 H5
Calthorpe Street Norfk ..77 N6
Calthwaite Cumb 101 N2
Calton N York 96 D9
Calton Staffs 71 L5
Calveley Ches E 69 Q3
Calver Derbys 84 B6
Calverhall Shrops 69 R7
Calver Hill Herefs 45 M5
Calverleigh Devon 9 M2
Calverley Leeds 90 G3
Calver Sough Derbys ..84 B6
Calvert Bucks 49 J10
Calverton M Keyn 49 L7
Calverton Notts 85 K11
Calvine P & K 141 K4
Calvo Cumb 109 P10
Calzeat Border 116 G3
Cam Gloucs 32 E5
Camasachoirce Highld ..138 D5
Camasine Highld 138 D5
Camas Luinie Highld ..146 A2
Camastianavaig Highld ..153 J10
Camault Muir Highld ..155 P9
Camber E Susx 26 G8
Camberley Surrey 23 N2
Camberwell Gt Lon 36 H5
Camblesforth N York ..91 Q5
Cambo Nthumb 112 F3
Cambois Nthumb 113 M4
Camborne Cnwll 2 G5
Camborne & Redruth
  Mining District Cnwll ..2 G5
Cambourne Cambs 62 D9
Cambridge Cambs 62 G9
Cambridge Gloucs 32 D4
Cambridge Airport
  Cambs 62 G9
Cambridge City
  Crematorium Cambs ..62 E8
Cambrose Cnwll 2 H4
Cambus Clacks 133 P9
Cambusavie Platform
  Highld 162 H7
Cambusbarron Stirlg ..133 M9
Cambuskenneth Stirlg ..133 N9
Cambuslang S Lans 125 Q5
Cambus o' May Abers ..150 C8
Cambuswallace S Lans ..116 E3
Camden Town Gt Lon ..36 G4
Cameley BaNES 20 B3
Camelford Cnwll 5 L5
Camelon Falk 133 P11
Camerory Highld 157 J11
Camer's Green Worcs ..46 E7
Camerton BaNES 20 C3
Camerton Cumb 100 D4
Camghouran P & K 140 E6
Camieston Border 117 R4
Cammachmore Abers ..151 N8
Cammeringham Lincs ..86 B4
Camore Highld 162 H9
Campbeltown Ag & B ..120 D7
Campbeltown Airport
  Ag & B 120 C7
Camperdown N Tyne ..113 L6
Cample D & G 109 J2
Campmuir P & K 142 C10
Camps W Loth 127 K4
Campsall Donc 91 N8
Campsea Ash Suffk 65 L10
Camps End Cambs 51 P2
Campton C Beds 50 D3
Camptown Border 118 C8
Camrose Pembks 40 H6
Camserney P & K 141 K8
Camusnagaul Highld ..139 K3
Camusnagaul Highld ..160 H9
Camusteel Highld 153 N9
Camusterrach Highld ..153 N9
Canada Hants 21 Q11
Canal Foot Cumb 94 G5

Canaston Bridge Pembks ..41 L7
Candacraig Abers 149 Q6
Candlesby Lincs 87 N7
Candle Street Suffk 64 E7
Candover Green Shrops ..57 J3
Candy Mill Border 116 F2
Cane End Oxon 35 J9
Canewdon Essex 38 F3
Canford Bottom Dorset ..12 H4
Canford Cliffs Poole 13 J7
Canford Crematorium
  Bristl 31 Q9
Canford Heath Poole 12 H6
Canford Magna Poole ..12 H5
Canhams Green Suffk ..64 F8
Canisbay Highld 167 P2
Cankley Covtry 59 M9
Canley Crematorium
  Covtry 59 M9
Cann Dorset 20 G10
Canna Highld 144 B6
Cann Common Dorset ..20 G10
Cannington Somset 19 J7
Canning Town Gt Lon ..37 K4
Cannock Staffs 58 E2
Cannock Chase Staffs ..70 H11
Cannock Wood Staffs ..58 F2
Cannon Bridge Herefs ..45 N6
Canonbie D & G 110 G5
Canon Frome Herefs 46 B6
Canon Pyon Herefs 45 P5
Canons Ashby Nhants ..48 G4
Canonstown Cnwll 2 E6
Canterbury Kent 39 K10
Canterbury Cathedral
  Kent 39 L10
Cantley Norfk 77 M11
Cantlop Shrops 57 J3
Canton Cardif 30 G9
Cantraywood Highld ..156 D9
Cantsfield Lancs 95 N6
Canvey Island Essex 38 C5
Canwick Lincs 86 C7
Canworthy Water Cnwll ..5 L3
Caol Highld 139 L2
Caolas Scalpaigh W Isls ..168 h8
Caoles Ag & B 136 D6
Caonich Highld 146 D9
Capel Kent 25 P2
Capel Surrey 24 E2
Capel Bangor Cerdgn ..54 F8
Capel Betws Lleucu
  Cerdgn 43 M3
Capel Coch IoA 78 H8
Capel Curig Conwy 67 N3
Capel Cynon Cerdgn ..42 G5
Capel Dewi Carmth 43 J10
Capel Dewi Cerdgn 43 J6
Capel-Dewi Cerdgn 54 E8
Capel Garmon Conwy ..67 Q3
Capel Green Suffk 53 Q2
Capel Gwyn Carmth 43 J10
Capel Gwyn IoA 78 E9
Capel Gwynfe Carmth ..43 P10
Capel Hendre Carmth ..28 G2
Capel Isaac Carmth 43 L9
Capel Iwan Carmth 41 Q3
Capel-le-Ferne Kent 27 N4
Capelles Guern 10 C1
Capel Llanilltern Cardif ..30 E9
Capel Mawr IoA 78 G10
Capel Parc IoA 78 G7
Capel St Andrew Suffk ..53 Q2
Capel St Mary Suffk 53 J4
Capel Seion Cerdgn 54 E9
Capel Trisant Cerdgn ..54 G9
Capeluchaf Gwynd 66 G5
Capelulo Conwy 79 N9
Capel-y-ffin Powys 45 K8
Capel-y-graig Gwynd ..79 J11
Capenhurst Ches W 81 M10
Capernwray Lancs 95 L6
Cape Wrath Highld 164 G1
Capheaton Nthumb 112 H4
Caplaw E Rens 125 L6
Capon's Green Suffk 65 K8
Cappercleuch Border ..117 J6
Capstone Medway 38 C8
Capton Devon 7 L8
Capton Somset 18 E7
Caputh P & K 141 Q9
Caradon Mining
  District Cnwll 5 M7
Caradon Town Cnwll 5 M7
Carbeth Inn Stirlg 125 N2
Carbis Cnwll 4 G10
Carbis Bay Cnwll 2 E6
Carbost Highld 152 F11
Carbost Highld 152 G8
Carbrook Sheff 84 E3
Carbrooke Norfk 76 C11
Carburton Notts 85 K6
Carclaze Cnwll 3 Q3
Car Colston Notts 73 J2
Carcroft Donc 91 N9
Cardenden Fife 134 G8
Cardeston Shrops 56 F2
Cardewlees Cumb 110 G10
Cardiff Cardif 30 G9
Cardiff Airport V Glam ..30 E11
Cardiff & Glamorgan
  Crematorium Cardif ..30 G8
Cardiff Gate Services
  Cardif 30 H8
Cardiff West Services
  Cardif 30 E9
Cardigan Cerdgn 42 C5
Cardinal's Green Cambs ..63 K11
Cardington Bed 61 N11
Cardington Shrops 57 J5
Cardinham Cnwll 5 J8
Cardrain D & G 106 F11
Cardross Ag & B 125 J2
Cardross Crematorium
  Ag & B 125 J2
Cardryne D & G 106 F11
Cardurnock Cumb 110 C9
Careby Lincs 73 Q7
Careston Angus 143 J5
Carew Pembks 41 K10
Carew Cheriton Pembks ..41 K10
Carew Newton Pembks ..41 K10
Carey Herefs 45 R8
Carfin N Lans 126 D6
Carfraemill Border 128 E9
Cargate Green Norfk 77 M9
Cargenbridge D & G 109 L6

Cargill P & K 142 B10
Cargo Cumb 110 G9
Cargreen Cnwll 6 C9
Cargurrel Cnwll 3 M6
Carham Nthumb 118 E3
Carhampton Somset 18 D6
Carharrack Cnwll 3 J5
Carie P & K 140 F6
Carinish W Isls 168 d11
Carisbrooke IoW 14 E9
Cark Cumb 94 H5
Carkeel Cnwll 5 Q9
Carland Cross Cnwll 3 M3
Carlbury Darltn 103 P7
Carlby Lincs 73 Q8
Carlcroft Nthumb 118 F8
Carlecotes Barns 83 Q4
Carleen Cnwll 2 G7
Carlesmoor N York 97 K6
Carleton Cumb 100 D9
Carleton Cumb 101 P5
Carleton Cumb 110 G10
Carleton Lancs 88 C3
Carleton Wakefd 91 M6
Carleton Crematorium
  Bpool 88 C3
Carleton Forehoe Norfk ..76 F10
Carleton-in-Craven
  N York 96 E11
Carleton Rode Norfk 64 G3
Carleton St Peter Norfk ..77 L11
Carlidnack Cnwll 3 K8
Carlincraig Abers 158 F9
Carlingcott BaNES 20 C3
Carlin How R & Cl 105 K7
Carlisle Cumb 110 H9
Carlisle Airport Cumb ..111 J8
Carlisle Crematorium
  Cumb 110 G10
Carloggas Cnwll 4 D8
Carlops Border 127 M6
Carloway W Isls 168 h3
Carlton Barns 91 K8
Carlton Bed 61 L9
Carlton Cambs 63 K10
Carlton Leeds 91 J5
Carlton Leics 72 B10
Carlton N York 91 Q6
Carlton N York 96 G4
Carlton N York 98 C3
Carlton Notts 72 G2
Carlton S on T 104 C6
Carlton Suffk 65 M9
Carlton Colville Suffk ..65 Q4
Carlton Curlieu Leics ..72 H11
Carlton Green Cambs ..63 K10
Carlton Husthwaite
  N York 97 Q5
Carlton-in-Cleveland
  N York 104 F10
Carlton in Lindrick Notts ..85 J4
Carlton-le-Moorland
  Lincs 86 B9
Carlton Miniott N York ..97 N4
Carlton-on-Trent Notts ..85 N8
Carlton Scroop Lincs ..86 B11
Carluke S Lans 126 E7
Carlyon Bay Cnwll 3 R3
Carmacoup S Lans 115 Q2
Carmarthen Carmth 42 H10
Carmel Carmth 43 L11
Carmel Flints 80 H9
Carmel Gwynd 66 H4
Carmichael S Lans 116 C3
Carmountside
  Crematorium C Stke ..70 G5
Carmunnock C Glas 125 P6
Carmyle C Glas 125 Q5
Carmyllie Angus 143 J9
Carnaby E R Yk 99 N7
Carnbee Fife 135 N6
Carnbo P & K 134 D7
Carn Brea Cnwll 2 H5
Carnbrogie Abers 151 M2
Carndu Highld 145 Q2
Carnduff S Lans 126 B8
Carne Cnwll 3 L5
Carne Cnwll 3 N6
Carne Cnwll 4 F10
Carnell E Ayrs 125 M11
Carnewas Cnwll 4 D8
Carnforth Lancs 95 K6
Carn-gorm Highld 146 B3
Carnhedryn Pembks 40 F5
Carnhell Green Cnwll 2 G6
Carnie Abers 151 L6
Carnkie Cnwll 2 H5
Carnkie Cnwll 3 J7
Carnkiet Cnwll 3 K3
Carno Powys 55 M5
Carnock Fife 134 C10
Carnon Downs Cnwll 3 K5
Carnousie Abers 158 G7
Carnoustie Angus 143 K11
Carnsmerry Cnwll 4 G10
Carnwath S Lans 126 H8
Carnyorth Cnwll 2 B7
Carol Green Solhll 59 L9
Carpalla Cnwll 3 P3
Carperby N York 96 F3
Carr Rothm 84 H2
Carradale Ag & B 120 F4
Carrbridge Highld 148 G3
Carrbrook Tamesd 83 L4
Carrefour Jersey 11 b1
Carreglefn IoA 78 F7
Carr Gate Wakefd 91 J6
Carrhouse N Linc 92 C9
Carrick Ag & B 131 J10
Carrick Castle Ag & B ..131 P9
Carrington Lincs 87 K9
Carrington Mdloth 127 Q5
Carrington Traffd 82 F6
Carrog Conwy 67 P5
Carrog Denbgs 68 F6
Carron Falk 133 P10
Carron Moray 157 N9
Carronbridge D & G 116 B10
Carron Bridge Stirlg ..133 L11
Carronshore Falk 133 P11
Carrow Hill Mons 31 M6
Carr Shield Nthumb 112 B11
Carruth House Inver ..125 K4
Carrutherstown D & G ..109 P6
Carr Vale Derbys 84 G7
Carrville Dur 104 B2
Carsaig Ag & B 137 N11
Carscreugh D & G 107 K5
Carse Gray Angus 143 J6
Carseriggan D & G 107 K4
Carsethorn D & G 109 L9

Carshalton Gt Lon 36 G8
Carsington Derbys 71 P4
Carskey Ag & B 120 C10
Carsluith D & G 107 N7
Carsphairn D & G 115 L9
Carstairs S Lans 126 G8
Carstairs Junction S Lans ..126 H8
Carswell Marsh Oxon ..34 B5
Carter's Clay Hants 22 B10
Carters Green Essex 51 M8
Carterton Oxon 33 Q3
Carterway Heads
  Nthumb 112 F10
Carthew Cnwll 4 G10
Carthorpe N York 97 M4
Cartington Nthumb 119 K10
Cartland S Lans 126 F8
Cartledge Derbys 84 D5
Cartmel Cumb 94 H5
Cartmel Fell Cumb 95 J3
Carway Carmth 28 E3
Carwinley Cumb 110 H6
Cashe's Green Gloucs ..32 F3
Cashmoor Dorset 12 G2
Cassington Oxon 34 E2
Cassop Dur 104 B3
Castallack Cnwll 2 C8
Castel Guern 10 b2
Casterton Cumb 95 N5
Castle Cnwll 4 H10
Castle Acre Norfk 75 R7
Castle Ashby Nhants ..61 J9
Castlebay W Isls 168 b18
Castle Bolton N York ..96 F2
Castle Bromwich Solhll ..58 H7
Castle Bytham Lincs ..73 P7
Castlebythe Pembks 41 K5
Castle Caereinion Powys ..56 B3
Castle Camps Cambs ..51 P2
Castle Carrock Cumb ..111 K10
Castlecary Falk 126 D2
Castle Cary Somset 20 B8
Castle Combe Wilts 32 F9
Castle Donington Leics ..72 C5
Castle Douglas D & G ..108 G8
Castle Eaton Swindn 33 M5
Castle Eden Dur 104 D3
Castle End C Pete 74 B9
Castleford Wakefd 91 L5
Castle Frome Herefs 46 C5
Castle Gate Cnwll 2 D7
Castle Green Cnwll 95 L2
Castle Green Surrey 23 Q2
Castle Gresley Derbys ..71 P11
Castle Hedingham Essex ..52 C4
Castlehill Border 117 J3
Castlehill Highld 167 L3
Castle Hill Kent 25 Q2
Castle Hill Suffk 53 K2
Castle Howard N York ..98 E6
Castle Kennedy D & G ..106 F6
Castle Lachlan Ag & B ..131 L8
Castlemartin Pembks ..40 H11
Castlemilk C Glas 125 P6
Castle Morris Pembks ..40 H4
Castlemorton Worcs ..46 E7
Castlemorton Common
  Worcs 46 E7
Castle O'er D & G 110 D2
Castle Rising Norfk 75 N6
Castleside Dur 112 G11
Castle Stuart Highld ..156 C8
Castlethorpe M Keyn ..49 M6
Castlethorpe N Linc ..92 G9
Castleton Border 111 K3
Castleton Derbys 83 Q8
Castleton N York 105 J9
Castleton Newpt 31 J8
Castleton Rochdl 89 P8
Castletown Ches W 69 M4
Castletown Dorset 11 P10
Castletown Highld 167 L3
Castletown IoM 80 c8
Castletown Sundld 113 N9
Castley N York 97 L11
Caston Norfk 64 D2
Castor C Pete 74 B11
Caswell Bay Swans 28 G7
Catacol N Ayrs 123 R10
Cat and Fiddle Derbys ..83 M10
Catbrain S Glos 31 Q8
Catbrook Mons 31 P4
Catch Flints 81 J10
Catchall Cnwll 2 C8
Catchem's Corner Solhll ..59 L9
Catchgate Dur 113 J10
Catcliffe Rothm 84 F3
Catcomb Wilts 33 K9
Catcott Somset 19 L7
Catcott Burtle Somset ..19 M6
Caterham Surrey 36 H9
Catfield Norfk 77 N7
Catfield Common Norfk ..77 N7
Catford Gt Lon 37 J6
Catforth Lancs 88 F3
Cathcart C Glas 125 P5
Cathedine Powys 44 G9
Catherine-de-Barnes
  Solhll 59 J8
Catherine Slack C Brad ..90 D5
Catherington Hants 15 J4
Catherston Leweston
  Dorset 10 H6
Catherton Shrops 57 M9
Catisfield Hants 14 G5
Catley Herefs 46 C5
Catley Lane Head Rochdl ..89 P7
Catlodge Highld 147 Q9
Catlow Lancs 89 P3
Catlowdy Cumb 111 J5
Catmere End Essex 51 L3
Catmore W Berk 34 E8
Caton Devon 7 K4
Caton Lancs 95 L8
Caton Green Lancs 95 M7
Cator Court Devon 8 G9
Catrine E Ayrs 115 K2
Cat's Ash Newpt 31 L6
Catsfield E Susx 26 B9
Catsfield Stream E Susx ..26 B9
Catsgore Somset 19 P9
Catsham Somset 19 Q8
Catshill Worcs 58 E10
Catstree Shrops 57 N5
Cattadale Ag & B 120 C9
Cattal N York 97 P10
Cattawade Suffk 53 K5
Catterall Lancs 88 F2

Catteralslane – Church End 263

Catteralslane Shrops 69 Q6
Catterick N York 103 P11
Catterick Bridge N York 103 P11
Catterick Garrison N York 103 N11
Catterlen Cumb 101 N4
Catterline Abers 143 R2
Catterton N York 97 R11
Catteshall Surrey 23 Q6
Catthorpe Leics 60 C5
Cattishall Suffk 64 B8
Cattistock Dorset 11 M5
Catton N York 97 N5
Catton Nthumb 112 B9
Catwick E R Yk 99 N11
Catworth Cambs 61 N6
Caudle Green Gloucs 32 H2
Caulcott C Beds 50 B2
Caulcott Oxon 48 F10
Cauldcots Angus 143 M8
Cauldhame Stirlg 133 J9
Cauldmill Border 117 Q7
Cauldon Staffs 71 K5
Cauldon Lowe Staffs 71 K5
Cauldwell Derbys 71 P11
Caulkerbush D & G 109 K9
Caulside D & G 110 H4
Caundle Marsh Dorset 11 P2
Caunsall Worcs 58 C8
Caunton Notts 85 M8
Causeway Hants 23 K10
Causeway End Cumb 95 K3
Causeway End D & G 107 M6
Causeway End Essex 51 Q7
Causewayend S Lans 116 E3
Causewayhead Cumb 109 P10
Causewayhead Stirlg 133 N8
Causeyend Abers 151 N4
Causey Park Nthumb 113 J2
Causey Park Bridge Nthumb 113 J2
Cavendish Suffk 63 P11
Cavenham Suffk 63 N6
Caversfield Oxon 48 G9
Caversham Readg 35 K10
Caverswall Staffs 70 H6
Caverton Mill Border 118 D5
Cavil E R Yk 92 C4
Cawdor Highld 156 E7
Cawkwell Lincs 87 J5
Cawood N York 91 P3
Cawsand Cnwll 6 C8
Cawston Norfk 76 G7
Cawston Warwks 59 Q10
Cawthorn N York 98 F3
Cawthorne Barns 90 H9
Cawton N York 98 C5
Caxton Cambs 62 D9
Caxton End Cambs 62 D9
Caxton Gibbet Cambs 62 C8
Caynham Shrops 57 K10
Caythorpe Lincs 86 B11
Caythorpe Notts 85 L11
Cayton N York 99 M4
Ceann a Bhaigh W Isls 168 c11
Ceannacroc Lodge Highld 146 G5
Cearsiadar W Isls 168 i5
Ceciliford Mons 31 P4
Cefn Newpt 31 J7
Cefn Berain Conwy 80 D11
Cefn-brîth Conwy 68 B4
Cefn-bryn-brain Carmth 29 K2
Cefn Byrle Powys 29 M2
Cefn Canel Powys 68 H8
Cefn Coch Powys 68 F9
Cefn-coed-y-cymmer Myr Td 30 D3
Cefn Cribwr Brdgnd 29 N8
Cefn Cross Brdgnd 29 N8
Cefn-ddwysarn Gwynd 68 C7
Cefn-Einion Shrops 56 D7
Cefneithin Carmth 28 G2
Cefngorwydd Powys 44 C5
Cefn-mawr Wrexhm 69 J6
Cefnpennar Rhondd 30 D4
Cefn-y-bedd Flints 69 K3
Cefn-y-pant Carmth 41 N5
Ceint IoA 78 H9
Cellan Cerdgn 43 M5
Cellardyke Fife 135 P7
Cellarhead Staffs 70 H5
Celleron Cumb 101 N5
Celynen Caerph 30 H5
Cemaes IoA 78 F6
Cemmaes Powys 55 J3
Cemmaes Road Powys 55 J4
Cenarth Cerdgn 41 Q2
Cerbyd Pembks 40 F5
Ceres Fife 135 L5
Cerne Abbas Dorset 11 P4
Cerney Wick Gloucs 33 L5
Cerrigceinwen IoA 78 G10
Cerrigydrudion Conwy 68 C5
Cess Norfk 77 N8
Ceunant Gwynd 67 J2
Chaceley Gloucs 46 G8
Chacewater Cnwll 3 K5
Chackmore Bucks 49 J7
Chacombe Nhants 48 E6
Chadbury Worcs 47 K5
Chadderton Oldham 89 Q9
Chadderton Fold Oldham 89 Q9
Chaddesden C Derb 72 B3
Chaddesley Corbett Worcs 58 C10
Chaddlehanger Devon 8 C9
Chaddleworth W Berk 34 D9
Chadlington Oxon 48 B10
Chadshunt Warwks 48 B4
Chadwell Leics 73 K6
Chadwell Shrops 57 P2
Chadwell End Bed 61 N7
Chadwell Heath Gt Lon 37 L3
Chadwell St Mary Thurr 37 P5
Chadwick Worcs 58 B11
Chadwick End Solhll 59 K10
Chadwick Green St Hel 82 B5
Chaffcombe Somset 10 H2
Chafford Hundred Thurr 37 P5
Chagford Devon 8 H7
Chailey E Susx 25 J7
Chainbridge Cambs 74 H10
Chainhurst Kent 26 B2
Chalbury Dorset 12 H3
Chalbury Common Dorset 12 H3
Chaldon Surrey 36 H9
Chaldon Herring Dorset 12 C8
Chale IoW 14 E11
Chale Green IoW 14 E11
Chalfont Common Bucks 36 B2
Chalfont St Giles Bucks 35 Q6
Chalfont St Peter Bucks 36 B2
Chalford Gloucs 32 G4
Chalford Oxon 35 K4
Chalford Wilts 20 G4
Chalgrave C Beds 50 B5
Chalgrove Oxon 34 H5
Chalk Kent 37 Q6
Chalk End Essex 51 P8
Chalkhouse Green Oxon 35 K9
Chalkway Somset 10 H3
Chalkwell Kent 38 E9
Challaborough Devon 6 H10
Challacombe Devon 17 M3
Challoch D & G 107 L4
Challock Kent 38 H11
Chalmington Dorset 11 M4
Chalton C Beds 50 B5
Chalton C Beds 61 P10
Chalton Hants 23 K11
Chalvey Slough 35 Q9
Chalvington E Susx 25 M9
Chambers Green Kent 26 F3
Chandler's Cross Herts 50 C11
Chandlers Cross Worcs 46 E7
Chandler's Ford Hants 22 D11
Channel's End Bed 61 P9
Channel Tunnel Terminal Kent 27 L4
Chanterlands Crematorium C KuH 93 J4
Chantry Somset 20 D5
Chantry Suffk 53 K3
Chapel Cumb 100 H4
Chapel Fife 134 H9
Chapel Allerton Leeds 91 J3
Chapel Allerton Somset 19 M4
Chapel Amble Cnwll 4 F6
Chapel Brampton Nhants 60 F7
Chapelbridge Cambs 62 C2
Chapel Chorlton Staffs 70 E7
Chapel Cross E Susx 25 P6
Chapel End Bed 61 P9
Chapel End C Beds 50 C2
Chapel End Cambs 61 P4
Chapel End Warwks 59 M6
Chapelend Way Essex 52 B4
Chapel-en-le-Frith Derbys 83 N8
Chapel Field Bury 89 M9
Chapelgate Lincs 74 H6
Chapel Green Warwks 48 E2
Chapel Green Warwks 59 L7
Chapel Haddlesey N York 91 P5
Chapelhall N Lans 126 D5
Chapel Hill Abers 159 Q10
Chapel Hill Lincs 86 H10
Chapel Hill Mons 31 P5
Chapel Hill N York 97 M11
Chapelhope Border 117 J7
Chapelknowe D & G 110 F6
Chapel Lawn Shrops 56 E9
Chapel-le-Dale N York 95 Q5
Chapel Leigh Somset 18 F9
Chapel Milton Derbys 83 N8
Chapel of Garioch Abers 151 J3
Chapel Rossan D & G 106 F9
Chapel Row E Susx 25 P8
Chapel Row Essex 52 C11
Chapel Row W Berk 34 G11
Chapels Cumb 94 E4
Chapel St Leonards Lincs 87 Q6
Chapel Stile Cumb 101 K9
Chapelton Abers 151 M9
Chapelton Angus 143 L8
Chapelton Devon 17 K6
Chapelton S Lans 126 B8
Chapeltown Bl w D 89 L7
Chapel Town Cnwll 4 D10
Chapeltown Moray 149 N3
Chapeltown Sheff 91 K11
Chapmanslade Wilts 20 F5
Chapmans Well Devon 5 P3
Chapmore End Herts 50 H7
Chappel Essex 52 E6
Charaton Cnwll 5 N8
Chard Somset 10 G3
Chard Junction Somset 10 G4
Chardleigh Green Somset 10 G2
Chardstock Devon 10 G4
Charfield S Glos 32 D6
Chargrove Gloucs 46 H11
Charing Kent 26 G2
Charing Crematorium Kent 26 G2
Charing Heath Kent 26 F2
Charing Hill Kent 38 G11
Charingworth Gloucs 47 N7
Charlbury Oxon 48 C11
Charlcombe BaNES 32 D11
Charlcutt Wilts 33 J9
Charlecote Warwks 47 Q3
Charlemont Sandw 58 F6
Charles Devon 17 M5
Charleshill Surrey 23 N6
Charleston Angus 142 F8
Charlestown C Aber 151 N7
Charlestown C Brad 90 F3
Charlestown Calder 90 B5
Charlestown Cnwll 3 Q3
Charlestown Cnwll 3 Q3
Charlestown Derbys 83 M6
Charlestown Dorset 11 P9
Charlestown Fife 134 D11
Charlestown Highld 153 Q3
Charlestown Highld 156 A8
Charlestown Salfd 82 H4
Charlestown of Aberlour Moray 157 P9
Charles Tye Suffk 64 E11
Charlesworth Derbys 83 M6
Charlinch Somset 18 H7
Charlottetown Fife 134 H5
Charlton Gt Lon 37 K5
Charlton Hants 22 C5
Charlton Herts 50 E5
Charlton Nhants 48 F7
Charlton Nthumb 112 B4
Charlton Oxon 34 D7
Charlton Somset 19 J9
Charlton Somset 20 B6
Charlton Somset 20 C4
Charlton Surrey 36 C7
Charlton W Susx 15 N4
Charlton Wilts 20 H10
Charlton Wilts 33 J7
Charlton Worcs 47 K5
Charlton Worcs 58 B10
Charlton Wrekin 57 K2
Charlton Abbots Gloucs 47 K10
Charlton Adam Somset 19 P9
Charlton All Saints Wilts 21 N10
Charlton Down Dorset 11 P5
Charlton Hill Shrops 57 K3
Charlton Horethorne Somset 20 C10
Charlton Kings Gloucs 47 J10
Charlton Mackrell Somset 19 P9
Charlton Marshall Dorset 12 F4
Charlton Musgrove Somset 20 D9
Charlton-on-Otmoor Oxon 48 G11
Charlton on the Hill Dorset 12 E4
Charlton St Peter Wilts 21 M3
Charlwood Hants 23 J8
Charlwood Surrey 24 F2
Charminster Dorset 11 P6
Charmouth Dorset 10 H6
Charndon Bucks 49 J10
Charney Bassett Oxon 34 C6
Charnock Green Lancs 88 H7
Charnock Richard Lancs 88 H7
Charnock Richard Crematorium Lancs 88 H7
Charnock Richard Services Lancs 88 G7
Charsfield Suffk 65 K10
Chart Corner Kent 38 C11
Charter Alley Hants 22 G3
Charterhall Border 129 K10
Charterhouse Somset 19 N3
Chartershall Stirlg 133 M9
Charterville Allotments Oxon 34 B2
Chartham Kent 39 K11
Chartham Hatch Kent 39 K10
Chart Hill Kent 26 C2
Chartridge Bucks 35 P4
Chart Sutton Kent 26 D2
Chartway Street Kent 38 D11
Charvil Wokham 35 L9
Charwelton Nhants 60 B9
Chase Terrace Staffs 58 F3
Chasetown Staffs 58 F3
Chastleton Oxon 47 P9
Chasty Devon 16 E11
Chatburn Lancs 89 M2
Chatcull Staffs 70 D8
Chatham Caerph 30 H7
Chatham Medway 38 C8
Chatham Green Essex 52 B8
Chathill Nthumb 119 N5
Chatley Worcs 46 G2
Chatsworth House Derbys 84 C6
Chattenden Medway 38 C7
Chatter End Essex 51 L5
Chatteris Cambs 62 E3
Chatterton Lancs 89 M7
Chattisham Suffk 53 J3
Chatto Border 118 E7
Chatton Nthumb 119 L5
Chaul End C Beds 50 C6
Chawleigh Devon 17 N9
Chawley Oxon 34 E4
Chawston Bed 61 Q9
Chawton Hants 23 K7
Chaxhill Gloucs 32 D2
Chazey Heath Oxon 35 J9
Cheadle Staffs 71 J6
Cheadle Stockp 83 J7
Cheadle Heath Stockp 83 J7
Cheadle Hulme Stockp 83 J7
Cheam Gt Lon 36 F8
Cheapside W & M 35 P11
Chearsley Bucks 35 K2
Chebsey Staffs 70 F9
Checkendon Oxon 35 J8
Checkley Ches E 70 C5
Checkley Herefs 46 A7
Checkley Staffs 71 J7
Checkley Green Ches E 70 C5
Chedburgh Suffk 63 N9
Cheddar Somset 19 N4
Cheddington Bucks 49 P11
Cheddleton Staffs 70 H4
Cheddleton Heath Staffs 70 H4
Cheddon Fitzpaine Somset 18 H9
Chedglow Wilts 32 H6
Chedgrave Norfk 65 M2
Chedington Dorset 11 K3
Chediston Suffk 65 M6
Chediston Green Suffk 65 M6
Chedworth Gloucs 33 L2
Chedzoy Somset 19 K7
Cheeseman's Green Kent 26 H4
Cheetham Hill Manch 82 H4
Cheldon Devon 8 H2
Chelford Ches E 82 H10
Chellaston C Derb 72 B4
Chellington Bed 61 L9
Chelmarsh Shrops 57 N7
Chelmick Shrops 56 H6
Chelmondiston Suffk 53 M4
Chelmorton Derbys 83 P11
Chelmsford Essex 52 B10
Chelmsford Crematorium Essex 51 Q9
Chelmsley Wood Solhll 59 J7
Chelsea Gt Lon 36 G5
Chelsfield Gt Lon 37 L8
Chelsham Surrey 37 J9
Chelston Somset 18 G10
Chelsworth Suffk 52 G2
Cheltenham Gloucs 46 H10
Cheltenham Crematorium Gloucs 47 J10
Chelveston Nhants 61 L7
Chelvey N Som 31 N11
Chelwood BaNES 20 B2
Chelwood Common E Susx 25 K5
Chelwood Gate E Susx 25 K4
Chelworth Wilts 33 J6
Chelworth Lower Green Wilts 33 L6
Chelworth Upper Green Wilts 33 L6
Cheney Longville Shrops 56 G8
Chenies Bucks 50 B11
Chepstow Mons 31 P6
Chequerbent Bolton 89 K9
Chequers Corner Norfk 75 J9
Cherhill Wilts 33 K10
Cherington Gloucs 32 H5
Cherington Warwks 47 Q7
Cheriton Devon 17 N2
Cheriton Hants 22 G9
Cheriton Kent 27 M4
Cheriton Pembks 41 J11
Cheriton Swans 28 E6
Cheriton Bishop Devon 9 J6
Cheriton Fitzpaine Devon 9 L3
Cherrington Wrekin 70 B11
Cherry Burton E R Yk 92 G2
Cherry Hinton Cambs 62 G9
Cherry Orchard Worcs 46 G4
Cherry Willingham Lincs 86 D6
Chertsey Surrey 36 B7
Cherwell Valley Services Oxon 48 F9
Cheselbourne Dorset 12 C5
Chesham Bucks 35 Q4
Chesham Bury 89 N8
Chesham Bois Bucks 35 Q5
Cheshunt Herts 51 J10
Chesil Beach Dorset 11 N9
Chesley Kent 38 E9
Cheslyn Hay Staffs 58 E3
Chessetts Wood Warwks 59 J10
Chessington Gt Lon 36 E8
Chessington World of Adventures Gt Lon 36 E8
Chester Ches W 81 N11
Chesterblade Somset 20 C6
Chester Crematorium Ches W 81 M11
Chesterfield Derbys 84 E6
Chesterfield Staffs 58 G3
Chesterfield Crematorium Derbys 84 E6
Chesterhill Mdloth 128 B7
Chester-le-Street Dur 113 L10
Chester Moor Dur 113 L11
Chesters Border 118 B6
Chesters Border 118 B8
Chester Services Ches W 81 P9
Chesterton Cambs 62 G8
Chesterton Cambs 74 B11
Chesterton Gloucs 33 K4
Chesterton Oxon 48 G10
Chesterton Shrops 57 P5
Chesterton Staffs 70 E5
Chesterton Green Warwks 48 C3
Chesterwood Nthumb 112 B7
Chester Zoo Ches W 81 N10
Chestfield Kent 39 K8
Chestnut Street Kent 38 E9
Cheston Devon 6 H7
Cheswardine Shrops 70 C8
Cheswick Nthumb 129 Q10
Cheswick Green Solhll 58 H9
Chetnole Dorset 11 N3
Chettiscombe Devon 9 N2
Chettisham Cambs 62 H4
Chettle Dorset 12 G2
Chetton Shrops 57 M6
Chetwode Bucks 48 H9
Chetwynd Wrekin 70 C10
Chetwynd Aston Wrekin 70 D11
Cheveley Cambs 63 L8
Chevening Kent 37 L9
Cheverton IoW 14 E10
Chevington Suffk 63 N9
Cheviot Hills 118 E9
Chevithorne Devon 18 C11
Chew Magna BaNES 19 Q2
Chew Moor Bolton 89 K9
Chew Stoke BaNES 19 Q2
Chewton Keynsham BaNES 32 C11
Chewton Mendip Somset 19 Q4
Chichacott Devon 8 F5
Chicheley M Keyn 49 P5
Chichester W Susx 15 N6
Chichester Crematorium W Susx 15 N5
Chickerell Dorset 11 N8
Chickering Suffk 65 J6
Chicklade Wilts 20 H8
Chicksands C Beds 50 D3
Chickward Herefs 45 K4
Chidden Hants 23 J11
Chiddingfold Surrey 23 Q7
Chiddingly E Susx 25 M8
Chiddingstone Kent 25 M2
Chiddingstone Causeway Kent 37 M11
Chideock Dorset 11 J6
Chidham W Susx 15 L6
Chidswell Kirk 90 H6
Chieveley W Berk 34 E10
Chieveley Services W Berk 34 E10
Chignall St James Essex 51 Q8
Chignall Smealy Essex 51 Q8
Chigwell Essex 37 K2
Chigwell Row Essex 37 L2
Chilbolton Hants 22 C6
Chilcomb Hants 22 F9
Chilcombe Dorset 11 L6
Chilcompton Somset 20 B4
Chilcote Leics 59 L2
Childer Thornton Ches W 81 M9
Child Okeford Dorset 12 D2
Childrey Oxon 34 C7
Child's Ercall Shrops 70 B9
Childswickham Worcs 47 L7
Childwall Lpool 81 N7
Childwick Bury Herts 50 D8
Childwick Green Herts 50 D8
Chilfrome Dorset 11 M5
Chilgrove W Susx 15 M4
Chilham Kent 39 J11
Chilla Devon 8 B4
Chillaton Devon 8 B8
Chillenden Kent 39 N11
Chillerton IoW 14 E10
Chillesford Suffk 65 M11
Chillingham Nthumb 119 L5
Chillington Devon 7 K10
Chillington Somset 10 H2
Chilmark Wilts 21 J8
Chilmington Green Kent 26 G3
Chilson Oxon 48 B11
Chilsworthy Cnwll 5 Q7
Chilsworthy Devon 16 E10
Chiltern Green C Beds 50 D7
Chiltern Hills 35 L5
Chilterns Crematorium Bucks 35 P5
Chilthorne Domer Somset 19 P11
Chilton Bucks 35 J2
Chilton Devon 9 L4
Chilton Dur 103 Q5
Chilton Kent 27 N3
Chilton Oxon 34 E7
Chilton Suffk 52 E3
Chilton Candover Hants 22 G6
Chilton Cantelo Somset 19 Q10
Chilton Foliat Wilts 34 B10
Chilton Polden Somset 19 L6
Chilton Street Suffk 63 N11
Chilton Trinity Somset 19 J7
Chilwell Notts 72 E3
Chilworth Hants 22 D11
Chilworth Surrey 36 B11
Chimney Oxon 34 C4
Chineham Hants 23 J3
Chingford Gt Lon 37 J2
Chinley Derbys 83 M8
Chinnor Oxon 35 L4
Chipchase Castle Nthumb 112 C5
Chipnall Shrops 70 C8
Chippenham Cambs 63 L7
Chippenham Wilts 32 H10
Chipperfield Herts 50 B10
Chipping Herts 51 J4
Chipping Lancs 89 J2
Chipping Campden Gloucs 47 N7
Chipping Hill Essex 52 D8
Chipping Norton Oxon 48 B9
Chipping Ongar Essex 51 N10
Chipping Sodbury S Glos 32 D8
Chipping Warden Nhants 48 E5
Chipshop Devon 8 B9
Chipstable Somset 18 D9
Chipstead Kent 37 M9
Chipstead Surrey 36 G9
Chirbury Shrops 56 D5
Chirk Wrexhm 69 J7
Chirnside Border 129 M8
Chirnsidebridge Border 129 M8
Chirton Wilts 21 L3
Chisbury Wilts 33 Q11
Chiselborough Somset 11 K2
Chiseldon Swindn 33 N8
Chiselhampton Oxon 34 G5
Chisholme Border 117 N8
Chislehurst Gt Lon 37 K6
Chislet Kent 39 M9
Chisley Calder 90 C5
Chiswell Green Herts 50 D10
Chiswick Gt Lon 36 F5
Chiswick End Cambs 62 E11
Chisworth Derbys 83 L6
Chitcombe E Susx 26 D7
Chithurst W Susx 23 M10
Chittering Cambs 62 G7
Chitterne Wilts 21 J6
Chittlehamholt Devon 17 M7
Chittlehampton Devon 17 L6
Chittoe Wilts 33 J11
Chivelstone Devon 7 K11
Chivenor Devon 17 J5
Chiverton Cross Cnwll 3 J4
Chlenry D & G 106 F5
Chobham Surrey 23 Q2
Cholderton Wilts 21 P6
Cholesbury Bucks 35 P3
Chollerford Nthumb 112 D6
Chollerton Nthumb 112 D6
Cholmondeston Ches E 70 A3
Cholsey Oxon 34 G7
Cholstrey Herefs 45 P3
Chop Gate N York 104 G11
Choppington Nthumb 113 L4
Chopwell Gatesd 112 H9
Chorley Ches E 69 Q4
Chorley Lancs 88 H7
Chorley Shrops 57 M8
Chorley Staffs 58 G2
Chorleywood Herts 50 B11
Chorleywood West Herts 50 B11
Chorlton Ches E 70 C4
Chorlton-cum-Hardy Manch 82 H6
Chorlton Lane Ches W 69 N5
Choulton Shrops 56 F7
Chowley Ches W 69 N3
Chrishall Essex 51 K3
Chrisswell Inver 124 G3
Christchurch Cambs 75 J11
Christchurch Dorset 13 L6
Christchurch Gloucs 31 Q2
Christchurch Newpt 31 K7
Christian Malford Wilts 33 J9
Christleton Ches W 81 N11
Christmas Common Oxon 35 K6
Christmas Pie Surrey 23 P5
Christon N Som 19 L3
Christon Bank Nthumb 119 P6
Christow Devon 9 K7
Christ's Hospital W Susx 24 D5
Chuck Hatch E Susx 25 L4
Chudleigh Devon 9 L9
Chudleigh Knighton Devon 9 K9
Chulmleigh Devon 17 M9
Chunal Derbys 83 M6
Church Lancs 89 L5
Churcham Gloucs 46 E11
Church Aston Wrekin 70 C11
Church Brampton Nhants 60 F7
Church Brough Cumb 102 E8
Church Broughton Derbys 71 N8
Church Cove Cnwll 3 J11
Church Crookham Hants 23 M4
Churchdown Gloucs 46 G11
Church Eaton Staffs 70 E11
Church End Bed 61 N9
Church End Bed 61 P9
Church End Bucks 35 K3
Church End C Beds 49 Q10
Church End C Beds 49 Q8
Church End C Beds 50 B4
Church End C Beds 50 B7
Church End C Beds 50 E3
Church End C Beds 61 Q10
Church End Cambs 61 N6
Church End Cambs 62 B4
Church End Cambs 62 D5
Churchend Essex 38 H3
Church End Essex 51 P6
Church End Essex 52 B6

Church End Essex....52 B8
Church End Gloucs....46 G7
Church End Gt Lon....36 F2
Church End Herts....50 D8
Church End Herts....50 G4
Church End Herts....51 K6
Church End Lincs....74 D4
Church End Lincs....93 R11
Church End Warwks....59 K6
Church End Warwks....59 L6
Church Enstone Oxon....48 C9
Church Fenton N York....91 N3
Churchfield Sandw....58 F6
Churchgate Herts....50 H10
Churchgate Street Essex....51 L8
Church Green Devon....10 D5
Church Gresley Derbys....71 P11
Church Hanborough Oxon....34 D2
Church Hill Staffs....58 F2
Church Houses N York....105 J11
Churchill Devon....10 F4
Churchill Devon....17 K3
Churchill N Som....19 M3
Churchill Oxon....47 Q10
Churchill Worcs....46 H4
Churchill Worcs....58 C9
Churchinford Somset....10 E2
Church Knowle Dorset....12 F8
Church Laneham Notts....85 P5
Church Langton Leics....60 F2
Church Lawford Warwks....59 Q9
Church Lawton Ches E....70 E3
Church Leigh Staffs....71 J7
Church Lench Worcs....47 K4
Church Mayfield Staffs....71 M6
Church Minshull Ches E....70 B2
Church Norton W Susx....15 N7
Churchover Warwks....60 B4
Church Preen Shrops....57 J5
Church Pulverbatch Shrops....56 G4
Churchstanton Somset....10 D2
Churchstoke Powys....56 D6
Churchstow Devon....7 J9
Church Stowe Nhants....60 D9
Church Street Essex....52 C3
Church Street Kent....38 B7
Church Street Suffk....65 P5
Church Stretton Shrops....56 H6
Churchthorpe Lincs....93 P11
Churchtown Bpool....88 C2
Churchtown Cnwll....4 H6
Churchtown Derbys....84 C8
Churchtown Devon....17 M3
Churchtown IoM....80 f3
Churchtown Lancs....88 F2
Church Town N Linc....92 C9
Churchtown Sefton....88 D7
Church Village Rhondd....30 E7
Church Warsop Notts....85 J7
Church Wilne Derbys....72 C4
Churnsike Lodge Nthumb....111 N5
Churston Ferrers Torbay....7 N7
Churt Surrey....23 N7
Churton Ches W....69 M3
Churwell Leeds....90 H5
Chwilog Gwynd....66 G7
Chyandour Cnwll....2 D7
Chyanvounder Cnwll....2 H9
Chyeowling Cnwll....3 K5
Chyvarloe Cnwll....2 H9
Cil Pembks....56 B4
Cilcain Flints....80 H11
Cilcennin Cerdgn....43 K2
Cilcewydd Powys....56 C4
Cilfrew Neath....29 L4
Cilfynydd Rhondd....30 E6
Cilgerran Pembks....41 N2
Cilgwyn Carmth....43 P9
Cilgwyn Gwynd....66 H4
Ciliau-Aeron Cerdgn....43 K3
Cilmaengwyn Neath....29 K3
Cilmery Powys....44 E4
Cilrhedyn Pembks....41 Q4
Cilsan Carmth....43 L10
Ciltalgarth Gwynd....68 A6
Cilycwm Carmth....43 Q7
Cimla Neath....29 L5
Cinderford Gloucs....32 C2
Cinder Hill Wolves....58 D6
Cippenham Slough....35 Q8
Cirencester Gloucs....33 K4
Citadilla N York....103 P11
City Gt Lon....36 H4
City V Glam....30 C9
City Airport Gt Lon....37 K4
City Dulas IoA....78 H7
City of London Crematorium Gt Lon....37 K3
Clabhach Ag & B....136 F4
Clachaig Ag & B....131 N11
Clachan Ag & B....123 N8
Clachan Ag & B....130 F4
Clachan Ag & B....131 M7
Clachan Ag & B....138 F9
Clachan Highld....153 J10
Clachan-a-Luib W Isls....168 d11
Clachan Mor Ag & B....136 B6
Clachan na Luib W Isls....168 d11
Clachan of Campsie E Duns....125 Q2
Clachan-Seil Ag & B....130 F4
Clachnaharry Highld....156 A8
Clachtoll Highld....164 B11
Clackavoid P & K....142 A5
Clacket Lane Services Surrey....37 K10
Clackmannan Clacks....133 Q9
Clackmannanshire Bridge Fife....133 Q10
Clackmarras Moray....157 N6
Clacton-on-Sea Essex....53 L8
Cladich Ag & B....131 M3
Cladswell Worcs....47 L3
Claggan Highld....138 C8
Claigan Highld....152 C7
Clandown BaNES....20 C3
Clanfield Hants....23 J11
Clanfield Oxon....33 Q4
Clannaborough Devon....8 H4
Clanville Hants....22 B5
Clanville Somset....20 B8
Claonaig Ag & B....123 Q8
Clapgate Dorset....12 H4
Clapgate Herts....51 K6
Clapham Bed....61 M10
Clapham Devon....9 L7
Clapham Gt Lon....36 G5
Clapham N York....95 Q7

Clapham W Susx....24 C9
Clapham Green Bed....61 M10
Clap Hill Kent....27 J4
Clappersgate Cumb....101 L10
Clapton Somset....11 J3
Clapton Somset....20 B4
Clapton-in-Gordano N Som....31 N10
Clapton-on-the-Hill Gloucs....47 N11
Clapworthy Devon....17 M7
Clarach Cerdgn....54 E8
Claravale Gatesd....112 H8
Clarbeston Pembks....41 L6
Clarbeston Road Pembks....41 K6
Clarborough Notts....85 M4
Clare Suffk....63 N11
Clarebrand D & G....108 G7
Clarencefield D & G....109 N7
Clarewood Nthumb....112 F7
Clarilaw Border....117 Q7
Clark's Green Surrey....24 E3
Clarkston E Rens....125 P6
Clashmore Highld....162 G9
Clashmore Highld....164 B10
Clashnessie Highld....164 C10
Clashnoir Moray....149 N3
Clathy P & K....134 B3
Clathymore P & K....134 C3
Clatt Abers....150 E2
Clatter Powys....55 M6
Clatterford End Essex....51 P8
Clatworthy Somset....18 E8
Claughton Lancs....88 G2
Claughton Lancs....95 M7
Claughton Wirral....81 L7
Clavelshay Somset....19 J8
Claverdon Warwks....59 J11
Claverham N Som....31 N11
Clavering Essex....51 L4
Claverley Shrops....57 P6
Claverton BaNES....20 E2
Claverton Down BaNES....20 E2
Clawdd-coch V Glam....30 E9
Clawdd-newydd Denbgs....68 E4
Clawthorpe Cumb....95 L5
Clawton Devon....5 P2
Claxby Lincs....86 F2
Claxby Lincs....87 N6
Claxton N York....98 D9
Claxton Norfk....77 L11
Claybrooke Magna Leics....59 Q7
Clay Common Suffk....65 P5
Clay Coton Nhants....60 C5
Clay Cross Derbys....84 E6
Claydon Oxon....48 E5
Claydon Suffk....53 K2
Clay End Herts....50 H6
Claygate D & G....110 G5
Claygate Kent....26 B3
Claygate Surrey....36 E8
Claygate Cross Kent....37 P9
Clayhall Gt Lon....37 K2
Clayhanger Devon....18 D10
Clayhanger Wsall....58 F4
Clayhidon Devon....18 G11
Clayhill E Susx....26 D7
Clayhill Hants....13 P3
Clayhithe Cambs....62 H8
Clayock Highld....167 L5
Claypit Hill Cambs....62 E10
Claypits Gloucs....32 E3
Claypole Lincs....85 P11
Claythorpe Lincs....87 M5
Clayton C Brad....90 E4
Clayton Donc....91 M9
Clayton W Susx....24 G8
Clayton Green Lancs....88 H4
Clayton-le-Moors Lancs....89 M4
Clayton-le-Woods Lancs....88 H4
Clayton West Kirk....90 H8
Clayworth Notts....85 M3
Cleadale Highld....144 G10
Cleadon S Tyne....113 N8
Clearbrook Devon....6 F4
Clearwell Gloucs....31 Q3
Clearwell Meend Gloucs....31 Q3
Cleasby N York....103 Q8
Cleat Ork....169 d8
Cleatlam Dur....103 M7
Cleator Cumb....100 D8
Cleator Moor Cumb....100 D7
Cleckheaton Kirk....90 F5
Cleedownton Shrops....57 K8
Cleehill Shrops....57 K8
Cleekhimin N Lans....126 D6
Clee St Margaret Shrops....57 K8
Cleestanton Shrops....57 K9
Cleethorpes NE Lin....93 P9
Cleeton St Mary Shrops....57 L9
Cleeve N Som....31 N11
Cleeve Oxon....34 H8
Cleeve Prior Worcs....47 L5
Cleghornie E Loth....128 F3
Clehonger Herefs....45 N7
Cleish P & K....134 D7
Cleland N Lans....126 D6
Clement's End C Beds....50 B8
Clement Street Kent....37 M6
Clenamacrie Ag & B....131 J2
Clench Common Wilts....33 N11
Clenchwarton Norfk....75 L6
Clenerty Abers....159 J5
Clent Worcs....58 D9
Cleobury Mortimer Shrops....57 M9
Cleobury North Shrops....57 L8
Cleongart Ag & B....120 C5
Clephanton Highld....156 E7
Clerkhill D & G....117 K3
Cleuch-head D & G....115 R7
Clevancy Wilts....33 L9
Clevedon N Som....31 M10
Cleveley Oxon....48 C10
Cleveleys Lancs....88 C2
Cleverton Wilts....33 J7
Clewer Somset....19 M4
Cley next the Sea Norfk....76 E3
Cliburn Cumb....101 R5
Cliddesden Hants....22 H5
Cliff Warwks....59 K5
Cliffe Lancs....89 L4
Cliffe Medway....38 B6
Cliffe N York....91 R4
Cliffe N York....103 P7
Cliff End E Susx....26 E9
Cliffe Woods Medway....38 B7
Clifford Herefs....45 J5
Clifford Leeds....91 L2

Clifford Chambers Warwks....47 N4
Clifford's Mesne Gloucs....46 D10
Cliffsend Kent....39 P9
Clifton Bristl....31 Q10
Clifton C Beds....50 E3
Clifton C Nott....72 E4
Clifton C York....98 B10
Clifton Calder....90 F6
Clifton Derbys....71 M6
Clifton Devon....17 L3
Clifton Donc....91 N11
Clifton Lancs....88 F4
Clifton N York....97 J11
Clifton Nthumb....113 K4
Clifton Oxon....48 E8
Clifton Salfd....82 G4
Clifton Worcs....46 F5
Clifton Campville Staffs....59 L2
Clifton Hampden Oxon....34 F5
Clifton Reynes M Keyn....49 P4
Clifton upon Dunsmore Warwks....60 B5
Clifton upon Teme Worcs....46 D2
Cliftonville Kent....39 Q7
Climping W Susx....24 Q6
Clink Somset....20 E5
Clint N York....97 L9
Clinterty C Aber....151 L5
Clint Green Norfk....76 E9
Clintmains Border....118 B4
Clipiau Gwynd....55 J2
Clippesby Norfk....77 N9
Clipsham Rutlnd....73 P7
Clipston Nhants....60 F5
Clipston Notts....72 G4
Clipstone C Beds....49 P9
Clipstone Notts....85 J8
Clitheroe Lancs....89 L2
Clive Shrops....69 P10
Clixby Lincs....93 J10
Cloatley Wilts....33 J6
Clocaenog Denbgs....68 E4
Clochan Moray....158 B5
Clock Face St Hel....82 B6
Cloddiau Powys....56 C3
Clodock Herefs....45 L9
Cloford Somset....20 D6
Clola Abers....159 P9
Clophill C Beds....50 C3
Clopton Nhants....61 N4
Clopton Suffk....65 J11
Clopton Corner Suffk....65 J11
Clopton Green Suffk....63 N10
Clopton Green Suffk....64 D10
Clos du Valle Guern....10 c1
Closeburn D & G....109 J11
Closeburnmill D & G....109 K2
Closeclark IoM....80 c6
Closworth Somset....11 M2
Clothall Herts....50 G4
Clotton Ches W....69 P2
Cloudesley Bush Warwks....59 Q7
Clouds Herefs....46 A7
Clough Oldham....89 Q9
Clough Foot Calder....89 Q6
Clough Head Calder....90 D7
Cloughton N York....99 L2
Cloughton Newlands N York....105 R11
Clousta Shet....169 q8
Clova Angus....142 E3
Clovelly Devon....16 E7
Clovenfords Border....117 P3
Clovulin Highld....139 J5
Clow Bridge Lancs....89 N5
Clowne Derbys....84 G5
Clows Top Worcs....57 N10
Cloy Wrexhm....69 L6
Cluanie Inn Highld....146 D5
Cluanie Lodge Highld....146 D5
Clubworthy Cnwll....5 M3
Clugston D & G....107 L6
Clun Shrops....56 E8
Clunas Highld....156 F8
Clunbury Shrops....56 F8
Clunderwen Carmth....41 M7
Clune Highld....148 D2
Clunes Highld....146 F10
Clungunford Shrops....56 F9
Clunton Shrops....56 E8
Cluny Fife....134 G8
Clutton BaNES....20 B3
Clutton Ches W....69 N4
Clutton Hill BaNES....20 C3
Clwt-y-bont Gwynd....67 K2
Clydach Mons....30 H2
Clydach Swans....29 J4
Clydach Vale Rhondd....30 C6
Clydebank W Duns....125 M3
Clydebank Crematorium W Duns....125 M3
Clydey Pembks....41 Q3
Clyffe Pypard Wilts....33 L9
Clynder Ag & B....131 Q11
Clyne Neath....29 M4
Clynnog-fawr Gwynd....66 G5
Clyro Powys....45 J6
Clyst Honiton Devon....9 N6
Clyst Hydon Devon....9 P4
Clyst St George Devon....9 N7
Clyst St Lawrence Devon....9 P4
Clyst St Mary Devon....9 N6
Cnoc W Isls....168 j4
Cnwch Coch Cerdgn....54 F10
Coad's Green Cnwll....5 M6
Coal Aston Derbys....84 E5
Coalbrookvale Blae G....30 G3
Coalburn S Lans....126 E11
Coalburns Gatesd....112 H8
Coaley Gloucs....32 E4
Coalhill Essex....38 C2
Coalmoor Wrekin....57 M3
Coalpit Heath S Glos....32 C8
Coalport Wrekin....57 M4
Coalsnaughton Clacks....133 Q8
Coal Street Suffk....65 J7
Coaltown of Balgonie Fife....134 H8
Coaltown of Wemyss Fife....135 J8
Coalville Leics....72 C8
Coanwood Nthumb....111 N9
Coat Somset....19 N10
Coatbridge N Lans....126 C4
Coatdyke N Lans....126 C4

Coate Swindn....33 N8
Coate Wilts....21 K2
Coates Cambs....74 F11
Coates Gloucs....33 J4
Coates Lincs....86 B4
Coates Notts....85 P4
Coates W Susx....23 Q5
Coatham R & Cl....104 G5
Coatham Mundeville Darltn....103 Q6
Cobbaton Devon....17 L6
Coberley Gloucs....47 J11
Cobhall Common Herefs....45 P7
Cobham Kent....37 Q8
Cobham Surrey....36 D8
Cobham Services Surrey....36 D9
Coblers Green Essex....51 Q7
Cobley Dorset....21 K10
Cobnash Herefs....45 P2
Cobo Guern....10 b1
Cobridge C Stke....70 F5
Coburby Abers....159 M5
Cock Alley Derbys....84 F6
Cockayne N York....104 H11
Cockayne Hatley C Beds....62 C11
Cock Bank Wrexhm....69 L5
Cock Bevington Warwks....47 L4
Cock Bridge Abers....149 P6
Cockburnspath Border....129 K5
Cock Clarks Essex....52 D11
Cockenzie and Port Seton E Loth....128 C4
Cocker Bar Lancs....88 G4
Cocker Brook Lancs....89 L5
Cockerham Lancs....95 K10
Cockermouth Cumb....100 F4
Cockernhoe Herts....50 D6
Cockersdale Leeds....90 G5
Cockett Swans....28 H6
Cockfield Dur....103 M6
Cockfield Suffk....64 C11
Cockfosters Gt Lon....50 G11
Cock Green Essex....51 Q7
Cocking W Susx....23 N11
Cocking Causeway W Susx....23 N11
Cockington Torbay....7 M6
Cocklake Somset....19 M5
Cockley Beck Cumb....100 H10
Cockley Cley Norfk....75 Q10
Cock Marling E Susx....26 E8
Cockpole Green Wokham....35 L8
Cocks Cnwll....3 K3
Cockshutford Shrops....57 K7
Cockshutt Shrops....69 M9
Cockthorpe Norfk....76 D3
Cockwells Cnwll....2 E7
Cockwood Devon....9 N8
Cockwood Somset....18 H6
Cockyard Derbys....83 M9
Cockyard Herefs....45 N8
Coddenham Suffk....64 G11
Coddington Ches W....69 N3
Coddington Herefs....46 D6
Coddington Notts....85 P10
Codford St Mary Wilts....21 J7
Codford St Peter Wilts....21 J7
Codicote Herts....50 F7
Codmore Hill W Susx....24 C6
Codnor Derbys....84 F11
Codrington S Glos....32 D9
Codsall Staffs....58 C3
Codsall Wood Staffs....58 B4
Coedely Rhondd....30 D7
Coedkernew Newpt....31 J8
Coed Morgan Mons....31 L2
Coedpoeth Wrexhm....69 J4
Coed Talon Flints....69 J3
Coedway Powys....69 K11
Coed-y-Bryn Cerdgn....42 G5
Coed-y-caerau Newpt....31 L6
Coed-y-paen Mons....31 K5
Coed-yr-ynys Powys....44 H10
Coed Ystumgwern Gwynd....67 K10
Coelbren Powys....29 N2
Coffinswell Devon....7 M5
Coffle End Bed....61 M9
Cofton Devon....9 N8
Cofton Hackett Worcs....58 F9
Cogan V Glam....30 G10
Cogenhoe Nhants....60 H8
Cogges Oxon....34 C3
Coggeshall Essex....52 E7
Coggin's Mill E Susx....25 N5
Coignafearn Highld....148 C4
Coilacriech Abers....149 Q8
Coilantogle Stirlg....132 H6
Coillore Highld....152 F10
Coity Brdgnd....29 P8
Col W Isls....168 j4
Colaboll Highld....162 D4
Colan Cnwll....4 D9
Colaton Raleigh Devon....10 B7
Colbost Highld....152 C8
Colburn N York....103 N11
Colby Cumb....102 C6
Colby IoM....80 b7
Colby Norfk....77 J5
Colchester Essex....52 G6
Colchester Crematorium Essex....52 F10
Colchester Zoo Essex....52 G7
Cold Ash W Berk....34 F11
Cold Ashby Nhants....60 E5
Cold Ashton S Glos....32 D10
Cold Aston Gloucs....47 M11
Coldbackie Highld....165 P4
Coldbeck Cumb....102 D10
Cold Blow Pembks....41 M8
Cold Brayfield M Keyn....49 P4
Cold Cotes N York....95 Q6
Coldean Br & H....24 H9
Coldeast Devon....7 L4
Colden Calder....90 B5
Colden Common Hants....22 E10
Coldfair Green Suffk....65 N9
Coldham Cambs....74 H10
Cold Hanworth Lincs....86 D4
Coldharbour Cnwll....3 K4
Coldharbour Devon....18 D11
Coldharbour Gloucs....31 Q4
Coldharbour Herts....50 D7
Cold Harbour Oxon....34 H9
Coldharbour Surrey....24 D2
Cold Hatton Wrekin....70 A10
Cold Hatton Heath Wrekin....70 A10
Cold Hesledon Dur....113 P11

Cold Hiendley Wakefd....91 K8
Cold Higham Nhants....49 J4
Coldingham Border....129 N6
Cold Kirby N York....98 A4
Coldmeece Staffs....70 F8
Cold Newton Leics....73 J9
Cold Northcott Cnwll....5 L4
Cold Norton Essex....52 E11
Cold Overton Leics....73 L8
Coldred Kent....27 N2
Coldridge Devon....17 M10
Coldstream Border....118 F3
Coldwaltham W Susx....24 B7
Coldwell Herefs....45 N7
Coldwells Abers....159 N10
Cold Weston Shrops....57 K8
Cole Somset....20 C8
Colebatch Shrops....56 F7
Colebrook C Plym....6 E7
Colebrook Devon....9 P3
Colebrooke Devon....9 J4
Coleby Lincs....86 C8
Coleby N Linc....92 E7
Cole End Warwks....59 K7
Coleford Devon....9 J4
Coleford Gloucs....31 Q2
Coleford Somset....20 C5
Coleford Water Somset....18 F7
Colegate End Norfk....64 H4
Cole Green Herts....50 G8
Cole Green Herts....51 K8
Cole Henley Hants....22 E4
Colehill Dorset....12 H4
Coleman Green Herts....50 E8
Coleman's Hatch E Susx....25 K4
Colemere Shrops....69 M8
Colemore Hants....23 K8
Colemore Green Shrops....57 N5
Colenden P & K....134 E2
Coleorton Leics....72 C7
Colerne Wilts....32 F10
Colesbourne Gloucs....33 K2
Cole's Cross Devon....7 K9
Coles Cross Dorset....10 H4
Colesden Bed....61 P9
Coles Green Suffk....53 K3
Coleshill Bucks....35 P5
Coleshill Oxon....33 P6
Coleshill Warwks....59 K7
Colestocks Devon....10 B4
Coley BaNES....19 Q3
Colgate W Susx....24 F4
Colinsburgh Fife....135 M7
Colinton C Edin....127 N4
Colintraive Ag & B....124 C3
Colkirk Norfk....76 C6
Coll Ag & B....136 G4
Coll W Isls....168 j4
Collace P & K....142 C11
Collafirth Shet....169 q5
Coll Airport Ag & B....136 F4
Collaton Devon....7 J11
Collaton St Mary Torbay....7 M6
College of Roseisle Moray....157 L4
College Town Br For....23 N2
Collessie Fife....134 H5
Colleton Mills Devon....17 M8
Collier Row Gt Lon....37 M2
Collier's End Herts....51 J6
Collier's Green E Susx....26 C7
Colliers Green Kent....26 C4
Collier Street Kent....26 B2
Colliery Row Sundld....113 M11
Collieston Abers....151 Q2
Collin D & G....109 M5
Collingbourne Ducis Wilts....21 P4
Collingbourne Kingston Wilts....21 P3
Collingham Leeds....97 N11
Collingham Notts....85 P8
Collington Herefs....46 B2
Collingtree Nhants....60 G9
Collins Green Warrtn....82 C6
Collins Green Worcs....46 D3
Colliston Angus....143 L8
Colliton Devon....10 B4
Collyweston Nhants....73 P10
Colmonell S Ayrs....114 B10
Colmworth Bed....61 P9
Colnabaichin Abers....149 P6
Colnbrook Slough....36 B5
Colne Cambs....62 E5
Colne Lancs....89 P3
Colne Bridge Kirk....90 F6
Colne Edge Lancs....89 P2
Colne Engaine Essex....52 D5
Colney Norfk....76 H10
Colney Heath Herts....50 F9
Colney Street Herts....50 E10
Coln Rogers Gloucs....33 L3
Coln St Aldwyns Gloucs....33 M3
Coln St Dennis Gloucs....33 L2
Colonsay Ag & B....136 b2
Colonsay Airport Ag & B....136 b3
Colpy Abers....158 F11
Colquhar Border....117 L2
Colquite Cnwll....4 H7
Colscott Devon....16 H9
Colsterdale N York....96 H4
Colsterworth Lincs....73 N6
Colston Bassett Notts....73 J4
Coltfield Moray....157 L4
Colt Hill Hants....23 L4
Coltishall Norfk....77 K8
Colton Cumb....94 G3
Colton Leeds....91 K4
Colton N York....91 N2
Colton Norfk....76 G10
Colton Staffs....71 J10
Colt's Hill Kent....25 P2
Columbjohn Devon....9 N5
Colva Powys....44 G4
Colvend D & G....109 J10
Colwall Herefs....46 E6
Colwell Nthumb....112 E5
Colwich Staffs....71 J10
Colwick Notts....72 G2
Colwinston V Glam....29 P9
Colworth W Susx....15 P6
Colwyn Bay Conwy....80 B9
Colwyn Bay Crematorium Conwy....79 Q9
Colyford Devon....10 F6
Colyton Devon....10 E6
Combe Devon....7 J11
Combe Herefs....45 L2
Combe Oxon....48 C11
Combe W Berk....22 C2
Combe Almer Dorset....12 G5

Combe Common Surrey......23 P7
Combe Down BaNES......20 E2
Combe Fishacre Devon......7 L5
Combe Florey Somset......18 G8
Combe Hay BaNES......20 D3
Combeinteignhead Devon......7 N4
Combe Martin Devon......17 K2
Combe Raleigh Devon......10 D4
Comberbach Ches W......82 D9
Comberford Staffs......59 J3
Comberton Cambs......62 E9
Comberton Herefs......56 H11
Combe St Nicholas Somset......10 G2
Combpyne Devon......10 F6
Combridge Staffs......71 K7
Combrook Warwks......48 B4
Combs Derbys......83 M9
Combs Suffk......64 E10
Combs Ford Suffk......64 E10
Combwich Somset......19 J6
Comers Abers......150 H6
Comhampton Worcs......58 B11
Commercial End Cambs......63 J8
Commins Coch Powys......55 J4
Commondale N York......105 J8
Common Edge Bpool......88 C4
Common End Cumb......100 D6
Common Moor Cnwll......5 L8
Common Platt Wilts......33 M7
Commonside Ches W......82 B10
Commonside Derbys......71 N6
Common Side Derbys......84 D5
Commonwood Shrops......69 N9
Commonwood Wrexhm......69 L4
Compass Somset......19 J8
Compstall Stockp......83 L6
Compstonend D & G......108 E10
Compton Devon......7 M6
Compton Hants......22 B9
Compton Hants......22 E9
Compton Staffs......57 Q8
Compton Surrey......23 Q5
Compton W Berk......34 F8
Compton W Susx......15 L4
Compton Wilts......21 M4
Compton Abbas Dorset......20 G11
Compton Abdale Gloucs......47 L11
Compton Bassett Wilts......33 K10
Compton Beauchamp Oxon......33 Q7
Compton Bishop Somset......19 L3
Compton Chamberlayne Wilts......21 K9
Compton Dando BaNES......20 B2
Compton Dundon Somset......19 N8
Compton Durville Somset......19 M11
Compton Greenfield S Glos......31 Q8
Compton Martin BaNES......19 P3
Compton Pauncefoot Somset......20 B9
Compton Valence Dorset......11 M6
Comrie Fife......134 C10
Comrie P & K......133 M3
Conaglen House Highld......139 J4
Conchra Highld......145 Q2
Concraigie P & K......141 Q9
Conder Green Lancs......95 K9
Conderton Worcs......47 J7
Condicote Gloucs......47 N9
Condorrat N Lans......126 C3
Condover Shrops......56 H3
Coneyhurst Common W Susx......24 D6
Coneysthorpe N York......98 E6
Coneythorpe N York......97 N9
Coney Weston Suffk......64 D6
Conford Hants......23 M8
Congdon's Shop Cnwll......5 M6
Congerstone Leics......72 B9
Congham Norfk......75 P6
Congleton Ches E......70 F2
Congl-y-wal Gwynd......67 N6
Congresbury N Som......19 M2
Congreve Staffs......58 D2
Conheath D & G......109 L7
Conicavel Moray......156 H7
Coningsby Lincs......86 H9
Conington Cambs......61 Q3
Conington Cambs......62 D7
Conisbrough Donc......91 N11
Conisholme Lincs......93 R11
Coniston Cumb......101 K11
Coniston E R Yk......93 L3
Coniston Cold N York......96 D10
Conistone N York......96 E7
Connah's Quay Flints......81 K11
Connel Ag & B......138 G11
Connel Park E Ayrs......115 M5
Connor Downs Cnwll......2 F6
Conon Bridge Highld......155 P6
Cononley N York......96 E11
Consall Staffs......70 H5
Consett Dur......112 H10
Constable Burton N York......97 J2
Constable Lee Lancs......89 N6
Constantine Cnwll......3 J8
Constantine Bay Cnwll......4 D7
Contin Highld......155 N6
Conwy Conwy......79 P9
Conwy Castle Conwy......79 P9
Conyer Kent......38 G9
Conyer's Green Suffk......64 B8
Cooden E Susx......26 B10
Cookbury Devon......16 G10
Cookbury Wick Devon......16 F10
Cookham W & M......35 N7
Cookham Dean W & M......35 N7
Cookham Rise W & M......35 N7
Cookhill Worcs......47 L3
Cookley Suffk......65 L6
Cookley Worcs......58 B8
Cookley Green Oxon......35 J6
Cooksbridge E Susx......25 K8
Cooksey Green Worcs......58 D11
Cook's Green Essex......53 L8
Cooks Green Suffk......64 D11
Cookshill Staffs......70 G6
Cooksland Cnwll......4 H8
Cooksmill Green Essex......51 P9
Cookson Green Ches W......82 C10
Coolham W Susx......24 D6
Cooling Medway......38 C6
Cooling Street Medway......38 B7
Coombe Cnwll......2 G5

Coombe Cnwll......3 L5
Coombe Cnwll......3 N3
Coombe Devon......7 N4
Coombe Devon......9 K8
Coombe Devon......10 C6
Coombe Gloucs......32 E6
Coombe Hants......23 J10
Coombe Wilts......21 M4
Combe Abbey Warwks......59 N9
Coombe Bissett Wilts......21 M9
Coombe Cellars Devon......7 N4
Coombe Cross Hants......23 J10
Coombe Hill Gloucs......46 G9
Coombe Keynes Dorset......12 D8
Coombe Pafford Torbay......7 N5
Coombes W Susx......24 E9
Coombes-Moor Herefs......45 M2
Coombe Street Somset......20 E8
Coombeswood Dudley......58 E7
Coopersale Common Essex......51 L10
Coopersale Street Essex......51 L10
Coopers Green E Susx......25 L6
Coopers Green Herts......50 E9
Cooper Street Kent......39 P9
Cooper Turning Bolton......89 J9
Cootham W Susx......24 C8
Copdock Suffk......53 K3
Copford Green Essex......52 F7
Copgrove N York......97 M8
Copister Shet......169 r6
Cople Bed......61 P11
Copley Calder......90 D6
Copley Dur......103 L5
Copley Tamesd......83 L5
Coplow Dale Derbys......83 Q9
Copmanthorpe C York......98 B11
Copmere End Staffs......70 E9
Copp Lancs......88 E3
Coppathorne Cnwll......16 C11
Coppenhall Staffs......70 G11
Coppenhall Moss Ches E......70 C3
Copperhouse Cnwll......2 F6
Coppicegate Shrops......57 N8
Coppingford Cambs......61 Q5
Coppins Corner Kent......26 F2
Copplestone Devon......9 J4
Coppull Lancs......88 H8
Coppull Moor Lancs......88 H8
Copsale W Susx......24 E6
Copster Green Lancs......89 K4
Copston Magna Warwks......59 Q7
Cop Street Kent......39 N9
Copthall Green Essex......51 K10
Copt Heath Solhll......59 J9
Copt Hewick N York......97 M6
Copthorne Cnwll......5 M3
Copthorne W Susx......24 H3
Copt Oak Leics......72 D8
Copy's Green Norfk......76 C4
Copythorne Hants......13 P2
Coram Street Suffk......52 H3
Corbets Tey Gt Lon......37 N3
Corbière Jersey......11 a2
Corbridge Nthumb......112 E8
Corby Nhants......61 J3
Corby Glen Lincs......73 Q6
Corby Hill Cumb......111 J9
Cordon N Ayrs......121 K5
Cordwell Derbys......84 D5
Coreley Shrops......57 L10
Cores End Bucks......35 P7
Corfe Somset......18 H11
Corfe Castle Dorset......12 G8
Corfe Mullen Dorset......12 G5
Corfton Shrops......56 H7
Corgarff Abers......149 P6
Corhampton Hants......22 H10
Corks Pond Kent......25 Q2
Corlae D & G......115 N8
Corley Warwks......59 M7
Corley Ash Warwks......59 L7
Corley Moor Warwks......59 L7
Corley Services Warwks......59 M7
Cormuir Angus......142 E4
Cornard Tye Suffk......52 F3
Corndon Devon......8 G7
Corner Row Lancs......88 E4
Corney Cumb......94 C2
Cornforth Dur......104 B4
Cornhill Abers......158 E6
Cornhill-on-Tweed Nthumb......118 G3
Cornholme Calder......89 Q5
Cornish Hall End Essex......51 Q3
Cornoigmore Ag & B......136 B6
Cornriggs Dur......102 F2
Cornsay Dur......103 M2
Cornsay Colliery Dur......103 N2
Corntown Highld......155 Q6
Corntown V Glam......29 P9
Cornwall Airport Newquay Cnwll......4 D9
Cornwell Oxon......47 Q9
Cornwood Devon......6 G7
Cornworthy Devon......7 L7
Corpach Highld......139 K2
Corpusty Norfk......76 G6
Corrachree Abers......150 D7
Corran Highld......139 J5
Corran Highld......145 P6
Corrany IoM......80 g4
Corrie D & G......110 D3
Corrie N Ayrs......121 K3
Corriecravie N Ayrs......120 H7
Corriegills N Ayrs......121 K4
Corriegour Lodge Hotel Highld......146 H9
Corriemoille Highld......155 L5
Corrimony Highld......155 L11
Corringham Lincs......85 Q2
Corringham Thurr......38 B5
Corris Gwynd......54 H3
Corris Uchaf Gwynd......54 G3
Corrow Ag & B......131 P7
Corry Highld......145 K3
Corscombe Devon......8 F5
Corscombe Dorset......11 L3
Corse Gloucs......46 E9
Corse Lawn Gloucs......46 F8
Corsham Wilts......32 G10
Corsindae Abers......150 H6
Corsley Wilts......20 F5
Corsley Heath Wilts......20 F5
Corsock D & G......108 G8
Corston BaNES......32 C11
Corston Wilts......32 H8
Corstorphine C Edin......127 M3
Cors-y-Gedol Gwynd......67 L10
Cortachy Angus......142 F6

Corton Suffk......65 Q2
Corton Wilts......20 H6
Corton Denham Somset......20 B10
Coruanan Highld......139 K4
Corwen Denbgs......68 C6
Coryates Dorset......11 N7
Coryton Devon......8 C8
Coryton Thurr......38 B5
Cosby Leics......72 E11
Coseley Dudley......58 D6
Cosford Shrops......57 Q3
Cosgrove Nhants......49 L6
Cosham C Port......15 J5
Cosheston Pembks......41 K10
Coshieville P & K......141 J8
Cossall Notts......72 D2
Cossall Marsh Notts......72 D2
Cossington Leics......72 G8
Cossington Somset......19 L6
Costessey Norfk......76 H9
Costock Notts......72 F5
Coston Leics......73 L6
Coston Norfk......76 F10
Cote Oxon......34 C4
Cote Somset......19 K6
Cotebrook Ches W......82 C11
Cotehill Cumb......111 J10
Cotes Cumb......95 K3
Cotes Leics......72 F6
Cotes Staffs......70 E8
Cotesbach Leics......60 B4
Cotes Heath Staffs......70 E8
Cotford St Luke Somset......18 G9
Cotgrave Notts......72 G3
Cothal Abers......151 M4
Cotham Notts......85 N11
Cothelstone Somset......18 G8
Cotherstone Dur......103 K7
Cothill Oxon......34 E5
Cotleigh Devon......10 E4
Cotmanhay Derbys......72 D2
Coton Cambs......62 F9
Coton Nhants......60 E6
Coton Shrops......69 P8
Coton Staffs......59 J4
Coton Staffs......70 E10
Coton Staffs......70 H8
Coton Clanford Staffs......70 F10
Coton Hayes Staffs......70 H8
Coton Hill Shrops......56 H2
Coton in the Clay Staffs......71 M9
Coton in the Elms Derbys......71 N11
Coton Park Derbys......71 P11
Cotswolds......33 J3
Cotswold Wildlife Park & Gardens Oxon......33 P3
Cott Devon......7 K6
Cottam E R Yk......99 K7
Cottam Lancs......88 G4
Cottam Notts......85 P5
Cottenham Cambs......62 F7
Cotterdale N York......96 B2
Cottered Herts......50 H5
Cotteridge Birm......58 F8
Cotterstock Nhants......61 M2
Cottesbrooke Nhants......60 F6
Cottesmore Rutlnd......73 N8
Cottingham E R Yk......92 H4
Cottingham Nhants......60 H2
Cottingley C Brad......90 E3
Cottingley Hall Crematorium Leeds......90 H4
Cottisford Oxon......48 G8
Cotton Suffk......64 F8
Cotton End Bed......61 N11
Cotton Tree Lancs......89 Q3
Cottown Abers......150 E2
Cottown Abers......151 K4
Cottown of Gight Abers......159 K9
Cotts Devon......6 C5
Cotwall Wrekin......69 R11
Cotwalton Staffs......70 G8
Couch's Mill Cnwll......5 J10
Coughton Herefs......46 A10
Coughton Warwks......47 L2
Coulaghailtro Ag & B......123 M6
Coulags Highld......154 C9
Coulderton Cumb......100 C9
Coull Abers......150 E7
Coulport Ag & B......131 Q10
Coulsdon Gt Lon......36 G9
Coulston Wilts......21 J4
Coulter S Lans......116 E4
Coultershaw Bridge W Susx......23 Q11
Coultings Somset......18 H6
Coulton N York......98 C6
Coultra Fife......135 K3
Cound Shrops......57 K3
Coundlane Shrops......57 K4
Coundon Dur......103 P5
Coundon Grange Dur......103 P5
Countersett N York......96 D3
Countess Wilts......21 N6
Countess Cross Essex......52 E5
Countess Wear Devon......9 M7
Countesthorpe Leics......72 F11
Counties Crematorium Nhants......60 F9
Countisbury Devon......17 N2
Coupar Angus P & K......142 C10
Coup Green Lancs......88 H5
Coupland Cumb......102 D7
Coupland Nthumb......118 H4
Cour Ag & B......123 P10
Court-at-Street Kent......27 J4
Courteachan Highld......145 L8
Courteenhall Nhants......49 L4
Court Henry Carmth......43 L10
Courtsend Essex......38 H3
Courtway Somset......18 H8
Cousland Mdloth......128 B6
Cousley Wood E Susx......25 Q4
Cove Ag & B......131 Q11
Cove Border......129 K5
Cove Devon......18 C11
Cove Hants......23 N3
Cove Highld......160 C8
Cove Bay C Aber......151 P7
Cove Bottom Suffk......65 P6
Covehithe Suffk......65 Q5
Coven Staffs......58 D3
Coveney Cambs......62 G4
Covenham St Bartholomew Lincs......87 K2
Covenham St Mary Lincs......87 K2
Coven Heath Staffs......58 D3
Coventry Covtry......59 M9
Coverack Cnwll......3 K10
Coverack Bridges Cnwll......2 H7

Coverham N York......96 H3
Covington Cambs......61 N6
Covington S Lans......116 D3
Cowan Bridge Lancs......95 N5
Cowbeech E Susx......25 P8
Cowbit Lincs......74 E7
Cowbridge V Glam......30 C10
Cowdale Derbys......83 N10
Cowden Kent......25 L2
Cowdenbeath Fife......134 F7
Cowden Pound Kent......25 L2
Cowden Station Kent......25 L2
Cowers Lane Derbys......71 Q5
Cowes IoW......14 F8
Cowesby N York......97 Q3
Cowesfield Green Wilts......21 Q10
Cowfold W Susx......24 F6
Cowgill Cumb......95 R3
Cow Green Suffk......64 F8
Cowhill S Glos......32 B6
Cowie Stirlg......133 N10
Cowlam E R Yk......99 K7
Cowley Devon......9 M5
Cowley Gloucs......33 J2
Cowley Gt Lon......36 C4
Cowley Oxon......34 F4
Cowling Lancs......88 H7
Cowling N York......90 B2
Cowling N York......97 K3
Cowlinge Suffk......63 M10
Cowmes Kirk......90 F7
Cowpe Lancs......89 N6
Cowpen Nthumb......113 L4
Cowpen Bewley S on T......104 E6
Cowplain Hants......15 J4
Cowshill Dur......102 G2
Cowslip Green N Som......19 N2
Cowthorpe N York......97 P10
Coxall Herefs......56 F10
Coxbank Ches E......70 B6
Coxbench Derbys......72 B2
Coxbridge Somset......19 P7
Cox Common Suffk......65 N5
Coxford Cnwll......5 K2
Coxford Norfk......76 B6
Coxgreen Staffs......57 Q7
Coxheath Kent......38 B11
Coxhoe Dur......104 B3
Coxley Somset......19 P6
Coxley Wakefd......90 H7
Coxley Wick Somset......19 P6
Coxpark Cnwll......5 Q7
Coxtie Green Essex......51 N11
Coxwold N York......98 A5
Coychurch Brdgnd......29 P9
Coychurch Crematorium Brdgnd......29 P8
Coylton S Ayrs......114 H4
Coylumbridge Highld......148 G5
Coytrahen Brdgnd......29 N7
Crabbs Cross Worcs......58 F11
Crab Orchard Dorset......13 J3
Crabtree W Susx......24 F5
Crabtree Green Wrexhm......69 K6
Crackenthorpe Cumb......102 C6
Crackington Haven Cnwll......5 J2
Crackley Staffs......70 E4
Crackley Warwks......59 L10
Crackleybank Shrops......57 P2
Crackpot N York......103 J11
Cracoe N York......96 E8
Craddock Devon......10 B2
Cradle End Herts......51 L6
Cradley Dudley......58 D7
Cradley Herefs......46 D5
Cradley Heath Sandw......58 D7
Cradoc Powys......44 E8
Crafthole Cnwll......5 P11
Crafton Bucks......49 N11
Crag Foot Lancs......95 K6
Craggan Highld......149 J2
Cragganmore Moray......157 M10
Cragg Hill Leeds......90 G3
Cragg Vale Calder......90 C6
Craghead Dur......113 K10
Cragside House & Garden Nthumb......119 L10
Crai Powys......44 B10
Craibstone Moray......158 C6
Craichie Angus......143 J8
Craig Angus......143 M6
Craig Highld......154 D8
Craigbank E Ayrs......115 L5
Craigburn Border......127 N7
Craigcefnparc Swans......29 J4
Craigcleuch D & G......110 F3
Craigdam Abers......159 K11
Craigdhu Ag & B......130 G6
Craigearn Abers......151 J5
Craigellachie Moray......157 P9
Craigend P & K......134 E3
Craigend Rens......125 M3
Craigendoran Ag & B......132 C11
Craigends Rens......125 L4
Craighlaw D & G......107 K5
Craighouse Ag & B......122 H6
Craigie P & K......141 R9
Craigie S Ayrs......125 L11
Craigiefold Abers......159 M4
Craigley D & G......108 G9
Craig Llangiwg Neath......29 K4
Craiglockhart C Edin......127 N3
Craigmillar C Edin......127 Q3
Craignant Shrops......69 J7
Craigneston D & G......115 Q10
Craigneuk N Lans......126 D4
Craigneuk N Lans......126 D4
Craignure Ag & B......138 C10
Craigo Angus......143 M5
Craig Penllyn V Glam......30 C9
Craigrothie Fife......135 K5
Craigruie Stirlg......132 F3
Craig's End Essex......52 B4
Craigton Angus......143 J10
Craigton C Aber......151 M7
Craigton E Rens......125 M7
Craigton Crematorium C Glas......125 N5
Craigton of Airlie Angus......142 E7
Craig-y-Duke Neath......29 K4
Craig-y-nos Powys......44 A11
Craik Border......117 L9
Crail Fife......135 Q6
Crailing Border......118 C6
Crailinghall Border......118 C6
Craiselound N Linc......92 C11
Crakehall N York......97 K3
Crakehill N York......97 P6
Crakemarsh Staffs......71 K7
Crambe N York......98 E8
Cramlington Nthumb......113 L5

Cramond C Edin......127 M2
Cramond Bridge C Edin......127 M2
Crampmoor Hants......22 C10
Cranage Ches E......82 G11
Cranberry Staffs......70 E7
Cranborne Dorset......13 J2
Cranbourne Br For......35 P10
Cranbrook Devon......9 N6
Cranbrook Kent......26 C4
Cranbrook Common Kent......26 C4
Crane Moor Barns......91 J10
Crane's Corner Norfk......76 C9
Cranfield C Beds......49 Q6
Cranford Devon......16 E7
Cranford Gt Lon......36 D5
Cranford St Andrew Nhants......61 K5
Cranford St John Nhants......61 K5
Cranham Gloucs......32 G2
Cranham Gt Lon......37 N3
Cranhill Warwks......47 M4
Crank St Hel......81 Q5
Cranleigh Surrey......24 C3
Cranmer Green Suffk......64 E7
Cranmore IoW......14 C8
Cranmore Somset......20 C6
Cranoe Leics......73 K11
Cransford Suffk......65 L9
Cranshaws Border......128 H7
Cranstal IoM......80 g1
Cranswick E R Yk......99 L10
Crantock Cnwll......4 B9
Cranwell Lincs......86 D11
Cranwich Norfk......63 N2
Cranworth Norfk......76 D11
Craobh Haven Ag & B......130 F6
Crapstone Devon......6 E5
Crarae Ag & B......131 K8
Crask Inn Highld......162 C2
Crask of Aigas Highld......155 N9
Craster Nthumb......119 Q7
Craswall Herefs......45 K7
Crateford Staffs......58 D3
Cratfield Suffk......65 L6
Crathes Abers......151 K8
Crathes Crematorium Abers......151 K8
Crathie Abers......149 P8
Crathie Highld......147 P9
Crathorne N York......104 D9
Craven Arms Shrops......56 G8
Crawcrook Gatesd......112 H8
Crawford Lancs......81 P4
Crawford S Lans......116 D6
Crawfordjohn S Lans......116 B6
Crawley Hants......22 D8
Crawley Oxon......34 B2
Crawley W Susx......24 G3
Crawley Down W Susx......24 H3
Crawleyside Dur......103 J2
Crawshawbooth Lancs......89 N5
Crawton Abers......143 R2
Craxe's Green Essex......52 E5
Cray N York......96 D5
Crayford Gt Lon......37 M5
Crayke N York......98 B6
Craymere Beck Norfk......76 F5
Crays Hill Essex......38 B3
Cray's Pond Oxon......34 H8
Craythorne Staffs......71 N9
Craze Lowman Devon......9 N2
Crazies Hill Wokam......35 L8
Creacombe Devon......17 Q8
Creagan Inn Ag & B......138 H9
Creag Ghoraidh W Isls......168 c13
Creagorry W Isls......168 c13
Creaguaineach Lodge Highld......139 Q4
Creamore Bank Shrops......69 P8
Creaton Nhants......60 F7
Creca D & G......110 D6
Credenhill Herefs......45 P6
Crediton Devon......9 K4
Creebank D & G......107 K2
Creebridge D & G......107 M4
Creech Dorset......12 F8
Creech Heathfield Somset......19 J9
Creech St Michael Somset......19 J9
Creed Cnwll......3 N4
Creekmoor Poole......12 H6
Creekmouth Gt Lon......37 L4
Creeksea Essex......38 F2
Creeting St Mary Suffk......64 F10
Creeton Lincs......73 Q6
Creetown D & G......107 N6
Cregneash IoM......80 a8
Creg ny Baa IoM......80 e5
Cregrina Powys......44 G4
Creich Fife......135 J3
Creigiau Cardif......30 E8
Cremyll Cnwll......6 C8
Cressage Shrops......57 K4
Cressbrook Derbys......83 Q10
Cresselly Pembks......41 L9
Cressex Bucks......35 M6
Cressing Essex......52 C7
Cresswell Nthumb......113 L2
Cresswell Pembks......41 L9
Cresswell Staffs......70 H7
Creswell Derbys......84 H6
Creswell Green Staffs......58 G2
Cretingham Suffk......65 J9
Cretshengan Ag & B......123 M6
Crewe Ches E......70 C3
Crewe-by-Farndon Ches E......69 M4
Crewe Crematorium Ches E......70 C3
Crewe Green Ches E......70 C3
Crew Green Powys......69 K11
Crewkerne Somset......11 J3
Crews Hill Station Gt Lon......50 H10
Crewton C Derb......72 B4
Crianlarich Stirlg......132 D2
Cribyn Cerdgn......43 K4
Criccieth Gwynd......66 H7
Crich Derbys......84 D10
Crich Carr Derbys......84 D10
Crichton Mdloth......128 B7
Crick Mons......31 N6
Crick Nhants......60 C6
Crickadarn Powys......44 F6
Cricket St Thomas Somset......10 H3
Crickheath Shrops......69 J10
Crickhowell Powys......45 J11
Cricklade Wilts......33 L6
Cricklewood Gt Lon......36 F3

266 Cridling Stubbs – Davington Hill

Cridling Stubbs N York 91 N6
Crieff P & K 133 P3
Criggan Cnwll 4 G9
Criggion Powys 69 J11
Crigglestone Wakefd 91 J7
Crimble Rochdl 89 P8
Crimond Abers 159 Q6
Crimplesham Norfk 75 N10
Crimscote Warwks 47 P5
Crinaglack Highld 155 M9
Crinan Ag & B 130 F9
Crindledyke N Lans 126 E6
Cringleford Norfk 76 H10
Cringles C Brad 96 F11
Crinow Pembks 41 M8
Cripplesease Cnwll 2 E6
Cripplestyle Dorset 13 J2
Cripp's Corner E Susx 26 C7
Croachy Highld 148 B2
Croanford Cnwll 4 G7
Crockenhill Kent 37 M7
Crocker End Oxon 35 K7
Crockerhill W Susx 15 P5
Crockernwell Devon 9 J6
Crocker's Ash Herefs 45 Q11
Crockerton Wilts 20 G6
Crocketford D & G 108 H6
Crockey Hill C York 98 C11
Crockham Hill Kent 37 K10
Crockhurst Street Kent 37 P11
Crockleford Heath Essex 52 H6
Crock Street Somset 10 G2
Croeserw Neath 29 N5
Croes-goch Pembks 40 F4
Croes-lan Cerdgn 42 G6
Croesor Gwynd 67 L6
Croesyceiliog Carmth 42 H11
Croesyceiliog Torfn 31 K5
Croes-y-mwyalch Torfn 31 K6
Croes-y-pant Mons 31 K4
Croft Leics 72 E11
Croft Lincs 87 P8
Croft Warrtn 82 D6
Croftamie Stirlg 132 F10
Croft Mitchell Cnwll 2 H6
Crofton Cumb 110 F10
Crofton Wakefd 91 K7
Crofton Wilts 21 Q2
Croft-on-Tees N York 103 Q9
Croftown Highld 161 K10
Crofts Moray 157 P7
Crofts Bank Traffd 82 G5
Crofts of Dipple Moray 157 Q6
Crofts of Savoch Abers 159 P5
Crofty Swans 28 F6
Crogen Gwynd 68 D7
Croggan Ag & B 130 E2
Croglin Cumb 111 L11
Croick Highld 162 B8
Cromarty Highld 156 D4
Crombie Fife 134 D11
Cromdale Highld 149 K2
Cromer Herts 50 G5
Cromer Norfk 77 J3
Cromford Derbys 84 C9
Cromhall S Glos 32 C6
Cromhall Common S Glos 32 C7
Cromor W Isls 168 j5
Crompton Fold Oldham 89 Q9
Cromwell Notts 85 N8
Cronberry E Ayrs 115 M3
Crondall Hants 23 L5
Cronkbourne IoM 80 e6
Cronk-y-Voddy IoM 80 d4
Cronton Knows 81 P7
Crook Cumb 101 N11
Crook Dur 103 N3
Crookdake Cumb 100 G2
Crooke Wigan 88 H9
Crooked End Gloucs 46 B11
Crookedholm E Ayrs 125 M10
Crooked Soley Wilts 34 B10
Crookes Sheff 84 D3
Crookhall Dur 112 H10
Crookham Nthumb 118 H3
Crookham W Berk 22 F2
Crookham Village Hants 23 L4
Crook Inn Border 116 G5
Crooklands Cumb 95 L4
Crook of Devon P & K 134 C7
Cropper Derbys 71 N7
Cropredy Oxon 48 E5
Cropston Leics 72 F8
Cropthorne Worcs 47 J5
Cropton N York 98 F3
Cropwell Bishop Notts 72 H3
Cropwell Butler Notts 72 H3
Cros W Isls 168 k1
Crosbost W Isls 168 i5
Crosby Cumb 100 E3
Crosby IoM 80 d6
Crosby N Linc 92 E8
Crosby Sefton 81 L5
Crosby Garret Cumb 102 D9
Crosby Ravensworth Cumb 102 B8
Crosby Villa Cumb 100 E3
Croscombe Somset 19 Q6
Crosemere Shrops 69 M9
Crosland Edge Kirk 90 E8
Crosland Hill Kirk 90 E8
Cross Somset 19 M4
Crossaig Ag & B 123 P9
Crossapol Ag & B 136 B7
Cross Ash Mons 45 N11
Cross-at-Hand Kent 26 C2
Crossbost W Isls 168 i5
Crossbush W Susx 24 B9
Crosscanonby Cumb 100 E3
Cross Coombe Cnwll 3 J3
Crossdale Street Norfk 77 J4
Cross End Bed 61 N9
Cross End Essex 52 E5
Crossens Sefton 88 D6
Cross Flatts C Brad 90 E2
Crossford Fife 134 D10
Crossford S Lans 126 E8
Crossgate Cnwll 5 N4
Crossgate Lincs 74 D5
Crossgate Staffs 70 G7
Crossgatehall E Loth 128 B6
Crossgates E Ayrs 125 K9
Crossgates Fife 134 E10
Cross Gates Leeds 91 K4
Crossgates N York 99 L4
Crossgates Powys 44 F2
Crossgill Lancs 95 M8
Cross Green Devon 5 P4
Cross Green Leeds 91 J4
Cross Green Staffs 58 D3
Cross Green Suffk 64 A11
Cross Green Suffk 64 B10
Cross Green Suffk 64 D11
Cross Hands Carmth 28 G2
Crosshands Carmth 41 N6
Crosshands E Ayrs 125 M11
Cross Hands Pembks 41 L8
Cross Hill Derbys 84 F11
Crosshill Fife 134 F8
Crosshill S Ayrs 114 F6
Cross Hills N York 96 F11
Crosshouse E Ayrs 125 K10
Cross Houses Shrops 57 J3
Cross Houses Shrops 57 M6
Cross in Hand E Susx 25 N6
Cross Inn Cerdgn 42 G3
Cross Inn Cerdgn 43 K2
Cross Inn Pembks 41 M9
Cross Inn Rhondd 30 E8
Cross Keys Ag & B 132 C10
Crosskeys Caerph 30 H6
Cross Keys Wilts 32 G10
Crosskirk Highld 166 H3
Crosslands Cumb 94 G3
Cross Lane IoW 14 F9
Cross Lane Head Shrops 57 N5
Cross Lanes Cnwll 2 H9
Cross Lanes Cnwll 3 K5
Cross Lanes N York 98 A8
Crosslanes Shrops 69 K11
Cross Lanes Wrexhm 69 L5
Crosslee Rens 125 L4
Crossley Kirk 90 G6
Crossmichael D & G 108 F7
Cross Oak Powys 44 G10
Cross of Jackston Abers 158 H11
Cross o' th' hands Derbys 71 P5
Crosspost W Susx 24 G6
Crossroads Abers 150 F6
Crossroads Abers 151 K9
Cross Roads C Brad 90 D3
Cross Street Suffk 64 H6
Crosston Angus 143 J6
Cross Town Ches E 82 G9
Crossway Mons 45 N11
Crossway Powys 44 F3
Crossway Green Mons 31 P6
Crossway Green Worcs 58 B11
Crossways Dorset 12 C7
Crosswell Pembks 41 M3
Crosthwaite Cumb 95 J2
Croston Lancs 88 F7
Crostwick Norfk 77 K8
Crostwight Norfk 77 L6
Crouch Kent 37 P9
Crouch Kent 39 J10
Crouch End Gt Lon 36 H3
Croucheston Wilts 21 L9
Crouch Hill Dorset 11 Q2
Crough House Green Kent 37 K11
Croughton Nhants 48 F8
Crovie Abers 159 K4
Crow Hants 13 L4
Crowan Cnwll 2 G7
Crowborough E Susx 25 M4
Crowborough Warren E Susx 25 M4
Crowcombe Somset 18 F7
Crowdecote Derbys 83 P11
Crowden Derbys 83 N5
Crowden Devon 8 C5
Crowdhill Hants 22 E10
Crowdleham Kent 37 N9
Crow Edge Barns 83 Q4
Crowell Oxon 35 K5
Crow End Cambs 62 D9
Crowfield Nhants 48 H6
Crowfield Suffk 64 G10
Crowfield Green Suffk 64 G10
Crowgate Street Norfk 77 L7
Crow Green Essex 51 N11
Crowhill E Loth 129 J5
Crow Hill Herefs 46 B9
Crowhole Derbys 84 D5
Crowhurst E Susx 26 C9
Crowhurst Surrey 37 J11
Crowhurst Lane End Surrey 37 J11
Crowland Lincs 74 D8
Crowland Suffk 64 E7
Crowlas Cnwll 2 E7
Crowle N Linc 92 C8
Crowle Worcs 46 H3
Crowle Green Worcs 46 H3
Crowmarsh Gifford Oxon 34 H7
Crown Corner Suffk 65 K7
Crownhill C Plym 6 D7
Crownhill Crematorium M Keyn 49 M7
Crownpits Surrey 23 Q6
Crownthorpe Norfk 76 F11
Crowntown Cnwll 2 G7
Crows-an-Wra Cnwll 2 B8
Crow's Green Essex 51 Q5
Crowshill Norfk 76 D10
Crow's Nest Cnwll 5 M8
Crowsnest Shrops 56 F4
Crowthorne Wokham 23 M2
Crowton Ches W 82 C10
Croxall Staffs 59 J2
Croxby Lincs 93 L11
Croxdale Dur 103 Q3
Croxden Staffs 71 K7
Croxley Green Herts 50 C11
Croxteth Lpool 81 N5
Croxton Cambs 62 B8
Croxton N Linc 93 J8
Croxton Norfk 64 B4
Croxton Norfk 76 D5
Croxton Staffs 70 D8
Croxtonbank Staffs 70 D8
Croxton Green Ches E 69 Q4
Croxton Kerrial Leics 73 L5
Croy Highld 156 D8
Croy N Lans 126 C2
Croyde Devon 16 G4
Croyde Bay Devon 16 G4
Croydon Cambs 62 D11
Croydon Gt Lon 36 H7
Croydon Crematorium Gt Lon 36 H7
Crubenmore Highld 148 B9
Cruckmeole Shrops 56 G3
Cruckton Shrops 56 G2
Cruden Bay Abers 159 Q10
Crudgington Wrekin 70 A11
Crudie Abers 159 J6
Crudwell Wilts 33 J6
Cruft Devon 8 D5
Crûg Powys 56 B10
Crugmeer Cnwll 4 E6
Crugybar Carmth 43 N7
Crug-y-byddar Powys 56 B8
Crumlin Caerph 30 H5
Crumplehorn Cnwll 5 L11
Crumpsall Manch 82 H4
Crundale Kent 27 J2
Crundale Pembks 41 J7
Crunwear Pembks 41 N8
Cruwys Morchard Devon 9 L2
Crux Easton Hants 22 D3
Cruxton Dorset 11 N5
Crwbin Carmth 28 E2
Cryers Hill Bucks 35 N5
Crymych Pembks 41 N4
Crynant Neath 29 L4
Crystal Palace Gt Lon 36 H6
Cuaig Highld 153 N6
Cuan Ag & B 130 F5
Cubbington Warwks 59 M11
Cubert Cnwll 4 B10
Cubley Barns 90 G10
Cublington Bucks 49 M10
Cublington Herefs 45 N7
Cuckfield W Susx 24 H5
Cucklington Somset 20 E9
Cuckney Notts 85 J6
Cuckoo Bridge Lincs 74 D6
Cuckoo's Corner Hants 23 K6
Cuckoo's Nest Ches W 69 L2
Cuddesdon Oxon 34 G4
Cuddington Bucks 35 K2
Cuddington Ches W 82 C10
Cuddington Heath Ches W 69 N5
Cuddy Hill Lancs 88 F3
Cudham Gt Lon 37 K9
Cudliptown Devon 8 D9
Cudnell Bmouth 13 J5
Cudworth Barns 91 K9
Cudworth Somset 10 H2
Cuerdley Cross Warrtn 82 B7
Cufaude Hants 23 J3
Cuffley Herts 50 H10
Cuil Highld 138 H6
Culbokie Highld 155 R6
Culbone Somset 17 Q2
Culburnie Highld 155 N9
Culcabock Highld 156 B9
Culcharry Highld 156 F7
Culcheth Warrtn 82 E6
Culdrain Abers 158 D11
Culduie Highld 153 N9
Culford Suffk 64 A7
Culgaith Cumb 102 B5
Culham Oxon 34 F5
Culkein Highld 164 B10
Culkein Drumbeg Highld 164 D10
Culkerton Gloucs 32 H5
Cullen Moray 158 D4
Cullercoats N Tyne 113 N6
Cullerlie Abers 151 K7
Cullicudden Highld 156 A5
Cullingworth C Brad 90 D3
Cuillin Hills Highld 144 G3
Cullipool Ag & B 130 E5
Cullivoe Shet 169 s3
Culloden Highld 156 C8
Cullompton Devon 9 P3
Cullompton Services Devon 9 P3
Culm Davy Devon 18 F11
Culmington Shrops 56 H8
Culmstock Devon 10 C2
Culnacraig Highld 160 H6
Culnaightrie D & G 108 G10
Culnaknock Highld 153 J5
Culpho Suffk 53 M2
Culrain Highld 162 D8
Culross Fife 134 B10
Culroy S Ayrs 114 F5
Culsalmond Abers 158 G11
Culscadden D & G 107 N8
Culshabbin D & G 107 K7
Culswick Shet 169 p9
Cultercullen Abers 151 N3
Cults C Aber 151 M7
Culverstone Green Kent 37 P8
Culverthorpe Lincs 73 Q2
Culworth Nhants 48 F5
Culzean Castle & Country Park S Ayrs 114 D5
Cumbernauld N Lans 126 D3
Cumbernauld Village N Lans 126 D2
Cumberworth Lincs 87 P6
Cumdivock Cumb 110 F11
Cuminestown Abers 159 K7
Cumledge Border 129 K8
Cummersdale Cumb 110 G10
Cummertrees D & G 109 P7
Cummingston Moray 157 L4
Cumnock E Ayrs 115 L3
Cumnor Oxon 34 E4
Cumrew Cumb 111 L10
Cumrue D & G 109 N3
Cumwhinton Cumb 111 J10
Cumwhitton Cumb 111 K10
Cundall N York 97 P6
Cunninghamhead N Ayrs 125 K9
Cunningsburgh Shet 169 r10
Cupar Fife 135 K5
Cupar Muir Fife 135 K5
Curbar Derbys 84 C6
Curbridge Hants 14 F4
Curbridge Oxon 34 B3
Curdridge Hants 14 F4
Curdworth Warwks 59 J6
Curland Somset 19 J11
Curridge W Berk 34 E10
Currie C Edin 127 M4
Curry Mallet Somset 19 K10
Curry Rivel Somset 19 L9
Curteis Corner Kent 26 E4
Curtisden Green Kent 26 B3
Curtisknowle Devon 7 J8
Cury Cnwll 2 H9
Cushnie Abers 150 E5
Cushuish Somset 18 G8
Cusop Herefs 45 J6
Cusworth Donc 91 N10
Cutcloy D & G 107 N11
Cutcombe Somset 18 B7
Cutgate Rochdl 89 P8
Cuthill Highld 162 H9
Cutiau Gwynd 67 L11
Cutler's Green Essex 51 N4
Cutmadoc Cnwll 4 H9
Cutmere Cnwll 5 N9
Cutnall Green Worcs 58 C11
Cutsdean Gloucs 47 L8
Cutsyke Wakefd 91 L6
Cutthorpe Derbys 84 D6
Cuttivett Cnwll 5 P9
Cuxham Oxon 35 J5
Cuxton Medway 38 B8
Cuxwold Lincs 93 L10
Cwm Blae G 30 G3
Cwm Denbgs 80 F9
Cwmafan Neath 29 L6
Cwmaman Rhondd 30 D5
Cwmann Carmth 43 L5
Cwmavon Torfn 31 J3
Cwmbach Carmth 28 E4
Cwmbach Carmth 41 Q5
Cwmbâch Powys 44 H7
Cwmbach Rhondd 30 D4
Cwmbach Llechrhyd Powys 44 E4
Cwmbelan Powys 55 L8
Cwmbran Torfn 31 J6
Cwmbrwyno Cerdgn 54 G8
Cwm Capel Carmth 28 E4
Cwmcarn Caerph 30 H6
Cwmcarvan Mons 31 N3
Cwm-celyn Blae G 30 H3
Cwm-Cewydd Gwynd 55 K2
Cwm-cou Cerdgn 41 Q2
Cwm Crawnon Powys 44 G11
Cwmdare Rhondd 30 C4
Cwmdu Carmth 43 M8
Cwmdu Powys 44 H10
Cwmdu Swans 28 H6
Cwmduad Carmth 42 G8
Cwm Dulais Swans 28 H4
Cwmdwr Carmth 43 P8
Cwmfelin Brdgnd 29 N7
Cwmfelin Myr Td 30 E4
Cwmfelin Boeth Carmth 41 N7
Cwmfelinfach Caerph 30 G6
Cwmfelin Mynach Carmth 41 P6
Cwmffrwd Carmth 42 H11
Cwmgiedd Powys 29 L2
Cwmgorse Carmth 29 K2
Cwm Gwaun Pembks 41 K4
Cwmgwili Carmth 28 G2
Cwmgwrach Neath 29 N4
Cwmhiraeth Carmth 42 F7
Cwm-Ifor Carmth 43 N9
Cwm Irfon Powys 44 B5
Cwmisfael Carmth 43 J11
Cwm Llinau Powys 55 J3
Cwmllynfell Neath 29 K2
Cwmmawr Carmth 28 F2
Cwm Morgan Carmth 41 Q4
Cwmparc Rhondd 29 P5
Cwmpengraig Carmth 42 G7
Cwm Penmachno Conwy 67 P5
Cwmpennar Rhondd 30 D4
Cwmrhos Powys 44 H10
Cwmrhydyceirw Swans 29 J5
Cwmsychbant Cerdgn 43 J5
Cwmtillery Blae G 30 H3
Cwm-twrch Isaf Powys 29 L2
Cwm-twrch Uchaf Powys 29 L2
Cwm-y-glo Carmth 28 G2
Cwm-y-glo Gwynd 67 K2
Cwmyoy Mons 45 K10
Cwmystwyth Cerdgn 54 H10
Cwrt Gwynd 54 F5
Cwrt-newydd Cerdgn 43 J5
Cwrt-y-gollen Powys 45 J11
Cyfarthfa Castle Museum Myr Td 30 D3
Cyfronydd Powys 55 Q3
Cylibebyll Neath 29 K4
Cymau Flints 69 J3
Cymer Neath 29 N5
Cymmer Rhondd 30 D6
Cynghordy Carmth 43 R6
Cynheidre Carmth 28 E3
Cynonville Neath 29 M5
Cynwyd Denbgs 68 E6
Cynwyl Elfed Carmth 42 G9

D

Daccombe Devon 7 N5
Dacre Cumb 101 N5
Dacre N York 97 J8
Dacre Banks N York 97 J8
Daddry Shield Dur 102 G3
Dadford Bucks 49 J7
Dadlington Leics 72 C11
Dafen Carmth 28 F4
Daffy Green Norfk 76 D10
Dagenham Gt Lon 37 M4
Daglingworth Gloucs 33 J3
Dagnall Bucks 49 Q11
Dagworth Suffk 64 E9
Dail bho Dheas W Isls 168 j1
Dailly S Ayrs 114 E7
Dainton Devon 7 M5
Dairsie Fife 135 L4
Daisy Hill Bolton 82 E4
Daisy Hill Leeds 90 H5
Dalabrog W Isls 168 c15
Dalavich Ag & B 131 K5
Dalbeattie D & G 108 H8
Dalbury Derbys 71 P8
Dalby IoM 80 b6
Dalby Lincs 87 M7
Dalby N York 98 C6
Dalcapon P & K 141 N7
Dalchalm Highld 163 L5
Dalchreichart Highld 146 H5
Dalchruin P & K 133 L4
Dalcrue P & K 134 C2
Dalderby Lincs 87 J7
Dalditch Devon 9 P8
Daldowie Crematorium C Glas 126 B5
Dale Cumb 101 P2
Dale Derbys 72 C3
Dale Pembks 40 F9
Dale Bottom Cumb 101 J6
Dale End Derbys 84 B8
Dale End N York 96 E11
Dale Hill E Susx 26 B5
Dalehouse N York 105 L7
Dalelia Highld 138 C4
Dalgarven N Ayrs 124 H8
Dalgety Bay Fife 134 F11
Dalgig E Ayrs 115 L5
Dalginross P & K 133 M3
Dalguise P & K 141 N8
Dalhalvaig Highld 166 E6
Dalham Suffk 63 M8
Daliburgh W Isls 168 c15
Dalkeith Mdloth 127 Q4
Dallas Moray 157 L7
Dallinghoo Suffk 65 K10
Dallington E Susx 25 Q7
Dallington Nhants 60 F8
Dallow N York 97 J6
Dalmally Ag & B 131 P2
Dalmary Stirlg 132 G8
Dalmellington E Ayrs 115 J6
Dalmeny C Edin 127 L2
Dalmore Highld 156 B4
Dalmuir W Duns 125 M3
Dalnabreck Highld 138 C4
Dalnacardoch P & K 140 H3
Dalnahaitnach Highld 148 F4
Dalnaspidal P & K 140 F3
Dalnawillan Lodge Highld 166 H8
Daloist P & K 141 J6
Dalqueich P & K 134 D7
Dalquhairn S Ayrs 114 F8
Dalreavoch Highld 162 H5
Dalry N Ayrs 124 H8
Dalrymple E Ayrs 114 G5
Dalserf S Lans 126 D7
Dalsmeran Ag & B 120 B9
Dalston Cumb 110 G10
Dalston Gt Lon 36 H4
Dalswinton D & G 109 K3
Dalton Cumb 95 L5
Dalton D & G 109 P6
Dalton Lancs 88 F9
Dalton N York 97 P5
Dalton N York 103 M9
Dalton Nthumb 112 H6
Dalton Rothm 84 G2
Dalton-in-Furness Cumb 94 E6
Dalton-le-Dale Dur 113 P11
Dalton Magna Rothm 84 G2
Dalton-on-Tees N York 103 Q9
Dalton Parva Rothm 84 G2
Dalton Piercy Hartpl 104 E4
Dalveich Stirlg 133 J3
Dalwhinnie Highld 147 Q11
Dalwood Devon 10 E4
Damask Green Herts 50 G5
Damerham Hants 21 M11
Damgate Norfk 77 N10
Dam Green Norfk 64 E4
Damnaglaur D & G 106 F10
Danaway Kent 38 E9
Danbury Essex 52 C10
Danby N York 105 K9
Danby Bottom N York 105 J10
Danby Wiske N York 104 B11
Dandaleith Moray 157 P8
Danderhall Mdloth 127 Q4
Danebridge Ches E 83 L11
Dane End Herts 50 H6
Danegate E Susx 25 N4
Danehill E Susx 25 K5
Dane Hills C Leic 72 F10
Danemoor Green Norfk 76 F10
Danesford Shrops 57 N6
Danesmoor Derbys 84 F8
Dane Street Kent 39 J11
Daniel's Water Kent 26 G3
Danshillock Abers 158 H6
Danskine E Loth 128 F6
Danthorpe E R Yk 93 N4
Danzey Green Warwks 58 H11
Dapple Heath Staffs 71 J9
Darby Green Hants 23 M2
Darcy Lever Bolton 89 L9
Dardy Powys 45 J11
Darenth Kent 37 N6
Daresbury Halton 82 C8
Darfield Barns 91 L10
Darfoulds Notts 85 J5
Dargate Kent 39 J9
Dargavel Rens 125 L3
Darite Cnwll 5 M8
Darland Medway 38 C8
Darland Wrexhm 69 L3
Darlaston Wsall 58 E5
Darlaston Green Wsall 58 E5
Darley N York 97 K9
Darley Abbey C Derb 72 B3
Darley Bridge Derbys 84 C8
Darley Dale Derbys 84 C8
Darley Green Solhll 59 J10
Darleyhall Herts 50 D6
Darley Head N York 97 J9
Darlingscott Warwks 47 P6
Darlington Darltn 103 Q8
Darlington Crematorium Darltn 103 Q8
Darliston Shrops 69 Q8
Darlton Notts 85 N6
Darnford Staffs 58 H3
Darnick Border 117 Q4
Darowen Powys 55 J4
Darra Abers 158 H8
Darracott Devon 16 C8
Darracott Devon 16 H4
Darras Hall Nthumb 113 J6
Darrington Wakefd 91 M7
Darsham Suffk 65 N8
Darshill Somset 20 B6
Dartford Kent 37 M6
Dartford Crossing Kent 37 N5
Dartington Devon 7 K6
Dartmeet Devon 6 H4
Dartmoor National Park Devon 8 G9
Dartmouth Devon 7 M8
Darton Barns 91 J8
Darvel E Ayrs 125 P10
Darwell Hole E Susx 25 Q7
Darwen Bl w D 89 K6
Datchet W & M 35 Q9
Datchworth Herts 50 G7
Datchworth Green Herts 50 G7
Daubhill Bolton 89 L9
Daugh of Kinermony Moray 157 N9
Dauntsey Wilts 33 J8
Dava Highld 157 J10
Davenham Ches W 82 E10
Davenport Stockp 83 K7
Davenport Green Ches E 82 H9
Davenport Green Traffd 82 H7
Daventry Nhants 60 C8
Davidson's Mains C Edin 127 N2
Davidstow Cnwll 5 K4
David Street Kent 37 P8
Davington D & G 117 J10
Davington Hill Kent 38 H9

Daviot – Dullingham 267

Daviot Abers 151 J2
Daviot Highld 156 C10
Daviot House Highld 156 C9
Davis's Town E Susx 25 M7
Davoch of Grange Moray 158 C7
Davyhulme Traffd 82 G5
Daw End Wsall 58 F4
Dawesgreen Surrey 36 F11
Dawley Wrekin 57 M3
Dawlish Devon 9 N9
Dawlish Warren Devon 9 N9
Dawn Conwy 80 B10
Daws Green Somset 18 G10
Daws Heath Essex 38 D4
Daw's House Cnwll 5 N5
Dawsmere Lincs 74 H4
Daybrook Notts 85 J11
Day Green Ches E 70 D3
Dayhills Staffs 70 H8
Dayhouse Bank Worcs 58 E9
Daylesford Gloucs 47 P9
Ddol Flints 80 G10
Ddol-Cownwy Powys 68 D11
Deal Kent 39 Q11
Dean Cumb 100 E5
Dean Devon 7 J6
Dean Devon 17 L2
Dean Devon 17 N2
Dean Dorset 21 J11
Dean Hants 22 D8
Dean Hants 22 G11
Dean Lancs 89 P5
Dean Oxon 48 B10
Dean Somset 20 C6
Dean Bottom Kent 37 N7
Deanburnhaugh Border 117 M8
Deancombe Devon 7 J6
Dean Court Oxon 34 E3
Deane Bolton 89 K9
Deane Hants 22 F4
Dean End Dorset 21 J11
Dean Head Barns 90 H10
Deanhead Kirk 90 C7
Deanland Dorset 21 J11
Deanlane End W Susx 15 K4
Dean Prior Devon 7 J6
Deanraw Nthumb 112 B8
Dean Row Ches E 83 J8
Deans W Loth 127 J4
Deanscales Cumb 100 E5
Deanshanger Nhants 49 L7
Deanshaugh Moray 157 R7
Deanston Stirlg 133 L7
Dean Street Kent 38 B11
Dearham Cumb 100 E3
Dearnley Rochdl 89 Q7
Debach Suffk 65 J11
Debden Essex 51 K11
Debden Essex 51 N4
Debden Green Essex 51 N4
Debenham Suffk 64 H9
Deblin's Green Worcs 46 F5
Dechmont W Loth 127 J3
Dechmont Road W Loth 127 J4
Deddington Oxon 48 E8
Dedham Essex 53 J5
Dedham Heath Essex 53 J5
Dedworth W & M 35 P9
Deene Nhants 61 K2
Deenethorpe Nhants 61 L2
Deepcar Sheff 90 H11
Deepcut Surrey 23 P3
Deepdale Cumb 95 Q4
Deepdale N York 96 C5
Deeping Gate C Pete 74 B9
Deeping St James Lincs 74 C9
Deeping St Nicholas Lincs 74 D7
Deerhurst Gloucs 46 G8
Deerhurst Walton Gloucs 46 G9
Deerton Street Kent 38 G9
Defford Worcs 46 H6
Defynnog Powys 44 C9
Deganwy Conwy 79 P9
Degnish Ag & B 130 F5
Deighton C York 91 Q2
Deighton N York 104 C10
Deiniolen Gwynd 67 K2
Delabole Cnwll 4 H5
Delamere Ches W 82 C11
Delfrigs Abers 151 P3
Delley Devon 17 J7
Delliefure Highld 157 K11
Dell Quay W Susx 15 M6
Delly End Oxon 34 C2
Delnabo Moray 149 M4
Delny Highld 156 C3
Delph Oldham 90 B9
Delves Dur 112 H11
Delvin End Essex 52 C4
Dembleby Lincs 73 Q3
Demelza Cnwll 4 F9
Denaby Donc 91 M11
Denaby Main Donc 91 M11
Denbies Surrey 36 D10
Denbigh Denbgs 80 F11
Denbighshire Crematorium Denbgs 80 E10
Denbrae Fife 135 K4
Denbury Devon 7 L5
Denby Derbys 84 E11
Denby Bottles Derbys 84 E11
Denby Dale Kirk 90 G9
Denchworth Oxon 34 C6
Dendron Cumb 94 E6
Denel End C Beds 50 B3
Denfield P & K 134 B4
Denford Nhants 61 L5
Dengie Essex 52 G11
Denham Bucks 36 B3
Denham Suffk 63 N8
Denham Suffk 64 H7
Denham End Suffk 63 N8
Denham Green Bucks 36 B3
Denham Green Suffk 64 H7
Denhead Abers 159 N7
Denhead Fife 135 M5
Denhead of Gray C Dund 142 F11
Denholm Border 117 R7
Denholme C Brad 90 D4
Denholme Clough C Brad 90 D4
Denio Gwynd 66 F7
Denmead Hants 15 J4
Denmore C Aber 151 N5
Denne Park W Susx 24 E5
Dennington Suffk 65 K8
Denny Falk 133 N11
Dennyloanhead Falk 133 N11
Den of Lindores Fife 134 H4
Denshaw Oldham 90 B8
Denside Abers 151 L8
Densole Kent 27 M3
Denston Suffk 63 N10
Denstone Staffs 71 K6
Denstroude Kent 39 K9
Dent Cumb 95 Q3
Denton Cambs 61 Q3
Denton Darltn 103 P7
Denton E Susx 25 L10
Denton Kent 27 M2
Denton Kent 37 Q6
Denton Lincs 73 M4
Denton N York 96 H11
Denton Nhants 60 H9
Denton Norfk 65 K4
Denton Oxon 34 G4
Denton Tamesd 83 K5
Denver Norfk 75 M10
Denwick Nthumb 119 P8
Deopham Norfk 76 E11
Deopham Green Norfk 64 E2
Depden Suffk 63 N9
Depden Green Suffk 63 N9
Deptford Gt Lon 37 J5
Deptford Wilts 21 K7
Derby C Derb 72 B3
Derby Devon 17 K5
Derbyhaven IoM 80 c8
Derculich P & K 141 L7
Dereham Norfk 76 D9
Deri Caerph 30 F4
Derril Devon 16 E11
Derringstone Kent 27 M2
Derrington Staffs 70 F10
Derriton Devon 16 E11
Derry Hill Wilts 33 J10
Derrythorpe N Linc 92 D9
Dersingham Norfk 75 N4
Dervaig Ag & B 137 L5
Derwen Denbgs 68 E4
Derwenlas Powys 54 G5
Derwent Valley Mills Derbys 84 D9
Derwent Water Cumb 101 J6
Derwydd Carmth 43 M11
Desborough Nhants 60 H4
Desford Leics 72 D10
Deskford Moray 158 D5
Detchant Nthumb 119 L3
Detling Kent 38 C10
Deuxhill Shrops 57 M7
Devauden Mons 31 N5
Devil's Bridge Cerdgn 54 G9
Devitts Green Warwks 59 L6
Devizes Wilts 21 K2
Devonport C Plym 6 D8
Devonside Clacks 133 Q8
Devoran Cnwll 3 K6
Devoran & Perran Cnwll 3 K6
Dewarton Mdloth 128 B7
Dewlish Dorset 12 C5
Dewsbury Kirk 90 G6
Dewsbury Moor Kirk 90 G6
Dewsbury Moor Crematorium Kirk 90 G6
Deytheur Powys 68 H11
Dial N Som 31 P11
Dial Green W Susx 23 P9
Dial Post W Susx 24 E7
Dibberford Dorset 11 K4
Dibden Hants 14 D5
Dibden Purlieu Hants 14 D5
Dickens Heath Solhll 58 H9
Dickleburgh Norfk 64 H5
Didbrook Gloucs 47 L8
Didcot Oxon 34 F6
Diddington Cambs 61 Q7
Diddlebury Shrops 57 J7
Didley Herefs 45 P8
Didling W Susx 23 M11
Didmarton Gloucs 32 F7
Didsbury Manch 82 H6
Didworthy Devon 6 H6
Digby Lincs 86 E10
Digg Highld 152 H4
Diggle Oldham 90 C9
Digmoor Lancs 88 F9
Digswell Herts 50 F7
Digswell Water Herts 50 G8
Dihewyd Cerdgn 43 J3
Dilham Norfk 77 L6
Dilhorne Staffs 70 H6
Dill Hall Lancs 89 M5
Dillington Cambs 61 P7
Dilston Nthumb 112 E8
Dilton Wilts 20 G5
Dilton Marsh Wilts 20 F5
Dilwyn Herefs 45 N4
Dimple Bolton 89 L7
Dimple Derbys 84 C8
Dinas Carmth 41 Q4
Dinas Cnwll 4 E7
Dinas Gwynd 66 D7
Dinas Pembks 41 K3
Dinas Rhondd 30 D6
Dinas Dinlle Gwynd 66 G3
Dinas-Mawddwy Gwynd 67 R11
Dinas Powys V Glam 30 G10
Dinder Somset 19 Q6
Dinedor Herefs 45 Q7
Dingestow Mons 31 N2
Dingle Lpool 81 M7
Dingleden Kent 26 D5
Dingley Nhants 60 G3
Dingwall Highld 155 P6
Dinmael Conwy 68 D6
Dinnet Abers 150 D8
Dinnington N u Ty 113 K6
Dinnington Rothm 84 H3
Dinnington Somset 11 J2
Dinorwic Gwynd 67 K2
Dinton Bucks 35 L2
Dinton Wilts 21 K8
Dinwoodie D & G 109 P2
Dinworthy Devon 16 E8
Dipford Somset 18 H10
Dipley Hants 23 K3
Dippen Ag & B 120 F4
Dippen N Ayrs 121 K7
Dippenhall Surrey 23 M5
Dippermill Devon 8 B3
Dippertown Devon 8 B8
Dipple Moray 157 Q6
Dipple S Ayrs 114 D7
Diptford Devon 7 J7
Dipton Dur 113 J10
Diptonmill Nthumb 112 D8
Dirleton E Loth 128 E3
Dirt Pot Nthumb 112 C11
Discoed Powys 45 K2
Diseworth Leics 72 D6
Dishforth N York 97 N6
Disley Ches E 83 L8
Diss Norfk 64 G5
Disserth Powys 44 E3
Distington Cumb 100 D6
Distington Hall Crematorium Cumb 100 D6
Ditchampton Wilts 21 L8
Ditcheat Somset 20 B7
Ditchingham Norfk 65 L3
Ditchling E Susx 24 H7
Ditherington Shrops 57 J2
Ditteridge Wilts 32 F11
Dittisham Devon 7 M7
Ditton Kent 38 B10
Ditton Green Cambs 63 L9
Ditton Priors Shrops 57 L7
Dixton Gloucs 47 J8
Dixton Mons 31 P2
Dizzard Cnwll 5 K2
Dobcross Oldham 90 B9
Dobwalls Cnwll 5 L8
Doccombe Devon 9 J7
Dochgarroch Highld 155 R9
Dockenfield Surrey 23 M6
Docker Lancs 95 M6
Docking Norfk 75 Q3
Docklow Herefs 45 R3
Dockray Cumb 101 L6
Dockray Cumb 110 E11
Dodbrooke Devon 7 J10
Doddinghurst Essex 51 N11
Doddington Cambs 62 F2
Doddington Kent 38 F10
Doddington Lincs 85 Q6
Doddington Nthumb 119 J4
Doddington Shrops 57 L9
Doddiscombsleigh Devon 9 L7
Dodd's Green Ches E 69 R6
Doddshill Norfk 75 N4
Doddy Cross Cnwll 5 N9
Dodford Nhants 60 D8
Dodford Worcs 58 D10
Dodington S Glos 32 E8
Dodington Somset 18 G6
Dodleston Ches W 69 L2
Dodscott Devon 17 J8
Dodside E Rens 125 N7
Dod's Leigh Staffs 71 J8
Dodworth Barns 91 J9
Dodworth Bottom Barns 91 J10
Dodworth Green Barns 91 J10
Doe Bank Birm 58 H5
Doe Lea Derbys 84 G7
Dogdyke Lincs 86 H9
Dogley Lane Kirk 90 F8
Dogmersfield Hants 23 L4
Dogridge Wilts 33 L7
Dogsthorpe C Pete 74 C10
Dog Village Devon 9 N5
Dolanog Powys 55 P2
Dolau Powys 55 Q11
Dolaucothi Carmth 43 N6
Dolbenmaen Gwynd 67 J6
Doley Staffs 70 C9
Dolfach Powys 55 L4
Dol-fôr Powys 55 J3
Dolfor Powys 55 Q7
Dolgarrog Conwy 79 P11
Dolgellau Gwynd 67 N11
Dolgoch Gwynd 54 F4
Dol-gran Carmth 42 H8
Doll Highld 163 K6
Dollar Clacks 134 B8
Dollarfield Clacks 134 B8
Dolley Green Powys 56 D11
Dollwen Cerdgn 54 F8
Dolphin Flints 80 H10
Dolphinholme Lancs 95 L10
Dolphinton S Lans 127 L8
Dolton Devon 17 K9
Dolwen Conwy 80 B10
Dolwyddelan Conwy 67 N4
Dolybont Cerdgn 54 E7
Dolyhir Powys 45 J3
Domgay Powys 69 J11
Donaldson's Lodge Nthumb 118 G2
Doncaster Donc 91 P10
Doncaster Carr Donc 91 P10
Doncaster North Services Donc 91 R8
Doncaster Sheffield Airport Donc 91 R11
Donhead St Andrew Wilts 20 H10
Donhead St Mary Wilts 20 H10
Donibristle Fife 134 F10
Doniford Somset 18 E6
Donington Lincs 74 D3
Donington on Bain Lincs 86 H4
Donington Park Services Leics 72 D5
Donington Southing Lincs 74 D4
Donisthorpe Leics 59 M2
Donkey Street Kent 27 K5
Donkey Town Surrey 23 P2
Donnington Gloucs 47 N9
Donnington Herefs 46 D8
Donnington Shrops 57 K3
Donnington W Berk 34 E11
Donnington W Susx 15 N6
Donnington Wrekin 57 N2
Donnington Wood Wrekin 57 N2
Donyatt Somset 10 G2
Doomsday Green W Susx 24 E5
Doonfoot S Ayrs 114 F4
Dora's Green Hants 23 M5
Dorback Lodge Highld 149 K4
Dorchester Dorset 11 P6
Dorchester-on-Thames Oxon 34 G6
Dordon Warwks 59 L4
Dore Sheff 84 D4
Dores Highld 155 Q11
Dorking Surrey 36 E11
Dorking Tye Suffk 52 F4
Dormansland Surrey 25 K2
Dormans Park Surrey 25 J2
Dormington Herefs 46 A6
Dormston Worcs 47 J3
Dorn Gloucs 47 P8
Dorney Bucks 35 P9
Dornie Highld 145 Q2
Dornoch Highld 162 H9
Dornock D & G 110 D7
Dorrery Highld 167 J6
Dorridge Solhll 59 J10
Dorrington Lincs 86 E10
Dorrington Shrops 56 H4
Dorrington Shrops 70 C6
Dorsington Warwks 47 M5
Dorstone Herefs 45 L6
Dorton Bucks 35 J2
Dosthill Staffs 59 K5
Dothan IoA 78 F10
Dottery Dorset 11 K5
Doublebois Cnwll 5 K9
Doughton Gloucs 32 G6
Douglas IoM 80 e6
Douglas S Lans 116 A4
Douglas and Angus C Dund 142 G11
Douglas Crematorium IoM 80 e6
Douglas Pier Ag & B 131 P8
Douglastown Angus 142 G8
Douglas Water S Lans 116 B3
Douglas West S Lans 126 E11
Doulting Somset 20 B6
Dounby Ork 169 b4
Doune Highld 161 Q6
Doune Stirlg 133 L7
Dounepark S Ayrs 114 C8
Dounie Highld 162 D8
Dousland Devon 6 E5
Dovaston Shrops 69 L10
Dove Dale Derbys 71 L4
Dove Green Notts 84 G10
Dove Holes Derbys 83 N9
Dovenby Cumb 100 E4
Dover Kent 27 P3
Dover Wigan 82 D4
Dover Castle Kent 27 P3
Dovercourt Essex 53 M5
Doverdale Worcs 58 C11
Doveridge Derbys 71 L8
Doversgreen Surrey 36 G11
Dowally P & K 141 P8
Dowbridge Lancs 88 E4
Dowdeswell Gloucs 47 K11
Dowlais Myr Td 30 E3
Dowland Devon 17 K9
Dowlish Ford Somset 10 H2
Dowlish Wake Somset 10 H2
Down Ampney Gloucs 33 L5
Downderry Cnwll 5 N11
Downe Gt Lon 37 K8
Downend Gloucs 32 F5
Downend IoW 14 F9
Downend S Glos 32 C9
Downend W Berk 34 E9
Downfield C Dund 142 F11
Downgate Cnwll 5 M7
Downgate Cnwll 5 P7
Downham Essex 38 B2
Downham Gt Lon 37 J6
Downham Lancs 89 M2
Downham Market Norfk 75 M10
Down Hatherley Gloucs 46 G10
Downhead Somset 19 Q9
Downhead Somset 20 C5
Downhill Cnwll 4 D8
Downhill P & K 134 D2
Downholland Cross Lancs 88 D9
Downholme N York 103 M11
Downicarey Devon 5 P3
Downies Abers 151 N9
Downing Flints 80 H9
Downley Bucks 35 M5
Down St Mary Devon 8 H4
Downs Crematorium Br & H 24 H9
Downs Crematorium Br & H 24 H9
Downside Somset 20 B4
Downside Somset 20 B6
Downside Surrey 36 D9
Down Thomas Devon 6 E8
Downton Hants 13 N6
Downton Wilts 21 N10
Dowsby Lincs 74 B5
Dowsdale Lincs 74 E8
Doxey Staffs 70 F10
Doxford Nthumb 119 N6
Doynton S Glos 32 D10
Draethen Caerph 30 H7
Draffan S Lans 126 D8
Dragonby N Linc 92 F8
Dragons Green W Susx 24 D6
Drakeholes Notts 85 M2
Drakelow Worcs 57 Q8
Drakemyre N Ayrs 124 H7
Drakes Broughton Worcs 46 H5
Drakewalls Cnwll 6 C4
Draughton N York 96 F10
Draughton Nhants 60 G5
Drax N York 92 A5
Drax Hales N York 91 R5
Draycote Warwks 59 P10
Draycot Foliat Swindn 33 N9
Draycott Derbys 72 C4
Draycott Gloucs 47 N7
Draycott Shrops 57 Q6
Draycott Somset 19 N4
Draycott Somset 19 Q10
Draycott Worcs 46 G5
Draycott in the Clay Staffs 71 M9
Draycott in the Moors Staffs 70 H6
Drayford Devon 9 J2
Drayton C Port 15 J5
Drayton Leics 60 H2
Drayton Lincs 74 D3
Drayton Norfk 76 H9
Drayton Oxon 34 E6
Drayton Oxon 48 D6
Drayton Somset 19 M10
Drayton Worcs 58 D9
Drayton Bassett Staffs 59 J4
Drayton Beauchamp Bucks 35 P2
Drayton Manor Park Staffs 59 J4
Drayton Parslow Bucks 49 M9
Drayton St Leonard Oxon 34 G5
Drebley N York 96 G9
Dreemskerry IoM 80 g3
Dreen Hill Pembks 40 H8
Drefach Carmth 28 F2
Drefach Carmth 42 G7
Drefach Cerdgn 43 J5
Drefelin Carmth 42 G7
Dreghorn N Ayrs 125 K10
Drellingore Kent 27 M3
Drem E Loth 128 E4
Dresden C Stke 70 G6
Drewsteignton Devon 8 H6
Driby Lincs 87 L6
Driffield E R Yk 99 L9
Driffield Gloucs 33 L5
Driffield Cross Roads Gloucs 33 L5
Drift Cnwll 2 C8
Drigg Cumb 100 E11
Drighlington Leeds 90 G5
Drimnin Highld 137 P5
Drimpton Dorset 11 J4
Drimsallie Highld 138 H2
Dringhouses C York 98 B11
Drinkstone Suffk 64 D9
Drinkstone Green Suffk 64 D9
Drive End Dorset 11 M3
Driver's End Herts 50 F6
Drointon Staffs 71 J9
Droitwich Spa Worcs 46 G2
Dron P & K 134 E4
Dronfield Derbys 84 E5
Dronfield Woodhouse Derbys 84 D5
Drongan E Ayrs 114 H4
Dronley Angus 142 E10
Droop Dorset 12 C3
Dropping Well Rothm 84 E2
Droxford Hants 22 H11
Droylsden Tamesd 83 K5
Druid Denbgs 68 D6
Druidston Pembks 40 G7
Druimarbin Highld 139 K3
Druimavuic Ag & B 139 J8
Druimdrishaig Ag & B 123 M5
Druimindarroch Highld 145 L11
Drum Ag & B 124 A2
Drum P & K 134 C7
Drumalbin S Lans 116 C3
Drumbeg Highld 164 D10
Drumblade Abers 158 E9
Drumbreddon D & G 106 E9
Drumbuie Highld 153 P11
Drumburgh Cumb 110 E9
Drumburn D & G 109 J10
Drumburn D & G 109 L8
Drumchapel C Glas 125 N3
Drumchastle P & K 140 G6
Drumclog S Lans 125 Q10
Drumeldrie Fife 135 L7
Drumelzier Border 116 G4
Drumfearn Highld 145 L4
Drumfrennie Abers 151 J8
Drumgley Angus 142 G7
Drumguish Highld 148 D7
Drumin Moray 157 M11
Drumjohn D & G 115 K8
Drumlamford S Ayrs 107 J2
Drumlasie Abers 150 G6
Drumleaning Cumb 110 E10
Drumlemble Ag & B 120 C8
Drumlithie Abers 151 K11
Drummoddie D & G 107 L8
Drummore D & G 106 F10
Drummuir Moray 158 A9
Drumnadrochit Highld 155 P11
Drumnagorrach Moray 158 D7
Drumpark D & G 109 J5
Drumrunie Lodge Highld 161 K6
Drumshang S Ayrs 114 E5
Drumuie Highld 152 H8
Drumuillie Highld 148 G3
Drumvaich Stirlg 133 K7
Drunzie P & K 134 E6
Druridge Nthumb 119 Q11
Drury Flints 69 J2
Drybeck Cumb 102 C7
Drybridge Moray 158 B5
Drybridge N Ayrs 125 K10
Drybrook Gloucs 46 B11
Dryburgh Border 118 A4
Dry Doddington Lincs 85 Q11
Dry Drayton Cambs 62 E8
Drymen Stirlg 132 F10
Drymuir Abers 159 M8
Drynoch Highld 152 G11
Dry Sandford Oxon 34 E4
Dryslwyn Carmth 43 L10
Dry Street Essex 37 Q3
Dryton Shrops 57 K3
Dubford Abers 159 J5
Dublin Suffk 64 H8
Duchally Highld 161 P3
Duck End Bed 50 C2
Duck End Cambs 62 B8
Duck End Essex 51 Q4
Duck End Essex 51 Q5
Duckend Green Essex 52 B7
Duckington Ches W 69 N4
Ducklington Oxon 34 C3
Duck's Cross Bed 61 P9
Duddenhoe End Essex 51 L3
Duddingston C Edin 127 P3
Duddington Nhants 73 P10
Duddlestone Somset 18 H10
Duddleswell E Susx 25 L5
Duddlewick Shrops 57 M8
Duddo Nthumb 118 H2
Duddon Ches W 69 P2
Duddon Bridge Cumb 94 D3
Duddon Common Ches W 81 Q11
Dudleston Shrops 69 K7
Dudleston Heath Shrops 69 L7
Dudley Dudley 58 D6
Dudley N Tyne 113 L6
Dudley Hill C Brad 90 F4
Dudley Port Sandw 58 E6
Dudnill Shrops 57 L10
Dudsbury Dorset 13 J5
Dudswell Herts 35 Q3
Duffield Derbys 72 A2
Duffryn Neath 29 M5
Dufftown Moray 157 Q9
Duffus Moray 157 M4
Dufton Cumb 102 C5
Duggleby N York 98 H7
Duirinish Highld 153 P11
Duisdalemore Highld 145 M5
Duisky Highld 139 J2
Dukestown Blae G 30 F2
Duke Street Suffk 53 J3
Dukinfield Tamesd 83 K5
Dukinfield Crematorium Tamesd 83 K5
Dulas IoA 78 H7
Dulcote Somset 19 Q6
Dulford Devon 9 Q3
Dull P & K 141 K8
Dullatur N Lans 126 C2
Dullingham Cambs 63 K9

268 Dullingham Ley – Ecclesall

Dullingham Ley Cambs 63 K9
Dulnain Bridge Highld 148 H3
Duloe Bed 61 Q8
Duloe Cnwll 5 L10
Dulsie Bridge Highld 156 G9
Dulverton Somset 18 B9
Dulwich Gt Lon 36 H6
Dumbarton W Duns 125 L2
Dumbleton Gloucs 47 K7
Dumfries D & G 109 L5
Dumgoyne Stirlg 132 G11
Dummer Hants 22 G5
Dumpton Kent 39 Q8
Dun Angus 143 M6
Dunalastair P & K 140 H6
Dunan Ag & B 124 F3
Dunan Highld 145 J2
Dunan P & K 140 C6
Dunaverty Ag & B 120 C10
Dunball Somset 19 K6
Dunbar E Loth 128 H4
Dunbeath Highld 167 L11
Dunbeg Ag & B 138 F11
Dunblane Stirlg 133 M7
Dunbog Fife 134 H4
Dunbridge Hants 22 B9
Duncanston Highld 155 Q6
Duncanstone Abers 150 F2
Dunchideock Devon 9 L7
Dunchurch Warwks 59 Q10
Duncote Nhants 49 J4
Duncow D & G 109 L4
Duncrievie P & K 134 E6
Duncton W Susx 23 Q11
Dundee C Dund 142 G11
Dundee Airport C Dund 135 K2
Dundee Crematorium
C Dund 142 F11
Dundon Somset 19 N8
Dundonald S Ayrs 125 K11
Dundonnell Highld 160 H9
Dundraw Cumb 110 D11
Dundreggan Highld 147 J5
Dundrennan D & G 108 F11
Dundry N Som 31 Q11
Dunecht Abers 151 K6
Dunfermline Fife 134 D10
Dunfermline
Crematorium Fife 134 E10
Dunfield Gloucs 33 M5
Dunford Bridge Barns 83 Q4
Dungate Kent 38 F10
Dungavel S Lans 126 B10
Dunge Wilts 20 G4
Dungeness Kent 27 J8
Dungworth Sheff 84 C3
Dunham Massey Traffd 82 F7
Dunham-on-the-Hill
Ches W 81 P10
Dunham-on-Trent Notts 85 P6
Dunhampstead Worcs 46 H2
Dunhampton Worcs 58 B11
Dunham Town Traffd 82 F7
Dunham Woodhouses
Traffd 82 F7
Dunholme Lincs 86 D5
Dunino Fife 135 N5
Dunipace Falk 133 N11
Dunkeld P & K 141 P9
Dunkerton BaNES 20 D3
Dunkeswell Devon 10 C3
Dunkeswick N York 97 M11
Dunkirk Ches W 81 M10
Dunkirk Kent 39 J10
Dunkirk S Glos 32 E7
Dunkirk Wilts 21 J2
Dunk's Green Kent 37 P10
Dunlappie Angus 143 K4
Dunley Hants 22 E4
Dunley Worcs 57 P11
Dunlop E Ayrs 125 L8
Dunmaglass Highld 147 P3
Dunmere Cnwll 4 G8
Dunmore Falk 133 P10
Dunnet Highld 167 M2
Dunnichen Angus 143 J8
Dunning P & K 134 C5
Dunnington C York 98 D10
Dunnington E R Yk 99 P10
Dunnington Warwks 47 L4
Dunnockshaw Lancs 89 N5
Dunn Street Kent 38 C9
Dunoon Ag & B 124 F2
Dunphail Moray 157 J8
Dunragit D & G 106 G6
Duns Border 129 K9
Dunsa Derbys 84 B6
Dunsby Lincs 74 B5
Dunscar Bolton 89 L8
Dunscore D & G 109 J4
Dunscroft Donc 91 Q9
Dunsdale R & Cl 104 H7
Dunsden Green Oxon 35 K9
Dunsdon Devon 16 E10
Dunsfold Surrey 24 B3
Dunsford Devon 9 K7
Dunshalt Fife 134 G5
Dunshillock Abers 159 N8
Dunsill Notts 84 G8
Dunsley N York 105 N8
Dunsley Staffs 58 C8
Dunsmore Bucks 35 N3
Dunsop Bridge Lancs 95 P11
Dunstable C Beds 50 B6
Dunstall Staffs 71 M10
Dunstall Common Worcs 46 G6
Dunstall Green Suffk 63 M8
Dunstan Nthumb 119 P7
Dunstan Steads Nthumb 119 P6
Dunster Somset 18 C6
Duns Tew Oxon 48 E9
Dunston Gatesd 113 K8
Dunston Lincs 86 E8
Dunston Norfk 77 J11
Dunston Staffs 70 G11
Dunstone Devon 6 F8
Dunstone Devon 8 H9
Dunston Heath Staffs 70 G11
Dunsville Donc 91 Q9
Dunswell E R Yk 93 J3
Dunsyre S Lans 127 K8
Dunterton Devon 5 P6
Dunthrop Oxon 48 C9
Duntisbourne Abbots
Gloucs 33 J3
Duntisbourne Leer
Gloucs 33 J3
Duntisbourne Rouse
Gloucs 33 J3
Duntish Dorset 11 P3
Duntocher W Duns 125 M3
Dunton Bucks 49 M10
Dunton C Beds 50 F2
Dunton Norfk 76 B5
Dunton Bassett Leics 60 B2
Dunton Green Kent 37 M9
Dunton Wayletts Essex 37 Q2
Duntulm Highld 152 G3
Dunure S Ayrs 114 E4
Dunvant Swans 28 G6
Dunvegan Highld 152 D8
Dunwich Suffk 65 P7
Dunwood Staffs 70 G3
Durdar Cumb 110 H10
Durgan Cnwll 3 K8
Durham Dur 103 Q2
Durham Cathedral Dur 103 Q2
Durham Crematorium
Dur 103 Q2
Durham Services Dur 103 R3
Durham Tees Valley
Airport S on T 104 C8
Durisdeer D & G 116 B10
Durisdeermill D & G 116 B10
Durkar Wakefd 91 J7
Durleigh Somset 19 J7
Durley Hants 22 F11
Durley Wilts 21 P2
Durley Street Hants 22 F11
Durlock Kent 39 N10
Durlock Kent 39 P9
Durlow Common Herefs 46 B7
Durn Rochdl 89 Q7
Durness Highld 165 K3
Durno Abers 151 J2
Duror Highld 138 H6
Durran Ag & B 131 K6
Durrington W Susx 24 D9
Durrington Wilts 21 N6
Durris Abers 151 K8
Dursley Gloucs 32 E5
Dursley Cross Gloucs 46 C10
Durston Somset 19 J9
Durweston Dorset 12 E3
Duston Nhants 60 F8
Duthil Highld 148 G3
Dutlas Powys 56 C9
Duton Hill Essex 51 P5
Dutson Cnwll 5 N4
Dutton Ches W 82 C9
Duxford Cambs 62 G11
Duxford Oxon 34 C5
Duxford IWM Cambs 62 G11
Dwygyfylchi Conwy 79 N9
Dwyran IoA 78 G11
Dyce C Aber 151 M5
Dyer's End Essex 52 B4
Dyfatty Carmth 28 E4
Dyffrydan Gwynd 54 F2
Dyffryn Brdgnd 29 N6
Dyffryn Myr Td 30 E4
Dyffryn V Glam 30 E10
Dyffryn Ardudwy Gwynd 67 K10
Dyffryn Castell Cerdgn 54 H8
Dyffryn Cellwen Neath 29 N2
Dyke Lincs 74 B6
Dyke Moray 156 H6
Dykehead Angus 142 C7
Dykehead Angus 142 F6
Dykehead N Lans 126 F6
Dykehead Stirlg 132 H8
Dykelands Abers 143 N4
Dykends Angus 142 D6
Dykeside Abers 158 H9
Dylife Powys 55 K6
Dymchurch Kent 27 K6
Dymock Gloucs 46 D8
Dyrham S Glos 32 D9
Dysart Fife 135 J9
Dyserth Denbgs 80 F9

E

Eachway Worcs 58 E9
Eachwick Nthumb 112 H6
Eagland Hill Lancs 95 J11
Eagle Lincs 85 Q7
Eagle Barnsdale Lincs 85 Q7
Eagle Moor Lincs 85 Q7
Eaglescliffe S on T 104 D7
Eaglesfield Cumb 100 E5
Eaglesfield D & G 110 D6
Eaglesham E Rens 125 P7
Eagley Bolton 89 L8
Eairy IoM 80 c6
Eakring Notts 85 L8
Ealand N Linc 92 C8
Ealing Gt Lon 36 E4
Eals Nthumb 111 N9
Eamont Bridge Cumb 101 P5
Earby Lancs 96 D11
Earcroft Bl w D 89 K6
Eardington Shrops 57 N6
Eardisland Herefs 45 N3
Eardisley Herefs 45 L5
Eardiston Shrops 69 L9
Eardiston Worcs 57 M11
Earith Cambs 62 E5
Earle Nthumb 119 J5
Earlestown St Hel 82 C5
Earley Wokham 35 K10
Earlham Norfk 76 H10
Earlham Crematorium
Norfk 77 J10
Earlish Highld 152 F5
Earls Barton Nhants 61 J8
Earls Colne Essex 52 E6
Earls Common Worcs 47 J3
Earl's Croome Worcs 46 G6
Earlsditton Shrops 57 L9
Earlsdon Covtry 59 M9
Earl's Down E Susx 25 P7
Earlsferry Fife 135 M7
Earlsfield Gt Lon 36 G6
Earlsford Abers 159 K11
Earl's Green Suffk 64 E8
Earlsheaton Kirk 90 H6
Earl Shilton Leics 72 D11
Earl Soham Suffk 65 J9
Earl Sterndale Derbys 83 N11
Earlston Border 117 R3
Earlston E Ayrs 125 L10
Earl Stonham Suffk 64 G10
Earlswood Surrey 36 G11
Earlswood Warwks 58 H10
Earlswood Common
Mons 31 N6
Earnley W Susx 15 M7
Earnshaw Bridge Lancs 88 G6
Earsdon N Tyne 113 M6
Earsdon Nthumb 113 J2
Earsham Norfk 65 L4
Earswick C York 98 C9
Eartham W Susx 15 P5
Earthcott S Glos 32 C7
Easby N York 104 G9
Easdale Ag & B 130 E4
Easebourne W Susx 23 P10
Easenhall Warwks 59 Q9
Eashing Surrey 23 P6
Easington Bucks 35 J2
Easington Dur 104 D2
Easington E R Yk 93 Q7
Easington Nthumb 119 M4
Easington Oxon 35 J5
Easington R & Cl 105 K7
Easington Colliery Dur 104 D2
Easington Lane Sundld 113 N11
Easingwold N York 98 A7
Easole Street Kent 39 N11
Eassie and Nevay Angus 142 E9
East Aberthaw V Glam 30 D11
East Allington Devon 7 K9
East Anstey Devon 17 R6
East Anton Hants 22 C5
East Appleton N York 103 P11
East Ashey IoW 14 G9
East Ashling W Susx 15 M5
East Aston Hants 22 D5
East Ayton N York 99 K3
East Balsdon Cnwll 5 M2
East Bank Blae G 30 H3
East Barkwith Lincs 86 G4
East Barming Kent 38 B11
East Barnby N York 105 M8
East Barnet Gt Lon 50 G11
East Barns E Loth 129 J4
East Barsham Norfk 76 C5
East Beckham Norfk 76 H4
East Bedfont Gt Lon 36 C6
East Bergholt Suffk 53 J5
East Bierley Kirk 90 F5
East Bilney Norfk 76 D8
East Blatchington E Susx 25 L10
East Bloxworth Dorset 12 E6
East Boldon S Tyne 113 N8
East Boldre Hants 14 C6
East Bolton Nthumb 119 M7
Eastbourne Darltn 104 B8
Eastbourne E Susx 25 P11
Eastbourne
Crematorium E Susx 25 P10
East Bower Somset 19 K7
East Bradenham Norfk 76 C10
East Brent Somset 19 K4
Eastbridge Suffk 65 P8
East Bridgford Notts 72 H2
East Briscoe Dur 103 J7
Eastbrook V Glam 30 G10
East Buckland Devon 17 M5
East Budleigh Devon 9 Q8
Eastburn C Brad 90 C2
Eastburn E R Yk 99 K9
East Burnham Bucks 35 Q8
East Burton Dorset 12 D7
Eastbury Herts 36 D2
Eastbury W Berk 34 B9
East Butsfield Dur 112 H11
East Butterwick N Linc 92 D9
Eastby N York 96 F10
East Calder W Loth 127 K4
East Carleton Norfk 76 H11
East Carlton Leeds 90 G2
East Carlton Nhants 60 H3
East Chaldon Dorset 12 C8
East Challow Oxon 34 C7
East Charleton Devon 7 K10
East Chelborough
Dorset 11 M3
East Chiltington E Susx 25 J7
East Chinnock Somset 11 K2
East Chisenbury Wilts 21 M4
East Cholderton Hants 21 Q5
Eastchurch Kent 38 G7
East Clandon Surrey 36 C10
East Claydon Bucks 49 K9
East Clevedon N Som 31 M10
East Coker Somset 11 L2
Eastcombe Gloucs 32 G4
Eastcombe Somset 18 G8
East Compton Somset 20 B6
East Cornworthy Devon 7 L7
East Cote Cumb 109 P9
Eastcote Gt Lon 36 D3
Eastcote Nhants 49 J4
Eastcote Solhll 59 J9
Eastcott Cnwll 16 D8
Eastcott Wilts 21 K3
East Cottingwith E R Yk 92 B2
Eastcourt Wilts 21 P2
Eastcourt Wilts 33 J6
East Cowes IoW 14 F7
East Cowick E R Yk 91 R6
East Cowton N York 104 B10
East Cramlington
Nthumb 113 L5
East Cranmore Somset 20 C6
East Creech Dorset 12 F8
East Curthwaite Cumb 110 F11
East Dean E Susx 25 N11
East Dean Gloucs 46 C10
East Dean Hants 21 Q9
East Dean W Susx 15 P4
East Devon
Crematorium Devon 9 Q5
Eastdown Devon 7 L9
East Down Devon 17 L3
East Drayton Notts 85 N5
East Dulwich Gt Lon 36 H5
East Dundry N Som 31 Q11
East Ella C KuH 93 J5
East End Bed 61 P9
East End C Beds 49 Q6
East End E R Yk 93 L4
East End E R Yk 93 N5
Eastend Essex 38 F3
East End Essex 51 K8
East End Hants 14 C7
East End Hants 22 D2
East End Herts 51 L5
East End Kent 26 D4
East End Kent 38 G7
East End M Keyn 49 P6
East End Oxon 48 C11
East End Somset 20 C5
East End Suffk 53 K4
Easter Balmoral Abers 149 P9
Easter Compton S Glos 31 Q8
Easter Dalziel Highld 156 D7
Eastergate W Susx 15 P5
Easterhouse C Glas 126 B4
Easter Howgate Mdloth 127 N5
Easter Kinkell Highld 155 Q6
Easter Moniack Highld 155 Q9
Eastern Green Covtry 59 L9
Easter Ord Abers 151 L7
Easter Pitkierie Fife 135 P6
Easter Skeld Shet 169 q9
Easter Softlaw Border 118 E4
Easterton Wilts 21 K4
Eastertown Somset 19 K4
East Everleigh Wilts 21 P4
East Farleigh Kent 38 B11
East Farndon Nhants 60 F4
East Ferry Lincs 92 D11
Eastfield N Lans 126 F5
Eastfield N York 99 L4
East Firsby Lincs 86 D3
East Fortune E Loth 128 E4
East Garforth Leeds 91 L4
East Garston W Berk 34 C9
Eastgate Dur 103 J3
Eastgate Lincs 74 B7
Eastgate Norfk 76 G7
East Ginge Oxon 34 D7
East Goscote Leics 72 G8
East Grafton Wilts 21 Q2
East Green Suffk 65 N8
East Grimstead Wilts 21 P9
East Grinstead W Susx 25 J3
East Guldeford E Susx 26 F7
East Haddon Nhants 60 E7
East Hagbourne Oxon 34 F7
East Halton N Linc 93 K7
East Ham Gt Lon 37 K4
Eastham Wirral 81 M8
Eastham Ferry Wirral 81 M8
Easthampstead Park
Crematorium Br For 35 M11
Easthampton Herefs 45 N2
East Hanney Oxon 34 D6
East Hanningfield Essex 52 C11
East Hardwick Wakefd 91 M7
East Harling Norfk 64 D4
East Harlsey N York 104 D11
East Harnham Wilts 21 M9
East Harptree BaNES 19 Q3
East Hartford Nthumb 113 L5
East Harting W Susx 23 L11
East Hatch Wilts 20 H9
East Hatley Cambs 62 C10
East Hauxwell N York 97 J2
East Haven Angus 143 K10
Eastheath Wokham 35 L11
East Heckington Lincs 74 C2
East Hedleyhope Dur 103 N2
East Helmsdale Highld 163 N3
East Hendred Oxon 34 E7
East Heslerton N York 99 J5
East Hewish N Som 19 M2
East Hoathly E Susx 25 M7
East Holme Dorset 12 E7
East Hope Dur 103 K9
Easthope Shrops 57 K5
Easthorpe Essex 52 F7
Easthorpe Notts 85 M10
East Horrington Somset 19 Q5
East Horsley Surrey 36 C10
East Horton Nthumb 119 K4
East Howe Bmouth 13 J5
East Huntington C York 98 C9
East Huntspill Somset 19 K5
East Hyde C Beds 50 D7
East Ilkerton Devon 17 N2
East Ilsley W Berk 34 E8
Eastington Devon 8 H3
Eastington Gloucs 32 E3
Eastington Gloucs 33 M2
East Keal Lincs 87 L8
East Kennett Wilts 33 M11
East Keswick Leeds 91 K2
East Kilbride S Lans 125 Q7
East Kimber Devon 8 C5
East Kirkby Lincs 87 K8
East Knighton Dorset 12 D7
East Knowstone Devon 17 Q7
East Knoyle Wilts 20 G8
East Lambrook Somset 19 M11
East Lancashire
Crematorium Bury 89 M9
Eastlands D & G 108 H6
East Langdon Kent 27 P2
East Langton Leics 60 F2
East Lavant W Susx 15 N5
East Lavington W Susx 23 P11
East Layton N York 103 N9
Eastleach Martin Gloucs 33 P4
Eastleach Turville Gloucs 33 N3
East Leake Notts 72 F5
East Learmouth Nthumb 118 G3
East Leigh Devon 6 H8
East Leigh Devon 7 K7
East Leigh Devon 8 G3
Eastleigh Devon 16 H6
Eastleigh Hants 22 E11
East Lexham Norfk 76 B8
Eastling Kent 38 G10
East Linton E Loth 128 F4
East Liss Hants 23 L9
East Lockinge Oxon 34 D7
East London
Crematorium Gt Lon 37 J4
East Lound N Linc 92 C11
East Lulworth Dorset 12 E8
East Lutton N York 99 J7
East Lydeard Somset 18 G9
East Lydford Somset 19 Q8
East Malling Kent 38 B10
East Malling Heath Kent 37 Q9
East Marden W Susx 15 M4
East Markham Notts 85 M6
East Martin Hants 21 L11
East Marton N York 96 D10
East Meon Hants 23 J10
East Mere Devon 18 C11
East Mersea Essex 52 H9
East Midlands Airport
Leics 72 D5
East Molesey Surrey 36 D7
Eastmoor Norfk 75 P10
East Morden Dorset 12 F6
East Morton C Brad 90 D2
East Morton D & G 116 B10
East Ness N York 98 D5
East Newton E R Yk 93 N3
Eastney C Port 15 J7
Eastnor Herefs 46 D7
East Norton Leics 73 K10
Eastoft N Linc 92 D7
East Ogwell Devon 7 L4
Easton Cambs 61 P6
Easton Cumb 110 E9
Easton Devon 8 H7
Easton Dorset 11 P10
Easton Hants 22 F8
Easton Lincs 73 N5
Easton Norfk 76 G9
Easton Somset 19 P5
Easton Suffk 65 K10
Easton W Berk 34 D10
Easton Wilts 32 G10
Easton Grey Wilts 32 G7
Easton-in-Gordano
N Som 31 P9
Easton Maudit Nhants 61 J9
Easton-on-the-Hill
Nhants 73 Q10
Easton Royal Wilts 21 P2
East Orchard Dorset 20 F11
East Ord Nthumb 129 P9
East Panson Devon 5 P3
East Parley Dorset 13 J5
East Peckham Kent 37 Q11
East Pennar Pembks 41 J10
East Pennard Somset 19 Q7
East Perry Cambs 61 Q7
East Portlemouth Devon 7 K11
East Prawle Devon 7 K11
East Preston W Susx 24 C10
East Pulham Dorset 11 Q3
East Putford Devon 16 F8
East Quantoxhead
Somset 18 F6
East Rainham Medway 38 D8
East Rainton Sundld 113 M11
East Ravendale NE Lin 93 M11
East Raynham Norfk 76 B6
Eastrea Cambs 74 E11
East Riding
Crematorium E R Yk 99 L7
Eastriggs D & G 110 D7
East Rigton Leeds 91 K2
Eastrington E R Yk 92 C5
East Rolstone N Som 19 L2
Eastrop Swindn 33 P6
East Rounton N York 104 D10
East Rudham Norfk 76 A6
East Runton Norfk 76 H3
East Ruston Norfk 77 L6
Eastry Kent 39 P11
East Saltoun E Loth 128 D6
Eastshaw W Susx 23 N10
East Sheen Gt Lon 36 F6
East Shefford W Berk 34 C10
East Sleekburn Nthumb 113 L4
East Somerton Norfk 77 P8
East Stockwith Lincs 85 N2
East Stoke Dorset 12 E7
East Stoke Notts 85 N11
East Stour Dorset 20 F10
East Stour Common
Dorset 20 F10
East Stourmouth Kent 39 N9
East Stowford Devon 17 L6
East Stratton Hants 22 F6
East Studdal Kent 27 P2
East Sutton Kent 26 D2
East Taphouse Cnwll 5 K9
East-the-Water Devon 16 H6
East Thirston Nthumb 119 N10
East Tilbury Thurr 37 Q5
East Tisted Hants 23 K8
East Torrington Lincs 86 F4
East Tuddenham Norfk 76 F9
East Tytherley Hants 21 Q9
East Tytherton Wilts 33 J10
East Village Devon 9 K3
Eastville Bristl 32 B10
Eastville Lincs 87 M9
East Wall Shrops 57 J6
East Walton Norfk 75 P7
East Water Somset 19 P4
East Week Devon 8 G6
Eastwell Leics 73 K5
East Wellow Hants 22 B10
East Wemyss Fife 135 J8
East Whitburn W Loth 126 H4
Eastwick Herts 51 K8
East Wickham Gt Lon 37 L5
East Williamston
Pembks 41 L10
East Winch Norfk 75 N7
East Winterslow Wilts 21 P8
East Wittering W Susx 15 L7
East Witton N York 96 H3
Eastwood Notts 84 G11
Eastwood Sthend 38 D4
East Woodburn Nthumb 112 D3
Eastwood End Cambs 62 F2
East Woodhay Hants 22 D2
East Woodlands Somset 20 E6
East Worldham Hants 23 L7
East Wretham Norfk 64 C3
East Youlstone Devon 16 D8
Eathorpe Warwks 59 N11
Eaton Ches E 83 J11
Eaton Ches W 69 Q2
Eaton Leics 73 K5
Eaton Norfk 77 J10
Eaton Notts 85 M5
Eaton Oxon 34 D4
Eaton Shrops 56 F7
Eaton Shrops 57 J7
Eaton Bishop Herefs 45 N7
Eaton Bray C Beds 49 Q10
Eaton Constantine
Shrops 57 K3
Eaton Ford Cambs 61 Q9
Eaton Green C Beds 49 Q10
Eaton Hastings Oxon 33 Q5
Eaton Mascott Shrops 57 J3
Eaton Socon Cambs 61 Q9
Eaton upon Tern Shrops 70 B10
Eaves Brow Warrtn 82 D6
Eaves Green Solhll 59 L8
Ebberston N York 98 H4
Ebbesborne Wake Wilts 21 J10
Ebbw Vale Blae G 30 G3
Ebchester Dur 112 H9
Ebdon N Som 19 L2
Ebford Devon 9 N7
Ebley Gloucs 32 F3
Ebnal Ches W 69 N5
Ebnall Herefs 45 P3
Ebrington Gloucs 47 N6
Ebsworthy Devon 8 D6
Ecchinswell Hants 22 E3
Ecclaw Border 129 K6
Ecclefechan D & G 110 C6
Eccles Border 118 E2
Eccles Kent 38 B9
Eccles Salfd 82 G5
Ecclesall Sheff 84 D4

Ecclesfield – Farne Islands 269

Ecclesfield Sheff 84 E2
Eccles Green Herefs 45 M5
Eccleshall Staffs 70 E9
Eccleshill C Brad 90 F3
Ecclesmachan W Loth 127 K3
Eccles on Sea Norfk 77 N6
Eccles Road Norfk 64 E4
Eccleston Ches W 69 M2
Eccleston Lancs 88 G7
Eccleston St Hel 81 P5
Eccleston Green Lancs 88 G7
Echt Abers 151 J6
Eckford Border 118 D5
Eckington Derbys 84 F5
Eckington Worcs 46 H6
Ecton Nhants 60 H8
Ecton Staffs 71 K3
Edale Derbys 83 P7
Eday Ork 169 e3
Eday Airport Ork 169 e3
Edburton W Susx 24 F8
Edderside Cumb 109 P11
Edderton Highld 162 G10
Eddington Kent 39 L8
Eddleston Border 127 N8
Eddlewood S Lans 126 C7
Edenbridge Kent 37 K11
Edenfield Lancs 89 N7
Edenhall Cumb 101 Q4
Edenham Lincs 73 R6
Eden Mount Cumb 95 J5
Eden Park Gt Lon 37 J7
Eden Project Cnwll 3 Q3
Edensor Derbys 84 B7
Edentaggart Ag & B 132 C9
Edenthorpe Donc 91 Q9
Edern Gwynd 66 D7
Edgarley Somset 19 P7
Edgbaston Birm 58 G8
Edgcombe Cnwll 3 J7
Edgcott Bucks 49 J10
Edgcott Somset 17 Q4
Edge Gloucs 32 F3
Edge Shrops 56 F3
Edgebolton Shrops 69 Q10
Edge End Gloucs 31 Q2
Edgefield Norfk 76 F5
Edgefield Green Norfk 76 F5
Edgefold Bolton 89 L9
Edge Green Ches W 69 N4
Edgehill Warwks 48 C5
Edgerley Shrops 69 L11
Edgerton Kirk 90 E7
Edgeside Lancs 89 N6
Edgeworth Gloucs 32 H3
Edgeworthy Devon 9 K2
Edginswell Torbay 7 M5
Edgiock Worcs 47 K2
Edgmond Wrekin 70 C11
Edgmond Marsh Wrekin 70 C10
Edgton Shrops 56 F7
Edgware Gt Lon 36 E2
Edgworth Bl w D 89 L7
Edinbane Highld 152 E7
Edinburgh C Edin 127 P3
Edinburgh Airport C Edin 127 L3
Edinburgh Castle C Edin 127 P3
Edinburgh Old & New Town C Edin 127 P3
Edinburgh Royal Botanic Gardens C Edin 127 N2
Edinburgh Zoo RZSS C Edin 127 N3
Edingale Staffs 59 K2
Edingham D & G 108 H8
Edingley Notts 85 L9
Edingthorpe Norfk 77 L5
Edingthorpe Green Norfk 77 L5
Edington Border 129 M9
Edington Nthumb 113 J4
Edington Somset 19 L7
Edington Wilts 20 H4
Edington Burtle Somset 19 L6
Edingworth Somset 19 L4
Edistone Devon 16 D7
Edithmead Somset 19 K5
Edith Weston Rutlnd 73 N9
Edlesborough Bucks 49 Q11
Edlingham Nthumb 119 M9
Edlington Lincs 86 H6
Edmond Castle Cumb 111 J9
Edmondsham Dorset 13 J2
Edmondsley Dur 113 K11
Edmondthorpe Leics 73 M7
Edmonton Cnwll 4 F7
Edmonton Gt Lon 36 H2
Edmundbyers Dur 112 F10
Ednam Border 118 D3
Ednaston Derbys 71 N6
Edney Common Essex 51 Q10
Edradynate P & K 141 L7
Edrom Border 129 L8
Edstaston Shrops 69 P8
Edstone Warwks 47 N2
Edvin Loach Herefs 46 C3
Edwalton Notts 72 F3
Edwardstone Suffk 52 F3
Edwardsville Myr Td 30 E5
Edwinsford Carmth 43 M8
Edwinstowe Notts 85 K7
Edworth C Beds 50 F2
Edwyn Ralph Herefs 46 B3
Edzell Angus 143 L4
Edzell Woods Abers 143 L5
Efail-fach Neath 29 L5
Efail Isaf Rhondd 30 E8
Efailnewydd Gwynd 66 F7
Efail-Rhyd Powys 68 G9
Efailwen Carmth 41 M5
Efenechtyd Denbgs 68 F3
Effgill D & G 110 F2
Effingham Surrey 36 D10
Effingham Junction Surrey 36 D9
Efflinch Staffs 71 M11
Efford Devon 9 L4
Efford Crematorium C Plym 6 E7
Egbury Hants 22 D4
Egdean W Susx 23 Q10
Egerton Bolton 89 L8
Egerton Kent 26 F2
Egerton Forstal Kent 26 E2
Eggborough N York 91 P6
Eggbuckland C Plym 6 E7
Eggesford Devon 17 M9
Eggington C Beds 49 Q9
Egginton Derbys 71 P9
Egglescliffe S on T 104 D8
Eggleston Dur 103 J6
Egham Surrey 36 B6
Egham Wick Surrey 35 Q10
Egleton Rutlnd 73 M9
Eglingham Nthumb 119 M7
Egloshayle Cnwll 4 G7
Egloskerry Cnwll 5 M4
Eglwysbach Conwy 79 Q10
Eglwys-Brewis V Glam 30 D11
Eglwys Cross Wrexhm 69 N6
Eglwys Fach Cerdgn 54 F5
Eglwyswrw Pembks 41 M3
Egmanton Notts 85 M7
Egremont Cumb 100 D8
Egremont Wirral 81 L6
Egton N York 105 M9
Egton Bridge N York 105 M10
Egypt Bucks 35 Q7
Egypt Hants 22 E6
Eigg Highld 144 G10
Eight Ash Green Essex 52 F6
Eilanreach Highld 145 P4
Eilean Donan Castle Highld 145 Q2
Eisteddfa Gurig Cerdgn 54 H8
Elan Valley Powys 44 B2
Elan Village Powys 44 C2
Elberton S Glos 32 B7
Elbridge W Susx 15 P6
Elburton C Plym 6 E8
Elcombe Swindn 33 M8
Elcot W Berk 34 C11
Eldernell Cambs 74 F11
Eldersfield Worcs 46 E8
Elderslie Rens 125 L5
Elder Street Essex 51 N4
Eldon Dur 103 P5
Eldwick C Brad 90 E2
Elerch Cerdgn 54 F7
Elfhill Abers 151 L10
Elford Nthumb 119 N4
Elford Staffs 59 J2
Elgin Moray 157 N5
Elgol Highld 144 H5
Elham Kent 27 L3
Elie Fife 135 M7
Elilaw Nthumb 119 J9
Elim IoA 78 F8
Eling Hants 14 C4
Elkesley Notts 85 L5
Elkstone Gloucs 33 J2
Ella Abers 158 F6
Ellacombe Torbay 7 N6
Elland Calder 90 E6
Elland Lower Edge Calder 90 E6
Ellary Ag & B 123 M4
Ellastone Staffs 71 L6
Ellel Lancs 95 K9
Ellemford Border 129 J7
Ellenabeich Ag & B 130 E4
Ellenborough Cumb 100 D3
Ellenbrook Salfd 82 F4
Ellenhall Staffs 70 E9
Ellen's Green Surrey 24 C3
Ellerbeck N York 104 D11
Ellerby N York 105 L8
Ellerdine Heath Wrekin 69 R10
Ellerhayes Devon 9 N4
Elleric Ag & B 139 J8
Ellerker E R Yk 92 F5
Ellers N York 90 C2
Ellerton E R Yk 92 B3
Ellerton N York 103 Q11
Ellerton Shrops 70 C9
Ellesborough Bucks 35 M3
Ellesmere Shrops 69 L8
Ellesmere Port Ches W 81 N9
Ellingham Hants 13 K3
Ellingham Norfk 65 M3
Ellingham Nthumb 119 N5
Ellingstring N York 97 J4
Ellington Cambs 61 Q6
Ellington Nthumb 113 L2
Ellington Thorpe Cambs 61 Q6
Elliots Green Somset 20 E5
Ellisfield Hants 22 H5
Ellishader Highld 153 J4
Ellistown Leics 72 C8
Ellon Abers 159 N11
Ellonby Cumb 101 M3
Ellough Suffk 65 N4
Elloughton E R Yk 92 F5
Ellwood Gloucs 31 Q3
Elm Cambs 75 J9
Elmbridge Worcs 58 D11
Elmdon Essex 51 L3
Elmdon Solhll 59 J8
Elmdon Heath Solhll 59 J8
Elmer W Susx 15 Q6
Elmers End Gt Lon 37 J7
Elmer's Green Lancs 88 G9
Elmesthorpe Leics 72 D11
Elm Green Essex 52 C10
Elmhurst Staffs 58 H2
Elmley Castle Worcs 47 J6
Elmley Lovett Worcs 58 C11
Elmore Gloucs 46 E11
Elmore Back Gloucs 46 E11
Elm Park Gt Lon 37 M3
Elmscott Devon 16 C7
Elmsett Suffk 53 J2
Elms Green Worcs 57 N11
Elmstead Heath Essex 53 J7
Elmstead Market Essex 53 J7
Elmstead Row Essex 53 J7
Elmsted Kent 27 K3
Elmstone Kent 39 N9
Elmstone Hardwicke Gloucs 46 H9
Elmswell E R Yk 99 K9
Elmswell Suffk 64 D9
Elmton Derbys 84 H6
Elphin Highld 161 L4
Elphinstone E Loth 128 B6
Elrick Abers 151 L6
Elrig D & G 107 K8
Elrington Nthumb 112 C8
Elsdon Nthumb 112 D2
Elsecar Barns 91 K11
Elsenham Essex 51 M5
Elsfield Oxon 34 F2
Elsham N Linc 92 H8
Elsing Norfk 76 F8
Elslack N York 96 D11
Elson Hants 14 H6
Elson Shrops 69 L7
Elsrickle S Lans 116 F2
Elstead Surrey 23 P6
Elsted W Susx 23 M11
Elsthorpe Lincs 73 R6
Elstob Dur 104 B6
Elston Lancs 88 H4
Elston Notts 85 N11
Elston Wilts 21 L6
Elstone Devon 17 M8
Elstow Bed 61 N11
Elstree Herts 50 E11
Elstronwick E R Yk 93 M4
Elswick Lancs 88 E3
Elswick N u Ty 113 K8
Elsworth Cambs 62 D8
Elterwater Cumb 101 K10
Eltham Gt Lon 37 K6
Eltham Crematorium Gt Lon 37 K6
Eltisley Cambs 62 C9
Elton Bury 89 M8
Elton Cambs 61 N2
Elton Ches W 81 P9
Elton Derbys 84 B8
Elton Gloucs 32 D2
Elton Herefs 56 H10
Elton Notts 73 K3
Elton S on T 104 D7
Elton Green Ches W 81 P10
Eltringham Nthumb 112 G8
Elvanfoot S Lans 116 D7
Elvaston Derbys 72 C4
Elveden Suffk 63 P4
Elvetham Heath Hants 23 M3
Elvingston E Loth 128 D5
Elvington C York 98 E11
Elvington Kent 39 N11
Elwell Devon 17 M5
Elwick Hartpl 104 E4
Elwick Nthumb 119 M3
Elworth Ches E 70 C2
Elworthy Somset 18 E8
Ely Cambs 62 H4
Ely Cardif 30 F9
Emberton M Keyn 49 N5
Embleton Cumb 100 G4
Embleton Dur 104 D5
Embleton Nthumb 119 P6
Embo Highld 163 J8
Emborough Somset 20 B4
Embo Street Highld 163 J8
Embsay N York 96 F10
Emery Down Hants 13 N3
Emley Kirk 90 G8
Emley Moor Kirk 90 G8
Emmbrook Wokham 35 M11
Emmer Green Readg 35 K9
Emmett Carr Derbys 84 G5
Emmington Oxon 35 K4
Emneth Norfk 75 J9
Emneth Hungate Norfk 75 K9
Empingham Rutlnd 73 N9
Empshott Hants 23 L8
Empshott Green Hants 23 K8
Emstrey Crematorium Shrops 57 J2
Emsworth Hants 15 K5
Enborne W Berk 34 D11
Enborne Row W Berk 22 D2
Enchmarsh Shrops 57 J5
Enderby Leics 72 E11
Endmoor Cumb 95 L4
Endon Staffs 70 G4
Endon Bank Staffs 70 G4
Enfield Gt Lon 51 J11
Enfield Crematorium Gt Lon 50 H11
Enfield Lock Gt Lon 51 J11
Enfield Wash Gt Lon 51 J11
Enford Wilts 21 M4
Engine Common S Glos 32 C8
England's Gate Herefs 45 Q4
Englefield W Berk 34 H10
Englefield Green Surrey 35 Q10
Engleseabrook Ches E 70 D4
English Bicknor Gloucs 46 A11
Englishcombe BaNES 20 D2
English Frankton Shrops 69 N9
Engollan Cnwll 4 D7
Enham-Alamein Hants 22 C5
Enmore Somset 18 H7
Enmore Green Dorset 20 G10
Ennerdale Bridge Cumb 100 E7
Enniscaven Cnwll 4 F10
Enochdhu P & K 141 Q5
Ensay Ag & B 137 K6
Ensbury Bmouth 13 J5
Ensdon Shrops 69 M11
Ensis Devon 17 K6
Enson Staffs 70 G9
Enstone Oxon 48 C10
Enterkinfoot D & G 116 B10
Enterpen N York 104 E9
Enville Staffs 58 B7
Eòlaigearraidh W Isls 168 c17
Eoligarry W Isls 168 c17
Epney Gloucs 32 E2
Epperstone Notts 85 L11
Epping Essex 51 L10
Epping Green Essex 51 K9
Epping Green Herts 50 G9
Epping Upland Essex 51 K10
Eppleby N York 103 N8
Eppleworth E R Yk 92 H4
Epsom Surrey 36 F8
Epwell Oxon 48 C6
Epworth N Linc 92 C10
Epworth Turbary N Linc 92 C10
Erbistock Wrexhm 69 L6
Erdington Birm 58 H6
Eridge Green E Susx 25 N3
Eridge Station E Susx 25 M4
Erines Ag & B 123 Q4
Eriska Ag & B 138 G9
Eriskay W Isls 168 c17
Eriswell Suffk 63 M5
Erith Gt Lon 37 M5
Erlestoke Wilts 21 J4
Ermington Devon 6 G8
Erpingham Norfk 76 H5
Erriottwood Kent 38 F10
Errogie Highld 147 P3
Errol P & K 134 G3
Erskine Rens 125 M3
Erskine Bridge Rens 125 M3
Ervie D & G 106 D4
Erwarton Suffk 53 M5
Erwood Powys 44 F6
Eryholme N York 104 B9
Eryrys Denbgs 68 H3
Escalls Cnwll 2 B8
Escomb Dur 103 N4
Escott Somset 18 E7
Escrick N York 91 Q2
Esgair Carmth 42 G9
Esgair Cerdgn 54 D11
Esgairgeiliog Powys 54 H3
Esgerdawe Carmth 43 M6
Esgyryn Conwy 79 Q9
Esh Dur 103 N2
Esher Surrey 36 D8
Esholt C Brad 90 F2
Eshott Nthumb 119 P11
Eshton N York 96 D9
Esh Winning Dur 103 N2
Eskadale Highld 155 N9
Eskbank Mdloth 127 Q4
Eskdale Green Cumb 100 F10
Eskdalemuir D & G 117 K11
Eske E R Yk 93 J2
Eskham Lincs 93 Q11
Eskholme Donc 91 Q7
Esperley Lane Ends Dur 103 M6
Esprick Lancs 88 E3
Essendine Rutlnd 73 Q8
Essendon Herts 50 G9
Essich Highld 156 A10
Essington Staffs 58 E4
Esslemont Abers 151 N2
Eston R & Cl 104 F7
Etal Nthumb 118 H3
Etchilhampton Wilts 21 K2
Etchingham E Susx 26 B6
Etchinghill Kent 27 L4
Etchinghill Staffs 71 J11
Etchingwood E Susx 25 M6
Etling Green Norfk 76 E9
Etloe Gloucs 32 C3
Eton W & M 35 Q9
Eton Wick W & M 35 P9
Etruria C Stke 70 F5
Etteridge Highld 148 B9
Ettersgill Dur 102 G5
Ettiley Heath Ches E 70 C2
Ettingshall Wolves 58 D5
Ettington Warwks 47 Q5
Etton C Pete 74 B9
Etton E R Yk 92 G2
Ettrick Border 117 K8
Ettrickbridge Border 117 M6
Ettrickhill Border 117 K8
Etwall Derbys 71 P8
Eudon George Shrops 57 M7
Euston Suffk 64 B6
Euximoor Drove Cambs 75 J11
Euxton Lancs 88 H7
Evancoyd Powys 45 K2
Evanton Highld 155 R4
Evedon Lincs 86 E11
Evelith Shrops 57 N3
Evelix Highld 162 H8
Evenjobb Powys 45 K2
Evenley Nhants 48 G8
Evenlode Gloucs 47 P9
Evenwood Dur 103 N6
Evenwood Gate Dur 103 N6
Evercreech Somset 20 B7
Everingham E R Yk 92 D2
Everleigh Wilts 21 P4
Everley N York 99 K3
Eversholt C Beds 49 Q8
Evershot Dorset 11 M4
Eversley Hants 23 L2
Eversley Cross Hants 23 L2
Everthorpe E R Yk 92 F4
Everton C Beds 62 B10
Everton Hants 13 N6
Everton Lpool 81 L6
Everton Notts 85 L2
Evertown D & G 110 G5
Evesbatch Herefs 46 C5
Evesham Worcs 47 K6
Evington C Leic 72 G10
Ewden Village Sheff 90 H11
Ewell Surrey 36 F8
Ewell Minnis Kent 27 N3
Ewelme Oxon 34 H6
Ewen Gloucs 33 K5
Ewenny V Glam 29 P9
Ewerby Lincs 86 F11
Ewerby Thorpe Lincs 86 F11
Ewhurst Surrey 24 C2
Ewhurst Green E Susx 26 C7
Ewhurst Green Surrey 24 C3
Ewloe Flints 81 L11
Ewloe Green Flints 81 K11
Ewood Bl w D 89 K5
Ewood Bridge Lancs 89 M6
Eworthy Devon 8 B5
Ewshot Hants 23 M5
Ewyas Harold Herefs 45 M9
Exbourne Devon 8 F4
Exbury Hants 14 D6
Exceat E Susx 25 M11
Exebridge Somset 18 B10
Exelby N York 97 L3
Exeter Devon 9 M6
Exeter Airport Devon 9 N6
Exeter & Devon Crematorium Devon 9 M6
Exeter Services Devon 9 N6
Exford Somset 17 R4
Exfordsgreen Shrops 56 H3
Exhall Warwks 47 M3
Exhall Warwks 59 N7
Exlade Street Oxon 35 J8
Exley Head C Brad 90 C2
Exminster Devon 9 M7
Exmoor National Park 17 R4
Exmouth Devon 9 P8
Exning Suffk 63 K7
Exted Kent 27 L3
Exton Devon 9 N7
Exton Hants 22 H10
Exton Rutlnd 73 N8
Exton Somset 18 B8
Exwick Devon 9 M6
Eyam Derbys 84 B5
Eydon Nhants 48 F5
Eye C Pete 74 D10
Eye Herefs 45 P2
Eye Suffk 64 G7
Eye Green C Pete 74 D10
Eye Kettleby Leics 73 J7
Eyemouth Border 129 N7
Eyeworth C Beds 62 C11
Eyhorne Street Kent 38 D11
Eyke Suffk 65 L11
Eynesbury Cambs 61 Q9
Eynsford Kent 37 M7
Eynsham Oxon 34 D3
Eype Dorset 11 J6
Eyre Highld 152 G7
Eythorne Kent 27 N2
Eyton Herefs 45 P2
Eyton Shrops 56 F2
Eyton Shrops 56 F7
Eyton Shrops 69 M10
Eyton Wrexhm 69 L6
Eyton on Severn Shrops 57 K3
Eyton upon the Weald Moors Wrekin 57 M2

F

Faccombe Hants 22 C3
Faceby N York 104 E10
Fachwen Powys 68 D11
Facit Lancs 89 P7
Fackley Notts 84 G8
Faddiley Ches E 69 Q4
Fadmoor N York 98 D3
Faerdre Swans 29 J4
Fagwyr Swans 29 J4
Faifley W Duns 125 M3
Failand N Som 31 P10
Failford S Ayrs 115 J2
Failsworth Oldham 83 J4
Fairbourne Gwynd 54 E2
Fairburn N York 91 M5
Fairfield Derbys 83 N10
Fairfield Kent 26 G6
Fairfield Worcs 58 D9
Fairfield Park Herts 50 F4
Fairford Gloucs 33 N4
Fairford Park Gloucs 33 N4
Fairgirth D & G 109 J9
Fair Green Norfk 75 N7
Fairhaven Lancs 88 C5
Fair Isle Shet 169 t14
Fair Isle Airport Shet 169 t14
Fairlands Surrey 23 Q4
Fairlie N Ayrs 124 G7
Fairlight E Susx 26 E9
Fairlight Cove E Susx 26 E9
Fairmile Devon 10 B5
Fairmile Surrey 36 D8
Fairnilee Border 117 P4
Fair Oak Hants 22 E11
Fairoak Staffs 70 D8
Fair Oak Green Hants 23 J2
Fairseat Kent 37 P8
Fairstead Essex 52 C8
Fairstead Norfk 75 M6
Fairstead Norfk 77 K7
Fairwarp E Susx 25 L5
Fairwater Cardif 30 F9
Fairy Cross Devon 16 G7
Fakenham Norfk 76 C6
Fakenham Magna Suffk 64 C6
Fala Mdloth 128 C7
Fala Dam Mdloth 128 C7
Falcut Nhants 48 G6
Faldingworth Lincs 86 E4
Faldouët Jersey 11 c2
Falfield S Glos 32 C6
Falkenham Suffk 53 N4
Falkirk Falk 133 P11
Falkirk Crematorium Falk 133 P11
Falkirk Wheel Falk 133 P11
Falkland Fife 134 H6
Fallburn S Lans 116 D3
Fallgate Derbys 84 E8
Fallin Stirlg 133 N9
Fallodon Nthumb 119 N6
Fallowfield Manch 83 J6
Fallowfield Nthumb 112 D7
Falls of Blarghour Ag & B 131 K5
Falmer E Susx 25 J9
Falmouth Cnwll 3 L7
Falnash Border 117 M9
Falsgrave N York 99 L3
Falstone Nthumb 111 P3
Fanagmore Highld 164 E7
Fancott C Beds 50 B5
Fanellan Highld 155 N9
Fangdale Beck N York 98 B2
Fangfoss E R Yk 98 F10
Fanmore Ag & B 137 L7
Fannich Lodge Highld 154 H4
Fans Border 118 B2
Far Bletchley M Keyn 49 N8
Farcet Cambs 62 B2
Far Cotton Nhants 60 G9
Farden Shrops 57 K9
Fareham Hants 14 G5
Farewell Staffs 58 G2
Far Forest Worcs 57 N9
Farforth Lincs 87 K5
Far Green Gloucs 32 E4
Faringdon Oxon 33 Q5
Farington Lancs 88 G5
Farlam Cumb 111 L9
Farleigh N Som 31 P11
Farleigh Surrey 37 J8
Farleigh Hungerford Somset 20 F3
Farleigh Wallop Hants 22 H5
Farlesthorpe Lincs 87 N6
Farleton Cumb 95 L4
Farleton Lancs 95 M7
Farley Derbys 84 C8
Farley Staffs 71 K6
Farley Wilts 21 P9
Farley Green Suffk 63 M10
Farley Green Surrey 36 C11
Farley Hill Wokham 23 K2
Farleys End Gloucs 32 E2
Farlington C Port 15 J5
Farlington N York 98 C7
Farlow Shrops 57 L8
Farmborough BaNES 20 C2
Farmbridge End Essex 51 P8
Farmcote Gloucs 47 L9
Farmcote Shrops 57 P6
Farmers Carmth 43 M6
Farmington Gloucs 47 M11
Farmoor Oxon 34 E3
Far Moor Wigan 82 B4
Farms Common Cnwll 2 H7
Farm Town Leics 72 B7
Farmtown Moray 158 D7
Farnah Green Derbys 84 D11
Farnborough Gt Lon 37 K8
Farnborough Hants 23 N4
Farnborough W Berk 34 D8
Farnborough Warwks 48 D5
Farnborough Park Hants 23 N3
Farncombe Surrey 23 Q6
Farndish Bed 61 K8
Farndon Ches W 69 M4
Farndon Notts 85 N10
Farne Islands Nthumb 119 P3

Farnell Angus 143 L6
Farnham Dorset 21 J11
Farnham Essex 51 L6
Farnham N York 97 M8
Farnham Suffk 65 M9
Farnham Surrey 23 M5
Farnham Common Bucks 35 Q7
Farnham Green Essex 51 L5
Farnham Royal Bucks 35 Q8
Farningham Kent 37 M7
Farnley Leeds 90 H4
Farnley N York 97 K11
Farnley Tyas Kirk 90 F8
Farnsfield Notts 85 K9
Farnworth Bolton 89 L9
Farnworth Halton 81 Q7
Far Oakridge Gloucs 32 H4
Farr Highld 148 E7
Farr Highld 156 B11
Farr Highld 166 B4
Farraline Highld 147 P3
Farrington Devon 9 P6
Farrington Gurney BaNES 20 B3
Far Sawrey Cumb 101 L11
Farsley Leeds 90 G3
Farther Howegreen Essex 52 D11
Farthing Green Kent 26 D2
Farthinghoe Nhants 48 F7
Farthingloe Kent 27 N3
Farthingstone Nhants 48 H4
Farthing Street Gt Lon 37 K8
Fartown Kirk 90 F7
Farway Devon 10 D5
Fasnacloich Ag & B 139 J8
Fasnakyle Highld 147 J2
Fassfern Highld 139 J2
Fatfield Sundld 113 L10
Faugh Cumb 111 K10
Fauld Staffs 71 M9
Fauldhouse W Loth 126 G5
Faulkbourne Essex 52 C8
Faulkland Somset 20 D4
Fauls Shrops 69 Q8
Faversham Kent 38 H9
Fawdington N York 97 P6
Fawdon N u Ty 113 K7
Fawdon Nthumb 119 K7
Fawfieldhead Staffs 71 K2
Fawkham Green Kent 37 N7
Fawler Oxon 48 C11
Fawley Bucks 35 L7
Fawley Hants 14 E6
Fawley W Berk 34 C8
Fawley Chapel Herefs 46 A9
Fawnog Flints 81 J11
Fawsley Nhants 60 C9
Faxfleet E R Yk 92 E6
Faygate W Susx 24 F4
Fazakerley Lpool 81 M5
Fazeley Staffs 59 K4
Fearby N York 97 J4
Fearn Highld 156 E2
Fearnan P & K 140 H9
Fearnbeg Highld 153 N6
Fearnhead Warrtn 82 D6
Fearnmore Highld 153 N5
Fearnoch Ag & B 124 A2
Featherstone Staffs 58 D3
Featherstone Wakefd 91 L7
Feckenham Worcs 47 K2
Feering Essex 52 E7
Feetham N York 103 J11
Feizor N York 96 A7
Felbridge Surrey 25 J3
Felbrigg Norfk 77 J4
Felcourt Surrey 25 J2
Felden Herts 50 B10
Felindre Carmth 42 G7
Felindre Carmth 43 L10
Felindre Carmth 43 P9
Felindre Cerdgn 43 L3
Felindre Powys 44 H10
Felindre Powys 56 B8
Felindre Swans 28 H4
Felindre Farchog Pembks 41 M3
Felin Fach Cerdgn 43 K3
Felinfach Powys 44 F8
Felinfoel Carmth 28 F4
Felingwm Isaf Carmth 43 K10
Felingwm Uchaf Carmth 43 K10
Felin-newydd Powys 44 G7
Felixkirk N York 97 Q4
Felixstowe Suffk 53 P5
Felixstowe Ferry Suffk 53 P4
Felkington Nthumb 118 H2
Felkirk Wakefd 91 K8
Felling Gatesd 113 L8
Fell Lane C Brad 90 C2
Fell Side Cumb 101 K3
Felmersham Bed 61 L9
Felmingham Norfk 77 K6
Felpham W Susx 15 P7
Felsham Suffk 64 C10
Felsted Essex 51 Q6
Feltham Gt Lon 36 D6
Felthamhill Surrey 36 C6
Felthorpe Norfk 76 H8
Felton Herefs 46 A5
Felton N Som 31 P11
Felton Nthumb 119 N10
Felton Butler Shrops 69 L11
Feltwell Norfk 63 M2
Fenay Bridge Kirk 90 F7
Fence Lancs 89 N3
Fence Rothm 84 F3
Fence Houses Sundld 113 M11
Fencott Oxon 48 G11
Fendike Corner Lincs 87 N8
Fen Ditton Cambs 62 G8
Fen Drayton Cambs 62 D7
Fen End Lincs 74 D6
Fen End Solhll 59 K10
Fenham Nthumb 119 L2
Feniscliffe Bl w D 89 K5
Feniscowles Bl w D 89 J5
Feniton Devon 10 C5
Fenland Crematorium Cambs 62 G2
Fenn Green Shrops 57 P8
Fenn Street Medway 38 C6
Fenny Bentley Derbys 71 M5
Fenny Bridges Devon 10 C5
Fenny Compton Warwks 48 D4
Fenny Drayton Leics 72 B11
Fenny Stratford M Keyn 49 N8
Fenrother Nthumb 113 J2
Fenstanton Cambs 62 D7

Fenstead End Suffk 63 P10
Fen Street Norfk 64 D2
Fen Street Suffk 64 H9
Fenton C Stke 70 F6
Fenton Cambs 62 D5
Fenton Cumb 111 K9
Fenton Lincs 85 P5
Fenton Lincs 85 Q10
Fenton Notts 85 N4
Fenton Nthumb 119 J4
Fenton Barns E Loth 128 E3
Fenwick Donc 91 P7
Fenwick E Ayrs 125 M9
Fenwick Nthumb 112 G6
Fenwick Nthumb 119 L2
Feock Cnwll 3 L6
Feolin Ferry Ag & B 122 F6
Fergushill N Ayrs 125 J9
Feriniquarrie Highld 152 B7
Fermain Bay Guern 10 c2
Fern Angus 142 H5
Ferndale Rhondd 30 C5
Ferndown Dorset 13 J4
Ferness Highld 156 H8
Fernham Oxon 33 Q6
Fernhill Heath Worcs 46 G3
Fernhurst W Susx 23 N9
Fernie Fife 135 J4
Ferniegair S Lans 126 C7
Fernilea Highld 152 F11
Fernilee Derbys 83 M9
Fernwood Notts 85 P10
Ferrensby N York 97 N8
Ferriby Sluice N Linc 92 G6
Ferrindonald Highld 145 L6
Ferring W Susx 24 C10
Ferrybridge Wakefd 91 M6
Ferrybridge Services Wakefd 91 M6
Ferryden Angus 143 N6
Ferryhill Dur 103 Q4
Ferryhill Station Dur 103 Q4
Ferry Point Highld 162 G9
Ferryside Carmth 28 C2
Ferrytown Highld 162 G9
Fersfield Norfk 64 F4
Fersit Highld 139 R2
Feshiebridge Highld 148 F5
Fetcham Surrey 36 D9
Fetlar Shet 169 t4
Fetterangus Abers 159 N7
Fettercairn Abers 143 M3
Fewcott Oxon 48 F9
Fewston N York 97 J10
Ffairfach Carmth 43 M10
Ffair Rhos Cerdgn 54 G11
Ffald-y-Brenin Carmth 43 M6
Ffawyddog Powys 45 J11
Ffestiniog Gwynd 67 N6
Ffestiniog Railway Gwynd 67 M6
Ffordd-las Denbgs 68 F2
Fforest Carmth 28 G4
Fforest Mons 45 K10
Fforest Fach Swans 28 H5
Fforest Gôch Neath 29 K4
Ffostrasol Cerdgn 42 G5
Ffrith Flints 69 J3
Ffynnonddewi Cerdgn 42 G4
Ffynnongroyw Flints 80 G8
Ffynnon-oer Cerdgn 43 K4
Fickleshole Surrey 37 J8
Fiddington Gloucs 46 H8
Fiddington Somset 18 H6
Fiddleford Dorset 12 D2
Fiddlers Green Cnwll 4 C10
Fiddlers Hamlet Essex 51 L10
Field Staffs 71 J8
Field Broughton Cumb 94 H4
Field Dalling Norfk 76 E4
Fieldhead Cumb 101 N3
Field Head Leics 72 D9
Fifehead Magdalen Dorset 20 E10
Fifehead Neville Dorset 12 C2
Fifehead St Quintin Dorset 12 C2
Fife Keith Moray 158 B7
Fifield Oxon 47 P11
Fifield W & M 35 P9
Fifield Wilts 21 M4
Figheldean Wilts 21 N5
Filands Wilts 32 H7
Filby Norfk 77 P9
Filey N York 99 N4
Filgrave M Keyn 49 N5
Filkins Oxon 33 P4
Filleigh Devon 8 H2
Filleigh Devon 17 M6
Fillingham Lincs 86 B3
Fillongley Warwks 59 L7
Filmore Hill Hants 23 J9
Filton S Glos 32 B9
Fimber E R Yk 98 H8
Finavon Angus 142 H6
Fincham Norfk 75 N9
Finchampstead Wokham 23 L2
Fincharn Ag & B 131 J7
Finchdean Hants 15 K4
Finchingfield Essex 51 Q4
Finchley Gt Lon 36 G2
Findern Derbys 71 Q8
Findhorn Moray 157 J5
Findhorn Bridge Highld 148 E2
Findochty Moray 158 C4
Findo Gask P & K 134 C4
Findon Abers 151 N8
Findon W Susx 24 D9
Findon Mains Highld 155 R5
Findrack House Abers 150 G7
Finedon Nhants 61 K6
Fingal Street Suffk 65 J8
Fingask P & K 134 F4
Fingest Bucks 35 L6
Finghall N York 97 J3
Fingland Cumb 110 G9
Finglesham Kent 39 P11
Fingringhoe Essex 52 H7
Finkle Green Essex 52 B3
Finkle Street Barns 91 J11
Finlarig Stirlg 140 E11
Finmere Oxon 48 H8
Finnart P & K 140 D6
Finningham Suffk 64 F8
Finningley Donc 91 R11
Finsbay W Isls 168 f9
Finstall Worcs 58 E10
Finsthwaite Cumb 94 H3
Finstock Oxon 48 C11
Finstown Ork 169 c5

Fintry Abers 159 J7
Fintry Stirlg 133 J10
Finzean Abers 150 G9
Fionnphort Ag & B 137 J11
Fionnsbhagh W Isls 168 f9
Firbank Cumb 95 N2
Firbeck Rothm 85 J3
Firby N York 97 L3
Firby N York 98 E7
Firgrove Rochdl 89 Q8
Firle E Susx 25 L9
Firsby Lincs 87 N8
Firsdown Wilts 21 P8
Fir Tree Dur 103 M4
Fishbourne IoW 14 G8
Fishbourne W Susx 15 M6
Fishbourne Roman Palace W Susx 15 M6
Fishburn Dur 104 C4
Fishcross Clacks 133 P8
Fisher W Susx 15 N6
Fisherford Abers 158 G10
Fisherrow E Loth 127 Q3
Fisher's Pond Hants 22 E10
Fisher's Row Lancs 95 J11
Fisherstreet W Susx 23 P8
Fisherton Highld 156 C7
Fisherton S Ayrs 114 E4
Fisherton de la Mere Wilts 21 K7
Fisherwick Staffs 59 J3
Fishery Estate W & M 35 N8
Fishguard Pembks 41 J3
Fishlake Donc 91 R8
Fishleigh Devon 8 D3
Fishmere End Lincs 74 E3
Fishnish Pier Ag & B 138 B9
Fishpond Bottom Dorset 10 H5
Fishponds Bristl 32 B9
Fishtoft Lincs 74 G2
Fishtoft Drove Lincs 87 K11
Fishwick Lancs 88 H5
Fiskavaig Highld 152 E11
Fiskerton Lincs 86 D6
Fiskerton Notts 85 M10
Fitling E R Yk 93 N4
Fittleton Wilts 21 M5
Fittleworth W Susx 24 B7
Fitton End Cambs 74 H8
Fitz Shrops 69 M11
Fitzhead Somset 18 F9
Fitzroy Somset 18 G9
Fitzwilliam Wakefd 91 L7
Five Ash Down E Susx 25 L6
Five Ashes E Susx 25 N5
Five Bells Somset 18 E6
Five Bridges Herefs 46 B5
Fivecrosses Ches W 82 B9
Five Lane Ends Lancs 95 K11
Fivehead Somset 19 L10
Fivelanes Cnwll 5 L5
Five Lanes Mons 31 M6
Five Oak Green Kent 37 P11
Five Oaks Jersey 11 c2
Five Oaks W Susx 24 C5
Five Roads Carmth 28 E3
Five Wents Kent 38 D11
Flack's Green Essex 52 C9
Flackwell Heath Bucks 35 N7
Fladbury Worcs 47 J5
Fladdabister Shet 169 r10
Flagg Derbys 83 P11
Flamborough E R Yk 99 Q6
Flamborough Head E R Yk 99 R6
Flamingo Land Theme Park N York 98 F5
Flamstead Herts 50 C8
Flamstead End Herts 50 H10
Flansham W Susx 15 Q6
Flanshaw Wakefd 91 J6
Flappit Spring C Brad 90 D3
Flasby N York 96 D9
Flash Staffs 83 M11
Flashader Highld 152 E7
Flaunden Herts 50 B10
Flawborough Notts 73 K2
Flawith N York 97 Q7
Flax Bourton N Som 31 P11
Flaxby N York 97 N9
Flaxley Gloucs 46 C11
Flaxmere Ches W 82 C10
Flaxpool Somset 18 F7
Flaxton N York 98 D8
Fleckney Leics 60 E2
Flecknoe Warwks 60 B8
Fledborough Notts 85 P6
Fleet Dorset 11 N8
Fleet Hants 15 K6
Fleet Hants 23 M4
Fleet Lincs 74 G6
Fleetend Hants 14 F5
Fleet Hargate Lincs 74 G6
Fleet Services Hants 23 L3
Fleetwood Lancs 94 G11
Fleggburgh Norfk 77 N9
Flemingston V Glam 30 D11
Flemington S Lans 126 B6
Flempton Suffk 63 P7
Fletchersbridge Cnwll 5 J8
Fletcher's Green Kent 37 M11
Fletchertown Cumb 100 H2
Fletching E Susx 25 K6
Fleur-de-lis Caerph 30 G5
Flexbury Cnwll 16 C10
Flexford Surrey 23 P4
Flimby Cumb 100 D4
Flimwell E Susx 26 B5
Flint Flints 81 J10
Flintham Notts 85 M11
Flint Mountain Flints 81 J10
Flinton E R Yk 93 M3
Flint's Green Solhll 59 L8
Flishinghurst Kent 26 C4
Flitcham Norfk 75 P5
Flitton C Beds 50 C3
Flitwick C Beds 50 B4
Flixborough N Linc 92 E8
Flixborough Stather N Linc 92 E8
Flixton N York 99 L5
Flixton Suffk 65 L4
Flixton Traffd 82 F6
Flockton Kirk 90 G8
Flockton Green Kirk 90 G8
Flodden Nthumb 118 H3
Flodigarry Highld 152 H3
Flookburgh Cumb 94 H5
Flordon Norfk 64 H2
Flore Nhants 60 D8
Flotterton Nthumb 119 J10
Flowers Green E Susx 25 P8

Flowton Suffk 53 J2
Flushdyke Wakefd 90 H6
Flushing Cnwll 3 L7
Fluxton Devon 10 B6
Flyford Flavell Worcs 47 J3
Fobbing Thurr 38 B3
Fochabers Moray 157 Q6
Fochriw Caerph 30 F3
Fockerby N Linc 92 E7
Foddington Somset 19 Q9
Foel Powys 55 N2
Foelgastell Carmth 28 F2
Foel y Dyffryn Brdgnd 29 N6
Foggathorpe E R Yk 92 C3
Fogo Border 129 K10
Fogwatt Moray 157 N6
Foindle Highld 164 E7
Folda Angus 142 B5
Fole Staffs 71 J7
Foleshill Covtry 59 N8
Folke Dorset 11 P2
Folkestone Kent 27 M4
Folkingham Lincs 73 R4
Folkington E Susx 25 N10
Folksworth Cambs 61 P3
Folkton N York 99 M5
Folla Rule Abers 158 H11
Follifoot N York 97 M10
Folly Gate Devon 8 E5
Folly Hill Surrey 23 M5
Fonmon V Glam 30 D11
Fonthill Bishop Wilts 20 H8
Fonthill Gifford Wilts 20 H8
Fontmell Magna Dorset 20 G11
Fontmell Parva Dorset 12 D2
Fontwell W Susx 15 P5
Font-y-gary V Glam 30 E11
Foolow Derbys 83 Q9
Foots Cray Gt Lon 37 L6
Forbestown Abers 150 B5
Forcett N York 103 N8
Ford Ag & B 130 H7
Ford Bucks 35 L3
Ford Derbys 84 F4
Ford Devon 6 G8
Ford Devon 7 K10
Ford Gloucs 47 L9
Ford Nthumb 118 H3
Ford Shrops 56 G2
Ford Somset 18 E9
Ford Somset 19 Q4
Ford Staffs 71 K4
Ford W Susx 15 Q6
Ford Wilts 21 N8
Ford Wilts 32 F9
Forda Devon 8 D8
Fordcombe Kent 25 M2
Fordell Fife 134 F10
Forden Powys 56 C4
Ford End Essex 51 Q7
Forder Green Devon 7 K5
Ford Green Lancs 95 K11
Fordham Cambs 63 K6
Fordham Essex 52 F6
Fordham Norfk 75 M11
Ford Heath Shrops 56 G2
Fordingbridge Hants 13 L3
Fordon E R Yk 99 L5
Fordoun Abers 143 N2
Ford's Green Suffk 64 F8
Fordstreet Essex 52 F6
Ford Street Somset 18 G11
Fordton Devon 9 K5
Fordwells Oxon 34 B2
Fordwich Kent 39 L10
Fordyce Abers 158 E5
Forebridge Staffs 70 G10
Foremark Derbys 72 A5
Forest Guern 10 b2
Forest N York 103 Q10
Forest Becks Lancs 96 A10
Forestburn Gate Nthumb 119 L11
Forest Chapel Ches E 83 L10
Forest Gate Gt Lon 37 K3
Forest Green Surrey 24 D2
Forest Hall N Tyne 113 L7
Forest Head Cumb 111 L9
Forest Hill Gt Lon 37 J6
Forest Hill Oxon 34 G3
Forest-in-Teesdale Dur 102 G4
Forest Lane Head N York 97 M9
Forest Mill Clacks 134 B9
Forest of Bowland Lancs 95 N10
Forest of Dean Gloucs 32 B2
Forest of Dean Crematorium Gloucs 32 B2
Forest Park Crematorium Gt Lon 37 L2
Forest Row E Susx 25 K4
Forest Side IoW 14 E9
Forestside W Susx 15 L4
Forest Town Notts 85 J8
Forfar Angus 142 H7
Forgandenny P & K 134 D4
Forge Powys 54 H5
Forge Hammer Torfn 31 J3
Forge Side Torfn 30 H3
Forgie Moray 158 A7
Forgieside Moray 158 B7
Forgue Abers 158 F8
Forhill Worcs 58 G9
Formby Sefton 88 C9
Forncett End Norfk 64 G3
Forncett St Mary Norfk 64 H3
Forncett St Peter Norfk 64 H3
Fornham All Saints Suffk 64 A8
Fornham St Martin Suffk 64 B8
Fornighty Highld 156 G7
Forres Moray 157 J6
Forsbrook Staffs 70 H6
Forse Highld 167 M10
Forshaw Heath Warwks 58 G10
Forsinard Highld 166 B8
Forss Highld 166 H3
Forston Dorset 11 P5
Fort Augustus Highld 147 K6
Forteviot P & K 134 D4
Forth S Lans 126 G7
Forthampton Gloucs 46 G8
Fort Hommet Guern 10 b1
Forth Rail Bridge C Edin 127 L2
Forth Road Bridge Fife 127 L2
Fortingall P & K 140 H8
Fort le Marchant Guern 10 c1
Forton Hants 22 D6
Forton Lancs 95 K10
Forton Shrops 69 M11
Forton Somset 10 G3

Forton Staffs 70 D10
Fortrie Abers 158 G8
Fortrose Highld 156 C6
Fortuneswell Dorset 11 P10
Fort William Highld 139 L3
Forty Green Bucks 35 P6
Forty Hill Gt Lon 50 H11
Forward Green Suffk 64 G10
Fosbury Wilts 22 B3
Foscot Oxon 47 P10
Foscote Nhants 49 J5
Fosdyke Lincs 74 F4
Fosdyke Bridge Lincs 74 F4
Foss P & K 141 J6
Fossebridge Gloucs 33 L2
Foss-y-ffin Cerdgn 42 H2
Fosterhouses Donc 91 R8
Foster Street Essex 51 L9
Foston Derbys 71 M8
Foston Leics 60 E2
Foston Lincs 73 M2
Foston N York 98 D7
Foston on the Wolds E R Yk 99 N9
Fotherby Lincs 87 K2
Fothergill Cumb 100 D4
Fotheringhay Nhants 61 N2
Foula Shet 169 k10
Foula Airport Shet 169 k10
Foulbridge Cumb 110 H11
Foulby Wakefd 91 K7
Foulden Border 129 N8
Foulden Norfk 75 Q11
Foul End Warwks 59 K6
Foul Mile E Susx 25 P8
Foulness Island Essex 38 G3
Foulon Vale Crematorium Guern 10 b2
Foulridge Lancs 89 P2
Foulsham Norfk 76 E7
Fountainhall Border 128 C10
Four Ashes Solhll 59 J9
Four Ashes Staffs 57 Q9
Four Ashes Staffs 58 D3
Four Ashes Suffk 64 E7
Four Cabots Guern 10 b2
Four Crosses Powys 69 J11
Four Crosses Staffs 58 E3
Four Elms Kent 37 L11
Four Foot Somset 19 Q8
Four Forks Somset 18 H7
Four Gates Bolton 89 J9
Four Gotes Cambs 75 J7
Four Lane End Barns 90 H10
Four Lane Ends Ches W 69 Q2
Four Lanes Cnwll 2 H6
Fourlanes End Ches E 70 E3
Four Marks Hants 23 J7
Four Mile Bridge IoA 78 D9
Four Oaks Birm 58 H5
Four Oaks E Susx 26 E7
Four Oaks Gloucs 46 C9
Four Oaks Solhll 59 K8
Fourpenny Highld 163 J8
Four Points W Berk 34 G9
Four Roads Carmth 28 D3
Four Shire Stone Warwks 47 P8
Fourstones Nthumb 112 C7
Four Throws Kent 26 C6
Four Wents Kent 37 P10
Fovant Wilts 21 K9
Foveran Abers 151 P3
Fowey Cnwll 5 J11
Fowley Common Warrtn 82 E5
Fowlhall Kent 37 Q11
Fowlis Angus 142 E11
Fowlis Wester P & K 133 Q3
Fowlmere Cambs 62 F11
Fownhope Herefs 46 A8
Foxbar Rens 125 M5
Foxcombe Devon 8 C7
Fox Corner Surrey 23 Q4
Foxcote Gloucs 47 K11
Foxcote Somset 20 D3
Foxdale IoM 80 c6
Foxearth Essex 52 D3
Foxendown Kent 37 P7
Foxfield Cumb 94 E3
Foxham Wilts 33 J9
Fox Hatch Essex 51 N11
Foxhills Hants 13 P2
Foxhole Cnwll 3 P3
Foxholes N York 99 L6
Foxhunt Green E Susx 25 M7
Foxley Nhants 48 H4
Foxley Norfk 76 E7
Foxley Wilts 32 G7
Foxlydiate Worcs 58 F11
Fox Street Essex 52 H6
Foxt Staffs 71 J5
Foxton Cambs 62 F11
Foxton Dur 104 C6
Foxton Leics 60 F3
Foxton N York 104 D11
Foxup N York 96 C5
Foxwist Green Ches W 82 D11
Foxwood Shrops 57 L9
Foy Herefs 46 A9
Foyers Highld 147 M3
Foynesfield Highld 156 F7
Fraddam Cnwll 2 F7
Fraddon Cnwll 4 E10
Fradley Staffs 59 J2
Fradswell Staffs 70 H8
Fraisthorpe E R Yk 99 P8
Framfield E Susx 25 L6
Framingham Earl Norfk 77 K11
Framingham Pigot Norfk 77 K11
Framlingham Suffk 65 K9
Frampton Dorset 11 N5
Frampton Lincs 74 F3
Frampton Cotterell S Glos 32 C8
Frampton Mansell Gloucs 32 H4
Frampton-on-Severn Gloucs 32 D3
Frampton West End Lincs 74 F2
Framsden Suffk 64 H10
Framwellgate Moor Dur 103 Q2
Franche Worcs 57 Q9
Frandley Ches W 82 D9
Frankaborough Devon 5 P3
Frankby Wirral 81 J7
Frankfort Norfk 77 L7
Franklands Gate Herefs 45 Q5
Frankley Worcs 58 E8
Frankley Services Worcs 58 E8
Franksbridge Powys 44 G4

Frankton – Glyntaff Crematorium 271

Frankton Warwks 59 P10
Frant E Susx 25 N3
Fraserburgh Abers 159 N4
Frating Essex 53 J7
Frating Green Essex 53 J7
Fratton C Port 15 J6
Freathy Cnwll 5 P11
Freckenham Suffk 63 L6
Freckleton Lancs 88 E5
Freebirch Derbys 84 D6
Freeby Leics 73 L6
Freefolk Hants 22 E5
Freehay Staffs 71 J6
Freeland Oxon 34 D2
Freethorpe Norfk 77 N10
Freethorpe Common Norfk 77 N11
Freiston Lincs 74 G2
Fremington Devon 17 J5
Fremington N York 103 K11
Frenchay S Glos 32 B9
Frenchbeer Devon 8 G7
French Street Kent 37 L10
Frenich P & K 141 K6
Frensham Surrey 23 M6
Freshfield Sefton 88 B9
Freshford Wilts 20 E2
Freshwater IoW 13 P7
Freshwater Bay IoW 13 P7
Freshwater East Pembks 41 K11
Fressingfield Suffk 65 K6
Freston Suffk 53 L4
Freswick Highld 167 Q3
Fretherne Gloucs 32 D2
Frettenham Norfk 77 J8
Freuchie Fife 134 H6
Freystrop Pembks 41 J8
Friar Park Sandw 58 F6
Friar's Gate E Susx 25 L4
Friars' Hill N York 98 E3
Friar Waddon Dorset 11 N7
Friday Bridge Cambs 75 J10
Friday Street Suffk 65 J10
Friday Street Suffk 65 L11
Friday Street Suffk 65 M9
Friday Street Surrey 36 D11
Fridaythorpe E R Yk 98 H9
Friden Derbys 71 M2
Friendly Calder 90 D6
Friern Barnet Gt Lon 36 G2
Friesthorpe Lincs 86 E4
Frieston Lincs 86 B11
Frieth Bucks 35 L6
Friezeland Notts 84 G10
Frilford Oxon 34 D5
Frilsham W Berk 34 F10
Frimley Surrey 23 N3
Frimley Green Surrey 23 N3
Frindsbury Medway 38 B8
Fring Norfk 75 P4
Fringford Oxon 48 H9
Frinsted Kent 38 E10
Frinton-on-Sea Essex 53 M7
Friockheim Angus 143 K8
Friog Gwynd 54 E2
Frisby on the Wreake Leics 72 H7
Friskney Lincs 87 N9
Friskney Eaudike Lincs 87 N9
Friston E Susx 25 N11
Friston Suffk 65 N9
Fritchley Derbys 84 E10
Fritham Hants 13 M2
Frith Bank Lincs 87 K11
Frith Common Worcs 57 M11
Frithelstock Devon 16 H8
Frithelstock Stone Devon 16 H8
Frithend Hants 23 M7
Frithsden Herts 50 B9
Frithville Lincs 87 K10
Frittenden Kent 26 D3
Frittiscombe Devon 7 L10
Fritton Norfk 65 J3
Fritton Norfk 77 P11
Fritwell Oxon 48 F9
Frizinghall C Brad 90 E3
Frizington Cumb 100 D7
Frocester Gloucs 32 E4
Frodesley Shrops 57 J4
Frodsham Ches W 81 Q9
Frogden Border 118 E5
Frog End Cambs 62 E11
Frog End Cambs 62 H9
Froggatt Derbys 84 B5
Froghall Staffs 71 J5
Frogham Hants 13 L2
Frogham Kent 39 N11
Frogmore Devon 7 K10
Frognall Lincs 74 C8
Frogpool Cnwll 3 K5
Frog Pool Worcs 57 Q11
Frogwell Cnwll 5 N8
Frolesworth Leics 60 B2
Frome Somset 20 E5
Frome St Quintin Dorset 11 M4
Fromes Hill Herefs 46 C5
Fron Denbgs 80 F11
Fron Gwynd 66 F7
Fron Gwynd 67 J4
Fron Powys 56 B5
Fron Powys 56 C4
Froncysyllte Denbgs 69 J6
Fron-goch Gwynd 68 B7
Fron Isaf Wrexhm 69 J6
Frostenden Suffk 65 P5
Frosterley Dur 103 K3
Froxfield C Beds 49 Q8
Froxfield Wilts 33 Q11
Froxfield Green Hants 23 K9
Fryern Hill Hants 22 D10
Fryerning Essex 51 P10
Fryton N York 98 D6
Fuinary Highld 137 Q6
Fulbeck Lincs 86 B10
Fulbourn Cambs 62 H9
Fulbrook Oxon 33 Q2
Fulflood Hants 22 E8
Fulford C York 98 C11
Fulford Somset 18 H9
Fulford Staffs 70 H7
Fulham Gt Lon 36 G5
Fulking W Susx 24 F8
Fullaford Devon 17 M4
Fullarton N Ayrs 125 J10
Fuller's End Essex 51 M5
Fuller's Moor Ches W 69 N4
Fuller Street Essex 52 B8
Fuller Street Kent 37 N9
Fullerton Hants 22 C7
Fulletby Lincs 87 J6
Fullready Warwks 47 Q5
Full Sutton E R Yk 98 E9
Fullwood E Ayrs 125 L7
Fulmer Bucks 35 Q7
Fulmodeston Norfk 76 D5
Fulnetby Lincs 86 E5
Fulney Lincs 74 E6
Fulstone Kirk 90 F9
Fulstow Lincs 93 P11
Fulwell Oxon 48 C10
Fulwell Sundld 113 N9
Fulwood Lancs 88 G4
Fulwood Notts 84 G9
Fulwood Sheff 84 D3
Fulwood Somset 18 H10
Fundenhall Norfk 64 H2
Funtington W Susx 15 M5
Funtley Hants 14 G5
Funtullich P & K 133 M2
Furley Devon 10 F4
Furnace Ag & B 131 L7
Furnace Carmth 28 F4
Furnace Cerdgn 54 F5
Furnace End Warwks 59 K6
Furner's Green E Susx 25 K5
Furness Vale Derbys 83 M8
Furneux Pelham Herts 51 K5
Further Quarter Kent 26 E4
Furtho Nhants 49 L6
Furzehill Devon 17 N2
Furzehill Dorset 12 H4
Furzehills Lincs 87 J6
Furzeley Corner Hants 15 J4
Furze Platt W & M 35 N8
Furzley Hants 21 Q11
Fyfett Somset 10 E2
Fyfield Essex 51 N9
Fyfield Hants 21 Q5
Fyfield Oxon 34 D5
Fyfield Wilts 21 N2
Fyfield Wilts 33 M11
Fyfield Bavant Wilts 21 K9
Fylingthorpe N York 105 P10
Fyning W Susx 23 M10
Fyvie Abers 159 J10

G

Gabroc Hill E Ayrs 125 M7
Gaddesby Leics 72 H8
Gaddesden Row Herts 50 C8
Gadfa IoA 78 H7
Gadgirth S Ayrs 114 H3
Gadlas Shrops 69 L7
Gaer Powys 44 H10
Gaerllwyd Mons 31 M5
Gaerwen IoA 78 H10
Gagingwell Oxon 48 D9
Gailes N Ayrs 125 J10
Gailey Staffs 58 D2
Gainford Dur 103 N7
Gainsborough Lincs 85 P3
Gainsford End Essex 52 B4
Gairloch Highld 153 Q2
Gairlochy Highld 146 F11
Gairneybridge P & K 134 E8
Gaisgill Cumb 102 B9
Gaitsgill Cumb 110 G11
Galashiels Border 117 P3
Galgate Lancs 95 K9
Galhampton Somset 20 B9
Gallanachbeg Ag & B 130 G2
Gallanachmore Ag & B 130 G2
Gallantry Bank Ches E 69 P4
Gallatown Fife 134 H9
Galley Common Warwks 59 M6
Galleywood Essex 52 B11
Gallovie Highld 147 P10
Galloway Forest Park 114 H10
Gallowfauld Angus 142 G9
Gallowhill P & K 142 B10
Gallows Green Essex 52 F6
Gallows Green Worcs 46 H2
Gallowstree Common Oxon 35 J8
Galltair Highld 145 P3
Gallt-y-foel Gwynd 67 K2
Gally Hill Hants 23 M4
Gallypot Street E Susx 25 L3
Galmisdale Highld 144 G11
Galmpton Devon 6 H10
Galmpton Torbay 7 M7
Galphay N York 97 L6
Galston E Ayrs 125 N10
Gamballs Green Staffs 83 M11
Gamblesby Cumb 102 B3
Gambles Green Essex 52 C9
Gamelsby Cumb 110 E10
Gamesley Derbys 83 M6
Gamlingay Cambs 62 B10
Gamlingay Cinques Cambs 62 B10
Gamlingay Great Heath Cambs 62 B10
Gammersgill N York 96 G4
Gamrie Abers 159 J5
Gamston Notts 72 F3
Gamston Notts 85 M5
Ganarew Herefs 45 Q11
Ganavan Bay Ag & B 138 F11
Gang Cnwll 5 N8
Ganllwyd Gwynd 67 N10
Gannachy Angus 143 K3
Ganstead E R Yk 93 K4
Ganthorpe N York 98 D6
Ganton N York 99 K5
Ganwick Corner Herts 50 G11
Gappah Devon 9 L9
Garbity Moray 157 Q7
Garboldisham Norfk 64 E5
Garbole Highld 148 D3
Garchory Abers 149 Q5
Garden City Flints 81 L11
Gardeners Green Wokham 35 M11
Garden of England Crematorium Kent 38 E8
Gardenstown Abers 159 K5
Garden Village Sheff 90 H11
Garderhouse Shet 169 q9
Gardham E R Yk 92 G2
Gare Hill Somset 20 E6
Garelochhead Ag & B 131 Q9
Garford Oxon 34 D5
Garforth Leeds 91 L4
Gargrave N York 96 D10
Gargunnock Stirlg 133 L9
Garizim Conwy 79 M9
Garlic Street Norfk 65 J5
Garlieston D & G 107 N8
Garlinge Kent 39 P8
Garlinge Green Kent 39 K11
Garlogie Abers 151 K6
Garmond Abers 159 K7
Garmouth Moray 157 Q5
Garmston Shrops 57 L3
Garnant Carmth 29 J2
Garn-Dolbenmaen Gwynd 66 H6
Garnett Bridge Cumb 101 P11
Garnfadryn Gwynd 66 D8
Garnswllt Swans 28 H3
Garn-yr-erw Torfn 30 H3
Garrabost W Isls 168 k4
Garrallan E Ayrs 115 K4
Garras Cnwll 3 J9
Garreg Gwynd 67 L6
Garrigill Cumb 102 D2
Garriston N York 97 J2
Garroch D & G 108 C4
Garrochtrie D & G 106 F10
Garrochty Ag & B 124 D7
Garros Highld 152 H5
Garsdale Cumb 95 Q3
Garsdale Head Cumb 96 A2
Garsdon Wilts 33 J7
Garshall Green Staffs 70 H8
Garsington Oxon 34 G4
Garstang Lancs 95 K11
Garston Herts 50 D10
Garston Lpool 81 N8
Garswood St Hel 82 C5
Gartachossan Ag & B 122 D7
Gartcosh N Lans 126 B4
Garth Brdgnd 29 N6
Garth Mons 31 K6
Garth Powys 44 D5
Garth Powys 56 D10
Garth Wrexhm 69 J6
Garthamlock C Glas 126 B4
Garthbrengy Powys 44 E8
Gartheli Cerdgn 43 L3
Garthmyl Powys 56 B5
Garthorpe Leics 73 L6
Garthorpe N Linc 92 D7
Garth Row Cumb 101 P11
Garths Cumb 95 L3
Gartly Abers 158 D11
Gartmore Stirlg 132 G8
Gartness N Lans 126 D5
Gartness Stirlg 132 G10
Gartocharn W Duns 132 E10
Garton E R Yk 93 N3
Garton-on-the-Wolds E R Yk 99 K9
Gartymore Highld 163 N4
Garva Bridge Highld 147 N9
Garvald E Loth 128 F5
Garvan Highld 138 H2
Garvard Ag & B 136 b3
Garve Highld 155 L5
Garvellachs Ag & B 130 D5
Garvestone Norfk 76 E10
Garvock Inver 124 H3
Garway Herefs 45 P10
Garway Common Herefs 45 P10
Garway Hill Herefs 45 N9
Garyvard W Isls 168 i6
Gasper Wilts 20 E8
Gastard Wilts 32 G11
Gasthorpe Norfk 64 D5
Gaston Green Essex 51 L7
Gatcombe IoW 14 E9
Gatebeck Cumb 95 L3
Gate Burton Lincs 85 P4
Gateford Notts 85 J4
Gateforth N York 91 P5
Gatehead E Ayrs 125 K10
Gate Helmsley N York 98 D9
Gatehouse Nthumb 111 Q3
Gatehouse of Fleet D & G 108 C9
Gateley Norfk 76 D7
Gatenby N York 97 M3
Gatesgarth Cumb 100 G7
Gateshaw Border 118 E6
Gateshead Gatesd 113 L8
Gates Heath Ches W 69 N2
Gateside Angus 142 G9
Gateside E Rens 125 M6
Gateside Fife 134 F6
Gateside N Ayrs 125 K7
Gateslack D & G 116 B10
Gathurst Wigan 88 G9
Gatley Stockp 82 H7
Gatton Surrey 36 G10
Gattonside Border 117 Q3
Gatwick Airport W Susx 24 G2
Gaufron Powys 55 M11
Gaulby Leics 72 H10
Gauldry Fife 135 K3
Gauldswell P & K 142 C7
Gaulkthorn Lancs 89 M5
Gaultree Norfk 75 J9
Gaunton's Bank Ches E 69 Q5
Gaunt's Common Dorset 12 H3
Gaunt's End Essex 51 N5
Gautby Lincs 86 G6
Gavinton Border 129 K9
Gawber Barns 91 J9
Gawcott Bucks 49 J8
Gawsworth Ches E 83 J11
Gawthorpe Wakefd 90 H6
Gawthrop Cumb 95 P3
Gawthwaite Cumb 94 F4
Gay Bowers Essex 52 C11
Gaydon Warwks 48 C4
Gayhurst M Keyn 49 M5
Gayle N York 96 C3
Gayles N York 103 M9
Gay Street W Susx 24 C6
Gayton Nhants 49 K4
Gayton Norfk 75 P7
Gayton Staffs 70 H9
Gayton Wirral 81 K8
Gayton le Marsh Lincs 87 M4
Gayton Thorpe Norfk 75 P7
Gaywood Norfk 75 M6
Gazeley Suffk 63 M8
Gear Cnwll 3 J9
Gearraidh Bhaird W Isls 168 i6
Geary Highld 152 D5
Gedding Suffk 64 C10
Geddington Nhants 61 J4
Gedling Notts 72 G2
Gedney Lincs 74 H6
Gedney Broadgate Lincs 74 H6
Gedney Drove End Lincs 75 J5
Gedney Dyke Lincs 74 H5
Gedney Hill Lincs 74 F8
Gee Cross Tamesd 83 L6
Geeston Rutlnd 73 P10
Geldeston Norfk 65 M3
Gelli Rhondd 30 C6
Gelli Torfn 31 J6
Gellifor Denbgs 68 F2
Gelligaer Caerph 30 F5
Gelligroes Caerph 30 G6
Gelligron Neath 29 K4
Gellilydan Gwynd 67 M7
Gellinudd Neath 29 K4
Gelly Pembks 41 L7
Gellyburn P & K 141 Q10
Gellywen Carmth 41 Q6
Gelston D & G 108 G9
Gelston Lincs 86 B11
Gembling E R Yk 99 N9
Gentleshaw Staffs 58 G2
Georgefield D & G 110 E2
George Green Bucks 35 Q8
Georgeham Devon 16 H4
Georgemas Junction Station Highld 167 L5
George Nympton Devon 17 N7
Georgetown Blae G 30 G3
Georgia Cnwll 2 D6
Georth Ork 169 c4
Gerlan Gwynd 79 L11
Germansweek Devon 8 B6
Germoe Cnwll 2 F8
Gerrans Cnwll 3 M6
Gerrards Cross Bucks 36 B3
Gerrick R & Cl 105 K8
Gestingthorpe Essex 52 D4
Geuffordd Powys 56 C2
Gib Hill Ches W 82 D9
Gibraltar Lincs 87 Q9
Gibsmere Notts 85 M11
Giddeahall Wilts 32 G10
Giddy Green Dorset 12 D7
Gidea Park Gt Lon 37 M2
Gidleigh Devon 8 G7
Giffnock E Rens 125 P6
Gifford E Loth 128 E6
Giffordtown Fife 134 H5
Giggleswick N York 96 B8
Gigha Ag & B 123 K10
Gilberdyke E R Yk 92 D5
Gilbert's End Worcs 46 F6
Gilbert Street Hants 22 H8
Gilchriston E Loth 128 D6
Gilcrux Cumb 100 F3
Gildersome Leeds 90 G5
Gildingwells Rothm 85 J3
Gilesgate Moor Dur 103 Q2
Gileston V Glam 30 D11
Gilfach Caerph 30 G5
Gilfach Goch Brdgnd 30 C6
Gilfachrheda Cerdgn 42 H3
Gilgarran Cumb 100 D6
Gill Cumb 101 M5
Gillamoor N York 98 D3
Gillan Cnwll 3 K8
Gillen Highld 152 D6
Gillesbie D & G 110 C2
Gilling East N York 98 C5
Gillingham Dorset 20 F9
Gillingham Medway 38 C8
Gillingham Norfk 65 N3
Gilling West N York 103 N9
Gillock Highld 167 M5
Gillow Heath Staffs 70 F3
Gills Highld 167 P2
Gill's Green Kent 26 C5
Gilmanscleuch Border 117 L6
Gilmerton C Edin 127 P4
Gilmerton P & K 133 P3
Gilmonby Dur 103 J8
Gilmorton Leics 60 C3
Gilroes Crematorium C Leic 72 F9
Gilsland Nthumb 111 M7
Gilson Warwks 59 J7
Gilstead C Brad 90 E3
Gilston Border 128 C8
Gilston Herts 51 K8
Gilston Park Herts 51 K8
Giltbrook Notts 84 G11
Gilwern Mons 30 H2
Gimingham Norfk 77 K4
Ginclough Ches E 83 L9
Gingers Green E Susx 25 P8
Gipping Suffk 64 F9
Gipsey Bridge Lincs 87 J11
Girdle Toll N Ayrs 125 J9
Girlington C Brad 90 E4
Girlsta Shet 169 r8
Girsby N York 104 C9
Girtford C Beds 61 Q11
Girthon D & G 108 D10
Girton Cambs 62 F8
Girton Notts 85 P7
Girvan S Ayrs 114 C8
Gisburn Lancs 96 B11
Gisleham Suffk 65 Q4
Gislingham Suffk 64 F7
Gissing Norfk 64 G4
Gittisham Devon 10 C5
Gladestry Powys 45 J3
Gladsmuir E Loth 128 D5
Glais Swans 29 K4
Glaisdale N York 105 L9
Glamis Angus 142 F8
Glanaber Gwynd 67 L4
Glanaman Carmth 29 J2
Glandford Norfk 76 E3
Glan-Duar Carmth 43 K6
Glandwr Pembks 41 N5
Glan-Dwyfach Gwynd 66 H6
Glandyfi Cerdgn 54 F5
Glangrwyney Powys 45 J11
Glanllynfi Brdgnd 29 N6
Glanmule Powys 56 B6
Glanrhyd Pembks 41 M2
Glan-rhyd Powys 29 L3
Glanton Nthumb 119 L8
Glanton Pike Nthumb 119 L8
Glanvilles Wootton Dorset 11 P3
Glan-y-don Flints 80 H9
Glan-y-llyn Rhondd 30 F8
Glan-y-nant Powys 55 L8
Glan-yr-afon Gwynd 68 B6
Glan-yr-afon Gwynd 68 D6
Glan-yr-afon IoA 79 L8
Glan-yr-afon Swans 28 H3
Glapthorn Nhants 61 M2
Glapwell Derbys 84 G7
Glasbury Powys 44 H7
Glascoed Denbgs 80 D10
Glascoed Mons 31 K4
Glascote Staffs 59 K4
Glascwm Powys 44 H4
Glasfryn Conwy 68 B4
Glasgow C Glas 125 P4
Glasgow Airport Rens 125 M4
Glasgow Prestwick Airport S Ayrs 114 G2
Glasgow Science Centre C Glas 125 P4
Glasinfryn Gwynd 79 K11
Glasnacardoch Bay Highld 145 L8
Glasnakille Highld 144 H5
Glaspwll Powys 54 G5
Glassenbury Kent 26 C4
Glassford S Lans 126 C8
Glass Houghton Wakefd 91 L6
Glasshouse Gloucs 46 D10
Glasshouse Hill Gloucs 46 D10
Glasshouses N York 97 J8
Glasslaw Abers 159 L6
Glasson Cumb 110 E8
Glasson Lancs 95 J9
Glassonby Cumb 101 Q3
Glasterlaw Angus 143 K7
Glaston Rutlnd 73 M10
Glastonbury Somset 19 P7
Glatton Cambs 61 Q3
Glazebrook Warrtn 82 E6
Glazebury Warrtn 82 E5
Glazeley Shrops 57 N7
Gleadless Sheff 84 E4
Gleadsmoss Ches E 82 H11
Gleaston Cumb 94 F6
Glebe Highld 147 N4
Gledhow Leeds 91 J3
Gledpark D & G 108 D10
Gledrid Shrops 69 K7
Glemsford Suffk 52 D2
Glenallachie Moray 157 P9
Glenancross Highld 145 L9
Glenaros House Ag & B 137 P7
Glen Auldyn IoM 80 f3
Glenbarr Ag & B 120 C4
Glenbarry Abers 158 E7
Glenbeg Highld 137 P3
Glenbervie Abers 151 K11
Glenboig N Lans 126 C4
Glenborrodale Highld 137 Q3
Glenbranter Ag & B 131 N8
Glenbreck Border 116 F6
Glenbrittle Highld 144 F3
Glenbuck E Ayrs 115 P2
Glencally Angus 142 F5
Glencaple D & G 109 L7
Glencarse P & K 134 F3
Glencoe Highld 139 L6
Glencothe Border 116 F5
Glencraig Fife 134 F9
Glencrosh D & G 115 Q10
Glendale Highld 152 B8
Glendaruel Ag & B 131 K11
Glendevon P & K 134 B7
Glendoe Lodge Highld 147 L6
Glendoick P & K 134 G3
Glenduckie Fife 134 H4
Glenegedale Ag & B 122 D9
Glenelg Highld 145 P4
Glenerney Moray 157 J8
Glenfarg P & K 134 E5
Glenfield Leics 72 E9
Glenfinnan Highld 145 R11
Glenfintaig Lodge Highld 146 G10
Glenfoot P & K 134 F4
Glenfyne Lodge Ag & B 131 Q4
Glengarnock N Ayrs 125 J7
Glengolly Highld 167 K3
Glengorm Castle Ag & B 137 L4
Glengrasco Highld 152 G9
Glenholm Border 116 G4
Glenhoul D & G 115 M10
Glenisla Angus 142 C5
Glenkin Ag & B 131 N11
Glenkindie Abers 150 C5
Glenlivet Moray 149 M2
Glenlochar D & G 108 F8
Glenlomond P & K 134 F7
Glenluce D & G 106 G6
Glenmassen Ag & B 131 N10
Glenmavis N Lans 126 D4
Glen Maye IoM 80 b6
Glen Mona IoM 80 g4
Glenmore Highld 152 G9
Glenmore Lodge Highld 148 H6
Glen Nevis House Highld 139 L3
Glenochil Clacks 133 P8
Glen Parva Leics 72 F11
Glenquiech Angus 142 G5
Glenralloch Ag & B 123 Q6
Glenridding Cumb 101 L7
Glenrothes Fife 134 H7
Glenshero Lodge Highld 147 P9
Glenstriven Ag & B 124 D2
Glentham Lincs 86 D2
Glentrool D & G 107 L2
Glen Trool Lodge D & G 114 H11
Glentruim Highld 148 B9
Glentworth Lincs 86 B3
Glenuig Highld 138 B2
Glenvarragill Highld 152 H10
Glen Vine IoM 80 d6
Glenwhilly D & G 106 G3
Glespin S Lans 115 R2
Glewstone Herefs 45 R10
Glinton C Pete 74 C9
Glooston Leics 73 K11
Glossop Derbys 83 M6
Gloster Hill Nthumb 119 Q10
Gloucester Gloucs 46 F11
Gloucester Crematorium Gloucs 46 G11
Gloucester Services Gloucs 32 F2
Gloucestershire Airport Gloucs 46 G10
Glusburn N York 96 F11
Glutt Lodge Highld 166 H9
Gluvian Cnwll 4 E9
Glympton Oxon 48 D10
Glynarthen Cerdgn 42 F5
Glyn Ceiriog Wrexhm 68 H7
Glyncorrwg Neath 29 N5
Glynde E Susx 25 L9
Glyndebourne E Susx 25 L8
Glyndyfrdwy Denbgs 68 F6
Glynneath Neath 29 N3
Glynn Valley Crematorium Cnwll 4 H8
Glyntaff Rhondd 30 E7
Glyntaff Crematorium Rhondd 30 E7

Glyntawe Powys....44 A11
Glynteg Carmth....42 G7
Gnosall Staffs....70 E10
Gnosall Heath Staffs....70 E10
Goadby Leics....73 K11
Goadby Marwood Leics....73 K5
Goatacre Wilts....33 K9
Gotham Green E Susx....26 D7
Goathill Dorset....20 C11
Goathland N York....105 M10
Goathurst Somset....19 J8
Goathurst Common Kent....37 L10
Goat Lees Kent....26 H2
Gobowen Shrops....69 K8
Godalming Surrey....23 Q6
Goddard's Corner Suffk....65 K8
Goddard's Green Kent....26 D5
Goddards Green W Susx....24 C6
Godford Cross Devon....10 C4
Godington Oxon....48 H9
Godley Tamesd....83 L5
Godmanchester Cambs....62 B6
Godmanstone Dorset....11 P5
Godmersham Kent....39 J11
Godney Somset....19 N6
Godolphin Cross Cnwll....2 G7
Godre'r-graig Neath....29 L3
Godshill Hants....21 N11
Godshill IoW....14 F10
Godstone Staffs....71 J8
Godstone Surrey....37 J10
Godsworthy Devon....8 D9
Godwinscroft Hants....13 L5
Goetre Mons....31 K3
Goff's Oak Herts....50 H10
Gogar C Edin....127 M3
Goginan Cerdgn....54 F8
Golan Gwynd....67 J6
Golant Cnwll....5 J11
Golberdon Cnwll....5 N7
Golborne Wigan....82 D5
Golcar Kirk....90 D7
Goldcliff Newpt....31 L8
Golden Cross E Susx....25 M8
Golden Green Kent....37 P11
Golden Grove Carmth....43 L11
Goldenhill C Stke....70 F4
Golden Hill Pembks....41 J10
Golden Pot Hants....23 K6
Golden Valley Derbys....84 F10
Golders Green Gt Lon....36 F3
Golders Green Crematorium Gt Lon....36 G3
Goldfinch Bottom W Berk....22 F2
Goldhanger Essex....52 F10
Gold Hill Cambs....62 H2
Gold Hill Dorset....12 D2
Golding Shrops....57 J4
Goldington Bed....61 N10
Goldsborough N York....97 N9
Goldsborough N York....105 M8
Golds Green Sandw....58 E6
Goldsithney Cnwll....2 E7
Goldstone Kent....39 N9
Goldstone Shrops....70 C9
Goldsworth Park Surrey....23 Q3
Goldthorpe Barns....91 M10
Goldworthy Devon....16 F7
Golford Kent....26 C4
Golford Green Kent....26 C4
Gollanfield Highld....156 E7
Gollinglith Foot N York....96 H4
Golly Wrexhm....69 K3
Golsoncott Somset....18 D7
Golspie Highld....163 J6
Gomeldon Wilts....21 N7
Gomersal Kirk....90 G5
Gomshall Surrey....36 C11
Gonalston Notts....85 L11
Gonerby Hill Foot Lincs....73 N3
Gonfirth Shet....169 q7
Goodameavy Devon....6 E6
Good Easter Essex....51 P8
Gooderstone Norfk....75 Q10
Goodleigh Devon....17 L5
Goodmanham E R Yk....92 E2
Goodmayes Gt Lon....37 L3
Goodnestone Kent....38 H9
Goodnestone Kent....39 N11
Goodrich Herefs....45 R11
Goodrington Torbay....7 M7
Goodshaw Lancs....89 N5
Goodshaw Fold Lancs....89 N5
Goodstone Devon....7 K4
Goodwick Pembks....40 H3
Goodworth Clatford Hants....22 C6
Goodyers End Warwks....59 M7
Goole E R Yk....92 B6
Goole Fields E R Yk....92 C6
Goom's Hill Worcs....47 K4
Goonbell Cnwll....3 J4
Goonhavern Cnwll....3 K3
Goonvrea Cnwll....3 J4
Goosecruives Abers....151 K11
Gooseford Devon....8 G6
Goose Green Essex....53 K6
Goose Green Kent....26 D4
Goose Green Kent....37 P10
Goose Green S Glos....32 C10
Goose Green W Susx....24 D7
Goose Green Wigan....82 C4
Gooseham Cnwll....16 C8
Gooseham Mill Cnwll....16 C8
Goosehill Green Worcs....46 H2
Goose Pool Herefs....45 P7
Goosey Oxon....34 C6
Goosnargh Lancs....88 H3
Goostrey Ches E....82 G10
Gordano Services N Som....31 P9
Gordding Conwy....79 M10
Gordon Border....118 B2
Gordon Arms Hotel Border....117 L5
Gordonstown Abers....158 E6
Gordonstown Abers....158 H10
Gore Powys....45 K3
Gorebridge Mdloth....127 Q5
Gorefield Cambs....74 H8
Gore Pit Essex....52 E8
Gores Wilts....21 M3
Gore Street Kent....39 N8
Gorey Jersey....11 c2
Goring Oxon....34 H8
Goring-by-Sea W Susx....24 D10
Goring Heath Oxon....35 J9
Gorleston on Sea Norfk....77 Q11

Gornal Wood Crematorium Dudley....58 D6
Gorrachie Abers....158 H6
Gorran Churchtown Cnwll....3 P5
Gorran Haven Cnwll....3 P5
Gorran High Lanes Cnwll....3 P5
Gorrig Cerdgn....42 H6
Gors Cerdgn....54 E9
Gorsedd Flints....80 H9
Gorse Hill Swindn....33 N7
Gorseinon Swans....28 G5
Gorseybank Derbys....71 P4
Gorslas Carmth....28 G2
Gorsley Gloucs....46 C9
Gorsley Common Herefs....46 C9
Gorstage Ches W....82 D10
Gorstan Highld....155 L5
Gorstella Ches W....69 L2
Gorsten Ag & B....138 C11
Gorst Hill Worcs....57 N10
Gorsty Hill Staffs....71 L9
Gorthleck Highld....147 N3
Gorton Manch....83 J5
Gosbeck Suffk....64 H10
Gosberton Lincs....74 D4
Gosberton Clough Lincs....74 C5
Gosfield Essex....52 C6
Gosford Devon....10 C5
Gosford Oxon....34 E2
Gosforth Cumb....100 E10
Gosforth N u Ty....113 K7
Gosling Street Somset....19 P8
Gosmore Herts....50 E5
Gospel End Staffs....58 C6
Gospel Green W Susx....23 P8
Gosport Hants....14 H7
Gossard's Green C Beds....49 Q6
Gossington Gloucs....32 D4
Goswick Nthumb....119 L2
Gotham Notts....72 E4
Gotherington Gloucs....47 J9
Gotton Somset....18 H9
Goudhurst Kent....26 B4
Goulceby Lincs....87 J5
Gourdas Abers....159 J9
Gourdie C Dund....142 F11
Gourdon Abers....143 Q3
Gourock Inver....124 G2
Govan C Glas....125 N4
Goveton Devon....7 K9
Govilon Mons....31 J2
Gowdall E R Yk....91 Q6
Gower Highld....155 P6
Gower Swans....28 F6
Gowerton Swans....28 G5
Gowkhall Fife....134 D10
Gowthorpe E R Yk....98 F10
Goxhill E R Yk....93 L2
Goxhill N Linc....93 K6
Goytre Neath....29 L7
Grabhair W Isls....168 i6
Graby Lincs....74 A5
Grade Cnwll....3 J11
Gradeley Green Ches E....69 Q4
Graffham W Susx....23 P11
Grafham Cambs....61 Q7
Grafham Surrey....24 B2
Grafton Herefs....45 P7
Grafton N York....97 P8
Grafton Oxon....33 Q4
Grafton Shrops....69 M11
Grafton Worcs....46 A2
Grafton Worcs....47 J7
Grafton Flyford Worcs....47 J3
Grafton Regis Nhants....49 L5
Grafton Underwood Nhants....61 K4
Grafty Green Kent....26 E2
Graianrhyd Denbgs....68 H3
Graig Conwy....79 Q10
Graig Denbgs....80 F10
Graigfechan Denbgs....68 F4
Grain Medway....38 E6
Grains Bar Oldham....90 B9
Grainsby Lincs....93 N11
Grainthorpe Lincs....93 Q11
Grampound Cnwll....3 N4
Grampound Road Cnwll....3 N3
Gramsdal W Isls....168 d12
Gramsdale W Isls....168 d12
Granborough Bucks....49 L9
Granby Notts....73 K3
Grandborough Warwks....59 Q11
Grand Chemins Jersey....11 c2
Grandes Rocques Guern....10 b1
Grandtully P & K....141 M7
Grange Cumb....101 J7
Grange Medway....38 C8
Grange P & K....134 H2
Grange Wirral....81 J7
Grange Crossroads Moray....158 C7
Grange Hall Moray....157 M5
Grangehall S Lans....116 D2
Grange Hill Essex....37 K2
Grangemill Derbys....84 B9
Grange Moor Kirk....90 G7
Grangemouth Falk....133 Q11
Grange of Lindores Fife....134 H4
Grange-over-Sands Cumb....95 J5
Grangepans Falk....134 C11
Grange Park Nhants....60 G9
Grangetown R & Cl....104 F6
Grangetown Sundld....113 P10
Grange Villa Dur....113 K10
Gransmoor E R Yk....99 N9
Gransmore Green Essex....51 Q6
Granston Pembks....40 G4
Grantchester Cambs....62 F9
Grantham Lincs....73 N3
Grantham Crematorium Lincs....73 N3
Granton C Edin....127 N2
Grantown-on-Spey Highld....149 J2
Grantsfield Herefs....45 Q2
Grantshouse Border....129 L6
Grappenhall Warrtn....82 D7
Grasby Lincs....93 J10
Grasmere Cumb....101 K9
Grasscroft Oldham....83 L4
Grassendale Lpool....81 M7
Grassgarth Cumb....101 K2
Grass Green Essex....52 B4
Grassington N York....96 F8
Grassmoor Derbys....84 F7
Grassthorpe Notts....85 N7
Grateley Hants....21 Q6

Gratwich Staffs....71 J8
Graveley Cambs....62 C8
Graveley Herts....50 F5
Gravelly Hill Birm....58 H6
Gravelsbank Shrops....56 E4
Graveney Kent....39 J9
Gravesend Kent....37 Q6
Gravir W Isls....168 i6
Grayingham Lincs....92 F11
Grayrigg Cumb....101 Q11
Grays Thurr....37 P5
Grayshott Hants....23 N7
Grayson Green Cumb....100 C5
Grayswood Surrey....23 P8
Graythorpe Hartpl....104 F5
Grazeley Wokham....35 J11
Greasbrough Rothm....91 L11
Greasby Wirral....81 K7
Greasley Notts....84 G11
Great Abington Cambs....62 H11
Great Addington Nhants....61 L5
Great Alne Warwks....47 M3
Great Altcar Lancs....88 C9
Great Amwell Herts....51 J8
Great Asby Cumb....102 C8
Great Ashfield Suffk....64 D8
Great Ayton N York....104 G8
Great Baddow Essex....52 B11
Great Badminton S Glos....32 F8
Great Bardfield Essex....51 Q4
Great Barford Bed....61 P10
Great Barr Sandw....58 F5
Great Barrington Gloucs....33 P2
Great Barrow Ches W....81 P11
Great Barton Suffk....64 B8
Great Barugh N York....98 F5
Great Bavington Nthumb....112 E4
Great Bealings Suffk....53 M2
Great Bedwyn Wilts....21 Q2
Great Bentley Essex....53 K7
Great Billing Nhants....60 H8
Great Bircham Norfk....75 Q4
Great Blakenham Suffk....64 G11
Great Blencow Cumb....101 N4
Great Bolas Wrekin....70 A10
Great Bookham Surrey....36 D10
Great Bosullow Cnwll....2 C7
Great Bourton Oxon....48 E5
Great Bowden Leics....60 F3
Great Bradley Suffk....63 L10
Great Braxted Essex....52 E9
Great Bricett Suffk....64 E11
Great Brickhill Bucks....49 P8
Great Bridgeford Staffs....70 F9
Great Brington Nhants....60 E7
Great Bromley Essex....53 J6
Great Broughton Cumb....100 E4
Great Broughton N York....104 F9
Great Budworth Ches W....82 E9
Great Burdon Darltn....104 B7
Great Burstead Essex....37 Q2
Great Busby N York....104 F9
Great Canfield Essex....51 N7
Great Carlton Lincs....87 M3
Great Casterton Rutlnd....73 Q9
Great Chalfield Wilts....20 G2
Great Chart Kent....26 G3
Great Chatwell Staffs....57 P2
Great Chell C Stke....70 F4
Great Chesterford Essex....51 M2
Great Cheverell Wilts....21 J4
Great Chishill Cambs....51 K3
Great Clacton Essex....53 L8
Great Cliffe Wakefd....91 J7
Great Clifton Cumb....100 D5
Great Coates NE Lin....93 M9
Great Comberton Worcs....47 J6
Great Comp Kent....37 P9
Great Corby Cumb....111 J10
Great Cornard Suffk....52 E3
Great Cowden E R Yk....93 M2
Great Coxwell Oxon....33 Q6
Great Cransley Nhants....60 H5
Great Cressingham Norfk....76 B11
Great Crosthwaite Cumb....101 J6
Great Cubley Derbys....71 M7
Great Cumbrae Island N Ayrs....124 F6
Great Dalby Leics....73 J8
Great Denham Bed....61 M11
Great Doddington Nhants....61 J8
Great Doward Herefs....45 Q11
Great Dunham Norfk....76 B9
Great Dunmow Essex....51 P6
Great Durnford Wilts....21 M7
Great Easton Essex....51 P5
Great Easton Leics....60 H2
Great Eccleston Lancs....88 E2
Great Edstone N York....98 E4
Great Ellingham Norfk....64 E2
Great Elm Somset....20 D5
Great Everdon Nhants....60 C9
Great Eversden Cambs....62 E10
Great Fencote N York....97 L2
Greatfield Wilts....33 L7
Great Finborough Suffk....64 E10
Greatford Lincs....74 A8
Great Fransham Norfk....76 B9
Great Gaddesden Herts....50 B8
Greatgate Staffs....71 K7
Great Gidding Cambs....61 P4
Great Givendale E R Yk....98 G10
Great Glemham Suffk....65 L9
Great Glen Leics....72 H11
Great Gonerby Lincs....73 M3
Great Gransden Cambs....62 C9
Great Green Cambs....50 C2
Great Green Norfk....65 K4
Great Green Suffk....64 C10
Great Green Suffk....64 C8
Great Habton N York....98 F5
Great Hale Lincs....74 B2
Great Hallingbury Essex....51 M7
Greatham Hants....23 L8
Greatham Hartpl....104 E5
Greatham W Susx....24 B7
Great Hampden Bucks....35 M4
Great Harrowden Nhants....61 J6
Great Harwood Lancs....89 L4
Great Haseley Oxon....34 H4
Great Hatfield E R Yk....93 L2
Great Haywood Staffs....70 H10
Great Heck N York....91 P6
Great Henny Essex....52 E4
Great Hinton Wilts....20 H3
Great Hockham Norfk....64 D3
Great Holland Essex....53 M8

Great Hollands Br For....35 N11
Great Horkesley Essex....52 G5
Great Hormead Herts....51 K5
Great Horton C Brad....90 E4
Great Horwood Bucks....49 L8
Great Houghton Barns....91 L9
Great Houghton Nhants....60 G9
Great Hucklow Derbys....83 Q9
Great Kelk E R Yk....99 N9
Great Kimble Bucks....35 M3
Great Kingshill Bucks....35 N5
Great Langdale Cumb....101 J9
Great Langton N York....103 Q11
Great Leighs Essex....52 B8
Great Limber Lincs....93 K9
Great Linford M Keyn....49 N6
Great Livermere Suffk....64 B7
Great Longstone Derbys....84 B6
Great Lumley Dur....113 L11
Great Lyth Shrops....56 H3
Great Malvern Worcs....46 E5
Great Maplestead Essex....52 D5
Great Marton Bpool....88 C3
Great Massingham Norfk....75 Q6
Great Melton Norfk....76 G10
Great Meols Wirral....81 J6
Great Milton Oxon....34 H4
Great Missenden Bucks....35 N4
Great Mitton Lancs....89 L3
Great Mongeham Kent....39 Q11
Great Moulton Norfk....64 H3
Great Munden Herts....51 J6
Great Musgrave Cumb....102 E8
Great Ness Shrops....69 L11
Great Notley Essex....52 B7
Great Oak Mons....31 L2
Great Oakley Essex....53 L6
Great Oakley Nhants....61 J3
Great Offley Herts....50 D5
Great Ormside Cumb....102 D7
Great Orton Cumb....110 F10
Great Ouseburn N York....97 P8
Great Oxendon Nhants....60 F4
Great Oxney Green Essex....51 Q10
Great Palgrave Norfk....76 A9
Great Park N u Ty....113 K6
Great Parndon Essex....51 K9
Great Pattenden Kent....26 B3
Great Paxton Cambs....62 B8
Great Plumpton Lancs....88 D4
Great Plumstead Norfk....77 L9
Great Ponton Lincs....73 N4
Great Potheridge Devon....17 J9
Great Preston Leeds....91 L5
Great Purston Nhants....48 F7
Great Raveley Cambs....62 C4
Great Rissington Gloucs....47 N11
Great Rollright Oxon....48 B8
Great Ryburgh Norfk....76 D6
Great Ryle Nthumb....119 K8
Great Ryton Shrops....56 H4
Great Saling Essex....51 Q5
Great Salkeld Cumb....101 Q3
Great Sampford Essex....51 P3
Great Saredon Staffs....58 E3
Great Saughall Ches W....81 M11
Great Saxham Suffk....63 N8
Great Shefford W Berk....34 C9
Great Shelford Cambs....62 G10
Great Smeaton N York....104 B10
Great Snoring Norfk....76 C5
Great Somerford Wilts....33 J8
Great Soudley Shrops....70 C9
Great Stainton Darltn....104 B6
Great Stambridge Essex....38 E3
Great Staughton Cambs....61 P8
Great Steeping Lincs....87 M8
Great Stoke S Glos....32 B8
Great Stonar Kent....39 P10
Greatstone-on-Sea Kent....27 J7
Great Strickland Cumb....101 Q6
Great Stukeley Cambs....62 B6
Great Sturton Lincs....86 H5
Great Sutton Ches W....81 M9
Great Sutton Shrops....57 J8
Great Swinburne Nthumb....112 D5
Great Tew Oxon....48 D9
Great Tey Essex....52 E6
Great Thurlow Suffk....63 L10
Great Torrington Devon....16 H8
Great Tosson Nthumb....119 K10
Great Totham Essex....52 E9
Great Totham Essex....52 E9
Great Tows Lincs....86 H2
Great Urswick Cumb....94 F6
Great Wakering Essex....38 F4
Great Waldingfield Suffk....52 F3
Great Walsingham Norfk....76 C4
Great Waltham Essex....51 Q8
Great Warford Ches E....82 H9
Great Warley Essex....37 N2
Great Washbourne Gloucs....47 J8
Great Weeke Devon....8 G6
Great Welnetham Suffk....64 B10
Great Wenham Suffk....53 J4
Great Whittington Nthumb....112 F6
Great Wigborough Essex....52 G8
Great Wilbraham Cambs....63 J9
Great Wilne Derbys....72 C4
Great Wishford Wilts....21 L7
Great Witchingham Norfk....76 G7
Great Witcombe Gloucs....32 H2
Great Witley Worcs....57 P11
Great Wolford Warwks....47 P7
Greatworth Nhants....48 G6
Great Wratting Suffk....63 L11
Great Wymondley Herts....50 F5
Great Wyrley Staffs....58 E3
Great Wytheford Shrops....69 Q11
Great Yarmouth Norfk....77 Q10
Great Yarmouth Crematorium Norfk....77 Q11
Great Yeldham Essex....52 C4
Grebby Lincs....87 M7
Greeba IoM....80 d5
Green Denbgs....80 F11
Green Bank Cumb....94 H4
Greenbottom Cnwll....3 J5
Greenburn W Loth....126 G5
Greencroft Hall Dur....113 J11
Green Cross Surrey....23 N7
Green Down Somset....19 Q4
Green End Bed....61 M11
Green End Bed....61 N8
Green End Bed....61 P10
Green End Bed....61 P8
Green End Cambs....61 Q4

Green End Cambs....62 B6
Green End Cambs....62 E9
Green End Cambs....62 G7
Green End Cambs....62 G8
Green End Herts....50 G4
Green End Herts....50 H4
Green End Herts....50 H6
Greenend Oxon....48 B10
Green End Warwks....59 L7
Greenfield Ag & B....131 Q9
Greenfield C Beds....50 C4
Greenfield Flints....80 H9
Greenfield Highld....146 G7
Greenfield Oldham....83 L4
Greenford Gt Lon....36 D4
Greengairs N Lans....126 D3
Greengates C Brad....90 F3
Greengill Cumb....100 F3
Greenhalgh Lancs....88 E3
Greenham Somset....18 E10
Greenham W Berk....34 E11
Green Hammerton N York....97 Q9
Greenhaugh Nthumb....111 Q3
Green Head Cumb....110 G11
Greenhead Nthumb....111 N7
Green Heath Staffs....58 E2
Greenheys Salfd....82 F4
Greenhill D & G....109 P5
Greenhill Falk....126 E2
Greenhill Herefs....46 D5
Greenhill Kent....39 L8
Greenhill S Lans....116 C10
Green Hill Wilts....33 L7
Greenhillocks Derbys....84 F11
Greenhills S Lans....125 Q7
Greenhithe Kent....37 N6
Greenholm E Ayrs....125 N10
Greenholme Cumb....101 Q9
Greenhouse Border....117 R6
Greenhow Hill N York....96 H9
Greenland Highld....167 M3
Greenland Sheff....84 E3
Greenlands Bucks....35 L7
Green Lane Devon....9 J9
Green Lane Worcs....47 L2
Greenlaw Border....129 J10
Greenlea D & G....109 M5
Greenloaning P & K....133 N6
Green Moor Barns....90 H11
Greenmount Bury....89 M8
Green Oak E R Yk....92 D5
Greenock Inver....124 H2
Greenodd Cumb....94 G4
Green Ore Somset....19 Q4
Green Quarter Cumb....101 N10
Greensgate Norfk....76 G8
Greenshields S Lans....116 E2
Greenside Gatesd....112 H8
Greenside Kirk....90 F7
Greens Norton Nhants....49 J5
Greenstead Green Essex....52 D6
Greensted Essex....51 M10
Green Street E Susx....26 C9
Green Street Gloucs....46 G11
Green Street Herts....50 E11
Green Street Herts....51 L6
Green Street Worcs....46 G5
Green Street Green Gt Lon....37 L8
Green Street Green Kent....37 N6
Greenstreet Green Suffk....52 H2
Green Tye Herts....51 K7
Greenway Gloucs....46 D8
Greenway Somset....19 K10
Greenway V Glam....30 E10
Greenway Worcs....57 N10
Greenwich Gt Lon....37 J5
Greenwich Maritime Gt Lon....37 J5
Greet Gloucs....47 K8
Greete Shrops....57 K10
Greetham Lincs....87 K6
Greetham Rutlnd....73 N8
Greetland Calder....90 D6
Gregson Lane Lancs....88 H5
Greinton Somset....19 M7
Grenaby IoM....80 c7
Grendon Nhants....61 J8
Grendon Warwks....59 L5
Grendon Green Herefs....46 A3
Grendon Underwood Bucks....49 J10
Grenofen Devon....6 D4
Grenoside Sheff....84 D2
Grenoside Crematorium Sheff....84 D2
Greosabhagh W Isls....168 g8
Gresford Wrexhm....69 K4
Gresham Norfk....76 H4
Greshornish Highld....152 E7
Gressenhall Norfk....76 D8
Gressenhall Green Norfk....76 D8
Gressingham Lancs....95 M7
Gresty Green Ches E....70 C4
Greta Bridge Dur....103 L8
Gretna D & G....110 F7
Gretna Green D & G....110 F7
Gretna Services D & G....110 F7
Gretton Gloucs....47 K8
Gretton Nhants....61 J2
Gretton Shrops....57 J5
Grewelthorpe N York....97 K5
Grey Friars Suffk....65 P7
Greygarth N York....96 H6
Grey Green N Linc....92 C9
Greylake Somset....19 L8
Greylees Lincs....73 Q2
Greyrigg D & G....109 N3
Greys Green Oxon....35 K8
Greysouthen Cumb....100 E5
Greystoke Cumb....101 N4
Greystone Angus....143 J9
Greywell Hants....23 K4
Gribb Dorset....10 H4
Gribthorpe E R Yk....92 C3
Griff Warwks....59 N7
Griffithstown Torfn....31 J5
Griffydam Leics....72 C7
Griggs Green Hants....23 M8
Grimeford Village Lancs....89 J8
Grimesthorpe Sheff....84 E3
Grimethorpe Barns....91 L9
Grimley Worcs....46 F2
Grimmet S Ayrs....114 F5
Grimoldby Lincs....87 L3
Grimpo Shrops....69 L9
Grimsargh Lancs....88 H4
Grimsby NE Lin....93 N9

Grimsby Crematorium – Harrow Hill 273

Grimsby Crematorium NE Lin 93 N9
Grimscote Nhants 49 J4
Grimscott Cnwll 16 D10
Grimshader W Isls 168 j5
Grimshaw Bl w D 89 L6
Grimshaw Green Lancs 88 F8
Grimsthorpe Lincs 73 Q6
Grimston E R Yk 93 N3
Grimston Leics 72 H6
Grimston Norfk 75 P6
Grimstone Dorset 11 N6
Grimstone End Suffk 64 C8
Grinacombe Moor Devon 5 Q3
Grindale E R Yk 99 N6
Grindle Shrops 57 P4
Grindleford Derbys 84 B5
Grindleton Lancs 95 R11
Grindley Brook Shrops 69 P6
Grindlow Derbys 83 Q9
Grindon Nthumb 118 H2
Grindon S on T 104 C5
Grindon Staffs 71 K4
Grindon Hill Nthumb 112 B7
Grindonrigg Nthumb 118 H2
Gringley on the Hill Notts 85 M2
Grinsdale Cumb 110 G9
Grinshill Shrops 69 P10
Grinton N York 103 K11
Griomaisiader W Isls 168 j5
Grishipoll Ag & B 136 F4
Grisling Common E Susx 25 K6
Gristhorpe N York 99 M4
Griston Norfk 64 C2
Gritley Ork 169 e6
Grittenham Wilts 33 K8
Grittleton Wilts 32 G8
Grizebeck Cumb 94 E4
Grizedale Cumb 94 G2
Groby Leics 72 E9
Groes Conwy 68 D2
Groes-faen Rhondd 30 E8
Groesffordd Gwynd 66 D7
Groesffordd Powys 44 F9
Groesffordd Marli Denbgs 80 E10
Groesllwyd Powys 56 C2
Groeslon Gwynd 66 H3
Groeslon Gwynd 67 J2
Groes-Wen Caerph 30 F7
Grogarry W Isls 168 c14
Grogport Ag & B 120 F3
Groigearraidh W Isls 168 c14
Gromford Suffk 65 M10
Gronant Flints 80 F8
Groombridge E Susx 25 M3
Grosebay W Isls 168 g8
Grosmont Mons 45 N10
Grosmont N York 105 M9
Groton Suffk 52 G3
Grotton Oldham 83 L4
Grouville Jersey 11 c2
Grove Bucks 49 P10
Grove Dorset 11 P10
Grove Kent 39 M9
Grove Notts 85 M5
Grove Oxon 34 D6
Grove Pembks 41 J10
Grove Green Kent 38 C10
Grovenhurst Kent 26 B3
Grove Park Gt Lon 37 K6
Grovesend S Glos 32 C7
Grovesend Swans 28 G4
Grubb Street Kent 37 N7
Gruinard Highld 160 E9
Gruinart Ag & B 122 C6
Grula Highld 144 E2
Gruline Ag & B 137 N7
Grumbla Cnwll 2 C8
Grundisburgh Suffk 65 J11
Gruting Shet 169 p9
Grutness Shet 169 r12
Gualachulain Highld 139 L8
Guanockgate Lincs 74 G8
Guardbridge Fife 135 M4
Guarlford Worcs 46 F5
Guay P & K 141 P8
Guernsey Guern 10 b2
Guernsey Airport Guern 10 b2
Guestling Green E Susx 26 E9
Guestling Thorn E Susx 26 E8
Guestwick Norfk 76 F6
Guide Bridge Tamesd 83 K5
Guide Post Nthumb 113 L3
Guilden Morden Cambs 50 G2
Guilden Sutton Ches W 81 N11
Guildford Surrey 23 Q5
Guildford Crematorium Surrey 23 Q5
Guildstead Kent 38 D9
Guildtown P & K 142 A11
Guilsborough Nhants 60 E6
Guilsfield Powys 56 C2
Guilton Kent 39 N10
Guiltreehill S Ayrs 114 G5
Guineaford Devon 17 K4
Guisborough R & Cl 104 H7
Guiseley Leeds 90 F2
Guist Norfk 76 E6
Guiting Power Gloucs 47 L10
Gullane E Loth 128 D3
Gulling Green Suffk 64 A10
Gulval Cnwll 2 D7
Gulworthy Devon 6 D4
Gumfreston Pembks 41 M10
Gumley Leics 60 E3
Gummow's Shop Cnwll 4 D10
Gunby E R Yk 92 B3
Gunby Lincs 73 N6
Gunby Lincs 87 N7
Gundleton Hants 22 H8
Gun Green Kent 26 C5
Gun Hill E Susx 25 N8
Gun Hill Warwks 59 L7
Gunn Devon 17 L5
Gunnerside N York 103 J11
Gunnerton Nthumb 112 D6
Gunness N Linc 92 D8
Gunnislake Cnwll 6 C4
Gunnista Shet 169 s9
Gunthorpe C Pete 74 C10
Gunthorpe N Linc 92 D11
Gunthorpe Norfk 76 E5
Gunthorpe Notts 72 H2
Gunton Suffk 65 Q2
Gunwalloe Cnwll 2 H9
Gupworthy Somset 18 C8
Gurnard IoW 14 E7
Gurnett Ches E 83 K10
Gurney Slade Somset 20 B5
Gurnos Powys 29 L3
Gushmere Kent 38 H10
Gussage All Saints Dorset 12 H2
Gussage St Andrew Dorset 12 G2
Gussage St Michael Dorset 12 G2
Guston Kent 27 P3
Gutcher Shet 169 s4
Guthrie Angus 143 K7
Guyhirn Cambs 74 H10
Guyhirn Gull Cambs 74 G10
Guy's Marsh Dorset 20 F10
Guyzance Nthumb 119 P10
Gwaenysgor Flints 80 F8
Gwalchmai IoA 78 F9
Gwastadnant Gwynd 67 L3
Gwaun-Cae-Gurwen Carmth 29 J2
Gwbert on Sea Cerdgn 42 C4
Gwealavellan Cnwll 2 G5
Gweek Cnwll 3 J8
Gwehelog Mons 31 L4
Gwenddwr Powys 44 F6
Gwennap Cnwll 3 J5
Gwennap Mining District Cnwll 3 K5
Gwent Crematorium Mons 31 K5
Gwenter Cnwll 3 J10
Gwernaffield Flints 81 J11
Gwernesney Mons 31 M4
Gwernogle Carmth 43 K8
Gwernymynydd Flints 68 H2
Gwersyllt Wrexhm 69 K4
Gwespyr Flints 80 G8
Gwindra Cnwll 3 P3
Gwinear Cnwll 2 F6
Gwithian Cnwll 2 F5
Gwredog IoA 78 G7
Gwrhay Caerph 30 G5
Gwyddelwern Denbgs 68 E5
Gwyddgrug Carmth 43 J7
Gwynfryn Wrexhm 69 J4
Gwystre Powys 55 P11
Gwytherin Conwy 68 A2
Gyfelia Wrexhm 69 K5
Gyrn-gôch Gwynd 66 G5

H

Habberley Shrops 56 F4
Habberley Worcs 57 Q9
Habergham Lancs 89 N4
Habertoft Lincs 87 P7
Habin W Susx 23 M10
Habrough NE Lin 93 K8
Hacconby Lincs 74 B5
Haceby Lincs 73 Q3
Hacheston Suffk 65 L10
Hackbridge Gt Lon 36 G7
Hackenthorpe Sheff 84 F4
Hackford Norfk 76 F11
Hackforth N York 97 K2
Hack Green Ches E 70 A5
Hackland Ork 169 c4
Hackleton Nhants 60 H9
Hacklinge Kent 39 P11
Hackman's Gate Worcs 58 C9
Hackness N York 99 K2
Hackness Somset 19 K5
Hackney Gt Lon 36 H4
Hackthorn Lincs 86 C4
Hackthorpe Cumb 101 P6
Hacton Gt Lon 37 N3
Hadden Border 118 E3
Haddenham Bucks 35 K3
Haddenham Cambs 62 G5
Haddington E Loth 128 E5
Haddington Lincs 86 B8
Haddiscoe Norfk 65 N2
Haddo Abers 159 K10
Haddon Cambs 61 P2
Hade Edge Kirk 83 P4
Hadfield Derbys 83 M5
Hadham Cross Herts 51 K7
Hadham Ford Herts 51 K6
Hadleigh Essex 38 D4
Hadleigh Suffk 52 H3
Hadleigh Heath Suffk 52 G3
Hadley Worcs 46 G2
Hadley Wrekin 57 M2
Hadley End Staffs 71 L10
Hadley Wood Gt Lon 50 G11
Hadlow Kent 37 P10
Hadlow Down E Susx 25 M6
Hadnall Shrops 69 P10
Hadrian's Wall 112 E7
Hadstock Essex 51 N2
Hadzor Worcs 46 H2
Haffenden Quarter Kent 26 E3
Hafodunos Conwy 80 B11
Hafod-y-bwch Wrexhm 69 K5
Hafod-y-coed Blae G 30 H4
Hafodyrynys Caerph 30 H5
Haggate Lancs 89 P3
Haggbeck Cumb 111 J6
Haggersta Shet 169 q9
Haggerston Nthumb 119 K2
Haggington Hill Devon 17 K2
Haggs Falk 126 D2
Hagley Herefs 45 R6
Hagley Worcs 58 D8
Hagmore Green Suffk 52 G4
Hagnaby Lincs 87 K8
Hagnaby Lincs 87 N5
Hagworthingham Lincs 87 K7
Haigh Wigan 89 J9
Haighton Green Lancs 88 H4
Haile Cumb 100 D9
Hailes Gloucs 47 K8
Hailey Herts 51 J8
Hailey Oxon 34 C2
Hailey Oxon 34 H7
Hailsham E Susx 25 N9
Hail Weston Cambs 61 Q8
Hainault Gt Lon 37 L2
Haine Kent 39 Q8
Hainford Norfk 77 J8
Hainton Lincs 86 G4
Hainworth C Brad 90 D3
Haisthorpe E R Yk 99 N8
Hakin Pembks 40 G9
Halam Notts 85 L10
Halbeath Fife 134 E10
Halberton Devon 9 P2
Halcro Highld 167 M4
Hale Cumb 95 L5
Hale Halton 81 P8
Hale Hants 21 N11
Hale Somset 20 D9
Hale Surrey 23 M5
Hale Traffd 82 G7
Hale Bank Halton 81 P8
Halebarns Traffd 82 G7
Hale Green E Susx 25 N8
Hale Nook Lancs 88 D2
Hales Norfk 65 M2
Hales Staffs 70 C8
Halesgate Lincs 74 F5
Hales Green Derbys 71 M6
Halesowen Dudley 58 E8
Hales Place Kent 39 K10
Hale Street Kent 37 Q11
Halesville Essex 38 F3
Halesworth Suffk 65 M6
Halewood Knows 81 P7
Halford Devon 7 L4
Halford Shrops 56 G8
Halford Warwks 47 Q5
Halfpenny Cumb 95 L3
Halfpenny Green Staffs 58 B6
Halfpenny Houses N York 97 K4
Halfway Carmth 43 M8
Halfway Carmth 44 A8
Halfway Sheff 84 F4
Halfway W Berk 34 D11
Halfway Bridge W Susx 23 P10
Halfway House Shrops 56 E2
Halfway Houses Kent 38 F7
Halifax Calder 90 D5
Halket E Ayrs 125 L7
Halkirk Highld 167 K5
Halkyn Flints 81 J10
Hall E Rens 125 L7
Hallam Fields Derbys 72 D3
Halland E Susx 25 L7
Hallaton Leics 73 K11
Hallatrow BaNES 20 B3
Hallbankgate Cumb 111 L9
Hallbeck Cumb 95 N3
Hall Cliffe Wakefd 90 H7
Hall Cross Lancs 88 E4
Hall Dunnerdale Cumb 100 H11
Hallen S Glos 31 Q8
Hall End Bed 61 M11
Hall End C Beds 50 C3
Hallfield Gate Derbys 84 E9
Hallgarth Dur 104 B2
Hallglen Falk 126 F2
Hall Green Birm 58 H8
Hallin Highld 152 D6
Halling Medway 38 B9
Hallington Lincs 87 K3
Hallington Nthumb 112 E5
Halliwell Bolton 89 K8
Halloughton Notts 85 L10
Hallow Worcs 46 F3
Hallow Heath Worcs 46 F3
Hallsands Devon 7 L11
Hall's Green Essex 51 K9
Hall's Green Herts 50 G5
Hallthwaites Cumb 94 D3
Hallworthy Cnwll 5 K4
Hallyne Border 116 H2
Halmer End Staffs 70 D5
Halmond's Frome Herefs 46 C5
Halmore Gloucs 32 D4
Halnaker W Susx 15 P5
Halsall Lancs 88 D8
Halse Nhants 48 G6
Halse Somset 18 F9
Halsetown Cnwll 2 E6
Halsham E R Yk 93 N5
Halsinger Devon 17 J4
Halstead Essex 52 D5
Halstead Kent 37 L8
Halstead Leics 73 K9
Halstock Dorset 11 L3
Halsway Somset 18 F7
Haltcliff Bridge Cumb 101 L3
Haltemprice Crematorium E R Yk 92 H4
Haltham Lincs 86 H8
Haltoft End Lincs 87 L11
Halton Bucks 35 N3
Halton Halton 82 B8
Halton Lancs 95 L8
Halton Leeds 91 K4
Halton Nthumb 112 E7
Halton Wrexhm 69 K7
Halton East N York 96 F10
Halton Fenside Lincs 87 M8
Halton Gill N York 96 C5
Halton Green Lancs 95 L7
Halton Holegate Lincs 87 M7
Halton Lea Gate Nthumb 111 M9
Halton Quay Cnwll 5 Q8
Halton Shields Nthumb 112 F7
Halton West N York 96 B10
Haltwhistle Nthumb 111 P8
Halvana Cnwll 5 L6
Halvergate Norfk 77 N10
Halwell Devon 7 K8
Halwill Devon 8 B5
Halwill Junction Devon 8 B4
Ham Devon 10 E4
Ham Gloucs 32 C5
Ham Gloucs 47 J10
Ham Gt Lon 36 E6
Ham Kent 39 P11
Ham Somset 19 J9
Ham Somset 20 C5
Ham Wilts 22 B2
Hambleden Bucks 35 L7
Hambledon Hants 14 H4
Hambledon Surrey 23 Q7
Hamble-le-Rice Hants 14 E5
Hambleton Lancs 88 D2
Hambleton N York 91 P4
Hambleton Moss Side Lancs 88 D2
Hambridge Somset 19 L10
Hambrook S Glos 32 B9
Hambrook W Susx 15 L5
Ham Common Dorset 20 F9
Hameringham Lincs 87 K7
Hamerton Cambs 61 P5
Ham Green Herefs 46 E6
Ham Green Kent 26 E6
Ham Green Kent 38 D8
Ham Green N Som 31 P9
Ham Green Worcs 47 K2
Ham Hill Kent 37 Q8
Hamilton S Lans 126 C6
Hamilton Services S Lans 126 C6
Hamlet Dorset 11 M3
Hamlins E Susx 25 N9
Hammerpot W Susx 24 C9
Hammersmith Gt Lon 36 F5
Hammerwich Staffs 58 G3
Hammerwood E Susx 25 K3
Hammond Street Herts 50 H10
Hammoon Dorset 12 D2
Hamnavoe Shet 169 q10
Hampden Park E Susx 25 P10
Hamperden End Essex 51 N4
Hampnett Gloucs 47 L11
Hampole Donc 91 N8
Hampreston Dorset 13 J5
Hampsfield Cumb 95 J4
Hampson Green Lancs 95 K10
Hampstead Gt Lon 36 G3
Hampstead Norreys W Berk 34 F9
Hampsthwaite N York 97 L9
Hampton C Pete 61 Q2
Hampton Devon 10 F5
Hampton Gt Lon 36 D7
Hampton Kent 39 L8
Hampton Shrops 57 N7
Hampton Swindn 33 N6
Hampton Worcs 47 K6
Hampton Bishop Herefs 45 R7
Hampton Court Palace Gt Lon 36 E7
Hampton Fields Gloucs 32 G5
Hampton Green Ches W 69 P5
Hampton Heath Ches W 69 P5
Hampton-in-Arden Solhll 59 K8
Hampton Loade Shrops 57 N7
Hampton Lovett Worcs 58 C11
Hampton Lucy Warwks 47 Q3
Hampton Magna Warwks 59 L11
Hampton on the Hill Warwks 47 Q2
Hampton Poyle Oxon 48 F11
Hampton Wick Gt Lon 36 E7
Hamptworth Wilts 21 P11
Hamrow Norfk 76 C7
Hamsey E Susx 25 K8
Hamsey Green Surrey 37 J9
Hamstall Ridware Staffs 71 L11
Hamstead Birm 58 G6
Hamstead IoW 14 D8
Hamstead Marshall W Berk 34 D11
Hamsterley Dur 103 M4
Hamsterley Dur 112 H9
Hamstreet Kent 26 H5
Ham Street Somset 19 Q8
Hamwood N Som 19 L3
Hamworthy Poole 12 G6
Hanbury Staffs 71 M9
Hanbury Worcs 47 J2
Hanby Lincs 73 Q4
Hanchet End Suffk 63 K11
Hanchurch Staffs 70 E6
Handa Island Highld 164 D7
Handale R & Cl 105 K7
Hand and Pen Devon 9 P5
Handbridge Ches W 81 N11
Handcross W Susx 24 G5
Handforth Ches E 83 J8
Hand Green Ches W 69 P2
Handley Ches W 69 N3
Handley Derbys 84 E8
Handley Green Essex 51 Q10
Handsacre Staffs 71 K11
Handsworth Birm 58 F7
Handsworth Sheff 84 F3
Handy Cross Bucks 35 N6
Hanford C Stke 70 F6
Hanford Dorset 12 D2
Hanging Heaton Kirk 90 H6
Hanging Houghton Nhants 60 G6
Hanging Langford Wilts 21 K7
Hangleton Br & H 24 G9
Hangleton W Susx 24 C10
Hanham S Glos 32 B10
Hankelow Ches E 70 B5
Hankerton Wilts 33 J6
Hankham E Susx 25 P9
Hanley C Stke 70 F5
Hanley Castle Worcs 46 F6
Hanley Child Worcs 57 M11
Hanley Swan Worcs 46 F6
Hanley William Worcs 57 M11
Hanlith N York 96 C8
Hanmer Wrexhm 69 N7
Hannaford Devon 17 L6
Hannah Lincs 87 N5
Hannington Hants 22 F3
Hannington Nhants 60 H6
Hannington Swindn 33 N6
Hannington Wick Swindn 33 N5
Hanscombe End C Beds 50 D4
Hanslope M Keyn 49 M5
Hanthorpe Lincs 74 A6
Hanwell Gt Lon 36 E5
Hanwell Oxon 48 D6
Hanwood Shrops 56 G3
Hanworth Gt Lon 36 D6
Hanworth Norfk 76 H4
Happendon S Lans 116 B4
Happendon Services S Lans 116 B4
Happisburgh Norfk 77 M5
Happisburgh Common Norfk 77 M6
Hapsford Ches W 81 P10
Hapton Lancs 89 M4
Hapton Norfk 64 H2
Harberton Devon 7 K7
Harbertonford Devon 7 K7
Harbledown Kent 39 K10
Harborne Birm 58 F8
Harborough Magna Warwks 59 Q9
Harbottle Nthumb 118 H10
Harbourneford Devon 7 J6
Harbours Hill Worcs 58 E11
Harbridge Hants 13 K2
Harbridge Green Hants 13 K2
Harbury Warwks 48 C3
Harby Leics 73 J4
Harby Notts 85 Q6
Harcombe Devon 9 L8
Harcombe Devon 10 D6
Harcombe Bottom Devon 10 G5
Harden C Brad 90 D3
Harden Wsall 58 F4
Hardendale Cumb 101 Q8
Hardenhuish Wilts 32 H10
Hardgate Abers 151 K7
Hardgate D & G 108 H7
Hardgate N York 97 L8
Hardgate W Duns 125 N3
Hardham W Susx 24 B7
Hardhorn Lancs 88 D3
Hardingham Norfk 76 E11
Hardingstone Nhants 60 G9
Hardington Somset 20 D4
Hardington Mandeville Somset 11 L2
Hardington Marsh Somset 11 L3
Hardington Moor Somset 11 L2
Hardisworthy Devon 16 C7
Hardley Hants 14 D6
Hardley Street Norfk 77 M11
Hardmead M Keyn 49 P5
Hardraw N York 96 C2
Hardsough Lancs 89 M6
Hardstoft Derbys 84 F8
Hardway Hants 14 H6
Hardway Somset 20 D8
Hardwick Bucks 49 M11
Hardwick Cambs 62 E9
Hardwick Nhants 60 H7
Hardwick Norfk 65 J4
Hardwick Oxon 34 C3
Hardwick Oxon 48 G9
Hardwick Rothm 84 G3
Hardwick Wsall 58 G5
Hardwicke Gloucs 32 E2
Hardwicke Gloucs 46 H9
Hardwick Hall Derbys 84 G8
Hardwick Village Notts 85 K5
Hardy's Green Essex 52 F7
Harebeating E Susx 25 N8
Hareby Lincs 87 K7
Hare Croft C Brad 90 D3
Harefield Gt Lon 36 C2
Hare Green Essex 53 K6
Hare Hatch Wokham 35 M9
Harehill Derbys 71 M7
Harehills Leeds 91 J4
Harehope Nthumb 119 L6
Harelaw Border 117 Q6
Harelaw D & G 110 H5
Harelaw Dur 113 J10
Hareplain Kent 26 D4
Harescaugh Cumb 102 B2
Harescombe Gloucs 32 F2
Haresfield Gloucs 32 F2
Harestock Hants 22 E8
Hare Street Essex 51 K9
Hare Street Essex 51 M10
Hare Street Herts 51 J5
Harewood Leeds 97 M11
Harewood End Herefs 45 Q9
Harford Devon 6 G7
Hargate Norfk 64 G3
Hargatewall Derbys 83 P9
Hargrave Ches W 69 N2
Hargrave Nhants 61 M6
Hargrave Suffk 63 N9
Harker Cumb 110 G8
Harkstead Suffk 53 L5
Harlaston Staffs 59 K2
Harlaxton Lincs 73 M4
Harlech Gwynd 67 K8
Harlech Castle Gwynd 67 K8
Harlescott Shrops 69 N11
Harlesden Gt Lon 36 F4
Harlesthorpe Derbys 84 G5
Harleston Devon 7 K9
Harleston Norfk 65 J5
Harleston Suffk 64 E9
Harlestone Nhants 60 F8
Harle Syke Lancs 89 P3
Harley Rothm 91 K11
Harley Shrops 57 K4
Harlington C Beds 50 B4
Harlington Donc 91 M10
Harlington Gt Lon 36 C5
Harlosh Highld 152 D9
Harlow Essex 51 K8
Harlow Carr RHS N York 97 L10
Harlow Hill Nthumb 112 G7
Harlthorpe E R Yk 92 B3
Harlton Cambs 62 E10
Harlyn Cnwll 4 D6
Harman's Cross Dorset 12 G8
Harmby N York 96 H3
Harmer Green Herts 50 G7
Harmer Hill Shrops 69 N10
Harmondsworth Gt Lon 36 C5
Harmston Lincs 86 C8
Harnage Shrops 57 K4
Harnham Nthumb 112 G4
Harnhill Gloucs 33 L4
Harold Hill Gt Lon 37 M2
Haroldston West Pembks 40 G7
Haroldswick Shet 169 t2
Harold Wood Gt Lon 37 N2
Harome N York 98 C4
Harpenden Herts 50 D8
Harpford Devon 10 B6
Harpham E R Yk 99 M8
Harpley Norfk 75 Q5
Harpley Worcs 46 C2
Harpole Nhants 60 E8
Harpsdale Highld 167 K5
Harpsden Oxon 35 L8
Harpswell Lincs 86 B3
Harpurhey Manch 83 J4
Harpur Hill Derbys 83 N10
Harraby Cumb 110 H10
Harracott Devon 17 K6
Harrapool Highld 145 L3
Harrietfield P & K 134 B2
Harrietsham Kent 38 E11
Harringay Gt Lon 36 H3
Harrington Cumb 100 C5
Harrington Lincs 87 L6
Harrington Nhants 60 G4
Harringworth Nhants 73 N11
Harris W Isls 168 f8
Harriseahead Staffs 70 F3
Harriston Cumb 100 G2
Harrogate N York 97 M9
Harrogate Crematorium N York 97 M10
Harrold Bed 61 K9
Harrop Dale Oldham 90 C9
Harrow Gt Lon 36 E3
Harrowbarrow Cnwll 5 Q7
Harrowden Bed 61 N11
Harrowgate Village Darltn 103 Q7
Harrow Green Suffk 64 B11
Harrow Hill Gloucs 46 C11

Harrow on the Hill – Heyshott

Harrow on the Hill Gt Lon 36 E3
Harrow Weald Gt Lon 36 E2
Harston Cambs 62 F10
Harston Leics 73 L4
Harswell E R Yk 92 D2
Hart Hartpl 104 E3
Hartburn Nthumb 112 G3
Hartburn S on T 104 D7
Hartest Suffk 64 A11
Hartfield E Susx 25 L3
Hartford Cambs 62 C6
Hartford Ches W 82 D10
Hartford Somset 18 C9
Hartfordbridge Hants 23 L3
Hartford End Essex 51 Q7
Hartforth N York 103 N9
Hartgrove Dorset 20 F11
Harthill Ches W 69 N3
Harthill N Lans 126 G5
Harthill Rothm 84 G4
Hartington Derbys 71 L2
Hartington Nthumb 112 F3
Hartland Devon 16 D7
Hartland Quay Devon 16 C7
Hartlebury Worcs 58 B10
Hartlepool Hartpl 104 F4
Hartlepool Crematorium Hartpl 104 F4
Hartley Cumb 102 E9
Hartley Kent 26 C5
Hartley Kent 37 P7
Hartley Nthumb 113 M5
Hartley Green Kent 37 P7
Hartley Green Staffs 70 H9
Hartley Wespall Hants 23 J3
Hartley Wintney Hants 23 L3
Hartlip Kent 38 D9
Hartoft End N York 98 E2
Harton N York 98 E8
Harton S Tyne 113 N7
Harton Shrops 56 H7
Hartpury Gloucs 46 E10
Hartshead Kirk 90 F6
Hartshead Moor Services Calder 90 F6
Hartshill C Stke 70 F5
Hartshill Warwks 59 M6
Hartshorne Derbys 71 Q10
Hartside Nthumb 119 J7
Hartsop Cumb 101 M8
Hart Station Hartpl 104 E3
Hartswell Somset 18 E9
Hartwell Nhants 49 L4
Hartwith N York 97 K8
Hartwood N Lans 126 E6
Hartwoodmyres Border 117 N6
Harvel Kent 37 Q8
Harvington Worcs 47 L5
Harvington Worcs 58 C10
Harwell Notts 85 L2
Harwell Oxon 34 E7
Harwich Essex 53 N5
Harwood Bolton 89 L8
Harwood Dur 102 F4
Harwood Dale N York 105 Q11
Harwood Lee Bolton 89 L8
Harwood Park Crematorium Herts 50 G6
Harworth Notts 85 K2
Hasbury Dudley 58 E8
Hascombe Surrey 24 B3
Haselbech Nhants 60 F5
Haselbury Plucknett Somset 11 K2
Haseley Warwks 59 K11
Haseley Green Warwks 59 K11
Haseley Knob Warwks 59 K10
Haselor Warwks 47 M3
Hasfield Gloucs 46 F9
Hasguard Pembks 40 G9
Hasholme E R Yk 92 D4
Haskayne Lancs 88 D9
Hasketon Suffk 65 J11
Hasland Derbys 84 E7
Haslemere Surrey 23 P8
Haslingden Lancs 89 M6
Haslingfield Cambs 62 F10
Haslington Ches E 70 C3
Hassall Ches E 70 D3
Hassall Green Ches E 70 D3
Hassell Street Kent 27 J2
Hassingham Norfk 77 M10
Hassness Cumb 100 G7
Hassocks W Susx 24 H7
Hassop Derbys 84 B6
Haste Hill Surrey 23 P8
Haster Highld 167 P6
Hasthorpe Lincs 87 N7
Hastingleigh Kent 27 J2
Hastings E Susx 26 D10
Hastings Somset 19 K11
Hastings Crematorium E Susx 26 D9
Hastingwood Essex 51 L9
Hastoe Herts 35 P3
Haswell Dur 104 C2
Haswell Plough Dur 104 C2
Hatch C Beds 61 Q11
Hatch Beauchamp Somset 19 K10
Hatch End Bed 61 N8
Hatch End Gt Lon 36 D2
Hatchet Gate Hants 14 C6
Hatching Green Herts 50 D8
Hatchmere Ches W 82 C10
Hatcliffe NE Lin 93 M10
Hatfield Donc 91 R9
Hatfield Herefs 46 A3
Hatfield Herts 50 F9
Hatfield Worcs 46 G4
Hatfield Broad Oak Essex 51 M7
Hatfield Heath Essex 51 M7
Hatfield Peverel Essex 52 C9
Hatfield Woodhouse Donc 92 A9
Hatford Oxon 34 B6
Hatherden Hants 22 B4
Hatherleigh Devon 8 D4
Hathern Leics 72 E6
Hatherop Gloucs 33 N3
Hathersage Derbys 84 B4
Hathersage Booths Derbys 84 B4
Hatherton Ches E 70 B5
Hatherton Staffs 58 E2
Hatley St George Cambs 62 C10
Hatt Cnwll 5 Q9
Hattersley Tamesd 83 L6
Hattingley Hants 22 H7
Hatton Abers 159 Q10
Hatton Angus 142 H9
Hatton Derbys 71 N8
Hatton Gt Lon 36 C5
Hatton Lincs 86 G5
Hatton Shrops 56 H6
Hatton Warrtn 82 C8
Hatton Warwks 59 K11
Hatton Heath Ches W 69 N2
Hatton of Fintray Abers 151 L4
Haugh E Ayrs 115 J2
Haugh Lincs 87 M5
Haugh Rochdl 89 Q8
Haugham Lincs 87 K4
Haughhead E Duns 125 Q2
Haugh Head Nthumb 119 K5
Haughley Suffk 64 E9
Haughley Green Suffk 64 E9
Haugh of Glass Moray 158 B10
Haugh of Urr D & G 108 H7
Haughs of Kinnaird Angus 143 L6
Haughton Ches E 69 Q3
Haughton Notts 85 L6
Haughton Powys 69 K11
Haughton Shrops 57 M5
Haughton Shrops 57 N3
Haughton Shrops 69 L9
Haughton Shrops 69 Q11
Haughton Staffs 70 F10
Haughton Green Tamesd 83 K6
Haughton le Skerne Darltn 104 B7
Haultwick Herts 50 H6
Haunton Staffs 59 K2
Hautes Croix Jersey 11 b1
Hauxton Cambs 62 F10
Havannah Ches E 70 F2
Havant Hants 15 K5
Havant Crematorium Hants 15 K5
Haven Herefs 45 N4
Haven Bank Lincs 86 H10
Haven Side E R Yk 93 L5
Havenstreet IoW 14 G8
Havercroft Wakefd 91 K8
Haverfordwest Pembks 41 J7
Haverhill Suffk 63 L11
Haverigg Cumb 94 D5
Havering-atte-Bower Gt Lon 37 M2
Haversham M Keyn 49 M6
Haverthwaite Cumb 94 G4
Haverton Hill S on T 104 E6
Havyatt N Som 19 N2
Havyatt Somset 19 P7
Hawarden Flints 81 L11
Hawbridge Worcs 46 H5
Hawbush Green Essex 52 C7
Hawcoat Cumb 94 E6
Hawen Cerdgn 42 F5
Hawes N York 96 C3
Hawe's Green Norfk 65 J2
Hawford Worcs 46 F2
Hawick Border 117 Q8
Hawkchurch Devon 10 G4
Hawkedon Suffk 63 N10
Hawkenbury Kent 26 D2
Hawkeridge Wilts 20 G4
Hawkerland Devon 9 Q7
Hawker's Cove Cnwll 4 E6
Hawkesbury S Glos 32 E7
Hawkesbury Warwks 59 N8
Hawkesbury Upton S Glos 32 E7
Hawkes End Covtry 59 L8
Hawk Green Stockp 83 L7
Hawkhill Nthumb 119 P8
Hawkhurst Kent 26 C5
Hawkhurst Common E Susx 25 M7
Hawkinge Kent 27 M4
Hawkinge Crematorium Kent 27 M3
Hawkley Hants 23 K9
Hawkley Wigan 82 C4
Hawkridge Somset 17 R5
Hawksdale Cumb 110 G11
Hawkshaw Bury 89 M7
Hawkshead Cumb 101 L11
Hawkshead Hill Cumb 101 K11
Hawksland S Lans 116 A3
Hawkspur Green Essex 51 Q4
Hawkstone Shrops 69 Q8
Hawkswick N York 96 E6
Hawksworth Leeds 90 F2
Hawksworth Notts 73 K2
Hawkwell Essex 38 E3
Hawkwell Nthumb 112 G6
Hawley Hants 23 N3
Hawley Kent 37 M6
Hawling Gloucs 47 L10
Hawnby N York 98 A3
Haworth C Brad 90 C3
Hawridge Bucks 35 P3
Hawstead Suffk 64 B10
Hawstead Green Suffk 64 B10
Hawthorn Dur 113 P11
Hawthorn Hants 23 J8
Hawthorn Rhondd 30 E7
Hawthorn Hill Br For 35 N10
Hawthorn Hill Lincs 86 H9
Hawthorpe Lincs 73 Q5
Hawton Notts 85 N10
Haxby C York 98 C9
Haxby Gates C York 98 C9
Haxey N Linc 92 C11
Haxey Carr N Linc 92 C10
Haxted Surrey 37 K11
Haxton Wilts 21 M5
Hay Cnwll 3 P3
Hay Cnwll 4 F7
Haycombe Crematorium BaNES 20 D2
Haydock St Hel 82 C5
Haydon BaNES 20 C4
Haydon Dorset 20 C11
Haydon Somset 19 J10
Haydon Bridge Nthumb 112 B8
Haydon Wick Swindn 33 M7
Haye Cnwll 5 P7
Hayes Gt Lon 36 C4
Hayes Gt Lon 37 K7
Hayes End Gt Lon 36 C4
Hayfield Ag & B 131 M3
Hayfield Derbys 83 M7
Hayfield Green Donc 91 R11
Haygate Wrekin 57 L2
Hay Green Norfk 75 K7
Hayhillock Angus 143 J9
Hayle Cnwll 2 F6
Hayle Port Cnwll 2 F6
Hayley Green Dudley 58 E8
Hayling Island Hants 15 K6
Haymoor Green Ches E 70 B4
Hayne Devon 9 J7
Hayne Devon 18 C11
Haynes (Church End) C Beds 50 C2
Haynes (Northwood End) C Beds 50 C2
Haynes (Silver End) C Beds 50 D2
Haynes (West End) C Beds 50 C2
Hay-on-Wye Powys 45 J6
Hayscastle Pembks 40 G5
Hayscastle Cross Pembks 40 H5
Haysden Kent 37 N11
Hay Street Herts 51 J5
Hayton Cumb 100 F2
Hayton Cumb 111 K9
Hayton E R Yk 98 G11
Hayton Notts 85 M4
Hayton's Bent Shrops 57 J8
Haytor Vale Devon 9 J9
Haytown Devon 16 F9
Haywards Heath W Susx 24 H6
Haywood Donc 91 P8
Haywood Herefs 45 P8
Haywood Oaks Notts 85 K9
Hazards Green E Susx 25 Q8
Hazelbank S Lans 126 E8
Hazelbury Bryan Dorset 12 B3
Hazeleigh Essex 52 D11
Hazeley Hants 23 K3
Hazelford Notts 85 M11
Hazel Grove Stockp 83 K7
Hazelhurst Tamesd 83 L4
Hazelslade Staffs 58 F2
Hazel Street Kent 25 Q3
Hazel Stub Suffk 51 Q2
Hazelton Walls Fife 135 J3
Hazelwood Derbys 84 D11
Hazlemere Bucks 35 N5
Hazlerigg N u Ty 113 K6
Hazles Staffs 71 J5
Hazleton Gloucs 47 L11
Heacham Norfk 75 N3
Headbourne Worthy Hants 22 E8
Headbrook Herefs 45 K3
Headcorn Kent 26 D3
Headingley Leeds 90 H3
Headington Oxon 34 F3
Headlam Dur 103 N7
Headlesscross N Lans 126 G6
Headless Cross Worcs 58 F11
Headley Hants 22 F2
Headley Hants 23 M7
Headley Surrey 36 F10
Headley Down Hants 23 M7
Headley Heath Worcs 58 G9
Headon Devon 16 F11
Headon Notts 85 M5
Heads Nook Cumb 111 K10
Heage Derbys 84 E10
Healaugh N York 97 R11
Healaugh N York 103 K11
Heald Green Stockp 82 H7
Heale Devon 17 L2
Heale Somset 18 H10
Heale Somset 19 L9
Healey N York 97 J4
Healey Nthumb 112 F9
Healey Rochdl 89 P7
Healey Wakefd 90 H7
Healeyfield Dur 112 G11
Healing NE Lin 93 M8
Heamoor Cnwll 2 D7
Heanor Derbys 84 F11
Heanton Punchardon Devon 17 J4
Heapham Lincs 85 Q3
Hearn Hants 23 M7
Heart of England Crematorium Warwks 59 N6
Heart of Scotland Services N Lans 126 G5
Hearts Delight Kent 38 E9
Heasley Mill Devon 17 N5
Heaste Highld 145 K4
Heath Derbys 84 G7
Heath Wakefd 91 K6
Heath and Reach C Beds 49 P9
Heath Common W Susx 24 C7
Heathcote Derbys 71 L2
Heathcote Shrops 70 B9
Heath End Bucks 35 N5
Heath End Hants 22 D2
Heath End Leics 72 B6
Heath End Warwks 47 P2
Heather Leics 72 B8
Heathfield Cambs 62 G11
Heathfield Devon 9 K9
Heathfield E Susx 25 N6
Heathfield N York 96 H7
Heathfield Somset 18 G9
Heathfield Village Oxon 48 F11
Heath Green Worcs 58 G10
Heath Hall D & G 109 L5
Heath Hayes & Wimblebury Staffs 58 F2
Heath Hill Shrops 57 P2
Heath House Somset 19 M5
Heathrow Airport Gt Lon 36 C5
Heathstock Devon 10 E4
Heathton Shrops 57 Q6
Heath Town Wolves 58 D5
Heathwaite N York 104 E10
Heatley Staffs 71 K9
Heatley Warrtn 82 F7
Heaton Bolton 89 K9
Heaton C Brad 90 E3
Heaton Lancs 95 J8
Heaton N u Ty 113 L7
Heaton Staffs 70 H2
Heaton Chapel Stockp 83 J6
Heaton Mersey Stockp 83 J6
Heaton Norris Stockp 83 J6
Heaton's Bridge Lancs 88 E8
Heaverham Kent 37 N9
Heaviley Stockp 83 K7
Heavitree Devon 9 M6
Hebburn S Tyne 113 M8
Hebden N York 96 F8
Hebden Bridge Calder 90 B5
Hebden Green Ches W 82 D11
Hebing End Herts 50 H6
Hebron Carmth 41 N5
Hebron IoA 78 H8
Hebron Nthumb 113 J3
Heckfield Hants 23 K2
Heckfield Green Suffk 64 H6
Heckfordbridge Essex 52 F7
Heckington Lincs 74 B2
Heckmondwike Kirk 90 G6
Heddington Wilts 33 J11
Heddon-on-the-Wall Nthumb 112 H7
Hedenham Norfk 65 L3
Hedge End Hants 14 E4
Hedgerley Bucks 35 Q7
Hedgerley Green Bucks 35 Q7
Hedging Somset 19 K9
Hedley on the Hill Nthumb 112 G9
Hednesford Staffs 58 E2
Hedon E R Yk 93 L5
Hedsor Bucks 35 P7
Heeley Sheff 84 E4
Hegdon Hill Herefs 46 A4
Heglibister Shet 169 q8
Heighington Darltn 103 P6
Heighington Lincs 86 D7
Heightington Worcs 57 P10
Heiton Border 118 D4
Hele Devon 7 J4
Hele Devon 9 N4
Hele Devon 17 J2
Hele Somset 18 G10
Helebridge Cnwll 16 C11
Hele Lane Devon 9 J2
Helensburgh Ag & B 132 B11
Helenton S Ayrs 125 K11
Helford Cnwll 3 K8
Helford Passage Cnwll 3 K8
Helhoughton Norfk 76 B6
Helions Bumpstead Essex 51 Q2
Hellaby Rothm 84 H2
Helland Cnwll 4 H7
Hellandbridge Cnwll 4 H7
Hell Corner W Berk 22 C2
Hellescott Cnwll 5 M4
Hellesdon Norfk 77 J9
Hellesveor Cnwll 2 E5
Hellidon Nhants 60 B9
Hellifield N York 96 C9
Hellingly E Susx 25 N8
Hellington Norfk 77 L11
Helm Nthumb 119 N11
Helmdon Nhants 48 G6
Helme Kirk 90 D8
Helmingham Suffk 64 H10
Helmington Row Dur 103 N3
Helmsdale Highld 163 N3
Helmshore Lancs 89 M6
Helmsley N York 98 C4
Helperby N York 97 P7
Helperthorpe N York 99 K6
Helpringham Lincs 74 B2
Helpston C Pete 74 B9
Helsby Ches W 81 P9
Helsey Lincs 87 P6
Helston Cnwll 2 H8
Helstone Cnwll 4 H5
Helton Cumb 101 P6
Helwith N York 103 L10
Helwith Bridge N York 96 B7
Hemblington Norfk 77 L9
Hembridge Somset 19 Q7
Hemel Hempstead Herts 50 C9
Hemerdon Devon 6 F7
Hemingbrough N York 91 R4
Hemingby Lincs 86 H6
Hemingfield Barns 91 K10
Hemingford Abbots Cambs 62 C6
Hemingford Grey Cambs 62 C6
Hemingstone Suffk 64 G11
Hemington Leics 72 D5
Hemington Nhants 61 N3
Hemington Somset 20 D4
Hemley Suffk 53 N3
Hemlington Middsb 104 F8
Hempholme E R Yk 99 M10
Hempnall Norfk 65 J3
Hempnall Green Norfk 65 J3
Hempriggs Moray 157 L5
Hempstead Essex 51 P3
Hempstead Medway 38 C9
Hempstead Norfk 76 G4
Hempstead Norfk 77 N6
Hempsted Gloucs 46 F11
Hempton Norfk 76 C6
Hempton Oxon 48 D8
Hemsby Norfk 77 P8
Hemswell Lincs 86 B2
Hemswell Cliff Lincs 86 B3
Hemsworth Wakefd 91 L8
Hemyock Devon 10 C2
Henbury Bristl 31 Q9
Henbury Ches E 83 J10
Hendham Devon 7 J8
Hendomen Powys 56 C5
Hendon Gt Lon 36 F3
Hendon Sundld 113 P9
Hendon Crematorium Gt Lon 36 F2
Hendra Cnwll 3 J6
Hendra Cnwll 4 G6
Hendre Brdgnd 29 P8
Hendre Flints 80 H11
Hendre Mons 31 N2
Hendy Carmth 28 G4
Heneglwys IoA 78 G9
Henfield W Susx 24 F7
Henford Devon 5 P3
Henfynyw Cerdgn 43 J2
Henghurst Kent 26 G4
Hengoed Caerph 30 G6
Hengoed Powys 45 J4
Hengoed Shrops 69 J8
Hengrave Suffk 63 P7
Henham Essex 51 M5
Heniarth Powys 55 Q3
Henlade Somset 19 J10
Henley Dorset 11 P4
Henley Gloucs 46 H11
Henley Shrops 56 H7
Henley Shrops 57 J9
Henley Somset 19 M8
Henley Suffk 64 H11
Henley W Susx 23 N9
Henley Green Covtry 59 N8
Henley-in-Arden Warwks 59 J11
Henley-on-Thames Oxon 35 L8
Henley Park Surrey 23 P4
Henley's Down E Susx 26 B9
Henley Street Kent 37 Q7
Henllan Cerdgn 42 G6
Henllan Denbgs 80 E11
Henllan Amgoed Carmth 41 N7
Henllys Torfn 31 J6
Henlow C Beds 50 E3
Hennock Devon 9 K8
Henny Street Essex 52 E4
Henryd Conwy 79 P10
Henry's Moat (Castell Hendre) Pembks 41 K5
Hensall N York 91 P6
Henshaw Nthumb 111 Q8
Hensingham Cumb 100 C7
Henstead Suffk 65 P4
Hensting Hants 22 E10
Henstridge Somset 20 D11
Henstridge Ash Somset 20 D10
Henstridge Marsh Somset 20 D10
Henton Oxon 35 L4
Henton Somset 19 N5
Henwick Worcs 46 F3
Henwood Cnwll 5 M7
Henwood Oxon 34 E4
Heol-las Swans 29 J5
Heol Senni Powys 44 C10
Heol-y-Cyw Brdgnd 29 P8
Hepburn Nthumb 119 L6
Hepple Nthumb 119 J10
Hepscott Nthumb 113 K4
Heptonstall Calder 90 B5
Hepworth Kirk 90 F9
Hepworth Suffk 64 D7
Herbrandston Pembks 40 G9
Hereford Herefs 45 Q7
Hereford Crematorium Herefs 45 P6
Hereson Kent 39 Q8
Heribusta Highld 152 F3
Heriot Border 128 C9
Hermiston C Edin 127 M3
Hermitage Border 117 Q11
Hermitage Dorset 11 P3
Hermitage W Berk 34 F10
Hermitage W Susx 15 L5
Hermit Hill Barns 91 J10
Hermon Carmth 42 G8
Hermon IoA 78 F11
Hermon Pembks 41 P4
Herne Kent 39 L8
Herne Bay Kent 39 L8
Herne Common Kent 39 L8
Herne Hill Gt Lon 36 H6
Herne Pound Kent 37 Q10
Herner Devon 17 K6
Hernhill Kent 39 J9
Herodsfoot Cnwll 5 L9
Heronden Kent 39 N11
Herongate Essex 37 P2
Heronsford S Ayrs 114 B11
Heronsgate Herts 36 B2
Herriard Hants 23 J5
Herringfleet Suffk 65 P2
Herring's Green Bed 50 C2
Herringswell Suffk 63 M6
Herringthorpe Rothm 84 F2
Herrington Sundld 113 N10
Hersden Kent 39 M9
Hersham Cnwll 16 D10
Hersham Surrey 36 D8
Herstmonceux E Susx 25 P8
Herston Dorset 12 H9
Herston Ork 169 d7
Hertford Herts 50 H8
Hertford Heath Herts 51 J8
Hertingfordbury Herts 50 H8
Hesketh Bank Lancs 88 E6
Hesketh Lane Lancs 89 J2
Hesket Newmarket Cumb 101 K3
Heskin Green Lancs 88 G7
Hesleden Dur 104 D3
Hesleden N York 96 C6
Hesley Donc 85 K2
Hesleyside Nthumb 112 B4
Heslington C York 98 C10
Hessay C York 97 R10
Hessenford Cnwll 5 N10
Hessett Suffk 64 C9
Hessle E R Yk 92 H5
Hessle Wakefd 91 L7
Hest Bank Lancs 95 K7
Hestley Green Suffk 64 H8
Heston Gt Lon 36 D5
Heston Services Gt Lon 36 D5
Hestwall Ork 169 b5
Heswall Wirral 81 K8
Hethe Oxon 48 G9
Hethersett Norfk 76 G11
Hethersgill Cumb 111 J7
Hetherside Cumb 110 H7
Hetherson Green Ches W 69 P4
Hethpool Nthumb 118 G5
Hett Dur 103 Q3
Hetton N York 96 E9
Hetton-le-Hole Sundld 113 N11
Hetton Steads Nthumb 119 K3
Heugh Nthumb 112 G6
Heughhead Abers 150 B5
Heugh Head Border 129 M7
Heveningham Suffk 65 L7
Hever Kent 37 L11
Heversham Cumb 95 K4
Hevingham Norfk 76 H7
Hewas Water Cnwll 3 P4
Hewelsfield Gloucs 31 Q4
Hewenden C Brad 90 D3
Hewish N Som 19 M2
Hewish Somset 11 J3
Hewood Dorset 10 H4
Hexham Nthumb 112 D8
Hextable Kent 37 M6
Hexthorpe Donc 91 P10
Hexton Herts 50 D4
Hexworthy Cnwll 5 P5
Hexworthy Devon 6 H4
Hey Lancs 89 P2
Heybridge Essex 51 P11
Heybridge Essex 52 E10
Heybridge Basin Essex 52 E10
Heybrook Bay Devon 6 D9
Heydon Cambs 51 K3
Heydon Norfk 76 G6
Heydour Lincs 73 Q3
Heyhead Manch 82 H7
Hey Houses Lancs 88 C5
Heylipoll Ag & B 136 B7
Heylor Shet 169 p5
Heyrod Tamesd 83 L5
Heysham Lancs 95 J8
Heyshaw N York 97 J8
Heyshott W Susx 23 N11

Heyside – Hook Green 275

Heyside Oldham 89 Q9
Heytesbury Wilts 20 H6
Heythrop Oxon 48 C9
Heywood Rochdl 89 P8
Heywood Wilts 20 G4
Hibaldstow N Linc 92 G10
Hickleton Donc 91 M9
Hickling Norfk 77 N7
Hickling Notts 72 H5
Hickling Green Norfk 77 N7
Hickling Heath Norfk 77 N7
Hickling Pastures Notts 72 H5
Hickmans Green Kent 39 J10
Hicks Forstal Kent 39 L9
Hickstead W Susx 24 G6
Hidcote Bartrim Gloucs 47 N6
Hidcote Boyce Gloucs 47 N6
High Ackworth Wakefd 91 L7
Higham Barns 91 J9
Higham Derbys 84 E9
Higham Kent 37 P11
Higham Kent 38 B7
Higham Lancs 89 N3
Higham Suffk 52 H4
Higham Suffk 63 M7
Higham Dykes Nthumb 112 H5
Higham Ferrers Nhants 61 L7
Higham Gobion C Beds 50 D4
Higham Hill Gt Lon 37 J2
Higham on the Hill Leics 72 B11
Highampton Devon 8 C4
Highams Park Gt Lon 37 J2
High Angerton Nthumb 112 G3
High Ardwell D & G 106 E8
High Auldgirth D & G 109 K3
High Bankhill Cumb 101 Q2
High Beach Essex 51 K11
High Bentham N York 95 P7
High Bewaldeth Cumb 100 H4
High Bickington Devon 17 L7
High Biggins Cumb 95 N5
High Birkwith N York 96 B5
High Blantyre S Lans 126 B6
High Bonnybridge Falk 126 E2
High Borrans Cumb 101 M10
High Bradley N York 96 F11
High Bray Devon 17 M5
Highbridge Hants 22 E10
Highbridge Somset 19 K5
Highbrook W Susx 25 J4
High Brooms Kent 25 N2
High Bullen Devon 17 J7
Highburton Kirk 90 F8
Highbury Gt Lon 36 H3
Highbury Somset 20 C5
High Buston Nthumb 119 P9
High Callerton Nthumb 113 J6
High Casterton Cumb 95 N5
High Catton E R Yk 98 E10
Highclere Hants 22 D3
Highcliffe Dorset 13 M6
High Close Dur 103 N7
High Cogges Oxon 34 C3
High Common Norfk 76 D10
High Coniscliffe Darltn 103 P7
High Crosby Cumb 111 J9
High Cross Cnwll 3 J8
High Cross E Ayrs 125 L8
High Cross Hants 23 K9
High Cross Herts 51 J7
Highcross Lancs 88 C3
High Cross W Susx 24 F7
High Cross Warwks 59 K11
High Drummore D & G 106 F10
High Dubmire Sundld 113 M11
High Easter Essex 51 P8
High Eggborough N York 91 P6
High Ellington N York 97 J4
Higher Alham Somset 20 C6
Higher Ansty Dorset 12 C4
Higher Ballam Lancs 88 D4
Higher Bartle Lancs 88 G4
Higher Berry End C Beds 49 Q8
Higher Bockhampton Dorset 12 B6
Higher Brixham Torbay 7 N8
Higher Burrowton Devon 9 P5
Higher Burwardsley Ches W 69 P3
High Ercall Wrekin 69 Q11
Higher Chillington Somset 10 H2
Higher Clovelly Devon 16 E7
Highercombe Somset 18 B8
Higher Coombe Dorset 11 L6
Higher Disley Ches E 83 L8
Higher Folds Wigan 82 E4
Higherford Lancs 89 P2
Higher Gabwell Devon 7 N5
Higher Halstock Leigh Dorset 11 L3
Higher Harpers Lancs 89 N3
Higher Heysham Lancs 95 J8
Higher Hurdsfield Ches E 83 K10
Higher Irlam Salfd 82 F5
Higher Kingcombe Dorset 11 L5
Higher Kinnerton Flints 69 K2
Higher Marston Ches W 82 E9
Higher Muddiford Devon 17 K4
Higher Nyland Dorset 20 D10
Higher Ogden Rochdl 90 B8
Higher Pentire Cnwll 2 H8
Higher Penwortham Lancs 88 G5
Higher Prestacott Devon 5 P2
Higher Studfold N York 96 B6
Higher Town Cnwll 3 L5
Higher Town Cnwll 4 G9
Higher Town IoS 2 c1
Higher Tregantle Cnwll 5 Q11
Higher Walton Lancs 88 H5
Higher Walton Warrtn 82 C7
Higher Wambrook Somset 10 F3
Higher Waterston Dorset 11 Q5
Higher Whatcombe Dorset 12 D4
Higher Wheelton Lancs 89 J6
Higher Whitley Ches W 82 D8
Higher Wincham Ches W 82 E9
Higher Wraxhall Dorset 11 M4
Higher Wych Ches W 69 N6
High Etherley Dur 103 N5
High Ferry Lincs 87 L11
Highfield E R Yk 92 B3
Highfield Gatesd 112 H9
Highfield N Ayrs 125 J7
Highfields Donc 91 N9
High Flats Kirk 90 G9
High Garrett Essex 52 C6
Highgate E Susx 25 K4
Highgate Gt Lon 36 G3
Highgate Kent 26 C5
High Grange Dur 103 N4
High Grantley N York 97 K7
High Green Cumb 101 M10
High Green Kirk 90 G8
High Green Norfk 64 H4
High Green Norfk 76 G10
High Green Sheff 91 J11
High Green Shrops 57 N8
High Green Suffk 64 B9
High Green Worcs 46 G5
Highgreen Manor Nthumb 112 B2
High Halden Kent 26 E4
High Halstow Medway 38 C6
High Ham Somset 19 M8
High Harrington Cumb 100 D5
High Harrogate N York 97 M9
High Haswell Dur 104 C2
High Hatton Shrops 69 R10
High Hauxley Nthumb 119 Q10
High Hawsker N York 105 P9
High Hesket Cumb 101 N2
High Hoyland Barns 90 H9
High Hunsley E R Yk 92 G3
High Hurstwood E Susx 25 L5
High Hutton N York 98 F7
High Ireby Cumb 100 H3
High Kelling Norfk 76 G3
High Kilburn N York 97 R5
High Killerby N York 99 M4
High Knipe Cumb 101 P7
High Lands Dur 103 M5
Highlane Ches E 83 J11
Highlane Derbys 84 F4
High Lane Stockp 83 L7
High Lanes Cnwll 2 F6
High Laver Essex 51 M9
Highlaws Cumb 109 P11
Highleadon Gloucs 46 E10
High Legh Ches E 82 F8
Highleigh W Susx 15 M7
High Leven S on T 104 E8
Highley Shrops 57 N8
High Littleton BaNES 20 B3
High Lorton Cumb 100 G5
High Marishes N York 98 G5
High Marnham Notts 85 P6
High Melton Donc 91 N10
High Mickley Nthumb 112 G8
Highmoor Cumb 110 E11
Highmoor Oxon 35 K8
Highmoor Cross Oxon 35 K8
Highmoor Hill Mons 31 N7
High Moorsley Sundld 113 M11
Highnam Gloucs 46 E11
Highnam Green Gloucs 46 E10
High Newport Sundld 113 N10
High Newton Cumb 95 J4
High Nibthwaite Cumb 94 F3
High Offley Staffs 70 D9
High Ongar Essex 51 N10
High Onn Staffs 70 E11
High Park Corner Essex 52 H7
High Pennyvenie E Ayrs 115 J6
High Post Wilts 21 N7
Highridge N Som 31 Q11
High Roding Essex 51 P7
High Row Cumb 101 L3
High Row Cumb 101 L6
High Salter Lancs 95 N8
High Salvington W Susx 24 D9
High Scales Cumb 110 C11
High Seaton Cumb 100 D4
High Shaw N York 96 C2
High Side Cumb 100 H4
High Spen Gatesd 112 H9
Highstead Kent 39 M8
Highsted Kent 38 F9
High Stoop Dur 103 M2
High Street Cnwll 3 P3
High Street Kent 26 B5
Highstreet Kent 39 J9
High Street Suffk 65 N10
High Street Suffk 65 N7
Highstreet Green Essex 52 C5
Highstreet Green Surrey 23 Q7
Hightae D & G 109 N5
Highter's Heath Birm 58 G9
High Throston Hartpl 104 E4
Hightown Ches E 70 F2
Hightown Hants 13 L4
Hightown Sefton 81 L4
High Town Staffs 58 E2
Hightown Green Suffk 64 D10
High Toynton Lincs 87 J7
High Trewhitt Nthumb 119 K9
High Urpeth Dur 113 K10
High Valleyfield Fife 134 C10
High Warden Nthumb 112 D7
Highway Herefs 45 P5
Highway Wilts 33 K10
Highweek Devon 7 L4
High Westwood Dur 112 H9
Highwood Essex 51 P10
Highwood Staffs 71 K8
Highwood Hill Gt Lon 36 F2
High Woolaston Gloucs 31 Q5
High Worsall N York 104 C9
Highworth Swindn 33 P6
High Wray Cumb 101 L11
High Wych Herts 51 L8
High Wycombe Bucks 35 N6
Hilborough Norfk 75 R10
Hilcote Derbys 84 G9
Hilcott Wilts 21 M3
Hildenborough Kent 37 N11
Hilden Park Kent 37 N11
Hildersham Cambs 62 H11
Hilderstone Staffs 70 H8
Hilderthorpe E R Yk 99 P7
Hilfield Dorset 11 N3
Hilgay Norfk 75 M11
Hill S Glos 32 B5
Hill Warwks 59 Q11
Hillam N York 91 N5
Hillbeck Cumb 102 E7
Hillborough Kent 39 M8
Hill Brow Hants 23 L9
Hillbutts Dorset 12 G4
Hill Chorlton Staffs 70 D7
Hillclifflane Derbys 71 P5
Hill Common Norfk 77 N7
Hill Common Somset 18 F9
Hill Deverill Wilts 20 G6
Hilldyke Lincs 87 K11
Hill End Dur 103 K3
Hill End Fife 134 C8
Hillend Fife 134 E11
Hill End Gloucs 46 H7
Hillend Mdloth 127 P4
Hillend N Lans 126 E4
Hillend Swans 28 D6
Hillersland Gloucs 31 Q2
Hillerton Devon 8 H5
Hillesden Bucks 49 J9
Hillesley Gloucs 32 E7
Hillfarrance Somset 18 G10
Hill Green Kent 38 D9
Hillgrove W Susx 23 P9
Hillhampton Herefs 46 A5
Hillhead Abers 158 E10
Hillhead Devon 7 N8
Hill Head Hants 14 F6
Hillhead S Lans 116 D2
Hillhead of Cocklaw Abers 159 Q9
Hilliard's Cross Staffs 59 J2
Hilliclay Highld 167 L4
Hillingdon Gt Lon 36 C4
Hillington C Glas 125 N5
Hillington Norfk 75 P5
Hillis Corner IoW 14 E8
Hillmorton Warwks 60 B6
Hillock Vale Lancs 89 M5
Hill of Beath Fife 134 F9
Hill of Fearn Highld 163 J11
Hillowton D & G 108 G8
Hillpool Worcs 58 C9
Hillpound Hants 22 G11
Hill Ridware Staffs 71 K11
Hillside Abers 151 N8
Hillside Angus 143 N5
Hillside Devon 7 J6
Hill Side Kirk 90 F7
Hill Side Worcs 46 E2
Hills Town Derbys 84 G7
Hillstreet Hants 22 B11
Hillswick Shet 169 p6
Hill Top Dur 103 J6
Hill Top Hants 14 D6
Hill Top Kirk 90 D8
Hill Top Rothm 84 E2
Hill Top Sandw 58 E6
Hill Top Wakefd 91 J7
Hillwell Shet 169 q12
Hilmarton Wilts 33 K9
Hilperton Wilts 20 G3
Hilperton Marsh Wilts 20 G3
Hilsea C Port 15 J6
Hilston E R Yk 93 N4
Hiltingbury Hants 22 D10
Hilton Border 129 M9
Hilton Cambs 62 C7
Hilton Cumb 102 D6
Hilton Derbys 71 N8
Hilton Dorset 12 C4
Hilton Dur 103 N6
Hilton Highld 156 F2
Hilton S on T 104 E8
Hilton Shrops 57 P5
Hilton Park Services Staffs 58 E4
Himbleton Worcs 46 H3
Himley Staffs 58 C6
Hincaster Cumb 95 L4
Hinchley Wood Surrey 36 E7
Hinckley Leics 59 P6
Hinderclay Suffk 64 E6
Hinderwell N York 105 L7
Hindford Shrops 69 K8
Hindhead Surrey 23 N7
Hindhead Tunnel Surrey 23 N7
Hindle Fold Lancs 89 L4
Hindley Nthumb 112 F9
Hindley Wigan 82 D4
Hindley Green Wigan 82 D4
Hindlip Worcs 46 G3
Hindolveston Norfk 76 E6
Hindon Wilts 20 H8
Hindringham Norfk 76 D4
Hingham Norfk 76 E11
Hinksford Staffs 58 C7
Hinstock Shrops 70 B9
Hintlesham Suffk 53 J3
Hinton Gloucs 32 C4
Hinton Hants 13 M5
Hinton Herefs 45 L7
Hinton S Glos 32 D9
Hinton Shrops 56 G3
Hinton Shrops 57 M8
Hinton Admiral Hants 13 M5
Hinton Ampner Hants 22 H9
Hinton Blewett BaNES 19 Q3
Hinton Charterhouse BaNES 20 E3
Hinton Green Worcs 47 K6
Hinton-in-the-Hedges Nhants 48 G7
Hinton Marsh Hants 22 G9
Hinton Martell Dorset 12 H3
Hinton on the Green Worcs 47 K6
Hinton Parva Swindn 33 P8
Hinton St George Somset 11 J2
Hinton St Mary Dorset 20 E11
Hinton Waldrist Oxon 34 C5
Hints Shrops 57 L10
Hints Staffs 59 J4
Hinwick Bed 61 K8
Hinxhill Kent 26 H3
Hinxton Cambs 62 G11
Hinxworth Herts 50 F2
Hipperholme Calder 90 E5
Hipsburn Nthumb 119 P8
Hipswell N York 103 N11
Hirn Abers 151 J7
Hirnant Powys 68 D10
Hirst Nthumb 113 L3
Hirst Courtney N York 91 Q6
Hirwaen Denbgs 68 F2
Hirwaun Rhondd 30 C3
Hiscott Devon 17 J6
Histon Cambs 62 F8
Hitcham Suffk 64 D11
Hitcham Causeway Suffk 64 D11
Hitcham Street Suffk 64 D11
Hitchin Herts 50 E5
Hither Green Gt Lon 37 J6
Hittisleigh Devon 8 H5
Hive E R Yk 92 D4
Hixon Staffs 71 J9
Hoaden Kent 39 N10
Hoar Cross Staffs 71 L10
Hoarwithy Herefs 45 Q9
Hoath Kent 39 M9
Hoathly Kent 25 Q3
Hobarris Shrops 56 E9
Hobbles Green Suffk 63 M10
Hobbs Cross Essex 51 L11
Hobbs Cross Essex 51 L8
Hobkirk Border 118 A8
Hobland Hall Norfk 77 Q11
Hobsick Notts 84 G11
Hobson Dur 113 J9
Hoby Leics 72 H7
Hoccombe Somset 18 F9
Hockering Norfk 76 F9
Hockerton Notts 85 M9
Hockley Ches E 83 K8
Hockley Covtry 59 L9
Hockley Essex 38 D3
Hockley Staffs 59 K4
Hockley Heath Solhll 59 J10
Hockliffe C Beds 49 Q9
Hockwold cum Wilton Norfk 63 M3
Hockworthy Devon 18 D11
Hoddesdon Herts 51 J9
Hoddlesden Bl w D 89 L6
Hoddom Cross D & G 110 C6
Hoddom Mains D & G 110 C6
Hodgehill Ches E 82 H11
Hodgeston Pembks 41 K11
Hodnet Shrops 69 R9
Hodsock Notts 85 K3
Hodsoll Street Kent 37 P8
Hodson Swindn 33 N8
Hodthorpe Derbys 84 H5
Hoe Hants 22 G11
Hoe Norfk 76 D8
Hoe Benham W Berk 34 D11
Hoe Gate Hants 14 H4
Hoff Cumb 102 C7
Hogben's Hill Kent 38 H10
Hoggards Green Suffk 64 B10
Hoggeston Bucks 49 M10
Hoggrill's End Warwks 59 K6
Hog Hill E Susx 26 E8
Hoghton Lancs 89 J5
Hoghton Bottoms Lancs 89 J5
Hognaston Derbys 71 N4
Hogsthorpe Lincs 87 P6
Holbeach Lincs 74 G6
Holbeach Bank Lincs 74 G5
Holbeach Clough Lincs 74 G5
Holbeach Drove Lincs 74 F8
Holbeach Hurn Lincs 74 G5
Holbeach St Johns Lincs 74 G7
Holbeach St Mark's Lincs 74 G4
Holbeach St Matthew Lincs 74 H4
Holbeck Notts 84 H6
Holbeck Woodhouse Notts 84 H6
Holberrow Green Worcs 47 K3
Holbeton Devon 6 G8
Holborn Gt Lon 36 H4
Holborough Kent 37 Q8
Holbrook Derbys 72 B2
Holbrook Sheff 84 F4
Holbrook Suffk 53 L4
Holbrook Moor Derbys 84 E11
Holbrooks Covtry 59 M8
Holburn Nthumb 119 K3
Holbury Hants 14 D6
Holcombe Devon 7 P4
Holcombe Somset 20 C5
Holcombe Rogus Devon 18 E11
Holcot Nhants 60 G7
Holden Lancs 96 A11
Holdenby Nhants 60 E7
Holden Gate Calder 89 P6
Holder's Green Essex 51 P5
Holdgate Shrops 57 K7
Holdingham Lincs 86 E11
Holditch Dorset 10 G4
Holdsworth Calder 90 D5
Holehouse Derbys 83 M6
Hole-in-the-Wall Herefs 46 B9
Holemoor Devon 16 G10
Hole Street W Susx 24 D8
Holford Somset 18 G6
Holgate C York 98 B10
Holker Cumb 94 H5
Holkham Norfk 76 B3
Hollacombe Devon 16 F11
Holland Fen Lincs 86 H11
Holland Lees Lancs 88 G9
Holland-on-Sea Essex 53 L8
Hollandstoun Ork 169 g1
Hollee D & G 110 E7
Hollesley Suffk 53 Q3
Hollicombe Torbay 7 M6
Hollingbourne Kent 38 D10
Hollingbury Br & H 24 H9
Hollingdon Bucks 49 N9
Hollingthorpe Leeds 91 K4
Hollington Derbys 71 N7
Hollington Staffs 71 K7
Hollingworth Tamesd 83 M5
Hollinlane Ches E 82 H8
Hollins Bury 89 N9
Hollins Derbys 84 D6
Hollins Staffs 70 H5
Hollinsclough Staffs 83 N11
Hollins End Sheff 84 E4
Hollins Green Warrtn 82 E6
Hollins Lane Lancs 95 K10
Hollinswood Wrekin 57 N3
Hollinwood Shrops 69 P7
Hollingrove E Susx 25 Q6
Hollocombe Devon 17 L9
Holloway Derbys 84 D9
Holloway Gt Lon 36 H3
Holloway Wilts 20 G8
Hollowell Nhants 60 E6
Hollowmoor Heath Ches W 81 P11
Hollows D & G 110 G5
Hollybush Caerph 30 G4
Hollybush E Ayrs 114 G4
Hollybush Herefs 46 E7
Holly End Norfk 75 J9
Holly Green Worcs 46 G6
Hollyhurst Ches E 69 Q6
Hollym E R Yk 93 P5
Hollywood Worcs 58 G9
Holmbridge Kirk 90 E9
Holmbury St Mary Surrey 24 D2
Holmbush Cnwll 3 Q3
Holmcroft Staffs 70 G10
Holme Cambs 61 Q3
Holme Cumb 95 L5
Holme Kirk 90 E9
Holme N Linc 92 F9
Holme N York 97 N4
Holme Notts 85 P9
Holme Chapel Lancs 89 P5
Holme Green N York 91 P2
Holme Hale Norfk 76 B10
Holme Lacy Herefs 45 R7
Holme Marsh Herefs 45 L4
Holme next the Sea Norfk 75 P2
Holme on the Wolds E R Yk 99 K11
Holme Pierrepont Notts 72 G3
Holmer Herefs 45 Q6
Holmer Green Bucks 35 P5
Holme St Cuthbert Cumb 109 P11
Holmes Chapel Ches E 82 G11
Holmesfield Derbys 84 D5
Holmes Hill E Susx 25 M8
Holmeswood Lancs 88 E7
Holmethorpe Surrey 36 G10
Holme upon Spalding Moor E R Yk 92 D3
Holmewood Derbys 84 F7
Holmfield Calder 90 D5
Holmfirth Kirk 90 E9
Holmhead E Ayrs 115 L3
Holmpton E R Yk 93 Q6
Holmrook Cumb 100 E11
Holmsford Bridge Crematorium N Ayrs 125 K10
Holmshurst E Susx 25 P5
Holmside Dur 113 K11
Holmwrangle Cumb 111 K11
Holne Devon 7 J5
Holnest Dorset 11 P3
Holnicote Somset 18 B5
Holsworthy Devon 16 E11
Holsworthy Beacon Devon 16 F10
Holt Dorset 12 H4
Holt Norfk 76 F4
Holt Wilts 20 G2
Holt Worcs 46 F2
Holt Wrexhm 69 M4
Holtby C York 98 D10
Holt End Worcs 58 G11
Holt Fleet Worcs 46 F2
Holt Green Lancs 88 D9
Holt Heath Dorset 13 J4
Holt Heath Worcs 46 F2
Holton Oxon 34 H3
Holton Somset 20 C9
Holton Suffk 65 N6
Holton cum Beckering Lincs 86 F4
Holton Heath Dorset 12 F6
Holton Hill E Susx 25 Q5
Holton le Clay Lincs 93 N10
Holton le Moor Lincs 93 J11
Holton St Mary Suffk 53 J4
Holt Street Kent 39 N11
Holtye E Susx 25 L3
Holway Flints 80 H9
Holwell Dorset 11 P2
Holwell Herts 50 E4
Holwell Leics 73 J6
Holwell Oxon 33 P3
Holwick Dur 102 H5
Holworth Dorset 12 C8
Holybourne Hants 23 K6
Holy Cross Worcs 58 D9
Holyfield Essex 51 J10
Holyhead IoA 78 C8
Holy Island IoA 78 D8
Holy Island Nthumb 119 M2
Holy Island Nthumb 119 M2
Holymoorside Derbys 84 D7
Holyport W & M 35 N9
Holystone Nthumb 119 J10
Holytown N Lans 126 D5
Holytown Crematorium N Lans 126 D5
Holywell C Beds 50 B7
Holywell Cambs 62 D6
Holywell Cnwll 4 B10
Holywell Dorset 11 M4
Holywell Flints 80 H9
Holywell Nthumb 113 M6
Holywell Warwks 59 K11
Holywell Green Calder 90 D7
Holywell Lake Somset 18 F10
Holywell Row Suffk 63 M5
Holywood D & G 109 K4
Holywood Village D & G 109 L5
Homer Shrops 57 L4
Homer Green Sefton 81 L4
Homersfield Suffk 65 K4
Homescales Cumb 95 M3
Hom Green Herefs 46 A10
Homington Wilts 21 M9
Honeyborough Pembks 40 H9
Honeybourne Worcs 47 M6
Honeychurch Devon 8 F4
Honey Hill Kent 39 K9
Honeystreet Wilts 21 M2
Honey Tye Suffk 52 G4
Honiley Warwks 59 K10
Honing Norfk 77 L6
Honingham Norfk 76 G9
Honington Lincs 73 N2
Honington Suffk 64 C7
Honington Warwks 47 Q6
Honiton Devon 10 D4
Honley Kirk 90 E8
Honnington Wrekin 70 C11
Honor Oak Crematorium Gt Lon 37 J6
Hoo Kent 39 N9
Hoobrook Worcs 58 B10
Hood Green Barns 91 J10
Hood Hill Rothm 91 K11
Hooe C Plym 6 E8
Hooe E Susx 25 Q8
Hoo End Herts 50 E6
Hoo Green Ches E 82 F8
Hoohill Bpool 88 C3
Hook Cambs 62 F2
Hook Devon 10 G3
Hook E R Yk 92 C5
Hook Gt Lon 36 E8
Hook Hants 14 F5
Hook Hants 23 K4
Hook Pembks 41 J8
Hook Wilts 33 L8
Hook-a-Gate Shrops 56 H3
Hook Bank Worcs 46 F6
Hooke Dorset 11 L4
Hook End Essex 51 N10
Hookgate Staffs 70 C7
Hook Green Kent 25 Q3
Hook Green Kent 37 P6

Hook Norton Oxon......48 C8
Hook Street Gloucs......32 C5
Hook Street Wilts......33 L8
Hookway Devon......9 L5
Hookwood Surrey......24 G2
Hooley Surrey......36 C9
Hooley Bridge Rochdl......89 P8
Hoo Meavy Devon......6 E5
Hoo St Werburgh
  Medway......38 C7
Hooton Ches W......81 M9
Hooton Levitt Rothm......84 H2
Hooton Pagnell Donc......91 M9
Hooton Roberts Rothm......91 M11
Hopcrofts Holt Oxon......48 E9
Hope Derbys......83 Q8
Hope Devon......6 H10
Hope Flints......69 K3
Hope Powys......56 D3
Hope Shrops......56 E4
Hope Staffs......71 L4
Hope Bagot Shrops......57 K10
Hope Bowdler Shrops......56 H6
Hope End Green Essex......51 N6
Hopehouse Border......117 K7
Hopeman Moray......157 L14
Hope Mansell Herefs......46 B11
Hopesay Shrops......56 F8
Hopetown Wakefd......91 K6
Hope under Dinmore
  Herefs......45 Q4
Hopgrove C York......98 C10
Hopperton N York......97 P9
Hop Pole Lincs......74 C8
Hopsford Warwks......59 P6
Hopstone Shrops......57 P6
Hopton Derbys......71 P4
Hopton Shrops......69 L10
Hopton Staffs......70 G9
Hopton Suffk......64 D6
Hopton Cangeford
  Shrops......57 J8
Hopton Castle Shrops......56 F9
Hoptonheath Shrops......56 F9
Hopton on Sea Norfk......65 Q2
Hopton Wafers Shrops......57 L9
Hopwas Staffs......59 J4
Hopwood Rochdl......89 P9
Hopwood Worcs......58 F9
Hopwood Park
  Services Worcs......58 F10
Horam E Susx......25 N7
Horbling Lincs......74 B3
Horbury Wakefd......90 H7
Horcott Gloucs......33 N4
Horden Dur......104 D2
Horderley Shrops......56 G7
Hordle Hants......13 N5
Hordley Shrops......69 L8
Horeb Carmth......28 E3
Horeb Cerdgn......42 G6
Horfield Bristl......31 Q9
Horham Suffk......65 J7
Horkesley Heath Essex......52 G6
Horkstow N Linc......92 G7
Horley Oxon......48 D6
Horley Surrey......24 G2
Hornblotton Green
  Somset......19 Q8
Hornby Lancs......95 M7
Hornby N York......97 K2
Hornby N York......104 C9
Horncastle Lincs......87 J7
Hornchurch Gt Lon......37 M3
Horncliffe Nthumb......129 N10
Horndean Border......129 N10
Horndean Hants......15 K4
Horndon Devon......8 D8
Horndon on the Hill
  Thurr......37 Q4
Horne Surrey......24 H2
Horner Somset......18 B5
Horne Row Essex......52 C11
Horners Green Suffk......52 G3
Horney Common E Susx......25 L5
Horn Hill Bucks......36 B2
Horning Norfk......77 L8
Horninghold Leics......73 L11
Horninglow Staffs......71 N9
Horningsea Cambs......62 G8
Horningsham Wilts......20 F6
Horningtoft Norfk......76 C7
Horningtops Cnwll......5 M9
Hornsbury Somset......10 G2
Hornsby Cumb......111 K10
Hornsbygate Cumb......111 K10
Horns Cross Devon......16 F7
Horns Cross E Susx......26 D7
Hornsea E R Yk......99 P11
Hornsey Gt Lon......36 H3
Horn's Green Gt Lon......37 L9
Horn Street Kent......27 L4
Hornton Oxon......48 C5
Horpit Swindn......33 P8
Horra Shet......169 r4
Horrabridge Devon......6 E5
Horringer Suffk......64 A9
Horringford IoW......14 F9
Horrocks Fold Bolton......89 L8
Horrocksford Lancs......89 M2
Horsacott Devon......17 J5
Horsebridge Devon......5 Q6
Horsebridge E Susx......25 N8
Horsebridge Hants......22 B8
Horsebridge Shrops......56 F3
Horsebridge Staffs......70 H4
Horsebrook Staffs......58 C2
Horsecastle N Som......31 M11
Horsedown Cnwll......2 G7
Horsehay Wrekin......57 M3
Horseheath Cambs......63 K11
Horsehouse N York......96 F4
Horsell Surrey......23 Q3
Horseman's Green
  Wrexhm......69 M6
Horsenden Bucks......35 L4
Horsey Norfk......77 P7
Horsey Somset......19 K7
Horsey Corner Norfk......77 P7
Horsford Norfk......76 H8
Horsforth Leeds......90 G3
Horsham W Susx......24 E4
Horsham Worcs......46 D3
Horsham St Faith Norfk......77 J8
Horsington Lincs......86 G7
Horsington Somset......20 D10
Horsley Derbys......72 B2
Horsley Gloucs......32 F5
Horsley Nthumb......112 G2
Horsley Nthumb......118 F11
Horsley Cross Essex......53 K6

Horsleycross Street
  Essex......53 K6
Horsley-Gate Derbys......84 D5
Horsleyhill Border......117 Q7
Horsley's Green Bucks......35 L6
Horsley Woodhouse
  Derbys......72 B2
Horsmonden Kent......26 B3
Horspath Oxon......34 G3
Horstead Norfk......77 K8
Horsted Keynes W Susx......25 J5
Horton Bucks......49 P11
Horton Dorset......12 H3
Horton Lancs......96 C10
Horton Nhants......49 M4
Horton S Glos......32 E8
Horton Shrops......69 N9
Horton Somset......10 G2
Horton Staffs......70 G3
Horton Surrey......36 E8
Horton Swans......28 E7
Horton W & M......36 B5
Horton Wilts......21 K2
Horton Wrekin......57 M2
Horton Cross Somset......19 K11
Horton-cum-Studley
  Oxon......34 G2
Horton Green Ches W......69 N5
Horton Heath Hants......22 E11
Horton-in-Ribblesdale
  N York......96 B6
Horton Kirby Kent......37 N7
Horwich Bolton......89 J8
Horwich End Derbys......83 M8
Horwood Devon......17 J6
Hoscar Lancs......88 F8
Hoscote Border......117 M8
Hose Leics......73 J5
Hosey Hill Kent......37 L10
Hosh P & K......133 P3
Hoswick Shet......169 r11
Hotham E R Yk......92 E4
Hothfield Kent......26 G3
Hoton Leics......72 F6
Hott Nthumb......111 Q3
Hough Ches E......70 C4
Hough Ches E......83 J9
Hougham Lincs......73 M2
Hough End Leeds......90 G4
Hough Green Halton......81 P7
Hough-on-the-Hill Lincs......86 B11
Houghton Cambs......62 C6
Houghton Cumb......110 H9
Houghton Hants......22 B8
Houghton Nthumb......112 H7
Houghton Pembks......41 J9
Houghton W Susx......24 B8
Houghton Conquest
  C Beds......50 B2
Houghton Gate Dur......113 M10
Houghton Green E Susx......26 F7
Houghton Green Warrtn......82 D6
Houghton le Side Darltn......103 P6
Houghton-le-Spring
  Sundld......113 M11
Houghton on the Hill
  Leics......72 H10
Houghton Regis C Beds......50 B6
Houghton St Giles Norfk......76 C4
Hound Green Hants......23 K3
Houndslow Border......128 G10
Houndsmoor Somset......18 F9
Houndwood Border......129 L7
Hounslow Gt Lon......36 D5
Househill Highld......156 F6
Houses Hill Kirk......90 F7
Housieside Abers......151 M2
Houston Rens......125 L4
Houstry Highld......167 L10
Houton Ork......169 c6
Hove Br & H......24 G10
Hove Edge Calder......90 E6
Hoveringham Notts......85 L11
Hoveton Norfk......77 L8
Hovingham N York......98 D5
Howbrook Barns......91 J11
How Caple Herefs......46 B8
Howden E R Yk......92 B5
Howden-le-Wear Dur......103 N4
Howe Highld......167 P4
Howe IoM......80 a8
Howe N York......97 N4
Howe Norfk......65 K2
Howe Bridge Wigan......82 E4
Howe Bridge
  Crematorium Wigan......82 E4
Howe Green Essex......52 B11
Howegreen Essex......52 D11
Howell Lincs......86 F11
How End C Beds......50 B2
Howe of Teuchar Abers......159 J8
Howes D & G......110 C7
Howe Street Essex......51 Q4
Howe Street Essex......51 Q8
Howey Powys......44 F3
Howgate Cumb......100 C6
Howgate Mdloth......127 N6
Howgill Lancs......96 B11
Howick Nthumb......119 Q7
Howle Wrekin......70 B10
Howle Hill Herefs......46 B10
Howlett End Essex......51 N4
Howley Somset......10 F3
How Mill Cumb......111 K9
Howmore W Isls......168 c14
Hownam Border......118 E4
Howrigg Cumb......110 F11
Howsham N Linc......92 H10
Howsham N York......98 E8
Howtel Nthumb......118 G4
Howt Green Kent......38 E8
Howton Herefs......45 N9
Howtown Cumb......101 M7
How Wood Herts......50 D10
Howwood Rens......125 K5
Hoxa Ork......169 d7
Hoxne Suffk......64 H6
Hoy Ork......169 b7
Hoylake Wirral......81 J7
Hoyland Barns......91 K10
Hoyland Common Barns......91 K10
Hoylandswaine Barns......90 H10
Hoyle W Susx......23 P11
Hoyle Mill Barns......91 K9
Hubberholme N York......96 D5
Hubberston Pembks......40 G9
Hubbert's Bridge Lincs......74 E2
Huby N York......97 L11
Huby N York......98 B7
Huccaby Devon......6 H4
Huccombe Gloucs......46 G11

Hucking Kent......38 D10
Hucknall Notts......84 H11
Huddersfield Kirk......90 E7
Huddersfield
  Crematorium Kirk......90 E7
Huddington Worcs......46 H3
Hudnall Herts......50 B8
Hudswell N York......103 M10
Huggate E R Yk......98 H9
Hugglescote Leics......72 C8
Hughenden Valley Bucks......35 N5
Hughley Shrops......57 K5
Hugh Town IoS......2 C2
Huish Devon......17 J9
Huish Wilts......21 M2
Huish Champflower
  Somset......18 E9
Huish Episcopi Somset......19 M9
Huisinis W Isls......168 e6
Huisinish W Isls......168 e6
Hulcote C Beds......49 P7
Hulcote Nhants......49 N5
Hulcott Bucks......49 N11
Hulham Devon......9 P8
Hulland Derbys......71 N5
Hulland Ward Derbys......71 P5
Hullavington Wilts......32 G8
Hull Bridge E R Yk......93 J2
Hullbridge Essex......38 D2
Hull, Kingston upon
  C KuH......93 J5
Hulme Manch......82 H5
Hulme Staffs......70 G5
Hulme Warrtn......82 D6
Hulme End Staffs......71 L3
Hulme Walfield Ches E......82 H11
Hulse Heath Ches E......82 F8
Hulton Lane Ends Bolton......89 K9
Hulverstone IoW......14 C10
Hulver Street Norfk......76 C9
Hulver Street Suffk......65 P4
Humber Devon......9 L9
Humber Herefs......45 Q3
Humber Bridge N Linc......92 H6
Humberside Airport
  N Linc......93 J8
Humberston NE Lin......93 P9
Humberstone C Leic......72 G9
Humberton N York......97 P7
Humbie E Loth......128 D7
Humbleton E R Yk......93 M4
Humbleton Nthumb......119 J5
Humby Lincs......73 Q4
Hume Border......118 D2
Humshaugh Nthumb......112 D6
Huna Highld......167 Q2
Huncoat Lancs......89 M4
Huncote Leics......72 E11
Hundalee Border......118 B7
Hundall Derbys......84 E5
Hunderthwaite Dur......103 J6
Hundleby Lincs......87 L7
Hundle Houses Lincs......86 H10
Hundleton Pembks......41 J10
Hundon Suffk......63 M11
Hundred End Lancs......88 E6
Hundred House Powys......44 G4
Hungarton Leics......72 H9
Hungerford Hants......13 L2
Hungerford Somset......18 D6
Hungerford W Berk......34 B11
Hungerford Newtown
  W Berk......34 C10
Hunger Hill Bolton......89 K9
Hunger Hill Lancs......88 G8
Hungerstone Herefs......45 N7
Hungerton Lincs......73 M5
Hungryhatton Shrops......70 B9
Hunmanby N York......99 M5
Hunningham Warwks......59 N14
Hunnington Worcs......58 E8
Hunsbury Hill Nhants......60 F9
Hunsdon Herts......51 K8
Hunsingore N York......97 P10
Hunslet Leeds......91 J4
Hunsonby Cumb......101 Q3
Hunstanton Norfk......75 N2
Hunstanworth Dur......112 D11
Hunsterson Ches E......70 B5
Hunston Suffk......64 D8
Hunston W Susx......15 N6
Hunston Green Suffk......64 D8
Hunstrete BaNES......20 B2
Hunsworth Kirk......90 F5
Hunt End Worcs......47 K2
Hunter's Inn Devon......17 M2
Hunter's Quay Ag & B......124 F2
Huntham Somset......19 K9
Hunthill Lodge Angus......142 H5
Huntingdon Cambs......62 B6
Huntingfield Suffk......65 L1
Huntingford Dorset......20 F9
Huntington C York......98 C9
Huntington Ches W......69 M2
Huntington E Loth......128 D5
Huntington Herefs......45 K4
Huntington Herefs......45 P6
Huntington Staffs......58 E2
Huntingtowerfield P & K......134 D2
Huntley Gloucs......46 D10
Huntly Abers......158 D10
Hunton Hants......22 E6
Hunton Kent......26 B2
Hunton N York......97 J2
Hunton Bridge Herts......50 C10
Hunt's Corner Norfk......64 F4
Huntscott Somset......18 B6
Hunt's Cross Lpool......81 N7
Hunts Green Bucks......35 N4
Hunts Green Warwks......59 J3
Huntsham Devon......18 D10
Huntshaw Devon......17 J7
Huntshaw Cross Devon......17 J7
Huntspill Somset......19 K5
Huntstile Somset......19 J8
Huntworth Somset......19 K8
Hunwick Dur......103 N4
Hunworth Norfk......76 F4
Hurdcott Wilts......21 N8
Hurdsfield Ches E......83 K10
Hurley W & M......35 M8
Hurley Warwks......59 K5
Hurley Bottom W & M......35 M8
Hurley Common Warwks......59 K5
Hurlford E Ayrs......125 M10
Hurlston Green Lancs......88 D8
Hurn Dorset......13 K5
Hursley Hants......22 D9
Hurst Dorset......12 C6

Hurst N York......103 K10
Hurst Somset......19 N11
Hurst Wokham......35 L10
Hurstbourne Priors
  Hants......22 D5
Hurstbourne Tarrant
  Hants......22 C4
Hurst Green E Susx......26 B6
Hurst Green Essex......53 J8
Hurst Green Lancs......89 K3
Hurst Green Surrey......37 K10
Hurst Hill Dudley......58 D6
Hurstley Herefs......45 M5
Hurstpierpoint W Susx......24 G7
Hurstwood Lancs......89 P4
Hurtiso Ork......169 e6
Hurtmore Surrey......23 P5
Hurworth Burn Dur......104 D4
Hurworth-on-Tees
  Darltn......104 B9
Hurworth Place Darltn......103 Q9
Hury Dur......103 J7
Husbands Bosworth
  Leics......60 D4
Husborne Crawley
  C Beds......49 Q7
Husthwaite N York......97 Q6
Hutcherleigh Devon......7 K8
Hutcliffe Wood
  Crematorium Sheff......84 D4
Hut Green N York......91 P6
Huthwaite Notts......84 G9
Huttoft Lincs......87 P5
Hutton Border......129 N9
Hutton Cumb......101 M5
Hutton E R Yk......99 L10
Hutton Essex......37 P2
Hutton Lancs......88 F5
Hutton N Som......19 L3
Hutton Bonville N York......104 B10
Hutton Buscel N York......99 K4
Hutton Conyers N York......97 M6
Hutton Cranswick E R Yk......99 L10
Hutton End Cumb......101 N3
Hutton Hang N York......97 J3
Hutton Henry Dur......104 D3
Hutton-le-Hole N York......98 E2
Hutton Lowcross R & Cl......104 G8
Hutton Magna Dur......103 M8
Hutton Mulgrave
  N York......105 M9
Hutton Roof Cumb......95 M5
Hutton Roof Cumb......101 L4
Hutton Rudby N York......104 E9
Hutton Sessay N York......97 Q5
Hutton Wandesley
  N York......97 R10
Huxham Devon......9 M6
Huxham Green Somset......19 Q7
Huxley Ches W......69 P2
Huyton Knows......81 N6
Hycemoor Cumb......94 B3
Hyde Gloucs......32 G4
Hyde Hants......13 L2
Hyde Tamesd......83 K6
Hyde Heath Bucks......35 P4
Hyde Lea Staffs......70 G11
Hydestile Surrey......23 Q6
Hykeham Moor Lincs......86 B7
Hylands House & Park
  Essex......51 Q10
Hyndford Bridge S Lans......116 C2
Hynish Ag & B......136 B8
Hyssington Powys......56 E6
Hystfield Gloucs......32 C5
Hythe Essex......52 H6
Hythe Hants......14 D5
Hythe Kent......27 L5
Hythe Somset......19 M4
Hythe End W & M......36 B6
Hyton Cumb......94 B3

I

Ibberton Dorset......12 C3
Ible Derbys......84 B9
Ibsley Hants......13 L3
Ibstock Leics......72 C9
Ibstone Bucks......35 L6
Ibthorpe Hants......22 C4
Iburndale N York......105 N9
Ibworth Hants......22 G4
Icelton N Som......31 L11
Ichrachan Ag & B......139 J11
Ickburgh Norfk......75 R11
Ickenham Gt Lon......36 C3
Ickford Bucks......34 H3
Ickham Kent......39 M10
Ickleford Herts......50 E4
Icklesham E Susx......26 E8
Ickleton Cambs......51 L2
Icklingham Suffk......63 N6
Ickornshaw N York......90 B2
Ickwell Green C Beds......61 Q11
Icomb Gloucs......47 P10
Idbury Oxon......47 P11
Iddesleigh Devon......17 K10
Ide Devon......9 L6
Ideford Devon......9 L9
Ide Hill Kent......37 L10
Iden E Susx......26 F7
Iden Green Kent......26 B4
Iden Green Kent......26 D5
Idle C Brad......90 F3
Idless Cnwll......3 L4
Idlicote Warwks......47 Q6
Idmiston Wilts......21 N7
Idole Carmth......42 H11
Idridgehay Derbys......71 P5
Idrigill Highld......152 F5
Idstone Oxon......33 Q8
Iffley Oxon......34 F4
Ifield W Susx......24 G3
Ifold W Susx......23 B4
Iford Bmouth......13 K6
Iford E Susx......25 K9
Ifton Mons......31 N7
Ifton Heath Shrops......69 K7
Ightfield Shrops......69 Q7
Ightham Kent......37 N9
Iken Suffk......65 N10
Ilam Staffs......71 L4
Ilchester Somset......19 P10
Ilderton Nthumb......119 K6
Ilford Gt Lon......37 K3
Ilford Somset......19 L11
Ilfracombe Devon......17 J2
Ilkeston Derbys......72 D2

Ilketshall St Andrew
  Suffk......65 M4
Ilketshall St John Suffk......65 M4
Ilketshall St Lawrence
  Suffk......65 M5
Ilketshall St Margaret
  Suffk......65 L4
Ilkley C Brad......96 H11
Illand Cnwll......5 M4
Illey Dudley......58 E8
Illidge Green Ches E......70 D2
Illingworth Calder......90 D5
Illogan Cnwll......2 H5
Illston on the Hill Leics......73 J11
Ilmer Bucks......35 L3
Ilmington Warwks......47 P6
Ilminster Somset......10 H2
Ilsington Devon......9 J9
Ilsington Dorset......12 C6
Ilston Swans......28 G6
Ilton N York......97 J5
Ilton Somset......19 L11
Imachar N Ayrs......120 G3
Immingham NE Lin......93 L8
Immingham Dock NE Lin......93 L7
Impington Cambs......62 F8
Ince Ches W......81 P9
Ince Blundell Sefton......81 L4
Ince-in-Makerfield
  Wigan......82 C4
Inchbae Lodge Hotel
  Highld......155 M4
Inchbare Angus......143 L4
Inchberry Moray......157 Q8
Incheril Highld......154 D5
Inchinnan Rens......125 M4
Inchlaggan Highld......146 F7
Inchmichael P & K......134 G2
Inchmore Highld......155 Q8
Inchnacardoch Hotel
  Highld......147 K5
Inchnadamph Highld......161 M2
Inchture P & K......134 H2
Inchvuilt Highld......154 H10
Inchyra P & K......134 F3
Indian Queens Cnwll......4 E10
Ingatestone Essex......51 P11
Ingbirchworth Barns......90 H9
Ingerthorpe N York......97 L7
Ingestre Staffs......71 H10
Ingham Lincs......86 B4
Ingham Norfk......77 M6
Ingham Suffk......64 B9
Ingham Corner Norfk......77 M6
Ingleborough Norfk......75 J7
Ingleby Derbys......72 A5
Ingleby Arncliffe
  N York......104 D10
Ingleby Barwick S on T......104 D8
Ingleby Cross N York......104 E10
Ingleby Greenhow
  N York......104 G9
Ingleigh Green Devon......8 F3
Inglesbatch BaNES......20 D2
Inglesham Swindn......33 P5
Ingleston D & G......109 L7
Ingleton Dur......103 N6
Ingleton N York......95 P6
Inglewhite Lancs......88 G3
Ingmanthorpe N York......97 P10
Ingoe Nthumb......112 F6
Ingol Lancs......88 G4
Ingoldisthorpe Norfk......75 N4
Ingoldmells Lincs......87 Q7
Ingoldsby Lincs......73 Q5
Ingram Nthumb......119 K7
Ingrave Essex......37 P2
Ingrow C Brad......90 D3
Ings Cumb......101 M11
Ingst S Glos......31 Q7
Ingthorpe Rutlnd......73 P9
Ingworth Norfk......76 H6
Inkberrow Worcs......47 K3
Inkerman Dur......103 M3
Inkhorn Abers......159 M10
Inkpen W Berk......22 C2
Inkstack Highld......167 N2
Inmarsh Wilts......20 H2
Innellan Ag & B......124 F3
Innerleithen Border......117 L3
Innerleven Fife......135 K7
Innermessan D & G......106 C5
Innerwick E Loth......129 J5
Innesmill Moray......157 P5
Innsworth Gloucs......46 G10
Insch Abers......150 G2
Insh Highld......148 E7
Inskip Lancs......88 F3
Inskip Moss Side Lancs......88 F3
Instow Devon......16 H5
Insworke Cnwll......6 C8
Intake Sheff......84 E4
Inver Abers......149 N6
Inver Highld......163 K10
Inver P & K......141 P9
Inverailort Highld......145 N11
Inveralligin Highld......153 Q6
Inverallochy Abers......159 P4
Inveran Highld......162 D7
Inverarary Ag & B......131 M6
Inverarish Highld......153 K10
Inverarity Angus......142 H9
Inverarnan Stirlg......132 C4
Inverasdale Highld......160 C10
Inverbeg Ag & B......132 C8
Inverbervie Abers......143 Q3
Invercreran House
  Hotel Ag & B......139 J8
Inverdruie Highld......148 F5
Inveresragan Ag & B......138 H10
Inverey Abers......141 K10
Inverfarigaig Highld......147 N3
Inverfolla Ag & B......138 H9
Invergarry Highld......147 J7
Invergeldie P & K......133 L2
Invergloy Highld......146 G10
Invergordon Highld......156 C4
Invergowrie P & K......142 E11
Inverguseran Highld......145 M6
Inverhadden P & K......140 G6
Inverherive Hotel Stirlg......132 D2
Inverie Highld......145 N7
Inverinan Ag & B......131 K4
Inverinate Highld......145 R3
Inverkeilor Angus......143 M8
Inverkeithing Fife......134 E11
Inverkeithny Abers......158 F8
Inverkip Inver......124 G3
Inverkirkaig Highld......160 H3

Inverlael – Kingshurst 277

Inverlael Highld 161 K9
Inverlair Highld 139 Q2
Inverliever Lodge Ag & B 130 H6
Inverlochy Ag & B 131 P2
Invermark Angus 150 C11
Invermoriston Highld 147 L4
Invernaver Highld 166 B4
Inverneill Ag & B 123 P3
Inverness Highld 156 B8
Inverness Airport Highld 156 D7
Inverness Crematorium Highld 156 A9
Invernettie Abers 159 R9
Invernoaden Ag & B 131 N8
Inveroran Hotel Ag & B 139 P9
Inverquharity Angus 142 G6
Inverquhomery Abers 159 P8
Inverroy Highld 146 H11
Inversanda Highld 138 G6
Invershiel Highld 146 A4
Invershin Highld 162 D7
Invershore Highld 167 M9
Inversnaid Hotel Stirlg 132 C6
Inverugie Abers 159 Q8
Inveruglas Ag & B 132 C6
Inveruglass Highld 148 E7
Inverurie Abers 151 K3
Inwardleigh Devon 8 E5
Inworth Essex 52 E8
Iochdar W Isls 168 c13
Iona Ag & B 136 H10
Iping W Susx 23 N10
iPort Logistics Park Donc 91 Q11
Ipplepen Devon 7 L5
Ipsden Oxon 34 H7
Ipstones Staffs 71 J5
Ipswich Suffk 53 L3
Ipswich Crematorium Suffk 53 L2
Irby Wirral 81 K8
Irby in the Marsh Lincs 87 N8
Irby upon Humber NE Lin 93 L10
Irchester Nhants 61 K7
Ireby Cumb 100 H3
Ireby Lancs 95 P5
Ireland C Beds 50 D2
Ireleth Cumb 94 E5
Ireshopeburn Dur 102 G3
Ireton Wood Derbys 71 P5
Irlam Salfd 82 F6
Irnham Lincs 73 Q5
Iron Acton S Glos 32 C8
Iron Bridge Cambs 75 J11
Ironbridge Wrekin 57 M4
Ironbridge Gorge Wrekin 57 M4
Iron Cross Warwks 47 L4
Ironmacannie D & G 108 E5
Irons Bottom Surrey 36 F11
Ironville Derbys 84 F10
Irstead Norfk 77 M7
Irthington Cumb 111 J8
Irthlingborough Nhants 61 K6
Irton N York 99 L4
Irvine N Ayrs 125 J10
Isauld Highld 166 G3
Isbister Shet 169 q4
Isbister Shet 169 s7
Isfield E Susx 25 K7
Isham Nhants 61 J6
Isington Hants 23 L6
Islandpool Worcs 58 C8
Islay Ag & B 122 E4
Islay Airport Ag & B 122 D9
Isle Abbotts Somset 19 L10
Isle Brewers Somset 19 L10
Isleham Cambs 63 K6
Isle of Dogs Gt Lon 37 J5
Isle of Grain Medway 38 E6
Isle of Lewis W Isls 168 i4
Isle of Man IoM 80 e4
Isle of Man Ronaldsway Airport IoM 80 c8
Isle of Mull Ag & B 137 Q8
Isle of Purbeck Dorset 12 H8
Isle of Sheppey Kent 38 G8
Isle of Skye Highld 152 G10
Isle of Thanet Kent 39 P8
Isle of Walney Cumb 94 D7
Isle of Whithorn D & G 107 N10
Isle of Wight IoW 14 F9
Isle of Wight Crematorium IoW 14 F8
Isleornsay Highld 145 M5
Isles of Scilly IoS 2 c2
Isles of Scilly St Mary's Airport IoS 2 c2
Islesteps D & G 109 L6
Islet Village Guern 10 c1
Isleworth Gt Lon 36 E5
Isley Walton Leics 72 C6
Islibhig W Isls 168 f5
Islington Gt Lon 36 H4
Islington Crematorium Gt Lon 36 G2
Islip Nhants 61 L5
Islip Oxon 34 F2
Islivig W Isls 168 f5
Isombridge Wrekin 57 L2
Istead Rise Kent 37 P6
Itchen Abbas Hants 22 F8
Itchen Stoke Hants 22 G8
Itchingfield W Susx 24 D5
Itchington S Glos 32 C7
Itteringham Norfk 76 G5
Itton Devon 8 G5
Itton Mons 31 N5
Itton Common Mons 31 N5
Ivegill Cumb 101 M2
Ivelet N York 102 H11
Iver Bucks 36 B4
Iver Heath Bucks 36 B4
Iveston Dur 112 H10
Ivinghoe Bucks 49 P11
Ivinghoe Aston Bucks 49 Q11
Ivington Herefs 45 P3
Ivington Green Herefs 45 P3
Ivybridge Devon 6 G7
Ivychurch Kent 26 H6
Ivy Cross Dorset 20 G10
Ivy Hatch Kent 37 N10
Ivy Todd Norfk 76 B10
Iwade Kent 38 F8
Iwerne Courtney Dorset 12 E2
Iwerne Minster Dorset 12 E2
Ixworth Suffk 64 C7
Ixworth Thorpe Suffk 64 C7

J

Jack Green Lancs 88 H5
Jack Hill N York 97 J10
Jack-in-the-Green Devon 9 P5
Jack's Bush Hants 21 Q7
Jacksdale Notts 84 F10
Jackson Bridge Kirk 90 F9
Jackton S Lans 125 P7
Jacobstow Cnwll 5 K2
Jacobstowe Devon 8 E4
Jacobs Well Surrey 23 Q4
Jameston Pembks 41 L11
Jamestown Highld 155 N6
Jamestown W Duns 132 D11
Janetstown Highld 167 L10
Janetstown Highld 167 Q6
Jardine Hall D & G 109 P3
Jarrow S Tyne 113 M8
Jarvis Brook E Susx 25 M5
Jasper's Green Essex 52 B6
Jawcraig Falk 126 E2
Jaywick Essex 53 L9
Jealott's Hill Br For 35 N10
Jeater Houses N York 97 P2
Jedburgh Border 118 B6
Jeffreyston Pembks 41 L9
Jemimaville Highld 156 C4
Jerbourg Guern 10 c2
Jersey Jersey 11 b1
Jersey Airport Jersey 11 a2
Jersey Crematorium Jersey 11 b2
Jersey Marine Neath 29 K6
Jerusalem Lincs 86 B6
Jesmond N u Ty 113 L7
Jevington E Susx 25 N10
Jingle Street Mons 31 N2
Jockey End Herts 50 B8
Jodrell Bank Ches E 82 G10
Johnby Cumb 101 M4
John Lennon Airport Lpool 81 N8
John o' Groats Highld 167 Q2
Johns Cross E Susx 26 B7
Johnshaven Abers 143 P4
Johnson Street Norfk 77 M8
Johnston Pembks 40 H8
Johnstone D & G 117 J10
Johnstone Rens 125 L5
Johnstonebridge D & G 109 P2
Johnstown Carmth 42 G11
Johnstown Wrexhm 69 K5
Joppa C Edin 127 Q3
Joppa Cerdgn 54 D11
Joppa S Ayrs 114 H4
Jordans Bucks 35 Q6
Jordanston Pembks 40 H4
Jordanthorpe Sheff 84 E4
Joyden's Wood Kent 37 M6
Jubilee Corner Kent 26 D2
Jump Barns 91 K10
Jumper's Town E Susx 25 L4
Juniper Nthumb 112 D9
Juniper Green C Edin 127 M4
Jura Ag & B 122 H3
Jurassic Coast Devon 10 G7
Jurby IoM 80 e2
Jurston Devon 8 G8

K

Kaber Cumb 102 E8
Kaimend S Lans 126 H8
Kames Ag & B 124 B3
Kames E Ayrs 115 N2
Kea Cnwll 3 L5
Keadby N Linc 92 D8
Keal Cotes Lincs 87 L8
Kearby Town End N York 97 M11
Kearsley Bolton 82 G4
Kearsley Nthumb 112 F5
Kearsney Kent 27 N3
Kearstwick Cumb 95 N5
Kearton N York 103 J11
Keasden N York 95 Q7
Keaton Devon 6 G8
Keckwick Halton 82 C8
Keddington Lincs 87 K3
Keddington Corner Lincs 87 L3
Kedington Suffk 63 M11
Kedleston Derbys 71 Q6
Keelby Lincs 93 L8
Keele Staffs 70 E5
Keele Services Staffs 70 E6
Keele University Staffs 70 E5
Keeley Green Bed 61 M11
Keelham C Brad 90 D4
Keeres Green Essex 51 N8
Keeston Pembks 40 H7
Keevil Wilts 20 H3
Kegworth Leics 72 D5
Kehelland Cnwll 2 G5
Keig Abers 150 G4
Keighley C Brad 90 D2
Keighley Crematorium C Brad 90 C3
Keilarsbrae Clacks 133 P9
Keillour P & K 134 B2
Keiloch Abers 149 M9
Keils Ag & B 122 H6
Keinton Mandeville Somset 19 P8
Keir Mill D & G 109 J2
Keirsleywell Row Nthumb 111 Q10
Keisby Lincs 73 Q5
Keisley Cumb 102 D6
Keiss Highld 167 P4
Keith Moray 158 B7
Keithick P & K 142 C10
Keithock Angus 143 L5
Keithtown Highld 155 P6
Kelbrook Lancs 89 Q2
Kelby Lincs 73 Q2
Keld Cumb 101 Q8
Keld N York 102 G10
Keld Head N York 98 F4
Keldholme N York 98 E3
Kelfield N Linc 92 D10
Kelfield N York 91 P3
Kelham Notts 85 N9
Kelhead D & G 109 P7
Kellacott Devon 5 Q4
Kellamergh Lancs 88 E5
Kellas Angus 142 H10
Kellas Moray 157 M7
Kellaton Devon 7 L11
Kelleth Cumb 102 C9
Kelling Norfk 76 F3
Kellington N York 91 P6
Kelloe Dur 104 B3
Kelloholm D & G 115 P5
Kells Cumb 100 C7
Kelly Devon 5 P5
Kelly Bray Cnwll 5 P7
Kelmarsh Nhants 60 F5
Kelmscott Oxon 33 P5
Kelsale Suffk 65 M8
Kelsall Ches W 81 Q11
Kelshall Herts 50 H3
Kelsick Cumb 110 C10
Kelso Border 118 D4
Kelstedge Derbys 84 D8
Kelstern Lincs 86 H3
Kelsterton Flints 81 K10
Kelston BaNES 32 D11
Keltneyburn P & K 141 J8
Kelton D & G 109 L6
Kelty Fife 134 E9
Kelvedon Essex 52 E8
Kelvedon Hatch Essex 51 N11
Kelynack Cnwll 2 B8
Kemacott Devon 17 M2
Kemback Fife 135 L5
Kemberton Shrops 57 N4
Kemble Gloucs 33 J5
Kemble Wick Gloucs 33 J5
Kemerton Worcs 47 J7
Kemeys Commander Mons 31 K4
Kemnay Abers 151 J4
Kempe's Corner Kent 26 H2
Kempley Gloucs 46 C9
Kempley Green Gloucs 46 C9
Kempsey Worcs 46 F5
Kempsford Gloucs 33 N5
Kemps Green Warwks 58 H10
Kempshott Hants 22 H4
Kempston Bed 61 M11
Kempston Hardwick Bed 50 B2
Kempton Shrops 56 F8
Kemp Town Br & H 24 H10
Kemsing Kent 37 N9
Kemsley Kent 38 F8
Kemsley Street Kent 38 D9
Kenardington Kent 26 G5
Kenchester Herefs 45 N6
Kencot Oxon 33 Q4
Kendal Cumb 95 L2
Kenderchurch Herefs 45 N9
Kendleshire S Glos 32 C9
Kenfig Brdgnd 29 M8
Kenfig Hill Brdgnd 29 M8
Kenilworth Warwks 59 L10
Kenley Gt Lon 36 H8
Kenley Shrops 57 K4
Kenmore Highld 153 P6
Kenmore P & K 141 J8
Kenn Devon 9 M7
Kenn N Som 31 M11
Kennacraig Ag & B 123 P7
Kennall Vale Cnwll 3 J6
Kennards House Cnwll 5 M5
Kenneggy Cnwll 2 F8
Kennerleigh Devon 9 K3
Kennessee Green Sefton 81 M4
Kennet Clacks 133 Q9
Kennethmont Abers 150 E2
Kennett Cambs 63 L7
Kennford Devon 9 M7
Kenninghall Norfk 64 E4
Kennington Kent 26 H2
Kennington Oxon 34 F4
Kennoway Fife 135 K7
Kenny Somset 19 K11
Kenny Hill Suffk 63 L5
Kennythorpe N York 98 F7
Kenovay Ag & B 136 B6
Kensaleyre Highld 152 G7
Kensington Gt Lon 36 G5
Kensington Palace Gt Lon 36 G4
Kensworth Common C Beds 50 B7
Kentallen Highld 139 J6
Kent and Sussex Crematorium Kent 25 N3
Kentchurch Herefs 45 N9
Kentford Suffk 63 M7
Kent Green Ches E 70 E3
Kentisbeare Devon 9 Q3
Kentisbury Devon 17 L3
Kentisbury Ford Devon 17 L3
Kentish Town Gt Lon 36 G4
Kentmere Cumb 101 N10
Kenton Devon 9 N8
Kenton Gt Lon 36 E3
Kenton N u Ty 113 K7
Kenton Suffk 64 H8
Kenton Bankfoot N u Ty 113 K7
Kentra Highld 138 B4
Kents Bank Cumb 94 H5
Kent's Green Gloucs 46 D10
Kent's Oak Hants 22 B10
Kent Street E Susx 26 C8
Kent Street Kent 37 Q10
Kenwick Shrops 69 M8
Kenwyn Cnwll 3 L4
Kenyon Warrtn 82 D5
Keoldale Highld 165 J3
Keppoch Highld 145 Q3
Kepwick N York 97 Q2
Keresley Covtry 59 M8
Kermincham Ches E 82 H11
Kernborough Devon 7 K10
Kerne Bridge Herefs 46 A11
Kerrera Ag & B 130 G2
Kerridge Ches E 83 K9
Kerridge-end Ches E 83 K9
Kerris Cnwll 2 C8
Kerry Powys 55 Q6
Kerrycroy Ag & B 124 E5
Kersall Notts 85 M8
Kersbrook Devon 9 Q8
Kerscott Devon 17 L6
Kersey Suffk 52 H3
Kersey Tye Suffk 52 G3
Kersey Upland Suffk 52 G3
Kershader W Isls 168 i5
Kershopefoot Cumb 111 J4
Kersoe Worcs 47 J6
Kerswell Devon 10 B3
Kerswell Green Worcs 46 G5
Kerthen Wood Cnwll 2 F7
Kesgrave Suffk 53 M2
Kessingland Suffk 65 Q4
Kessingland Beach Suffk 65 Q4
Kestle Cnwll 3 P4
Kestle Mill Cnwll 4 C10
Keston Gt Lon 37 K8
Keswick Cumb 101 J6
Keswick Norfk 77 J11
Ketsby Lincs 87 L5
Kettering Nhants 61 J5
Kettering Crematorium Nhants 61 J5
Ketteringham Norfk 76 H11
Kettins P & K 142 C10
Kettlebaston Suffk 64 D11
Kettlebridge Fife 135 J6
Kettlebrook Staffs 59 K4
Kettleburgh Suffk 65 K9
Kettle Green Herts 51 K7
Kettleholm D & G 109 P5
Kettleness N York 105 M7
Kettleshulme Ches E 83 L9
Kettlesing N York 97 K9
Kettlesing Bottom N York 97 K9
Kettlestone Norfk 76 D5
Kettlethorpe Lincs 85 P5
Kettletoft Ork 169 f3
Kettlewell N York 96 E6
Ketton Rutlnd 73 P10
Kew Gt Lon 36 E5
Kew Royal Botanic Gardens Gt Lon 36 E5
Kewstoke N Som 19 K2
Kexbrough Barns 91 J9
Kexby C York 98 E10
Kexby Lincs 85 Q3
Key Green Ches E 70 F2
Key Green N York 105 M10
Keyham Leics 72 H9
Keyhaven Hants 13 P6
Keyingham E R Yk 93 M5
Keymer W Susx 24 H7
Keynsham BaNES 32 C11
Keysoe Bed 61 N8
Keysoe Row Bed 61 N8
Keyston Cambs 61 M5
Key Street Kent 38 E9
Keyworth Notts 72 G4
Kibbear Somset 18 H10
Kibblesworth Gatesd 113 K9
Kibworth Beauchamp Leics 60 E2
Kibworth Harcourt Leics 60 E2
Kidbrooke Gt Lon 37 K5
Kidburngill Cumb 100 E6
Kiddemore Green Staffs 58 C3
Kidderminster Worcs 58 B9
Kiddington Oxon 48 D10
Kidd's Moor Norfk 76 G11
Kidlington Oxon 34 E2
Kidmore End Oxon 35 J9
Kidsdale D & G 107 M10
Kidsgrove Staffs 70 E4
Kidstones N York 96 E4
Kidwelly Carmth 28 D3
Kiel Crofts Ag & B 138 G10
Kielder Nthumb 111 M2
Kielder Forest 111 M3
Kiells Ag & B 122 F6
Kilbarchan Rens 125 L5
Kilbeg Highld 145 L6
Kilberry Ag & B 123 M7
Kilbirnie N Ayrs 125 J7
Kilbride Ag & B 123 M4
Kilbride Ag & B 124 C4
Kilbuiack Moray 157 K5
Kilburn Derbys 84 E11
Kilburn Gt Lon 36 F4
Kilburn N York 97 R5
Kilby Leics 72 G11
Kilchamaig Ag & B 123 P7
Kilchattan Ag & B 124 E7
Kilchattan Ag & B 136 b2
Kilcheran Ag & B 138 E10
Kilchoan Highld 137 M3
Kilchoman Ag & B 122 B7
Kilchrenan Ag & B 131 L3
Kilconquhar Fife 135 M7
Kilcot Gloucs 46 C9
Kilcoy Highld 155 Q7
Kilcreggan Ag & B 131 Q11
Kildale N York 104 H9
Kildalloig Ag & B 120 E8
Kildary Highld 156 D3
Kildavaig Ag & B 124 B4
Kildavanan Ag & B 124 C4
Kildonan Highld 163 L2
Kildonan N Ayrs 121 K7
Kildonan Lodge Highld 163 L2
Kildonnan Highld 144 G10
Kildrochet House D & G 106 E6
Kildrummy Abers 150 D4
Kildwick N York 96 F11
Kilfinan Ag & B 124 A2
Kilfinnan Highld 146 H8
Kilford Denbgs 80 F11
Kilgetty Pembks 41 M9
Kilgrammie S Ayrs 114 E7
Kilgwrrwg Common Mons 31 N5
Kilham E R Yk 99 M8
Kilham Nthumb 118 G4
Kilkenneth Ag & B 136 A7
Kilkenzie Ag & B 120 C7
Kilkerran Ag & B 120 D8
Kilkhampton Cnwll 16 D9
Killamarsh Derbys 84 G4
Killay Swans 28 H6
Killearn Stirlg 132 G10
Killen Highld 156 B6
Killerby Darltn 103 N7
Killerton Devon 9 N4
Killichonan P & K 140 D6
Killiechonate Highld 146 G11
Killiechronan Ag & B 137 N7
Killiecrankie P & K 141 M5
Killilan Highld 154 B11
Killimster Highld 167 P5
Killin Stirlg 140 E11
Killinghall N York 97 L9
Killington Cumb 95 N3
Killington Devon 17 M2
Killington Lake Services Cumb 95 M2
Killingworth N Tyne 113 L6
Killiow Cnwll 3 L5
Killochyett Border 128 D10
Kilmacolm Inver 125 K3
Kilmahog Stirlg 133 J6
Kilmahumaig Ag & B 130 F9
Kilmaluag Highld 152 G3
Kilmany Fife 135 K3
Kilmarnock E Ayrs 125 L10
Kilmartin Ag & B 130 G8
Kilmaurs E Ayrs 125 L9
Kilmelford Ag & B 130 H5
Kilmersdon Somset 20 C4
Kilmeston Hants 22 G9
Kilmichael Ag & B 120 C7
Kilmichael Glassary Ag & B 130 H9
Kilmichael of Inverlussa Ag & B 130 F10
Kilmington Devon 10 F5
Kilmington Wilts 20 E7
Kilmington Common Wilts 20 E7
Kilmington Street Wilts 20 E7
Kilmorack Highld 155 N9
Kilmore Ag & B 130 H2
Kilmore Highld 145 L6
Kilmory Ag & B 123 M5
Kilmory Highld 137 N1
Kilmory N Ayrs 121 J7
Kilmuir Highld 152 D8
Kilmuir Highld 152 F3
Kilmuir Highld 156 B8
Kilmuir Highld 156 D3
Kilmun Ag & B 131 P11
Kilnave Ag & B 122 C5
Kilncadzow S Lans 126 F8
Kilndown Kent 26 B4
Kiln Green Wokham 35 M9
Kilnhill Cumb 100 H4
Kilnhouses Ches W 82 D11
Kilnhurst Rothm 91 M11
Kilninver Ag & B 130 G3
Kiln Pit Hill Nthumb 112 F9
Kilnsea E R Yk 93 R7
Kilnsey N York 96 E7
Kilnwick E R Yk 99 K11
Kilnwick Percy E R Yk 98 G11
Kiloran Ag & B 136 b2
Kilpatrick N Ayrs 120 H6
Kilpeck Herefs 45 N8
Kilpin E R Yk 92 C5
Kilpin Pike E R Yk 92 C5
Kilrenny Fife 135 P7
Kilsby Nhants 60 C6
Kilspindie P & K 134 G2
Kilstay D & G 106 F10
Kilsyth N Lans 126 C2
Kiltarlity Highld 155 P9
Kilton R & Cl 105 K7
Kilton Thorpe R & Cl 105 J7
Kilvaxter Highld 152 F4
Kilve Somset 18 F6
Kilvington Notts 73 L2
Kilwinning N Ayrs 125 J9
Kimberley Norfk 76 F11
Kimberley Notts 72 D2
Kimberworth Rothm 84 F2
Kimblesworth Dur 113 L11
Kimble Wick Bucks 35 M3
Kimbolton Cambs 61 P7
Kimbolton Herefs 45 Q2
Kimcote Leics 60 C3
Kimmeridge Dorset 12 F9
Kimmerston Nthumb 119 J3
Kimpton Hants 21 Q5
Kimpton Herts 50 E7
Kimworthy Devon 16 E9
Kinbrace Highld 166 E10
Kinbuck Stirlg 133 M6
Kincaple Fife 135 M4
Kincardine Fife 133 Q10
Kincardine Highld 162 E9
Kincardine Bridge Fife 133 Q10
Kincardine O'Neil Abers 150 F8
Kinclaven P & K 142 B10
Kincorth C Aber 151 N7
Kincorth House Moray 157 J5
Kincraig Highld 148 E6
Kincraigie P & K 141 N8
Kindallachan P & K 141 N8
Kinerarach Ag & B 123 L9
Kineton Gloucs 47 L9
Kineton Warwks 48 B4
Kinfauns P & K 134 F3
Kingarth Ag & B 124 D6
Kingcausie Abers 151 M8
Kingcoed Mons 31 M3
Kingerby Lincs 86 E2
Kingford Devon 16 D10
Kingham Oxon 47 Q10
Kingholm Quay D & G 109 L6
Kinghorn Fife 134 H10
Kinglassie Fife 134 G8
Kingoodie P & K 135 J2
King's Acre Herefs 45 P6
Kingsand Cnwll 6 C8
Kingsash Bucks 35 N3
Kingsbarns Fife 135 P5
Kingsbridge Devon 7 J10
Kingsbridge Somset 18 C7
Kings Bridge Swans 28 G5
King's Bromley Staffs 71 L11
Kingsburgh Highld 152 F6
Kingsbury Gt Lon 36 E3
Kingsbury Warwks 59 K5
Kingsbury Episcopi Somset 19 M10
King's Caple Herefs 45 R9
Kingsclere Hants 22 F3
King's Cliffe Nhants 73 Q11
Kings Clipstone Notts 85 K8
Kingscote Gloucs 32 F5
Kingscott Devon 17 J8
King's Coughton Warwks 47 L3
Kingscross N Ayrs 121 K6
Kingsdon Somset 19 P9
Kingsdown Kent 27 Q2
Kingsdown Swindn 33 N7
Kingsdown Wilts 32 F11
Kingsdown Crematorium Swindn 33 N7
Kingseat Abers 151 N4
Kingseat Fife 134 E9
Kingsey Bucks 35 K3
Kingsfold W Susx 24 E3
Kingsford C Aber 151 M6
Kingsford E Ayrs 125 L8
Kingsford Worcs 57 Q8
Kingsgate Kent 39 Q7
Kings Green Gloucs 46 E8
Kingshall Street Suffk 64 C9
Kingsheanton Devon 17 K4
King's Heath Birm 58 G8
Kings Hill Kent 37 Q9
King's Hill Wsall 58 E5
Kings House Hotel Highld 139 P7
Kingshouse Hotel Stirlg 132 H3
Kingshurst Solhll 59 J7

Kingside Hill Cumb 110 C10
Kingskerswell Devon 7 M5
Kingskettle Fife 135 J6
Kingsland Dorset 11 K5
Kingsland Herefs 45 N2
Kingsland IoA 78 D8
Kings Langley Herts 50 C10
Kingsley Ches W 82 C10
Kingsley Hants 23 L1
Kingsley Staffs 71 J5
Kingsley Green W Susx 23 N8
Kingsley Park Nhants 60 G8
Kingslow Shrops 57 P5
King's Lynn Norfk 75 M6
Kings Meaburn Cumb 102 B6
Kingsmead Hants 14 G4
King's Mills Guern 10 b2
King's Moss St Hel 81 Q4
Kingsmuir Angus 142 H8
Kings Muir Border 117 K3
Kingsmuir Fife 135 N6
Kings Newnham Warwks 59 N4
King's Newton Derbys 72 B5
Kingsnorth Kent 26 H4
King's Norton Birm 58 G9
King's Norton Leics 72 H10
Kings Nympton Devon 17 M8
King's Pyon Herefs 45 N4
Kings Ripton Cambs 62 C5
King's Somborne Hants 22 C8
King's Stag Dorset 11 Q2
King's Stanley Gloucs 32 F4
King's Sutton Nhants 48 E7
Kingstanding Birm 58 G6
Kingsteignton Devon 7 M4
King Sterndale Derbys 83 N10
Kingsthorne Herefs 45 P8
Kingsthorpe Nhants 60 G8
Kingston Cambs 62 D9
Kingston Cnwll 5 P6
Kingston Devon 6 G9
Kingston Devon 9 Q7
Kingston Dorset 12 C3
Kingston Dorset 12 G9
Kingston E Loth 128 E3
Kingston Hants 13 K4
Kingston IoW 14 E10
Kingston Kent 39 L1
Kingston W Susx 24 C10
Kingston Bagpuize Oxon 34 D5
Kingston Blount Oxon 35 K6
Kingston Deverill Wilts 20 F7
Kingstone Herefs 45 N7
Kingstone Somset 10 H2
Kingstone Staffs 71 K9
Kingstone Winslow
   Oxon 33 Q7
Kingston Lacy House &
   Gardens Dorset 12 G4
Kingston Lisle Oxon 34 B7
Kingston near Lewes
   E Susx 25 J9
Kingston on Soar Notts 72 E5
Kingston on Spey Moray 157 Q4
Kingston Russell Dorset 11 M6
Kingston St Mary
   Somset 18 H9
Kingston Seymour
   N Som 31 M11
Kingston Stert Oxon 35 K4
Kingston upon Hull
   C KuH 93 J5
Kingston upon Thames
   Gt Lon 36 E7
Kingston upon Thames
   Crematorium Gt Lon 36 E7
King's Walden Herts 50 E6
Kingswear Devon 7 M8
Kingswells C Aber 151 M6
Kings Weston Bristl 31 P9
Kingswinford Dudley 58 C7
Kingswood Bucks 49 J11
Kingswood Gloucs 32 D6
Kingswood Kent 38 D11
Kingswood Powys 56 C4
Kingswood S Glos 32 B10
Kingswood Somset 18 F7
Kingswood Surrey 36 F9
Kingswood Warwks 59 J10
Kingswood Brook
   Warwks 59 J10
Kingswood Common
   Herefs 45 K4
Kingswood Common
   Staffs 58 B4
Kings Worthy Hants 22 E8
Kingthorpe Lincs 86 F5
Kington Herefs 45 K3
Kington S Glos 32 B6
Kington Worcs 47 J3
Kington Langley Wilts 32 H9
Kington Magna Dorset 20 E10
Kington St Michael Wilts 32 H9
Kingussie Highld 148 D7
Kingweston Somset 19 P8
Kinharrachie Abers 159 M11
Kinharvie D & G 109 K7
Kinkell Bridge P & K 133 Q4
Kinknockie Abers 159 P9
Kinleith C Edin 127 M4
Kinlet Shrops 57 N8
Kinloch Highld 144 F8
Kinloch Highld 164 H10
Kinloch Highld 165 N6
Kinloch P & K 142 A9
Kinlochard Stirlg 132 F7
Kinlochbervie Highld 164 F5
Kinlocheil Highld 138 H2
Kinlochewe Highld 154 D5
Kinloch Hourn Highld 146 B6
Kinlochlaggan Highld 147 N10
Kinlochleven Highld 139 M5
Kinlochmoidart Highld 138 C3
Kinlochnanuagh Highld 145 M11
Kinloch Rannoch P & K 140 C2
Kinloss Moray 157 K5
Kinmel Bay Conwy 80 D8
Kinmuck Abers 151 L4
Kinmundy Abers 151 M4
Kinnabus Ag & B 122 C11
Kinnadie Abers 159 N9
Kinnaird P & K 141 N6
Kinneff Abers 143 Q2
Kinnelhead D & G 116 E10
Kinnell Angus 143 L7
Kinnerley Shrops 69 K10
Kinnersley Herefs 45 L5
Kinnersley Worcs 46 G6
Kinnerton Powys 45 J2
Kinnerton Shrops 56 F5

Kinnerton Green Flints 69 K2
Kinnesswood P & K 134 F7
Kininvie Dur 103 L6
Kinnordy Angus 142 F6
Kinoulton Notts 72 H4
Kinross P & K 134 E7
Kinrossie P & K 142 B11
Kinross Services P & K 134 E7
Kinsbourne Green Herts 50 D7
Kinsey Heath Ches E 70 B6
Kinsham Herefs 56 F11
Kinsham Worcs 46 H7
Kinsley Wakefd 91 L8
Kintail Highld 146 B4
Kintbury W Berk 34 C11
Kintessack Moray 157 J5
Kintillo P & K 134 E4
Kinton Herefs 56 G10
Kinton Shrops 69 L11
Kintore Abers 151 K4
Kintour Ag & B 122 G9
Kintra Ag & B 122 D10
Kintra Ag & B 137 J10
Kintraw Ag & B 130 G7
Kintyre Ag & B 120 D4
Kinveachy Highld 148 G4
Kinver Staffs 58 B8
Kiplin N York 103 Q11
Kippax Leeds 91 L4
Kippen Stirlg 133 J9
Kippford D & G 108 H10
Kipping's Cross Kent 25 P2
Kirbister Ork 169 c6
Kirby Bedon Norfk 77 K10
Kirby Bellars Leics 73 J7
Kirby Cane Norfk 65 M3
Kirby Corner Covtry 59 L9
Kirby Cross Essex 53 M7
Kirby Fields Leics 72 E10
Kirby Grindalythe N York 99 J7
Kirby Hill N York 97 N7
Kirby Hill N York 103 M9
Kirby Knowle N York 97 Q3
Kirby-le-Soken Essex 53 M7
Kirby Misperton N York 98 F5
Kirby Muxloe Leics 72 E10
Kirby Sigston N York 97 P2
Kirby Underdale E R Yk 98 G9
Kirby Wiske N York 97 N4
Kirdford W Susx 24 B5
Kirk Highld 167 N5
Kirkabister Shet 169 r10
Kirkandrews D & G 108 D11
Kirkandrews upon
   Eden Cumb 110 G9
Kirkbampton Cumb 110 F9
Kirkbean D & G 109 L9
Kirk Bramwith Donc 91 Q8
Kirkbride Cumb 110 D9
Kirkbridge N York 97 L2
Kirkbuddo Angus 143 J9
Kirkburn Border 117 K3
Kirkburn E R Yk 99 K9
Kirkburton Kirk 90 F8
Kirkby Knows 81 N5
Kirkby Lincs 86 E2
Kirkby N York 104 F9
Kirkby Fleetham N York 97 L2
Kirkby Green Lincs 86 E9
Kirkby-in-Ashfield Notts 84 H9
Kirkby-in-Furness Cumb 94 E4
Kirkby la Thorpe Lincs 86 E11
Kirkby Lonsdale Cumb 95 N5
Kirkby Malham N York 96 C8
Kirkby Mallory Leics 72 D10
Kirkby Malzeard N York 97 K6
Kirkby Mills N York 98 E3
Kirkbymoorside N York 98 D3
Kirkby on Bain Lincs 86 H8
Kirkby Overblow N York 97 M11
Kirkby Stephen Cumb 102 E9
Kirkby Thore Cumb 102 B5
Kirkby Underwood Lincs 73 R5
Kirkby Wharf N York 91 N2
Kirkby Woodhouse
   Notts 84 G10
Kirkcaldy Fife 134 H9
Kirkcaldy Crematorium
   Fife 134 H9
Kirkcambeck Cumb 111 K7
Kirkchrist D & G 108 E10
Kirkcolm D & G 106 D4
Kirkconnel D & G 115 P5
Kirkconnell D & G 109 L7
Kirkcowan D & G 107 K5
Kirkcudbright D & G 108 E10
Kirkdale Lpool 81 L6
Kirk Deighton N York 97 N10
Kirk Ella E R Yk 92 H5
Kirkfieldbank S Lans 116 B2
Kirkgunzeon D & G 109 J7
Kirk Hallam Derbys 72 D2
Kirkham Lancs 88 E4
Kirkham N York 98 E7
Kirkhamgate Wakefd 90 H6
Kirk Hammerton N York 97 Q9
Kirkharle Nthumb 112 F4
Kirkhaugh Nthumb 111 N11
Kirkheaton Kirk 90 F7
Kirkheaton Nthumb 112 F5
Kirkhill Highld 155 Q8
Kirkhope S Lans 116 D9
Kirkhouse Cumb 111 L9
Kirkhouse Green Donc 91 Q8
Kirkibost Highld 145 L4
Kirkinch P & K 142 E9
Kirkinner D & G 107 M7
Kirkintilloch E Duns 126 B3
Kirk Ireton Derbys 71 P4
Kirkland Cumb 100 E7
Kirkland Cumb 102 B4
Kirkland D & G 109 M3
Kirkland D & G 115 P5
Kirkland D & G 115 R9
Kirkland Guards Cumb 100 G2
Kirk Langley Derbys 71 P7
Kirkleatham R & Cl 104 G6
Kirkleatham
   Crematorium R & Cl 104 G6
Kirklevington S on T 104 D9
Kirkley Suffk 65 Q3
Kirklington N York 97 M4
Kirklington Notts 85 L9
Kirklinton Cumb 110 H7
Kirkliston C Edin 127 L3
Kirkmabreck D & G 107 N6
Kirkmaiden D & G 106 F10
Kirk Merrington Dur 103 Q4
Kirk Michael IoM 80 d3
Kirkmichael P & K 141 Q6

Kirkmichael S Ayrs 114 F6
Kirkmuirhill S Lans 126 D9
Kirknewton Nthumb 118 H4
Kirknewton W Loth 127 L4
Kirkney Abers 158 D11
Kirk of Shotts N Lans 126 E5
Kirkoswald Cumb 101 Q2
Kirkoswald S Ayrs 114 D6
Kirkpatrick D & G 109 K2
Kirkpatrick Durham
   D & G 108 G6
Kirkpatrick-Fleming
   D & G 110 E8
Kirk Sandall Donc 91 Q9
Kirksanton Cumb 94 C4
Kirk Smeaton N York 91 N7
Kirkstall Leeds 90 H3
Kirkstead Lincs 86 G8
Kirkstile Abers 158 D10
Kirkstile D & G 110 G2
Kirkstone Pass Inn
   Cumb 101 M9
Kirkstyle Highld 167 P2
Kirkthorpe Wakefd 91 K6
Kirkton Abers 150 G2
Kirkton D & G 109 L4
Kirkton Fife 135 K4
Kirkton Highld 145 P2
Kirkton Highld 154 B9
Kirkton P & K 134 B4
Kirkton Manor Border 117 J3
Kirkton of Airlie Angus 142 E7
Kirkton of
   Auchterhouse Angus 142 E10
Kirkton of Barevan
   Highld 156 E8
Kirkton of Collace P & K 142 B11
Kirkton of Glenbuchat
   Abers 150 B4
Kirkton of Kingoldrum
   Angus 142 E6
Kirkton of Logie
   Buchan Abers 151 P2
Kirkton of Maryculter
   Abers 151 M8
Kirkton of Menmuir
   Angus 143 J5
Kirkton of Monikie
   Angus 143 J10
Kirkton of Rayne Abers 158 G11
Kirkton of Skene Abers 151 L6
Kirkton of Tealing Angus 142 G10
Kirkton of Tough Abers 150 G5
Kirktown Abers 159 N4
Kirktown Abers 159 Q7
Kirktown of Alvah Abers 158 G5
Kirktown of Bourtie
   Abers 151 L2
Kirktown of Fetteresso
   Abers 151 M10
Kirktown of Mortlach
   Moray 157 Q10
Kirktown of Slains Abers 151 Q2
Kirkurd Border 116 G2
Kirkwall Ork 169 d5
Kirkwall Airport Ork 169 d6
Kirkwhelpington
   Nthumb 112 E4
Kirk Yetholm Border 118 F5
Kirmington N Linc 93 K8
Kirmond le Mire Lincs 86 G2
Kirn Ag & B 124 F2
Kirriemuir Angus 142 F7
Kirstead Green Norfk 65 K2
Kirtlebridge D & G 110 D6
Kirtling Cambs 63 L9
Kirtling Green Cambs 63 L9
Kirtlington Oxon 48 E11
Kirtomy Highld 166 B4
Kirton Lincs 74 F3
Kirton Notts 85 L7
Kirton Suffk 53 N3
Kirton End Lincs 74 E2
Kirtonhill W Duns 125 K2
Kirton Holme Lincs 74 E2
Kirton in Lindsey N Linc 92 F11
Kirwaugh D & G 107 M7
Kishorn Highld 153 Q10
Kislingbury Nhants 60 E9
Kitebrook Warwks 47 P8
Kite Green Warwks 59 J11
Kites Hardwick Warwks 59 Q11
Kitleigh Cnwll 5 L2
Kitt Green Wigan 88 G9
Kittisford Somset 18 E10
Kittle Swans 28 G7
Kitt's Green Birm 59 J7
Kittybrewster C Aber 151 N6
Kitwood Hants 23 J8
Kivernoll Herefs 45 P8
Kiveton Park Rothm 84 G4
Knaith Lincs 85 P4
Knaith Park Lincs 85 P3
Knap Corner Dorset 20 F10
Knaphill Surrey 23 Q3
Knapp Somset 19 K9
Knapp Hill Hants 22 D10
Knapthorpe Notts 85 M9
Knapton C York 98 B10
Knapton N York 98 H5
Knapton Norfk 77 L5
Knapton Green Herefs 45 N4
Knapwell Cambs 62 D8
Knaresborough N York 97 N9
Knarsdale Nthumb 111 N10
Knaven Abers 159 L9
Knayton N York 97 P3
Knebworth Herts 50 G6
Knedlington E R Yk 92 B5
Kneesall Notts 85 M8
Kneesworth Cambs 62 F11
Kneeton Notts 85 M11
Knelston Swans 28 E7
Knenhall Staffs 70 G7
Knettishall Suffk 64 D5
Knightacott Devon 17 M4
Knightcote Warwks 48 D4
Knightley Staffs 70 E9
Knightley Dale Staffs 70 E10
Knighton C Leic 72 G10
Knighton Devon 6 E9
Knighton Dorset 11 N2
Knighton Poole 12 H5
Knighton Powys 56 D10
Knighton Somset 18 G6
Knighton Staffs 70 C7
Knighton Staffs 70 D9
Knighton on Teme
   Worcs 57 L11
Knightsbridge Gloucs 46 G9
Knightsmill Cnwll 4 H5

Knightwick Worcs 46 D3
Knill Herefs 45 K3
Knipoch Ag & B 130 G3
Knipton Leics 73 L4
Knitsley Dur 112 H11
Kniveton Derbys 71 N4
Knock Cumb 102 C5
Knock Highld 145 L6
Knock Moray 158 D7
Knock W Isls 168 j4
Knockally Highld 167 K11
Knockan Highld 161 L4
Knockando Moray 157 M9
Knockbain Highld 155 Q9
Knockbain Highld 156 A6
Knock Castle N Ayrs 124 F5
Knockdee Highld 167 L4
Knockdow Ag & B 124 E3
Knockdown Wilts 32 F7
Knockeen S Ayrs 114 F8
Knockenkelly N Ayrs 121 K6
Knockentiber E Ayrs 125 L10
Knockhall Kent 37 N6
Knockholt Kent 37 L9
Knockholt Pound Kent 37 L9
Knockin Shrops 69 K10
Knockinlaw E Ayrs 125 L10
Knockmill Kent 37 N8
Knocknain D & G 106 C5
Knockrome Ag & B 123 J5
Knocksharry IoM 80 c4
Knocksheen D & G 108 C4
Knockvennie Smithy
   D & G 108 G6
Knodishall Suffk 65 N9
Knodishall Common
   Suffk 65 N9
Knole Somset 19 N9
Knole Park S Glos 31 Q8
Knolls Green Ches E 82 H9
Knolton Wrexhm 69 L7
Knook Wilts 20 H6
Knossington Leics 73 L9
Knott End-on-Sea Lancs 94 H11
Knotting Bed 61 M8
Knotting Green Bed 61 M8
Knottingley Wakefd 91 N6
Knotty Ash Lpool 81 N6
Knotty Green Bucks 35 P6
Knowbury Shrops 57 K9
Knowe D & G 107 K3
Knowehead D & G 115 M9
Knoweside S Ayrs 114 E5
Knowle Bristl 32 B10
Knowle Devon 9 J4
Knowle Devon 9 P3
Knowle Devon 16 H4
Knowle Shrops 57 K10
Knowle Solhll 59 J9
Knowle Somset 18 C6
Knowle Cross Devon 9 P5
Knowlefield Cumb 110 H9
Knowle Green Lancs 89 J3
Knowle Hill Surrey 35 Q10
Knowle St Giles Somset 10 G2
Knowle Village Hants 14 G5
Knowle Wood Calder 89 Q6
Knowl Green Essex 52 C3
Knowl Hill W & M 35 M9
Knowlton Dorset 12 H3
Knowlton Kent 39 N11
Knowsley Knows 81 N5
Knowsley Safari Park
   Knows 81 P6
Knowstone Devon 17 Q7
Knox N York 97 L9
Knox Bridge Kent 26 C3
Knoydart Highld 145 P7
Knuckles Powys 56 D10
Knuston Nhants 61 K7
Knutsford Ches E 82 G9
Knutsford Services
   Ches E 82 F9
Knutton Staffs 70 E5
Krumlin Calder 90 D7
Kuggar Cnwll 3 J10
Kyleakin Highld 145 N2
Kyle of Lochalsh Highld 145 N2
Kylerhea Highld 145 N3
Kylesku Highld 164 F10
Kylesmorar Highld 145 P9
Kyles Scalpay W Isls 168 h8
Kylestrome Highld 164 F10
Kynaston Herefs 46 B7
Kynaston Shrops 69 L10
Kynnersley Wrekin 70 B11
Kyre Green Worcs 46 B2
Kyre Park Worcs 46 B2
Kyrewood Worcs 57 K11
Kyrle Somset 18 E10

L

La Bellieuse Guern 10 b2
Lacasaigh W Isls 168 i5
Lacasdal W Isls 168 j4
Laceby NE Lin 93 M9
Lacey Green Bucks 35 M4
Lach Dennis Ches W 82 F10
Lackenby R & Cl 104 G7
Lackford Suffk 63 N6
Lackford Green Suffk 63 N6
Lacock Wilts 32 H11
Ladbroke Warwks 48 D3
Ladderedge Staffs 70 H4
Laddingford Kent 37 Q11
Lade Bank Lincs 87 L10
Ladock Cnwll 3 M3
Lady Ork 169 f2
Ladybank Fife 135 J6
Ladycross Cnwll 5 P5
Ladygill S Lans 116 C5
Lady Hall Cumb 94 E3
Ladykirk Border 129 M10
Ladyridge Herefs 46 A8
Lady's Green Suffk 63 N9
Ladywood Birm 58 G7
Ladywood Worcs 46 G2
La Fontenelle Guern 10 c1
La Fosse Guern 10 b2
Lag D & G 109 J3
Laga Highld 138 A5
Lagavulin Ag & B 122 F10
Lagg N Ayrs 121 J7
Laggan Highld 146 H8
Laggan Highld 147 P2
Lagganlia Highld 148 F7
La Greve Guern 10 c1

La Grève de Lecq Jersey 11 a1
La Hougue Bie Jersey 11 c2
La Houguette Guern 10 b2
Laid Highld 165 K5
Laide Highld 160 E8
Laig Highld 144 G10
Laigh Clunch E Ayrs 125 K4
Laigh Fenwick E Ayrs 125 M9
Laigh Glenmuir E Ayrs 115 M3
Laighstonehall S Lans 126 C7
Laindon Essex 37 Q3
Lairg Highld 162 D5
Laisterdyke C Brad 90 F4
Laithes Cumb 101 N4
Lake Devon 8 D7
Lake Devon 17 K5
Lake IoW 14 G10
Lake Wilts 21 M7
Lake District Cumb 100 H8
Lake District National
   Park Cumb 100 H8
Lakenheath Suffk 63 M4
Laker's Green Surrey 24 B3
Lakesend Norfk 75 K11
Lakeside Cumb 94 H3
Laleham Surrey 36 C7
Laleston Brdgnd 29 N9
Lamanva Cnwll 3 K7
Lamarsh Essex 52 E4
Lamas Norfk 77 J7
Lambden Border 118 D2
Lamberhurst Kent 25 Q3
Lamberhurst Down Kent 25 Q3
Lamberton Border 129 P8
Lambeth Gt Lon 36 H5
Lambeth Crematorium
   Gt Lon 36 G6
Lambfair Green Suffk 63 M10
Lambley Notts 85 K11
Lambley Nthumb 111 N9
Lambourn W Berk 34 B9
Lambourne End Essex 37 L2
Lambourn Woodlands
   W Berk 34 B9
Lamb Roe Lancs 89 L3
Lambs Green W Susx 24 F4
Lambston Pembks 40 H7
Lamellion Cnwll 5 L9
Lamerton Devon 8 C9
Lamesley Gatesd 113 L9
Lamington S Lans 116 D4
Lamlash N Ayrs 121 K5
Lamonby Cumb 101 M3
Lamorick Cnwll 4 G9
Lamorna Cnwll 2 C9
Lamorran Cnwll 3 M5
Lampen Cnwll 5 K8
Lampeter Cerdgn 43 L5
Lampeter Velfrey
   Pembks 41 N8
Lamphey Pembks 41 K10
Lamplugh Cumb 100 E6
Lamport Nhants 60 G6
Lamyatt Somset 20 C7
Lana Devon 5 N2
Lana Devon 16 E10
Lanark S Lans 116 B2
Lancaster &
   Morecambe
   Crematorium Lancs 95 K8
Lancaster Services Lancs 95 L10
Lancaut Gloucs 31 P5
Lanchester Dur 113 J11
Lancing W Susx 24 E10
L'Ancresse Guern 10 c1
Landbeach Cambs 62 G7
Landcross Devon 16 H7
Landerberry Abers 151 J7
Landford Wilts 21 Q11
Land-hallow Highld 167 L10
Landican Crematorium
   Wirral 81 K7
Landimore Swans 28 E6
Landkey Devon 17 K5
Landore Swans 29 J5
Landrake Cnwll 5 P9
Landscove Devon 7 K5
Land's End Cnwll 2 A8
Land's End Airport Cnwll 2 B8
Landshipping Pembks 41 K8
Landue Cnwll 5 P6
Landulph Cnwll 6 C7
Landwade Suffk 63 K7
Lane Cnwll 4 C9
Laneast Cnwll 5 L5
Lane Bottom Lancs 89 P3
Lane End Bucks 35 M6
Lane End Cnwll 4 G8
Lane End Hants 22 G9
Lane End Kent 37 N6
Lane End Lancs 96 C11
Lane End Warrtn 82 E6
Lane End Wilts 20 F5
Lane Ends Derbys 71 N8
Lane Ends Lancs 89 M4
Lane Ends N York 90 B2
Lane Green Staffs 58 C4
Laneham Notts 85 P5
Lanehead Dur 102 F2
Lane Head Dur 103 M8
Lanehead Nthumb 111 Q3
Lane Head Wigan 82 D5
Lane Head Wsall 58 E4
Lane Heads Lancs 88 E3
Lanercost Cumb 111 L8
Laneshaw Bridge Lancs 89 Q2
Lane Side Lancs 89 M6
Langaford Devon 16 Q2
Langal Highld 138 C4
Langaller Somset 19 J9
Langar Notts 73 J4
Langbank Rens 125 K3
Langbar N York 96 G10
Langbaurgh N York 104 G8
Langcliffe N York 96 B8
Langdale End N York 99 J2
Langdon Cnwll 5 P4
Langdon Beck Dur 102 G4
Langdown Hants 14 D5
Langdyke Fife 135 J7
Langenhoe Essex 52 H8
Langford C Beds 50 E2
Langford Devon 9 P4
Langford Essex 52 D10
Langford N Som 19 N2
Langford Notts 85 P9
Langford Oxon 33 P4
Langford Budville
   Somset 18 F10
Langham Dorset 20 E8

Langham – Little Bourton 279

Langham Essex 52 H5
Langham Norfk 76 E3
Langham Rutlnd 73 L8
Langham Suffk 64 D8
Langho Lancs 89 L4
Langholm D & G 110 G4
Langland Swans 28 H7
Langlee Border 117 Q3
Langley Ches E 83 K10
Langley Derbys 84 F11
Langley Gloucs 47 K9
Langley Hants 14 D6
Langley Herts 50 F6
Langley Kent 38 D11
Langley Nthumb 112 B8
Langley Oxon 47 Q11
Langley Rochdl 89 P9
Langley Slough 36 B5
Langley Somset 18 E9
Langley W Susx 23 M9
Langley Warwks 47 N2
Langley Burrell Wilts 32 H9
Langley Castle Nthumb 112 B8
Langley Common Derbys 71 P7
Langley Green Derbys 71 P7
Langley Green Essex 52 E7
Langley Green Warwks 47 N2
Langley Heath Kent 38 D11
Langley Lower Green Essex 51 K4
Langley Marsh Somset 18 E9
Langley Mill Derbys 84 F11
Langley Moor Dur 103 Q2
Langley Park Dur 113 K11
Langley Street Norfk 77 M11
Langley Upper Green Essex 51 K4
Langney E Susx 25 P10
Langold Notts 85 J3
Langore Cnwll 5 M4
Langport Somset 19 M9
Langrick Lincs 87 J11
Langridge BaNES 32 D11
Langridgeford Devon 17 K7
Langrigg Cumb 110 C11
Langrish Hants 23 K10
Langsett Barns 90 G10
Langside P & K 133 M5
Langstone Hants 15 K6
Langstone Newpt 31 L7
Langthorne N York 97 K2
Langthorpe N York 97 N7
Langthwaite N York 103 K10
Langtoft E R Yk 99 L7
Langtoft Lincs 74 B8
Langton Dur 103 N7
Langton Lincs 86 H7
Langton Lincs 87 L6
Langton N York 98 F7
Langton by Wragby Lincs 86 F5
Langton Green Kent 25 M3
Langton Green Suffk 64 G7
Langton Herring Dorset 11 N8
Langton Long Blandford Dorset 12 F3
Langton Matravers Dorset 12 H9
Langtree Devon 16 H8
Langtree Week Devon 16 H8
Langwathby Cumb 101 Q4
Langwell House Highld 163 Q2
Langwith Derbys 84 H7
Langwith Junction Derbys 84 H7
Langworth Lincs 86 E5
Lanhydrock House & Gardens Cnwll 4 H9
Lanivet Cnwll 4 G9
Lanjeth Cnwll 3 P3
Lank Cnwll 4 H6
Lanlivery Cnwll 4 H10
Lanner Cnwll 3 J6
Lanoy Cnwll 5 M6
Lanreath Cnwll 5 K10
Lansallos Cnwll 5 K11
Lanteglos Cnwll 4 H5
Lanteglos Highway Cnwll 5 J11
Lanton Border 118 B6
Lanton Nthumb 118 H4
La Passee Guern 10 b1
Lapford Devon 8 H3
Laphroaig Ag & B 122 E10
Lapley Staffs 58 C2
La Pulente Jersey 11 a2
Lapworth Warwks 59 J10
Larachbeg Highld 138 B8
Larbert Falk 133 P11
Larbreck Lancs 88 E2
Largie Abers 158 F11
Largiemore Ag & B 131 J10
Largoward Fife 135 M6
Largs N Ayrs 124 G6
Largybeg N Ayrs 121 K7
Largymore N Ayrs 121 K7
Larkbeare Devon 9 Q5
Larkfield Inver 124 G2
Larkfield Kent 38 B10
Larkhall S Lans 126 D7
Larkhill Wilts 21 M6
Larling Norfk 64 D4
La Rocque Jersey 11 c2
La Rousaillerie Guern 10 b1
Lartington Dur 103 K7
Lasborough Gloucs 32 F6
Lasham Hants 23 J6
Lashbrook Devon 8 B3
Lashbrook Devon 16 G10
Lashenden Kent 26 D3
Lask Edge Staffs 70 G3
Lasswade Mdloth 127 Q4
Lastingham N York 98 E2
Latcham Somset 19 M5
Latchford Herts 51 J6
Latchford Oxon 35 J4
Latchford Warrtn 82 D7
Latchingdon Essex 52 E11
Latchley Cnwll 5 Q7
Lately Common Warrtn 82 E5
Lathbury M Keyn 49 N6
Latheron Highld 167 M10
Latheronwheel Highld 167 L10
Lathones Fife 135 M6
Latimer Bucks 50 B11
Latteridge S Glos 32 C8
Lattiford Somset 20 C9
Latton Wilts 33 L5
Lauder Border 128 E10
Laugharne Carmth 28 B2
Laughterton Lincs 85 P5
Laughton E Susx 25 L8
Laughton Leics 60 E3
Laughton Lincs 74 A4
Laughton Lincs 92 D11
Laughton-en-le-Morthen Rothm 84 H3
Launcells Cnwll 16 C10
Launcells Cross Cnwll 16 D10
Launceston Cnwll 5 N5
Launton Oxon 48 H10
Laurencekirk Abers 143 N3
Laurieston D & G 108 E8
Laurieston Falk 126 G2
Lavendon M Keyn 49 P4
Lavenham Suffk 52 F2
Lavernock V Glam 30 G11
Laversdale Cumb 111 J8
Laverstock Wilts 21 N8
Laverstoke Hants 22 E5
Laverton Gloucs 47 L7
Laverton N York 97 K6
Laverton Somset 20 E4
La Villette Guern 10 b2
Lavister Wrexhm 69 L3
Law S Lans 126 E7
Lawers P & K 140 G10
Lawford Essex 53 J5
Lawford Somset 18 F7
Law Hill S Lans 126 E7
Lawhitton Cnwll 5 P5
Lawkland N York 95 R7
Lawkland Green N York 96 A7
Lawley Wrekin 57 M3
Lawnhead Staffs 70 E9
Lawns Wood Crematorium Leeds 90 H3
Lawrenny Pembks 41 K9
Lawshall Suffk 64 B11
Lawshall Green Suffk 64 B11
Lawton Herefs 45 N3
Laxay W Isls 168 i5
Laxdale W Isls 168 j4
Laxey IoM 80 f5
Laxfield Suffk 65 K7
Laxford Bridge Highld 164 F7
Laxo Shet 169 r7
Laxton E R Yk 92 C5
Laxton Nhants 73 P11
Laxton Notts 85 M7
Laycock C Brad 90 C2
Layer Breton Essex 52 F8
Layer-de-la-Haye Essex 52 G7
Layer Marney Essex 52 F8
Layham Suffk 52 H3
Layland's Green W Berk 34 C11
Laymore Dorset 10 H4
Layter's Green Bucks 35 Q6
Laytham E R Yk 92 B3
Laythes Cumb 110 D9
Lazenby R & Cl 104 G7
Lazonby Cumb 101 P3
Lea Derbys 84 D9
Lea Herefs 46 C10
Lea Lincs 85 P3
Lea Shrops 56 F7
Lea Shrops 56 G3
Lea Wilts 33 J7
Leachkin Highld 156 A9
Leadburn Border 127 N6
Leadenham Lincs 86 B10
Leaden Roding Essex 51 N8
Leadgate Dur 112 H10
Leadgate Nthumb 112 H9
Leadhills S Lans 116 B7
Leadingcross Green Kent 38 E11
Leadmill Derbys 84 B4
Leafield Oxon 48 B11
Leagrave Luton 50 C6
Leahead Ches W 70 B2
Lea Heath Staffs 71 J9
Leake N York 97 P2
Leake Common Side Lincs 87 L10
Lealholm N York 105 L9
Lealholm Side N York 105 L9
Lealt Highld 153 J5
Leam Derbys 84 B5
Lea Marston Warwks 59 K6
Leamington Hastings Warwks 59 P11
Leamington Spa Warwks 59 M11
Leamside Dur 113 M11
Leap Cross E Susx 25 N8
Leasgill Cumb 95 K4
Leasingham Lincs 86 E11
Leasingthorne Dur 103 Q4
Leatherhead Surrey 36 E9
Leathley N York 97 K11
Leaton Shrops 69 N11
Leaton Wrekin 57 L2
Lea Town Lancs 88 F4
Leaveland Kent 38 H11
Leavenheath Suffk 52 G4
Leavening N York 98 F8
Leaves Green Gt Lon 37 K8
Lea Yeat Cumb 95 R3
Lebberston N York 99 M4
Le Bigard Guern 10 b2
Le Bourg Guern 10 b2
Le Bourg Jersey 11 c2
Lechlade on Thames Gloucs 33 P5
Lecht Gruinart Ag & B 122 C6
Leck Lancs 95 N5
Leckbuie P & K 140 H9
Leckford Hants 22 C7
Leckhampstead Bucks 49 K7
Leckhampstead W Berk 34 D9
Leckhampstead Thicket W Berk 34 D9
Leckhampton Gloucs 46 H11
Leckmelm Highld 161 K9
Leckwith V Glam 30 G10
Leconfield E R Yk 92 H2
Ledaig Ag & B 138 G10
Ledburn Bucks 49 P10
Ledbury Herefs 46 D7
Leddington Gloucs 46 C8
Ledgemoor Herefs 45 N4
Ledicot Herefs 45 N2
Ledmore Junction Highld 161 L4
Ledsham Ches W 81 M10
Ledsham Leeds 91 M5
Ledston Leeds 91 L5
Ledstone Devon 7 J9
Ledston Luck Leeds 91 L4
Ledwell Oxon 48 D9
Lee Devon 16 H2
Lee Gt Lon 37 J5
Lee Hants 22 C11
Lee Shrops 69 M8
Leebotwood Shrops 56 H5
Lee Brockhurst Shrops 69 P9
Leece Cumb 94 E7
Lee Chapel Essex 37 Q3
Lee Clump Bucks 35 P4
Lee Common Bucks 35 P4
Leeds Kent 38 D11
Leeds Leeds 90 H4
Leeds Bradford Airport Leeds 90 G2
Leeds Castle Kent 38 D11
Leedstown Cnwll 2 G7
Lee Green Ches E 70 B2
Leek Staffs 70 H3
Leek Wootton Warwks 59 L11
Lee Mill Devon 6 F7
Leeming C Brad 90 C4
Leeming N York 97 L3
Leeming Bar N York 97 L3
Lee Moor Devon 6 F6
Lee-on-the-Solent Hants 14 G6
Lees C Brad 90 C3
Lees Derbys 71 P7
Lees Oldham 83 L4
Lees Green Derbys 71 P7
Leesthorpe Leics 73 K8
Leeswood Flints 69 J2
Leetown P & K 134 G3
Leftwich Ches W 82 E10
Legar Powys 45 J11
Legbourne Lincs 87 L4
Legburthwaite Cumb 101 K7
Legerwood Border 118 A2
Legoland W & M 35 P10
Le Gron Guern 10 b2
Legsby Lincs 86 F3
Le Haguais Jersey 11 c2
Le Hocq Jersey 11 c2
Leicester C Leic 72 F10
Leicester Forest East Leics 72 E10
Leicester Forest East Services Leics 72 E10
Leigh Devon 17 N9
Leigh Dorset 11 N3
Leigh Gloucs 46 G9
Leigh Kent 37 M11
Leigh Shrops 56 E4
Leigh Surrey 36 F11
Leigh Wigan 82 E5
Leigh Wilts 33 L6
Leigh Worcs 46 E4
Leigh Beck Essex 38 D5
Leigh Delamere Wilts 32 G9
Leigh Delamere Services Wilts 32 G9
Leigh Green Kent 26 F5
Leigh Knoweglass S Lans 125 Q7
Leighland Chapel Somset 18 D7
Leigh-on-Sea Sthend 38 D4
Leigh Park Dorset 12 H5
Leigh Park Hants 15 K5
Leigh Sinton Worcs 46 E4
Leighswood Wsall 58 G4
Leighterton Gloucs 32 F6
Leighton N York 97 J5
Leighton Powys 56 C3
Leighton Shrops 57 L3
Leighton Somset 20 D6
Leighton Bromswold Cambs 61 P5
Leighton Buzzard C Beds 49 P9
Leigh upon Mendip Somset 20 C5
Leigh Woods N Som 31 Q10
Leinthall Earls Herefs 56 G11
Leinthall Starkes Herefs 56 G11
Leintwardine Herefs 56 G10
Leire Leics 60 B3
Leiston Suffk 65 N9
Leith C Edin 127 P2
Leitholm Border 118 E2
Lelant Cnwll 2 E6
Lelley E R Yk 93 M4
Lem Hill Worcs 57 N9
Lempitlaw Border 118 E4
Lemreway W Isls 168 i6
Lemsford Herts 50 F8
Lenchwick Worcs 47 K5
Lendalfoot S Ayrs 114 B9
Lendrick Stirlg 132 H6
Lendrum Terrace Abers 159 R9
Lenham Kent 38 E11
Lenham Heath Kent 26 F2
Lenie Highld 147 N2
Lennel Border 118 G2
Lennox Plunton D & G 108 D10
Lennoxtown E Duns 125 Q2
Lent Bucks 35 P8
Lenton C Nott 72 F3
Lenton Lincs 73 Q4
Lenwade Norfk 76 F8
Lenzie E Duns 126 B3
Leochel-Cushnie Abers 150 E5
Leomansley Staffs 58 H3
Leominster Herefs 45 P3
Leonard Stanley Gloucs 32 F4
Leoville Jersey 11 a1
Lepe Hants 14 D7
Lephin Highld 152 B8
Leppington N York 98 F8
Lepton Kirk 90 G7
Lerags Ag & B 130 H2
L'Erée Guern 10 a2
Lerryn Cnwll 5 J10
Lerwick Shet 169 r9
Les Arquêts Guern 10 b2
Lesbury Nthumb 119 P8
Les Hubits Guern 10 c2
Leslie Abers 150 F3
Leslie Fife 134 H7
Les Lohiers Guern 10 b2
Lesmahagow S Lans 126 E10
Les Murchez Guern 10 b2
Lesnewth Cnwll 5 J3
Les Nicolles Guern 10 b2
Les Quartiers Guern 10 c1
Les Quennevais Jersey 11 a2
Les Sages Guern 10 b2
Lessingham Norfk 77 M6
Lessonhall Cumb 110 D10
Lestowder Cnwll 3 K9
Les Villets Guern 10 b2
Leswalt D & G 106 D5
L'Etacq Jersey 11 a1
Letchmore Heath Herts 50 E11
Letchworth Garden City Herts 50 F4
Letcombe Bassett Oxon 34 C8
Letcombe Regis Oxon 34 C7
Letham Angus 143 J8
Letham Border 118 C9
Letham Falk 133 P10
Letham Fife 135 J5
Letham Grange Angus 143 L8
Lethendy P & K 142 A9
Lethenty Abers 150 F3
Lethenty Abers 159 K9
Letheringham Suffk 65 K10
Letheringsett Norfk 76 F4
Lettaford Devon 8 H8
Letterewe Highld 154 C3
Letterfearn Highld 145 Q3
Letterfinlay Lodge Hotel Highld 146 H9
Lettermorar Highld 145 M10
Letters Highld 161 K9
Lettershaw S Lans 116 B6
Letterston Pembks 40 H5
Lettoch Highld 149 J4
Lettoch Highld 157 L11
Letton Herefs 45 L5
Letton Herefs 56 F10
Lett's Green Kent 37 L9
Letty Green Herts 50 G8
Letwell Rothm 85 J3
Leuchars Fife 135 M3
Leumrabhagh W Isls 168 i6
Leurbost W Isls 168 i5
Levalsa Meor Cnwll 3 Q4
Levedale Staffs 70 F11
Level's Green Essex 51 L6
Leven E R Yk 99 N11
Leven Fife 135 K7
Levens Cumb 95 K3
Levens Green Herts 51 J6
Levenshulme Manch 83 J6
Levenwick Shet 169 r11
Leverburgh W Isls 168 f9
Leverington Cambs 74 H8
Leverstock Green Herts 50 C9
Leverton Lincs 87 M11
Le Villocq Guern 10 b1
Levington Suffk 53 M4
Levisham N York 98 G2
Lew Oxon 34 B3
Lewannick Cnwll 5 M5
Lewdown Devon 8 C7
Lewes E Susx 25 K8
Leweston Pembks 40 H6
Lewisham Gt Lon 37 J6
Lewisham Crematorium Gt Lon 37 J6
Lewiston Highld 147 N2
Lewistown Brdgnd 29 P7
Lewis Wych Herefs 45 L3
Lewknor Oxon 35 K5
Leworthy Devon 16 E11
Leworthy Devon 17 M4
Lewson Street Kent 38 G9
Lewth Lancs 88 F3
Lewtrenchard Devon 8 C7
Lexden Essex 52 G6
Lexworthy Somset 19 J7
Ley Cnwll 5 K8
Leybourne Kent 37 Q9
Leyburn N York 96 H2
Leycett Staffs 70 D5
Leygreen Herts 50 E6
Ley Hill Bucks 35 Q4
Leyland Lancs 88 G6
Leyland Green St Hel 82 C4
Leylodge Abers 151 K5
Leys Abers 159 P7
Leys P & K 142 D10
Leysdown-on-Sea Kent 38 H7
Leysmill Angus 143 L8
Leys of Cossans Angus 142 F8
Leysters Herefs 45 R2
Leyton Gt Lon 37 J3
Leytonstone Gt Lon 37 J3
Lezant Cnwll 5 N6
Lezerea Cnwll 2 H7
Lhanbryde Moray 157 P5
Libanus Powys 44 D9
Libberton S Lans 116 D2
Libbery Worcs 47 J3
Liberton C Edin 127 P4
Lichfield Staffs 58 H3
Lichfield & District Crematorium Staffs 59 J2
Lickey Worcs 58 E9
Lickey End Worcs 58 E10
Lickey Rock Worcs 58 E10
Lickfold W Susx 23 P9
Liddaton Green Devon 8 C8
Liddesdale Highld 138 D6
Liddington Swindn 33 P8
Lidgate Derbys 84 D5
Lidgate Suffk 63 M9
Lidget Donc 91 R10
Lidgett Notts 85 K7
Lidham Hill E Susx 26 D8
Lidlington C Beds 49 Q7
Lidsey W Susx 15 P6
Lidsing Kent 38 C9
Liff Angus 142 E11
Lifford Birm 58 G8
Lifton Devon 5 P4
Liftondown Devon 5 P4
Lighthorne Warwks 48 B3
Lighthorne Heath Warwks 48 C3
Lightwater Surrey 23 P2
Lightwater Valley Theme Park N York 97 L5
Lightwood C Stke 70 G6
Lightwood Green Ches E 70 A6
Lightwood Green Wrexhm 69 L6
Lilbourne Nhants 60 C5
Lilburn Tower Nthumb 119 K6
Lilleshall Wrekin 70 C11
Lilley Herts 50 D5
Lilley W Berk 34 D9
Lilliesleaf Border 117 Q5
Lillingstone Dayrell Bucks 49 K7
Lillingstone Lovell Bucks 49 K6
Lillington Dorset 11 N2
Lilliput Poole 12 H7
Lilstock Somset 18 G5
Lilyhurst Shrops 57 N2
Limbrick Lancs 89 J7
Limbury Luton 50 C6
Limebrook Herefs 56 F11
Limefield Bury 89 N8
Limekilnburn S Lans 126 C7
Limekilns Fife 134 D11
Limerigg Falk 126 F3
Limerstone IoW 14 D10
Limestone Brae Nthumb 111 Q11
Lime Street Worcs 46 F8
Limington Somset 19 P10
Limmerhaugh E Ayrs 115 M2
Limpenhoe Norfk 77 M11
Limpley Stoke Wilts 20 E2
Limpsfield Surrey 37 K10
Limpsfield Chart Surrey 37 K10
Linby Notts 84 H10
Linchmere W Susx 23 N8
Lincluden D & G 109 L5
Lincoln Lincs 86 C6
Lincoln Crematorium Lincs 86 C6
Lincomb Worcs 57 Q11
Lincombe Devon 7 J10
Lincombe Devon 16 H2
Lindale Cumb 95 J4
Lindal in Furness Cumb 94 E5
Lindfield W Susx 24 H5
Lindford Hants 23 M7
Lindley Kirk 90 E7
Lindley N York 97 K11
Lindores Fife 134 H4
Lindow End Ches E 82 H9
Lindridge Worcs 57 M11
Lindsell Essex 51 P5
Lindsey Suffk 52 G2
Lindsey Tye Suffk 52 G2
Liney Somset 19 L7
Linford Hants 13 L3
Linford Thurr 37 Q5
Lingbob C Brad 90 D3
Lingdale R & Cl 105 J7
Lingen Herefs 56 F11
Lingfield Surrey 25 J2
Lingwood Norfk 77 M10
Liniclate W Isls 168 c13
Linicro Highld 152 F4
Linkend Worcs 46 F8
Linkenholt Hants 22 C3
Linkhill Kent 26 D6
Linkinhorne Cnwll 5 N7
Linktown Fife 134 H9
Linkwood Moray 157 N5
Linley Shrops 56 F6
Linley Green Herefs 46 C4
Linleygreen Shrops 57 M5
Linlithgow W Loth 126 H2
Linn Crematorium E Rens 125 P6
Linshiels Nthumb 118 G9
Linsidemore Highld 162 C7
Linslade C Beds 49 P9
Linstead Parva Suffk 65 L6
Linstock Cumb 110 H9
Linthurst Worcs 58 E10
Linthwaite Kirk 90 E8
Lintlaw Border 129 L8
Lintmill Moray 158 D4
Linton Border 118 E5
Linton Cambs 63 J11
Linton Derbys 71 P11
Linton Herefs 46 C9
Linton Kent 38 C11
Linton Leeds 97 N11
Linton N York 96 E8
Linton Nthumb 113 L2
Linton Heath Derbys 71 P11
Linton Hill Herefs 46 C10
Linton-on-Ouse N York 97 Q8
Linwood Hants 13 L3
Linwood Lincs 86 F3
Linwood Rens 125 L5
Lionacleit W Isls 168 c13
Lional W Isls 168 k1
Lions Green E Susx 25 N7
Liphook Hants 23 M8
Lipley Shrops 70 C8
Liscard Wirral 81 K6
Liscombe Somset 18 A8
Liskeard Cnwll 5 M9
Lismore Ag & B 138 E9
Liss Hants 23 L9
Lissett E R Yk 99 N9
Liss Forest Hants 23 L9
Lissington Lincs 86 F4
Liston Essex 52 E3
Lisvane Cardif 30 G8
Liswerry Newpt 31 K7
Litcham Norfk 76 B8
Litchard Brdgnd 29 P8
Litchborough Nhants 48 H4
Litchfield Hants 22 E4
Litherland Sefton 81 L5
Litlington Cambs 50 H2
Litlington E Susx 25 M10
Little Abington Cambs 62 H11
Little Addington Nhants 61 L6
Little Airies D & G 107 M8
Little Almshoe Herts 50 F5
Little Alne Warwks 47 M2
Little Altcar Sefton 88 C9
Little Amwell Herts 51 J8
Little Asby Cumb 102 C9
Little Aston Staffs 58 G5
Little Atherfield IoW 14 E11
Little Ayton N York 104 G8
Little Baddow Essex 52 C10
Little Badminton S Glos 32 F8
Little Bampton Cumb 110 E9
Little Bardfield Essex 51 Q4
Little Barford Bed 61 Q9
Little Barningham Norfk 76 G5
Little Barrington Gloucs 33 P2
Little Barrow Ches W 81 P11
Little Barugh N York 98 F5
Little Bavington Nthumb 112 E5
Little Bealings Suffk 53 M2
Littlebeck N York 105 N10
Little Bedwyn Wilts 33 Q11
Little Bentley Essex 53 K6
Little Berkhamsted Herts 50 G9
Little Billing Nhants 60 H8
Little Billington C Beds 49 P10
Little Birch Herefs 45 Q8
Little Bispham Bpool 88 C2
Little Blakenham Suffk 53 K2
Little Blencow Cumb 101 N4
Little Bloxwich Wsall 58 F4
Little Bognor W Susx 24 B6
Little Bolehill Derbys 71 P4
Little Bollington Ches E 82 F7
Little Bookham Surrey 36 D10
Littleborough Devon 9 K2
Littleborough Notts 85 P4
Littleborough Rochdl 89 Q7
Littlebourne Kent 39 M10
Little Bourton Oxon 48 E6

Little Bowden Leics 60 F3
Little Bradley Suffk 63 L10
Little Brampton Herefs 45 L2
Little Brampton Shrops 56 F8
Little Braxted Essex 52 D9
Little Brechin Angus 143 K5
Littlebredy Dorset 11 M7
Little Brickhill M Keyn 49 P8
Little Bridgeford Staffs 70 F9
Little Brington Nhants 60 E8
Little Bromley Essex 53 J6
Little Broughton Cumb 100 E4
Little Budworth Ches W 82 C11
Littleburn Highld 156 A7
Little Burstead Essex 37 Q2
Littlebury Essex 51 M3
Littlebury Green Essex 51 L3
Little Bytham Lincs 73 Q7
Little Canfield Essex 51 N6
Little Carlton Lincs 87 L3
Little Carlton Notts 85 N9
Little Casterton Rutlnd 73 Q9
Little Catwick E R Yk 93 K2
Little Catworth Cambs 61 P6
Little Cawthorpe Lincs 87 L4
Little Chalfont Bucks 35 Q5
Little Chart Kent 26 F2
Little Chesterford Essex 51 M2
Little Cheveney Kent 26 B3
Little Cheverell Wilts 21 J4
Little Chishill Cambs 51 K3
Little Clacton Essex 53 L8
Little Clanfield Oxon 33 Q4
Little Clifton Cumb 100 E6
Little Coates NE Lin 93 M9
Little Comberton Worcs 47 J6
Little Common E Susx 26 B10
Little Comp Kent 37 P9
Little Compton Warwks 47 Q8
Little Corby Cumb 111 J9
Little Cornard Suffk 52 F4
Littlecott Wilts 21 M4
Little Cowarne Herefs 46 B4
Little Coxwell Oxon 33 Q6
Little Crakehall N York 97 K2
Little Cransley Nhants 60 H5
Little Cressingham Norfk 76 B11
Little Crosby Sefton 81 L4
Little Crosthwaite Cumb 100 H5
Little Cubley Derbys 71 M7
Little Dalby Leics 73 K8
Littledean Gloucs 32 C2
Little Dewchurch Herefs 45 Q8
Little Ditton Cambs 63 L9
Little Doward Herefs 45 Q10
Littledown Hants 22 B3
Little Downham Cambs 62 H4
Little Driffield E R Yk 99 L9
Little Dunham Norfk 76 B9
Little Dunkeld P & K 141 P9
Little Dunmow Essex 51 Q6
Little Durnford Wilts 21 M8
Little Easton Essex 51 P6
Little Eaton Derbys 72 B2
Little Ellingham Norfk 64 E2
Little Elm Somset 20 D5
Little Everdon Nhants 60 C9
Little Eversden Cambs 62 E10
Little Faringdon Oxon 33 P4
Little Fencote N York 97 L2
Little Fenton N York 91 N3
Little Fransham Norfk 76 C9
Little Gaddesden Herts 35 Q2
Little Garway Herefs 45 N10
Little Gidding Cambs 61 P4
Little Glemham Suffk 65 L10
Little Gorsley Herefs 46 C10
Little Gransden Cambs 62 C9
Little Green Notts 73 J2
Little Green Somset 20 D5
Little Grimsby Lincs 87 K2
Little Gringley Notts 85 M4
Little Habton N York 98 E5
Little Hadham Herts 51 K6
Little Hale Lincs 74 B2
Little Hallam Derbys 72 D2
Little Hallingbury Essex 51 M7
Littleham Devon 9 P8
Littleham Devon 16 G7
Little Hampden Bucks 35 N4
Littlehampton W Susx 24 B10
Little Hanford Dorset 12 D2
Little Harrowden Nhants 61 J6
Little Haseley Oxon 34 H4
Little Hatfield E R Yk 93 L2
Little Hautbois Norfk 77 K7
Little Haven Pembks 40 G8
Littlehaven W Susx 24 E4
Little Hay Staffs 58 H4
Little Hayfield Derbys 83 M7
Little Haywood Staffs 71 J10
Little Heath Staffs 70 F11
Little Heath W Berk 35 J10
Littlehempston Devon 7 L6
Little Hereford Herefs 57 K11
Little Horkesley Essex 52 G5
Little Hormead Herts 51 K5
Little Horsted E Susx 25 L7
Little Horton C Brad 90 F4
Little Horton Wilts 21 K2
Little Horwood Bucks 49 L8
Little Houghton Barns 91 L9
Little Houghton Nhants 60 H9
Littlehoughton Nthumb 119 P7
Little Hucklow Derbys 83 Q9
Little Hulton Salfd 82 F4
Little Hungerford W Berk 34 F10
Little Hutton N York 97 Q5
Little Irchester Nhants 61 K7
Little Kelk E R Yk 99 M8
Little Keyford Somset 20 E5
Little Kimble Bucks 35 M3
Little Kineton Warwks 48 B4
Little Kingshill Bucks 35 N5
Little Knox D & G 108 H8
Little Langdale Cumb 101 K10
Little Langford Wilts 21 K7
Little Laver Essex 51 M9
Little Leigh Ches W 82 D9
Little Leighs Essex 52 B8
Little Lever Bolton 89 M9
Little Linford M Keyn 49 N6
Little Load Somset 19 N10
Little London Bucks 34 H2
Little London Cambs 74 H11
Little London E Susx 25 N6
Little London Essex 51 L5
Little London Essex 51 Q3
Little London Gloucs 46 D11
Little London Hants 22 C5
Little London Hants 22 H3

Little London Leeds 90 G3
Little London Lincs 74 D6
Little London Lincs 74 H6
Little London Lincs 87 K6
Little London Norfk 75 L6
Little London Powys 55 N7
Little Longstone Derbys 83 Q10
Little Madeley Staffs 70 D5
Little Malvern Worcs 46 E6
Little Mancot Flints 81 L11
Little Maplestead Essex 52 D5
Little Marcle Herefs 46 C7
Little Marland Devon 17 J9
Little Marlow Bucks 35 N7
Little Massingham Norfk 75 Q6
Little Melton Norfk 76 H10
Littlemill Abers 149 Q8
Littlemill Highld 156 G7
Little Mill Mons 31 K4
Little Milton Oxon 34 H4
Little Missenden Bucks 35 P5
Little Mongeham Kent 39 P11
Littlemoor Derbys 84 E8
Little Moor Somset 19 K8
Littlemore Oxon 34 F4
Little Musgrave Cumb 102 E8
Little Ness Shrops 69 M11
Little Neston Ches W 81 K9
Little Newcastle Pembks 41 J5
Little Newsham Dur 103 M7
Little Norton Somset 19 N11
Little Oakley Essex 53 M6
Little Oakley Nhants 61 J3
Little Odell Bed 61 L9
Little Offley Herts 50 D5
Little Ormside Cumb 102 D7
Little Orton Cumb 110 G9
Little Ouse Cambs 63 K3
Little Ouseburn N York 97 P8
Littleover C Derb 72 A4
Little Oxendon Nhants 60 F4
Little Packington Warwks 59 K8
Little Pattenden Kent 26 B2
Little Paxton Cambs 61 Q8
Little Petherick Cnwll 4 E7
Little Plumpton Lancs 88 D4
Little Plumstead Norfk 77 L9
Little Ponton Lincs 73 N4
Littleport Cambs 63 J3
Littleport Bridge Cambs 63 J3
Little Posbrook Hants 14 F6
Little Potheridge Devon 17 J9
Little Preston Leeds 91 K4
Little Preston Nhants 48 G4
Little Raveley Cambs 62 C5
Little Reedness E R Yk 92 D6
Little Ribston N York 97 N10
Little Rissington Gloucs 47 N11
Little Rollright Oxon 47 Q8
Little Rowsley Derbys 84 C7
Little Ryburgh Norfk 76 D6
Little Ryle Nthumb 119 K8
Little Ryton Shrops 56 H4
Little Salkeld Cumb 101 Q3
Little Sampford Essex 51 Q4
Little Sandhurst Br For 23 M2
Little Saredon Staffs 58 D3
Little Saughall Ches W 81 M11
Little Saxham Suffk 63 P8
Little Scatwell Highld 155 L6
Little Shelford Cambs 62 G10
Little Shrewley Warwks 59 K11
Little Silver Devon 9 M3
Little Singleton Lancs 88 D3
Little Skipwith N York 91 R3
Little Smeaton N York 91 N7
Little Snoring Norfk 76 D5
Little Sodbury S Glos 32 E8
Little Sodbury End S Glos 32 D8
Little Somborne Hants 22 C8
Little Somerford Wilts 33 J8
Little Soudley Shrops 70 C9
Little Stainforth N York 96 B7
Little Stainton Darltn 104 B6
Little Stanion Nhants 61 J3
Little Stanney Ches W 81 N10
Little Staughton Bed 61 P8
Little Steeping Lincs 87 M8
Little Stoke Staffs 70 G8
Littlestone-on-Sea Kent 27 J7
Little Stonham Suffk 64 G9
Little Stretton Leics 72 H10
Little Stretton Shrops 56 G6
Little Strickland Cumb 101 Q7
Little Stukeley Cambs 62 B5
Little Sugnall Staffs 70 E8
Little Sutton Ches W 81 M9
Little Sutton Shrops 57 J8
Little Swinburne Nthumb 112 D5
Little Sypland D & G 108 F10
Little Tew Oxon 48 C9
Little Tey Essex 52 E7
Little Thetford Cambs 62 H5
Little Thirkleby N York 97 Q5
Little Thornage Norfk 76 F4
Little Thornton Lancs 88 D2
Little Thorpe Dur 104 D2
Littlethorpe Leics 72 E11
Littlethorpe N York 97 M7
Little Thurlow Suffk 63 L10
Little Thurlow Green Suffk 63 L10
Little Thurrock Thurr 37 P5
Littleton Angus 142 E7
Littleton BaNES 19 Q2
Littleton Ches W 81 N11
Littleton D & G 108 D9
Littleton Dorset 12 E4
Littleton Hants 22 E7
Littleton Somset 19 N8
Littleton Surrey 23 Q5
Littleton Surrey 36 C7
Littleton Drew Wilts 32 F8
Littleton-on-Severn S Glos 31 Q7
Littleton Pannell Wilts 21 K4
Little Torrington Devon 16 H8
Little Totham Essex 52 E9
Little Town Cumb 100 H7
Littletown Dur 104 B2
Little Town Lancs 89 K3
Little Town Warrtn 82 D6
Little Twycross Leics 72 A9
Little Urswick Cumb 94 F6
Little Wakering Essex 38 F4
Little Walden Essex 51 M4
Little Waldingfield Suffk 52 F2
Little Walsingham Norfk 76 C4

Little Waltham Essex 52 B9
Little Warley Essex 37 P2
Little Washbourne Gloucs 47 J8
Little Weighton E R Yk 92 G4
Little Welnetham Suffk 64 B10
Little Welton Lincs 87 K3
Little Wenham Suffk 53 J4
Little Wenlock Wrekin 57 L3
Little Weston Somset 20 B9
Little Whitefield IoW 14 G9
Little Whittingham Green Suffk 65 K6
Little Whittington Nthumb 112 E7
Littlewick Green W & M 35 M9
Little Wilbraham Cambs 62 H9
Littlewindsor Dorset 11 J4
Little Witcombe Gloucs 46 H11
Little Witley Worcs 46 E2
Little Wittenham Oxon 34 G6
Little Wolford Warwks 47 Q7
Littlewood Staffs 58 E3
Little Woodcote Gt Lon 36 G8
Littleworth Bucks 49 N10
Littleworth Oxon 34 B5
Littleworth Staffs 58 F2
Littleworth Staffs 70 G10
Littleworth W Susx 24 E6
Littleworth Worcs 46 G4
Littleworth Worcs 47 J2
Littleworth Common Bucks 35 P7
Little Wratting Suffk 63 L11
Little Wymington Bed 61 L8
Little Wymondley Herts 50 F5
Little Wyrley Staffs 58 F3
Little Wytheford Shrops 69 Q11
Little Yeldham Essex 52 C4
Littley Green Essex 51 Q7
Litton Derbys 83 Q9
Litton N York 96 D6
Litton Somset 19 Q4
Litton Cheney Dorset 11 L6
Liurbost W Isls 168 I5
Liverpool Lpool 81 L6
Liverpool Maritime Mercantile City Lpool 81 L7
Liversedge Kirk 90 F6
Liverton Devon 9 K9
Liverton R & Cl 105 K7
Liverton Mines R & Cl 105 K7
Liverton Street Kent 38 E11
Livingston W Loth 127 K4
Livingston Village W Loth 127 J4
Lixwm Flints 80 H10
Lizard Cnwll 3 J11
Llaingoch IoA 78 C8
Llaithddu Powys 55 P8
Llan Powys 55 K4
Llanaber Gwynd 67 L11
Llanaelhaearn Gwynd 66 F6
Llanafan Cerdgn 54 F10
Llanafan-Fawr Powys 44 D3
Llanafan-fechan Powys 44 D4
Llanallgo IoA 79 H7
Llanarmon Gwynd 66 G7
Llanarmon Dyffryn Ceiriog Wrexhm 68 G8
Llanarmon-yn-Ial Denbgs 68 G3
Llanarth Cerdgn 42 H3
Llanarth Mons 31 L2
Llanarthne Carmth 43 K11
Llanasa Flints 80 G8
Llanbabo IoA 78 F7
Llanbadarn Fawr Cerdgn 54 E8
Llanbadarn Fynydd Powys 55 P9
Llanbadarn-y-garreg Powys 44 G5
Llanbadoc Mons 31 L5
Llanbadrig IoA 78 F6
Llanbeder Newpt 31 L6
Llanbedr Gwynd 67 K9
Llanbedr Powys 44 G5
Llanbedr Powys 45 J10
Llanbedr-Dyffryn-Clwyd Denbgs 68 F3
Llanbedrgoch IoA 79 J8
Llanbedrog Gwynd 66 E8
Llanbedr-y-Cennin Conwy 79 P11
Llanberis Gwynd 67 K2
Llanbethêry V Glam 30 D11
Llanbister Powys 55 Q10
Llanblethian V Glam 30 C10
Llanboidy Carmth 41 P6
Llanbradach Caerph 30 F6
Llanbrynmair Powys 55 K4
Llancadle V Glam 30 D11
Llancarfan V Glam 30 D10
Llancayo Mons 31 L4
Llancloudy Herefs 45 P10
Llancynfelyn Cerdgn 54 E6
Llandaff Cardif 30 G9
Llandanwg Gwynd 67 K9
Llandarcy Neath 29 K5
Llandawke Carmth 41 Q8
Llanddaniel Fab IoA 78 H10
Llanddarog Carmth 43 K11
Llanddeiniol Cerdgn 54 D10
Llanddeiniolen Gwynd 79 J11
Llanddderfel Gwynd 68 C7
Llanddeusant Carmth 43 Q10
Llanddeusant IoA 78 E7
Llanddew Powys 44 F8
Llanddewi Swans 28 E7
Llanddewi Brefi Cerdgn 43 N3
Llanddewi'r Cwm Powys 44 E5
Llanddewi Rhydderch Mons 31 L2
Llanddewi Velfrey Pembks 41 M7
Llanddewi Ystradenni Powys 55 Q11
Llanddoget Conwy 67 Q2
Llanddona IoA 79 K9
Llanddowror Carmth 41 Q8
Llanddulas Conwy 80 C9
Llanddwywe Gwynd 67 K10
Llandecwyn Gwynd 67 L7
Llandefaelog Powys 44 E8
Llandefaelog-Tre'r-Graig Powys 44 G7
Llandefalle Powys 44 F7
Llandegai Gwynd 79 K10
Llandegfan IoA 79 J10
Llandegla Denbgs 68 G4
Llandegley Powys 44 G4

Llandegveth Mons 31 K5
Llandegwning Gwynd 66 D9
Llandeilo Carmth 43 M10
Llandeilo Graban Powys 44 F6
Llandeilo'r Fan Powys 44 B8
Llandenny Mons 31 M4
Llandevaud Newpt 31 M6
Llandevenny Mons 31 M7
Llandinabo Herefs 45 Q9
Llandinam Powys 55 N7
Llandissilio Pembks 41 M6
Llandogo Mons 31 P4
Llandough V Glam 30 C10
Llandough V Glam 30 G10
Llandovery Carmth 43 Q8
Llandow V Glam 29 P10
Llandre Carmth 43 N6
Llandre Cerdgn 54 E7
Llandre Isaf Pembks 41 M5
Llandrillo Denbgs 68 D7
Llandrillo-yn-Rhos Conwy 79 Q8
Llandrindod Wells Powys 44 F2
Llandrinio Powys 69 J11
Llandudno Conwy 79 P8
Llandudno Junction Conwy 79 P9
Llandulas Powys 44 B6
Llandwrog Gwynd 66 H3
Llandybie Carmth 43 M11
Llandyfaelog Carmth 28 Q2
Llandyfriog Cerdgn 42 F6
Llandyfrydog IoA 78 G7
Llandygai Gwynd 79 K10
Llandygwydd Cerdgn 41 P2
Llandynan Denbgs 68 G5
Llandyrnog Denbgs 80 G11
Llandyssil Powys 56 B5
Llandysul Cerdgn 42 H6
Llanedeyrn Cardif 30 H8
Llanedi Carmth 28 G3
Llaneglwys Powys 44 F7
Llanegryn Gwynd 54 E3
Llanegwad Carmth 43 K10
Llaneilian IoA 78 H6
Llanelian-yn-Rhôs Conwy 80 B9
Llanelidan Denbgs 68 F4
Llanelieu Powys 44 H8
Llanellen Mons 31 K2
Llanelli Carmth 28 C4
Llanelli Crematorium Carmth 28 C4
Llanelltyd Gwynd 67 N11
Llanelly Mons 30 H2
Llanelly Hill Mons 30 H2
Llanelwedd Powys 44 E4
Llanenddwyn Gwynd 67 K10
Llanengan Gwynd 66 D9
Llanerch Gwynd 56 A11
Llanerch Powys 56 E6
Llanerchymedd IoA 78 G8
Llanerfyl Powys 55 M3
Llanfachraeth IoA 78 E8
Llanfachreth Gwynd 67 P10
Llanfaelog IoA 78 E10
Llanfaelrhys Gwynd 66 C9
Llanfaenor Mons 45 N11
Llanfaes IoA 79 L9
Llanfaes Powys 44 E9
Llanfaethlu IoA 78 E7
Llanfair Gwynd 67 K9
Llanfair Caereinion Powys 55 Q3
Llanfair Clydogau Cerdgn 43 M4
Llanfair Dyffryn Clwyd Denbgs 68 F3
Llanfairfechan Conwy 79 M10
Llanfair Kilgeddin Mons 31 L3
Llanfair-Nant-Gwyn Pembks 41 N3
Llanfairpwllgwyngyll IoA 79 J10
Llanfair Talhaiarn Conwy 80 C10
Llanfair Waterdine Shrops 56 C9
Llanfairynghornwy IoA 78 E6
Llanfair-yn-Neubwll IoA 78 E9
Llanfallteg Carmth 41 N6
Llanfallteg West Carmth 41 M7
Llanfarian Cerdgn 54 D9
Llanfechain Powys 68 G10
Llanfechell IoA 78 F6
Llanferres Denbgs 68 G2
Llanfflewyn IoA 78 F7
Llanfigael IoA 78 E8
Llanfihangel-ar-arth Carmth 43 J7
Llanfihangel Glyn Myfyr Conwy 68 C5
Llanfihangel Nant Bran Powys 44 C8
Llanfihangel-nant-Melan Powys 44 H3
Llanfihangel Rhydithon Powys 56 B11
Llanfihangel Rogiet Mons 31 N7
Llanfihangel Tal-y-llyn Powys 44 G9
Llanfihangel-uwch-Gwili Carmth 43 J10
Llanfihangel-y-Creuddyn Cerdgn 54 F9
Llanfihangel-yng-Ngwynfa Powys 68 E11
Llanfihangel yn Nhowyn IoA 78 E9
Llanfihangel-y-pennant Gwynd 54 F3
Llanfihangel-y-pennant Gwynd 67 J6
Llanfihangel-y-traethau Gwynd 67 K8
Llanfilo Powys 44 G8
Llanfoist Mons 31 J2
Llanfor Gwynd 68 B7
Llanfrechfa Torfn 31 K6
Llanfrothen Gwynd 67 L6
Llanfrynach Powys 44 F9
Llanfwrog Denbgs 68 F3
Llanfwrog IoA 78 E8
Llanfyllin Powys 68 F11
Llanfynydd Carmth 43 L9
Llanfynydd Flints 69 J3
Llanfyrnach Pembks 41 P4
Llangadfan Powys 55 N2
Llangadog Carmth 28 D3

Llangadog Carmth 43 P9
Llangadwaladr IoA 78 F11
Llangadwaladr Powys 68 G8
Llangaffo IoA 78 G11
Llangain Carmth 42 G11
Llangammarch Wells Powys 44 C5
Llangan V Glam 30 C9
Llangarron Herefs 45 Q10
Llangasty-Talyllyn Powys 44 G9
Llangathen Carmth 43 L10
Llangattock Powys 31 J11
Llangattock Lingoed Mons 45 M10
Llangattock-Vibon-Avel Mons 45 P11
Llangedwyn Powys 68 G10
Llangefni IoA 78 H9
Llangeinor Brdgnd 29 P7
Llangeitho Cerdgn 43 M3
Llangeler Carmth 42 G7
Llangelynin Gwynd 54 D3
Llangendeirne Carmth 28 E2
Llangennech Carmth 28 G4
Llangennith Swans 28 D6
Llangenny Powys 45 J11
Llangernyw Conwy 80 B11
Llangian Gwynd 66 D9
Llangiwg Neath 29 K3
Llangloffan Pembks 40 H4
Llanglydwen Carmth 41 N5
Llangoed IoA 79 L9
Llangoedmor Cerdgn 42 D5
Llangollen Denbgs 68 H6
Llangolman Pembks 41 M5
Llangors Powys 44 G9
Llangovan Mons 31 N3
Llangower Gwynd 68 B8
Llangrannog Cerdgn 42 F4
Llangristiolus IoA 78 G10
Llangrove Herefs 45 Q11
Llangua Mons 45 M9
Llangunllo Powys 56 C10
Llangunnor Carmth 42 H10
Llangurig Powys 55 L9
Llangwm Conwy 68 C6
Llangwm Mons 31 M5
Llangwm Pembks 41 J9
Llangwnnadl Gwynd 66 C8
Llangwyfan Denbgs 80 G11
Llangwyllog IoA 78 G9
Llangwyryfon Cerdgn 54 D10
Llangybi Cerdgn 43 M4
Llangybi Gwynd 66 G6
Llangybi Mons 31 L5
Llangyfelach Swans 28 H5
Llangynhafal Denbgs 68 F2
Llangynidr Powys 44 H11
Llangynin Carmth 41 Q7
Llangynllo Cerdgn 42 G6
Llangynog Carmth 28 B2
Llangynog Powys 68 E9
Llangynwyd Brdgnd 29 N7
Llanhamlach Powys 44 F9
Llanharan Rhondd 30 D8
Llanharry Rhondd 30 D8
Llanhennock Mons 31 L6
Llanhilleth Blae G 30 H3
Llanidan IoA 78 H11
Llanidloes Powys 55 M8
Llaniestyn Gwynd 66 D8
Llanigon Powys 45 J7
Llanilar Cerdgn 54 E9
Llanilid Rhondd 30 C8
Llanina Cerdgn 42 H3
Llanio Cerdgn 43 M3
Llanishen Cardif 30 G8
Llanishen Mons 31 N4

Llanllechid Gwynd 79 L11
Llanlleonfel Powys 44 C4
Llanllowell Mons 31 L5
Llanllugan Powys 55 P4
Llanllwch Carmth 42 G11
Llanllwchaiarn Powys 55 Q6
Llanllwni Carmth 42 J7
Llanllyfni Gwynd 66 H4
Llanmadoc Swans 28 D6
Llanmaes V Glam 30 C11
Llanmartin Newpt 31 L7
Llanmerewig Powys 56 B6
Llanmihangel V Glam 30 C10
Llanmiloe Carmth 41 P9
Llanmorlais Swans 28 F6
Llannefydd Conwy 80 D10
Llannon Carmth 28 F3
Llannor Gwynd 66 F7
Llanon Cerdgn 54 C11
Llanover Mons 31 K3
Llanpumsaint Carmth 42 H9
Llanrhaeadr-ym-Mochnant Powys 68 F9
Llanrhian Pembks 40 F4
Llanrhidian Swans 28 E6
Llanrhos Conwy 79 P8
Llanrhychwyn Conwy 67 P2
Llanrhyddlad IoA 78 E7
Llanrhystud Cerdgn 54 C11
Llanrothal Herefs 45 P11
Llanrug Gwynd 67 J2
Llanrumney Cardif 30 H8
Llanrwst Conwy 67 Q2
Llansadurnen Carmth 41 Q8
Llansadwrn Carmth 43 N8
Llansadwrn IoA 79 K9
Llansaint Carmth 28 C3
Llansamlet Swans 29 J5
Llansanffraid Glan Conwy Conwy 79 Q9
Llansannan Conwy 80 C11
Llansannor V Glam 30 C9
Llansantffraed Powys 44 G10
Llansantffraed-Cwmdeuddwr Powys 55 M11
Llansantffraed-in-Elvel Powys 44 F4
Llansantffraid Cerdgn 54 C11
Llansantffraid-ym-Mechain Powys 68 H10
Llansawel Carmth 43 M7
Llansilin Powys 68 H9
Llansoy Mons 31 M4
Llanspyddid Powys 44 E9
Llanstadwell Pembks 40 H10
Llansteffan Carmth 28 C2
Llanstephan Powys 44 G6
Llantarnam Torfn 31 K6
Llanteg Pembks 41 N8
Llanthewy Skirrid Mons 45 L2
Llanthony Mons 45 K9
Llantilio-Crossenny Mons 31 L2

Llantilio Pertholey Mons....45 L11
Llantood Pembks....41 L9
Llantrisant IoA....78 F8
Llantrisant Mons....31 L5
Llantrisant Rhondd....30 D8
Llantrithyd V Glam....30 D10
Llantwit Fardre Rhondd....30 E7
Llantwit Major V Glam....30 C11
Llantysilio Denbgs....68 G6
Llanuwchllyn Gwynd....68 A8
Llanvaches Newpt....31 M6
Llanvair Discoed Mons....31 M6
Llanvapley Mons....31 L2
Llanvetherine Mons....45 M11
Llanveynoe Herefs....45 L8
Llanvihangel Crucorney Mons....45 L10
Llanvihangel Gobion Mons....31 K3
Llanvihangel-Ystern-Llewern Mons....31 M2
Llanwarne Herefs....45 Q9
Llanwddyn Powys....68 D11
Llanwenarth Mons....31 J2
Llanwenog Cerdgn....43 J5
Llanwern Newpt....31 L7
Llanwinio Carmth....41 Q5
Llanwnda Gwynd....66 H3
Llanwnda Pembks....40 H3
Llanwnnen Cerdgn....43 K5
Llanwnog Powys....55 N6
Llanwonno Rhondd....30 D5
Llanwrda Carmth....43 P8
Llanwrin Powys....54 H4
Llanwrthwl Powys....44 D2
Llanwrtyd Powys....44 B5
Llanwrtyd Wells Powys....44 B5
Llanwyddelan Powys....55 P4
Llanyblodwel Shrops....68 H10
Llanybri Carmth....28 B2
Llanybydder Carmth....43 K6
Llanycefn Pembks....41 L6
Llanychaer Pembks....41 J3
Llanycil Gwynd....68 B8
Llanycrwys Carmth....43 M5
Llanymawddwy Gwynd....68 B11
Llanymynech Powys....69 J10
Llanynghenedl IoA....78 E8
Llanynys Denbgs....68 F2
Llan-y-pwll Wrexhm....69 L4
Llanyre Powys....44 E2
Llanystumdwy Gwynd....66 H7
Llanywern Powys....44 G9
Llawhaden Pembks....41 L7
Llawnt Shrops....68 H4
Llawryglyn Powys....55 L6
Llay Wrexhm....69 K3
Llechcynfarwy IoA....78 F8
Llechfaen Powys....44 F9
Llechrhyd Caerph....30 F3
Llechryd Cerdgn....41 P2
Llechylched IoA....78 E9
Lledrod Cerdgn....54 E10
Lleyn Peninsula Gwynd....66 E7
Llidiardau Gwynd....68 A4
Llidiartnenog Carmth....43 K7
Llidiart-y-parc Denbgs....68 F6
Llithfaen Gwynd....66 F6
Lloc Flints....80 G9
Llowes Powys....44 H6
Llwydcoed Rhondd....30 C4
Llwydcoed Crematorium Rhondd....30 C3
Llwydiarth Powys....68 D11
Llwyn Denbgs....68 E2
Llwyncelyn Cerdgn....42 H3
Llwyndafydd Cerdgn....42 G3
Llwynderw Powys....56 C4
Llwyn-drain Pembks....41 Q4
Llwyn-du Mons....45 K11
Llwyndyrys Gwynd....66 F6
Llwyngwril Gwynd....54 P3
Llwynhendy Carmth....28 F5
Llwynmawr Wrexhm....68 H7
Llwyn-on Myr Td....30 D2
Llwyn-y-brain Carmth....41 N8
Llwyn-y-groes Cerdgn....43 L3
Llwynypia Rhondd....30 C6
Llynclys Shrops....69 J10
Llynfaes IoA....78 G9
Llyn-y-pandy Flints....81 J11
Llysfaen Conwy....80 B9
Llyswen Cerdgn....43 J2
Llyswen Powys....44 G2
Llysworney V Glam....30 C10
Llys-y-frân Pembks....41 K6
Llywel Powys....44 B8
Load Brook Sheff....84 C3
Loan Falk....126 H2
Loanend Nthumb....129 N9
Loanhead Mdloth....127 P4
Loaningfoot D & G....109 L9
Loans S Ayrs....125 J11
Lobb Devon....16 H4
Lobhillcross Devon....8 C7
Lochailort Highld....145 N11
Lochaline Highld....138 B9
Lochans D & G....106 E6
Locharbriggs D & G....109 L4
Lochavich Ag & B....131 J4
Lochawe Ag & B....131 N2
Loch Baghasdail W Isls....168 c16
Lochboisdale W Isls....168 c16
Lochbuie Ag & B....137 Q10
Lochcarron Highld....154 A10
Lochdon Ag & B....138 C11
Lochdonhead Ag & B....138 C11
Lochearnhead Stirlg....132 H3
Lochee C Dund....142 F11
Locheilside Station Highld....138 H2
Lochend Highld....155 Q10
Locheport W Isls....168 d11
Loch Euphoirt W Isls....168 d11
Lochfoot D & G....109 J6
Lochgair Ag & B....131 J9
Lochgelly Fife....134 F9
Lochgilphead Ag & B....130 H10
Lochgoilhead Ag & B....131 Q7
Lochieheads Fife....134 H5
Lochill Moray....157 P9
Lochindorb Lodge Highld....156 H10
Lochinver Highld....160 H2
Loch Lomond and The Trossachs National Park....132 E5
Loch Loyal Lodge Highld....165 P7
Lochluichart Highld....155 K5
Lochmaben D & G....109 N4

Lochmaddy W Isls....168 e11
Loch nam Madadh W Isls....168 e11
Loch Ness Highld....147 N2
Lochore Fife....134 F8
Lochranza N Ayrs....124 A7
Loch Sgioport W Isls....168 d14
Lochside Abers....143 N5
Lochside D & G....109 L5
Lochside Highld....156 E7
Lochslin Highld....163 J10
Lochton S Ayrs....107 J2
Lochty Angus....143 J5
Lochty Fife....135 N6
Lochuisge Highld....138 D6
Lochwinnoch Rens....125 K6
Lochwood D & G....116 F11
Lockengate Cnwll....4 G9
Lockerbie D & G....109 P4
Lockeridge Wilts....33 M11
Lockerley Hants....22 B9
Locking N Som....19 L3
Locking Stumps Warrtn....82 D6
Lockington E R Yk....99 K11
Lockington Leics....72 D5
Lockleywood Shrops....70 B9
Locksbottom Gt Lon....37 K7
Locksgreen IoW....14 D8
Locks Heath Hants....14 F5
Lockton N York....98 G3
Loddington Leics....73 K10
Loddington Nhants....60 H5
Loddiswell Devon....7 J3
Loddon Norfk....65 M2
Lode Cambs....62 H8
Lode Heath Solhll....59 J8
Loders Dorset....11 K6
Lodge Hill Crematorium Birm....58 F8
Lodsworth W Susx....23 P10
Lofthouse Leeds....91 J3
Lofthouse N York....96 H6
Lofthouse Gate Wakefd....91 J6
Loftus R & Cl....105 K7
Logan E Ayrs....115 L3
Loganbeck Cumb....94 D2
Loganlea W Loth....126 H5
Loggerheads Staffs....70 C7
Logie Angus....143 M5
Logie Fife....135 L3
Logie Moray....157 J7
Logie Coldstone Abers....150 C7
Logie Newton Abers....158 G10
Logie Pert Angus....143 M5
Logierait P & K....141 N7
Logierieve Abers....151 N2
Login Carmth....41 N6
Lolworth Cambs....62 E8
Lonbain Highld....153 M7
Londesborough E R Yk....98 H11
London Gt Lon....36 H4
London Apprentice Cnwll....3 Q4
London Beach Kent....26 E4
London Colney Herts....50 E10
Londonderry N York....97 M3
London End Nhants....61 K7
London Gateway Services Gt Lon....36 E2
London Gatwick Airport W Susx....24 G2
London Heathrow Airport Gt Lon....36 C5
London Luton Airport Luton....50 D6
London Oxford Airport Oxon....48 E11
London Southend Airport Essex....38 E4
London Stansted Airport Essex....51 N6
Londonthorpe Lincs....73 P3
London Zoo ZSL Gt Lon....36 G4
Londubh Highld....160 D10
Lonemore Highld....153 P2
Long Ashton N Som....31 P10
Long Bank Worcs....57 P10
Long Bennington Lincs....73 L2
Longbenton N Tyne....113 L7
Longborough Gloucs....47 N9
Long Bredy Dorset....11 M6
Longbridge Birm....58 F9
Longbridge Warwks....47 Q2
Longbridge Deverill Wilts....20 G6
Long Buckby Nhants....60 D7
Longburgh Cumb....110 F9
Longburton Dorset....11 N2
Long Cause Devon....7 K4
Long Clawson Leics....73 J5
Longcliffe Derbys....84 B9
Longcombe Devon....7 L7
Long Common Hants....14 F4
Long Compton Staffs....70 F10
Long Compton Warwks....47 Q8
Longcot Oxon....33 Q6
Long Crendon Bucks....35 J3
Long Crichel Dorset....12 G2
Longcroft Cumb....110 D9
Longcross Surrey....35 Q11
Longden Shrops....56 G3
Longden Common Shrops....56 G3
Long Ditton Surrey....36 E7
Longdon Staffs....58 G2
Longdon Worcs....46 F7
Longdon Green Staffs....58 G2
Longdon Heath Worcs....46 F7
Longdon upon Tern Wrekin....69 R11
Longdown Devon....9 L6
Longdowns Cnwll....3 J7
Long Drax N York....92 A5
Long Duckmanton Derbys....84 F6
Long Eaton Derbys....72 D4
Longfield Kent....37 P7
Longford Covtry....59 N8
Longford Derbys....71 N7
Longford Gloucs....46 F10
Longford Gt Lon....36 C5
Longford Kent....37 M9
Longford Shrops....70 A8
Longford Wrekin....70 C11
Longforgan P & K....134 H2
Longformacus Border....128 H7
Longframlington Nthumb....119 M10
Long Green Ches W....81 P10
Long Green Worcs....46 F8
Longham Dorset....13 J5

Longham Norfk....76 C8
Long Hanborough Oxon....34 D2
Longhaven Abers....159 R10
Long Hedges Lincs....87 L11
Longhirst Nthumb....113 K3
Longhope Gloucs....46 C11
Longhope Ork....169 c7
Longhorsley Nthumb....112 H2
Longhoughton Nthumb....119 P7
Long Itchington Warwks....59 P11
Longlands Cumb....101 J3
Longlane Derbys....71 N7
Long Lawford Warwks....59 Q9
Longleat Safari & Adventure Park Wilts....20 F6
Longlevens Gloucs....46 G11
Longley Calder....90 D6
Longley Kirk....90 E9
Longley Green Worcs....46 D4
Longleys P & K....142 D9
Long Load Somset....19 N10
Longmanhill Abers....158 H5
Long Marston Herts....49 N11
Long Marston N York....97 R10
Long Marston Warwks....47 N5
Long Marton Cumb....102 C6
Long Meadowend Shrops....56 G8
Long Melford Suffk....52 E2
Longmoor Camp Hants....23 L8
Longmorn Moray....157 N6
Longmoss Ches E....83 J10
Long Newnton Gloucs....32 H6
Long Newton Border....118 A5
Long Newton E Loth....128 C7
Longney Gloucs....32 E2
Longniddry E Loth....128 C4
Longnor Shrops....56 H4
Longnor Staffs....71 K2
Longparish Hants....22 D5
Longpark Cumb....110 H8
Long Preston N York....96 B9
Longridge Lancs....89 J3
Longridge Staffs....70 G11
Longridge W Loth....126 G5
Longriggend N Lans....126 E3
Long Riston E R Yk....93 K2
Longrock Cnwll....2 E7
Longsdon Staffs....70 H4
Longshaw Wigan....82 B4
Longside Abers....159 P8
Long Sight Oldham....89 Q9
Longslow Shrops....70 B7
Longstanton Cambs....62 E7
Longstock Hants....22 C7
Longstone Pembks....41 M9
Longstowe Cambs....62 D10
Long Stratton Norfk....64 H3
Long Street M Keyn....49 L5
Longstreet Wilts....21 M4
Long Sutton Hants....23 K5
Long Sutton Lincs....74 H6
Long Sutton Somset....19 N9
Longthorpe C Pete....74 C11
Long Thurlow Suffk....64 E8
Longthwaite Cumb....101 M6
Longton C Stke....70 G6
Longton Lancs....88 F5
Longtown Cumb....110 G7
Longtown Herefs....45 L9
Longueville Jersey....11 c2
Longville in the Dale Shrops....57 J6
Long Waste Wrekin....69 R11
Long Whatton Leics....72 D6
Longwick Bucks....35 L3
Long Wittenham Oxon....34 F6
Longwitton Nthumb....112 G3
Longwood D & G....108 F8
Longwood Shrops....57 L3
Longworth Oxon....34 C5
Longyester E Loth....128 E7
Lôn-las Swans....29 K5
Lonmay Abers....159 P6
Lonmore Highld....152 D8
Looe Cnwll....5 M11
Loose Kent....38 C11
Loosebeare Devon....8 H3
Loosegate Lincs....74 F5
Loosley Row Bucks....35 M4
Lootcherbrae Abers....158 F7
Lopcombe Corner Wilts....21 Q7
Lopen Somset....11 J2
Loppington Shrops....69 N9
Lorbottle Nthumb....119 K9
Lordington W Susx....15 L5
Lordsbridge Norfk....75 J9
Lordshill C Sotn....22 C11
Lords Wood Medway....38 C9
Lornty P & K....142 B8
Loscoe Derbys....84 F11
Loscombe Dorset....11 K5
Losgaintir W Isls....168 f8
Lossiemouth Moray....157 N3
Lostford Shrops....69 R8
Lostock Gralam Ches W....82 E10
Lostock Green Ches W....82 E10
Lostock Hall Lancs....88 G5
Lostock Hall Fold Bolton....89 K9
Lostock Junction Bolton....89 K9
Lostwithiel Cnwll....5 J10
Lothbeg Highld....163 L4
Lothersdale N York....96 E11
Lothmore Highld....163 M4
Loudwater Bucks....35 P6
Loughborough Leics....72 E7
Loughborough Crematorium Leics....72 E7
Loughor Swans....28 G5
Loughton Essex....51 K11
Loughton M Keyn....49 M7
Loughton Shrops....57 L8
Lound Lincs....73 R7
Lound Notts....85 L4
Lound Suffk....65 Q2
Lounston Devon....9 J9
Lount Leics....72 B7
Louth Lincs....87 K3
Loveclough Lancs....89 N5
Lovedean Hants....15 J4
Lover Wilts....21 P10
Loversall Donc....91 P11
Loves Green Essex....51 P10
Lovesome Hill N York....104 C11
Loveston Pembks....41 L9
Lovington Somset....19 Q8
Low Ackworth Wakefd....91 M7
Low Angerton Nthumb....112 G4
Lowbands Gloucs....46 E8
Low Barbeth D & G....106 D4

Low Barlings Lincs....86 E6
Low Bell End N York....105 K11
Low Bentham N York....95 N7
Low Biggins Cumb....95 N5
Low Borrowbridge Cumb....102 B10
Low Bradfield Sheff....84 C2
Low Bradley N York....96 F11
Low Braithwaite Cumb....101 M2
Low Burnham N Linc....92 C10
Low Buston Nthumb....119 P9
Lowca Cumb....100 C6
Low Catton E R Yk....98 E10
Low Conscliffe Darltn....103 Q8
Low Crosby Cumb....110 H9
Lowdham Notts....85 L11
Low Dinsdale Darltn....104 B8
Lowe Shrops....69 N8
Lowe Hill Staffs....70 H3
Low Ellington N York....97 K4
Lower Aisholt Somset....18 H7
Lower Ansty Dorset....12 C4
Lower Apperley Gloucs....46 G9
Lower Arncott Oxon....48 H11
Lower Ashton Devon....9 K8
Lower Assendon Oxon....35 K8
Lower Ballam Lancs....88 D4
Lower Bartle Lancs....88 F4
Lower Basildon W Berk....34 H9
Lower Bearwood Herefs....45 M3
Lower Beeding W Susx....24 F5
Lower Benefield Nhants....61 L3
Lower Bentley Worcs....58 E11
Lower Beobridge Shrops....57 P6
Lower Birchwood Derbys....84 F10
Lower Boddington Nhants....48 E4
Lower Boscaswell Cnwll....2 B7
Lower Bourne Surrey....23 M6
Lower Brailes Warwks....48 B7
Lower Breakish Highld....145 L3
Lower Bredbury Stockp....83 K6
Lower Broadheath Worcs....46 F3
Lower Broxwood Herefs....45 M4
Lower Buckenhill Herefs....46 B8
Lower Bullingham Herefs....45 Q7
Lower Burgate Hants....21 N11
Lower Burrowton Devon....9 P5
Lower Burton Herefs....45 N3
Lower Caldecote C Beds....61 Q11
Lower Cam Gloucs....32 D4
Lower Canada N Som....19 L3
Lower Catesby Nhants....60 B9
Lower Chapel Powys....44 E7
Lower Chicksgrove Wilts....21 J9
Lower Chute Wilts....22 B4
Lower Clapton Gt Lon....36 H3
Lower Clent Worcs....58 D9
Lower Common Hants....23 L2
Lower Creedy Devon....9 K4
Lower Crossings Derbys....83 M8
Lower Cumberworth Kirk....90 G9
Lower Darwen Bl w D....89 K5
Lower Dean Bed....61 N7
Lower Denby Kirk....90 G9
Lower Diabaig Highld....153 P5
Lower Dicker E Susx....25 N8
Lower Dinchope Shrops....56 H8
Lower Down Shrops....56 E8
Lower Dunsforth N York....97 P8
Lower Egleton Herefs....46 B5
Lower Elkstone Staffs....71 K3
Lower Ellastone Staffs....71 L6
Lower End Bucks....35 J3
Lower End M Keyn....49 P7
Lower End Nhants....60 H9
Lower End Nhants....61 J8
Lower Everleigh Wilts....21 N4
Lower Exbury Hants....14 D7
Lower Eythorne Kent....27 N2
Lower Failand N Som....31 P10
Lower Farringdon Hants....23 K7
Lower Feltham Gt Lon....36 C6
Lower Fittleworth W Susx....24 B7
Lower Foxdale IoM....80 C6
Lower Frankton Shrops....69 L8
Lower Freystrop Pembks....41 J8
Lower Froyle Hants....23 L6
Lower Gabwell Devon....7 N5
Lower Gledfield Highld....162 D4
Lower Godney Somset....19 N6
Lower Gornal Dudley....58 D6
Lower Gravenhurst C Beds....50 D3
Lower Green Herts....50 E4
Lower Green Herts....51 K4
Lower Green Kent....25 N2
Lower Green Kent....25 P2
Lower Green Norfk....76 D4
Lower Green Staffs....58 D3
Lower Green Suffk....63 M7
Lower Hacheston Suffk....65 L10
Lower Halliford Surrey....36 C7
Lower Halstock Leigh Dorset....11 L3
Lower Halstow Kent....38 E8
Lower Hamworthy Poole....12 G6
Lower Hardres Kent....39 L11
Lower Harpton Herefs....45 K2
Lower Hartlip Kent....38 D9
Lower Hartshay Derbys....84 E10
Lower Hartwell Bucks....35 J2
Lower Hatton Staffs....70 E7
Lower Hawthwaite Cumb....94 E3
Lower Hergest Herefs....45 K3
Lower Heyford Oxon....48 E10
Lower Heysham Lancs....95 J8
Lower Higham Kent....38 B7
Lower Holbrook Suffk....53 L4
Lower Hordley Shrops....69 K11
Lower Horncroft W Susx....24 B7
Lower Houses Kirk....90 F7
Lower Howsell Worcs....46 E5
Lower Irlam Salfd....82 F6
Lower Kilburn Derbys....72 B2
Lower Kilcott Gloucs....32 E7
Lower Killeyan Ag & B....122 C11
Lower Kingcombe Dorset....11 M5
Lower Kingswood Surrey....36 F10
Lower Kinnerton Ches W....69 K2

Lower Langford N Som....19 N2
Lower Largo Fife....135 L7
Lower Leigh Staffs....71 J7
Lower Lemington Gloucs....47 P8
Lower Llanfadog Powys....55 M11
Lower Lovacott Devon....17 J6
Lower Loxhore Devon....17 L4
Lower Lydbrook Gloucs....46 A11
Lower Lye Herefs....56 G11
Lower Machen Newpt....30 H7
Lower Maes-coed Herefs....45 L8
Lower Mannington Dorset....13 J4
Lower Marston Somset....20 E6
Lower Meend Gloucs....31 Q4
Lower Merridge Somset....18 H8
Lower Middleton Cheney Nhants....48 F6
Lower Milton Somset....19 P5
Lower Moor Worcs....47 J5
Lower Morton S Glos....32 B6
Lower Nazeing Essex....51 J9
Lower Norton Warwks....47 P2
Lower Nyland Dorset....20 E10
Lower Penarth V Glam....30 G11
Lower Penn Staffs....58 C5
Lower Pennington Hants....13 P6
Lower Penwortham Lancs....88 G5
Lower Peover Ches E....82 F10
Lower Place Rochdl....89 Q8
Lower Pollicott Bucks....35 K2
Lower Quinton Warwks....47 N5
Lower Rainham Medway....38 D8
Lower Raydon Suffk....52 H4
Lower Roadwater Somset....18 D7
Lower Salter Lancs....95 N8
Lower Seagry Wilts....33 J8
Lower Sheering Essex....51 L8
Lower Shelton C Beds....49 Q6
Lower Shiplake Oxon....35 L9
Lower Shuckburgh Warwks....48 E2
Lower Slaughter Gloucs....47 N10
Lower Soothill Kirk....90 H6
Lower Soudley Gloucs....32 C3
Lower Standen Kent....27 M3
Lower Stanton St Quintin Wilts....32 H8
Lower Stoke Medway....38 D6
Lower Stone Gloucs....32 C6
Lower Stonnall Staffs....58 G4
Lower Stow Bedon Norfk....64 D3
Lower Street Dorset....12 D5
Lower Street E Susx....26 B9
Lower Street Norfk....77 K4
Lower Street Suffk....63 N10
Lower Street Suffk....64 G11
Lower Stretton Warrtn....82 D8
Lower Stroud Dorset....11 K5
Lower Sundon C Beds....50 C5
Lower Swanwick Hants....14 E5
Lower Swell Gloucs....47 N9
Lower Tadmarton Oxon....48 D7
Lower Tale Devon....9 Q4
Lower Tean Staffs....71 J7
Lower Thurlton Norfk....65 N2
Lower Town Cnwll....2 H8
Lower Town Devon....7 J4
Lower Town Herefs....46 B6
Lower Town Pembks....41 J3
Lower Trebullett Cnwll....5 N6
Lower Treluswell Cnwll....3 K6
Lower Tysoe Warwks....48 B5
Lower Ufford Suffk....65 K11
Lower Upcott Devon....9 L8
Lower Upham Hants....22 F11
Lower Upnor Medway....38 C7
Lower Vexford Somset....18 F7
Lower Walton Warrtn....82 D7
Lower Waterston Dorset....12 B5
Lower Weare Somset....19 M4
Lower Weedon Nhants....60 D9
Lower Welson Herefs....45 K4
Lower Westmancote Worcs....46 H7
Lower Whatcombe Dorset....12 D4
Lower Whatley Somset....20 D5
Lower Whitley Ches W....82 D9
Lower Wick Gloucs....32 D5
Lower Wick Worcs....46 F4
Lower Wield Hants....22 H6
Lower Willingdon E Susx....25 N10
Lower Withington Ches E....82 H11
Lower Woodend Bucks....35 M7
Lower Woodford Wilts....21 M7
Lower Wraxhall Dorset....11 M4
Lower Wyche Worcs....46 E6
Lower Wyke C Brad....90 F5
Lowesby Leics....73 J9
Lowestoft Suffk....65 Q3
Loweswater Cumb....100 F6
Low Fell Gatesd....113 L9
Lowfield Heath W Susx....24 G3
Low Gartachorrans Stirlg....132 F10
Low Gate Nthumb....112 D8
Low Gettbridge Cumb....111 K9
Lowgill Cumb....102 B11
Lowgill Lancs....95 P8
Low Grantley N York....97 K6
Low Green N York....97 K9
Low Habberley Worcs....57 Q9
Low Ham Somset....19 M9
Low Harrogate N York....97 L9
Low Hawsker N York....105 P9
Low Hesket Cumb....111 J11
Low Hutton N York....98 F7
Lowick Cumb....94 F3
Lowick Nhants....61 L4
Lowick Nthumb....119 K3
Lowick Bridge Cumb....94 F3
Lowick Green Cumb....94 F3
Low Knipe Cumb....101 P7
Low Laithe N York....97 J8
Lowlands Dur....103 M5
Lowlands Torfn....31 J5
Low Langton Lincs....86 G5
Low Leighton Derbys....83 M7
Low Lorton Cumb....100 G5
Low Marishes N York....98 G5
Low Marnham Notts....85 P7
Low Middleton Nthumb....119 M3
Low Mill N York....105 J11
Low Moor C Brad....90 F5
Low Moorsley Sundld....113 M11
Low Moresby Cumb....100 C6
Low Newton Cumb....95 J4

Low Row Cumb....100 G2
Low Row Cumb....101 L3
Low Row Cumb....111 L8
Low Row N York....103 J11
Low Salchrie D & G....106 D4
Low Santon N Linc....92 F8
Lowsonford Warwks....59 J11
Low Street Norfk....77 L7
Low Street Thurr....37 Q5
Low Tharston Norfk....64 H2
Lowther Cumb....101 P6
Lowther Castle Cumb....101 P6
Lowthorpe E R Yk....99 M8
Lowton Devon....8 G4
Lowton Somset....18 G11
Lowton Wigan....82 D5
Lowton Common Wigan....82 D5
Lowton St Mary's Wigan....82 D5
Low Torry Fife....134 C10
Low Toynton Lincs....87 J6
Low Valley Barns....91 L10
Low Wood Cumb....94 G4
Low Worsall N York....104 C9
Low Wray Cumb....101 L10
Loxbeare Devon....18 B11
Loxhill Surrey....24 B3
Loxhore Devon....17 L4
Loxhore Cott Devon....17 L4
Loxley Warwks....47 Q4
Loxley Green Staffs....71 K8
Loxter Herefs....46 D6
Loxton N Som....19 L3
Loxwood W Susx....24 B4
Lubenham Leics....60 F3
Lucasgate Lincs....87 M11
Lucas Green Surrey....23 P2
Luccombe Somset....18 B6
Luccombe Village IoW....14 G10
Lucker Nthumb....119 N4
Luckett Cnwll....5 P7
Lucking Street Essex....52 D5
Luckington Wilts....32 F8
Lucklawhill Fife....135 L3
Lucknam Wilts....32 F10
Luckwell Bridge Somset....18 B7
Lucton Herefs....45 N2
Lucy Cross N York....103 P8
Ludag W Isls....168 c16
Ludborough Lincs....93 N11
Ludbrook Devon....6 H8
Ludchurch Pembks....41 M8
Luddenden Calder....90 C5
Luddenden Foot Calder....90 C5
Luddenham Court Kent....38 G9
Luddesdown Kent....37 Q7
Luddington N Linc....92 D7
Luddington Warwks....47 N4
Luddington in the Brook Nhants....61 P4
Ludford Lincs....86 G3
Ludford Shrops....57 J10
Ludgershall Bucks....49 J11
Ludgershall Wilts....21 Q4
Ludgvan Cnwll....2 E7
Ludham Norfk....77 M8
Ludlow Shrops....57 J9
Ludney Somset....10 H2
Ludwell Wilts....20 H10
Ludworth Dur....104 C2
Luffenhall Herts....50 G5
Luffincott Devon....5 N3
Luffness E Loth....128 D4
Lugar E Ayrs....115 L3
Luggate Burn E Loth....128 F5
Luggiebank N Lans....126 D3
Lugton E Ayrs....125 L7
Lugwardine Herefs....45 R6
Luib Highld....145 J2
Luing Ag & B....130 E5
Lulham Herefs....45 N6
Lullington Derbys....59 K2
Lullington E Susx....25 M10
Lullington Somset....20 E4
Lulsgate Bottom N Som....31 P11
Lulsley Worcs....46 D3
Lumb Calder....90 C6
Lumb Lancs....89 N6
Lumbutts Calder....90 B6
Lumby N York....91 M4
Lumphanan Abers....150 F7
Lumphinnans Fife....134 F9
Lumsden Abers....150 D3
Lunan Angus....143 M7
Lunanhead Angus....142 H7
Luncarty P & K....134 D2
Lund E R Yk....99 K11
Lund N York....91 R4
Lundie Angus....142 D10
Lundin Links Fife....135 L7
Lundin Mill Fife....135 L7
Lundy Devon....16 A2
Lundy Green Norfk....65 J3
Lunga Ag & B....130 E6
Lunna Shet....169 r7
Lunsford Kent....37 Q9
Lunsford's Cross E Susx....26 B9
Lunt Sefton....81 L4
Luntley Herefs....45 M3
Luppitt Devon....10 D3
Lupridge Devon....7 J8
Lupset Wakefd....91 J7
Lupton Cumb....95 M4
Lurgashall W Susx....23 P9
Lurley Devon....18 B11
Lusby Lincs....87 K7
Luscombe Devon....7 K7
Luson Devon....6 G8
Luss Ag & B....132 D9
Lussagiven Ag & B....130 C10
Lusta Highld....152 D6
Lustleigh Devon....9 J8
Luston Herefs....45 P2
Luthermuir Abers....143 M4
Luthrie Fife....135 J4
Lutley Dudley....58 D8
Luton Devon....9 M9
Luton Devon....10 B4
Luton Luton....50 C6
Luton Medway....38 C8
Luton Airport Luton....50 D6
Lutterworth Leics....60 B4
Lutton Devon....6 F7
Lutton Devon....6 H6
Lutton Lincs....74 H5
Lutton Nhants....61 P3
Luxborough Somset....18 C7
Luxulyan Cnwll....4 H10
Luxulyan Valley Cnwll....4 H10
Luzley Tamesd....83 L4

Lybster Highld....167 M9
Lydbury North Shrops....56 E7
Lydcott Devon....17 M4
Lydd Kent....26 H7
Lydd Airport Kent....27 J7
Lydden Kent....27 N2
Lydden Kent....39 Q8
Lyddington Rutlnd....73 M11
Lydd-on-Sea Kent....27 J8
Lydeard St Lawrence Somset....18 F8
Lyde Green Hants....23 K3
Lydford Devon....8 D7
Lydford on Fosse Somset....19 Q8
Lydgate Calder....89 Q5
Lydgate Rochdl....90 B7
Lydham Shrops....56 E6
Lydiard Green Wilts....33 L7
Lydiard Millicent Wilts....33 L7
Lydiard Tregoze Swindn....33 M8
Lydiate Sefton....81 M4
Lydiate Ash Worcs....58 E9
Lydlinch Dorset....12 B2
Lydney Gloucs....32 B4
Lydstep Pembks....41 L11
Lye Dudley....58 D8
Lye Cross N Som....19 N2
Lye Green Bucks....35 Q4
Lye Green E Susx....25 M4
Lye Green Warwks....59 J11
Lye Head Worcs....57 P10
Lye's Green Wilts....20 F5
Lyford Oxon....34 C6
Lymbridge Green Kent....27 K3
Lyme Regis Dorset....10 G6
Lyminge Kent....27 L3
Lymington Hants....13 P5
Lyminster W Susx....24 B10
Lymm Warrtn....82 E7
Lymm Services Warrtn....82 E8
Lympne Kent....27 K4
Lympsham Somset....19 K4
Lympstone Devon....9 N8
Lynbridge Devon....17 N2
Lynchat Highld....148 D7
Lynch Green Norfk....76 H10
Lyndhurst Hants....13 P3
Lyndon Rutlnd....73 N10
Lyndon Green Birm....58 H7
Lyne Border....117 J2
Lyne Surrey....36 B7
Lyneal Shrops....69 M8
Lyne Down Herefs....46 B8
Lyneham Devon....9 L9
Lyneham Oxon....47 Q10
Lyneham Wilts....33 K9
Lyneholmford Cumb....111 K6
Lynemouth Nthumb....113 L2
Lyne of Skene Abers....151 K5
Lynesack Dur....103 L5
Lyness Ork....169 c7
Lyng Norfk....76 F8
Lyng Somset....19 K9
Lynmouth Devon....17 N2
Lynn Staffs....58 G4
Lynn Wrekin....70 D11
Lynsted Kent....38 F9
Lynstone Cnwll....16 C10
Lynton Devon....17 N2
Lynton Cross Devon....17 J3
Lyon's Gate Dorset....11 P3
Lyonshall Herefs....45 L3
Lytchett Matravers Dorset....12 F5
Lytchett Minster Dorset....12 G6
Lyth Highld....167 N4
Lytham Lancs....88 D5
Lytham St Anne's Lancs....88 C5
Lythbank Shrops....56 H3
Lythe N York....105 M8
Lythmore Highld....167 J3

M

Mabe Burnthouse Cnwll....3 K7
Mablethorpe Lincs....87 P4
Macclesfield Ches E....83 K10
Macclesfield Crematorium Ches E....83 K10
Macduff Abers....158 H5
Macharioch Ag & B....120 D10
Machen Caerph....30 H7
Machrie N Ayrs....120 G5
Machrihanish Ag & B....120 B7
Machrins Ag & B....136 b3
Machynlleth Powys....54 G4
Machynys Carmth....28 F5
Mackworth Derbys....71 Q7
Macmerry E Loth....128 C5
Maddaford Devon....8 D6
Madderty P & K....134 B3
Maddington Wilts....21 L6
Maddiston Falk....126 G2
Madehurst W Susx....15 Q4
Madeley Staffs....70 D6
Madeley Wrekin....57 M4
Madeley Heath Staffs....70 D5
Madford Devon....10 C2
Madingley Cambs....62 E8
Madley Herefs....45 N7
Madresfield Worcs....46 F5
Madron Cnwll....2 D7
Maenaddwyn IoA....78 H8
Maenan Conwy....79 P11
Maenclochog Pembks....41 L5
Maendy V Glam....30 D9
Maenporth Cnwll....3 K8
Maentwrog Gwynd....67 M6
Maen-y-groes Cerdgn....42 G3
Maer Cnwll....16 C10
Maer Staffs....70 D7
Maerdy Carmth....43 N9
Maerdy Rhondd....30 C5
Maesbrook Shrops....69 K10
Maesbury Shrops....69 K9
Maesbury Marsh Shrops....69 K9
Maes-glas Newpt....31 J7
Maesgwynne Carmth....41 P6
Maeshafn Denbgs....68 H2
Maesllyn Cerdgn....42 G6
Maesmynis Powys....44 E5
Maesmynis Powys....44 E5
Maesteg Brdgnd....29 N6
Maesybont Carmth....43 L11
Maesycwmmer Caerph....30 G6
Magdalen Laver Essex....51 M9
Maggieknockater Moray....157 Q8
Maggots End Essex....51 L5

Magham Down E Susx....25 P8
Maghull Sefton....81 M4
Magna Park Leics....60 B4
Magor Mons....31 M7
Magor Services Mons....31 M7
Maidenbower W Susx....24 G3
Maiden Bradley Wilts....20 F7
Maidencombe Torbay....7 N5
Maidenhayne Devon....10 F5
Maiden Head N Som....31 Q11
Maidenhead W & M....35 N8
Maiden Law Dur....113 J11
Maiden Newton Dorset....11 M5
Maidens S Ayrs....114 D6
Maiden's Green Br For....35 P10
Maidenwell Lincs....87 K5
Maiden Wells Pembks....41 J11
Maidford Nhants....48 H4
Maids Moreton Bucks....49 K7
Maidstone Kent....38 C10
Maidstone Services Kent....38 D10
Maidwell Nhants....60 F5
Mail Shet....169 r9
Maindee Newpt....31 K7
Mainland Ork....169 d6
Mainland Shet....169 r8
Mainsforth Dur....104 B4
Mains of Balhall Angus....143 J5
Mains of Balnakettle Abers....143 L3
Mains of Dalvey Highld....157 L11
Mains of Haulkerton Abers....143 N3
Mains of Lesmoir Abers....150 D2
Mains of Melgunds Angus....143 J6
Mainsriddle D & G....109 K9
Mainstone Shrops....56 D7
Maisemore Gloucs....46 F10
Major's Green Worcs....58 H9
Makeney Derbys....72 B2
Malborough Devon....7 J11
Malcoff Derbys....83 N8
Malden Rushett Gt Lon....36 E8
Maldon Essex....52 E10
Malham N York....96 D8
Maligar Highld....152 H5
Mallaig Highld....145 L8
Mallaigvaig Highld....145 L8
Malleny Mills C Edin....127 M4
Mallows Green Essex....51 L5
Malltraeth IoA....78 G11
Mallwyd Gwynd....55 L2
Malmesbury Wilts....32 H7
Malmsmead Devon....17 P2
Malpas Ches W....69 N5
Malpas Cnwll....3 L5
Malpas Newpt....31 K6
Malshanger Hants....22 G4
Malswick Gloucs....46 D10
Maltby Lincs....87 K4
Maltby Rothm....84 H2
Maltby S on T....104 E8
Maltby le Marsh Lincs....87 N4
Malting Green Essex....52 G7
Maltman's Hill Kent....26 F3
Malton N York....98 F6
Malvern Worcs....46 E5
Malvern Hills....46 E6
Malvern Link Worcs....46 E5
Malvern Wells Worcs....46 E6
Mamble Worcs....57 M10
Mamhilad Mons....31 K4
Manaccan Cnwll....3 K9
Manafon Powys....55 Q4
Manais W Isls....168 g9
Manaton Devon....9 J8
Manby Lincs....87 L3
Mancetter Warwks....59 M5
Manchester Manch....82 H5
Manchester Airport Manch....82 H7
Manchester Crematorium Manch....82 H6
Mancot Flints....81 L11
Mandally Highld....146 H7
Manea Cambs....62 G3
Maney Birm....58 H5
Manfield N York....103 P8
Mangerton Dorset....11 K5
Mangotsfield S Gloucs....32 C9
Mangrove Green Herts....50 D6
Manhay Cnwll....2 H7
Manish W Isls....168 g9
Mankinholes Calder....90 B6
Manley Ches W....81 Q10
Manmoel Caerph....30 G4
Mannal Ag & B....136 B7
Manningford Bohune Wilts....21 M3
Manningford Bruce Wilts....21 M3
Manningham C Brad....90 E3
Mannings Heath W Susx....24 F5
Mannington Dorset....13 J3
Manningtree Essex....53 K5
Mannofield C Aber....151 N7
Manorbier Pembks....41 K10
Manorbier Newton Pembks....41 K10
Manordeilo Carmth....43 N9
Manorhill Border....118 C4
Manorowen Pembks....40 H3
Manor Park Gt Lon....37 K3
Manor Park Crematorium Gt Lon....37 J3
Mansell Gamage Herefs....45 M6
Mansell Lacy Herefs....45 N5
Mansergh Cumb....95 N4
Mansfield E Ayrs....115 M5
Mansfield Notts....84 H8
Mansfield & District Crematorium Notts....84 H9
Mansfield Woodhouse Notts....84 H8
Mansriggs Cumb....94 F4
Manston Dorset....20 F11
Manston Kent....39 P8
Manston Leeds....91 K4
Manswood Dorset....12 G3
Manthorpe Lincs....73 N3
Manthorpe Lincs....73 R7
Manton N Linc....92 F10
Manton Notts....85 K5
Manton Rutlnd....73 M10
Manton Wilts....33 N11
Manuden Essex....51 L5
Manwood Green Essex....51 M8
Maperton Somset....20 C9
Maplebeck Notts....85 M8
Maple Cross Herts....36 B2
Mapledurham Oxon....35 J9

Mapledurwell Hants....23 J4
Maplehurst W Susx....24 E6
Maplescombe Kent....37 N8
Mapleton Derbys....71 M5
Mapleton Kent....37 L11
Mapperley Derbys....72 C2
Mapperley Park C Nott....72 F2
Mapperton Dorset....11 L5
Mappleborough Green Warwks....58 G11
Mappleton E R Yk....93 M2
Mapplewell Barns....91 J8
Mappowder Dorset....12 B3
Marazanvose Cnwll....3 K3
Marazion Cnwll....2 E7
Marbury Ches E....69 Q5
March Cambs....74 H11
March S Lans....116 D8
Marcham Oxon....34 E5
Marchamley Shrops....69 Q9
Marchamley Wood Shrops....69 Q8
Marchington Staffs....71 L8
Marchington Woodlands Staffs....71 L9
Marchros Gwynd....66 E9
Marchwiel Wrexhm....69 L5
Marchwood Hants....14 C4
Marcross V Glam....29 P11
Marden Herefs....45 Q5
Marden Kent....26 B3
Marden Wilts....21 L3
Marden Ash Essex....51 N10
Marden Beech Kent....26 B3
Marden's Hill E Susx....25 M4
Marden Thorn Kent....26 C3
Mardlebury Herts....50 G7
Mardy Mons....45 L11
Marefield Leics....73 J9
Mareham le Fen Lincs....87 J8
Mareham on the Hill Lincs....87 J7
Marehay Derbys....84 E11
Marehill W Susx....24 C7
Maresfield E Susx....25 L6
Marfleet C KuH....93 K5
Marford Wrexhm....69 L3
Margam Neath....29 L7
Margam Crematorium Neath....29 L7
Margaret Marsh Dorset....20 F11
Margaret Roding Essex....51 N8
Margaretting Essex....51 Q10
Margaretting Tye Essex....51 Q10
Margate Kent....39 Q7
Margnaheglish N Ayrs....121 K5
Margrie D & G....108 C10
Margrove Park R & Cl....105 J7
Marham Norfk....75 P9
Marhamchurch Cnwll....16 C11
Marholm C Pete....74 B10
Marian-glas IoA....79 J8
Mariansleigh Devon....17 N7
Marine Town Kent....38 F7
Marionburgh Abers....151 J6
Marishader Highld....152 H5
Maristow Devon....6 D6
Marjoriebanks D & G....109 N4
Mark Somset....19 L5
Markbeech Kent....25 L2
Markby Lincs....87 N5
Mark Causeway Somset....19 L5
Mark Cross E Susx....25 N4
Markeaton C Derb....72 A3
Markeaton Crematorium C Derb....72 A3
Market Bosworth Leics....72 C10
Market Deeping Lincs....74 B8
Market Drayton Shrops....70 B8
Market Harborough Leics....60 F3
Market Lavington Wilts....21 L4
Market Overton Rutlnd....73 M7
Market Rasen Lincs....86 F3
Market Stainton Lincs....86 H5
Market Warsop Notts....85 J7
Market Weighton E R Yk....92 E2
Market Weston Suffk....64 D6
Markfield Leics....72 D9
Markham Caerph....30 G4
Markham Moor Notts....85 M6
Markinch Fife....134 H7
Markington N York....97 L7
Markle E Loth....128 F4
Marksbury BaNES....20 C2
Mark's Corner IoW....14 E8
Marks Tey Essex....52 F7
Markwell Cnwll....5 P10
Markyate Herts....50 C7
Marlborough Wilts....33 N11
Marlbrook Herefs....45 Q4
Marlbrook Worcs....58 E10
Marlcliff Warwks....47 L4
Marldon Devon....7 M6
Marle Green E Susx....25 N7
Marlesford Suffk....65 L10
Marley Kent....39 L11
Marley Kent....39 P11
Marley Green Ches E....69 Q5
Marley Hill Gatesd....113 K9
Marlingford Norfk....76 H10
Marloes Pembks....40 E9
Marlow Bucks....35 M7
Marlow Herefs....56 G9
Marlow Bottom Bucks....35 M7
Marlpit Hill Kent....37 K11
Marlpits E Susx....25 L5
Marlpits E Susx....25 B9
Marlpool Derbys....84 F11
Marnhull Dorset....20 D11
Marple Stockp....83 L7
Marple Bridge Stockp....83 L7
Marr Donc....91 N9
Marrick N York....103 L11
Marros Carmth....41 P9
Marsden Kirk....90 C8
Marsden S Tyne....113 N8
Marsden Height Lancs....89 P3
Marsett N York....96 D3
Marsh Bucks....35 M3
Marsh C Brad....90 C3
Marsh Devon....10 F2
Marshall's Heath Herts....50 E8
Marshalswick Herts....50 D9
Marsham Norfk....76 H7
Marsh Baldon Oxon....34 G5
Marsh Benham W Berk....34 D11
Marshborough Kent....39 P10
Marshbrook Shrops....56 G7
Marshchapel Lincs....93 Q11
Marsh Farm Luton....50 C6

Marshfield Newpt....31 J8
Marshfield S Glos....32 E9
Marshgate Cnwll....5 K3
Marsh Gibbon Bucks....48 H10
Marsh Green Devon....9 P6
Marsh Green Kent....25 K2
Marsh Green Wrekin....57 L2
Marshland St James Norfk....75 K9
Marsh Lane Derbys....84 F5
Marsh Lane Gloucs....31 Q3
Marshside Sefton....88 D7
Marsh Street Somset....18 C6
Marshwood Dorset....10 H5
Marske N York....103 M10
Marske-by-the-Sea R & Cl....104 H6
Marsland Green Wigan....82 E5
Marston Ches W....82 E9
Marston Herefs....45 M3
Marston Lincs....73 M2
Marston Oxon....34 F3
Marston Staffs....58 B2
Marston Staffs....70 G9
Marston Warwks....59 K6
Marston Wilts....21 J3
Marston Green Solhll....59 J7
Marston Jabbet Warwks....59 N7
Marston Magna Somset....19 Q10
Marston Meysey Wilts....33 M5
Marston Montgomery Derbys....71 L7
Marston Moretaine C Beds....49 Q6
Marston on Dove Derbys....71 N9
Marston St Lawrence Nhants....48 F6
Marston Stannett Herefs....45 R3
Marston Trussell Nhants....60 E3
Marstow Herefs....45 R11
Marsworth Bucks....35 P2
Marten Wilts....21 Q2
Marthall Ches E....82 G9
Martham Norfk....77 P8
Martin Hants....21 L11
Martin Kent....27 P2
Martin Lincs....86 F9
Martin Lincs....86 H7
Martindale Cumb....101 M7
Martin Dales Lincs....86 G8
Martin Drove End Hants....21 L10
Martinhoe Devon....17 M2
Martin Hussingtree Worcs....46 G2
Martinscroft Warrtn....82 E7
Martinstown Dorset....11 N7
Martlesham Suffk....53 M2
Martlesham Heath Suffk....53 M2
Martletwy Pembks....41 K8
Martley Worcs....46 E2
Martock Somset....19 N11
Marton Ches E....83 J11
Marton Ches W....82 D11
Marton Cumb....94 E5
Marton E R Yk....93 L3
Marton E R Yk....99 Q7
Marton Lincs....85 P4
Marton Middsb....104 F7
Marton N York....97 P4
Marton N York....98 E4
Marton Shrops....56 D4
Marton Warwks....59 P11
Marton-le-Moor N York....97 N6
Martyr's Green Surrey....36 C9
Martyr Worthy Hants....22 F8
Marwell Wildlife Hants....22 F10
Marwick Ork....169 b4
Marwood Devon....17 J4
Marybank Highld....155 N7
Maryburgh Highld....155 P6
Marygold Border....129 L8
Maryhill C Glas....125 P4
Maryhill Crematorium C Glas....125 P4
Marykirk Abers....143 M4
Maryland Mons....31 P3
Marylebone Gt Lon....36 G4
Marylebone Wigan....88 H9
Marypark Moray....157 M10
Maryport Cumb....100 D3
Maryport D & G....106 F11
Marystow Devon....8 B8
Mary Tavy Devon....8 B8
Maryton Angus....143 M6
Marywell Abers....150 F8
Marywell Abers....151 N8
Marywell Angus....143 M9
Masham N York....97 K4
Mashbury Essex....51 Q8
Mason N u Ty....113 K6
Masongill N York....95 P5
Masonhill Crematorium S Ayrs....114 G3
Mastin Moor Derbys....84 G5
Matching Essex....51 M8
Matching Green Essex....51 M8
Matching Tye Essex....51 M8
Matfen Nthumb....112 F6
Matfield Kent....25 Q2
Mathern Mons....31 P6
Mathon Herefs....46 D5
Mathry Pembks....40 G4
Matlask Norfk....76 H5
Matlock Derbys....84 D9
Matlock Bank Derbys....84 D8
Matlock Bath Derbys....84 C9
Matlock Dale Derbys....84 C9
Matson Gloucs....46 G11
Matterdale End Cumb....101 L6
Mattersey Notts....85 L3
Mattersey Thorpe Notts....85 L3
Mattingley Hants....23 K3
Mattishall Norfk....76 F9
Mattishall Burgh Norfk....76 F9
Mauchline E Ayrs....115 J2
Maud Abers....159 M8
Maufant Jersey....11 C1
Maugersbury Gloucs....47 P9
Maughold IoM....80 g3
Mauld Highld....155 M10
Maulden C Beds....50 C3
Maulds Meaburn Cumb....102 B7
Maunby N York....97 N3
Maund Bryan Herefs....45 R4
Maundown Somset....18 E9
Mautby Norfk....77 P9
Mavesyn Ridware Staffs....71 K11
Mavis Enderby Lincs....87 K7
Mawbray Cumb....109 N11
Mawdesley Lancs....88 F7
Mawdlam Brdgnd....29 M8

Mawgan – Molescroft 283

Mawgan Cnwll 3 J8
Mawgan Porth Cnwll 4 D8
Maw Green Ches E 70 C3
Mawla Cnwll 3 J4
Mawnan Cnwll 3 K8
Mawnan Smith Cnwll 3 K8
Mawsley Nhants 60 H5
Mawthorpe Lincs 87 N6
Maxey C Pete 74 B9
Maxstoke Warwks 59 K7
Maxted Street Kent 27 K3
Maxton Border 118 B4
Maxton Kent 27 P3
Maxwelltown D & G 109 L5
Maxworthy Cnwll 5 M3
Mayals Swans 28 H7
May Bank Staffs 70 F5
Maybole S Ayrs 114 E6
Maybury Surrey 36 B9
Mayes Green Surrey 24 D3
Mayfield E Susx 25 N5
Mayfield Mdloth 128 B7
Mayfield Staffs 71 M5
Mayford Surrey 23 Q3
May Hill Gloucs 46 D10
Mayland Essex 52 F11
Maylandsea Essex 52 F11
Maynard's Green E Susx 25 N7
Maypole Birm 58 G9
Maypole Kent 39 M9
Maypole Mons 45 P11
Maypole Green Norfk 65 N2
Maypole Green Suffk 64 C10
Maypole Green Suffk 65 K8
May's Green Oxon 35 K8
May's Green Surrey 36 C9
Mead Devon 16 C8
Meadgate BaNES 20 C3
Meadle Bucks 35 M3
Meadowfield Dur 103 P3
Meadowtown Shrops 56 E4
Meadwell Devon 5 Q5
Meaford Staffs 70 F7
Meal Bank Cumb 101 P11
Mealrigg Cumb 109 P11
Mealsgate Cumb 100 H2
Meanwood Leeds 90 H3
Mearbeck N York 96 B8
Meare Somset 19 N6
Meare Green Somset 19 J10
Meare Green Somset 19 K9
Mearns E Rens 125 N6
Mears Ashby Nhants 60 H7
Measham Leics 72 A8
Meath Green Surrey 24 G2
Meathop Cumb 95 J4
Meaux E R Yk 93 J3
Meavaig W Isls 168 f4
Meavy Devon 6 E5
Medbourne Leics 60 H2
Medburn Nthumb 112 H6
Meddon Devon 16 D8
Meden Vale Notts 85 J7
Medlam Lincs 87 K9
Medlar Lancs 88 E3
Medmenham Bucks 35 M8
Medomsley Dur 112 H10
Medstead Hants 23 J7
Medway Crematorium Kent 38 B9
Medway Services Medway 38 D9
Meerbrook Staffs 70 H2
Meer Common Herefs 45 M4
Meesden Herts 51 K4
Meeson Wrekin 70 A10
Meeth Devon 17 J10
Meeting Green Suffk 63 M9
Meeting House Hill Norfk 77 L6
Meidrim Carmth 41 Q6
Meifod Powys 56 B2
Meigle P & K 142 D9
Meikle Carco D & G 115 Q5
Meikle Earnock S Lans 126 C7
Meikle Kilmory Ag & B 124 D5
Meikle Obney P & K 141 P10
Meikleour P & K 142 B10
Meikle Wartle Abers 158 H11
Meinciau Carmth 28 E2
Meir C Stke 70 G6
Meir Heath Staffs 70 G6
Melbourn Cambs 51 J2
Melbourne Derbys 72 B5
Melbourne E R Yk 92 C2
Melbur Cnwll 3 N3
Melbury Devon 16 F8
Melbury Abbas Dorset 20 G10
Melbury Bubb Dorset 11 M3
Melbury Osmond Dorset 11 M3
Melbury Sampford Dorset 11 M3
Melchbourne Bed 61 M7
Melcombe Bingham Dorset 12 C4
Meldon Devon 8 E6
Meldon Nthumb 112 H4
Meldon Park Nthumb 112 H3
Meldreth Cambs 62 E11
Meldrum Stirlg 133 L8
Melfort Ag & B 130 G5
Meliden Denbgs 80 F8
Melinau Pembks 41 N8
Melin-byrhedyn Powys 55 J5
Melincourt Neath 29 M4
Melin-y-coed Conwy 67 Q2
Melin-y-ddol Powys 55 P3
Melin-y-wîg Denbgs 68 D5
Melkinthorpe Cumb 101 Q5
Melkridge Nthumb 111 P8
Melksham Wilts 20 H2
Mellangoose Cnwll 2 H8
Mell Green W Berk 34 E9
Mellguards Cumb 110 H11
Melling Lancs 95 M6
Melling Sefton 81 M4
Melling Mount Sefton 81 N4
Mellis Suffk 64 F7
Mellon Charles Highld 160 C8
Mellon Udrigle Highld 160 D7
Mellor Lancs 89 K4
Mellor Stockp 83 L7
Mellor Brook Lancs 89 J4
Mells Somset 20 D5
Mells Suffk 65 N6
Melmerby Cumb 102 B3
Melmerby N York 96 G3
Melmerby N York 97 M5
Melness Highld 165 N4
Melon Green Suffk 64 A10
Melplash Dorset 11 K5
Melrose Border 117 Q4
Melsetter Ork 169 b8
Melsonby N York 103 N9
Meltham Kirk 90 E8
Meltham Mills Kirk 90 E8
Melton E R Yk 92 G5
Melton Suffk 65 K11
Meltonby E R Yk 98 F10
Melton Constable Norfk 76 E5
Melton Mowbray Leics 73 K7
Melton Ross N Linc 93 J8
Melvaig Highld 160 A9
Melverley Shrops 69 K11
Melverley Green Shrops 69 K11
Melvich Highld 166 E4
Membury Devon 10 F4
Membury Services W Berk 34 B9
Memsie Abers 159 N5
Memus Angus 142 G6
Menabilly Cnwll 4 H11
Menagissey Cnwll 3 J4
Menai Bridge IoA 79 K10
Mendham Suffk 65 K5
Mendip Crematorium Somset 19 Q6
Mendip Hills 19 P4
Mendlesham Suffk 64 G8
Mendlesham Green Suffk 64 F9
Menheniot Cnwll 5 M9
Menithwood Worcs 57 N11
Menna Cnwll 3 N3
Mennock D & G 115 R6
Menston C Brad 90 F2
Menstrie Clacks 133 P8
Menthorpe N York 92 B4
Mentmore Bucks 49 P11
Meoble Highld 145 N10
Meole Brace Shrops 56 H2
Meonstoke Hants 22 H11
Meopham Kent 37 P7
Meopham Green Kent 37 P7
Meopham Station Kent 37 P7
Mepal Cambs 62 F4
Meppershall C Beds 50 D3
Merbach Herefs 45 L5
Mere Ches E 82 F8
Mere Wilts 20 F8
Mere Brow Lancs 88 E7
Mereclough Lancs 89 P4
Mere Green Birm 58 H5
Mere Green Worcs 47 J2
Mere Heath Ches W 82 E10
Meresborough Medway 38 D9
Mereworth Kent 37 Q10
Meriden Solhll 59 K8
Merkadale Highld 152 F11
Merley Poole 12 H5
Merlin's Bridge Pembks 40 H8
Merrington Shrops 69 N10
Merrion Pembks 40 H11
Merriott Somset 11 J2
Merrivale Devon 8 D9
Merrow Surrey 36 B10
Merry Field Hill Dorset 12 H4
Merry Hill Herts 36 D2
Merryhill Wolves 58 C5
Merry Lees Leics 72 D9
Merrymeet Cnwll 5 M8
Mersea Island Essex 52 H8
Mersey Crossing Halton 81 Q8
Mersham Kent 27 J3
Merstham Surrey 36 G10
Merston W Susx 15 N6
Merstone IoW 14 F9
Merther Cnwll 3 M5
Merthyr Carmth 42 G10
Merthyr Cynog Powys 44 D7
Merthyr Dyfan V Glam 30 F11
Merthyr Mawr Brdgnd 29 N9
Merthyr Tydfil Myr Td 30 D3
Merthyr Vale Myr Td 30 E5
Merton Devon 17 J9
Merton Gt Lon 36 G6
Merton Norfk 64 C2
Merton Oxon 48 G11
Meshaw Devon 17 P8
Messing Essex 52 E8
Messingham N Linc 92 E10
Metfield Suffk 65 K5
Metherell Cnwll 5 Q8
Metheringham Lincs 86 E8
Methil Fife 135 K8
Methilhill Fife 135 K7
Methley Leeds 91 K5
Methley Junction Leeds 91 K5
Methlick Abers 159 L10
Methven P & K 134 C2
Methwold Norfk 63 M2
Methwold Hythe Norfk 63 M2
Mettingham Suffk 65 M4
Metton Norfk 76 J4
Mevagissey Cnwll 3 Q5
Mexborough Donc 91 M10
Mey Highld 167 N2
Meysey Hampton Gloucs 33 M4
Miabhaig W Isls 168 f4
Michaelchurch Herefs 45 Q9
Michaelchurch Escley Herefs 45 L8
Michaelchurch-on-Arrow Powys 45 J4
Michaelstone-y-Fedw Newpt 30 H8
Michaelston-le-Pit V Glam 30 G10
Michaelstow Cnwll 4 H6
Michaelwood Services Gloucs 32 D5
Michelcombe Devon 6 H5
Micheldever Hants 22 F7
Micheldever Station Hants 22 F6
Michelmersh Hants 22 B9
Mickfield Suffk 64 G9
Micklebring Donc 84 H2
Mickleby N York 105 M8
Micklefield Leeds 91 L4
Micklefield Green Herts 50 B11
Mickleham Surrey 36 E10
Mickleover C Derb 71 Q8
Micklethwaite C Brad 90 E2
Micklethwaite Cumb 110 E10
Mickleton Dur 103 J6
Mickleton Gloucs 47 N6
Mickletown Leeds 91 L5
Mickle Trafford Ches W 81 N11
Mickley Derbys 84 D5
Mickley N York 97 L5
Mickley Green Suffk 64 A10
Mickley Square Nthumb 112 G8
Mid Ardlaw Abers 159 M5
Midbea Ork 169 d2
Mid Beltie Abers 150 G7
Mid Bockhampton Dorset 13 L5
Mid Calder W Loth 127 K4
Mid Clyth Highld 167 N9
Mid Culbeuchly Abers 158 G5
Middle Assendon Oxon 35 K7
Middle Aston Oxon 48 E9
Middle Barton Oxon 48 D9
Middlebie D & G 110 D5
Middlebridge P & K 141 L4
Middle Chinnock Somset 11 K2
Middle Claydon Bucks 49 K9
Middlecliffe Barns 91 L9
Middlecott Devon 8 H7
Middle Duntisbourne Gloucs 33 J3
Middleham N York 96 H3
Middle Handley Derbys 84 F5
Middle Harling Norfk 64 D4
Middlehill Cnwll 5 M8
Middlehill Wilts 32 F11
Middlehope Shrops 56 H7
Middle Kames Ag & B 131 J10
Middle Littleton Worcs 47 L5
Middle Madeley Staffs 70 D5
Middle Maes-coed Herefs 45 L8
Middlemarsh Dorset 11 P3
Middle Mayfield Staffs 71 L6
Middle Mill Pembks 40 F5
Middlemore Devon 6 D4
Middle Quarter Kent 26 E4
Middle Rasen Lincs 86 E3
Middle Rocombe Devon 7 N5
Middle Salter Lancs 95 N8
Middlesbrough Middsb 104 E7
Middlesceugh Cumb 101 M2
Middleshaw Cumb 95 M3
Middlesmoor N York 96 G6
Middle Stoford Somset 18 G10
Middle Stoke Medway 38 D6
Middlestone Dur 103 Q4
Middlestone Moor Dur 103 P4
Middle Stoughton Somset 19 M5
Middlestown Wakefd 90 H7
Middle Street Gloucs 32 E4
Middle Taphouse Cnwll 5 K9
Middlethird Border 118 C2
Middleton Ag & B 136 A7
Middleton Cumb 95 N3
Middleton Derbys 71 M2
Middleton Derbys 84 C9
Middleton Essex 52 E4
Middleton Hants 22 D6
Middleton Herefs 57 J11
Middleton Lancs 95 J9
Middleton Leeds 91 J5
Middleton N York 96 H11
Middleton N York 98 F3
Middleton Nhants 60 H3
Middleton Norfk 75 N7
Middleton Nthumb 112 G4
Middleton Nthumb 119 M3
Middleton P & K 134 E6
Middleton Rochdl 89 P9
Middleton Shrops 57 J9
Middleton Shrops 69 K9
Middleton Suffk 65 N8
Middleton Swans 28 D7
Middleton Warwks 59 J5
Middleton Cheney Nhants 48 E6
Middleton Crematorium Rochdl 89 P9
Middleton Green Staffs 70 H7
Middleton Hall Nthumb 119 J5
Middleton-in-Teesdale Dur 102 H5
Middleton Moor Suffk 65 N8
Middleton One Row Darltn 104 C8
Middleton-on-Leven N York 104 E9
Middleton-on-Sea W Susx 15 Q6
Middleton on the Hill Herefs 45 Q2
Middleton on the Wolds E R Yk 99 J11
Middleton Park C Aber 151 N5
Middleton Priors Shrops 57 L6
Middleton Quernhow N York 97 M5
Middleton St George Darltn 104 B8
Middleton Scriven Shrops 57 M7
Middleton Stoney Oxon 48 F10
Middleton Tyas N York 103 P9
Middletown Cumb 100 C9
Middle Town IoS 2 b3
Middletown N Som 31 N10
Middletown Powys 56 E2
Middle Tysoe Warwks 48 B6
Middle Wallop Hants 21 Q7
Middlewich Ches E 82 F11
Middle Winterslow Wilts 21 P8
Middlewood Cnwll 5 M6
Middlewood Herefs 45 K6
Middle Woodford Wilts 21 M7
Middlewood Green Suffk 64 F9
Middleyard E Ayrs 125 N11
Middle Yard Gloucs 32 F4
Middlezoy Somset 19 L8
Middridge Dur 103 P5
Midford BaNES 20 E2
Midge Hall Lancs 88 G6
Midgeholme Cumb 111 M9
Midgham W Berk 34 G11
Midgley Calder 90 C5
Midgley Wakefd 90 H8
Mid Holmwood Surrey 36 E11
Midhopestones Sheff 90 G11
Midhurst W Susx 23 N10
Mid Lavant W Susx 15 N5
Midlem Border 117 Q5
Mid Mains Highld 155 M10
Midney Somset 19 N9
Midpark Ag & B 124 C6
Midsomer Norton BaNES 20 C4
Midtown Highld 165 N4
Midville Lincs 87 L9
Mid Warwickshire Crematorium Warwks 48 B3
Midway Ches E 83 K8
Mid Yell Shet 169 s4
Migvie Abers 150 C6
Milborne Port Somset 20 C11
Milborne St Andrew Dorset 12 D5
Milborne Wick Somset 20 C10
Milbourne Nthumb 112 H5
Milbourne Wilts 33 J7
Milburn Cumb 102 C5
Milbury Heath S Glos 32 C6
Milby N York 97 P7
Milcombe Oxon 48 D8
Milden Suffk 52 G2
Mildenhall Suffk 63 M6
Mildenhall Wilts 33 P11
Milebrook Powys 56 E10
Milebush Kent 26 C2
Mile Elm Wilts 33 J11
Mile End Essex 52 G6
Mile End Gloucs 31 Q2
Mile End Suffk 65 L4
Mileham Norfk 76 C8
Mile Oak Br & H 24 F9
Mile Oak Kent 25 Q2
Mile Oak Staffs 59 J4
Miles Hope Herefs 45 R2
Milesmark Fife 134 D10
Miles Platting Manch 83 J5
Mile Town Kent 38 F7
Milfield Nthumb 118 H4
Milford Derbys 84 E11
Milford Devon 16 C7
Milford Powys 55 P6
Milford Staffs 70 H10
Milford Surrey 23 P6
Milford Haven Pembks 40 H9
Milford on Sea Hants 13 N6
Milkwall Gloucs 31 Q3
Millais Jersey 11 a1
Milland W Susx 23 M9
Milland Marsh W Susx 23 M9
Mill Bank Calder 90 C6
Millbeck Cumb 101 J5
Millbreck Abers 159 P9
Millbridge Surrey 23 M6
Millbrook C Beds 50 B3
Millbrook C Sotn 14 C4
Millbrook Cnwll 6 C8
Millbrook Jersey 11 b2
Millbrook Tamesd 83 L5
Mill Brow Stockp 83 L7
Millbuie Abers 151 K6
Millbuie Highld 155 Q7
Millcombe Devon 7 L9
Mill Common Norfk 77 L11
Mill Common Suffk 65 N5
Millcorner E Susx 26 D7
Millcraig Highld 156 B3
Mill Cross Devon 7 J6
Milldale Staffs 71 L4
Mill End Bucks 35 L7
Mill End Cambs 62 D4
Millend Gloucs 32 D5
Mill End Herts 50 H4
Millerhill Mdloth 127 Q4
Miller's Dale Derbys 83 P10
Millers Green Derbys 71 P4
Miller's Green Essex 51 N9
Millerston C Glas 125 Q4
Millgate Lancs 89 P7
Mill Green Cambs 63 K11
Mill Green Essex 51 P10
Mill Green Herts 50 F8
Mill Green Lincs 74 D6
Mill Green Norfk 64 G5
Millgreen Shrops 70 B9
Mill Green Staffs 58 G4
Mill Green Staffs 71 K10
Mill Green Suffk 52 G3
Mill Green Suffk 64 D10
Mill Green Suffk 64 G9
Mill Green Suffk 65 L9
Millhalf Herefs 45 K5
Millhayes Devon 10 E4
Millhead Lancs 95 K6
Millheugh S Lans 126 C7
Mill Hill E Susx 25 P9
Mill Hill Gt Lon 36 F2
Millhouse Ag & B 124 B3
Millhouse Cumb 101 L3
Millhousebridge D & G 109 P3
Millhouse Green Barns 90 G10
Millhouses Barns 91 L10
Millhouses Sheff 84 D4
Milliken Park Rens 125 L5
Millin Cross Pembks 41 J8
Millington E R Yk 98 G10
Mill Lane Hants 23 L4
Millmeece Staffs 70 E8
Millness Cumb 95 L4
Mill of Drummond P & K 133 N4
Mill of Haldane W Duns 132 D11
Millom Cumb 94 D4
Millook Cnwll 5 K2
Millpool Cnwll 2 F7
Millpool Cnwll 5 J7
Millport N Ayrs 124 F7
Mill Side Cumb 95 J4
Mill Street Kent 37 Q9
Mill Street Norfk 76 F8
Mill Street Suffk 64 F7
Millthorpe Derbys 84 D5
Millthrop Cumb 95 P2
Milltimber C Aber 151 M7
Milltown Abers 149 P6
Milltown Abers 150 D4
Milltown Cnwll 5 J10
Milltown D & G 110 F5
Milltown Derbys 84 E8
Milltown Devon 17 K4
Milltown of Auchindoun Moray 157 R9
Milltown of Campfield Abers 150 H7
Milltown of Edinvillie Moray 157 P9
Milltown of Learney Abers 150 G7
Milltown of Rothiemay Moray 158 E8
Milnathort P & K 134 E7
Milngavie E Duns 125 P3
Milnrow Rochdl 89 Q8
Milnthorpe Cumb 95 K4
Milnthorpe Wakefd 91 J7
Milovaig Highld 152 B8
Milson Shrops 57 L10
Milstead Kent 38 F10
Milston Wilts 21 N5
Milthorpe Lincs 74 B4
Milthorpe Nhants 48 G5
Milton C Stke 70 G4
Milton Cambs 62 G8
Milton Cumb 111 L8
Milton D & G 106 H7
Milton D & G 108 H6
Milton Derbys 71 Q9
Milton Highld 153 N9
Milton Highld 155 N11
Milton Highld 155 Q8
Milton Highld 156 D3
Milton Highld 167 P6
Milton Inver 125 K4
Milton Kent 37 Q6
Milton Moray 149 M4
Milton Moray 158 D5
Milton N Som 19 K2
Milton Newpt 31 L7
Milton Notts 85 M6
Milton Oxon 34 E6
Milton Oxon 48 E7
Milton P & K 141 Q5
Milton Pembks 41 K10
Milton Somset 19 N10
Milton Stirlg 132 G7
Milton W Duns 125 L3
Milton Abbas Dorset 12 D4
Milton Abbot Devon 5 Q6
Milton Bridge Mdloth 127 P5
Milton Bryan C Beds 49 Q8
Milton Clevedon Somset 20 C7
Milton Combe Devon 6 D5
Milton Common Oxon 35 J4
Milton Damerel Devon 16 F9
Milton End Gloucs 32 D2
Milton End Gloucs 33 M4
Milton Ernest Bed 61 M9
Milton Green Ches W 69 N3
Milton Hill Oxon 34 E6
Milton Keynes M Keyn 49 N7
Milton Lilbourne Wilts 21 N2
Milton Malsor Nhants 60 F9
Milton Morenish P & K 140 F10
Milton of Auchinhove Abers 150 F7
Milton of Balgonie Fife 135 J7
Milton of Buchanan Stirlg 132 E9
Milton of Campsie E Duns 126 B2
Milton of Finavon Angus 142 H6
Milton of Leys Highld 156 B9
Milton of Murtle C Aber 151 M7
Milton on Stour Dorset 20 E9
Milton Regis Kent 38 F9
Milton Street E Susx 25 M10
Milton-under-Wychwood Oxon 47 Q11
Milverton Somset 18 F9
Milverton Warwks 59 M11
Milwich Staffs 70 H8
Milwr Flints 80 H10
Minard Ag & B 131 K8
Minchington Dorset 12 G2
Minchinhampton Gloucs 32 G4
Mindrum Nthumb 118 F4
Minehead Somset 18 C5
Minera Wrexhm 69 J4
Minety Wilts 33 K6
Minffordd Gwynd 67 K7
Mingarrypark Highld 138 B4
Miningsby Lincs 87 K8
Minions Cnwll 5 M7
Minishant S Ayrs 114 F5
Minllyn Gwynd 55 K2
Minnigaff D & G 107 M4
Minnonie Abers 159 J5
Minshull Vernon Ches E 70 B2
Minskip N York 97 N8
Minstead Hants 13 N2
Minsted W Susx 23 N10
Minster Kent 39 P9
Minsterley Shrops 56 F3
Minster Lovell Oxon 34 B2
Minster-on-Sea Kent 38 G7
Minsterworth Gloucs 46 E11
Minterne Magna Dorset 11 P4
Minterne Parva Dorset 11 P4
Minting Lincs 86 G6
Mintlaw Abers 159 N8
Mintlyn Crematorium Norfk 75 N7
Minto Border 117 R6
Minton Shrops 56 G6
Minwear Pembks 41 K8
Minworth Birm 59 J6
Mirehouse Cumb 100 C7
Mireland Highld 167 P4
Mirfield Kirk 90 G7
Miserden Gloucs 32 H3
Miskin Rhondd 30 D5
Miskin Rhondd 30 D8
Misson Notts 85 L2
Misterton Leics 60 C4
Misterton Notts 85 N2
Misterton Somset 11 K3
Mistley Essex 53 K5
Mistley Heath Essex 53 K5
Mitcham Gt Lon 36 G7
Mitcheldean Gloucs 46 C11
Mitchell Cnwll 3 M3
Mitchellslacks D & G 116 D11
Mitchel Troy Mons 31 N2
Mitford Nthumb 113 J3
Mithian Cnwll 3 J3
Mitton Staffs 70 F11
Mixbury Oxon 48 H8
Mixenden Calder 90 D5
Moats Tye Suffk 64 E10
Mobberley Ches E 82 G9
Mobberley Staffs 71 J6
Moccas Herefs 45 M6
Mochdre Conwy 79 Q9
Mochdre Powys 55 P7
Mochrum D & G 107 K8
Mockbeggar Hants 13 L3
Mockbeggar Kent 26 B2
Mockerkin Cumb 100 E6
Modbury Devon 6 H8
Moddershall Staffs 70 G7
Moelfre IoA 79 J7
Moelfre Powys 68 G9
Moel Tryfan Gwynd 67 J3
Moffat D & G 116 F9
Mogador Surrey 36 F10
Moggerhanger C Beds 61 P11
Moira Leics 71 Q11
Molash Kent 38 H11
Mol-chlach Highld 144 G5
Mold Flints 68 H2
Moldgreen Kirk 90 F7
Molehill Green Essex 51 N6
Molehill Green Essex 52 B7
Molescroft E R Yk 92 H2

Molesden Nthumb 112 H4
Molesworth Cambs 61 N5
Moll Highld 153 K11
Molland Devon 17 Q6
Mollington Ches W 81 M10
Mollington Oxon 48 D5
Mollinsburn N Lans 126 C3
Monachty Cerdgn 43 K2
Mondynes Abers 143 P2
Monewden Suffk 65 J10
Moneydie P & K 134 D2
Moneyrow Green W & M 35 N9
Moniaive D & G 115 Q9
Monifieth Angus 142 H11
Monikie Angus 142 H10
Monimail Fife 134 H5
Monington Pembks 41 M2
Monk Bretton Barns 91 K9
Monken Hadley Gt Lon 50 F11
Monk Fryston N York 91 N5
Monkhide Herefs 46 B6
Monkhill Cumb 110 F9
Monkhopton Shrops 57 L6
Monkland Herefs 45 P3
Monkleigh Devon 16 H7
Monknash V Glam 29 P10
Monkokehampton
Devon 8 E3
Monkseaton N Tyne 113 M6
Monks Eleigh Suffk 52 G2
Monk's Gate W Susx 24 F5
Monks Heath Ches E 82 H10
Monk Sherborne Hants 22 H3
Monksilver Somset 18 E7
Monks Kirby Warwks 59 Q8
Monk Soham Suffk 65 J8
Monkspath Solhll 58 H9
Monks Risborough
Bucks 35 M4
Monksthorpe Lincs 87 M7
Monk Street Essex 51 P5
Monkswood Mons 31 K4
Monkton Devon 10 D4
Monkton Kent 39 N9
Monkton S Ayrs 114 G2
Monkton S Tyne 113 M8
Monkton V Glam 29 P10
Monkton Combe BaNES 20 E2
Monkton Deverill Wilts 20 G7
Monkton Farleigh Wilts 32 F11
Monkton Heathfield
Somset 19 J9
Monkton Up Wimborne
Dorset 12 H2
Monkton Wyld Dorset 10 G5
Monkwearmouth Sundld 113 N9
Monkwood Hants 23 J8
Monmore Green Wolves 58 D5
Monmouth Mons 31 P2
Monnington on Wye
Herefs 45 M6
Monreith D & G 107 L9
Montacute Somset 19 N11
Montcliffe Bolton 89 K8
Montford Shrops 56 G2
Montford Bridge Shrops 69 M11
Montgarrie Abers 150 F4
Montgomery Powys 56 C5
Monton Salfd 82 G5
Montrose Angus 143 N6
Mont Saint Guern 10 b2
Monxton Hants 22 B6
Monyash Derbys 83 Q11
Monymusk Abers 150 H4
Monzie P & K 133 P2
Moodiesburn N Lans 126 B3
Moonzie Fife 135 J4
Moor Allerton Leeds 91 J3
Moorbath Dorset 11 J5
Moorby Lincs 87 J8
Moorcot Herefs 45 M3
Moor Crichel Dorset 12 G3
Moordown Bmouth 13 J6
Moore Halton 82 C8
Moor End C Beds 49 Q10
Moor End Calder 90 D5
Moor End Devon 17 M10
Moorends Gloucs 32 D4
Moor End Lancs 88 D2
Moor End N York 91 Q3
Moorends Donc 92 A7
Moorgreen Hants 22 E11
Moor Green Herts 50 H5
Moorgreen Notts 84 G11
Moorhall Derbys 84 D6
Moorhampton Herefs 45 M5
Moorhead C Brad 90 E3
Moor Head Leeds 90 G5
Moorhouse Cumb 110 E10
Moorhouse Cumb 110 F9
Moorhouse Donc 91 M8
Moorhouse Notts 85 N7
Moorhouse Bank Surrey 37 K10
Moorland Somset 19 K8
Moorlinch Somset 19 L7
Moor Monkton N York 97 R9
Moor Row Cumb 100 D8
Moor Row Cumb 110 D11
Moorsholm R & Cl 105 J8
Moorside Dorset 20 E11
Moorside Dur 112 G11
Moor Side Lancs 88 E4
Moor Side Lancs 88 F3
Moorside Leeds 90 G3
Moor Side Lincs 87 J9
Moorside Oldham 89 Q9
Moorstock Kent 27 K4
Moor Street Birm 58 E8
Moor Street Medway 38 D8
Moorswater Cnwll 5 L9
Moorthorpe Wakefd 91 M8
Moortown Devon 6 E4
Moortown Hants 13 L4
Moortown IoW 14 D10
Moortown Leeds 90 H3
Moortown Lincs 93 J11
Moortown Wrekin 69 R11
Morangie Highld 162 H10
Morar Highld 145 L9
Moray Crematorium
Moray 158 A5
Morborne Cambs 61 P2
Morchard Bishop Devon 9 J3
Morchard Road Devon 9 J3
Morcombelake Dorset 11 J5
Morcott Rutlnd 73 N10
Morda Shrops 69 J9
Morden Dorset 12 F5
Morden Gt Lon 36 G7
Mordiford Herefs 45 R7

Mordon Dur 104 B5
More Shrops 56 E6
Morebath Devon 18 C9
Morebattle Border 118 E6
Morecambe Lancs 95 J8
Moredon Swindn 33 M7
Morefield Highld 161 J7
Morehall Kent 27 M4
Moreleigh Devon 7 K8
Morenish P & K 140 F10
Moresby Parks Cumb 100 C7
Morestead Hants 22 F9
Moreton Dorset 12 D7
Moreton Essex 51 M9
Moreton Herefs 45 Q2
Moreton Oxon 35 J4
Moreton Staffs 70 D11
Moreton Staffs 71 L9
Moreton Wirral 81 K7
Moreton Corbet Shrops 69 Q10
Moretonhampstead
Devon 9 J7
Moreton-in-Marsh
Gloucs 47 P8
Moreton Jeffries Herefs 46 B5
Moretonmill Shrops 69 Q10
Moreton Morrell Warwks 48 B3
Moreton on Lugg Herefs 45 Q5
Moreton Paddox Warwks 48 B4
Moreton Pinkney Nhants 48 G5
Moreton Say Shrops 70 A8
Moreton Valence Gloucs 32 E3
Morfa Cerdgn 42 F4
Morfa Bychan Gwynd 67 J7
Morfa Dinlle Gwynd 66 G3
Morfa Glas Neath 29 N3
Morfa Nefyn Gwynd 66 D6
Morganstown Cardif 30 F8
Morgan's Vale Wilts 21 N10
Morham E Loth 128 F5
Moriah Cerdgn 54 E9
Morland Cumb 102 B6
Morley Ches E 82 H8
Morley Derbys 72 B2
Morley Dur 103 M5
Morley Leeds 90 H5
Morley Green Ches E 82 H8
Morley St Botolph Norfk 64 F2
Mornick Cnwll 5 N7
Morningside C Edin 127 N3
Morningside N Lans 126 E6
Morningthorpe Norfk 65 J3
Morpeth Nthumb 113 J3
Morphie Abers 143 N5
Morrey Staffs 71 L11
Morridge Side Staffs 71 J4
Morriston Swans 29 J5
Morston Norfk 76 E3
Mortehoe Devon 16 H2
Morthen Rothm 84 G3
Mortimer W Berk 23 J2
Mortimer Common
W Berk 35 J11
Mortimer's Cross Herefs 45 N2
Mortimer West End
Hants 22 H2
Mortlake Gt Lon 36 F5
Mortlake Crematorium
Gt Lon 36 E5
Morton Cumb 101 N3
Morton Cumb 110 G10
Morton Derbys 84 F8
Morton IoW 14 H9
Morton Lincs 74 A6
Morton Lincs 85 P2
Morton Notts 85 M10
Morton Shrops 69 J10
Morton Hall Lincs 85 Q8
Mortonhall
Crematorium C Edin 127 P4
Morton-on-Swale N York 97 M2
Morton on the Hill Norfk 76 G8
Morton Tinmouth Dur 103 N6
Morvah Cnwll 2 C6
Morval Cnwll 5 M10
Morvich Highld 146 B3
Morville Shrops 57 M6
Morville Heath Shrops 57 M6
Morwenstow Cnwll 16 C8
Mosborough Sheff 84 F4
Moscow E Ayrs 125 M9
Mose Shrops 57 P6
Mosedale Cumb 101 L4
Moseley Birm 58 G8
Moseley Wolves 58 D5
Moseley Worcs 46 F3
Moses Gate Bolton 89 L9
Moss Ag & B 136 B7
Moss Donc 91 P8
Moss Wrexhm 69 K4
Mossat Abers 150 D4
Mossbank Shet 169 r6
Moss Bank St Hel 81 Q5
Mossbay Cumb 100 C5
Mossblown S Ayrs 114 H3
Mossbrow Traffd 82 F7
Mossburnford Border 118 C7
Mossdale D & G 108 G6
Mossdale E Ayrs 115 J7
Moss Edge Lancs 88 E2
Moss End Ches E 82 E9
Mossend N Lans 126 C5
Mosser Mains Cumb 100 F5
Mossley Ches E 70 F2
Mossley Tamesd 83 L4
Mosspaul Hotel Border 117 M11
Moss Side Cumb 110 C10
Moss-side Highld 156 F6
Moss Side Lancs 88 D4
Moss Side Sefton 81 M4
Mosstodloch Moray 157 Q6
Mossyard D & G 107 P7
Mossy Lea Lancs 88 G8
Mosterton Dorset 11 K3
Moston Manch 83 J4
Moston Shrops 69 Q9
Moston Green Ches E 70 C2
Mostyn Flints 80 H8
Motcombe Dorset 20 G9
Mothecombe Devon 6 H9
Motherby Cumb 101 M5
Motherwell N Lans 126 C6
Motspur Park Gt Lon 36 F7
Mottingham Gt Lon 37 K6
Mottisfont Hants 22 B9
Mottistone IoW 14 D10
Mottram in
Longdendale Tamesd 83 L5
Mottram St Andrew
Ches E 83 J9

Mouilpied Guern 10 b2
Mouldsworth Ches W 81 Q10
Moulin P & K 141 M6
Moulsecoomb Br & H 24 H9
Moulsford Oxon 34 G8
Moulsoe M Keyn 49 P6
Moultavie Highld 156 A3
Moulton Ches W 82 E11
Moulton Lincs 74 F6
Moulton N York 103 P10
Moulton Nhants 60 G7
Moulton Suffk 63 L8
Moulton V Glam 30 E11
Moulton Chapel Lincs 74 E7
Moulton St Mary Norfk 77 M10
Moulton Seas End Lincs 74 F5
Mount Cnwll 4 B10
Mount Cnwll 5 J8
Mount Kirk 90 D7
Mountain C Brad 90 D4
Mountain Ash Rhondd 30 D5
Mountain Cross Border 127 M8
Mountain Street Kent 39 J11
Mount Ambrose Cnwll 3 J4
Mount Bures Essex 52 F5
Mountfield E Susx 26 B5
Mountgerald Highld 155 Q5
Mount Hawke Cnwll 3 J4
Mount Hermon Cnwll 2 H10
Mountjoy Cnwll 4 D9
Mount Lothian Mdloth 127 P6
Mountnessing Essex 51 P11
Mounton Mons 31 P6
Mount Pleasant Ches E 70 E3
Mount Pleasant Derbys 71 P11
Mount Pleasant Derbys 84 D11
Mount Pleasant Dur 103 Q4
Mount Pleasant E R Yk 93 N3
Mount Pleasant E Susx 25 K7
Mount Pleasant Norfk 64 D3
Mount Pleasant Suffk 63 M11
Mount Pleasant Worcs 47 K2
Mountsett
Crematorium Dur 113 J10
Mountsorrel Leics 72 F8
Mount Sorrel Wilts 21 K10
Mount Tabor Calder 90 D5
Mousehole Cnwll 2 D8
Mouswald D & G 109 N6
Mow Cop Ches E 70 F3
Mowhaugh Border 118 F6
Mowmacre Hill C Leic 72 F9
Mowsley Leics 60 D3
Moy Highld 147 L11
Moy Highld 156 D11
Moyle Highld 145 Q4
Moylegrove Pembks 41 M2
Muasdale Ag & B 120 C3
Muchalls Abers 151 N9
Much Birch Herefs 45 Q8
Much Cowarne Herefs 46 B5
Much Dewchurch Herefs 45 P8
Muchelney Somset 19 M10
Muchelney Ham Somset 19 M10
Much Hadham Herts 51 K7
Much Hoole Lancs 88 F5
Much Hoole Town Lancs 88 F6
Muchlarnick Cnwll 5 L10
Much Marcle Herefs 46 C8
Much Wenlock Shrops 57 L5
Muck Highld 144 F12
Mucking Thurr 37 Q4
Muckingford Thurr 37 Q5
Muckleburgh
Collection Norfk 76 G3
Muckleford Dorset 11 N6
Mucklestone Staffs 70 C7
Muckton Lincs 87 L4
Muddiford Devon 17 K4
Muddles Green E Susx 25 M8
Mudeford Dorset 13 L6
Mudford Somset 19 Q11
Mudford Sock Somset 19 Q11
Mudgley Somset 19 N5
Mud Row Kent 38 H7
Mugdock Stirlg 125 P2
Mugeary Highld 152 G10
Mugginton Derbys 71 P6
Muggintonlane End
Derbys 71 P6
Muggleswick Dur 112 H11
Muirden Abers 158 H7
Muirdrum Angus 143 K10
Muiresk Abers 158 F8
Muirhead Angus 142 E11
Muirhead Fife 134 H6
Muirhead N Lans 126 B4
Muirkirk E Ayrs 115 N2
Muirmill Stirlg 133 L11
Muir of Fowlis Abers 150 F5
Muir of Miltonduff
Moray 157 M6
Muir of Ord Highld 155 P7
Muirshearlich Highld 146 E11
Muirtack Abers 159 N10
Muirton P & K 133 Q5
Muirton Mains Highld 155 N7
Muirton of Ardblair
P & K 142 B9
Muker N York 102 H11
Mulbarton Norfk 76 H11
Mulben Moray 157 R7
Mulfra Cnwll 2 D7
Mull Ag & B 137 Q9
Mullacott Cross Devon 17 J3
Mullion Cnwll 2 H10
Mullion Cove Cnwll 2 H10
Mumby Lincs 87 P6
Munderfield Row Herefs 46 B4
Munderfield Stocks
Herefs 46 C4
Mundesley Norfk 77 L4
Mundford Norfk 63 P2
Mundham Norfk 65 L2
Mundon Hill Essex 52 E11
Mundy Bois Kent 26 F2
Mungrisdale Cumb 101 L4
Munlochy Highld 156 A7
Munnoch N Ayrs 124 H8
Munsley Herefs 46 C6
Munslow Shrops 57 J7
Murchington Devon 8 G7
Murcot Worcs 47 L6
Murcott Oxon 48 G11
Murcott Wilts 33 J5
Murkle Highld 167 L3
Murlaggan Highld 146 C9
Murrell Green Hants 23 K3
Murroes Angus 142 H10
Murrow Cambs 74 G9

Mursley Bucks 49 M9
Murston Kent 38 F9
Murthill Angus 142 H6
Murthly P & K 141 Q10
Murton C York 98 C10
Murton Cumb 102 D6
Murton Dur 113 N11
Murton N Tyne 113 M6
Murton Nthumb 129 P10
Murton Swans 28 G7
Musbury Devon 10 F6
Muscoates N York 98 D5
Musselburgh E Loth 127 Q3
Muston Leics 73 L3
Muston N York 99 M5
Mustow Green Worcs 58 C10
Muswell Hill Gt Lon 36 G3
Mutehill D & G 108 E11
Mutford Suffk 65 P4
Muthill P & K 133 P4
Mutterton Devon 9 P3
Muxton Wrekin 57 N2
Mybster Highld 167 L6
Myddfai Carmth 43 Q8
Myddle Shrops 69 N10
Mydroilyn Cerdgn 43 J3
Myerscough Lancs 88 F3
Mylor Cnwll 3 L6
Mylor Bridge Cnwll 3 L6
Mynachlog ddu Pembks 41 M4
Myndd-llan Flints 80 H10
Myndtown Shrops 56 F7
Mynydd-bach Mons 31 N6
Mynydd-Bach Swans 29 J5
Mynydd Buch Cerdgn 54 G9
Mynyddgarreg Carmth 28 D3
Mynydd Isa Flints 69 J2
Mynydd Llandygai
Gwynd 79 L11
Mynytho Gwynd 66 E8
Myrebird Abers 151 J8
Myredykes Border 118 A11
Mytchett Surrey 23 N3
Mytholm Calder 90 B5
Mytholmroyd Calder 90 C5
Mythop Lancs 88 D4
Myton-on-Swale N York 97 P7

N

Naast Highld 160 C10
Nab's Head Lancs 89 J5
Na Buirgh W Isls 168 f8
Naburn C York 98 B11
Nab Wood
Crematorium C Brad 90 E3
Naccolt Kent 27 J3
Nackington Kent 39 L11
Nacton Suffk 53 M3
Nafferton E R Yk 99 M9
Nag's Head Gloucs 32 G5
Nailbridge Gloucs 46 B11
Nailsbourne Somset 18 H9
Nailsea N Som 31 N10
Nailstone Leics 72 C9
Nailsworth Gloucs 32 F5
Nairn Highld 156 F6
Nalderswood Surrey 36 F11
Nancegollan Cnwll 2 G7
Nancledra Cnwll 2 D6
Nanhoron Gwynd 66 D8
Nannerch Flints 80 H11
Nanpantan Leics 72 E7
Nanpean Cnwll 4 F10
Nanquidno Cnwll 2 B8
Nanstallon Cnwll 4 G8
Nant-ddu Powys 30 D2
Nanternis Cerdgn 42 G3
Nantgaredig Carmth 43 J10
Nantgarw Rhondd 30 F7
Nant-glas Powys 55 M11
Nantglyn Denbgs 68 D2
Nantgwyn Powys 55 M9
Nant Gwynant Gwynd 67 J4
Nantlle Gwynd 67 J4
Nantmawr Shrops 69 J10
Nantmel Powys 55 N11
Nantmor Gwynd 67 L5
Nant Peris Gwynd 67 L3
Nantwich Ches E 70 B4
Nant-y-Bwch Blae G 30 F2
Nantycaws Carmth 43 J11
Nant-y-derry Mons 31 K3
Nantyffyllon Brdgnd 29 M6
Nantyglo Blae G 30 G2
Nant-y-gollen Shrops 68 H9
Nant-y-moel Brdgnd 29 N6
Nant-y-pandy Conwy 79 M10
Naphill Bucks 35 M5
Napleton Worcs 46 G5
Nappa N York 96 C10
Napton on the Hill
Warwks 48 C2
Narberth Pembks 41 M8
Narborough Leics 72 E11
Narborough Norfk 75 P8
Narkurs Cnwll 5 N10
Nasareth Gwynd 66 H5
Naseby Nhants 60 E5
Nash Bucks 49 L8
Nash Gt Lon 37 K8
Nash Herefs 45 L2
Nash Newpt 31 K8
Nash Shrops 57 L10
Nash End Worcs 57 P8
Nashes Green Hants 23 J5
Nash Lee Bucks 35 M3
Nash Street Kent 37 P7
Nassington Nhants 73 R11
Nastend Gloucs 32 E3
Nasty Herts 51 J6
Nateby Cumb 102 E9
Nateby Lancs 88 F2
National Memorial
Arboretum Staffs 59 J2
National Motor
Museum (Beaulieu)
Hants 14 C6
National Space Centre
C Leic 72 G9
Natland Cumb 95 L3
Naughton Suffk 52 H2
Naunton Gloucs 47 M10
Naunton Worcs 47 G7
Naunton Beauchamp
Worcs 47 J4
Navenby Lincs 86 C9
Navestock Essex 51 M11
Navestock Side Essex 51 N11

Navidale Highld 163 N3
Navity Highld 156 D5
Nawton N York 98 D4
Nayland Suffk 52 G5
Nazeing Essex 51 K9
Nazeing Gate Essex 51 K9
Neacroft Hants 13 L5
Neal's Green Warwks 59 M8
Neap Shet 169 s8
Near Cotton Staffs 71 K5
Near Sawrey Cumb 101 L11
Neasden Gt Lon 36 F3
Neasham Darltn 104 B8
Neath Neath 29 L5
Neatham Hants 23 K6
Neatishead Norfk 77 L7
Nebo Cerdgn 54 C11
Nebo Conwy 67 Q3
Nebo Gwynd 66 H4
Nebo IoA 78 H6
Necton Norfk 76 B10
Nedd Highld 164 D10
Nedderton Nthumb 113 K4
Nedging Suffk 52 G3
Nedging Tye Suffk 52 H2
Needham Norfk 65 J3
Needham Market Suffk 64 F10
Needham Street Suffk 63 M7
Needingworth Cambs 62 D6
Neen Savage Shrops 57 M9
Neen Sollars Shrops 57 M10
Neenton Shrops 57 L7
Nefyn Gwynd 66 E6
Neilston E Rens 125 M6
Nelson Caerph 30 F5
Nelson Lancs 89 P3
Nemphlar S Lans 116 B2
Nempnett Thrubwell
BaNES 19 P2
Nenthall Cumb 111 Q11
Nenthead Cumb 102 E2
Nenthorn Border 118 C3
Neopardy Devon 9 J7
Nep Town W Susx 24 F7
Nercwys Flints 68 H2
Nereabolls Ag & B 122 B8
Nerston S Lans 125 Q6
Nesbit Nthumb 119 J4
Nesfield N York 96 G11
Ness Ches W 81 L9
Nesscliffe Shrops 69 L11
Neston Ches W 81 K9
Neston Wilts 32 G11
Netchwood Shrops 57 L6
Nether Alderley Ches E 82 H9
Netheravon Wilts 21 M5
Nether Blainslie Border 117 Q2
Netherbrae Abers 159 J6
Nether Broughton Leics 72 H5
Netherburn S Lans 126 D8
Netherbury Dorset 11 K5
Netherby Cumb 110 G6
Netherby N York 97 M11
Nether Cerne Dorset 11 P5
Nethercleuch D & G 109 P3
Nether Compton Dorset 19 Q11
Nethercote Warwks 60 B8
Nethercott Devon 5 P2
Nethercott Devon 16 H4
Nether Crimond Abers 151 L3
Nether Dallachy Moray 157 R5
Netherend Gloucs 31 Q4
Nether Exe Devon 9 M4
Netherfield E Susx 26 B8
Netherfield Leics 72 F7
Netherfield Notts 72 G2
Nether Fingland S Lans 116 C8
Nethergate N Linc 92 C11
Nethergate Norfk 76 F6
Netherhampton Wilts 21 M9
Nether Handley Derbys 84 F5
Nether Handwick Angus 142 F9
Nether Haugh Rothm 91 L11
Netherhay Dorset 11 J3
Nether Headon Notts 85 M5
Nether Heage Derbys 84 E10
Nether Heyford Nhants 60 E9
Nether Howcleugh
S Lans 116 E8
Nether Kellet Lancs 95 L7
Nether Kinmundy Abers 159 Q9
Netherland Green Staffs 71 L8
Nether Langwith Notts 84 H6
Netherlaw D & G 108 F12
Netherley Abers 151 M9
Nethermill D & G 109 M3
Nethermuir Abers 159 M9
Netherne-on-the-Hill
Surrey 36 G9
Netheroyd Hill Kirk 90 E7
Nether Padley Derbys 84 B5
Nether Poppleton C York 98 B10
Nether Row Cumb 101 L3
Netherseal Derbys 59 L2
Nether Silton N York 97 Q2
Nether Skyborry Shrops 56 D10
Nether Stowey Somset 18 G7
Netherstreet Wilts 21 J2
Netherthong Kirk 90 E9
Netherthorpe Derbys 84 F6
Netherton Angus 143 J6
Netherton Devon 7 M4
Netherton Dudley 58 D7
Netherton Hants 22 C3
Netherton Herefs 45 Q9
Netherton Kirk 90 F7
Netherton N Lans 126 D7
Netherton Nthumb 119 J9
Netherton Oxon 34 D5
Netherton P & K 142 A7
Netherton Sefton 81 M5
Netherton Shrops 57 N8
Netherton Stirlg 125 P2
Netherton Wakefd 90 H7
Netherton Worcs 47 J6
Nethertown Cumb 100 C9
Nethertown Highld 167 Q1
Nethertown Lancs 89 L3
Nethertown Staffs 71 L11
Nether Wallop Hants 22 B7
Nether Wasdale Cumb 100 F10
Nether Welton Cumb 110 G11
Nether Westcote Gloucs 47 P10
Nether Whitacre Warwks 59 K6
Nether Whitecleuch
S Lans 116 A7
Nether Winchendon
Bucks 35 K2
Netherwitton Nthumb 112 H2

Nethy Bridge – Northcott 285

Nethy Bridge Highld 149 J3
Netley Hants 14 E5
Netley Marsh Hants 13 P2
Nettlebed Oxon 35 J7
Nettlebridge Somset 20 B5
Nettlecombe Dorset 11 L5
Nettlecombe IoW 14 F11
Nettleden Herts 50 B8
Nettleham Lincs 86 D5
Nettlestead Kent 37 Q10
Nettlestead Green Kent 37 Q10
Nettlestone IoW 14 H8
Nettlesworth Dur 113 L11
Nettleton Lincs 93 K10
Nettleton Wilts 32 F9
Nettleton Shrub Wilts 32 F9
Netton Devon 6 F9
Netton Wilts 21 M7
Neuadd Carmth 43 P10
Neuadd-ddu Powys 55 L9
Nevendon Essex 38 C3
Nevern Pembks 41 L2
Nevill Holt Leics 60 H2
New Abbey D & G 109 L7
New Aberdour Abers 159 L5
New Addington Gt Lon 37 J8
Newall Leeds 97 J11
New Alresford Hants 22 G8
New Alyth P & K 142 C8
Newark C Pete 74 D10
Newark Ork 169 g2
Newark-on-Trent Notts 85 N10
New Arram E R Yk 92 H2
Newarthill N Lans 126 D6
New Ash Green Kent 37 P7
New Balderton Notts 85 P10
Newbarn Kent 27 L3
New Barn Kent 37 P7
New Barnet Gt Lon 50 G11
New Barton Nhants 61 J8
Newbattle Mdloth 127 Q4
New Bewick Nthumb 119 L6
Newbie D & G 110 C7
Newbiggin Cumb 94 B2
Newbiggin Cumb 94 F7
Newbiggin Cumb 101 N5
Newbiggin Cumb 102 B5
Newbiggin Cumb 111 L11
Newbiggin Dur 102 H5
Newbiggin Dur 112 H11
Newbiggin N York 96 E2
Newbiggin N York 96 F3
Newbiggin-by-the-Sea Nthumb 113 M3
Newbigging Angus 142 D9
Newbigging Angus 142 G10
Newbigging Angus 142 H10
Newbigging S Lans 127 J8
Newbiggin-on-Lune Cumb 102 D10
New Bilton Warwks 59 Q9
Newbold Derbys 84 E6
Newbold Leics 72 C7
Newbold on Avon Warwks 59 Q9
Newbold on Stour Warwks 47 P5
Newbold Pacey Warwks 47 Q3
Newbold Revel Warwks 59 Q8
Newbold Verdon Leics 72 C10
New Bolingbroke Lincs 87 K9
Newborough C Pete 74 D9
Newborough IoA 78 G11
Newborough Staffs 71 L9
Newbottle Nhants 48 F7
Newbottle Sundld 113 M10
New Boultham Lincs 86 C6
Newbourne Suffk 53 N3
New Bradwell M Keyn 49 M6
New Brampton Derbys 84 E6
New Brancepeth Dur 103 P2
Newbridge C Edin 127 L3
Newbridge Caerph 30 H5
Newbridge Cerdgn 43 K3
Newbridge Cnwll 2 C7
Newbridge Cnwll 3 K5
Newbridge D & G 109 K5
Newbridge Hants 21 Q11
Newbridge IoW 14 D9
New Bridge N York 98 G3
Newbridge Oxon 34 D4
Newbridge Wrexhm 69 J6
Newbridge Green Worcs 46 F7
Newbridge-on-Usk Mons 31 L6
Newbridge-on-Wye Powys 44 E3
New Brighton Flints 81 K11
New Brighton Wirral 81 L6
New Brinsley Notts 84 G10
New Brotton R & Cl 105 J6
Newbrough Nthumb 112 C7
New Broughton Wrexhm 69 K4
New Buckenham Norfk 64 F3
Newbuildings Devon 9 J4
Newburgh Abers 151 P2
Newburgh Abers 159 N6
Newburgh Fife 134 G4
Newburgh Lancs 88 F8
Newburgh Priory N York 98 A5
Newburn N u Ty 113 J7
New Bury Bolton 82 F4
Newbury Somset 20 C5
Newbury W Berk 34 E11
Newbury Wilts 20 F6
Newbury Park Gt Lon 37 K3
Newby Cumb 101 Q6
Newby Lancs 96 B11
Newby N York 95 Q7
Newby N York 99 L2
Newby N York 104 F8
Newby Bridge Cumb 94 H3
Newby Cross Cumb 110 G10
Newby East Cumb 111 J9
Newby Head Cumb 101 Q6
New Byth Abers 159 K7
Newby West Cumb 110 G10
Newby Wiske N York 97 N3
Newcastle Mons 45 N11
Newcastle Shrops 56 D8
Newcastle Airport Nthumb 113 J6
Newcastle Emlyn Carmth 42 F6
Newcastleton Border 111 J3
Newcastle-under-Lyme Staffs 70 E5
Newcastle upon Tyne N u Ty 113 K8
Newchapel Pembks 41 P3
Newchapel Staffs 70 F4
Newchapel Surrey 25 J2
Newchurch Blae G 30 G2
Newchurch Herefs 45 M4
Newchurch IoW 14 G9
Newchurch Kent 27 J5
Newchurch Mons 31 N5
Newchurch Powys 45 J4
Newchurch Staffs 71 L10
Newchurch in Pendle Lancs 89 N3
New Costessey Norfk 76 H9
New Cowper Cumb 109 P11
Newcraighall C Edin 127 Q3
New Crofton Wakefd 91 K7
New Cross Cerdgn 54 E9
New Cross Gt Lon 37 J5
New Cross Somset 19 M11
New Cumnock E Ayrs 115 M5
New Cut E Susx 26 D8
New Deer Abers 159 L8
New Delaval Nthumb 113 L5
New Delph Oldham 90 B9
New Denham Bucks 36 B4
Newdigate Surrey 24 E2
New Duston Nhants 60 F8
New Earswick C York 98 C9
New Eastwood Notts 84 G11
New Edlington Donc 91 N11
New Elgin Moray 157 N5
New Ellerby E R Yk 93 L3
Newell Green Br For 35 N10
New Eltham Gt Lon 37 K6
New End Worcs 47 L2
Newenden Kent 26 D6
New England C Pete 74 C10
New England Essex 52 B3
Newent Gloucs 46 D9
New Farnley Leeds 90 H4
New Ferry Wirral 81 L7
Newfield Dur 103 P4
Newfield Dur 113 K10
Newfield Highld 156 D2
New Fletton C Pete 74 C11
New Forest National Park 13 N3
Newfound Hants 22 G4
New Fryston Wakefd 91 M5
Newgale Pembks 40 G6
New Galloway D & G 108 D5
Newgate Norfk 76 E3
Newgate Street Herts 50 H9
New Gilston Fife 135 L6
New Grimsby IoS 2 b1
Newhall Ches E 69 R5
Newhall Derbys 71 P10
Newham Nthumb 119 N5
New Hartley Nthumb 113 M5
Newhaven C Edin 127 P2
Newhaven Derbys 71 M2
Newhaven E Susx 25 K10
New Haw Surrey 36 C8
New Hedges Pembks 41 M10
New Herrington Sundld 113 M10
Newhey Rochdl 89 Q8
New Holkham Norfk 76 B4
New Holland N Linc 93 J6
Newholm N York 105 N8
New Houghton Derbys 84 G7
New Houghton Norfk 75 Q5
Newhouse N Lans 126 D5
New Houses N York 96 B6
New Houses Wigan 82 C4
New Hutton Cumb 95 M2
New Hythe Kent 38 B10
Newick E Susx 25 K6
Newingreen Kent 27 K4
Newington Kent 27 L4
Newington Kent 38 E9
Newington Oxon 34 H5
Newington Shrops 56 G8
Newington Bagpath Gloucs 32 F6
New Inn Carmth 43 J7
New Inn Torfn 31 K5
New Invention Shrops 56 D9
New Lakenham Norfk 77 J10
New Lanark S Lans 116 B2
New Lanark Village S Lans 116 B2
Newland C KuH 93 J4
Newland Cumb 94 G5
Newland E R Yk 92 D5
Newland Gloucs 31 Q3
Newland N York 92 A6
Newland Oxon 34 C3
Newland Somset 17 Q4
Newland Worcs 46 E5
Newlandrig Mdloth 128 B7
Newlands Border 111 K2
Newlands Cumb 101 K3
Newlands Nthumb 112 G9
Newlands of Dundurcas Moray 157 P7
New Lane Lancs 88 E8
New Lane End Warrtn 82 D6
New Langholm D & G 110 G4
New Leake Lincs 87 M9
New Leeds Abers 159 N7
New Lodge Barns 91 K9
New Longton Lancs 88 G5
New Luce D & G 106 G5
Newlyn Cnwll 2 D8
Newmachar Abers 151 M4
Newmains N Lans 126 E6
New Malden Gt Lon 36 F7
Newman's End Essex 51 M8
Newman's Green Suffk 52 E3
Newmarket Suffk 63 K8
Newmarket W Isls 168 j4
New Marske R & Cl 104 H6
New Marston Oxon 34 F3
New Marton Shrops 69 K8
New Mill Abers 151 K11
Newmill Border 117 P8
New Mill Cnwll 2 D7
New Mill Herts 35 P2
New Mill Kirk 90 F9
Newmill Moray 158 B7
Newmillerdam Wakefd 91 J7
Newmill of Inshewan Angus 142 G5
Newmills C Edin 127 M4
New Mills Cnwll 3 M3
New Mills Derbys 83 M7
Newmills Fife 134 C10
Newmills Mons 31 P3
New Mills Powys 55 P4
Newmiln P & K 142 A11
Newmilns E Ayrs 125 N10
New Milton Hants 13 M5
New Mistley Essex 53 K5
New Moat Pembks 41 L5
Newnes Shrops 69 L8
Newney Green Essex 51 Q9
Newnham Hants 23 K4
Newnham Herts 50 F3
Newnham Kent 38 G10
Newnham Nhants 60 C9
Newnham Bridge Worcs 57 L11
Newnham on Severn Gloucs 32 C2
New Ollerton Notts 85 L7
New Oscott Birm 58 G6
New Pitsligo Abers 159 L6
New Polzeath Cnwll 4 E6
Newport Cnwll 5 N4
Newport Dorset 12 E5
Newport E R Yk 92 E4
Newport Essex 51 M4
Newport Gloucs 32 D5
Newport Highld 163 Q2
Newport IoW 14 F9
Newport Newpt 31 K7
Newport Norfk 77 Q8
Newport Pembks 41 L3
Newport Wrekin 70 C11
Newport-on-Tay Fife 135 L2
Newport Pagnell M Keyn 49 N6
Newport Pagnell Services M Keyn 49 N6
Newpound Common W Susx 24 C5
New Prestwick S Ayrs 114 F3
New Quay Cerdgn 42 G3
Newquay Cnwll 4 C9
New Quay Essex 52 H7
Newquay Zoo Cnwll 4 C9
New Rackheath Norfk 77 K9
New Radnor Powys 45 J2
New Rent Cumb 101 N3
New Ridley Nthumb 112 G9
New Road Side N York 90 B2
New Romney Kent 27 J7
New Rossington Donc 91 Q11
New Row Cerdgn 54 G10
New Row Lancs 89 J3
New Sauchie Clacks 133 P9
Newsbank Ches E 82 H11
Newseat Abers 158 H11
Newsham Lancs 88 G3
Newsham N York 97 N4
Newsham N York 103 M8
Newsham Nthumb 113 M5
New Sharlston Wakefd 91 K7
Newsholme E R Yk 92 B5
Newsholme Lancs 96 B10
New Shoreston Nthumb 119 N4
New Silksworth Sundld 113 N10
New Skelton R & Cl 105 J7
Newsome Kirk 90 F8
New Somerby Lincs 73 N3
New Southgate Crematorium Gt Lon 36 G2
New Springs Wigan 88 H9
Newstead Border 117 R4
Newstead Notts 84 H10
Newstead Nthumb 119 N5
New Stevenston N Lans 126 D6
New Street Herefs 45 L3
New Swannington Leics 72 C7
Newthorpe N York 91 M4
Newthorpe Notts 84 G11
New Thundersley Essex 38 C4
Newtimber W Susx 24 G8
Newtoft Lincs 86 D3
Newton Ag & B 131 L8
Newton Border 118 B6
Newton Brdgnd 29 M9
Newton C Beds 50 F2
Newton Cambs 62 F11
Newton Cambs 74 H8
Newton Cardif 30 H9
Newton Ches W 69 P3
Newton Ches W 81 N11
Newton Ches W 82 B9
Newton Cumb 94 E6
Newton Derbys 84 F9
Newton Herefs 45 L8
Newton Herefs 45 Q4
Newton Herefs 56 F11
Newton Highld 155 Q7
Newton Highld 156 C8
Newton Highld 156 D4
Newton Highld 167 P7
Newton Lancs 88 C3
Newton Lancs 95 M6
Newton Lincs 73 Q3
Newton Mdloth 127 Q4
Newton Moray 157 M5
Newton Moray 157 Q5
Newton N York 98 H6
Newton Nhants 61 J4
Newton Norfk 76 A8
Newton Notts 72 H2
Newton Nthumb 112 F8
Newton Nthumb 118 H9
Newton S Lans 116 C4
Newton S Lans 126 B5
Newton Sandw 58 F6
Newton Shrops 69 M8
Newton Somset 18 F7
Newton Staffs 71 J9
Newton Suffk 52 F3
Newton W Loth 127 K2
Newton Warwks 60 B5
Newton Wilts 21 P10
Newton Abbot Devon 7 M4
Newton Arlosh Cumb 110 D9
Newton Aycliffe Dur 103 Q6
Newton Bewley Hartpl 104 E5
Newton Blossomville M Keyn 49 P4
Newton Bromswold Nhants 61 L7
Newton Burgoland Leics 72 B9
Newton-by-the-Sea Nthumb 119 P5
Newton by Toft Lincs 86 D3
Newton Ferrers Devon 6 F9
Newton Ferry W Isls 168 d10
Newton Flotman Norfk 65 J2
Newtongrange Mdloth 127 Q5
Newton Green Mons 31 P6
Newton Harcourt Leics 72 G11
Newton Heath Manch 83 J4
Newtonhill Abers 151 N9
Newton Hill Wakefd 91 J6
Newton-in-Bowland Lancs 95 P10
Newton Kyme N York 91 M2
Newton-le-Willows N York 97 K3
Newton-le-Willows St Hel 82 C5
Newtonloan Mdloth 127 Q5
Newton Longville Bucks 49 M8
Newton Mearns E Rens 125 N6
Newtonmill Angus 143 L5
Newtonmore Highld 148 C8
Newton Morrell N York 103 P9
Newton Mountain Pembks 41 J9
Newton Mulgrave N York 105 L7
Newton of Balcanquhal P & K 134 F5
Newton of Balcormo Fife 135 N7
Newton-on-Ouse N York 97 R9
Newton-on-Rawcliffe N York 98 G2
Newton on the Hill Shrops 69 N10
Newton-on-the-Moor Nthumb 119 N9
Newton on Trent Lincs 85 P6
Newton Poppleford Devon 10 B7
Newton Purcell Oxon 48 H8
Newton Regis Warwks 59 L3
Newton Reigny Cumb 101 N4
Newton St Cyres Devon 9 L5
Newton St Faith Norfk 77 J8
Newton St Loe BaNES 20 D2
Newton St Petrock Devon 16 G9
Newton Solney Derbys 71 P9
Newton Stacey Hants 22 D6
Newton Stewart D & G 107 M4
Newton Tony Wilts 21 P6
Newton Tracey Devon 17 J6
Newton under Roseberry R & Cl 104 G8
Newton Underwood Nthumb 112 H3
Newton upon Derwent E R Yk 98 E11
Newton Valence Hants 23 K8
Newton Wamphray D & G 109 P2
Newton with Scales Lancs 88 F4
Newtown Blae G 30 G3
Newtown Ches W 82 B9
Newtown Cnwll 2 F8
Newtown Cnwll 5 M6
Newtown Cumb 101 P6
Newtown Cumb 109 P11
Newtown Cumb 110 G8
Newtown Cumb 111 K8
Newtown D & G 115 Q5
Newtown Derbys 83 L8
Newtown Devon 9 Q5
Newtown Devon 17 P6
Newtown Dorset 11 K4
New Town Dorset 12 G3
New Town Dorset 21 J11
New Town Dorset 21 J11
New Town E Susx 25 L6
Newtown Gloucs 32 C4
Newtown Hants 13 N2
Newtown Hants 14 H4
Newtown Hants 22 E2
Newtown Herefs 45 P3
Newtown Herefs 45 Q8
Newtown Herefs 46 B5
Newtown Highld 147 K7
Newtown IoW 14 D8
Newtown Lancs 88 G7
New Town Nhants 61 L5
Newtown Nthumb 119 J4
Newtown Nthumb 119 K10
Newtown Nthumb 119 K5
Newtown Poole 12 H6
Newtown Powys 55 Q6
Newtown Rhondd 30 E5
Newtown Shrops 69 M10
Newtown Shrops 69 N8
Newtown Somset 10 F2
Newtown Staffs 58 E4
Newtown Staffs 70 G2
Newtown Wigan 88 H9
Newtown Wilts 20 H9
Newtown Wilts 21 Q2
New Town Wilts 33 Q10
Newtown Worcs 46 G3
Newtown Worcs 58 D9
Newtown-in-St Martin Cnwll 3 J9
Newtown Linford Leics 72 E9
Newtown of Beltrees Rens 125 K6
Newtown St Boswells Border 117 R4
Newtown Unthank Leics 72 D10
New Tredegar Caerph 30 F4
New Trows S Lans 126 E10
New Tupton Derbys 84 E7
Newtyle Angus 142 D9
New Walsoken Cambs 75 J9
New Waltham NE Lin 93 N10
New Whittington Derbys 84 E5
New Winton E Loth 128 C5
New Yatt Oxon 34 C2
Newyears Green Gt Lon 36 C3
Newyork Ag & B 131 K5
New York Lincs 86 H9
New York N Tyne 113 M6
New York N York 97 J8
Nextend Herefs 45 L3
Neyland Pembks 41 J9
Niarbyl IoM 80 b6
Nibley Gloucs 32 C3
Nibley S Glos 32 C8
Nibley Green Gloucs 32 D5
Nicholashayne Devon 18 F11
Nicholaston Swans 28 F7
Nickies Hill Cumb 111 K7
Nidd N York 97 M8
Nigg C Aber 151 N7
Nigg Highld 156 E3
Nigg Ferry Highld 156 D4
Nimlet BaNES 32 D10
Ninebanks Nthumb 111 Q10
Nine Elms Swindn 33 M7
Nine Wells Pembks 40 E6
Ninfield E Susx 26 B9
Ningwood IoW 14 C9
Nisbet Border 118 C5
Nisbet Hill Border 129 K9
Niton IoW 14 F11
Nitshill C Glas 125 N5
Noah's Ark Kent 37 N9
Noak Bridge Essex 37 Q2
Noak Hill Gt Lon 37 M2
Noblethorpe Barns 90 H9
Nobold Shrops 56 H2
Nobottle Nhants 60 E8
Nocton Lincs 86 E8
Nogdam End Norfk 77 M11
Noke Oxon 34 F2
Nolton Pembks 40 G7
Nolton Haven Pembks 40 G7
No Man's Heath Ches W 69 P5
No Man's Heath Warwks 59 L3
No Man's Land Cnwll 5 M10
Nomansland Devon 9 K2
Nomansland Wilts 21 Q11
Noneley Shrops 69 N9
Nonington Kent 39 N11
Nook Cumb 95 L4
Nook Cumb 111 J5
Norbiton Gt Lon 36 E7
Norbreck Bpool 88 C2
Norbridge Herefs 46 D6
Norbury Ches E 69 Q5
Norbury Derbys 71 L6
Norbury Gt Lon 36 H7
Norbury Shrops 56 F6
Norbury Staffs 70 D10
Norbury Common Ches E 69 Q5
Norbury Junction Staffs 70 D10
Norchard Worcs 58 B11
Norcott Brook Ches W 82 D8
Norcross Lancs 88 C2
Nordelph Norfk 75 L10
Norden Rochdl 89 P8
Nordley Shrops 57 M5
Norfolk Broads Norfk 77 P10
Norham Nthumb 129 N10
Norland Town Calder 90 D6
Norley Ches W 82 C10
Norleywood Hants 14 C7
Norlington E Susx 25 K8
Normanby Lincs 86 C3
Normanby N Linc 92 E7
Normanby N York 98 E4
Normanby R & Cl 104 F7
Normanby le Wold Lincs 93 K11
Norman Cross Cambs 61 Q2
Normandy Surrey 23 P4
Normans Bay E Susx 25 Q9
Norman's Green Devon 9 Q4
Normanton C Derb 72 A4
Normanton Leics 73 L2
Normanton Notts 85 M10
Normanton Rutlnd 73 N9
Normanton Wakefd 91 K6
Normanton Wilts 21 M6
Normanton le Heath Leics 72 B8
Normanton on Cliffe Lincs 86 B11
Normanton on Soar Notts 72 E6
Normanton on the Wolds Notts 72 G4
Normanton on Trent Notts 85 N7
Normoss Lancs 88 C3
Norney Surrey 23 P6
Norrington Common Wilts 20 G2
Norris Green Cnwll 5 Q8
Norris Green Lpool 81 M6
Norris Hill Leics 72 A7
Norristhorpe Kirk 90 G6
Northacre Norfk 64 D2
Northall Bucks 49 Q10
Northallerton N York 97 N2
Northall Green Norfk 76 D9
Northam C Sotn 14 D4
Northam Devon 16 H6
Northampton Nhants 60 G8
Northampton Worcs 58 B11
Northampton Services Nhants 60 F9
North Anston Rothm 84 H4
North Ascot Br For 35 P11
North Aston Oxon 48 E9
Northaw Herts 50 G10
Northay Somset 10 F2
North Baddesley Hants 22 C10
North Ballachulish Highld 139 K5
North Barrow Somset 20 B9
North Barsham Norfk 76 C4
Northbay W Isls 168 c17
North Benfleet Essex 38 C4
North Berwick E Loth 128 E3
North Bitchburn Dur 103 N4
North Blyth Nthumb 113 M4
North Boarhunt Hants 14 H4
North Bockhampton Dorset 13 L5
Northborough C Pete 74 C9
Northbourne Kent 39 P11
North Bovey Devon 8 H8
North Bradley Wilts 20 G3
North Brentor Devon 8 C8
North Brewham Somset 20 D7
North Bridge Surrey 23 Q7
Northbridge Street E Susx 26 B7
Northbrook Hants 22 F7
Northbrook Oxon 48 E10
North Brook End Cambs 50 G2
North Buckland Devon 16 H3
North Burlingham Norfk 77 M10
North Cadbury Somset 20 B9
North Carlton Lincs 86 B5
North Carlton Notts 85 J4
North Cave E R Yk 92 E4
North Cerney Gloucs 33 K3
North Chailey E Susx 25 J6
Northchapel W Susx 23 Q9
North Charford Hants 21 N11
North Charlton Nthumb 119 N6
North Cheam Gt Lon 36 F7
North Cheriton Somset 20 C9
North Chideock Dorset 11 J6
Northchurch Herts 35 Q3
North Cliffe E R Yk 92 E3
North Clifton Notts 85 P6
North Close Dur 103 Q4
North Cockerington Lincs 87 L2
North Connel Ag & B 138 G11
North Cornelly Brdgnd 29 M8
North Corner Cnwll 3 K10
North Cotes Lincs 93 P10
Northcott Devon 5 N3
Northcott Devon 10 B2

Northcott Devon 10 C3
North Country Cnwll 2 H5
Northcourt Oxon 34 E5
North Cove Suffk 65 P4
North Cowton N York 103 Q10
North Crawley M Keyn 49 P6
North Creake Norfk 76 B4
North Curry Somset 19 K9
North Dalton E R Yk 99 J10
North Deighton N York 97 N10
North Devon Crematorium Devon 17 J5
Northdown Kent 39 Q7
North Downs 38 F10
North Duffield N York 92 A3
North East Surrey Crematorium Gt Lon 36 F7
Northedge Derbys 84 E7
North Elham Kent 27 L3
North Elkington Lincs 87 J2
North Elmham Norfk 76 D7
North Elmsall Wakefd 91 M8
Northend Bucks 35 K6
North End C Port 15 J6
North End Cumb 110 F9
North End Dorset 20 F9
North End E R Yk 93 L2
North End E R Yk 93 N4
North End Essex 51 Q7
North End Hants 21 M11
North End Hants 22 G9
North End Leics 72 F7
North End Lincs 74 D2
North End Lincs 87 M3
North End Lincs 92 H11
North End Lincs 93 P10
North End N Linc 93 K6
North End N Som 31 M11
North End Nhants 61 L7
North End Norfk 64 D3
North End Nthumb 119 M10
North End Sefton 81 L4
North End W Susx 15 Q6
North End W Susx 24 D9
Northend Warwks 48 C4
Northenden Manch 82 H7
Northend Woods Bucks 35 P7
North Erradale Highld 160 A10
North Evington C Leic 72 G10
North Fambridge Essex 38 E2
North Featherstone Wakefd 91 L6
North Ferriby E R Yk 92 G5
Northfield Birm 58 F9
Northfield C Aber 151 N6
Northfield E R Yk 92 H5
Northfields Lincs 73 Q9
Northfleet Kent 37 P6
North Frodingham E R Yk 99 N10
North Gorley Hants 13 L2
North Green Norfk 65 J4
North Green Suffk 65 L9
North Green Suffk 65 M8
North Greetwell Lincs 86 D6
North Grimston N York 98 G7
North Halling Medway 38 B8
North Haven Shet 169 t14
North Hayling Hants 15 K6
North Hazelrigg Nthumb 119 L4
North Heasley Devon 17 N5
North Heath W Susx 24 C6
North Hele Devon 18 D10
North Hertfordshire Memorial Park & Crematorium Herts 50 E4
North Hill Cnwll 5 M6
North Hillingdon Gt Lon 36 C4
North Hinksey Village Oxon 34 E3
North Holmwood Surrey 36 E11
North Huish Devon 7 J7
North Hykeham Lincs 86 B7
Northiam E Susx 26 D7
Northill C Beds 61 P11
Northington Gloucs 32 D3
Northington Hants 22 G7
North Kelsey Lincs 92 H10
North Kessock Highld 156 B8
North Killingholme N Linc 93 K7
North Kilvington N York 97 P3
North Kilworth Leics 60 D4
North Kingston Hants 13 L4
North Kyme Lincs 86 G10
North Lancing W Susx 24 E9
North Landing E R Yk 99 Q6
Northlands Lincs 87 K10
Northleach Gloucs 33 M2
North Lee Bucks 35 M3
North Lees N York 97 L6
Northleigh Devon 10 D5
Northleigh Devon 17 L5
North Leigh Kent 27 K2
North Leigh Oxon 34 C2
North Leverton with Habblesthorpe Notts 85 N4
Northlew Devon 8 D5
North Littleton Worcs 47 L5
Northload Bridge Somset 19 N7
North Lopham Norfk 64 E5
North Luffenham Rutlnd 73 N10
North Marden W Susx 23 M11
North Marston Bucks 49 L10
North Middleton Mdloth 128 B8
North Middleton Nthumb 119 J6
North Millbrex Abers 159 K9
North Milmain D & G 106 E7
North Molton Devon 17 N6
Northmoor Oxon 34 D4
North Moreton Oxon 34 G7
Northmuir Angus 142 F7
North Mundham W Susx 15 N6
North Muskham Notts 85 N9
North Newbald E R Yk 92 F3
North Newington Oxon 48 D6
North Newnton Wilts 21 M3
North Newton Somset 19 K8
Northney Hants 15 K6
North Nibley Gloucs 32 D5
North Oakley Hants 22 F4
North Ockendon Gt Lon 37 N3
Northolt Gt Lon 36 D4
Northolt Airport Gt Lon 36 C3
Northop Flints 81 J11
Northop Hall Flints 81 K11
North Ormesby Middsb 104 F7
North Ormsby Lincs 87 J2

Northorpe Kirk 90 G6
Northorpe Lincs 74 A7
Northorpe Lincs 74 D3
Northorpe Lincs 92 E11
North Otterington N York 97 N3
Northover Somset 19 N7
Northover Somset 19 P10
North Owersby Lincs 86 E2
Northowram Calder 90 E5
North Perrott Somset 11 K3
North Petherton Somset 19 J8
North Petherwin Cnwll 5 M4
North Pickenham Norfk 76 B10
North Piddle Worcs 47 J4
North Poorton Dorset 11 L5
Northport Dorset 12 F7
North Poulner Hants 13 L3
North Queensferry Fife 134 E11
North Radworthy Devon 17 P5
North Rauceby Lincs 86 D11
Northrepps Norfk 77 J4
North Reston Lincs 87 L4
North Rigton N York 97 L11
North Ripley Hants 13 L5
North Rode Ches E 83 J11
North Ronaldsay Ork 169 g1
North Ronaldsay Airport Ork 169 g1
North Row Cumb 100 H4
North Runcton Norfk 75 M7
North Scale Cumb 94 D7
North Scarle Lincs 85 P7
North Seaton Nthumb 113 L3
North Seaton Colliery Nthumb 113 L3
North Shian Ag & B 138 G9
North Shields N Tyne 113 N7
North Shoebury Sthend 38 F4
North Shore Bpool 88 C3
North Side C Pete 74 E11
North Side Cumb 100 C5
North Skelton R & Cl 105 J7
North Somercotes Lincs 93 R11
North Stainley N York 97 L5
North Stainmore Cumb 102 F8
North Stifford Thurr 37 P4
North Stoke BaNES 32 D11
North Stoke Oxon 34 H7
North Stoke W Susx 24 B8
Northstowe Cambs 62 F7
North Street Cambs 63 J7
North Street Hants 21 N11
North Street Hants 22 H8
North Street Kent 38 H10
North Street Medway 38 D7
North Street W Berk 34 H10
North Sunderland Nthumb 119 P4
North Tamerton Cnwll 5 N2
North Tawton Devon 8 G4
North Third Stirlg 133 M10
North Thoresby Lincs 93 N11
North Togston Nthumb 119 P10
North Tolsta W Isls 168 k3
Northton W Isls 168 e9
North Town Devon 17 J10
North Town Somset 19 Q6
North Town W & M 35 N8
North Tuddenham Norfk 76 E9
North Uist W Isls 168 c10
Northumberland National Park Nthumb 118 G10
North Walbottle N u Ty 113 J7
North Walsham Norfk 77 K5
North Waltham Hants 22 G5
North Warnborough Hants 23 K4
Northway Somset 18 F9
North Weald Bassett Essex 51 L10
North Wheatley Notts 85 N3
North Whilborough Devon 7 M5
Northwich Ches W 82 E10
North Wick BaNES 31 Q11
Northwick S Glos 31 Q7
Northwick Somset 19 L5
Northwick Worcs 46 F3
North Widcombe BaNES 19 Q3
North Willingham Lincs 86 G3
North Wingfield Derbys 84 F7
North Witham Lincs 73 N6
Northwold Norfk 75 Q11
Northwood C Stke 70 F5
Northwood Derbys 84 C8
Northwood Gt Lon 36 C2
Northwood IoW 14 E8
Northwood Shrops 69 N8
Northwood Green Gloucs 46 D11
North Wootton Dorset 11 P2
North Wootton Norfk 75 M6
North Wootton Somset 19 Q6
North Wraxall Wilts 32 F9
North Wroughton Swindn 33 M8
North York Moors National Park 105 K10
Norton Donc 91 N7
Norton E Susx 25 L10
Norton Gloucs 46 G10
Norton Halton 82 C8
Norton Hants 22 E6
Norton Herts 50 F4
Norton IoW 13 P7
Norton Mons 45 N10
Norton N Som 19 K2
Norton Nhants 60 C8
Norton Notts 85 J6
Norton Powys 56 E11
Norton S on T 104 D6
Norton Sheff 84 E4
Norton Shrops 56 H8
Norton Shrops 57 K3
Norton Shrops 57 L4
Norton Shrops 57 N4
Norton Suffk 64 D8
Norton Swans 28 H7
Norton W Susx 15 P5
Norton Wilts 32 G8
Norton Worcs 46 G4
Norton Worcs 47 K5
Norton Bavant Wilts 20 H6
Norton Bridge Staffs 70 F8
Norton Canes Staffs 58 F3
Norton Canes Services Staffs 58 F3
Norton Canon Herefs 45 M5
Norton Corner Norfk 76 F7
Norton Disney Lincs 85 Q9

Norton Ferris Wilts 20 E7
Norton Fitzwarren Somset 18 G9
Norton Green IoW 13 P7
Norton Hawkfield BaNES 19 Q2
Norton Heath Essex 51 P10
Norton in Hales Shrops 70 C7
Norton-Juxta-Twycross Leics 59 M3
Norton-le-Clay N York 97 P6
Norton-le-Moors C Stke 70 F4
Norton Lindsey Warwks 47 P2
Norton Little Green Suffk 64 D8
Norton Malreward BaNES 20 B2
Norton Mandeville Essex 51 N10
Norton-on-Derwent N York 98 F6
Norton St Philip Somset 20 E3
Norton Subcourse Norfk 65 N2
Norton sub Hamdon Somset 19 N11
Norton Wood Herefs 45 M5
Norwell Notts 85 N8
Norwell Woodhouse Notts 85 M8
Norwich Norfk 77 J10
Norwich Airport Norfk 77 J9
Norwich (St Faith) Crematorium Norfk 77 J8
Norwick Shet 169 t2
Norwood Clacks 133 P9
Norwood Derbys 84 G4
Norwood Kent 27 J5
Norwood End Essex 51 N9
Norwood Green Calder 90 E5
Norwood Green Gt Lon 36 D5
Norwood Hill Surrey 24 F2
Norwoodside Cambs 74 H11
Noseley Leics 73 J11
Noss Mayo Devon 6 F9
Nosterfield N York 97 L4
Nosterfield End Cambs 51 P2
Nostie Highld 145 Q2
Notgrove Gloucs 47 M9
Nottage Brdgnd 29 M9
Notter Cnwll 5 P9
Nottingham C Nott 72 F3
Nottington Dorset 11 P8
Notton Wakefd 91 J8
Notton Wilts 32 H11
Nounsley Essex 52 C9
Noutard's Green Worcs 57 Q11
Nowton Suffk 64 B9
Nox Shrops 56 G2
Nuffield Oxon 35 J7
Nunburnholme E R Yk 98 G11
Nuncargate Notts 84 H10
Nunclose Cumb 111 J11
Nuneaton Warwks 59 N6
Nuneham Courtenay Oxon 34 G5
Nunhead Gt Lon 36 H5
Nunkeeling E R Yk 99 N11
Nun Monkton N York 97 R9
Nunney Somset 20 D5
Nunney Catch Somset 20 D5
Nunnington Herefs 45 R6
Nunnington N York 98 D5
Nunsthorpe NE Lin 93 N9
Nunthorpe C York 98 C10
Nunthorpe Middsb 104 F8
Nunthorpe Village Middsb 104 F8
Nunton Wilts 21 N9
Nunwick N York 97 M6
Nunwick Nthumb 112 C6
Nupdown S Glos 32 B5
Nup End Bucks 49 N11
Nupend Gloucs 32 E3
Nuptown Br For 35 N10
Nursling Hants 22 C11
Nursted Hants 23 L10
Nursteed Wilts 21 K2
Nurton Staffs 58 B5
Nutbourne W Susx 15 L5
Nutbourne W Susx 24 C7
Nutfield Surrey 36 H10
Nuthall Notts 72 E2
Nuthampstead Herts 51 K4
Nuthurst W Susx 24 E5
Nutley E Susx 25 K5
Nutley Hants 22 H6
Nuttall Bury 89 M7
Nutwell Donc 91 Q10
Nybster Highld 167 Q4
Nyetimber W Susx 15 N7
Nyewood W Susx 23 M10
Nymans W Susx 24 G5
Nymet Rowland Devon 17 N10
Nymet Tracey Devon 8 H4
Nympsfield Gloucs 32 F4
Nynehead Somset 18 F10
Nythe Somset 19 M8
Nyton W Susx 15 P5

O

Oadby Leics 72 G10
Oad Street Kent 38 E9
Oakall Green Worcs 46 F2
Oakamoor Staffs 71 J6
Oakbank W Loth 127 K4
Oak Cross Devon 8 D9
Oakdale Caerph 30 G5
Oaken Somset 18 G9
Oaken Staffs 58 C4
Oakenclough Lancs 95 L11
Oakengates Wrekin 57 N2
Oakenholt Flints 81 K10
Oakenshaw Dur 103 N3
Oakenshaw Kirk 90 F5
Oakerthorpe Derbys 84 E10
Oakford Cerdgn 43 J3
Oakford Devon 18 B10
Oakfordbridge Devon 18 B10
Oakgrove Ches E 83 K11
Oakham Rutlnd 73 M9
Oakhanger Ches E 70 C4
Oakhanger Hants 23 L7
Oakhill Somset 20 B5
Oakhurst Kent 37 N10
Oakington Cambs 62 F8
Oaklands Powys 44 E4
Oakle Street Gloucs 46 E11
Oakley Bed 61 M10
Oakley Bucks 34 H2
Oakley Fife 134 C10
Oakley Hants 22 G4

Oakley Oxon 35 L4
Oakley Poole 12 H5
Oakley Suffk 64 H6
Oakley Green W & M 35 P9
Oakley Park Powys 55 M7
Oakridge Lynch Gloucs 32 H4
Oaks Lancs 89 K4
Oaks Shrops 56 G4
Oaks Green Derbys 71 M8
Oakshaw Ford Cumb 111 K5
Oakshott Hants 23 K8
Oakthorpe Leics 59 M2
Oak Tree Darltn 104 C8
Oakwood C Derb 72 B3
Oakwood Nthumb 112 D6
Oakworth C Brad 90 C3
Oare Kent 38 H9
Oare Somset 17 P2
Oare Wilts 21 N2
Oasby Lincs 73 Q3
Oath Somset 19 L9
Oathlaw Angus 142 H6
Oatlands Park Surrey 36 C7
Oban Ag & B 130 H2
Oban Airport Ag & B 138 G10
Obley Shrops 56 E9
Oborne Dorset 20 C11
Obthorpe Lincs 74 B8
Occold Suffk 64 H7
Occumster Highld 167 N9
Ochiltree E Ayrs 115 K3
Ockbrook Derbys 72 C3
Ocker Hill Sandw 58 E6
Ockeridge Worcs 46 E2
Ockham Surrey 36 C9
Ockle Highld 137 P1
Ockley Surrey 24 D2
Ocle Pychard Herefs 46 A5
Octon E R Yk 99 L7
Odcombe Somset 19 N11
Odd Down BaNES 20 D2
Oddendale Cumb 101 Q8
Oddingley Worcs 46 H3
Oddington Oxon 48 G11
Odell Bed 61 L9
Odham Devon 8 C4
Odiham Hants 23 K4
Odsal C Brad 90 F5
Odsey Cambs 50 G3
Odstock Wilts 21 M9
Odstone Leics 72 B9
Offchurch Warwks 59 N11
Offenham Worcs 47 L5
Offerton Stockp 83 K7
Offerton Sundld 113 M9
Offham E Susx 25 K8
Offham Kent 37 Q9
Offham W Susx 24 B9
Offleymarsh Staffs 70 D9
Offord Cluny Cambs 62 B7
Offord D'Arcy Cambs 62 B7
Offton Suffk 53 J2
Offwell Devon 10 D5
Ogbourne Maizey Wilts 33 N10
Ogbourne St Andrew Wilts 33 N10
Ogbourne St George Wilts 33 P10
Ogden Calder 90 D4
Ogle Nthumb 112 H5
Oglet Lpool 81 N8
Ogmore V Glam 29 N9
Ogmore-by-Sea V Glam 29 N9
Ogmore Vale Brdgnd 29 P6
Ogwen Bank Gwynd 79 L11
Okeford Fitzpaine Dorset 12 D2
Okehampton Devon 8 E5
Oker Side Derbys 84 C8
Okewood Hill Surrey 24 D3
Olchard Devon 9 L5
Old Nhants 60 G6
Old Aberdeen C Aber 151 N6
Old Alresford Hants 22 G8
Oldany Highld 164 C10
Old Auchenbrack D & G 115 Q8
Old Basford C Nott 72 F2
Old Basing Hants 23 J4
Old Beetley Norfk 76 D8
Oldberrow Warwks 58 H11
Old Bewick Nthumb 119 L6
Old Bolingbroke Lincs 87 L8
Old Bramhope Leeds 90 G2
Old Brampton Derbys 84 D6
Old Bridge of Urr D & G 108 G7
Old Buckenham Norfk 64 F3
Old Burghclere Hants 22 E3
Oldbury Kent 37 N9
Oldbury Sandw 58 E7
Oldbury Shrops 57 N6
Oldbury Warwks 59 M6
Oldbury Naite S Glos 32 B6
Oldbury-on-Severn S Glos 32 B6
Oldbury on the Hill Gloucs 32 F7
Old Byland N York 98 B3
Old Cantley Donc 91 Q10
Old Cassop Dur 104 B3
Oldcastle Mons 45 L10
Oldcastle Heath Ches W 69 N5
Old Catton Norfk 77 J9
Old Churchstoke Powys 56 D6
Old Clee NE Lin 93 N9
Old Cleeve Somset 18 D6
Old Colwyn Conwy 80 B9
Oldcotes Notts 85 J3
Old Coulsdon Gt Lon 36 H9
Old Dailly S Ayrs 114 D4
Old Dalby Leics 72 H6
Old Dam Derbys 83 P9
Old Deer Abers 159 N8
Old Ditch Somset 19 P5
Old Edlington Donc 91 N11
Old Eldon Dur 103 P5
Old Ellerby E R Yk 93 L3
Old Felixstowe Suffk 53 P4
Oldfield C Brad 90 C3
Oldfield Worcs 46 F2
Old Fletton C Pete 74 C11
Oldford Somset 20 E4
Old Forge Herefs 45 R10
Old Furnace Herefs 45 P10
Old Glossop Derbys 83 M6
Old Goole E R Yk 92 B6
Old Grimsby IoS 2 b1
Old Hall Green Herts 51 J6
Oldhall Green Suffk 64 B10

Old Hall Street Norfk 77 L5
Oldham Oldham 83 K4
Oldham Crematorium Oldham 83 K4
Oldhamstocks E Loth 129 J5
Old Harlow Essex 51 L8
Old Heath Essex 52 H7
Old Hunstanton Norfk 75 N2
Old Hurst Cambs 62 D5
Old Hutton Cumb 95 M3
Old Inns Services N Lans 126 D3
Old Kea Cnwll 3 L5
Old Kilpatrick W Duns 125 M3
Old Knebworth Herts 50 F6
Old Lakenham Norfk 77 J10
Oldland S Glos 32 C10
Old Langho Lancs 89 L3
Old Laxey IoM 80 f5
Old Leake Lincs 87 M10
Old Malton N York 98 F5
Oldmeldrum Abers 151 L2
Oldmill Cnwll 5 P7
Old Milverton Warwks 59 L11
Old Mixon N Som 19 K3
Old Newton Suffk 64 F9
Old Oxted Surrey 37 J10
Old Portlethen Abers 151 N8
Old Quarrington Dur 104 B3
Old Radford C Nott 72 F2
Old Radnor Powys 45 K3
Old Rayne Abers 150 H2
Old Romney Kent 26 H7
Old Shoreham W Susx 24 F9
Oldshoremore Highld 164 F5
Old Soar Kent 37 P10
Old Sodbury S Glos 32 E8
Old Somerby Lincs 73 P4
Oldstead N York 98 A3
Old Stratford Nhants 49 L6
Old Struan P & K 141 K4
Old Swarland Nthumb 119 N10
Old Swinford Dudley 58 D8
Old Tebay Cumb 102 B9
Old Thirsk N York 97 P3
Old Town Calder 90 C5
Old Town Cumb 95 M4
Old Town Cumb 101 N2
Old Town E Susx 25 N11
Old Town IoS 2 c2
Old Trafford Traffd 82 H5
Old Tupton Derbys 84 E7
Oldwall Cumb 111 J8
Oldwalls Swans 28 E6
Old Warden C Beds 50 D2
Oldways End Somset 17 R7
Old Weston Cambs 61 N5
Old Wick Highld 167 Q6
Old Windsor W & M 35 Q10
Old Wives Lees Kent 39 J11
Old Woking Surrey 36 B9
Old Wolverton M Keyn 49 M6
Old Woodhall Lincs 86 H7
Old Woods Shrops 69 N10
Olgrinmore Highld 167 J6
Olive Green Staffs 71 L11
Oliver's Battery Hants 22 E9
Ollaberry Shet 169 q5
Ollach Highld 153 J10
Ollerton Ches E 82 G9
Ollerton Notts 85 L7
Ollerton Shrops 70 A9
Olmarch Cerdgn 43 M3
Olmstead Green Cambs 51 P2
Olney M Keyn 49 N4
Olrig House Highld 167 L3
Olton Solhll 58 H8
Olveston S Glos 32 B7
Ombersley Worcs 46 F2
Ompton Notts 85 L7
Once Brewed Nthumb 111 P7
Onchan IoM 80 e6
Onecote Staffs 71 J3
Onehouse Suffk 64 E10
Onen Mons 31 M2
Ongar Street Herefs 56 F11
Onibury Shrops 56 H9
Onich Highld 139 J5
Onllwyn Neath 29 M2
Onneley Staffs 70 D6
Onslow Green Essex 51 Q7
Onslow Village Surrey 23 Q5
Onston Ches W 82 C10
Openwoodgate Derbys 84 E11
Opinan Highld 153 N3
Orbliston Moray 157 Q6
Orbost Highld 152 D9
Orby Lincs 87 N7
Orchard Portman Somset 18 H10
Orcheston Wilts 21 L5
Orcop Herefs 45 P9
Orcop Hill Herefs 45 P9
Ord Abers 158 F6
Ordhead Abers 150 H5
Ordie Abers 150 D7
Ordiequish Moray 157 Q6
Ordley Nthumb 112 D9
Ordsall Notts 85 M5
Ore E Susx 26 D9
Oreleton Common Herefs 56 H11
Oreton Shrops 57 M8
Orford Suffk 65 N11
Orford Warrtn 82 D6
Organford Dorset 12 F6
Orgreave Staffs 71 L11
Orkney Islands Ork 169 d6
Orkney Neolithic Ork 169 b5
Orlestone Kent 26 H5
Orleton Herefs 56 H11
Orleton Worcs 57 N11
Orlingbury Nhants 61 J6
Ormathwaite Cumb 101 J5
Ormesby St Margaret Norfk 77 P9
Ormesby St Michael Norfk 77 P9
Ormiscaig Highld 160 D8
Ormiston E Loth 128 C6
Ormsaigmore Highld 137 M3
Ormsary Ag & B 123 N8
Ormskirk Lancs 88 E9
Ornsby Hill Dur 113 J11
Oronsay Ag & B 136 b4
Orphir Ork 169 c6
Orpington Gt Lon 37 L7
Orrell Sefton 81 L5
Orrell Wigan 82 B4
Orrell Post Wigan 88 B3
Orrisdale IoM 80 d3

Orroland D & G 108 G11
Orsett Thurr 37 P4
Orsett Heath Thurr 37 P4
Orslow Staffs 70 E11
Orston Notts 73 K2
Orthwaite Cumb 101 J4
Ortner Lancs 95 L10
Orton Cumb 102 B9
Orton Nhants 60 H5
Orton Staffs 58 C5
Orton Longueville C Pete .74 C11
Orton Rigg Cumb 110 F10
Orton-on-the-Hill Leics ..59 M4
Orton Waterville C Pete ..74 C11
Orwell Cambs 62 E10
Osbaldeston Lancs 89 J4
Osbaldeston Green
   Lancs 89 J4
Osbaldwick C York 98 C10
Osbaston Leics 72 C10
Osbaston Shrops 69 K10
Osborne IoW 14 F8
Osborne House IoW 14 F8
Osbournby Lincs 73 R3
Oscroft Ches W 81 Q11
Ose Highld 152 E9
Osgathorpe Leics 72 C7
Osgodby Lincs 86 E2
Osgodby N York 91 Q4
Osgodby N York 99 M4
Oskaig Highld 153 J10
Oskamull Ag & B 137 M7
Osmaston Derbys 71 M6
Osmington Dorset 11 Q8
Osmington Mills Dorset ..12 B8
Osmondthorpe Leeds 91 J4
Osmotherley N York 104 E11
Osney Oxon 34 E3
Ospringe Kent 38 H9
Ossett Wakefd 90 H6
Ossington Notts 85 N8
Ostend Essex 38 F2
Osterley Gt Lon 36 E5
Oswaldkirk N York 98 C5
Oswaldtwistle Lancs 89 L5
Oswestry Shrops 69 J9
Otford Kent 37 M9
Otham Kent 38 C11
Otham Hole Kent 38 D11
Othery Somset 19 L8
Otley Leeds 97 K11
Otley Suffk 65 J10
Otley Green Suffk 65 J10
Otterbourne Hants 22 E10
Otterburn N York 96 C9
Otterburn Nthumb 112 C2
Otter Ferry Ag & B 131 J11
Otterham Cnwll 5 K3
Otterhampton Somset 18 H6
Otterham Quay Kent 38 D8
Otterham Station Cnwll 5 K4
Otternish W Isls 168 e10
Ottershaw Surrey 36 B8
Otterswick Shet 169 s5
Otterton Devon 10 B7
Otterwood Hants 14 D6
Ottery St Mary Devon 10 C5
Ottinge Kent 27 L3
Ottringham E R Yk 93 N6
Oughterby Cumb 110 E9
Oughtershaw N York 96 C4
Oughterside Cumb 100 F2
Oughtibridge Sheff 84 D2
Oughtrington Warrtn 82 E7
Oulston N York 98 A6
Oulton Cumb 110 D10
Oulton Leeds 91 K5
Oulton Norfk 76 G6
Oulton Staffs 70 D10
Oulton Staffs 70 G7
Oulton Suffk 65 Q3
Oulton Broad Suffk 65 Q3
Oulton Street Norfk 76 H6
Oundle Nhants 61 M3
Ounsdale Staffs 58 C6
Our Dynamic Earth
   C Edin 127 P3
Ousby Cumb 102 B4
Ousden Suffk 63 M9
Ousefleet E R Yk 92 D6
Ouston Dur 113 L10
Outchester Nthumb 119 M4
Out Elmstead Kent 39 M11
Outgate Cumb. 101 L11
Outhgill Cumb 102 E10
Outhill Warwks 58 H11
Outlands Staffs 70 D8
Outlane Kirk 90 D7
Out Newton E R Yk 93 Q6
Out Rawcliffe Lancs 88 E2
Outwell Norfk 75 K10
Outwick Hants 21 M11
Outwood Surrey 36 H11
Outwood Wakefd 91 J6
Outwood Gate Bury 89 M9
Outwoods Leics 72 C7
Outwoods Staffs 70 D11
Ouzlewell Green Leeds ...91 J5
Ovenden Calder 90 D5
Over Cambs 62 E6
Over Ches W 82 D11
Over Gloucs 46 F11
Over S Glos 31 Q8
Over Burrows Derbys 71 P7
Overbury Worcs 47 J7
Overcombe Dorset 11 P8
Over Compton Dorset 19 Q11
Overdale Crematorium
   Bolton 89 K9
Over End Cambs 61 N2
Overgreen Derbys 84 D6
Over Green Warwks 59 J6
Over Haddon Derbys 84 B7
Over Kellet Lancs 95 L7
Over Kiddington Oxon 48 D10
Overleigh Somset 19 N7
Overley Staffs 71 M11
Over Monnow Mons 31 P2
Over Norton Oxon 48 B9
Over Peover Ches E 82 G10
Overpool Ches W 81 M9
Overscaig Highld 161 Q2
Overseal Derbys 71 P11
Over Silton N York 97 P2
Oversland Kent 39 J10
Overstone Nhants 60 G7
Overstrand Norfk 77 J3
Over Stowey Somset 18 G7
Over Stratton Somset 19 M11
Overstreet Wilts 21 L7

Over Tabley Ches E 82 F9
Overthorpe Nhants 48 E5
Overton C Aber 151 M5
Overton Ches W 81 Q9
Overton Hants 22 F5
Overton Lancs 95 J9
Overton N York 98 B9
Overton Shrops 57 J10
Overton Swans 28 E7
Overton Wakefd 90 H7
Overton Wrexhm 69 L6
Overton Bridge Wrexhm ..69 L6
Overton Green Ches E 70 E2
Overtown Lancs 89 P5
Overtown Lancs 95 N5
Overtown N Lans 126 E7
Overtown Swindn 33 N9
Overtown Wakefd 91 K7
Over Wallop Hants 21 Q7
Over Whitacre Warwks ...59 L6
Over Woodhouse Derbys ..84 G6
Over Worton Oxon 48 D9
Overy Oxon 34 G6
Oving Bucks 49 L10
Oving W Susx 15 P6
Ovingdean Br & H 25 J10
Ovingham Nthumb 112 G8
Ovington Dur 103 M8
Ovington Essex 52 C3
Ovington Hants 22 G8
Ovington Norfk 76 C11
Ovington Nthumb 112 G8
Ower Hants 14 E6
Ower Hants 22 B11
Owermoigne Dorset 12 C7
Owlbury Shrops 56 E6
Owlerton Sheff 84 D3
Owlpen Gloucs 32 E5
Owl's Green Suffk 65 K8
Owlsmoor Br For 23 M2
Owlswick Bucks 35 L3
Owmby Lincs 86 D3
Owmby Lincs 93 J10
Owslebury Hants 22 F10
Owston Donc 91 P8
Owston Leics 73 K9
Owston Ferry N Linc 92 D10
Owstwick E R Yk 93 N4
Owthorne E R Yk 93 P5
Owthorpe Notts 72 H4
Owton Manor Hartpl 104 E5
Oxborough Norfk 75 P10
Oxbridge Dorset 11 K5
Oxcombe Lincs 87 K5
Oxcroft Derbys 84 G6
Oxen End Essex 51 Q5
Oxenholme Cumb 95 L3
Oxenhope C Brad 90 C4
Oxen Park Cumb 94 G3
Oxenpill Somset 19 M6
Oxenton Gloucs 47 J8
Oxenwood Wilts 22 B3
Oxford Oxon 34 F3
Oxford Airport Oxon 48 E11
Oxford Crematorium
   Oxon 34 G3
Oxford Services Oxon 34 H4
Oxhey Herts 50 D11
Oxhill Dur 113 J10
Oxhill Warwks 48 B5
Oxley Wolves 58 D4
Oxley Green Essex 52 F9
Oxley's Green E Susx 25 Q6
Oxlode Cambs 62 G3
Oxnam Border 118 C7
Oxnead Norfk 77 J7
Oxshott Surrey 36 D8
Oxshott Heath Surrey 36 D8
Oxspring Barns 90 H10
Oxted Surrey 37 J10
Oxton Border 128 D9
Oxton N York 91 N2
Oxton Notts 85 K10
Oxton Wirral 81 L7
Oxwich Swans 28 E7
Oxwich Green Swans 28 E7
Oxwick Norfk 76 C6
Oykel Bridge Highld 161 P6
Oyne Abers 150 H2
Oystermouth Swans 28 H7
Ozleworth Gloucs 32 E6

P

Pabail W Isls 168 k4
Packers Hill Dorset 11 Q2
Packington Leics 72 B8
Packmoor C Stke 70 F4
Packmores Warwks 59 L11
Padanaram Angus 142 G7
Padbury Bucks 49 K8
Paddington Gt Lon 36 G4
Paddington Warrtn 82 D7
Paddlesworth Kent 27 L4
Paddlesworth Kent 37 Q8
Paddock Wood Kent 25 Q2
Paddolgreen Shrops 69 P8
Padgate Warrtn 82 D7
Padiham Lancs 89 M4
Padside N York 97 J9
Padstow Cnwll 4 E6
Padworth W Berk 34 H11
Page Bank Dur 103 P3
Pagham W Susx 15 N7
Paglesham Essex 38 F3
Paignton Torbay 7 M6
Pailton Warwks 59 Q8
Paine's Cross E Susx 25 P6
Painleyhill Staffs 71 J8
Painscastle Powys 44 H5
Painshawfield Nthumb ...112 G8
Painsthorpe E R Yk 98 G9
Painswick Gloucs 32 G3
Painter's Forstal Kent 38 G10
Paisley Rens 125 M5
Paisley Woodside
   Crematorium Rens 125 M5
Pakefield Suffk 65 Q3
Pakenham Suffk 64 C8
Pale Gwynd 68 C7
Pale Green Essex 51 Q2
Palestine Hants 21 Q6
Paley Street W & M 35 N9
Palfrey Wsall 58 F5
Palgrave Suffk 64 G6
Pallington Dorset 12 C6
Palmersbridge Cnwll 5 K6

Palmers Green Gt Lon 36 H2
Palmerston E Ayrs 115 K4
Palmerstown V Glam 30 F11
Palnackie D & G 108 H9
Palnure D & G 107 N5
Palterton Derbys 84 G7
Pamber End Hants 22 H3
Pamber Green Hants 22 H3
Pamber Heath Hants 22 H2
Pamington Gloucs 46 H8
Pamphill Dorset 12 G4
Pampisford Cambs 62 G11
Panborough Somset 19 N5
Panbride Angus 143 K10
Pancrasweek Devon 16 D10
Pancross V Glam 30 D11
Pandy Caerph 30 G7
Pandy Gwynd 54 E4
Pandy Gwynd 68 A9
Pandy Mons 45 L10
Pandy Powys 55 L4
Pandy Wrexhm 68 G7
Pandy'r Capel Denbgs 68 E4
Pandy Tudur Conwy 67 R2
Panfield Essex 52 B6
Pangbourne W Berk 34 H9
Pangdean W Susx 24 G8
Panks Bridge Herefs 46 B5
Pannal N York 97 M10
Pannal Ash N York 97 L10
Pant Shrops 69 J10
Pantasaph Flints 80 H9
Panteg Pembks 40 H4
Pantersbridge Cnwll 5 K8
Pant-ffrwyth Brdgnd 29 P8
Pant Glas Gwynd 66 H5
Pantglas Powys 54 H5
Pant-Gwyn Carmth 43 L9
Pant-lasau Swans 29 J4
Pant Mawr Powys 55 J8
Panton Lincs 86 G5
Pant-pastynog Denbgs ...68 D2
Pantperthog Gwynd 54 G4
Pant-y-dwr Powys 55 M10
Pant-y-ffridd Powys 56 B4
Pantyffynnon Carmth 28 H2
Pantygaseg Torfn 31 J5
Pant-y-gog Brdgnd 29 P6
Pantymenyn Carmth 41 M5
Pant-y-mwyn Flints 68 G2
Panxworth Norfk 77 M9
Papa Stour Airport Shet ...169 n8
Papa Westray Airport Ork .169 d1
Papcastle Cumb 100 F4
Papigoe Highld 167 Q6
Papple E Loth 128 F5
Papplewick Notts 84 H10
Papworth Everard
   Cambs 62 C8
Papworth St Agnes
   Cambs 62 C8
Par Cnwll 3 R3
Paramour Street Kent 39 N9
Parbold Lancs 88 F8
Parbrook Somset 19 Q7
Parbrook W Susx 24 C5
Parc Gwynd 68 A8
Parc Gwyn
   Crematorium Pembks ...41 M8
Parcllyn Cerdgn 42 D4
Parc Seymour Newpt 31 M6
Pardshaw Cumb 100 E6
Parham Suffk 65 L9
Park D & G 109 K2
Park Nthumb 111 N8
Park Bottom Cnwll 2 H5
Park Bridge Tamesd 83 K4
Park Corner E Susx 25 M3
Park Corner Oxon 35 J7
Park Corner W & M 35 N8
Park Crematorium Hants ..23 N5
Park Crematorium Lancs ..88 D5
Park End Bed 49 Q4
Parkend Gloucs 32 B3
Park End Nthumb 112 C5
Parker's Green Kent 37 P11
Parkeston Essex 53 M5
Parkeston Quay Essex 53 M5
Park Farm Kent 26 H4
Parkgate Ches W 81 K9
Parkgate Cumb 110 D11
Parkgate D & G 109 M3
Parkgate E Susx 26 B9
Parkgate Essex 51 Q5
Park Gate Hants 14 F5
Parkgate Kent 26 E5
Parkgate Kent 37 M8
Park Gate Leeds 90 F2
Parkgate Surrey 24 F2
Park Gate Worcs 58 D10
Park Green Essex 51 L5
Park Green Suffk 64 G9
Parkgrove
   Crematorium Angus ...143 L8
Parkhall W Duns 125 M3
Parkham Devon 16 F7
Parkham Ash Devon 16 F7
Park Head Derbys 84 E10
Park Hill Gloucs 31 Q5
Parkhouse Mons 31 P4
Parkmill Swans 28 F7
Park Royal Gt Lon 36 E4
Parkside Dur 113 P11
Parkside N Lans 126 E6
Parkside Wrexhm 69 L3
Parkstone Poole 12 H6
Park Street Herts 50 D10
Park Street W Susx 24 D4
Parkway Herefs 46 D7
Park Wood
   Crematorium Calder 90 E6
Parley Green Dorset 13 K5
Parmoor Bucks 35 L7
Parndon Wood
   Crematorium Essex 51 K9
Parracombe Devon 17 M2
Parrog Pembks 41 L3
Parsonby Cumb 100 F3
Parson Cross Sheff 84 D2
Parson Drove Cambs 74 G9
Parson's Heath Essex 52 H6
Parson's Hill Derbys 71 P9
Partick C Glas 125 N4
Partington Traffd 82 F6
Partney Lincs 87 M7
Parton Cumb 100 C6
Partridge Green W Susx ..24 E7
Partrishow Powys 45 K10
Parwich Derbys 71 M4
Paslow Wood Common
   Essex 51 N10

Passenham Nhants 49 L7
Passfield Hants 23 M8
Passingford Bridge
   Essex 51 M11
Paston C Pete 74 C10
Paston Norfk 77 L5
Pasturefields Staffs 70 H10
Patchacott Devon 8 C5
Patcham Br & H 24 H9
Patchetts Green Herts 50 D11
Patching W Susx 24 C9
Patchole Devon 17 L3
Patchway S Glos 32 B8
Pateley Bridge N York 97 J7
Paternoster Heath Essex ..52 F8
Pathe Somset 19 L8
Pathhead Fife 134 H9
Pathhead Mdloth 128 B7
Pathlow Warwks 47 N3
Path of Condie P & K 134 D5
Patmore Heath Herts 51 K5
Patna E Ayrs 114 H5
Patney Wilts 21 L3
Patrick IoM 80 b5
Patrick Brompton
   N York 97 K2
Patricroft Salfd 82 G5
Patrington E R Yk 93 P6
Patrington Haven E R Yk ..93 P6
Patrixbourne Kent 39 L10
Patterdale Cumb 101 L7
Pattingham Staffs 57 Q5
Pattishall Nhants 49 J4
Pattiswick Green Essex ...52 D7
Patton Shrops 57 K5
Patton Bridge Cumb 101 Q11
Paul Cnwll 2 D8
Paulerspury Nhants 49 K5
Paull E R Yk 93 P5
Paulton BaNES 20 C3
Paunton Herefs 46 C4
Pauperhaugh Nthumb ...119 M11
Pave Lane Wrekin 70 D11
Pavenham Bed 61 L9
Pawlett Somset 19 J6
Pawston Nthumb 118 G4
Paxford Gloucs 47 N7
Paxton Border 129 N9
Payden Street Kent 38 F11
Payhembury Devon 10 B4
Paynter's Lane End
   Cnwll 2 H5
Paythorne Lancs 96 B10
Paytoe Herefs 56 G10
Peacehaven E Susx 25 K10
Peak Dale Derbys 83 N9
Peak District National
   Park 83 Q6
Peak Forest Derbys 83 P9
Peak Hill Lincs 74 D10
Peakirk C Pete 74 C9
Pearson's Green Kent 25 Q2
Peartree Green Herefs 46 A8
Peasedown St John
   BaNES 20 D3
Peasehill Derbys 84 F11
Peaseland Green Norfk ...76 F8
Peasemore W Berk 34 E9
Peasenhall Suffk 65 M8
Pease Pottage W Susx 24 G4
Pease Pottage Services
   W Susx 24 G4
Peaslake Surrey 24 C2
Peasley Cross St Hel 81 Q6
Peasmarsh E Susx 26 E7
Peasmarsh Somset 10 G2
Peasmarsh Surrey 23 Q5
Peathill Abers 159 M4
Peat Inn Fife 135 M6
Peatling Magna Leics 60 C2
Peatling Parva Leics 60 C3
Peaton Shrops 57 J7
Pebmarsh Essex 52 E5
Pebsham E Susx 26 C10
Pebworth Worcs 47 M5
Pecket Well Calder 90 B5
Peckforton Ches E 69 P3
Peckham Gt Lon 36 H5
Peckleton Leics 72 D10
Pedairffordd Powys 68 F10
Pedlinge Kent 27 K4
Pedmore Dudley 58 D8
Pedwell Somset 19 M7
Peebles Border 117 K2
Peel IoM 80 b5
Peel Lancs 88 D4
Peel Common Hants 14 G6
Peel Green
   Crematorium Salfd 82 F5
Peene Kent 27 L4
Peening Quarter Kent 26 E6
Peggs Green Leics 72 C7
Pegsdon C Beds 50 D4
Pegswood Nthumb 113 K3
Pegwell Kent 39 Q9
Peinchorran Highld 153 J11
Peinlich Highld 152 G6
Pelcomb Pembks 40 H7
Pelcomb Bridge Pembks ..40 H7
Pelcomb Cross Pembks ...40 H7
Peldon Essex 52 G8
Pell Green E Susx 25 P4
Pelsall Wsall 58 F4
Pelsall Wood Wsall 58 F4
Pelton Dur 113 L10
Pelton Fell Dur 113 L10
Pelutho Cumb 109 P11
Pelynt Cnwll 5 L10
Pemberton Carmth 28 F4
Pemberton Wigan 82 C4
Pembles Cross Kent 26 E2
Pembrey Carmth 28 D4
Pembridge Herefs 45 M3
Pembroke Pembks 41 J10
Pembroke Dock Pembks ..41 J10
Pembrokeshire Coast
   National Park Pembks ..40 F6
Pembury Kent 25 P2
Pen-allt Herefs 45 R9
Penallt Mons 31 P2
Penally Pembks 41 M11
Penare Cnwll 3 P5
Penarth V Glam 30 G10
Penblewin Pembks 41 M7
Pen-bont
   Rhydybeddau Cerdgn ..54 F8
Penbryn Cerdgn 42 D4
Pencader Carmth 42 H4
Pencaenewydd Gwynd ...66 G6
Pencaitland E Loth 128 C6
Pencarnisiog IoA 78 F10

Pencarreg Carmth 43 K5
Pencarrow Cnwll 5 J5
Pencelli Powys 44 F9
Penclawdd Swans 28 F5
Pencoed Brdgnd 30 C8
Pencombe Herefs 46 A4
Pencoyd Herefs 45 R10
Pencraig Herefs 45 R10
Pencraig Powys 68 D9
Pendeen Cnwll 2 B7
Penderyn Rhondd 29 P3
Pendine Carmth 41 P9
Pendlebury Salfd 82 G4
Pendleton Lancs 89 M3
Pendock Worcs 46 E8
Pendoggett Cnwll 4 G6
Pendomer Somset 11 L2
Pendoylan V Glam 30 E9
Penegoes Powys 54 H4
Penelewey Cnwll 3 L5
Pen-ffordd Pembks 41 L6
Pengam Caerph 30 G5
Pengam Cardif 30 H9
Penge Gt Lon 37 J6
Pengelly Cnwll 4 H5
Pengorffwysfa IoA 78 H6
Pengover Green Cnwll 5 M8
Pen-groes-oped Mons 31 K3
Pengwern Denbgs 80 E9
Penhale Cnwll 2 H10
Penhale Cnwll 4 E10
Penhale Cnwll 4 H9
Penhale Cnwll 5 Q11
Penhallow Cnwll 3 K3
Penhalurick Cnwll 3 J6
Penhalvean Cnwll 3 J6
Penhill Swindn 33 N7
Penhow Newpt 31 M6
Penhurst E Susx 25 Q7
Peniarth Gwynd 54 E3
Penicuik Mdloth 127 N6
Peniel Carmth 42 H10
Peniel Denbgs 68 D2
Penifiler Highld 152 H9
Peninver Ag & B 120 E7
Penisarwaun Gwynd 67 K2
Penistone Barns 90 G10
Penjerrick Cnwll 3 K7
Penketh Warrtn 82 C7
Penkill S Ayrs 114 D8
Penkridge Staffs 58 D2
Penlean Cnwll 5 L2
Penleigh Wilts 20 H4
Penley Wrexhm 69 M6
Penllergaer Swans 28 H5
Pen-llyn IoA 78 F8
Penllyn V Glam 30 C9
Pen-lôn IoA 78 G11
Penmachno Conwy 67 P4
Penmaen Caerph 30 G5
Penmaen Swans 28 F7
Penmaenan Conwy 79 N9
Penmaenmawr Conwy 79 N9
Penmaenpool Gwynd 67 M11
Penmark V Glam 30 E11
Penmon IoA 79 L8
Penmorfa Gwynd 67 J6
Penmount
   Crematorium Cnwll 3 L4
Penmynydd IoA 79 J10
Penn Bucks 35 P6
Penn Wolves 58 C5
Pennal Gwynd 54 F4
Pennan Abers 159 K4
Pennant Cerdgn 43 K2
Pennant Denbgs 68 D8
Pennant Powys 55 K5
Pennant-Melangell
   Powys 68 D9
Pennard Swans 28 G7
Pennerley Shrops 56 F5
Pennicott Devon 9 L4
Pennines 90 B3
Pennington Cumb 94 F5
Pennington Hants 13 P5
Pennington Green
   Wigan 89 J9
Pennorth Powys 44 G9
Penn Street Bucks 35 P5
Pennsylvania S Glos 32 D10
Penny Bridge Cumb 94 G4
Pennycross Ag & B 137 N10
Pennygate Norfk 77 L7
Pennyghael Ag & B 137 N10
Pennyglen S Ayrs 114 D4
Penny Green Derbys 84 H5
Penny Hill Lincs 74 D7
Pennymoor Devon 9 L2
Pennywell Sundld 113 N9
Penparc Cerdgn 42 D5
Penparcau Cerdgn 54 D8
Penpedairheol Caerph 30 F5
Penpedairheol Mons 31 K4
Penpergwm Mons 31 K2
Penperlleni Mons 31 K4
Penpethy Cnwll 4 H4
Penpillick Cnwll 4 H10
Penpol Cnwll 3 L6
Penpoll Cnwll 5 J11
Penponds Cnwll 2 G6
Penpont Cnwll 4 H7
Penpont D & G 108 H2
Penpont Powys 44 D9
Penquit Devon 6 G8
Penrest Cnwll 5 N6
Penrherber Carmth 41 Q3
Pen-rhiw Pembks 41 P2
Penrhiwceiber Rhondd 30 E5
Pen Rhiwfawr Neath 29 K2
Penrhiwllan Cerdgn 42 F5
Penrhiw-pal Cerdgn 42 F5
Penrhos Gwynd 66 E8
Penrhos IoA 78 D8
Penrhos Mons 31 M2
Penrhos Powys 29 M2
Penrhos garnedd Gwynd ..79 K10
Penrhyn Bay Conwy 79 Q8
Penrhyncoch Cerdgn 54 E8
Penrhyn-coch Cerdgn 54 E8
Penrhyndeudraeth
   Gwynd 67 L7
Penrhyn-side Conwy 79 Q8
Penrice Swans 28 E7
Penrioch N Ayrs 120 G3
Penrith Cumb 101 P4
Penrose Cnwll 4 D7
Penruddock Cumb 101 M5
Penryn Cnwll 3 K7
Pensarn Conwy 80 D9
Pensax Worcs 57 N11
Pensby Wirral 81 K8

Penselwood Somset....20 E8
Pensford BaNES....20 B2
Pensham Worcs....46 H6
Penshaw Sundld....113 M10
Penshurst Kent....25 M2
Penshurst Station Kent....37 M11
Pensilva Cnwll....5 M7
Pensnett Dudley....58 D7
Penstone Devon....9 J4
Penstrowed Powys....55 P6
Pentewan Cnwll....3 Q4
Pentir Gwynd....79 K11
Pentire Cnwll....4 B9
Pentlepoir Pembks....41 M9
Pentlow Essex....63 P11
Pentlow Street Essex....63 P11
Pentney Norfk....75 P8
Pentonbridge Cumb....110 H5
Penton Grafton Hants....22 B5
Penton Mewsey Hants....22 B5
Pentraeth IoA....79 J9
Pentre Denbgs....68 E2
Pentre Flints....81 L11
Pentre Mons....31 K3
Pentre Mons....31 M4
Pentre Powys....55 P7
Pentre Powys....56 B7
Pentre Powys....56 D6
Pentre Rhondd....30 C5
Pentre Shrops....69 L11
Pentre Wrexhm....69 J6
Pentre-bâch Cerdgn....43 L5
Pentre Bach Flints....81 J9
Pentrebach Myr Td....30 E4
Pentre-bach Powys....44 C8
Pentrebeirdd Powys....56 B2
Pentre Berw IoA....78 H10
Pentre-bont Conwy....67 N4
Pentrebychan Crematorium Wrexhm....69 K5
Pentre-cagel Carmth....42 F6
Pentrecelyn Denbgs....68 F4
Pentre-celyn Powys....55 K3
Pentre-chwyth Swans....29 J6
Pentre-clawdd Shrops....69 J8
Pentredwr Denbgs....68 G5
Pentrefelin Gwynd....67 J7
Pentrefelin IoA....78 G6
Pentre Ffwrndan Flints....81 K10
Pentrefoelas Conwy....67 R4
Pentregalar Pembks....41 N4
Pentregat Cerdgn....42 G4
Pentre-Gwenlais Carmth....43 M11
Pentre Gwynfryn Gwynd....67 K9
Pentre Halkyn Flints....81 J10
Pentre Hodrey Shrops....56 E9
Pentre Isaf Conwy....80 D10
Pentre Llanrhaeadr Denbgs....68 E2
Pentre Llifior Powys....56 B5
Pentre-llwyn-llwyd Powys....44 D4
Pentre-llyn Cerdgn....54 E9
Pentre-llyn-cymmer Conwy....68 C4
Pentre-Maw Powys....55 K4
Pentre Meyrick V Glam....30 C9
Pentre-piod Torfn....31 J4
Pentre-poeth Newpt....31 J7
Pentre'rbryn Cerdgn....42 G4
Pentre'r-felin Cerdgn....43 M5
Pentre'r Felin Conwy....79 Q11
Pentre'r Felin Powys....44 C8
Pentre Saron Denbgs....68 D2
Pentre-tafarn-y-fedw Conwy....67 Q2
Pentre ty gwyn Carmth....43 R7
Pentrich Derbys....84 E10
Pentridge Dorset....21 K11
Pen-twyn Caerph....30 H4
Pen-twyn Mons....31 P3
Pen-twyn Torfn....31 J4
Pentwynmaur Caerph....30 G5
Pentyrch Cardif....30 F8
Penwithick Cnwll....4 G10
Penwood Hants....22 D2
Penwyllt Powys....44 B11
Penybanc Carmth....43 M10
Penybont Powys....44 G2
Pen-y-bont Powys....68 H10
Pen-y-bont-fawr Powys....68 E10
Pen-y-bryn Pembks....41 N2
Pen-y-cae Powys....29 M2
Penycae Wrexhm....69 J5
Pen-y-cae-mawr Mons....31 M5
Penycaerau Gwynd....66 B9
Pen-y-cefn Flints....80 G9
Pen-y-clawdd Mons....31 N3
Pen-y-coedcae Rhondd....30 E7
Penycwm Pembks....40 G5
Pen-y-fai Brdgnd....29 N8
Pen-y-felin Flints....80 H11
Penyffordd Flints....69 K2
Penyffridd Gwynd....67 J3
Pen-y-garn Cerdgn....54 E7
Pen-y-Garnedd Powys....68 F10
Pen-y-genffordd Powys....44 H9
Pen-y-graig Gwynd....66 C8
Penygraig Rhondd....30 D6
Pen-y-graigwen Gwynd....66 H4
Pen-y-Gwryd Gwynd....67 M3
Pen-y-lan V Glam....30 C9
Pen-y-Mynydd Carmth....28 D2
Penymynydd Flints....69 K2
Pen-y-pass Gwynd....67 L3
Pen-yr-Heol Mons....31 M2
Pen-yr-Heolgerrig Myr Td....30 D3
Penysarn IoA....78 H6
Pen-y-stryt Denbgs....68 H4
Penywaun Rhondd....30 C4
Penzance Cnwll....2 D7
Peopleton Worcs....46 H4
Peover Heath Ches E....82 G10
Peper Harow Surrey....23 P6
Peplow Shrops....70 A10
Pepper's Green Essex....51 P8
Pepperstock C Beds....50 C7
Perceton N Ayrs....125 K9
Percyhorner Abers....159 N4
Perelle Guern....10 b2
Perham Down Wilts....21 Q5
Periton Somset....18 C5
Perivale Gt Lon....36 E4
Perkins Village Devon....9 P6
Perkinsville Dur....113 L10
Perlethorpe Notts....85 K6
Perranarworthal Cnwll....3 K6

Perranporth Cnwll....3 K3
Perranuthnoe Cnwll....2 E9
Perranwell Cnwll....3 K5
Perranwell Cnwll....3 K6
Perran Wharf Cnwll....3 K6
Perranzabuloe Cnwll....3 K5
Perrott's Brook Gloucs....33 K3
Perry Birm....58 G6
Perry Barr Birm....58 G6
Perry Barr Crematorium Birm....58 G6
Perry Green Essex....52 D7
Perry Green Herts....51 K7
Perry Green Wilts....33 J7
Perrystone Hill Herefs....46 B9
Perry Street Somset....10 G3
Pershall Staffs....70 E9
Pershore Worcs....46 H5
Pertenhall Bed....61 N7
Perth P & K....134 E3
Perth Crematorium P & K....134 D2
Perthy Shrops....69 L8
Perton Herefs....46 A6
Perton Staffs....58 C5
Pertwood Wilts....20 G7
Peterborough C Pete....74 C11
Peterborough Crematorium C Pete....74 C10
Peterborough Services Cambs....61 P2
Peterchurch Herefs....45 L7
Peterculter C Aber....151 L7
Peterhead Abers....159 R8
Peterlee Dur....104 D2
Petersfield Hants....23 K10
Peter's Green Herts....50 D7
Petersham Gt Lon....36 E6
Peters Marland Devon....16 H9
Peterstone Wentlooge Newpt....31 J9
Peterston-super-Ely V Glam....30 E9
Peterstow Herefs....45 R10
Peters Village Kent....38 B9
Peter Tavy Devon....8 D9
Petham Kent....39 K11
Petherwin Gate Cnwll....5 M4
Petrockstow Devon....17 J10
Petsoe End M Keyn....49 N5
Pet Street Kent....27 J2
Pett E Susx....26 E9
Pettaugh Suffk....64 H10
Pett Bottom Kent....39 L11
Petterden Angus....142 G9
Pettistree Suffk....65 L10
Petton Devon....18 D10
Petton Shrops....69 M9
Petts Wood Gt Lon....37 L7
Pettycur Fife....134 H10
Petty France S Glos....32 E7
Pettymuk Abers....151 N3
Petworth W Susx....23 Q10
Pevensey E Susx....25 P9
Pevensey Bay E Susx....25 Q10
Pewsey Wilts....21 N2
Pheasant's Hill Bucks....35 L7
Phepson Worcs....46 H3
Philadelphia Sundld....113 M10
Philham Devon....16 D7
Philiphaugh Border....117 N5
Phillack Cnwll....2 F6
Philleigh Cnwll....3 M6
Philpot End Essex....51 P7
Philpstoun W Loth....127 K2
Phocle Green Herefs....46 B9
Phoenix Green Hants....23 L3
Pibsbury Somset....19 M9
Pica Cumb....100 D6
Piccadilly Warwks....59 K5
Piccotts End Herts....50 B9
Pickburn Donc....91 N9
Pickering N York....98 F4
Picket Piece Hants....22 C5
Picket Post Hants....13 L3
Picket Twenty Hants....22 C5
Pickford Covtry....59 L8
Pickford Green Covtry....59 L8
Pickhill N York....97 M4
Picklescott Shrops....56 G5
Pickmere Ches E....82 E9
Pickney Somset....18 G9
Pickstock Wrekin....70 C10
Pickup Bank Bl w D....89 L6
Pickwell Devon....16 H3
Pickwell Leics....73 K8
Pickwick Wilts....32 G10
Pickworth Lincs....73 Q4
Pickworth Rutlnd....73 P8
Picton Ches W....81 N10
Picton Flints....80 G8
Picton N York....104 D9
Piddinghoe E Susx....25 K10
Piddington Bucks....35 M6
Piddington Nhants....49 M4
Piddington Oxon....48 H11
Piddlehinton Dorset....11 Q5
Piddletrenthide Dorset....11 Q5
Pidley Cambs....62 D5
Piercebridge Darltn....103 P7
Pierowall Ork....169 d2
Piff's Elm Gloucs....46 H9
Pigdon Nthumb....113 J3
Pigeon Green Warwks....47 P2
Pig Oak Dorset....12 H4
Pig Street Herefs....45 M5
Pikehall Derbys....71 M3
Pilford Dorset....12 H4
Pilgrims Hatch Essex....51 N11
Pilham Lincs....85 Q2
Pill N Som....31 P9
Pillaton Cnwll....5 P9
Pillatonmill Cnwll....5 P9
Pillerton Hersey Warwks....47 Q5
Pillerton Priors Warwks....47 Q5
Pilleth Powys....56 D11
Pilley Barns....91 J11
Pilley Hants....13 P5
Pilley Bailey Hants....13 P5
Pillgwenlly Newpt....31 K7
Pillhead Devon....16 H6
Pilling Lancs....95 J11
Pilling Lane Lancs....94 H11
Pilning S Glos....31 Q7
Pilot Inn Kent....27 J8
Pilsbury Derbys....71 L2
Pilsdon Dorset....11 J5
Pilsgate C Pete....73 R9
Pilsley Derbys....84 B6
Pilsley Derbys....84 F8

Pilson Green Norfk....77 M9
Piltdown E Susx....25 K5
Pilton Devon....17 K5
Pilton Nhants....61 M4
Pilton Rutlnd....73 N10
Pilton Somset....19 Q6
Pilton Green Swans....28 D7
Pimbo Lancs....81 P4
Pimlico Herts....50 C9
Pimlico Lancs....89 L2
Pimlico Nhants....48 H6
Pimperne Dorset....12 F3
Pinchbeck Lincs....74 D5
Pinchbeck Bars Lincs....74 C5
Pincheon Green Donc....91 R7
Pinchinthorpe R & Cl....104 G8
Pincock Lancs....88 G7
Pinfold Lancs....88 D8
Pinford End Suffk....64 A10
Pinged Carmth....28 D4
Pingewood W Berk....35 J11
Pin Green Herts....50 G5
Pinhoe Devon....9 N6
Pinkett's Booth Covtry....59 L8
Pinkney Wilts....32 G7
Pinkneys Green W & M....35 N8
Pinley Covtry....59 N9
Pinley Green Warwks....59 K11
Pin Mill Suffk....53 M4
Pinminnoch S Ayrs....114 C9
Pinmore S Ayrs....114 D9
Pinn Devon....10 C7
Pinner Gt Lon....36 D3
Pinner Green Gt Lon....36 D3
Pinsley Green Ches E....69 Q5
Pinvin Worcs....47 J5
Pinwherry S Ayrs....114 D10
Pinxton Derbys....84 G10
Pipe and Lyde Herefs....45 Q6
Pipe Aston Herefs....56 H10
Pipe Gate Shrops....70 C6
Pipehill Staffs....58 G3
Piperhill Highld....156 F7
Pipers Pool Cnwll....5 M4
Pipewell Nhants....60 H3
Pippacott Devon....17 J4
Pippin Street Lancs....88 H6
Pipton Powys....44 H7
Pirbright Surrey....23 P3
Pirbright Camp Surrey....23 P3
Pirnie Border....118 C5
Pirnmill N Ayrs....120 H3
Pirton Herts....50 D4
Pirton Worcs....46 G5
Pisgah Cerdgn....54 F9
Pistyll Gwynd....66 E6
Pitblae Abers....159 N5
Pitcairngreen P & K....134 D2
Pitcalnie Highld....156 E3
Pitcaple Abers....151 J2
Pitcarity Angus....142 E4
Pitchcombe Gloucs....32 G3
Pitchcott Bucks....49 L10
Pitcher Row Lincs....74 E4
Pitchford Shrops....57 J4
Pitch Green Bucks....35 L4
Pitch Place Surrey....23 N7
Pitch Place Surrey....23 Q4
Pitchroy Moray....157 M10
Pitcombe Somset....20 C8
Pitcot V Glam....29 N10
Pitcox E Loth....128 G5
Pitfichie Abers....150 H4
Pitglassie Abers....158 G9
Pitgrudy Highld....162 H3
Pitlessie Fife....135 J6
Pitlochry P & K....141 M6
Pitmachie Abers....150 H2
Pitmain Highld....148 C7
Pitmedden Abers....151 M2
Pitmedden Garden Abers....151 M2
Pitminster Somset....18 H11
Pitmuies Angus....143 K8
Pitmunie Abers....150 H5
Pitney Somset....19 N9
Pitroddie P & K....134 G2
Pitscottie Fife....135 L5
Pitsea Essex....38 B4
Pitses Oldham....83 K4
Pitsford Nhants....60 G7
Pitstone Bucks....49 P11
Pitt Devon....18 D11
Pitt Hants....22 E9
Pittarrow Abers....143 N3
Pitt Court Gloucs....32 D5
Pittenweem Fife....135 P7
Pitteuchar Fife....134 H8
Pittington Dur....104 B2
Pittodrie House Hotel Abers....150 H3
Pitton Wilts....21 P8
Pitt's Wood Kent....37 P11
Pittulie Abers....159 N4
Pityme Cnwll....4 F6
Pity Me Dur....113 L11
Pivington Kent....26 F2
Pixey Green Suffk....65 J6
Pixham Surrey....36 E10
Plains N Lans....126 D4
Plain Street Cnwll....4 F6
Plaish Shrops....57 J5
Plaistow Gt Lon....37 K4
Plaistow W Susx....24 B4
Plaitford Hants....21 Q11
Plank Lane Wigan....82 D5
Plas Cymyran IoA....78 D9
Plastow Green Hants....22 F2
Platt Bridge Wigan....82 D4
Platt Lane Shrops....69 P7
Platts Heath Kent....38 E11
Plawsworth Dur....113 L11
Plaxtol Kent....37 P10
Playden E Susx....26 F7
Playford Suffk....53 M2
Play Hatch Oxon....35 K9
Playing Place Cnwll....3 L5
Playley Green Gloucs....46 E8
Plealey Shrops....56 G3
Plean Stirlg....133 N10
Pleasance Fife....134 G5
Pleasington Bl w D....89 J5
Pleasington Crematorium Bl w D....89 J5
Pleasley Derbys....84 H8
Pleasleyhill Notts....84 H8
Pleasurewood Hills Suffk....65 Q2
Pleck Dorset....11 Q2
Pledgdon Green Essex....51 N5
Pledwick Wakefd....91 J7

Pleinheaume Guern....10 b1
Plemont Jersey....11 a1
Plemstall Ches W....81 P10
Plenmeller Nthumb....111 P8
Plesley Essex....51 Q8
Plockton Highld....153 Q11
Plowden Shrops....56 F7
Plox Green Shrops....56 F3
Pluckley Kent....26 F2
Pluckley Station Kent....26 F3
Pluckley Thorne Kent....26 F3
Plucks Gutter Kent....39 N9
Plumbland Cumb....100 G3
Plumgarths Cumb....95 K2
Plumley Ches E....82 F10
Plump Hill Gloucs....46 C11
Plumpton Cumb....94 G5
Plumpton Cumb....101 N3
Plumpton E Susx....25 J8
Plumpton Nhants....48 G5
Plumpton End Nhants....49 K6
Plumpton Green E Susx....25 J7
Plumpton Head Cumb....101 P3
Plumstead Gt Lon....37 K5
Plumstead Norfk....76 G4
Plumstead Green Norfk....76 G4
Plumtree Notts....72 G4
Plumtree Green Kent....26 D2
Plungar Leics....73 K4
Plurenden Kent....26 F4
Plush Dorset....11 Q4
Plusha Cnwll....5 M5
Plushabridge Cnwll....5 N7
Plwmp Cerdgn....42 G4
Plymouth C Plym....6 D8
Plympton C Plym....6 E7
Plymstock C Plym....6 E8
Plymtree Devon....9 Q4
Pockley N York....98 C3
Pocklington E R Yk....98 G11
Pode Hole Lincs....74 D6
Podimore Somset....19 P10
Podington Bed....61 K8
Podmore Staffs....70 D7
Point Clear Essex....53 K9
Pointon Lincs....74 B4
Pokesdown Bmouth....13 K6
Polbain Highld....160 H4
Polbathic Cnwll....5 N10
Polbeth W Loth....127 J5
Polbrock Cnwll....4 G8
Poldark Mine Cnwll....2 H7
Polebrook Nhants....61 N3
Pole Elm Worcs....46 F4
Polegate E Susx....25 N10
Pole Moor Kirk....90 D7
Polesden Lacey Surrey....36 D10
Polesworth Warwks....59 L4
Polgigga Cnwll....2 B9
Polglass Highld....160 G5
Polgooth Cnwll....3 P3
Polgown D & G....115 P7
Poling W Susx....24 B10
Poling Corner W Susx....24 B9
Polkerris Cnwll....4 H11
Pollard Street Norfk....77 L5
Pollington E R Yk....91 Q7
Polloch Highld....138 D4
Pollokshaws C Glas....125 P5
Pollokshields C Glas....125 P5
Polmassick Cnwll....3 P4
Polmear Cnwll....4 H11
Polmont Falk....126 G2
Polnish Highld....145 N11
Polperro Cnwll....5 L11
Polruan Cnwll....5 J5
Polsham Somset....19 P6
Polstead Suffk....52 G4
Polstead Heath Suffk....52 G3
Poltalloch Ag & B....130 G8
Poltescoe Cnwll....3 J10
Poltimore Devon....9 N5
Polton Mdloth....127 P5
Polwarth Border....129 J9
Polyphant Cnwll....5 M5
Polzeath Cnwll....4 E6
Pomathorn Mdloth....127 N6
Pomeroy Derbys....83 P11
Ponde Powys....44 G7
Pondersbridge Cambs....62 C2
Ponders End Gt Lon....51 J11
Ponsanooth Cnwll....3 K6
Ponsonby Cumb....100 E9
Ponsongath Cnwll....3 K10
Ponsworthy Devon....7 J4
Pont Abraham Services Carmth....28 G3
Pontamman Carmth....28 H2
Pontantwn Carmth....28 D2
Pontardawe Neath....29 K4
Pontarddulais Swans....28 G4
Pont-ar-gothi Carmth....43 K10
Pont-ar-Hydfer Powys....44 B9
Pont-ar-llechau Carmth....43 P10
Pontarsais Carmth....42 H9
Pontblyddyn Flints....69 J2
Pont Cyfyng Conwy....67 N3
Pontcysyllte Aqueduct Wrexhm....69 J6
Pont Dolgarrog Conwy....79 P10
Pontdolgoch Powys....55 N6
Pont-Ebbw Newpt....31 J7
Pontefract Wakefd....91 M6
Pontefract Crematorium Wakefd....91 L6
Ponteland Nthumb....113 J6
Ponterwyd Cerdgn....54 G8
Pontesbury Shrops....56 F3
Pontesbury Hill Shrops....56 F3
Pontesford Shrops....56 G3
Pontfadog Wrexhm....68 H7
Pontfaen Pembks....41 K4
Pont-faen Powys....44 D8
Pontgarreg Cerdgn....42 F4
Pontgarreg Pembks....41 M2
Ponthenri Carmth....28 E3
Ponthir Torfn....31 K6
Ponthirwaun Cerdgn....42 E5
Pontlanfraith Caerph....30 G5
Pontliiw Swans....28 H5
Pontlottyn Caerph....30 F4
Pontlyfni Gwynd....66 G4
Pont Morlais Carmth....28 G3
Pontnêddfechan Neath....29 P3
Pontnewydd Torfn....31 J5
Pontnewynydd Torfn....31 J4
Pont Pen-y-benglog Gwynd....67 M2
Pontrhydfendigaid Cerdgn....54 G11

Pont Rhyd-sarn Gwynd....67 R9
Pont Rhyd-y-cyff Brdgnd....29 N7
Pont-rhyd-y-fen Neath....29 L6
Pontrhydygroes Cerdgn....54 G10
Pontrhydyrun Torfn....31 J5
Pontrilas Herefs....45 M9
Pont Robert Powys....55 Q2
Pont-rug Gwynd....67 J2
Ponts Green E Susx....25 Q7
Pontshaen Cerdgn....42 H5
Pontshill Herefs....46 B10
Pontsticill Myr Td....30 E2
Pont Walby Neath....29 N3
Pontwelly Carmth....42 H6
Pontyates Carmth....28 E3
Pontyberem Carmth....28 F2
Pont-y-blew Wrexhm....69 K7
Pontybodkin Flints....69 J3
Pontyclun Rhondd....30 D8
Pontycymer Brdgnd....29 P6
Pontyglasier Pembks....41 M3
Pontygwaith Rhondd....30 D6
Pontygynon Pembks....41 M3
Pont-y-pant Conwy....67 N4
Pontypool Torfn....31 J4
Pontypridd Rhondd....30 E7
Pont-yr-hafod Pembks....40 H5
Pont-yr-Rhyl Brdgnd....29 P7
Pontywaun Caerph....30 H6
Pool Cnwll....2 H5
Pool IoS....2 b2
Poole Poole....12 H6
Poole Crematorium Poole....12 H5
Poole Keynes Gloucs....33 J5
Poolewe Highld....160 D10
Pooley Bridge Cumb....101 N6
Pooley Street Norfk....64 F5
Poolfold Staffs....70 F3
Pool Head Herefs....45 R4
Poolhill Gloucs....46 D9
Pool in Wharfedale Leeds....97 K11
Pool of Muckhart Clacks....134 C7
Pool Quay Powys....56 D2
Pool Street Essex....52 C4
Pooting's Kent....37 L11
Popham Hants....22 G6
Poplar Gt Lon....37 J4
Poplar Street Suffk....65 M8
Porchfield IoW....14 D8
Poringland Norfk....77 K11
Porkellis Cnwll....2 H7
Porlock Somset....18 A5
Porlock Weir Somset....17 R2
Portachoillan Ag & B....123 N8
Port-an-Eorna Highld....153 Q10
Port Appin Ag & B....138 G8
Port Askaig Ag & B....122 F6
Portavadie Ag & B....124 A4
Port Bannatyne Ag & B....124 D4
Portbury N Som....31 P9
Port Carlisle Cumb....110 D8
Port Charlotte Ag & B....122 C8
Portchester Hants....14 H5
Portchester Crematorium Hants....14 H5
Port Clarence S on T....104 E6
Port Driseach Ag & B....124 B3
Port Ellen Ag & B....122 E10
Port Elphinstone Abers....151 K3
Portencalzie D & G....106 D3
Portencross N Ayrs....124 F9
Port Erin IoM....80 a8
Portesham Dorset....11 N7
Portessie Moray....158 B4
Port e Vullen IoM....80 g3
Port Eynon Swans....28 E7
Portfield Gate Pembks....40 H7
Portgate Devon....5 Q4
Port Gaverne Cnwll....4 G5
Port Glasgow Inver....125 J3
Portgordon Moray....158 A5
Portgower Highld....163 N4
Porth Cnwll....4 C9
Porth Rhondd....30 D6
Porthallow Cnwll....3 K9
Porthallow Cnwll....5 L11
Porthcawl Brdgnd....29 M9
Porthcothan Cnwll....4 D7
Porthcurno Cnwll....2 B9
Port Henderson Highld....153 P3
Porthgain Pembks....40 F4
Porthgwarra Cnwll....2 B9
Porthill Staffs....70 E5
Porthkea Cnwll....3 L5
Porthkerry V Glam....30 E11
Porthleven Cnwll....2 G8
Porthmadog Gwynd....67 K7
Porthmeor Cnwll....2 C6
Porth Navas Cnwll....3 K8
Portholland Cnwll....3 P5
Porthoustock Cnwll....3 L9
Porthpean Cnwll....3 Q3
Porthtowan Cnwll....2 H4
Porthwgan Wrexhm....69 L5
Porthyrhyd Carmth....43 K11
Porth-y-Waen Shrops....69 J10
Portincaple Ag & B....131 Q9
Portinfer Jersey....11 a1
Portington E R Yk....92 C4
Portinnisherrich Ag & B....131 K5
Portinscale Cumb....101 J6
Port Isaac Cnwll....4 F5
Portishead N Som....31 N9
Portknockie Moray....158 C4
Portland Dorset....11 P10
Portlethen Abers....151 N8
Portling D & G....109 J10
Portloe Cnwll....3 N6
Port Logan D & G....106 C9
Portlooe Cnwll....5 L11
Portmahomack Highld....163 L10
Portmeirion Gwynd....67 K7
Portmellon Cnwll....3 Q4
Port Mòr Highld....144 F12
Portmore Hants....13 P5
Portnacroish Ag & B....138 G8
Portnaguran W Isls....168 k4
Portnahaven Ag & B....122 A9
Portnalong Highld....152 E11
Port nan Giuran W Isls....168 k4
Port nan Long W Isls....168 d10
Port Nis W Isls....168 k1
Portobello Edinb....127 Q3
Portobello Gatesd....113 L9
Portobello Wolves....58 E5
Port of Menteith Stirlg....132 H7
Port of Ness W Isls....168 k1

Porton – Red Street 289

Porton Wilts 21 N7
Portontown Devon 5 Q6
Portpatrick D & G 106 C7
Port Quin Cnwll 4 F5
Port Ramsay Ag & B 138 F8
Portreath Cnwll 2 H4
Portreath Harbour Cnwll 2 H4
Portree Highld 152 H9
Port Righ Ag & B 120 F4
Port St Mary IoM 80 b8
Portscatho Cnwll 3 M6
Portsea C Port 14 H6
Portskerra Highld 166 E3
Portskewett Mons 31 N7
Portslade Br & H 24 G9
Portslade-by-Sea Br & H 24 G9
Portslogan D & G 106 C6
Portsmouth C Port 14 H7
Portsmouth Calder 89 Q5
Portsmouth Arms Devon 17 L8
Portsmouth Dockyard C Port 14 H6
Port Soderick IoM 80 d7
Port Solent C Port 14 H5
Portsonachan Hotel Ag & B 131 L3
Portsoy Abers 158 E4
Port Sunlight Wirral 81 L8
Portswood C Sotn 14 D4
Port Talbot Neath 29 L7
Port Tennant Swans 29 J6
Portuairk Highld 137 L2
Portway Herefs 45 P6
Portway Herefs 45 P7
Portway Sandw 58 E7
Portway Worcs 58 G10
Port Wemyss Ag & B 122 A9
Port William D & G 107 K9
Portwrinkle Cnwll 5 P11
Portyerrock D & G 107 N10
Posbury Devon 9 K5
Posenhall Shrops 57 M4
Poslingford Suffk 63 N11
Posso Border 117 J4
Postbridge Devon 8 G9
Postcombe Oxon 35 K4
Post Green Dorset 12 G6
Postling Kent 27 K4
Postwick Norfk 77 K10
Potarch Abers 150 G8
Potsgrove C Beds 49 Q8
Potten End Herts 50 B9
Potten Street Kent 39 N8
Potter Brompton N York 99 K5
Pottergate Street Norfk 64 H3
Potterhanworth Lincs 86 E7
Potterhanworth Booths Lincs 86 E7
Potter Heigham Norfk 77 N8
Potterne Wilts 21 J3
Potterne Wick Wilts 21 J3
Potter Row Bucks 35 P4
Potters Bar Herts 50 F10
Potters Brook Lancs 95 K10
Potter's Cross Staffs 58 B8
Potters Crouch Herts 50 D9
Potter's Forstal Kent 26 E2
Potters Green Covtry 59 N8
Potter's Green E Susx 25 M6
Potter's Green Herts 51 J6
Pottersheath Herts 50 F7
Potters Marston Leics 72 D11
Potter Somersal Derbys 71 L7
Potterspury Nhants 49 L6
Potter Street Essex 51 L9
Potterton Abers 151 N4
Potterton Leeds 91 L3
Potthorpe Norfk 76 C7
Pottle Street Wilts 20 F6
Potto N York 104 E10
Potton C Beds 62 B11
Pott Row Norfk 75 P6
Pott's Green Essex 52 F7
Pott Shrigley Ches E 83 K9
Poughill Cnwll 16 C10
Poughill Devon 9 L3
Poulner Hants 13 L3
Poulshot Wilts 21 J3
Poulton Gloucs 33 L4
Poulton Wirral 81 L6
Poulton-le-Fylde Lancs 88 C3
Poulton Priory Gloucs 33 L5
Pound Bank Worcs 57 N10
Poundbury Dorset 11 P6
Poundffald Swans 28 G6
Poundgate E Susx 25 L5
Pound Green E Susx 25 M6
Pound Green Suffk 63 M10
Pound Green Worcs 57 P9
Pound Hill W Susx 24 G3
Poundon Bucks 48 H9
Poundsbridge Kent 25 M2
Poundsgate Devon 7 J4
Poundstock Cnwll 5 L2
Pound Street Hants 22 E2
Pounsley E Susx 25 M6
Pouton D & G 107 N8
Pouy Street Suffk 65 M7
Povey Cross Surrey 24 G2
Powburn Nthumb 119 L7
Powderham Devon 9 N8
Powerstock Dorset 11 L5
Powfoot D & G 109 P7
Pow Green Herefs 46 D6
Powhill Cumb 110 D9
Powick Worcs 46 F4
Powmill P & K 134 C8
Poxwell Dorset 12 B8
Poyle Slough 36 B5
Poynings W Susx 24 G8
Poyntington Dorset 20 C10
Poynton Ches E 83 K8
Poynton Wrekin 69 Q11
Poynton Green Wrekin 69 Q11
Poyston Cross Pembks 41 J7
Poystreet Green Suffk 64 D10
Praa Sands Cnwll 2 F8
Pratt's Bottom Gt Lon 37 L8
Praze-an-Beeble Cnwll 2 G6
Predannack Wollas Cnwll 2 H10
Prees Shrops 69 Q8
Preesall Lancs 94 H11
Prees Green Shrops 69 Q8
Preesgweene Shrops 69 J7
Prees Heath Shrops 69 Q7
Prees Higher Heath Shrops 69 Q7
Prees Lower Heath Shrops 69 Q8
Prendwick Nthumb 119 K8
Pren-gwyn Cerdgn 42 H6
Prenteg Gwynd 67 K6
Prenton Wirral 81 L7
Prescot Knows 81 P6
Prescott Devon 10 B2
Prescott Shrops 57 M8
Prescott Shrops 69 M10
Presnerb Angus 142 B4
Pressen Nthumb 118 F3
Prestatyn Denbgs 80 F8
Prestbury Ches E 83 J9
Prestbury Gloucs 47 J10
Presteigne Powys 45 L2
Prestleigh Somset 20 B6
Prestolee Bolton 89 M9
Preston Border 129 K8
Preston Br & H 24 H9
Preston Devon 7 M4
Preston Dorset 11 Q8
Preston E R Yk 93 L4
Preston Gloucs 33 K4
Preston Herts 50 E6
Preston Kent 38 H9
Preston Kent 39 M9
Preston Lancs 88 G5
Preston Nthumb 119 N5
Preston Rutlnd 73 M10
Preston Shrops 57 J2
Preston Somset 18 E7
Preston Torbay 7 M6
Preston Wilts 33 K9
Preston Wilts 33 Q10
Preston Bagot Warwks 59 J11
Preston Bissett Bucks 49 J9
Preston Bowyer Somset 18 F9
Preston Brockhurst Shrops 69 P10
Preston Brook Halton 82 C8
Preston Candover Hants 22 H6
Preston Capes Nhants 48 G4
Preston Crematorium Lancs 88 H4
Preston Crowmarsh Oxon 34 H6
Preston Deanery Nhants 60 G9
Preston Green Warwks 59 J11
Preston Gubbals Shrops 69 N11
Preston Montford Shrops 56 G2
Preston on Stour Warwks 47 P5
Preston on Tees S on T 104 D7
Preston on the Hill Halton 82 C8
Preston on Wye Herefs 45 M6
Prestonpans E Loth 128 B5
Preston Patrick Cumb 95 L4
Preston Plucknett Somset 19 P11
Preston St Mary Suffk 64 C11
Preston Street Kent 39 N9
Preston-under-Scar N York 96 G2
Preston upon the Weald Moors Wrekin 70 B11
Preston Wynne Herefs 45 R5
Prestwich Bury 82 H4
Prestwick Nthumb 113 J6
Prestwick S Ayrs 114 G2
Prestwick Airport S Ayrs 114 G2
Prestwood Bucks 35 N4
Prestwood Staffs 58 C7
Price Town Brdgnd 29 P6
Prickwillow Cambs 63 J4
Priddy Somset 19 P4
Priestacott Devon 8 B3
Priestcliffe Derbys 83 P10
Priestcliffe Ditch Derbys 83 P10
Priest Hutton Lancs 95 L6
Priestland E Ayrs 125 P10
Priestley Green Calder 90 E5
Priest Weston Shrops 56 D5
Priestwood Green Kent 37 Q8
Primethorpe Leics 60 B2
Primrose Green Norfk 76 F8
Primrosehill Border 129 K8
Primrose Hill Cambs 62 E3
Primrose Hill Derbys 84 F9
Primrose Hill Dudley 58 D7
Primrose Hill Lancs 88 D9
Primsidemill Border 118 F5
Princes Gate Pembks 41 M8
Princes Risborough Bucks 35 M4
Princethorpe Warwks 59 P10
Princetown Devon 6 F4
Prinsted W Susx 15 L5
Prion Denbgs 68 E2
Prior Rigg Cumb 111 J7
Priors Halton Shrops 56 H9
Priors Hardwick Warwks 48 E3
Priorslee Wrekin 57 N2
Priors Marston Warwks 48 E3
Priors Norton Gloucs 46 G10
Priory Wood Herefs 45 K5
Prisk V Glam 30 D9
Priston BaNES 20 C2
Pristow Green Norfk 64 G4
Prittlewell Sthend 38 E4
Privett Hants 23 J9
Prixford Devon 17 K4
Probus Cnwll 3 M4
Prora E Loth 128 E4
Prospect Cumb 100 F2
Prospidnick Cnwll 2 G7
Protstonhill Abers 159 K5
Prudhoe Nthumb 112 G8
Prussia Cove Cnwll 2 F8
Publow BaNES 20 B2
Puckeridge Herts 51 J6
Puckington Somset 19 L11
Pucklechurch S Glos 32 C9
Puckrup Gloucs 46 G7
Puddinglake Ches W 82 F11
Puddington Ches W 81 L10
Puddington Devon 9 K2
Puddledock Norfk 64 F3
Puddletown Dorset 12 C6
Pudleston Herefs 45 R3
Pudsey Leeds 90 G4
Pulborough W Susx 24 B7
Puleston Wrekin 70 C10
Pulford Ches W 69 L3
Pulham Dorset 11 Q3
Pulham Market Norfk 64 H4
Pulham St Mary Norfk 65 J4
Pullens Green S Glos 32 B6
Pulloxhill C Beds 50 C4
Pulverbatch Shrops 56 G4
Pumpherston W Loth 127 K4
Pumsaint Carmth 43 N6
Puncheston Pembks 41 K5
Puncknowle Dorset 11 L7
Punnett's Town E Susx 25 P6
Purbrook Hants 15 J5
Purfleet Thurr 37 N5
Puriton Somset 19 K6
Purleigh Essex 52 D11
Purley Gt Lon 36 H8
Purley W Berk 35 J9
Purlogue Shrops 56 D9
Purlpit Wilts 32 G11
Purls Bridge Cambs 62 G3
Purse Caundle Dorset 20 C11
Purshull Green Worcs 58 C10
Purslow Shrops 56 F8
Purston Jaglin Wakefd 91 L7
Purtington Somset 10 H3
Purton Gloucs 32 C3
Purton Gloucs 32 C4
Purton Wilts 33 L7
Purton Stoke Wilts 33 L6
Pury End Nhants 49 K5
Pusey Oxon 34 C5
Putley Herefs 46 B7
Putley Green Herefs 46 B7
Putloe Gloucs 32 E3
Putney Gt Lon 36 F6
Putney Vale Crematorium Gt Lon 36 F6
Putsborough Devon 16 G3
Puttenham Herts 35 N2
Puttenham Surrey 23 P5
Puttock End Essex 52 D3
Putton Dorset 11 N8
Putts Corner Devon 10 C5
Puxley Nhants 49 L6
Puxton N Som 19 M2
Pwll Carmth 28 E4
Pwllcrochan Pembks 40 H10
Pwll-du Mons 30 H2
Pwll-glâs Denbgs 68 F4
Pwllgloyw Powys 44 E8
Pwllheli Gwynd 66 F7
Pwllmeyric Mons 31 P6
Pwll-trap Carmth 41 Q7
Pwll-y-glaw Neath 29 L6
Pydew Conwy 79 Q9
Pye Bridge Derbys 84 F10
Pyecombe W Susx 24 G8
Pye Corner Newpt 31 K7
Pye Green Staffs 58 E2
Pyle Brdgnd 29 M8
Pyleigh Somset 18 F8
Pylle Somset 20 B7
Pymoor Cambs 62 G3
Pymore Dorset 11 K6
Pyrford Surrey 36 B9
Pyrton Oxon 35 J5
Pytchley Nhants 61 J6
Pyworthy Devon 16 E11

Q

Quabbs Shrops 56 C8
Quadring Lincs 74 D4
Quadring Eaudike Lincs 74 D4
Quainton Bucks 49 K10
Quaker's Yard Myr Td 30 E5
Quaking Houses Dur 113 J10
Quantock Hills Somset 18 G7
Quarff Shet 169 r10
Quarley Hants 21 Q6
Quarndon Derbys 72 A2
Quarr Hill IoW 14 G8
Quarrier's Village Inver 125 K4
Quarrington Lincs 73 R2
Quarrington Hill Dur 104 B3
Quarrybank Ches W 82 C11
Quarry Bank Dudley 58 D7
Quarrywood Moray 157 M5
Quarter N Ayrs 124 F5
Quarter S Lans 126 C7
Quatford Shrops 57 N6
Quatt Shrops 57 P7
Quebec Dur 103 N2
Quedgeley Gloucs 32 F2
Queen Adelaide Cambs 63 J4
Queenborough Kent 38 F7
Queen Camel Somset 19 Q10
Queen Charlton BaNES 32 B11
Queen Dart Devon 17 Q8
Queen Elizabeth Forest Park Stirlg 132 G7
Queenhill Worcs 46 G7
Queen Oak Dorset 20 E8
Queen's Bower IoW 14 G10
Queensbury C Brad 90 E4
Queensferry Flints 81 L11
Queensferry Crossing Fife 134 E11
Queen's Head Shrops 69 K9
Queen's Hills Norfk 76 H9
Queenslie C Glas 126 B4
Queen's Park Bed 61 M11
Queen's Park Nhants 60 G8
Queen Street Kent 37 Q11
Queen Street Wilts 33 K7
Queenzieburn N Lans 126 B2
Quendon Essex 51 M4
Queniborough Leics 72 G8
Quenington Gloucs 33 M4
Quernmore Lancs 95 L9
Queslett Birm 58 G6
Quethiock Cnwll 5 N9
Quick's Green W Berk 34 G9
Quidenham Norfk 64 E4
Quidhampton Hants 22 F4
Quidhampton Wilts 21 M8
Quina Brook Shrops 69 P8
Quinbury End Nhants 48 H4
Quinton Dudley 58 E8
Quinton Nhants 49 L4
Quinton Green Nhants 49 L4
Quintrell Downs Cnwll 4 C9
Quixhall Staffs 71 L6
Quixwood Border 129 K7
Quoditch Devon 5 Q2
Quoig P & K 133 N3
Quorn Leics 72 F7
Quothquan S Lans 116 D3
Quoyburray Ork 169 e6
Quoyloo Ork 169 b4

R

Raasay Highld 153 K9
Rabbit's Cross Kent 26 C2
Rableyheath Herts 50 F7
Raby Cumb 110 C10
Raby Wirral 81 L9
Rachan Mill Border 116 G4
Rachub Gwynd 79 L11
Rackenford Devon 17 R8
Rackham W Susx 24 B8
Rackheath Norfk 77 K9
Racks D & G 109 M6
Rackwick Ork 169 b7
Radbourne Derbys 71 P7
Radcliffe Bury 89 M9
Radcliffe Nthumb 119 Q10
Radcliffe on Trent Notts 72 G3
Radclive Bucks 49 J8
Radcot Oxon 33 Q5
Raddery Highld 156 C6
Raddington Somset 18 D9
Radernie Fife 135 M6
Radford Covtry 59 M8
Radford Semele Warwks 48 B2
Radlet Somset 18 H7
Radlett Herts 50 E10
Radley Devon 17 N7
Radley Oxon 34 F5
Radley W Berk 34 C11
Radley Green Essex 51 P9
Radmore Green Ches E 69 Q3
Radnage Bucks 35 L5
Radstock BaNES 20 C4
Radstone Nhants 48 G6
Radway Warwks 48 C5
Radwell Bed 61 M9
Radwell Herts 50 F3
Radwinter Essex 51 P3
Radwinter End Essex 51 P3
Radyr Cardif 30 F8
RAF College (Cranwell) Lincs 86 D11
Rafford Moray 157 K6
RAF Museum Cosford Shrops 57 P3
RAF Museum Hendon Gt Lon 36 F2
Ragdale Leics 72 H7
Ragdon Shrops 56 H6
Raginnis Cnwll 2 D8
Raglan Mons 31 M3
Ragnall Notts 85 P6
Raigbeg Highld 148 E2
Rainbow Hill Worcs 46 G3
Rainford St Hel 81 P4
Rainham Gt Lon 37 M4
Rainham Medway 38 D8
Rainhill St Hel 81 P6
Rainhill Stoops St Hel 81 Q6
Rainow Ches E 83 K9
Rainsbrook Crematorium Warwks 60 B6
Rainsough Bury 82 H4
Rainton N York 97 N5
Rainworth Notts 85 J9
Raisbeck Cumb 102 B9
Raise Cumb 111 P11
Raisthorpe N York 98 H8
Rait P & K 134 G2
Raithby Lincs 87 K4
Raithby Lincs 87 L7
Raithwaite N York 105 N8
Rake Hants 23 M9
Rakewood Rochdl 89 Q8
Ralia Highld 148 C8
Ram Carmth 43 L5
Ramasaig Highld 152 B9
Rame Cnwll 3 J7
Rame Cnwll 6 C9
Ram Hill S Glos 32 C9
Ram Lane Kent 26 G2
Rampisham Dorset 11 M4
Rampside Cumb 94 E7
Rampton Cambs 62 F7
Rampton Notts 85 P5
Ramsbottom Bury 89 M7
Ramsbury Wilts 33 Q10
Ramscraigs Highld 167 K11
Ramsdean Hants 23 K10
Ramsdell Hants 22 G3
Ramsden Oxon 48 C11
Ramsden Worcs 46 H5
Ramsden Bellhouse Essex 38 B3
Ramsden Heath Essex 38 B2
Ramsey Cambs 62 C3
Ramsey Essex 53 M5
Ramsey IoM 80 g3
Ramsey Forty Foot Cambs 62 D3
Ramsey Heights Cambs 62 B4
Ramsey Island Essex 52 F10
Ramsey Island Pembks 40 D6
Ramsey Mereside Cambs 62 C3
Ramsey St Mary's Cambs 62 C3
Ramsgate Kent 39 Q8
Ramsgill N York 96 H6
Ramshaw Dur 103 M5
Ramshaw Dur 112 E11
Ramsholt Suffk 53 P3
Ramshope Nthumb 118 D10
Ramshorn Staffs 71 K5
Ramsley Devon 8 G6
Ramsnest Common Surrey 23 P8
Ranby Lincs 86 H5
Ranby Notts 85 L4
Rand Lincs 86 F5
Randalls Park Crematorium Surrey 36 E9
Randwick Gloucs 32 F3
Ranfurly Rens 125 K4
Rangemore Staffs 71 M10
Rangeworthy S Glos 32 C7
Rankinston E Ayrs 115 J5
Ranksborough Rutlnd 73 L8
Rank's Green Essex 52 B8
Rannoch Station P & K 140 B6
Ranscombe Somset 18 B6
Ranskill Notts 85 L3
Ranton Staffs 70 F10
Ranton Green Staffs 70 E10
Ranworth Norfk 77 M9
Raploch Stirlg 133 M9
Rapness Ork 169 e2
Rapps Somset 19 K11
Rascarrel D & G 108 G11
Rashfield Ag & B 131 N11
Rashwood Worcs 58 D11
Raskelf N York 97 Q6
Rassau Blae G 30 G2
Rastrick Calder 90 E6
Ratagan Highld 145 R4
Ratby Leics 72 E9
Ratcliffe Culey Leics 72 A11
Ratcliffe on Soar Notts 72 D5
Ratcliffe on the Wreake Leics 72 G8
Rathen Abers 159 N5
Rathillet Fife 135 K3
Rathmell N York 96 B9
Ratho C Edin 127 L3
Ratho Station C Edin 127 L3
Rathven Moray 158 B4
Ratlake Hants 22 D10
Ratley Warwks 48 C5
Ratling Kent 39 M11
Ratlinghope Shrops 56 G5
Rattar Highld 167 N2
Ratten Row Cumb 101 K2
Ratten Row Cumb 110 G11
Ratten Row Lancs 88 E2
Rattery Devon 7 J6
Rattlesden Suffk 64 D10
Ratton Village E Susx 25 N10
Rattray P & K 142 B8
Raughton Cumb 110 G11
Raughton Head Cumb 110 G11
Raunds Nhants 61 L6
Ravenfield Rothm 91 M11
Ravenglass Cumb 100 E11
Ravenhills Green Worcs 46 D4
Raveningham Norfk 65 M2
Ravenscar N York 105 Q10
Ravenscraig N Lans 126 D6
Ravensdale IoM 80 e3
Ravensden Bed 61 N10
Ravenseat N York 102 G10
Ravenshead Notts 85 J10
Ravensmoor Ches E 69 R4
Ravensthorpe Kirk 90 G6
Ravensthorpe Nhants 60 E6
Ravenstone Leics 72 C8
Ravenstone M Keyn 49 M4
Ravenstonedale Cumb 102 D10
Ravenstruther S Lans 126 G8
Ravensworth N York 103 M9
Raw N York 105 P9
Rawcliffe C York 98 B10
Rawcliffe E R Yk 92 A6
Rawcliffe Bridge E R Yk 92 A6
Rawdon Leeds 90 G3
Rawdon Crematorium Leeds 90 G3
Rawling Street Kent 38 F10
Rawmarsh Rothm 91 L11
Rawnsley Staffs 58 F2
Rawreth Essex 38 C3
Rawridge Devon 10 E3
Rawtenstall Lancs 89 N6
Raydon Suffk 52 H4
Raylees Nthumb 112 D2
Rayleigh Essex 38 D3
Raymond's Hill Devon 10 G5
Rayne Essex 52 B7
Raynes Park Gt Lon 36 F7
Reach Cambs 63 J7
Read Lancs 89 M4
Reading Readg 35 K10
Reading Crematorium Readg 35 K9
Reading Services W Berk 35 J11
Reading Street Kent 26 F5
Reading Street Kent 39 Q8
Reagill Cumb 102 B7
Realwa Cnwll 2 G6
Rearquhar Highld 162 G8
Rearsby Leics 72 H8
Rease Heath Ches E 70 A4
Reay Highld 166 G4
Reculver Kent 39 M8
Red Ball Devon 18 E11
Redberth Pembks 41 L10
Redbourn Herts 50 D8
Redbourne N Linc 92 G11
Redbrook Gloucs 31 P3
Redbrook Wrexhm 69 P6
Redbrook Street Kent 26 F4
Redburn Highld 156 G8
Redburn Nthumb 111 Q8
Redcar R & Cl 104 H6
Redcastle D & G 108 H7
Redcastle Highld 155 Q8
Red Dial Cumb 110 E11
Redding Falk 126 G2
Reddingmuirhead Falk 126 G2
Reddish Stockp 83 J6
Redditch Worcs 58 F11
Redditch Crematorium Worcs 58 F11
Rede Suffk 63 P9
Redenhall Norfk 65 K5
Redenham Hants 22 B5
Redesmouth Nthumb 112 C4
Redford Abers 143 P3
Redford Angus 143 K9
Redford W Susx 23 N9
Redfordgreen Border 117 M7
Redgate Rhondd 30 D7
Redgorton P & K 134 D2
Redgrave Suffk 64 E6
Redhill Abers 151 K7
Red Hill Bmouth 13 J5
Redhill Herts 50 H4
Redhill N Som 19 N2
Redhill Surrey 36 G10
Red Hill Warwks 47 M3
Redisham Suffk 65 N5
Redland Bristl 31 Q9
Redland Ork 169 c4
Redlingfield Suffk 64 H7
Redlingfield Green Suffk 64 H7
Red Lodge Suffk 63 L6
Red Lumb Rochdl 89 N7
Redlynch Somset 20 D8
Redlynch Wilts 21 P10
Redmain Cumb 100 F4
Redmarley Worcs 57 P11
Redmarley D'Abitot Gloucs 46 E8
Redmarshall S on T 104 C6
Redmile Leics 73 K3
Redmire N York 96 F2
Redmyre Abers 143 P2
Rednal Birm 58 F9
Rednal Shrops 69 L9
Redpath Border 118 A3
Redpoint Highld 153 N4
Red Post Cnwll 16 D10
Red Rock Wigan 88 H9
Red Roses Carmth 41 P8
Red Row Nthumb 119 Q11
Redruth Cnwll 2 H5
Redstocks Wilts 20 H2
Redstone P & K 142 B11
Redstone Cross Pembks 41 M7
Red Street Staffs 70 E4

Redvales Bury 89 N9
Red Wharf Bay IoA 79 J8
Redwick Newpt 31 M8
Redwick S Glos 31 P7
Redworth Darltn 103 P6
Reed Herts 51 J3
Reedham Norfk 77 N11
Reedness E R Yk 92 C6
Reeds Beck Lincs 86 H7
Reeds Holme Lancs 89 N6
Reepham Lincs 86 D6
Reepham Norfk 76 G7
Reeth N York 103 K11
Reeves Green Solhll 59 L9
Regaby IoM 80 f2
Regil N Som 19 P2
Reiff Highld 160 F4
Reigate Surrey 36 G10
Reighton N York 99 N5
Reisque Abers 151 M4
Reiss Highld 167 P6
Rejerrah Cnwll 4 B10
Releath Cnwll 2 H7
Relubbus Cnwll 2 F7
Relugas Moray 156 H8
Remenham Wokham 35 L8
Remenham Hill Wokham 35 L8
Rempstone Notts 72 F6
Rendcomb Gloucs 33 K3
Rendham Suffk 65 L9
Rendlesham Suffk 65 L11
Renfrew Rens 125 N4
Renishaw Derbys 84 G5
Rennington Nthumb 119 P7
Renton W Duns 125 K2
Renwick Cumb 101 Q2
Repps Norfk 77 N8
Repton Derbys 71 Q9
Reraig Highld 145 P2
Resaurie Highld 156 C8
Rescassa Cnwll 3 P5
Rescorla Cnwll 3 P4
Resipole Burn Highld 138 C5
Reskadinnick Cnwll 2 G5
Resolis Highld 156 B4
Resolven Neath 29 M4
Rest and be thankful Ag & B 131 Q6
Reston Border 129 M7
Restronguet Cnwll 3 L6
Reswallie Angus 143 J7
Reterth Cnwll 4 E9
Retford Notts 85 M4
Retire Cnwll 4 G9
Rettendon Essex 38 C2
Retyn Cnwll 4 D10
Revesby Lincs 87 J8
Rew Devon 7 J11
Rew Devon 7 K4
Rewe Devon 9 M5
Rew Street IoW 14 E8
Rexon Devon 5 Q4
Reydon Suffk 65 P6
Reymerston Norfk 76 E10
Reynalton Pembks 41 L9
Reynoldston Swans 28 E7
Rezare Cnwll 5 P6
Rhadyr Mons 31 L4
Rhandirmwyn Carmth 43 Q6
Rhayader Powys 55 M11
Rheindown Highld 155 P8
Rhes-y-cae Flints 80 H10
Rhewl Denbgs 68 F2
Rhewl Denbgs 68 G6
Rhewl-fawr Flints 80 G8
Rhewl Mostyn Flints 80 H8
Rhicarn Highld 164 C11
Rhiconich Highld 164 G6
Rhicullen Highld 156 B3
Rhigos Rhondd 29 P3
Rhireavach Highld 160 G2
Rhives Highld 163 J6
Rhiwbina Cardif 30 G8
Rhiwbryfdir Gwynd 67 M5
Rhiwderyn Newpt 31 J7
Rhiwen Gwynd 67 K2
Rhiwinder Rhondd 30 D7
Rhiwlas Gwynd 68 B7
Rhiwlas Gwynd 79 K11
Rhiwlas Powys 68 G8
Rhiwsaeson Rhondd 30 E8
Rhode Somset 19 J8
Rhoden Green Kent 37 Q11
Rhodes Notts 85 J5
Rhodes Minnis Kent 27 L3
Rhodiad-y-brenin Pembks 40 E5
Rhonehouse D & G 108 F9
Rhoose V Glam 30 E11
Rhos Carmth 42 G7
Rhos Denbgs 68 F2
Rhos Neath 29 K4
Rhosaman Carmth 29 K2
Rhosbeirio IoA 78 F6
Rhoscefnhir IoA 79 J9
Rhoscolyn IoA 78 D9
Rhoscrowther Pembks 40 H10
Rhosesmor Flints 81 J11
Rhos-fawr Gwynd 66 F7
Rhosgadfan Gwynd 67 J3
Rhosgoch IoA 78 G7
Rhosgoch Powys 44 H5
Rhos Haminiog Cerdgn 43 K2
Rhoshill Pembks 41 N2
Rhoshirwaun Gwynd 66 C9
Rhoslan Gwynd 66 H6
Rhoslefain Gwynd 54 D3
Rhosllanerchrugog Wrexhm 69 J5
Rhôs Lligwy IoA 78 H7
Rhosmaen Carmth 43 M10
Rhosmeirch IoA 78 H9
Rhosneigr IoA 78 E10
Rhosnesni Wrexhm 69 L4
Rhôs-on-Sea Conwy 79 Q8
Rhosrobin Wrexhm 69 K4
Rhossili Swans 28 D7
Rhostryfan Gwynd 66 H3
Rhostyllen Wrexhm 69 K5
Rhosybol IoA 78 G7
Rhos y-brithdir Powys 68 F10
Rhos-y-garth Cerdgn 54 E10
Rhos-y-gwaliau Gwynd 68 B8
Rhos-y-llan Gwynd 66 C9
Rhosymedre Wrexhm 69 J6
Rhos-y-meirch Powys 56 D11
Rhu Ag & B 132 B11
Rhualt Denbgs 80 F9
Rhubodach Ag & B 124 C3

Rhuddall Heath Ches W 69 Q2
Rhuddlan Cerdgn 43 J8
Rhuddlan Denbgs 80 E9
Rhulen Powys 44 H3
Rhunahaorine Ag & B 123 M10
Rhyd Gwynd 67 L6
Rhydargaeau Carmth 42 H9
Rhydcymerau Carmth 43 L7
Rhydd Worcs 46 F5
Rhyd-Ddu Gwynd 67 K4
Rhydding Neath 29 K5
Rhydgaled Conwy 68 C2
Rhydlanfair Conwy 67 Q4
Rhydlewis Cerdgn 42 F5
Rhydlios Gwynd 66 B9
Rhyd-lydan Conwy 68 A4
Rhydowen Cerdgn 42 H5
Rhydrosser Cerdgn 54 D11
Rhydspence Herefs 45 J5
Rhydtalog Flints 68 H4
Rhyd-uchaf Gwynd 68 B7
Rhydycroesau Shrops 68 H8
Rhydyfelin Cerdgn 54 D9
Rhydyfelin Rhondd 30 E7
Rhyd-y-foel Conwy 80 C9
Rhydyfro Neath 29 K3
Rhyd-y-groes Gwynd 79 K11
Rhydymain Gwynd 67 Q10
Rhyd-y-meirch Mons 31 K3
Rhydymwyn Flints 81 J11
Rhyd-y-pennau Cerdgn 54 E7
Rhyd-yr-onnen Gwynd 54 E4
Rhyd-y-sarn Gwynd 67 M6
Rhyl Denbgs 80 E8
Rhymney Caerph 30 F3
Rhynd P & K 134 F3
Rhynie Abers 150 D2
Rhynie Highld 163 J11
Ribbesford Worcs 57 P10
Ribbleton Lancs 88 H4
Ribby Lancs 88 E4
Ribchester Lancs 89 K3
Riber Derbys 84 D9
Riby Lincs 93 L9
Riccall N York 91 Q3
Riccarton Border 111 K2
Riccarton E Ayrs 125 L10
Richards Castle Herefs 56 H11
Richings Park Bucks 36 B5
Richmond Gt Lon 36 E6
Richmond N York 103 N10
Richmond Sheff 84 F3
Richmond Fort Guern 10 b2
Rich's Holford Somset 18 F8
Rickerscote Staffs 70 G10
Rickford N Som 19 N3
Rickham Devon 5 K11
Rickinghall Suffk 64 E6
Rickling Essex 51 L4
Rickling Green Essex 51 M5
Rickmansworth Herts 36 C2
Riddell Border 117 Q6
Riddings Derbys 84 F10
Riddlecombe Devon 17 L9
Riddlesden C Brad 90 D2
Ridge BaNES 19 Q3
Ridge Dorset 12 F7
Ridge Herts 50 F10
Ridge Wilts 21 J8
Ridgebourne Powys 44 F2
Ridge Green Surrey 36 H11
Ridge Lane Warwks 59 L6
Ridge Row Kent 27 M3
Ridgeway Derbys 84 F4
Ridgeway Worcs 47 K2
Ridgeway Cross Herefs 46 D5
Ridgewell Essex 52 B3
Ridgewood E Susx 25 L7
Ridgmont C Beds 49 Q7
Riding Mill Nthumb 112 F8
Ridley Kent 37 P8
Ridley Nthumb 111 Q8
Ridley Green Ches E 69 Q4
Ridlington Norfk 77 L5
Ridlington Rutlnd 73 L10
Ridlington Street Norfk 77 L5
Ridsdale Nthumb 112 D4
Rievaulx N York 98 B3
Rigg D & G 110 E2
Riggend N Lans 126 D3
Righoul Highld 156 F7
Rigmadon Park Cumb 95 N4
Rigsby Lincs 87 M5
Rigside S Lans 116 B3
Riley Green Lancs 89 J5
Rileyhill Staffs 58 H2
Rilla Mill Cnwll 5 M7
Rillaton Cnwll 5 M7
Rillington N York 98 H6
Rimington Lancs 96 B11
Rimpton Somset 20 B10
Rimswell E R Yk 93 P5
Rinaston Pembks 41 J5
Rindleford Shrops 57 N5
Ringford D & G 108 E9
Ringinglow Sheff 84 C4
Ringland Norfk 76 G9
Ringles Cross E Susx 25 L6
Ringlestone Kent 38 E10
Ringley Bolton 89 M9
Ringmer E Susx 25 K8
Ringmore Devon 6 H9
Ringmore Devon 7 N4
Ring o'Bells Lancs 88 F8
Ringorm Moray 157 P9
Ring's End Cambs 74 G10
Ringsfield Suffk 65 N4
Ringsfield Corner Suffk 65 N4
Ringshall Herts 35 Q2
Ringshall Suffk 64 E11
Ringshall Stocks Suffk 64 F11
Ringstead Nhants 61 L5
Ringstead Norfk 75 P2
Ringwood Hants 13 L3
Ringwould Kent 27 Q2
Rinmore Abers 150 C4
Rinsey Cnwll 2 F8
Rinsey Croft Cnwll 2 G8
Ripe E Susx 25 M8
Ripley Derbys 84 E10
Ripley Hants 13 L5
Ripley N York 97 L8
Ripley Surrey 36 C9
Riplingham E R Yk 92 G4
Riplington Hants 23 J10
Ripon N York 97 M6
Rippingale Lincs 74 A5
Ripple Kent 39 Q11
Ripple Worcs 46 G7
Ripponden Calder 90 C7

Risabus Ag & B 122 D11
Risbury Herefs 45 Q4
Risby N Linc 92 F8
Risby Suffk 63 P7
Risca Caerph 30 H6
Rise E R Yk 93 L2
Riseden E Susx 25 P4
Riseden Kent 26 B4
Risegate Lincs 74 D5
Riseholme Lincs 86 C5
Risehow Cumb 100 D4
Riseley Bed 61 M8
Riseley Wokham 23 K2
Rishangles Suffk 64 H8
Rishton Lancs 89 L4
Rishworth Calder 90 C7
Rising Bridge Lancs 89 M5
Risley Derbys 72 D3
Risley Warrtn 82 E6
Risplith N York 97 K7
Rivar Wilts 22 B2
Rivenhall End Essex 52 D8
River Kent 27 N3
River W Susx 23 P10
River Bank Cambs 62 H7
Riverford Highld 155 P7
Riverhead Kent 37 M9
Rivers Corner Dorset 12 C2
Rivington Lancs 89 J8
Rivington Services Lancs 89 J8
Roachill Devon 17 R7
Roade Nhants 49 L4
Road Green Norfk 65 K3
Roadhead Cumb 111 K6
Roadmeetings S Lans 126 F4
Roadside E Ayrs 115 L4
Roadside Highld 167 L4
Roadwater Somset 18 D7
Roag Highld 152 D9
Roa Island Cumb 94 E7
Roan of Craigoch S Ayrs 114 E7
Roast Green Essex 51 L4
Roath Cardif 30 G9
Roberton Border 117 M8
Roberton S Lans 116 C5
Robertsbridge E Susx 26 B7
Roberttown Kirk 90 F6
Robeston Wathen Pembks 41 L7
Robgill Tower D & G 110 D6
Robin Hill Staffs 70 G3
Robin Hood Lancs 88 G8
Robin Hood Leeds 91 J5
Robin Hood Crematorium Solhll 58 H8
Robinhood End Essex 52 B4
Robin Hood's Bay N York 105 P9
Roborough Devon 6 E6
Roborough Devon 17 K8
Robroyston C Glas 125 Q4
Roby Knows 81 N6
Roby Mill Lancs 88 G9
Rocester Staffs 71 L7
Roch Pembks 40 G6
Rochdale Rochdl 89 P8
Rochdale Crematorium Rochdl 89 P8
Roche Cnwll 4 F9
Rochester Medway 38 B8
Rochester Nthumb 118 F11
Rochford Essex 38 E3
Rochford Worcs 57 L11
Roch Gate Pembks 40 G6
Rock Cnwll 4 E6
Rock Neath 29 L6
Rock Nthumb 119 P6
Rock W Susx 24 D8
Rock Worcs 57 N10
Rockbeare Devon 9 P6
Rockbourne Hants 21 M11
Rockcliffe Cumb 110 G8
Rockcliffe D & G 108 H10
Rockcliffe Cross Cumb 110 F8
Rock End Staffs 70 F3
Rockend Torbay 7 N6
Rock Ferry Wirral 81 L7
Rockfield Highld 163 L10
Rockfield Mons 31 N2
Rockford Devon 17 P2
Rockford Hants 13 L3
Rockgreen Shrops 57 J9
Rockhampton S Glos 32 C6
Rockhead Cnwll 4 H5
Rockhill Shrops 56 D9
Rock Hill Worcs 58 E11
Rockingham Nhants 61 J2
Rockland All Saints Norfk 64 D2
Rockland St Mary Norfk 77 L11
Rockland St Peter Norfk 64 D2
Rockley Notts 85 M6
Rockley Wilts 33 N10
Rockliffe Lancs 89 P6
Rockville Ag & B 131 Q9
Rockwell End Bucks 35 L7
Rockwell Green Somset 18 F10
Rodborough Gloucs 32 F4
Rodbourne Swindn 33 M7
Rodbourne Wilts 32 H8
Rodd Herefs 45 L2
Roddam Nthumb 119 K6
Rodden Dorset 11 M8
Roddymoor Dur 103 N3
Rode Somset 20 F4
Rode Heath Ches E 70 E3
Rode Heath Ches E 83 J11
Rodel W Isls 168 f9
Roden Wrekin 69 Q11
Rodhuish Somset 18 D7
Rodington Wrekin 57 K2
Rodington Heath Wrekin 57 K2
Rodley Gloucs 32 D2
Rodley Leeds 90 G3
Rodmarton Gloucs 32 H5
Rodmell E Susx 25 K9
Rodmersham Kent 38 F9
Rodmersham Green Kent 38 F9
Rodney Stoke Somset 19 N5
Rodsley Derbys 71 N6
Rodway Somset 19 J6
Roecliffe N York 97 N7
Roe Cross Tamesd 83 L5
Roe Green Herts 50 F9
Roe Green Herts 51 H4
Roehampton Gt Lon 36 F6
Roffey W Susx 24 E4
Rogart Highld 162 G6
Rogate W Susx 23 M10
Roger Ground Cumb 101 L11

Rogerstone Newpt 31 J7
Roghadal W Isls 168 f9
Rogiet Mons 31 N7
Roke Oxon 34 H6
Roker Sundld 113 P9
Rollesby Norfk 77 N8
Rolleston Leics 73 J10
Rolleston Notts 85 M10
Rolleston on Dove Staffs 71 N9
Rolston E R Yk 93 M2
Rolstone N Som 19 L2
Rolvenden Kent 26 D5
Rolvenden Layne Kent 26 E5
Romaldkirk Dur 103 J6
Romanby N York 97 N1
Romanno Bridge Border 127 M4
Romansleigh Devon 17 N7
Romdesal Highld 152 G7
Romford Dorset 13 J3
Romford Gt Lon 37 M3
Romiley Stockp 83 K6
Romney Street Kent 37 N8
Romsey Cambs 62 G9
Romsey Hants 22 C10
Romsley Shrops 57 P8
Romsley Worcs 58 E8
Rona Highld 153 L6
Ronachan Ag & B 123 M9
Rood Ashton Wilts 20 G3
Rookhope Dur 102 H2
Rookley IoW 14 F10
Rookley Green IoW 14 F10
Rooks Bridge Somset 19 L4
Rooks Nest Somset 18 E8
Rookwith N York 97 K3
Roos E R Yk 93 N4
Roose Cumb 94 E7
Roosebeck Cumb 94 F7
Roothams Green Bed 61 N9
Ropley Hants 22 H8
Ropley Dean Hants 22 H8
Ropley Soke Hants 23 J8
Ropsley Lincs 73 P4
Rora Abers 159 Q7
Rorrington Shrops 56 E4
Rosarie Moray 158 A7
Rose Cnwll 3 K3
Roseacre Lancs 88 E3
Rose Ash Devon 17 P7
Rosebank S Lans 126 E5
Rosebush Pembks 41 L5
Rosecare Cnwll 5 K2
Rosecliston Cnwll 4 C10
Rosedale Abbey N York 105 K11
Rose Green Essex 52 F6
Rose Green Suffk 52 F4
Rose Green Suffk 52 G3
Rose Green W Susx 15 P7
Rosehall Highld 162 B6
Rosehearty Abers 159 M4
Rose Hill E Susx 25 L7
Rose Hill Lancs 89 N4
Rosehill Shrops 69 N11
Rose Hill Crematorium Donc 91 Q10
Roseisle Moray 157 L4
Roselands E Susx 25 P10
Rosemarket Pembks 41 J9
Rosemarkie Highld 156 C6
Rosemary Lane Devon 10 D2
Rosemount P & K 142 B9
Rosenannon Cnwll 4 F7
Rosenithon Cnwll 3 L9
Roser's Cross E Susx 25 M6
Rosevean Cnwll 4 G10
Rosevine Cnwll 3 M6
Rosewarne Cnwll 2 G6
Rosewell Mdloth 127 P5
Roseworth S on T 104 D6
Roseworthy Cnwll 2 G6
Rosgill Cumb 101 P7
Roskestal Cnwll 2 B9
Roskhill Highld 152 D9
Roskorwell Cnwll 3 K9
Rosley Cumb 110 F11
Roslin Mdloth 127 P5
Rosliston Derbys 71 N11
Rosneath Ag & B 132 B11
Ross D & G 108 D12
Ross Nthumb 119 M3
Rossett Wrexhm 69 L3
Rossett Green N York 97 L10
Rossington Donc 91 Q11
Ross-on-Wye Herefs 46 A10
Roster Highld 167 N9
Rostherne Ches E 82 F8
Rosthwaite Cumb 101 J8
Roston Derbys 71 L6
Rosudgeon Cnwll 2 F8
Rosyth Fife 134 E11
Rothbury Nthumb 119 L10
Rotherby Leics 72 H7
Rotherfield E Susx 25 N5
Rotherfield Greys Oxon 35 K8
Rotherfield Peppard Oxon 35 K8
Rotherham Crematorium Rothm 84 G2
Rothersthorpe Nhants 60 F9
Rotherwick Hants 23 K3
Rothes Moray 157 P8
Rothesay Ag & B 124 D5
Rothiebrisbane Abers 158 H10
Rothiemurchus Lodge Highld 148 H6
Rothienorman Abers 158 H10
Rothley Leics 72 F8
Rothley Nthumb 112 F3
Rothmaise Abers 158 F10
Rothwell Leeds 91 J5
Rothwell Lincs 93 K11
Rothwell Nhants 60 H4
Rotsea E R Yk 99 M10
Rottal Lodge Angus 142 F4
Rottingdean Br & H 25 J10
Rottington Cumb 100 C8
Roucan D & G 109 M5
Roucan Loch Crematorium D & G 109 M10
Roud IoW 14 F10
Rougham Norfk 76 A7
Rougham Suffk 64 C9
Rough Close Staffs 70 G7
Rough Common Kent 39 K10
Roughlee Lancs 89 N2
Roughpark Abers 149 Q5
Roughton Lincs 86 H8
Roughton Norfk 77 K4

Roughton Shrops 57 P6
Roughway Kent 37 P10
Roundbush Essex 52 E11
Round Bush Herts 50 D11
Roundbush Green Essex 51 N8
Round Green Luton 50 D6
Roundham Somset 11 J3
Roundhay Leeds 91 J3
Rounds Green Sandw 58 E7
Round Street Kent 37 Q7
Roundstreet Common W Susx 24 C5
Roundswell Devon 17 J5
Roundway Wilts 21 K2
Roundyhill Angus 142 F7
Rousay Ork 169 c3
Rousdon Devon 10 F6
Rousham Oxon 48 E9
Rous Lench Worcs 47 K4
Routenburn N Ayrs 124 F5
Routh E R Yk 93 J2
Rout's Green Bucks 35 L5
Row Cnwll 4 H6
Row Cumb 95 K3
Row Cumb 102 B4
Rowanburn D & G 110 H5
Rowardennan Stirlg 132 D8
Rowarth Derbys 83 M7
Row Ash Hants 14 F4
Rowberrow Somset 19 N3
Rowborough IoW 14 E10
Rowde Wilts 21 J2
Rowden Devon 8 F5
Rowen Conwy 79 P10
Rowfield Derbys 71 M5
Rowfoot Nthumb 111 N8
Rowford Somset 18 H9
Row Green Essex 52 B7
Rowhedge Essex 52 H7
Rowhook W Susx 24 D4
Rowington Warwks 59 K11
Rowland Derbys 84 B6
Rowland's Castle Hants 15 K4
Rowlands Gill Gatesd 113 J9
Rowledge Surrey 23 M6
Rowley Dur 112 G10
Rowley E R Yk 92 G4
Rowley Shrops 56 E3
Rowley Hill Kirk 90 F8
Rowley Regis Sandw 58 E7
Rowley Regis Crematorium Sandw 58 E7
Rowlstone Herefs 45 M9
Rowly Surrey 24 B2
Rowner Hants 14 G6
Rowney Green Worcs 58 F10
Rownhams Hants 22 C11
Rownhams Services Hants 22 C11
Rowrah Cumb 100 E7
Rowsham Bucks 49 M11
Rowsley Derbys 84 C7
Rowstock Oxon 34 E7
Rowston Lincs 86 E9
Rowthorne Derbys 84 G8
Rowton Ches W 69 M2
Rowton Shrops 56 F2
Rowton Shrops 56 G8
Rowton Wrekin 69 R11
Row Town Surrey 36 B8
Roxburgh Border 118 C4
Roxby N Linc 92 F7
Roxby N York 105 L7
Roxton Bed 61 Q10
Roxwell Essex 51 P4
Royal Leamington Spa Warwks 59 M11
Royal Oak Darltn 103 P6
Royal Oak Lancs 81 N4
Royal's Green Ches E 69 R6
Royal Sutton Coldfield Birm 58 H5
Royal Tunbridge Wells Kent 25 N3
Royal Wootton Bassett Wilts 33 L8
Royal Yacht Britannia C Edin 127 P2
Roy Bridge Highld 146 H11
Roydhouse Kirk 90 G8
Roydon Essex 51 K8
Roydon Norfk 64 G5
Roydon Norfk 75 P6
Roydon Hamlet Essex 51 K9
Royston Barns 91 K8
Royston Herts 51 J2
Royton Oldham 89 Q9
Rozel Jersey 11 c1
Ruabon Wrexhm 69 K6
Ruaig Ag & B 136 D6
Ruan High Lanes Cnwll 3 N6
Ruan Lanihorne Cnwll 3 M5
Ruan Major Cnwll 3 J10
Ruan Minor Cnwll 3 J10
Ruardean Gloucs 46 B11
Ruardean Hill Gloucs 46 B11
Ruardean Woodside Gloucs 46 B11
Rubery Birm 58 E9
Rubha Ban W Isls 168 c16
Ruckcroft Cumb 101 P2
Ruckhall Herefs 45 P7
Ruckinge Kent 26 H5
Ruckland Lincs 87 K5
Ruckley Shrops 57 J4
Rudbaxton Pembks 41 J6
Rudby N York 104 E9
Rudchester Nthumb 112 H7
Ruddington Notts 72 F4
Ruddle Gloucs 32 C2
Ruddlemoor Cnwll 3 Q3
Rudford Gloucs 46 E10
Rudge Somset 20 F4
Rudgeway S Glos 32 B7
Rudgwick W Susx 24 B4
Rudhall Herefs 46 B9
Rudheath Ches W 82 E10
Rudheath Woods Ches E 82 F10
Rudley Green Essex 52 D11
Rudloe Wilts 32 F10
Rudry Caerph 30 G7
Rudston E R Yk 99 M7
Rudyard Staffs 70 H3
Ruecastle Border 118 B6
Rufford Lancs 88 F7
Rufford Abbey Notts 85 K8
Rufforth C York 98 A10
Rugby Warwks 60 B5
Rugeley Staffs 71 J11
Ruishton Somset 19 J9

Ruislip Gt Lon....36 C3
Rùm Highld....144 E8
Rumbach Moray....158 A7
Rumbling Bridge P & K....134 C8
Rumburgh Suffk....65 L5
Rumby Hill Dur....103 N4
Rumford Cnwll....4 D7
Rumford Falk....126 G2
Rumney Cardif....30 H9
Rumwell Somset....18 G10
Runcorn Halton....81 Q8
Runcton W Susx....15 N6
Runcton Holme Norfk....75 M9
Runfold Surrey....23 N5
Runhall Norfk....76 F10
Runham Norfk....77 P9
Runham Norfk....77 Q10
Runnington Somset....18 F10
Runsell Green Essex....52 C10
Runshaw Moor Lancs....88 G7
Runswick N York....105 M7
Runtaleave Angus....142 D4
Runwell Essex....38 C3
Ruscombe Wokham....35 L9
Rushall Herefs....46 B7
Rushall Norfk....64 H5
Rushall Wilts....21 M3
Rushall Wsall....58 F4
Rushbrooke Suffk....64 B9
Rushbury Shrops....57 J6
Rushden Herts....50 H4
Rushden Nhants....61 L7
Rushenden Kent....38 F7
Rusher's Cross E Susx....25 P5
Rushford Devon....8 C9
Rushford Norfk....64 C5
Rush Green Essex....53 L8
Rush Green Gt Lon....37 M3
Rush Green Herts....50 F6
Rush Green Warrtn....82 G7
Rushlake Green E Susx....25 P7
Rushmere Suffk....65 P4
Rushmere St Andrew Suffk....53 L2
Rushmoor Surrey....23 N6
Rushock Herefs....45 L3
Rushock Worcs....58 C10
Rusholme Manch....83 J6
Rushton Ches W....69 Q2
Rushton Nhants....60 H4
Rushton Shrops....57 L3
Rushton Spencer Staffs....70 G2
Rushwick Worcs....46 F4
Rushyford Dur....103 Q5
Ruskie Stirlg....133 J7
Ruskington Lincs....86 E10
Rusland Cross Cumb....94 G3
Rusper W Susx....24 F3
Ruspidge Gloucs....32 C2
Russell Green Essex....52 B9
Russell's Water Oxon....35 K7
Russel's Green Suffk....65 K7
Russ Hill Surrey....24 F2
Rusthall Kent....25 N3
Rustington W Susx....24 B10
Ruston N York....99 K4
Ruston Parva E R Yk....99 M8
Ruswarp N York....105 N9
Ruthall Shrops....57 K6
Rutherford Border....118 B4
Rutherglen S Lans....125 Q5
Ruthernbridge Cnwll....4 G8
Ruthin Denbgs....68 F3
Ruthrieston C Aber....151 N7
Ruthven Abers....158 D8
Ruthven Angus....142 D8
Ruthven Highld....148 D8
Ruthven Highld....156 E11
Ruthvoes Cnwll....4 E9
Ruthwaite Cumb....100 H3
Ruthwell D & G....109 N7
Ruxley Corner Gt Lon....37 L6
Ruxton Green Herefs....45 Q11
Ruyton-XI-Towns Shrops....69 L10
Ryal Nthumb....112 F6
Ryall Dorset....11 J5
Ryall Worcs....46 G6
Ryarsh Kent....37 Q8
Rycote Oxon....35 J3
Rydal Cumb....101 L9
Ryde IoW....14 G8
Rye E Susx....26 F7
Ryebank Shrops....69 P8
Ryeford Herefs....46 B10
Rye Foreign E Susx....26 E7
Rye Harbour E Susx....26 F8
Ryehill E R Yk....93 M5
Ryeish Green Wokham....35 K11
Rye Street Worcs....46 E7
Ryhall Rutlnd....73 Q8
Ryhill Wakefd....91 K8
Ryhope Sundld....113 P10
Rylah Derbys....84 G7
Ryland Lincs....86 D5
Rylands Notts....72 E4
Rylstone N York....96 E9
Ryme Intrinseca Dorset....11 M2
Ryther N York....91 P3
Ryton Gatesd....113 J8
Ryton N York....98 F5
Ryton Shrops....57 P4
Ryton Warwks....59 P7
Ryton-on-Dunsmore Warwks....59 N10
Ryton Woodside Gatesd....112 H8
RZSS Edinburgh Zoo C Edin....127 N3

S

Sabden Lancs....89 M3
Sabine's Green Essex....51 M11
Sacombe Herts....50 H7
Sacombe Green Herts....50 H7
Sacriston Dur....113 K11
Sadberge Darltn....104 B7
Saddell Ag & B....120 E5
Saddington Leics....60 E2
Saddle Bow Norfk....75 M7
Saddlescombe W Susx....24 G8
Sadgill Cumb....101 N9
Saffron Walden Essex....51 M3
Sageston Pembks....41 L10
Saham Hills Norfk....76 C11
Saham Toney Norfk....76 B11
Saighton Ches W....69 M2
St Abbs Border....129 N6
St Agnes Border....128 H7
St Agnes Cnwll....3 J3

St Agnes IoS....2 b3
St Agnes Mining District Cnwll....3 J4
St Albans Herts....50 D9
St Allen Cnwll....3 L3
St Andrew Guern....10 b2
St Andrews Fife....135 N4
St Andrews Botanic Garden Fife....135 N4
St Andrews Major V Glam....30 F10
St Andrews Well Dorset....11 K6
St Anne's Lancs....88 C5
St Ann's D & G....109 N2
St Ann's Chapel Cnwll....5 Q7
St Ann's Chapel Devon....6 H9
St Anthony-in-Meneage Cnwll....3 K8
St Anthony's Hill E Susx....25 P10
St Arvans Mons....31 P5
St Asaph Denbgs....80 E10
St Athan V Glam....30 D11
St Aubin Jersey....11 b2
St Austell Cnwll....3 Q3
St Bees Cumb....100 C8
St Blazey Cnwll....3 R3
St Blazey Gate Cnwll....3 R3
St Boswells Border....118 A4
St Brelade Jersey....11 a2
St Brelade's Bay Jersey....11 a2
St Breock Cnwll....4 F7
St Breward Cnwll....4 H6
St Briavels Gloucs....31 Q4
St Brides Pembks....40 F8
St Bride's Major V Glam....29 N10
St Brides Netherwent Mons....31 M7
St Brides-super-Ely V Glam....30 E9
St Brides Wentlooge Newpt....31 J8
St Budeaux C Plym....6 D7
Saintbury Gloucs....47 M7
St Buryan Cnwll....2 C8
St Catherine BaNES....32 E11
St Catherines Ag & B....131 N6
St Chloe Gloucs....32 F4
St Clears Carmth....41 Q7
St Cleer Cnwll....5 L8
St Clement Cnwll....3 M5
St Clement Jersey....11 c2
St Clether Cnwll....5 L5
St Colmac Ag & B....124 C4
St Columb Major Cnwll....4 E9
St Columb Minor Cnwll....4 C9
St Columb Road Cnwll....4 E10
St Combs Abers....159 Q5
St Cross South Elmham Suffk....65 K5
St Cyrus Abers....143 N5
St David's P & K....133 Q3
St Davids Pembks....40 E5
St Davids Cathedral Pembks....40 E5
St Day Cnwll....3 J5
St Decumans Somset....18 E6
St Dennis Cnwll....4 F10
St Devereux Herefs....45 N8
St Dogmaels Pembks....42 C5
St Dogwells Pembks....41 J5
St Dominick Cnwll....5 Q8
St Donats V Glam....29 P11
St Edith's Marsh Wilts....21 J2
St Endellion Cnwll....4 F6
St Enoder Cnwll....4 D10
St Erme Cnwll....3 L4
St Erney Cnwll....5 P10
St Erth Cnwll....2 F6
St Erth Praze Cnwll....2 F6
St Ervan Cnwll....4 D7
St Eval Cnwll....4 D8
St Ewe Cnwll....3 P4
St Fagans Cardif....30 F9
St Fagans: National History Museum Cardif....30 F9
St Fergus Abers....159 Q7
St Fillans P & K....133 K3
St Florence Pembks....41 L10
St Gennys Cnwll....5 J2
St George Conwy....80 D9
St Georges N Som....19 L2
St George's V Glam....30 F9
St George's Hill Surrey....36 C8
St Germans Cnwll....5 P10
St Giles in the Wood Devon....17 J8
St Giles-on-the-Heath Devon....5 P3
St Gluvia's Cnwll....3 K7
St Harmon Powys....55 M10
St Helen Auckland Dur....103 N5
St Helens Cumb....100 D4
St Helen's E Susx....26 D9
St Helens IoW....14 H9
St Helens St Hel....81 Q5
St Helens Crematorium St Hel....81 P5
St Helier Gt Lon....36 G7
St Helier Jersey....11 b2
St Hilary Cnwll....2 E7
St Hilary V Glam....30 D10
Saint Hill Devon....10 B3
Saint Hill W Susx....25 J3
St Illtyd Blae G....30 H4
St Ippollitts Herts....50 E5
St Ishmael's Pembks....40 F9
St Issey Cnwll....4 E7
St Ive Cnwll....5 N8
St Ive Cross Cnwll....5 N8
St Ives Cambs....62 D6
St Ives Cnwll....2 E5
St Ives Dorset....13 K4
St James Norfk....77 K7
St James's End Nhants....60 F8
St James South Elmham Suffk....65 L5
St Jidgey Cnwll....4 E8
St John Cnwll....5 Q11
St John Jersey....11 b1
St Johns Dur....103 L4
St John's E Susx....25 M4
St John's IoM....80 c5
St John's Kent....37 M9
St Johns Surrey....23 Q3
St Johns Worcs....46 F4
St John's Chapel Devon....17 J4
St John's Chapel Dur....102 G3
St John's Fen End Norfk....75 K8
St John's Highway Norfk....75 K8
St John's Kirk S Lans....116 D3

St John's Town of Dalry D & G....108 D4
St John's Wood Gt Lon....36 G4
St Judes IoM....80 e2
St Just Cnwll....2 B7
St Just-in-Roseland Cnwll....3 L6
St Just Mining District Cnwll....2 B7
St Katherines Abers....159 J11
St Keverne Cnwll....3 K9
St Kew Cnwll....4 G6
St Kew Highway Cnwll....4 G6
St Keyne Cnwll....5 L9
St Lawrence Cnwll....4 G8
St Lawrence Essex....52 G11
St Lawrence IoW....14 F11
St Lawrence Jersey....11 b1
St Lawrence Kent....39 Q8
St Leonards Bucks....35 P3
St Leonards Dorset....13 K4
St Leonards E Susx....26 D10
St Leonard's Street Kent....37 Q9
St Levan Cnwll....2 B9
St Lythans V Glam....30 F10
St Madoes P & K....134 F3
St Margarets Herefs....45 M8
St Margarets Herts....51 J8
St Margaret's at Cliffe Kent....27 Q3
St Margaret's Hope Ork....169 d7
St Margaret South Elmham Suffk....65 L5
St Marks IoM....80 c7
St Martin Cnwll....3 J9
St Martin Cnwll....5 M10
St Martin Guern....10 b2
St Martin Jersey....11 c1
St Martin's IoS....2 c1
St Martin's P & K....142 B11
St Martin's Shrops....69 K7
St Martin's Moor Shrops....69 K7
St Mary Jersey....11 a1
St Mary Bourne Hants....22 D4
St Marychurch Torbay....7 N5
St Mary Church V Glam....30 D10
St Mary Cray Gt Lon....37 L7
St Mary Hill V Glam....30 C9
St Mary in the Marsh Kent....27 J6
St Marylebone Crematorium Gt Lon....36 G2
St Mary's IoS....2 c2
St Mary's Ork....169 d6
St Mary's Bay Kent....27 J6
St Mary's Hoo Medway....38 D6
St Mary's Platt Kent....37 P9
St Maughans Mons....45 P11
St Maughans Green Mons....45 P11
St Mawes Cnwll....3 L7
St Mawgan Cnwll....4 D8
St Mellion Cnwll....5 P8
St Mellons Cardif....30 H8
St Merryn Cnwll....4 D7
St Mewan Cnwll....3 P3
St Michael Caerhays Cnwll....3 P5
St Michael Church Somset....19 K8
St Michael Penkevil Cnwll....3 M5
St Michaels Kent....26 E4
St Michaels Worcs....57 K11
St Michael's Mount Cnwll....2 E8
St Michael's on Wyre Lancs....88 F2
St Michael South Elmham Suffk....65 L5
St Minver Cnwll....4 F6
St Monans Fife....135 N7
St Neot Cnwll....5 K8
St Neots Cambs....61 Q8
St Newlyn East Cnwll....4 C10
St Nicholas Pembks....40 H3
St Nicholas V Glam....30 E10
St Nicholas-at-Wade Kent....39 N8
St Ninians Stirlg....133 M9
St Olaves Norfk....65 P2
St Osyth Essex....53 K8
St Ouen Jersey....11 a1
St Owen's Cross Herefs....45 Q10
St Paul's Cray Gt Lon....37 L7
St Paul's Walden Herts....50 E6
St Peter Jersey....11 a1
St Peter Port Guern....10 c2
St Peter's Guern....10 b2
St Peter's Kent....39 Q8
St Peter's Hill Cambs....62 B6
St Petrox Pembks....41 J11
St Pinnock Cnwll....5 L9
St Quivox S Ayrs....114 G3
St Ruan Cnwll....3 J10
St Sampson Guern....10 c1
St Saviour Guern....10 b2
St Saviour Jersey....11 b2
St Stephen Cnwll....3 N3
St Stephens Cnwll....5 N4
St Stephens Cnwll....5 Q10
St Teath Cnwll....4 H5
St Thomas Devon....9 M6
St Margaret's Bay Kent....27 Q3
St Tudy Cnwll....4 H6
St Twynnells Pembks....41 J11
St Veep Cnwll....5 J10
St Vigeans Angus....143 L9
St Wenn Cnwll....4 F9
St Weonards Herefs....45 P10
St y-Nyll V Glam....30 E9
Salcombe Devon....7 J11
Salcombe Regis Devon....10 D7
Salcott-cum-Virley Essex....52 F9
Sale Traffd....82 G6
Saleby Lincs....87 N5
Sale Green Worcs....46 H3
Salehurst E Susx....26 C7
Salem Carmth....43 M9
Salem Cerdgn....54 F8
Salen Ag & B....137 P7
Salen Highld....138 B5
Salesbury Lancs....89 K4
Salford C Beds....49 P7
Salford Oxon....47 Q9
Salford Salfd....82 H5
Salford Priors Warwks....47 L4
Salfords Surrey....36 G11
Salhouse Norfk....77 L9
Saline Fife....134 C9
Salisbury Wilts....21 M9

Salisbury Crematorium Wilts....21 N8
Salisbury Plain Wilts....21 L6
Salkeld Dykes Cumb....101 P3
Salle Norfk....76 G7
Salmonby Lincs....87 K6
Salperton Gloucs....47 L10
Salph End Bed....61 N10
Salsburgh N Lans....126 E5
Salt Staffs....70 H9
Salta Cumb....109 N11
Saltaire C Brad....90 E3
Saltaire C Brad....90 E3
Saltash Cnwll....6 C7
Saltburn Highld....156 C3
Saltburn-by-the-Sea R & Cl....105 J6
Saltby Leics....73 M5
Salt Coates Cumb....110 C10
Saltcoats Cumb....100 E11
Saltcoats N Ayrs....124 G9
Saltcotes Lancs....88 D5
Saltdean Br & H....25 J10
Salterbeck Cumb....100 C5
Salterforth Lancs....96 C11
Salterswall Ches W....82 D11
Salterton Wilts....21 M7
Saltfleet Lincs....87 N2
Saltfleetby All Saints Lincs....87 N2
Saltfleetby St Clement Lincs....87 N2
Saltfleetby St Peter Lincs....87 M3
Saltford BaNES....32 C11
Salthouse Norfk....76 F3
Saltley Birm....58 H7
Saltmarsh Newpt....31 K8
Saltmarshe E R Yk....92 C6
Saltney Flints....69 L2
Salton N York....98 E5
Saltrens Devon....16 H7
Saltwell Crematorium Gatesd....113 L8
Saltwick Nthumb....113 J4
Saltwood Kent....27 L4
Salvington W Susx....24 D9
Salwarpe Worcs....46 G2
Salway Ash Dorset....11 K5
Sambourne Warwks....47 L2
Sambrook Wrekin....70 C10
Samlesbury Lancs....88 H4
Samlesbury Bottoms Lancs....89 J5
Sampford Arundel Somset....18 F11
Sampford Brett Somset....18 E6
Sampford Courtenay Devon....8 F4
Sampford Moor Somset....18 F11
Sampford Peverell Devon....9 P2
Sampford Spiney Devon....6 E4
Samsonlane Ork....169 f4
Samson's Corner Essex....53 J8
Samuelston E Loth....128 D5
Sanaigmore Ag & B....122 B5
Sancreed Cnwll....2 C8
Sancton E R Yk....92 E3
Sand Somset....19 M5
Sandaig Highld....145 M7
Sandale Cumb....100 H2
Sandal Magna Wakefd....91 J7
Sanday Ork....169 f2
Sanday Airport Ork....169 f2
Sandbach Ches E....70 D2
Sandbach Services Ches E....70 D2
Sandbank Ag & B....131 P11
Sandbanks Poole....12 H7
Sandend Abers....158 E4
Sanderstead Gt Lon....36 H8
Sandford Cumb....102 D7
Sandford Devon....9 K4
Sandford Dorset....12 F7
Sandford Hants....13 L4
Sandford IoW....14 F10
Sandford N Som....19 M3
Sandford S Lans....126 C9
Sandford Shrops....69 K10
Sandford Shrops....69 Q8
Sandford-on-Thames Oxon....34 F4
Sandford Orcas Dorset....20 B10
Sandford St Martin Oxon....48 B9
Sandgate Kent....27 M4
Sandhaven Abers....159 N4
Sandhead D & G....106 E8
Sandhill Rothm....91 L11
Sandhills Dorset....11 M4
Sandhills Dorset....11 P2
Sandhills Leeds....91 K3
Sandhills Oxon....34 G3
Sandhills Surrey....23 P7
Sandhoe Nthumb....112 E7
Sandhole Ag & B....131 L8
Sand Hole E R Yk....92 D3
Sandholme E R Yk....92 D4
Sandholme Lincs....74 F3
Sandhurst Br For....35 M2
Sandhurst Gloucs....46 F10
Sandhurst Kent....26 D6
Sandhurst Cross Kent....26 C6
Sandhutton N York....97 N4
Sand Hutton N York....98 D9
Sandiacre Derbys....72 D3
Sandilands Lincs....87 P4
Sandiway Ches W....82 D10
Sandleheath Hants....21 M11
Sandleigh Oxon....34 E4
Sandley Dorset....20 E10
Sandling Kent....38 C10
Sandlow Green Ches E....82 G11
Sandness Shet....169 n8
Sandon Essex....52 B11
Sandon Herts....50 H4
Sandon Staffs....70 G9
Sandon Bank Staffs....70 G9
Sandown IoW....14 G10
Sandplace Cnwll....5 M10
Sandridge Herts....50 E8
Sandridge Wilts....32 H11
Sandringham Norfk....75 N5
Sands Bucks....35 M6
Sandsend N York....105 N8
Sand Side Cumb....94 E4
Sandside Cumb....95 K4
Sandtoft N Linc....92 B9
Sandway Kent....38 E11
Sandwell Valley Crematorium Sandw....58 F6

Sandwich Kent....39 P10
Sandwich Bay Kent....39 Q10
Sandwick Cumb....101 M7
Sandwick Shet....169 r11
Sandwick W Isls....168 j4
Sandwith Cumb....100 C8
Sandwith Newtown Cumb....100 C8
Sandy C Beds....61 Q11
Sandy Bank Lincs....87 J9
Sandycroft Flints....81 L11
Sandy Cross E Susx....25 N6
Sandy Cross Herefs....46 C3
Sandyford D & G....110 D2
Sandygate Devon....7 M4
Sandygate IoM....80 e2
Sandy Haven Pembks....40 G9
Sandyhills D & G....109 J9
Sandylands Lancs....95 J8
Sandy Lane C Brad....90 E3
Sandylane Staffs....70 C7
Sandylane Swans....28 G7
Sandy Lane Wilts....33 J11
Sandy Lane Wrexhm....69 M6
Sandy Park Devon....8 H7
Sandysike Cumb....110 G2
Sandyway Herefs....45 P9
Sangobeg Highld....165 K3
Sangomore Highld....165 K3
Sankey Bridges Warrtn....82 C7
Sankyn's Green Worcs....57 P11
Sanna Highld....137 L2
Sanndabhaig W Isls....168 j4
Sannox N Ayrs....124 C8
Sanquhar D & G....115 Q6
Santon Cumb....100 F10
Santon IoM....80 d7
Santon Bridge Cumb....100 F10
Santon Downham Suffk....63 P3
Sapcote Leics....59 Q6
Sapey Common Herefs....46 D2
Sapiston Suffk....64 C6
Sapley Cambs....62 B6
Sapperton Derbys....71 M8
Sapperton Gloucs....32 H4
Sapperton Lincs....73 Q4
Saracen's Head Lincs....74 F5
Sarclet Highld....167 P8
Sarisbury Hants....14 F5
Sarn Brdgnd....29 P8
Sarn Powys....55 M5
Sarn Powys....56 C6
Sarnau Carmth....42 F11
Sarnau Cerdgn....42 F4
Sarnau Gwynd....68 C7
Sarnau Powys....44 E8
Sarnau Powys....68 H11
Sarn Bach Gwynd....66 E9
Sarnesfield Herefs....45 M4
Sarn Meyllteyrn Gwynd....66 C8
Sarn Park Services Brdgnd....29 P8
Sarn-wen Powys....69 J11
Saron Carmth....28 H2
Saron Carmth....42 G7
Saron Gwynd....66 H3
Saron Gwynd....79 J11
Sarratt Herts....50 B11
Sarre Kent....39 N8
Sarsden Oxon....47 Q10
Sarson Hants....22 B6
Satley Dur....103 M2
Satmar Kent....27 N4
Satron N York....102 H11
Satterleigh Devon....17 M7
Satterthwaite Cumb....94 G2
Satwell Oxon....35 K8
Sauchen Abers....151 J5
Saucher P & K....142 B11
Sauchieburn Abers....143 M4
Saul Gloucs....32 D3
Saundby Notts....85 M4
Saundersfoot Pembks....41 M10
Saunderton Bucks....35 L4
Saunderton Station Bucks....35 M5
Saunton Devon....16 H4
Sausthorpe Lincs....87 L7
Saverley Green Staffs....70 H7
Savile Town Kirk....90 G6
Sawbridge Warwks....59 B7
Sawbridgeworth Herts....51 L8
Sawdon N York....99 J4
Sawley Derbys....72 D4
Sawley Lancs....96 A11
Sawley N York....97 K7
Sawston Cambs....62 G11
Sawtry Cambs....61 Q4
Saxby Leics....73 L7
Saxby Lincs....86 D3
Saxby All Saints N Linc....92 G7
Saxelbye Leics....72 H6
Saxham Street Suffk....64 F9
Saxilby Lincs....85 Q5
Saxlingham Norfk....76 E4
Saxlingham Green Norfk....65 J2
Saxlingham Nethergate Norfk....65 J2
Saxlingham Thorpe Norfk....65 J2
Saxmundham Suffk....65 M9
Saxondale Notts....72 H3
Saxon Street Cambs....63 L9
Saxtead Suffk....65 K8
Saxtead Green Suffk....65 K9
Saxtead Little Green Suffk....65 J8
Saxthorpe Norfk....76 G5
Saxton N York....91 M3
Sayers Common W Susx....24 G7
Scackleton N York....98 C6
Scafell Pike Cumb....100 H9
Scaftworth Notts....85 L2
Scagglethorpe N York....98 G6
Scalasaig Ag & B....136 b3
Scalby E R Yk....92 D5
Scalby N York....99 L2
Scald End Bed....61 M9
Scaldwell Nhants....60 G6
Scaleby Cumb....110 H8
Scalebyhill Cumb....110 H8
Scale Houses Cumb....111 L11
Scales Cumb....94 F6
Scales Cumb....101 K5
Scalesceugh Cumb....110 H11
Scalford Leics....73 K6
Scaling N York....105 K8
Scaling Dam R & Cl....105 K8
Scalloway Shet....169 r10
Scalpay Highld....153 L11
Scamblesby Lincs....87 J5

Scammonden Kirk 90 D7
Scamodale Highld 138 E3
Scampston N York 98 H5
Scampton Lincs 86 C5
Scaniport Highld 156 A10
Scapegoat Hill Kirk 90 D7
Scarba Ag & B 130 D7
Scarborough N York 99 L3
Scarcewater Cnwll 3 N3
Scarcliffe Derbys 84 G7
Scarcroft Leeds 91 K2
Scarfskerry Highld 167 N2
Scargill Dur 103 L8
Scarinish Ag & B 136 C7
Scarisbrick Lancs 88 D8
Scarness Cumb 100 H4
Scarning Norfk 76 D9
Scarrington Notts 73 J2
Scarth Hill Lancs 88 E9
Scarthingwell N York 91 M3
Scartho NE Lin 93 N9
Scatsta Airport Shet 169 q6
Scaur D & G 108 H10
Scawby N Linc 92 G9
Scawsby Donc 91 N10
Scawthorpe Donc 91 P9
Scawton N York 98 A4
Scayne's Hill W Susx 25 J6
Scethrog Powys 44 G9
Scholar Green Ches E 70 E3
Scholemoor
    Crematorium C Brad 90 E4
Scholes Kirk 90 F5
Scholes Kirk 90 F9
Scholes Leeds 91 K3
Scholes Rothm 91 K11
Scholes Wigan 88 H9
School Aycliffe Dur 103 Q6
School Green C Brad 90 E4
School Green Ches W 70 A2
Schoolgreen Wokham 35 K11
School House Dorset 10 H4
Scissett Kirk 90 G8
Scleddau Pembks 40 H4
Scofton Notts 85 K4
Scole Norfk 64 H6
Scone P & K 134 E2
Sconser Highld 153 J11
Scoonie Fife 135 K7
Scopwick Lincs 86 E9
Scoraig Highld 160 G7
Scorborough E R Yk 99 L11
Scorrier Cnwll 3 J5
Scorriton Devon 7 J5
Scorton Lancs 95 L11
Scorton N York 103 Q10
Sco Ruston Norfk 77 K7
Scotby Cumb 110 H9
Scotch Corner N York 103 P9
Scotch Corner Rest
    Area N York 103 P9
Scotforth Lancs 95 K9
Scot Hay Staffs 70 D5
Scothern Lincs 86 D5
Scotland Lincs 73 Q4
Scotland Gate Nthumb 113 L4
Scotlandwell P & K 134 F7
Scot Lane End Bolton 89 J9
Scotscalder Station
    Highld 167 J5
Scotsdike Cumb 110 G6
Scot's Gap Nthumb 112 F3
Scotsmill Abers 150 F4
Scotstoun C Glas 125 N4
Scotswood N u Ty 113 K8
Scotter Lincs 92 E10
Scotterthorpe Lincs 92 E10
Scottish Seabird Centre
    E Loth 128 F2
Scottish Wool Centre
    Stirlg 132 G7
Scottlethorpe Lincs 73 R6
Scotton Lincs 92 E11
Scotton N York 97 M9
Scotton N York 103 N11
Scottow Norfk 77 K7
Scott Willoughby Lincs 73 R3
Scoulton Norfk 76 D11
Scounslow Green Staffs 71 K9
Scourie Highld 164 E8
Scourie More Highld 164 D8
Scousburgh Shet 169 q12
Scouthead Oldham 90 B9
Scrabster Highld 167 K2
Scraesburgh Border 118 C2
Scrafield Lincs 87 K7
Scrainwood Nthumb 119 J9
Scrane End Lincs 74 G2
Scraptoft Leics 72 G9
Scratby Norfk 77 Q8
Scrayingham N York 98 E9
Scrays E Susx 26 C8
Scredington Lincs 74 A2
Scremby Lincs 87 M7
Scremerston Nthumb 129 Q10
Screveton Notts 73 J2
Scrivelsby Lincs 87 J7
Scriven N York 97 M9
Scrooby Notts 85 L2
Scropton Derbys 71 M8
Scrub Hill Lincs 86 H9
Scruton N York 97 L2
Scuggate Cumb 110 H6
Scullomie Highld 165 P4
Sculthorpe Norfk 76 B5
Scunthorpe N Linc 92 E8
Scurlage Swans 28 E7
Sea Somset 10 G2
Seaborough Dorset 11 J3
Seabridge Staffs 70 E6
Seabrook Kent 27 L4
Seaburn Sundld 113 P9
Seacombe Wirral 81 L6
Seacroft Leeds 91 K3
Seacroft Lincs 87 Q8
Seadyke Lincs 74 F3
Seafield W Loth 127 J4
Seafield Crematorium
    C Edin 127 P2
Seaford E Susx 25 L11
Seaforth Sefton 81 L5
Seagrave Leics 72 G7
Seagry Heath Wilts 33 J8
Seaham Dur 113 P11
Seahouses Nthumb 119 P4
Seal Kent 37 N9
Sealand Flints 81 M11
Seale Surrey 23 N5
Seamer N York 99 L4
Seamer N York 98 E8
Seamill N Ayrs 124 G8

Sea Palling Norfk 77 N6
Searby Lincs 93 J9
Seasalter Kent 39 J9
Seascale Cumb 100 D10
Seathwaite Cumb 100 H11
Seathwaite Cumb 100 H8
Seatle Cumb 94 H4
Seatoller Cumb 100 H8
Seaton Cnwll 5 N11
Seaton Cumb 100 D4
Seaton Devon 10 E6
Seaton Dur 113 N11
Seaton E R Yk 99 P11
Seaton Kent 39 M10
Seaton Nthumb 113 M5
Seaton Rutlnd 73 N11
Seaton Burn N Tyne 113 K6
Seaton Carew Hartpl 104 F5
Seaton Delaval Nthumb 113 M5
Seaton Ross E R Yk 92 C2
Seaton Sluice Nthumb 113 M5
Seatown Dorset 11 J6
Seave Green N York 104 G10
Seaview IoW 14 H8
Seaville Cumb 110 C10
Seavington St Mary
    Somset 11 J2
Seavington St Michael
    Somset 19 M11
Sebastopol Torfn 31 J5
Sebergham Cumb 101 L2
Seckington Warwks 59 L3
Second Severn
    Crossing Mons 31 P7
Sedbergh Cumb 95 P2
Sedbury Gloucs 31 P6
Sedbusk N York 96 C2
Sedgeberrow Worcs 47 K7
Sedgebrook Lincs 73 M3
Sedge Fen Suffk 63 L4
Sedgefield Dur 104 C5
Sedgeford Norfk 75 P3
Sedgehill Wilts 20 G9
Sedgemoor
    Crematorium Somset 19 J6
Sedgemoor Services
    Somset 19 L4
Sedgley Dudley 58 D6
Sedgley Park Bury 82 H4
Sedgwick Cumb 95 L3
Sedlescombe E Susx 26 C8
Sedrup Bucks 35 M2
Seed Kent 38 F10
Seend Wilts 20 H2
Seend Cleeve Wilts 20 H2
Seer Green Bucks 35 Q6
Seething Norfk 65 L2
Sefton Sefton 81 M4
Seghill Nthumb 113 L6
Seighford Staffs 70 F9
Seion Gwynd 79 J11
Seisdon Staffs 58 B5
Selattyn Shrops 69 J8
Selborne Hants 23 K8
Selby N York 91 Q4
Selham W Susx 23 P10
Selhurst Gt Lon 36 H7
Selkirk Border 117 P5
Sellack Herefs 45 R9
Sellafield Station Cumb 100 D10
Sellafirth Shet 169 s4
Sellan Cnwll 2 C7
Sellick's Green Somset 18 H11
Sellindge Kent 27 J4
Selling Kent 38 H10
Sells Green Wilts 20 H2
Selly Oak Birm 58 F8
Selmeston E Susx 25 M9
Selsdon Gt Lon 37 J8
Selsey W Susx 15 N8
Selsfield Common
    W Susx 24 H4
Selside Cumb 101 P11
Selside N York 96 A5
Selsley Gloucs 32 F4
Selsted Kent 27 M3
Selston Notts 84 G10
Selworthy Somset 18 B5
Semer Suffk 52 G2
Semington Wilts 20 G2
Semley Wilts 20 G9
Sempringham Lincs 74 B4
Send Surrey 36 B9
Send Marsh Surrey 36 B9
Senghenydd Caerph 30 F6
Sennen Cnwll 2 B8
Sennen Cove Cnwll 2 B8
Sennybridge Powys 44 C9
Serlby Notts 85 K3
Sessay N York 97 Q5
Setchey Norfk 75 M8
Setley Hants 13 P4
Seton Mains E Loth 128 C4
Settle N York 96 B8
Settrington N York 98 G6
Seven Ash Somset 18 G8
Sevenhampton Gloucs 47 K10
Sevenhampton Swindn 33 P6
Seven Hills
    Crematorium Suffk 53 M3
Seven Kings Gt Lon 37 L3
Sevenoaks Kent 37 M9
Sevenoaks Weald Kent 37 M10
Seven Sisters Neath 29 M3
Seven Springs Gloucs 47 J11
Seven Star Green Essex 52 F6
Severn Beach S Glos 31 P8
Severn Bridge S Glos 31 Q6
Severn Stoke Worcs 46 G6
Severn View Services
    S Glos 31 Q7
Sevick End Bed 61 N10
Sevington Kent 26 H3
Sewards End Essex 51 N3
Sewardstonebury Essex 51 J11
Sewell C Beds 49 Q10
Sewerby E R Yk 99 P7
Seworgan Cnwll 3 J7
Sewstern Leics 73 M6
Sexhow N York 104 E9
Sezincote Gloucs 47 N8
Shabbington Bucks 35 J3
Shackerley Shrops 57 Q3
Shackerstone Leics 72 B9
Shacklecross Derbys 72 C4
Shackleford Surrey 23 P5
Shade Calder 89 Q6
Shader W Isls 168 i2
Shadforth Dur 104 B2
Shadingfield Suffk 65 N5

Shadoxhurst Kent 26 G4
Shadwell Leeds 91 J3
Shadwell Norfk 64 C5
Shaftenhoe End Herts 51 K3
Shaftesbury Dorset 20 G10
Shaftholme Donc 91 P9
Shafton Barns 91 K8
Shafton Two Gates
    Barns 91 K8
Shakerley Wigan 82 E4
Shalbourne Wilts 22 B2
Shalcombe IoW 14 C9
Shalden Hants 23 J6
Shalden Green Hants 23 K6
Shaldon Devon 7 N4
Shalfleet IoW 14 D9
Shalford Essex 52 B6
Shalford Surrey 36 B11
Shalford Green Essex 52 B6
Shallowford Staffs 70 F9
Shalmsford Street Kent 39 J11
Shalstone Bucks 48 H7
Shamley Green Surrey 24 B2
Shandford Angus 142 H5
Shandon Ag & B 132 B10
Shandwick Highld 156 F2
Shangton Leics 73 J11
Shankhouse Nthumb 113 L5
Shanklin IoW 14 G10
Shantron Ag & B 132 C10
Shap Cumb 101 Q7
Shapinsay Ork 169 e5
Shapwick Dorset 12 H4
Shapwick Somset 19 M7
Shard End Birm 59 J7
Shardlow Derbys 72 C4
Shareshill Staffs 58 D3
Sharlston Wakefd 91 K7
Sharlston Common
    Wakefd 91 K7
Sharman's Cross Solhll 58 H9
Sharnal Street Medway 38 C2
Sharnbrook Bed 61 L9
Sharneyford Lancs 89 P6
Sharnford Leics 59 Q6
Sharnhill Green Dorset 11 Q3
Sharoe Green Lancs 88 G4
Sharow N York 97 M6
Sharpenhoe C Beds 50 C4
Sharperton Nthumb 119 J10
Sharp Green Norfk 77 M7
Sharpness Gloucs 32 C4
Sharpthorne W Susx 25 J4
Sharptor Cnwll 5 M7
Sharpway Gate Worcs 58 E11
Sharrington Norfk 76 E4
Shatterford Worcs 57 P8
Shatterling Kent 39 N10
Shatton Derbys 84 B4
Shaugh Prior Devon 6 E6
Shave Cross Dorset 11 J5
Shavington Ches E 70 B4
Shaw C Brad 90 C3
Shaw Oldham 89 Q9
Shaw Swindn 33 M7
Shaw W Berk 34 E11
Shaw Wilts 32 G11
Shawbirch Wrekin 57 L2
Shawbost W Isls 168 h3
Shawbury Shrops 69 Q10
Shawclough Rochdl 89 P8
Shaw Common Gloucs 46 C9
Shawdon Hill Nthumb 119 L8
Shawell Leics 60 B4
Shawford Hants 22 E9
Shawforth Lancs 89 P6
Shaw Green Herts 50 H4
Shaw Green Lancs 88 G7
Shaw Green N York 97 L10
Shawhead D & G 109 J3
Shaw Mills N York 97 L8
Shawsburn S Lans 126 D7
Shear Cross Wilts 20 G6
Shearington D & G 109 M7
Shearsby Leics 60 D2
Shearston Somset 19 J8
Shebbear Devon 16 G10
Shebdon Staffs 70 D9
Shebster Highld 166 H4
Sheddens E Rens 125 P6
Shedfield Hants 14 G4
Sheen Staffs 71 L2
Sheepbridge Derbys 84 E6
Sheep Hill Dur 113 J9
Sheepridge Kirk 90 F7
Sheepscar Leeds 91 J4
Sheepscombe Gloucs 32 G2
Sheepstor Devon 6 F5
Sheepwash Devon 8 C3
Sheepwash Nthumb 113 L3
Sheepway N Som 31 N9
Sheepy Magna Leics 72 A10
Sheepy Parva Leics 72 A10
Sheering Essex 51 M8
Sheerness Kent 38 F7
Sheerwater Surrey 36 B8
Sheet Hants 23 L10
Sheffield Cnwll 2 D8
Sheffield Sheff 84 E3
Sheffield Bottom W Berk 34 H11
Sheffield City Road
    Crematorium Sheff 84 E3
Sheffield Green E Susx 25 K5
Sheffield Park E Susx 25 K6
Shefford C Beds 50 D3
Shefford Woodlands
    W Berk 34 C10
Sheigra Highld 164 E4
Sheinton Shrops 57 L4
Shelderton Shrops 56 G9
Sheldon Birm 58 J8
Sheldon Derbys 83 Q11
Sheldon Devon 10 C3
Sheldwich Kent 38 H10
Sheldwich Lees Kent 38 H10
Shelf Calder 90 E5
Shelfanger Norfk 64 G5
Shelfield Warwks 47 M2
Shelfield Wsall 58 F4
Shelfield Green Warwks 47 M2
Shelford Notts 72 H2
Shelford Warwks 59 P7
Shellacres Nthumb 118 G2
Shelley Essex 51 N9
Shelley Kirk 90 G8
Shelley Suffk 52 H4
Shelley Far Bank Kirk 90 G8
Shellingford Oxon 34 B5
Shellow Bowells Essex 51 P9
Shelsley Beauchamp
    Worcs 46 D2

Shelsley Walsh Worcs 46 D2
Shelton Bed 61 M7
Shelton Norfk 65 J3
Shelton Notts 73 K2
Shelton Shrops 56 H2
Shelton Green Norfk 65 J3
Shelton Lock C Derb 72 B4
Shelton Under Harley
    Staffs 70 E7
Shelve Shrops 56 E5
Shelwick Herefs 45 Q6
Shenfield Essex 51 P11
Shenington Oxon 48 C6
Shenley Herts 50 E10
Shenley Brook End
    M Keyn 49 M7
Shenleybury Herts 50 E10
Shenley Church End
    M Keyn 49 M7
Shenmore Herefs 45 M7
Shennanton D & G 107 K5
Shenstone Staffs 58 H4
Shenstone Worcs 58 C10
Shenstone Woodend
    Staffs 58 H4
Shenton Leics 72 B11
Shenval Moray 149 N2
Shepeau Stow Lincs 74 F8
Shephall Herts 50 G6
Shepherd's Bush Gt Lon 36 F4
Shepherd's Green Oxon 35 K8
Shepherds Patch Gloucs 32 C4
Shepherdswell Kent 27 N2
Shepley Kirk 90 F9
Shepperdine S Glos 32 B5
Shepperton Surrey 36 C7
Shepperton Green
    Surrey 36 C7
Shepreth Cambs 62 E11
Shepshed Leics 72 D7
Shepton Beauchamp
    Somset 19 M11
Shepton Mallet Somset 20 B6
Shepton Montague
    Somset 20 C8
Shepway Kent 38 C11
Sheraton Dur 104 D3
Sherborne Dorset 20 B11
Sherborne Gloucs 33 N2
Sherborne Somset 19 Q3
Sherborne St John Hants 22 H3
Sherbourne Warwks 47 Q2
Sherburn Dur 104 B2
Sherburn N York 99 K5
Sherburn Hill Dur 104 B2
Sherburn in Elmet
    N York 91 M4
Shere Surrey 36 C11
Shereford Norfk 76 B6
Sherfield English Hants 21 Q10
Sherfield on Loddon
    Hants 23 J3
Sherfin Lancs 89 M5
Sherford Devon 7 K10
Sherford Dorset 12 H5
Sheriffhales Shrops 57 P2
Sheriff Hutton N York 98 D7
Sheringham Norfk 76 H3
Sherington M Keyn 49 N5
Shermanbury W Susx 24 F7
Shernborne Norfk 75 P4
Sherrington Wilts 21 J7
Sherston Wilts 32 G7
Sherwood C Nott 72 F2
Sherwood Forest Notts 85 K8
Sherwood Forest
    Crematorium Notts 85 L7
Shetland Islands Shet 169 r8
Shettleston C Glas 125 Q5
Shevington Wigan 88 G9
Shevington Moor Wigan 88 G8
Shevington Vale Wigan 88 G9
Sheviock Cnwll 5 P10
Shibden Head C Brad 90 D5
Shide IoW 14 F9
Shidlaw Nthumb 118 F3
Shiel Bridge Highld 146 A4
Shieldaig Highld 153 Q7
Shieldhill D & G 109 M3
Shieldhill Falk 126 F2
Shieldhill House Hotel
    S Lans 116 E2
Shields N Lans 126 D6
Shielfoot Highld 138 B3
Shielhill Angus 142 G6
Shielhill Inver 124 G3
Shifford Oxon 34 C4
Shifnal Shrops 57 N3
Shilbottle Nthumb 119 N9
Shildon Dur 103 P5
Shillford E Rens 125 M6
Shillingford Devon 18 C10
Shillingford Oxon 34 G6
Shillingford Abbot
    Devon 9 M7
Shillingford St George
    Devon 9 M7
Shillingstone Dorset 12 D2
Shillington C Beds 50 D4
Shillmoor Nthumb 118 G9
Shilton Oxon 33 Q3
Shilton Warwks 59 P8
Shimpling Norfk 64 H5
Shimpling Suffk 64 B11
Shimpling Street Suffk 64 B11
Shincliffe Dur 103 Q2
Shiney Row Sundld 113 M10
Shinfield Wokham 35 K11
Shingay Cambs 62 D11
Shingle Street Suffk 53 Q3
Shinnersbridge Devon 7 K6
Shinness Highld 162 C4
Shipbourne Kent 37 N10
Shipdham Norfk 76 D10
Shipham Somset 19 M3
Shiphay Torbay 7 M5
Shiplake Oxon 35 L9
Shiplake Row Oxon 35 K9
Shiplate N Som 19 L3
Shipley C Brad 90 F3
Shipley Derbys 72 C2
Shipley Shrops 57 Q5
Shipley W Susx 24 E6
Shipley Bridge Surrey 24 H2
Shipley Hatch Kent 26 H4
Shipmeadow Suffk 65 M3
Shippea Hill Station
    Cambs 63 K4
Shippon Oxon 34 E5
Shipston-on-Stour
    Warwks 47 Q6

Shipton Bucks 49 L9
Shipton Gloucs 47 K11
Shipton N York 98 B9
Shipton Shrops 57 K6
Shipton Bellinger Hants 21 P5
Shipton Gorge Dorset 11 K6
Shipton Green W Susx 15 M5
Shipton Moyne Gloucs 32 G7
Shipton-on-Cherwell
    Oxon 48 E11
Shiptonthorpe E R Yk 92 E2
Shipton-under-
    Wychwood Oxon 47 Q11
Shirburn Oxon 35 J5
Shirdley Hill Lancs 88 D8
Shire Cumb 102 B11
Shirebrook Derbys 84 H7
Shiregreen Sheff 84 E2
Shirehampton Bristl 31 P9
Shiremoor N Tyne 113 M6
Shirenewton Mons 31 N6
Shire Oak Wsall 58 G4
Shireoaks Notts 85 J4
Shirkoak Kent 26 F4
Shirland Derbys 84 F9
Shirlett Shrops 57 L5
Shirley C Sotn 14 D4
Shirley Derbys 71 N6
Shirley Gt Lon 37 J7
Shirley Solhll 58 H9
Shirl Heath Herefs 45 N3
Shirrell Heath Hants 14 G4
Shirvan Ag & B 123 Q3
Shirwell Devon 17 L4
Shiskine N Ayrs 120 H6
Shittlehope Dur 103 K3
Shobdon Herefs 45 N2
Shobley Hants 13 L3
Shobrooke Devon 9 L4
Shoby Leics 72 H6
Shocklach Ches W 69 M5
Shocklach Green Ches W 69 M5
Shoeburyness Sthend 38 F4
Sholden Kent 39 Q11
Sholing C Sotn 14 E4
Shoot Hill Shrops 56 G2
Shop Cnwll 4 D7
Shop Cnwll 16 C9
Shopwyke W Susx 15 N5
Shore Rochdl 89 Q7
Shoreditch Gt Lon 36 H4
Shoreditch Somset 18 H10
Shoreham Kent 37 M8
Shoreham-by-Sea
    W Susx 24 F9
Shoreswood Nthumb 129 N10
Shorley Hants 22 G9
Shorncote Gloucs 33 K5
Shorne Kent 37 Q6
Shortacross Cnwll 5 M10
Shortbridge E Susx 25 L6
Shortfield Common
    Surrey 23 M6
Shortgate E Susx 25 L7
Short Heath Birm 58 G6
Shortheath Hants 23 L7
Short Heath Wsall 58 E4
Shortlanesend Cnwll 3 L4
Shortlees E Ayrs 125 L10
Shortstown Bed 61 N11
Shorwell IoW 14 E10
Shoscombe BaNES 20 D3
Shotesham Norfk 65 J2
Shotgate Essex 38 C3
Shotley Suffk 53 M4
Shotley Bridge Dur 112 G10
Shotleyfield Nthumb 112 G10
Shotley Gate Suffk 53 M5
Shotley Street Suffk 53 M4
Shottenden Kent 38 H11
Shottermill Surrey 23 N7
Shottery Warwks 47 N4
Shotteswell Warwks 48 C5
Shottisham Suffk 53 P3
Shottle Derbys 71 Q5
Shottlegate Derbys 71 Q5
Shotton Dur 104 C5
Shotton Dur 104 D3
Shotton Flints 81 L11
Shotton Nthumb 113 K5
Shotton Nthumb 118 F4
Shotton Colliery Dur 104 C2
Shotts N Lans 126 F6
Shotwick Ches W 81 L11
Shougle Moray 157 N6
Shouldham Norfk 75 N9
Shouldham Thorpe
    Norfk 75 N9
Shoulton Worcs 46 F3
Shover's Green E Susx 25 Q4
Shraleybrook Staffs 70 D5
Shrawardine Shrops 69 L11
Shrawley Worcs 57 Q11
Shreding Green Bucks 36 B4
Shrewley Warwks 59 K11
Shrewsbury Shrops 56 H2
Shrewton Wilts 21 L6
Shripney W Susx 15 P6
Shrivenham Oxon 33 P7
Shropham Norfk 64 D3
Shroton Dorset 12 D2
Shrub End Essex 52 G7
Shucknall Herefs 46 A6
Shudy Camps Cambs 51 P2
Shuna Ag & B 130 C6
Shurdington Gloucs 46 H11
Shurlock Row W & M 35 M10
Shurnock Worcs 47 K2
Shurrery Highld 166 H5
Shurrery Lodge Highld 166 H5
Shurton Somset 18 H6
Shustoke Warwks 59 K6
Shute Devon 10 F5
Shute Devon 9 L4
Shutford Oxon 48 C6
Shut Heath Staffs 70 F10
Shuthonger Gloucs 46 G7
Shutlanger Nhants 49 K5
Shutterton Devon 9 N8
Shutt Green Staffs 58 C3
Shuttington Warwks 59 L3
Shuttlewood Derbys 84 G6
Shuttleworth Bury 89 N7
Siabost W Isls 168 h3
Siadar W Isls 168 i2
Sibbertoft Nhants 60 E4
Sibdon Carwood Shrops 56 G8
Sibford Ferris Oxon 48 C7
Sibford Gower Oxon 48 C7
Sible Hedingham Essex 52 B4
Sibley's Green Essex 51 P5

Siblyback Cnwll 5 L7
Sibsey Lincs 87 L10
Sibsey Fenside Lincs 87 K10
Sibson Cambs 74 A11
Sibson Leics 72 B10
Sibster Highld 167 P6
Sibthorpe Notts 85 M6
Sibthorpe Notts 85 N11
Sibton Suffk 65 M8
Sicklesmere Suffk 64 B9
Sicklinghall N York 97 N11
Sidbrook Somset 19 J9
Sidbury Devon 10 C6
Sidbury Shrops 57 M7
Sid Cop Barns 91 K9
Sidcot N Som 19 M3
Sidcup Gt Lon 37 L6
Siddick Cumb 100 D4
Siddington Ches E 82 H10
Siddington Gloucs 33 K5
Sidemoor Worcs 58 E10
Sidestrand Norfk 77 K4
Sidford Devon 10 C6
Sidlesham W Susx 15 N7
Sidlesham Common
    W Susx 15 N7
Sidley E Susx 26 B10
Sidmouth Devon 10 C7
Siefton Shrops 56 H8
Sigford Devon 7 K4
Sigglesthorne E R Yk 99 P11
Sigingstone V Glam 30 C10
Signet Oxon 33 P2
Silchester Hants 22 H2
Sileby Leics 72 G7
Silecroft Cumb 94 C4
Silfield Norfk 64 G2
Silian Cerdgn 43 L4
Silkstead Hants 22 D10
Silkstone Barns 90 H9
Silkstone Common Barns ...90 H10
Silk Willoughby Lincs 73 R2
Silloth Cumb 109 P10
Silpho N York 99 K2
Silsden C Brad 96 F11
Silsoe C Beds 50 C3
Silton Dorset 20 E9
Silverburn Mdloth 127 N5
Silverdale Lancs 95 K6
Silverdale Staffs 70 E5
Silver End Essex 52 D8
Silvergate Norfk 76 H6
Silverford Abers 159 J5
Silverlace Green Suffk 65 L9
Silverley's Green Suffk 65 K6
Silverstone Nhants 49 J6
Silver Street Kent 38 E9
Silver Street Somset 19 P8
Silverton Devon 9 N4
Silverwell Cnwll 3 J4
Silvington Shrops 57 L9
Simister Bury 89 N9
Simmondley Derbys 83 M6
Simonburn Nthumb 112 C6
Simonsbath Somset 17 P4
Simonsburrow Devon 18 F11
Simonstone Lancs 89 M4
Simonstone N York 96 C2
Simprim Border 129 L11
Simpson M Keyn 49 N7
Simpson Cross Pembks 40 G7
Sinclair's Hill Border 129 L9
Sinclairston E Ayrs 115 J4
Sinderby N York 97 M4
Sinderhope Nthumb 112 B10
Sinderland Green Traffd 82 F7
Sindlesham Wokham 35 L11
Sinfin C Derb 72 A4
Singleborough Bucks 49 L8
Single Street Gt Lon 37 K9
Singleton Kent 26 H3
Singleton Lancs 88 D3
Singleton W Susx 15 N4
Singlewell Kent 37 Q6
Sinkhurst Green Kent 26 D3
Sinnarhard Abers 150 D5
Sinnington N York 98 E3
Sinope Leics 72 C7
Sinton Worcs 46 F2
Sinton Worcs 46 F2
Sinton Green Worcs 46 F2
Sipson Gt Lon 36 C5
Sirhowy Blae G 30 F2
Sissinghurst Kent 26 C4
Siston S Glos 32 C9
Sitcott Devon 5 P3
Sithney Cnwll 2 G8
Sithney Common Cnwll 2 G8
Sithney Green Cnwll 2 G8
Sittingbourne Kent 38 F9
Six Ashes Shrops 57 P7
Six Bells Blae G 30 H4
Six Hills Leics 72 G6
Sixhills Lincs 86 G3
Six Mile Bottom Cambs 63 J9
Sixmile Cottages Kent 27 K3
Sixpenny Handley
    Dorset 21 J11
Six Rues Jersey 11 b1
Sizewell Suffk 65 P9
Skaill Ork 169 e6
Skara Brae Ork 169 b5
Skares E Ayrs 115 K4
Skateraw Abers 151 N9
Skateraw E Loth 129 J3
Skeabost Highld 152 G8
Skeeby N York 103 N10
Skeffington Leics 73 J10
Skeffling E R Yk 93 Q7
Skegby Notts 84 G8
Skegby Notts 85 N7
Skegness Lincs 87 Q8
Skelbo Highld 162 H7
Skelbo Street Highld 162 H8
Skelbrooke Donc 91 N8
Skeldyke Lincs 74 F3
Skellingthorpe Lincs 86 B6
Skellorn Green Ches E 83 K8
Skellow Donc 91 N8
Skelmanthorpe Kirk 90 G8
Skelmersdale Lancs 88 F9
Skelmorlie N Ayrs 124 F4
Skelpick Highld 166 B5
Skelton C York 98 B9
Skelton Cumb 101 M3
Skelton E R Yk 92 C5
Skelton N York 103 L10
Skelton R & Cl 105 J2
Skelton on Ure N York 97 N7
Skelwith Bridge Cumb 101 K10

Skendleby Lincs 87 M7
Skene House Abers 151 K5
Skenfrith Mons 45 P10
Skerne E R Yk 99 L9
Skerray Highld 165 Q4
Skerricha Highld 164 F6
Skerries Airport Shet 169 t6
Skerton Lancs 95 K8
Sketchley Leics 59 P6
Sketty Swans 28 H6
Skewen Neath 29 K5
Skewsby N York 98 C6
Skeyton Norfk 77 J6
Skeyton Corner Norfk 77 K6
Skiall Highld 166 H3
Skidbrooke Lincs 87 M2
Skidbrooke North End
    Lincs 93 R11
Skidby E R Yk 92 H4
Skigersta W Isls 168 k1
Skilgate Somset 18 C9
Skillington Lincs 73 M5
Skinburness Cumb 109 P9
Skinflats Falk 133 Q11
Skinidin Highld 152 C8
Skinners Green W Berk 34 D11
Skinningrove R & Cl 105 K7
Skipness Ag & B 123 R8
Skipper's Bridge D & G 110 G4
Skiprigg Cumb 110 G11
Skipsea E R Yk 99 P10
Skipsea Brough E R Yk 99 P10
Skipton N York 96 E10
Skipton-on-Swale N York ...97 N5
Skipwith N York 91 R3
Skirlaugh E R Yk 93 K3
Skirling Border 116 F3
Skirmett Bucks 35 L6
Skirpenbeck E R Yk 98 E9
Skirwith Cumb 102 B4
Skirwith N York 95 Q6
Skirza Highld 167 Q3
Skitby Cumb 110 H7
Skittle Green Bucks 35 L4
Skokholm Island Pembks ...40 D10
Skomer Island Pembks 40 D9
Skulamus Highld 145 L3
Skyborry Green Shrops 56 D10
Skye Green Essex 52 E7
Skye of Curr Highld 148 H3
Skyreholme N York 96 G8
Slack Calder 90 B5
Slackcote Oldham 90 B9
Slack Head Cumb 95 K5
Slackholme End Lincs 87 P6
Slacks of Cairnbanno
    Abers 159 K8
Slad Gloucs 32 G3
Slade Devon 10 C3
Slade Devon 17 J2
Slade Devon 17 Q6
Slade End Oxon 34 G6
Slade Green Gt Lon 37 M5
Slade Heath Staffs 58 D3
Slade Hooton Rothm 84 H3
Sladesbridge Cnwll 4 G7
Slades Green Worcs 46 F8
Slaggyford Nthumb 111 N10
Slaidburn Lancs 95 Q10
Slaithwaite Kirk 90 D8
Slaley Derbys 84 C9
Slaley Nthumb 112 E9
Slamannan Falk 126 F3
Slapton Bucks 49 P10
Slapton Devon 7 L9
Slapton Nhants 48 H5
Slattocks Rochdl 89 P9
Slaugham W Susx 24 G5
Slaughterford Wilts 32 F10
Slawston Leics 60 G2
Sleaford Hants 23 M7
Sleaford Lincs 86 E11
Sleagill Cumb 101 Q7
Sleap Shrops 69 N9
Sleapford Wrekin 70 A11
Sleapshyde Herts 51 E9
Sleasdairidh Highld 162 E7
Slebech Pembks 41 K7
Sledge Green Worcs 46 F8
Sledmere E R Yk 99 J8
Sleetbeck Cumb 111 K5
Sleight Dorset 12 G5
Sleightholme Dur 103 J8
Sleights N York 105 N9
Slepe Dorset 12 F6
Slickly Highld 167 N3
Sliddery N Ayrs 120 H7
Sligachan Highld 144 G2
Sligrachan Ag & B 131 P9
Slimbridge Gloucs 32 D4
Slindon Staffs 70 E8
Slindon W Susx 15 Q5
Slinfold W Susx 15 M3
Sling Gwynd 79 L11
Slingsby N York 98 D6
Slip End C Beds 50 C7
Slip End Herts 50 G3
Slipton Nhants 61 L5
Slitting Mill Staffs 71 J11
Slockavullin Ag & B 130 G8
Sloley Norfk 77 K7
Sloncombe Devon 8 H7
Sloothby Lincs 87 N6
Slough Slough 35 Q9
Slough Crematorium
    Bucks 35 Q8
Slough Green Somset 19 J11
Slough Green W Susx 24 G5
Slumbay Highld 154 A10
Slyfield Green Surrey 23 Q4
Slyne Lancs 95 K7
Smailholm Border 118 B3
Smallbridge Rochdl 89 Q7
Smallbrook Devon 9 L5
Smallbrook Gloucs 31 Q4
Smallburgh Norfk 77 L7
Smalldale Derbys 83 N9
Smalldale Derbys 83 Q8
Small Dole W Susx 24 F8
Smalley Derbys 72 C2
Smalley Common Derbys 72 C2
Smalley Green Derbys 72 C2
Smallfield Surrey 24 H2
Small Heath Birm 58 H7
Small Hythe Kent 26 E5
Smallridge Devon 10 G4
Smallthorne C Stke 70 F4
Smallways N York 103 M8
Smallwood Ches E 70 E2
Small Wood Hey Lancs 94 H11
Smallworth Norfk 64 E5

Smannell Hants 22 C5
Smardale Cumb 102 D9
Smarden Kent 26 E3
Smarden Bell Kent 26 E3
Smart's Hill Kent 25 M2
Smeafield Nthumb 119 L3
Smearisary Highld 138 A2
Smeatharpe Devon 10 D2
Smeeth Kent 27 J4
Smeeton Westerby Leics 60 E2
Smelthouses N York 97 J8
Smerral Highld 167 L10
Smestow Staffs 58 C6
Smethwick Sandw 58 F7
Smethwick Green Ches E 70 E2
Smisby Derbys 72 A7
Smithaclose IoW 14 F8
Smith End Green Worcs 46 E4
Smithfield Cumb 110 H7
Smith Green Lancs 95 K9
Smithies Barns 91 K9
Smithincott Devon 9 Q2
Smith's End Herts 51 K3
Smith's Green Essex 51 N6
Smith's Green Essex 51 Q2
Smithstown Highld 160 B11
Smithton Highld 156 C8
Smithy Bridge Rochdl 89 Q7
Smithy Green Ches E 82 F10
Smithy Green Stockp 83 J7
Smithy Houses Derbys 84 E11
Smockington Leics 59 Q7
Smoo Highld 165 K3
Smythe's Green Essex 52 F8
Snade D & G 108 H3
Snailbeach Shrops 56 F4
Snailwell Cambs 63 K7
Snainton N York 99 J4
Snaith E R Yk 91 Q6
Snake Pass Inn Derbys 83 P6
Snape N York 97 L4
Snape Suffk 65 M10
Snape Green Lancs 88 D8
Snape Street Suffk 65 M10
Snaresbrook Gt Lon 37 K3
Snarestone Leics 72 A9
Snarford Lincs 86 D4
Snargate Kent 26 G6
Snave Kent 26 H6
Sneachill Worcs 46 H4
Snead Powys 56 E6
Sneath Common Norfk 64 H4
Sneaton N York 105 N9
Sneatonthorpe N York 105 P9
Snelland Lincs 86 E4
Snelson Ches E 82 H10
Snelston Derbys 71 M6
Snetterton Norfk 64 D3
Snettisham Norfk 75 N4
Snibston Leics 72 C8
Snig's End Gloucs 46 E9
Snitter Nthumb 119 K10
Snitterby Lincs 86 C2
Snitterfield Warwks 47 P3
Snitterton Derbys 84 C8
Snitton Shrops 57 K9
Snodhill Herefs 45 L6
Snodland Kent 38 B9
Snoll Hatch Kent 37 Q11
Snowden Hill Barns 90 H10
Snowdon Gwynd 67 L4
Snowdon Kent 39 M11
Snowdonia National
    Park 67 Q9
Snow End Herts 51 K4
Snowshill Gloucs 47 L8
Snow Street Norfk 64 F5
Soake Hants 15 J4
Soar Cardif 30 E8
Soar Devon 7 J11
Soar Powys 44 D8
Soay Highld 144 F5
Soberton Hants 22 H11
Soberton Heath Hants 14 H4
Sockbridge Cumb 101 N5
Sockburn Darltn 104 B9
Sodom Denbgs 80 F10
Sodylt Bank Shrops 69 K7
Soham Cambs 63 J6
Soham Cotes Cambs 63 J5
Solas W Isls 168 d10
Soldon Devon 16 E9
Soldon Cross Devon 16 E9
Soldridge Hants 23 J7
Sole Street Kent 27 J2
Sole Street Kent 37 Q7
Solihull Solhll 59 J9
Sollers Dilwyn Herefs 45 N3
Sollers Hope Herefs 46 B8
Sollom Lancs 88 F7
Solva Pembks 40 F6
Solwaybank D & G 110 F5
Somerby Leics 73 K8
Somerby Lincs 93 J9
Somercotes Derbys 84 F10
Somerford Dorset 13 L6
Somerford Keynes
    Gloucs 33 K5
Somerley W Susx 15 M7
Somerleyton Suffk 65 P2
Somersal Herbert Derbys ...71 L7
Somersby Lincs 87 K6
Somersham Cambs 62 E5
Somersham Suffk 53 J2
Somerton Oxon 48 E9
Somerton Somset 19 N9
Somerton Suffk 63 P10
Somerwood Shrops 57 K2
Sompting W Susx 24 E9
Sompting Abbotts
    W Susx 24 E9
Sonning Wokham 35 L9
Sonning Common Oxon 35 K8
Sonning Eye Oxon 35 K9
Sontley Wrexhm 69 K5
Sopley Hants 13 L5
Sopwell Herts 50 E9
Sopworth Wilts 32 F7
Sorbie D & G 107 M8
Sordale Highld 167 K4
Sorisdale Ag & B 136 H3
Sorn E Ayrs 115 L2
Sortat Highld 167 N4
Sotby Lincs 86 H5
Sots Hole Lincs 86 F8
Sotterley Suffk 65 N5
Soughton Flints 81 J11
Soulbury Bucks 49 N9
Soulby Cumb 101 N5

Soulby Cumb 102 D8
Souldern Oxon 48 F8
Souldrop Bed 61 L8
Sound Ches E 70 A5
Sound Muir Moray 157 R7
Soundwell S Glos 32 C9
Sourton Devon 8 D6
Soutergate Cumb 94 E4
South Acre Norfk 75 R8
South Alkham Kent 27 M3
Southall Gt Lon 36 D5
South Allington Devon 7 K11
South Alloa Falk 133 P9
Southam Gloucs 47 J9
Southam Warwks 48 D2
South Ambersham
    W Susx 23 P10
Southampton C Sotn 14 D4
Southampton Airport
    Hants 22 E11
Southampton
    Crematorium Hants 22 D11
South Anston Rothm 84 H4
South Ascot W & M 35 P11
South Ashford Kent 26 H3
South Baddesley Hants 14 C7
South Ballachulish
    Highld 139 K6
South Bank C York 98 B10
South Bank R & Cl 104 F6
South Barrow Somset 20 B9
South Beddington
    Gt Lon 36 G8
South Beer Cnwll 5 N3
South Benfleet Essex 38 C4
South Bockhampton
    Dorset 13 L5
Southborough Gt Lon 37 K7
Southborough Kent 25 N2
Southbourne Bmouth 13 K6
Southbourne W Susx 15 L5
South Bowood Dorset 11 J5
South Bramwith Donc 91 Q8
South Brent Devon 6 H6
South Brewham Somset 20 D7
South Bristol
    Crematorium Bristl 31 Q11
South Broomhill
    Nthumb 119 P11
Southburgh Norfk 76 E10
South Burlingham Norfk 77 M10
Southburn E R Yk 99 K10
South Cadbury Somset 20 B9
South Carlton Lincs 86 B5
South Carlton Lincs 85 J4
South Cave E R Yk 92 F4
South Cerney Gloucs 33 K5
South Chailey E Susx 25 J7
South Chard Somset 10 G3
South Charlton Nthumb 119 N6
South Cheriton Somset 20 C10
South Church Dur 103 P5
Southchurch Sthend 38 F4
South Cleatlam Dur 103 M7
South Cliffe E R Yk 92 E3
South Clifton Notts 85 P6
South Cockerington
    Lincs 87 L3
South Cornelly Brdgnd 29 M8
Southcott Cnwll 5 K2
Southcott Devon 8 D5
Southcott Devon 9 J8
Southcott Devon 16 G8
Southcott Wilts 21 N3
Southcourt Bucks 35 M2
South Cove Suffk 65 P5
South Creake Norfk 76 B4
South Crosland Kirk 90 E8
South Croxton Leics 72 H8
South Dalton E R Yk 99 K11
South Darenth Kent 37 N7
South Dell W Isls 168 j1
South Downs National
    Park 25 J9
South Duffield N York 92 A4
South Earlswood Surrey 36 G11
Southease E Susx 25 K9
South Elkington Lincs 87 J3
South Elmsall Wakefd 91 M8
Southend Ag & B 120 C10
South End E R Yk 93 Q7
South End Hants 21 M11
South End Herefs 46 D6
South End N Linc 93 K6
South End Norfk 64 D3
Southend Wilts 33 N10
Southend Airport Essex 38 E4
Southend
    Crematorium Sthend 38 E4
Southend-on-Sea
    Sthend 38 E4
Southernby Cumb 101 L3
Southernden Kent 26 E2
Southerndown V Glam 29 N10
Southerness D & G 109 L10
South Erradale Highld 153 N3
Southerton Devon 10 B6
Southery Norfk 63 K2
South Essex
    Crematorium Gt Lon 37 N3
South Fambridge Essex 38 E3
South Fawley W Berk 34 C8
South Ferriby N Linc 92 G6
South Field E R Yk 92 H5
Southfield Falk 126 E3
Southfleet Kent 37 P6
Southford IoW 14 F11
Southgate Gt Lon 36 G2
Southgate Norfk 75 N4
Southgate Norfk 76 B4
Southgate Norfk 76 G7
Southgate Swans 28 G7
South Godstone Surrey 37 J11
South Gorley Hants 13 L2
South Gosforth N u Ty 113 K7
South Green Essex 37 Q2
South Green Essex 52 H8
South Green Kent 26 E9
South Green Kent 76 F9
South Green Suffk 64 H6
South Gyle C Edin 127 M3
South Hanningfield
    Essex 38 B2
South Harting W Susx 23 L11
South Hayling Hants 15 K7
South Hazelrigg Nthumb 119 L4
South Heath Bucks 35 P4
South Heighton E Susx 25 K10
South Hetton Dur 113 N11
South Hiendley Wakefd 91 K8
South Hill Cnwll 5 N7

South Hill Somset 19 N9
South Hinksey Oxon 34 F4
South Hole Devon 16 C7
South Holmwood Surrey 24 E2
South Hornchurch
    Gt Lon 37 M4
South Horrington
    Somset 19 Q5
South Huish Devon 6 H10
South Hykeham Lincs 86 B8
South Hylton Sundld 113 N9
Southill C Beds 50 E2
Southington Hants 22 F5
South Kelsey Lincs 92 H11
South Kessock Highld 156 B8
South Killingholme
    N Linc 93 K7
South Kilvington N York 97 P4
South Kilworth Leics 60 D4
South Kirkby Wakefd 91 L8
South Knighton Devon 7 L2
South Kyme Lincs 86 G11
South Lanarkshire
    Crematorium S Lans 126 B6
South Leicestershire
    Crematorium Leics 72 F11
Southleigh Devon 10 E6
South Leigh Oxon 34 C3
South Leverton Notts 85 N4
South Lincolnshire
    Crematorium Lincs 74 D5
South Littleton Worcs 47 L5
South London
    Crematorium Gt Lon 36 G7
South Lopham Norfk 64 E5
South Luffenham Rutlnd 73 N10
South Lynn Norfk 75 M7
South Malling E Susx 25 K8
South Marston Swindn 33 N7
South Merstham Surrey 36 G10
South Middleton
    Nthumb 119 J6
South Milford N York 91 M4
South Milton Devon 6 J10
South Mimms Herts 50 F10
South Mimms Services
    Herts 50 F10
Southminster Essex 38 G2
South Molton Devon 17 N6
South Moor Dur 113 J10
Southmoor Oxon 34 C5
South Moreton Oxon 34 G7
Southmuir Angus 142 F7
South Mundham W Susx 15 N6
South Muskham Notts 85 N9
South Newbald E R Yk 92 F3
South Newington Oxon 48 D8
South Newton Wilts 21 L8
South Normanton
    Derbys 84 F9
South Norwood Gt Lon 36 H7
South Nutfield Surrey 36 H11
South Ockendon Thurr 37 N4
Southoe Cambs 61 Q8
Southolt Suffk 64 H8
South Ormsby Lincs 87 L5
Southorpe C Pete 74 A10
South Ossett Wakefd 90 H7
South Otterington
    N York 97 N3
Southover Dorset 11 N6
Southover E Susx 25 Q5
South Owersby Lincs 86 E2
Southowram Calder 90 E6
South Oxfordshire
    Crematorium Oxon 34 D6
South Park Surrey 36 F11
South Perrott Dorset 11 K3
South Petherton Somset 19 M11
South Petherwin Cnwll 5 N5
South Pickenham Norfk 76 B11
South Pill Cnwll 5 Q10
South Pool Devon 7 K10
South Poorton Dorset 11 L5
Southport Sefton 88 C7
Southport
    Crematorium Lancs 88 D8
South Queensferry
    C Edin 127 L2
South Radworthy Devon 17 N5
South Rauceby Lincs 86 D11
South Raynham Norfk 76 B7
South Reddish Stockp 83 J6
Southrepps Norfk 77 K4
South Reston Lincs 87 M4
Southrey Lincs 86 F7
South Ronaldsay Ork 169 d8
Southrop Gloucs 33 N4
Southrope Hants 23 J6
South Runcton Norfk 75 M9
South Scarle Notts 85 P8
Southsea C Port 15 J7
Southsea Wrexhm 69 K4
South Shian Ag & B 138 G9
South Shields S Tyne 113 N7
South Shields
    Crematorium S Tyne 113 M8
South Shore Bpool 88 C4
Southside Dur 103 M5
South Somercotes Lincs 87 M2
South Stainley N York 97 M8
South Stifford Thurr 37 N5
South Stoke BaNES 20 D2
South Stoke Oxon 34 G8
South Stoke W Susx 24 B9
South Stour Kent 26 H4
South Street Kent 37 P8
South Street Kent 39 J10
South Street Kent 39 K8
South Tarbrax S Lans 127 J7
South Tawton Devon 8 G6
South Tehidy Cnwll 2 H5
South Thoresby Lincs 87 M5
South Thorpe Dur 103 M8
South Town Hants 23 J7
Southtown Norfk 77 Q10
Southtown Somset 19 K11
South Uist W Isls 168 d14
Southwaite Cumb 110 H11
Southwaite Services
    Cumb 110 H11
South Walsham Norfk 77 M9
Southwark Gt Lon 36 H5
South Warnborough
    Hants 23 K5
Southwater W Susx 24 E5
Southwater Street
    W Susx 24 D5
Southway Somset 19 P6
South Weald Essex 37 N2
Southwell Dorset 11 P10

Place	County	Page	Grid
Southwell	Notts	85	L10
South West Middlesex Crematorium	Gt Lon	36	D6
South Weston	Oxon	35	K5
South Wheatley	Cnwll	5	L3
South Wheatley	Notts	85	N3
Southwick	Hants	14	H5
Southwick	Nhants	61	M2
Southwick	Somset	19	L5
Southwick	Sundld	113	N9
Southwick	W Susx	24	F9
Southwick	Wilts	20	F3
South Widcombe	BaNES	19	Q3
South Wigston	Leics	72	F11
South Willesborough	Kent	26	H3
South Willingham	Lincs	86	G4
South Wingate	Dur	104	D4
South Wingfield	Derbys	84	E9
Southwold	Suffk	65	Q6
South Witham	Lincs	73	N7
Southwood	Norfk	77	M10
Southwood	Somset	19	Q8
South Wonston	Hants	22	E7
South Woodham Ferrers	Essex	38	D2
South Wootton	Norfk	75	M6
South Wraxall	Wilts	20	F2
South Zeal	Devon	8	G6
Sovereign Harbour	E Susx	25	P10
Sowerby	Calder	90	C6
Sowerby	N York	97	P4
Sowerby Bridge	Calder	90	D6
Sowerby Row	Cumb	101	L2
Sower Carr	Lancs	88	D2
Sowerhill	Somset	18	A10
Sowhill	Torfn	31	J4
Sowley Green	Suffk	63	M10
Sowood	Calder	90	D7
Sowton	Devon	6	E5
Sowton	Devon	9	N6
Soyland Town	Calder	90	C6
Spa Common	Norfk	77	K5
Spain's End	Essex	51	Q3
Spalding	Lincs	74	D6
Spaldington	E R Yk	92	C4
Spaldwick	Cambs	61	P6
Spalford	Notts	85	P7
Spanby	Lincs	74	A3
Spanish Green	Hants	23	J3
Sparham	Norfk	76	F8
Sparhamill	Norfk	76	F8
Spark Bridge	Cumb	94	G4
Sparket	Cumb	101	M5
Sparkford	Somset	20	B9
Sparkhill	Birm	58	H8
Sparkwell	Devon	6	F7
Sparrow Green	Norfk	76	C9
Sparrowpit	Derbys	83	N8
Sparrows Green	E Susx	25	P4
Sparsholt	Hants	22	D8
Sparsholt	Oxon	34	B7
Spartylea	Nthumb	112	C11
Spath	Staffs	71	K7
Spaunton	N York	98	E3
Spaxton	Somset	18	H7
Spean Bridge	Highld	146	G11
Spear Hill	W Susx	24	D7
Spearywell	Hants	22	B9
Speen	Bucks	35	M5
Speen	W Berk	34	E11
Speeton	N York	99	P6
Speke	Lpool	81	N9
Speldhurst	Kent	25	N2
Spellbrook	Herts	51	L7
Spelmonden	Kent	26	B4
Spelsbury	Oxon	48	B10
Spen	Kirk	90	F5
Spencers Wood	Wokham	35	K11
Spen Green	Ches E	70	E2
Spennithorne	N York	96	H3
Spennymoor	Dur	103	Q4
Spernall	Warwks	47	L2
Spetchley	Worcs	46	G4
Spetisbury	Dorset	12	F4
Spexhall	Suffk	65	M5
Spey Bay	Moray	157	N4
Speybridge	Highld	149	J2
Speyview	Moray	157	P9
Spilsby	Lincs	87	M7
Spindlestone	Nthumb	119	N4
Spinkhill	Derbys	84	G5
Spinningdale	Highld	162	F9
Spion Kop	Notts	85	J7
Spirthill	Wilts	33	J9
Spital	Wirral	81	L8
Spital Hill	Donc	85	K2
Spital in the Street	Lincs	86	C2
Spithurst	E Susx	25	K7
Spittal	E Loth	128	D4
Spittal	E R Yk	98	F10
Spittal	Highld	167	L6
Spittal	Nthumb	129	Q9
Spittal	Pembks	41	J6
Spittalfield	P & K	141	R9
Spittal of Glenmuick	Abers	149	Q10
Spittal of Glenshee	P & K	141	R4
Spittal-on-Rule	Border	118	A7
Spixworth	Norfk	77	J8
Splatt	Cnwll	4	E6
Splatt	Cnwll	5	L4
Splatt	Devon	8	F3
Splayne's Green	E Susx	25	K6
Splottlands	Cardif	30	H9
Spofforth	N York	97	N10
Spondon	C Derb	72	C3
Spon Green	Flints	69	J2
Spooner Row	Norfk	64	F2
Sporle	Norfk	76	A9
Spott	E Loth	128	H4
Spottiswoode	Border	128	G10
Spratton	Nhants	60	F7
Spreakley	Surrey	23	M6
Spreyton	Devon	8	G5
Spriddlestone	Devon	6	E8
Spridlington	Lincs	86	D4
Springburn	C Glas	125	Q4
Springfield	D & G	110	F7
Springfield	Essex	52	B10
Springfield	Fife	135	J3
Springhill	Staffs	58	E4
Springhill	Staffs	58	G3
Springholm	D & G	108	H6
Springside	N Ayrs	125	K10
Springthorpe	Lincs	85	Q3
Spring Vale	Barns	90	H10
Springwell	Sundld	113	L9
Springwood Crematorium	Lpool	81	N7
Sproatley	E R Yk	93	L4
Sproston Green	Ches W	82	F11
Sprotbrough	Donc	91	N10
Sproughton	Suffk	53	K3
Sprouston	Border	118	E3
Sprowston	Norfk	77	K9
Sproxton	Leics	73	M6
Sproxton	N York	98	C4
Spunhill	Shrops	69	M8
Spurstow	Ches E	69	Q3
Spyway	Dorset	11	L6
Square & Compass	Pembks	40	F4
Stableford	Shrops	57	P5
Stableford	Staffs	70	E7
Stacey Bank	Sheff	84	C2
Stackhouse	N York	96	B7
Stackpole	Pembks	41	J11
Stackpole Elidor	Pembks	41	J11
Stacksford	Norfk	64	F3
Stacksteads	Lancs	89	P6
Staddiscombe	C Plym	6	E8
Staddlethorpe	E R Yk	92	D5
Staden	Derbys	83	N10
Stadhampton	Oxon	34	H5
Stadhlaigearraidh	W Isls	168	C14
Staffield	Cumb	101	P2
Staffin	Highld	152	H4
Stafford	Staffs	70	G10
Stafford Crematorium	Staffs	70	H10
Stafford Services (northbound)	Staffs	70	F8
Stafford Services (southbound)	Staffs	70	F8
Stagsden	Bed	49	Q5
Stainborough	Barns	91	J10
Stainburn	Cumb	100	D5
Stainburn	N York	97	L11
Stainby	Lincs	73	N6
Staincross	Barns	91	J8
Staindrop	Dur	103	M6
Staines-upon-Thames	Surrey	36	B6
Stainfield	Lincs	74	A6
Stainfield	Lincs	86	F6
Stainforth	Donc	91	Q8
Stainforth	N York	96	B7
Staining	Lancs	88	C3
Stainland	Calder	90	D7
Stainsacre	N York	105	P9
Stainsby	Derbys	84	G7
Stainton	Cumb	95	L3
Stainton	Cumb	101	N5
Stainton	Cumb	110	Q8
Stainton	Donc	85	J2
Stainton	Dur	103	L7
Stainton	Middsb	104	E8
Stainton	N York	103	M11
Stainton by Langworth	Lincs	86	E5
Staintondale	N York	105	Q11
Stainton le Vale	Lincs	86	G2
Stainton with Adgarley	Cumb	94	E6
Stair	Cumb	100	H6
Stair	E Ayrs	114	H3
Stairfoot	Barns	91	K9
Stairhaven	D & G	106	H7
Staithes	N York	105	L7
Stakeford	Nthumb	113	L3
Stake Pool	Lancs	95	J11
Stakes	Hants	15	J5
Stalbridge	Dorset	20	D11
Stalbridge Weston	Dorset	20	D11
Stalham	Norfk	77	M6
Stalham Green	Norfk	77	M7
Stalisfield Green	Kent	38	G11
Stalland Common	Norfk	64	E2
Stallen	Dorset	20	B11
Stallingborough	NE Lin	93	L8
Stalling Busk	N York	96	D3
Stallington	Staffs	70	G7
Stalmine	Lancs	94	H11
Stalmine Moss Side	Lancs	94	H11
Stalybridge	Tamesd	83	L5
Stambourne	Essex	52	B4
Stambourne Green	Essex	51	Q3
Stamford	Lincs	73	Q9
Stamford	Nthumb	119	P7
Stamford Bridge	Ches W	81	P11
Stamford Bridge	E R Yk	98	E9
Stamfordham	Nthumb	112	G6
Stamford Hill	Gt Lon	36	H3
Stanah	Lancs	88	D2
Stanborough	Herts	50	F8
Stanbridge	C Beds	49	Q10
Stanbridge	Dorset	12	H4
Stanbury	C Brad	90	C3
Stand	Bury	89	M9
Stand	N Lans	126	D4
Standburn	Falk	126	G3
Standeford	Staffs	58	D3
Standen	Kent	26	E3
Standen Street	Kent	26	D5
Standerwick	Somset	20	F4
Standford	Hants	23	M8
Standingstone	Cumb	100	C8
Standish	Gloucs	32	E3
Standish	Wigan	88	H8
Standish Lower Ground	Wigan	88	H9
Standlake	Oxon	34	C4
Standon	Hants	22	D9
Standon	Herts	51	J6
Standon	Staffs	70	E7
Standon Green End	Herts	51	J7
Standwell Green	Suffk	64	G8
Stane	N Lans	126	F6
Stanfield	Norfk	76	C7
Stanford	C Beds	50	E2
Stanford	Kent	27	K4
Stanford	Shrops	56	E2
Stanford Bishop	Herefs	46	C4
Stanford Bridge	Worcs	57	N11
Stanford Bridge	Wrekin	70	C10
Stanford Dingley	W Berk	34	G10
Stanford in the Vale	Oxon	34	B6
Stanford le Hope	Thurr	37	Q4
Stanford on Avon	Nhants	60	C5
Stanford on Soar	Notts	72	E6
Stanford on Teme	Worcs	57	N11
Stanford Rivers	Essex	51	M10
Stanfree	Derbys	84	G6
Stanghow	R & Cl	105	J7
Stanground	C Pete	74	D11
Stanhill	Lancs	89	L5
Stanhoe	Norfk	75	R3
Stanhope	Border	116	G5
Stanhope	Dur	103	J3
Stanhope	Kent	26	H3
Stanhope Bretby	Derbys	71	P10
Stanion	Nhants	61	K3
Stanklin	Worcs	58	C10
Stanley	Derbys	72	C2
Stanley	Dur	113	J10
Stanley	Notts	84	G8
Stanley	P & K	141	R11
Stanley	Shrops	57	N8
Stanley	Staffs	70	G4
Stanley	Wakefd	91	J6
Stanley Common	Derbys	72	C2
Stanley Crook	Dur	103	N3
Stanley Ferry	Wakefd	91	K6
Stanley Gate	Lancs	88	E9
Stanley Moor	Staffs	70	G4
Stanley Pontlarge	Gloucs	47	K8
Stanmer	Br & H	24	H9
Stanmore	Gt Lon	36	E2
Stanmore	Hants	22	E9
Stanmore	W Berk	34	E9
Stannersburn	Nthumb	111	P3
Stanningfield	Suffk	64	B10
Stanningley	Leeds	90	G4
Stannington	Nthumb	113	K5
Stannington	Sheff	84	C3
Stannington Station	Nthumb	113	K4
Stansbatch	Herefs	45	L2
Stansfield	Suffk	63	N10
Stanshope	Staffs	71	L4
Stanstead	Suffk	52	D2
Stanstead Abbotts	Herts	51	J8
Stansted	Kent	37	P8
Stansted Airport	Essex	51	N6
Stansted Mountfitchet	Essex	51	M5
Stanton	Derbys	71	P11
Stanton	Gloucs	47	L8
Stanton	Mons	45	L10
Stanton	Nthumb	112	H2
Stanton	Staffs	71	L5
Stanton	Suffk	64	D7
Stanton by Bridge	Derbys	72	B5
Stanton by Dale	Derbys	72	D3
Stanton Drew	BaNES	19	Q2
Stanton Fitzwarren	Swindn	33	N6
Stanton Harcourt	Oxon	34	D3
Stanton Hill	Notts	84	G8
Stanton in Peak	Derbys	84	B8
Stanton Lacy	Shrops	56	H9
Stanton Lees	Derbys	84	C8
Stanton Long	Shrops	57	K6
Stanton-on-the-Wolds	Notts	72	G4
Stanton Prior	BaNES	20	C2
Stanton St Bernard	Wilts	21	L2
Stanton St John	Oxon	34	G3
Stanton St Quintin	Wilts	32	H9
Stanton Street	Suffk	64	D8
Stanton under Bardon	Leics	72	D8
Stanton upon Hine Heath	Shrops	69	Q10
Stanton Wick	BaNES	20	B2
Stantway	Gloucs	32	D2
Stanwardine in the Field	Shrops	69	M10
Stanwardine in the Wood	Shrops	69	M9
Stanway	Essex	52	F7
Stanway	Gloucs	47	L8
Stanway Green	Essex	52	G7
Stanway Green	Suffk	65	J7
Stanwell	Surrey	36	C6
Stanwell Moor	Surrey	36	B6
Stanwick	Nhants	61	L6
Stanwick St John	N York	103	N8
Stanwix	Cumb	110	H9
Staoinebrig	W Isls	168	C14
Stape	N York	98	F2
Stapehill	Dorset	13	J4
Stapeley	Ches E	70	B5
Stapenhill	Staffs	71	P10
Staple	Kent	39	N10
Staple Cross	Devon	18	D10
Staplecross	E Susx	26	C7
Staplefield	W Susx	24	G5
Staple Fitzpaine	Somset	19	J11
Stapleford	Cambs	62	G10
Stapleford	Herts	50	H7
Stapleford	Leics	73	L7
Stapleford	Lincs	85	Q9
Stapleford	Notts	72	D3
Stapleford	Wilts	21	L7
Stapleford Abbotts	Essex	37	M2
Stapleford Tawney	Essex	51	M11
Staplegrove	Somset	18	H9
Staplehay	Somset	18	H10
Staple Hill	Worcs	58	E10
Staplehurst	Kent	26	C3
Staplers	IoW	14	F9
Staplestreet	Kent	39	J9
Stapleton	Cumb	111	K6
Stapleton	Herefs	56	E11
Stapleton	Leics	72	C11
Stapleton	N York	103	Q8
Stapleton	Shrops	56	H4
Stapleton	Somset	19	N10
Stapley	Somset	10	D2
Staploe	Bed	61	Q8
Staplow	Herefs	46	C6
Star	Fife	135	J7
Star	IoA	79	J10
Star	Pembks	41	P4
Star	Somset	19	M3
Starbeck	N York	97	M9
Starbotton	N York	96	E6
Starcross	Devon	9	N8
Stareton	Warwks	59	M10
Starkholmes	Derbys	84	D9
Starlings Green	Essex	51	L4
Starr's Green	E Susx	26	C8
Starston	Norfk	65	J5
Start	Devon	7	L10
Startforth	Dur	103	K7
Startley	Wilts	32	H8
Statenborough	Kent	39	P10
Statham	Warrtn	82	E7
Stathe	Somset	19	L9
Stathern	Leics	73	K4
Station Town	Dur	104	D3
Staughton Green	Cambs	61	P7
Staughton Highway	Cambs	61	P8
Staunton	Gloucs	31	Q2
Staunton	Gloucs	46	E9
Staunton in the Vale	Notts	73	L2
Staunton on Arrow	Herefs	45	M2
Staunton on Wye	Herefs	45	M6
Staveley	Cumb	101	N11
Staveley	Derbys	84	F6
Staveley	N York	97	N8
Staveley-in-Cartmel	Cumb	94	H3
Staverton	Devon	7	K6
Staverton	Gloucs	46	G10
Staverton	Nhants	60	B8
Staverton	Wilts	20	G2
Staverton Bridge	Gloucs	46	G10
Stawell	Somset	19	L7
Stawley	Somset	18	E10
Staxigoe	Highld	167	Q6
Staxton	N York	99	L5
Staylittle	Cerdgn	54	E7
Staylittle	Powys	55	K6
Staynall	Lancs	88	D2
Staythorpe	Notts	85	N10
Stead	C Brad	96	H11
Stean	N York	96	G6
Stearsby	N York	98	C6
Steart	Somset	19	J5
Stebbing	Essex	51	Q6
Stebbing Green	Essex	51	Q6
Stechford	Birm	58	H7
Stedham	W Susx	23	N10
Steel	Nthumb	112	D9
Steel Cross	E Susx	25	M4
Steelend	Fife	134	C9
Steele Road	Border	111	K2
Steel Green	Cumb	94	D5
Steel Heath	Shrops	69	Q7
Steen's Bridge	Herefs	45	Q3
Steep	Hants	23	K9
Steephill	IoW	14	F11
Steep Lane	Calder	90	C6
Steeple	Dorset	12	F8
Steeple	Essex	52	F11
Steeple Ashton	Wilts	20	H3
Steeple Aston	Oxon	48	E9
Steeple Barton	Oxon	48	D10
Steeple Bumpstead	Essex	51	Q2
Steeple Claydon	Bucks	49	K9
Steeple Gidding	Cambs	61	P4
Steeple Langford	Wilts	21	K7
Steeple Morden	Cambs	50	G2
Steep Marsh	Hants	23	L9
Steeton	C Brad	90	C2
Stein	Highld	152	D6
Stella	Gatesd	113	J8
Stelling Minnis	Kent	27	K2
Stembridge	Somset	19	M10
Stenalees	Cnwll	4	G10
Stenhouse	D & G	115	R9
Stenhousemuir	Falk	133	P11
Stenigot	Lincs	86	H4
Stenscholl	Highld	152	H4
Stenson Fields	Derbys	72	A4
Stenton	E Loth	128	G4
Steornabhagh	W Isls	168	j4
Stepaside	Pembks	41	M9
Stepford	D & G	109	J4
Stepney	Gt Lon	37	J4
Stepping Hill	Stockp	83	K7
Steppingley	C Beds	50	B3
Stepps	N Lans	126	B4
Sternfield	Suffk	65	M9
Stert	Wilts	21	K3
Stetchworth	Cambs	63	K9
Stevenage	Herts	50	F5
Steven's Crouch	E Susx	26	B8
Stevenston	N Ayrs	124	H9
Steventon	Hants	22	F5
Steventon	Oxon	34	E6
Steventon End	Essex	51	N2
Stevington	Bed	49	Q4
Stewartby	Bed	50	B2
Stewartfield	S Lans	125	Q6
Stewarton	Ag & B	120	C8
Stewarton	E Ayrs	125	L8
Stewkley	Bucks	49	N9
Stewley	Somset	19	K11
Stewton	Lincs	87	L3
Steyne Cross	IoW	14	H9
Steyning	W Susx	24	E8
Steynton	Pembks	40	H9
Stibb	Cnwll	16	C9
Stibbard	Norfk	76	D6
Stibb Cross	Devon	16	G9
Stibb Green	Wilts	21	P2
Stibbington	Cambs	74	A11
Stichill	Border	118	D3
Sticker	Cnwll	3	P3
Stickford	Lincs	87	L8
Sticklepath	Devon	8	F6
Sticklepath	Somset	18	D7
Stickling Green	Essex	51	L4
Stickney	Lincs	87	K9
Stiffkey	Norfk	76	D3
Stifford Clays	Thurr	37	P4
Stifford's Bridge	Herefs	46	D5
Stiff Street	Kent	38	E9
Stile Bridge	Kent	26	C2
Stileway	Somset	19	N6
Stilligarry	W Isls	168	c14
Stillingfleet	N York	91	P2
Stillington	N York	98	B7
Stillington	S on T	104	C6
Stilton	Cambs	61	Q3
Stinchcombe	Gloucs	32	D5
Stinsford	Dorset	11	Q6
Stiperstones	Shrops	56	F4
Stirchley	Birm	58	G8
Stirchley	Wrekin	57	M3
Stirling	Abers	159	R9
Stirling	Stirlg	133	M9
Stirling Castle	Stirlg	133	M9
Stirling Services	Stirlg	133	N10
Stirtloe	Cambs	61	Q7
Stirton	N York	96	E10
Stisted	Essex	52	D7
Stitchcombe	Wilts	33	P11
Stithians	Cnwll	2	J6
Stivichall	Covtry	59	M9
Stixwould	Lincs	86	G7
St Michaels	Fife	135	K4
Stoak	Ches W	81	N10
Stobo	Border	116	H3
Stoborough	Dorset	12	F7
Stoborough Green	Dorset	12	F7
Stobs Castle	Border	117	Q9
Stobswood	Nthumb	119	P11
Stock	Essex	51	Q11
Stock	N Som	19	L2
Stockbridge	Hants	22	C7
Stockbriggs	S Lans	126	D10
Stockbury	Kent	38	D9
Stockcross	W Berk	34	D11
Stockdalewath	Cumb	110	G11
Stocker's Hill	Kent	38	C11
Stockerston	Leics	73	L11
Stock Green	Worcs	47	J3
Stocking	Herefs	46	B8
Stockingford	Warwks	59	M6
Stocking Pelham	Herts	51	L5
Stockland	Devon	10	E4
Stockland Bristol	Somset	18	H6
Stockland Green	Kent	25	N2
Stockleigh English	Devon	9	L3
Stockleigh Pomeroy	Devon	9	L4
Stockley	Wilts	33	J11
Stockley Hill	Herefs	45	M7
Stocklinch	Somset	19	L11
Stockmoor	Herefs	45	M4
Stockport	Stockp	83	J6
Stockport Crematorium	Stockp	83	J7
Stocksbridge	Sheff	90	H11
Stocksfield	Nthumb	112	G8
Stockton	Herefs	45	Q2
Stockton	Norfk	65	M2
Stockton	Shrops	56	D4
Stockton	Shrops	57	N5
Stockton	Warwks	48	D2
Stockton	Wilts	21	J7
Stockton	Wrekin	70	D11
Stockton Brook	Staffs	70	G4
Stockton Heath	Warrtn	82	D7
Stockton-on-Tees	S on T	104	D7
Stockton on Teme	Worcs	57	N11
Stockton on the Forest	C York	98	D9
Stockwell	Gloucs	32	H2
Stockwell End	Wolves	58	C4
Stockwell Heath	Staffs	71	K10
Stockwood	Bristl	32	B11
Stockwood	Dorset	11	M3
Stock Wood	Worcs	47	K3
Stodday	Lancs	95	K9
Stodmarsh	Kent	39	M9
Stody	Norfk	76	F4
Stoer	Highld	164	B11
Stoford	Somset	11	M2
Stoford	Wilts	21	L7
Stogumber	Somset	18	E7
Stogursey	Somset	18	H6
Stoke	Covtry	59	N9
Stoke	Devon	16	C7
Stoke	Hants	15	K6
Stoke	Hants	22	D4
Stoke	Medway	38	D7
Stoke Abbott	Dorset	11	K4
Stoke Albany	Nhants	60	H3
Stoke Ash	Suffk	64	G7
Stoke Bardolph	Notts	72	G2
Stoke Bliss	Worcs	46	C2
Stoke Bruerne	Nhants	49	K5
Stoke-by-Clare	Suffk	52	B3
Stoke-by-Nayland	Suffk	52	G4
Stoke Canon	Devon	9	M5
Stoke Charity	Hants	22	E7
Stoke Climsland	Cnwll	5	P7
Stoke Cross	Herefs	46	B4
Stoke D'Abernon	Surrey	36	D9
Stoke Doyle	Nhants	61	M3
Stoke Dry	Rutlnd	73	M11
Stoke Edith	Herefs	46	B6
Stoke End	Warwks	59	J5
Stoke Farthing	Wilts	21	L9
Stoke Ferry	Norfk	75	P10
Stoke Fleming	Devon	7	M9
Stokeford	Dorset	12	E7
Stoke Gabriel	Devon	7	M7
Stoke Gifford	S Glos	32	B9
Stoke Golding	Leics	72	B11
Stoke Goldington	M Keyn	49	M5
Stoke Green	Bucks	35	Q8
Stokeham	Notts	85	N5
Stoke Hammond	Bucks	49	N9
Stoke Heath	Shrops	70	B9
Stoke Heath	Worcs	58	D11
Stoke Holy Cross	Norfk	77	J11
Stokeinteignhead	Devon	7	N4
Stoke Lacy	Herefs	46	B5
Stoke Lyne	Oxon	48	G9
Stoke Mandeville	Bucks	35	M2
Stokenchurch	Bucks	35	L5
Stoke Newington	Gt Lon	36	H3
Stokenham	Devon	7	L10
Stoke-on-Trent	C Stke	70	F5
Stoke Orchard	Gloucs	46	H9
Stoke Poges	Bucks	35	Q8
Stoke Pound	Worcs	58	E11
Stoke Prior	Herefs	45	Q3
Stoke Prior	Worcs	58	D11
Stoke Rivers	Devon	17	L4
Stoke Rochford	Lincs	73	N5
Stoke Row	Oxon	35	J8
Stoke St Gregory	Somset	19	K9
Stoke St Mary	Somset	19	J10
Stoke St Michael	Somset	20	C5
Stoke St Milborough	Shrops	57	K8
Stokesay	Shrops	56	G8
Stokesby	Norfk	77	N9
Stokesley	N York	104	F9
Stoke sub Hamdon	Somset	19	N11
Stoke Talmage	Oxon	35	J5
Stoke Trister	Somset	20	D9
Stoke upon Tern	Shrops	70	A9
Stoke-upon-Trent	C Stke	70	F5
Stoke Wake	Dorset	12	C3
Stoke Wharf	Worcs	58	E11
Stolford	Somset	18	H5
Stondon Massey	Essex	51	N10
Stone	Bucks	35	L2
Stone	Gloucs	32	C5
Stone	Kent	37	N6
Stone	Rothm	85	J3
Stone	Somset	19	Q8
Stone	Staffs	70	G8
Stone	Worcs	58	C9
Stonea	Cambs	62	G2
Stone Allerton	Somset	19	L4

Ston Easton Somset 20 B4
Stonebridge N Som 19 L3
Stonebridge Norfk 64 C3
Stonebridge Warwks 59 K8
Stone Bridge Corner
 C Pete 74 E10
Stonebroom Derbys 84 F9
Stone Chair Calder 90 E5
Stone Cross E Susx 25 M5
Stone Cross E Susx 25 P10
Stone Cross E Susx 25 P4
Stone Cross Kent 25 M3
Stone Cross Kent 26 H4
Stone Cross Kent 39 P10
Stonecross Green Suffk 63 P9
Stonecrouch Kent 26 B5
Stone-edge-Batch
 N Som 31 N10
Stoneferry C KuH 93 K4
Stonefield Castle Hotel
 Ag & B 123 Q5
Stonegate E Susx 25 Q5
Stonegate N York 105 L9
Stonegrave N York 98 D5
Stonehall Worcs 46 Q5
Stonehaugh Nthumb 111 Q5
Stonehaven Abers 151 M10
Stonehenge Wilts 21 M6
Stone Hill Donc 92 A9
Stonehouse C Plym 6 D8
Stone House Cumb 95 R3
Stonehouse Gloucs 32 F3
Stonehouse Nthumb 111 N9
Stonehouse S Lans 126 D8
Stone in Oxney Kent 26 F6
Stoneleigh Warwks 59 M10
Stoneley Green Ches E 69 R4
Stonely Cambs 61 P7
Stoner Hill Hants 23 K9
Stonesby Leics 73 L6
Stonesfield Oxon 48 C11
Stones Green Essex 53 L6
Stone Street Kent 37 N10
Stone Street Suffk 52 G4
Stone Street Suffk 52 H3
Stone Street Suffk 65 M5
Stonestreet Green Kent 27 J4
Stonethwaite Cumb 101 J8
Stonewells Moray 157 P4
Stonewood Kent 37 N6
Stoneybridge W Isls 168 c14
Stoneybridge Worcs 58 D9
Stoneyburn W Loth 126 H5
Stoney Cross Hants 13 N2
Stoneygate C Leic 72 G10
Stoneyhills Essex 38 G2
Stoneykirk D & G 106 E7
Stoney Middleton
 Derbys 84 B5
Stoney Stanton Leics 59 Q6
Stoney Stoke Somset 20 D8
Stoney Stratton Somset 20 C7
Stoney Stretton Shrops 56 F3
Stoneywood C Aber 151 M5
Stoneywood Falk 133 M11
Stonham Aspal Suffk 64 G10
Stonnall Staffs 58 G4
Stonor Oxon 35 K7
Stonton Wyville Leics 73 J11
Stony Cross Herefs 46 D5
Stony Cross Herefs 57 J11
Stonyford Hants 22 B11
Stony Houghton Derbys 84 G7
Stony Stratford M Keyn 49 L6
Stonywell Staffs 58 G2
Stoodleigh Devon 17 M5
Stoodleigh Devon 18 B11
Stop 24 Services Kent 27 K4
Stopham W Susx 24 B7
Stopsley Luton 50 D6
Stoptide Cnwll 4 E6
Storeton Wirral 81 L8
Storeyard Green Herefs 46 D6
Storey Arms Powys 44 D10
Stornoway W Isls 168 j4
Stornoway Airport W Isls 168 j4
Storridge Herefs 46 E5
Storrington W Susx 24 C8
Storth Cumb 95 K5
Storwood E R Yk 92 B2
Stotfield Moray 157 N3
Stotfold C Beds 50 F3
Stottesdon Shrops 57 M8
Stoughton Leics 72 G10
Stoughton Surrey 23 Q4
Stoughton W Susx 15 M4
Stoulton Worcs 46 H5
Stourbridge Dudley 58 C8
Stourbridge
 Crematorium Dudley 58 C8
Stourhead Wilts 20 E8
Stourpaine Dorset 12 E3
Stourport-on-Severn
 Worcs 57 Q10
Stour Provost Dorset 20 E10
Stour Row Dorset 20 F10
Stourton Leeds 91 J4
Stourton Staffs 58 C8
Stourton Warwks 47 Q7
Stourton Wilts 20 E8
Stourton Caundle Dorset 20 D11
Stout Somset 19 M8
Stove Shet 169 r11
Stoven Suffk 65 N5
Stow Border 117 P2
Stow Lincs 85 Q4
Stow Bardolph Norfk 75 M9
Stow Bedon Norfk 64 D2
Stowbridge Norfk 75 M9
Stow-cum-Quy Cambs 62 H8
Stowe Gloucs 31 Q3
Stowe Shrops 56 F10
Stowe by Chartley Staffs 71 J9
Stowehill Nhants 60 D9
Stowell Somset 20 C10
Stowey BaNES 19 Q3
Stowford Devon 8 B5
Stowford Devon 8 H5
Stowford Devon 10 C7
Stowford Devon 17 M3
Stowlangtoft Suffk 64 D8
Stow Longa Cambs 61 P6
Stow Maries Essex 38 D2
Stowmarket Suffk 64 E10
Stow-on-the-Wold
 Gloucs 47 N9
Stowting Kent 27 K4
Stowting Common Kent 27 K3
Stowupland Suffk 64 F9
Straanruie Highld 148 H4
Strachan Abers 150 H9

Strachur Ag & B 131 M7
Stradbroke Suffk 65 J7
Stradbrook Wilts 20 H4
Stradishall Suffk 63 N10
Stradsett Norfk 75 N9
Stragglethorpe Lincs 86 B10
Stragglethorpe Notts 72 H3
Straight Soley Wilts 34 B10
Straiton Mdloth 127 P4
Straiton S Ayrs 114 G7
Straloch Abers 151 M3
Straloch P & K 141 P5
Stramshall Staffs 71 K7
Strang IoM 80 e6
Strangeways Salfd 82 H5
Strangford Herefs 46 A9
Stranraer D & G 106 E5
Strata Florida Cerdgn 54 G11
Stratfield Mortimer
 W Berk 23 J2
Stratfield Saye Hants 23 J2
Stratfield Turgis Hants 23 J3
Stratford C Beds 61 Q11
Stratford Gt Lon 37 J4
Stratford St Andrew
 Suffk 65 M9
Stratford St Mary Suffk 52 H5
Stratford sub Castle
 Wilts 21 M8
Stratford Tony Wilts 21 L9
Stratford-upon-Avon
 Warwks 47 P3
Strath Highld 160 B11
Strathan Highld 160 H2
Strathan Highld 165 N4
Strathaven S Lans 126 C9
Strathblane Stirlg 125 P2
Strathcanaird Highld 161 K6
Strathcarron Highld 154 B9
Strathcoil Ag & B 138 B11
Strathdon Abers 150 B5
Strathkinness Fife 135 M4
Strathloanhead W Loth 126 G3
Strathmashie House
 Highld 147 P9
Strathmiglo Fife 134 G6
Strathpeffer Highld 155 N6
Strathtay P & K 141 M4
Strathwhillan N Ayrs 121 K4
Strathy Highld 166 D4
Strathy Inn Highld 166 D3
Strathyre Stirlg 132 H4
Stratton Cnwll 16 C10
Stratton Dorset 11 P6
Stratton Gloucs 33 K4
Stratton Audley Oxon 48 H9
Stratton-on-the-Fosse
 Somset 20 C4
Stratton St Margaret
 Swindn 33 N7
Stratton St Michael
 Norfk 65 J3
Stratton Strawless Norfk 77 J7
Stream Somset 18 E7
Streat E Susx 25 J7
Streatham Gt Lon 36 H6
Streatley C Beds 50 C5
Streatley W Berk 34 G8
Street Devon 10 D7
Street Lancs 95 L10
Street N York 105 K10
Street Somset 19 N7
Street Ashton Warwks 59 Q8
Street Dinas Shrops 69 K7
Street End E Susx 25 P6
Street End Kent 39 K11
Street End W Susx 15 N7
Street Gate Gatesd 113 K9
Streethay Staffs 58 H2
Street Houses N York 98 A11
Streetlam N York 104 B11
Street Lane Derbys 84 E11
Streetly Wsall 58 G5
Streetly Crematorium
 Wsall 58 G5
Streetly End Cambs 63 K11
Street on the Fosse
 Somset 20 B7
Strefford Shrops 56 G7
Strelitz P & K 142 B10
Strelley Notts 72 E2
Strensall C York 98 C8
Strensham Worcs 46 H6
Strensham Services
 (northbound) Worcs 46 G6
Strensham Services
 (southbound) Worcs 46 H6
Stretcholt Somset 19 J6
Strete Devon 7 L9
Stretford Herefs 45 N3
Stretford Herefs 45 Q3
Stretford Traffd 82 G6
Strethall Essex 51 L3
Stretham Cambs 62 H6
Strettington W Susx 15 N5
Stretton Ches W 69 M4
Stretton Derbys 84 E8
Stretton Rutlnd 73 N7
Stretton Staffs 58 C2
Stretton Staffs 71 P9
Stretton Warrtn 82 D8
Stretton en le Field Leics 59 M2
Stretton Grandison
 Herefs 46 B6
Stretton-on-Dunsmore
 Warwks 59 P10
Stretton on Fosse
 Warwks 47 P7
Stretton Sugwas Herefs 45 P6
Stretton under Fosse
 Warwks 59 Q8
Stretton Westwood
 Shrops 57 K5
Strichen Abers 159 M6
Strines Stockp 83 L7
Stringston Somset 18 G6
Strixton Nhants 61 K8
Stroat Gloucs 31 Q5
Strollamus Highld 145 J2
Stroma Highld 167 Q1
Stromeferry Highld 153 R11
Stromness Ork 169 b6
Stronaba Highld 146 G11
Stronachlachar Stirlg 132 E5
Stronafian Ag & B 131 L11
Stronchrubie Highld 161 L3
Strone Ag & B 131 P11
Strone Highld 146 E11
Strone Highld 147 N2
Stronmilchan Ag & B 131 P2
Stronsay Ork 169 f4

Stronsay Airport Ork 169 f4
Strontian Highld 138 E5
Strood Kent 26 E5
Strood Medway 38 B8
Strood Green Surrey 36 F11
Strood Green W Susx 24 B6
Stroud Gloucs 32 G3
Stroud Hants 23 K10
Stroude Surrey 36 B7
Stroud Green Essex 38 E3
Stroud Green Gloucs 32 F3
Stroxton Lincs 73 N4
Struan Highld 152 E10
Struan P & K 141 K4
Strubby Lincs 87 N4
Strumpshaw Norfk 77 L10
Strutherhill S Lans 126 D8
Struthers Fife 135 K6
Struy Highld 155 M9
Stryd-y-Facsen IoA 78 E8
Stryt-issa Wrexhm 69 J5
Stuartfield Abers 159 N8
Stubbers Green Wsall 58 F4
Stubbington Hants 14 G6
Stubbins Lancs 89 M7
Stubbs Green Norfk 65 K2
Stubhampton Dorset 12 F2
Stubley Derbys 84 D5
Stubshaw Cross Wigan 82 C5
Stubton Lincs 85 Q11
Stuckton Hants 13 L2
Studfold N York 96 B7
Stud Green W & M 35 N9
Studham C Beds 50 B7
Studholme Cumb 110 E9
Studland Dorset 12 H8
Studley Warwks 47 L2
Studley Wilts 33 J10
Studley Common
 Warwks 47 L2
Studley Roger N York 97 L7
Studley Royal N York 97 L6
Studley Royal Park &
 Fountains Abbey
 N York 97 L7
Stuntney Cambs 63 J5
Stunts Green E Susx 25 P8
Sturbridge Staffs 70 E8
Sturgate Lincs 85 Q3
Sturmer Essex 51 Q2
Sturminster Common
 Dorset 12 C1
Sturminster Marshall
 Dorset 12 G4
Sturminster Newton
 Dorset 12 C2
Sturry Kent 39 L9
Sturton by Stow Lincs 85 Q4
Sturton le Steeple Notts 85 N4
Stuston Suffk 64 G6
Stutton N York 91 M2
Stutton Suffk 53 L5
Styal Ches E 82 H8
Stydd Lancs 89 K3
Stynie Moray 157 Q5
Styrrup Notts 85 K2
Succoth Ag & B 132 B6
Suckley Worcs 46 D4
Suckley Green Worcs 46 D4
Sudborough Nhants 61 L4
Sudbourne Suffk 65 N11
Sudbrook Lincs 73 P2
Sudbrook Mons 31 P7
Sudbrooke Lincs 86 D5
Sudbury Derbys 71 M8
Sudbury Gt Lon 36 E3
Sudbury Suffk 52 E3
Sudden Rochdl 89 P8
Sudgrove Gloucs 32 H3
Suffield Norfk 99 K2
Suffield N York 77 J5
Sugdon Wrekin 69 R11
Sugnall Staffs 70 D8
Sugwas Pool Herefs 45 P6
Suisnish Highld 145 J4
Sulby IoM 80 e3
Sulgrave Nhants 48 G6
Sulham W Berk 34 H10
Sulhamstead W Berk 34 H11
Sulhamstead Abbots
 W Berk 34 H11
Sulhamstead Bannister
 W Berk 34 H11
Sullington W Susx 24 C8
Sullom Shet 169 q6
Sullom Voe Shet 169 r6
Sully V Glam 30 G11
Sumburgh Airport Shet 169 q12
Summerbridge N York 97 K8
Summercourt Cnwll 4 D10
Summerfield Norfk 75 Q3
Summerfield Worcs 58 B10
Summer Heath Bucks 35 K6
Summerhill Pembks 41 N9
Summerhill Staffs 58 G3
Summer Hill Wrexhm 69 K4
Summerhouse Darltn 103 P7
Summerlands Cumb 95 L3
Summerley Derbys 84 E5
Summersdale W Susx 15 N5
Summerseat Bury 89 M8
Summertown Oxon 34 F3
Summit Oldham 89 Q9
Summit Rochdl 89 Q7
Sunbiggin Cumb 102 C9
Sunbury-on-Thames
 Surrey 36 D7
Sundaywell D & G 108 H4
Sunderland Ag & B 122 B7
Sunderland Cumb 100 G3
Sunderland Lancs 95 J9
Sunderland Sundld 113 N9
Sunderland Bridge Dur 103 Q3
Sunderland
 Crematorium Sundld 113 N9
Sundhope Border 117 L5
Sundon Park Luton 50 C5
Sundridge Kent 37 L9
Sunk Island E R Yk 93 N7
Sunningdale W & M 35 Q11
Sunninghill W & M 35 P11
Sunningwell Oxon 34 E4
Sunniside Dur 103 M3
Sunniside Gatesd 113 K9
Sunny Brow Dur 103 N4
Sunnyhill C Derb 72 A4
Sunnyhurst Bl w D 89 K6
Sunnylaw Stirlg 133 M8
Sunnymead Oxon 34 F3
Sunton Wilts 21 P4

Surbiton Gt Lon 36 E7
Surfleet Lincs 74 E5
Surfleet Seas End Lincs 74 E5
Surlingham Norfk 77 L10
Surrex Essex 52 E7
Surrey & Sussex
 Crematorium W Susx 24 G3
Sustead Norfk 76 H4
Susworth Lincs 92 D10
Sutcombe Devon 16 E9
Sutcombemill Devon 16 E9
Suton Norfk 64 F2
Sutterby Lincs 87 L6
Sutterton Lincs 74 E3
Sutton C Beds 62 B11
Sutton C Pete 74 A11
Sutton Cambs 62 F5
Sutton Devon 7 J10
Sutton Devon 8 H4
Sutton Donc 91 P8
Sutton E Susx 25 L11
Sutton Gt Lon 36 G8
Sutton Kent 27 P2
Sutton N York 91 M5
Sutton Norfk 77 M7
Sutton Notts 73 K3
Sutton Oxon 34 D3
Sutton Pembks 40 H7
Sutton Shrops 57 J2
Sutton Shrops 57 N7
Sutton Shrops 69 L9
Sutton Shrops 70 B8
Sutton St Hel 82 B6
Sutton Staffs 70 D10
Sutton Suffk 53 P2
Sutton W Susx 23 Q11
Sutton Abinger Surrey 36 D11
Sutton-at-Hone Kent 37 N7
Sutton Bassett Nhants 60 G2
Sutton Benger Wilts 32 H9
Sutton Bingham Somset 11 L2
Sutton Bonington Notts 72 E6
Sutton Bridge Lincs 75 J6
Sutton Cheney Leics 72 C10
Sutton Coldfield Birm 58 H5
Sutton Coldfield
 Crematorium Birm 58 H5
Sutton Courtenay Oxon 34 F6
Sutton Crosses Lincs 74 H6
Sutton cum Lound Notts 85 L4
Sutton Fields Notts 72 D5
Sutton Green Surrey 36 B10
Sutton Green Wrexhm 69 M5
Sutton Howgrave N York 97 M5
Sutton-in-Ashfield Notts 84 G9
Sutton-in-Craven N York 90 C2
Sutton in the Elms Leics 60 B2
Sutton Lane Ends Ches E 83 K10
Sutton Maddock Shrops 57 N4
Sutton Mallet Somset 19 L7
Sutton Mandeville Wilts 21 J9
Sutton Manor St Hel 81 Q6
Sutton Marsh Herefs 45 R6
Sutton Montis Somset 20 B10
Sutton-on-Hull C KuH 93 K4
Sutton on Sea Lincs 87 P4
Sutton-on-the-Forest
 N York 98 B8
Sutton on the Hill Derbys 71 N8
Sutton on Trent Notts 85 N7
Sutton Poyntz Dorset 11 Q8
Sutton St Edmund Lincs 74 G8
Sutton St James Lincs 74 G7
Sutton St Nicholas
 Herefs 45 Q5
Sutton Scotney Hants 22 E7
Sutton Street Kent 38 D10
Sutton-under-Brailes
 Warwks 48 B7
Sutton-under-
 Whitestonecliffe
 N York 97 Q4
Sutton upon Derwent
 E R Yk 98 E11
Sutton Valence Kent 26 D2
Sutton Veny Wilts 20 H6
Sutton Waldron Dorset 20 G11
Sutton Weaver Ches W 82 B9
Sutton Wick BaNES 19 Q3
Sutton Wick Oxon 34 E6
Swaby Lincs 87 L5
Swadlincote Derbys 71 P11
Swaffham Norfk 77 R9
Swaffham Bulbeck
 Cambs 63 J8
Swaffham Prior Cambs 63 J8
Swafield Norfk 77 K5
Swainby N York 104 E10
Swainshill Herefs 45 P6
Swainsthorpe Norfk 77 J11
Swainswick BaNES 32 E11
Swalcliffe Oxon 48 C7
Swalecliffe Kent 39 K8
Swallow Lincs 93 L10
Swallow Beck Lincs 86 B7
Swallowcliffe Wilts 21 J9
Swallowfield Wokham 23 K2
Swallownest Rothm 84 G3
Swallows Cross Essex 51 P11
Swampton Hants 22 D4
Swanage Dorset 12 H9
Swanbourne Bucks 49 M9
Swanbridge V Glam 30 G11
Swancote Shrops 57 N6
Swan Green Ches W 82 F10
Swanland E R Yk 92 G5
Swanley Kent 37 M7
Swanley Village Kent 37 M7
Swanmore Hants 22 G11
Swannington Leics 72 C7
Swannington Norfk 76 G8
Swanpool Lincs 86 C7
Swanscombe Kent 37 P6
Swansea Swans 29 J6
Swansea Airport Swans 28 G6
Swansea Crematorium
 Swans 29 J5
Swansea West Services
 Swans 28 H5
Swan Street Essex 52 E6
Swanton Abbot Norfk 77 K6
Swanton Morley Norfk 76 E8
Swanton Novers Norfk 76 E5
Swanton Street Kent 38 E10
Swan Valley Nhants 60 F9
Swan Village Sandw 58 E6
Swanwick Derbys 84 F10
Swanwick Hants 14 F5
Swarby Lincs 73 Q2
Swardeston Norfk 77 J11
Swarkestone Derbys 72 B5

Swarland Nthumb 119 N10
Swarraton Hants 22 G7
Swartha C Brad 96 G11
Swarthmoor Cumb 94 F5
Swaton Lincs 74 B3
Swavesey Cambs 62 E7
Sway Hants 13 N5
Swayfield Lincs 73 P6
Swaythling C Sotn 22 D11
Sweet Green Worcs 46 B2
Sweetham Devon 9 L5
Sweethaws E Susx 25 M5
Sweetlands Corner Kent 26 C2
Sweets Cnwll 5 K2
Sweetshouse Cnwll 4 H9
Swefling Suffk 65 L9
Swepstone Leics 72 B8
Swerford Oxon 48 C9
Swettenham Ches E 82 H11
Swffryd Blae G 30 H5
Swift's Green Kent 26 E3
Swilland Suffk 64 H11
Swillbrook Lancs 88 F4
Swillington Leeds 91 K4
Swimbridge Devon 17 L5
Swimbridge Newland
 Devon 17 L5
Swinbrook Oxon 33 Q2
Swincliffe Kirk 90 G5
Swincliffe N York 97 K9
Swincombe Devon 17 M3
Swinden N York 96 C10
Swinderby Lincs 85 Q8
Swindon Gloucs 46 H9
Swindon Nthumb 119 J11
Swindon Staffs 58 C6
Swindon Swindn 33 M8
Swine E R Yk 93 K3
Swinefleet E R Yk 92 C6
Swineford S Glos 32 C11
Swineshead Bed 61 N7
Swineshead Lincs 74 D2
Swineshead Bridge Lincs 74 D2
Swiney Highld 167 M9
Swinford Leics 60 C5
Swinford Oxon 34 D3
Swingfield Minnis Kent 27 M3
Swingfield Street Kent 27 M3
Swingleton Green Suffk 52 G2
Swinhoe Nthumb 119 P5
Swinhope Lincs 93 M11
Swinithwaite N York 96 F3
Swinmore Common
 Herefs 46 C6
Swinscoe Staffs 71 L5
Swinside Cumb 100 H6
Swinstead Lincs 73 Q6
Swinthorpe Lincs 86 E4
Swinton Border 129 L10
Swinton N York 97 K5
Swinton N York 98 F6
Swinton Rothm 91 M11
Swinton Salfd 82 G4
Swithland Leics 72 F8
Swordale Highld 155 Q4
Swordland Highld 145 N9
Swordly Highld 166 B4
Sworton Heath Ches E 82 E8
Swyddffynnon Cerdgn 54 F11
Swyncombe Oxon 35 J6
Swynnerton Staffs 70 F7
Swyre Dorset 11 L7
Sycharth Powys 68 H9
Sychnant Powys 55 M9
Sychtyn Powys 55 M3
Sydallt Wrexhm 69 K3
Syde Gloucs 33 J2
Sydenham Gt Lon 37 J6
Sydenham Oxon 35 K4
Sydenham Damerel
 Devon 5 Q6
Sydenhurst Surrey 23 Q8
Syderstone Norfk 76 A5
Sydling St Nicholas
 Dorset 11 N5
Sydmonton Hants 22 E3
Sydnal Lane Shrops 57 Q3
Syerston Notts 85 M11
Syke Rochdl 89 P7
Sykehouse Donc 91 Q7
Syleham Suffk 65 J6
Sylen Carmth 28 F3
Symbister Shet 169 s7
Symington S Ayrs 125 K11
Symington S Lans 116 D3
Symondsbury Dorset 11 J6
Symonds Yat (East)
 Herefs 45 R11
Symonds Yat (West)
 Herefs 45 R11
Sympson Green C Brad 90 F3
Synderford Dorset 10 H4
Synod Inn Cerdgn 42 H4
Syre Highld 165 Q8
Syreford Gloucs 47 K10
Syresham Nhants 48 H6
Syston Leics 72 G8
Syston Lincs 73 N2
Sytchampton Worcs 58 B11
Sywell Nhants 60 H7

T

Tabley Hill Ches E 82 F9
Tackley Oxon 48 E11
Tacolneston Norfk 64 G2
Tadcaster N York 91 M2
Taddington Derbys 83 P10
Taddington Gloucs 47 L8
Taddiport Devon 16 H8
Tadley Hants 22 H2
Tadlow Cambs 62 C11
Tadmarton Oxon 48 C7
Tadwick BaNES 32 D10
Tadworth Surrey 36 F9
Tafarnaubach Blae G 30 F2
Tafarn-y-bwlch Pembks 41 L4
Tafarn-y-Gelyn Denbgs 68 G2
Taff's Well Rhondd 30 F8
Tafolwern Powys 55 K4
Taibach Neath 29 L7
Tain Highld 162 H10
Tain Highld 167 M3
Tai'n Lôn Gwynd 66 G4
Tairbeart W Isls 168 g7
Tai'r Bull Powys 44 D9
Tairgwaith Neath 29 K2
Takeley Essex 51 N6
Takeley Street Essex 51 M6

Talachddu Powys 44 F8
Talacre Flints 80 G8
Talaton Devon 9 Q5
Talbenny Pembks 40 F8
Talbot Green Rhondd 30 D8
Talbot Village Bmouth 13 J6
Taleford Devon 10 B5
Talerddig Powys 55 L4
Talgarreg Cerdgn 42 H4
Talgarth Powys 44 H8
Talisker Highld 152 E11
Talke Staffs 70 E4
Talke Pits Staffs 70 E4
Talkin Cumb 111 L9
Talladale Highld 154 B3
Talla Linnfoots Border 116 G6
Tallaminnock S Ayrs 114 H8
Tallarn Green Wrexhm 69 M6
Tallentire Cumb 100 F3
Talley Carmth 43 M8
Tallington Lincs 74 A9
Tallwrn Wrexhm 69 J5
Talmine Highld 165 N4
Talog Carmth 42 F9
Talsarn Cerdgn 43 K3
Talsarnau Gwynd 67 K3
Talskiddy Cnwll 4
Talwin IoA 78 H9
Talwrn Wrexhm 69 L5
Tal-y-bont Cerdgn 54 F7
Tal-y-bont Conwy 79 P11
Tal-y-bont Gwynd 67 K10
Tal-y-bont Gwynd 79 L10
Talybont-on-Usk Powys 44 G10
Tal-y-Cafn Conwy 79 P10
Tal-y-coed Mons 45 N11
Tal-y-garn Rhondd 30 D9
Tal-y-llyn Gwynd 54 G3
Talysarn Gwynd 66 H4
Tal-y-Waun Torfn 31 J4
Talywern Powys 55 J4
Tamar Valley Mining District Devon 6 C5
Tamer Lane End Wigan 82 D4
Tamerton Foliot C Plym 6 D4
Tamworth Staffs 59 K4
Tamworth Green Lincs 74 G2
Tamworth Services Warwks 59 K4
Tancred N York 97 Q9
Tancredston Pembks 40 G4
Tandridge Surrey 37 J10
Tanfield Dur 113 J9
Tanfield Lea Dur 113 J10
Tangasdale W Isls 168 b17
Tangiers Pembks 41 J7
Tangley Hants 22 B4
Tangmere W Susx 15 P5
Tan Hill N York 102 G9
Tankerness Ork 169 e6
Tankersley Barns 91 J11
Tankerton Kent 39 K8
Tannach Highld 167 P7
Tannachie Abers 151 K11
Tannadice Angus 142 H6
Tanner's Green Worcs 58 G10
Tannington Suffk 65 J8
Tannochside N Lans 126 C5
Tansley Derbys 84 D9
Tansor Nhants 61 N2
Tantobie Dur 113 J10
Tanton N York 104 F8
Tanwood Worcs 58 D10
Tanworth in Arden Warwks 58 H10
Tan-y-Bwlch Gwynd 67 M6
Tan-y-fron Conwy 68 C2
Tan-y-fron Wrexhm 69 J4
Tan-y-grisiau Gwynd 67 M5
Tan-y-groes Cerdgn 42 E5
Taobh Tuath W Isls 168 e9
Taplow Bucks 35 P8
Tarbert Ag & B 123 L9
Tarbert Ag & B 123 Q6
Tarbert W Isls 168 g7
Tarbet Ag & B 132 C7
Tarbet Highld 145 N9
Tarbet Highld 164 E7
Tarbock Green Knows 81 P7
Tarbolton S Ayrs 114 H2
Tarbrax S Lans 127 J6
Tardebigge Worcs 58 E11
Tarfside Angus 142 H2
Tarland Abers 150 D7
Tarleton Lancs 88 F6
Tarlscough Lancs 88 E8
Tarlton Gloucs 33 J5
Tarnock Somset 19 L4
Tarns Cumb 109 P11
Tarnside Cumb 95 J2
Tarporley Ches W 69 Q2
Tarr Somset 17 R5
Tarrant Crawford Dorset 12 F4
Tarrant Gunville Dorset 12 F2
Tarrant Hinton Dorset 12 F2
Tarrant Keyneston Dorset 12 F4
Tarrant Launceston Dorset 12 F3
Tarrant Monkton Dorset 12 F3
Tarrant Rawston Dorset 12 F3
Tarrant Rushton Dorset 12 F3
Tarring Neville E Susx 25 K10
Tarrington Herefs 46 B6
Tarskavaig Highld 145 J5
Tarves Abers 159 L11
Tarvin Ches W 81 P11
Tarvin Sands Ches W 81 P11
Tasburgh Norfk 64 H2
Tasley Shrops 57 M6
Taston Oxon 48 C10
Tatenhill Staffs 71 N10
Tathall End M Keyn 49 M5
Tatham Lancs 95 N7
Tathwell Lincs 87 K4
Tatsfield Surrey 37 K9
Tattenhall Ches W 69 N3
Tatterford Norfk 76 B6
Tattersett Norfk 76 A6
Tattershall Lincs 86 H9
Tattershall Bridge Lincs 86 G9
Tattershall Thorpe Lincs 86 H9
Tattingstone Suffk 53 K4
Tattingstone White Horse Suffk 53 K4
Tatton Park Ches E 82 F9
Tauchers Moray 157 R8
Taunton Somset 18 H10
Taunton Deane Crematorium Somset 18 H10

Taunton Deane Services Somset 18 G10
Taverham Norfk 76 H9
Taverners Green Essex 51 N3
Tavernspite Pembks 41 N8
Tavistock Devon 6 D4
Tavistock Devon 6 D4
Taw Green Devon 8 G5
Tawstock Devon 17 K6
Taxal Derbys 83 M9
Tay Bridge C Dund 135 L2
Taychreggan Hotel Ag & B 131 L3
Tay Forest Park P & K 141 J5
Tayinloan Ag & B 123 L10
Taynton Gloucs 46 D10
Taynton Oxon 33 P2
Taynuilt Ag & B 139 J11
Tayport Fife 135 M2
Tayvallich Ag & B 130 E10
Tealby Lincs 86 G2
Tealing Angus 142 G10
Team Valley Gatesd 113 K9
Teangue Highld 145 L6
Teanord Highld 155 Q5
Tebay Cumb 102 B10
Tebay Services Cumb 102 B10
Tebworth C Beds 49 Q9
Tedburn St Mary Devon 9 K6
Teddington Gloucs 47 J8
Teddington Gt Lon 36 E6
Tedstone Delamere Herefs 46 C3
Tedstone Wafer Herefs 46 C3
Teesport R & Cl 104 F6
Teesside Crematorium Middsb 104 E7
Teesside Park S on T 104 E7
Teeton Nhants 60 E6
Teffont Evias Wilts 21 J8
Teffont Magna Wilts 21 J8
Tegryn Pembks 41 P4
Teigh Rutlnd 73 M7
Teigncombe Devon 8 G7
Teigngrace Devon 7 M4
Teignmouth Devon 7 N4
Teindside Border 117 N9
Telford Wrekin 57 M3
Telford Crematorium Wrekin 57 N2
Telford Services Shrops 57 N3
Tellisford Somset 20 F3
Telscombe E Susx 25 K10
Telscombe Cliffs E Susx 25 K10
Tempar P & K 140 G6
Templand D & G 109 N3
Temple Cnwll 5 J7
Temple Mdloth 127 Q6
Temple Balsall Solhll 59 K9
Temple Bar Cerdgn 43 K4
Temple Cloud BaNES 20 B3
Templecombe Somset 20 D10
Temple End Suffk 63 L10
Temple Ewell Kent 27 N3
Temple Grafton Warwks 47 M3
Temple Guiting Gloucs 47 L9
Temple Herdewyke Warwks 48 C4
Temple Hirst N York 91 Q6
Temple Normanton Derbys 84 F7
Temple of Fiddes Abers 151 L11
Temple Sowerby Cumb 102 B5
Templeton Devon 9 L2
Templeton Pembks 41 M8
Templetown Dur 112 H10
Tempsford C Beds 61 Q10
Tenbury Wells Worcs 57 K11
Tenby Pembks 41 M10
Tendring Essex 53 K7
Tendring Green Essex 53 K6
Tendring Heath Essex 53 K6
Ten Mile Bank Norfk 75 L11
Tenpenny Heath Essex 53 J7
Tenterden Kent 26 E5
Terling Essex 52 C8
Tern Wrekin 69 R11
Ternhill Shrops 70 A8
Terregles D & G 109 K5
Terrington N York 98 D6
Terrington St Clement Norfk 75 L6
Terrington St John Norfk 75 K8
Terry's Green Warwks 58 H10
Teston Kent 38 B11
Testwood Hants 14 C4
Tetbury Gloucs 32 G6
Tetbury Upton Gloucs 32 G5
Tetchill Shrops 69 L8
Tetcott Devon 5 N2
Tetford Lincs 87 K6
Tetney Lincs 93 P10
Tetney Lock Lincs 93 P10
Tetsworth Oxon 35 J4
Tettenhall Wolves 58 C4
Tettenhall Wood Wolves 58 C5
Teversal Notts 84 G8
Teversham Cambs 62 G9
Teviothead Border 117 N9
Tewin Herts 50 G8
Tewin Wood Herts 50 G7
Tewkesbury Gloucs 46 G8
Teynham Kent 38 G9
Thackley C Brad 90 F3
Thackthwaite Cumb 100 F6
Thackthwaite Cumb 101 M5
Thainstone Abers 151 K4
Thakeham W Susx 24 D7
Thame Oxon 35 K3
Thames Ditton Surrey 36 E7
Thamesmead Gt Lon 37 L4
Thamesport Medway 38 E7
Thanet Crematorium Kent 39 Q8
Thanington Kent 39 K10
Thankerton S Lans 116 D3
Tharston Norfk 64 H3
Thatcham W Berk 34 F11
Thatto Heath St Hel 81 Q6
Thaxted Essex 51 P4
Theakston N York 97 M3
Thealby N Linc 92 E7
Theale Somset 19 N5
Theale W Berk 34 H10
Thearne E R Yk 93 J3
The Bank Ches E 70 E3
The Beeches Gloucs 33 K4
Theberton Suffk 65 N8
The Blythe Staffs 71 J9
The Bog Shrops 56 F5
The Bourne Worcs 47 J3

The Braes Highld 153 J11
The Bratch Staffs 58 C6
The Broad Herefs 45 P2
The Broads 77 P10
The Brunt E Loth 128 H5
The Bryn Mons 31 K3
The Bungalow IoM 80 e4
The Burf Worcs 57 Q11
The Camp Gloucs 32 H3
The Chequer Wrexhm 69 N6
The City Bed 61 P9
The City Bucks 35 L5
The Common Oxon 47 Q9
The Common Wilts 21 P8
The Common Wilts 33 K7
The Corner Kent 26 B3
The Cronk IoM 80 d2
The Deep C KuH 93 J5
The Den N Ayrs 125 J7
The Forge Herefs 45 L3
The Forstal Kent 26 H4
The Fouralls Shrops 70 B8
The Green Cumb 94 D4
The Green Essex 52 C8
The Green N York 105 L9
The Green Wilts 20 G8
The Grove Worcs 46 G6
The Haven W Susx 24 C4
The Haw Gloucs 46 F9
The Headland Hartpl 104 F4
The Hill Cumb 94 D4
The Holt Wokham 35 M9
The Hundred Herefs 45 Q2
Thelbridge Cross Devon 9 J2
The Leacon Kent 26 G5
The Lee Bucks 35 P4
The Lhen IoM 80 e1
Thelnetham Suffk 64 E6
The Lochs Moray 157 Q5
Thelveton Norfk 64 H5
Thelwall Warrtn 82 E7
The Marsh Powys 56 E5
Themelthorpe Norfk 76 F7
The Middles Dur 113 K10
The Moor Kent 26 C6
The Mumbles Swans 28 H7
The Murray S Lans 125 Q7
The Mythe Gloucs 46 G8
The Narth Mons 31 P3
The Neuk Abers 151 J3
Thenford Nhants 48 F6
Theobald's Green Wilts 33 K11
The Quarry Gloucs 32 D5
The Quarter Kent 26 E3
The Reddings Gloucs 46 H10
Therfield Herts 50 H4
The Rhôs Powys 44 H8
The Ross P & K 133 M3
The Sands Surrey 23 N5
The Shoe Wilts 32 F10
The Smithies Shrops 57 M5
The Spring Warwks 59 L10
The Square Torfn 31 J5
The Stair Kent 37 P11
The Stocks Kent 26 F6
The Straits Hants 23 L7
The Strand Wilts 20 H3
Thetford Norfk 64 B5
Thetford Forest Park 63 P3
Thethwaite Cumb 101 L2
The Towans Cnwll 2 F6
The Vauld Herefs 45 Q5
The Wyke Shrops 57 N3
Theydon Bois Essex 51 K11
Theydon Mount Essex 51 L11
Thicket Priory N York 92 A2
Thickwood Wilts 32 F10
Thimbleby Lincs 86 H6
Thimbleby N York 104 D11
Thingwall Wirral 81 K8
Thirkleby N York 97 Q5
Thirlby N York 97 Q4
Thirlestane Border 128 F10
Thirn N York 97 K3
Thirsk N York 97 P4
Thirtleby E R Yk 93 K4
Thistleton Lancs 88 E3
Thistleton Rutlnd 73 N7
Thistley Green Suffk 63 L5
Thixendale N York 98 G8
Thockrington Nthumb 112 H5
Tholomas Drove Cambs 74 H9
Tholthorpe N York 97 Q7
Thomas Chapel Pembks 41 M9
Thomas Close Cumb 101 M2
Thomastown Abers 158 E10
Thomas Town Warwks 47 L2
Thompson Norfk 64 C2
Thong Kent 37 Q6
Thongsbridge Kirk 90 F9
Thoralby N York 96 F3
Thoresby Notts 85 K6
Thoresthorpe Lincs 87 N5
Thoreswell Lincs 93 L11
Thorganby Lincs 93 M11
Thorganby N York 92 A2
Thorgill N York 105 K11
Thorington Suffk 65 N7
Thorington Street Suffk 52 H4
Thorlby N York 96 E10
Thorley Herts 51 L7
Thorley IoW 14 C9
Thorley Houses Herts 51 L6
Thorley Street IoW 14 C9
Thormanby N York 97 Q6
Thornaby-on-Tees S on T 104 E7
Thornage Norfk 76 F4
Thornborough Bucks 49 K8
Thornborough N York 97 L5
Thornbury C Brad 90 F4
Thornbury Devon 16 G10
Thornbury Herefs 46 B3
Thornbury S Glos 32 B3
Thornby Cumb 110 E10
Thornby Nhants 60 E5
Thorncliff Staffs 71 J3
Thorncliffe Crematorium Cumb 94 D6
Thorncombe Dorset 10 H4
Thorncombe Street Surrey 23 Q6
Thorncott Green C Beds 61 Q11
Thorncross IoW 14 D10
Thorndon Suffk 64 G8
Thorndon Cross Devon 8 D6
Thorne Donc 92 A8

Thorne Coffin Somset 19 P11
Thornecroft Devon 7 K5
Thornehillhead Devon 16 G8
Thorner Leeds 91 K2
Thornes Staffs 58 G4
Thornes Wakefd 91 J7
Thorne St Margaret Somset 18 F10
Thorney Bucks 36 B5
Thorney C Pete 74 E10
Thorney Notts 85 Q6
Thorney Somset 19 M10
Thorney Hill Hants 13 M5
Thorney Island W Susx 15 L6
Thorney Toll Cambs 74 F10
Thornfalcon Somset 19 J10
Thornford Dorset 11 N2
Thorngrafton Nthumb 111 Q7
Thorngrove Somset 19 L8
Thorngumbald E R Yk 93 M5
Thornham Norfk 75 P2
Thornham Magna Suffk 64 G7
Thornham Parva Suffk 64 G7
Thornhaugh C Pete 73 R10
Thornhill C Sotn 14 E4
Thornhill Caerph 30 G8
Thornhill Cumb 100 D9
Thornhill D & G 116 B11
Thornhill Derbys 83 Q8
Thornhill Kirk 90 H7
Thornhill Stirlg 133 K7
Thornhill Lees Kirk 90 G7
Thornhills Calder 90 F6
Thornholme E R Yk 99 N8
Thornicombe Dorset 12 E4
Thornington Nthumb 118 G4
Thornley Dur 103 M3
Thornley Dur 104 C3
Thornley Gate Nthumb 112 B9
Thornliebank E Rens 125 P6
Thorns Suffk 63 M9
Thornsett Derbys 83 M7
Thorns Green Ches E 82 G8
Thornthwaite Cumb 100 H5
Thornthwaite N York 97 J9
Thornton Angus 142 F8
Thornton Bucks 49 K7
Thornton C Brad 90 D4
Thornton E R Yk 98 F11
Thornton Fife 134 H8
Thornton Lancs 88 C2
Thornton Leics 72 C9
Thornton Lincs 86 H7
Thornton Middsb 104 E8
Thornton Nthumb 129 P10
Thornton Pembks 40 H9
Thornton Sefton 81 L4
Thornton Curtis N Linc 93 J7
Thornton Garden of Rest Crematorium Sefton 81 L4
Thorntonhall S Lans 125 P6
Thornton Heath Gt Lon 36 H7
Thornton Hough Wirral 81 L8
Thornton-in-Craven N York 96 D11
Thornton in Lonsdale N York 95 P6
Thornton-le-Beans N York 97 N2
Thornton-le-Clay N York 98 D7
Thornton-le-Dale N York 98 G4
Thornton le Moor Lincs 92 H11
Thornton-le-Moor N York 97 N3
Thornton-le-Moors Ches W 81 N10
Thornton-le-Street N York 97 P3
Thorntonloch E Loth 129 K5
Thornton Rust N York 96 E3
Thornton Steward N York 97 J3
Thornton Watlass N York 97 L3
Thornwood Common Essex 51 L10
Thornydykes Border 128 G10
Thornythwaite Cumb 101 L6
Thoroton Notts 73 K2
Thorp Arch Leeds 97 P11
Thorpe Derbys 71 M4
Thorpe E R Yk 99 K11
Thorpe Lincs 87 N4
Thorpe N York 96 F8
Thorpe Norfk 65 N2
Thorpe Notts 85 N11
Thorpe Surrey 36 B7
Thorpe Abbotts Norfk 64 H6
Thorpe Acre Leics 72 E7
Thorpe Arnold Leics 73 K6
Thorpe Audlin Wakefd 91 M7
Thorpe Bassett N York 98 H6
Thorpe Bay Sthend 38 F4
Thorpe by Water Rutlnd 73 M11
Thorpe Common Rothm 91 K11
Thorpe Constantine Staffs 59 L3
Thorpe End Norfk 77 K9
Thorpe Green Essex 53 L7
Thorpe Green Lancs 88 H6
Thorpe Green Suffk 64 D10
Thorpe Hesley Rothm 91 K11
Thorpe in Balne Donc 91 P8
Thorpe Langton Leics 60 F2
Thorpe Larches Dur 104 C5
Thorpe Lea Surrey 36 B6
Thorpe le Fallows Lincs 86 B4
Thorpe-le-Soken Essex 53 L7
Thorpe le Street E R Yk 92 D2
Thorpe Malsor Nhants 60 H6
Thorpe Mandeville Nhants 48 F6
Thorpe Market Norfk 77 J4
Thorpe Marriot Norfk 76 H8
Thorpe Morieux Suffk 64 C11
Thorpeness Suffk 65 P10
Thorpe on the Hill Leeds 91 J5
Thorpe on the Hill Lincs 86 B7
Thorpe Park Surrey 36 B7
Thorpe St Andrew Norfk 77 K10
Thorpe St Peter Lincs 87 N8
Thorpe Salvin Rothm 84 H4
Thorpe Satchville Leics 73 J8
Thorpe Thewles S on T 104 C6
Thorpe Tilney Lincs 86 F9
Thorpe Underwood N York 97 Q9
Thorpe Underwood Nhants 60 G4
Thorpe Waterville Nhants 61 M4

Thorpe Willoughby N York 91 P4
Thorpland Norfk 75 M9
Thorrington Essex 53 J8
Thorverton Devon 9 M4
Thrales End C Beds 50 D7
Thrandeston Suffk 64 G6
Threapland Cumb 100 G3
Threapland N York 96 E8
Threapwood Ches W 69 N6
Threapwood Staffs 71 J6
Threapwood Head Staffs 71 J6
Threave S Ayrs 114 F6
Three Ashes Herefs 45 Q10
Three Bridges W Susx 24 G3
Three Burrows Cnwll 3 J4
Three Chimneys Kent 26 D4
Three Cocks Powys 44 H7
Three Counties Crematorium Essex 52 C6
Three Crosses Swans 28 G6
Three Cups Corner E Susx 25 P6
Threehammer Common Norfk 77 L8
Three Gates Worcs 46 C2
Three Hammers Cnwll 5 L4
Three Holes Norfk 75 K10
Threekingham Lincs 74 A3
Three Leg Cross E Susx 25 Q4
Three Legged Cross Dorset 13 J3
Three Mile Cross Wokham 35 K11
Threemilestone Cnwll 3 K4
Threemiletown W Loth 127 K2
Three Oaks E Susx 26 D9
Threlkeld Cumb 101 K5
Threshers Bush Essex 51 L9
Threshfield N York 96 E8
Thrigby Norfk 77 P9
Thringarth Dur 102 H6
Thringstone Leics 72 C7
Thrintoft N York 97 M2
Thriplow Cambs 62 F11
Throapham Rothm 84 H3
Throckenhalt Lincs 74 C9
Throcking Herts 50 H4
Throckley N u Ty 113 J7
Throckmorton Worcs 47 J4
Throop Bmouth 13 K5
Throop Dorset 12 D6
Throphill Nthumb 112 H3
Thropton Nthumb 119 K10
Throsk Stirlg 133 P9
Througham Gloucs 32 H3
Throughgate D & G 109 J4
Throwleigh Devon 8 G6
Throwley Kent 38 G10
Throwley Forstal Kent 38 G10
Thrumpton Notts 72 E4
Thrumpton Notts 85 M4
Thrumster Highld 167 P7
Thrunscoe NE Lin 93 P9
Thrunton Nthumb 119 L8
Thrup Oxon 33 Q5
Thrupp Gloucs 32 G4
Thrupp Oxon 48 E11
Thruscross N York 97 J9
Thrushelton Devon 8 B7
Thrussington Leics 72 H7
Thruxton Hants 21 Q5
Thruxton Herefs 45 N8
Thrybergh Rothm 91 M11
Thulston Derbys 72 C4
Thundersley Essex 38 C4
Thurcaston Leics 72 F8
Thurcroft Rothm 84 G3
Thurdon Cnwll 16 D9
Thurgarton Norfk 76 H5
Thurgarton Notts 85 L11
Thurgoland Barns 90 H10
Thurlaston Leics 72 E11
Thurlaston Warwks 59 Q10
Thurlbear Somset 19 J10
Thurlby Lincs 74 A7
Thurlby Lincs 86 B8
Thurlby Lincs 87 N5
Thurleigh Bed 61 N9
Thurlestone Devon 6 H10
Thurloxton Somset 19 J8
Thurlstone Barns 90 G10
Thurlton Norfk 65 N2
Thurlwood Ches E 70 E3
Thurmaston Leics 72 G9
Thurnby Leics 72 G10
Thurne Norfk 77 N8
Thurnham Kent 38 D10
Thurning Nhants 61 N4
Thurning Norfk 76 F6
Thurnscoe Barns 91 M9
Thurrock Services Thurr 37 N5
Thursby Cumb 110 F10
Thursden Lancs 89 Q4
Thursford Norfk 76 D5
Thursley Surrey 23 P7
Thurso Highld 167 K3
Thurstaston Wirral 81 J8
Thurston Suffk 64 C8
Thurston Clough Oldham 90 B9
Thurstonfield Cumb 110 F9
Thurstonland Kirk 90 F8
Thurton Norfk 77 L11
Thurvaston Derbys 71 N7
Thuxton Norfk 76 E10
Thwaite N York 102 G11
Thwaite Suffk 64 G8
Thwaite Head Cumb 94 G3
Thwaites C Brad 90 D2
Thwaite St Mary Norfk 65 L2
Thwaites Brow C Brad 90 D2
Thwing E R Yk 99 L6
Tibbermore P & K 134 C3
Tibbers D & G 116 B11
Tibberton Gloucs 46 E10
Tibberton Worcs 47 H3
Tibberton Wrekin 70 B10
Tibbie Shiels Inn Border 117 J6
Tibenham Norfk 64 G4
Tibshelf Derbys 84 F8
Tibshelf Services Derbys 84 F8
Tibthorpe E R Yk 99 K9
Ticehurst E Susx 25 Q4
Tichborne Hants 22 G8
Tickencote Rutlnd 73 P9
Tickenham N Som 31 N10
Tickford End M Keyn 49 N6
Tickhill Donc 85 J2
Ticklerton Shrops 56 H6
Ticknall Derbys 72 B6

Place	Page	Grid
Tickton E R Yk	93	J2
Tidbury Green Solhll	58	H9
Tidcombe Wilts	21	Q3
Tiddington Oxon	34	H4
Tiddington Warwks	47	P3
Tiddleywink Wilts	32	G9
Tidebrook E Susx	25	P4
Tideford Cnwll	5	P10
Tideford Cross Cnwll	5	N9
Tidenham Gloucs	31	Q5
Tideswell Derbys	83	Q9
Tidmarsh W Berk	34	H10
Tidmington Warwks	47	Q7
Tidpit Hants	21	L11
Tidworth Wilts	21	P5
Tiers Cross Pembks	40	H8
Tiffield Nhants	49	K4
Tigerton Angus	143	J5
Tigh a' Ghearraidh W Isls	168	C10
Tigharry W Isls	168	C10
Tighnabruaich Ag & B	124	B3
Tigley Devon	7	K6
Tilbrook Cambs	61	N7
Tilbury Thurr	37	P5
Tilbury Dock Thurr	37	P5
Tilbury Green Essex	52	B3
Tilbury Juxta Clare Essex	52	C3
Tile Cross Birm	59	J7
Tile Hill Covtry	59	L9
Tilehouse Green Solhll	59	J9
Tilehurst Readg	35	J10
Tilford Surrey	23	N6
Tilgate W Susx	24	G4
Tilgate Forest Row W Susx	24	G4
Tilham Street Somset	19	Q7
Tillers Green Gloucs	46	C8
Tillicoultry Clacks	133	Q8
Tillietudlem S Lans	126	E8
Tillingham Essex	52	G11
Tillington Herefs	45	P6
Tillington W Susx	23	Q10
Tillington Common Herefs	45	P5
Tillybirloch Abers	150	H6
Tillyfourie Abers	150	G5
Tillygreig Abers	151	M3
Tillyrie P & K	134	E6
Tilmanstone Kent	39	P11
Tilney All Saints Norfk	75	L7
Tilney High End Norfk	75	L7
Tilney St Lawrence Norfk	75	K8
Tilshead Wilts	21	K5
Tilstock Shrops	69	P7
Tilston Ches W	69	N4
Tilstone Bank Ches W	69	Q3
Tilstone Fearnall Ches W	69	Q2
Tilsworth C Beds	49	Q10
Tilton on the Hill Leics	73	J9
Tiltups End Gloucs	32	F5
Tilty Essex	51	N5
Timberland Lincs	86	F9
Timbersbrook Ches E	70	F2
Timberscombe Somset	18	C6
Timble N York	97	J10
Timewell Devon	18	C9
Timpanheck D & G	110	F6
Timperley Traffd	82	G7
Timsbury BaNES	20	C3
Timsbury Hants	22	B10
Timsgarry W Isls	168	f4
Timsgearraidh W Isls	168	f4
Timworth Suffk	64	B8
Timworth Green Suffk	64	B8
Tincleton Dorset	12	C6
Tindale Cumb	111	M9
Tingewick Bucks	49	J8
Tingley Leeds	90	H5
Tingrith C Beds	50	B4
Tingwall Airport Shet	169	r9
Tingwell Ork	169	d4
Tinhay Devon	5	P4
Tinker's Hill Hants	22	D5
Tinkersley Derbys	84	C8
Tinsley Sheff	84	F2
Tinsley Green W Susx	24	G3
Tintagel Cnwll	4	H4
Tintern Mons	31	P4
Tintinhull Somset	19	N11
Tintwistle Derbys	83	M5
Tinwald D & G	109	M4
Tinwell Rutlnd	73	Q9
Tippacott Devon	17	P2
Tipp's End Norfk	75	K11
Tiptoe Hants	13	N5
Tipton Sandw	58	E6
Tipton Green Sandw	58	E6
Tipton St John Devon	10	B6
Tiptree Essex	52	E8
Tiptree Heath Essex	52	E8
Tirabad Powys	44	B6
Tiree Ag & B	136	C7
Tiree Airport Ag & B	136	C7
Tiretigan Ag & B	123	M7
Tirley Gloucs	46	F9
Tiroran Ag & B	137	M10
Tirphil Caerph	30	F4
Tirril Cumb	101	P5
Tir-y-fron Flints	69	J3
Tisbury Wilts	20	H9
Tisman's Common W Susx	24	C4
Tissington Derbys	71	M4
Titchberry Devon	16	C6
Titchfield Hants	14	F5
Titchfield Common Hants	14	F5
Titchmarsh Nhants	61	M5
Titchwell Norfk	75	Q2
Tithby Notts	72	H3
Titley Herefs	45	L2
Titmore Green Herts	50	F5
Titsey Surrey	37	K10
Titson Cnwll	16	C11
Tittensor Staffs	70	F7
Tittleshall Norfk	76	B7
Titton Worcs	58	B11
Tiverton Ches W	69	Q2
Tiverton Devon	9	N2
Tivetshall St Margaret Norfk	64	H4
Tivetshall St Mary Norfk	64	H4
Tivington Somset	18	B5
Tivy Dale Barns	90	H9
Tixall Staffs	70	H10
Tixover Rutlnd	73	P10
Toab Shet	169	q12
Toadhole Derbys	84	E10
Toadmoor Derbys	84	D10
Tobermory Ag & B	137	N4
Toberonochy Ag & B	130	E6
Tobha Mòr W Isls	168	c14
Tocher Abers	158	G11
Tochieneal Moray	158	D4
Tockenham Wilts	33	K9
Tockenham Wick Wilts	33	K8
Tocketts R & Cl	104	H7
Tockholes Bl w D	89	K6
Tockington S Glos	32	B7
Tockwith N York	97	Q10
Todber Dorset	20	E11
Todburn Nthumb	119	M11
Toddington C Beds	50	B5
Toddington Gloucs	47	K8
Toddington Services C Beds	50	B5
Todds Green Herts	50	F5
Todenham Gloucs	47	P7
Todhills Angus	142	G10
Todhills Cumb	110	G8
Todhills Dur	103	P4
Todhills Rest Area Cumb	110	G8
Todmorden Calder	89	Q6
Todwick Rothm	84	G4
Toft Cambs	62	E9
Toft Ches E	82	G9
Toft Lincs	73	R7
Toft Shet	169	r6
Toft Warwks	59	Q10
Toft Hill Dur	103	N5
Toft Hill Lincs	86	H8
Toft Monks Norfk	65	N3
Toft next Newton Lincs	86	D3
Toftrees Norfk	76	B6
Toftwood Norfk	76	D9
Togston Nthumb	119	P10
Tokavaig Highld	145	K5
Tokers Green Oxon	35	K9
Tolastadh bho Thuath W Isls	168	k3
Toldish Cnwll	4	E10
Tolland Somset	18	F8
Tollard Farnham Dorset	21	J11
Tollard Royal Wilts	20	H11
Toll Bar Donc	91	P9
Tollbar End Covtry	59	N9
Toller Fratrum Dorset	11	M5
Toller Porcorum Dorset	11	M5
Tollerton N York	97	R8
Tollerton Notts	72	G4
Toller Whelme Dorset	11	L4
Tollesbury Essex	52	G9
Tolleshunt D'Arcy Essex	52	F9
Tolleshunt Knights Essex	52	F9
Tolleshunt Major Essex	52	F9
Tollingham E R Yk	92	D3
Toll of Birness Abers	159	P11
Tolpuddle Dorset	12	C6
Tolworth Gt Lon	36	E7
Tomatin Highld	148	E2
Tomchrasky Highld	146	H5
Tomdoun Highld	146	F7
Tomich Highld	147	J2
Tomich Highld	155	P8
Tomich Highld	156	B3
Tomich Highld	162	E5
Tomintoul Moray	149	M4
Tomlow Warwks	48	E2
Tomnacross Highld	155	P9
Tomnavoulin Moray	149	N2
Tompkin Staffs	70	G4
Ton Mons	31	K4
Ton Mons	31	L5
Tonbridge Kent	37	N11
Tondu Brdgnd	29	N8
Tonedale Somset	18	F10
Ton fanau Gwynd	54	D4
Tong C Brad	90	G4
Tong Kent	38	G10
Tong Shrops	57	P3
Tong W Isls	168	j4
Tonge Leics	72	C6
Tong Green Kent	38	G11
Tongham Surrey	23	N5
Tongland D & G	108	E10
Tong Norton Shrops	57	P3
Tongue Highld	165	N5
Tongue End Lincs	74	C7
Tongwynlais Cardif	30	F8
Tonmawr Neath	29	M5
Tonna Neath	29	L5
Ton-teg Rhondd	30	E7
Tonwell Herts	50	H7
Tonypandy Rhondd	30	C6
Tonyrefail Rhondd	30	D7
Toot Baldon Oxon	34	G4
Toot Hill Essex	51	M10
Toothill Hants	22	C11
Toothill Swindn	33	M8
Tooting Gt Lon	36	G6
Tooting Bec Gt Lon	36	G6
Topcliffe N York	97	N5
Topcroft Norfk	65	K3
Topcroft Street Norfk	65	K3
Top End Bed	61	M8
Topham Donc	91	Q7
Top of Hebers Rochdl	89	P9
Toppesfield Essex	52	B4
Toprow Norfk	64	H2
Topsham Devon	9	N7
Top-y-rhos Flints	69	J3
Torbeg N Ayrs	120	G6
Torboll Highld	162	H7
Torbreck Highld	156	A9
Torbryan Devon	7	L5
Torcastle Highld	139	L2
Torcross Devon	7	L10
Tore Highld	155	R7
Torfrey Cnwll	5	J11
Torinturk Ag & B	123	P7
Torksey Lincs	85	P5
Torlundy Highld	139	L2
Tormarton S Glos	32	E9
Tormore N Ayrs	120	G5
Tornagrain Highld	156	D7
Tornaveen Abers	150	G6
Torness Highld	147	P2
Toronto Dur	103	N4
Torpenhow Cumb	100	H3
Torphichen W Loth	126	H3
Torphins Abers	150	G7
Torpoint Cnwll	6	C7
Torquay Torbay	7	N6
Torquay Crematorium Torbay	7	N5
Torquhan Border	128	C10
Torr Devon	6	F8
Torran Highld	153	K8
Torrance E Duns	125	Q3
Torranyard N Ayrs	125	K9
Torre Somset	18	D7
Torridon Highld	154	B6
Torridon House Highld	153	R6
Torrin Highld	145	J3
Torrisdale Ag & B	120	E4
Torrisdale Highld	165	Q4
Torrish Highld	163	M3
Torrisholme Lancs	95	K8
Torrobull Highld	162	D6
Torry C Aber	151	N6
Torryburn Fife	134	C10
Torteval Guern	10	a2
Torthorwald D & G	109	M5
Tortington W Susx	24	B10
Torton Worcs	58	B10
Tortworth S Glos	32	D6
Torvaig Highld	152	H9
Torver Cumb	94	F2
Torwood Falk	133	N10
Torwoodlee Border	117	P3
Torworth Notts	85	L3
Tosberry Devon	16	D7
Toscaig Highld	153	N10
Toseland Cambs	62	B8
Tosside Lancs	95	R9
Tostock Suffk	64	D9
Totaig Highld	152	C7
Tote Highld	152	G8
Tote Highld	152	J5
Tote Hill W Susx	23	N10
Totford Hants	22	G7
Tothill Lincs	87	M4
Totland IoW	13	P7
Totley Sheff	84	D5
Totley Brook Sheff	84	D4
Totnes Devon	7	L6
Toton Notts	72	E4
Totronald Ag & B	136	F4
Totscore Highld	152	F4
Tottenham Gt Lon	36	H2
Tottenhill Norfk	75	M8
Totteridge Gt Lon	36	F2
Totternhoe C Beds	49	Q10
Tottington Bury	89	M8
Tottleworth Lancs	89	L4
Totton Hants	14	C4
Touchen End W & M	35	N9
Toulston N York	91	M2
Toulton Somset	18	G8
Toulvaddie Highld	163	K10
Tovil Kent	38	C11
Towan Cnwll	3	Q4
Towan Cnwll	4	D7
Toward Ag & B	124	E4
Toward Quay Ag & B	124	E4
Towcester Nhants	49	J5
Towednack Cnwll	2	D6
Towend Cumb	95	J4
Town End Cumb	101	K9
Town End Cumb	102	B5
Townend W Duns	125	K2
Towngate Cumb	111	K11
Towngate Lincs	74	B8
Town Green Lancs	88	E9
Town Green Norfk	77	M9
Townhead Barns	83	Q4
Townhead Cumb	100	E3
Town Head Cumb	101	M10
Townhead Cumb	102	B4
Townhead D & G	109	M3
Town Head N York	96	B9
Townhead of Greenlaw D & G	108	F8
Townhill Fife	134	E10
Town Kelloe Dur	104	C3
Townlake Devon	5	Q7
Town Lane Wigan	82	E5
Town Littleworth E Susx	25	K7
Town of Lowton Wigan	82	D5
Town Row E Susx	25	N4
Towns End Hants	22	G3
Townsend Somset	10	H2
Townshend Cnwll	2	F7
Town Street Suffk	63	N3
Townwell S Glos	32	D6
Town Yetholm Border	118	F5
Towthorpe C York	98	C9
Towthorpe E R Yk	98	H8
Towton N York	91	M3
Towyn Conwy	80	D9
Toxteth Lpool	81	M7
Toynton All Saints Lincs	87	L8
Toynton Fen Side Lincs	87	L8
Toynton St Peter Lincs	87	M8
Toy's Hill Kent	37	L10
Trabboch E Ayrs	114	H3
Trabbochburn E Ayrs	115	J3
Traboe Cnwll	3	J9
Tracebridge Somset	18	E10
Tradespark Highld	156	F6
Trafford Park Traffd	82	G5
Trallong Powys	44	D9
Tranent E Loth	128	C5
Tranmere Wirral	81	L7
Trantelbeg Highld	166	E6
Trantlemore Highld	166	E6
Tranwell Nthumb	113	J4
Trap Carmth	43	N11
Traprain E Loth	128	F4
Trap's Green Warwks	58	H11
Trapshill W Berk	22	C2
Traquair Border	117	L4
Trash Green W Berk	35	J11
Trawden Lancs	89	Q3
Trawscoed Cerdgn	54	F10
Trawsfynydd Gwynd	67	N7
Trealaw Rhondd	30	D6
Treales Lancs	88	E4
Trearddur Bay IoA	78	D9
Treaslane Highld	152	F7
Treator Cnwll	4	E6
Tre Aubrey V Glam	30	D10
Trebanog Rhondd	30	D6
Trebanos Neath	29	K4
Trebartha Cnwll	5	M6
Trebarwith Cnwll	4	H4
Trebeath Cnwll	5	M4
Trebetherick Cnwll	4	E6
Treborough Somset	18	D7
Trebudannon Cnwll	4	D9
Trebullett Cnwll	5	N6
Treburgett Cnwll	4	H6
Treburley Cnwll	5	P6
Treburrick Cnwll	4	D7
Trebyan Cnwll	4	H9
Trecastle Powys	44	B9
Trecogo Cnwll	5	N5
Trecott Devon	8	F4
Trecwn Pembks	41	J4
Trecynon Rhondd	30	C4
Tredaule Cnwll	5	L5
Tredavoe Cnwll	2	D8
Tredegar Blae G	30	F3
Tredethy Cnwll	4	H7
Tredington Gloucs	46	H9
Tredington Warwks	47	Q6
Tredinnick Cnwll	4	E7
Tredinnick Cnwll	4	G10
Tredinnick Cnwll	5	K8
Tredinnick Cnwll	5	L10
Tredinnick Cnwll	5	M10
Tredomen Powys	44	G8
Tredrissi Pembks	41	L2
Tredrizzick Cnwll	4	F6
Tredunnock Mons	31	L6
Tredustan Powys	44	G8
Treen Cnwll	2	B9
Treen Cnwll	2	C6
Treesmill Cnwll	4	H10
Treeton Rothm	84	F3
Trefasser Pembks	40	G3
Trefdraeth IoA	78	G10
Trefecca Powys	44	G8
Trefeglwys Powys	55	M6
Trefenter Cerdgn	54	E11
Treffgarne Pembks	41	J6
Treffgarne Owen Pembks	40	G5
Trefforest Rhondd	30	E7
Treffynnon Pembks	40	G5
Trefil Blae G	30	F2
Trefilan Cerdgn	43	K3
Trefin Pembks	40	F4
Treflach Wood Shrops	69	J9
Trefnannau Powys	68	H11
Trefnant Denbgs	80	F10
Trefonen Shrops	69	J9
Trefor Gwynd	66	F5
Trefor IoA	78	F8
Trefrew Cnwll	5	J5
Trefriw Conwy	67	P2
Tregadillett Cnwll	5	M5
Tre-gagle Mons	31	P3
Tregaian IoA	78	H8
Tregare Mons	31	M2
Tregarne Cnwll	3	K9
Tregaron Cerdgn	43	N3
Tregarth Gwynd	79	L11
Tregaswith Cnwll	4	D9
Tregatta Cnwll	4	H4
Tregawne Cnwll	4	G8
Tregeare Cnwll	5	L4
Tregeiriog Wrexhm	68	G8
Tregele IoA	78	F6
Tregellist Cnwll	4	G6
Tregenna Cnwll	3	M5
Tregeseal Cnwll	2	B7
Tregew Cnwll	3	L7
Tre-Gibbon Rhondd	30	C3
Tregidden Cnwll	3	K9
Tregiskey Cnwll	3	Q4
Treglemais Pembks	40	F5
Tregole Cnwll	5	K2
Tregolls Cnwll	3	J6
Tregonce Cnwll	4	E7
Tregonetha Cnwll	4	F9
Tregonning & Gwinear Mining District Cnwll	2	F7
Tregony Cnwll	3	N5
Tregoodwell Cnwll	5	J5
Tregorrick Cnwll	3	Q3
Tregoss Cnwll	4	F9
Tregoyd Powys	44	H7
Tregrehan Mills Cnwll	3	Q3
Tre-groes Cerdgn	42	H6
Tregullon Cnwll	4	H9
Tregunna Cnwll	4	F7
Tregunnon Cnwll	5	L5
Tregurrian Cnwll	4	D8
Tregynon Powys	55	P5
Tre-gynwr Carmth	42	H11
Trehafod Rhondd	30	D6
Trehan Cnwll	5	Q10
Treharris Myr Td	30	E5
Treharrock Cnwll	4	G6
Trehemborne Cnwll	4	D7
Treherbert Carmth	43	L5
Treherbert Rhondd	29	P5
Trehunist Cnwll	5	N9
Trekenner Cnwll	5	N6
Treknow Cnwll	4	H4
Trelan Cnwll	3	J10
Trelash Cnwll	5	K3
Trelassick Cnwll	3	L4
Trelawne Cnwll	5	L9
Trelawnyd Flints	80	F9
Treleague Cnwll	3	K9
Treleaver Cnwll	3	K10
Trelech Carmth	41	Q4
Trelech a'r Betws Carmth	42	F9
Treleddyd-fawr Pembks	40	E5
Trelew Cnwll	3	L7
Trelewis Myr Td	30	F5
Treligga Cnwll	4	F6
Trelights Cnwll	4	F6
Trelill Cnwll	4	G6
Trelinnoe Cnwll	5	N5
Trelion Cnwll	3	N3
Trelissick Cnwll	3	L6
Trellech Mons	31	P3
Trelleck Grange Mons	31	N4
Trelogan Flints	80	G8
Trelow Cnwll	4	E8
Trelowarren Cnwll	3	J9
Trelowia Cnwll	5	M10
Treluggan Cnwll	5	M8
Trelystan Powys	56	D4
Tremadog Gwynd	67	K6
Tremail Cnwll	5	K4
Tremaine Cnwll	5	L4
Tremar Cnwll	5	M8
Trematon Cnwll	5	P10
Trembraze Cnwll	5	M8
Tremeirchion Denbgs	80	F10
Tremethick Cross Cnwll	2	C7
Tremore Cnwll	4	G8
Tre-Mostyn Flints	80	G9
Trenance Cnwll	4	D8
Trenance Cnwll	4	D9
Trenance Cnwll	4	E7
Trenarren Cnwll	3	Q4
Trench Wrekin	57	M2
Trench Green Oxon	35	J9
Trendeal Cnwll	3	M3
Trendrine Cnwll	2	D6
Treneague Cnwll	4	F7
Trenear Cnwll	2	H7
Treneglos Cnwll	5	L4
Trenerth Cnwll	2	G6
Trenewan Cnwll	5	K11
Trenewth Cnwll	4	H6
Trengune Cnwll	5	K3
Treninnick Cnwll	4	C9
Trenoweth Cnwll	3	B10
Trenoweth Cnwll	4	K7
Trent Dorset	19	Q11
Trentham C Stke	70	F6
Trentishoe Devon	17	L2
Trentlock Derbys	72	D4
Trent Port Lincs	85	P4
Trent Vale C Stke	70	F6
Trenwheal Cnwll	2	G7
Treoes V Glam	29	P9
Treorchy Rhondd	30	C5
Trequite Cnwll	4	G6
Tre'r-ddol Cerdgn	54	F6
Trerhyngyll V Glam	30	D9
Trerulefoot Cnwll	5	N10
Tresaith Cerdgn	42	E4
Tresawle Cnwll	3	M4
Tresco IoS	2	b2
Trescott Staffs	58	C5
Trescowe Cnwll	2	F7
Tresean Cnwll	4	B10
Tresham Gloucs	32	E6
Treshnish Isles Ag & B	136	G7
Tresillian Cnwll	3	M4
Tresinney Cnwll	5	J5
Treskinnick Cross Cnwll	5	L2
Tresmeer Cnwll	5	L4
Tresparrett Cnwll	5	J3
Tressait P & K	141	K5
Tresta Shet	169	q8
Tresta Shet	169	t4
Treswell Notts	85	N5
Treswithian Cnwll	2	G5
Treswithian Downs Crematorium Cnwll	2	G5
Tre Taliesin Cerdgn	54	F6
Trethevey Cnwll	4	H4
Trethewey Cnwll	2	B9
Trethomas Caerph	30	G7
Trethosa Cnwll	3	N3
Trethurgy Cnwll	4	G10
Tretio Pembks	40	E5
Tretire Herefs	45	Q10
Tretower Powys	44	H10
Treuddyn Flints	69	J3
Trevadlock Cnwll	5	M6
Trevalga Cnwll	4	H3
Trevalyn Wrexhm	69	L3
Trevanger Cnwll	4	F6
Trevanson Cnwll	4	E7
Trevarrack Cnwll	2	D7
Trevarren Cnwll	4	E9
Trevarrian Cnwll	4	D8
Trevarrick Cnwll	3	P5
Trevarth Cnwll	3	J6
Trevaughan Carmth	41	P7
Tre-vaughan Carmth	42	G10
Treveal Cnwll	2	D6
Treveal Cnwll	4	B10
Treveighan Cnwll	4	H6
Trevellas Downs Cnwll	3	J3
Trevelmond Cnwll	5	L9
Trevemper Cnwll	4	C10
Trevescan Cnwll	2	B9
Trevethin Torfn	31	J4
Trevia Cnwll	4	H5
Trevigro Cnwll	5	N8
Trevilla Cnwll	3	L7
Trevilson Cnwll	4	C10
Treviscoe Cnwll	4	E10
Treviskey Cnwll	3	N5
Trevithick Cnwll	3	P4
Trevithick Cnwll	4	C10
Trevoll Cnwll	4	C10
Trevone Cnwll	4	D6
Trevor Wrexhm	69	J6
Trevorgans Cnwll	2	C8
Trevorrick Cnwll	4	E7
Trevose Cnwll	4	D6
Trew Cnwll	2	G8
Trewalder Cnwll	4	H5
Trewalkin Powys	44	H8
Trewarmett Cnwll	4	H4
Trewassa Cnwll	5	J4
Trewavas Cnwll	2	F8
Trewavas Mining District Cnwll	2	F8
Treween Cnwll	5	L5
Trewellard Cnwll	2	B7
Trewen Cnwll	5	M5
Trewennack Cnwll	2	H8
Trewent Pembks	41	K11
Trewern Powys	56	D2
Trewetha Cnwll	4	G6
Trewethern Cnwll	4	G6
Trewidland Cnwll	5	M10
Trewillis Cnwll	3	K10
Trewint Cnwll	5	L5
Trewint Cnwll	5	M9
Trewithian Cnwll	3	M6
Trewoodloe Cnwll	5	N7
Trewoon Cnwll	2	H10
Trewoon Cnwll	3	P3
Treworga Cnwll	3	M5
Treworgan Cnwll	3	L4
Treworlas Cnwll	3	M6
Treworld Cnwll	5	J3
Tre-wyn Mons	45	L10
Treyarnon Cnwll	4	D7
Treyford W Susx	23	M11
Trickett's Cross Dorset	13	J4
Triermain Cumb	111	L7
Triffleton Pembks	41	J6
Trillacott Cnwll	5	M4
Trimdon Dur	104	C4
Trimdon Colliery Dur	104	C3
Trimdon Grange Dur	104	C3
Trimingham Norfk	77	K4
Trimley Lower Street Suffk	53	N4
Trimley St Martin Suffk	53	N4
Trimley St Mary Suffk	53	N4
Trimpley Worcs	57	P9
Trimsaran Carmth	28	E4
Trims Green Herts	51	L7
Trimstone Devon	17	J3
Trinafour P & K	140	H5
Trinant Caerph	30	H5
Tring Herts	35	P2

Tringford Herts 35 P2
Tring Wharf Herts 35 P2
Trinity Angus 143 L5
Trinity Jersey 11 b1
Trinity Gask P & K 134 B4
Triscombe Somset 18 G7
Trislaig Highld 139 K3
Trispen Cnwll 3 L3
Tritlington Nthumb 113 K2
Troan Cnwll 4 D10
Trochry P & K 141 N9
Troedrhiwfuwch Caerph 30 F4
Troedyraur Cerdgn 42 F5
Troedyrhiw Myr Td 30 E4
Trofarth Conwy 80 B10
Trois Bois Jersey 11 b1
Troon Cnwll 2 H6
Troon S Ayrs 125 J11
Tropical World
  Roundhay Park Leeds 91 J3
Trossachs Stirlg 132 G6
Trossachs Pier Stirlg 132 F6
Troston Suffk 64 B7
Troswell Cnwll 5 M3
Trotshill Worcs 46 G3
Trottiscliffe Kent 37 P8
Trotton W Susx 23 M10
Troughend Nthumb 112 C2
Trough Gate Lancs 89 P6
Troutbeck Cumb 101 L5
Troutbeck Cumb 101 M10
Troutbeck Bridge Cumb 101 M10
Troway Derbys 84 E5
Trowbridge Wilts 20 G3
Trowell Notts 72 D3
Trowell Services Notts 72 D2
Trowle Common Wilts 20 F3
Trowley Bottom Herts 50 C8
Trowse Newton Norfk 77 J10
Troy Leeds 90 G3
Trudoxhill Somset 20 D6
Trull Somset 18 H10
Trumfleet Donc 91 Q8
Trumpan Highld 152 C5
Trumpet Herefs 46 C7
Trumpington Cambs 62 F10
Trumpsgreen Surrey 35 Q11
Trunch Norfk 77 K5
Trunnah Lancs 88 C2
Truro Cnwll 3 L5
Truscott Cnwll 5 M4
Trusham Devon 9 L8
Trusley Derbys 71 P7
Trusthorpe Lincs 87 P4
Trysull Staffs 58 C6
Tubney Oxon 34 D5
Tuckenhay Devon 7 L7
Tuckhill Shrops 57 P7
Tuckingmill Cnwll 2 H5
Tuckingmill Wilts 20 H9
Tuckton Bmouth 13 K6
Tucoyse Cnwll 3 P4
Tuddenham Suffk 53 L2
Tuddenham Suffk 63 M6
Tudeley Kent 37 P11
Tudhoe Dur 103 Q3
Tudorville Herefs 46 A10
Tudweiliog Gwynd 66 C7
Tuesley Surrey 23 Q6
Tuffley Gloucs 32 F2
Tufton Hants 22 E5
Tufton Pembks 41 K5
Tugby Leics 73 K10
Tugford Shrops 57 K7
Tughall Nthumb 119 P5
Tullibody Clacks 133 P8
Tullich Abers 150 B8
Tullich Highld 147 Q2
Tullich Highld 156 F7
Tulliemet P & K 141 P7
Tulloch Abers 159 K11
Tullochgorm Ag & B 131 K8
Tulloch Station Highld 147 K11
Tullymurdoch P & K 142 B7
Tullynessle Abers 150 F4
Tulse Hill Gt Lon 36 H6
Tumble Carmth 28 F2
Tumbler's Green Essex 52 D6
Tumby Lincs 86 H9
Tumby Woodside Lincs 87 J9
Tummel Bridge P & K 141 J6
Tunbridge Wells Kent 25 N3
Tundergarth D & G 110 C4
Tunga W Isls 168 j4
Tungate Norfk 77 K6
Tunley BaNES 20 C3
Tunstall C Stke 70 F4
Tunstall E R Yk 93 P4
Tunstall Kent 38 E9
Tunstall Lancs 95 N6
Tunstall N York 103 P11
Tunstall Norfk 77 N10
Tunstall Staffs 70 D9
Tunstall Suffk 65 M10
Tunstall Sundld 113 N10
Tunstead Derbys 83 P10
Tunstead Norfk 77 K7
Tunstead Milton Derbys 83 M8
Tunworth Hants 23 J5
Tupsley Herefs 45 Q6
Turgis Green Hants 23 J3
Turkdean Gloucs 47 M11
Tur Langton Leics 60 F2
Turleigh Wilts 20 F2
Turleygreen Shrops 57 P7
Turn Lancs 89 N7
Turnastone Herefs 45 M7
Turnberry S Ayrs 114 D8
Turnchapel C Plym 6 D6
Turnditch Derbys 71 P5
Turner Green Lancs 89 J4
Turner's Green E Susx 25 P7
Turner's Green Warwks 59 J11
Turner's Hill W Susx 24 H3
Turners Puddle Dorset 12 D6
Turnford Herts 51 J10
Turnhouse C Edin 127 M3
Turnworth Dorset 12 D3
Turriff Abers 158 H7
Turton Bottoms Bl w D 89 L7
Turves Cambs 74 F11
Turvey Bed 49 P4
Turville Bucks 35 L6
Turville Heath Bucks 35 K6
Turweston Bucks 48 H7
Tushielaw Inn Border 117 L7
Tutbury Staffs 71 N9
Tutnall Worcs 58 E10
Tutshill Gloucs 31 P6
Tuttington Norfk 77 J6
Tutwell Cnwll 5 P6

Tuxford Notts 85 M6
Twatt Ork 169 b4
Twatt Shet 169 q8
Twechar E Duns 126 B2
Tweedbank Border 117 Q4
Tweedmouth Nthumb 129 P9
Tweedsmuir Border 116 C6
Twelveheads Cnwll 3 K5
Twelve Oaks E Susx 25 Q6
Twemlow Green Ches E 82 G11
Twenty Lincs 74 C6
Twerton BaNES 20 D2
Twickenham Gt Lon 36 E6
Twigworth Gloucs 46 F10
Twineham W Susx 24 G7
Twineham Green W Susx 24 G6
Twinhoe BaNES 20 E3
Twinstead Essex 52 E4
Twitchen Devon 17 P5
Twitchen Shrops 56 F9
Twitham Kent 39 N10
Two Bridges Devon 6 G4
Two Dales Derbys 84 C8
Two Gates Staffs 59 K4
Two Mile Oak Cross
  Devon 7 L5
Two Pots Devon 17 J3
Two Waters Herts 50 C9
Twycross Leics 72 A10
Twycross Zoo Leics 59 M3
Twyford Bucks 49 J9
Twyford Hants 22 E10
Twyford Leics 73 J8
Twyford Lincs 73 N6
Twyford Norfk 76 E7
Twyford Wokham 35 L9
Twyford Common
  Herefs 45 Q7
Twyn-carno Caerph 30 F3
Twynholm D & G 108 E10
Twyning Green Gloucs 46 H7
Twynllanan Carmth 43 Q10
Twyn-yr-Odyn V Glam 30 F10
Twyn-y-Sheriff Mons 31 M3
Twywell Nhants 61 L5
Tyberton Herefs 45 M7
Tyburn Birm 58 H6
Tycroes Carmth 28 H2
Ty Croes IoA 78 E10
Tycrwyn Powys 68 F11
Tydd Gote Lincs 75 J7
Tydd St Giles Cambs 74 H7
Tydd St Mary Lincs 74 H7
Tye Hants 15 K6
Tye Green Essex 51 M6
Tye Green Essex 51 N3
Tye Green Essex 52 C7
Tyersal C Brad 90 F4
Tyldesley Wigan 82 E4
Tyler Hill Kent 39 K9
Tylers Green Bucks 35 P6
Tyler's Green Essex 51 M9
Tylers Green Surrey 37 J10
Tylorstown Rhondd 30 D5
Tylwch Powys 55 M8
Ty-nant Conwy 68 C6
Ty-nant Gwynd 68 B9
Tyndrum Stirlg 139 Q11
Ty'n-dwr Denbgs 68 H6
Tyneham Dorset 12 E8
Tynemouth N Tyne 113 N7
Tynemouth
  Crematorium N Tyne 113 M7
Tyne Tunnel S Tyne 113 M7
Tynewydd Rhondd 29 P5
Tyninghame E Loth 128 G4
Tynron D & G 115 R9
Ty'n-y-bryn Rhondd 30 D7
Ty'n-y-coedcae Caerph 30 G7
Tynygongl IoA 79 J8
Tyngraig Cerdgn 54 F11
Ty'n-y-Groes Conwy 79 P10
Tyn-y-nant Rhondd 30 E7
Tyrie Abers 159 M5
Tyringham M Keyn 49 N5
Tyseley Birm 58 H8
Tythegston Brdgnd 29 N9
Tytherington Ches E 83 K9
Tytherington S Glos 32 C7
Tytherington Somset 20 E6
Tytherington Wilts 20 H6
Tytherleigh Devon 10 G4
Tytherton Lucas Wilts 32 H10
Tyttenhanger Herts 50 E9
Tywardreath Cnwll 4 H11
Tywardreath Highway
  Cnwll 4 H10
Tywyn Conwy 79 P9
Tywyn Gwynd 54 D4

U

Ubbeston Green Suffk 65 L7
Ubley BaNES 19 P3
Uckerby N York 103 P10
Uckfield E Susx 25 L6
Uckinghall Worcs 46 G7
Uckington Gloucs 46 H10
Uckington Shrops 57 K2
Uddingston S Lans 126 B5
Uddington S Lans 116 B4
Udimore E Susx 26 E8
Udny Green Abers 151 M2
Udny Station Abers 151 N3
Uffcott Wilts 33 M9
Uffculme Devon 9 Q2
Uffington Lincs 73 R9
Uffington Oxon 34 B7
Uffington Shrops 57 J2
Ufford C Pete 74 A10
Ufford Suffk 65 K11
Ufton Warwks 48 C2
Ufton Nervet W Berk 34 H11
Ugadale Ag & B 120 E6
Ugborough Devon 6 H7
Uggeshall Suffk 65 N5
Ugglebarnby N York 105 N9
Ughill Sheff 84 C2
Ugley Essex 51 M5
Ugley Green Essex 51 M5
Ugthorpe N York 105 L8
Uibhist A Deas W Isls 168 d14
Uibhist A Tuath W Isls 168 c10
Uig Ag & B 136 F5
Uig Highld 152 E10
Uig Highld 152 F5
Uig W Isls 168 f4
Uigshader Highld 152 G8
Uisken Ag & B 137 K12

Ulbster Highld 167 P8
Ulcat Row Cumb 101 M6
Ulceby Lincs 87 M6
Ulceby N Linc 93 K8
Ulceby Skitter N Linc 93 K7
Ulcombe Kent 26 D2
Uldale Cumb 100 H3
Uley Gloucs 32 E5
Ulgham Nthumb 113 K2
Ullapool Highld 161 J8
Ullenhall Warwks 58 H11
Ullenwood Gloucs 46 H11
Ulleskelf N York 91 N3
Ullesthorpe Leics 60 B3
Ulley Rothm 84 G3
Ullingswick Herefs 46 A5
Ullinish Lodge Hotel
  Highld 152 E10
Ullock Cumb 100 E6
Ullswater Cumb 101 M6
Ullswater Steamers
  Cumb 101 L7
Ulpha Cumb 94 D2
Ulpha Cumb 95 K4
Ulrome E R Yk 99 P9
Ulsta Shet 169 r5
Ulting Wick Essex 52 D10
Ulva Ag & B 137 K7
Ulverley Green Solhll 58 H8
Ulverston Cumb 94 F5
Ulwell Dorset 12 H8
Ulzieside D & G 115 Q6
Umberleigh Devon 17 L7
Unapool Highld 164 F10
Underbarrow Cumb 95 K2
Under Burnmouth
  Border 111 J4
Undercliffe C Brad 90 F4
Underdale Shrops 57 J2
Underling Green Kent 26 C2
Underriver Kent 37 N10
Underwood Newpt 31 L7
Underwood Notts 84 G10
Undley Suffk 63 L4
Undy Mons 31 M7
Union Mills IoM 80 e6
Union Street E Susx 26 B5
Unst Shet 169 s3
Unstone Derbys 84 E5
Unstone Green Derbys 84 E5
Unthank Cumb 101 N3
Unthank Cumb 102 B2
Unthank Cumb 110 G11
Unthank Derbys 84 D5
Unthank Nthumb 129 P10
Upavon Wilts 21 M4
Up Cerne Dorset 11 P4
Upchurch Kent 38 D8
Upcott Devon 17 P6
Upcott Herefs 45 L4
Upend Cambs 63 M9
Up Exe Devon 9 M4
Upgate Norfk 76 G8
Upgate Street Norfk 64 F3
Upgate Street Norfk 65 K3
Uphall Dorset 11 M4
Uphall W Loth 127 K3
Upham Devon 9 L3
Upham Hants 22 F10
Uphampton Herefs 45 M2
Uphampton Worcs 46 F2
Uphill N Som 19 K3
Up Holland Lancs 88 G9
Uplawmoor E Rens 125 L6
Upleadon Gloucs 46 E9
Upleatham R & Cl 104 H7
Uplees Kent 38 H9
Uploders Dorset 11 L6
Uplowman Devon 18 D11
Uplyme Devon 10 G6
Up Marden W Susx 15 L4
Upminster Gt Lon 37 N3
Up Mudford Somset 19 Q11
Up Nately Hants 23 J4
Upottery Devon 10 E3
Upper Affcot Shrops 56 G7
Upper Ardchronie Highld 162 E9
Upper Arley Worcs 57 P8
Upper Arncott Oxon 48 H11
Upper Astrop Nhants 48 F7
Upper Basildon W Berk 34 G9
Upper Batley Kirk 90 G5
Upper Beeding W Susx 24 E8
Upper Benefield Nhants 61 L3
Upper Bentley Worcs 58 E11
Upper Bighouse Highld 166 E5
Upper Birchwood
  Derbys 84 F9
Upper Boat Rhondd 30 F7
Upper Boddington
  Nhants 48 E4
Upper Borth Cerdgn 54 E7
Upper Brailes Warwks 48 B5
Upper Breinton Herefs 45 P6
Upper Broadheath
  Worcs 46 F3
Upper Broughton Notts 72 H5
Upper Bucklebury
  W Berk 34 F11
Upper Burgate Hants 21 N11
Upper Bush Medway 37 Q7
Upperby Cumb 110 H10
Upper Caldecote C Beds 61 Q11
Upper Canada N Som 19 L3
Upper Canterton Hants 13 N2
Upper Catesby Nhants 60 B9
Upper Catshill Worcs 58 E10
Upper Chapel Powys 44 E6
Upper Cheddon Somset 18 H9
Upper Chicksgrove Wilts 21 J9
Upper Chute Wilts 21 Q4
Upper Clapton Gt Lon 36 H3
Upper Clatford Hants 22 C6
Upper Coberley Gloucs 46 J11
Upper Cotton Staffs 71 K5
Upper Cound Shrops 57 K3
Upper Cudworth Barns 91 K9
Upper Cumberworth
  Kirk 90 G9
Upper Dallachy Moray 157 R5
Upper Deal Kent 39 Q11
Upper Dean Bed 61 M7
Upper Denby Kirk 90 G8
Upper Denton Cumb 111 M7
Upper Dicker E Susx 25 N9
Upper Dinchope Shrops 56 H8
Upper Dounreay Highld 166 H3
Upper Dovercourt Essex 53 M5
Upper Drumbane Stirlg 133 L6
Upper Dunsforth N York 97 P8
Upper Eashing Surrey 23 Q6

Upper Eathie Highld 156 D5
Upper Egleton Herefs 46 B6
Upper Elkstone Staffs 71 K3
Upper Ellastone Staffs 71 L6
Upper End Derbys 83 N9
Upper Enham Hants 22 C4
Upper Farmcote Shrops 57 P6
Upper Farringdon Hants 23 J7
Upper Framilode Gloucs 32 E2
Upper Froyle Hants 23 L6
Upper Godney Somset 19 N6
Upper Gravenhurst
  C Beds 50 D3
Upper Green Mons 45 M11
Upper Green Suffk 63 M8
Upper Green W Berk 22 C2
Upper Grove Common
  Herefs 45 R9
Upper Hackney Derbys 84 C8
Upper Hale Surrey 23 M5
Upper Halliford Surrey 36 C7
Upper Halling Medway 37 Q8
Upper Hambleton
  Rutlnd 73 N9
Upper Harbledown Kent 39 K10
Upper Hardres Court
  Kent 39 L11
Upper Hardwick Herefs 45 N3
Upper Hartfield E Susx 25 L4
Upper Hartshay Derbys 84 E10
Upper Hatherley Gloucs 46 H10
Upper Hatton Staffs 70 E7
Upper Haugh Rothm 91 L11
Upper Hayton Shrops 57 J8
Upper Heaton Kirk 90 F7
Upper Helmsley N York 98 D9
Upper Hergest Herefs 45 K4
Upper Heyford Nhants 60 E9
Upper Heyford Oxon 48 E9
Upper Hill Herefs 45 P4
Upper Hockenden Kent 37 M7
Upper Hopton Kirk 90 F7
Upper Howsell Worcs 46 E5
Upper Hulme Staffs 71 J2
Upper Ifold Surrey 24 B4
Upper Inglesham Swindn 33 P5
Upper Kilcott Gloucs 32 E7
Upper Killay Swans 28 G6
Upper Kinchrackine
  Ag & B 131 P2
Upper Knockando Moray 157 M9
Upper Lambourn W Berk 34 B8
Upper Landywood Staffs 58 E3
Upper Langford N Som 19 N3
Upper Langwith Derbys 84 H7
Upper Largo Fife 135 L7
Upper Leigh Staffs 71 J7
Upper Littleton N Som 19 Q2
Upper Lochton Abers 150 H8
Upper Longdon Staffs 58 G2
Upper & Lower
  Stondon C Beds 50 E3
Upper Ludstone Shrops 57 Q5
Upper Lybster Highld 167 N9
Upper Lydbrook Gloucs 46 B11
Upper Lyde Herefs 45 P6
Upper Lye Herefs 56 F11
Upper Maes-coed Herefs 45 L8
Upper Midhope Sheff 90 G11
Uppermill Oldham 90 B9
Upper Milton Worcs 57 Q10
Upper Minety Wilts 33 K6
Upper Moor Worcs 47 J5
Upper Moor Side Leeds 90 G4
Upper Mulben Moray 157 R7
Upper Netchwood
  Shrops 57 L6
Upper Nobut Staffs 71 J7
Upper Norwood W Susx 23 P11
Upper Padley Derbys 84 B5
Upper Pennington Hants 13 P5
Upper Pollicott Bucks 35 K2
Upper Poppleton C York 98 B10
Upper Quinton Warwks 47 N5
Upper Ratley Hants 22 B10
Upper Rissington Gloucs 47 P11
Upper Rochford Worcs 57 L11
Upper Ruscoe D & G 108 C2
Upper Sapey Herefs 46 C2
Upper Saxondale Notts 72 H3
Upper Seagry Wilts 32 H8
Upper Shelton C Beds 49 Q6
Upper Sheringham
  Norfk 76 G3
Upper Skelmorlie N Ayrs 124 G4
Upper Slaughter Gloucs 47 N10
Upper Soudley Gloucs 32 C2
Upper Spond Herefs 45 L4
Upper Standen Kent 27 M3
Upper Staploe Bed 61 P9
Upper Stoke Norfk 77 K11
Upper Stowe Nhants 60 D9
Upper Street Hants 21 N11
Upper Street Norfk 64 H6
Upper Street Norfk 77 L8
Upper Street Norfk 77 M8
Upper Street Suffk 53 K5
Upper Street Suffk 63 N10
Upper Street Suffk 64 G7
Upper Strensham Worcs 46 G7
Upper Sundon C Beds 50 B5
Upper Swell Gloucs 47 N9
Upper Tankersley Barns 91 J11
Upper Tasburgh Norfk 65 J2
Upper Tean Staffs 71 J7
Upperthong Kirk 90 E9
Upperthorpe Derbys 84 G6
Upperthorpe N Linc 92 C10
Upper Threapwood
  Ches W 69 M5
Upperton W Susx 23 Q10
Upper Town Derbys 71 N4
Uppertown Derbys 84 D8
Upper Town Dur 103 L3
Upper Town Herefs 46 A5
Uppertown Highld 167 Q1
Upper Town N Som 31 P11
Upper Town Suffk 64 C8
Upper Tumble Carmth 28 F2
Upper Tysoe Warwks 48 B6
Upper Ufford Suffk 65 K11
Upperup Gloucs 33 K5
Upper Upham Wilts 33 P9
Upper Upnor Medway 38 C7
Upper Victoria Angus 143 J10
Upper Vobster Somset 20 D6
Upper Wardington Oxon 48 E5
Upper Weald M Keyn 49 M7
Upper Weedon Nhants 60 D9
Upper Welland Worcs 46 E6

Upper Wellingham
  E Susx 25 K8
Upper Weston BaNES 32 D11
Upper Weybread Suffk 65 K6
Upper Wick Worcs 46 F4
Upper Wield Hants 22 H7
Upper Winchendon
  Bucks 35 K2
Upperwood Derbys 84 C9
Upper Woodford Wilts 21 M8
Upper Wootton Hants 22 G4
Upper Wraxall Wilts 32 F10
Upper Wyche Worcs 46 E6
Uppincott Devon 9 M3
Uppingham Rutlnd 73 M11
Uppington Dorset 12 H3
Uppington Shrops 57 K3
Upsall N York 97 Q3
Upsettlington Border 129 M10
Upshire Essex 51 K10
Up Somborne Hants 22 C8
Upstreet Kent 39 M9
Up Sydling Dorset 11 N4
Upthorpe Suffk 64 D7
Upton Bucks 35 L2
Upton C Pete 74 B10
Upton Cambs 61 Q5
Upton Ches W 81 N11
Upton Cnwll 5 M7
Upton Cnwll 16 C11
Upton Cumb 101 K3
Upton Devon 7 J10
Upton Devon 10 D4
Upton Dorset 12 B8
Upton Dorset 12 G6
Upton E R Yk 99 N10
Upton Halton 81 P7
Upton Hants 22 C11
Upton Hants 22 C3
Upton Leics 72 B11
Upton Lincs 85 Q3
Upton Nhants 60 F9
Upton Norfk 77 M9
Upton Notts 85 M10
Upton Notts 85 M5
Upton Oxon 33 P2
Upton Oxon 34 F7
Upton Pembks 41 K10
Upton R & Cl 105 K7
Upton Slough 35 Q9
Upton Somset 18 C9
Upton Somset 19 N9
Upton Wakefd 91 M8
Upton Warwks 47 M3
Upton Wilts 20 G8
Upton Wirral 81 K7
Upton Bishop Herefs 46 C9
Upton Cheyney S Glos 32 C10
Upton Cressett Shrops 57 M6
Upton Crews Herefs 46 B9
Upton Cross Cnwll 5 M7
Upton End C Beds 50 D4
Upton Grey Hants 23 J5
Upton Heath Ches W 81 N11
Upton Hellions Devon 9 K4
Upton Lovell Wilts 20 H6
Upton Magna Shrops 57 K2
Upton Noble Somset 20 D7
Upton Pyne Devon 9 M5
Upton St Leonards
  Gloucs 46 G11
Upton Scudamore Wilts 20 G5
Upton Snodsbury Worcs 46 H4
Upton Towans Cnwll 2 F5
Upton-upon-Severn
  Worcs 46 G6
Upton Warren Worcs 58 D11
Upwaltham W Susx 15 P4
Upware Cambs 62 H6
Upwell Norfk 75 J10
Upwey Dorset 11 P7
Upwick Green Herts 51 L6
Upwood Cambs 62 C4
Urchfont Wilts 21 K3
Urdimarsh Herefs 45 Q5
Ure Bank N York 97 M6
Urlay Nook S on T 104 D8
Urmston Traffd 82 G6
Urpeth Dur 113 L10
Urquhart Moray 157 P5
Urquhart Castle Highld 147 N2
Urra N York 104 G10
Urray Highld 155 P7
Usan Angus 143 N7
Ushaw Moor Dur 103 P2
Usk Mons 31 L4
Usselby Lincs 86 E2
Usworth Sundld 113 M9
Utkinton Ches W 82 B11
Utley C Brad 90 D2
Uton Devon 9 K5
Utterby Lincs 87 K2
Uttoxeter Staffs 71 K8
Uwchmynydd Gwynd 66 B9
Uxbridge Gt Lon 36 C4
Uyeasound Shet 169 s3
Uzmaston Pembks 41 J8

V

Vale Guern 10 c1
Vale Crematorium
  Luton 50 D6
Vale of Glamorgan
  Crematorium V Glam 30 F10
Valley IoA 78 D9
Valley End Surrey 23 Q2
Valley Truckle Cnwll 4 H3
Valtos Highld 153 J5
Valtos W Isls 168 f4
Vange Essex 38 B4
Varteg Torfn 31 J3
Vatsetter Shet 169 s5
Vatten Highld 152 D9
Vaynor Myr Td 30 D2
Vazon Bay Guern 10 b2
Veensgarth Shet 169 r9
Velindre Powys 44 H7
Vellow Somset 18 E7
Velly Devon 16 D7
Venngreen Devon 16 F9
Vennington Shrops 56 E3
Venn Ottery Devon 10 B6
Venny Tedburn Devon 9 K5
Venterdon Cnwll 5 P7
Ventnor IoW 14 G11
Venton Devon 6 F6
Vernham Dean Hants 22 B3
Vernham Street Hants 22 B3

Vernolds Common
  Shrops....56 H8
Verwood Dorset....13 J3
Veryan Cnwll....3 N6
Veryan Green Cnwll....3 N5
Vicarage Devon....10 E7
Vickerstown Cumb....94 D7
Victoria Barns....F9
Victoria Blae G....30 G3
Victoria Cnwll....4 F9
Vidlin Shet....169 r7
Viewfield Moray....157 P5
Viewpark N Lans....126 C5
Vigo Kent....37 P8
Village de Putron Guern....10 c2
Ville la Bas Jersey....11 a1
Villiaze Guern....10 b2
Vinehall Street E Susx....26 C7
Vines Cross E Susx....25 N7
Vinters Park
  Crematorium Kent....38 C10
Virginia Water Surrey....36 B7
Virginstow Devon....5 P3
Vobster Somset....20 D5
Voe Shet....169 r7
Vowchurch Herefs....45 M7
Vulcan Village St Hel....82 C6

W

Waberthwaite Cumb....94 C2
Wackerfield Dur....103 N6
Wacton Norfk....64 H3
Wadborough Worcs....46 H5
Waddesdon Bucks....49 K11
Waddesdon Manor
  Bucks....49 K11
Waddeton Devon....7 M7
Waddicar Sefton....81 M5
Waddingham Lincs....92 G11
Waddington Lancs....89 L2
Waddington Lincs....86 C8
Waddon Devon....9 L9
Waddon Dorset....11 N7
Waddon Gt Lon....36 H8
Wadebridge Cnwll....4 F7
Wadeford Somset....10 G2
Wadenhoe Nhants....61 M4
Wadesmill Herts....51 J7
Wadhurst E Susx....25 P4
Wadshelf Derbys....84 D6
Wadswick Wilts....32 F11
Wadworth Donc....91 P11
Waen Denbgs....68 C2
Waen Denbgs....80 G11
Waen Powys....68 H11
Waen Fach Powys....68 H11
Waen-pentir Gwynd....79 K11
Waen-wen Gwynd....79 K11
Wagbeach Shrops....56 F4
Wainfelin Torfn....31 J4
Wainfleet All Saints Lincs....87 N9
Wainfleet Bank Lincs....87 N9
Wainfleet St Mary Lincs....87 N9
Wainford Norfk....65 L3
Wainhouse Corner
  Cnwll....5 K2
Wainscott Medway....38 B7
Wain's Hill N Som....31 L10
Wainstalls Calder....90 C5
Waitby Cumb....102 E9
Waithe Lincs....93 N10
Wakefield Wakefd....91 J6
Wakefield
  Crematorium Wakefd....91 J7
Wake Green Birm....58 G8
Wakehurst Place W Susx....24 H4
Wakerley Nhants....73 P11
Wakes Colne Essex....52 E6
Walberswick Suffk....65 P7
Walberton W Susx....15 Q5
Walbottle N u Ty....113 J7
Walbutt D & G....108 F7
Walby Cumb....110 H8
Walcombe Somset....19 Q5
Walcot Lincs....73 R3
Walcot N Linc....92 E6
Walcot Shrops....56 E7
Walcot Shrops....57 K2
Walcot Swindn....33 N8
Walcot Warwks....47 M3
Walcote Leics....60 C4
Walcot Green Norfk....64 G5
Walcott Lincs....86 F9
Walcott Norfk....77 M5
Walden N York....96 F4
Walden Head N York....96 E4
Walden Stubbs N York....91 P7
Walderslade Medway....38 C9
Walderton W Susx....15 L4
Walditch Dorset....11 K6
Waldley Derbys....71 L7
Waldridge Dur....113 L11
Waldringfield Suffk....53 N2
Waldron E Susx....25 M7
Wales Rothm....84 G4
Wales Somset....19 Q10
Walesby Lincs....86 F2
Walesby Notts....85 L6
Walford Herefs....46 A10
Walford Herefs....45 P5
Walford Shrops....69 M10
Walford Staffs....70 E8
Walford Heath Shrops....69 M11
Walgherton Ches E....70 B5
Walgrave Nhants....60 H6
Walhampton Hants....13 P5
Walkden Salfd....82 F4
Walker N u Ty....113 L8
Walkerburn Border....117 M3
Walker Fold Lancs....89 K2
Walkeringham Notts....85 N2
Walkerith Lincs....85 N2
Walkern Herts....50 G5
Walker's Green Herefs....45 Q5
Walker's Heath Birm....58 G9
Walkerton Fife....134 G7
Walkford Dorset....13 M6
Walkhampton Devon....6 E5
Walkington E R Yk....92 G3
Walkley Sheff....84 D3
Walk Mill Lancs....89 P5
Walkwood Worcs....47 K2
Wall Nthumb....112 D7
Wall Staffs....58 H3
Wallacetown S Ayrs....114 E7
Wallacetown S Ayrs....114 F3
Wallands Park E Susx....25 K8
Wallasey Wirral....81 K6

Wallasey (Kingsway)
  Tunnel Wirral....81 L6
Wall End Cumb....94 E4
Wall End Herefs....45 N3
Wallend Medway....38 E6
Waller's Green Herefs....46 C7
Wallhead Cumb....111 J8
Wall Heath Dudley....58 C7
Wall Houses Nthumb....112 F7
Wallingford Oxon....34 H7
Wallington Gt Lon....36 G8
Wallington Hants....14 G5
Wallington Herts....50 G4
Wallington Heath Wsall....58 E4
Wallis Pembks....41 K5
Wallisdown Poole....13 J6
Walliswood Surrey....24 D3
Walls Shet....169 p9
Wallsend N Tyne....113 L7
Wallthwaite Cumb....101 L5
Wall under Haywood
  Shrops....57 J6
Wallyford E Loth....128 B5
Walmer Kent....39 Q11
Walmer Bridge Lancs....88 F6
Walmersley Bury....89 N8
Walmestone Kent....39 N10
Walmley Birm....58 H6
Walmley Ash Birm....58 H6
Walmsgate Lincs....87 L5
Walney Cumb....94 D7
Walpole Somset....19 K6
Walpole Suffk....65 M7
Walpole Cross Keys
  Norfk....75 K7
Walpole Highway Norfk....75 K8
Walpole St Andrew
  Norfk....75 K7
Walpole St Peter Norfk....75 K7
Walrow Somset....19 K5
Walsall Wsall....58 F5
Walsall Wood Wsall....58 F4
Walsden Calder....89 Q6
Walsgrave on Sowe
  Covtry....59 N8
Walsham le Willows
  Suffk....64 E7
Walshaw Bury....89 M8
Walshford N York....97 P10
Walsoken Norfk....75 J8
Walston S Lans....127 K8
Walsworth Herts....50 E4
Walter's Ash Bucks....35 M5
Walters Green Kent....25 M2
Walterston V Glam....30 E10
Walterstone Herefs....45 L9
Waltham Kent....27 K2
Waltham NE Lin....93 N10
Waltham Abbey Essex....51 J10
Waltham Chase Hants....14 G4
Waltham Cross Herts....51 J10
Waltham on the Wolds
  Leics....73 L6
Waltham St Lawrence
  W & M....35 M9
Waltham's Cross Essex....51 Q4
Walthamstow Gt Lon....37 J3
Walton C Pete....74 C10
Walton Cumb....111 K8
Walton Derbys....84 E7
Walton Leeds....97 P11
Walton Leics....60 C3
Walton M Keyn....49 N7
Walton Powys....45 K3
Walton Shrops....56 H9
Walton Somset....19 N7
Walton Staffs....70 F8
Walton Staffs....70 F9
Walton Suffk....53 N4
Walton W Susx....15 M6
Walton Wakefd....91 K7
Walton Warwks....47 Q4
Walton Wrekin....69 Q11
Walton Cardiff Gloucs....46 H8
Walton East Pembks....41 K6
Walton Elm Dorset....20 E11
Walton Grounds Nhants....48 F8
Walton Highway Norfk....75 J8
Walton-in-Gordano
  N Som....31 M10
Walton Lea
  Crematorium Warrtn....82 D7
Walton-le-Dale Lancs....88 H5
Walton-on-Thames
  Surrey....36 D7
Walton-on-the-Hill Staffs....70 H10
Walton on the Hill Surrey....36 F9
Walton-on-the-Naze
  Essex....53 N7
Walton on the Wolds
  Leics....72 F7
Walton-on-Trent Derbys....71 N11
Walton Park N Som....31 M10
Walton West Pembks....40 G8
Waltonwrays
  Crematorium N York....96 E10
Walwen Flints....80 G9
Walwen Flints....80 H10
Walwen Flints....81 J9
Walwick Nthumb....112 D6
Walworth Darltn....103 P7
Walworth Gt Lon....36 H5
Walworth Gate Darltn....103 P6
Walwyn's Castle Pembks....40 G8
Wambrook Somset....10 F3
Wampool Cumb....110 D10
Wanborough Surrey....23 P5
Wanborough Swindn....33 P8
Wandon End Herts....50 D6
Wandsworth Gt Lon....36 G6
Wangford Suffk....65 P6
Wanlip Leics....72 F8
Wanlockhead D & G....116 B8
Wannock E Susx....25 N10
Wansford C Pete....73 R11
Wansford E R Yk....99 M9
Wanshurst Green Kent....26 C2
Wanstead Gt Lon....37 K3
Wanstrow Somset....20 D6
Wanswell Gloucs....32 C4
Wantage Oxon....34 C7
Wants Green Worcs....46 E3
Wapley S Glos....32 D9
Wappenbury Warwks....59 N11
Wappenham Nhants....48 H5
Warbleton E Susx....25 P7
Warborough Oxon....34 G6
Warboys Cambs....62 D4
Warbreck Bpool....88 C3
Warbstow Cnwll....5 L3
Warburton Traffd....82 F7

Warcop Cumb....102 D7
Warden Kent....38 H7
Warden Nthumb....112 D7
Ward End Birm....58 H7
Ward Green Suffk....64 E9
Ward Green Cross Lancs....89 J3
Wardhedges C Beds....50 C3
Wardington Oxon....48 E5
Wardle Ches E....69 R3
Wardle Rochdl....89 Q7
Wardley Gatesd....113 M8
Wardley Rutlnd....73 L10
Wardley Salfd....82 G4
Wardlow Derbys....83 Q10
Wardsend Ches E....83 K8
Wardy Hill Cambs....62 G4
Ware Herts....51 J8
Wareham Dorset....12 F7
Warehorne Kent....26 G5
Warenford Nthumb....119 M5
Waren Mill Nthumb....119 M4
Warenton Nthumb....119 M4
Wareside Herts....51 J7
Waresley Cambs....62 C10
Waresley Worcs....58 B10
Ware Street Kent....38 C10
Warfield Br For....35 N10
Warfleet Devon....7 M8
Wargate Lincs....74 D4
Wargrave Wokham....35 L9
Warham Herefs....45 P7
Warham Norfk....76 D3
Wark Nthumb....112 C5
Wark Nthumb....118 F3
Warkleigh Devon....17 L7
Warkton Nhants....61 J5
Warkworth Nhants....48 E6
Warkworth Nthumb....119 P9
Warlaby N York....97 M2
Warland Calder....89 Q6
Warleggan Cnwll....5 K8
Warleigh BaNES....20 E2
Warley Town Calder....90 D6
Warlingham Surrey....37 J9
Warmbrook Derbys....71 P4
Warmfield Wakefd....91 K6
Warmingham Ches E....70 C2
Warmington Nhants....61 N2
Warmington Warwks....48 D5
Warminster Wilts....20 G5
Warmley S Glos....32 C10
Warmsworth Donc....91 N10
Warmwell Dorset....12 C7
Warndon Worcs....46 G3
Warner Bros. Studio
  Tour Herts....50 C10
Warnford Hants....22 H10
Warnham W Susx....24 E4
Warnham Court W Susx....24 E4
Warningcamp W Susx....24 B9
Warninglid W Susx....24 F5
Warren Ches E....83 J10
Warren Pembks....40 H11
Warrenby R & Cl....104 G5
Warrenhill S Lans....116 C3
Warren Row W & M....35 M8
Warren's Green Herts....50 G5
Warren Street Kent....38 F11
Warrington M Keyn....49 N4
Warrington Warrtn....82 D7
Warriston C Edin....127 P2
Warriston
  Crematorium C Edin....127 P2
Warsash Hants....14 E5
Warslow Staffs....71 K3
Warsop Vale Notts....84 H7
Warter E R Yk....98 H10
Warthermaske N York....97 K5
Warthill N York....98 D9
Wartling E Susx....25 Q9
Wartnaby Leics....73 J6
Warton Lancs....88 E5
Warton Lancs....95 K6
Warton Nthumb....119 K10
Warton Warwks....59 L4
Warwick Warwks....59 L11
Warwick Bridge Cumb....111 J9
Warwick Castle Warwks....47 Q2
Warwick-on-Eden Cumb....111 J9
Warwick Services
  Warwks....48 B3
Warwicksland Cumb....111 J5
Wasbister Ork....169 c3
Wasdale Head Cumb....100 G9
Wash Derbys....83 N8
Washall Green Herts....51 K4
Washaway Cnwll....4 G8
Washbourne Devon....7 K8
Washbrook Somset....19 M4
Washbrook Suffk....53 K3
Washfield Devon....18 B11
Washfold N York....103 L10
Washford Somset....18 E6
Washford Pyne Devon....9 K2
Washingborough Lincs....86 D6
Washington Sundld....113 M9
Washington W Susx....24 D8
Washington Services
  Gatesd....113 L9
Washwood Heath Birm....58 H7
Wasing W Berk....22 G2
Waskerley Dur....112 F11
Wasperton Warwks....47 Q3
Wasps Nest Lincs....86 E8
Wass N York....98 B5
Wast Water Cumb....100 G9
Watchet Somset....18 E6
Watchfield Oxon....33 P6
Watchfield Somset....19 K5
Watchgate Cumb....101 P11
Watchhill Cumb....100 G2
Watcombe Torbay....7 N5
Watendlath Cumb....101 J7
Water Devon....9 J8
Water Lancs....89 N5
Waterbeach Cambs....62 G7
Waterbeach W Susx....15 N5
Waterbeck D & G....110 D5
Waterden Norfk....76 B4
Water Eaton Oxon....34 F2
Water Eaton Staffs....58 D2
Water End Bed....61 P10
Water End Bed....61 P11
Water End C Beds....50 C3
Waterend Cumb....100 F6
Water End E R Yk....92 C3
Water End Essex....51 N2
Water End Herts....50 B8
Water End Herts....50 F10
Waterfall Staffs....71 K4

Waterfoot Ag & B....120 F4
Waterfoot E Rens....125 P6
Waterford Herts....50 H8
Water Fryston Wakefd....91 M3
Watergate Cnwll....5 J5
Waterhead Cumb....101 L10
Waterheads Border....127 N7
Waterhouses Dur....103 N2
Waterhouses Staffs....71 K4
Wateringbury Kent....37 Q10
Waterlane Gloucs....32 H4
Waterloo Cnwll....5 J7
Waterloo Derbys....84 F8
Waterloo Herefs....45 L5
Waterloo Highld....145 L3
Waterloo N Lans....126 E7
Waterloo P & K....141 Q10
Waterloo Pembks....41 J10
Waterloo Sefton....81 L5
Waterloo Cross Devon....9 G2
Waterloo Port Gwynd....66 H2
Waterlooville Hants....15 J5
Watermead Bucks....49 M11
Watermillock Cumb....101 M6
Water Newton Cambs....74 B11
Water Orton Warwks....59 J6
Waterperry Oxon....34 H3
Waterrow Somset....18 E9
Watersfield W Susx....24 B7
Waterside Bl w D....89 L6
Waterside Bucks....35 Q4
Waterside Cumb....110 D11
Waterside Donc....91 R8
Waterside E Ayrs....114 H6
Waterside E Ayrs....125 M9
Waterside E Duns....126 B3
Water's Nook Bolton....89 K9
Waterstein Highld....152 A8
Waterstock Oxon....34 H3
Waterston Pembks....40 H9
Water Stratford Bucks....49 J8
Water Street Neath....29 M8
Waters Upton Wrekin....70 A11
Water Yeat Cumb....94 F3
Watford Herts....50 D11
Watford Nhants....60 D7
Watford Gap Services
  Nhants....60 D7
Wath N York....96 H7
Wath N York....97 M5
Wath upon Dearne
  Rothm....91 L10
Watlington Norfk....75 M8
Watlington Oxon....35 J6
Watnall Notts....84 H11
Watten Highld....167 M6
Wattisfield Suffk....64 E7
Wattisham Suffk....64 E11
Watton Dorset....11 K6
Watton E R Yk....99 L11
Watton Norfk....76 C11
Watton-at-Stone Herts....50 H7
Watton Green Norfk....76 C11
Wattons Green Essex....51 M11
Wattston N Lans....126 D3
Wattstown Rhondd....30 D6
Wattsville Caerph....30 H6
Wauldby E R Yk....92 G5
Waulkmill Abers....150 G9
Waunarlwydd Swans....28 H5
Waunfawr Cerdgn....54 E8
Waunfawr Gwynd....67 J3
Waungron Swans....28 G4
Waunlwyd Blae G....30 G3
Wavendon M Keyn....49 P7
Waveney Crematorium
  Suffk....65 P4
Waverbridge Cumb....110 D11
Waverton Ches W....69 N2
Waverton Cumb....110 D11
Wawne E R Yk....93 J3
Waxham Norfk....77 N6
Waxholme E R Yk....93 P5
Way Kent....39 P8
Waye Devon....7 K4
Wayford Somset....11 J3
Waytown Dorset....11 K5
Way Village Devon....9 L2
Way Wick N Som....19 L2
Weacombe Somset....18 F6
Weald Oxon....34 B4
Wealdstone Gt Lon....36 E3
Weardley Leeds....90 H2
Weare Somset....19 M4
Weare Giffard Devon....16 H7
Wearhead Dur....102 G3
Wearne Somset....19 M9
Wear Valley
  Crematorium Dur....103 Q4
Weasdale Cumb....102 C10
Weasenham All Saints
  Norfk....76 A7
Weasenham St Peter
  Norfk....76 B7
Weaste Salfd....82 H5
Weatheroak Hill Worcs....58 G10
Weaverham Ches W....82 D10
Weaverslake Staffs....71 L11
Weaverthorpe N York....99 K6
Webbington Somset....19 L3
Webb's Heath S Glos....32 C10
Webheath Worcs....58 F11
Webton Herefs....45 N7
Wedderlairs Abers....159 L11
Wedding Hall Fold
  N York....96 D11
Weddington Kent....39 N10
Weddington Warwks....59 N6
Wedhampton Wilts....21 M3
Wedmore Somset....19 M5
Wednesbury Sandw....58 E5
Wednesfield Wolves....58 D4
Weecar Notts....85 P7
Weedon Bucks....49 M11
Weedon Bec Nhants....60 D9
Weedon Lois Nhants....48 H5
Weeford Staffs....58 H4
Week Devon....7 K6
Week Devon....17 K6
Week Devon....17 N8
Weeke Devon....9 K4
Weeke Hants....22 E8
Weekley Nhants....61 J4
Week St Mary Cnwll....5 L2
Weel E R Yk....93 J3
Weeley Essex....53 K7
Weeley Crematorium
  Essex....53 K7
Weeley Heath Essex....53 L7
Weem P & K....141 K8

Weeping Cross Staffs....70 G10
Weethley Warwks....47 L3
Weeting Norfk....63 N3
Weeton E R Yk....93 Q6
Weeton Lancs....88 D4
Weeton N York....97 L11
Weetwood Leeds....90 H3
Weir Lancs....89 P5
Weirbrook Shrops....69 K10
Weir Quay Devon....6 C5
Weisdale Shet....169 q8
Welborne Norfk....76 F9
Welbourn Lincs....86 C10
Welburn N York....98 E7
Welbury N York....104 C10
Welby Lincs....73 P3
Welches Dam Cambs....62 G3
Welcombe Devon....16 C8
Weldon Nhants....61 K3
Weldon Bridge Nthumb....119 M11
Welford Nhants....60 D4
Welford W Berk....34 D10
Welford-on-Avon
  Warwks....47 M4
Welham Leics....60 G2
Welham Notts....85 M4
Welham Bridge E R Yk....92 C4
Welham Green Herts....50 F9
Well Hants....23 L5
Well Lincs....87 M6
Well N York....97 L4
Welland Worcs....46 E6
Wellbank Angus....142 H10
Well End Bucks....35 N7
Well End Herts....50 F11
Wellesbourne Warwks....47 Q3
Wellesbourne
  Mountford Warwks....47 Q3
Well Head Herts....50 E5
Well Hill Kent....37 L8
Wellhouse W Berk....34 F10
Welling Gt Lon....37 L5
Wellingborough Nhants....61 J7
Wellingham Norfk....76 B7
Wellingore Lincs....86 C9
Wellington Cumb....100 E10
Wellington Herefs....45 P5
Wellington Somset....18 F10
Wellington Wrekin....57 M2
Wellington Heath Herefs....46 D6
Wellington Marsh Herefs....45 P5
Wellow BaNES....20 D3
Wellow IoW....14 C9
Wellow Notts....85 L7
Wellpond Green Herts....51 K6
Wells Somset....19 P5
Wellsborough Leics....72 B10
Wells Green Ches E....70 B4
Wells Head C Brad....90 D4
Wells-next-the-Sea
  Norfk....76 C3
Wellstye Green Essex....51 P7
Well Town Devon....9 M3
Welltree P & K....134 B3
Wellwood Fife....134 D10
Welney Norfk....62 H2
Welshampton Shrops....69 M7
Welsh Bicknor Herefs....46 A11
Welsh End Shrops....69 P7
Welsh Frankton Shrops....69 L8
Welsh Hook Pembks....40 H5
Welsh Newton Herefs....45 Q11
Welshpool Powys....56 C3
Welsh St Donats V Glam....30 D9
Welton Cumb....101 L2
Welton E R Yk....92 G5
Welton Lincs....86 D5
Welton Nhants....60 C7
Welton le Marsh Lincs....87 N7
Welton le Wold Lincs....87 J3
Welwick E R Yk....93 P6
Welwyn Herts....50 F7
Welwyn Garden City
  Herts....50 F8
Wem Shrops....69 P9
Wembdon Somset....19 J7
Wembley Gt Lon....36 E3
Wembury Devon....6 E9
Wembworthy Devon....17 M10
Wemyss Bay Inver....124 F4
Wenallt Cerdgn....54 F10
Wendens Ambo Essex....51 M3
Wendlebury Oxon....48 G11
Wendling Norfk....76 C9
Wendover Bucks....35 N3
Wendron Cnwll....2 H7
Wendron Mining
  District Cnwll....2 H7
Wendy Cambs....62 D11
Wenfordbridge Cnwll....4 H6
Wenhaston Suffk....65 N6
Wennington Cambs....62 B5
Wennington Gt Lon....37 M4
Wennington Lancs....95 N7
Wensley Derbys....84 C8
Wensley N York....96 G3
Wentbridge Wakefd....91 M7
Wentnor Shrops....56 F6
Wentworth Cambs....62 G5
Wentworth Rothm....91 K11
Wentworth Castle Barns....91 J10
Wenvoe V Glam....30 F10
Weobley Herefs....45 N4
Weobley Marsh Herefs....45 N4
Wepham W Susx....24 B9
Wereham Norfk....75 N10
Wergs Wolves....58 C4
Wern Gwynd....67 J7
Wern Powys....44 G11
Wern Powys....56 D2
Wern Shrops....69 J8
Werneth Low Tamesd....83 L6
Wernffrwd Swans....28 F6
Wern-y-gaer Flints....81 J11
Werrington C Pete....74 C10
Werrington Cnwll....5 N4
Werrington Staffs....70 G5
Wervin Ches W....81 N10
Wesham Lancs....88 E4
Wessex Vale
  Crematorium Hants....22 E11
Wessington Derbys....84 E8
West Aberthaw V Glam....30 D11
West Acre Norfk....75 Q7
West Allerdean Nthumb....129 P10
West Alvington Devon....7 J10
West Amesbury Wilts....21 M6
West Anstey Devon....17 R6
West Appleton N York....97 K2
West Ashby Lincs....87 J6
West Ashling W Susx....15 M5

300 West Ashton – Whitcott Keysett

West Ashton Wilts 20 G3
West Auckland Dur 103 N5
West Ayton N York 99 K4
West Bagborough Somset 18 G8
West Bank Blae G 30 H3
West Bank Halton 81 Q8
West Barkwith Lincs 86 G4
West Barnby N York 105 M8
West Barns E Loth 128 H4
West Barsham Norfk 76 C5
West Bay Dorset 11 K6
West Beckham Norfk 76 G4
West Bedfont Surrey 36 C6
Westbere Kent 39 L9
West Bergholt Essex 52 G6
West Berkshire Crematorium W Berk 34 F11
West Bexington Dorset 11 L7
West Bilney Norfk 75 P7
West Blatchington Br & H 24 G9
West Boldon S Tyne 113 N8
Westborough Lincs 73 M2
Westbourne Bmouth 13 J6
Westbourne W Susx 15 L5
West Bourton Dorset 20 E9
West Bowling C Brad 90 F4
West Brabourne Kent 27 J3
West Bradenham Norfk 76 C10
West Bradford Lancs 89 L2
West Bradley Somset 19 Q7
West Bretton Wakefd 90 H8
West Bridgford Notts 72 F3
West Briscoe Dur 103 J7
West Bromwich Sandw 58 F6
Westbrook Kent 39 P7
Westbrook W Berk 34 D10
Westbrook Wilts 33 J11
West Buckland Devon 17 M5
West Buckland Somset 18 G10
West Burrafirth Shet 169 p8
West Burton N York 96 F3
West Burton W Susx 15 Q4
Westbury Bucks 48 H7
Westbury Shrops 56 F3
Westbury Wilts 20 G4
Westbury Leigh Wilts 20 G5
Westbury-on-Severn Gloucs 32 D2
Westbury-on-Trym Bristl 31 Q9
Westbury-sub-Mendip Somset 19 P5
West Butsfield Dur 103 M2
West Butterwick N Linc 92 D9
Westby Lancs 88 D4
West Byfleet Surrey 36 B8
West Cairngaan D & G 106 F11
West Caister Norfk 77 Q9
West Calder W Loth 127 J5
West Camel Somset 19 Q10
West Chaldon Dorset 12 C8
West Challow Oxon 34 C7
West Charleton Devon 7 K10
West Chelborough Dorset 11 L3
West Chevington Nthumb 119 P11
West Chiltington W Susx 24 C7
West Chinnock Somset 11 K2
West Chisenbury Wilts 21 M4
West Clandon Surrey 36 B10
West Cliffe Kent 27 P3
Westcliff-on-Sea Sthend 38 E4
West Coker Somset 11 L2
West Combe Devon 7 K6
Westcombe Somset 20 C7
West Compton Somset 19 Q6
West Compton Abbas Dorset 11 M6
Westcote Gloucs 47 P10
Westcote Barton Oxon 48 D9
Westcott Bucks 49 K11
Westcott Devon 9 P4
Westcott Surrey 36 D11
West Cottingwith N York 92 A2
Westcourt Wilts 21 P2
West Cowick E R Yk 91 Q6
West Cross Swans 28 H7
West Curry Cnwll 5 M3
West Curthwaite Cumb 110 F11
Westdean E Susx 25 M11
West Dean W Susx 15 N4
West Dean Wilts 21 Q9
West Deeping Lincs 74 B9
West Derby Lpool 81 M6
West Dereham Norfk 75 N10
West Ditchburn Nthumb 119 M6
West Down Devon 17 J3
Westdown Camp Wilts 21 K5
Westdowns Cnwll 4 H5
West Drayton Gt Lon 36 C5
West Drayton Notts 85 M6
West Dunnet Highld 167 M2
Wested Kent 37 M7
West Ella E R Yk 92 H5
West End Bed 49 Q4
West End Br For 35 N10
West End Caerph 30 H5
West End Cambs 62 D7
West End Cumb 110 F9
West End E R Yk 92 F4
West End E R Yk 93 L4
West End E R Yk 93 N5
Westend Gloucs 32 E3
West End Hants 14 E4
West End Hants 22 H7
West End Herts 50 G9
West End Herts 50 H9
West End Lancs 89 L5
West End Leeds 90 G3
West End Lincs 93 Q11
West End N Som 31 N11
West End N York 91 N2
West End Norfk 76 C10
West End Norfk 77 Q9
West End Oxon 34 G7
West End S Glos 32 D7
West End Somset 20 C8
West End Surrey 23 P2
West End Surrey 36 D8
West End W & M 35 M9
West End W Susx 24 F7
West End Wilts 20 H10
West End Wilts 21 J10
West End Wilts 33 J9
West End Green Hants 23 J2
Westend Town Nthumb 111 Q7
Westenhanger Kent 27 K4
Wester Aberchalder Highld 147 P3
Westerdale Highld 167 K6
Westerdale N York 105 J9
Westerfield Suffk 53 L2
Westergate W Susx 15 P5
Westerham Kent 37 K10
Westerhope N u Ty 113 J7
Westerland Devon 7 M6
Westerleigh S Glos 32 C9
Westerleigh Crematorium S Glos 32 D9
Western Isles W Isls 168 f8
Wester Ochiltree W Loth 127 J3
Wester Pitkierie Fife 135 P6
Wester Ross Highld 160 F11
Westerton W Susx 15 N5
Westerton of Rossie Angus 143 M7
Westerwick Shet 169 p9
West Ewell Surrey 36 F8
West Farleigh Kent 38 B11
West Farndon Nhants 48 F4
West Felton Shrops 69 K9
Westfield BaNES 20 C4
Westfield Cumb 100 C5
Westfield E Susx 26 D8
Westfield Highld 167 J4
Westfield N Lans 126 C3
Westfield Norfk 76 D10
Westfield W Loth 126 G3
Westfields Dorset 12 B3
Westfields Herefs 45 P6
Westfields of Rattray P & K 142 B8
Westfield Sole Kent 38 C9
West Flotmanby N York 99 M5
Westford Somset 18 F10
Westgate Dur 102 H3
Westgate N Linc 92 C9
Westgate Norfk 76 D3
Westgate Hill C Brad 90 G5
Westgate-on-Sea Kent 39 P7
Westgate Street Norfk 76 H7
West Ginge Oxon 34 D7
West Grafton Wilts 21 P2
West Green Hants 23 K3
West Grimstead Wilts 21 P9
West Grinstead W Susx 24 E6
West Haddlesey N York 91 P5
West Haddon Nhants 60 D6
West Hagbourne Oxon 34 F7
West Hagley Worcs 58 D8
Westhall Suffk 65 N5
West Hallam Derbys 72 C2
West Hallam Common Derbys 72 C2
West Halton N Linc 92 F6
Westham Dorset 11 P9
Westham E Susx 25 P10
West Ham Gt Lon 37 J4
Westham Somset 19 M5
Westhampnett W Susx 15 N5
West Handley Derbys 84 E5
West Hanney Oxon 34 D6
West Hanningfield Essex 38 B2
West Harnham Wilts 21 M9
West Harptree BaNES 19 Q3
West Harting W Susx 23 L10
West Hatch Somset 19 J10
West Hatch Wilts 20 H9
West Haven Angus 143 K10
Westhay Somset 19 M6
Westhead Lancs 88 E9
West Head Norfk 75 L9
West Heath Birm 58 F9
West Heath Hants 22 G3
West Helmsdale Highld 163 N3
West Hendred Oxon 34 D7
West Hertfordshire Crematorium Herts 50 D10
West Heslerton N York 99 J5
West Hewish N Som 19 L2
Westhide Herefs 46 A6
Westhill Abers 151 L6
West Hill Devon 9 Q6
West Hoathly W Susx 25 J4
West Holme Dorset 12 E7
Westholme Somset 19 Q6
Westhope Herefs 45 P4
Westhope Shrops 56 H7
West Horndon Essex 37 P3
Westhorp Nhants 48 F4
Westhorpe Lincs 74 D4
Westhorpe Suffk 64 E8
West Horrington Somset 19 Q5
West Horsley Surrey 36 C10
West Horton Nthumb 119 K4
West Hougham Kent 27 N3
Westhoughton Bolton 89 K9
Westhouse N York 95 P6
Westhouses Derbys 84 F9
West Howe Bmouth 13 J5
West Howetown Somset 18 B8
Westhumble Surrey 36 E10
West Huntingtower P & K 134 D3
West Huntspill Somset 19 K6
West Hyde C Beds 50 D7
West Hyde Herts 36 B2
West Hythe Kent 27 K5
West Ilkerton Devon 17 N2
West Ilsley W Berk 34 E8
West Itchenor W Susx 15 L6
West Keal Lincs 87 L8
West Kennett Wilts 33 M11
West Kilbride N Ayrs 124 G8
West Kingsdown Kent 37 N8
West Kington Wilts 32 F9
West Kirby Wirral 81 J7
West Knapton N York 98 H5
West Knighton Dorset 12 B7
West Knoyle Wilts 20 G8
West Kyloe Nthumb 119 L2
Westlake Devon 6 G8
West Lambrook Somset 19 M11
West Lancashire Crematorium Lancs 88 E8
Westland Green Herts 51 K6
West Langdon Kent 27 P2
West Lavington W Susx 23 N10
West Lavington Wilts 21 K4
West Layton N York 103 M8
West Leake Notts 72 E5
West Learmouth Nthumb 118 F3
West Lees N York 104 E10
West Leigh Devon 8 G3
Westleigh Devon 16 H6
Westleigh Devon 18 E11
West Leigh Somset 18 F8
Westleton Suffk 65 N8
West Lexham Norfk 76 A8
Westley Shrops 56 F3
Westley Suffk 63 P8
Westley Waterless Cambs 63 K9
West Lilling N York 98 C8
Westlington Bucks 35 L2
Westlinton Border 127 M7
Westlinton Cumb 110 G8
West Littleton S Glos 32 E9
West Lockinge Oxon 34 D7
West London Crematorium Gt Lon 36 F4
West Lothian Crematorium W Loth 127 J4
West Lulworth Dorset 12 D8
West Lutton N York 99 J7
West Lydford Somset 19 Q8
West Lyn Devon 17 N2
West Lyng Somset 19 K9
West Lynn Norfk 75 M6
West Malling Kent 37 Q9
West Malvern Worcs 46 E5
West Marden W Susx 15 L4
West Markham Notts 85 M6
Westmarsh Kent 39 N9
West Marsh NE Lin 93 N9
West Marton N York 96 C10
West Melbury Dorset 20 G10
West Melton Rothm 91 L10
West Meon Hants 22 H10
West Meon Hut Hants 23 J9
West Meon Woodlands Hants 22 H9
West Mersea Essex 52 H9
Westmeston E Susx 24 H8
West Mickley Nthumb 112 G8
West Midland Safari Park Worcs 57 Q9
Westmill Herts 50 H7
Westmill Herts 51 J5
West Milton Dorset 11 L5
Westminster Gt Lon 36 G5
Westminster Abbey & Palace Gt Lon 36 G5
West Molesey Surrey 36 D7
West Monkton Somset 19 J9
West Moors Dorset 13 J4
West Morden Dorset 12 F5
West Morriston Border 118 B2
West Morton C Brad 90 D2
West Mudford Somset 19 Q10
Westmuir Angus 142 F7
West Ness N York 98 D5
West Newbiggin Darltn 104 C7
Westnewton Cumb 100 F2
West Newton E R Yk 93 M3
West Newton Norfk 75 N5
West Newton Somset 19 J9
West Norwood Gt Lon 36 H6
West Norwood Crematorium Gt Lon 36 H6
Westoe S Tyne 113 N7
West Ogwell Devon 7 L4
Weston BaNES 32 D11
Weston Ches E 70 C4
Weston Devon 10 C4
Weston Devon 10 D7
Weston Dorset 11 P10
Weston Halton 81 Q8
Weston Hants 23 K10
Weston Herefs 45 M3
Weston Herts 50 G4
Weston Lincs 74 E6
Weston N York 97 J11
Weston Nhants 48 G5
Weston Notts 85 N7
Weston Shrops 56 E10
Weston Shrops 57 L6
Weston Shrops 69 J9
Weston Staffs 70 H9
Weston W Berk 34 C10
Weston Beggard Herefs 46 A6
Westonbirt Gloucs 32 G7
Weston by Welland Nhants 60 G2
Weston Colley Hants 22 F7
Weston Colville Cambs 63 K10
Weston Corbett Hants 23 J5
Weston Coyney C Stke 70 G6
Weston Favell Nhants 60 G8
Weston Green Cambs 63 K10
Weston Heath Shrops 57 P2
Weston Hills Lincs 74 E6
Weston in Arden Warwks 59 N7
Westoning C Beds 50 B4
Weston-in-Gordano N Som 31 M10
Westoning Woodend C Beds 50 B4
Weston Jones Staffs 70 D10
Weston Longville Norfk 76 G8
Weston Lullingfields Shrops 69 M10
Weston Mill Crematorium C Plym 6 D7
Weston-on-Avon Warwks 47 N4
Weston-on-the-Green Oxon 48 F11
Weston Park Staffs 57 Q2
Weston Patrick Hants 23 J5
Weston Rhyn Shrops 69 J7
Weston-sub-Edge Gloucs 47 M6
Weston-super-Mare N Som 19 K2
Weston-super-Mare Crematorium N Som 19 L2
Weston Turville Bucks 35 N2
Weston-under-Lizard Staffs 57 Q2
Weston under Penyard Herefs 46 B10
Weston-under-Redcastle Shrops 69 Q9
Weston under Wetherley Warwks 59 N11
Weston Underwood Derbys 71 P6
Weston Underwood M Keyn 49 N4
Weston-upon-Trent Derbys 72 C5
Westonzoyland Somset 19 L8
West Orchard Dorset 20 F11
West Overton Wilts 33 M11
Westow N York 98 F7
West Panson Devon 5 N3
West Park Abers 151 K8
West Parley Dorset 13 J5
West Peckham Kent 37 P10
West Peeke Devon 5 N3
West Pelton Dur 113 K10
West Pennard Somset 19 P7
West Pentire Cnwll 4 B9
West Perry Cambs 61 P7
West Pinchbeck Lincs 74 D6
West Porlock Somset 17 R2
Westport Somset 19 L10
West Pulham Dorset 11 Q3
West Putford Devon 16 F8
West Quantoxhead Somset 18 F6
Westquarter Falk 126 G2
Westra V Glam 30 F10
West Raddon Devon 9 L4
West Rainton Dur 113 M11
West Rasen Lincs 86 E3
West Ravendale NE Lin 93 M11
Westray Ork 169 d2
Westray Airport Ork 169 d1
West Raynham Norfk 76 B6
West Retford Notts 85 L4
Westridge Green W Berk 34 G9
Westrigg W Loth 126 G4
West Road Crematorium N u Ty 113 K7
Westrop Swindn 33 P6
West Rounton N York 104 D10
West Row Suffk 63 L5
West Rudham Norfk 75 R5
West Runton Norfk 76 H3
Westruther Border 128 G10
Westry Cambs 74 H11
West Saltoun E Loth 128 D6
West Sandford Devon 9 K4
West Sandwick Shet 169 r5
West Scrafton N York 96 G4
West Sleekburn Nthumb 113 L4
West Somerton Norfk 77 P7
West Stafford Dorset 11 Q7
West Stockwith Notts 92 C11
West Stoke W Susx 15 M5
West Stonesdale N York 102 G10
West Stoughton Somset 19 M5
West Stour Dorset 20 E10
West Stourmouth Kent 39 N9
West Stow Suffk 63 P6
West Stowell Wilts 21 M2
West Stratton Hants 22 F6
West Street Kent 38 F11
West Street Kent 39 P11
West Street Medway 38 B6
West Street Suffk 64 D7
West Suffolk Crematorium Suffk 63 P7
West Tanfield N York 97 L5
West Taphouse Cnwll 5 J9
West Tarbert Ag & B 123 Q6
West Tarring W Susx 24 D10
West Thirston Nthumb 119 N11
West Thorney W Susx 15 L6
Westthorpe Derbys 84 G5
West Thorpe Notts 72 G5
West Thurrock Thurr 37 N5
West Tilbury Thurr 37 Q5
West Tisted Hants 23 J9
West Torrington Lincs 86 F4
West Town BaNES 19 P2
West Town Hants 15 K7
West Town Herefs 45 N2
West Town N Som 31 N11
West Town Somset 19 P7
West Town Somset 20 D6
West Tytherley Hants 21 Q9
West Walton Norfk 75 J8
Westward Cumb 101 J2
Westward Ho! Devon 16 G6
Westwell Kent 26 G2
Westwell Oxon 33 P3
Westwell Leacon Kent 26 G2
West Wellow Hants 21 Q11
West Wembury Devon 6 E9
West Wemyss Fife 135 J9
Westwick Cambs 62 F7
Westwick Dur 103 L7
West Wick N Som 19 L2
Westwick Norfk 77 K6
West Wickham Cambs 63 K11
West Wickham Gt Lon 37 J7
West Williamston Pembks 41 K9
West Wiltshire Crematorium Wilts 20 H3
West Winch Norfk 75 M7
West Winterslow Wilts 21 P8
West Wittering W Susx 15 L7
West Witton N York 96 G3
Westwood Devon 9 P5
Westwood Kent 37 P6
Westwood Kent 39 Q8
Westwood Notts 84 G10
Westwood Nthumb 111 Q7
Westwood Wilts 20 F3
West Woodburn Nthumb 112 C3
West Woodhay W Berk 22 C2
Westwood Heath Covtry 59 L9
West Woodlands Somset 20 E6
Westwoodside N Linc 92 B10
West Worldham Hants 23 K7
West Worthing W Susx 24 D10
West Wratting Cambs 63 K10
West Wycombe Bucks 35 M6
West Wylam Nthumb 112 H8
West Yatton Wilts 32 G9
West Yoke Kent 37 P7
West Youlstone Cnwll 16 D8
Wetham Green Kent 38 D8
Wetheral Cumb 111 J10
Wetherby Leeds 97 P11
Wetherby Services N York 97 P10
Wetherden Suffk 64 E9
Wetheringsett Suffk 64 G8
Wethersfield Essex 52 B5
Wetherup Street Suffk 64 G9
Wetley Rocks Staffs 70 H5
Wettenhall Ches E 69 R2
Wetton Staffs 71 L3
Wetwang E R Yk 99 J9
Wetwood Staffs 70 D8
Wexcombe Wilts 21 Q3
Wexham Slough 35 Q8
Wexham Street Bucks 35 Q8
Weybourne Norfk 76 G3
Weybourne Surrey 23 N5
Weybread Suffk 65 J5
Weybread Street Suffk 65 J6
Weybridge Surrey 36 C8
Weycroft Devon 10 G5
Weydale Highld 167 L4
Weyhill Hants 22 B5
Weymouth Dorset 11 P9
Weymouth Crematorium Dorset 11 P9
Whaddon Bucks 49 M8
Whaddon Cambs 62 E11
Whaddon Gloucs 32 F2
Whaddon Wilts 20 G2
Whaddon Wilts 21 N9
Whale Cumb 101 P6
Whaley Derbys 84 H6
Whaley Bridge Derbys 83 M8
Whaley Thorns Derbys 84 H6
Whaligoe Highld 167 P8
Whalley Lancs 89 L3
Whalley Banks Lancs 89 L3
Whalsay Shet 169 s7
Whalton Nthumb 112 H4
Whaplode Lincs 74 F6
Whaplode Drove Lincs 74 F8
Wharf Warwks 48 D4
Wharfe N York 96 A7
Wharles Lancs 88 E3
Wharley End C Beds 49 P6
Wharncliffe Side Sheff 84 C2
Wharram-le-Street N York 98 H7
Wharton Ches W 82 E11
Wharton Herefs 45 Q3
Whashton N York 103 N9
Whasset Cumb 95 L4
Whatcote Warwks 47 Q6
Whateley Warwks 59 K5
Whatfield Suffk 52 H2
Whatley Somset 10 H3
Whatley Somset 20 D5
Whatley's End S Glos 32 C8
Whatlington E Susx 26 C8
Whatsole Street Kent 27 K3
Whatstandwell Derbys 84 D10
Whatton Notts 73 J3
Whauphill D & G 107 M8
Whaw N York 103 J10
Wheal Peevor Cnwll 3 J5
Wheal Rose Cnwll 3 J5
Wheatacre Norfk 65 P3
Wheatfield Oxon 35 J5
Wheathampstead Herts 50 E8
Wheathill Shrops 57 L8
Wheathill Somset 19 Q8
Wheatley Calder 90 D5
Wheatley Hants 23 L6
Wheatley Oxon 34 G3
Wheatley Hill Dur 104 C3
Wheatley Hills Donc 91 P10
Wheatley Lane Lancs 89 N3
Wheaton Aston Staffs 58 C2
Wheatsheaf Wrexhm 69 K4
Wheddon Cross Somset 18 B7
Wheelbarrow Town Kent 27 K2
Wheeler End Bucks 35 M6
Wheeler's Green Wokham 35 L10
Wheelerstreet Surrey 23 P6
Wheelock Ches E 70 D3
Wheelock Heath Ches E 70 D3
Wheelton Lancs 89 J6
Wheldale Wakefd 91 M5
Wheldrake C York 92 A2
Whelford Gloucs 33 N5
Whelpley Hill Bucks 35 Q4
Whelpo Cumb 101 K3
Whelston Flints 81 J9
Whempstead Herts 50 H6
Whenby N York 98 C7
Whepstead Suffk 64 A10
Wherstead Suffk 53 L3
Wherwell Hants 22 C6
Wheston Derbys 83 P9
Whetsted Kent 37 Q11
Whetstone Gt Lon 36 G2
Whetstone Leics 72 F11
Wheyrigg Cumb 110 C11
Whicham Cumb 94 C4
Whichford Warwks 48 B8
Whickham Gatesd 113 K8
Whiddon Devon 8 C5
Whiddon Down Devon 8 G6
Whigstreet Angus 142 H9
Whilton Nhants 60 D8
Whimble Devon 16 F11
Whimple Devon 9 P5
Whimpwell Green Norfk 77 M6
Whinburgh Norfk 76 E10
Whin Lane End Lancs 88 D2
Whinnieliggate D & G 108 F10
Whinnow Cumb 110 F10
Whinnyfold Abers 159 Q11
Whinny Hill S on T 104 C7
Whippingham IoW 14 F8
Whipsnade C Beds 50 B7
Whipsnade Zoo ZSL C Beds 50 B7
Whipton Devon 9 M6
Whirlow Sheff 84 D4
Whisby Lincs 86 B7
Whissendine Rutlnd 73 L8
Whissonsett Norfk 76 C7
Whistlefield Ag & B 131 Q9
Whistlefield Inn Ag & B 131 N9
Whistley Green Wokham 35 L10
Whiston Knows 81 P6
Whiston Nhants 60 H8
Whiston Rothm 84 F3
Whiston Staffs 58 C2
Whiston Staffs 71 J5
Whiston Cross Shrops 57 P4
Whiston Eaves Staffs 71 J5
Whitacre Fields Warwks 59 L6
Whitbeck Cumb 94 C4
Whitbourne Herefs 46 D3
Whitburn S Tyne 113 P8
Whitburn W Loth 126 G5
Whitby Ches W 81 M9
Whitby N York 105 N8
Whitbyheath Ches W 81 M10
Whitchester Border 129 J8
Whitchurch BaNES 32 B11
Whitchurch Bucks 49 M10
Whitchurch Cardif 30 G9
Whitchurch Devon 6 D4
Whitchurch Hants 22 E5
Whitchurch Herefs 45 R11
Whitchurch Oxon 34 H9
Whitchurch Pembks 40 F5
Whitchurch Shrops 69 P6
Whitchurch Canonicorum Dorset 10 H5
Whitchurch Hill Oxon 34 H9
Whitcombe Dorset 11 Q7
Whitcot Shrops 56 F6
Whitcott Keysett Shrops 56 D8

Whiteacre – Wolverhampton 301

Whiteacre Kent 27 K2
Whiteacre Heath Warwks 59 K6
Whiteash Green Essex 52 C5
White Ball Somset 18 F11
Whitebridge Highld 147 M4
Whitebrook Mons 31 P3
Whitebushes Surrey 36 G11
Whitecairns Abers 151 N4
Whitechapel Gt Lon 36 H4
White Chapel Lancs 88 H2
Whitechurch Pembks 41 N3
Whitecliffe Gloucs 31 Q3
White Colne Essex 52 E6
White Coppice Lancs 89 J7
Whitecraig E Loth 127 Q3
Whitecroft Gloucs 32 B3
Whitecrook D & G 106 G6
Whitecross Cnwll 2 E7
White Cross Cnwll 2 H9
Whitecross Cnwll 4 F7
Whitecross Falk 126 H2
White End Worcs 46 E8
Whiteface Highld 162 G9
Whitefarland N Ayrs 120 G3
Whitefaulds S Ayrs 114 E6
Whitefield Bury 89 N9
Whitefield Devon 17 N4
Whitefield Somset 18 E9
Whitefield Lane End Knows 81 P7
Whiteford Abers 151 J2
Whitegate Ches W 82 D11
Whitehall Hants 23 K4
Whitehall Ork 169 f4
Whitehall W Susx 24 D6
Whitehaven Cumb 100 C7
Whitehill Kent 38 H10
Whitehill Leics 72 C8
Whitehill and Bordon Hants 23 L8
Whitehills Abers 158 G4
Whitehouse Abers 150 G5
Whitehouse Ag & B 123 P7
Whitehouse Common Birm 58 H5
Whitekirk E Loth 128 F3
White Kirkley Dur 103 K3
White Lackington Dorset 11 Q5
Whitelackington Somset 19 L11
White Ladies Aston Worcs 46 H4
Whiteleaf Bucks 35 M4
White-le-Head Dur 113 J10
Whiteley Hants 14 F5
Whiteley Bank IoW 14 G10
Whiteley Green Ches E 83 K9
Whiteley Village Surrey 36 C8
Whitemans Green W Susx 24 H5
White Mill Carmth 43 J10
Whitemire Moray 156 H7
Whitemoor C Nott 72 E2
Whitemoor Cnwll 4 F10
Whitemoor Derbys 84 E11
Whitemoor Staffs 70 F2
Whiteness Shet 169 q9
White Notley Essex 52 C8
Whiteoak Green Oxon 34 B2
White Ox Mead BaNES 20 D3
Whiteparish Wilts 21 P10
White Pit Lincs 87 L5
Whiterashes Abers 151 M3
White Roding Essex 51 N8
Whiterow Highld 167 Q7
Whiterow Moray 157 J6
Whiteshill Gloucs 32 F3
Whitesmith E Susx 25 M8
White Stake Lancs 88 G5
Whitestaunton Somset 10 F2
Whitestone Devon 9 L6
White Stone Herefs 45 R6
Whitestone Cross Devon 9 L6
Whitestreet Green Suffk 52 G4
Whitewall Corner N York 98 F7
White Waltham W & M 35 M9
Whiteway BaNES 20 D2
Whiteway Gloucs 32 H2
Whitewell Lancs 95 P11
Whiteworks Devon 6 G4
Whitfield C Dund 142 G11
Whitfield Kent 27 P2
Whitfield Nhants 48 H7
Whitfield Nthumb 111 Q9
Whitfield S Glos 32 C6
Whitfield Hall Nthumb 111 Q9
Whitford Devon 10 F5
Whitford Flints 80 G9
Whitgift E R Yk 92 D6
Whitgreave Staffs 70 G9
Whithorn D & G 107 M9
Whiting Bay N Ayrs 121 K6
Whitkirk Leeds 91 K4
Whitland Carmth 41 N7
Whitlaw Border 117 Q8
Whitletts S Ayrs 114 G3
Whitley N York 91 P6
Whitley Readg 35 K10
Whitley Sheff 84 D2
Whitley Wilts 32 G11
Whitley Bay N Tyne 113 N6
Whitley Bay Crematorium N Tyne 113 M6
Whitley Chapel Nthumb 112 D9
Whitley Heath Staffs 70 E9
Whitley Lower Kirk 90 G7
Whitley Row Kent 37 L10
Whitlock's End Solhll 58 H9
Whitminster Gloucs 32 E3
Whitmore Dorset 13 J3
Whitmore Staffs 70 E6
Whitnage Devon 18 D11
Whitnash Warwks 48 B2
Whitney-on-Wye Herefs 45 K5
Whitrigg Cumb 100 H3
Whitrigg Cumb 110 D9
Whitrigglees Cumb 110 D9
Whitsbury Hants 21 M11
Whitsome Border 129 M9
Whitson Newpt 31 L8
Whitstable Kent 39 K8
Whitstone Cnwll 5 M2
Whittingham Nthumb 119 L8
Whittingslow Shrops 56 G7
Whittington Derbys 84 E5
Whittington Gloucs 47 K10
Whittington Lancs 95 N5
Whittington Norfk 75 P11
Whittington Shrops 69 K8
Whittington Staffs 58 C8
Whittington Staffs 59 J3
Whittington Warwks 59 L5
Whittington Worcs 46 G4
Whittington Moor Derbys 84 E6
Whittlebury Nhants 49 J6
Whittle-le-Woods Lancs 88 H6
Whittlesey Cambs 74 E11
Whittlesford Cambs 62 G11
Whittlestone Head Bl w D 89 L7
Whitton N Linc 92 F6
Whitton Nthumb 119 L10
Whitton Powys 56 D11
Whitton S on T 104 C6
Whitton Shrops 57 K10
Whitton Suffk 53 K2
Whittonditch Wilts 33 Q10
Whittonstall Nthumb 112 G9
Whitway Hants 22 E3
Whitwell Derbys 84 H5
Whitwell Herts 50 E6
Whitwell IoW 14 F11
Whitwell N York 103 Q11
Whitwell Rutlnd 73 N9
Whitwell-on-the-Hill N York 98 E7
Whitwell Street Norfk 76 G7
Whitwick Leics 72 C7
Whitwood Wakefd 91 L6
Whitworth Lancs 89 P7
Whixall Shrops 69 P8
Whixley N York 97 P9
Whorlton Dur 103 M8
Whorlton N York 104 E10
Whyle Herefs 45 R2
Whyteleafe Surrey 36 H9
Wibdon Gloucs 31 Q5
Wibsey C Brad 90 E4
Wibtoft Warwks 59 Q7
Wichenford Worcs 46 E2
Wichling Kent 38 F10
Wick Bmouth 13 L6
Wick Devon 10 D4
Wick Highld 167 Q6
Wick S Glos 32 D10
Wick Somset 18 H6
Wick Somset 19 M9
Wick V Glam 29 P10
Wick W Susx 24 B10
Wick Wilts 21 N10
Wick Worcs 47 J5
Wicken Cambs 63 J6
Wicken Nhants 49 K7
Wicken Bonhunt Essex 51 L4
Wickenby Lincs 86 E4
Wick End Bed 49 Q4
Wicken Green Village Norfk 76 A5
Wickersley Rothm 84 G2
Wicker Street Green Suffk 52 G3
Wickford Essex 38 B3
Wickham Hants 14 G4
Wickham W Berk 34 C10
Wickham Bishops Essex 52 D9
Wickhambreaux Kent 39 M10
Wickhambrook Suffk 63 N10
Wickhamford Worcs 47 L6
Wickham Green Suffk 64 F8
Wickham Green W Berk 34 D10
Wickham Heath W Berk 34 D11
Wickham Market Suffk 65 L10
Wickhampton Norfk 77 N10
Wickham St Paul Essex 52 D4
Wickham Skeith Suffk 64 F8
Wickham Street Suffk 63 N10
Wickham Street Suffk 64 F8
Wickhurst Green W Susx 24 D4
Wick John o' Groats Airport Highld 167 Q6
Wicklewood Norfk 76 F11
Wickmere Norfk 76 H5
Wick St Lawrence N Som 31 L11
Wicksteed Park Nhants 61 J5
Wickstreet E Susx 25 M9
Wickwar S Glos 32 D7
Widdington Essex 51 M4
Widdop Calder 89 Q4
Widdrington Nthumb 119 Q11
Widdrington Station Nthumb 113 K2
Widecombe in the Moor Devon 8 H9
Widegates Cnwll 5 M10
Widemouth Bay Cnwll 16 C11
Wide Open N Tyne 113 K6
Widford Essex 51 Q10
Widford Herts 51 K7
Widham Wilts 33 L7
Widley Hants 15 J5
Widmer End Bucks 35 N5
Widmerpool Notts 72 G5
Widmore Gt Lon 37 K7
Widnes Halton 81 Q7
Widnes Crematorium Halton 81 Q7
Widworthy Devon 10 E5
Wigan Wigan 88 H9
Wigan Crematorium Wigan 82 C4
Wigborough Somset 19 M11
Wiggaton Devon 10 C6
Wiggenhall St Germans Norfk 75 L8
Wiggenhall St Mary Magdalen Norfk 75 L8
Wiggenhall St Mary the Virgin Norfk 75 L8
Wiggenhall St Peter Norfk 75 M8
Wiggens Green Essex 51 Q2
Wiggenstall Staffs 71 K2
Wiggington Shrops 69 K7
Wigginton C York 98 C9
Wigginton Herts 35 P2
Wigginton Oxon 48 C8
Wigginton Staffs 59 K3
Wigginton Bottom Herts 35 P3
Wigglesworth N York 96 B9
Wiggonby Cumb 110 E10
Wiggonholt W Susx 24 C7
Wighill N York 97 Q11
Wighton Norfk 76 C4
Wightwick Wolves 58 C5
Wigley Derbys 84 D6
Wigley Hants 22 B11
Wigmore Herefs 56 G11
Wigmore Medway 38 C9
Wigsley Notts 85 Q6
Wigsthorpe Nhants 61 M4
Wigston Leics 72 G11
Wigston Fields Leics 72 G10
Wigston Parva Leics 59 Q7
Wigthorpe Notts 85 J4
Wigtoft Lincs 74 E3
Wigton Cumb 110 E11
Wigtown D & G 107 M6
Wigtwizzle Sheff 90 G11
Wike Leeds 91 J2
Wilbarston Nhants 60 H3
Wilberfoss E R Yk 98 E10
Wilburton Cambs 62 G5
Wilby Nhants 61 J7
Wilby Norfk 64 E4
Wilby Suffk 65 J7
Wilcot Wilts 21 M2
Wilcott Shrops 69 L11
Wilcrick Newpt 31 M7
Wilday Green Derbys 84 D6
Wildboarclough Ches E 83 L11
Wilden Bed 61 N9
Wilden Worcs 58 B10
Wilde Street Suffk 63 M5
Wildhern Hants 22 C4
Wildhill Herts 50 G9
Wildmanbridge S Lans 126 E7
Wildmill Brdgnd 29 P8
Wildmoor Hants 23 J3
Wildmoor Worcs 58 E9
Wildsworth Lincs 92 D11
Wilford C Nott 72 F3
Wilford Hill Crematorium Notts 72 F3
Wilkesley Ches E 70 A6
Wilkhaven Highld 163 L9
Wilkieston W Loth 127 L4
Wilkin's Green Herts 50 E9
Wilksby Lincs 87 J8
Willand Devon 9 P2
Willards Hill E Susx 26 B7
Willaston Ches E 70 B4
Willaston Ches W 81 L9
Willen M Keyn 49 N6
Willenhall Covtry 59 N9
Willenhall Wsall 58 E5
Willerby E R Yk 92 H4
Willerby N York 99 L5
Willersey Gloucs 47 M7
Willersley Herefs 45 L5
Willesborough Kent 26 H3
Willesborough Lees Kent 26 H3
Willesden Gt Lon 36 F4
Willesleigh Devon 17 K5
Willesley Wilts 32 G7
Willett Somset 18 F8
Willey Shrops 57 M5
Willey Warwks 59 Q8
Willey Green Surrey 23 P4
Williamscot Oxon 48 E5
Williamstown Rhondd 30 D6
Willian Herts 50 F4
Willicote Warwks 47 N5
Willingale Essex 51 N9
Willingdon E Susx 25 N10
Willingham Cambs 62 F6
Willingham by Stow Lincs 85 Q4
Willingham Green Cambs 63 K10
Willington Bed 61 P10
Willington Derbys 71 P9
Willington Dur 103 N3
Willington Kent 38 C11
Willington N Tyne 113 M7
Willington Warwks 47 Q7
Willington Corner Ches W 82 B11
Willitoft E R Yk 92 B4
Williton Somset 18 E6
Willoughby Lincs 87 N6
Willoughby Warwks 60 B7
Willoughby Hills Lincs 87 L11
Willoughby-on-the-Wolds Notts 72 G5
Willoughby Waterleys Leics 60 C2
Willoughton Lincs 86 B2
Willow Green Ches W 82 D9
Willows Green Essex 52 B8
Willsbridge S Glos 32 C10
Willsworthy Devon 8 D8
Willtown Somset 19 L10
Wilmcote Warwks 47 N3
Wilmington BaNES 20 C2
Wilmington Devon 10 E5
Wilmington E Susx 25 M10
Wilmington Kent 37 M6
Wilmslow Ches E 82 H8
Wilnecote Staffs 59 K4
Wilpshire Lancs 89 K4
Wilsden C Brad 90 D3
Wilsford Lincs 73 Q2
Wilsford Wilts 21 M3
Wilsford Wilts 21 M7
Wilsham Devon 17 P2
Wilshaw Kirk 90 E9
Wilsill N York 97 J8
Wilsley Green Kent 26 C4
Wilsley Pound Kent 26 C4
Wilson Herefs 45 R10
Wilson Leics 72 C6
Wilsontown S Lans 126 G6
Wilstead Bed 50 C2
Wilsthorpe Lincs 74 A8
Wilstone Herts 35 P2
Wilstone Green Herts 35 P2
Wilton Cumb 100 D8
Wilton Herefs 46 A10
Wilton N York 98 H4
Wilton R & Cl 104 G7
Wilton Wilts 21 L8
Wilton Wilts 21 Q2
Wilton Dean Border 117 P8
Wimbish Essex 51 N3
Wimbish Green Essex 51 P3
Wimbledon Gt Lon 36 F6
Wimblington Cambs 62 F2
Wimboldsley Ches W 70 B2
Wimborne Minster Dorset 12 H5
Wimborne St Giles Dorset 12 H2
Wimbotsham Norfk 75 M9
Wimpole Cambs 62 E11
Wimpstone Warwks 47 P5
Wincanton Somset 20 D9
Winceby Lincs 87 K7
Wincham Ches W 82 E9
Winchburgh W Loth 127 K3
Winchcombe Gloucs 47 K9
Winchelsea E Susx 26 F8
Winchelsea Beach E Susx 26 F8
Winchester Hants 22 E9
Winchester Services Hants 22 F7
Winchet Hill Kent 26 B3
Winchfield Hants 23 L4
Winchmore Hill Bucks 35 P5
Winchmore Hill Gt Lon 36 H2
Wincle Ches E 83 L11
Wincobank Sheff 84 E2
Winder Cumb 100 D7
Windermere Cumb 101 M11
Windermere Steamboats & Museum Cumb 101 M11
Winderton Warwks 48 B6
Windhill Highld 155 P8
Windlehurst Stockp 83 L7
Windlesham Surrey 23 P2
Windmill Cnwll 4 D7
Windmill Derbys 83 Q9
Windmill Hill E Susx 25 P8
Windmill Hill Somset 19 K11
Windrush Gloucs 33 N2
Windsole Abers 158 E5
Windsor W & M 35 Q9
Windsor Castle W & M 35 Q9
Windsoredge Gloucs 32 F4
Windsor Green Suffk 64 B11
Windygates Fife 135 J7
Windyharbour Ches E 82 H10
Windy Hill Wrexhm 69 K4
Wineham W Susx 24 F6
Winestead E R Yk 93 N6
Winewall Lancs 89 Q2
Winfarthing Norfk 64 G4
Winford IoW 14 G10
Winford N Som 19 P2
Winforton Herefs 45 K5
Winfrith Newburgh Dorset 12 D8
Wing Bucks 49 N10
Wing Rutlnd 73 M10
Wingate Dur 104 D3
Wingates Bolton 89 K9
Wingates Nthumb 119 L11
Wingerworth Derbys 84 E7
Wingfield C Beds 50 B5
Wingfield Suffk 65 J6
Wingfield Wilts 20 F3
Wingfield Green Suffk 65 J6
Wingham Kent 39 M10
Wingland Lincs 75 J6
Wingmore Kent 27 L2
Wingrave Bucks 49 N11
Winkburn Notts 85 M9
Winkfield Br For 35 P10
Winkfield Row Br For 35 N10
Winkhill Staffs 71 K4
Winkhurst Green Kent 37 L11
Winkleigh Devon 17 L10
Winksley N York 97 L6
Winkton Dorset 13 L5
Winlaton Gatesd 113 J8
Winlaton Mill Gatesd 113 J8
Winless Highld 167 P6
Winllan Powys 68 H10
Winmarleigh Lancs 95 K11
Winnall Hants 22 E9
Winnersh Wokham 35 L10
Winnington Ches W 82 D10
Winscales Cumb 100 D5
Winscombe N Som 19 M3
Winsford Ches W 82 E11
Winsford Somset 18 B8
Winsham Devon 17 J4
Winsham Somset 10 H3
Winshill Staffs 71 P10
Winshwen Swans 29 J5
Winskill Cumb 101 Q4
Winslade Hants 23 J5
Winsley Wilts 20 E2
Winslow Bucks 49 L9
Winson Gloucs 33 L3
Winsor Hants 13 P2
Winster Cumb 95 J2
Winster Derbys 84 B8
Winston Dur 103 M7
Winston Suffk 64 H9
Winstone Gloucs 33 J3
Winswell Devon 16 H9
Winterborne Came Dorset 11 Q7
Winterborne Clenston Dorset 12 D4
Winterborne Herringston Dorset 11 P7
Winterborne Houghton Dorset 12 D4
Winterborne Kingston Dorset 12 E5
Winterborne Monkton Dorset 11 P7
Winterborne Stickland Dorset 12 D4
Winterborne Tomson Dorset 12 E5
Winterborne Whitechurch Dorset 12 D4
Winterborne Zelston Dorset 12 E5
Winterbourne S Glos 32 B8
Winterbourne W Berk 34 E10
Winterbourne Abbas Dorset 11 N6
Winterbourne Bassett Wilts 33 L10
Winterbourne Dauntsey Wilts 21 N8
Winterbourne Earls Wilts 21 N8
Winterbourne Gunner Wilts 21 N7
Winterbourne Monkton Wilts 33 L10
Winterbourne Steepleton Dorset 11 N7
Winterbourne Stoke Wilts 21 L6
Winterbrook Oxon 34 H7
Winterburn N York 96 D9
Winteringham N Linc 92 F6
Winterley Ches E 70 C3
Wintersett Wakefd 91 K7
Winterslow Wilts 21 P8
Winterton N Linc 92 F7
Winterton-on-Sea Norfk 77 P8
Winthorpe Lincs 87 Q7
Winthorpe Notts 85 P9
Winton Bmouth 13 J6
Winton Cumb 102 E8
Winton E Susx 25 M10
Winton N York 104 D11
Wintringham N York 98 H6
Winwick Cambs 61 P4
Winwick Nhants 60 D6
Winwick Warrtn 82 D6
Wirksworth Derbys 71 P4
Wirral 81 K7
Wirswall Ches E 69 P6
Wisbech Cambs 75 J9
Wisbech St Mary Cambs 74 H9
Wisborough Green W Susx 24 C5
Wiseman's Bridge Pembks 41 M9
Wiseton Notts 85 M3
Wishanger Gloucs 32 H3
Wishaw N Lans 126 D6
Wisley Surrey 36 C9
Wisley Garden RHS Surrey 36 C9
Wispington Lincs 86 H6
Wissenden Kent 26 F3
Wissett Suffk 65 M6
Wissington Norfk 75 N11
Wissington Suffk 52 G5
Wistanstow Shrops 56 G7
Wistanswick Shrops 70 B9
Wistaston Ches E 70 B4
Wistaston Green Ches E 70 B4
Wisterfield Ches E 82 H10
Wiston Pembks 41 K7
Wiston S Lans 116 D4
Wiston W Susx 24 D8
Wistow Cambs 62 C4
Wistow Leics 72 G11
Wistow N York 91 P3
Wiswell Lancs 89 L3
Witcham Cambs 62 G4
Witchampton Dorset 12 G3
Witchford Cambs 62 H5
Witcombe Somset 19 N10
Witham Essex 52 D9
Witham Friary Somset 20 D6
Witham on the Hill Lincs 73 R7
Witham St Hughs Lincs 85 Q8
Withcall Lincs 87 J4
Withdean Br & H 24 H9
Witherenden Hill E Susx 25 P5
Witheridge Devon 9 K2
Witherley Leics 72 A11
Withern Lincs 87 M4
Withernsea E R Yk 93 P5
Withernwick E R Yk 93 L2
Withersdale Street Suffk 65 K5
Withersfield Suffk 63 L11
Witherslack Cumb 95 J4
Withiel Cnwll 4 F8
Withiel Florey Somset 18 C8
Withielgoose Cnwll 4 G8
Withington Gloucs 47 K11
Withington Herefs 45 R6
Withington Manch 82 H6
Withington Shrops 57 K2
Withington Staffs 71 J7
Withington Green Ches E 82 H10
Withington Marsh Herefs 45 R6
Withleigh Devon 9 M2
Withnell Lancs 89 J6
Withnell Fold Lancs 89 J6
Withybed Green Worcs 58 F10
Withybrook Warwks 59 P8
Withycombe Somset 18 D6
Withyham E Susx 25 L3
Withy Mills BaNES 20 C3
Withypool Somset 17 Q4
Withywood Bristl 31 Q11
Witley Surrey 23 P7
Witnesham Suffk 64 H11
Witney Oxon 34 C2
Wittering C Pete 73 R10
Wittersham Kent 26 F6
Witton Birm 58 G6
Witton Norfk 77 L10
Witton Norfk 77 L5
Witton Gilbert Dur 113 K11
Witton Green Norfk 77 N11
Witton le Wear Dur 103 M4
Witton Park Dur 103 N4
Wiveliscombe Somset 18 E9
Wivelrod Hants 23 J7
Wivelsfield E Susx 24 H6
Wivelsfield Green E Susx 25 J7
Wivelsfield Station W Susx 24 H7
Wivenhoe Essex 52 H7
Wivenhoe Cross Essex 52 H7
Wiveton Norfk 76 E3
Wix Essex 53 L6
Wixams Bed 50 C2
Wixford Warwks 47 L4
Wix Green Essex 53 L6
Wixhill Shrops 69 Q9
Wixoe Suffk 52 B3
Woburn C Beds 49 P8
Woburn Safari Park C Beds 49 Q8
Woburn Sands M Keyn 49 P7
Wokefield Park W Berk 35 J11
Woking Surrey 36 B9
Woking Crematorium Surrey 23 Q3
Wokingham Wokham 35 M11
Wolborough Devon 7 M4
Woldingham Surrey 37 J9
Wold Newton E R Yk 99 L6
Wold Newton NE Lin 93 M11
Wolfclyde S Lans 116 E3
Wolferlow Herefs 46 C2
Wolferton Norfk 75 N5
Wolfhampcote Warwks 60 B7
Wolfhill P & K 142 B11
Wolf Hills Nthumb 111 P9
Wolf's Castle Pembks 41 J5
Wolfsdale Pembks 40 H6
Wollaston Dudley 58 C8
Wollaston Nhants 61 K8
Wollaston Shrops 56 E2
Wollaton C Nott 72 E3
Wollaton Hall & Park C Nott 72 E3
Wolleigh Devon 9 K8
Wollerton Shrops 69 R8
Wollescote Dudley 58 D8
Wolseley Bridge Staffs 71 J10
Wolsingham Dur 103 L3
Wolstanton Staffs 70 F5
Wolstenholme Rochdl 89 N8
Wolston Warwks 59 P9
Wolsty Cumb 109 P10
Wolvercote Oxon 34 E2
Wolverhampton Wolves 58 D5

Wolverhampton Halfpenny Green Airport Staffs....58 B6
Wolverley Shrops....69 N8
Wolverley Worcs....58 B9
Wolverton Hants....22 G3
Wolverton Kent....27 N3
Wolverton M Keyn....49 M6
Wolverton Warwks....47 P2
Wolverton Wilts....20 E8
Wolverton Common Hants....22 G3
Wolvesnewton Mons....31 N5
Wolvey Warwks....59 P7
Wolvey Heath Warwks....59 P7
Wolviston S on T....104 E5
Wombleton N York....98 D4
Wombourne Staffs....58 C6
Wombwell Barns....91 L10
Womenswold Kent....39 M11
Womersley N York....91 N7
Wonastow Mons....31 N2
Wonersh Surrey....36 B11
Wonford Devon....9 M6
Wonson Devon....8 G7
Wonston Dorset....12 B3
Wonston Hants....22 E7
Wooburn Green Bucks....35 P7
Wooburn Moor Bucks....35 P7
Woodacott Devon....16 F10
Woodale N York....96 F5
Woodall Rothm....84 G4
Woodall Services Rothm....84 G4
Woodbank Ches W....81 M10
Woodbastwick Norfk....77 L8
Woodbeck Notts....85 N5
Wood Bevington Warwks....47 L4
Woodborough Notts....85 K11
Woodborough Wilts....21 M3
Woodbridge Devon....10 D5
Woodbridge Dorset....20 G11
Woodbridge Suffk....53 N2
Wood Burcote Nhants....49 J5
Woodbury Devon....9 P7
Woodbury Salterton Devon....9 P7
Woodchester Gloucs....32 F4
Woodchurch Kent....26 F5
Woodchurch Wirral....81 K7
Woodcombe Somset....18 C5
Woodcote Gt Lon....36 G8
Woodcote Oxon....34 H8
Woodcote Wrekin....70 D11
Woodcote Green Worcs....58 D10
Woodcott Hants....22 D4
Woodcroft Gloucs....31 P5
Woodcutts Dorset....21 J11
Wood Dalling Norfk....76 F6
Woodditton Cambs....63 L9
Woodeaton Oxon....34 F2
Wood Eaton Staffs....70 E11
Wooden Pembks....41 M9
Wood End Bed....61 M11
Wood End Bed....61 N7
Wood End C Beds....49 Q6
Wood End Cambs....62 E5
Wood End Gt Lon....36 D4
Wood End Herts....50 H5
Woodend Highld....138 D5
Woodend Nhants....48 H5
Woodend Staffs....71 M9
Woodend W Loth....126 H4
Woodend W Susx....15 M5
Wood End Warwks....58 H10
Wood End Warwks....59 K5
Wood End Warwks....59 L7
Wood End Wolves....58 D4
Wood Enderby Lincs....87 J8
Woodend Green Essex....51 N5
Woodfalls Wilts....21 N10
Woodford Cnwll....16 C9
Woodford Devon....7 K8
Woodford Gloucs....32 C5
Woodford Gt Lon....37 K2
Woodford Nhants....61 L5
Woodford Stockp....83 J8
Woodford Bridge Gt Lon....37 K2
Woodford Green Gt Lon....37 K2
Woodford Halse Nhants....48 F4
Woodford Wells Gt Lon....37 K2
Woodgate Birm....58 E8
Woodgate Devon....18 F11
Woodgate Norfk....76 B8
Woodgate Norfk....76 E8
Woodgate W Susx....15 P6
Woodgate Worcs....58 E11
Wood Green Gt Lon....36 H2
Woodgreen Hants....21 N11
Woodgreen Oxon....34 C2
Woodhall N York....96 E2
Woodhall Hill Leeds....90 G3
Woodhall Spa Lincs....86 G8
Woodham Bucks....49 K11
Woodham Dur....103 Q5
Woodham Surrey....36 B8
Woodham Ferrers Essex....38 C2
Woodham Mortimer Essex....52 D11
Woodham Walter Essex....52 D10
Wood Hayes Wolves....58 D4
Woodhead Abers....159 J10
Woodhill Shrops....57 N8
Woodhill Somset....19 L9
Woodhorn Nthumb....113 L3
Woodhorn Demesne Nthumb....113 M3
Woodhouse Leeds....90 H4
Woodhouse Leics....72 E8
Woodhouse Sheff....84 F4
Woodhouse Wakefd....91 K6
Woodhouse Eaves Leics....72 E8
Woodhouse Green Staffs....70 G2
Woodhouselee Mdloth....127 N5
Woodhouselees D & G....110 G6
Woodhouse Mill Sheff....84 F3
Woodhouses Cumb....110 F10
Woodhouses Oldham....83 K4
Woodhouses Staffs....58 G3
Woodhouses Staffs....71 M11
Woodhuish Devon....7 N8
Woodhurst Cambs....62 D5
Woodingdean Br & H....25 J9
Woodkirk Leeds....90 H5
Woodland Abers....151 M3
Woodland Devon....6 G7
Woodland Devon....7 K5
Woodland Dur....103 L5
Woodland Kent....27 K4
Woodland S Ayrs....114 C8
Woodland Head Devon....9 J5
Woodlands Abers....151 K8

Woodlands Donc....91 N9
Woodlands Dorset....13 J3
Woodlands Hants....13 P2
Woodlands Kent....37 N8
Woodlands N York....97 M10
Woodlands Somset....18 G6
Woodlands (Coleshill) Crematorium Warwks....59 J7
Woodlands Park W & M....35 N9
Woodlands St Mary W Berk....34 B9
Woodlands (Scarborough) Crematorium N York....99 L3
Woodlands (Scunthorpe) Crematorium N Linc....92 E8
Woodland Street Somset....19 P7
Woodland View Sheff....84 D3
Wood Lane Shrops....69 M8
Wood Lane Staffs....70 E5
Woodleigh Devon....7 J9
Woodlesford Leeds....91 K5
Woodley Stockp....83 K6
Woodley Wokham....35 L10
Woodmancote Gloucs....32 E5
Woodmancote Gloucs....33 K3
Woodmancote Gloucs....47 J9
Woodmancote W Susx....15 L5
Woodmancote W Susx....24 F8
Woodmancote Worcs....46 H6
Woodmancott Hants....22 G6
Woodmansey E R Yk....93 J3
Woodmansgreen W Susx....23 N9
Woodmansterne Surrey....36 G9
Woodmanton Devon....9 P7
Woodmarsh Wilts....20 G3
Woodmill Staffs....71 L10
Woodminton Wilts....21 K10
Woodnesborough Kent....39 P10
Woodnewton Nhants....61 M2
Woodnook Notts....84 G10
Wood Norton Norfk....76 E6
Woodplumpton Lancs....88 F4
Woodrising Norfk....76 D11
Wood Row Leeds....91 K5
Woodrow Worcs....58 C9
Wood's Corner E Susx....25 Q7
Woods Eaves Herefs....45 K5
Woodseaves Shrops....70 B8
Woodseaves Staffs....70 D9
Woodsend Wilts....33 P9
Woodsetts Rothm....84 H4
Woodsford Dorset....12 C6
Wood's Green E Susx....25 Q4
Woodside Br For....35 P10
Woodside Cumb....100 D4
Woodside Essex....51 L10
Woodside Fife....135 L6
Woodside Gt Lon....36 H7
Woodside Hants....13 M5
Woodside Herts....50 F9
Woodside P & K....142 C10
Woodside Crematorium Inver....124 H2
Woodside Green Kent....38 F11
Woodstock Oxon....48 D11
Woodstock Pembks....41 K5
Woodston C Pete....74 C11
Wood Street Norfk....77 M7
Wood Street Village Surrey....23 Q4
Woodthorpe Derbys....84 G6
Woodthorpe Leics....72 E7
Woodthorpe Lincs....87 M4
Woodton Norfk....65 K3
Woodtown Devon....16 G7
Woodvale Sefton....88 C8
Woodvale Crematorium Br & H....24 H9
Woodville Derbys....71 Q11
Woodwall Green Staffs....70 D8
Wood Walton Cambs....62 B4
Woodyates Dorset....21 K11
Woody Bay Devon....17 M2
Woofferton Shrops....57 J11
Wookey Somset....19 P5
Wookey Hole Somset....19 P5
Wool Dorset....12 D7
Woolacombe Devon....16 H3
Woolage Green Kent....27 M2
Woolage Village Kent....39 M11
Woolaston Gloucs....31 Q5
Woolaston Common Gloucs....31 Q4
Woolavington Somset....19 K6
Woolbeding W Susx....23 N10
Woolbrook Devon....10 C7
Woolcotts Somset....18 C8
Wooldale Kirk....90 F9
Wooler Nthumb....119 J5
Woolfardisworthy Devon....9 K3
Woolfardisworthy Devon....16 E7
Woolfold Bury....89 M8
Woolfords S Lans....127 J6
Woolhampton W Berk....34 G11
Woolhope Herefs....46 B7
Woolland Dorset....12 C3
Woollard BaNES....20 B2
Woollensbrook Herts....51 J9
Woolley BaNES....32 D11
Woolley Cambs....61 Q6
Woolley Cnwll....16 D8
Woolley Derbys....84 E8
Woolley Wakefd....91 J8
Woolley Bridge Derbys....83 M6
Woolley Edge Services Wakefd....91 J8
Woolley Green W & M....35 N8
Woolmere Green Worcs....47 J2
Woolmer Green Herts....50 G7
Woolmerston Somset....19 J8
Woolminstone Somset....11 J3
Woolpack Kent....26 E4
Woolpit Suffk....64 D9
Woolpit Green Suffk....64 D9
Woolscott Warwks....60 B7
Woolsgrove Devon....9 J4
Woolsington N u Ty....113 J6
Woolstaston Shrops....56 H5
Woolsthorpe Lincs....73 L4
Woolsthorpe-by-Colsterworth Lincs....73 N6
Woolston C Sotn....14 D4
Woolston Devon....7 J10
Woolston Devon....7 J8
Woolston Shrops....56 G7
Woolston Shrops....69 K10
Woolston Somset....18 E7

Woolston Somset....20 C9
Woolston Warrtn....82 D7
Woolstone Gloucs....47 J8
Woolstone M Keyn....49 N7
Woolstone Oxon....33 Q7
Woolston Green Devon....7 J5
Woolton Lpool....81 N7
Woolton Hill Hants....22 D2
Woolverstone Suffk....53 L4
Woolverton Somset....20 E4
Woolwich Gt Lon....37 K5
Woonton Herefs....45 M4
Woonton Herefs....45 R2
Wooperton Nthumb....119 K6
Woore Shrops....70 C6
Wootten Green Suffk....65 J7
Wootton Bed....50 B2
Wootton Hants....13 M5
Wootton Herefs....45 L4
Wootton IoW....14 F8
Wootton Kent....27 M2
Wootton N Linc....93 J7
Wootton Nhants....60 G9
Wootton Oxon....34 E4
Wootton Oxon....48 D11
Wootton Shrops....69 K9
Wootton Staffs....70 E9
Wootton Staffs....71 L6
Wootton Bassett Wilts....33 L8
Wootton Bridge IoW....14 F8
Wootton Broadmead Bed....50 B2
Wootton Common IoW....14 F8
Wootton Courtenay Somset....18 B6
Wootton Fitzpaine Dorset....10 H5
Wootton Rivers Wilts....21 N2
Wootton St Lawrence Hants....22 G4
Wootton Wawen Warwks....47 N2
Worcester Worcs....46 G4
Worcester Crematorium Worcs....46 G3
Worcester Park Gt Lon....36 F7
Wordsley Dudley....58 C7
Worfield Shrops....57 P5
Worgret Dorset....12 F7
Workhouse End Bed....61 N10
Workhouse Green Suffk....52 F4
Workington Cumb....100 D5
Worksop Notts....85 J5
Worlaby Lincs....87 K5
Worlaby N Linc....92 H8
Worlds End Bucks....35 N3
Worlds End Hants....14 H4
World's End W Berk....34 E9
World's End W Susx....24 H6
Worle N Som....19 L2
Worleston Ches E....70 B3
Worlingham Suffk....65 N4
Worlington Devon....9 J2
Worlington Suffk....63 L6
Worlingworth Suffk....65 J8
Wormald Green N York....97 M7
Wormbridge Herefs....45 N8
Wormegay Norfk....75 N8
Wormelow Tump Herefs....45 P8
Wormhill Derbys....83 P10
Wormhill Herefs....45 N7
Wormingford Essex....52 F5
Worminghall Bucks....34 H3
Wormington Gloucs....47 K7
Worminster Somset....19 Q6
Wormit Fife....135 L2
Wormleighton Warwks....48 E4
Wormley Herts....51 J9
Wormley Surrey....23 P7
Wormleybury Herts....51 J9
Wormley Hill Donc....91 R7
Wormshill Kent....38 E10
Wormsley Herefs....45 N5
Worplesdon Surrey....23 Q4
Worrall Sheff....84 D2
Worrall Hill Gloucs....32 B2
Worsbrough Barns....91 K10
Worsbrough Bridge Barns....91 K10
Worsbrough Dale Barns....91 K10
Worsley Salfd....82 G4
Worstead Norfk....77 L6
Worsthorne Lancs....89 P4
Worston Devon....6 F8
Worston Lancs....89 M2
Worth Kent....39 P10
Worth Somset....19 P6
Worth W Susx....24 H3
Wortham Suffk....64 F6
Worthen Shrops....56 E4
Worthenbury Wrexhm....69 M5
Worthing Norfk....76 D8
Worthing W Susx....24 D10
Worthing Crematorium W Susx....24 D9
Worthington Leics....72 C6
Worth Matravers Dorset....12 G9
Worthybrook Mons....31 N2
Worting Hants....22 G4
Wortley Barns....91 J11
Wortley Leeds....90 H4
Worton N York....96 E3
Worton Wilts....21 J3
Wortwell Norfk....65 K5
Wotherton Shrops....56 D4
Wothorpe C Pete....73 Q9
Wotter Devon....6 F6
Wotton Surrey....36 D11
Wotton-under-Edge Gloucs....32 E6
Wotton Underwood Bucks....49 J11
Woughton on the Green M Keyn....49 N7
Wouldham Kent....38 B9
Woundale Shrops....57 P6
Wrabness Essex....53 L5
Wrafton Devon....16 H4
Wragby Lincs....86 F5
Wragby Wakefd....91 L7
Wramplingham Norfk....76 G10
Wrangaton Devon....6 H7
Wrangbrook Wakefd....91 M8
Wrangle Lincs....87 M10
Wrangle Common Lincs....87 M10
Wrangle Lowgate Lincs....87 M10
Wrangway Somset....18 F11
Wrantage Somset....19 K10
Wrawby N Linc....92 H9
Wraxall N Som....31 N10
Wraxall Somset....20 B7

Woolston Somset....20 C9
Wray Lancs....95 N7
Wray Castle Cumb....101 L10
Wraysbury W & M....36 B6
Wrayton Lancs....95 N6
Wrea Green Lancs....88 D4
Wreaks End Cumb....94 E3
Wreay Cumb....101 M6
Wreay Cumb....110 H11
Wrecclesham Surrey....23 M6
Wrekenton Gatesd....113 L9
Wrelton N York....98 F3
Wrenbury Ches E....69 Q5
Wrench Green N York....99 K3
Wreningham Norfk....64 H2
Wrentham Suffk....65 P5
Wrenthorpe Wakefd....91 J6
Wrentnall Shrops....56 G4
Wressle E R Yk....92 B4
Wressle N Linc....92 G9
Wrestlingworth C Beds....62 C11
Wretton Norfk....75 N10
Wrexham Wrexhm....69 K4
Wrexham Industrial Estate Wrexhm....69 L4
Wribbenhall Worcs....57 P9
Wrickton Shrops....57 L7
Wrightington Bar Lancs....88 G8
Wright's Green Essex....51 M7
Wrinehill Staffs....70 D5
Wrington N Som....19 N2
Writhlington BaNES....20 C4
Writtle Essex....51 Q9
Wrockwardine Wrekin....57 L2
Wroot N Linc....92 B10
Wrose C Brad....90 F3
Wrotham Kent....37 P9
Wrotham Heath Kent....37 P9
Wrottesley Staffs....58 B4
Wroughton Swindn....33 M8
Wroxall IoW....14 G11
Wroxall Warwks....59 K10
Wroxeter Shrops....57 K3
Wroxham Norfk....77 L8
Wroxton Oxon....48 D6
Wyaston Derbys....71 M6
Wyatt's Green Essex....51 N11
Wyberton East Lincs....74 F2
Wyberton West Lincs....74 F2
Wyboston Bed....61 Q9
Wybunbury Ches E....70 B5
Wychbold Worcs....58 D11
Wych Cross E Susx....25 K4
Wychnor Staffs....71 M11
Wyck Hants....23 L7
Wyck Rissington Gloucs....47 N10
Wycliffe Dur....103 M8
Wycoller Lancs....89 Q3
Wycomb Leics....73 K6
Wycombe Marsh Bucks....35 N6
Wyddial Herts....51 J4
Wye Kent....27 J2
Wyesham Mons....31 P2
Wyfordby Leics....73 K7
Wyke C Brad....90 F5
Wyke Devon....9 L5
Wyke Devon....10 F5
Wyke Dorset....20 E9
Wyke Shrops....57 L4
Wyke Surrey....23 P4
Wyke Champflower Somset....20 C8
Wykeham N York....99 K4
Wyken Covtry....59 N8
Wyken Shrops....57 P5
Wyke Regis Dorset....11 P9
Wykey Shrops....69 L10
Wykin Leics....72 C11
Wylam Nthumb....112 H8
Wylde Green Birm....58 H6
Wylye Wilts....21 K7
Wymeswold Leics....72 G6
Wymington Bed....61 L8
Wymondham Leics....73 L7
Wymondham Norfk....76 G11
Wyndham Brdgnd....29 P6
Wynford Eagle Dorset....11 M5
Wynyard Park S on T....104 D5
Wynyard Village S on T....104 D5
Wyre Forest Crematorium Worcs....57 Q10
Wyre Piddle Worcs....47 J5
Wysall Notts....72 G5
Wyson Herefs....57 J11
Wythall Worcs....58 G9
Wytham Oxon....34 E3
Wythburn Cumb....101 K8
Wythenshawe Manch....82 H7
Wythop Mill Cumb....100 G5
Wyton Cambs....62 C6
Wyton E R Yk....93 L4
Wyverstone Suffk....64 E8
Wyverstone Street Suffk....64 E8
Wyville Lincs....73 M5

Y

Yaddlethorpe N Linc....92 E9
Yafford IoW....14 D10
Yafforth N York....97 M2
Yalberton Torbay....7 M7
Yalding Kent....37 Q10
Yanwath Cumb....101 P5
Yanworth Gloucs....33 L2
Yapham E R Yk....98 F10
Yapton W Susx....15 Q6
Yarborough N Som....19 L3
Yarbridge IoW....14 H9
Yarburgh Lincs....87 L2
Yarcombe Devon....10 E3
Yard Devon....17 P7
Yardley Birm....58 H7
Yardley Crematorium Birm....58 H8
Yardley Gobion Nhants....49 L6
Yardley Hastings Nhants....61 J9
Yardley Wood Birm....58 H9
Yardro Powys....45 J3
Yarford Somset....18 H9
Yarkhill Herefs....46 B6
Yarley Somset....19 P6
Yarlington Somset....20 C9
Yarm S on T....104 D8
Yarmouth IoW....14 C9
Yarnacott Devon....17 L5
Yarnbrook Wilts....20 G4
Yarner Devon....9 J9
Yarnfield Staffs....70 F8
Yarnscombe Devon....17 K7
Yarnton Oxon....34 E2

Yarpole Herefs....45 P2
Yarrow Border....117 M5
Yarrow Somset....19 L5
Yarrow Feus Border....117 L5
Yarrowford Border....117 N4
Yarsop Herefs....45 N5
Yarwell Nhants....73 R11
Yate S Glos....32 D8
Yateley Hants....23 M2
Yatesbury Wilts....33 L10
Yattendon W Berk....34 G10
Yatton Herefs....56 H11
Yatton N Som....31 M11
Yatton Keynell Wilts....32 G9
Yaverland IoW....14 H9
Yawl Devon....10 G6
Yawthorpe Lincs....85 Q2
Yaxham Norfk....76 E9
Yaxley Cambs....61 Q2
Yaxley Suffk....64 G7
Yazor Herefs....45 N5
Yeading Gt Lon....36 D4
Yeadon Leeds....90 G2
Yealand Conyers Lancs....95 L6
Yealand Redmayne Lancs....95 L5
Yealand Storrs Lancs....95 K5
Yealmbridge Devon....6 F8
Yealmpton Devon....6 F8
Yearby R & Cl....104 G6
Yearngill Cumb....100 F2
Yearsley N York....98 B6
Yeaton Shrops....69 M11
Yeaveley Derbys....71 M6
Yeavering Nthumb....118 H4
Yedingham N York....98 H5
Yelford Oxon....34 C4
Yell Shet....169 q15
Yelland Devon....16 H5
Yelling Cambs....62 C8
Yelvertoft Nhants....60 C5
Yelverton Devon....6 E5
Yelverton Norfk....77 K11
Yenston Somset....20 D10
Yeoford Devon....9 J5
Yeolmbridge Cnwll....5 N4
Yeo Mill Devon....17 Q6
Yeo Vale Devon....16 G7
Yeovil Somset....19 Q11
Yeovil Crematorium Somset....19 P11
Yeovil Marsh Somset....19 P11
Yeovilton Somset....19 P10
Yerbeston Pembks....41 L9
Yesnaby Ork....169 b5
Yetlington Nthumb....119 K9
Yetminster Dorset....11 M2
Yetson Devon....7 L7
Yettington Devon....9 Q7
Yetts o'Muckhart Clacks....134 C7
Yews Green C Brad....90 D4
Yew Tree Sandw....58 F5
Y Felinheli Gwynd....79 J11
Y Ferwig Cerdgn....42 C5
Y Ffôr Gwynd....66 F7
Y Gyffylliog Denbgs....68 E3
Yielden Bed....61 M7
Yieldingtree Worcs....58 C9
Yieldshields S Lans....126 F7
Yiewsley Gt Lon....36 C4
Y Maerdy Conwy....68 D6
Y Nant Wrexhm....69 J4
Ynysboeth Rhondd....30 E5
Ynysddu Caerph....30 G5
Ynysforgan Swans....29 J5
Ynyshir Rhondd....30 D6
Ynyslas Cerdgn....54 E6
Ynysmaerdy Rhondd....30 D8
Ynysmeudwy Neath....29 K3
Ynystawe Swans....29 J4
Ynyswen Powys....29 M2
Ynyswen Rhondd....30 C5
Ynysybwl Rhondd....30 E6
Ynysymaengwyn Gwynd....54 D4
Yockenthwaite N York....96 D5
Yockleton Shrops....56 F2
Yokefleet E R Yk....92 D6
Yoker C Glas....125 N4
York C York....98 C10
York Lancs....89 L4
York City Crematorium C York....98 B11
Yorkletts Kent....39 J9
Yorkley Gloucs....32 B3
Yorkshire Dales National Park....96 C5
York Town Surrey....23 N2
Yorton Heath Shrops....69 P10
Youlgreave Derbys....84 B8
Youlthorpe E R Yk....98 F9
Youlton N York....97 Q8
Youngsbury Herts....51 J7
Young's End Essex....52 B8
Yoxall Staffs....71 L11
Yoxford Suffk....65 M8
Y Rhiw Gwynd....66 C9
Ysbyty Cynfyn Cerdgn....54 H9
Ysbyty Ifan Conwy....67 Q5
Ysbyty Ystwyth Cerdgn....54 G10
Ysceifiog Flints....80 H10
Ysgubor-y-Coed Cerdgn....54 F5
Ystalyfera Neath....29 L3
Ystrad Rhondd....30 C5
Ystrad Aeron Cerdgn....43 K3
Ystradfellte Powys....29 P2
Ystrad Ffin Carmth....43 Q5
Ystradgynlais Powys....29 L2
Ystrad Meurig Cerdgn....54 G11
Ystrad Mynach Caerph....30 F6
Ystradowen V Glam....30 D9
Ystumtuen Cerdgn....54 G9
Ythanbank Abers....159 M11
Ythanwells Abers....158 F10
Ythsie Abers....159 L11

Z

Zeal Monachorum Devon....8 H4
Zeals Wilts....20 E8
Zelah Cnwll....3 L3
Zennor Cnwll....2 D6
Zoar Cnwll....3 K10
Zouch Notts....72 E6
ZSL London Zoo Gt Lon....36 G4
ZSL Whipsnade Zoo C Beds....50 B7